INVESTMENTS

Zvi Bodie
Boston University

Alex Kane
University of California, San Diego

Alan J. Marcus
Boston College

Stylianos Perrakis
University of Ottawa

Peter J. Ryan
University of Ottawa

with **244** *illustrations*

IRWIN

BURR RIDGE, ILLINOIS
BOSTON, MASSACHUSETTS
SYDNEY, AUSTRALIA

This symbol indicates that the paper in this book is made of recycled paper. Its fiber content exceeds the recommended minimum of 50% waste paper fibers as specified by the EPA.

Cover Photos:

Executives: Douglas E. Walker/Masterfile
Gold coins: Bob Anderson/Masterfile
Bay Street: Derek Caron/Masterfile
Wheat: Sherman Hines/Masterfile
Oil rig: Toby Rankin/Masterfile

Senior sponsoring editor: Roderick T. Banister
Product manager: Murray D. Moman
Project editor: Rebecca Dodson
Production manager: Bob Lange
Designer: Mercedes Santos
Art coordinator: Mark Malloy
Compositor: Bi-Comp, Inc.
Typeface: 10/12 Times Roman
Printer: R. R. Donnelley & Sons Company

ISBN 0-256-12214-8

Library of Congress Catalog Number 92-75979

Printed in the United States of America
2 3 4 5 6 7 8 9 0   DOC   0 9 8 7 6 5 4

Foreword

Along with the explosive growth in world financial markets has come an inter-action between scholarly theory and day-to-day business practice that is un-precedented in the history of economics. Not only are the tools of modern finance the accepted modes of analysis for sophisticated investors and traders, they are also the sources of many of the new products that are dramatically altering the financial markets. For the teacher of investments, however, the excitement and relevance of the field are matched by its dangers. A teacher must carefully craft a course for the student that balances the ever-changing and often unsettled background of scholarly theories against the temptation to titillate with the latest fad to hit the securities markets. The only way to teach successfully in such a minefield is to take a firm grasp of what is truly funda-mental and to utilize what is happening in the financial markets to illustrate the workings of these fundamentals. *Investments* accomplishes that difficult task with consummate skill.

Investments sensibly begins with an overview that lays out the workings of the securities markets in a thorough but lively fashion. After the student has been exposed to the institutional structure of the securities markets, the funda-mental intuitions of the trade-off between return and risk and the role of infor-mation are developed and used to clarify the workings of the markets. The major asset-pricing models are all treated with a commendable clarity that should make teaching them a pleasure.

A central theme of the book is the investor's perspective on using securities to form portfolios. The fine treatments of the stock and fixed-income markets further this theme with their emphasis on the empirical properties of these markets, and derivative securities such as options and futures become natural topics from the perspective of how they fit into investor portfolios. A careful distinction is drawn between passive and active investment management, and this distinction is used to great advantage to deal with such troublesome mat-ters as the reconciliation of the efficient market hypotheses with active manage-ment. As with all the material, a clear presentation of the theory is accompa-nied by a rich matrix of institutional material within which it is applied.

Students and teachers will welcome this thoroughly modern and well exe-cuted treatment of investments. I believe that it will become the central text in the field.

Stephen A. Ross

ABOUT THE AUTHORS

Zvi Bodie
Boston University

Zvi Bodie is Professor of Finance and Economics at the Boston University School of Management. He is the director of Boston University's Chartered Financial Analysts Examination Review Program and has served as consultant to many private and governmental organizations. Professor Bodie is a research associate of the National Bureau of Economic Research, where he was director of the NBER Project on Financial Aspects of the U.S. Pension System, and he is a member of the Pension Research Council of The Wharton School. He is widely published in leading professional journals, and his previous books include *Pensions in the U.S. Economy, Issues in Pension Economics,* and *Financial Aspects of the U.S. Pension System.*

Alex Kane
University of California, San Diego

Alex Kane is Professor of Finance and Economics at the University of California, San Diego, and is a fellow of the National Bureau of Economic Research in the Financial Markets and Monetary Economics Group. The author of many articles published in finance and management journals, Professor Kane has research interests in the areas of capital market theory, corporate finance, and portfolio management.

Alan J. Marcus
Boston College

Alan Marcus is Professor of Finance at Boston College. He is a research fellow of the National Bureau of Economic Research, where he participates in the Financial Markets and Monetary Economics Group. He also took part in the NBER project on pension economics. Professor Marcus has been a research fellow of the Center for the Study of Futures Markets at Columbia University. His main research interests are futures and options markets, and he has published more than 20 articles in these and related areas. Professor Marcus recently was a member of the Financial Research department at Freddie Mac, the Federal Home Loan Mortgage Corporation.

Stylianos Perrakis
University of Ottawa

Stylianos Perrakis is Professor of Finance and Economics, with a joint appointment at the Faculty of Administration and the Department of Economics of the University of Ottawa. He holds an engineering diploma from Athens, Greece, and a Ph.D. from the University of California at Berkeley. Professor Perrakis is the author of many articles published in leading academic and professional journals in economics and finance, especially in the areas of industrial organization, corporate finance, and option pricing. He has served as a consultant to many private and governmental organizations, including the Institute of Canadian Bankers and the World Bank. He is also the author of *Canadian Industrial Organization*. Professor Perrakis has taught as a visiting professor in universities in Switzerland, France, and the United States.

Peter J. Ryan
University of Ottawa

Peter Ryan is Associate Professor of Finance at the University of Ottawa. His research interests include both contingent claims in general and the incentive effects of financial claims in corporate structures. His articles on the subject of options and financial instruments have been published in a number of international journals in finance and management science.

To our families with love and gratitude.

Preface

In teaching and practice, the field of investments has experienced many changes over the last 2 decades. This is due in part to an abundance of newly designed securities, in part to the creation of new trading strategies that would have been impossible without concurrent advances in computer technology, and in part to rapid advances in the theory of investments that have come out of the academic community. In no other field, perhaps, is the transmission of theory to real-world practice as rapid as is now commonplace in the financial industry. These developments place new burdens on practitioners and teachers of investments far beyond what was required only a short while ago.

Investments is intended primarily as a textbook for courses in investment analysis. Its guiding principle has been to present the material in a framework that is organized by a central core of consistent fundamental principles. Every attempt was made to strip away unnecessary mathematical and technical detail, and to provide the intuition that may guide students and practitioners as they confront new ideas and challenges in their professional lives.

The primary goal is to present material of practical value, but all five co-authors are active researchers in the science of financial economics and find virtually all of the material in this book to be of great intellectual interest. Fortunately, we think, there is no contradiction in the field of investments between the pursuit of truth and the pursuit of wealth. Quite the opposite. The capital asset pricing model, the arbitrage pricing model, the efficient markets hypothesis, the option pricing model, and the other centerpieces of modern financial research are as much intellectually satisfying subjects of scientific inquiry as they are of immense practical importance for the sophisticated investor.

Since 1983 the three U.S. authors have conducted an annual review program at Boston University for candidates from all over the world preparing for the Chartered Financial Analyst examinations. The book has benefited from this CFA experience in two ways. First, the text has incorporated much of the content of the readings and other study materials in the official CFA curriculum. As a result, the book includes some material not found in most other investments texts. Most notably, Part VIII presents material on portfolio management principles and techniques for both the individual and institutional investor that stems largely from the CFA curriculum. Second, questions from CFA examinations have been included in the end-of-chapter problem sets throughout the book.

Realistic Presentation of Modern Portfolio Theory

The exposition of modern portfolio theory in this text differs from its presentation in all other major investments texts in that it develops the basic model starting with a risk-free asset such as a Treasury bill, and a single risky asset such as a common stock mutual fund.[1] Not until later are other risky assets added. Other texts develop the model by first assuming that the investor has to choose from two risky assets; only later do they introduce the possibility of investing in a risk-free asset. Ultimately both approaches reach the same end point, a model in which there are many risky assets in addition to a risk-free asset.

We think our approach is better for two important reasons. First, it corresponds to the actual procedure that most individual investors follow. Typically, one starts with all of one's money invested in a bank account and only then considers how much to invest in something riskier that may offer the prospect of a higher expected return. The next logical step is to consider the addition of other risky assets such as real estate or gold, which requires determining whether the benefits of such increased diversification are worth the additional transaction costs involved in including them in one's portfolio.

The second advantage of our approach is that it vastly simplifies exposition of the mathematics for deriving the menu of risk-return combinations open to the investor. Portfolio optimization techniques are mathematically complex, ultimately requiring a computer. Anything that can help to simplify their presentation should be welcome. In short, we believe our approach is both more realistic and analytically simpler than the conventional one.

Changes in the Canadian Edition

This Canadian edition is both an adaptation of the U.S. text for a Canadian audience and an extension of the material to incorporate several topics of specific Canadian interest. The adaptation has changed the presentation and examples of the basic material with respect to currency, macroeconomic environment, tax rates and legislation, and other legal and institutional features of the Canadian economy. Thus, the first three chapters include a description of the Canadian environment, markets, instruments, and institutions, as well as a summary description of the same concepts in the U.S. context.

---

[1] We define and discuss mutual funds in Chapter 3. For now it is sufficient to know that a common stock mutual fund is a diversified portfolio of stocks in which an investor can invest as much money as desired.

The inclusion of the U.S. material was motivated by several factors. In the first place, much of the investment activity by Canadian investors takes place in U.S. markets, implying that Canadian investment professionals cannot afford to ignore the situation south of their country's border. Furthermore, not only does the U.S. market set the standards for most of the financial innovation and research in Canada, but it also paces many of the economic developments that underlie the performance of the Canadian financial system.

Nevertheless, several Canadian financial aspects are unique, and deserve more extended coverage in their theoretical and empirical aspects. What follows is a summary of major additions and innovations from the first and second U.S. editions; however, we cannot mention in this brief preface all the differences from these editions.

Equilibrium in Capital Markets

This section has been compressed and reorganized from the U.S. edition. The multifactor CAPM has been included as an appendix of the single-factor CAPM in Chapter 8. Index models and arbitrage pricing theory have been combined into a single chapter, Chapter 9, in order to facilitate a unified treatment and shorten what was, in our view, too long an exposition. Due to the importance of international investments for Canadian investors, we included the subject of international diversification as Chapter 10 (Chapter 25 in the first U.S. edition). This chapter was also expanded by the inclusion of a section on the key issue of integration vs. segmentation of Canadian and U.S. financial markets.

Empirical Studies of Risk and Return

Chapter 11 includes a new discussion of time-varying volatility, as well as a discussion of available Canadian studies on capital market equilibrium. This chapter includes also an extended presentation of the issue of thin trading, which is present in all Canadian financial markets. The presentation of market efficiency in Chapter 12 covers the considerable literature that has appeared since the first U.S. edition concerning Canadian and U.S. markets, with emphasis on the question of predictability of stock market returns.

Active Management

Chapters 13 and 14 are an adaptation of the material on portfolio management found in Chapters 23 and 24 of the first U.S. edition. This material was moved forward and combined with the presentation of market efficiency because of its close relation to the preceding topic of capital market equilibrium. Both chapters contain extensive reviews of Canadian studies and practices.

Equity of Fixed-Income Management

The analysis of fixed-income portfolio management in Chapter 17 now includes considerable coverage of bond indexing. Chapter 18, on security analysis, includes an expanded treatment of macroeconomics, as well as industry analysis. This chapter has also been revised to emphasize practical application of the techniques and models actually used by security analysts. Chapter 19 presents a revised treatment of financial statement analysis, including new discussions on how analysts use cash flow statements. Chapter 20 is a new chapter containing the main elements of technical analysis, as well as a discussion of the topic in the light of the efficient markets hypothesis.

Derivative Markets

Chapter 22 contains a new section on option pricing in incomplete markets as a generalization of binomial option pricing, as well as a review of empirical studies in Canadian option markets. Chapter 23 combines Chapters 21 and 22 of the first U.S. edition, and provides new coverage of swaps.

Players and Strategies

Chapter 24 presents portfolio management policy with a revised discussion of hedging against inflation that reflects new developments in this field. The treatment of retirement asset selection and pension fund management has been revised in Chapter 25 to emphasize the investment motives and unique trading strategies appropriate to various pension funds and retirement savings accounts.

Acknowledgments

As Canadian authors, we would like first to express our gratitude to Professors Bodie, Kane, and Marcus for their production of what we recognized as an outstanding text in its original form, and for agreeing to our collaboration in the production of a Canadian edition. In addition a large number of reviewers read both the first and the revised editions of the American text. Of these, coincidentally, Jean Masson is now our colleague and has contributed information used in our version. All of these deserve thanks for their particular insights. We should also like to note the extensive contributions and comments of our Canadian reviewers; almost all of their suggestions were incorporated into the final draft, as they led to clarifications and more effective presentations. These reviewers were:

Ben Amoako-Adu	Wilfred Laurier University
Giovanni Barone-Adesi	University of Alberta
Abraham Brodt	Concordia University
Harry Turtle	University of Manitoba

A great quantity of material and information was contributed by Gilles Gagné of Burns Fry Ltd. over the course of the writing of the text. Other institutions giving considerable support were Scotia McLeod and the Export Development Corporation. For granting permission to include many of their examination questions in the text, we are grateful to the Institute of Chartered Financial Analysts.

Many of the tables and graphs have been compiled from information provided through the cooperation of Statistics Canada. Readers wishing further information may obtain copies of related publications by mail from Publications Sales, Statistics Canada, Ottawa, Ontario K1A 0T6, by phone at 613-951-7277 or national toll-free 800-267-6677. They may also facsimile their orders by dialing 613-951-1548.

Much of the work of obtaining data, locating articles, reproduction and collation was performed by Shalene Curtis and Dan Perrakis; we are happy to acknowledge their assistance.

Much credit is due also to the development and production team: our special thanks go to Rod Banister, senior sponsoring editor; Becky Dodson, project editor; Bob Lange; production manager; and Mark Malloy, art coordinator.

Stylianos Perrakis
Peter J. Ryan

List of Boxes

Title	Source	Page
Montreal Exchange to Draw on Past for Futures	*The Globe and Mail*	798
Watching the Witching	*The Financial Post*	825
Diversity Is More Than Stocks and Bonds	*The Wall Street Journal*	891
Illustration of a Variable Annuity		897
Battle Rages over Pension Surplus Ownership	*The Financial Post*	901

Table of Contents in Brief

Contents

PART I

INTRODUCTION

Prologue

Prologue

This is a book about investing in securities such as stocks, bonds, options, and futures contracts. It is intended to provide an understanding of how to analyze these securities, how to determine whether they are appropriate for inclusion in your **investment portfolio*** (the set of securities you choose to hold), and how to buy and sell them.

We can usefully divide the process of investing, both in theory and in practice, into two parts: security analysis and portfolio management. **Security analysis** is the attempt to determine whether an individual security is correctly valued in the marketplace; that is, it is the search for mispriced securities. **Portfolio management** is the process of combining securities into a portfolio tailored to the investor's preferences and needs, monitoring that portfolio, and evaluating its performance. This book is intended to provide a thorough treatment of both parts of the investment process.

This book is designed first and foremost to impart knowledge of practical value to anyone interested in becoming an investment professional or a sophisticated private investor. It provides a lot of institutional detail, but of necessity it also contains a lot of theory. It is impossible to be a sophisticated investor or investment professional today without a sound basis in valuation theory, modern portfolio theory, and option pricing theory at the level presented in the following chapters.

---

* Throughout this text key terms are denoted in boldface, summarized at the end of each chapter, and defined in the Glossary.

The Main Themes of Investments

The Risk-Return Trade-off

One simple strategy for an investor to pursue is to keep all of his or her money invested in a bank account. This strategy has a number of advantages. It is safe, and it requires no expertise and little effort on the part of the investor.

However, if an investor is willing to consider the possibility of taking on some risk, there is the potential reward of higher expected returns. A considerable part of this book is devoted to exploring the nature of this **risk-return trade-off** and the principles of rational portfolio choice associated with it. The approach we present is known as **modern portfolio theory** (MPT).

The main organizing principle of MPT is **efficient diversification**. The basic idea is that any investor who is averse to risk, that is, who requires a higher expected return in order to increase exposure to risk, will be made better off by reorganizing the portfolio so as to increase its expected return without taking on additional risk.

In this book we devote considerable space to explaining the principles of efficient diversification and applying them to the issue of **asset allocation**. Asset allocation is the choice of how much to invest in each of the broad asset classes—stocks, bonds, cash, real estate, foreign securities, *derivative securities,*[1] gold, and possibly others to achieve the best portfolio given the investor's objectives and constraints.

Active vs. Passive Management

We define **passive management** as a strategy of holding a well-diversified portfolio of generic security types without attempting to outperform other investors through superior market forecasting or superior ability to find mispriced securities. Depending on the approach used to find the best portfolio mix, passive management can be quite sophisticated. Indeed, as we show in our exposition of the asset allocation decision, efficient diversification can be a rather complex process, requiring many inputs and the aid of a computer.

Active management can take two forms: market timing and security selection. The most popular kind of **market timing** is trying to time the stock market, increasing one's commitment to stocks when one is "bullish" (when one thinks the market will do relatively well), and moving out of stocks when one is "bearish." But market timing is potentially just as profitable in the markets for fixed-income securities, where the name of the game is forecasting interest

---

[1] Derivative securities include options and futures contracts. They are described briefly in Chapter 2 and then discussed in much greater detail in Part VII.

rates. Successful market timing, whether in the market for stocks or for bonds, requires superior forecasting ability.

Security selection is the attempt to find mispriced securities and to improve one's risk-return trade-off by concentrating on such securities. Security selection can involve both buying those securities believed to be underpriced and selling those believed to be overpriced. Successful security selection requires the sacrifice of some amount of diversification.

There is a large body of empirical evidence to support a theory called the **efficient markets hypothesis** (EMH), which among other things says that active management of both types should not be expected to work for very long. The basic reasoning behind the EMH is that in a competitive financial environment successful trading strategies tend to "self-destruct." Bargains may exist for brief periods, but with so many talented, highly paid analysts scouring the markets for them, by the time you or I "discover" them, they are no longer bargains.

To be sure, there are some extremely successful investors, but according to the EMH one can account for some or all of them on the basis of luck rather than skill. And even if their success in the past derived from skill at finding some extraordinary bargains, the EMH would say that their chances to continue to find more in the future are slight. Even the legendary Benjamin Graham,[2] the father of modern security analysis and the teacher of some of today's investment giants, has said that the job of finding true bargains has become difficult if not impossible in today's competitive environment. In part, this situation is testimony to the success Graham and his followers have had in teaching the principles of fundamental analysis.

Our view is that markets are nearly efficient. Nevertheless, even in this competitive environment profit opportunities may exist for especially diligent and creative investors. This idea motivates our treatment of active portfolio management in Part IV, which is a section unique to this textbook.

Equilibrium Pricing Relationships

A fascinating feature of financial markets, and one that is not at all apparent to the untrained observer, is that the prices of securities must often have a specific relationship to each other, because if the relationships are violated market forces will come into play to restore them. Financial economists refer to these as *equilibrium pricing relationships,* and in this text we explain them in detail.

Perhaps the best known of these relationships are the following:

1. The security market line (expected return-beta) relationship.
2. The put-call parity relationship.
3. The Black-Scholes option pricing model.
4. The spot-futures parity relationship.
5. The international interest rate parity relationship.

---

[2] We will have much more to say about Graham and his ideas about investing in Chapter 19.

These relationships are more than just intellectually pleasing theoretical constructs. In most cases if they are violated, the first investors to discover the violation have opportunities for large profits with little or no risk. For example, the recent practice of *program trading* is primarily a systematic method of profiting from violations of equilibrium pricing relationships in the market for the Standard & Poor's 500 stock-index futures contract.

A well-trained investment professional must not only be aware of these equilibrium relationships, but also must understand why they exist and how to profit from any violation of them. We have tried to provide the basis for this knowledge throughout the book, as well as in the specific chapters in which these relationships are presented and explained.

The Use of Options and Futures Contracts in Implementing Investment Strategy

In today's securities markets, there are a variety of ways sophisticated investors can tailor the set of possible investment outcomes to their specific knowledge or preferences regarding security returns. The emergence of markets for so-called derivative securities such as options and futures contracts has made it possible to implement strategies unheard of only a few short years ago. Perhaps in no other area of investments is the recent business school graduate at a greater advantage over the investment veteran who studied investments several years ago.

Probably the most well known of these strategies is *portfolio insurance*. There are a variety of ways an investor can combine stocks and/or bonds with derivative securities to eliminate the possibility of loss of principal while preserving much of the upside potential of an investment in the stock market. These securities and strategies are here to stay. The investment professional must understand and master them if he or she is to avoid technological obsolescence.

In our chapters on derivative securities we explain in some detail and with a minimum of mathematics the use of options and futures in implementing portfolio insurance and other investment strategies.

Text Organization

The text has eight parts, which are fairly independent and may be studied in a variety of sequences. Part I is introductory and contains much institutional material. Part II contains the core of modern portfolio theory as it relates to optimal portfolio selection. Part III contains the core of modern portfolio theory as it relates to the equilibrium structure of expected rates of return on risky assets. It builds on the material in Part II and therefore must be preceded by it.

Part IV is devoted to active portfolio management and performance measurement. It has as a prerequisite the material on MPT in Part II. Part V, which is on the analysis and valuation of fixed-income securities, is the first of three parts on security valuation. Part VI is devoted to equity securities. Part VII covers derivative assets such as options, futures contracts, and convertible securities. Finally, Part VIII is about the process of portfolio management.

Canadian and U.S. Content

The main object of our study is the Canadian investment environment. Thus, whenever we refer to unspecified securities, financial markets, or investment professionals, it should be implicitly understood that we refer to Canadian ones. Likewise, we have tried to report extensively on the main Canadian studies on each topic.

Nonetheless, this book is addressed to the problems of Canadian investors. It cannot, therefore, ignore the fact that much Canadian investing takes place abroad, especially in the United States. Accordingly, we have covered in detail all relevant U.S. features of every topic discussed in this book. This is particularly true for those topics where significant differences exist between Canada and the United States, or where there are no Canadian counterparts. As we shall see, the existence of an investment opportunity in the United States can also frequently serve the needs of Canadian investors and, thus, precludes the establishment of a comparable opportunity in Canada.

Other Features

A unique feature is the inclusion of self-test questions and problems within the following chapters. These Concept Checks are designed to provide the student with a means for determining whether he or she has understood the preceding material and for reinforcing that understanding. Detailed solutions to all Concept Checks are provided at the end of the book.

These in-chapter questions may be used in a variety of ways. They may be skipped altogether in a first reading of the chapter with no loss in continuity. They can then be done with any degree of diligence and intensity upon the second reading. Finally, they can serve as models for solving the end-of-chapter problems.

The end-of-chapter problems progress from the simple to the complex. We strongly believe that practice in solving problems is a critical part of learning investments, so we have provided many opportunities. Many are taken from past (U.S.) chartered financial analyst examinations and therefore represent the kinds of questions that professionals in the field believe are relevant to the "real world." The *Study Guide*, which accompanies the text, provides many more practice problems, with solutions.

The Investments Field and Career Opportunities

As with any other field of scientific inquiry, the theory of investments is constantly changing and, we believe, advancing. In that sense we too are always learning something new. What makes it especially exciting is that the lag between discovery and application in investments is extraordinarily short. For example, the Black-Scholes option pricing formula and the dynamic hedging strategy that is its mainspring were developed in 1973.[3] Just a few years later practitioners were busy applying it on the Chicago Board Options Exchange.

Far from being an exception, the example of the Black-Scholes formula has become the paradigm for the relationship between the academic and applied worlds in investments. Indeed, Fischer Black himself is an example of this development, moving from a professorship at MIT's Sloan School of Management to a full partnership in the investment banking firm of Goldman Sachs.

We believe that the field of investments offers great opportunities for careers that are both fascinating and lucrative, but the competition is fierce. A mastery of the material in this text will, we hope, give you a competitive advantage.

Key terms

Investment portfolio	Asset allocation
Security analysis	Passive management
Portfolio management	Active management
Risk-return trade-off	Market timing
Modern portfolio theory	Security selection
Efficient diversification	Efficient markets hypothesis

---

[3] See Fischer Black and M. Scholes, "The Pricing of Options and Corporate Liabilities," *Journal of Political Economy,* May–June 1973.

Rocket Scientists Are Revolutionizing Wall Street

Former Academics Are Pioneering Ways to Make More Money with Less Risk

Before coming to Wall Street in 1980, Henry Nicholas Hanson was a physicist at Brown University, where he researched the properties of helium at low temperatures. Now, Hanson, a Salomon Brothers vice-president, is one of Wall Street's leading authorities on stock-index futures.

Stanley Diller is a former economics professor. In the mid-1970s, at the age of 40, he started a bond research department at Goldman, Sachs & Co. Now at Bear, Stearns & Co., Diller is said to earn at least $500,000 a year and tells his colleagues: "Never call me doctor. It would cut my salary by 75%."

Fischer Black, one of the nation's leading finance academics, left a tenured full professorship at Massachusetts Institute of Technology in early 1984 to become a vice-president at Goldman Sachs. Black is internationally known for developing an option-pricing model that traders use to value stock options.

The three men represent Wall Street's new breed, known as the "rocket scientists" or "quants." These former academics, trained in mathematics, and the whiz kids, most from the physical sciences, who have come after them, are revolutionizing the stock and bond markets. They are the brains behind program trading—the controversial use of stock-index futures to lock in high risk-free yields. They have introduced a plethora of new financial products, including interest rate swaps, zero-coupon bonds, and new types of mortgage-backed securities. In the process, they've made hundreds of millions of dollars for the brokerage houses that employ them and for the firms' clients.

Today the top firms employ more than 1,000 rocket scientists and usually pay them well over six figures. Indeed, the Wall Street whiz kids—just like top traders and salesmen—can become millionaires in only a few years. "There is no other way a technical guy is going to make that kind of money," says Diller.

Pigeonholed

The first rocket scientists on Wall Street were cut from a different mold. In the early 1970s they and their computer programs were used for back-office functions such as data processing to handle increased trading volume. Although they vastly increased the efficiency of the brokerage industry, they were pigeonholed by top management.

But by the end of that decade, as interest rates began fluctuating wildly and the deregulation of the financial markets was picking up steam, Wall Street houses turned to the quants in increasing numbers. The firms desperately needed ways to protect against the calamitous movements in bond prices that could wipe out their capital. To their horror, they found that the old way of hedging one bond against another of a different maturity was often producing big losses. Rocket scientists solved the problem using "convexity," a tool from calculus that describes the behavior of bond prices when interest rates move violently. They also designed new hedges using options and futures contracts.

James A. Tilley's Ph.D. thesis was titled *The Effects of Spin-Orbit Interactions in Itinerant Ferromagnets*. Now at Morgan Stanley & Co., Tilley helps insurance companies meet their policyholder obligations by matching those cash needs with the flows generated from investments. He exhibits the polish of the typical investment banker—not the dishevelment of the stereotyped technician.

More and more rocket scientists, like Tilley, are getting directly involved with corporate clients. Kennedy of Merrill Lynch recalls a client that had a series of payments totaling $45 million to make over five years and owned bonds whose cash flows precisely matched those obligations. Merrill's rocket scientists were asked whether there might be a less expensive way to do it. They constructed a new portfolio that would save the client $1 million. They also developed a solution that could save the company even more money if the client was

(Continued)

willing to borrow money for a short period. The company did, and saved $3 million.

The successful Wall Street rocket scientists have learned to operate within time and budget constraints.

Some analytical problems, such as matching the cash flows of assets and liabilities, "if run to completion, would occupy the largest computer mainframes for weeks," says First Boston's Senft. "Rocket scientists get the computer to give answers that are close enough in a short time—like 15 minutes—to reduce the risk of a change in market prices during the analysis."

The message that Wall Street wants rocket scientists is being heard on university campuses. From MIT to the University of California at Berkeley, big firms are actively courting students with advanced degrees in all scientific fields. Meanwhile, investment managers around the country are struggling to keep up with the latest techniques of the quants. "We make sure we make a quarterly pilgrimage to the esoteric pillars of money management," says Bruce P. Bedford, chairman of Flagship Financial Inc. in Dayton, Ohio. "Some of it is above our heads, yeah." But "that's where the action is."

CHAPTER 1

The Investment Environment

Even a cursory glance at the financial pages of daily newspapers reveals a bewildering collection of securities, markets, and financial institutions. Although it may appear chaotic, the financial environment is not so: there is rhyme and reason behind the array of instruments and markets. The central message we want to convey in this chapter is that financial markets and institutions evolve in response to the desires, technologies, and regulatory constraints of the investors in the economy. In fact, we could *predict* the general shape of the investment environment (if not the design of particular securities) if we knew nothing more than these desires, technologies, and constraints.

Competition and liquidity are major factors of the investment environment, and their interplay helps to define the resultant structure. If government regulations do not prohibit competition, then more attractive instruments and markets will draw both capital and companies seeking capital away from their illiquid counterparts. We see the impact of this in Canadian markets, where many innovative instruments available in the United State do not have Canadian equivalents; insufficient liquidity in Canada either precludes the establishment of markets or has caused their demise. Competition implies that these U.S. instruments are available to Canadian investors; thus a presentation of both U.S. instruments and available Canadian equivalents is necessary for a complete appreciation of the environment.

This chapter provides a broad overview of the investment environment. We begin by examining the differences between financial assets and real assets. We proceed to the four broad sectors of the financial environment: households, businesses, government, and the foreign sector. We then give a brief description of how taxation affects investment returns. We see how many features of the investment environment are natural responses of profit-seeking firms and individuals to opportunities created by the demands of these sectors, and we examine the driving forces behind financial innovation. Next, we discuss recent trends in financial markets. Finally, we conclude with a discussion of the relationship between households and the business sector.

1.1 *Real Assets vs. Financial Assets*

The material wealth of a society is determined ultimately by the productive capacity of its economy—the goods and services that can be provided to its members. This productive capacity is a function of the **real assets** of the economy: the land, buildings, knowledge, and machines that are used to produce goods, and the workers whose skills are necessary to use those resources. Together, physical and human assets generate the entire spectrum of output produced and consumed by the society.

In contrast to real assets are **financial assets**, such as stocks or bonds. These assets, per se, do not represent a society's wealth. Shares of stock are no more than sheets of paper; they do not directly contribute to the productive capacity of the economy. Instead, financial assets contribute to the productive capacity of the economy *indirectly*, because they allow for separation of the ownership and management of the firm and facilitate the transfer of funds to enterprises with attractive investment opportunities. Financial assets certainly contribute to the wealth of the individuals or firms holding them, because they are *claims* to the income generated by real assets or claims on income from the government.

When the real assets used by a firm ultimately generate income, that income is allocated to investors according to their ownership of financial assets, or securities, issued by the firm. Bondholders, for example, are entitled to a flow of income based on the interest rate and par value of the bond. Equityholders or stockholders are entitled to any residual income after bondholders and other creditors are paid. In this way the values of financial assets are derived from and depend on the values of the underlying real assets of the firm.

Real assets are income-generating assets, whereas financial assets define the allocation of income or wealth among investors. Individuals can choose between consuming their current endowments of wealth today and investing for the future. When they invest for the future, they may choose to hold financial assets. The money a firm receives when it issues securities (sells them to investors) is used to purchase real assets. Ultimately, then, the returns on a financial asset come from the income produced by the real assets that are financed by the issuance of the security. In this way, it is useful to view financial assets as the means by which individuals hold their claims on real assets in well-developed economies. Most of us cannot personally own a bank, but we can hold shares of the Royal Bank or the Bank of Nova Scotia, which provide us with income derived from providing banking services.

An operational distinction between real and financial assets involves the balance sheets of individuals and firms in the economy. Real assets appear only on the asset side of the balance sheet. In contrast, financial assets always appear on both sides of balance sheets. Your financial claim on a firm is an asset, but the firm's issuance of that claim is the firm's liability. When we aggregate over all balance sheets, financial assets will cancel out, leaving only the sum of real assets as the net wealth of the aggregate economy.

Another way of distinguishing between financial and real assets is to note that financial assets are created *and destroyed* in the ordinary course of doing business. For example, when a loan is paid off, both the creditor's claim (a financial asset) and the debtor's obligation (a financial liability) cease to exist. In contrast, real assets are destroyed only by accident or by wearing out over time.

The distinction between real and financial assets is apparent when we compare the composition of national wealth in Canada, presented in Table 1.1, with the financial assets and liabilities of Canadian households and small businesses, shown in Table 1.2. National wealth consists of structures, equipment, inventories of goods, and land. (It does not include the value of "human capital," the value of the earnings potential of the work force.) In contrast, Table 1.2 includes financial assets such as bank accounts, corporate equity, bonds, and mortgages.

Individuals in Canada tend to hold their financial claims in an indirect form. In fact, only a small proportion of the adult Canadian population holds shares directly. The claims of most individuals on firms are mediated through institutions that hold shares on their behalf: institutional investors such as pension funds, insurance companies, mutual funds, and college endowments.

Concept Check	Question 1. Are the following assets real or financial?
	a. Patents.
	b. Lease obligations.
	c. Customer good will.
	d. A college education.
	e. A $5 bill.

TABLE 1.1   National Net Worth, 1990

Assets	$ Billion
Residential structures	607
Plant and equipment	900
Consumer durables	242
Inventories	118
Land	+ 438
Net claims on foreigners	− 259
TOTAL	**2,046***

* Column sum may differ from total because of rounding errors.

Data from *Statistics Canada cat. # 13-214 Financial Flow and Balance Sheets Accounts*, 1990.

TABLE 1.2   Balance Sheet of Canadian Households and Unincorporated Businesses, 1990

Assets	$ Billion	% Total	Liabilities and Net Worth	$ Billion	% Total
Tangible Assets					
Residential structures	513	23.1	Consumer credit	98	4.4
Nonresidential			Other loans	51	2.3
structures	34	1.5	Mortgages	269	12.1
Machinery and			Other	1	.1
equipment	14	.6	**Total liabilities**	419	18.9
Consumer durables	242	10.9			
Inventories	15	.7			
Land	240	10.8			
Total tangibles	1,058	47.6			
Financial Assets					
Deposits and cash	423	19.0			
Short-term debt	46	2.1			
Mortgages	21	.9			
Long-term debt	58	2.6			
Life insurance and					
pensions	324	14.6			
Equity and foreign					
investments	242	10.9			
Other financial assets	50	2.2			
Total financial assets	1,165	52.4	**Net Worth**	1,804	81.1
TOTAL	2,223	100.0		2,223	100.0

Data from *Statistics Canada cat. # 13-214 Financial Flow and Balance Sheets Accounts,* 1990, table 02-27.

1.2   *Clients of the Financial System*

We start our analysis with a broad view of the major clients that place demands on the financial system. By considering the needs of these clients, we can gain considerable insight into why organizations and institutions evolved as they have.

We can classify the clientele of the investment environment into four groups: the household sector, the corporate sector, the government sector, and the foreign sector. This classification is not perfect. It excludes some organizations, such as not-for-profit agencies, and has difficulty with some hybrids, such as unincorporated or family-run businesses and public corporations. Nevertheless, from the standpoint of capital markets, the four-group classification is useful.

The Household Sector

Households constantly make economic decisions concerning such activities as work, job training, retirement planning, and savings versus consumption. We will consider most of these decisions as already made, and focus on financial decisions specifically. Essentially, we concern ourselves only with what financial assets households desire to hold.

Even this limited focus, however, leaves a broad range of issues to consider. Most households are potentially interested in a wide array of assets, and the assets that are attractive can vary considerably depending on the household's economic situation. Even a limited consideration of taxes and risk preferences can lead to widely varying asset demands, and this demand for variety is, as we shall see, a driving force behind financial innovation.

Taxes lead to varying asset demands because people in different tax brackets "transform" before-tax income into after-tax income at different rates. For example, income from dividends and capital gains is taxed at a lower rate than interest income. High tax-bracket investors naturally will seek securities that generate income from capital gains and dividends, compared with low tax-bracket investors who may prefer fully taxable interest-bearing instruments. There are also some types of shares issued by natural resource companies that transfer unused tax benefits to their owners; these are also highly favoured by high tax-bracket investors. A desire to minimize taxes also leads to demand for portfolios of such securities. In other words, differential tax status creates "tax clienteles" that in turn give rise to demand for a range of assets with a variety of tax implications. The demand of investors encourages entrepreneurs to offer such portfolios (for a fee, of course!).

Risk considerations also create demand for a diverse set of investment alternatives. At an obvious level, differences in risk tolerance create demand for assets with a variety of risk-return combinations. Individuals also have particular hedging requirements that contribute to diverse investment demands.

Consider, for example, a resident of Toronto who plans to sell her house and retire to Miami, Florida, in 15 years. Such a plan seems feasible if real estate prices in the two cities do not diverge before her retirement. How can one hedge Miami real estate prices now, short of purchasing a home there immediately rather than at retirement? One way to hedge the risk is to purchase securities that will increase in value if Florida real estate becomes more expensive. This creates a hedging demand for an asset with a particular risk characteristic. Such demands lead profit-seeking financial corporations to supply the desired goods: observe Florida real estate investment trusts (REITs) that allow individuals to invest in securities whose performance is tied to Florida real estate prices. If Florida real estate becomes more expensive, the REIT will increase in value. The Toronto woman's loss as a potential purchaser of Florida real estate is offset by her gain as an investor in that real estate. This is only one example of how a myriad of risk-specific assets are demanded *and created* by agents in the financial environment.

Risk motives also lead to demand for ways that investors can easily diversify their portfolios and even out their risk exposure. We will see that these diversification motives inevitably give rise to mutual funds that offer small individual investors the ability to invest in a wide range of stocks, bonds, precious metals, and virtually all other financial instruments.

The Business Sector

Whereas household financial decisions are concerned with how to invest money, businesses typically need to raise money to finance their investments in real assets: plant, equipment, technological know-how, and so forth. Table 1.3 presents balance sheets of Canadian private corporations and government enterprises as a whole for 1990. The heavy concentration on tangible assets is obvious. Broadly speaking, there are two ways for private businesses to raise money—they can borrow it, either from banks or directly from households by issuing bonds, or they can "take in new partners" by issuing stocks, which are ownership shares in the firm. Public enterprises can, in addition, also obtain money from the government budget, which is financed through taxes.

Businesses issuing securities to the public have several objectives. First, they want to get the best price possible for their securities. Second, they want to market the issues to the public at the lowest possible cost. This has two implications. First, businesses might want to farm out the marketing of their securities to firms that specialize in such security issuance, because it is unlikely that any single firm is in the market often enough to justify a full-time security issuance division. Issue of securities requires immense effort. The security issue must be brought to the attention of the public. Buyers then must subscribe to the issue, and records of subscriptions and deposits must be kept. The allocation of the security to each buyer must be determined, and subscribers finally must exchange money for the securities. These activities clearly call for specialists. The complexities of security issuance have been the catalyst for creation of an investment banking industry catering to business demands. (We will return to this industry shortly.)

The second implication of the desire for low-cost security issuance is that most businesses will prefer to issue fairly simple securities that require the least extensive incremental analysis and, correspondingly, are the least expensive to arrange. Such a demand for simplicity or uniformity by business-sector security issuers is likely to be at odds with the household sector's demand for a wide variety of risk-specific securities. This mismatch of objectives gives rise to an industry of middlemen who act as intermediaries between the two sectors, specializing in transforming simple securities to complex issues that suit particular market niches.

The Government Sector

Like businesses, governments often need to finance their expenditures by borrowing. Unlike businesses, governments cannot sell equity shares; they are restricted to borrowing to raise funds when tax revenues are not sufficient to cover expenditures. The federal government can also print money, of course,

TABLE 1.3   Balance Sheet of Nonfinancial Canadian Corporations, 1990
(Private, Public)*

Assets	$ Billion	% Total	Liabilities and Net Worth	$ Billion	% Total
Tangible Assets					
Residential structures	87	6.4	Finance and other		
Nonresidential structures	390	28.5	short-term paper	56	4.1
Machinery and equipment	197	14.4	Trade payables	94	6.9
Inventories	103	7.5	Bank loans	103	7.5
Land	135	9.9	Other loans	47	3.4
Total tangibles	**911**	**66.5**	Bonds and		
			mortgages	212	15.5
Financial Assets			Corporate claims	577	42.1
			Other liabilities	47	3.4
Deposits and cash	59	4.3	**Total liabilities**	**1,135**	**82.8**
Consumer credit	2	0.1			
Trade receivables	105	7.7			
Short-term debt securities	34	2.5			
Mortgages and long-term					
debt securities	14	1.0			
Corporate claims	188	13.7			
Equity and foreign					
investments	8	0.6			
Other financial assets	49	3.6			
Total financial assets	**459**	**33.5**	**Net worth**	**235**	**17.2**
TOTAL	1,370	100.0		1,370	100.0

* Column sum may differ from total because of rounding errors.

Data from *Statistics Canada cat. # 13-214 Financial Flow and Balance Sheet Accounts,* 1990, table 02-27.

but this source of funds is limited by its inflationary implications, and so most national governments usually try to avoid excessive use of the printing press.

Governments have a special advantage in borrowing money because their taxing power makes them very creditworthy and therefore able to borrow at the lowest rates. The financial component of the consolidated balance sheet of all levels of government is presented in Table 1.4. Notice that the major liabilities are government securities.

Although all levels of government have the power to tax, the federal government has special powers not available to the others, through its control over the Bank of Canada. The latter is the main institution responsible for Canada's monetary policy. This policy is a major determinant of Canada's economic performance, including output growth, price level, and interest rates.

A second, special role of the government is to regulate the financial environment. This is fulfilled in Canada by both federal and provincial governments,

TABLE 1.4   Financial Assets and Liabilities of Canadian Governments, 1990

Assets	$ Billion	% Total	Liabilities	$ Billion	% Total
Deposits and currency	12	4.5	Currency and reports	2	0.4
Trade receivables	3	1.0	Payables and loans	24	4.3
Loans	12	4.5	Short-term paper	153	27.1
Short-term paper	20	7.3	Federal, provincial,		
Mortgages	4	1.3	municipal, and other		
Federal, provincial,			bonds	343	60.7
municipal, and other			Life insurance and		
bonds	79	28.7	pensions	1	0.1
Government enter-			Government enter-		
prise claims	117	42.6	prise claims	8	1.4
Equity and foreign			Other liabilities	34	6.0
investments	7	2.6			
Other financial assets	21	7.5			
TOTAL	**274**	**100.0**	**TOTAL**	**565**	**100.0**

Data from *Statistics Canada cat. 34-214 Financial Flow and Balance Sheet Accounts,* 1990, table 02-27.

resulting in a fragmented regulatory system. Since trading in Canadian financial markets often transcends interprovincial borders, the fragmentation of the regulatory system has at times created inefficiencies and problems of law enforcement.

Some government regulations are relatively innocuous. For example, the Ontario Securities Commission is responsible for disclosure laws that are designed to enforce truthfulness in various financial transactions that take place in that province. Other types of government intervention in the financial markets, however, have been more controversial. For instance, both federal and provincial governments have instituted programs to encourage investment in certain sectors. One example is the *flow-through* share program, that transfers tax benefits from resource expenditures to investors in mineral and petroleum firms. This program allowed many small exploration companies to raise capital at much lower rates than would have been available under normal circumstances; it also encouraged unprofitable exploratory activity. The 1990 tax reform sharply reduced the transferable tax benefits and, consequently, the attractiveness of these shares.

The Foreign Sector

Recall the previous example of the Torontonian who plans to retire to Florida and hedges Miami real estate prices by purchasing Florida REITs. She is an example of a Canadian resident holding U.S. assets. Conversely, a Japanese furniture manufacturer who uses imported Canadian lumber as raw material faces the risk of rising production costs every time Canadian forest product prices rise. He can hedge this risk by purchasing a portfolio of shares of Cana-

TABLE 1.5 Foreign Sector Balance Sheet, 1990

	Assets ($ billion)	Liabilities ($ billion)	Net Canadian Holdings ($ billion)
United States	101.9	209.3	(107.4)
Rest of world	149.436	301.21	(151.774)
TOTAL	**251.336**	**510.510**	**(259.174)**

Data provided by *Statistics Canada*, Balance of Payments Department.

dian forest products firms, whose price would also rise with that of their products. These two examples illustrate how demand is created for financial assets that transcend a country's frontier. Such assets carry an additional risk, associated with the fluctuations of the exchange rates between Canadian and foreign currencies.

Table 1.5 shows the foreign sector's balance sheet for 1990, broken down by U.S. and other foreign holdings. In both cases the Canadian position is highly negative, reflecting the importance of foreign firms in the Canadian economy. The relatively large numbers reflected in these reciprocal holdings show the need for the creation of financial instruments that can be used to hedge against foreign exchange risk. We will see that the market has responded by offering both Canadian and foreign investors a large number of alternatives from which to choose.

1.3 *The Canadian Tax System*

Investment choice by individuals is a process of placing funds temporarily under the control of others in the hope of obtaining a future cash flow greater than the amount invested. Governments consider the increase in funds, or the return on investment, to be taxable, like earned income. For the investor, the return available after tax is what is relevant. Frequently, the tax payable may reflect the risk involved in the investment; hence, the government may encourage risky investments by exempting part, or even all, of their returns from income tax. In order to stimulate investment in certain areas or of certain types, the government may legislate particularly favourable tax treatment. Thus tax policy is often (many would say always) a reflection of social policy.

In Canada, the three major characteristics of income tax that are relevant to investment are the treatment of interest, dividends, and capital gains. The receipt of interest is predictable and relatively certain (barring default by the borrower), leading the government to tax it as ordinary income. In order to promote savings and investment by households, the first $1,000 of interest income used to be exempt from tax. Since equity capital is safer for corporations than is debt, purchase of equity was encouraged by giving dividends a lower effective tax rate; this was accomplished by a complicated procedure that first "grossed up" the actual dividend to a larger amount to be included in income, and then allowed a credit against tax payable. Prior to 1972, capital gains were completely exempt from income tax; as of January 1, 1972, 50 percent of the gain was exempted, with the remainder taxed as ordinary income. The result of this system was that $1 of interest was worth less than $1 of dividends, which was worth less than $1 of capital gains. Thus the system rewarded long-term equity investment for the purpose of growth more than equity investment for income, in turn more than interest income; risk-taking paid off.

The Canadian system at that time somewhat resembled the U.S. system, in the level of capital gains exemption and the more favourable treatment of growth equity; the United States did not, however, give any preference to dividend income, nor did it exempt some interest income. The United States currently has a system that does not distinguish between any kind of investment income, derived from equity or debt. Under their tax reform, all marginal income tax rates were lowered, but the price paid was the elimination of the capital gains exemption.

Under Canadian tax reform, a number of significant changes occurred over the last 15 years. The $1,000 interest exemption was lost; the effective tax rate on dividends was increased; and the exemption of part of the capital gain was reduced. For a brief period, a lifetime exemption of $500,000 on capital gains was given to each investor; thus for the great majority of investors (classified as small or medium), capital gains were free of tax. Social pressures have reduced the lifetime exemption to a current level of $100,000 per individual; at this level, while for small investors no tax is payable, the limit is certainly attainable for most investors over a lifetime of investment. This is significant since it means that investment choices must be made on the basis of eventual taxation of capital gains; every capital gain taken today that is tax free has the effect of making a later one taxable. Those investors whose gains are taxable face income tax on 75 percent of the capital gain. Currently, dividends are grossed up by 25 percent, and 13⅓ percent of the grossed-up amount is taken as a tax credit.

Let us examine how taxes affect the returns of investments for the purpose of gaining interest, dividends, and capital gains. Suppose that $1,000 of income is gained in each case. In these calculations, it is normal to assume that investors are in the top marginal bracket and have exhausted their capital gains exemptions; the last dollar invested in one instrument or another is an incremental dollar that faces the highest rate applicable to an investor. We use the combined 1992 federal and provincial tax rate for Ontario, 50.46 percent. The after-tax return on the debt investment is then:

$$(1 - .5046) \times \$1,000 = \$495.40$$

For the dividend income, $1,000 is increased to $1,250 and then taxed at the basic federal rate of 29 percent, or:

$$.29 \times \$1,250 = \$362.50$$

The tax credit of $13\frac{1}{3}$ percent of the grossed-up $1,250, or $166.67, reduces this to $195.80 of basic federal tax. Then both federal surtax (8 percent) and provincial tax (66 percent of basic federal tax) are added for a total tax payable of:

$$(1 + .08 + .66) \times \$195.80 = \$340.69$$

The after-tax return on the dividend income is then:

$$\$1,000 - \$340.69 = \$659.31$$

Finally, a $1,000 capital gain is only 75 percent taxable at 50.46 percent, so the after-tax gain is:

$$\$1,000 \times (1 - .5046 \times .75) = \$621.55$$

We see that currently in Ontario, dividends actually have a less than 4 percent advantage over capital gains and more than 16 percent advantage over interest.

Table 1.6 displays the after-tax return on income from interest, dividends, and capital gains from Ontario, Quebec, and British Columbia, using 1991 rates. Note that the difference between current income and growth in equity investment is relatively inconsequential. This is equivalent to the current situation in the United States, and is of interest to corporate management in its dividend policy.

One other important detail of taxation involves timing. Generally, income is taxed in the year that it is received, although corporations may account for income on an accrual basis. Bond interest is then taxed when received, which is determined as the payment date by the issuer; similarly, dividends are taxed as of the payment date (not to be confused with the declaration or record dates). Capital gains are based on the years of purchase and sale; because of transfer

TABLE 1.6 After-Tax Retention of Income from Interest, Dividends, and Capital Gains, 1991

Province	Ontario	Quebec	British Columbia
Combined federal and provincial tax rate	49.11%	51.12%	48.33%
Retention rate on:			
Interest	50.89	48.88	51.67
Dividends	66.83	62.77	67.36
Capital gains	63.16	61.66	63.75

delays, the date for tax purposes—the **settlement date**—is formally five business days after the actual trade date (this makes the days prior to Christmas an active period of trading, as annual gains and losses are established).

One exception to the actual receipt of cash occurs for so-called **zero-coupon bonds**, or **zeroes** (described in Section 1.4), and similarly for compound interest savings bonds. Although no actual interest is paid, interest is imputed from the increase in value over the life of the zero-coupon bond; similarly, the savings bond interest is not received until redemption. In both cases, the income tax is paid annually on the imputed interest, making these negative cash flow instruments. Note that the government is precluding the possibility of an investor claiming the increase in value of the zero, from its initial discounted value to its redemption value, as a capital gain to be taxed at the preferential rate.

The significance of the after-tax returns on different forms of investment is that the prices of financial assets are determined by the returns, on an after-tax basis, that are required by investors in recompense for the risks posed by the assets. Investment choices in response to tax policies must be made from the available set of instruments that are competitively priced to appeal to the investing public. As previously mentioned, occasionally governments may judge that the investment appeal of certain assets does not attract sufficient capital; in such cases, additional incentives may be offered to increase their appeal.

1.4   *The Environment Responds to Clientele Demands*

When enough clients demand and are willing to pay for a service, it is likely in a capitalistic economy that a profit-seeking supplier will find a way to provide and charge for that service. This is the mechanism that leads to the diversity of financial markets. Let us consider the market responses to the disparate demands of the three sectors.

Financial Intermediation

Recall that the financial problem facing households is how best to invest their funds. The relative smallness of most households makes direct investment intrinsically difficult. A small investor obviously cannot advertise in the local newspaper his or her willingness to lend money to businesses that need to finance investments. Instead, **financial intermediaries** such as banks, investment companies, insurance companies, or credit unions naturally evolve to bring the two sectors together. Financial intermediaries sell their own liabilities to raise funds that are used to purchase liabilities of other corporations.

For example, a bank raises funds by borrowing (taking in deposits) and lending that money to (purchasing the loans of) other borrowers. The spread between the rates paid to depositors and the rates charged to borrowers is the source of the bank's profit. In this way, lenders and borrowers do not need to contact each other directly. Instead, each goes to the bank, which acts as an intermediary between the two. The problem of matching lenders with borrowers is solved when each comes independently to the common intermediary. The convenience and cost savings the bank offers the borrowers and lenders allow it to profit on the spread between the rates on its loans and the rates on its deposits. In other words, the problem of coordination creates a market niche for the bank as intermediary. Profit opportunities alone dictate that banks will emerge in a trading economy.

Financial intermediaries are distinguished from other businesses in that both their assets and their liabilities are overwhelmingly financial. Table 1.7 shows that the balance sheets of financial institutions include very small amounts of tangible assets. Compare Table 1.7 with Table 1.3, the balance sheet of the

TABLE 1.7 Balance Sheet of Financial Institutions, 1990

Assets	$ Billion	% Total	Liabilities and Net Worth	$ Billion	% Total
Equipment and structures	47	3.1	Deposits	583	38.4
Land	9	0.6	Loans	26	1.7
Total tangibles	**56**	**3.7**	Money market securities	17	1.1
			Bonds and mortgages	48	3.2
Financial Assets			Life insurance and pensions	324	21.3
Deposits and cash	71	4.7	Corporate claims	432	28.4
Consumer credit	96	6.3	Other	72	4.7
Loans	204	13.4	**Total liabilities**	**1,502**	**98.8**
Money market securities	109	7.2			
Mortgages and long-term debt securities	517	34.0			
Corporate equity and foreign investments	422	27.8			
Other	45	3.0			
Total financial assets	**1,464**	**96.4**	**Net worth**	**18**	**1.2**
TOTAL	**1,520**	**100.0**		**1,520**	**100.0**

Data from *Statistics Canada cat. # 34-214 Financial Flow and Balance Sheet Accounts*, 1990, table 02-27.

nonfinancial corporate sector. The contrast arises precisely because intermediaries are middlemen, simply moving funds from one sector to another. In fact, from a bird's-eye view, this is the primary social function of such intermediaries, to channel household savings to the business sector.

Other examples of financial intermediaries are investment companies, insurance companies, and credit unions. All these firms offer similar advantages, in addition to playing a middleman role. First, by pooling the resources of many small investors, they are able to lend considerable sums to large borrowers. Second, by lending to many borrowers, intermediaries achieve significant diversification, meaning they can accept loans that individually might be risky. Third, intermediaries build expertise through the volume of business they do. One individual trying to borrow or lend directly would have much less specialized knowledge of how to structure and execute the transaction with another party.

Investment companies, which pool together and manage the money of many investors, also arise out of the "smallness problem." Here, the problem is that most household portfolios are not large enough to be spread among a wide variety of securities. It is very expensive in terms of brokerage fees to purchase one or two shares of many different firms, and it clearly is more economical for stocks and bonds to be purchased and sold in large blocks. This observation reveals a profit opportunity that has been filled by mutual funds offered by many investment companies. **Mutual funds** pool the limited funds of small investors into large amounts, thereby gaining the advantages of large-scale trading; investors are assigned a prorated share of the total funds according to the size of their investment. This system gives small investors advantages that they are willing to pay for via a management fee to the mutual fund operator. Mutual funds are logical extensions of an investment club or cooperative, in which individuals themselves team up and pool funds. The fund sets up shop as a firm that accepts the assets of many investors, acting as an investment agent on their behalf. Again, the advantages of specialization are sufficiently large that the fund can provide a valuable service and still charge enough for it to clear a handsome profit.

Investment companies also can design portfolios specifically for large investors with particular goals. In contrast, mutual funds are sold in the retail market, and their investment philosophies are differentiated mainly by strategies that are likely to attract a large number of clients. Some investment companies manage *commingled funds,* in which the monies of different clients with similar goals are merged into a *mini-mutual fund,* which is run according to the common preferences of those clients.

Economies of scale also explain the proliferation of analytic services available to investors. Newsletters, data bases, and brokerage house research services all exploit the fact that the expense of collecting information is best borne by having a few agents engage in research to be sold to a large client base. This set-up arises naturally. Investors clearly want information, but with only small portfolios to manage, they do not find it economical to incur the expense of collecting it. Hence, a profit opportunity emerges: a firm can perform this service for many clients and charge for it.

Investment Banking

Just as economies of scale and specialization create profit opportunities for financial intermediaries, so too do these economies create niches for firms that perform specialized services for businesses. We said before that firms raise much of their capital by selling securities such as stocks and bonds to the public. Because these firms do not do so frequently, however, investment banking firms that specialize in such activities are able to offer their services at a cost below that of running an in-house security issuance division.

Investment bankers or, as they are known in Canada, **investment dealers,** such as Scotia McLeod, RBC Dominion, or Burns Fry, advise the issuing firm on the prices it can charge for the securities issued, market conditions, appropriate interest rates, and so forth. Ultimately, the investment banking firm handles the marketing of the security issue to the public.

Investment dealers also can help firms design securities with special, desirable properties. As an example of this practice, consider a pharmaceutical company undertaking a risky research and development (R&D) project for a new drug. It needs to raise money for research costs, and realizes that if the research is successful the company will need to build a new manufacturing plant requiring still more financing. To deal with this contingency, the investment dealer might design a bond-with-warrant issue. (A *warrant* is a security giving its holder the option to purchase stock from the firm at a specified price up until the warrant's expiration date.) The bonds and warrants are issued, and the research commences. If the research is eventually successful, the stock price will increase, the warrant holders will find it advantageous to exercise their options to purchase additional shares, and as they purchase those shares, additional funds will flow to the firm precisely as they are needed to finance the new manufacturing plant. The design of the financing scheme lets the firm avoid two separate security offerings and saves the considerable costs of the second offering. The exercise of the warrants provides additional financing at no additional flotation costs.

Financial Innovation

The example of the pharmaceutical company illustrates one source of financial innovation. The company's need for initial and contingent financing led to a creative packaging of securities that met the particular needs of the firm. The investment diversity desired by households, however, is far greater than most businesses have a desire to satisfy. Most firms find it simpler to issue "plain vanilla" securities, leaving exotic variants to others who specialize in financial markets. This, of course, creates a profit opportunity for innovative security design and repackaging that investment dealers are only too happy to fill.

Consider the astonishing changes in the mortgage markets since 1970, when mortgage **pass-through securities** were first introduced in the United States by the Government National Mortgage Association (GNMA, or Ginnie Mae). In Canada, these same instruments became available as National Housing Act (NHA) mortgage-backed securities (MBSs); this occurred in 1986, when the government took direct action to improve the liquidity of the mortgage market. The NHA MBS represents an undivided interest in a relatively homogeneous pool of residential mortgages insured and guaranteed by the Canada Mortgage and Housing Corporation (CMHC). MBS holders receive prorated shares of all the principal and interest payments made on the underlying mortgage pool. For example, the pool might total $10 million of 12 percent, 30-year amortization, 5-year term mortgages. The rights to the cash flows could then be sold as 500 units, each worth $20,000. Each unit holder would then receive 1/500 of all monthly interest and principal payments made on the pool. The banks that originated the mortgages continue to service them, but no longer own the mortgage investments; these have been passed through to the MBS holders.

Mortgage-backed securities were a tremendous innovation in mortgage markets. The *securitization* of mortgages meant that mortgages could be traded just like other securities in national financial markets. Availability of funds no longer depended on local credit conditions; with mortgage pass-throughs trading in national markets, mortgage funds could flow from any region to wherever demand was greatest.

The next round of innovation began when it became apparent that investors might be interested in mortgage-backed securities with different effective times to maturity. Thus was born the *collateralized mortgage obligation* (CMO), for which an active market exists in the United States but not in Canada. The CMO meets the demand for mortgage-backed securities with a range of maturities by dividing the overall pool into a series of classes, called *tranches*. The so-called fast-pay tranche receives all the principal payments made on the entire mortgage pool until the total investment of the investors in the tranche is repaid. In the meantime, investors in the other tranches receive only interest on their investment. In this way the fast-pay tranche is retired first and is the shortest-term mortgage-backed security. The next tranche then receives all of the principal payments until it is retired, and so on, until the slow-pay tranche, the longest-term class, finally receives payback of principal after all other tranches have been retired.

Although these securities are relatively complex, the message here is that security demand elicited a market response. The waves of product development in the last two decades are responses to perceived profit opportunities created by as-yet unsatisfied demands for securities with particular risk, return, tax, and timing attributes. As the investment banking industry becomes even more sophisticated, security creation and customization become more routine. Most new securities are created by dismantling and rebundling more basic securities. A Wall Street joke asks how many investment bankers it takes to sell a light bulb. The answer is 100—one to break the bulb and 99 to sell off the individual fragments.

This discussion leads to the notion of primitive versus derivative securities. A **primitive security** offers returns based only on the status of the issuer, who is generally a corporation or government. For example, corporate bonds make stipulated interest payments depending only on the solvency of the issuing firm. Dividends paid to stockholders depend as well on the board of directors' assessment of the firm's financial position. In contrast, **derivative securities** yield returns that depend on additional factors pertaining to the prices of other assets. For example, the payoff to stock options depends on the price of the underlying stock, and not on the financial conditions of the writer (issuer) of the option. In our mortgage examples the derivative mortgage-backed securities offer payouts that depend on the original mortgages, which are the primitive securities. Much of the innovation in security design may be viewed as the continual creation of new types of derivative securities from the available set of primitive securities.

Concept Check	Question 2. If you take out a car loan, is the loan a primitive security or a derivative security?
	Question 3. Explain how a car loan from a bank creates both financial assets and financial liabilities.

Response to Taxation and Regulation

We have seen that much financial innovation and security creation may be viewed as a natural market response to unfulfilled investor needs. Another driving force behind innovation is the ongoing game played between governments and investors on taxation and regulation. Many financial innovations are direct responses to government attempts either to regulate or to tax investments of various sorts. We already saw one such example in the case of the flow-through shares. We can also provide several other examples, originating in the United States and subsequently appearing in Canada to serve investment needs.

Prior to 1980, U.S. banking was restricted by Regulation Q, which put a ceiling on interest rates that banks were allowed to pay to their depositors. This regulation spurred the growth of the money market industry, but it also was one reason for the birth of the Eurodollar market. Because Regulation Q did not apply to dollar-denominated time deposits in foreign accounts, many U.S. banks and foreign competitors established branches in Western Europe, where they could offer competitive rates outside the jurisdiction of U.S. regulators. The growth of the Eurodollar market was also the result of another U.S. regulation: reserve requirements. Foreign branches were exempt from such requirements and were thus better able to compete for deposits. Ironically, despite the fact that Regulation Q no longer exists, not only does the Eurodollar market continue to thrive, but other markets in the world's major currencies (Eurocurrencies) have been created as well.

Another innovation attributable largely to tax avoidance motives is the long-term deep discount, or zero-coupon, bond. These bonds pay little or no interest, instead providing most or all of the return to investors through a redemption price that is higher than the initial sales price. Corporations were allowed, for tax purposes, to impute an implied interest expense based on this built-in price appreciation. Originally, the technique for imputing tax-deductible interest expenses was excessively advantageous to corporations, resulting in a large number of issues of these bonds; ultimately, the interest imputation procedures were amended, and the issue of zeroes for tax purposes ended.

Meanwhile, however, the financial markets had discovered that zeroes were useful ways to lock in a long-term investment return. When the supply of primitive zero-coupon bonds ended, financial innovators created derivative zeroes by purchasing Government of Canada bonds, "stripping" off the coupons, and selling them separately as zeroes. The major Canadian investment dealers combined to institutionalize these stripped bonds by selling claims against a pool of government bonds under the name of *Sentinels*. Various instruments with catchy names such as *Cougars, TIGRs,* and *LYONS* were issued by other financial institutions, using acronyms such as the LYONS, Merrill Lynch's liquid-yield option notes, which are zero-coupon convertible bonds for corporate issuers.

Another tax-induced innovation is the **dual fund**. Under old U.S. tax laws, capital gains were taxed at lower rates than were dividends. The differential meant high tax-bracket investors preferred capital gains, whereas tax-exempt investors were happy to receive dividends. Entrepreneurs then created dual funds (the derivative asset) in which *income* and *capital* shares on a portfolio of stocks (the primitive assets) were sold separately. The income shareholders receive the dividends on the portfolio, plus their share of the initial value when the portfolio is cashed in. The capital shareholders receive their share of initial value plus any accumulated capital gains. More recently, this splitting of income and capital shares has been effected on individual stocks in both the United States and Canada. With tax reform, the only interest in such instruments lies in the new risk-return characteristics that they create. Accordingly, sophisticated investors have maintained activity in the markets for the split shares, by trading in bank capital shares (created for the major Canadian banks) and capital shares of Bell Canada Enterprises.

There are plenty of other examples. The Eurobond market came into existence as a response to changes in U.S. tax laws. Financial futures markets were

TABLE 1.8 Innovative Instruments Managed by Merrill Lynch in 1991 for Canadian Issuers

Issuer	Size of Issue ($ millions)	Type of Instrument (yield)	Maturity	Characteristic
Ontario Hydro	$1,250 (Cdn)	Global bonds (10⅞%)	1996	First global debt offering by a Canadian issuer
Rogers Communications	$718.75 (US)	LYONS (variable)	2011	First LYONS offering by a Canadian issuer and first debt offering under the Multijurisdictional Disclosure System
Hydro-Quebec	$900 (US)	Debentures (9.4%)	2021	Largest Yankee debt offering by a Canadian issuer
Rogers Cantel Mobile	$460 (US)	Senior secured guaranteed notes (10¾%)	2001	Largest noninvestment grade offering by a Canadian company
Ontario Hydro	$3,990 (Cdn)	Zero coupon global bonds (discounted)	1992–2031	First global offering of zero coupon debt by a Canadian issuer
PanCanadian Petroleum	$300 (US)	Medium-term notes (by term)	1992–2021	First cross-border medium-term note program under the Multijurisdictional Disclosure System

stimulated by abandonment in the early 1970s of the system of fixed exchange rates, and by new U.S. federal regulations that overrode state laws treating some financial futures as gambling arrangements. Now these financial futures are traded actively in all the world's major financial centres.

The general tendency is clear: tax and regulatory pressures on the financial system very often lead to unanticipated financial innovations when profit-seeking investors make an end run around a government's restrictions. The constant game of regulatory catch-up sets off another flow of new innovations.

Table 1.8 summarizes an advertisement by Merrill Lynch of announcements of innovative instruments issued through them and other investment dealers. These include LYONs and zero-coupon bonds as well as other securities that we will describe later.

1.5 *Markets and Market Structure*

Just as securities and financial institutions come into existence as natural responses to investor demands, so too do markets evolve to meet needs. Consider what would happen if organized markets did not exist. Households that wanted to borrow would need to find others that wanted to lend. Inevitably, a meeting place for borrowers and lenders would be settled on, and that meeting place would evolve into a financial market. A pub in old London called Lloyd's launched the maritime insurance industry. A Manhattan curb on Wall Street became synonymous with the financial world.

We can differentiate four types of markets: direct search markets, brokered markets, dealer markets, and auction markets.

A **direct search market** is the least organized market. Here, buyers and sellers must seek each other out directly. One example of a transaction taking place in such a market would be the sale of a used refrigerator in which the seller advertises for buyers in a local newspaper. Such markets are characterized by sporadic participation and low-priced and nonstandard goods. It does not pay for most people or firms to seek profits by specializing in such an environment.

The next level of organization is a **brokered market.** In markets where trading in a good is sufficiently active, brokers can find it profitable to offer search services to buyers and sellers. A good example is the real estate market, where economies of scale in searches for available homes and for prospective buyers make it worthwhile for participants to pay brokers to conduct the searches for them. Brokers in given markets develop specialized knowledge on valuing assets traded in that given market.

An important brokered investment market is the so-called **primary market,** where new issues of securities are offered to the public. In the primary market, investment dealers act as brokers; they seek out investors to purchase securities directly from the issuing corporation. By contrast, purchase and sale of existing securities among investors take place in the **secondary market**, which means on established security exchanges or in the over-the-counter market.

Another brokered market is that for large **block transactions,** in which very large blocks of stock are bought or sold. These blocks are so large (more than 10,000 shares) that brokers (or ''block houses'') often are engaged to search directly for other large traders, rather than bringing the trade directly to the stock exchange where relatively smaller investors trade. Attempting to sell a large block normally on the exchange would cause the trade price to fall as successive small purchase orders were matched against the block. The block can be recorded, however, as being ''crossed'' on the exchange, when the shares are traded as a block.

When trading activity in a particular type of asset increases, **dealer markets** arise. Here, dealers specialize in various commodities, purchase assets for their own inventory, and sell goods for a profit from their inventory. Dealers, unlike brokers, trade assets for their own accounts. The dealer's profit margin is the ''bid-asked'' spread, the difference between the price at which the dealer buys for and sells from inventory. Dealer markets save traders on search costs because market participants are easily able to look up the prices at which they can buy from or sell to dealers. Obviously, a fair amount of market activity is required before dealing in a market is an attractive source of income. The over-the-counter securities market is one example of a dealer market.

The most integrated market is an **auction market,** in which all transactors in a good converge at one place to bid on or offer a good. The New York Stock Exchange (NYSE) is an example of an auction market, as are all the major Canadian markets. An advantage of auction markets over dealer markets is that one need not search to find the best price for a good. If all participants converge, they can arrive at mutually agreeable prices and thus save the bid-asked spread.[1] Continuous auction markets (as opposed to periodic auctions such as in the art world) require very heavy and frequent trading to cover the expense of maintaining the market. For this reason, larger exchanges set up listing requirements, which limit the shares traded on the exchange to those of firms in which sufficient trading interest is likely to exist.

Concept Check	Question 4. Many assets trade in more than one type of market. What types of markets do the following trade in? *a*. Used cars. *b*. Paintings. *c*. Rare coins.

---

[1] Of course, an observed bid-asked spread is characteristic of the NYSE and TSE, as we see in Chapter 3.

1.6 *Recent Trends*

We have recently seen three trends in the contemporary investment environment:

1. Globalization.
2. Issuing derivative securities.
3. Securitization and credit enhancement.

Each is a logical consequence of the demand and supply forces that give rise to specialized markets and instruments. Although the smaller-sized Canadian financial system has not fostered the growth of the last and more recent of these developments, globalization has always been a feature of Canadian investment and derivative securities have become quite common in Canada.

Globalization

If a wider array of investment choices can improve welfare, why should we limit ourselves to purely domestic assets? **Globalization** requires efficient communication technology and the dismantling of regulatory constraints. These tendencies in worldwide investment environments have encouraged international investing in recent years.

Canadian investors can invest in mutual funds specifically designed to hold shares in foreign assets. The most common of these hold either purely U.S. or internationally diversified portfolios. More recently we have seen mutual funds devoted to single countries, or to specific geographical areas such as Southeast Asia. Canadians can also take advantage of foreign investment opportunities in a number of ways:

1. Purchase of foreign securities (several U.S. firms and a small number of overseas companies), which are cross-listed on Canadian stock markets.
2. Purchase of U.S. securities on U.S. exchanges through Canadian brokers.
3. Purchase of overseas firms whose shares are listed on U.S. exchanges, or for which American Depository Receipts (ADRs) exist; ADRs are U.S.-traded securities representing claims to shares of non-American companies.

Purchasing foreign securities on Canadian exchanges is no more difficult than purchasing Canadian shares. The investor must, however, take care to distinguish foreign firms' securities from those issued by closely held Canadian subsidiaries of foreign parent firms. For instance, while IBM shares on the TSE are claims against the U.S. parent, the shares in Ford Motors represent stock in the subsidiary.

Many foreign firms are so eager to lure U.S. investors that they will save these investors the expense of paying the higher commissions that are associated with the ADRs. This is achieved by a firm's issuing the ADR itself; the instrument is then known as a *sponsored* ADR. Since 1983, only sponsored ADRs have been eligible for listing on the major exchanges. Originally ADRs were *unsponsored,* being created by a depository bank; new unsponsored ADRs must be traded over the counter. A few British firms, such as British Gas (the parent of Consumer Gas), have ADRs that are listed on the TSE, although trading is very illiquid.

It should be noted that the investment implications of holding foreign securities may be significantly different from those of domestic firms. Even U.S. securities traded on the TSE expose their holders to exchange rate risk. Holding U.S. ADRs implies a double exposure to such risk: between foreign currency and U.S. dollars, and between U.S. and Canadian dollars.

Globalization is a major factor in the raising of capital by Canadian corporations and government issuers. Issues and instruments are now described as global when they simultaneously appear domestically and in foreign markets; portions of the total issue are allocated to different markets and, in the case of equities, may be denominated in both the Canadian dollar and the currency of the other market, where the shares will continue to trade quoted in that currency. Magna International offered shares under the Multijurisdictional Disclosure System at $16.50 Canadian and $14.60 U.S.; two global bond issues were reported in Table 1.8. Certain global offerings of the past, particularly privatizations of British corporations, have given rise to trading in their shares on the TSE; the lack of liquidity after the initial offering means that investors will usually do better to trade these in New York.

The federal and provincial governments, their agencies, and larger Canadian corporations have long been engaged in issuing debt or equity instruments in foreign markets, and, in particular, debt denominated in foreign currencies. Foreign currencies expose the issuer to foreign exchange risk, for example a deutschemark bond becomes expensive if the mark appreciates against the dollar; this may be controlled, however, if the issuer takes steps to hedge against currency fluctuations or even uses the bond to offset foreign currency receipts.

The Export Development Corporation (EDC) has been especially active in issuing innovative instruments. Figure 1.1 shows an instance where EDC issued a bond denominated in the European currency unit, known as the ECU. Canadian or other investors purchasing this bond will be protected against depreciation of their domestic currency with respect to the basket of European currencies still used in the European Common Market.

An idea of the size and diversity of the international debt markets can be gained from Table 1.9, drawn from an announcement by the Union Bank of Switzerland of financings arranged by it for Canadian issuers in the first half of 1991. A similar announcement by Merrill Lynch noted that it ranked first (followed by Goldman Sachs, Morgan Stanley, Deutsche Bank, and CS First Boston—all foreign investment bankers) in international debt and equity issues by Canadians in 1991. They reported having offered $7.292 billion (U.S.), repre-

FIGURE 1.1
Globalization: A bond issue denominated in European Currency Units.

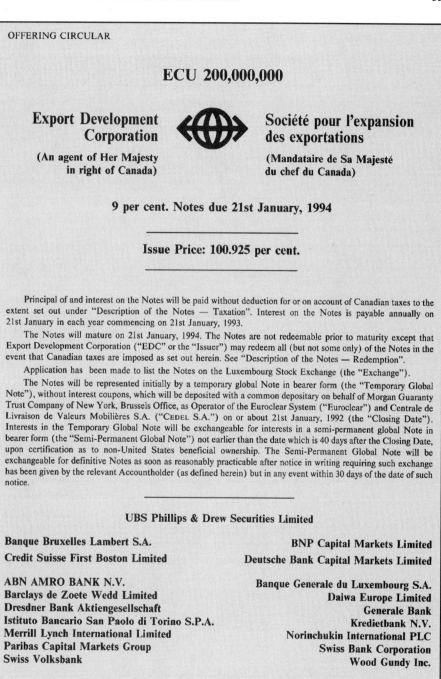

OFFERING CIRCULAR

ECU 200,000,000

Export Development Corporation

(An agent of Her Majesty in right of Canada)

Société pour l'expansion des exportations

(Mandataire de Sa Majesté du chef du Canada)

9 per cent. Notes due 21st January, 1994

Issue Price: 100.925 per cent.

Principal of and interest on the Notes will be paid without deduction for or on account of Canadian taxes to the extent set out under "Description of the Notes — Taxation". Interest on the Notes is payable annually on 21st January in each year commencing on 21st January, 1993.

The Notes will mature on 21st January, 1994. The Notes are not redeemable prior to maturity except that Export Development Corporation ("EDC" or the "Issuer") may redeem all (but not some only) of the Notes in the event that Canadian taxes are imposed as set out herein. See "Description of the Notes — Redemption".

Application has been made to list the Notes on the Luxembourg Stock Exchange (the "Exchange").

The Notes will be represented initially by a temporary global Note in bearer form (the "Temporary Global Note"), without interest coupons, which will be deposited with a common depositary on behalf of Morgan Guaranty Trust Company of New York, Brussels Office, as Operator of the Euroclear System ("Euroclear") and Centrale de Livraison de Valeurs Mobilières S.A. ("CEDEL S.A.") on or about 21st January, 1992 (the "Closing Date"). Interests in the Temporary Global Note will be exchangeable for interests in a semi-permanent global Note in bearer form (the "Semi-Permanent Global Note") not earlier than the date which is 40 days after the Closing Date, upon certification as to non-United States beneficial ownership. The Semi-Permanent Global Note will be exchangeable for definitive Notes as soon as reasonably practicable after notice in writing requiring such exchange has been given by the relevant Accountholder (as defined herein) but in any event within 30 days of the date of such notice.

UBS Phillips & Drew Securities Limited

Banque Bruxelles Lambert S.A.

Credit Suisse First Boston Limited

BNP Capital Markets Limited

Deutsche Bank Capital Markets Limited

ABN AMRO BANK N.V.
Barclays de Zoete Wedd Limited
Dresdner Bank Aktiengesellschaft
Istituto Bancario San Paolo di Torino S.P.A.
Merrill Lynch International Limited
Paribas Capital Markets Group
Swiss Volksbank

Banque Generale du Luxembourg S.A.
Daiwa Europe Limited
Generale Bank
Kredietbank N.V.
Norinchukin International PLC
Swiss Bank Corporation
Wood Gundy Inc.

The date of this Offering Circular is 15th January, 1992

TABLE 1.9   Issues managed or underwritten by Union Bank of Switzerland for Canadian issuers, January to August 1990

Issuer	Description of Issue
Toronto Dominion Bank	SFR 100,000,000 10-year bond
Province of Manitoba	US $250,000,000 30-year Yankee bond
General Motors Acceptance of Canada	SFR 150,000,000 7-year notes
Hydro Quebec	SFR 200,000,000 10-year bond
Province of Manitoba	SFR 200,000,000 10-year bond
Export Development Corporation	ECU 150,000,000 1-year Eurobond
Province of Quebec	US $500,000,000 10-year Yankee bond
Province of Nova Scotia	US $300,000,000 30-year Yankee bond
Trizec Corporation Ltd.	SFR 150,000,000 7-year financial credit
Hydro Quebec	SFR 100,000,000 10-year notes
Province of Manitoba	US $300,000,000 30-year Yankee bond
Hydro Quebec	DM 500,000,000 10-year Euro FRN
Province of Alberta	US $500,000,000 10-year Yankee bond
Hydro Quebec	US $500,000,000 40-year Yankee bond
Province of Newfoundland	US $150,000,000 30-year Yankee bond
Bell Canada	C $125,000,000 10-year Eurobond
Province of Manitoba	SFR 200,000,000 10-year bond
Province of Nova Scotia	SFR 250,000,000 10-year bond
Province of Nova Scotia	US $300,000,000 12-year Yankee bond
Province of Saskatchewan	SFR 250,000,000 10-year bond
Montreal Trustco Inc.	SFR 100,000,000 5-year bond

senting 25.9 percent of the market; they also noted ranking first in both Yankee debt ($4.171 billion or 40.9 percent) and Euro-debt ($3.002 billion or 27.8 percent) offerings by Canadian issuers.

A more common opportunity is for investors to receive payments in U.S. dollars from securities issued by Canadian firms. In some cases, such as Moore Corp. (the largest business forms company in the world), the bulk of the income is generated in the United States or abroad, and financial results are presented in U.S. dollars; Moore can be bought on the TSE or the NYSE in the corresponding currency. Alternatively, several Canadian banks, such as the Royal Bank, issue preferred shares paying dividends eligible for the dividend tax credit but denominated in U.S. dollars and traded on the TSE. In both these cases, purchase of the U.S. dollar securities provides a hedge against Canadian dollar depreciation against the U.S. dollar.

Issuing Derivative Securities

Derivative securities may be relatively simple instruments such as warrants or options on a single company's stock, or they may be quite complicated—taking their value from a number of underlying instruments. Effectively, the foreign-denominated securities mentioned above are derivatives because their value depends on the exchange rate. Canadian issuers can appeal to the wishes of investors to have their investment returns depend on more than the financial results of companies operating in the Canadian economy.

Once again, EDC provides some interesting examples of derivative securities. Figure 1.2 describes EDC's issue of a dual currency bond with payment in either Australian dollars or Japanese yen, at the option of the holder. These will

FIGURE 1.2
Derivative
Securities: A
Dual-Currency
Bond Issue

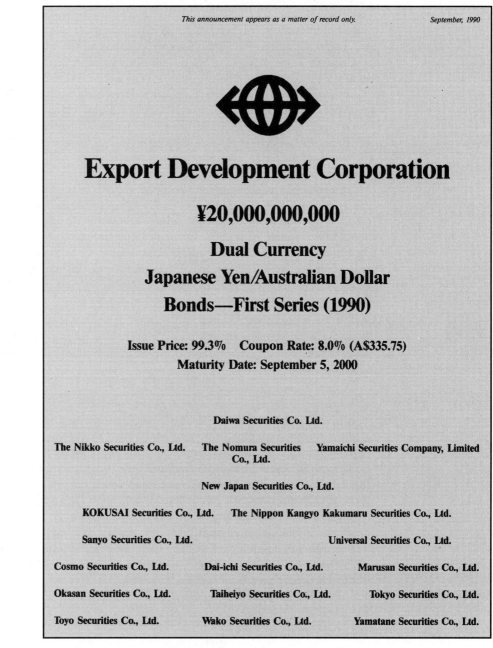

This announcement appears as a matter of record only.   *September, 1990*

Export Development Corporation

¥20,000,000,000

Dual Currency
Japanese Yen/Australian Dollar
Bonds—First Series (1990)

Issue Price: 99.3%   Coupon Rate: 8.0% (A$335.75)
Maturity Date: September 5, 2000

Daiwa Securities Co. Ltd.

The Nikko Securities Co., Ltd.   The Nomura Securities   Yamaichi Securities Company, Limited
Co., Ltd.

New Japan Securities Co., Ltd.

KOKUSAI Securities Co., Ltd.   The Nippon Kangyo Kakumaru Securities Co., Ltd.

Sanyo Securities Co., Ltd.   Universal Securities Co., Ltd.

Cosmo Securities Co., Ltd.   Dai-ichi Securities Co., Ltd.   Marusan Securities Co., Ltd.

Okasan Securities Co., Ltd.   Taiheiyo Securities Co., Ltd.   Tokyo Securities Co., Ltd.

Toyo Securities Co., Ltd.   Wako Securities Co., Ltd.   Yamatane Securities Co., Ltd.

obviously have appeal to Australian and Japanese investors; however, they also provide an opportunity to Canadian or other investors to speculate on the appreciation of either of the currencies against the dollar. Figure 1.3 reproduces the cover page of the prospectus for PINS, or protected index notes. Each PIN on issue cost $10 in U.S. dollars and promised, at the option of the holder, to repay the $10 upon maturity after five-and-a-half years, or, at any time up to maturity, an amount based on the value of the S&P 500[2] relative to its value at issue. The holder is guaranteed a minimum repayment of the initial investment without interest, but also can participate in any appreciation in the U.S. equity market—in both cases speculating on the exchange rate.

Creative security design often calls for **bundling** primitive and derivative securities into one composite security. The long-established example of this is the convertible preferred share or bond, by which the holder has the right to exchange the convertible for a number of common shares in the company; this is usually done when the converted value is higher than the value of the original instrument as a fixed-income security. PINS can be considered as an example of bundling; for a much more intricate case, we can consider the prospectus of the Chubb Corporation in Figure 1.4.

Quite often, creating a security that appears to be attractive requires **unbundling** of an asset. An example is given by the strip bonds such as Sentinels—the composite bond cash flow of regular interest payments and principal is unbundled into single payments. Other examples of unbundling were given in the discussion on financial innovation in Section 1.4. Both CMOs and the bank capital shares permit investors to concentrate on the payment stream, and its risk, which appeal to their particular interests.

Concept Check

Question 5. How can tax motives contribute to the desire for unbundling?

Securitization and Credit Enhancement

Until recently, financial intermediaries served to channel funds from national capital markets to smaller local ones. **Securitization,** however, now allows borrowers to enter capital markets directly. In this procedure pools of loans typically are aggregated into pass-through securities, such as mortgage pass-throughs. Then investors can invest in securities backed by those pools. The transformation of these pools into standardized securities enables issuers to deal in a volume large enough that they can bypass intermediaries engaged in and charging for matching investors with the original issuers of the mortgages. We have already discussed this phenomenon in the context of the securitization of the mortgage market.

---

[2] The S&P 500 is a stock market index based on the value of the 500 largest firms in the United States; see the discussion in Chapter 2.

FIGURE 1.3

Derivative
Securities:
Prospectus for a
Minimum-Return
Index Investment

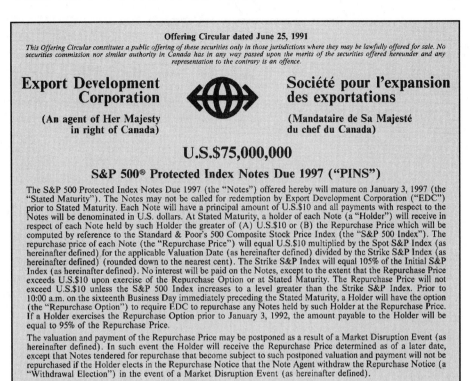

Offering Circular dated June 25, 1991

This Offering Circular constitutes a public offering of these securities only in those jurisdictions where they may be lawfully offered for sale. No securities commission nor similar authority in Canada has in any way passed upon the merits of the securities offered hereunder and any representation to the contrary is an offence.

Export Development Corporation

(An agent of Her Majesty in right of Canada)

Société pour l'expansion des exportations

(Mandataire de Sa Majesté du chef du Canada)

U.S.$75,000,000

S&P 500® Protected Index Notes Due 1997 ("PINS")

The S&P 500 Protected Index Notes Due 1997 (the "Notes") offered hereby will mature on January 3, 1997 (the "Stated Maturity"). The Notes may not be called for redemption by Export Development Corporation ("EDC") prior to Stated Maturity. Each Note will have a principal amount of U.S.$10 and all payments with respect to the Notes will be denominated in U.S. dollars. At Stated Maturity, a holder of each Note (a "Holder") will receive in respect of each Note held by such Holder the greater of (A) U.S.$10 or (B) the Repurchase Price which will be computed by reference to the Standard & Poor's 500 Composite Stock Price Index (the "S&P 500 Index"). The repurchase price of each Note (the "Repurchase Price") will equal U.S.$10 multiplied by the Spot S&P Index (as hereinafter defined) for the applicable Valuation Date (as hereinafter defined) divided by the Strike S&P Index (as hereinafter defined) (rounded down to the nearest cent). The Strike S&P Index will equal 105% of the Initial S&P Index (as hereinafter defined). No interest will be paid on the Notes, except to the extent that the Repurchase Price exceeds U.S.$10 upon exercise of the Repurchase Option or at Stated Maturity. The Repurchase Price will not exceed U.S.$10 unless the S&P 500 Index increases to a level greater than the Strike S&P Index. Prior to 10:00 a.m. on the sixteenth Business Day immediately preceding the Stated Maturity, a Holder will have the option (the "Repurchase Option") to require EDC to repurchase any Notes held by such Holder at the Repurchase Price. If a Holder exercises the Repurchase Option prior to January 3, 1992, the amount payable to the Holder will be equal to 95% of the Repurchase Price.

The valuation and payment of the Repurchase Price may be postponed as a result of a Market Disruption Event (as hereinafter defined). In such event the Holder will receive the Repurchase Price determined as of a later date, except that Notes tendered for repurchase that become subject to such postponed valuation and payment will not be repurchased if the Holder elects in the Repurchase Notice that the Note Agent withdraw the Repurchase Notice (a "Withdrawal Election") in the event of a Market Disruption Event (as hereinafter defined).

PRICE: U.S.$10.00 per Note
Minimum Subscription: 100 Notes

	Price to the Public (1)(2)	Agents' Commission	Proceeds to EDC (3)
Per Note	U.S.$10.00	U.S.$0.30	U.S.$9.70
Total Offering (4)	U.S.$75,000,000	U.S.$2,250,000	U.S.$72,750,000

Notes:

(1) The subscription price has been determined by negotiation between EDC and the Agents (as hereinafter defined).

(2) On June 24, 1991, the Canadian dollar purchase price of each Note would have been C$11.43 based on the noon exchange rate of C$1.1427 for each U.S.$1.00.

(3) The expenses of the issue of approximately C$350,000 are being borne by the Issuer and the Agents.

(4) EDC has granted to the Agents an overallotment option, exercisable from time to time up to the Date of Closing (as hereinafter defined) with the concurrence of EDC, to distribute an additional 1,000,000 Notes on the same terms and conditions as the other Notes offered hereby. To the extent such option is exercised, the Agents will offer to the public such additional Notes at the price shown above.

Investment in the Notes is speculative and a Holder may sustain a substantial loss of its investment if such Holder elects to exercise the Repurchase Option and the Notes are repurchased prior to Stated Maturity. Since the return to a Holder on exercise of the Repurchase Option or at Stated Maturity is determined solely by reference to the S&P 500 Index, the Notes are not suitable for persons unfamiliar with the risks of investing in equity securities. (See "Risk Factors".) In order for a Holder to avoid a loss of principal on the Notes, the level of the S&P 500 Index must increase to the Breakeven Point (as hereinafter defined) or the Notes must be held to Stated Maturity. (See "Description of Notes — Breakeven Point" and "Description of the Notes — Repurchase Price".) The Notes will constitute direct unsecured obligations of EDC and, as such, will constitute direct obligations of Her Majesty in right of Canada. (See "Description of the Notes — Status".)

The Repurchase Option will be exercisable on any Business Day (as hereinafter defined) after the Date of Closing and will expire at 10:00 a.m. on the sixteenth Business Day immediately preceding the Stated Maturity of the Notes. Any Holder who does not exercise the Repurchase Option will receive in respect of each Note held by such Holder the greater of (A) U.S.$10 or (B) the Repurchase Price, at the Stated Maturity. The Repurchase Option may not be exercised by or on behalf of any Holder in respect of fewer than 100 Notes or integral multiples thereof. (See "Description of the Notes — Repurchase Option".)

FIGURE 1.4
Bundling creates a
complex security.

3,000,000 Shares
The Chubb Corporation
$4.25 Convertible Exchangeable Preferred Stock

(Stated Value $50 Per Share)

The $4.25 Convertible Exchangeable Preferred Stock (the "Preferred Stock"), $1.00 par value, of The Chubb Corporation (the "Corporation") offered hereby is convertible at the option of the holder at any time, unless previously redeemed, into Common Stock, $1.00 par value, of the Corporation (the "Common Stock") at the rate of .722 shares of Common Stock for each share of Preferred Stock (equivalent to a conversion price of $69.25 per share), subject to adjustment under certain conditions. On March 25, 1985, the last reported sale price of the Common Stock on the New York Stock Exchange was $57 1/4 per share.

The Preferred Stock also is exchangeable in whole at the sole option of the Corporation on any dividend payment date beginning April 15, 1988 for the Corporation's 8 1/2 % Convertible Subordinated Debentures due April 15, 2010 (the "Debentures") at the rate of $50 principal amount of Debentures for each share of Preferred Stock. See "Description of Debentures".

The Preferred Stock is redeemable for cash at any time, in whole or in part, at the option of the Corporation at redemption prices declining to $50 on April 15, 1995, plus accrued and unpaid dividends to the redemption date. However, the Preferred Stock is not redeemable prior to April 15, 1988 unless the closing price of the Common Stock on the New York Stock Exchange shall have equaled or exceeded 140% of the then effective conversion price per share for at least 20 consecutive trading days ending within 5 days prior to the notice of redemption. Dividends on the Preferred Stock will be cumulative and are payable quarterly on January 15, April 15, July 15 and October 15. The initial dividend will be payable on July 15, 1985 and will accrue from the date of issuance. See "Description of Preferred Stock".

Application will be made to list the Preferred Stock on the New York Stock Exchange.

THESE SECURITIES HAVE NOT BEEN APPROVED OR DISAPPROVED BY THE
SECURITIES AND EXCHANGE COMMISSION NOR HAS THE COMMISSION
PASSED UPON THE ACCURACY OR ADEQUACY OF THIS PROSPECTUS.
ANY REPRESENTATION TO THE CONTRARY IS A CRIMINAL OFFENSE.

	Initial Public Offering Price	Underwriting Discount	Proceeds to Corporation(1)
Per Share	$50.00	$1.375	$48.625
Total	$150,000,000	$4,125,000	$145,875,000

(1) Before deducting expenses payable by the Corporation estimated at $500,000.

The shares of Preferred Stock are offered severally by the Underwriters, as specified herein, subject to receipt and acceptance by them and subject to their right to reject any order in whole or in part. It is expected that certificates for the shares of Preferred Stock will be ready for delivery at the offices of Goldman, Sachs & Co., New York, New York on or about April 2, 1985.

Goldman, Sachs & Co.

The date of this Prospectus is March 26, 1985.

FIGURE 1.5

Aetna's credit enhancement of the Rockefeller Group's bond.

Offering Circular

$100,000,000

Rockefeller Group International Finance N.V.

13¼% Notes Due 1989

Unconditionally Guaranteed as to Payment of Principal and Interest by

Rockefeller Group, Inc.

and under a Surety Bond Issued by

The Ætna Casualty and Surety Company

Issue Price 99¾%

Principal of, premium, if any, and interest on the Notes will be payable without deduction for, or on account of, United States or Netherlands Antilles withholding taxes, all as set forth herein. Interest will be payable annually on June 21, commencing in 1985.

The Notes will mature on June 21, 1989. The Notes are redeemable (i) as a whole or from time to time in part, on or after June 21, 1987 at a redemption price equal to 101¼% of the principal amount of the Notes if made prior to June 21, 1988 and 100½% of the principal amount of the Notes if made on or after June 21, 1988, plus, in each case, accrued interest to the date fixed for redemption, and (ii) as a whole at any time in the event of certain developments involving United States or Netherlands Antilles withholding taxes, at their principal amount plus accrued interest to the date fixed for redemption. See "Description of the Notes". The Notes may also be redeemed as a whole, at a redemption price equal to their principal amount plus accrued interest to the date fixed for redemption, at the option of The Ætna Casualty and Surety Company ("Ætna") upon the occurrence of certain events. See "Description of the Surety Bond".

The Notes will be unconditionally guaranteed as to the payment of principal, premium, if any, and interest and certain other amounts by Rockefeller Group, Inc. As a private corporation, Rockefeller Group, Inc., does not disclose financial information to the public. Accordingly, arrangements have been made for payments of principal of, premium, if any, and interest on, and certain other amounts with respect to, the Notes to be guaranteed under a Surety Bond issued by Ætna. See "Description of the Notes" and "Description of the Surety Bond".

Application has been made to list the Notes on the Luxembourg Stock Exchange.

The Notes have not been registered under the United States Securities Act of 1933 and may not be offered or sold, directly or indirectly, in the United States of America, or its territories or possessions or to citizens, nationals or residents thereof, except as set forth herein. See "Underwriting".

A temporary global Note without interest coupons in the amount of $100,000,000 will be delivered to a depositary in London for the account of participants in Euro-clear and CEDEL S.A. on or about June 21, 1984 and will be exchangeable for definitive Notes not earlier than 90 days after the completion of the distribution upon certification that such Notes are not beneficially owned by United States citizens, nationals or residents, as set forth herein. Interest on the Notes will not be payable until issuance of the definitive Notes. See "Description of the Notes—Denominaton and Transfer".

MORGAN GUARANTY LTD

AMRO INTERNATIONAL LIMITED	**CHASE MANHATTAN LIMITED**
CREDIT SUISSE FIRST BOSTON LIMITED	**DEUTSCHE BANK AKTIENGESELLSCHAFT**
DRESDNER BANK AKTIENGESELLSCHAFT	**ENSKILDA SECURITIES** SKANDINAVISKA ENSKILDA LIMITED
LEHMAN BROTHERS INTERNATIONAL SHEARSON LEHMAN/AMERICAN EXPRESS INC	**SAMUEL MONTAGU & CO. LIMITED**
ORION ROYAL BANK LIMITED	**SOCIÉTÉ GÉNÉRALE**
SOCIÉTÉ GÉNÉRALE DE BANQUE S.A.	**SWISS BANK CORPORATION INTERNATIONAL LIMITED**
UNION BANK OF SWITZERLAND (SECURITIES) LIMITED	**S. G. WARBURG & CO. LTD.**

May 25, 1984

Another type of securitization is the issue of securities that are backed up by portfolios of short-term loans rather than long-term mortgages. One example is a collateralized automobile receivable, a pass-through arrangement for car loans, such as the $25 million issue in 1987 by the First Boston Corporation. The other typical case securitizes credit card receivables; in 1991, Chase Manhattan Bank made an issue of $1 billion of credit card-backed securities. In these cases, the originator passes the loan payments through to the holder of the instrument.

In the past, a corporation that was not in the best of financial conditions would be able to obtain loans only through commercial banks. The banks' credit departments scrutinized each customer. A business shopping around for a loan might be sized up simultaneously by several different banks. Today, the credit-hungry corporation can arrange for **credit enhancement.** It engages an insurance company to put its credit behind the corporation's, for a fee. The firm can then float a bond of "enhanced" credit rating directly to the public. Figure 1.5 shows an example of credit enhancement in a joint financial venture between the Rockefeller Group and Aetna Casualty and Surety. The Rockefeller Group is a privately held corporation and thus exempt from a large part of typical disclosure rules. It cannot issue publicly traded bonds at reasonably low yields without revealing information to the public that it wishes to keep private. Instead, it purchases Aetna's backing. Aetna can perform its own credit analysis, keeping the information revealed confidential.

1.7 *Corporate Control and Concentration*

Occasional waves of takeovers, particularly with the development of exotic defenses, have brought to the surface public misgivings about "unproductive speculation" in the stock markets. Many see a need to curb such activities that supposedly divert funds from productive use and cause plant shutdowns and unemployment. An important related issue that may not come up in the public debate is the inherent conflict among households, the direct and indirect shareholders of businesses, and the professional managers who run them. This issue is an important feature of the investment environment.

The control structure of a standard, publicly traded firm is modeled on a democratic arrangement. Its main features are, in theory, as follows:

1. No one has to own shares. Willing investors buy shares, satisfied shareholders can buy more, and unsatisfied shareholders can unload the stock at any time.
2. Management has to disclose to the public a great deal of information, which is audited by independent experts.
3. Important decisions of management must be approved by voting in shareholder meetings.

4. The normal rule is one share/one vote, but Canadian law also allows multiple-voting shares;[3] thus, shareholder voting power is proportional to the shareholder's stake in the corporation. (Absentee shareholders can vote by proxy.)

5. Corporate management, from the president down, is subject to control by the board of directors led by the chairman. Individual directors are elected by shareholders, who can unseat directors in any meeting. Shareholder meetings can be called by shareholders, as well as by management. One annual meeting is mandatory.

Given such a system, what can go wrong? If management is unsatisfactory, the board in principle will oust it. If the board members are not on their toes, shareholders will oust them. In the end, if all works as intended, the corporation will be run by management that executes the (aggregate) will of the shareholders.

Management, however, can hurt shareholders in two ways. First, incompetent managers may be very expensive to shareholders (and to corporate employees, who also are stakeholders). Second, management's control of pecuniary rewards and other perquisites comes directly from the pockets of shareholders. This creates a conflict between management and shareholders, which is called the **agency problem.** A great deal of financial theory is dedicated to the analysis of this problem. Corporate executives are probably the best-compensated professionals in the nation, which is fine as long as shareholders are happy. After all, competition itself should ensure that managerial resource compensation is allocated as efficiently as any production factor in the economy. The necessary information for the smooth functioning of this competitive process is ensured in the United States by the annual disclosure of executive salaries; in Canada, this protection is unfortunately absent.

Corporate control is not a minor issue, because a lot of shareholder wealth is at stake. When we have large corporations and many diversified investors, control is very dispersed. In many cases, even the largest shareholder holds less than 2 percent of the shares. Management, as a whole, through executive stock options and compensation shares, may become important shareholders. By and by, one finds that management controls the board, rather than vice versa.

What about proxy fights to wrest control of the firm from current management? Evidence shows that the cost of an average proxy fight is millions of dollars. Shareholders who attempt such a fight have to use their own funds. Management that defends against it uses corporate coffers, in addition to already existing communication channels to shareholders at large. Little wonder that few such attempts are made. When they are, 75 percent fail. Dissidents win some seats on the board of directors in a majority of cases, but seldom enough seats to assume control of the company. Ousting the management of a large corporation is a modern-day version of David's battle with Goliath.

---

[3] See the discussion of restricted shares in Chapter 2.

Are shareholders in trouble? Not yet. Their greatest protection is the hunger and might of other businesses. How does this sword of Damocles work? A bad management team, whether incompetent or excessively greedy, presumably causes the firm's shares to sell at a price that reflects its poor performance. Now imagine the management of one business observing another that is underperforming. All it has to do is acquire the underperforming business, fire current management, put in place its own (presumably better) people, and the stock price should reflect the acquiring business's expectations of improved performance. The acquiring firm might therefore be willing to bid up the price of shares of the target firm by as much as 50 percent to acquire it. In the process, the economy gets rid of one bad management team and becomes more efficient.

Just the threat of this mechanism ought to keep management on its toes. However, give management the ability to engage in expensive takeover defenses (at shareholder expense, of course), and their vulnerability is limited. The danger of antitakeover regulation that allows poor managers to protect their positions is clear.

What about the arguments that takeovers lead to shutdowns and unemployment, and that funds for takeovers are diverted from productive resources? A firm that takes over another one must believe that it can improve operations. If it pays a premium for the acquisition, the acquiring firm must believe it can create additional value to justify the purchase price. Potential efficiency gains might therefore be expected to be an impetus for mergers and acquisitions. Of course, one might argue that some acquisitions are motivated more by tax motives than true economic efficiency, but this seems more a reason to modify tax law than intrude in the market for corporate control.

The argument that takeover funds are diverted from productive uses is without merit. After all, the money that is paid by the acquirer to the target firm's shareholders does not disappear; it is reinvested in financial markets. If shareholders had needed the money for food, they would have sold their shares in the first place. In the end, the displacement of bad management ought to bring in, if anything, more investment funds in this newly created opportunity.

On the other hand, control of Canadian corporations is quite distinct from the U.S. situation. Canadian corporate assets are controlled by individuals and families, by conglomerates, by financial institutions, and even by the government to a significant degree. A recent count showed 32 family empires (such as the Bronfmans and the Westons) and 5 publicly held conglomerates (such as Bell Canada and Canadian Pacific) controlling approximately one third of the non-financial assets in Canada. Comparable U.S. statistics show that one-third share of assets to be controlled by the 100 largest corporations, with very few of those effectively controlled by individuals (such as the control of Ford Motors by the Ford family).

More precise Canadian statistics from 1985 indicate that 33.5 percent of non-financial assets and 31.5 percent of profits were controlled by 25 corporations owned by foreign firms (e.g., Imperial Esso owned by Exxon), the federal government, and Canadian corporations. The latter 11 corporations actually controlled 11.3 percent of assets and 7.3 percent of profits.[4]

The structure of control is through holding companies. The prime example is that of the Edper Bronfman network, the now partially publicly owned creation of a branch of the Bronfman family. This corporation owns controlling interests in other corporations that hold others in a bewildering entanglement, down to the final levels where products and services are sold and physical assets exist. The holdings might be as small as 10 percent or complete, but generally debt and the equity of small investors is used to leverage the initial capital in Edper. This enables the management of Edper to direct the resources of dozens of companies ranging across natural resources (forest products and mining), financial services (investments, insurance, and banking), and real estate.

Why is this **concentration** of control a matter of concern? Leaving aside the political question of the desirability of government ownership, the major corporations in Canada are controlled by a minute number of individuals or by foreign corporations (controlled obviously by foreigners). Should the interests of Canadians as a whole diverge from those of the owners of the significant factors of production for the nation, there is no remedy besides government intervention. Such a possibility does not exist for the U.S. economy.[5]

Summary

1. Real assets are used to produce the goods and services created by an economy. Financial assets are claims to the income generated by real assets. Securities are financial assets. Financial assets are part of an investor's wealth, but not part of national wealth. Instead, financial assets determine how the "national pie" is split up among investors.

2. The four sectors of the financial environment are households, businesses, government, and foreign. Households decide on investing their funds. Businesses and government, in contrast, typically need to raise funds. The foreign sector is a net supplier of funds to the Canadian economy.

3. The Canadian tax system is designed to make investment in equity more favourable than in debt, by offering a dividend tax credit. Capital gains and dividends are taxed at approximately the same effective rate.

4. The diverse tax and risk preferences of households create a demand for a wide variety of securities. In contrast, businesses typically find it more efficient

---

[4] Edward G. Grabb, "Who Owns Canada? Concentration of Ownership and the Distribution of Economic Assets 1975–1985," *Journal of Canadian Studies* vol. 25, no. 2 (Summer 1990), pp. 72–93.

[5] A different problem arises in Japan, where banks and industrial conglomerates own each other in complicated arrangements that involve both business and financial dealings.

to offer relatively uniform forms of securities. This conflict gives rise to an industry that creates complex derivative securities from primitive ones.

5. The smallness of households leads to a market niche for financial intermediaries, mutual funds, and investment companies. Economies of scale and specialization are factors supporting the investment banking industry.

6. Four types of markets may be distinguished: direct search, brokered, dealer, and auction markets. Securities are sold in all but direct search markets.

7. Three recent trends in the financial environment are globalization, issuing derivative securities (especially by bundling and unbundling), and securitization and credit enhancement.

8. Stockholders own the corporation and, in principle, can oust an unsatisfactory management team. In practice, ouster may be difficult because of the advantage that management has in proxy fights. The threat of takeover helps keep management doing its best for the firm.

9. The Canadian economy is characterized by an extreme degree of concentration of equity holdings, with effective control of one third of all non-financial assets by a small number of corporations and family empires.

Key terms

Real assets	Primary market
Financial assets	Secondary market
Settlement date	Block transactions
Zero-coupon bonds	Dealer markets
Financial intermediaries	Auction market
Mutual funds	Globalization
Investment dealers	Bundling
Pass-through security	Unbundling
Primitive security	Securitization
Derivative security	Credit enhancement
Dual fund	Agency problem
Direct search market	Concentration
Brokered market	

Selected Readings

An excellent discussion of financial innovation may be found in:
  Miller, Merton H. "Financial Innovation: The Last Twenty Years and the Next." *Journal of Financial and Quantitative Analysis* 21 (December 1986), pp. 459–471.
Detailed discussions of a variety of financial markets and market structures are provided in:
  Garbade, Kenneth D. *Securities Markets.* New York: McGraw-Hill, 1982.
  Wood, John H.; and Wood, Norm L. *Financial Markets.* San Diego: Harcourt Brace Jovanovich, 1985.
Several trends in the capital market are discussed in:
  Recent Innovations in International Banking. Basel: Bank for International Settlements, 1986.

The subject of Canadian corporate control is discussed in:

Eckbo, Espen B. "Mergers and the Market for Corporate Control: The Canadian Evidence." *Canadian Journal of Economics* 19, (May 1986), pp. 236–260.

A broad range of non-technical articles on the subject of investing in Canada and by Canadians appear semi-annually in the Canadian Investment Review (CIR). *These articles are usually organized by themes. Some examples of interest to our discussion would be:*

"Market Innovation in Canada" (theme). *CIR* vol. 3, no. 2 (Fall 1990).

"Investment Perspectives on Ethics, Ownership and Control" (theme). *CIR* vol. 4, no. 2 (Fall 1991).

Poapst, James V. "Households as Financial Managers: An Assessment." *CIR* vol. 2, no. 2 (Fall 1989).

Halpern, Paul; and Heath, Frederick. "Canada's Securities Investment Universe: The Size of It." *CIR* vol. 2, no. 2 (Fall 1989).

Problems

1. Suppose you discover a treasure chest of $10 billion in cash.
   a. Is this a real or financial asset?
   b. Is society any richer for the discovery?
   c. Are you wealthier?
   d. Can you reconcile your answers to b and c? Is anyone worse off as a result of the discovery?
2. Examine the balance sheet of the financial sector. What is the ratio of tangible assets to total assets? What is that ratio for non-financial firms? Why should this difference be expected?
3. In the 1960s, the U.S. government instituted a 30 percent withholding tax on interest payments on bonds sold in the United States to overseas investors. (It has since been repealed.) What connection does this have to the contemporaneous growth of the huge Eurobond market, where U.S. firms issue dollar-denominated bonds overseas?
4. A corporation issues the following three types of securities: bonds paying 10 percent, preferred shares paying 8 percent, and common shares paying no dividend but growing at 7.5 percent per annum. If you are an Ontario investor in the top tax bracket and are ignoring risk issues, which security do you prefer to own? If the bonds were zero-coupon bonds maturing in five years and you intended to hold each of the three securities for five years, would you answer differently?
5. Why would you expect securitization to take place only in highly developed capital markets?
6. Suppose that you are an executive of Ford Motor Canada, and that a large share of your potential income is derived from year-end bonuses that depend on your firm's annual profits.
   a. Would purchase of Ford Canada's stock be an effective hedging strategy for the executive who is worried about the uncertainty surrounding his or her bonus?
   b. Would purchase of Toyota stock be an effective hedging strategy?

7. Consider again the Ford executive in question 6. In light of the fact that the design of the annual bonus exposes the executive to risk that he or she would like to shed, why doesn't Ford instead pay him or her a fixed salary that doesn't entail this uncertainty?

8. What is the relationship between securitization and the role of financial intermediaries in the economy? What happens to financial intermediaries as securitization progresses?

9. Although we stated that real assets comprise the true productive capacity of an economy, it is hard to conceive of a modern economy without well-developed financial markets and security types. How would the productive capacity of the Canadian economy be affected if there were no markets in which one could trade financial assets?

10. In Section 1.6 the securitization of various debt contracts was raised. How might a third-world debt pass-through security be designed?

11. Why does it make sense that the first futures markets introduced in 19th-century America were for trades in agricultural products? For example, why did we not see instead futures markets for goods such as paper or pencils?

CHAPTER 2

Markets and Instruments

This chapter covers a range of financial securities and the markets in which they trade. Our goal is to introduce you to the features of various security types. This foundation will be necessary to understand the more analytic material that follows in later chapters.

We refer to the traditional classification of securities, money market instruments, or capital market instruments. The **money market** includes short-term, marketable, liquid, low-risk debt securities. Money market instruments sometimes are called *cash equivalents* because of their safety and liquidity. **Capital markets,** in contrast, include longer-term and riskier securities. Securities in the capital market are much more diverse than those found within the money market. For this reason, we will subdivide the capital market into four segments. Accordingly, this chapter contains a discussion of five markets overall: the money market, longer-term fixed income capital markets, equity markets, and the two so-called derivative markets—options and futures markets.

2.1   *The Money Market*

The money market is a subsector of the bond market. It consists of very short-term debt securities that usually are highly marketable. Many of these securities trade in large denominations, and so are out of reach of individual investors. Money market funds, however, are easily accessible to small investors. These mutual funds pool the resources of many investors and purchase a wide variety of money market securities on their behalf.

Figure 2.1 is a reprint of a money rates listing from *The Toronto Globe and Mail*. It includes the various instruments of the money market that we will describe in detail. Table 2.1 lists total trading volume in 1990 of the major instruments of the money market.

FIGURE 2.1

Rates on money
market securities.

From *The Globe and
Mail,* October 17, 1991.
Reprinted by permission.

MONEY MARKETS

ADMINISTERED RATES

Bank of Canada	8.33%
Canadian prime	9-9.50%

MONEY MARKET RATES
(for transactions
of $1-million or more)

3-month treasury bills	8.12%
6-month treasury bills	8.08%
1-year treasury bills	8.08%
2001 Canada bonds	9.05%
2021 Canada bonds	9.41%
30-day comm. paper	8.75%
60-day comm. paper	8.60%
90-day comm. paper	8.40%
30-day banker's accept.	8.55%
60-day banker's accept.	8.45%
90-day banker's accept.	8.23%
1-month dollar swaps	8.54%
2-month dollar swaps	8.45%
3-month dollar swaps	8.20%
6-month dollar swaps	8.06%
1-year dollar swaps	8.02%
Call money	8.75%

UNITED STATES

NEW YORK (AP) — Money rates for Wednesday as reported by Telerate Systems Inc:

Telerate interest rate index: 5.345

Prime Rate: 8.00

Discount Rate: 5.00

Broker call loan rate: 7.00-7.50

Federal funds market rate: High 7.00, low 5.75, last 6.25

Dealers commercial paper: 30-180 days: 5.20-5.15

Commercial paper by finance company: 30-270 days: 5.15-5.14

Bankers acceptances dealer indications: 30 days, 5.17; 60 days, 5.12; 90 days, 5.19; 120 days, 5.17; 150 days, 5.14; 180 days, 5.12

Certificates of Deposit Primary: 30 days, 4.76; 90 days, 4.85; 180 days, 4.87

Certificates of Deposit by dealer: 30 days, 5.20; 60 days, 5.20; 90 days, 5.32; 120 days, 5.32; 150 days, 5.32; 180 days, 5.32

Eurodollar rates: Overnight, 6.00-6.25; 1 month, 5.1875-5.1875; 3 months, 5.3125-5.4375; 6 months, 5.3125-5.4325; 1 year, 5.4375-5.5625

London Interbank Offered Rate: 3 months, 5.3125; 6 months, 5.3125

Treasury Bill auction results: average discount rate: 3-month as of Oct 15: 4.99; 6-month as of Oct 15: 5.03

Treasury Bill, annualized rate on weekly average basis, yield adjusted for constant maturity, 1-year, as of Oct.15 5.36

Treasury Bill market rate, 1-year: 5.00-4.98

Treasury Bond market rate, 30-year: 7.88

Treasury Bills

Treasury bills (T-bills) are the most marketable of all Canadian money market instruments. T-bills represent the simplest form of borrowing: the government raises money by selling bills to the public. Investors buy the bills at a discount from the stated maturity value. At the bill's maturity, the holder receives from the government a payment equal to the face value of the bill. The difference between the purchase price and ultimate maturity value constitutes the investor's earnings.

TABLE 2.1   Components of the Money Market, 1990

	$ Millions
Canada bills	522,147
Provincial securities	42,097
Municipal bills	457
Canadian banker's acceptances: Schedule I	137,510
Canadian banker's acceptances: Schedule II	55,168
Canadian bank paper	161,753
Corporate paper	240,950
Trust & mortgage company paper	21,942
Other	34,500
Total money market trading	**1,216,524**

Data from Investment Dealers of Canada *Report,* Fall 1991.

T-bills with initial maturities of 3, 6, and 12 months are issued weekly. Sales are conducted via auction, at which chartered banks and authorized dealers can submit only *competitive* bids. A competitive bid is an order for a given quantity of bills at a specific offered price. The order is filled only if the bid is high enough relative to other bids to be accepted. By contrast, a noncompetitive bid is an unconditional offer to purchase at the average price of the successful competitive bids; such bids can be submitted only for bonds. The government rank-orders bids by offering price, and accepts bids in order of descending price until the entire issue is absorbed. Competitive bidders face two dangers: they may bid too high and overpay for the bills, or they may bid too low and be shut out of the auction.

T-bills are purchased primarily by chartered banks, by the Bank of Canada (as part of its monetary policy), and by individuals who obtain them on the secondary market from a government securities dealer. T-bills are highly liquid; that is, they are easily converted to cash and sold at low transaction cost with not much price risk. Unlike most other money market instruments, which sell in minimum denominations of $100,000, T-bills are offered in denominations of $1,000, $5,000, $25,000, $100,000 and $1 million.

T-bill yields

T-bill yields are not quoted in the financial pages as effective annual rates of return. Instead, the **bond equivalent yield** is used. To illustrate this method, consider a $10,000 par value T-bill sold at $9,600 with a maturity of a half year, or 182 days. With the bond equivalent yield method, the bill's discount from par value, which here equals $400, is "annualized" based on a 365-day year. The $400 discount is annualized as

$$\$400 \times (365/182) = \$802.20$$

The result is divided by the $9,600 purchase price to obtain a bond equivalent yield of 8.356 percent per year. Rather than report T-bill prices, the financial pages report these bond equivalent yields.

The bond equivalent yield is not an accurate measure of the effective annual rate of return. To see this, note that the half-year holding period return on the bill is 4.17 percent: the $9,600 investment provides $400 in earnings, and $400/9,600 = .0417$. The compound interest-annualized rate of return, or **effective annual yield,** is therefore

$$(1.0417)^2 - 1 = .0851 = 8.51\%$$

We can highlight the source of the discrepancy between the bond equivalent yield and effective annual yield by examining the bond equivalent yield formula:

$$r_{\text{BEY}} = \frac{10,000 - P}{P} \times \frac{365}{n} \qquad \textbf{(2.1)}$$

where P is the bond price, n is the maturity of the bill in days, and r_{BEY} is the bond equivalent yield. The bond equivalent formula thus takes the bill's discount from par as a fraction of price and then annualizes by the factor $365/n$.

The annualization technique uses simple interest rather than compound interest. Multiplication by 365/n does not account for the ability to earn interest on interest, which is the essence of compounding. The discrepancy is, therefore, greater for a 91-day bill and disappears for a one-year bill.

The quoted yields for U.S. T-bills use a formula similar to that in equation 2.1, with a 360-day year and the par value of 10,000 in the denominator instead of P. The resulting yield is known as the **bank discount yield.** As a result, the quoted U.S. rate for the example would have been 7.912 percent. Part of the difference in yields between Canadian and U.S. bills can thus be attributed to the method of quoting yields. A convenient formula relating the bond equivalent yield to the bank discount yield is

$$r_{BEY} = \frac{365 \times d}{360 - (d \times n)}$$

where d is the discount yield. Suppose $d = .07912$; then

$$r_{BEY} = \frac{365 \times .07912}{360 - (.07912 \times 61)} = .08356$$

the previously derived yield. Hence, in this case about 0.4 percentage points of the differential between Canadian and U.S. quoted yields stem from the method of calculation.

In Figure 2.1, the money market listings include Treasury bills for closing prices on October 16, 1991. Three-month T-bills show a bond equivalent yield of 8.12 percent. To determine a bill's true market price, we must solve equation 2.1 for P. Rearranging equation 2.1, we obtain

$$P = 10,000/[1 + r_{BEY} \times (n/365)] \qquad \textbf{(2.2)}$$

Equation 2.2 in effect first "deannualizes" the bond equivalent yield to obtain the actual proportional interest rate, then discounts the par value of $10,000 to obtain the T-bill's sale price. In the case at hand, $n = 91$ days, and the yield is 8.12 percent for the bill, so that the price is

$$\$10,000/[1 + .0812 \times (91/365)] = \$9,801.57$$

Concept Check

Question 1. Find the price of the six-month bill from Figure 2.1.

The bond equivalent yield is the bill's yield over its life, assuming that it is purchased for the auction bid price, and annualized using simple interest techniques. Note that this yield uses a simple interest procedure to annualize, also known as *annual percentage rate* (APR), and so there are problems in comparing yields on bills with different maturities. Nevertheless, yields on most securities with less than a year to maturity are annualized using a simple interest approach.

Finally, the effective annual yield on the quoted bill based on the market price, $9,801.57, is 8.37 percent. The bond's 91-day return equals $(10,000 - 9,801.57)/9,801.57$, or 1.020245 percent. Annualizing this return, we obtain $(1.020245)^{365/91} = 1.0837$, implying an effective annual interest rate of 8.37 percent.

Certificates of Deposit and Bearer Deposit Notes

A *certificate of deposit* (CD), is a time deposit with a chartered bank. Time deposits may not be withdrawn on demand. The bank pays interest and principal to the depositor only at the end of the fixed term of the deposit. Similar time deposits offered by trust companies are known as *guaranteed investment certificates* (GICs).

Although both CDs and GICs are non-transferable in Canada, some bank time deposits issued in denominations greater than $100,000 are negotiable; that is, they can be sold to another investor if the owner needs to cash in the deposit before its maturity date. In Canada these marketable CDs are known as *bearer deposit notes* (BDN). By contrast, a CD in the United States is a marketable instrument, similar to BDNs. Recently some trust companies have also issued transferable GICs. CDs and GICs are treated as bank deposits by the Canada Deposit Insurance Corporation (CDIC), so they are insured for up to $60,000 in the event of a bank insolvency.

Commercial Paper

Large, well-known companies often issue their own short-term unsecured debt notes rather than borrow directly from banks. These notes are called *commercial paper*. Very often, commercial paper is backed by a bank line of credit, which gives the borrower access to cash that can be used (if needed) to pay off the paper at maturity. Commercial paper maturities range up to one year; longer maturities would require registration under the Ontario Securities Act and so are almost never issued. Most often, commercial paper is issued with maturities of less than one or two months and minimum denominations of $50,000. Therefore, small investors can invest in commercial paper only indirectly, via money market mutual funds.

Commercial paper is considered to be a fairly safe asset, because a firm's condition presumably can be monitored and predicted over a term as short as one month. Many firms issue commercial paper intending to roll it over at maturity, that is, issue new paper to obtain the funds necessary to retire the old paper. If in the meantime there are doubts raised about their creditworthiness, then the borrowers may be forced to turn to other, more expensive, sources of financing. For instance, in the recent Olympia and York bankruptcy case the firm was forced to retire its outstanding commercial paper several weeks before it became insolvent.

If lenders become complacent about a firm's prospects and grant rollovers heedlessly, they can suffer big losses. When Penn Central defaulted in the United States in 1970, it had $82 million of commercial paper outstanding.

However, very few such defaults on commercial paper have been observed in the past 40 years.

Bankers' Acceptances

A *bankers' acceptance* starts as an order to a bank by a bank's customer to pay a sum of money at a future date, typically within six months. At this stage, it is similar to a postdated check. When the bank endorses the order for payment as "accepted," it assumes responsibility for ultimate payment to the holder of the acceptance. At this point, the acceptance may be traded in secondary markets like any other claim on the bank. Bankers' acceptances are considered very safe assets because traders can substitute the bank's credit standing for their own. They are used widely in foreign trade where the creditworthiness of one trader is unknown to the trading partner. Acceptances sell at a discount from the face value of the payment order, just as T-bills sell at a discount from par value.

Eurodollars

Eurodollars are U.S. dollar-denominated deposits at foreign banks or foreign branches of American banks. By locating outside the United States, these banks escape regulation by the Federal Reserve Board. Despite the tag "Euro," these accounts need not be in European banks, although that is where the practice of accepting dollar-denominated deposits outside the United States began.

Most Eurodollar deposits are for large sums, and most are time deposits of less than six months' maturity. A variation on the Eurodollar time deposit is the Eurodollar certificate of deposit. A Eurodollar CD resembles a U.S. domestic bank CD, except that it is the liability of a non-U.S. branch of a bank (typically a London branch). The advantage of Eurodollar CDs over Eurodollar time deposits is that the holder can sell the asset to realize its cash value before maturity. Eurodollar CDs are considered less liquid and riskier than U.S. domestic CDs, however, and thus offer higher yields. Firms also issue Eurodollar bonds, which are dollar-denominated bonds in Europe, although bonds are not a money market investment because of their long maturities.

All of the above instruments—time deposits, CDs, and bonds—also exist denominated in all major currencies; these are labelled Eurocurrency instruments when located outside the country of currency. When issued in Canadian dollar denominations then they are referred to as *Euro-Canadian* dollars; these constitute a minor proportion of the Eurocurrency market, which is dominated by Eurodollar trading.

Repos and Reverses

Dealers in government securities use *repurchase agreements* (also called *repos* or *RPs*) as a form of short-term, usually overnight, borrowing. The dealer sells government securities to an investor on an overnight basis, with an agreement to buy back those securities the next day at a slightly higher price. The increase in the price is the overnight interest. The dealer thus takes out a one-day loan from the investor, and the securities serve as collateral.

A *term repo* is essentially an identical transaction, except that the term of the implicit loan can be 30 days or more. Repos are considered very safe in terms of credit risk because the loans are backed by the government securities. A *reverse repo* is the mirror image of a repo. Here, the dealer finds an investor holding government securities and buys them, agreeing to sell them back at a specified higher price on a future date.

The U.S. repo market was upset by several failures of government security dealers in 1985. In these cases the dealers had entered into the typical repo arrangements with investors, pledging government securities as collateral. The investors did not take physical possession of the securities as they could have under the purchase and resale arrangement. Some of the dealers, unfortunately, fraudulently pledged the same securities as collateral in different repos; when the dealers went under, the investors found that they could not collect the securities that they had ''purchased'' in the first phase of the repo transaction. In the wake of the scandal repo rates for nonprimary dealers increased, whereas rates for some well-capitalized firms fell as investors became more sensitive to credit risk.[1] Investors can best protect themselves by taking delivery of the securities, either directly or through an agent such as a bank custodian.

Brokers' Calls

Individuals who buy stocks on margin borrow part of the funds to pay for the stocks from their broker. The broker in turn may borrow the funds from a bank, agreeing to repay the bank immediately (on call) if the bank requests it. Chartered banks make such call loans to investment firms that use them to finance their inventory of securities. The rate paid on these loans is usually closely related to the rate on short-term T-bills.

The LIBOR Market

The **London Interbank Offered Rate** (LIBOR) is the rate at which large banks in London are willing to lend money among themselves. This rate has become the premier short-term interest rate quoted in the European money market, and it serves as a reference rate for a wide range of transactions. For example, a corporation might borrow at a rate equal to LIBOR plus 2 percent.

Yields on Money Market Instruments

Although most money market securities are of low risk, they are not risk-free. For example, as we noted earlier, the U.S. commercial paper market was

---

[1] Stephen A. Lumpkin, "Repurchase and Reverse Repurchase Agreements," in T. Cook and T. Rowe (editors), *Instruments of the Money Market* (Richmond, Va.: Federal Reserve Bank of Richmond, 1986).

FIGURE 2.2
The spread between
short-term corporate
paper and T-bill
rates.

Constructed from
CANSIM data.

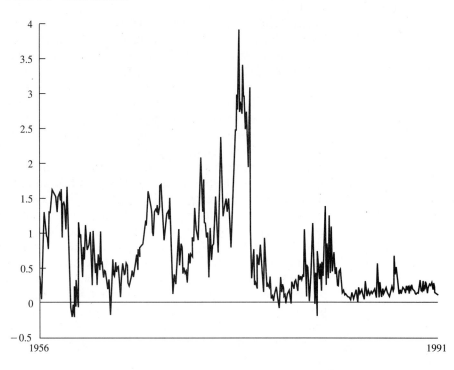

rocked by the Penn Central bankruptcy, which precipitated a default on $82 million of commercial paper. Money market investors in that country became more sensitive to creditworthiness after this episode, and the yield spread between low- and high-quality paper widened.

The securities of the money market do promise yields greater than those on default-free T-bills, at least in part because of greater relative riskiness. In addition, many investors require more liquidity; thus they will accept lower yields on securities such as T-bills that can be quickly and cheaply sold for cash. Figure 2.2 shows that commercial paper, for example, has consistently paid a risk premium over T-bills of approximately equal maturity. Moreover, that risk premium increased with economic crises such as the energy price shocks associated with the two OPEC disturbances, even though it has been lower overall in more recent years, as compared to earlier periods.

2.2 *The Fixed-Income Capital Market*

The fixed-income capital market is composed of longer-term borrowing instruments than those that trade in the money market. This market includes Government of Canada bonds, provincial and municipal bonds, corporate bonds, and mortgage securities. Bonds can be *callable* during a given period; this feature allows the issuer to redeem the bond at par value, or at a stated premium prior to maturity.

Government of Canada Bonds

The Canadian government borrows funds in large part by selling both nonmarketable and marketable debt securities. The nonmarketable securities are known as *Canada Savings Bonds* (CSB); they are issued each year on November 1st, generally for a seven-year term. Although these bonds are nontransferable, they are perfectly liquid, since they can be cashed any time prior to maturity at face value plus accrued interest. Because of this latter feature, the valuation of CSBs is quite complex and transcends the level of this text.

Government of Canada Bonds or simply *Canada Bonds* are longer-term marketable debt securities issued by the Canadian federal government. These bonds have varying maturities at issue date, ranging up to 40 years. They are considered part of the money market when their term becomes less than three years. Canada bonds are generally non-callable, and make semi-annual coupon payments that are set at a competitive level designed to ensure their issue at or near par value.

Figure 2.3 is a listing of actively traded Canada bonds as they appear in *The Globe and Mail*. Under the Government of Canada section, note the bond (*arrow*) that matures in June 2001. The coupon income, or interest, paid by the bond is 9.75 percent of par value, meaning that for a $1,000 face value bond $97.50 in annual interest payments will be made in two semi-annual installments of $48.75 each. In the trading of a security, bid and asked prices are quoted; these represent, respectively, the price at which an investor can sell or buy the asset. These prices are not shown separately in this listing, but their average is given as 104.350, denoting a percentage of par value. Thus the price shown should be interpreted as 104.35 percent of par, or $1,043.50 for a $1,000 face value bond. This price decreased by $2.50 from the previous day's closing price, or $.250 per $100 of par value. Finally, the yield to maturity on the bond is 9.059 percent.

The **yield to maturity** reported in the financial pages is calculated by determining the semiannual yield and then doubling it, rather than compounding it for two half-year periods. This use of a simple interest technique to annualize means that the yield is quoted on an annual percentage rate (APR) basis, rather than as an effective annual yield. The APR method in this context is also called the *bond equivalent yield*. From Figure 2.3 we can see that the yields on Government of Canada bonds are generally rising with term to maturity; this is not true uniformly, due to the different coupons of bonds with similar maturities. Listings for callable bonds trading at a premium (selling above par value) show the yield calculated to the first call date, while for discount bonds the yield is calculated to the redemption date. (No such callable bonds appear in Figure 2.3.)

FIGURE 2.3
Canadian bonds.

From *The Globe and Mail*, October 17, 1991. Reprinted by permission.

The Globe and Mail, Thursday, October 17, 1991

CANADIAN BONDS

Selected quotations, with changes since the previous day, on actively traded bond issues, provided by RBC Dominion Securities. Yields are calculated to full maturity, unless marked C to indicate callable date. Price is the midpoint between final bid and ask quotations Oct. 16, 1991.

Issuer	Coupon	Maturity	Price	Yield	$ Chg	Issuer	Coupon	Maturity	Price	Yield	$ Chg
GOVERNMENT OF CANADA						N S POWER	11.00	26 FEB 31	106.725	10.291	-0.200
CANADA	10.25	5 DEC 92	102.250	8.110	-0.050	ONTARIO HYD	10.00	16 JUN 93	102.675	8.217	-0.050
CANADA	9.50	1 SEP 93	102.375	8.096	-0.050	ONTARIO HYD	10.75	19 NOV 95	106.075	8.934	-0.150
CANADA	8.75	6 SEP 93	101.325	7.970	NC	ONTARIO HYD	10.88	8 JAN 96	106.225	9.055	-0.100
CANADA	10.25	1 FEB 94	104.150	8.211	-0.150	ONTARIO HYD	9.63	3 AUG 99	101.275	9.385	-0.250
CANADA	9.25	1 OCT 94	102.750	8.180	-0.100	ONTARIO HYD	10.00	19 MAR 01	102.725	9.552	-0.200
CANADA	10.50	1 JUN 95	106.225	8.455	-0.100	ONTARIO HYD	10.75	6 AUG 21	106.775	10.028	-0.200
CANADA	9.25	1 OCT 96	102.550	8.603	-0.150	ONTARIO HYD	10.13	15 OCT 21	101.075	10.011	-0.200
CANADA	8.25	1 MAR 97	98.600	8.577	-0.100	ONTARIO	10.25	3 OCT 96	104.725	9.041	-0.100
CANADA	9.75	1 OCT 97	104.650	8.728	-0.150	ONTARIO	10.20	27 AUG 98	104.500	9.292	-0.200
CANADA	9.50	1 OCT 98	103.450	8.823	-0.250	ONTARIO	10.50	12 DEC 01	105.625	9.615	-0.200
CANADA	9.25	1 DEC 99	101.900	8.913	-0.300	P E I	11.00	19 SEP 11	105.250	10.369	-0.200
CANADA	9.75	1 JUN 01	104.350	9.059	-0.250	QUEBEC	10.25	7 APR 98	103.575	9.495	-0.200
CANADA	9.50	1 OCT 01	102.725	9.076	-0.250	QUEBEC	10.25	15 OCT 01	102.800	9.803	-0.250
CANADA	9.75	1 DEC 01	104.500	9.058	-0.250	SASKATCHEWAN	10.00	21 NOV 94	103.575	8.647	-0.150
CANADA	10.00	1 MAY 02	105.825	9.126	-0.150	SASKATCHEWAN	10.13	3 JUL 98	103.450	9.413	-0.200
CANADA	11.75	1 FEB 03	116.275	9.376	-0.200	SASKATCHEWAN	10.25	10 APR 14	100.625	10.178	-0.200
CANADA	10.25	1 FEB 04	107.300	9.239	-0.200	TORONTO -MET	10.38	4 SEP 01	104.275	9.689	-0.150
CANADA	10.00	1 JUN 08	104.950	9.403	-0.200	**CORPORATE**					
CANADA	9.50	1 JUN 10	101.400	9.338	-0.200	BELL CANADA	10.50	15 MAY 98	105.625	9.332	-0.250
CANADA	9.00	1 MAR 11	97.550	9.272	-0.200	BELL CANADA	11.45	15 APR 10	110.750	10.150	-0.375
CANADA	10.25	15 MAR 14	107.300	9.458	-0.200	BC TELEPHONE	10.50	12 JUN 00	104.625	9.693	NC
CANADA	10.50	15 MAR 21	109.500	9.530	-0.200	BC TELEPHONE	10.65	19 JUN 21	104.625	10.151	-0.250
CANADA	9.75	1 JUN 21	103.400	9.406	-0.200	BANK OF N S	10.75	26 MAR 01	105.000	9.919	-0.250
PROVINCIAL						CONSUMER GAS	10.80	15 APR 11	104.000	10.319	-0.375
ALBERTA	9.75	8 MAY 98	102.925	9.144	-0.200	CDN IMP BANK	10.38	31 JAN 00	103.750	9.700	-0.250
ALBERTA	10.25	22 AUG 01	104.950	9.461	-0.200	CDN PACIFIC	10.50	30 APR 01	103.125	9.983	-0.250
B C	9.60	12 SEP 94	102.725	8.509	-0.100	CP SECURITIE	10.50	2 AUG 96	103.625	9.530	-0.125
B C	10.15	29 AUG 01	103.775	9.546	-0.200	CDN UTIL	11.40	15 AUG 10	110.000	10.191	-0.375
B C	10.75	21 FEB 11	106.475	9.984	-0.250	GAZ METRO	10.45	31 OCT 16	100.375	10.407	-0.125
HYDRO QUEBEC	9.25	2 DEC 96	100.225	9.189	-0.100	IMPERIAL OIL	9.88	15 DEC 99	101.875	9.535	-0.250
HYDRO QUEBEC	10.88	25 JUL 01	106.525	9.815	-0.250	IMASCO LTD	11.85	15 FEB 96	108.125	9.501	-0.125
HYDRO QUEBEC	11.00	15 AUG 20	106.925	10.245	-0.200	NOVA CORP	10.75	14 APR 99	101.875	10.382	-0.375
MANITOBA	11.25	17 OCT 00	109.250	9.684	-0.150	PANCDN PETE	10.55	4 JAN 00	104.750	9.692	-0.125
MANITOBA	10.50	5 MAR 31	103.775	10.108	-0.200	ROYAL BANK	10.75	15 AUG 01	105.750	9.819	-0.375
NEW BRUNSWIC	11.25	18 OCT 95	107.075	9.093	-0.150	ROYAL BANK	10.50	1 MAR 02	104.500	9.795	-0.250
NEW BRUNSWIC	10.13	31 OCT 11	100.025	10.121	-0.200	TRANSALTA UT	11.38	1 AUG 00	109.125	9.795	-0.250
NEWFOUNDLAND	10.13	22 NOV 14	96.975	10.473	-0.200	THOMSON CORP	10.55	10 MAY 01	104.500	9.811	-0.250
NFLD&LAB HYD	10.75	17 SEP 01	104.625	10.000	-0.250						
N S POWER	11.85	24 OCT 95	108.875	9.152	-0.150						

Concept Check

Question 2. Why does it make sense to calculate yields on discount bonds to maturity and yields on premium bonds to the first call date?

Provincial and Municipal Bonds

Figure 2.3 shows a representative sample of bonds issued by provincial governments and by provincial Crown Corporations; the latter are generally guaranteed by the corresponding provincial government. One municipal bond, Metro Toronto, also appears in the listings. All these bonds are similar in their characteristics to federal government issues, with a variety of maturities and coupon rates, and are available to investors at any given time. These securities are considered extremely safe assets, even though not as safe as comparable Government of Canada bonds. Consequently, a small yield spread can be observed in Figure 2.3 between Canada's and provincials, as well as yield spreads between the various provinces. For instance, bonds maturing in 2001 yield 9.059 percent for Canada's, 9.615 percent for Ontario's, and 9.803 percent for Quebec's.

U.S. municipal bonds are exempt from federal income tax, and from state and local tax in the issuing state. Hence, the quoted yield is an after-tax yield, which should be compared with after-tax yields on other bonds. This explains why the quoted yields on municipals are lower than the quoted (before-tax) yields on other comparable bonds. Since the tax advantage is not available to Canadian investors, U.S. municipal bonds would generally not be attractive to them.

Corporate Bonds

Corporate bonds enable private firms to borrow money directly from the public. These bonds are similar in structure to government issues—they typically pay semi-annual coupons over their lives and return the face value to the bondholder at maturity. However, they differ most importantly from government bonds in degree of risk. Default risk is a real consideration in the purchase of corporate bonds, and Chapter 15 discusses this issue in considerable detail. For now, we distinguish only among *secured bonds*, which have specific collateral backing them in the event of firm bankruptcy, unsecured bonds called *debentures*, which have no collateral, and *subordinated debentures,* which have a lower priority claim to the firm's assets in the event of bankruptcy. Referring to Figure 2.3 again, we see a Canadian Pacific bond maturing in 2001 and paying a coupon of 10.50 percent; its yield of 9.983 percent compares with the above-mentioned government bonds with yields ranging from 9.05 percent to 9.80 percent.

Corporate bonds usually come with options attached. *Callable bonds* give the firm the option to repurchase the bond from the holder at a stipulated call price. *Retractable* and *extendible bonds* give the holder the option, respectively, to redeem the bonds earlier and later than the stated maturity date. *Convertible bonds* give the bondholder the option to convert each bond into a stipulated number of shares of stock. These options are treated in more detail in Chapter 15.

Mortgages and Mortgage-Backed Securities

An investments text of 20 years ago probably would not include a section on mortgage loans, since at that time investors could not invest in them. Now, because of the explosion in mortgage-backed securities, almost anyone can invest in a portfolio of mortgage loans, and these securities have become a major component of a fixed-income market.

Home mortgages are usually written with a long-term (25- to 30-year maturity) amortization of the principal. Until the 1970s, almost all such mortgages had a fixed interest rate over the life of the loan, and with equal fixed monthly payments. Since then these so-called conventional mortgages became renewable at one- to five-year intervals, at which point their interest rates were renegotiated. More recently, a diverse set of alternative mortgage designs has developed.

Fixed-rate mortgages pose difficulties to banks in years of increasing interest rates because of the mismatching of the maturities of assets and liabilities. Banks commonly issue short-term liabilities (the deposits of their customers) and hold long-term assets such as fixed-rate mortgages. Hence, they suffer losses when interest rates increase: the rates they pay on deposits increase while their mortgage income remains fixed. The five-year renewal period helps to alleviate this problem.

A relatively recent introduction is the *adjustable rate mortgage*. These mortgages require the borrower to pay an interest rate that varies with some measure of the current market interest rate. For example, the interest rate might be set at two points above the current rate on one-year Treasury bills and might be adjusted once a year. Often, a contract sets a limit, or cap, on the maximum size of an interest rate change within a year and over the life of the contract. The adjustable rate contract shifts the risk of fluctuations in interest rates from the lender to the borrower.

Because of the shifting of interest rate risk to their customers, banks are willing to offer lower rates on adjustable rate mortgages than on conventional fixed-rate mortgages. This proved to be a great inducement to borrowers during a period of high interest rates in the early 1980s. As interest rates fell, however, conventional mortgages appeared to regain popularity.

A *mortgage-backed security* (MBS) is either an ownership claim in a pool of mortgages or an obligation that is secured by such a pool. These claims represent securitization of mortgage loans. Mortgage lenders originate loans and then sell packages of these loans in the secondary market. Specifically, they sell their claim to the cash inflows from the mortgages as those loans are paid off. The mortgage originator continues to service the loan, collecting principal and interest payments, and passes these payments along to the purchaser of the mortgage. For this reason, these mortgage-backed securities are called *passthroughs*. Like the adjustable rate mortgages, they were designed to deal with the mismatching of maturities of bank assets and liabilities. Mortgage-backed pass-through securities were first introduced in Canada by the Canada Mortgage and Housing Corporation (CMHC, a federal Crown Corporation) in 1987. CMHC pass-throughs carry a federal government guarantee under the National Housing Act (NHA), which insures the timely payment of principal and interest. Thus the cash flow can be considered risk-free even if individual borrowers default on their mortgages. This guarantee increases the marketability of the pass-through. Thus, investors can buy or sell NHA MBSs like any other bond.

Although pass-through securities often guarantee payment of interest and principal, they do not guarantee the rate of return. Holders of mortgage pass-throughs therefore can be severely disappointed in their returns in years when interest rates drop significantly. This is because homeowners usually have an option to prepay, or pay ahead of schedule, the remaining principal outstanding

FIGURE 2.4

Mortgage-backed
securities.

From *The Globe and
Mail*, May 25, 1992.
Reprinted by permission.

MORTGAGE-BACKED SECURITIES

Mortgage-backed securities are investments in pools of residential mortgages guaranteed by the Canadian government under the National Housing Act. This representative list of actively traded pools is provided by Wood Gundy Inc. and shows the gross bid price for transactions of at least $1-million at Friday's close. The list is divided between open mortgages that are prepayable, and are likely to produce accelerated return of principal, and closed mortgages, on which unscheduled principal payments are not permitted.

PREPAYABLE

Pool	Issuer	Maturity	Coupon	Price	Yield
96400809	Shoppers	Jul.93	10.000	102.13783	7.61
96401682	Shoppers	Aug.94	9.385	102.93667	8.29
96402045	Standard	Oct.94	9.750	102.69917	8.27
96402169	FirstLine	Jan.95	9.875	103.11331	8.33
96402300	Central Guar.	Jan.95	10.250	103.92418	8.34
96402797	Shoppers	Jun.95	10.250	103.57052	8.70
96403639	FirstLine	May.96	10.125	103.01223	9.05
96403944	CIBC	Jun.96	10.250	103.59164	9.01
96404314	Canada Trust	Nov.96	9.125	100.53830	8.87
96404629	Nat. Bank	Dec.96	8.375	98.18847	8.80

NONPREPAYABLE

Pool	Issuer	Maturity	Coupon	Price	Yield
99000010	TD	Jul.93	10.000	102.50431	7.28
99000036	CIBC	Aug.93	10.000	102.70317	7.28
99002891	Sun Life	Nov.93	7.875	100.51440	7.28
99000614	Central Guar.	Apr.94	10.375	104.29081	7.61
99001042	FirstLine	Nov.94	9.875	103.63495	8.02
99001018	Nat. Trust	Dec.94	10.000	104.01121	8.02
99001075	CIBC	Jan.95	10.250	104.38486	8.15
99002305	Nat. Trust	May.96	9.500	102.47397	8.62
99002867	TD	Nov.96	9.250	101.95192	8.60
99003196	CIBC	Feb.97	7.750	96.54077	8.62

on their mortgages. This right is essentially an option held by the borrower to "call back" the loan for the remaining principal balance, quite analogous to the option held by government or corporate issuers of callable bonds. The prepayment option gives the borrower the right to buy back the loan at the outstanding principal amount rather than at the present discounted value of the *scheduled* remaining payments. The exercise of this option usually requires the payment of a penalty or bonus by the borrower, which is also passed through to the MBS investors; prepayments may also occur due to the sale of the underlying property. When interest rates fall, causing the present value of the scheduled mortgage payments to increase, the borrower may choose to take out a new loan at today's lower interest rate and use the proceeds of the loan to prepay or retire the outstanding mortgage. This refinancing may disappoint pass-through investors, who are liable to "receive a call" just when they might have anticipated capital gains from interest rate declines. Figure 2.4 is a recent listing from *The Globe and Mail* of both prepayable and nonprepayable MBSs.

2.3 *Equity Securities*

Common Stock as Ownership Shares

Common stocks, also known as *equity securities* or *equities,* represent ownership shares in a corporation. Each share of common stock entitles its owner to one vote on any matters of corporate governance that are put to a vote at the corporation's annual meeting, as well as to a share in the financial benefits of ownership.

The corporation is controlled by a board of directors elected by the shareholders. The board, which meets only a few times each year, selects managers who actually run the corporation on a day-to-day basis. Managers have the authority to make most business decisions without the board's specific approval. The board's mandate is overseeing the management to ensure that it acts in the best interests of shareholders. The members of the board are elected at the annual meeting. Shareholders who do not attend the annual meeting can vote by *proxy,* empowering another party to vote in their name. Management usually solicits the proxies of shareholders and normally gets a vast majority of these proxy votes. Occasionally, however, a group of shareholders intent on unseating the current management or altering its policies will wage a proxy fight to gain the voting rights of shareholders not attending the annual meeting. Thus, although management usually has considerable discretion to run the firm as it sees fit—without daily scrutiny from the equityholders who actually own the firm—both scrutiny from the board and the possibility of a proxy fight serve as checks on management's jurisdiction.

Another related check on management's discretion is the possibility of a corporate takeover. In these episodes, an outside investor who believes that the firm is mismanaged will attempt to acquire the firm. Usually, this is accomplished with a *tender offer,* which is an offer made to purchase, at a stipulated price (usually substantially above the current market price), some or all of the shares held by the current stockholders. If the tender is successful, the acquiring investor purchases enough shares to obtain control of the firm and can replace the existing management.

Several Canadian firms have at times issued a special type of common stock (**restricted shares**) that has no voting rights, or only restricted voting rights, but otherwise participates fully in the financial benefits of share ownership. For instance, a company may issue two classes of shares, only one of which has the right to vote; alternatively, the senior class may have five votes and the subordinate class only one vote per share. Such shares accounted for about 15 percent of the market on the Toronto Stock Exchange at the end of 1989. They were issued by firms that wanted to expand without diluting the holdings of a controlling group. Occasionally, restricted shares were issued to comply with regulatory requirements, such as those restricting foreign ownership in Canadian broadcasting.

Restricted shares sometimes carry different (generally higher) financial benefits for their holders than regular common stock. Otherwise, the loss of the right to vote should be reflected in a lower market value for restricted than for ordinary shares; this loss is the market value of the right to vote. Restricted shareholders also have some legal protection in case of tender offers. Several studies have examined this value of the voting rights, as well as other implications of restricted shares.[2]

---

[2] See, for instance, Vijay Jog and Allan Riding, "Price Effects of Dual-Class Shares," *Financial Analysts Journal,* January/February 1986, and "Market Reactions of Return, Risk, and Liquidity to the Creation of Restricted Voting Shares," *Canadian Journal of Administrative Sciences* 6, no. 1 (March 1989); Elizabeth Maynes, Chris Robinson, and Alan White, "How Much Is a Share Vote Worth?" *Canadian Investment Review* 3, no. 1 (Spring

The common stock of most large corporations can be bought or sold freely on one or more stock exchanges. A corporation whose stock is not publicly traded is said to be *closely held*. In most closely held corporations, the owners of the firm also take an active role in its management. Takeovers, therefore, are generally not an issue.

Thus, although there is substantial separation of the ownership and the control of large corporations, there are at least some implicit controls on management that tend to force it to act in the interests of the shareholders.

Characteristics of Common Stock

The two most important characteristics of common stock as an investment are its **residual claim** and **limited liability** features.

Residual claim means that stockholders are the last in line of all those who have a claim on the assets and income of the corporation. In a liquidation of the firm's assets, the shareholders have a claim to what is left after all other claimants such as the tax authorities, employees, suppliers, bondholders, and other creditors have been paid. For a firm not in liquidation, shareholders have claim to the part of operating income left over after interest and taxes have been paid. Management can either pay this residual as cash dividends to shareholders or reinvest it in the business to increase the value of the shares.

Limited liability means that the greatest amount shareholders can lose in event of failure of the corporation is their original investment. Unlike owners of unincorporated businesses, whose creditors can lay claim to the personal assets of the owner (e.g., house, car, furniture), corporate shareholders may at worst have worthless stock. They are not personally liable for the firm's obligations.

Concept Check	Question 3.
	a. If you buy 100 shares of Alcan stock, to what are you entitled?
	b. What is the most money you can make on this investment over the next year?
	c. If you pay $50 per share, what is the most money you could lose over the year?

Stock Market Listings

Figure 2.5 is a partial listing from *The Globe and Mail* weekly report of stocks traded on the Toronto Stock Exchange. The TSE is one of several Canadian

1990); Chris Robinson and Alan White, "Empirical Evidence on the Relative Valuation of Voting and Restricted Voting Shares," *Canadian Journal of Administrative Sciences* 7, no. 4 (December 1990); and Elizabeth Maynes, "Evidence on the Value of a Stock Exchange Listing," *Canadian Journal of Administrative Sciences* 8, no. 3 (September 1991).

FIGURE 2.5
Stock market listings.

From *The Globe and Mail*, October 19, 1991. Reprinted by permission.

53-week			WEEK TRADING				Sales	Ind.		Share	
High	Low	Company	High	Low	Close	Chg	000s	Div.	Yield	profit	P/E
33	21⅝	CIBC	$30¾	30¼	30¾	+ ⅜	773	1.32	4.3	3.84	8.0
103	95¼	CIBC 3 FLTG PR D	$100¼	100¼	100¼	+ ⅛	.522	8.90	8.9		
87	80¼	CIBC 4 PR F	$86½	86	86½	+ 1	.975	6.82	7.9		
22¼	20⅜	CIBC 5 FLTG PR E	$21¼	20¾	21	− ½	2	1.66	7.9		
26⅜	22⅛	CIBC 6 PR G	$26⅜	25⅞	26⅜	+ ⅜	24	2.25	8.5		
26¼	21¾	CIBC 8 PR H	$26¼	25¾	26¼	+ ½	12	2.22	8.5		
27	24⅞	CIBC 9 PR I	$26⅝	26⅛	26½	− ⅛	30	2.28	8.6		
195	105	CDN JOREX	195	185	190	− 4	52			0.14	13.6
14¼	9	CDN MARCONI	$13⅜	13¼	13⅜	+ ¼	1	0.14	1.0	0.63	21.2
6⅞	325	CDN NATURAL RES	$6⅞	6⅛	6⅞	+ ⅝	282			0.34	20.2
160	57	CDN NEWSCOPE RES J	60	60	60		2			-0.55	
5½	390	CDN NORTHSTAR	390	390	390		1			-0.81	
24¾	13⅜	CDN OCC PETROL	$23¼	22⅛	22¾	− ½	203	0.40	1.8	0.37	61.5
35	27	CDN PACIFC FRST PRD	$28½	27¾	28	− ¼	10	0.40	1.4	-2.93	
23¼	17	CDN PACIFIC	$19⅛	18⅛	18⅝	+ ⅝	2152	0.64	3.4	0.63	29.6
200	101	CDN PACIF 4% UK PR C	115	110	110		.606	0.01	1.2		
7⅜	490	CDN ROXY PETROL	$6¾	6⅝	6⅝		24			0.07	94.6
13¾	11	CDN SATELL COMM J	$12¼	11¾	12¼	+ ¾	10	0.20	1.6	0.72	17.0
20	4	CDN SPOONER RES			10		z.334			-0.03	
27½	21½	CDN TIRE	$25	25	25	+ 1	.325	0.40	1.6	1.56	16.0
26	19¾	CDN TIRE A NV	$23½	22⅜	23⅜	+ ⅞	384	0.40	1.7	1.56	15.0
440	155	CDN TURBO	190	165	180	+ 15	207			-0.28	
70	60	CDN UTIL 6.00% PR C	$67⅛	67⅛	67⅛	− 2⅞	.150	6.00	8.9		
24½	21¼	CDN UTIL C 2ND PR G	$23½	23½	23½		.300	1.83	7.8		
21⅛	18⅝	CDN UTIL CL A NV	$20¼	20	20	− ¼	61	1.38	6.9	1.63	12.3
21¼	18⅝	CDN UTIL CL B X	$20⅜	20¼	20¼	+ ⅜	7	1.38	6.8	1.63	12.4
25¾	24¾	CDN UTIL I 2ND PR N	$25¼	25⅛	25⅛		103	2.18	8.7		
25½	23¾	CDN UTIL K 2ND PR O	$25½	25½	25½	+ ½	3	1.95	7.6		
25¾	25	CDN UTIL P PR S	$25¾	25½	25¾	+ ¼	3	2.00	7.8		
5⅞	370	CDN WESTERN BANK	410	410	410	+ 5	.700			0.37	11.1
425	205	CANAM MANAC GRP A SV	205	205	205	− 30	.300	0.10	4.9	-2.03	
65	26	CANAMAX RES	28	27	28	+ 1	20			-1.86	
7	250	CANBRA FOODS	400	400	400	+ 50	.400			-0.75	
29¾	19⅜	CANFOR	$23½	22	22¾	+ 1	49	0.40	1.8	-3.25	
23	18½	CANFOR $2.25 PR A	$21½	20⅝	20⅝	+ ⅛	3	2.25	10.9		
54	12½	CANHORN MNG J	15	15	15		3			-0.63	
325	125	CANLAN INVESTMENT	255	250	255		.800			0.23	11.0
6	260	CANSTAR SPORTS	480	470	480	− 10	6			0.43	11.2
25¼	23⅜	CANUTILITIES PR A	$24⅞	24⅞	24⅞	− ⅜	2	1.94	7.8		
11⅝	11½	CANWEST GLOBAL SV	$11⅝	11½	11⅝	+ 11⅝	65				
200	180	CANWEST GLOBAL WT	200	180	190	+ 190	12				
345	74	CAPILANO INTL J	93	90	90		13			0.20	4.6
5⅝	450	CARA OPERATIONS	$5½	5⅛	5½	+ ¼	288	0.09	1.6	0.26	21.0
6½	435	CARA OPERATIONS A NV	$5½	5¼	5⅜	+ ¼	819	0.09	1.6	0.26	20.5
15⅝	9	CARENA DEVEL	$9⅝	9⅛	9¼	− ¼	2	0.50	5.4	0.60	15.4
225	60	CARENA DEV WT	62	62	62	− 13	2				
6¼	310	CASCADES	$6¼	6	6¼	+ ½	6			0.31	20.2
165	85	CASCADES WT	165	144	165	+ 23	3				
110	32	CATHEDRAL GOLD J	50	32	50	− 2	65			-1.08	
39¼	30½	CELANESE CDA	$38⅝	38½	38⅝	+ ¼	28	1.85	4.8	2.24	17.2
34	26¾	CELANESE CDA S1 PR B	$31	31	31		.120	2.16	7.0		
8	90	CENTRAL CAP	140	126	139	− 1	21			-1.92	
6¾	70	CENTRAL CAP A SV	115	105	110	− 10	37			-1.92	
22⅛	400	CENTRAL CAP PR A	$6¼	5½	6¼	+ ⅜	19	1.91	30.5		
21¾	350	CENTRAL CAP PR B	$6	5¼	5¼	− ¾	5	1.91	36.3		
495	85	CENTRAL CRUDE J	120	120	120	− 13	1			-0.09	
5½	430	CENTRAL FND CDA A NV	445	435	435	− 5	9	0.01	0.2	-0.06	
17	9	CNT GRNTY TR CO1 PR A	$13⅜	13⅜	13⅜	+ ⅜	.150	1.60	12.0	1.59	8.4
17½	10	CNT GRNTY TR CO2 PR B	$14¾	14	14¾	+ ⅝	2	2.06	14.0		
24½	18	CNT GRNTY TR CO3 PR C	$23	22¼	23	+ ¾	2	2.31	10.1	1.59	14.5
9¼	5	CNTRL GRNTY TRUSTCO	$6⅜	6	6⅛		19	0.50	8.2	-0.03	
21	11	CNTRL GRNTY TRUSTCO PR A	$15⅝	15⅝	15⅝	− 4⅜	.400	1.60	10.2		
255	133	CHAI-NA-TA GINSNG	250	230	250	+ 10	35	0.12	4.7	0.09	28.8
71	23	CHANCELLOR E RES J	43	35	43	+ 10	100				
475	45	CHANCELLOR GROUP	55	50	50	− 10	4			-2.45	

markets in which investors may buy or sell shares of stock. We will examine these markets in detail in Chapter 3.

To interpret the information provided for each traded stock, consider the two listings for Canadian Tire, CDN TIRE and CDN TIRE A NV. These two shares are otherwise identical, except that the second or class A listing has no voting rights; for this reason, its quoted prices are somewhat lower than the

CDN TIRE, with the difference representing the value of the voting privilege. For the class A shares, the first two columns provide the highest and lowest price at which the stock has traded in the last 52 weeks, 26 and 19¾, respectively. The 0.40 figure following the name means that the dividend payout to its shareholders in each class over the last quarter was $0.40 per share on an annual basis. Thus Canadian Tire class A stock, which is selling at 23⅜ (the last recorded, or *close* price, in the sixth column), has a dividend yield of 0.40/23.375 = .017, or 1.7 percent; this is higher than the yield on the voting shares, 1.6 percent of the price of 25. A cursory analysis of the stock listings shows that dividend yields vary widely among firms. It is important to recognize that high dividend-yield stocks are not necessarily better investments than low-yield stocks. Total return to an investor comes from dividends and **capital gains,** or appreciation in the value of the stock. Low dividend-yield firms presumably offer greater prospects for capital gains, or investors would not be willing to hold the low-yield firms in their portfolios.

The share profit, or earnings per share, represents the corporate earnings for the last four quarters divided by the number of shares outstanding. P-E ratio, or **price-earnings ratio,** is the ratio of the closing stock price to last year's earnings per share. The P-E ratio tells us how much stock purchasers must pay per dollar of earnings that the firm generates for each share. The P-E ratio also varies widely across firms. Where the dividend yield or P-E ratio are not reported in Figure 2.5, the firms have zero dividends, or zero or negative earnings. We shall have much to say about P-E ratios in Chapter 18.

The sales column shows that 384,000 shares of the stock were traded in the week ending October 18, 1991. Shares commonly are traded in **board lots** of 100 shares each; however, a board lot consists of 1,000 shares for stocks selling below $5, while it falls to 25 shares for stocks above $100. Investors who wish to trade in smaller odd lots can expect to pay higher commissions to their stock brokers, although many brokers are not charging an odd-lot differential in order to attract the small investor. The commission structure actually makes trading in a small number of higher-priced stocks (say 25 shares at $120) cheaper on a percentage basis than the same value of a low-priced stock (say 1,000 shares at $3). The highest price and lowest price per share at which the stock traded in that week were 23½ and 22⅜, respectively. The last, or closing, price of 23⅜ was up ⅞ from the closing price of the previous week.

Preferred Stock

Preferred stock has features similar to both equity and debt. Like a bond, it promises to pay to its holder fixed dividends each year. In this sense preferred stock is similar to an infinite-maturity bond, that is, a perpetuity. It also resembles a bond in that it does not convey voting power regarding the management of the firm. Preferred stock is an equity investment, however, in the sense that failure to pay the dividend does not precipitate corporate bankruptcy. Instead, preferred dividends are usually *cumulative;* that is, unpaid dividends cumulate and must be paid in full before any dividends may be paid to holders of common stock.

Preferred stock also differs from bonds in terms of its tax treatment for the firm. Because preferred stock payments are treated as dividends rather than interest, they are not tax-deductible expenses for the firm. This disadvantage is somewhat offset by the fact that corporations may exclude dividends received from domestic corporations in the computation of their taxable income. Preferred stocks, therefore, make desirable fixed-income investments for some corporations. Similarly, preferred dividends are taxed like common dividends for individual investors, which confers them a higher after-tax yield than bonds with the same pre-tax yield. Hence, even though they rank after bonds in the event of corporate bankruptcy, preferred stocks generally sell at lower yields than do corporate bonds.

Preferred stock is issued in variations similar to those of corporate bonds. It can be callable by the issuing firm, in which case it is said to be *redeemable*. It also can be convertible into common stock at some specified conversion ratio. A firm often issues different series of preferreds, with different dividends, over time. In Figure 2.5 there are five different issues of Canadian Utilities (CDN UTIL), in addition to two classes of common. A recent innovation in the market is adjustable rate preferred stock, which, similar to adjustable rate mortgages, ties the dividend rate to current market interest rates.

2.4 *Stock and Bond Market Indices*

Stock Market Indices

The daily performance of the Dow Jones Industrial Average and the Toronto Stock Exchange (TSE) Composite Index are staple portions of the Canadian evening news report. Although these indices are, respectively, the best-known measures of the performances of the U.S. and Canadian stock markets, they are only two of several indicators of stock market performance in the two countries. Other indices are computed and published daily. In addition, several indices of bond market performance are widely available.

Dow Jones Averages

The Dow Jones Industrial Average of 30 large blue-chip corporations has been computed since 1896. Its long history probably accounts for its preeminence in the public mind. (The average covered only 20 stocks until 1928). The Dow is a **price-weighted average,** which means that it is computed by adding the prices of the 30 companies and dividing by a divisor.

Originally, the divisor was simply 20 when 20 stocks were included in the index; thus the index was no more than the average price of the 20 stocks. This makes the index performance a measure of the performance of a particular portfolio strategy that buys one share of each firm in the index. Therefore, the weight of each firm in the index is proportional to the share price rather than the total outstanding market value of the shares. For example, if shares of firm XYZ sell for $100 each and it has 1 million shares outstanding, while shares of firm ABC sell for $25 each but there are 20 million shares outstanding, the "Dow portfolio" would have four times as much invested in XYZ as in ABC ($100 compared with $25) despite the fact that ABC is a more prominent firm in the market ($500 million market value of equity versus only $100 million for XYZ).

Table 2.2 illustrates this point. Suppose that ABC increases by 20 percent, from $25 to $30, while XYZ increases by only 10 percent, from $100 to $110. The return on a price-weighted average of the two stocks would come to only 12 percent, whereas the combined market value of the two stocks actually increases by more than 18 percent. Because of its lower price, the superior performance of ABC relative to XYZ has a smaller effect on the price-weighted average than it does on the actual combined value of the stocks.

Concept Check	Question 4. Suppose that shares of XYZ increase in price to $110 while shares of ABC fall to $20. Find the percentage change in the price-weighted average of these two stocks. Compare that to the percentage change in their combined market value.

As stocks are added to or dropped from the average, or stocks split over time, the Dow divisor is continually adjusted to leave the average unaffected by the change. For example, if XYZ were to split two for one, and its share price were therefore to fall to $50, we would not want the average to fall, because that would incorrectly indicate a fall in the general level of market prices. Following a split, the divisor must be reduced to a value that leaves the average unaffected by the split. Table 2.3 illustrates this point. The initial share price of XYZ, which was $100 in Table 2.2, falls to $50 if the stock splits at the beginning of the period. Notice that the number of shares outstanding doubles,

TABLE 2.2 Price-Weighted Returns

Stock	Initial Price	Final Price	Shares (million)	Initial Value of Outstanding Stock ($ million)	Final Value of Outstanding Stock ($ million)
ABC	25	30	20	500	600
XYZ	100	110	1	100	110
Average	62.5	70	**Total market value 600**		**710**

Increase in average price = 12% = 70/62.5 − 1
Increase in market value = 18.3% = 710/660 − 1

TABLE 2.3   Price-Weighted Returns after a Stock Split

Stock	Initial Price	Final Price	Shares (million)	Initial Value of Outstanding Stock ($ million)	Final Value of Outstanding Stock ($ million)
ABC	25	30	20	500	600
XYZ	50	55	2	100	110
Index value	$\frac{75}{1.20} = 62.5$	$\frac{85}{1.2} = 70.83$			
Market value				600	710

leaving the market value of total shares unaffected. The divisor, d, which originally was 2.0 when the two-stock average was initiated, must be reset to a value that leaves the average unchanged. Because the sum of the post-split stock prices is 75 and the pre-split average price was 62.5, we calculate the new value of d by solving $75/d = 62.5$. The value of d therefore falls from its original value of 2.0 to $75/62.5 = 1.20$, and the initial value of the average in indeed unaffected by the split: $75/1.20 = 62.5$. At period end, shares of ABC will sell for $30, while shares of XYZ will sell for $55, representing the same 10 percent return it was assumed to earn in Table 2.2. The new value of the price-weighted average is $(30 + 55)/1.20 = 70.83$, and the rate of return on the average is $70.83/62.5 - 1 = .133$, or 13.3 percent. Notice that this return is greater than that calculated in Table 2.2. The relative weight of XYZ, which is the poorer-performing stock, is lower after the split because its price is lower; the performance of the average therefore improves. This example illustrates again that the implicit weighting scheme of a price-weighted average is somewhat arbitrary, being determined by the prices rather than the outstanding market values of the shares in the average.

In the same way that the divisor is updated for stock splits, if one firm is dropped from the average and another firm with a different price is added, the divisor has to be updated to leave the average unchanged by the substitution. By now, the divisor for the Dow Jones Industrial Average has fallen to a value of about .75.

Dow Jones & Company also computes a Transportation Average of 20 airline, trucking, and railroad stocks; a Public Utility Average of 15 electric and natural gas utilities; and a Composite Average combining the 65 firms of the three separate averages. Each is a price-weighted average, and thus overweights the performance of high-priced stocks.

Figure 2.6 reproduces some of the data reported on the TSE Index and the Dow Jones Industrial Average from *The Globe and Mail*. The bars show the range of values assumed by the average on each day. The small boxes indicate the highs, lows, and closing averages of both exchanges.

FIGURE 2.6 TSE 300 Indices and Dow Jones Averages.

From *The Globe and Mail*, October 17, 1991. Reprinted by permission.

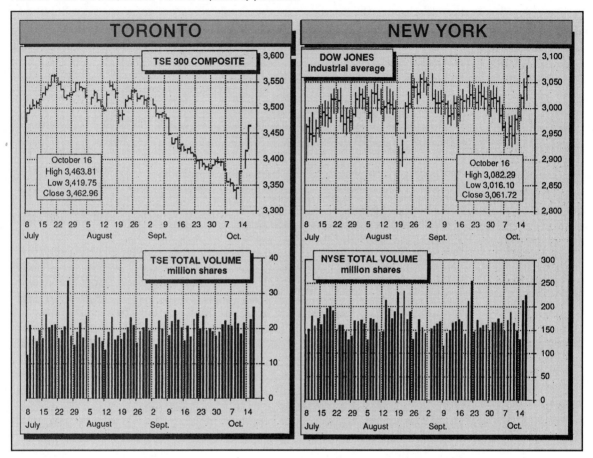

Toronto Stock Exchange indices

The TSE 300 Composite Index is Canada's best-known stock market indicator. It contains the 300 largest securities (in terms of market value) traded on the TSE, regardless of industry group, but excluding *control blocks* composed of more than 20 percent of outstanding shares. Besides being more broadly based than the Dow, it differs also in being a **market value-weighted index**. In the case of the firms XYZ and ABC that we mentioned above, the TSE 300 would give ABC five times the weight given to XYZ because the market value of its outstanding equity is five times larger. The TSE 300 is computed by calculating the total market value of the 300 stocks in the index and the total market value of those stocks on the previous day of trading, always excluding the control blocks. The percentage increase in the total market value from one day to the next represents the increase in the index. The rate of return of the index therefore equals the rate of return that would be earned by an investor holding a portfolio of all 300 stocks in the index in proportion to their market value, except that the index does not reflect cash dividends paid out by those stocks.

To illustrate, look again at Table 2.2. If the initial level of a market value-weighted index of stocks ABC and XYZ were set equal to an arbitrarily chosen starting value such as 100, the index value at year-end would be 100 × (710/600) = 118.3. The increase in the index reflects the 18.3 percent return earned on a portfolio consisting of those two stocks held in proportion to outstanding market values.

Note also from Tables 2.2 and 2.3 that market value-weighted indices are unaffected by stock splits. The total market value of outstanding XYZ stock increases from $100 million to $110 million regardless of the stock split, thereby rendering the split irrelevant to the performance of the index.

A nice feature of both market value-weighted and price-weighted indices is that they reflect the returns to buy-and-hold portfolio strategies. If one were to buy each share in the index in proportion to its outstanding market value, the value-weighted index would perfectly track capital gains on the underlying portfolio. Similarly, a price-weighted index tracks the returns on a portfolio composed of an equal number of shares in each firm.

Investors today can purchase shares in mutual funds that hold shares in proportion to their representation in the TSE 300. These **index funds** yield a return equal to that of the TSE 300 index and so provide a low-cost passive investment strategy for equity investors.

The Toronto Stock Exchange also computes the TSE 35, a 35-stock index composed of 35 of the largest Canadian companies drawn from a variety of industry groups; as well, it presents several stock indices based on narrow industry groupings, such as the Oil and Gas Index and the High Technology Index. The Montreal Stock Exchange computes the 25-stock Canadian Market Portfolio Index and several industry stock indices. The Vancouver Stock Exchange calculates its own VSE Index, based on the low-capitalization stocks traded there. Figure 2.7 reproduces a listing from *The Globe and Mail* of the performance of industry group and subgroup stock indices from the TSE.

The TSE 35 was introduced in 1987 and is aimed especially at the trading of derivative products such as index options and futures (see the next section). The 35 firms whose stocks are represented in the index are some of the largest and most actively traded Canadian firms. The TSE 35 is a modified market value-weighted index, with a ceiling of 10 percent placed on any one stock so that it doesn't dominate the index. All major industry groupings in the TSE 300 are also represented in the TSE 35, with the exception of Real Estate and Construction. Table 2.4 compares the relative weights of the industry groups in the TSE 300 and TSE 35 indices.

The TIP (Toronto 35 Index Participation) is a derivative product based on the TSE 35. It is sold in units representing participation in a trust created by the TSE. The trust holds a portfolio of the stocks in the TSE 35, which is designed to track accurately the performance of that index. TIPs are like listed common

FIGURE 2.7

TSE stock indices

From *The Globe and Mail*, October 19, 1991. Reprinted by permission.

TSE COMPOSITE INDEX

	300 Index	Exchange volume		
Net change	+ 16.19			
Close	3482.34	29,268,139	Yesterdays high	3482.83
3 p.m.	3478.75	24,041,170	Yesterdays low	3470.98
2 p.m.	3473.32	20,415,345	Previous high	3467.98
1 p.m.	3475.21	18,154,371	Previous low	3451.58
Noon	3477.49	14,342,410	1991 high	3598.05
11 a.m.	3472.96	9,970,573	1991 low	3150.88
10 a.m.	3471.48	5,608,992	52-week high	3598.05
9:45 a.m.	3472.85	4,687,762	52-week low	3030.37
Previous close	3466.15	30,397,484	P/E ratio	33.92
Week ago	3375.43	21,453,159	Div. yield	3.25
Month ago	3418.48	17,557,034	300 volume	17,442,737
Year ago	3060.02	60,362,745	Total return index	6186.43

TSE 300 INDEX COMPARISONS

(Intra-day highs and lows)

	Close	Chng	% Chng	Index volume	52 wk high	52 wk low
Metals & Minerals	3031.99	+ 16.30	+ 0.54	1543776	3324.89	2475.31
Integrated mines	3272.79	+ 14.36	+ 0.44	865006	3584.61	2604.50
Metal mines	1685.93	+ 27.60	+ 1.66	486270	2018.54	1638.59
Uranium & coal	1199.22	+ 16.15	+ 1.37	192500	1405.52	1030.04
Gold & silver	5031.36	+ 72.32	+ 1.46	2883680	5764.82	4468.45
Gold & silver mines	5064.63	+ 72.81	+ 1.46	2866230	5806.05	4493.07
Prec. metal funds	594.38	+ 8.40	+ 1.43	17450	716.91	553.49
Oil and gas	3637.27	+ 17.62	+ 0.49	1454435	4175.45	3504.90
Integrated oils	4214.05	− 14.96	− 0.35	109033	4923.65	4183.69
Oil & gas prodcrs	3431.62	+ 31.33	+ 0.92	1345402	3938.65	3247.87
Paper, forestry	3237.80	+ 32.35	+ 1.01	219004	3879.61	2926.48
Consumer products	5882.64	+ 49.67	+ 0.85	805944	5884.49	4174.42
Food processing	6590.60	+ 96.87	+ 1.49	65127	6615.17	4293.13
Tobacco	8545.85	+ 101.16	+ 1.20	109475	8560.27	6713.58
Distilleries	8077.35	+ 62.31	+ 0.78	52330	8384.21	5346.94
Breweries & bev.	5759.93	+ 36.88	+ 0.64	140130	5759.93	4083.48
Household goods	1051.30	+ 16.28	+ 1.57	25635	1270.13	699.54
Autos and parts	3582.67	+ 24.65	+ 0.69	393831	3639.42	1262.99
Packaging prod.	2385.92	− 15.62	− 0.65	19416	2650.04	1885.85
Industrial products	1967.27	+ 12.49	+ 0.64	1597303	2038.08	1521.36
Steel	970.31	+ 6.60	+ 0.68	560871	1165.72	881.58
Metal fabricators	2828.85	+ 42.59	+ 1.53	76298	2954.23	1927.37
Machinery	273.72	− 5.59	− 2.00	200	314.67	186.67
Trans. equipment	12368.11	+ 141.30	+ 1.16	128320	12580.89	6352.46
Elec/electronic	4923.04	+ 13.80	+ 0.28	364416	5017.50	3017.94
Cement/concrete	4559.23	− 15.93	− 0.35	9800	5434.74	3729.99
Chemicals	2451.03	+ 36.97	+ 1.53	346166	2864.10	2232.20
Bus. forms&equip.	1646.38	+ 4.69	+ 0.29	111230	1884.80	1400.80
Real estate & const	7659.32	+ 165.53	+ 2.21	201686	9954.77	7043.09
Devl. & contractors	1853.55	− 6.30	− 0.34	8300	2209.49	1486.59
Property mgmt.	9653.59	+ 269.94	+ 2.88	193386	13330.04	9103.97
Transportation	4707.55	− 351.16	− 6.94	2643564	8974.53	4669.29
Pipelines	3558.15	+ 45.76	+ 1.30	406211	4068.07	3445.06
Oil pipelines	2292.89	+ 8.44	+ 0.37	10491	3553.02	2122.43
Gas pipelines	3994.34	+ 57.44	+ 1.46	395720	4290.32	3787.27
Utilities	3159.60	+ 8.60	+ 0.27	830997	3161.91	2571.99
Gas utilities	2427.77	+ 24.08	+ 1.00	128229	2743.39	2280.08
Elec. utilities	3613.14	− 4.99	− 0.14	216790	3847.70	3266.05
Telephone	3048.05	+ 9.72	+ 0.32	465978	3050.69	2403.86
Communicatn & Media	6659.63	+ 75.08	+ 1.14	642740	7178.85	5491.73
Broadcasting	3664.81	− 10.52	− 0.29	500	4102.41	3123.71
Cable & entertnmnt	14980.00	+ 145.72	+ 0.98	261112	15095.00	7701.77
Publish/printing	6641.16	+ 85.35	+ 1.30	381128	7453.57	5826.67
Merchandising	4334.62	+ 36.10	+ 0.84	1275765	4558.24	3458.80
Wholesale dist.	3562.64	+ 14.67	+ 0.41	1500	4188.05	3011.22
Food stores	7171.52	+ 73.34	+ 1.03	305685	8343.92	6696.80
Department stores	1705.41	+ 8.96	+ 0.53	93040	2020.46	1137.01
Clothing stores	1987.08	+ 38.31	+ 1.97	21700	2544.42	1492.29
Specialty stores	2629.42	+ 17.76	+ 0.68	148962	2921.96	2214.83
Lodge/food/hlth	33968.96	+ 296.44	+ 0.88	704878	33968.96	19385.44
Financial services	2726.44	+ 8.37	+ 0.31	1662653	2828.04	2088.35
Banks	3004.00	+ 9.78	+ 0.33	1104217	3100.00	2196.82
Trust,svgs & loan	2201.17	− 22.45	− 1.01	322468	2960.99	2045.86
Invest compny & fnd	4019.21	+ 18.87	+ 0.47	68589	4465.19	3092.53
Insurance	1645.00	− 3.01	− 0.18	68103	1814.33	1281.03
Fin. mgmt. cos.	1099.20	+ 10.08	+ 0.93	99276	1274.70	1043.94
Management cos.	4284.23	+ 13.87	+ 0.32	1274979	4901.71	3774.69
High tech comp.	1110.49	+ 7.31	+ 0.66	1507201	1111.04	648.11
Computer industry	19.68	+ 0.20	+ 1.03	612064	20.58	9.17
Systems & softwr	18.65	+ 0.20	+ 1.08	570514	20.72	9.25
Manufactrs & serv.	23.16	+ 0.19	+ 0.83	41550	25.05	7.25
Distributors	7.12	unch	unch	0	9.79	5.12
Electronics	1629.34	+ 8.57	+ 0.40	284761	1735.27	1065.59
Component Mnfctrs	46.86	+ 0.43	+ 0.93	20353	47.12	30.43
System Manufctrs	1733.01	+ 6.25	+ 0.36	264406	1858.90	1125.20
Communications	1191.63	+ 2.92	+ 0.25	277779	1237.72	730.49
Telecommunications	1245.15	+ 3.07	+ 0.25	268178	1293.01	760.83
Data communications	16.51	unch	unch	9600	26.29	13.76
Biotech & pharm.	587.59	+ 21.32	+ 3.76	332598	589.38	166.17

TSE 35 INDEX

Open	191.82	Close	192.01	P/E ratio		18.93
High	192.07	Change	+ 0.98	Volume		8,520,235
Low	190.97	Yield	3.43	Value		$164,105,131

TABLE 2.4 Toronto 35 vs. TSE 300 Relative Weights, August 30, 1991

	TSE 300 Group Code	Toronto 35 (%)	TSE 300 (%)	Toronto 35 over/under Weighting (%)
Metals and minerals	MM	9.54	8.11	1.43
Gold and silver	GL	7.07	7.11	−0.04
Oil and gas	OG	7.82	7.75	0.07
Paper and forest products	PF	1.94	2.40	−0.46
Consumer products	CP	9.94	9.24	0.70
Industrial products	IP	10.46	10.89	−0.43
Real estate and construction	RC	0.00	1.05	−1.05
Transportation/environmental services	TR	2.69	2.48	0.21
Pipelines	PP	1.71	2.00	−0.29
Utilities	UT	11.85	12.26	−0.41
Communications and media	CM	4.04	4.27	−0.23
Merchandising	MR	6.19	5.70	0.49
Financial services	FS	21.24	20.48	0.76
Conglomerates	MG	5.52	6.25	−0.73

shares, which pay dividends and can be bought on margin. They allow small investors to hold a diversified portfolio of senior Canadian firms representing most sectors of the Canadian economy. Effectively, TIPS are like a mutual fund without the management fee.

Concept Check

> Question 5. Reconsider the stock of firms XYZ and ABC from question 4. Calculate the percentage change in the market value-weighted index. Compare that to the rate of return of a portfolio that holds $500 of ABC stock for every $100 of XYZ stock, that is, an index portfolio.

Other U.S. market value indices

Standard & Poor's publishes the widely used S&P Composite 500-Stock Index, a 500-Stock Industrial Index, as well as transportation, utility, and financial stock indices. The New York Stock Exchange publishes a market value-weighted composite index of all NYSE-listed stocks, in addition to sub-indices for industrial, utility, transportation, and financial stocks. The American Stock Exchange, or Amex, also computes a market value-weighted index of its stocks. These indices are even more broadly based than the S&P 500. The National Association of Securities Dealers publishes an index of nearly 3,000 OTC firms using the NASDAQ quotation service.

The ultimate equity index so far computed is the Wilshire 5,000 index of the market value of all NYSE and Amex stocks plus actively traded OTC stocks.

Figure 2.8 reproduces a listing from *The Wall Street Journal* of stock index performance.

Equally weighted indices

Market performance is sometimes measured by an equally weighted average of the returns of each stock in an index. Such an averaging technique, by placing equal weight on each return, corresponds to an implicit portfolio strategy that places equal dollar values on each stock. This is in contrast to both price

FIGURE 2.8 Performance of U.S. stock indices.

STOCK MARKET DATA BANK											May 24, 1988
Major Indexes											
HIGH	LOW	(12 MOS)	CLOSE	NET CH	% CH	12 MO CH	%		FROM 12/31		%
DOW JONES AVERAGES											
2722.42	1738.74	30 Industrials	×1962.53	+ 21.05	+ 1.08	− 335.41	− 14.60		+ 23.70		+ 1.22
1101.16	661.00	20 Transportation	794.95	+ 10.90	+ 1.39	− 162.43	− 16.97		+ 46.09		+ 6.15
213.79	160.98	15 Utilities	169.16	+ 1.19	+ 0.71	− 29.31	− 14.77		− 5.92		− 3.38
992.21	653.76	65 Composite	× 727.29	+ 7.99	+ 1.11	− 132.49	− 15.41		+ 13.02		+ 1.82
NEW YORK STOCK EXCHANGE											
187.99	125.91	Composite	143.53	+ 1.32	+ 0.93	− 19.19	− 11.79		+ 5.30		+ 3.83
231.05	149.43	Industrials	173.71	+ 1.49	+ 0.87	− 24.64	− 12.42		+ 6.67		+ 3.99
80.22	61.63	Utilities	68.75	+ 0.67	+ 0.98	− 2.62	− 3.67		+ 1.44		+ 2.14
168.20	104.76	Transportation	123.89	+ 1.62	+ 1.32	− 17.14	− 12.15		+ 5.32		+ 4.49
165.36	107.39	Finance	120.29	+ 1.42	+ 1.19	− 26.32	− 17.95		+ 5.72		+ 4.99
STANDARD & POOR'S INDEXES											
336.77	223.92	500 Index	253.51	+ 2.68	+ 1.07	− 35.60	− 12.31		+ 6.43		+ 2.60
393.17	255.43	Industrials	293.49	+ 2.75	+ 0.95	− 42.41	− 12.63		+ 7.63		+ 2.67
274.20	167.59	Transportation	191.05	+ 3.29	+ 1.75	− 40.06	− 17.33		+ 0.88		+ 0.46
121.11	91.80	Utilities	103.66	+ 1.44	+ 1.41	− 4.01	− 3.72		+ 1.54		+ 1.51
32.56	20.39	Financials	22.42	+ 0.37	+ 1.68	− 5.78	− 20.50		+ 0.79		+ 3.65
NASDAQ											
455.26	291.88	Composite	365.16	+ 1.90	+ 0.52	− 46.28	− 11.25		+ 34.69		+ 10.50
488.92	288.30	Industrials	374.87	+ 2.28	+ 0.61	− 67.05	− 15.17		+ 35.93		+ 10.60
475.78	333.66	Insurance	386.28	+ 1.76	+ 0.46	− 24.16	− 5.89		+ 35.22		+ 10.03
510.24	365.63	Banks	437.84	+ 2.42	+ 0.56	− 26.49	− 5.70		+ 47.18		+ 12.08
195.37	124.98	Nat. Mkt. Comp.	157.74	+ 0.86	+ 0.55	− 17.96	− 10.22		+ 15.15		+ 10.62
187.94	110.21	Nat. Mkt. Indus.	144.98	+ 0.93	+ 0.65	− 23.49	− 13.94		+ 13.87		+ 10.58
OTHERS											
365.01	231.90	AMEX	290.52	− 0.16	− 0.06	− 34.82	− 10.70		+ 30.17		+ 11.59
1926.2	1232.0	Fln. Times Indus.	1428.3	+ 20.7	+ 1.47	− 249.5	− 14.87		+ 55.0		+ 4.00
27819.98	21036.80	Nikkei Stock Avg.	27312.66	+ 62.90	+ 0.23	+ 2731.76	+ 11.11		+ 5748.66		+ 26.66
289.02	181.09	Value-Line(geom)	222.09	+ 1.33	+ 0.60	− 35.87	− 13.91		+ 20.47		+ 10.15
3299.44	2188.11	Wilshire 5000	2528.15	+ 21.21	+ 0.85	− 334.96	− 11.70		+ 111.02		+ 4.59

weighting (which requires equal numbers of shares of each stock) and market value weighting (which requires investments in proportion to outstanding value). The Montreal Exchange's Canadian Market Portfolio Index and the Value Line Index in the United States are examples of equally weighted indices.

Unlike price- or market value-weighted indices, equally weighted indices do not correspond to buy-and-hold portfolio strategies. Suppose that you start with equal dollar investments in the two stocks of Table 2.2, ABC and XYZ. Because ABC increases in value by 20 percent over the year while XYZ increases by only 10 percent, your portfolio no longer is equally weighted; it is now more heavily invested in ABC. To reset the portfolio to equal weights, you would need to rebalance: either sell off some ABC stock and/or purchase more XYZ stock. Such rebalancing would be necessary to align the return on your portfolio with that on the equally weighted index.

Bond Market Indicators

Just as stock market indices provide guidance concerning the performance of the overall stock market, bond market indicators measure the performance of various categories of bonds. ScotiaMcLeod publishes the main Canadian bond market indices, while in the United States the two most well-known groups of indices are those of Shearson-Lehman Hutton and Salomon Brothers. Table 2.5 lists some of the indices compiled by ScotiaMcLeod, as well as some characteristics of those indices as of October 1991.

The indices are all computed monthly, and all measure total returns as the sum of capital gains plus interest income derived from the bonds during the month. Any intra-month cash distributions received from the bonds are assumed to be reinvested weekly during the month back into the bond market.

TABLE 2.5   ScotiaMcLeod Debt Market Indices, October 31, 1991 (averages)

Universe Bond Index	Duration*	Coupon	Term	Price	Yield	Total Return Index	Sector Weight (%)
All governments	5.17	10.61	9.2	102.71	8.67	187.84	89.4
Canadas	5.15	10.54	8.9	102.46	8.44	186.62	57.1
Provincials	5.16	10.73	9.7	102.85	9.06	189.14	30.2
Municipals	5.74	11.00	9.9	103.72	9.37	196.32	2.1
All corporates	5.53	10.65	10.0	104.42	9.64	188.56	10.6
AAA	6.30	10.12	11.8	106.35	9.38	186.24	1.5
AA	5.60	10.67	10.0	103.76	9.44	187.52	3.6
A	5.44	10.75	10.0	105.24	9.71	190.19	3.8
BBB	4.90	10.82	8.6	101.89	10.15	187.79	1.7
Overall	**5.20**	**10.62**	**9.3**	**103.08**	**8.77**	**188.26**	**100.0**

* Duration is defined and discussed in Chapter 17.
Modified from *Debt Market Indices*, ScotiaMcLeod, October 31, 1991.

The major problem with these indices is that true rates of return on many bonds are difficult to compute because the infrequency with which the bonds trade make reliable up-to-date prices difficult to obtain. In practice, prices often must be estimated from bond valuation models. These ''matrix'' prices may differ substantially from true market values.

2.5 *Derivative Markets*

One of the most significant developments in financial markets in recent years has been the growth of futures and options markets. These instruments provide payoffs that depend on the values of other assets such as commodity prices, bond and stock prices, or market index values. For this reason, these instruments sometimes are called **derivative assets,** or **contingent claims.** Their values derive from or are contingent on the values of other assets.

Options

A *call option* gives its holder the right to purchase an asset for a specified price, called the *exercise* or *strike price,* on or before a specified expiration date. For example, a February call option on Alcan Aluminium stock with an exercise price of $25 entitles its owner to purchase Alcan stock for a price of $25 at any time up to and including the expiration date in February. Each option contract is for the purchase of 100 shares. However, quotations are made on a per-share basis. The holder of the call need not exercise the option; it will be profitable to exercise only if the market value of the asset that may be purchased exceeds the exercise price.

When the market price exceeds the exercise price, the option holder may ''call away'' the asset for the exercise price and reap a profit equal to the difference between the stock price and the exercise price. Otherwise, the option will be left unexercised. If not exercised before the expiration date of the contract, the option simply expires and no longer has value. Calls therefore provide greater profits when stock prices increase and thus represent bullish investment vehicles.

In contrast, a *put option* gives its holder the right to sell an asset for a specified exercise price on or before a specified expiration date. A February put on Alcan with an exercise price of $25 thus entitles its owner to sell Alcan stock (''put the stock'') to the put writer at a price of $25 at any time before expiration in February, even if the market price of Alcan is lower than $25. Whereas profits on call options increase when the asset increases in value, profits on put options increase when the asset value falls. The put is exercised only if its holder can deliver an asset worth less than the exercise price in return for the exercise price.

Figure 2.9 gives listed stock option quotations from *The Globe and Mail.* The quotations cover Montreal, Toronto, and Vancouver option trading. The sixth option listed in Trans Canada Options is for shares of Bombardier. The number on the same line as the company name indicates that the closing (C) price for Bombardier stock was 25¾ per share. The total number of all option contracts on Bombardier traded the previous day is given next. Options were traded on Bombardier with exercise prices of 16, 19, 20, 22, 25, and 26. (Options with other exercise prices might exist but were not traded the previous day.) These values, the exercise price or strike price, are given in the second column of numbers, after the expiration month.

The next three columns of numbers provide the bid, ask, and last trade prices of call options on Bombardier shares with expiration dates of January, April, and July. The prices of call options decrease in successive rows for a given expiration date, corresponding to progressively higher exercise prices. This makes sense, because the right to purchase a share at a given exercise price is worth less as the exercise price increases. For example, with an exercise price of 16, the January call lists for 9¾ per share, whereas the option to purchase the stock for an exercise price of 25 is worth only $1.80. The exercise

FIGURE 2.9
Trans Canada options market listings.

From *The Globe and Mail,* October 26, 1991. Reprinted by permission.

Trans Canada Options combine Montreal, Toronto and Vancouver option trading. P is a put.

Five most active TCO option classes

	Volume	Op Int
TSE 35 Index	1575	10320
IAF Biochem Intl	1278	25119
Echo Bay Mines	894	3619
Laidlaw Inc B	642	10121
TransCda Pipe	380	3861

Series		Bid	Ask	Last	Vol	Op Int
Air Canada		**C**	**$8¼**	**Opt**	**Vol**	**13**
JA $8		60	75	75	8	218
AP $7		155	170	170	5	30
Alcan Aluminiu		**C**	**$23½**	**Opt**	**Vol**	**151**
NV $22½	P	20	25	20	10	1407
$25		8	10	15	85	1597
DC $25		40	50	45	32	257
FB $25		100	110	100	17	1224
$25	P	210	235	210	2	317
MY $22½	P	120	135	120	5	340
Amer Barrick		**C**	**$27⅝**	**Opt**	**Vol**	**15**
JA $27½		195	220	230	15	1093
Bk of Montreal		**C**	**$36⅜**	**Opt**	**Vol**	**175**
JA $34		250	275	265	10	65
$36	P	80	95	75	110	118
AP $38		70	90	70	5	141
$39		45	55	50	50	123
Bk of Nova Scoti		**C**	**$18¾**	**Opt**	**Vol**	**155**
NV $18		75	95	80	25	25
MR $18	P	40	60	40	130	100
Bombardier B		**C**	**$25¾**	**Opt**	**Vol**	**94**
JA $16		$9½	$9⅞	$9¾	10	19
$19		$6½	$6⅞	$6⅞	6	12
$20		$5½	$5⅞	$5⅞	6	45
$25		165	190	180	15	124
AP $22		455	480	465	15	25
JY $26		235	260	240	42	92
Bow Valley Ind		**C**	**$14½**	**Opt**	**Vol**	**100**
JA $14	P	10	35	30	100	260
BC Telephone		**C**	**$20¼**	**Opt**	**Vol**	**9**
DC $20		55	75	70	9	609
BCE Inc		**C**	**$44¾**	**Opt**	**Vol**	**95**
NV $45		30	55	60	75	972

Series		Bid	Ask	Last	Vol	Op Int
DC $45	P	90	100	95	10	10
FB $42½		295	320	325	10	826
Cambior Inc		**C**	**$10⅝**	**Opt**	**Vol**	**19**
FB $10		130	155	140	10	57
$11		80	105	90	9	121
Canadian Pacific		**C**	**$18½**	**Opt**	**Vol**	**184**
NV $19		20	30	20	20	214
$19	P	45	70	50	4	69
DC $19		50	60	50	40	197
MY $20		75	80	80	120	120
Cascades Inc		**C**	**$6¼**	**Opt**	**Vol**	**20**
JN $5	P	10	30	20	20	20
Cdn Impl Bk Co		**C**	**$29⅜**	**Opt**	**Vol**	**90**
DC $31		40	60	40	80	175
MR $32		70	90	85	10	24
Cominco Ltd		**C**	**$21⅞**	**Opt**	**Vol**	**20**
MR $20	P	60	75	65	20	20
Corel Systems C		**C**	**$15**	**Opt**	**Vol**	**40**
JA $20		15	25	25	20	20
AP $15		250	285	275	20	23
CAE Industries		**C**	**$6¾**	**Opt**	**Vol**	**119**
MR $6		90	110	90	3	3
$7		35	50	45	11	108
JN $6		105	120	120	30	40
$7		65	80	65	30	134
$8		30	50	30	45	120
CDA Mar 2011 9		**C**	**$98⅛**	**Opt**	**Vol**	**118**
NV $90		7.80	8.30	$8	30	8
$100	P	185	210	200	20	40
DC $98		95	120	95	2	89
$98	P	85	110	125	4	111
$100		25	50	35	3	3
MR $100		90	115	95	59	131
CDA Oct 2001 9.5		**C**	**103⅛**	**Opt**	**Vol**	**85**
NV $101		205	230	205	40	42
DC $101		215	240	240	8	80
$103		85	110	100	7	65
$104		40	65	55	10	35
MR $102		195	220	235	20	53
Deprenyl Resear		**C**	**$19⅛**	**Opt**	**Vol**	**243**
NV $19	P	75	100	75	10	10

Series		Bid	Ask	Last	Vol	Op Int
$20		65	90	75	20	30
DC $22		70	95	80	5	5
JA $15		475	490	500	5	91
$17		325	345	360	54	113
$18		270	290	310	64	169
$20		190	200	210	15	183
$22		125	135	150	50	215
AP $20		275	300	300	20	52
Dofasco Inc		**C**	**$18¾**	**Opt**	**Vol**	**44**
DC $17		195	210	195	5	105
MR $18		160	185	170	6	36
$18	P	90	115	105	3	10
$19	P	130	155	150	30	40
Echo Bay Mines		**C**	**$9⅛**	**Opt**	**Vol**	**894**
JA $8		150	175	175	21	29
$8	P	25	45	20	29	210
$9		90	110	100	20	163
$9	P	65	75	50	100	301
$10		50	65	50	143	538
$10	P	120	130	100	44	159
$11		40	45	25	17	180
$11	P	195	200	175	30	146
$12		10	30	15	83	268
$13		5	20	20	116	386
AP $8	P	50	60	40	12	30
$9		130	150	135	7	20
$9	P	90	100	80	30	105
$10		90	100	85	20	175
$10	P	145	155	130	48	196
$11		60	75	65	42	200
$11	P	210	220	195	20	88
$12		25	40	40	7	70
$13		30	35	25	56	217
JY $9	P	100	125	100	10	10
$11		85	110	95	18	28
$12		60	75	65	13	54
$12	P	300	315	275	8	30
Gulf Canada Res		**C**	**$6¾**	**Opt**	**Vol**	**10**
MY $10		5	30	25	10	10
Hemlo Gold Min		**C**	**$10⅝**	**Opt**	**Vol**	**26**
JA $9		180	200	195	10	25

FIGURE 2.9
Continued

TRANS CANADA OPTIONS

Series	Bid	Ask	Last	Vol	Op Int
$10	105	125	110	13	185
$10 P	25	50	45	3	280
Inco Ltd	C $38¾		Opt Vol		109
NV $37½	45	55	45	15	300
$37⅛ P	165	180	165	10	475
FB $40	100	115	110	74	664
MY $32½ P	115	130	120	10	121
Intl Corona A	C $7¼		Opt Vol		15
$30	130	155	150	16	15
MY $7	C $7⅞		Opt Vol		15
Intl Corona Corp	C $7⅞		Opt Vol		5
FB $10	240	280	240	20	10
IAF Biochem Int	C $43¾		Opt Vol		1278
NV $38	56⅞/57⅞/59⅛			30	88

(Trans Canada Options listing — stock option quotations for numerous series; full tabular data continues across columns.)

Total contract volume 8,776
Total open interest 221,512

price indicates the range of prices at which the stock has traded during the life of the option; thus we see that Bombardier has had a price near $16 in the last six months. The last two columns give an indication of the liquidity of the option as they record the volume traded and the "open interest," which refers to the total number of contracts outstanding in that option.

Put options, with various strike prices and times to maturity, are denoted with a P next to the exercise price. Put prices, of course, increase with the exercise price. The right to sell a share of Dofasco at a price of 18 is less valuable than the right to sell it at 19.

Concept Check	Question 6. What would be the profit or loss per share of stock to an investor who bought the February maturity Alcan call option with exercise price 25 on October 25, 1991, if the stock price at the expiration of the option was 27? What about a purchaser of the put option with the same exercise price and maturity?

Futures Contracts

The *futures contract* calls for delivery of an asset or its cash value at a specified delivery or maturity date for an agreed-upon price, called the *futures price,* to be paid at contract maturity. The *long position* is held by the trader who commits to purchasing the commodity on the delivery date. The trader who takes the short position commits to delivering the commodity at contract maturity.

Figure 2.10 illustrates the listing of several financial futures contracts as they appear in *The Globe and Mail*. The listings include commodity futures traded on the Winnipeg Exchange, as well as bond futures and stock index futures from the Montreal and Toronto Exchanges. The top line in boldface type gives the contract name and size. Thus the last contract listed on the right is for the TSE 35 index, traded on the Toronto Stock Exchange. Each contract calls for delivery of 500 times the value of the TSE 35 stock price index.

The next three rows detail price data for contracts expiring on various dates. The November 1991 maturity contract's highest futures price during the day was 193.50, the lowest was 192.30, and the settlement price (a representative trading price during the last few minutes of trading) was 193.50. The settlement price rose by 1.30 from the previous trading day. The highest and lowest futures prices over the contract's life to date have been 193.50 and 185.58, respectively. Finally, open interest was 651. Corresponding information is given for the other maturity dates.

The trader holding the long position profits from price increases. Suppose that at expiration the TSE 35 index is at 195. The long position trader who entered the contract at the futures price of 192.50 on October 18 would pay the previously agreed-upon 192.50 for each unit of the index, which at contract maturity would be worth 195. Because each contract calls for delivery of $500

FIGURE 2.10

Canadian financial futures listings.

From *The Globe and Mail*, October 19, 1991. Reprinted by permission.

WINNIPEG COMMODITY EXCHANGE

WHEAT 20 metric tons- can $ per ton

SeaHi	SeaLow	Mth.	Open	High	Low	Settle	Chg.	OpInt
110.00	84.10	Oct	97.00	98.30	97.00	98.30	+.30	496
104.00	86.00	Dec	95.00	95.90	94.30	95.70	+.70	4,965
106.00	89.80	Mar	98.00	99.00	97.70	98.60	+.60	4,243
103.90	95.00	May	100.00	101.00	100.00	101.20	+1.20	1,066
102.90	96.00	Jul				103.00	+.50	153

Est Sales — Prv Sales 1,059 — Prv Open Int 10,923 — Chg. —55

OATS 20 metric tons- can $ per ton

SeaHi	SeaLow	Mth.	Open	High	Low	Settle	Chg.	OpInt
101.20	80.00	Oct	91.00	91.00	91.00	91.00	...	212
103.50	84.00	Dec	93.00	94.00	93.00	94.00	+1.00	921
107.60	89.50	Mar				99.80	...	527
104.00	92.00	May				103.50	...	20
106.00	100.00	Jul	104.50	104.50	104.50	104.50	...	

Est Sales — Prv Sales 103 — Prv Open Int 1,680 — Chg. —104

RYE 20 metric tons- can $ per ton

SeaHi	SeaLow	Mth.	Open	High	Low	Settle	Chg.	OpInt
107.50	73.50	Oct				97.20	+1.70	25
102.00	78.90	Dec	98.00	98.00	98.00	98.20	+.20	1,241
106.00	87.50	Mar	101.50	101.50	101.50	101.70	—.30	552
108.20	89.50	May				103.90	...	10

Est Sales — Prv Sales 225 — Prv Open Int 1,828 — Chg. +56

BARLEY 20 metric tons- can $ per ton

SeaHi	SeaLow	Mth.	Open	High	Low	Settle	Chg.	OpInt
890.00	74.80	Oct	83.30	83.30	82.30	82.70	—1.10	475
95.80	77.20	Dec	85.20	85.30	85.00	85.50	—.10	2,411
96.50	81.00	Mar	89.80	90.20	89.60	90.00	...	2,153
94.60	84.50	May	92.20	92.30	92.10	92.10	—.30	473
97.00	90.00	Jul				95.00	+.40	20

Est Sales — Prv Sales 241 — Prv Open Int 5,532 — Chg. —61

CANOLA 20 metric tons- can $ per ton

SeaHi	SeaLow	Mth.	Open	High	Low	Settle	Chg.	OpInt
325.20	248.10	Nov	274.00	274.00	271.00	272.30	—2.10	10,732
317.50	255.00	Jan	280.00	280.50	277.10	278.60	—2.00	11,308
319.80	261.30	Mar	285.80	286.50	283.00	284.60	—1.80	4,578
321.00	267.00	Jun	294.00	294.00	292.20	293.30	—2.20	3,343
299.30	299.30	Sep				299.80	—1.80	15

Est Sales — Prv Sales 2,626 — Prv Open Int 29,976 — Chg. +391

FLAXSEED 20 metric tons- can $ per ton

SeaHi	SeaLow	Mth.	Open	High	Low	Settle	Chg.	OpInt
350.00	183.00	Oct	192.00	192.10	192.00	192.10	—1.90	200
273.40	187.10	Dec	197.00	197.20	196.30	196.70	—.50	3,745
233.50	193.50	Mar	205.10	205.10	204.40	204.30	—.90	1,925
232.00	200.70	May				209.40	—.60	659
219.80	205.50	Jul	214.50	214.50	214.50	214.80	—.20	93

Est Sales — Prv Sales 1,443 — Prv Open Int 6,622 — Chg. +323

MONTREAL FUTURES

Bankers' acceptances; $1-million; pts of 100%.
Change of 0.01 equals $25 a contract.

Season High	Season Low	Month	High	Low	Settle Price	Change	Open Interest
92.33	89.00	Dec	92.25	92.21	92.23	+ 0.05	4497
92.45	88.30	Mar	92.33	92.31	92.31	+ 0.08	3892
92.62	88.40	Jun	92.31	92.28	92.28	+ 0.06	3028
92.25	88.00	Sep	0.00	0.00	92.07	+ 0.06	1169
91.95	88.15	Dec	0.00	0.00	91.86	+ 0.06	1292
91.55	89.25	Mar	91.48	91.48	91.48	+ 0.15	677
91.00	88.99	Jun	91.09	91.05	91.09	+ 0.16	256
90.75	89.94	Sep	0.00	0.00	90.93	+ 0.16	55

Estimated volume: 659
Previous day's volume: 1,447
Previous day's open interest: 14,866

Government of Canada bond futures
$100,000; pts of 100%.

Season High	Season Low	Month	High	Low	Settle Price	Change	Open Interest
99.24	92.85	Dec	99.00	98.55	98.95	+ 0.66	6204

Estimated volume: 3,089
Previous day's volume: 4,765
Previous day's open interest: 6,204

Canada bond futures option; $100,000; pts of 100%

Strike Price	Calls Dec	Calls Mar	Calls Jun	Puts Dec	Puts Mar	Puts Jun
92	6.90	6.60	0.00	0.00	0.00	0.00
93	5.90	5.60	0.00	0.03	0.00	0.00
94	4.90	4.60	0.00	0.05	0.00	0.00
95	3.93	3.65	0.00	0.03	0.06	0.00
96	2.90	2.82	0.00	0.04	0.20	0.00
97	1.95	2.08	0.00	0.09	0.43	0.00
98	1.17	1.46	0.00	0.25	0.78	0.00
99	0.49	0.95	0.00	0.65	1.24	0.00
100	0.15	0.57	0.00	1.30	1.83	0.00
101	0.00	0.30	0.00	2.04	2.54	0.00
102	0.00	0.13	0.00	3.00	3.33	0.00

Estimated volume: 1
Prev. call volume: 61 — Prev. call open interest: 281
Prev. put volume: 10 — Prev. put open interest: 429

MINNEAPOLIS GRAIN EXCHANGE

WHEAT 5,000 bu minimum- dollars per bushel

SeaHi	SeaLow	Mth.	Open	High	Low	Settle	Chg.	OpInt
3.38¼	2.69½	Dec	3.38	3.44¾	3.38	3.43½	+.05¾	9,263
3.45¾	2.79½	Mar	3.45	3.50½	3.44¾	3.50¼	+.05¾	3,929
3.47	2.84	May	3.47	3.51	3.47	3.51½	+.05	759
3.36	3.08	Jul	3.40	3.42½	3.40	3.43	+.05	87
3.40	3.22	Sep	3.40	3.41½	3.40	3.41½	+.04½	48

Est Sales — Prv Sales 2,587 — Prv Open Int 14,088 — Chg. —809

OATS 5,000 bu minimum- dollars per bushel

SeaHi	SeaLow	Mth.	Open	High	Low	Settle	Chg.	OpInt
1.24	1.24	Dec				1.25¼	...	2

Est Sales — Prv Sales — Prv Open Int — Chg. unch

WHITE WHEAT 1,000 bu minimum- dollars per bushel

SeaHi	SeaLow	Mth.	Open	High	Low	Settle	Chg.	OpInt
4.00	3.39	Dec	4.02	4.03	4.02	4.04	+.03	725
4.08	3.93	Mar	4.09	4.09	4.09	4.11	+.03	445

Est Sales — Prv Sales — Prv Open Int — Chg. unch

TORONTO FUTURES

Toronto 35 (TXF); $500 times index.
Change of 0.02 equals $10 a contract.

Season High	Season Low	Month	High	Low	Settle price	Change	Open Interest
192.76	183.00	Oct 91	.00	.00	191.82	+.32	560
193.50	185.58	Nov 91	193.50	192.30	193.50	+1.3	651
197.50	184.84	Dec 91	.00	.00	194.00	+1.3	1156

Sales: 157
Prev. day's open interest: 2,367; change from 2 days ago: +55

times the index, ignoring brokerage fees, the profit to the long position would equal $500 × (195 − 192.50) = $1,250. Conversely, the short position must deliver 500 times the value of the index for the previously agreed-upon futures price. The short position's loss equals the long position's profit.

The right to purchase the asset at an agreed-upon price, as opposed to the obligation, distinguishes call options from long positions in futures contracts. A futures contract *obliges* the long position to purchase the asset at the futures price; the call option, in contrast, *conveys the right* to purchase the asset at the exercise price. The purchase will be made only if it yields a profit.

Clearly, a holder of a call has a better position than does the holder of a long position on a futures contract with a futures price equal to the option's exercise price. This advantage, of course, comes only at a price. Call options must be purchased; futures investments may be entered into without cost. The purchase price of an option is called the premium. It represents the compensation the holder of the call must pay for the ability to exercise the option only when it is profitable to do so. Similarly, the difference between a put option and a short futures position is the right, as opposed to the obligation, to sell an asset at an agreed-upon price.

Summary

1. Money market securities are very short-term debt obligations. They are usually highly marketable and have relatively low credit risk. Their low maturities and low credit risk ensure minimal capital gains or losses. These securities trade in large denominations, but may be purchased indirectly through money market funds.

2. Much of the Canadian government borrowing is in the form of Canada bonds. These are coupon-paying bonds usually issued at or near par value. Canada bonds are similar in design to coupon-paying corporate bonds. Provincial governments and Crown Corporations also issue similar default-free coupon-paying bonds.

3. Mortgage pass-through securities are pools of mortgages sold in one package. Owners of pass-throughs receive all principal and interest payments made by the borrower. The bank that originally issued the mortgage merely services the mortgage, simply "passing through" the payments to the purchasers of the mortgage. The government guarantees the timely payment of interest and principal on mortgages pooled into these pass-through securities.

4. Common stock is an ownership share in a corporation. Each voting share entitles its owner to a vote on matters of corporate governance and to a pro-rated share of the dividends paid to shareholders. Restricted shares have a lower number of votes, or no right to vote. Stock, or equity, owners are the residual claimants on the income earned by the firm.

5. Preferred stock usually pays fixed dividends for the life of the firm; it is a perpetuity. A firm's failure to pay the dividend due on preferred stock, however, does not precipitate corporate bankruptcy. Instead, unpaid dividends simply cumulate. New varieties of preferred stock include convertible and adjustable-rate issues.

6. Many stock market indices measure the performance of the overall market in Canada and the United States. The Dow Jones Averages, the oldest and best-known indicators, are U.S. price-weighted indices. Today, many broad-based, market value-weighted indices are computed daily. These include the main Canadian index, Toronto Stock Exchange's 300-Stock Index, as well as the U.S. Standard & Poor's 500-Stock Index, the NYSE and Amex indices, the NASDAQ index, and the Wilshire 5000 Index. The Montreal Exchange's Canadian Market Portfolio Index and the Value Line index are equally weighted averages of individual firms' returns.

7. A call option is a right to purchase an asset at a stipulated exercise price on or before a maturity date. A put option is the right to sell an asset at some exercise price. Calls increase in value while puts decrease in value as the value of the underlying asset increases.

8. A futures contract is an obligation to buy or sell an asset at a stipulated futures price on a maturity date. The long position, which commits to purchasing, gains if the asset value increases, while the short position, which commits to delivering the asset, loses.

Key Terms

Money market	Limited liability
Capital markets	Capital gains
Bond equivalent yield	Price-earnings ratio
Effective annual yield	Board lots
Bank discount yield	Price-weighted average
London Interbank Offered Rate	Market value-weighted index
Yield to maturity	Index funds
Restricted shares	Derivative assets
Residual claim	Contingent claims

Selected Readings

The standard reference to the securities, terminology, and organization of the U.S. money market is:

Stigum, Marcia. *The Money Market.* Homewood, Ill.: Dow Jones-Irwin, 1983.

A more detailed treatment of money market securities is contained in the following collection of articles:

Cook, Timothy Q.; and Rowe, Timothy D. *Instruments of the Money Market.* Richmond, Va.: Federal Reserve Bank of Richmond, 1986.

The Canadian money market is described in:

Sarpkaya, S. *The Money Market in Canada,* 4th ed. Toronto, Ont.: CCH Canadian, 1989.

A collection of essays on a wide variety of fixed-income securities is:

Fabozzi, Frank J.; T. Dessa; and Pollack, Irving M. *The Handbook of Fixed Income Securities*. 3rd ed. Homewood, Ill.: Business One Irwin, 1991.

A reference to Canadian and international fixed-income instruments is the annual publication:

Guide to International Investing. Toronto, Ont.: CCH Canadian.

An extended coverage of restricted voting shares is in:

Smith, Brian; and Amoako-Adu, Ben. *Financing Canadian Corporations with Restricted Shares*. (Monograph). London, Ont.: National Centre for Management Research and Development, University of Western Ontario, 1990.

A good treatment of the institutional organization of option markets is contained in:

Reference Manual. Chicago: The Chicago Board Options Exchange, 1982.

Institutional details of Canadian options markets are provided by:

The prospectus of Trans Canada Options Inc., 1980.

Institutional features of futures markets are provided by:

Kolb, Robert. *Understanding Futures Markets*. Glenview, Ill.: Scott, Foresman & Co., 1991.

Hore, John E. *Trading on Canadian Futures Markets,* 4th ed. Toronto, Ont.: The Canadian Securities Institute, 1989.

Problems

1. The following multiple-choice problems are based on questions that appeared in the 1986 CFA examination.
    a. Preferred stock:
        i. Is actually a form of equity.
        ii. Pays dividends not taxable to Canadian corporations.
        iii. Is normally considered a fixed-income security.
        iv. All of the above.
    b. Straight preferred stock yields are usually lower than yields on straight bonds of the same quality because of:
        i. Marketability.
        ii. Risk.
        iii. Taxation.
        iv. Call protection.
2. The investment manager of a corporate pension fund has purchased a Treasury bill with 180 days to maturity at a price of $9,600 per $10,000 face value. The manager has computed the bank discount yield at 8 percent (CFA examination, Level II, 1986).
    a. Calculate the bond equivalent yield for the Treasury bill. Show your calculations.
    b. Briefly state two reasons why a Treasury bill's bond equivalent yield is always different from the discount yield.
3. The following questions deal with yields.
    a. Which security offers a higher effective annual yield?
        i. A three-month bill selling at $9,764.
        ii. A six-month bill selling at $9,539.
    b. Calculate the bond equivalent yield on each bill.
4. Find the after-tax return to a corporation that buys a share of preferred

stock at $40, sells it at year-end at $40, and receives a $4 year-end dividend. The firm is in the 45 percent tax bracket.

5. Consider the three stocks in the following table. P_t represents price at time t, and Q_t represents shares outstanding at time t. Stock C splits two for one in the last period.

	P_0	Q_0	P_1	Q_1	P_2	Q_2
A	90	100	95	100	95	100
B	50	200	45	200	45	200
C	100	200	110	200	55	400

   a. Calculate the rate of return on a price-weighted index of the three stocks for the first period ($t = 0$ to $t = 1$).
   b. What must happen to the divisor for the price-weighted index in year 2?
   c. Calculate the price-weighted index for the second period ($t = 1$ to $t = 2$).

6. Using the data in problem 5, calculate the first period rates of return on the following indices of the three stocks:
   a. A market value-weighted index.
   b. An equally weighted index.

7. Which of the following securities should sell at a greater price?
   a. A 10-year Canada bond with a 9 percent coupon rate versus a 10-year Canada bond with a 10 percent coupon.
   b. A three-month maturity call option with an exercise price of $40 versus a three-month call on the same stock with an exercise price of $35.
   c. A put option on a stock selling at $50, or a put option on another stock selling at $60 (all other relevant features of the stocks and options may be assumed to be identical).
   d. A three-month T-bill with a discount yield of 6.1 percent versus a three-month bill with a discount yield of 6.2 percent.

8. Why do call options with exercise prices greater than the price of the underlying stock sell for positive prices?

9. Both a call and a put currently are traded on stock XYZ; both have strike prices of $50 and maturities of six months. What will be the profit to an investor who buys the call for $4 in the following scenarios for stock prices in six months?
   a. $40.
   b. $45.
   c. $50.
   d. $55.
   e. $60.
   What will be the profit in each scenario to an investor who buys the put for $6?

10. Explain the difference between a put option and a short position in a futures contract.

11. Examine the first 25 stocks listed in Figure 2.5 For how many of these stocks is the 52-week high price at least 50 percent greater than the 52-week low price? What do you conclude about the volatility of prices on individual stocks?

CHAPTER 3

How Securities Are Traded

We examine in this chapter how securities are bought and sold, how firms issue securities, and how they are traded on various exchanges or in the over-the-counter markets. We explain short sales and buying securities on margin. We also examine the role of regulatory agencies and explain how an individual can invest in securities through either a broker or a mutual fund.

3.1 *How Firms Issue Securities*

When firms need to raise capital they may choose to sell (or *float*) new securities. These new issues of stock, bonds, or other securities typically are marketed to the public by investment bankers in what is called the **primary market.** Purchase and sale of already issued securities among private investors take place in the **secondary market.**

There are two types of primary market issues of common stock. *Initial public offerings,* or *IPOs,* are stocks issued by a formerly privately owned company selling stock to the public for the first time. *Seasoned new issues* are offered by companies that already have floated equity. A sale by Canadian Pacific of new shares of stock, for example, would constitute a seasoned new issue. A *secondary offering* is a stock sale that has all the characteristics of a primary market issue, but is in fact a secondary market transaction. These offerings are relatively common in Canada, arising when a company that holds a significant interest in another firm chooses to sell all or part of that holding. The shares are sold to the general public as in a new equity issue; however, the parent firm receives the cash proceeds and no new shares are issued.

In the case of bonds we also distinguish between two types of primary market issues. A *public offering* is an issue of bonds sold to the general investing public that can then be traded on the secondary market. A *private place-ment* is an issue that is sold to a few institutional investors at most, and is generally held to maturity.

Investment Bankers

Public offerings of both stocks and bonds typically are marketed via an **under-writing** by investment bankers, often known in Canada as *investment dealers*. In fact, more than one investment dealer usually markets the securities. A lead firm forms an *underwriting syndicate* of other investment dealers to share the responsibility for the stock issue.

The bankers advise the firm regarding the terms on which it should attempt to sell the securities. A preliminary registration statement describing the issue and the prospects of the company must be filed with the provincial securities commission in the provinces in which the securities will be offered for sale. This *preliminary prospectus* is known as a *red herring* because of a statement, printed in red, that the company is not attempting to sell the security before the registration is approved. When the statement is finalized and approved by the commission, it is called the **prospectus.** At this time the price at which the securities will be offered to the public is announced.

There are two methods of underwriting a securities issue. In a *firm commit-ment* underwriting arrangement, the investment bankers purchase the securi-ties from the issuing company and then resell them to the public. The issuing firm sells the securities to the underwriting syndicate for the public offering price less a spread that serves as compensation to the underwriters. In such an arrangement the underwriters assume the full risk that the shares cannot in fact be sold to the public at the stipulated offering price. Under significant changes in market conditions the underwriters can escape from the firm commitment, if a *market-out* clause exists. By contrast, in a *bought deal* the underwriter takes full responsibility for the issue under any circum-stances.

An alternative to this arrangement is the *best-efforts* agreement. In this case, the investment banker agrees to help the firm sell the issue to the public, but does not actually purchase the securities. The banker simply acts as an inter-mediary between the public and the firm and thus does not bear the risk of being unable to resell purchased securities at the offering price. The best-efforts procedure is more common for initial public offerings of common stock, for which the appropriate share price is less certain.

Corporations engage investment bankers either by negotiation or by compet-itive bidding. Negotiation is more common. Besides being compensated by the spread between the purchase and public offering prices, an investment banker may receive shares of common stock or other securities of the firm. In the case of competitive bidding, a firm may announce its intent to issue securities and invite investment bankers to submit bids for the underwriting. Such a bidding process may reduce the cost of the issue; it might also bring fewer services from the investment banker. Many public utilities are required to solicit com-petitive bids from underwriters.

Prompt Offering Prospectus

The Ontario Securities Commission (OSC) permits the preparation of a prospectus for a new issue, with only minor additions to available financial information. This information, filed annually with OSC, contains virtually all required information for a prospectus. The approval of the supplementary
material requires only a few days instead of weeks, thus allowing the prompt
placement of the issue with the underwriters; this is known as the *prompt
offering prospectus* (POP). This system reduces the underwriters' risk and
makes bought deals more attractive. The sale to the public, however, still
requires a full prospectus.

Underpricing

Underwriters face a peculiar conflict of interest. On the one hand, acting in the
best interest of the issuing firm, they should attempt to market securities to the
public at the highest possible price, thereby maximizing the revenue realized
from the offering. On the other hand, if they set the offering price higher than
the public will pay, they will be unable to market the securities to customers.
Underwriters left with unmarketable securities will be forced to sell them at a
loss on the secondary market. Underwriters therefore must balance their own
interests against those of their clients. The lower the public offering price, the
less capital the firm raises, but the greater the chance that the securities can be
sold at that price. Also, the lower the price, the less effort is needed to find
investors to purchase the securities. If the offering is made at a low enough
price, investors will beat down the doors of the underwriters to purchase the
securities.

   In fact, there is some evidence that IPOs of common stock often are underpriced compared with the price at which they could be marketed. In a U.S.
study of the pricing of 112 IPOs, Ibbotson[1] found that an investor who purchased shares of each issue at the initial offering price and then resold the stock
one month later would have earned an average *abnormal* return of 11.4 percent.[2] Such an abnormal return would indicate that the stock was offered to the
public at a price substantially below that which investors were willing to pay.
Such underpricing means that IPOs commonly are oversubscribed; that is,
there is demand from the public for more of the shares at the offering price than
there are shares being offered. Competitive bidding for an issue by underwriters is required for some issues by many American regulators; this is not true in
Canada, where negotiation between the issuer and underwriter is a more common practice. There is evidence that the competitive process leads to a higher
price for the issuer.[3]

---

[1] Roger G. Ibbotson, "Price Performance of Common Stock New Issues," *Journal of Financial Economics* 2
(September 1975).

[2] Abnormal return measures the return on the investment net of the portion that can be attributed to general
market movements. See the discussion of this concept in Chapter 13.

[3] D. Logue and R. Jarrow, "Negotiation vs. Competitive Bidding in the Sale of Securities by Public Utilities,"
Financial Management, Autumn 1978.

3.2 *Where Securities Are Traded*

Once securities are issued to the public, investors may trade them among themselves. Purchase and sale of already issued securities take place in the secondary markets, which consist of (1) national and local securities exchanges, (2) the over-the-counter market, and (3) direct trading between two parties.

The Secondary Markets

There are five **stock exchanges** in Canada. Three of these, the Toronto Stock Exchange (TSE), the Montreal Exchange (ME), and the Vancouver Stock Exchange (VSE), are national in scope. The other two are regional exchanges, which list firms located in a particular geographic area (Manitoba and Alberta). There also are several exchanges for the trading of options and futures contracts, which we will discuss in the options and futures chapters.

The ME is the oldest organized securities market in Canada. It was officially granted a charter in 1874, when it was known under the name Montreal Stock Exchange. The TSE was formally incorporated in 1878. It became the largest Canadian financial market in the 1930s, and remains so today (see discussion below). Nonetheless, the ME has shown signs of increased activity in the last decade, and has pioneered the introduction of many derivative products and other financial innovations (albeit not always successfully).

The VSE was incorporated in 1907. From the very beginning it specialized in small, resource-oriented firms, primarily in Western Canada. In recent years it has tried to diversify its activities and become more North American in scope. As for the Alberta and Winnipeg stock exchanges, they have remained regionally oriented in their activities, even though they were formed at about the same time as the VSE.

An exchange provides a facility for its members to trade securities, and only members of the exchange may trade there. Therefore memberships, or *seats,* on the exchange are valuable assets. The exchange member charges investors for executing trades on their behalf. This is the means by which brokerage firms operate. They own seats on exchanges and advertise their willingness to execute trades for customers for a fee. The commissions that can be earned through this activity determine the market value of a seat. Hence, the price of a seat is taken as an indicator of the buoyancy of the market. For instance, a seat on the New York Stock Exchange (NYSE), which sold for more than U.S. $1 million prior to the October 1987 crash, was worth only U.S. $625,000 by January 1988. The highest price of a seat on the TSE was $175,000 in 1991.

The TSE is by far the largest Canadian exchange. The shares of approximately 1,150 firms trade there, and over 1,500 stock issues (common and preferred stock) are listed. Daily trading volume on the TSE regularly exceeds 25

TABLE 3.1   North American Stock Exchanges, 1990

Exchange	Value of Securities Traded ($ million annually)	% of Total Canadian	Volume of Securities Traded (thousands of shares annually)	% of Total Canadian
New York	1,537,386	—	39,664,516	—
Midwest	82,713	—	2,440,126	—
Toronto	64,009	76.1	5,660,401	47.9
Pacific	48,045	—	1,615,573	—
American	43,749	—	3,328,918	—
Philadelphia	32,420	—	922,587	—
Boston	30,786	—	917,330	—
Montreal	15,405	18.3	1,364,689	11.5
Cincinnati	13,934	—	287,263	—
Vancouver	4,063	4.8	4,128,099	34.9
Alberta	621	0.7	663,304	5.6
Spokane	6	—	7,576	—
Winnipeg	0.4	0.0	197	0.0
TOTAL	**1,873,137**	**100.0**	**61,000,579**	**100.0**

Data from *TSE Review*, June 1991.

million shares. Table 3.1 shows the value and the volume of market trading for securities listed on the five Canadian and eight U.S. stock exchanges as of 1990.

From Table 3.1 you can see that the TSE accounts for about 76 percent of the value of shares traded on Canadian exchanges. The ME trades many of the same stocks as the TSE, but in much smaller volumes. The VSE is also national in scope; originally focused on resource stocks, it has recently expanded as a market for younger hi-tech or other start-up companies. Regional exchanges provide a market for trading shares of local firms that do not meet the listing requirements of the national exchanges. While the NYSE dominates North American trading, the TSE is the second highest in volume and third in value of trading. On a worldwide basis, the NYSE and the Tokyo stock exchange account for the vast majority of trading, while the TSE is seventh in value.

The national exchanges are willing to list a stock (allow trading in that stock on the exchange) only if it meets certain criteria of size and stability. Table 3.2 gives the initial listing requirements of the TSE for industrial companies. Unlike the NYSE, the TSE has different requirements for the various kinds of companies. The next most important (after industrial) types of companies listed on the TSE include mining and energy companies; these are required to have both capital and either reserves or potential for mineral production. These requirements ensure that a firm is of significant trading interest before the TSE will allocate facilities for it to be traded on the floor of the exchange. If a listed company suffers a decline and fails to meet the criteria in Table 3.2 (or those applicable), it may be delisted from the exchange.

TABLE 3.2 Minimum Listing Requirements for the TSE

Financial Requirements	
Pre-tax cash flow in last year	$200,000
Average annual pre-tax cash flow in previous 2 years	$150,000
Net tangible assets	$1,000,000
Adequate working capital	
Public Distribution	
Market value of publicly held stock	$350,000
Shares publicly held	200,000
Number of holders of board lot or more	200

Data from the Toronto Stock Exchange, 1986.

Although most common and preferred stocks are traded on the exchanges, bonds are not. Corporate and all federal, provincial, and municipal government bonds are traded only over the counter.

The Over-the-Counter Market

There are several hundred issues traded on the Canadian **over-the-counter market** (OTC) on a regular basis, and, in fact, any security may be traded there. The OTC market, however, is not a formal exchange; there are no membership requirements for trading, nor are there listing requirements for securities. In the OTC market, brokers registered with the provincial Securities Commission act as dealers in OTC securities. Security dealers quote prices at which they are willing to buy or sell securities. A broker can execute a trade by contacting a dealer listing an attractive quote.

The Canadian OTC market has developed similarly to that of the United States. Prior to automation, quotations of stock were recorded manually and published daily. The so-called pink sheets were the means by which dealers communicated their interest in trading at various prices. This was a cumbersome and inefficient technique, and published quotes were a full day out of date. In 1971, the U.S. National Association of Securities Dealers Automated Quotation system, or **NASDAQ,** began to offer immediate information on a computer-linked system of bid and asked prices for stocks offered by various dealers. The **bid price** is that at which a dealer is willing to purchase a security; the **asked price** is that at which the dealer will sell a security. The system allows a dealer who receives a buy or a sell order from an investor to examine all current quotes, call the dealer with the best quote, and execute a trade.

The Canadian Over-the-Counter Automated Trading System **(COATS)** was patterned after NASDAQ and introduced in 1986. In 1991, responsibility for operation and regulation of COATS was transferred to the Canadian Dealing Network Inc. (CDN), a subsidiary of the TSE. To be quoted by the **CDN system** a firm must satisfy a number of criteria, involving primarily the disclosure of financial information. Other conditions refer to the financial position of the issuer, the size of the public float, the number of public investors, etc. Although no precise requirements are stated for each one of these criteria, they are all taken into account when the board of directors of CDN examines a firm's application to be included in the system. By contrast, NASDAQ sets minimum size requirements for several financial variables of a firm before it will allow it to become part of its network.

There are two levels of interaction with CDN. A *user* has access to the network in order to receive current market information (bids and offers) and statistics for the previous trading day. Such users are brokers who accept bid or asked prices in executing a trade on behalf of their clients; they may also act as principals for their own accounts. Information on any trade is automatically recorded by the system.

The higher level is for a user who has been approved as a *market-maker* in a CDN security. This grants access to the CDN system for listing bid and asked quotations. These market-makers must maintain inventories of a security and continually stand ready to buy these shares from or sell them to the public at the quoted bid and asked prices. They earn profits from the spread between the bid price and the asked price. These higher-level subscribers may enter the bid and asked prices at which they are willing to buy or sell stocks into the computer network and update these quotes as desired.

For bonds, the over-the-counter market is a loosely organized network of dealers linked together by a computer quotation system for a number of bellwether bonds. In practice, the corporate bond market often is quite "thin," in that there are few investors interested in trading a particular bond at any particular time. The bond market is subject to a type of liquidity risk, because it can be difficult to sell holdings quickly if the need arises.

The Third and Fourth Markets

The **third market** refers to trading of exchange-listed securities on the OTC market. The development of this phenomenon followed its evolution in the United States. Until recently, members of an exchange were required to execute all their trades of exchange-listed securities on the exchange itself, and to charge commissions according to a fixed schedule. This schedule was disadvantageous to large traders, who were prevented from realizing economies of scale on large trades. The restriction led brokerage firms that were not members of the NYSE, and so not bound by its rules, to establish trading in the OTC market on large NYSE-listed firms. These trades took place at lower commissions than would have been charged on the NYSE, and the third market grew dramatically until 1975, when commissions on all orders became negotiable in the United States. Negotiated commissions became a common practice in Canada after April 1983, together with the growing popularity of discount brokerage houses.

The **fourth market** refers to direct trading between investors in exchange-listed securities without benefit of a broker. Large institutions who wish to avoid brokerage fees altogether may engage in direct trading.

3.3 *Trading on Exchanges*

Most of the material in this section applies to all securities traded on exchanges. Some of it, however, applies just to stocks, and in such cases we use the terms *stocks* or *shares*.

The Participants

When an investor instructs a broker to buy or sell securities, a number of players must act to consummate the trade. We start our discussion of the mechanics of exchange trading with a brief description of the potential parties to a trade.

The investor places an order with a broker. The latter contacts a brokerage firm owning a seat on the exchange (a *commission broker*) to execute the order. *Floor traders* (also known as floor attorneys) are representatives of members of the exchange charged with executing the trades on behalf of their firms' clients.

Registered traders are floor traders entrusted with **market-making** in specific stocks. A registered trader, who is known as a *specialist* in the NYSE, is central to the trading process. Registered traders maintain a market in one or more listed securities. We will examine their role in detail shortly.

Types of Orders

Investors may issue several types of orders to their brokers. *Market orders* are simple buy or sell orders that are to be executed immediately at current market prices. In contrast, investors can issue *limit orders,* whereby they specify prices at which they are willing to buy or sell a security. If the stock falls below the limit on a limit-buy order, then the trade is to be executed. If stock XYZ is selling at $45, for example, a limit-buy order may instruct the broker to buy the stock if and when the share price falls below $43. Correspondingly, a limit-sell order instructs the broker to sell as soon as the stock price goes above the specified limit. Orders also can be limited by a time period. Day orders, for example, expire at the close of the trading day. If it is not executed on that day, the order is canceled. *Open* or *good-till-cancelled orders,* in contrast, remain in force for up to six months unless cancelled by the customer.

Stop-loss orders are similar to limit orders in that the trade is not to be executed unless the stock hits a price limit. In this case however, the stock is to be sold if its price falls *below* a stipulated level. As the name suggests, the order lets the stock be sold to stop further losses from accumulating. Symmetrically, *stop-buy orders* specify that the stock should be bought when its price rises above a given limit. These trades often accompany short sales, and they are used to limit potential losses from the short position. Short sales are discussed in greater detail in Section 3.6.

The Execution of Trades

The registered trader, who is the central figure in the execution of trades, makes a market in the shares of one or more firms. Part of this task is simply mechanical. It involves maintaining a ''book'' listing all outstanding unexecuted limit orders entered by brokers on behalf of clients. Actually, the book is now a computer console. When limit orders can be executed at market prices, the registered trader sees to the trade; in this role he or she merely acts as a facilitator. As buy and sell orders at mutually agreeable prices cross the trading desk, the market-maker matches the two parties to the trade.

The registered trader is required to use the highest outstanding offered purchase price and lowest outstanding offered selling price when matching trades. Therefore, this system results in an auction market—all buy orders and all sell orders come to one location, and the best bids ''win'' the trades.

The most interesting function of the market-maker is to maintain a ''fair and orderly market'' by dealing personally in the stock. In return for the exclusive right to make the market in a specific stock on the exchange, the registered trader is required to maintain an orderly market by buying and selling shares from inventory. Registered traders maintain bid and asked prices, within a maximum spread specified by TSE regulations, at which they are obligated to meet at least a limited amount of market orders. If market buy orders come in, the registered traders must sell shares from their own accounts at the maintained asked price; if sell orders come in, they must be willing to buy at the listed bid price.

Ordinarily, in an active market registered traders can cross buy and sell orders without direct participation on their own accounts. That is, the trader's own inventory need not be the primary means of order execution. However, sometimes the market-maker's bid and asked prices will be better than those offered by any other market participant. Therefore, at any point the effective asked price in the market is the lower of either the registered trader's offered asked price or the lowest of the unfilled limit-sell orders. Similarly, the effective bid price is the highest of unfilled limit-buy orders or the trader's bid. These procedures ensure that the registered trader provides liquidity to the market.

By standing ready to trade at quoted bid and asked prices, the market-maker is exposed somewhat to exploitation by other traders. Large traders with ready access to late-breaking news will trade with market-makers only if the latters' quoted prices are temporarily out of line with assessments based on the traders' (possibly superior) information. Registered traders who cannot match the information resources of large traders will be at a disadvantage when their quoted prices offer profit opportunities to more-informed traders.

You might wonder why market-makers do not protect their interests by setting a low bid price and a high asked price. A registered trader using that strategy would not suffer losses by maintaining a too-low asked price or a too-high bid price in a period of dramatic movements in the stock price. Traders who offer a narrow spread between the bid and the asked prices have little leeway for error and must constantly monitor market conditions to avoid offering other investors advantageous terms.

There are two reasons why large bid-asked spreads are not viable options for the market-maker. First, one source of his or her income is derived from frequent trading at the bid and asked prices, with the spread as a trading profit. A too-large spread would tend to discourage investors from trading, and the market-maker's business would dry up. Another reason registered traders cannot use large bid-ask spreads to protect their interests is that they are obligated to provide price continuity to the market.

To illustrate the principle of price continuity, suppose that the highest limit-buy order for a stock is $30, while the lowest limit-sell order is $32. When a market buy order comes in, it is matched to the best limit-sell at $32. A market sell order would be matched to the best limit-buy at $30. As market buys and sells come to the floor randomly, the stock price would fluctuate between $30 and $32. The exchange authorities would consider this excessive volatility, and the market-maker would be expected to step in with bid and/or asked prices in between these values to reduce the bid-asked spread to an acceptable level, such as ¼ or ½ point.

Registered traders earn income both from commissions for acting as brokers for orders, and from the spread between the bid and asked prices at which they buy and sell securities. It also appears that their "book" of limit orders gives them unique knowledge about the probable direction of price movement over short periods of time. For example, suppose the market-maker sees that a stock now selling for $45 has limit-buy orders for over 100,000 shares at prices ranging from $44.50 to $44.75. This latent buying demand provides a cushion of support, because it is unlikely that enough sell pressure could come in during the next few hours to cause the price to drop below $44.50. If there are very few limit-sell orders above $45, some transient buying demand could raise the price substantially. The trader in such circumstances realizes that a position in the stock offers little downside risk and substantial upside potential. Such unique access to the trading intentions of other market participants seems to allow a market-maker to earn substantial profits on personal transactions.

Specific regulations of the TSE govern the registered traders' ability to profit from their superior information and their responsibility to maintain an orderly market. Such a market should respond to changes in information affecting the value of the stock by adjusting the price without excessive fluctuations. The trader achieves this result by making *stabilizing* trades. As defined by the TSE, a stabilizing trade is one in which a purchase (sale) is made at a price lower (higher) than the last price on an *uptick* (*downtick*); an uptick is an upward move in the share price. Registered traders are required to make a minimum 70–30 superiority of stabilizing over destabilizing trades, where the latter is defined as the reverse of a stabilizing trade.[4]

The effectiveness of the market-making system was challenged by the market crash of October 19, 1987, when NYSE stock prices fell about 25 percent on one day. In the face of overwhelming sell pressure, market-makers were called upon to purchase huge amounts of stock. In buying $486 million of stock on this

---

[4] *Toronto Stock Exchange Member's Manual*, Division G, Part XIX, p. G19-3.

single day, specialists suffered large losses, thereby eliminating much of their net worth. This precluded further share purchases by specialist firms and brought the stock market close to a halt. Since the crash, the NYSE has sharply increased the capital requirements for its specialist firms.

Moreover, in the wake of the market collapse many specialists apparently decided not to sacrifice their own capital in a seemingly hopeless effort to shore up prices. Although specialists as a whole were net purchasers of stock, fully 30 percent of the specialists in a sample of large stocks were net sellers on October 19. These firms came under criticism for failing to live up to their mandate to attempt to support an orderly market.

Block Sales

Institutional investors frequently trade blocks of several thousand shares of stock. Table 3.3 shows that **block transactions** of over 10,000 shares now account for more than one third of all trading on the TSE; on the NYSE block trading represents about one half. Such transactions are often too large to be handled comfortably by registered traders, who do not wish to hold such large blocks of stock in their inventory. Moreover, registered traders are prohibited from soliciting interest in shares from other institutional traders, and so cannot easily lay off large positions that they might assume in dealing with institutional traders.

In response to this problem, "block houses" have evolved in the United States to aid in the placement of block trades. Block houses are brokerage firms that help to find potential buyers or sellers of large block trades. With the absorption of independent major broker firms by the commercial banks in Canada, blocks are still handled by most large brokerages. Figure 3.1 shows an example of the daily report on block trading activity on the three major exchanges. Gordon Capital is noted for its role as a block house on the TSE.

Settlement

An order executed on the exchange must be settled within five working days. The purchaser must deliver the cash, and the seller must deliver the stock to

TABLE 3.3   Block Transactions on the Toronto Stock Exchange, 1989

	Transactions	Shares (millions)	% of TSE Volume
First quarter	14,910	576	37.45
Second quarter	15,595	605	39.23
Third quarter	16,539	692	38.59
Fourth quarter	15,471	635	37.13
Year	**62,515**	**2,508**	**38.58**

Data from *Official Trading Statistics*, 1989.

FIGURE 3.1

The daily block trading report.

From *The Globe and Mail*, December 18, 1991.

Reprinted by permission.

TSE BLOCK TRADES

(Trades of 50,000 or more shares worth at least $1-million)

Stock	Buyer	Seller	Volume	Price
Air Canada	Gordon	Gordon	322,100	$7.00
Amer Barrick	Gordon	Gordon	65,000	$29.63
Atco Cl I X f	Loewen	Loewen	205,400	$11.88
BCE Mobile	Gordon	Gordon	65,000	$28.50
BNT Ltd	Burns Fry	Burns Fry	115,000	$18.50
Bank of Mtl	Richardson	Richardson	81,000	$42.50
Bank of NS	Gordon	Gordon	155,000	$20.25
Bombardier B f	Gordon	Gordon	80,000	$25.38
Cdn Occ Petrol	Gordon	Gordon	65,000	$23.50
CHUM B f	First Mara	First Mara	89,000	$21.00
Cominco	Gordon	Gordon	50,000	$20.13
Domtar Inc	Richardson	Richardson	165,300	$7.13
Imasco	Deacon B	Deacon B	50,000	$35.50
Intrprv Pipe	ScotiaMcL	ScotiaMcL	50,000	$30.50
Labatt John	Research	Research	52,000	$25.75
Laidlaw B f	Burns Fry	Burns Fry	246,000	$8.88
Laidlaw B f	Gordon	Gordon	200,000	$8.75
Mackenzie Fin	Gordon	Gordon	350,000	$5.50
Maple Leaf Fds	Gordon	Gordon	100,000	$16.38
Mark Res	RBC Dom	RBC Dom	202,800	$5.75
Mark Res	RBC Dom	RBC Dom	270,200	$5.75
Natl Bk of Cda	Maison	Maison	96,400	$11.25
Natl Bk of Cda	RBC Dom	RBC Dom	1,358,200	$11.25
Norcen Ener A f	Gordon	Gordon	70,000	$22.25
Northern Tel	Gordon	Gordon	65,000	$49.88
Philip Envir	McLean	McLean	450,000	$9.50
Placer Dome	Burns Fry	Burns Fry	100,000	$11.75
Placer Dome	Burns Fry	Burns Fry	200,000	$11.50
Placer Dome	Gordon	Gordon	100,000	$11.63
Placer Dome	Gordon	Gordon	100,000	$11.63
Placer Dome	Gordon	Gordon	89,000	$11.63
Placer Dome	Levesque	Levesque	100,000	$11.63
Poco Pete	Gordon	Gordon	345,050	$5.00
Quebecor B f	Gordon	Gordon	80,000	$19.25
Renaissance	Gordon	Gordon	110,000	$12.50
Royal Bank	Gordon	Gordon	120,000	$25.50
Sask Oil & Gas	First Mara	First Mara	230,000	$6.50
TNT Financial E	RBC Dom	RBC Dom	100,000	$11.88
Telus Corp I	BBNCapel	BBNCapel	128,000	$8.38
Telus Corp I	Green Line	Green Line	130,000	$8.38
Telus Corp I	RBC Dom	RBC Dom	136,300	$8.38
Telus Corp I	RBC Dom	RBC Dom	250,000	$8.38
Telus Corp I	Richardson	Richardson	134,900	$8.38
Telus Corp	Richardson	Richardson	100,000	$15.25
TransAlta p T	Nesbitt	Nesbitt	200,000	$25.00
TransAlta p T	Nesbitt	Nesbitt	200,000	$25.00
TransAlta Util	RBC Dom	RBC Dom	100,000	$13.50
Ultramar Cap D	Nesbitt	Nesbitt	50,000	$95.00

MONTREAL BLOCKS

(Trades of 50,000 or more shares worth at least $1-million)

Stock	Buyer	Seller	Volume	Price
BCE Inc	Gordon	Gordon	60,000	$46.75
BCE Inc	RBC Dom	RBC Dom	60,000	$46.63
Bruncor	RBC Dom	RBC Dom	60,300	$18.63
Cdn Pacific	Gordon	Gordon	60,000	$16.88
Cdn Pacific	RBC Dom	RBC Dom	60,000	$16.88
DuPont Cda A	ScotiaMcl	ScotiaMcl	50,000	$39.63
Moore	Research	Research	552,600	$21.88
Onex Cp f	First Mara	First Mara	200,000	$10.13
Onex Cp f	First Mara	First Mara	200,000	$6.63
Royal Bank	Gordon	Gordon	60,000	$25.75
Royal Bank	RBC Dom	RBC Dom	60,000	$25.63
Teck B f	RBC Dom	RBC Dom	60,000	$18.50
Telus Corp I	Richardson	Richardson	200,000	$8.38
Tor-Dom Bk	Gordon	Gordon	60,000	$17.38
Tor-Dom Bk	RBC Dom	RBC Dom	100,000	$17.38

VANCOUVER BLOCKS

(Trades of 50,000 or more shares worth at least $1-million)

Stock	Buyer	Seller	Volume	Price
Cdn Pacific	Burns Fry	Burns Fry	79,500	$16.88
Molson Co A	Bunting	Bunting	60,000	$28.88
TD Bank	First Mara	First Mara	68,800	$17.25

the broker, who in turn delivers it to the buyer's broker. Transfer of the shares is made easier when the firm's clients keep their securities in *street name,* meaning that the broker holds the shares registered in the firm's own name on behalf of the client.

Settlement is simplified further by a clearinghouse. The trades of all exchange members are recorded each day, with members' transactions netted out, so that each member need only transfer or receive the net number of shares sold or bought that day. Each member settles only with the clearinghouse, instead of with each firm with whom trades were executed.

3.4 *Trading on the OTC Market*

On the exchanges, all trading takes place through a registered trader. Trades on the OTC market, however, are negotiated directly through dealers. Each dealer maintains an inventory of selected securities. Dealers sell from their inventories at asked prices and buy for them at bid prices.

An investor wishing to purchase or sell shares engages a broker who tries to locate the dealer offering the best deal on the security. This contrasts with exchange trading, where all buy or sell orders are negotiated through the registered trader, who arranges for the best bids to get the trade. In the OTC market, brokers must search the offers of dealers directly to find the best trading opportunity.

Exchange trading is effectively conducted in an auction market, whereas OTC trading is conducted in a **dealer market**. The CDN system facilitates access for users in obtaining a full set of dealer bid and asked quotes provided by the approved market-makers.

Because this system bypasses the registered trader system, OTC trades do not require a centralized trading floor as do exchange-listed stocks. Dealers can be located anywhere, as long as they can communicate effectively with other buyers and sellers.

3.5 *Buying on Margin*

Investors who purchase stocks on **margin** borrow part of the purchase price of the stock from their brokers. The brokers in turn borrow money from banks at the call money rate to finance these purchases, and charge their clients that rate plus a service charge for the loan. All securities purchased on margin must be left with the brokerage firm in street name, because the securities are used as collateral for the loan.

The regulators of the various exchanges set limits on the extent to which stock purchases can be financed via margin loans. Currently, the margin is 30 percent for optionable stocks, meaning that at most 70 percent of the purchase price may be borrowed; however, on the TSE, ME, and Alberta Stock Exchange this margin rises to as much as 100 percent on low-price stocks.

The percentage margin is defined as the ratio of the net worth, or "equity value" of the account to the market value of the securities. To demonstrate, suppose that the investor initially pays $6,000 toward the purchase of $10,000 worth of stock (100 shares at $100 per share), borrowing the remaining $4,000 from the broker. The account will have a balance sheet as follows:

Assets		Liabilities and Owner's Equity	
Value of stock	$10,000	Loan from broker	$4,000
		Equity	$6,000

The initial percentage margin is $6,000/$10,000 = 60 percent. If the stock's price declines to $70 per share, the account balance becomes:

Value of stock	$7,000	Loan from broker	$4,000
		Equity	$3,000

The equity in the account falls by the full decrease in the stock value, and the percentage margin is now $3,000/$7,000 = 43 percent.

If the stock value were to fall below $4,000, equity would become negative, meaning that the value of the stock is no longer sufficient collateral to cover the loan from the broker. To guard against this possibility, the broker sets a *maintenance margin*. If the percentage margin falls below the maintenance level, the broker will issue a *margin call* requiring the investor to add new cash or securities to the margin account. If the investor does not act, the broker may sell the securities from the account to pay off enough of the loan to restore the percentage margin to an acceptable level.

An example will show how the maintenance margin works. Suppose the maintenance margin is 30 percent. How far could the stock price fall before the investor would get a margin call? To answer this question requires some algebra.

Let P be the price of the stock. The value of the investor's 100 shares is then $100P$, and the equity in his or her account is $100P - \$4,000$. The percentage margin is therefore $(100P - \$4,000)/100P$. The price at which the percentage margin equals the maintenance margin of .3 is found by solving the equation:

$$\frac{100P - \$4,000}{100P} = .3$$
$$100P - \$4,000 = 30P$$
$$70P = \$4,000$$
$$P = \$57.14$$

If the price of the stock were to fall below $57.14 per share, the investor would get a margin call.

Concept Check	Question 1. If the maintenance margin in the example we have discussed were 40 percent, how far could the stock price fall before the investor would get a margin call?

Why do investors buy stock (or bonds) on margin? They do so when they wish to invest an amount greater than their own money alone would allow. Thus they can achieve greater upside potential, but they also expose themselves to greater downside risk.

To see how, let us suppose that an investor is bullish (optimistic) on Seagram's stock, which is currently selling at $100 per share. The investor has $10,000 to invest and expects Seagram's stock to go up in price by 30 percent during the next year. Ignoring any dividends, the expected rate of return would thus be 30 percent if the investor spent only $10,000 to buy 100 shares.

But now let us assume that the investor also borrows another $10,000 from the broker and invests it in Seagram's also. The total investment in Seagram's would thus be $20,000 (for 200 shares). Assuming an interest rate on the margin loan of 9 percent per year, what will be the investor's rate of return now (again ignoring dividends) if Seagram's stock does go up 30 percent by year's end?

The 200 shares will be worth $26,000. Paying off $10,900 of principal and interest on the margin loan leaves $15,100 ($26,000 − $10,900). The rate of return therefore will be

$$\frac{\$15,100 - \$10,000}{\$10,000} = 51\%$$

The investor has parlayed a 30 percent rise in the stock's price into a 51 percent rate of return on the $10,000 investment.

Doing so, however magnifies the downside risk. Suppose that instead of going up by 30 percent the price of Seagram's stock goes down by 30 percent to $70 per share. In that case the 200 shares will be worth $14,000, and the investor is left with $3,100 after paying off the $10,900 of principal and interest on the loan. The result is a disastrous rate of return:

$$\frac{\$3,100 - \$10,000}{\$10,000} = -69\%$$

Table 3.4 summarizes the possible results of these hypothetical transactions. Note that if there is no change in Seagram's stock price, the investor loses 9 percent, the cost of the loan.

TABLE 3.4   Illustration of Buying Stock on Margin

Change in Stock Price	End of Year Value of Shares	Repayment of Principal and Interest	Investor's Rate of Return*
30% increase	$26,000	$10,900	51%
No change	20,000	10,900	−9%
30% decrease	14,000	10,900	−69%

* Assuming the investor buys $20,000 worth of stock by borrowing $10,000 at an interest rate of 9% per year.

Concept Check

> Question 2. Suppose that in the previous example the investor borrows only $5,000 at the same interest rate of 9 percent per year. What will be the rate of return if the price of Seagram's stock goes up by 30 percent? If it goes down by 30 percent? If it remains unchanged?

3.6   *Short Sales*

A **short sale** allows investors to profit from a decline in a security's price. In this procedure, an investor borrows shares of stock from another investor through a broker and sells the shares. Later, the investor (the short seller) must repurchase the shares in the market in order to replace the shares that were borrowed. This is called *covering* the short position. If the stock price has fallen, the shares will be repurchased at a lower price than that at which they were initially sold, and the short seller reaps a profit. Short sellers must not only return the shares but also give the lender any dividends paid on the shares during the period of the short sale, because the lender of the shares would have received the dividends directly from the firm had the shares not been lent.

Exchange rules permit short sales only after an *uptick,* that is, only when the last recorded change in the stock price is positive. This rule apparently is meant to prevent waves of speculation against the stock. In other words, the votes of ''no confidence'' in the stock that short sales represent may be entered only after a price increase.

Finally, exchange rules require that proceeds from a short sale must be kept on account with the broker. The short seller therefore cannot invest these funds to generate income. In addition, short sellers are required to post margin (which is essentially collateral) with the broker to ensure that the trader can cover any losses sustained should the stock price rise during the period of the short sale.[5]

To illustrate the actual mechanics of short selling, suppose that you are bearish (pessimistic) on Seagram's stock, and that its current market price is $100 per share. You tell your broker to sell short 1,000 shares. The broker borrows 1,000 shares either from another customer's account or from another broker.

The $100,000 cash proceeds from the short sale are credited to your account. Suppose the broker has a 50 percent margin requirement on short sales. This

---

[5] We should note that although we have been describing a short sale of a stock, bonds also may be sold short.

means that you must have other cash or securities in your account worth at least $50,000 that can serve as margin (that is, collateral) on the short sale. Let us suppose that you have $50,000 in Treasury bills. Your account with the broker after the short sale will then be:

Assets		Liabilities and Owner's Equity	
Cash	$100,000	Short position in Seagram's stock	$100,000
T-bills	$ 50,000	(1,000 shares owned)	
		Equity	$ 50,000

Now if you are right, and Seagram's stock falls to $70 per share, you can cover your short sale for a profit of $30,000. If the price of Seagram's stock goes up while you are short, however, you may get a margin call from your broker.

Let us suppose that the broker has a maintenance margin of 30 percent on short sales. This means that the equity in your account must be at least 30 percent of the value of your short position at all times. How far can the price of Seagram's stock go up before you get a margin call?

Let P be the price Seagram's stock. Then the value of your short position is $1,000P$, and the equity in your account is $150,000 - 1,000P$. Your short position margin ratio is $(\$150,000 - 1,000P)/1,000P$. The critical value of P is thus

$$\frac{\$150,000 - 1,000P}{1,000P} = .3$$
$$\$150,000 - 1,000P = 300P$$
$$1,300P = \$150,000$$
$$P = \$115.38 \text{ per share}$$

If Seagram's stock should rise above $115.38 per share, you will get a margin call, and you will either have to put up additional cash or cover your short position.

Concept Check

Question 3. If the short position maintenance margin in the preceding example were 40 percent, how far could the stock price rise before the investor would get a margin call?

3.7 *Regulation of Securities Markets*

Trading in securities markets in Canada is regulated under a number of laws. Laws such as the federal Canada Business Corporations Act govern the conduct of business firms, while the various provincial Securities Acts regulate trading of securities. Most legislation is at the provincial level, even though historically the first Canadian laws concerning securities were introduced at the federal level in the late 19th century. Provincial legislation in the Maritime Provinces followed shortly thereafter, while the Ontario Companies Act was established in 1907. The Ontario Securities Act, Canada's first provincial securities act, was passed in 1945, and has been revised repeatedly since that time. Other provinces have generally tended to follow Ontario's lead. Although the federal government doesn't have a Securities Act, portions of the Criminal Code of Canada are specifically directed to securities trading.

In addition to the laws, there is also considerable self-regulation in the financial services industry. It takes place via regulations governing membership in various associations of professionals participating in the industry. Thus the Investment Dealers Association of Canada encompasses stock exchange members and bond dealers, while the Investment Funds Institute of Canada is the association of Canadian mutual funds. Self-regulation also occurs through the organized stock exchanges. (See the accompanying box for a discussion of the TSE's concern for transparency.)

What's Right with the TSE?

by Martin Mayer

Beneath the glossy and widely reported surface of the world's financial markets, a hidden battle rages today between the forces of light and darkness, of modernity and of tradition. Out in front, leading the cohorts of light and modernity, rides the Toronto Stock Exchange, slashing through opposition from England and the United States in a bid to sell its software and processes to the world's hundred-odd stock markets. It's a remarkable transformation for an institution that only a quarter of a century ago was described by Mr. Justice Arthur Kelly as "a private gaming club."

The TSE's weapon in this war is CATS, for Computer Assisted Trading System. Like any screen-based market communications system, CATS is a way for participants in a market to deliver information about their desire to purchase or sell what this market trades. It thus has a family resemblance to the NASDAQ system by which members of the National Association of Securities Dealers in the United States broadcast to other dealers their bid and asked quotes for stocks traded over-the-counter, and to the Telerate and Reuters systems by which government bond dealers and foreign-currency traders get the word out to their in-groups.

What makes CATS better is that the Toronto system is actually a way to do business with justice for all—and also a way to report to the brokerage community and to the investing and trading publics more details of what actually happens than are available through any other procedure now in use.

What is right with the Toronto system is probably best described by contrast to the NASDAQ procedure, which was (unfortunately) adopted by the London Stock Exchange in the form of SEAQ at the time of Big Bang in 1986. As the names indicate—the letters AQ stand for "Automated Quote"—the NASDAQ and SEAQ systems are "quote driven." The bids and offers on the screen

(Continued)

are from dealers who stand ready to buy at the lower price and sell at the higher one. The system sorts these out, and for each stock presents a ranked list of offers from the lowest up (or a ranked list of bids from the highest down) with the code name of the dealer beside his number. All bids and offers at the same price are equal: a purchaser (or seller) can legitimately do business with any of a number of firms quoting the "best" price.

The dealer placing the quote in the system may specify how many shares he's prepared to buy or sell at this price, or he may enter only a pro forma "100 shares," what is called a "board lot" in Canada or a "round lot" in the United States. The broker with the customer has to call to find out how much he can buy or sell at the price on the screen. Transactions do not necessarily change what appears on the screen: dealers must take an action to change their publicized quotes.

CATS, by contrast, is "order driven." The prices on the screen are accompanied by a statement of the number of shares to buy or to sell. It's first come, first served: the computer establishes by "time priority" a queue of bidders and offerers at each price. When the offer at the head of the queue is taken or the bid is hit, the entry vanishes from the screen, to be replaced by another offer or bid at the same (or another) price from the next order in the queue.

For each security, a "registered trader" (in U.S. terminology, "specialist") has committed himself to sell or buy for his own account, up to a stated limit, the shares necessary to satisfy a customer's order when the number of shares offered or bid on the screen at the best price is insufficient to complete the "fill." Nobody has to pick up a telephone: a touch on the keyboard does the business—and automatically generates the record that the business has been done. That record includes not only the ticker tape that informs the world of the course of trading, but also a monthly magnetic tape that allows any interested party to track the course of trading in any of the CATS-traded stock.

In the United States, the Department of Labor has been charged by law with making sure that pension fund moneys are not wasted or stolen in the process of their investment. Among the scams that

are believed to occur are transactions where a fund's broker trades with friendly brokers in ways that generate buy prices to the fund near the top of the day's range and sell prices near the bottom. With volatility often at a rate of 2 percent and 3 percent a day, purchase or sale at the wrong time can wipe out the dividend yield for a year.

A number of funds, and consultants to the Labor Department, have tried to get from the New York Stock Exchange information on patterns of trading identifying the brokers in specified purchases and sales, and the exchange has refused to supply the reports. By contrast, trades on the Toronto Stock Exchange come with a full boat of information. Anyone who wants to know which brokers did what can buy a tape, which includes the identity of the brokers on both sides of every transaction.

Touch another key and CATS reveals the total number of shares offered or bid for at each price, at this instant, by all brokers together, in any stock in the system. Someone thinking of buying or selling can see where the weight of interest in this stock lies right now, and make judgments accordingly. To date, these aggregate screens have been available only on the "inside," to the numbers of the exchange. This summer [1989], however, the public will be able to see the same data, and CATS screens will be wired into the trading desks of the institutional customers, the banks, pension funds and insurance companies that put in the big orders.

At present, 850 stocks, representing just 20 percent of Toronto's volume and 15 percent of the value of listed securities, are in the CATS stable. The other stocks trade only on the exchange floor. But that floor, in a tower that is part of the First Canadian Place complex, was wired from the start for electronic trading. At each "post" where a stock is trading, a screen shows the "book" of bids (and offers) lower (higher) than the current market price. A broker who is working a big order at another post may leave his order for this stock on the screen, and the "registered trader" on the floor executes it for him should the market move to bring it in line.

"By the end of the year," says J. Pearce Bunting, the white-haired and unflappable chairman of the TSE, "electronic trading will be on the floor,

(Continued)

too.'' Brokers will have a choice of entering orders through their screens upstairs or by the traditional system of telephone calls to clerks on the floor. To give the bidding and negotiating process of the floor time to work, upstairs orders will acquire priority in the ''crowd'' around the post only after a brief delay. This will also give independent floor traders a chance to compete with the registered trader, presumably making for a market with a narrower spread between the bid and asked quotations.

There are sceptics on both sides. A mixed CATS/floor system has been about to be launched for more than two years. Don Bainbridge, whose Gordon Capital is the largest and most aggressive trading operation at the TSE, feels strongly that computerized systems will not be able to handle the business in the more active stocks. ''Trading is not just putting numbers up,'' he says. ''Floor trading is a way for bridging capital to be put to proper use. On the floor, I can mobilize people's capital to assist me when I need it, and there's no way I can do that on CATS. You can't feel on a screen that a market's crapping out.''

John Kolosky, who used to work for the TSE as director of market operations but now works for Gordon Capital, finds the very equality of CATS a handicap: ''There's a cost to having people call a continuous auction market. If somebody is taking a risk, he's entitled to be paid for it.''

In London, upstairs trading on screens killed the exchange floor in a matter of weeks after its introduction as part of Big Bang. Stanley Beck, chairman of the Ontario Securities Commission, would not be surprised if something similar happens in Toronto and doesn't worry about it. ''Whenever anything changes,'' he says, ''extravagant claims are made for what's being lost. What we know is that CATS is the most open system in the world.''

Of course, real life is not as simple as schematic descriptions. NASDAQ and all the exchanges have automated execution systems that allow small customers to buy anywhere from a hundred to several thousand shares without getting involved in the complexities of ''quote driven'' versus ''order driven'' systems. The aggregate screens in Toronto will not tell as much of the story as appears on the surface, because traders need not and will not enter

into the system the total of their orders when they are planning a big move. They may be willing to pay the price in a lost priority for the rest of their order (because each time they place a new order they return to the end of the queue at that price) so as not to tip their hand. And while time takes precedence for deals done with traders and other brokers' customers, a broker may fill a customer's order from his own bid or offer even if someone else has priority on the screen.

But there is no question that Toronto is moving steadily toward greater ''transparency''—while both London and New York are retreating. In London, new rules promulgated by the so-called ''International Stock Exchange'' relieve dealers from reporting until tomorrow (and maybe not even then) all trades of more than 100,000 pounds. In the United States, the Securities and Exchange Commission is about to announce a rule that trading between institutions worth more than $100 million does not have to be reported to anyone.

In effect, these new rules in Britain and the United States will create separate markets for institutional and individual investors. And as we already know from the bond market and the currency markets, such separations, not monitored by regulators, create situations where traders can ''paint the tape''—publicizing whatever trades they wish at whatever prices suit them—to gain an edge on the rest of the market.

Until quite recently, the dominant opinion in the United States was that information improves not only the quality of stock markets but also people's desire to use them as basic tools for investing and trading. ''Sunshine,'' said Justice Louis D. Brandeis, ''is the best disinfectant.'' Since the late 1970s, unfortunately, it has become fashionable to say that if governments try to make markets open and honest the business will move to the Caymans or Luxembourg or the Far East.

Toronto has put its money on the old faith, that investors both individual and institutional will be drawn to the markets where they know what's going on. An age of information should demand no less. Donald Unruh, the TSE's vice-president for international trading, who is selling CATS around the world, a man with a military mustache behind a

(Continued)

busy desk, says the bet is being won: "When Paris started to use our system in 1985 I told my chairman their volume would grow four to eight times what it was. They put all their shares into CATS, and put the aggregate order book on satellite, for distribution throughout Europe. In 1984, the value of their trading was 38 percent of the value of trading on the TSE. Last year, it was 1.93 times the value of trading on the TSE, and so far this year, it's two and a half times. And only 20 percent of that can be accounted for by the privatization of state-owned companies."

Originally only in Paris, CATS has now been adopted by the French regional exchanges, too, in a nationwide market system. The same movement, from Madrid out, has made CATS a national system in Spain. This year, the São Paulo stock exchange will move its trading onto CATS screens under license from Toronto.

Hugh Cleland, who was in charge of this project at the TSE from 1978 to 1981, reports that it cost about $1 million to develop. The drive to sell internationally began in an effort to recoup the investment. Unruh recently supervised an investigation of the trading of Canadian stocks in the London market, with examiners going from firm to firm and examining the "blotters" on which all the trades they handled were registered. He had started with the belief that only 21 Canadian stocks were active in London, and found 600. Six foreign firms in London were making markets for 50 or more Canadian stocks every day (mostly for Canadian customers) before the Toronto market had opened for business.

The mission, therefore, is to get this trading home, and to establish links with stock exchanges elsewhere in the world, that will expand both the ownership of Canadian equities and Canadian investment abroad. The first such link, with the American Stock Exchange in New York for stocks listed both in Toronto and on the ASE, was less than a triumph; the ASE, according to Ivers Riley of that exchange, got 90 percent of the volume, and the TSE unilaterally backed out of the contract last year. But the ASE link was floor-to-floor, and computer-to-computer may be a very different game. "The more people there are on comparable systems," says Pearce Bunting contentedly, "the greater the opportunity for people to do business together."

From *Challenges*, Spring 1989. Reprinted by permission of *Challenges* and the author.

Provincial securities legislation exists in all Canadian provinces and territories, but provincial securities commissions exist only in six provinces, the five provinces with organized stock exchanges plus Saskatchewan. These commissions are responsible for administering and enforcing the provincial securities laws. The key purpose of these laws is to protect investors from fraud. They achieve this by controlling (through registration) the people participating in the financial services industry, and by ensuring that investors have all material facts at their disposal in order to make their own investment decisions. The approval, however, by a securities commission of a prospectus or financial report does not mean that it views the security as a good investment. The commission cares only that the relevant facts are disclosed; investors make their own evaluations of the security's value.

Relevant facts are revealed for prospective investors when a primary issue takes place, through the prospectus. Investors must also be kept informed, on a continuous basis, about all important changes to a company's status, such as changes in the control structure of the corporation, acquisitions or disposals of major assets, proposed takeovers or mergers, etc. Companies must also issue several financial reports on a quarterly basis, and more complete reports annually.

Several problems are created by the fragmentation along provincial lines of the regulatory system for Canadian securities markets. Financial transactions in such markets may involve parties residing in different provinces; for instance, a group of Ontario investors purchases the shares of a Quebec company, traded on the TSE. Such a transaction would fall under the jurisdiction of two provinces' regulatory bodies, implying that it should simultaneously comply with the Quebec and Ontario regulatory regimes. Apart from the fact that this may create multiple (and costly) investigations of the same transaction, it would also generate uncertainty among the investors about the set of rules governing their investment.

Such problems are avoided in the United States, where the securities industry is regulated by national agencies. The most important of these is the Securities and Exchange Commission (SEC), established by the 1934 Securities Exchange Act, to ensure the full disclosure of relevant information relating to the issue of new securities and the periodic release of financial information for secondary trading. The act also empowered the SEC to register and regulate securities exchanges, OTC trading, brokers, and dealers. It thus established the SEC as the administrative agency responsible for broad oversight of the securities markets. The SEC, however, shares oversight with other regulatory bodies. For example, the Commodity Futures Trading Commission (CFTC) regulates trading in futures markets, whereas the Federal Reserve Bank (the Fed) has broad responsibility for the health of the U.S. financial system. In this role, the Fed sets margin requirements on stocks and stock options and regulates bank lending to securities markets participants.

The Investment Dealers Association and the stock exchanges have established the Canadian Investor Protection Fund (CIPF) to protect investors from losses if their brokerage firms fail. Just as the Canadian Deposit Insurance Corporation provides federal protection to depositors against bank failure, the CIPF ensures that investors will receive the value of their accounts up to a maximum of $250,000. Securities held for their account in street name by the failed brokerage firm, and cash balances up to a limit of $60,000, will be replaced by equivalent securities, or by their cash value. The CIPF is financed by levying an "insurance premium" on its participating, or member, brokerage firms.

One of the important restrictions on trading involves *insider trading*. It is illegal for anyone to transact in securities to profit from **inside information,** that is, private information held by senior officers, directors, or major stockholders (with a direct or indirect interest of at least 10 percent of the voting shares) that has not yet been divulged to the public. The difficulty is that the definition of insiders can be ambiguous. Although it is obvious that the chief financial officer of a firm is an insider, it is less clear whether the firm's biggest supplier can be considered one as well. However, the supplier may deduce the firm's near-term prospects from significant changes in orders. This gives the supplier a unique form of private information, yet the supplier does not necessarily qualify as an insider. These ambiguities plague security analysts, whose job is to uncover as much information as possible concerning the firm's expected prospects. The distinction between legal private information and illegal inside information can be fuzzy.

The OSC requires officers, directors, and major stockholders of all publicly held firms to report all of their transactions in their firm's stock within 10 days of the end of the month of the transaction. A compendium of insider trades is published monthly in the OSC's insider trading bulletin, extracts of which are published promptly by *The Globe and Mail*. The idea is to inform the public of any implicit votes of confidence or no confidence made by insiders.

Do insiders exploit their knowledge? The answer seems to be, to a limited degree, yes. Two forms of evidence support this conclusion. First, there is massive evidence of "leakage" of useful information to some traders before any public announcement of that information. For example, share prices of firms announcing dividend increases (which the market interprets as good news concerning the firm's prospects) commonly increase in value a few days *before* the public announcement of the increase.[6] Clearly, some investors are acting on the good news before it is released to the public. Similarly, share prices tend to increase a few days before the public announcement of above-trend earnings growth.[7] At the same time, share prices still rise substantially on the day of the public release of good news, indicating that insiders, or their associates, have not fully bid up the price of the stock to the level commensurate with that news.

The second sort of evidence on insider trading is based on returns earned on trades by insiders. Researchers have examined the SEC's summary of insider trading to measure the performance of insiders. A Canadian study by Baesel and Stein[8] investigated the abnormal return on stocks over the months following purchases or sales by insiders. They found that a simulated policy of buying a portfolio of stocks purchased by insiders yielded an abnormal return in the following eight months of about 3.8 percent. If the insiders were also directors of Canadian banks (presumed to be even better informed), the abnormal return persisted for 12 months and rose to 7.8 percent. In both cases, the major part of the gain occurred after publication of the insiders' actions. Insider sales, however, did not generate information leading to abnormal gains.

---

[6] See, for example, J. Aharony and I. Swary, "Quarterly Dividend and Earnings Announcement and Stockholders' Return: An Empirical Analysis," *Journal of Finance* 35 (March 1980).

[7] See, for example, George Foster, Chris Olsen, and Terry Shevlin, "Earnings Releases, Anomalies, and the Behavior of Security Returns," *The Accounting Review,* October 1984.

[8] Jerome Baesel and Garry Stein, "The Value of Information: Inferences from the Profitability of Insider Trading," *Journal of Financial and Quantitative Analysis,* September 1979. See also Jean-Marc Suret and Elise Cormier, "Insiders and the Stock Market," *Canadian Investment Review* 3, no. 2 (Fall 1990).

3.8 *Selecting a Broker*

Basically, individuals may choose from two kinds of brokers: *full-service* or *discount*. Full-service brokers, who provide a variety of services, often are referred to as *account executives* or *financial consultants*. Besides carrying out the basic services of executing orders, holding securities for safekeeping, extending margin loans, and facilitating short sales, normally they also provide information and advice relating to investment alternatives. Full-service brokers usually are supported by a research staff that issues analyses and forecasts of general economic, industry, and company conditions and often makes specific buy or sell recommendations. Some customers take the ultimate leap of faith and allow a full-service broker to make buy and sell decisions for them by establishing a *discretionary account*. This step requires an unusual degree of trust on the part of the customer, because an unscrupulous broker can "churn" an account, that is, trade securities excessively in order to generate commissions.

Discount brokers, on the other hand, provide no-frills services. They buy and sell securities, hold them for safekeeping, offer margin loans, and facilitate short sales, and that is all. The only information they provide about the securities they handle consists of price quotations.

In recent years, discount brokerage services have become increasingly available. Today, many banks and mutual fund management companies offer such services to the investing public as part of a general trend toward the creation of one-stop financial "supermarkets." In addition, some of the major Canadian banks have acquired full-service brokerages as subsidiaries; the Royal Bank has both a full-service subsidiary and a discount brokerage service.

One important service that most brokers, both full-service and discount, offer their customers is an automatic cash management feature allowing cash generated from the sale of securities or the receipt of dividends or interest to be almost immediately invested in a money market fund. This ensures that there will never be idle (uninvested) cash in the investor's account.

3.9 *Cost of Trading*

We can look at the cost of buying or selling securities as having an explicit part—the broker's commission—and an implicit part—the dealer's **bid-asked**

Cheaper Fees Come in a Wide Range at the Discount Brokers

By Rudy Luukko

You pick up the telephone. You call your discount broker. You place your trade. The transaction is the same no matter which discounter you use, as are the basic qualifications of the person on the other end of the line. But, as the chart below illustrates, the fees charged by different brokerages vary widely.

Discount brokerages generally charge a flat fee—currently ranging from $25 to $40—for each transaction, plus a fee for each share traded. The

HOW THE DISCOUNTERS COMPARE

(A random sample of stock trades shows that fees vary widely among brokerages)

Stock Example*	No. of Shares	Recent Stock Price	Trade Value	Typical Full-Service **Fee	Royal Bank Action Direct	Bank of Montreal Investors Line	Green Line Direct Trading	Marathon Discount	National Bank Investel	Disnat Invest-ments	Scotia Discount Brokerage
Intl. Praxis Resources	5,000	$ 0.04	$ 200	$65	$40	$25	$45	$43	$65	$35	$25
Consolidated Bel-Air	5,000	0.64	3,200	108	90	50	65	60	90	60	50
Hillcrest Resources	1,000	2.00	2,000	65	70	45	70	60	70	60	45
Arbor Capital A	500	9.00	4,500	140	60	40	60	55	60	53	40
ConWest Explorations A	400	13.00	5,200	150	60	41	60	55	60	53	41
Royal Bank	300	25.38	7,614	170	58	40	58	53	56	52	40
Inco Ltd.	100	34.88	3,488	65	47	31	47	41	47	42	31
TOTAL			26,202	763	425	272	405	367	450	354	272
Flat fee for trades under $2,000					40	25	45	43	N/A	35	25
Hours of Service					8 A.M. to 5:30 P.M. Mon.–Fri.	8 A.M. to 8 P.M. Mon.–Fri.	24 hrs. daily	24 hrs. daily	8 A.M. to 8 P.M. Mon.–Fri.	8 A.M. to 8 P.M. Mon.–Fri.	8 A.M. to 8 P.M. Mon.–Fri.
Location					Ont., Que.	Ont., Que., Man., N.B., Nfld, P.E.I.	throughout Canada	Ont., Que., B.C., Alta., Man., Sask., N.S.	Que.	Que.	Ont., Que., B.C., N.S., N.B., Nfld., P.E.I., Alta.

* Chosen for their price within trading ranges only   ** Based on Scotia McLeod Inc. commission structure.   N/A not available

(Continued)

per-share fee rises with the price of the stock. For instance, the per-share fees charged by Toronto Dominion Bank's Green Line Investor Services Inc. range from half a cent a share for shares worth less than $1 apiece to seven cents a share for shares over $30.13. So for a trade of 10,000 shares of 40-cent stock, Green Line would charge $90—a $40 flat fee plus $50 in per-share fees (or half a cent multiplied by 10,000).

On shares worth less than $1, all the major discount brokerages charge half a cent a share. But the per-share charges vary with higher-priced stocks. For instance, on shares of more than $30.13, the Bank of Nova Scotia's Scotia Discount Brokerage charges six cents a share. Disnat Investment Inc. charges six and a half cents and Green Line charges seven cents. So the cost on a 1,000-share transaction, including the flat fees, ranges from $85 at Scotia to $100 at Disnat to $110 at Green Line.

The chart on page 106 lists the commissions charged by various discounters on a sample portfolio of small-volume stock trades totalling $26,202. The largest discounters, Green Line and Marathon Brokerage, charged $405 (or 1.5 percent of the value of the trades) and $367 (1.4 percent), respectively. Tied for the lowest trading fees were the Bank of Montreal's InvestorLine and Scotia at $272 apiece (1 percent). At $25, InvestorLine and Scotia also have the cheapest flat rates for trades under $2,000. The larger the trade, the less significant the flat fee is.

In general, the brokerages that charge more provide more services. For instance, Toronto Dominion's Green Line and Marathon, the nation's two largest discounters, offer 24-hour-a-day service. All of the other discount shops operate Monday to Friday, under varying hours.

Additional services also bump up the fees—even for investors who don't make use of them. For instance, Green Line offers discounts on research reports, data bases and software. It also offers an automated service accessible by touch-tone phone that allows investors to obtain quotes or review their portfolios at any time. Marathon has a similar service, but it is available only in Ontario. It also offers a program that provides guidelines on how to select a mutual fund.

Unfortunately, there is no similar program for selecting a discount broker. It's up to the vigilant investor to decide which firm offers the combination of fee structure and services best suited to him.

From *The Financial Times of Canada*, March 4, 1991. Reprinted by permission of the author and *The Financial Times of Canada*.

spread. Sometimes the broker is a dealer in the security being traded and will charge no commission, but will collect the fee entirely in the form of the bid-asked spread.

Another implicit cost of trading that some observers would distinguish is the price concession an investor may be forced to make for trading in any quantity that exceeds the quantity the dealer is willing to trade at the posted bid or asked price.

The commission for trading common stocks is generally around 2 percent of the value of the transaction, but it can vary significantly. Before 1983 the schedule of commissions was fixed, but in today's environment of negotiated commissions there is substantial flexibility. On some trade, full-service brokers will offer even lower commissions than will discount brokers. In general, it pays the investor to shop around.

Total trading costs consisting of the commission, the dealer bid-asked spread, and the price concession can be substantial. According to one U.S.

study, the round-trip costs (costs of purchase and resale) of trading large blocks of stocks of small companies can be as high as 30 percent.[9]

There is one Canadian phenomenon that deserves mention. A number of brokerage houses act as exclusive market-makers for low-capitalization stocks. Under such circumstances the stocks are extremely illiquid, with bid-asked spreads as high as 50 percent of the asked value. These stocks are generally thought to be poor investment prospects.

In most cases, however, costs of trades are far smaller. Because of the existence of negotiated commissions, the quoted rates are not representative of actual fees paid on larger orders. The commissions can be as low as .25 percent of the value of stocks traded for large transactions made through discount houses. The box on pages 106–107 illustrates comparative commissions.

3.10 *Mutual Funds and Other Investment Companies*

As an alternative to investing in securities through a broker (or in addition to it), many individuals invest in mutual funds sponsored by investment companies. This section explains how these institutions work.

Mutual Funds

Mutual funds are firms that manage pools of other people's money. Individuals buy shares of mutual funds, and the funds invest the money in certain specified types of assets (e.g., common stocks, tax-exempt bonds, and mortgages). The shares issued to the investors entitle them to a pro rata portion of the income generated by these assets.

Mutual funds perform several important functions for their shareholders:

1. *Record keeping and administration.* The funds prepare periodic status reports and reinvest dividends and interest.
2. *Diversification and divisibility.* By pooling their money, investment companies enable shareholders to hold fractional shares of many different securities. Funds can act as large investors even if any individual shareholder cannot.
3. *Professional management.* Many, but not all, mutual funds have full-time staffs of security analysts and portfolio managers who attempt to achieve superior investment results for their shareholders.
4. *Lower transaction costs.* By trading large blocks of securities, investment companies can achieve substantial savings on brokerage fees and commissions.

---

[9] T. F. Loeb, "Trading Cost: The Critical Link between Investment Information and Results," *Financial Analysts Journal,* May-June 1983.

There are two types of mutual funds: **closed-end funds** and **open-end funds.** Open-end funds stand ready to redeem or issue shares at their net asset value (NAV), which is the market value of all securities held divided by the number of shares outstanding. The number of shares outstanding of an open-end fund changes daily, as investors buy new shares or redeem old ones. Closed-end funds do not redeem or issue shares at net asset value. Shares of closed-end funds are traded through brokers, as are other common stocks, and their price can therefore differ from NAV.[10]

The prices of closed-end funds are listed with other shares in the financial pages; *The Globe and Mail* also includes some of them in the section called "Trust Units" following the TSE listings. Single-country funds are generally closed-end. The NAV must be obtained from other sources offering specific information about funds; the majority of closed-end funds trade at a discount, typically of about 10 percent of NAV.

Many investors consider closed-end fund shares selling at a discount to their NAV to be a true bargain. Even if the market price never rises to the level of NAV, the dividend yield on an investment in the fund would exceed the dividend yield on the same securities held outside of the fund. To see this, imagine a fund with a NAV of $10 per share and a market price of $9 that pays an annual dividend of $1 per share. Its dividend yield based on NAV is 10 percent per year, which is the yield obtainable by buying the securities directly. But the dividend yield to someone buying shares in the fund at $9 would be 11.11 percent per year.

The market price of open-end funds, on the other hand, cannot fall below NAV because these funds redeem shares at NAV. The price at which the fund can be bought or sold will differ from NAV, however, if the fund carries a load. Shares of a **load fund** are sold by security brokers, many insurance brokers, and others. A load is in effect a sales commission, usually from 3 percent to 8.5 percent of NAV, which is paid to the seller. More recently, the practice has arisen of charging the load upon redemption, if the fund is cashed in within less than five years. Thus the load also serves to deter movement in and out of the fund.

Shares of a **no-load fund** are bought directly from the fund at NAV and carry no sales charge. The investment performance of no-load funds does not differ systematically from that of load funds, so it would seem that an investor who buys into a load fund is simply paying the retail price for an equivalent item readily available wholesale.

Figure 3.2 shows part of the listings for mutual funds published every weekday in *The Globe and Mail.* As explained, funds are identified as charging a front-end or redemption load, or none. Some are seen to be unavailable or closed; this indicates that the managers do not wish to pool further capital with that fund due to excessive size.

---

[10] The divergence of the market price of a closed-end fund's shares from NAV constitutes a major puzzle, which has yet to be satisfactorily explained by finance theorists.

FIGURE 3.2

Part of the daily listing of mutual funds.

From *The Globe and Mail,* December 18, 1991. Reprinted by permission.

CANADIAN MUTUAL FUNDS

Recent prices of investment funds supplied by Fundata Canada at 5:15 p.m. Dec. 17. Prices reported by funds are the net asset value per share or unit last calculated and are for information purposes only. Confirmation of price should be obtained from the fund. Chg—change from last valuation; D—distributed by fund sponsor; G—redemption charge; I—distributed by independent dealers; L—sales charge; M—minimum purchase of $150,000; N—no sales charge; O—optional front—end or redemption charge; R—eligible for RRSPs; S—stock split; U—U.S. currency; X—ex-dividend; Y—delayed NAVPS; Z—not available for purchase.

MEMBERS

Fund	Load	RSP	Dist	Value	Chg
ABC FUNDS					
ymFully-Mgd	N	RD		5.77	+.05
ymFund-Value	N	RD		5.87	+.06
ADMAX INV.					
uAme Perf$US	O	D		4.56	+.03
Ame Perform	O	D		5.23	+.04
yCanadian Inc	O	RD		5.32	+.01
Cdn Perform	O	RD		4.82	−.03
Polymetric	O	R I		5.12	−.00
US Poly	O	I		5.03	+.01
uUS Poly $US	O	I		4.39	−.00
AGF GROUP					
AGF Asian	O	I		6.04	−.01
Amer Grth	O	I		8.06	−.04
Cdn Bond	O	R I		4.84	+.01
Cdn Equ	O	R I		8.25	−.06
Cdn Res	O	R I		7.18	−.04
Conv Inc	O	R I		8.53	−.05
Corp Inv	L	R I		12.13	+.02
Crp Inv Stk	L	R I		5.47	−.06
Global	O	I		9.79	+.01
Grth Equ	O	R I		10.05	−.07
Hilncome	O	I		9.60	—
Japan	O	I		4.68	+.01
Special	O	I		7.04	−.04

Fund	Load	RSP	Value	Chg
Global Eq.	O	I	12.68	+.04
Global Inc.	O	I	9.39	+.01
High Yield	O	R I	9.06	+.03
One DecisnFd	O	R I	10.73	+.01
BULLOCK GROUP				
American C$	O	I	17.28	−.13
uAmerican US$	O	I	15.05	−.18
Balanced	O	R I	10.09	−.02
CIF	O	R I	6.27	−.03
Growth	O	R I	2.25	−.03
CANADA TRUST				
yCTIF Equity	N	RD	56.92	+.04
yCTIF Income	N	RD	10.20	−.04
Ev Balanced	N	RD	11.54	−.05
Ev Bond	N	RD	11.19	+.03
yEv Int'l	N	D	15.10	+.01
Ev Nor Ame	N	D	25.60	−.20
Ev Spec Eq	N	RD	12.15	−.04
Ev Stock	N	RD	10.33	−.09
Ev US Bond	N	D	9.74	+.05
Ev US Equity	N	D	10.55	−.04
yRSP Equity	N	RD	123.34	−1.65
yRSP Income	N	RD	62.36	+.59
yRSP Mtg	N	RD	56.11	+.97
CENTRAL GUARANTY				
yFut Cd. Gth	N	RD	11.46	−.14
yFut Gov. Bd.	N	RD	10.51	+.01
yFut Income	N	D	10.97	−.01
yFut Mortgage	N	RD	10.61	+.01
yFut Select	N	RD	10.73	−.05
CENTRAL GUARANTY				
yInv Equity	N	D	6.63	—
yInv Income	N	D	4.82	+.01
yMortgage	N	RD	10.74	+.05
yProp Fund	O	R I	10.08	—
CENTURY				
DJ	L	I	10.36	−.01
uDJ-U.S.	L	I	9.04	−.04
CHOU ASSOC MGT				
yAssociates	L	I	22.28	+.11
yRRSP	L	R I	9.70	+.02
CHURCH STREET				
yBalanced	N	RD	11.10	−.04
yEquity	N	RD	10.16	−.15
yIncome	N	RD	10.75	+.05
CIBC FUNDS				

Fund	Load	RSP	Value	Chg
yFar East CD	O	I	10.47	+.07
yuFar East US	O	I	9.17	+.06
Gov't Bond	O	R I	11.20	+.02
Gr + Inc	O	RD	11.21	−.03
Gr America CD	O	RD	13.77	−.05
uGr America US	O	RD	12.02	−.07
yIntP'folio	O	I	12.18	+.04
FINSCO FUNDS				
JF Bal	L	RD	8.91	−.02
JF Bond	L	RD	9.32	+.02
JF Cdn Equ	L	RD	10.07	−.06
JFAmEq C$	L	D	12.09	+.03
uJFAmEq US$	L	D	10.55	—
FIRST CITY FUNDS				
Growth	N	RD	4.92	−.00
Income	N	RD	5.25	+.01
yRealFund	G	R I	5.98	+.00
FONDS DESJARDINS				
yActions	N	RD	17.08	−.34
yEnviro	N	RD	10.08	−.11
yEquilibre	N	RD	10.22	−.06
yHypo	N	RD	4.53	+.01
yIntern'tl	N	D	17.95	+.32
yOblig	N	RD	4.71	+.01
FONDS FICADRE				
yActions	L	RD	10.67	−.11
yEquilibre	L	RD	10.55	−.13
yObligations	L	RD	10.99	−.02
FONDS SNF				
yActions	L	RD	5.93	−.07
yEquilibree	L	RD	9.18	−.12
yObligations	L	RD	10.43	−.06
GBC FUNDS				
yBond	N	RD	11.36	+.02
yCanada	N	RD	7.59	−.11
yNor Ame	N	D	3.44	−.01
GLOBAL STRATEGY				
Americas	O	R I	10.46	−.05
Canadian	O	R I	9.10	−.01
Europe	O	I	8.70	+.07
Far East	O	I	11.63	+.05
Global Fund	O	I	15.15	+.04
Income Fund	O	R I	10.49	+.03
Real Estate	O	I	7.70	−.04
World Bond	O	I	9.89	+.06
World Money	O	R I	10.08	+.03
GUARDIAN GROUP				

At the end of September 1991, there were 594 open-end mutual funds with assets of $51,935.5 million. Of these, 77 were money market funds with assets of $8,798.6 million. Table 3.5 gives a breakdown of the number of mutual funds and their assets by size and type of fund at the end of September 1991.

Management Companies and Mutual Fund Investment Policies

Management companies are firms that manage a family of mutual funds. They typically organize the funds and then collect a management fee for operating them. Some of the best-known management companies are AGF, Bolton Tremblay, Guardian, and Investors; also, most major banks and trust companies direct a variety of funds. Each offers an array of open-end mutual funds

TABLE 3.5   Classification of Mutual Funds by Type (as of September 30, 1991)

	Number of Funds	Combined Assets ($ millions)	% of Total Assets
Type of Fund			
Canadian equity	150	13,494.6	26.0
U.S. equity	44	1,967.4	3.8
International equity	56	5,537.2	10.7
Specialty equity	23	319.9	0.6
Balanced	100	6,305.8	12.1
Preferred dividends	16	1,736.7	3.3
Bond	88	6,625.9	12.8
Mortgage	18	5,137.8	9.9
Bond & mortgage	9	627.7	1.2
Money market	77	8,798.6	16.9
Real estate	13	1,383.9	2.7
TOTAL	**594**	**51,935.5**	**100.0**

From *Mutual Fund Sourcebook*, 1991.

with different investment policies. Table 3.6 lists the 12 largest mutual fund families and discusses some of their features.

Figure 3.3 gives a listing of the funds offered by the Investors Group. Generally, the name of each fund describes its investment policy; thus, there are funds that are formed to provide income from dividends (both preferred and ordinary), to pursue growth, to give security for retirement, or to invest in

TABLE 3.6   The Major Mutual Fund Families

Family	Total Net Assets ($ millions)*	Number of Funds*	Range of Up-Front or Deferred Sales Charges (%)	Basic Switching Charges
AGF Group	1180.6	10	0–9	2% max
Altamira	135.4	9	None	None
Bolton Tremblay	329.7	10	2.5–9	2% max
Dynamic Group	566.1	10	0–9	2% max
Global Strategy	196.1	5	0–4.5	2% max (negotiable)
Industrial Group	5057.5	11	1–9	Subject to normal sales charges
Investors Group	8075.7	25	0–5	None
Metropolitan Group	138.9	10	0–5	One free transfer between funds per policy year ($25 each)
Mutual Group	364.6	7	2–6	None
Templeton Group	1028.5	7	0–8.5 (negotiable)	$10 plus up to 2% NAV (dealer's discretion)
United Group	495.2	11	0–9	2% max
Universal Group	398.2	13	0–9	2% max

* As of September 1990.
Data from *Mutual Fund Sourcebook*, 1990.

FIGURE 3.3

The Investors
Group listing of
mutual funds.

From *The Globe and
Mail,* December 18, 1991.
Reprinted by permission.

INVESTORS GROUP			
yBond	G ¼D	4.56	–.01
yCdn Equity	L RD	6.25	–.01
yDividend	L D	10.10	–.01
yEuropean Fund	L D	5.07	+.02
yGlobal	L D	6.22	+.02
yGro P'folio	L D	5.41	+.05
yGroPlus P'fol	L D	5.32	+.03
yInc P'folio	G RD	5.32	+.01
yIncPlus P'fol	L RD	5.35	–.01
yJapan	L D	12.33	+.04
yMtge	G RD	5.10	–.01
yMutual	L D	8.02	–.03
yN.A. Growth	L D	9.72	+.01
yPacificFund	L D	5.69	+.05
yReal Prop	L RD	5.21	–.05
yRetGro P'fol	L RD	5.08	–.10
yRetPlus P'fol	L RD	5.21	–.05
yRetiremnt	L RD	9.12	–.04
ySpecial	L D	11.80	–.01
ySumma	L RD	4.89	+.02
yU.S. Growth	L D	13.27	+.07

various geographical areas. Some funds have names that provide little indication as to their investment policies (such as the Summa fund); one must consult
the fund prospectus for a clear definition in these cases.

Some funds are designed as candidates for an individual's whole investment
portfolio. Such funds, which hold both equities and fixed-income securities,
can be classified as *income* or *balanced funds.* Wiesenberger's manual,[11] which
provides information on U.S. funds, comments that income funds "provide as
liberal a current income from investments as possible," whereas balanced
funds "minimize investment risks so far as this is possible without unduly
sacrificing possibilities for long-term growth and current income."

Finally, an **index fund** tries to match the performance of a broad market
index. For example, First Canadian Equity Index Fund is a no-load mutual
fund that replicates the composition of the TSE 300 Index, thus providing a
relatively low-cost way for small investors to pursue a passive common stock
investment strategy. (The Investors Group does not offer an index fund.)

When choosing a mutual fund, an individual investor should consider not
only the fund's stated investment policy, but also its management fees and
other expenses. Comparative data on virtually all important aspects of U.S.
mutual funds are available in the annual volumes prepared by Wiesenberger
Investment Companies Services. Similar services are available in Canada. For
instance, Portfolio Analytics Limited has prepared for the discount broker
Marathon Brokerage a Mutual Fund Disk. The disk, using the Financial Post
data base, gives information on over 200 funds (including also U.S. and international funds). The data provided include performance, management expense
ratios and load structures, characterization as to purpose, asset allocation,
NAV, dividend payouts, and other relevant material.

---

[11] *Investment Companies 1987,* Wiesenberger Investment Companies Services.

Commingled Funds

Commingled funds are investment pools managed by financial and insurance companies, and by other fund managers for trust or retirement accounts that are too small to warrant managing on a separate basis; they are also used for portions of pension funds restricted to certain areas. A commingled fund is similar in form to an open-end mutual fund. Instead of shares, though, the fund offers units that are bought and sold at net asset value. The manager may offer an array of different commingled funds for trust or retirement accounts to choose from, for example, a money market fund, a bond fund, and a common stock fund. In certain cases, these funds may be formed as *unit investment trusts* as a means of avoiding realization of gains when assets are sold and the proceeds reinvested. The holding in the trust is not deemed to be realized, so that tax or other regulatory consequences can be avoided, but the composition of the portfolio can be adjusted to meet market conditions. (The concept of unit investment trust has another interpretation in the United States.)

Real Estate Limited Partnerships and Mortgage Funds

A real estate limited partnership functions similarly to a closed-end mutual fund, using leverage to purchase real estate. Partnership units are sold to the public to raise equity capital, which is leveraged by borrowing from banks and issuing mortgages. Mortgage funds invest directly in mortgages by purchasing pass-through securities of different maturities; they tend to be managed by banks or trust companies.

A limited partnership, by its very construction, pays no income taxes; all income or loss is recognized in the hands of its unit holders. The mortgage funds are treated as any other mutual fund.

The equivalent U.S. institution is the real estate investment trust (REIT), which can take the form of either an equity or a mortgage trust. REITs generally are established by banks, insurance companies, or mortgage companies, which then serve as investment managers to earn a fee.

Summary

1. Firms issue securities to raise the capital necessary to finance their investments. Investment bankers market these securities to the public on the primary market. Investment bankers generally act as underwriters who purchase the securities from the firm and resell them to the public at a markup. Before the securities may be sold to the public, the firm must publish a securities commission-approved prospectus that provides information on the firm's prospects.

2. Issued securities are traded on the secondary market, that is, on organized stock exchanges. Securities also trade on the over-the-counter market and, for large traders, through direct negotiation. Only members of exchanges may trade on the exchange. Brokerage firms holding seats on the exchange sell their services to individuals, charging commissions for executing trades on their behalf. The TSE and ME have fairly strict listing requirements; the VSE is much less restrictive. The two regional exchanges provide listing opportunities for local firms who do not meet the requirements of the national exchanges.

3. Trading of common stocks in exchanges takes place through registered traders or market-makers; these act to maintain an orderly market in the shares of one or more firms, maintaining ''books'' of limit-buy and limit-sell orders and matching trades at mutually acceptable prices. Market-makers also will accept market orders by selling from or buying for their own inventory of stocks when an imbalance of buy and sell orders exists.

4. The over-the-counter market is not a formal exchange but an informal network of brokers and dealers who negotiate sales of securities. The CDN system provides on-line computer quotes offered by dealers in the stock. When an individual wishes to purchase or sell a share, the broker can search the listing of offered bid and asked prices, call the dealer who has the best quote, and execute the trade.

5. Block transactions are a fairly recent but fast-growing segment of the securities market, which currently accounts for over one third of trading volume. These trades often are too large to be handled readily by specialists, and thus block houses have developed that specialize in these transactions, identifying potential trading partners for their clients.

6. Buying on margin means borrowing money from a broker in order to buy more securities. By buying securities on margin, an investor magnifies both the upside potential and the downside risk. If the equity in a margin account falls below the required maintenance level, the investor will get a margin call from the broker.

7. Short selling is the practice of selling securities that the seller does not own. The short seller borrows the securities sold through a broker and may be required to cover the short position at any time on demand. The cash proceeds of a short sale are always kept in escrow by the broker, and the broker usually requires that the short seller deposit additional cash or securities to serve as margin (collateral) for the short sale.

8. Securities trading is regulated by the provincial securities commissions, as well as by self-regulation of the exchanges and the dealer associations. Many of the important regulations have to do with full disclosure of relevant information concerning the securities in question. Insider trading rules also prohibit traders from attempting to profit from inside information.

9. In addition to providing the basic services of executing buy and sell orders, holding securities for safekeeping, making margin loans, and facilitating short sales, full-service brokers offer investors information, advice, and even investment decisions. Discount brokers offer only the basic brokerage services but usually charge less.

10. Total trading costs consist of commissions, the dealer's bid-asked spread, and price concessions. These costs can represent as much as 30 percent of the value of the securities traded.

11. As an alternative to investing in securities through a broker, many individuals invest in mutual funds and other investment companies. Mutual funds free the individual from many of the administrative burdens of owning individual securities, and offer the prospect of superior investment results. Mutual funds are classified according to whether they are open-end or closed-end, load or no-load, and by the type of securities in which they invest. Real estate limited partnerships are specialized investment companies that invest in real estate; mortgage funds invest in loans secured by real estate.

Key terms

Primary market	Registered trader (market-maker)
Secondary market	Block transactions
Underwriting	Dealer market
Prospectus	Margin
Stock exchanges	Short sale
Over-the-counter market	Inside information
NASDAQ	Bid-asked spread
Bid price	Closed-end fund
Asked price	Open-end fund
CDN system (COATS)	Load fund
Third market	No-load fund
Fourth market	Index fund

Selected readings

A good treatment of investment banking is found in:
Smith, Clifford W. "Investment Banking and the Capital Acquisition Process." *Journal of Financial Economics* 15 (January-February 1986).
An overview of securities markets is provided in:
Garbade, Kenneth D. *Securities Markets.* New York: McGraw-Hill, 1982.
The American specialist system is examined in:
Stoll, Hans R. "The Stock Exchange Specialist System: An Economic Analysis." *Monograph Series in Finance and Economics,* Graduate School of Business Administration, New York University, 1985.
An examination of market functioning during the October 1987 crash is:
The Brady Commission Report, or formally, the *Report of the Presidential Task Force on Market Mechanisms.* Washington, D.C.: United States Government Printing Office, 1988.

Material facts about listing and trading on Canadian markets are available in:
   The Toronto Stock Exchange Fact Book, published annually, and *The TSE Review,*
   published monthly. Produced by the Toronto Stock Exchange, Toronto, Ontario.
Guide to International Investing (annual). Don Mills, Ontario: CCH Canadian, 1991.
A discussion on automated trading, complementary to that in the box, is given in:
   Boyd, Greg. "Who Will Be the Winner in the Battle Being Fought for the Trading
   Floor?" *Investment Executive, Financial Times of Canada,* December 1991.
*An examination of the pros and cons of a national Canadian securities regulatory
system is in:*
   Daniels, Ronald. "How 'Broke' Is the System of Provincial Securities Regulation?"
   Canadian Investment Review 5, no. 1 (Spring 1992).

Problems

1. FBN, Inc. has just sold 100,000 shares in an initial public offering. The
   underwriter's explicit fees were $70,000. The offering price for the shares
   was $50, but immediately upon issue the share price jumped to $53.
   a. What is your best guess as to the total cost to FBN of the equity issue?
   b. Is the entire cost of the underwriting a source of profit to the underwriters?
2. Suppose that you sell short 100 shares of Seagram's, now selling at $120
   per share.
   a. What is your maximum possible loss?
   b. What happens to the maximum loss if you simultaneously place a stop-
   buy order at $128?
3. An expiring put will be exercised and the stock will be sold if the stock
   price is below the exercise price. A stop-loss order causes a stock sale
   when the stock price falls below some limit. Compare and contrast the two
   strategies of purchasing put options versus issuing a stop-loss order.
4. Compare call options and stop-buy orders.
5. Do you think it is possible to replace market-makers by a fully automated
   computerized trade-matching system?
6. Consider the following limit-order book of a specialist. The last trade in the
   stock took place at a price of $50.

Limit-Buy Orders		Limit-Sell Orders	
Price ($)	Shares	Price ($)	Shares
49.75	500	50.25	100
49.50	800	51.50	100
49.25	500	54.75	300
49.00	200	58.25	100
48.50	600		

   a. If a market-buy order for 100 shares comes in, at what price will it be
   filled?
   b. At what price would the next market-buy order be filled?
   c. If you were the specialist, would you desire to increase or decrease your
   inventory of this stock?

7. Consider the following data*:

Year	Market Value of Shares Traded on NYSE ($ millions)	Price of an NYSE Seat ($)	
		High	Low
1960	37,960	162,000	135,000
1965	73,200	250,000	190,000
1970	103,063	320,000	130,000
1975	133,819	138,000	55,000
1980	397,670	275,000	175,000
1985	1,023,202	480,000	310,000

a. What do you conclude about the relationship between trading volume and the price of a seat?

b. What happened in 1975 to upset this relationship?

8. You are bullish on BCE stock. The current market price is $50 per share, and you have $5,000 of your own to invest. You borrow an additional $5,000 from your broker at an interest rate of 8 percent per year, and invest $10,000 in the stock.

a. What will be your rate of return if the price of BCE stock goes up by 10 percent during the next year? (Ignore the expected dividend.)

b. How far does the price of BCE stock have to fall for you to get a margin call if the maintenance margin is 30 percent?

9. You are bearish on BCE stock and decide to sell short 100 shares at the current market price of $50 per share.

a. How much in cash or securities must you put into your brokerage account if the broker's initial margin requirement is 50 percent of the value of the short position?

b. How high can the price of the stock go before you get a margin call if the maintenance margin is 30 percent of the value of the short position?

10. Call one full-service broker and one discount broker and find out the transaction costs of implementing the following strategies:

a. Buying 100 shares of Seagram's now and selling them six months from now.

b. Investing an equivalent amount in six-month at-the-money call options (calls with strike price equal to the stock price) on Seagram's stock now and selling them six months from now.

Questions 11 and 12 are from the 1986 Level I CFA examination:

11. If you place a stop-loss order to sell 100 shares of stock at $55 when the current price is $62, how much will you receive for each share if the price drops to $50?

a. $50.

b. $55.

c. $54⅞.

d. Cannot tell from the information given.

---

* Data from the New York Stock Exchange *Fact Book*, 1986.

12. You wish to sell short 100 shares of XYZ Corporation stock. If the last two transactions were at 34⅛ followed by 34¼, you only can sell short on the next transaction at a price of:

a. 34⅛ or higher.

b. 34¼ or higher.

c. 34¼ or lower.

d. 34⅛ or lower.

Concepts and Issues

This chapter introduces some key concepts and issues that are central to informed investment decision making. The material presented is basic to the development of the theory in subsequent parts of the book. We start with the determination of real and nominal interest rates and risk premiums on risky securities. Then we review the historical record of rates of return on bills, bonds, and stocks, as well as the relationship between bill rates and inflation. We also distinguish between real and nominal risk. We conclude by introducing the law of one price, which states that securities or combinations of securities will be priced so that no investor can make riskless arbitrage profits by trading them.

4.1 Determinants of the Level of Interest Rates

The Equilibrium Real Rate of Interest

Perhaps the single most important factor in investment decision making is the level of interest rates. Decisions depend to a great extent on what investors think interest rates will do.

For example, suppose that you have $10,000 in a savings account. The bank pays you a variable interest rate tied to some short-term reference rate such as the 30-day Treasury bill rate. You have the option of moving some or all of your money into a longer-term Guaranteed Investment Certificate (GIC) that offers a fixed rate over the term of the deposit.

Your decision depends critically on your outlook for interest rates. If you think rates will fall, you will want to lock in the current higher rates by investing in a relatively long-term GIC. If, on the other hand, you expect rates to rise, you will want to postpone committing any funds to long-term GICs.

Forecasting interest rates is one of the most notoriously difficult parts of applied macroeconomics. Nonetheless, we do have a good understanding of the following fundamental factors that determine the level of interest rates:

1. The supply of funds from savers, primarily households.
2. The demand from businesses for funds to be used to finance physical investments in plant, equipment, and inventories (real assets or capital formation).
3. The government's net supply and/or demand for funds as modified by actions of the monetary authority.

These three basic factors determine the level of the **real interest rate,** that is, the interest rate in a no-inflation world. The level of nominal interest rates, which is the rate we actually observe, is the real rate plus the expected rate of inflation. Thus a fourth factor affecting the interest rate is the expected rate of inflation.

Until recently we could not observe what the risk-free real rate of interest in the Canadian economy was. However, in late 1991 the Canadian government issued the so-called Real Return Bonds, or RRBs, which offer a guaranteed real rate of interest for a 30-year maturity. The RRBs pay a real coupon of 4.25 percent on a principal amount that is adjusted by the Consumer Price Index (CPI). Hence, the actual nominal rate of interest earned by investors is the promised real rate plus the rate of inflation as measured by the proportional increase in the CPI. It is, however, too early to judge whether these new instruments will be successful. A similar innovation was introduced in early 1988 in the United States by the Franklin Savings and Loan Association of Ottawa, Kansas, but did not find much success. The issuer has since gone under, and the instruments are no longer available to U.S. investors.

Although there are many different interest rates economywide (as many indeed as there are different types of securities), economists frequently talk as if there were a single representative rate. We can use this abstraction to gain some insight into the determination of the real rate of interest if we consider the supply and demand curves for funds.

Figure 4.1 shows a downward sloping demand curve and an upward sloping supply curve. On the horizontal axis we measure the quantity of funds, and on the vertical axis we measure the real rate of interest.

The supply curve slopes up from left to right because the higher the real interest rate, the greater the supply of household savings. The assumption is that at higher real interest rates households will choose to postpone some current consumption and set aside or invest more of their disposable income for future use.[1]

The demand curve slopes down from left to right because the lower the real interest rate, the more businesses will want to invest in physical capital. As-

---

[1] There is a considerable amount of controversy among experts on the issue of whether household saving does in fact go up in response to an increase in the real interest rate. See, for example, Gerald Carlino, "Interest Rate Effects and Intertemporal Consumption," *Journal of Monetary Economics,* March 1982.

FIGURE 4.1

Determination of
the equilibrium real
rate of interest.

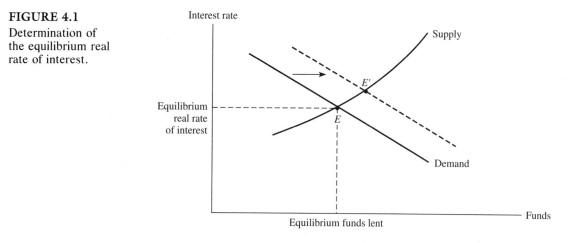

suming that businesses rank projects by the expected real return on invested capital, the lower the real interest rate on the funds needed to finance those projects, the more of them firms will undertake.

Equilibrium is at the point of intersection of the supply and demand curves, point *E* in Figure 4.1. The government can shift these supply and demand curves either to the right or to the left through its fiscal and monetary policies. For example, consider an increase in the government's budget deficit. This increases the government's borrowing demand and shifts the demand curve to the right up to the dashed line, which causes the equilibrium real interest rate to rise to point *E'*. Hence a revised forecast indicating higher than expected government borrowing might increase expected future interest rates. The monetary authority may offset such a rise through an expansionary monetary policy, which will shift the supply to the right.

Thus the fundamental determinants of the real interest rate are the propensity of households to save and the expected productivity (or profitability) of investment in physical capital. However, the real rate can be affected as well by government fiscal and monetary policies.

The Equilibrium Nominal Rate of Interest

Conventional certificates of deposit offer a guaranteed **nominal rate of interest.** Thus you can only infer what the expected real rate is by subtracting your expectation of what the rate of inflation will be. For example, if the interest rate on one-year conventional CDs is 8 percent, we can only infer what the expected real rate is by subtracting an estimate of the expected rate of inflation over the next year. Thus, if we estimate expected inflation to be 5 percent, the expected real rate would be 3 percent.

Actually, the exact relationship between the real and nominal interest rates on a conventional CD is given by

$$1 + R = (1 + r)/(1 + i)$$

or equivalently,

$$R = (r - i)/(1 + i)$$

where R is the real rate, r is the nominal rate,[2] and i is the rate of inflation. The relationship $R = r - i$ holds exactly only for continuously compounded rates; otherwise, it is only an approximation. See the appendix to this chapter for further details.

4.2 *Risk and Risk Premiums*

Risk means uncertainty about future rates of return. We quantify that uncertainty using probability distributions. For example, suppose you are considering investing some of your money, which is all currently in a bank account, in a stock market index fund. The price of a share in the fund is currently $100, and your *time horizon* is one year. You expect the cash dividend during the year to be $4, and therefore your expected *dividend yield* is 4 percent.

Your total **holding period return** (HPR) will depend on the price you expect to prevail one year from now. Suppose your best guess is that it will be $110 per share. Then your *capital gain* will be $10, and your HPR will be 14 percent. The definition of the holding period return is

$$HPR = \frac{\text{Ending price of a share} - \text{Beginning price} + \text{Cash dividend}}{\text{Beginning price}}$$

In our case we have

$$HPR = \frac{\$110 - \$100 + \$4}{\$100}$$
$$= .14$$
$$= 14\%$$

However, there is considerable uncertainty about the price of a share a year from now and, therefore, about the HPR. Let us assume that we can quantify our beliefs about the state of the economy and the stock market in terms of three possible scenarios with the probabilities presented in Table 4.1.

How can we evaluate this probability distribution? Throughout this book we will characterize probability distributions of rates of return in terms of their expected or mean return, $E(r)$, and their standard deviation, σ. The expected rate of return is a probability-weighted average of the rates of return in all scenarios. Calling $Pr(s)$ the probability of each scenario and $r(s)$ the HPR in

---

[2] To be more exact, r is the effective annual rate of interest on the CD.

TABLE 4.1   Probability Distribution of HPR on the Stock Market

State of the Economy	Probability	Ending Price ($)	HPR (%)
Boom	.25	140	44
Normal growth	.50	110	14
Recession	.25	80	−16

each scenario, where scenarios are labelled, or "indexed," by the variable s, we may write the expected return as

$$E(r) = \Sigma Pr(s)r(s) \tag{4.1}$$

Applying this formula to Table 4.1, we find that the expected rate of return on the index fund is

$$E(r) = .25 \times 44\% + .5 \times 14\% + .25 \times -16\%$$
$$= 14\%$$

The standard deviation of the rate of return, σ, is a measure of risk. It is defined as the square root of the variance, which in turn is defined as the expected value of the squared deviations from the expected return. Symbolically,

$$\sigma^2 = \Sigma Pr(s)[r(s) - E(r)]^2 \tag{4.2}$$

Therefore in our example,

$$\sigma^2 = .25 \times (44 - 14)^2 + .5 \times (14 - 14)^2 + .25 \times (-16 - 14)^2$$
$$= 450$$

and

$$\sigma = 21\%$$

Clearly, what troubles us as potential investors in the index fund is the downside risk of a −16 percent rate of return, not the upside potential of a 44 percent rate of return. The standard deviation of the rate of return does not distinguish between these two; it treats both as deviations from the mean. As long as the probability distribution is more or less symmetric about the mean, σ is an adequate measure of risk. In the special case where we can assume that the probability distribution is normal—that is, the well-known bell-shaped curve—$E(r)$ and σ are perfectly adequate to completely characterize the distribution.

Now getting back to our example, how much, if anything, should we invest in the index fund? First, we must ask how much of a reward there is for our taking on risk by investing some of our money in stocks.

We measure the reward as the difference between the expected HPR on the index fund and the **risk-free rate** we can earn by leaving our money in the bank. We call this difference the **risk premium** on common stocks. If the risk-free rate in our example is 6 percent per year, then the risk premium on stocks is 8 percent per year.

The degree to which we are willing to commit funds to stocks depends on our *risk aversion*. Finance theorists generally assume that investors are risk-averse in the sense that, if the risk premium were zero, they would not be willing to invest any money at all in stocks. In theory, then, there must always be a positive risk premium on stocks to induce risk-averse investors to hold the existing supply.

Although this simple scenario analysis serves to illustrate the concepts behind the quantification of risk and return, the next question is how can we get a more realistic estimate of $E(r)$ and σ for common stocks and other types of securities?

4.3 *The Historical Record*

Bills, Bonds, and Stocks: 1957–1990

The record of past rates of return is one possible source of information about risk premiums and standard deviations. We can estimate the historical risk premium by taking an average of the past differences between the HPRs on the asset type and the risk-free rate. Table 4.2 presents the annual HPRs on three asset classes for the period 1957–1990.

The first column shows the one-year HPR on a policy of "rolling-over" 91-day Treasury bills as they mature. Because this rate changes from month to month, it is risk-free only for a 91-day holding period. The second column presents the annual HPR an investor would have earned by investing in Canadian bonds with maturities higher than 10 years. The third column illustrates the HPR on the TSE 300 Index of common stocks, which is a value-weighted stock portfolio of 300 of the largest corporations in Canada. (We discussed the TSE 300 stock index in Chapter 2.) Finally, the last column gives the annual inflation rate as measured by the rate of change in the consumer price index.

At the bottom of each column are five descriptive statistics. The first is the arithmetic mean or average HPR. For bills it is 7.65 percent, for bonds it is 7.86 percent, and for common stock it is 10.59 percent. These numbers imply an average risk premium of 0.21 percent per year on bonds and 2.94 percent on stocks (the average HPR less the risk-free rate of 7.65 percent).

The third statistic reported at the bottom of Table 4.2 is the standard deviation. The higher the standard deviation, the higher the variability of the HPR. This standard deviation is based on historical data rather than forecasts of *future* scenarios, as in equation 4.2. The formula for historical variance, however, is similar to equation 4.2. It is as follows:

$$\sigma^2 = \frac{n}{n-1} \sum_{t=1}^{n} \frac{(r_t - \bar{r})^2}{n} \qquad (4.3)$$

TABLE 4.2   Rates of Return, 1957–1990

Date	T-bill	LT Bond	Stock	CPI Change
1957	0.038322	0.079399	−0.20584	0.017937
1958	0.02507	0.019218	0.312471	0.026432
1959	0.046196	−0.05072	0.045861	0.012876
1960	0.033117	0.121918	0.017815	0.012712
1961	0.028913	0.091575	0.327455	0.004184
1962	0.04215	0.050336	−0.07094	0.016667
1963	0.036342	0.045793	0.156011	0.016393
1964	0.037896	0.061609	0.254329	0.020161
1965	0.039237	0.00048	0.066819	0.031621
1966	0.050341	−0.01055	−0.07067	0.034483
1967	0.045931	−0.00484	0.180884	0.040741
1968	0.064439	0.021422	0.224451	0.039146
1969	0.070852	−0.0286	−0.00809	0.047945
1970	0.067002	0.163886	−0.03566	0.013072
1971	0.038069	0.148398	0.080077	0.051613
1972	0.035539	0.081131	0.273834	0.04908
1973	0.051114	0.019694	0.002736	0.093567
1974	0.078499	−0.04529	−0.25927	0.122995
1975	0.074074	0.080223	0.184831	0.095238
1976	0.092654	0.236358	0.110223	0.058696
1977	0.076564	0.090363	0.10706	0.094456
1978	0.083355	0.040958	0.297202	0.084428
1979	0.114118	−0.0283	0.447698	0.096886
1980	0.149736	0.021785	0.301336	0.111987
1981	0.184056	−0.02086	−0.10246	0.121986
1982	0.154204	0.458225	0.055413	0.092288
1983	0.096237	0.096088	0.354871	0.045139
1984	0.115866	0.168962	−0.02393	0.037652
1985	0.09878	0.266785	0.250654	0.043757
1986	0.0933	0.1721	0.08954	0.041922
1987	0.084789	0.017661	0.058788	0.041217
1988	0.094098	0.113011	0.110814	0.039585
1989	0.123613	0.151702	0.213728	0.051677
1990	0.134842	0.043231	−0.14798	0.05
Mean	0.07645	0.078622	0.105884	0.051722
Variance	0.001635	0.010619	0.028382	0.00114
Standard deviation	0.040432	0.103049	0.16847	0.033766
Minimum	0.02507	−0.05072	−0.25927	0.004184
Maximum	0.184056	0.458225	0.447698	0.122995

Data from *ScotiaMcLeod's Handbook of Canadian Debt Market Indices, 1947–1990*.

Here, each year's outcome is taken as a possible scenario.[3] Deviations are simply taken from the historical average, $\bar{r}$, instead of the expected value $E(r)$. Each historical outcome is taken as equally likely, and given a "probability" of $1/n$.

---

[3] We multiply by $n/(n - 1)$ in equation 4.3 to eliminate statistical bias in the estimate of variance.

FIGURE 4.2

Rates of return on bills, bonds, and stocks, 1957–1990.

Data from *ScotiaMcLeod's Handbook of Canadian Debt Market Indices, 1947–1990,* February 1991.

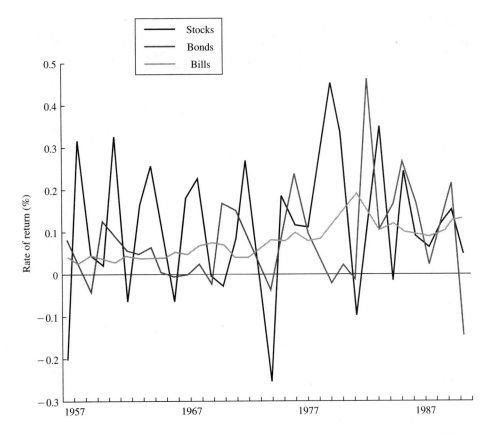

Figure 4.2 gives a graphic representation of the relative variabilities of the annual HPR on the three different asset classes. We have plotted the three time series on the same set of axes, each in a different manner. Clearly, the annual HPR on stocks is the most variable series. The standard deviation of stock returns has been 16.85 percent, compared to 10.30 percent for bonds and 4.04 percent for bills. Here is evidence of the risk-return trade-off that characterizes security markets: the markets with the highest average returns also are the most volatile.

Comparable figures for U.S. stocks show that they have both a higher return and a higher risk than their Canadian counterparts. Thus, over the period 1926–1990 the average annual HPR for the 500 stocks that made the S&P 500 index was 12.13 percent, with a standard deviation of 20.64 percent. Similarly, a recent study by Roll[4] that used daily data covering the period April 1988–March 1991 gives average annual HPR's of 4.20 percent and 12.27 percent for Canada and the United States, with corresponding standard deviations of 9.97

---

[4] See R. Roll, "Industrial Structure and the Comparative Behavior of International Stock Market Indexes," *Journal of Finance* 47, no. 1 (March 1992).

FIGURE 4.3
The normal distribution.

(From Stephen A. Ross and Randolph Westerfield, *Corporate Finance*. St. Louis: The C.V. Mosby Co., 1988.)

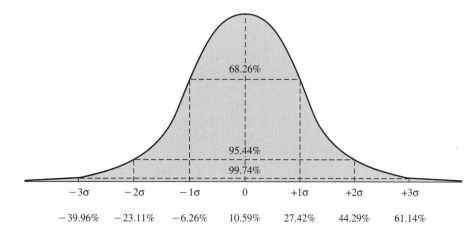

-3σ	-2σ	-1σ	0	$+1\sigma$	$+2\sigma$	$+3\sigma$
-39.96%	-23.11%	-6.26%	10.59%	27.42%	44.29%	61.14%

68.26%
95.44%
99.74%

percent and 14.37 percent. Part of the Canada–U.S. difference is due to the different industrial composition of their respective economies.

The other summary measures at the bottom of Table 4.2 show the highest and lowest annual HPR (the range) for each asset over the 33-year period. The size of this range is another possible measure of the relative riskiness of each asset class. It too confirms the ranking of stocks as the riskiest and bills as the least risky of the three asset classes.

An all-stock portfolio with a standard deviation of 16.85 percent would constitute a very volatile investment. For example, if stock returns are normally distributed with that standard deviation and an expected rate of return of 10.59 percent (the historical average), then in roughly one year out of three, returns will be less than −6.26 percent (10.59 percent − 16.85 percent) or greater than 27.44 percent (10.59 percent + 16.85 percent).

Figure 4.3 is a graph of the normal curve with a mean of 10.59 percent and a standard deviation of 16.85 percent. The graph shows the theoretical probability of rates of return within various ranges given these parameters.

Figure 4.4 presents another view of the historical data, the actual frequency distribution of returns on various asset classes over the period 1957–1990. Notice the greater range of stock returns relative to bill or bond returns.

We should stress that variability of HPR in the past can be an unreliable guide to risk, at least in the case of the risk-free asset. For an investor with a holding period of one year, for example, a one-year T-bill is risk-free with a σ of zero, despite the fact that the standard deviation of the one-year T-bill rate estimated from historical data is not zero.

Bills and Inflation: 1957–1990

A very important empirical relationship is the connection between inflation and the rate of return on T-bills. This is apparent in Figure 4.5, which plots both of the time series on the same set of axes. Both series tend to move together,

FIGURE 4.4A
Frequency
distributions of the
annual HPR on
three asset
classes—stocks.

Modified from
*ScotiaMcLeod's
Handbook of Canadian
Debt Market Indices,
1947–1990,* February
1991.

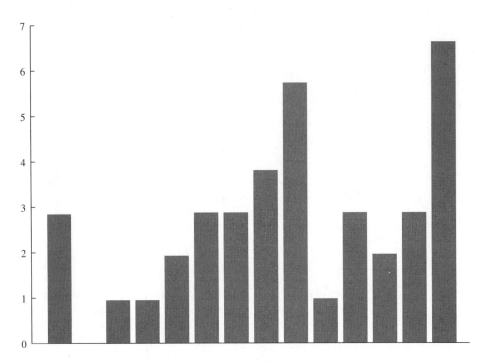

FIGURE 4.4B
Frequency
distributions of the
annual HPR on
three asset
classes—LT bonds.

Modified from
*ScotiaMcLeod's
Handbook of Canadian
Debt Market Indices,
1947–1990,* February
1991.

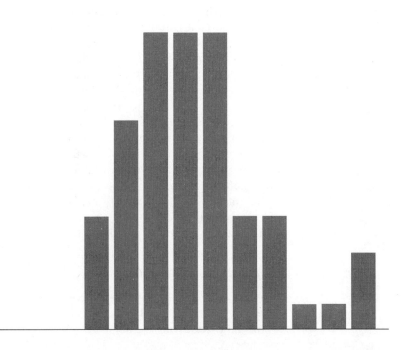

FIGURE 4.4C
Frequency distributions of the annual HPR on three asset classes—T-bills.

Modified from *ScotiaMcLeod's Handbook of Canadian Debt Market Indices, 1947–1990*, February 1991.

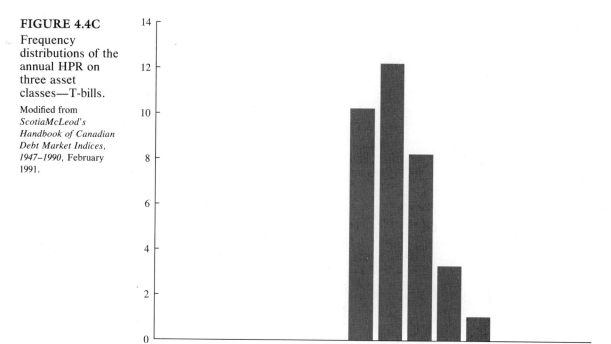

Figure 4.4D
Frequency distributions of the annual HPR on three asset classes—inflation.

Modified from *ScotiaMcLeod's Handbook of Canadian Debt Market Indices, 1947–1990*, February 1991.

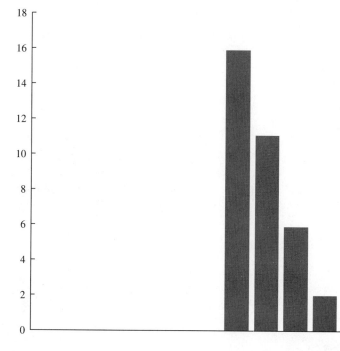

FIGURE 4.5
Bills and inflation,
1957–1990.

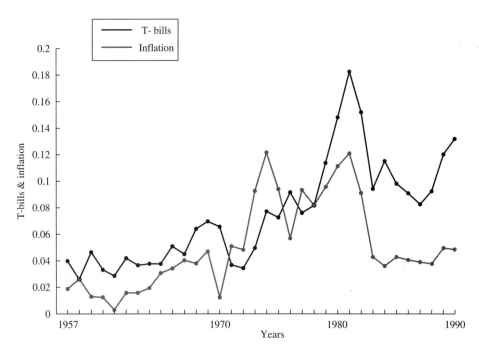

which is consistent with our previous statement that expected inflation is a significant force determining the nominal rate of interest.[5]

In the case of a holding period of 91 days, the difference between actual and expected inflation is not large. The 91-day bill rate will adjust rapidly to changes in expected inflation induced by observed changes in actual inflation. It is not surprising that over time we see nominal rates on bills move roughly in tandem with inflation.

Concept Check

Question 1.
a. Suppose the real interest rate is 3 percent per year and the expected inflation rate is 8 percent. What is the nominal interest rate?
b. Suppose the expected inflation rate rises to 10 percent, but the real rate is unchanged. What happens to the nominal interest rate?

---

[5] See Nabil T. Khoury and Guy Melard, "The Relationship between the Canadian Treasury-Bill Rate and Expected Inflation in Canada and the United States," *Canadian Journal of Administrative Sciences* 2, no. 1 (June 1985).

4.4   *Real Risk vs. Nominal Risk*

The distinction between the real and the nominal rate of interest is crucial in making investment choices, assuming, of course, that investors have any interest in the future purchasing power of their wealth. Consider the way that a Canada bond that offers a "risk-free" nominal rate of return is not truly a risk-free investment—it does not guarantee the future purchasing power of its cash flow.

An example might be a bond that pays $1,000 20 years from now but nothing in the interim. Many people have seen such a zero coupon bond as a convenient way for individuals to lock in attractive, risk-free, long-term interest rates (particularly in RRSP [Registered Retirement Savings Plan] accounts). However, see Table 4.3 for what the value of the $1,000 will be in 20 years in terms of today's purchasing power. If we assume that the purchase price of the bond is $103.67, giving a nominal rate of return of 12 percent per year (since $103.67 \times 1.12^{20} = 1,000$), then the real annualized HPR can be computed for each inflation rate.

A simple comparison is at the rate of inflation of 12 percent per year. At that rate, Table 4.3 shows that the purchasing power of the $1,000 to be received in 20 years would be $103.67, just what was paid initially for the bond. The real HPR in these circumstances is zero: when the rate of inflation equals the nominal rate of interest, the price of goods increases as fast as the money accumulated from the investment, and there is no growth in purchasing power.

TABLE 4.3   Purchasing Power of $1,000 20 Years from Now and 20-Year Real Annualized HPR

Assumed Annual Rate of Inflation (%)	Number of Dollars Required 20 Years from Now to Buy What $1 Buys Today	Purchasing Power of $1,000 to Be Received in 20 Years	Annualized Real HPR (%)
4	$2.19	$456.39	7.69
6	$3.21	$311.80	5.66
8	$4.66	$214.55	3.70
10	$6.73	$148.64	1.82
12	$9.65	$103.67	0

Purchase price of bond is $103.67.
Nominal 20-year annualized HPR is 12% per year.
Purchasing power = $1,000/(1 + inflation rate)^{20}.
Real HPR, R, is computed from the following relationship:

$$R = (1 + r)/(1 + i) - 1$$
$$= 1.12/(1 + i) - 1$$

At an inflation rate of only 4 percent per year, however, the purchasing power of $1,000 will be $456.39 in terms of today's prices; that is, the investment of $103.67 grows to a real value of $456.39, for a real 20-year annualized HPR of 7.69 percent per year.

Even professional economic forecasters admit that their inflation forecasts are hardly certain even for the next year, not to mention the next 20 years. When we look at an asset from the perspective of its future purchasing power, we realize that an asset that is risk-free in nominal terms can be very risky in real terms.

Again, looking at Table 4.3, we see that an investor expecting an inflation rate of 8 percent per year anticipates a real annualized HPR of 3.70 percent. If the actual rate of inflation turns out to be 10 percent per year, the resulting real HPR is only 1.82 percent per year. These differences show the important distinction between expected and actual inflation rates.

Concept Check

Question 2. Suppose the rate of inflation turns out to be 13 percent per year. What will be the real annualized 20-year HPR on the nominally risk-free bond?

4.5   *Risk in a Portfolio Context*

The riskiness of a security should never be judged in isolation from an investor's entire portfolio of assets. Sometimes adding a seemingly risky asset to a portfolio actually reduces the risk of the portfolio as a whole. Investing in an asset that reduces the overall risk of a portfolio is called **hedging.**

The most direct example of hedging is an insurance contract, which is a legal arrangement transferring a specific risk from the insured to the insurer for a specified cost (the insurance premium). Suppose you own a $100,000 house and have total net worth of $300,000. There is a small distinct possibility that your house will burn to the ground within the coming year. If it does, your net wealth will be reduced by $100,000. If it does not, your wealth remains unchanged (independent of any income from this and other investments, which we shall ignore to simplify the example).

Let us say that your probability assessment of your house burning to the ground during the coming year is .002. Your expected loss (.002 × $100,000 = $200) is small in terms of your overall wealth. On the other hand, fire will reduce your wealth by a full one third. An insurance contract to cover this risk might cost $220, a price that exceeds the expected loss and thereby provides expected profit to the insurer. Consider the payoff to the insurance contract evaluated in isolation as a seemingly risky security. Not only is the expected

Investing: What to Buy When?

In making broad-scale investment decisions, investors may want to know how various types of investments have performed during booms, recessions, high inflation, and low inflation. The table shows how 10 asset categories performed during representative years since World War II. But history rarely repeats itself, so historical performance is only a rough guide to the future.

Average Annual Return on Investment*

Investment	Recession (%)	Boom (%)	High Inflation (%)	Low Inflation (%)
Bonds (long-term government)	17	4	−1	8
Commodity index	1	−6	15	−5
Diamonds (1-carat investment grade)	−4	8	79	15
Gold† (bullion)	−8	−9	105	19
Private home	4	6	6	5
Real estate‡ (commercial)	9	13	18	6
Silver (bullion)	3	−6	94	4
Stocks (blue chip)	14	7	−3	21
Stocks (small-growth company)	17	14	7	12
Treasury bills (three-month)	6	5	7	3

Modified from *The Wall Street Journal*, November 13, 1987. Reprinted by permission of *The Wall Street Journal*. © Dow Jones & Company, Inc. 1987. All rights reserved.
* In most cases, figures are computed as follows: Recession—average of performance during calendar years 1946, 1975, and 1982; boom—average of 1951, 1965, and 1984; high inflation—average of 1947, 1974, and 1980; low inflation—average of 1955, 1961, and 1986.
† Gold figures are based on data since 1971 and may be less reliable than others.
‡ Commercial real estate figures are based only on data since 1978 and may be less reliable than others.
Sources: Commerce Dept.; Commodity Research Bureau; DeBeers Inc.; Diamond Registry; Dow Jones & Co.; Dun & Bradstreet; Handy & Harman; Ibbotson Associates; Charles Kroll (Diversified Investor's Forecast); Merrill Lynch; National Council of Real Estate Investment Fiduciaries; Frank B. Russell Co.; Shearson Lehman Bros.; T. Rowe Price New Horizons Fund.

profit of the policy negative (−$20), and the expected rate of return negative (−$20/$220 = −9.09 percent), but the risk also seems to be substantial. The standard deviation of the policy's payoff is identical to that of the uninsured house. You receive either $100,000 (with probability .002) or nothing (with probability .998). Does this mean that only risk-lovers should purchase insurance? Clearly not. Instead, the example illustrates the fallacy of evaluating the risk of an asset (the insurance contract) in isolation.

Consider the insured house as a portfolio that includes the insurance contract and the house:

Portfolio Component	Value if No Fire	Value if Fire
House	$100,000	0
Insurance contract	0	$100,000

The *portfolio* payoff in the two outcomes is identical, and equal to $100,000, because the house is insured for its precise value, and the insurance pays only when the value of the house goes to zero (in the event of a fire). Thus the portfolio's overall risk has been reduced to zero.

People are concerned about the overall volatility of the value of their portfolios. They do not necessarily dislike volatility in individual components of their portfolios, though. Indeed, most risk-averse persons would invest in the "risky" insurance policy in this example even with its negative expected HPR.

4.6   *The Law of One Price and Arbitrage*

One of the most fundamental concepts in investments is arbitrage, as you will see again and again throughout this book. **Arbitrage** is the act of buying an asset at one price and simultaneously selling it or its equivalent at a higher price.

If you can buy Seagram's stock over-the-counter (OTC) for $128 per share and sell it on the Toronto Stock Exchange for $128.50, you can make a risk-free arbitrage profit of 50 cents per share. Furthermore, by synchronizing the purchase and sale you might not have to tie up any of your own funds in the transaction. You can use the proceeds from the sale at $128.50 to finance the purchase at $128, and clear the 50 cents without actually investing any of your own money.

Pure arbitrage opportunities of this sort are very rare, because it requires only the participation of a few (maybe only one) arbitrageurs to eliminate the price differential. The increased demand for Seagram's by arbitrageurs buying on the OTC market would tend to drive the price above $128, and the increased supply of Seagram's on the TSE would drive the price down, until the stock would reach a single price in both markets.

This is a somewhat simplified example of arbitrage and the activity of arbitrageurs. In practice, there are transaction costs to deal with, and often the arbitrage opportunity involves not one security but combinations of them. We will see in later chapters that Seagram's stock can be created synthetically, using Seagram's options plus T-bills, and arbitrage considerations therefore dictate a pricing relationship that must hold among these securities.

Practitioners and academicians may often disagree about the right way to characterize equilibrium yield and price relationships, but almost everyone would agree that the *law of one price* holds almost all of the time in the securities markets. Stated simply, the law of one price is that equivalent securities or bundles of securities are priced so that risk-free arbitrage is not possible.

Summary

1. The economy's equilibrium level of real interest rates depends on the willingness of households to save (as reflected in the supply curve of funds), and on the expected profitability of business investment in plant, equipment, and inventories, as reflected in the demand curve for funds. It depends also on government fiscal and monetary policy.

2. In Canada investors can invest in securities offering a guaranteed nominal rate of interest. Their real rate of return depends on the actual rate of inflation. A recently marketed issue of Canada bonds offers a guaranteed real rate of return.

3. The equilibrium expected rate of return on any security is the sum of the risk-free rate and a security-specific risk premium.

4. Investors face a trade-off between risk and expected return. Historical data confirm our intuition that assets with low degrees of risk provide lower returns on average than do those of higher risk.

5. Assets with guaranteed nominal interest rates are risky in real terms because the future inflation rate is uncertain.

6. The riskiness of a security should always be viewed in the context of an investor's total portfolio of assets. Some securities, such as insurance contracts, that would seem quite risky in isolation actually help reduce the risk of an investor's overall portfolio.

7. The law of one price says that two securities or groups of securities with the same payoff structure must sell for the same price. If two identical securities are selling in two markets at different prices it should be profitable to simultaneously buy the security in the low-priced market and sell it in the high-priced market. In the process arbitrageurs, who engage in this activity for a profit, drive up the price in the low-priced market and drive down the price in the high-priced market, eliminating the price differential.

Key terms

Real interest rate
Nominal rate of interest
Holding period return
Risk-free rate

Risk premium
Hedging
Arbitrage

Selected readings

The classic article on the determination of the level of interest rates is:
Fisher, Irving. *The Theory of Interest: As Determined by Impatience to Spend Income and Opportunity to Invest It.* New York: Augustus M. Kelley, Publishers, 1965 (originally published in 1930).

Historical returns on a variety of Canadian instruments, updated on an ongoing basis, are found in the following publications:

ScotiaMcLeod's Handbook of Canadian Debt Market Indices 1947–1990. Scotia-McLeod, February 1991.

Report on Canadian Economic Statistics 1924–1990. Canadian Institute of Actuaries, June 1991.

Hatch, James E.; and Robert W. White. *Canadian Stocks, Bonds, Bills and Inflation.* Charlottesville, Va.: The Financial Analysts Research Foundation, 1988.

An early Canadian study on bond returns is:

Khoury, Nabil T. "Historical Return Distributions of Investments in Canadian Bonds: 1950–1976." *Journal of Business Administration* 12, no. 1 (Fall 1980).

For an in-depth treatment of the distinction between real and nominal risk, read:

Bodie, Zvi. "Investment Strategy in an Inflationary Environment." In Benjamin M. Friedman (editor), *The Changing Roles of Debt and Equity in Financing U.S. Capital Formation.* Chicago: University of Chicago Press, 1982.

Problems

1. You have $5,000 to invest for the next year and are considering the following three alternatives:
   a. A money market fund with an average maturity of 30 days offering a current yield of 6 percent per year.
   b. A one-year savings deposit at a bank offering an interest rate of 7.5 percent.
   c. A 20-year Canada bond offering a yield to maturity of 9 percent per year.

   What role does your forecast of future interest rates play in your decision?

2. Use Figure 4.1 in this chapter to analyze the effect of the following on the level of real interest rates:
   a. Businesses become more optimistic about future demand for their products and decide to increase their capital spending.
   b. Households are induced to save more because of increased uncertainty about their future Canada Pension Plan benefits.
   c. The Bank of Canada undertakes open-market sales of Canada Treasury securities to reduce the supply of money.

3. You are considering the choice between investing $50,000 in a conventional one-year bank CD offering an interest rate of 8 percent and a one-year Inflation-Plus CD offering 3 percent per year plus the rate of inflation.
   a. Which is the safer investment?
   b. Which offers the higher expected return?
   c. If you expect the rate of inflation to be 4 percent over the next year, which is the better investment? Why?
   d. If we observe a risk-free nominal interest rate of 8 percent per year and a risk-free real rate of 3 percent, can we infer that the market's expected rate of inflation is 5 percent per year?

4. Suppose that you revise your expectations regarding the stock market (which were summarized in Table 4.1 in the chapter) as follows:

State of the Economy	Probability	Ending Price ($)	HPR (%)
Boom	.3	140	44
Normal growth	.4	110	14
Recession	.3	80	−16

Use equations 4.1 and 4.2 to compute the mean and standard deviation of the HPR on stocks. Compare your revised parameters with your previous ones.

5. Derive the probability distribution of the one-year holding period return on a 30-year Canada bond with a 9 percent coupon if it is currently selling at par and the probability distribution of its yield to maturity (YTM) a year from now is as follows:

State of the Economy	Probability	YTM (%)
Boom	.25	12.0
Normal growth	.50	9.0
Recession	.25	7.5

For simplicity, assume that the entire 9 percent coupon is paid at the end of the year rather than every six months.

6. Using the historical risk premiums as your guide, if the current risk-free interest rate is 8 percent, what is your estimate of the expected annual HPR on the TSE 300 stock portfolio?

7. Compute the means and standard deviations of the annual holding period returns listed in Table 4.2 of the chapter using only the last 17 years, 1974–1990. How do they compare with these same statistics computed from data for the period 1957–1973? Which do you think are the most relevant statistics to use for projecting into the future?

8. During a period of severe inflation, a bond offered a nominal HPR of 80 percent per year. The inflation rate was 70 percent per year.
   a. What was the real HPR on the bond over the year?
   b. Compare this real HPR to the approximation $R = r - i$.

9. You own a house worth $250,000 and intend to insure it fully against fire for the next year. Suppose that the probability of its burning to the ground during the year is .001 and that an insurance policy covering the full value costs $500. Consider the insurance policy as a security.
   a. What is its expected holding period return?
   b. What is the standard deviation of its HPR?
   c. Is the policy a risky asset? Why?

10. You own an export business for which the only source of risk is foreign currency fluctuations. This year your main contract is to ship $1 million worth of goods to Germany. You have already invested your own money in the goods and signed a contract for the delivery 90 days from now for 2.2 million deutsche marks (DM). The exchange rate is currently 1.4 DM to the Canadian dollar. Suppose the 90-day risk-free interest rate in Canada is

now 8 percent per year and in Germany it is 6 percent per year (for loans denominated in DM).

   a. If you can borrow and lend at the risk-free interest rates in each country, how could you completely eliminate the risk of fluctuations in the dollar value of your 2.2 million DM to be received 90 days from now?

   b. If you can sell the DM in the forward market, what is the minimum price you would require?

   c. What general conclusion can you draw from this about the relationship between the interest rates in both countries and the forward price of the currencies?

11. You are faced with the probability distribution of the holding period return on the stock market index fund given in Table 4.1 of the chapter. Suppose the price of a put option on a share of the index fund with an exercise price of $110 and a maturity of one year is $12.

   a. What is the probability distribution of the HPR on the put option?

   b. What is the probability distribution of the HPR on a portfolio consisting of one share of the index fund and a put option?

   c. In what sense does buying the put option constitute a purchase of insurance in this case?

   d. Explain why the market price of the put option cannot be less than $10 as long as the market price of the underlying stock is $100.

12. Take as given the conditions described in the previous question, and suppose that the risk-free interest rate is 6 percent per year. You are contemplating investing $114/1.06 in a one-year CD and simultaneously buying a call option on the stock market index fund with an exercise price of $110 and a maturity of one year.

   a. What is the probability distribution of your dollar return at the end of the year?

   b. What must the market price of the call option be, and why?

Appendix: Continuous Compounding

Suppose your money earns interest at an annual percentage rate (APR) of 6 percent compounded semiannually. What is your *effective* annual rate of return, accounting for compound interest?

We find the answer by first computing the per-period rate, 3 percent per half-year, and then computing the future value (FV) at the end of the year per dollar invested at the beginning of the year. In this example we get

$$FV = (1.03)^2$$
$$= 1.0609$$

The effective annual rate (r_{EFF}) is just this number minus 1.0.

$$r_{EFF} = 1.0609 - 1$$
$$= .0609$$
$$= 6.09\% \text{ per year}$$

The general formula for the effective annual rate is

$$r_{EFF} = \left(1 + \frac{r}{n}\right)^n - 1$$

where r is the annual percentage rate, and n is the number of compounding periods per year. Table 4A.1 presents the effective annual rates corresponding to an annual percentage rate of 6 percent for different compounding frequencies.

As the compounding frequency increases, $(1 + r/n)^n$ gets closer and closer to e^r, where e is the number 2.71828 (rounded off to the fifth decimal place). In our example, $e^{.06} = 1.0618365$. Therefore, if interest is continuously compounded, $r_{EFF} = .0618365$, or 6.18365 percent per year.

As we noted in Section 4.1 of this chapter, using continuously compounded rates simplifies the algebraic relationship between real and nominal rates of return. To see how, let us compute the real rate of return, first using annual compounding and then using the continuous compounding. Assume the nominal interest rate is 6 percent compounded annually and the rate of inflation is 4 percent compounded annually. Using the relationship

$$\text{Real rate} = \frac{1 + \text{Nominal rate}}{1 + \text{Inflation rate}} - 1$$

$$R = \frac{(1 + r)}{(1 + i)} - 1$$
$$= \frac{(r - i)}{(1 + i)}$$

we find that the real rate is

$$R = \frac{1.06}{1.04} - 1$$
$$= .01923$$
$$= 1.923\% \text{ per year}$$

TABLE 4A.1 Effective Annual Rates for an APR of 6%

Compounding Frequency	n	r_{EFF} (%)
Annually	1	6.00
Semiannually	2	6.09
Quarterly	4	6.13636
Monthly	12	6.16778
Weekly	52	6.17998
Daily	365	6.18313

With continuous compounding the relationship becomes

$$e^R = e^r/e^i = e^{r-i}$$

Taking the natural logarithm we get

$$R = r - i$$

Real rate = Nominal rate − Inflation rate

all expressed as annual percentage rates, continuously compounded.

Thus, if we assume a nominal interest rate of 6 percent per year compounded continuously and an inflation rate of 4 percent per year compounded continuously, the real rate is 2 percent per year compounded continuously.

PART II

PORTFOLIO THEORY

CHAPTER 5

Risk and Risk Aversion

The investment process consists of two broad tasks. One task is security and market analysis, by which we assess the risk and expected-return attributes of the entire set of possible investment vehicles. The second task is the formation of an optimal portfolio of assets. This task involves the determination of the best risk-return opportunities available from feasible investment portfolios and the choice of the best portfolio from that feasible set. We start our formal analysis of investments with this latter task, called *portfolio theory*. We return to the security analysis task in later chapters.

This chapter introduces three themes in portfolio theory, all centering on risk. The first is the basic tenet that investors avoid risk and demand a reward for engaging in risky investments. The reward is taken as a risk premium, an expected rate of return higher than that available on alternative risk-free investments.

The second theme allows us to summarize and quantify investors' personal tradeoffs between portfolio risk and expected return. To do this we introduce the utility function, which assumes that investors can assign a welfare, or "utility," score to any investment portfolio depending on its risk and return.

Finally, the third fundamental principle is that we cannot evaluate the risk of an asset separate from the portfolio of which it is a part; that is, the proper way to measure the risk of an individual asset is to assess its impact on the volatility of the entire portfolio of investments. Taking this approach, we find that seemingly risky securities may be portfolio stabilizers and actually low-risk assets.

Appendix A to this chapter describes the theory and practice of measuring portfolio risk by the variance or standard deviation of returns. We discuss other potentially relevant characteristics of the probability distribution of portfolio returns, as well as the circumstances in which variance is sufficient to measure risk. Appendix B discusses the classical theory of risk aversion.

5.1   *Risk and Risk Aversion*

Risk with Simple Prospects

The presence of risk means that more than one outcome is possible. A *simple prospect* is an investment opportunity in which a certain initial wealth is placed at risk, and there are only two possible outcomes. For the sake of simplicity, it is useful to begin our analysis and elucidate some basic concepts using simple prospects.[1]

Take as an example initial wealth, W, of $100,000, and assume two possible results. With a probability, p, of .6, the favourable outcome will occur, leading to final wealth, W_1, of $150,000. Otherwise, with probability $1 - p = .4$, a less favourable outcome, $W_2 = \$80,000$, will occur. We can represent the simple prospect using an event tree:

$$W = \$100,000 \qquad \begin{array}{l} \overset{p = .6}{\diagup} \quad W_1 = \$150,000 \\ \underset{1 - p = .4}{\diagdown} \quad W_2 = \$80,000 \end{array}$$

Suppose that an investor, Susan, is offered an investment portfolio with a payoff in one year that is described by such a simple prospect. How can she evaluate this portfolio?

First, she could try to summarize it using descriptive statistics. For instance, her mean or expected end-of-year wealth, denoted $E(W)$, is

$$\begin{aligned} E(W) &= pW_1 + (1 - p)W_2 \\ &= .6 \times 150,000 + .4 \times 80,000 \\ &= \$122,000 \end{aligned}$$

The expected profit on the $100,000 investment portfolio is $22,000: 122,000 − 100,000. The variance, σ^2, of the portfolio's payoff is calculated as the expected value of the squared deviations of each possible outcome from the mean:

$$\begin{aligned} \sigma^2 &= p[W_1 - E(W)]^2 + (1 - p)\,[W_2 - E(W)]^2 \\ &= .6(150,000 - 122,000)^2 + .4(80,000 - 122,000)^2 \\ &= 1,176,000,247 \end{aligned}$$

The standard deviation, σ, which is the square root of the variance, is therefore $34,292.86.

---

[1] Chapters 5 through 7 rely on some basic results from elementary statistics. For a refresher, see the Quantitative Review in the Appendix at the end of the book.

Clearly, this is risky business: the standard deviation of the payoff is large, much larger than the expected profit of $22,000. Whether the expected profit is large enough to justify such risk depends on the alternative portfolios.

Let us suppose Treasury bills are one alternative to Susan's risky portfolio. Suppose that at the time of the decision, a one-year T-bill offers a rate of return of 5 percent; $100,000 can be invested to yield a sure profit of $5,000. We can now draw Susan's decision tree:

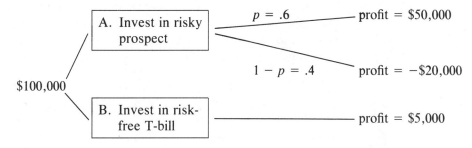

Earlier, we showed the expected profit on the portfolio to be $22,000. Therefore the expected marginal, or incremental, profit of the risky portfolio over investing in safe T-bills is

$$\$22,000 - \$5,000 = \$17,000$$

meaning that one can earn an expected **risk premium** of $17,000 as compensation for the risk of the investment.

The question of whether a given risk premium provides adequate compensation for the investment's risk is age-old. Indeed, one of the central concerns of finance theory (and much of this text) is the measurement of risk and the determination of the risk premiums that investors can expect of risky assets in well-functioning capital markets.

Concept Check	Question 1. What is the risk premium of Susan's risky portfolio in terms of rate of return rather than dollars?

Risk, Speculation, and Gambling

One definition of *speculation* is "the assumption of considerable business risk in obtaining commensurate gain." Although this definition is fine linguistically, it is useless without first specifying what is meant by "commensurate gain" and "considerable risk."

By *commensurate gain* we mean a positive expected profit beyond the risk-free alternative. This is the risk premium. In our example the dollar risk premium is the profit net of the alternative, which is the sure T-bill profit. The risk premium is the incremental expected gain from taking on the risk. By *considerable risk* we mean that the risk is sufficient to affect the decision. An individual might reject a prospect that has a positive risk premium because the added gain is insufficient to make up for the risk involved.

To gamble is "to bet or wager on an uncertain outcome." If you compare this definition to that of speculation, you will see that the central difference is the lack of "good profit." Economically speaking, a gamble is the assumption of risk for no purpose but enjoyment of the risk itself, whereas speculation is undertaken because one perceives a favourable risk-return trade-off. To turn a gamble into a speculative prospect requires an adequate risk premium for compensation to risk-averse investors for the risks that they bear. Hence *risk aversion and speculation are not inconsistent.*

In some cases a gamble may appear to the participants as speculation. Suppose that two investors disagree sharply about the future exchange rate of the Canadian dollar against the British pound. They may choose to bet on the outcome. Suppose that Paul will pay Mary $100 if the value of one pound exceeds $2.00 one year from now, whereas Mary will pay Paul if the pound is worth less than $2.00. There are only two relevant outcomes: (1) the pound will exceed $2.00, or (2) it will fall below $2.00. If both Paul and Mary agree on the probabilities of the two possible outcomes, and if neither party anticipates a loss, it must be that they assign $p = .5$ to each outcome. In that case the expected profit to both is zero and each has entered one side of a gambling prospect.

What is more likely, however, is that the bet results from differences in the probabilities that Paul and Mary assign to the outcome. Mary assigns it $p > .5$, whereas Paul's assessment is $p < .5$. They perceive, subjectively, two different prospects. Economists call this case of differing beliefs *heterogeneous expectations*. In such cases investors on each side of a financial position see themselves as speculating rather than gambling.

Both Paul and Mary should be asking, "Why is the other willing to invest in the side of a risky prospect that I believe offers a negative expected profit?" The ideal way to resolve heterogeneous beliefs is for Paul and Mary to "merge their information," that is, for each party to verify that he or she possesses all relevant information and processes the information properly. Of course, the acquisition of information and the extensive communication that is required to eliminate all heterogeneity in expectations is costly, and thus up to a point heterogeneous expectations cannot be taken as irrational. If, however, Paul and Mary enter such contracts frequently, they would recognize the information problem in one of two ways: either they will realize that they are creating gambles when each wins half of the bets, or the consistent loser will admit that he or she has been betting on inferior forecasts.

Risk Aversion and Utility Values

We have discussed risk with simple prospects and how risk premiums bear on speculation. A prospect that has a zero risk premium is called a *fair game*. Investors who are **risk averse** reject investment portfolios that are fair games or worse. Risk-averse investors are willing to consider only risk-free or speculative prospects. Loosely speaking, a risk-averse investor "penalizes" the ex-

Concept Check

> **Question 2.** Assume that dollar-denominated T-bills in Canada and pound-denominated bills in the United Kingdom offer equal yields to maturity. Both are short-term assets, and both are free of default risk. Neither offers investors a risk premium. However, a Canadian investor who holds U.K. bills is subject to the exchange rate risk since the pounds earned on the U.K. bills eventually will be exchanged for dollars at the future exchange rate. What expectation about future exchange rates would determine whether a Canadian investor who purchases U.K. bills is engaging in speculation or gambling?

pected rate of return of a risky portfolio by a certain percentage (or penalizes the expected profit by a dollar amount) to account for the risk involved. The greater the risk the investor perceives, the larger the penalization. (One might wonder why we assume risk aversion as fundamental. We believe that most investors accept this view from simple introspection, but we discuss the question more fully in Appendix B of this chapter.)

We can formalize this notion of a risk-penalty system. To do so, we will assume that each investor can assign a welfare, or **utility,** score to competing investment portfolios based on the expected return and risk of those portfolios. The utility score may be viewed as a means of ranking portfolios. Higher utility values are assigned to portfolios with more attractive risk-return profiles. Portfolios receive higher utility scores for higher expected returns and lower scores for higher volatility. Many particular "scoring" systems are legitimate. One reasonable function that is commonly employed by financial theorists assigns a portfolio with expected return $E(r)$ and variance of returns σ^2 the following utility score:

$$U = E(r) - \tfrac{1}{2}A\sigma^2 \tag{5.1}$$

where U is the utility value and A is an index of the investor's aversion to taking on risk. (The factor of $\tfrac{1}{2}$ is a scaling convention that will simplify calculations in later chapters. It has no economic significance, and we could eliminate it simply by defining a "new" A with half the value of the A used here.)

Equation 5.1 is consistent with the notion that utility is enhanced by high expected returns and diminished by high risk. (Whether variance is an adequate measure of portfolio risk is discussed in Appendix A.) The extent to which variance lowers utility depends on A, the investor's degree of risk aversion. More risk-averse investors (who have the larger As) penalize risky investments more severely. Investors choosing among competing investment portfolios will select the one providing the highest utility level.

Notice in equation 5.1 that the utility provided by a risk-free portfolio is simply the rate of return on the portfolio, since there is no penalization for risk. This provides us with a convenient benchmark for evaluating portfolios. For example, recall Susan's investment problem, choosing between a portfolio with expected return .22 (22 percent) and standard deviation $\sigma = .34$, and T-bills, providing a risk-free return of 5 percent. Although the risk premium on the risky portfolio is large, 17 percent, the risk of the project is so great that Susan does not need to be very risk averse to choose the safe all-bills strategy. Even for $A = 3$, a moderate risk-aversion parameter, equation 5.1 shows the risky portfolio's utility value as $.22 - \frac{1}{2} \times 3 \times .34^2 = .0466$, or 4.66 percent, which is slightly lower than the risk-free rate. In this case Susan would reject the portfolio in favor of T-bills.

The downward adjustment of the expected return as a penalty for risk is $\frac{1}{2} \times 3 \times .34^2 = .1734$, or 17.34 percent. If Susan were less risk averse (more risk tolerant), for example with $A = 2$, she would adjust the expected rate of return downward by only 11.56 percent. In that case the utility level of the portfolio would be 10.44 percent, higher than the risk-free rate, leading her to accept the prospect.

Concept Check

Question 3. A portfolio has an expected rate of return of .20, and standard deviation of .20. Bills offer a sure rate of return of .07. Which investment alternative will be chosen by an investor whose $A = 4$? What if $A = 8$? *Note:* Treat the interest rates as decimals (for example, $E(r) = .20$, not 20 percent) to answer this question.

Because we can compare utility values to the rate offered on risk-free investments when choosing between a risky portfolio and a safe one, we may interpret a portfolio's utility value as its "certainty equivalent" rate of return to an investor. That is, the **certainty equivalent rate** of a portfolio is the rate that risk-free investments would need to offer with certainty to be considered equally attractive to the risky portfolio.

Now we can say that a portfolio is desirable only if its certainty equivalent return exceeds that of the risk-free alternative. A sufficiently risk-averse investor may assign any risky portfolio, even one with a positive risk premium, a certainty equivalent rate of return that is below the risk-free rate, which will cause the investor to reject the portfolio. At the same time a less risk-averse (more risk-tolerant) investor will assign the same portfolio a certainty equivalent rate that exceeds the risk-free rate and thus will prefer the portfolio to the risk-free alternative. If the risk premium is zero or negative to begin with, any downward adjustment to utility only makes the portfolio look worse. Its certainty equivalent rate will be below that of the risk-free alternative for all risk-averse investors.

In contrast to risk-averse investors, **risk-neutral** investors judge risky prospects solely by their expected rates of return. The level of risk is irrelevant to the risk-neutral investor, meaning that there is no penalization for risk. For this investor a portfolio's certainty equivalent rate is simply its expected rate of return.

A **risk lover** is willing to engage in fair games and gambles; this investor adjusts the expected return upward to take into account the "fun" of confronting the prospect's risk. Risk lovers will always take a fair game because their upward adjustment of utility for risk gives the fair game a certainty equivalent that exceeds the alternative of the risk-free investment.

We can depict the individual's trade-off between risk and return by plotting the characteristics of potential investment portfolios that the individual would view as equally attractive on a graph with axes measuring the expected value and standard deviation of portfolio returns. Figure 5.1 plots the characteristics of one portfolio.

Portfolio P, which has expected return $E(r_P)$ and standard deviation σ_p, is preferred by risk-averse investors to any portfolio in quadrant IV because it has an expected return equal to or greater than any portfolio in that quadrant and a standard deviation equal to or smaller than any portfolio in that quadrant. Conversely, any portfolio in quadrant I is preferable to portfolio P because its expected return is equal to or greater than P's and its standard deviation is equal to or smaller than P's.

This is the mean-standard deviation, or equivalently, **mean-variance (M-V) criterion.** It can be stated as A dominates B if

$$E(r_A) \geq E(r_B)$$

and

$$\sigma_A \leq \sigma_B$$

and at least one inequality is strict.

In the expected return–standard deviation graph the preferred direction is northwest, because in this direction we simultaneously increase the expected return *and* decrease the variance of the rate of return. This means that any portfolio that lies northwest of P is superior to P.

What can be said about portfolios in the quadrants II and III? Their desirability, compared with P, depends on the exact nature of the investor's risk aver-

FIGURE 5.1

The trade-off between risk and return of a potential investment portfolio.

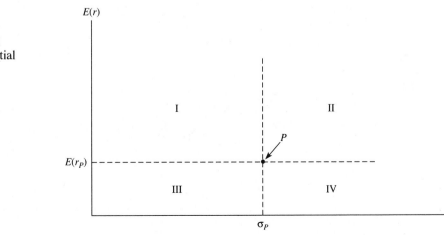

FIGURE 5.2
The indifference
curve.

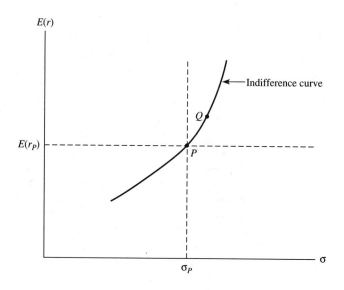

sion. Suppose an investor identifies all portfolios that are equally attractive as portfolio P. Starting at P, an increase in standard deviation lowers utility; it must be compensated for by an increase in expected return. Thus point Q is equally desirable to this investor as P. Investors will be equally attracted to portfolios with high risk and high expected returns compared with other portfolios with lower risk but lower expected returns.

These equally preferred portfolios will lie on a curve in the mean-standard deviation graph that connects all portfolio points with the same utility value (Figure 5.2). This is called the **indifference curve.**

To determine some of the points that appear on the indifference curve, examine the utility values of several possible portfolios for an investor with $A = 4$, presented in Table 5.1. Note that each portfolio offers identical utility, since the high-return portfolios also have high risk. Although in practice the exact indifference curves of various investors cannot be known, this analysis can take us a long way in determining appropriate principles for portfolio selection strategy.

TABLE 5.1   Utility Values of Possible Portfolios

Expected Return, $E(r)$	Standard Deviation, σ	Utility = $E(r) - \frac{1}{2}A\sigma^2$
.10	.200	$.10 - .5 \times 4 \times .04 = .02$
.15	.255	$.15 - .5 \times 4 \times .065 = .02$
.20	.300	$.20 - .5 \times 4 \times .09 = .02$
.25	.339	$.25 - .5 \times 4 \times .115 = .02$

Concept Check	Question 4.
	a. How will the indifference curve of a less risk-averse investor compare to the indifference curve drawn in Figure 5.2?
	b. Draw both indifference curves passing through point *P*.

5.2   *Portfolio Risk*

Asset Risk vs. Portfolio Risk

We have focused so far on the return and risk of an individual's overall investment portfolio. Such portfolios are composed of diverse types of assets. In addition to their direct investment in financial markets, investors have stakes in pension funds, life insurance policies with savings components, homes, and, not least, the earning power of their skills (human capital).

We saw in Chapter 4 that, sometimes, adding a seemingly risky asset to a portfolio actually reduces the risk of the overall portfolio. The example we cited was that of a fire insurance policy. Although the policy viewed in isolation had a very uncertain and volatile payoff, it clearly was a portfolio risk reducer because it provided a positive payoff precisely when another major part of the portfolio, the investor's house, fared poorly. Investing in an asset with a payoff pattern that offsets your exposure to a particular source of risk is called **hedging.**

Insurance contracts are obvious hedging vehicles. In many contexts financial markets offer similar, although perhaps less direct, hedging opportunities. For example, consider two firms, one producing suntan lotion, the other producing umbrellas. The shareholders of each firm face weather risk of an opposite nature. A rainy summer lowers the return on the suntan-lotion firm but raises it on the umbrella firm. Shares of the umbrella firm act as "weather insurance" for the suntan-lotion firm shareholders in precisely the same way that fire insurance policies insure houses. When the lotion firm does poorly (bad weather), the "insurance" asset (umbrella shares) provides a high payoff that offsets the loss.

Another means to control portfolio risk is **diversification,** by which we mean that investments are made in a wide variety of assets so that the exposure to the risk of any particular security is limited. By placing one's eggs in many baskets, overall portfolio risk actually may be less than the risk of any component security considered in isolation.

To examine these effects more precisely, and to lay a foundation for the mathematical properties that will be used in coming chapters, we will consider an example with less than perfect hedging opportunities, and in the process review the statistics underlying portfolio risk and return characteristics.

A Review of Portfolio Mathematics

Consider the problem of Humanex, a non-profit organization deriving most of its income from the return of its endowment. Years ago, the founders of Best Candy willed a large block of Best Candy stock to Humanex with the provision that Humanex may never sell it. This block of shares now comprises 50 percent of Humanex's endowment. Humanex has free choice as to where to invest the remainder of its portfolio.[2]

The value of Best Candy stock is sensitive to the price of sugar. In years when the Caribbean sugar crop fails, the price of sugar rises significantly and Best Candy suffers considerable losses. We can describe the fortunes of Best Candy stock using the following scenario analysis:

| | Normal Year for Sugar | | Abnormal Year |
	Bullish Stock Market	Bearish Stock Market	Sugar Crisis
Probability	.5	.3	.2
Rate of return	.25	.10	−.25

To summarize these three possible outcomes using conventional statistics, we review some of the key rules governing the properties of risky assets and portfolios.

Rule 1. The mean or **expected return** of an asset is a probability-weighted average of its return in all scenarios. Calling $Pr(s)$ the probability of scenario s and $r(s)$ the return in scenario s, we may write the expected return, $E(r)$, as

$$E(r) = \sum_s Pr(s)r(s) \tag{5.2}$$

Applying this formula to the case at hand, with three possible scenarios, we find that the expected rate of return of Best Candy's stock is

$$E(r_{Best}) = .5 \times .25 + .3 \times .10 + .2(-.25)$$
$$= .105$$
$$= 10.5\%$$

Rule 2. The **variance** of an asset's returns is the expected value of the squared deviations from the expected return. Symbolically,

$$\sigma^2 = \sum_s Pr(s)[r(s) - E(r)]^2 \tag{5.3}$$

---

[2] The portfolio restriction is admittedly unrealistic. We use this example only to illustrate the various strategies that might be used to control risk and to review some useful results from statistics.

Therefore, in our example

$$\sigma_{\text{Best}}^2 = .5(.25 - .105)^2 + .3(.10 - .105)^2 + .2(-.25 - .105)^2$$
$$= .035725$$

The **standard deviation** of Best's return, which is the square root of the variance, is $\sqrt{.035725} = .189$, or 18.9 percent.

Humanex has 50 percent of its endowment in Best's stock. To reduce the risk of the overall portfolio, it could invest the remainder in T-bills, which yield a sure rate of return of 5 percent. To derive the return of the overall portfolio, we apply rule 3:

Rule 3. The rate of return on a portfolio is a weighted average of the rates of return of each asset comprising the portfolio, with portfolio proportions as weights. This implies that the *expected* rate of return on a portfolio is a weighted average of the *expected* rate of return on each component asset.

In this case the portfolio proportions in each asset are .5, and the portfolio's expected rate of return is

$$E(r_{\text{Humanex}}) = .5E(r_{\text{Best}}) + .5r_{\text{Bills}}$$
$$= .5 \times .105 + .5 \times .05$$
$$= .0775$$
$$= 7.75\%$$

The standard deviation of the portfolio may be derived from the following:

Rule 4. When a risky asset is combined with a risk-free asset, the portfolio standard deviation equals the risky asset's standard deviation multiplied by the portfolio proportion invested in the asset.

In this case, the Humanex portfolio is 50 percent invested in Best stock and 50 percent invested in risk-free bills. Therefore

$$\sigma_{\text{Humanex}} = .5\sigma_{\text{Best}}$$
$$= .5 \times .189$$
$$= .0945$$
$$= 9.45\%$$

By reducing its exposure to the risk of Best by half, Humanex reduces its portfolio standard deviation by half. The cost of this risk reduction, however, is a reduction in expected return. The expected rate of return on Best stock is 10.5 percent. The expected return on the one-half T-bill portfolio is 7.75 percent. This makes the risk premiums over the 5 percent rate on risk-free bills 5.5 percent for Best stock and 2.75 percent for the half T-bill portfolio. By reducing the share of Best stock in the portfolio by one half, Humanex reduces its portfolio risk premium by one half, from 5.5 percent to 2.75 percent.

In an effort to improve the contribution of the endowment to the operating budget, Humanex's trustees hire Sally, a recent MBA, as a consultant. Investigating the sugar and candy industry, Sally discovers, not surprisingly, that during years of sugar crisis in the Caribbean basin, SugarBeet, a Canadian sugar refiner that uses beets as raw material, reaps unusual profits and its stock price soars. A scenario analysis of SugarBeet's stock looks like this:

| | Normal Year for Sugar | | Abnormal Year |
	Bullish Stock Market	Bearish Stock Market	Sugar Crisis
Probability	.5	.3	.2
Rate of return	.01	−.05	.35

The expected rate of return on SugarBeet's stock is 6 percent, and its standard deviation is 14.73 percent. Thus SugarBeet is almost as volatile as Best, yet its expected return is only a notch better than the T-bill rate. This cursory analysis makes SugarBeet appear to be an unattractive investment. For Humanex, however, the stock holds great promise.

SugarBeet offers excellent hedging potential for holders of Best stock because its return is highest precisely when Best's return is lowest—during a Caribbean sugar crisis. Consider Humanex's portfolio when it splits its investment evenly between Best and SugarBeet. The rate of return for each scenario is the simple average of the rates on Best and SugarBeet because the portfolio is split evenly between the two stocks (see Rule 3).

| | Normal Year for Sugar | | Abnormal Year |
	Bullish Stock Market	Bearish Stock Market	Sugar Crisis
Probability	.5	.3	.2
Rate of return	.13	.025	.05

The expected rate of return on Humanex's hedged portfolio is .0825 with a standard deviation of 0.483, or 4.83 percent.

Sally now summarizes the reward and risk of the three alternatives:

Portfolio	Expected Return	Standard Deviation
All in Best Candy	.105	.1890
Half in T-bills	.0775	.0945
Half in SugarBeet	.0825	.0483

The numbers speak for themselves. The hedge portfolio including SugarBeet clearly dominates the simple risk-reduction strategy of investing in safe T-bills. It has higher expected return *and* lower standard deviation than the one-half T-bill portfolio. The point is that, despite SugarBeet's large standard deviation of return, it is a risk reducer for some investors—in this case those holding Best stock.

The risk of the individual assets in the portfolio must be measured in the context of the effect of their return on overall portfolio variability. This example demonstrates that assets with returns that are inversely associated with the initial risky position are the most powerful risk reducers.

Concept Check

To quantify the hedging or diversification potential of an asset, we use the concepts of covariance and correlation. The **covariance** measures how much the returns on two risky assets move in tandem. A positive covariance means that asset returns move together. A negative covariance means that they vary inversely, as in the case of Best and SugarBeet.

To measure covariance, we look at return "surprises" or deviations from expected value in each scenario. Consider the product of each stock's deviation from expected return in a particular scenario:

$$[r_{Best} - E(r_{Best})][r_{Beet} - E(r_{Beet})]$$

This product will be positive if the returns of the two stocks move together across scenarios, that is, if both returns exceed their expectations or both fall short of those expectations in the scenario in question. On the other hand, if one stock's return exceeds its expected value when the other's falls short, the product will be negative. Thus a good measure of how much the returns move together is the *expected value* of this product across all scenarios, which is defined as the covariance:

$$\text{Cov}(r_{Best}, r_{Beet}) = \sum_s Pr(s) \, [r_{Best}(s) - E(r_{Best})][r_{Beet}(s) - E(r_{Beet})] \quad \textbf{(5.4)}$$

In this example, with $E(r_{Best}) = .105$ and $E(r_{Beet}) = .06$ and with returns in each scenario summarized as follows, we find the covariance from a simple application of equation 5.4.

	Normal Year for Sugar		Abnormal Year
	Bullish Stock Market	Bearish Stock Market	Sugar Crisis
Probability	.5	.3	.2
Stock			
Best Candy	˙25	.10	−.25
SugarBeet	.01	−.05	.35

The covariance between the two stocks is

$$\begin{aligned}
\text{Cov}(r_{Best}, r_{Beet}) &= .5(.25 - .105)(.01 - .06) \\
&+ .3(.10 - .105)(-.05 - .06) + .2(-.25 - .105)(.35 - .06) \\
&= -.02405
\end{aligned}$$

The negative covariance confirms the hedging quality of SugarBeet stock relative to Best Candy. SugarBeet's returns move inversely with Best's.

An easier statistic to interpret than the covariance is the **correlation coefficient,** which scales the covariance to a value between -1 (perfect negative correlation) and $+1$ (perfect positive correlation). The correlation coefficient between two variables equals their covariance divided by the product of the standard deviations. Denoting the correlation by the Greek letter ρ, we find that

$$\rho(\text{Best, SugarBeet}) = \frac{\text{Cov}[r_{\text{Best}}, r_{\text{SugarBeet}}]}{\sigma_{\text{Best}}\sigma_{\text{SugarBeet}}}$$

$$= \frac{-.0240}{.189 \times .1473}$$

$$= -.86$$

This large negative correlation (close to -1) confirms the strong tendency of Best and SugarBeet stocks to move inversely, or "out of phase" with one another.

The impact of the covariance of asset returns on portfolio risk is apparent in the following formula for portfolio variance.

> *Rule 5.* When two risky assets with variances σ_1^2 and σ_2^2, respectively, are combined into a portfolio with portfolio weights w_1 and w_2, respectively, the portfolio variance σ_P^2 is given by

$$\sigma_P^2 = w_1^2\sigma_1^2 + w_2^2\sigma_2^2 + 2w_1w_2\text{Cov}(r_1,r_2)$$

In this example, with equal weights in Best and SugarBeet, $w_1 = w_2 = .5$, and with $\sigma_{\text{Best}} = .189$, $\sigma_{\text{Beet}} = .1473$, and Cov $(r_{\text{Best}}, r_{\text{Beet}}) = -.02405$, we find that

$$\sigma_P^2 = .5^2 \times .189^2 + .5^2 \times .1473^2 + 2 \times .5 \times .5\,(-.02405) = .00233$$

or that $\sigma_P = \sqrt{.00233} = .0483$, precisely the same answer for the standard deviation of the returns on the hedged portfolio that we derived directly from the scenario analysis.

Rule 5 for portfolio variance highlights the effect of covariance on portfolio risk. A positive covariance increases portfolio variance, and a negative covariance acts to reduce portfolio variance. This makes sense because returns on negatively correlated assets tend to be offsetting, which stabilizes portfolio returns.

Basically, hedging involves the purchase of a risky asset that is negatively correlated with the existing portfolio. This negative correlation makes the volatility of the hedge asset a risk-reducing feature. A hedge strategy is a powerful alternative to the simple risk-reduction strategy of including a risk-free asset in the portfolio.

In later chapters we will see that, in a rational equilibrium, hedge assets must offer relatively low expected rates of return. The perfect hedge, an insurance contract, is by design perfectly negatively correlated with a specified risk. As one would expect in a "no free lunch" world, the insurance premium reduces the portfolio's expected rate of return.

Concept Check

Question 6. Suppose that the distribution of SugarBeet stock is as follows:

Bullish Stock Market	Bearish Stock Market	Sugar Crisis
.07	−.05	.20

a. What would be its correlation with Best?
b. Is SugarBeet stock a useful hedge asset now?
c. Calculate the portfolio rate of return in each scenario and the standard deviation of the portfolio from the scenario returns. Then evaluate σ_P using rule 5.
d. Are the two methods of computing portfolio standard deviation consistent?

Summary

1. Speculation is the undertaking of a risky investment for its risk premium. The risk premium has to be large enough to compensate a risk-averse investor for the risk of the investment.

2. A fair game is a risky prospect that has a zero-risk premium. It will not be undertaken by a risk-averse investor.

3. Investors' preferences toward the expected return and volatility of a portfolio may be expressed by a utility function that is higher for higher expected returns and lower for higher portfolio variances. More risk-averse investors will apply greater penalties for risk. We can describe these preferences graphically using indifference curves.

4. The desirability of a risky portfolio to a risk-averse investor may be summarized by the certainty equivalent value of the portfolio. The certainty equivalent rate of return is a value that, if it is received with certainty, would yield the same utility as the risky portfolio.

5. Hedging is the purchase of a risky asset to reduce the risk of a portfolio. The negative correlation between the hedge asset and the initial portfolio turns the volatility of the hedge asset into a risk-*reducing* feature. When a hedge asset is perfectly negatively correlated with the initial portfolio, it serves as a perfect hedge and works like an insurance contract on the portfolio.

Key terms

Risk premium	Utility
Risk averse	Certainty equivalent rate

Risk neutral
Risk lover
Mean-variance criterion
Indifference curve
Hedging
Diversification

Expected return
Variance
Standard deviation
Covariance
Correlation coefficient

Selected readings

A classic work on risk and risk aversion is:
  Arrow, Kenneth. *Essays in the Theory of Risk Bearing.* Amsterdam: North Holland, 1971.
Some good statistics texts with business applications are:
  Levy, Haim; and Ben-Horim, Moshe. *Statistics: Decisions and Applications in Business and Economics.* New York: Random House, 1984.
  Wonnacott, Thomas H.; and Wonnacott, Ronald J. *Introductory Statistics for Business and Economics.* New York: John Wiley & Sons, 1984.

Problems

1. Consider a risky portfolio. The end-of-year cash flow derived from the portfolio will be either $50,000 or $150,000 with equal probabilities of .5. The alternative risk-free investment in T-bills pays 5 percent per year.
   a. If you require a risk premium of 10 percent, how much will you be willing to pay for the portfolio?
   b. Suppose that the portfolio can be purchased for the amount you found in (a). What will be the expected rate of return on the portfolio?
   c. Now suppose that you require a risk premium of 15 percent. What is the price that you will be willing to pay?
   d. Comparing your answers to (a) and (c), what do you conclude about the relationship between the required risk premium on a portfolio and the price at which the portfolio will sell?
2. Consider a portfolio that offers an expected rate of return of 10 percent and a standard deviation of 15 percent. T-bills offer a risk-free 8 percent rate of return. What is the maximum level of risk aversion for which the risky portfolio is still preferred to bills?
3. Draw the indifference curve in the expected return–standard deviation plane corresponding to a utility level of .05 for an investor with a risk aversion coefficient of 3. *Hint:* Choose several possible standard deviations, ranging from .05 to .25, and find the expected rates of return providing a utility level of .05. Then plot the expected return–standard deviation points so derived.

4. Now draw the indifference curve corresponding to a utility level of .04 for an investor with risk aversion coefficient $A = 4$. Comparing your answers to questions 3 and 4, what do you conclude?
5. Draw an indifference curve for a risk-neutral investor providing utility level .05.
6. What must be true about the sign of the risk aversion coefficient, A, for a risk lover? Draw the indifference curve for a utility level of .05 for a risk lover.

Consider historical data showing that the average annual rate of return on the TSE 300 portfolio over the past 34 years has averaged about 2.9 percent more than the Treasury bill return, and that the TSE 300 standard deviation has been about 16.8 percent per year. Assume that these values are representative of investors' expectations for future performance and that the current T-bill rate is 7 percent. Use these values to answer questions 7 to 9.

7. Calculate the expected return and variance of portfolios invested in T-bills and the TSE 300 index with weights as follows:

W_{bills}	W_{market}
0	1.0
.2	.8
.4	.6
.6	.4
.8	.2
1.0	0

8. Calculate the utility levels of each portfolio of question 7 for an investor with $A = 3$. What do you conclude?
9. Repeat question 8 for an investor with $A = 5$. What do you conclude?

Reconsider the Best and SugarBeet stock market hedging example in the text, but assume for questions 10 to 12 that the probability distribution of the rate of return on SugarBeet stock is as follows:

	Bullish Stock Market	Bearish Stock Market	Sugar Crisis
Probability	.5	.3	.2
Rate of return	.10	−.05	.20

10. If Humanex's portfolio is half Best stock and half SugarBeet, what are its expected return and standard deviation? Calculate the standard deviation from the portfolio returns in each scenario.
11. What is the covariance between Best and SugarBeet?
12. Calculate the portfolio standard deviation using rule 5 and show that the result is consistent with your answer to question 10.

Appendix A: *A Defense of Mean-Variance Analysis*

Describing Probability Distributions

The axiom of risk aversion needs little defense. So far, however, our treatment of risk has been limiting in that it took the variance (or equivalently, the standard deviation) of portfolio returns as an adequate risk measure. In situations in which variance alone is not adequate to measure risk this assumption is potentially restrictive. Here, we provide some justification for mean-variance analysis.

The basic question is how one can best describe the uncertainty of portfolio rates of return. In principle, one could list all possible outcomes for the portfolio over a given period. If each outcome results in a payoff such as a dollar profit or rate of return, then this payoff value is the *random variable* in question. A list assigning a probability to all possible values of the random variable is called the probability distribution of the random variable.

The reward for holding a portfolio is typically measured by the expected rate of return across all possible scenarios, which equals

$$E(r) = \sum_{s=1}^{n} Pr(s)r_s$$

where $s = 1, \ldots, n$ are the possible outcomes or scenarios, r_s is the rate of return for outcome s, and $Pr(s)$ is the probability associated with it.

Actually, the expected value or mean is not the only candidate for the central value of a probability distribution. Other candidates are the median and the mode.

The median is defined as the outcome value that exceeds the outcome values for half the population and is exceeded by the other half. Whereas the expected rate of return is a weighted average of the outcomes, the weights being the probabilities, the median is based on the rank order of the outcomes and takes into account only the order of the outcome values rather than the values themselves.

The median differs significantly from the mean in cases where the expected value is dominated by extreme values. One example is the income (or wealth) distribution in a population. A relatively small number of households command a disproportionate share of total income (and wealth). The mean income is "pulled up" by these extreme values, which makes it nonrepresentative. The median is free of this effect, since it equals the income level that is exceeded by half the population, regardless of by how much.

Finally, a third candidate for the measure of central value is the mode, which is the most likely value of the distribution or the outcome with the highest probability. However, the expected value is by far the most widely used measure of central or average tendency.

We now turn to the characterization of the risk implied by the nature of the probability distribution of returns. In general, it is impossible to quantify risk by a single number. We can, however, describe the probabilities and magnitudes of the possible deviations from the mean, or the "surprises," in a concise fashion, to illuminate the risk-return trade-off. The easiest way to accomplish this is to answer a set of questions in order of their informational value and to stop at the point where additional questions would not affect our notion of the risk-return trade-off.

The first question is, "What is a typical deviation from the expected value?" A natural answer would be, "The expected deviation from the expected value is _____." Unfortunately, this answer is meaningless because it is necessarily zero: positive deviations from the mean are offset exactly by negative deviations.

There are two ways of getting around this problem. The first is to use the expected *absolute* value of the deviation. This is known as MAD (mean absolute deviation), which is given by

$$\sum_{s=1}^{n} Pr(s) \times \text{Absolute Value}[r_s - E(r)]$$

The second is to use the expected *squared* deviation from the expected, or mean, value, which is simply the variance of the probability distribution:

$$\sigma^2 = \sum_{s=1}^{n} Pr(s) [r_s - E(r)]^2$$

Note that the unit of measurement of the variance is percent squared. To return to our original units, we compute the standard deviation as the square root of the variance, which is measured in percentage terms, as is the expected value.

The variance also is called the *second central moment* around the mean, with the expected return itself being the first moment. Although the variance measures the average squared deviation from the expected value, it does not provide a full description of risk. To see why, consider the two probability distributions for rates of return on a portfolio, in Figure 5A.1.

A and B are probability distributions with identical expected values and variances. The graphs show that the variances are identical because probability distribution B is the mirror image of A.

What is the principal difference between A and B? A is characterized by more likely but small losses and less likely but extreme gains. This pattern is reversed in B. The difference is important. When we talk about risk, we really mean "*bad* surprises." The bad surprises in A, although they are more likely, are small (and limited) in magnitude. The bad surprises in B could be extreme, indeed unbounded. A risk-averse investor will prefer A to B on these grounds; hence it is worthwhile to quantify this characteristic. The asymmetry of the

FIGURE 5A.1
Skewed probability
distributions for
rates of return on a
portfolio.

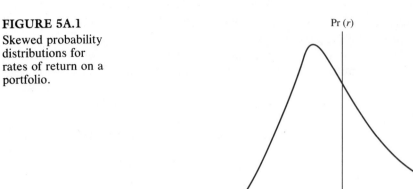

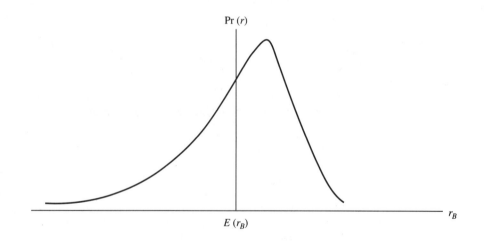

distribution is called *skewness*, which we measure by the *third central moment*, given by

$$M_3 = \sum_{s=1}^{n} Pr(s) \, [r_s - E(r)]^3$$

Cubing the deviations from expected value preserves their signs, which allows us to distinguish good from bad surprises. Because this procedure gives greater weight to larger deviations, it causes the "long tail" of the distribution to dominate the measure of skewness. Thus the skewness of the distribution will be positive for a right-skewed distribution such as *A* and negative for a left-skewed distribution such as *B*. The asymmetry is a relevant characteristic, although it is not as important as the magnitude of the standard deviation.

To summarize, the first moment (expected value) represents the expected reward. The second and higher central moments characterize the uncertainty of the reward. All the even moments (variance, M_4, and so on) represent the likelihood of extreme values. Larger values for these moments indicate greater uncertainty. The odd moments (M_3, M_5, and so on) represent measures of asymmetry. Positive numbers are associated with positive skewness and hence are desirable.

We can characterize the risk aversion of any investor by the preference scheme that the investor assigns to the various moments of the distribution. In other words, we can write the utility value derived from the probability distribution as

$$U = E(r) - b_0\sigma^2 + b_1M_3 - b_2M_4 + b_3M_5 - \ldots$$

where the importance of the terms lessens as we proceed to higher moments. Notice that the "good" (odd) moments have positive coefficients, whereas the "bad" (even) moments have minus signs in front of the coefficients.

How many moments are needed to describe the investor's assessment of the probability distribution adequately? Samuelson's "Fundamental Approximation Theorem of Portfolio Analysis in Terms of Means, Variances, and Higher Moments"[a] proves that in many important circumstances:

1. The importance of all moments beyond the variance is much smaller than that of the expected value and variance. In other words, disregarding moments higher than the variance will not affect portfolio choice.
2. The variance is as important as the mean to investor welfare.

Samuelson's proof is the major theoretical justification for mean-variance analysis. Under the conditions of this proof mean and variance are equally important, and we can overlook all other moments without harm.

The major assumption that Samuelson makes to arrive at this conclusion concerns the "compactness" of the distribution of stock returns. The distribution of the rate of return on a portfolio is said to be compact if the risk can be controlled by the investor. Practically speaking, we test for compactness of the distribution by posing a question: Will the risk of my position in the portfolio decline if I hold it for a shorter period, or will the risk approach zero if I hold the risky portfolio for only an instant? If the answer is yes, then the distribution is compact.

In general, compactness may be seen as being equivalent to continuity of stock prices. If stock prices do not take sudden jumps, then the uncertainty of stock returns over smaller and smaller time periods decreases. Under these circumstances investors who can rebalance their portfolios frequently will act so as to make higher moments of the stock return distribution so small as to be unimportant. It is not that skewness, for example, does not matter in principle.

---

[a] Paul A. Samuelson, "The Fundamental Approximation Theorem of Portfolio Analysis in Terms of Means, Variances, and Higher Moments," *Review of Economic Studies,* 37, 1970.

It is, instead, that the actions of investors in frequently revising their portfolios will limit higher moments to negligible levels.

Continuity or compactness is not, however, an innocuous assumption. Portfolio revisions entail transaction costs, meaning that rebalancing must of necessity be somewhat limited and that skewness and other higher moments cannot entirely be ignored. Compactness also rules out such phenomena as the major stock price jumps that occur in response to takeover attempts. It also rules out such dramatic events as the 25 percent one-day decline of the stock market on October 19, 1987. Except for these relatively unusual events, however, mean-variance analysis is adequate. In most cases, if the portfolio may be revised frequently, we need to worry about the mean and variance only.

Portfolio theory, for the most part, is built on the assumption that the conditions for mean-variance (or mean-standard deviation) analysis are satisfied. Accordingly, we typically ignore higher moments.

Concept Check
═══════════
═══════════

Question 5A.1. How does the simultaneous popularity of both lotteries and insurance policies confirm the notion that individuals prefer positive to negative skewness of portfolio returns?

Normal and Lognormal Distributions

Modern portfolio theory, for the most part, assumes that asset returns are normally distributed. This is a convenient assumption because the normal distribution can be described completely by its mean and variance, which provides another justification for mean-variance analysis. The argument has been that, even if individual asset returns are not exactly normal, the distribution of returns of a large portfolio will resemble a normal distribution quite closely.

The data support this argument. Table 5A.1 shows summaries of the results of one-year investments in many portfolios selected randomly from NYSE stocks. The portfolios are listed in order of increasing degrees of diversification; that is, the numbers of stocks in each portfolio sample are 1, 8, 32, and 128. The percentiles of the distribution of returns for each portfolio are compared to what one would have expected from portfolios identical in mean and variance but drawn from a normal distribution.

Looking first at the single stock portfolio ($n = 1$), the departure of the return distribution from normality is significant. The mean of the sample is 28.2 percent, and the standard deviation is 41.0 percent. In the case of a normal distribution with the same mean and standard deviation, we would expect the fifth percentile stock to lose 39.2 percent, but the fifth percentile stock actually lost 14.4 percent. In addition, while the normal distribution's mean coincides with its median, the actual sample median of the single stock was 19.6 percent, far below the sample mean of 28.2 percent.

In contrast, the returns of the 128-stock portfolios are virtually identical in distribution to the hypothetical normally distributed portfolio. The normal dis-

TABLE 5A.1   Frequency Distributions of Rates of Return from a One-Year Investment in Randomly Selected Portfolios from NYSE-Listed Stocks

Statistic	N = 1 Observed	N = 1 Normal	N = 8 Observed	N = 8 Normal	N = 32 Observed	N = 32 Normal	N = 128 Observed	N = 128 Normal
Minimum	−71.1	NA	−12.4	NA	6.5	NA	16.4	NA
5th centile	−14.4	−39.2	8.1	4.6	17.4	16.7	22.7	22.6
20th centile	−.5	−6.3	16.3	16.1	22.2	22.3	25.3	25.3
50th centile	19.6	28.2	26.4	28.2	27.8	28.2	28.1	28.2
70th centile	38.7	49.7	33.8	35.7	31.6	32.9	30.0	30.0
95th centile	96.3	95.6	54.3	51.8	40.9	39.9	34.1	33.8
Maximum	442.6	NA	136.7	NA	73.7	NA	43.1	NA
Mean	28.2	28.2	28.2	28.2	28.2	28.2	28.2	28.2
Standard deviation	41.0	41.0	14.4	14.4	7.1	7.1	3.4	3.4
Skewness (M_3)	255.4	0.0	88.7	0.0	44.5	0.0	17.7	0.0
Sample size	1,227	—	131,072	—	32,768	—	16,384	—

From Lawrence Fisher and James H. Lorie, "Some Studies of Variability of Returns on Investments in Common Stocks," *Journal of Business*, 43 (April 1970); published by the University of Chicago.

tribution therefore is a pretty good working assumption for well-diversified portfolios. How large a portfolio must be for this result to take hold depends on how far the distribution of the individual stocks is from normality. It appears that a portfolio typically must include at least 32 stocks for the one-year return to be close to normally distributed.

There remain theoretical objections to the assumption that individual stock returns are normally distributed. Given that a stock price cannot be negative, the normal distribution cannot be truly representative of the behavior of a holding period rate of return because it allows for any outcome, including the whole range of negative prices. Specifically, rates of return lower than −100 percent are theoretically impossible because they imply the possibility of negative security prices. The failure of the normal distribution to rule out such outcomes must be viewed as a shortcoming.

An alternative assumption is that the continuously compounded annual rate of return is normally distributed. If we call this rate r and we call the effective annual rate r_e, then $r_e = e^r - 1$, and since e^r can never be negative, the smallest possible value for r_e is −1 or −100 percent. Thus this assumption nicely rules out the troublesome possibility of negative prices while still conveying the advantages of working with normal distributions.

Under this assumption the distribution of r_e will be *lognormal*. This distribution is depicted in Figure 5A.2.

For *short* holding periods, that is, where t is small, the approximation of $r_e(t) = e^{rt} - 1$ by rt is quite accurate and the normal distribution provides a good approximation to the lognormal. With rt normally distributed, the effective annual return over short time periods may be taken as approximately normally distributed.

FIGURE 5A.2

The lognormal distribution for three values of σ^2.

(From J. Atchison and J. A. C. Brown, *The Lognormal Distribution*. New York: Cambridge University Press, 1976.)

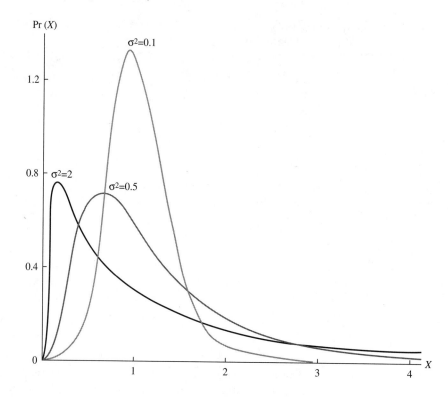

For short holding periods, therefore, the mean and standard deviation of the effective holding period returns are proportional to the mean and standard deviation of the annual, continuously compounded rate of return on the stock and to the time interval.

Therefore, if the standard deviation of the annual continuously compounded rate of return on a stock is 40 percent ($\sigma = .40$), then the variance of the holding period return for one month, for example, is for all practical purposes

$$\sigma^2(\text{monthly}) = \frac{\sigma^2}{12} = \frac{.16}{12} = .0133$$

and the standard deviation is $\sqrt{.0133} = .1155$.

To illustrate this principle, suppose that the Dow Jones Industrials went up one day by 50 points from 3,200 to 3,250. Is this a "large" move? Looking at annual, continuously compounded rates on the Dow Jones portfolio, we find that the annual standard deviation historically has been about 27 percent. Under the assumption that the return on the Dow Jones portfolio is lognormally distributed and that returns between successive subperiods are uncorrelated, the one-day distribution has a standard deviation (based on 250 trading days per year) of

$$\sigma(day) = \sigma(year) \sqrt{1/250}$$
$$= \frac{.27}{\sqrt{250}}$$
$$= .0171$$
$$= 1.71\% \text{ per day}$$

Applying this to the opening level of the Dow Jones on that trading day, 3,200, we find that the daily standard deviation of the Dow Jones index is 3,200 × .0171 = 54.7 points per day.

Since the daily rate on the Dow Jones portfolio is approximately normal, we know that in one day out of three, the Dow Jones will move (from a starting level of 3,200) by more than 54 points either way. Thus a move of 50 points is hardly an unusual event.

| Concept Check | Question 5A.2. Look again at Table 5A.1. Are you surprised that the minimum rates of return are less negative for more diversified portfolios? Is your explanation consistent with the behaviour of the sample's maximum rates of return? |

Summary: Appendix A

1. The probability distribution of the rate of return can be characterized by its moments. The reward from taking the risk is measured by the first moment, which is the mean of the return distribution. Higher moments characterize the risk. Even moments provide information on the likelihood of extreme values, and odd moments provide information on the asymmetry of the distribution.

2. Investors' risk preferences can be characterized by their preferences for the various moments of the distribution. The fundamental approximation theorem shows that when portfolios are revised often enough, and prices are continuous, the desirability of a portfolio can be measured by its mean and variance alone.

3. The rates of return on well-diversified portfolios for holding periods that are not too long can be approximated by a normal distribution. For short holding periods (up to one month), the normal distribution is a good approximation for the lognormal.

Problem: Appendix A

1. The Smartstock investment consulting group prepared the following scenario analysis for the end-of-year dividend and stock price of Klink Inc., which is selling now at $12 per share:

| | | End-of-Year | |
Scenario	Probability	Dividend ($)	Price ($)
1	.10	0	0
2	.20	.25	2.00
3	.40	.40	14.00
4	.25	.60	20.00
5	.05	.85	30.00

Compute the rate of return for each scenario and
a. The mean, median, and mode.
b. The standard deviation and mean absolute deviation.
c. The first moment, and the second and third moments around the mean. Is the probability distribution of Klink stock positively skewed?

Appendix B: Risk Aversion and Expected Utility

We digress here to examine the rationale behind our contention that investors are risk averse. Recognition of risk aversion as central in investment decisions goes back at least to 1738. Daniel Bernoulli, one of a famous Swiss family of distinguished mathematicians, spent the years 1725 through 1733 in St. Petersburg, where he analyzed the following coin-toss game. To enter the game one pays an entry fee. Thereafter, a coin is tossed until the *first* head appears. The number of tails, denoted by n, that appears until the first head is tossed is used to compute the payoff, R, to the participant, as

$$R(n) = 2^n$$

The probability of no tails before the first head ($n = 0$) is ½ and the corresponding payoff is $2^0 = \$1$. The probability of one tail and then heads ($n = 1$) is ½ × ½ with payoff $2^1 = \$2$, the probability of two tails and then heads ($n = 2$) is ½ × ½ × ½, and so forth.

The following table illustrates the probabilities and payoffs for various outcomes:

Tails	Probability	Payoff = $R(n)$	Probability × Payoff
0	½	$1	$1/2
1	¼	$2	$1/2
2	⅛	$4	$1/2
3	1⁄16	$8	$1/2
.	.	.	.
.	.	.	.
n	$(½)^{n+1}$	2^n	$1/2

The expected payoff is therefore

$$E(R) = \sum_{n=0}^{\infty} Pr(n)R(n)$$

$$= \tfrac{1}{2} + \tfrac{1}{2} + \ldots$$

$$= \infty$$

This game is called the "St. Petersburg Paradox." Although the expected payoff is infinite, participants obviously will be willing to purchase tickets to play the game only at a finite, and possibly quite modest, entry fee.

Bernoulli resolved the paradox by noting that investors do not assign the same value per dollar to all payoffs. Specifically, the greater their wealth, the less their "appreciation" for each extra dollar. We can make this insight mathematically precise by assigning a welfare or utility value to any level of investor wealth. Our utility function should increase as wealth is higher, but each extra dollar of wealth should increase utility by progressively smaller amounts.[b] (Modern economists would say that investors exhibit "decreasing marginal utility" from an additional payoff dollar.) One particular function that assigns a subjective value to the investor from a payoff of R, which has a smaller value per dollar the greater the payoff, is the function $\log(R)$. If this function measures utility values of wealth, the subjective utility value of the game is indeed finite.[c] The certain wealth level necessary to yield this utility value is $2.38, because log (2.38) = .866. Hence the certainty equivalent value of the risky payoff is $2.38, which is the maximum amount that this investor will pay to play the game.

Von Neumann and Morgenstern adapted this approach to investment theory in a complete axiomatic system in 1946. Avoiding unnecessary technical detail, we restrict ourselves here to an intuitive exposition of the rationale for risk aversion.

Imagine two individuals who are identical twins, except that one of them is less fortunate than the other. Peter has only $1,000 to his name while Paul has a net worth of $200,000. How many hours of work would each twin be willing to offer to earn one extra dollar? It is likely that Peter (the poor twin) has more essential uses for the extra money than does Paul. Therefore Peter will offer more hours. In other words, Peter derives a greater personal welfare or assigns a greater "utility" value to the 1,0001st dollar than Paul does to the 200,001st.

---

[b] This utility function is similar in spirit to the one that assigns a satisfaction level to portfolios with given risk-and-return attributes. However, the utility function here refers not to investor's satisfaction with alternative portfolio choices but only to the subjective welfare they derive from different levels of wealth.

[c] If we substitute the "utility" value, $\log(R)$, for the dollar payoff, R, to obtain an expected utility value of the game (rather than expected dollar value), we have, calling $V(R)$ the expected utility,

$$V(R) = \sum_{n=0}^{\infty} Pr(n) \log[R(n)] = \sum_{n=0}^{\infty} (\tfrac{1}{2})^{n+1} \log(2^n) \approx 0.866$$

Figure 5B.1 depicts graphically the relationship between wealth and the utility value of wealth that is consistent with this notion of decreasing marginal utility.

Individuals have different rates of decrease in their marginal utility of wealth. What is constant is the *principle* that per-dollar utility decreases with wealth. Functions that exhibit the property of decreasing per-unit value as the number of units grows are called concave. A simple example is the log function, familiar from high school mathematics. Of course, a log function will not fit all investors, but it is consistent with the risk aversion that we assume for all investors.

Now consider the following simple prospect:

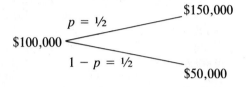

This is a fair game in that the expected profit is zero. Suppose, however, that the curve in Figure 5B.1 represents the investor's utility value of wealth, assuming a log utility function. Figure 5B.2 shows this curve with the numerical values marked.

Figure 5B.2 shows that the loss in utility from losing $50,000 exceeds the gain from winning $50,000. Consider the gain first. With probability $p = .5$, wealth goes from $100,000 to $150,000. Using the log utility function, utility goes from $\log(100,000) = 11.51$ to $\log(150,000) = 11.92$, the distance G on the graph. This gain is $G = 11.92 - 11.51 = .41$. In expected utility terms, then, the gain is $pG = .5 \times .41 = .21$.

FIGURE 5B.1

Utility of wealth with a log utility function.

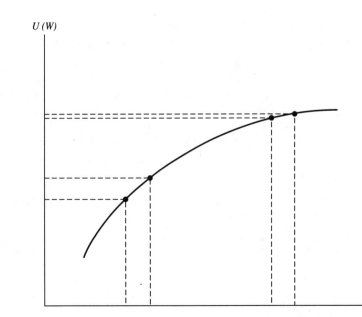

FIGURE 5B.2

Fair games and expected utility.

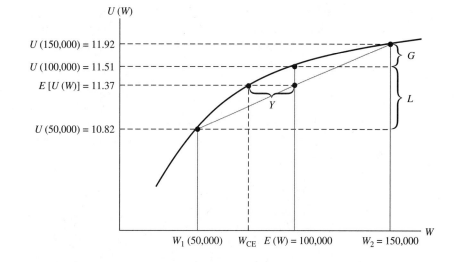

Now consider the possibility of coming up on the short end of the prospect. In that case, wealth goes from $100,000 to $50,000. The loss in utility, the distance L on the graph, is $L = \log(100,000) - \log(50,000) = 11.51 - 10.82 = .69$. Thus the loss in expected utility terms is $(1 - p)L = .5 \times .69 = .35$, which exceeds the gain in expected utility from the possibility of winning the game.

We compute the expected utility from the risky prospect:

$$E[U(W)] = pU(W_1) + (1 - p)U(W_2)$$
$$= \tfrac{1}{2}\log(50,000) + \tfrac{1}{2}\log(150,000)$$
$$= 11.37$$

If the prospect is rejected, the utility value of the (sure) $100,000 is $\log(100,000) = 11.51$, greater than that of the fair game (11.37). Hence the risk-averse investor will reject the fair game.

Using a specific investor utility function (such as the log utility) allows us to compute the certainty equivalent value of the risky prospect to a given investor, Mary Smith. This is the amount that, if received with certainty, the investor would consider equally attractive as the risky prospect.

If log utility describes the investor's preferences toward wealth outcomes, then Figure 5B.2 can also tell us what is, for her, the dollar value of the prospect. We ask, "What sure level of wealth has a utility value of 11.37 (which equals the expected utility from the prospect)?" A horizontal line drawn at the level 11.37 intersects the utility curve at the level of wealth W_{CE}. This means that

$$\log(W_{CE}) = 11.37$$

which implies that

$$W_{CE} = e^{11.37}$$
$$= \$86,681.86$$

W_{CE} is therefore the certainty equivalent of the prospect. The distance Y in Figure 5B.2 is the penalty, or the downward adjustment, to the expected profit that is attributable to the risk of the prospect.

$$
\begin{aligned}
Y &= E(W) - W_{CE} \\
&= \$100,000 - \$86,681.86 \\
&= \$13,318.13
\end{aligned}
$$

Smith views $86,681.56 for certain as being equal in utility value as $100,000 at risk. Therefore she would be indifferent between the two.

Concept Check

Question 5B.1. Suppose the utility function is $U(W) = \sqrt{W}$.
a. What is the utility level at wealth levels $50,000 and $150,000?
b. What is expected utility if p still equals .5?
c. What is the certainty equivalent of the risky prospect?
d. Does this utility function also display risk aversion?
e. Does this utility function display more or less risk aversion than the log utility function?

Does revealed behaviour of investors demonstrate risk aversion? Looking at prices and past rates of return in financial markets, we can answer with a resounding "yes." With remarkable consistency, riskier bonds are sold at lower prices than are safer ones with otherwise similar characteristics. Riskier stocks also have provided higher average rates of return over long periods of time than less risky assets such as T-bills. For example, over the 1957–1990 period, the average rate of return on the TSE 300 portfolio exceeded the T-bill return by about 2.9 percent per year.

It is abundantly clear from financial data that the average, or representative, investor exhibits substantial risk aversion. For readers who recognize that financial assets are priced to compensate for risk by providing a risk premium and at the same time feel the urge for some gambling, we have a constructive recommendation: Direct your gambling desire to investment in financial markets. As Von Neumann once said, "The stock market is a casino with the odds in your favour." A small risk-seeking investment may provide all the excitement you want with a positive expected return to boot!

Problems: Appendix B

1. Suppose that your wealth is $250,000. You buy a $200,000 house and invest the remainder in a risk-free asset paying an annual interest rate of 6 percent. There is a probability of .001 that your house will burn to the ground and its value be reduced to zero. With a log utility of end-of-year wealth, how much would you be willing to pay for insurance (at the beginning of the year)?

(Assume that, if the house does not burn down, its end-of-year value still will be $200,000.)

2. If the cost of insuring your house is $1 per $1,000 of value, what will be the certainty equivalent of your end-of-year wealth if you insure your house at:
   a. ½ its value.
   b. Its full value.
   c. 1½ times its value.

CHAPTER 6

Capital Allocation Between the Risky Asset and the Risk-Free Asset

Portfolio managers seek to achieve the best possible trade-off between risk and return. A top-down analysis of their strategies starts with the broadest decisions concerning portfolio composition and progresses to ever-finer details about the exact make-up of the portfolio.

For example, the **capital allocation decision** is the choice of the proportion of the overall portfolio to place in safe but low-return money market securities versus in risky but higher-return securities like stocks. Given the fraction of funds apportioned to risky investments, the investor next makes an **asset allocation decision,** which describes the distribution of risky investments across broad asset classes like stocks, bonds, real estate, foreign assets, and so on. Finally, the **security selection decision** describes the choice of which particular securities to hold within each asset class.

The top-down analysis of portfolio construction has much to recommend it. Most institutional investors follow a top-down approach. Capital allocation and asset allocation decisions will be made at a high organizational level with the choice of the specific securities to hold within each asset class delegated to particular portfolio managers. Individual investors typically follow a less structured approach to investment management, but they too typically give priority to broader allocation issues. For example, an individual's first decision is usually how much of his or her wealth must be left in a safe bank or money market account. The box on page 175 describes asset allocation for the individual.

This chapter treats the broadest investment decision, capital allocation between risk-free assets versus the risky portion of the portfolio. We will take the composition of the risky portfolio as given and refer to it as ''the'' risky asset. In Chapter 7 we will examine how the composition of the risky portfolio may best be determined. For now, however, we start our top-down journey by asking how an investor decides how much to invest in the risky versus the risk-free asset.

Asset Allocation Works Once Confusion Cleared

Greater Return at Less Risk Is Possible with Right Strategy

"Asset allocation"—an overused, misused, confused term.

Ever since Harry Markowitz won a Nobel Prize in 1990 for his work on diversification in an investment portfolio, asset allocation has been a buzzword of the financial community.

Once of interest only to pension plan managers, its appeal now is recognized by mutual fund and investment dealers. The result is a proliferation of products and services for the small investor.

Does it work? Yes, unequivocally.

However, because there is so much misinformation about asset allocation and what it can do, you can easily conclude otherwise.

Critics routinely make two mistakes: They focus on investment return and equate asset allocation with computer-driven market timing.

Return on investment is obviously important and many asset allocation services do rely on computer models. Nevertheless, the fundamental goal of asset allocation is to reduce risk in a portfolio.

The objective is lower volatility for a targeted rate of return—or higher return for a given level of risk.

If we define asset allocation as the distribution of investments among various asset classes, the first question is, "What should be included in the mix?"

Typically, the answer will be cash, bonds and stocks and, perhaps, some real estate. Some investors may add limited partnerships, options, collectibles and other personal favourites.

Once this decision is made, the next question is, "How much of each asset should be in the portfolio?" The answer is crucial to long-term performance.

A study of 91 large U.S. pension plans looked at three determinants of investment performance—asset allocation, market timing and security selection—to see which had the greatest impact. The conclusion? Over 90 percent of a portfolio's performance can be attributed to how the money was apportioned among cash, bonds and stocks.

By far, asset allocation outweighed the contribution of market timing and security selection.

How do you make the asset mix decision? Basically, there are two approaches, frequently known as strategic and tactical.

At the strategic level, your own risk tolerance and personal objectives influence the choices.

What is your investment time horizon? One year, five, 10, 25 years? For most investors, it is much longer than typically assumed, because it should also include the period after retirement.

Do you have cash or income needs? How much volatility can you bear? These kinds of considerations should drive your decision.

Tactical asset allocation is an attempt to change the asset mix, within the overall strategic guidelines, if you feel the ability exists to predict which way the markets are headed.

Using the tactical approach, a particular asset class would be overweighted or underweighted to improve overall portfolio return or minimize the downside. Market timing and sector rotation are examples of tactical asset allocation.

The research of Harry Markowitz, along with fellow Nobel Prize winner Bill Sharpe, is commonly referred to as Modern Portfolio Theory. MPT is the statistical foundation for asset allocation. It suggests that combining assets with different performance characteristics into a portfolio will increase total return or decrease volatility.

The key to this "magic of diversification" lies in the fact that all investment assets do not go up and down at the same rate or the same time. If you hold assets that do not correlate with each other, the increases in one can offset losses in another.

It is possible to quantify the expected outcome of such a combination by considering historical returns, volatility and cross-correlations of various alternatives. This takes some work but a good financial planner or investment adviser should be able to help. There are also software packages that can do the job.

If you do not want to be so involved in the deci-

(continued)

This capital allocation problem may be solved in two stages. First, we determine the risk-return trade-off encountered when choosing between the risky and risk-free assets. Then we show how risk aversion determines the optimal mix of the two assets. This analysis leads us to examine so-called passive strategies, which call for allocation of the portfolio between a (risk-free) money market fund and an index fund of common stocks.

6.1   *Risk Reduction with the Risk-Free Asset*

Throughout this chapter we will consider investors holding a risky portfolio, called *P*, and some risk-free securities such as T-bills. When we shift wealth from the risky portfolio to the risk-free asset, we do not change the relative proportions of the various risky assets within the risky portfolio. Rather, we reduce the relative weight of the risky portfolio as a whole in favour of risk-free assets.

For example, assume that the total market value of an initial portfolio is $300,000, of which $90,000 is invested in the Ready Asset money market fund, a risk-free asset for practical purposes. The remaining $210,000 is invested in risky equity securities—$113,400 in Seagram's (VO) and $96,600 in Canadian Tire (CT). The VO and CT holding is "the" risky portfolio, 54 percent in VO and 46 percent in CT:

$$\text{VO:} \quad w_1 = \frac{113{,}400}{210{,}000}$$
$$= .54$$

$$\text{CT:} \quad w_2 = \frac{96{,}600}{210{,}000}$$
$$= .46$$

The weight of the risky portfolio, P, in the **complete portfolio,** including risk-free investments, is denoted by y:

$$y = \frac{210,000}{300,000} = .7 \text{ (risky assets)}$$

$$1 - y = \frac{90,000}{300,000} = .3 \text{ (risk-free assets)}$$

The weights of each stock in the complete portfolio are as follows:

$$\text{VO:} \quad \frac{\$113,400}{\$300,000} = .378$$

$$\text{CT:} \quad \frac{\$96,600}{\$300,000} = .322$$

$$\text{Risky portfolio} \quad = .700$$

The risky portfolio is 70 percent of the complete portfolio.

Suppose that the owner of this portfolio wishes to decrease risk by reducing the allocation to the risky portfolio from $y = .7$ to $y = .56$. The risky portfolio would total only $168,000 (.56 × $300,000 = $168,000), requiring the sale of $42,000 of the original $210,000 risky holdings, with the proceeds used to purchase more shares in Ready Asset (the money market fund). Total holdings in the risk-free asset will increase to $300,000(1 − .56) = $132,000$, or the original holdings plus the new contribution to the money market fund:

$$\$90,000 + \$42,000 = \$132,000$$

The key point, however, is that we leave the proportions of each stock in the risky portfolio unchanged. Because the weights of VO and CT in the risky portfolio are .54 and .46, respectively, we sell .54 × $42,000 = $22,680 of VO and .46 × $42,000 = $19,320 of CT. After the sale the proportions of each share in the risky portfolio are in fact unchanged:

$$\text{VO:} \quad w_1 = \frac{113,400 - 22,680}{210,000 - 42,000}$$
$$= .54$$

$$\text{CT:} \quad w_2 = \frac{96,600 - 19,320}{210,000 - 42,000}$$
$$= .46$$

Rather than thinking of our risky holdings as VO and CT stock separately, we may view our holdings as if they were in a single fund that holds VO and CT in fixed proportions. In this sense we treat the risky fund as a single risky asset, that asset being a particular bundle of securities. As we shift in and out of safe assets, we simply alter our holdings of that bundle of securities commensurately.

Given this assumption, we can now turn to the desirability of reducing risk by changing the risky/risk-free asset mix, that is, reducing risk by decreasing the proportion y. As long as we do not alter the weights of each stock within the risky portfolio, the probability distribution of the rate of return on the risky portfolio remains unchanged by the asset reallocation. What will change is the probability distribution of the rate of return on the complete portfolio that consists of the risky asset and the risk-free asset.

Concept Check

> Question 1. What will be the dollar value of your position in VO, and its proportion in your overall portfolio, if you decide to hold 50 percent of your investment budget in Ready Asset?

6.2 The Risk-Free Asset

By virtue of its power to tax and control the money supply, only the government can issue default-free bonds. Actually, the default-free guarantee by itself is not sufficient to make the bonds risk-free in real terms. The only risk-free asset in real terms would be a perfectly price-indexed bond. Moreover, a default-free perfectly indexed bond offers a guaranteed real rate to an investor only if the maturity of the bond is identical to the investor's desired holding period. Even indexed bonds are subject to interest rate risk, because real interest rates change unpredictably through time. When future real rates are uncertain, so is the future price of perfectly indexed bonds.

Nevertheless, it is common practice to view Treasury bills as "the" **risk-free asset.** Their short-term nature makes their values insensitive to interest rate fluctuations. Indeed, an investor can lock in a short-term nominal return by buying a bill and holding it to maturity. The inflation uncertainty over the course of a few weeks, or even months, is negligible compared with the uncertainty of stock market returns.

In practice, most investors use a broader range of money market instruments as a risk-free asset. All the money market instruments are virtually free of interest rate risk because of their short maturities, and are fairly safe in terms of default or credit risk.

Most money market funds hold, for the most part, three types of securities: Treasury bills, bearer deposit notes (BDNs), and commercial paper (CP), differing slightly in their default risk. The yields to maturity on BDNs and CP for identical maturity, for example, are always slightly higher than those of T-bills. The pattern of this yield spread for short-term high-quality commercial paper is shown in Figure 6.1.

Money market funds have changed their relative holdings of these securities over time, but by and large, T-bills make up only about 15 percent of their portfolios. Nevertheless, the risk of such blue-chip short-term investments as BDNs and CP is miniscule compared with that of most other assets, such as

FIGURE 6.1

The pattern of the yield spread for high-quality corporate paper versus 3-month Treasury bills.

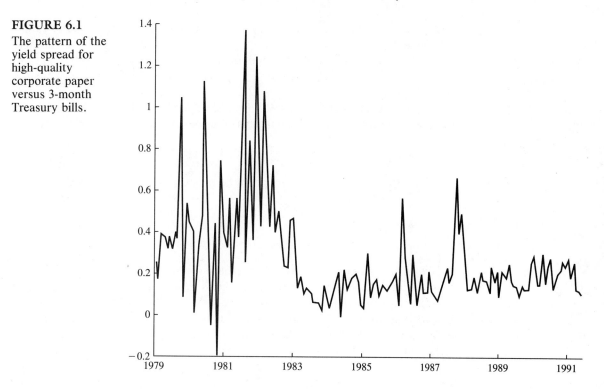

long-term corporate bonds, common stocks, or real estate. Hence, we treat money market funds as the most easily accessible risk-free asset for most investors.

6.3 *Portfolios of One Risky Asset and One Risk-Free Asset*

In this section we examine the risk-return combinations available to investors. This is the "technological" part of asset allocation; it deals with only the opportunities available to investors given the features of the broad asset markets in which they can invest. In the next section we will address the "personal" part of the problem—the specific individual's choice of the best risk-return combination from the set of feasible combinations.

Suppose that the investor has already decided on the composition of the optimal risky portfolio. The investment proportions in all the available risky assets are known. Now the final concern is with the proportion of the investment budget, y, to be allocated to the risky portfolio, P. The remaining proportion, $1 - y$, is to be invested in the risk-free asset, F.

Denote the risky rate of return by r_P and denote the expected rate of return on P by $E(r_P)$ and its standard deviation by σ_P. The rate of return on the risk-free asset is denoted as r_f. In the numerical example we assume that $E(r_P) = 15$ percent, $\sigma_P = 22$ percent, and that the risk-free rate is $r_f = 7$ percent. Thus the risk premium on the risky asset is $E(r_P) - r_f = 8$ percent.

With a proportion, y, in the risky portfolio, and $1 - y$ in the risk-free asset, the rate of return on the *complete* portfolio, denoted C, is r_C where

$$r_C = yr_P + (1 - y)r_f$$

Taking the expectation of this portfolio's rate of return,

$$\begin{aligned} E(r_C) &= yE(r_P) + (1 - y)r_f \\ &= r_f + y[E(r_P) - r_f] \\ &= .07 + y(.15 - .07) \end{aligned} \qquad \textbf{(6.1)}$$

This result is easily interpreted. The base rate of return for any portfolio is the risk-free rate. In addition, the portfolio is *expected* to earn a risk premium that depends on the risk premium of the risky portfolio, $E(r_P) - r_f$, and the investor's exposure to the risky asset, denoted by y. Investors are assumed to be risk averse and thus unwilling to take on a risky position without a positive risk premium.

As we noted in Chapter 5, when we combine a risky asset and a risk-free asset in a portfolio, the standard deviation of that portfolio is the standard deviation of the risky asset multiplied by the weight of the risky asset in that portfolio. In our case, the complete portfolio consists of the risky asset and the risk-free asset. Since the standard deviation of the risky portfolio is $\sigma_P = .22$,

$$\begin{aligned} \sigma_C &= y\sigma_P \\ &= .22y \end{aligned} \qquad \textbf{(6.2)}$$

which makes sense because the standard deviation of the portfolio is proportional to both the standard deviation of the risky asset and the proportion invested in it. In sum, the rate of return of the complete portfolio will have expected return $E(r_C) = r_f + y[E(r_P) - r_f] = .07 + .08y$ and standard deviation $\sigma_C = .22y$.

The next step is to plot the portfolio characteristics (as a function of y) in the expected return–standard deviation plane. This is done in Figure 6.2. The expected return–standard deviation combination for the risk-free asset, F, appears on the vertical axis because the standard deviation is zero. The risky asset, P, is plotted with a standard deviation, $\sigma_P = .22$, and expected return of .15. If an investor chooses to invest solely in the risky asset, then $y = 1.0$, and the resulting portfolio is P. If the chosen position is $y = 0$, then $1 - y = 1.0$, and the resulting portfolio is the risk-free portfolio F.

What about the more interesting midrange portfolios where y lies between zero and 1? These portfolios will graph on the straight line connecting points F and P. The slope of that line is simply $[E(r_P) - r_f]/\sigma_P$ (or rise/run), in this case $.08/.22$.

FIGURE 6.2
Expected
return–standard
deviation
combinations.

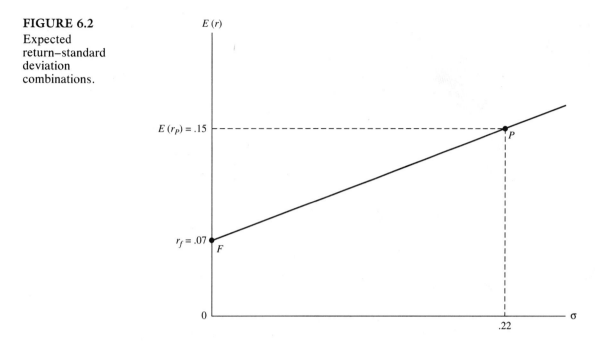

The conclusion is straightforward. Increasing the fraction of the overall portfolio invested in the risky asset increases the expected return by the risk premium of equation 6.1, which is .08. It also increases portfolio standard deviation according to equation 6.2 at the rate .22. The extra return per extra risk is thus .08/.22 = .36.

To derive the exact equation for the straight line between F and P, we rearrange equation 6.2 to find that $y = \sigma_C/\sigma_P$, and substitute for y in equation 6.1 to describe the expected return–standard deviation trade-off:

$$E[r_C(y)] = r_f + y[E(r_P) - r_f]$$

$$= r_f + \frac{\sigma_C}{.22} [E(r_P) - r_f]$$

$$= .07 + \frac{.08}{.22} \sigma_C$$

Thus the expected return of the portfolio as a function of its standard deviation is a straight line, with intercept r_f and slope as follows:

$$S = \frac{E(r_P) - r_f}{\sigma_P}$$

$$= \frac{.08}{.22}$$

Figure 6.3 graphs the *investment opportunity set*, which is the set of feasible expected return and standard deviation pairs of all portfolios resulting from different values of y. The graph is a straight line originating at r_f and going through the point labelled P.

FIGURE 6.3

The investment opportunity set with a risky asset and a risk-free asset.

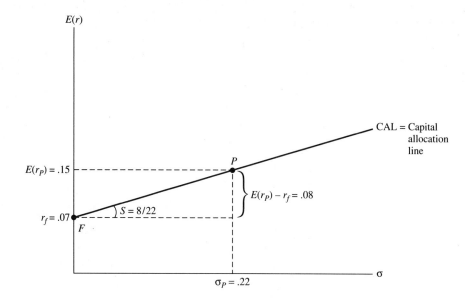

This straight line is called the **capital allocation line** (CAL). It depicts all the risk-return combinations available to investors. The slope of the CAL, S, equals the increase in the expected return of the chosen portfolio per unit of additional standard deviation—in other words, the measure of extra return per extra risk. For this reason, the slope also is called the **reward-to-variability ratio.**

A portfolio equally divided between the risky asset and the risk-free asset, that is, where $y = .5$, will have an expected rate of return of $E(r_C) = .07 + .5 \times .08 = .11$, implying a risk premium of 4 percent, and a standard deviation of $\sigma_C = .5 \times .22 = .11$, or 11 percent. It will plot on the line FP midway between F and P. The reward-to-variability ratio is $S = .08/.22 = .36$.

Concept Check	Question 2. Can the reward-to-variability ratio, $S = [E(r_C) - r_f]/\sigma$, of any combination of the risky asset and the risk-free asset be different from the ratio for the risky asset taken alone, $[E(r_P) - r_f]/\sigma$, which in this case is .36?

What about points on the line to the right of portfolio P in the investment opportunity set? If investors can borrow at the (risk-free) rate of $r_f = 7$ percent, they can construct portfolios that may be plotted on the CAL to the right of P.

Suppose the investment budget is $300,000, and our investor borrows an additional $120,000, investing the total available funds in the risky asset. This is a *leveraged* position in the risky asset; it is financed in part by borrowing. In that case

$$y = \frac{420,000}{300,000}$$
$$= 1.4$$

and $1 - y = 1 - 1.4 = -.4$, reflecting a short position in the risk-free asset, which is a borrowing position. Rather than lending at a 7 percent interest rate, the investor borrows at 7 percent. The distribution of the portfolio rate of return still exhibits the same reward-to-variability ratio:

$$E(r_C) = .07 + (1.4 \times .08) = .182$$
$$\sigma_C = 1.4 \times .22 = .308$$
$$S = \frac{E(r_C) - r_f}{\sigma_C}$$
$$= \frac{.182 - .07}{.308} = .36$$

As one might expect, the leveraged portfolio has a higher standard deviation than does an unleveraged position in the risky asset.

Of course, nongovernment investors cannot borrow at the risk-free rate. The risk of a borrower's default causes lenders to demand higher interest rates on loans. Therefore, the nongovernment investor's borrowing cost will exceed the lending rate of $r_f = 7$ percent. Suppose that the borrowing rate is $r_f^B = 9$ percent. Then, in the borrowing range the reward-to-variability ratio, the slope of the CAL will be $[E(r_P) - r_f^B]/\sigma_P = .06/.22 = .27$. The CAL will therefore be "kinked" at point P as shown in Figure 6.4. To the left of P the investor is

FIGURE 6.4

The opportunity set with differential borrowing and lending rates.

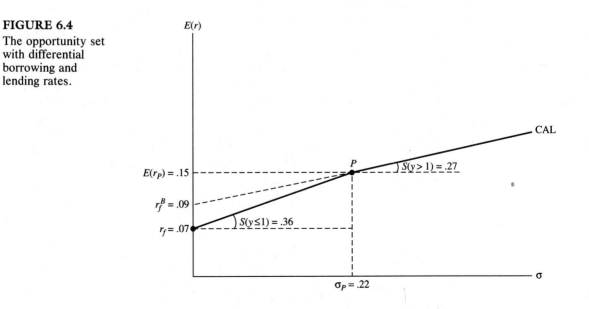

lending at 7 percent, and the slope of the CAL is .36. To the right of P, where $y > 1$, the investor is borrowing to finance extra investments in the risky asset, and the slope is .27.

In practice, borrowing to invest in the risky portfolio is easy and straightforward if you have a margin account with a broker. All you have to do is tell your broker that you want to buy "on margin." Margin purchases may not exceed 50 percent of the purchase value. Therefore, if your net worth in the account is $300,000, the broker is allowed to lend you up to $300,000 to purchase additional stock.[1] You would then have $600,000 on the asset side of your account and $300,000 on the liability side, resulting in $y = 2.0$.

Concept Check
========

> Question 3. Suppose that there is a shift upward in the expected rate of return on the risky asset, from 15 percent to 17 percent. If all other parameters remain unchanged, what will be the slope of the CAL for $y \leqslant 1$ and $y > 1$?

6.4 *Risk Tolerance and Asset Allocation*

We have shown how to develop the CAL, the graph of all feasible risk-return combinations available from different asset-allocation choices. The investor confronting the CAL now must choose one optimal combination from the set of feasible choices. This choice entails a trade-off between risk and return. Individual investor differences in risk aversion imply that, given an identical opportunity set (as described by a risk-free rate and a reward-to-variability ratio), different investors will choose different positions in the risky asset. In particular, the more risk-averse investors will choose to hold less of the risky asset and more of the risk-free asset.

In Chapter 5 we showed that the utility an investor derives from a portfolio with a given probability distribution of rates of return can be described by the expected return and variance of the portfolio rate of return. Specifically, we developed the following representation:

$$U = E(r) - \tfrac{1}{2}A\sigma^2$$

---

[1] Margin purchases require the investor to maintain the securities in a margin account with the broker. If the value of the securities declines below a maintenance margin, a *margin call* is sent out, requiring a deposit to bring the net worth of the account up to the appropriate level. If the margin call is not met, regulations mandate that some or all of the securities be sold by the broker and the proceeds used to reestablish the required margin. See Chapter 3, Section 3.5, for a further discussion.

where A is the coefficient of risk aversion. We interpret this expression to say that the utility from a portfolio increases as the expected rate of return increases, and it decreases when the variance increases. The relative magnitude of these changes is governed by the coefficient of risk aversion A. For risk-neutral investors, $A = 0$. Higher levels of risk aversion are reflected in larger values for A.

An investor who faces a risk-free rate, r_f, and a risky portfolio with expected return $E(r_P)$ and standard deviation σ_P will find that, for any choice of y, the expected return of the complete portfolio is given by equation 6.1, part of which we repeat here:

$$E(r_C) = r_f + y[E(r_P) - r_f]$$

From equation 6.2, the variance of the overall portfolio is

$$\sigma_C^2 = y^2 \sigma_P^2$$

The investor attempts to maximize his or her utility level, U, by choosing the best allocation to the risky asset, y. Typically, we write this problem as follows:

$$\underset{y}{\text{Max}}\ U = E(r_C) - \tfrac{1}{2} A \sigma_C^2 = r_f + y[E(r_P) - r_f] - \tfrac{1}{2} y^2 A \sigma_P^2$$

where A is the coefficient of risk aversion.

Students of calculus will remember that the maximization problem is solved by setting the derivative of this expression to zero. Doing so and solving for y yields the optimal position for risk-averse investors in the risky asset, y^*, as follows:[2]

$$y^* = \frac{E(r_P) - r_f}{A \sigma_P^2} \tag{6.3}$$

This solution shows that the optimal position in the risky asset is, as one would expect, *inversely* proportional to the level of risk aversion and the level of risk, as measured by the variance, and directly proportional to the risk premium offered by the risky asset.

Going back to our numerical example [$r_f = 7$ percent, $E(r_P) = 15$ percent, and $\sigma_P = 22$ percent], the optimal solution for an investor with a coefficient of risk aversion, $A = 4$, is

$$y^* = \frac{.15 - .07}{4 \times .22^2}$$
$$= .41$$

In other words, this particular investor will invest 41 percent of the investment budget in the risky asset and 59 percent in the risk-free asset. (Note that r_f, $E(r_P)$, and σ_P must be expressed as decimals, or else it is necessary to change the scale of A.)

---

[2] The derivative with respect to y equals $E(r_P) - r_f - yA\sigma_P^2$. Setting this expression equal to zero and solving for y yields equation 6.3.

With 41 percent invested in the risky portfolio, the rate of return of the complete portfolio will have an expected return and standard deviation as follows:

$$E(r_C) = .07 + .41 \times (.15 - .07)$$
$$= .1028$$
$$\sigma_C = .41 \times .22$$
$$= .0902$$

The risk premium of the complete portfolio is $E(r_C) - r_f = 3.28$ percent, which is obtained by taking on a portfolio with a standard deviation of 9.02 percent. Notice that $3.28/9.02 = .36$, which is the reward-to-variability ratio assumed for this problem.

A less mathematical way of presenting this decision problem is to use indifference curve analysis. Recall from Chapter 5 that the indifference curve is a graph in the expected return–standard deviation plane of all points that result in a given level of utility. The curve then displays the investor's required trade-off between expected return and standard deviation.

For example, suppose that the initial portfolio under consideration is the risky asset itself, $y = 1$. The dark curve in Figure 6.5 represents the indifference curve for an investor with a degree of risk aversion, $A = 4$, that passes through the risky asset with $E(r_P) = 15$ percent and $\sigma_P = 22$ percent. The light curve, by contrast, shows an indifference curve going through P with a smaller degree of risk aversion, $A = 2$. The dashed indifference curve is flatter, that is, the more risk-tolerant (less risk-averse) investor requires a smaller increase in expected return to compensate for a given increase in standard deviation. The intercept of the indifference curve with the vertical axis is the *certainty equivalent* of the risky portfolio's expected rate of return because it gives a risk-free return with

FIGURE 6.5

Two indifference curves through a risky asset.

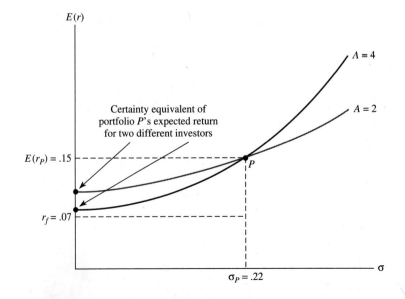

FIGURE 6.6

A set of indifference curves.

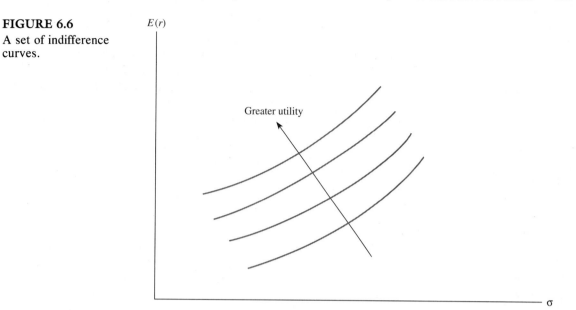

the same utility as the risky portfolio. Notice in Figure 6.5 that the less risk-averse investor (with $A = 2$) has a higher certainty equivalent for a risky portfolio such as P than the more risk-averse investor ($A = 4$).

Indifference curves can be drawn for many benchmark portfolios, representing various levels of utility. Figure 6.6 shows this set of indifference curves.

To show how to use indifference curve analysis to determine the choice of the optimal portfolio for a specific CAL, Figure 6.7 superimposes the graphs of

FIGURE 6.7

The graphical solution to the portfolio decision.

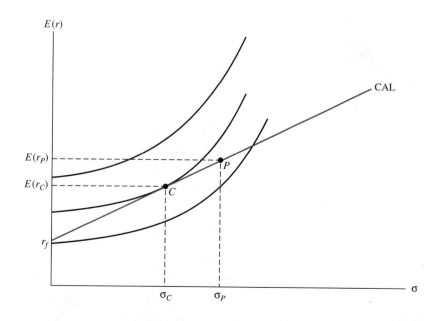

the indifference curves on the graph of the investment opportunity set, the CAL.

The investor seeks the position with the highest feasible level of utility, represented by the highest possible indifference curve that touches the investment opportunity set. This is the indifference curve tangent to the CAL.

This optimal overall portfolio is represented by point C on the investment opportunity set. Such a graphical approach yields the same solution as the algebraic approach:

$$E(r_C) = .1028$$

and

$$\sigma_C = .0902$$

which yields $y^* = .41$.

In summary, the asset allocation process can be broken down into two steps: (1) determine the CAL, and (2) find the point of highest utility along that line.

Concept Check

Question 4.
a. If an investor's coefficient of risk aversion is $A = 3$, how does the optimal asset mix change? What are the new $E(r_C)$ and σ_C?
b. Suppose that the borrowing rate, $r_f^B = 9$ percent, is greater than the lending rate, $r_f = 7$ percent. Show, graphically, how the optimal portfolio choice of some investors will be affected by the higher borrowing rate. Which investors will *not* be affected by the borrowing rate?

6.5   *Passive Strategies: The Capital Market Line*

The CAL is derived with the risk-free asset and "the" risky portfolio P. Determination of the assets to include in risky portfolio P may result from a passive or an active strategy. A **passive strategy** describes a portfolio decision that avoids *any* direct or indirect security analysis.[3] At first blush, a passive strategy would appear to be naive. As will become apparent, however, forces of supply and demand in large capital markets may make such a strategy a reasonable choice for many investors.

---

[3] By "indirect security analysis" we mean the delegation of that responsibility to an intermediary, such as a professional money manager.

TABLE 6.1   Annual Rates of Return for Common Stocks and 3-Month Bills, and the Risk Premium Over Bills on Common Stock

	Common Stocks		3-Month Bills		Risk Premium over Bills on Common Stocks	
	Mean	Standard Deviation	Mean	Standard Deviation	Mean	Standard Deviation
1957–1967	9.22	17.10	3.85	.76	5.37	17.53
1968–1978	8.89	16.11	6.66	1.82	.23	16.47
1979–1990	13.40	18.34	12.03	3.03	1.37	19.60
1957–1990	**10.59**	**16.85**	**7.65**	**.16**	**2.94**	**17.50**

Data from *ScotiaMcLeod's Handbook of Canadian Debt Market Indices, 1947–1990*. Reprinted by permission.

A natural candidate for a passively held risky asset would be a well-diversified portfolio of common stocks. We have already said that a passive strategy requires that we devote no resources to acquiring information on any individual stock or group of stocks, so we must follow a "neutral" diversification strategy. One way is to select a diversified portfolio of stocks that mirrors the value of the corporate sector of the Canadian economy. This results in a value-weighted portfolio in which, for example, the proportion invested in Seagram's stock will be the ratio of Seagram's total market value to the market value of all listed stocks.

The most frequently used value-weighted stock portfolio in Canada is the Toronto Stock Exchange's composite index of the 300 large capitalization Canadian corporations[4] (TSE 300). Table 6.1 shows the historical record of this portfolio. The last pair of columns shows the average risk premium over T-bills and its standard deviation. The risk premium of 2.94 percent and standard deviation of 17.5 percent over the entire period correspond to the figures of 8 percent and 22 percent we assumed for the risky portfolio that we used as an example in Section 6.4.

We call the capital allocation line provided by one-month T-bills and a broad index of common stocks the **capital market line** (CML). A passive strategy generates an investment opportunity set that is represented by the CML.

How reasonable is it for an investor to pursue a passive strategy? Of course, we cannot answer such a question without comparing the strategy to the costs and benefits accruing to an active portfolio strategy. Some thoughts are relevant at this point, however.

First, the alternative active strategy is not free. Whether you choose to invest the time and cost to acquire the information needed to generate an

---

[4] For a discussion of value-weighted Canadian stock portfolios in asset allocation see Paul Potvin, "Passive Management, the TSE 300 and the Toronto 35 Stock Indexes," *Canadian Investment Review* 5, 1 (Spring 1992).

optimal active portfolio of risky assets, or whether you delegate the task to a professional who will charge a fee, construction of an active portfolio is more expensive than construction of a passive one. The passive portfolio requires only small commissions on purchases of T-bills (or zero commissions if you purchase bills directly from the government) and management fees to a mutual fund company that offers a market index fund to the public. First Canadian's Equity Index Fund, for example, mimics the TSE 300 index. It purchases shares of the firms constituting the TSE 300 in proportion to the market values of the outstanding equity of each firm, and therefore essentially replicates the TSE 300 index. The fund thus duplicates the performance of this market index. It has low operating expenses (as a percentage of assets) when compared to other mutual stock funds precisely because it requires minimal managerial effort.

A second reason supporting a passive strategy is the free-rider benefit. If we assume there are many active, knowledgeable investors who quickly bid up prices of undervalued assets and bid down overvalued assets (by selling), we have to conclude that at any time most assets will be fairly priced. Therefore, a well-diversified portfolio of common stock will be a reasonably fair buy, and the passive strategy may not be inferior to that of the average active investor. (We will explain this assumption and provide a more comprehensive analysis of the relative success of passive strategies in later chapters.)

To summarize, however, a passive strategy involves investment in two passive portfolios: virtually risk-free, short-term T-bills (or, alternatively, a money market fund), and a fund of common stocks that mimics a broad market index. The capital allocation line representing such a strategy is called the *capital market line*. Historically, based on data from 1957 to 1990, the passive risky portfolio offered an average risk premium of 2.94 percent and a standard deviation of 17.5 percent, resulting in a reward-to-variability ratio of .17. Passive investors allocate their investment budgets among instruments according to their degree of risk aversion.

We can use our analysis to deduce a typical investor's risk-aversion parameter. In October 1991, the total market value of the TSE 300 stocks was about 1.7 times the market value of all outstanding T-bills of less than a year's maturity. If we ignore all other assets (e.g., long-term bonds, foreign securities, and real estate), and pretend that all investors followed a passive strategy, then the average investor's position in the risky asset (the TSE 300) was

$$y = \frac{1.7}{1 + 1.7}$$
$$= .63$$

What degree of risk aversion must investors have for this portfolio to be optimal? Assuming that the average investor uses the historical average risk premium (2.94 percent) and standard deviation (17.5 percent) to forecast future return and standard deviation, and noting that the weight in the risky portfolio was .63, we can work out the average investor's risk tolerance as follows:

$$y^* = \frac{E(r_M) - r_f}{A\sigma_M^2}$$
$$= .63$$
$$= \frac{.0294}{A \times .175^2}$$

which implies a coefficient of risk aversion of

$$A = \frac{.0294}{.63 \times .175^2}$$
$$= 1.52$$

This is, of course, mere speculation. We have assumed without basis that the average 1991 investor held the naive view that historical average rates of return and standard deviations are the best estimates of expected rates of return and risk, looking to the future. To the extent that in 1991 the average investor took advantage of contemporary information in addition to simple historical data, our estimate of $A = 1.52$ would be an unjustified inference.[5]

The equivalent figures for the United States, if Standard & Poor's composite index of the 500 largest corporations (S&P 500) is used as the value-weighted portfolio, yield a significantly different picture. Over the period 1926–1987, the risk premium of that portfolio over one-month T-bills averaged 8.5 percent, with a standard deviation of 21.4 percent. In 1987, the total market value of the S&P 500 stocks was about four times as large as the market value of all outstanding T-bills of less than six months' maturity. These numbers correspond to an average investor position of .8 in the risky asset (the S&P 500), yielding a coefficient of risk aversion of 2.32. It should be noted that the broad range of studies that take into account the full range of available assets places the degree of risk aversion for the representative U.S. investor in the range of 2.0–4.0.[6]

Concept Check	Question 5. Suppose that expectations about the TSE 300 index and the T-bill rate are the same as they were in 1991, but you find that a greater proportion is invested in T-bills today than in 1991. What can you conclude about the change in risk tolerance over the years since 1991?

---

[5] A study by Kryzanowski and To estimated the risk-aversion coefficient for a variety of Canadian households. Their analysis is cross-sectional, and takes into account the effects of differential tax rates and inflation. Hence, the estimates are not directly comparable to the value of *A* that we found. See Lawrence Kryzanowski and Minh Chau To, "Revealed Preferences for Risky Assets in Imperfect Markets," *Canadian Journal of Administrative Sciences,* 3, 2 (December 1986).

[6] See for example, I. Friend and M. Blume, "The Demand for Risky Assets," *American Economic Review* 64 (1974); or S. J. Grossman and R. J. Shiller, "The Determinants of the Variability of Stock Market Prices," *American Economic Review* 71 (1981).

Summary

1. Shifting funds from the risky portfolio to the risk-free asset is the simplest way to reduce risk. Other methods involve diversification of the risky portfolio (we take up these methods in later chapters).

2. T-bills provide a perfectly risk-free asset in nominal terms only. Nevertheless, the standard deviation of real rates on short-term T-bills is small compared to that of other assets such as long-term bonds and common stocks, so for the purpose of our analysis we consider T-bills as the risk-free asset. Money market funds hold, in addition to T-bills, short-term and relatively safe obligations such as CP and CDs. These entail some default risk, but again the additional risk is small relative to most other risky assets. For convenience, we often refer to money market funds as risk-free assets.

3. An investor's risky portfolio (the risky asset) can be characterized by its reward-to-variability ratio, $S = [E(r_P) - r_f]/\sigma_P$. This ratio is also the slope of the CAL, the line that, when graphed, goes from the risk-free asset through the risky asset. All combinations of the risky asset and the risk-free asset lie on this line. All things considered, an investor would prefer a steeper-sloping CAL, because that means higher expected return for any level of risk. If the borrowing rate is greater than the lending rate, the CAL will be "kinked" at the point of the risky asset.

4. The investor's degree of risk aversion is characterized by the slope of his or her indifference curve. Indifference curves show, at any level of expected return and risk, the required risk premium for taking on one additional percentage of standard deviation. More risk-averse investors have steeper indifference curves; that is, they require a greater risk premium for taking on more risk.

5. The exact optimal position, y^*, in the risky asset, is proportional to the risk premium and inversely proportional to the variance and degree of risk aversion:

$$y^* = \frac{E(r_P) - r_f}{A\sigma_P^2}$$

Graphically, this portfolio represents the point at which the indifference curve is tangent to the CAL.

6. A passive investment strategy disregards security analysis, targeting instead the risk-free asset and a broad portfolio of risky assets, such as the TSE 300 stock portfolio. If in 1991 investors took the mean historical return and standard deviation of the TSE 300 as proxies for its expected return and standard deviation, then the market values of outstanding T-bills and the TSE 300 stocks would imply a degree of risk aversion of about $A = 1.5$ for the average investor. The equivalent figure for U.S. investors in 1987 was 2.3, which is in line with other studies that estimate typical risk aversion for U.S. investors in the range of 2.0 through 4.0.

Key terms

Capital allocation decision	Risk-free asset
Asset allocation decision	Capital allocation line
Security selection decision	Reward-to-variability ratio
Risky asset	Passive strategy
Complete portfolio	Capital market line

Selected readings

The classic article describing the asset allocation choice, whereby investors choose the optimal fraction of their wealth to place in risk-free assets, is:

Tobin, James. "Liquidity Preference as Behavior towards Risk." *Review of Economic Studies* 25 (February 1958).

A three-asset class asset allocation problem is considered in:

Bodie, Zvi; Kane, Alex; and McDonald, Robert. "Inflation and the Role of Bonds in Investor Portfolios." In Benjamin Friedman (editor), *Corporate Capital Structures in the United States.* Chicago: University of Chicago Press, 1985.

Practitioner-oriented approaches to asset allocation may be found in:

Maginn, John L.; and Tuttle, Donald L. *Managing Investment Portfolios: A Dynamic Process,* 2nd edition. New York: Warren, Gorham, & Lamont, Inc., 1990.

Similar practitioner-oriented Canadian contributions include:

Auger, Robert; and Denis Parisien. "Understanding Asset Allocation." *Canadian Investment Review* 4, 1 (Spring 1991).

Potvin, Paul. "Passive Management, the TSE 300, and the Toronto 35 Stock Indexes." *Canadian Investment Review* 5, 1 (Spring 1992).

Problems

You manage a risky portfolio with an expected rate of return of 17 percent and a standard deviation of 27 percent. The T-bill rate is 7 percent.

1. Your client chooses to invest 70 percent of a portfolio in your fund and 30 percent in a T-bill money market fund. What is the expected value and standard deviation of the rate of return on your client's portfolio?

2. Suppose that your risky portfolio includes the following investments in the given proportions:
   Stock *A:* 27 percent
   Stock *B:* 33 percent
   Stock *C:* 40 percent
   What are the investment proportions of your client's overall portfolio, including the position in T-bills?

3. What is the reward-to-variability ratio (*S*) of your risky portfolio?

4. Draw the CAL of your portfolio on an expected return–standard deviation diagram. What is the slope of the CAL? Show the position of your client on your fund's CAL.

5. Suppose that your client decides to invest in your portfolio a proportion *y* of the total investment budget so that the overall portfolio will have an expected rate of return of 15 percent.

    a. What is the proportion *y*?

    b. What are your client's investment proportions in your three stocks and the T-bill fund?

    c. What is the standard deviation of the rate of return on your client's portfolio?

  6. Suppose that your client prefers to invest in your fund a proportion *y* that maximizes the expected return on the overall portfolio subject to the constraint that the overall portfolio's standard deviation will not exceed 20 percent.

    a. What is the investment proportion (*y*)?

    b. What is the expected rate of return on the overall portfolio?

  7. Your client's degree of risk aversions is $A = 3.5$.

    a. What proportion (*y*) of the total investment should be invested in your fund?

    b. What is the expected value and standard deviation of the rate of return on your client's optimized portfolio?

You estimate that a passive portfolio (i.e., one invested in a risky portfolio that mimics the TSE 300 stock index) yields an expected rate of return of 13 percent with a standard deviation of 25 percent.

  8. Draw the CML and your fund's CAL on an expected return–standard deviation diagram.

    a. What is the slope of the CML?

    b. Characterize in one short paragraph the advantage(s) of your fund over the passive fund.

  9. Your client ponders whether to switch the 70 percent that is invested in your fund to the passive portfolio.

    a. Explain to your client the disadvantage(s) of the switch.

    b. Show your client the maximum fee you could charge (as a percentage of the investment in your fund deducted at the end of the year) that would still leave him or her at least as well off investing in your fund as in the passive one. (Hint: The fee will lower the slope of your client's CAL by reducing the expected return net of the fee.)

  10. Consider the client in question 7 with $A = 3.5$.

    a. If the client chose to invest in the passive portfolio, what proportion (*y*) would be selected?

    b. What fee (percentage of the investment in your fund, deducted at the end of the year) can you charge to make the client indifferent between your fund and the passive strategy?

  11. Look at the data in Table 6.1 on the average risk premium of the TSE 300 over T-bills, and the standard deviation of that risk premium. Suppose that the TSE 300 is your risky portfolio.

    a. If your risk-aversion coefficient is 2 and you believe that the entire 1957–1990 period is representative of future expected performance, what fraction of your portfolio should be allocated to T-bills and what fraction to equity?

    b. What if you believe that the 1979–1990 period is representative?

    c. What do you conclude upon comparing your answers to (a) and (b)?

12. What do you think would happen to the expected return on stocks if investors perceived higher volatility in the equity market? Relate your answer to equation 6.3.

CHAPTER 7

Optimal Risky Portfolios

In Chapter 6 we discussed the capital allocation decision. That decision governs how an investor chooses between risk-free assets and "the" optimal portfolio of risky assets. This chapter explains how to construct that optimal risky portfolio.

We begin at the simplest level, with a discussion of how diversification can reduce the variability of portfolio returns. After establishing this basic point, we examine efficient diversification strategies at the asset allocation and security selection levels. We start with a simple, restricted example of asset allocation that excludes the risk-free asset. To that effect we use two risky mutual funds: a long-term bond fund and a stock fund. With this example we investigate the relationship between investment proportions and the resulting portfolio expected return and standard deviation. We then add a risk-free asset (e.g., T-bills) to the menu of assets and determine the optimal asset allocation. We do so by combining the principles of optimal allocation between risky assets and risk-free assets (from Chapter 6) with the risky portfolio construction methodology.

Moving from asset allocation to security selection we first generalize our discussion of restricted asset allocation (with only two risky assets) to a universe of many risky securities. This generalization relies on the celebrated Markowitz portfolio selection model[1] that identifies the set of efficient stock portfolios from the available universe of securities. Proceeding to capital allocation we show how the best attainable capital allocation line emerges from the Markowitz algorithm. We pause to explain why portfolio optimization is often conducted in two stages, asset allocation and security selection, and discuss the potential inefficiency that may result from separating the asset allocation decision from security selection.

Finally, in the last two appendices to this chapter, we examine common fallacies regarding the power of diversification in the contexts of the insurance principle and the notion of time diversification.

---

[1] Harry Markowitz, *Portfolio Selection: Efficient Diversification of Investments* (New York: John Wiley, 1959).

7.1 *Diversification and Portfolio Risk*

Suppose that your risky portfolio is composed of only one stock, Dominion Computing Corporation (DCC). What would be the sources of risk to this "portfolio"? You might think of two broad sources of uncertainty. First, there is the risk that comes from conditions in the general economy, such as the business cycle, the inflation rate, interest rates, and exchange rates. None of these macroeconomic factors can be predicted with certainty, and all affect the rate of return that DCC stock eventually will provide. In addition to these macroeconomic factors there are firm-specific influences, such as DCC's success in research and development, and personnel changes. These factors affect DCC without noticeably affecting other firms in the economy.

Now consider a naive **diversification** strategy, in which you include additional securities in your risky portfolio. For example, suppose that you place half of your risky portfolio in an oil and minerals firm, Energy Resources Ltd (ERL), leaving the other half in DCC. What should happen to portfolio risk? To the extent that the firm-specific influences on the two stocks differ, we should reduce portfolio risk. For example, when oil prices fall, hurting ERL, computer prices might rise, helping DCC. The two effects are off-setting, and stabilize portfolio return.

But why end diversification at only two stocks? If we diversify into many more securities, we continue to spread out our exposure to firm-specific factors, and portfolio volatility should continue to fall. Ultimately, however, even if we include a large number of risky securities in our portfolio we cannot avoid risk altogether. To the extent that virtually all securities are affected by the common macroeconomic factors, we cannot eliminate our exposure to these risk sources. For example, if all stocks are affected by the business cycle, we cannot avoid exposure to business cycle risk no matter how many stocks we hold.

When all risk is firm-specific, as in Figure 7.1**A**, diversification can reduce risk to arbitrarily low levels. The reason is that with all risk sources independent, and with the portfolio spread across many securities, the exposure to any particular source of risk is reduced to a negligible level. This is just an application of the well-known law of averages. The reduction of risk to very low levels in the case of independent risk sources is sometimes called the **insurance principle,** because of the conventional belief that an insurance company depends on the risk reduction achieved through diversification when it writes many policies insuring against many independent sources of risk, each policy being a small part of the company's overall portfolio. (See Appendix B for a discussion of the insurance principle.)

When common sources of risk affect all firms, however, even extensive diversification cannot eliminate risk. In Figure 7.1**B**, portfolio standard deviation falls as the number of securities increases, but it cannot be reduced to

FIGURE 7.1

Portfolio risk as a function of the number of stocks in the portfolio.

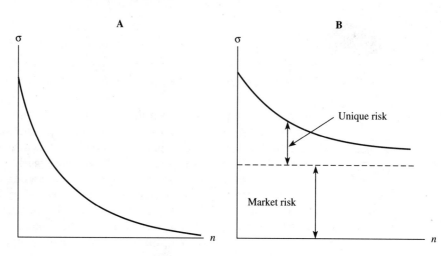

FIGURE 7.2

Portfolio diversification. The average standard deviation of returns of portfolios composed of only one stock was 49.2 percent. The average portfolio risk fell rapidly as the number of stocks included in the portfolio increased. In the limit, portfolio risk could be reduced to only 19.2 percent.

Source: Edwin J. Elton and Martin J. Gruber, *Modern Portfolio Theory and Investment Analysis,* 2d Edition (New York: John Wiley and Sons, 1989), p. 35, adapted by Meir Stotman, ''How Many Stocks Make a Diversified Portfolio,'' *Journal of Financial and Quantitative Analysis* 22 (September 1987).

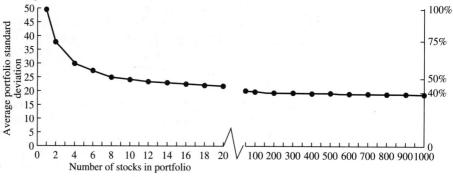

zero.[2] The risk that remains even after extensive diversification is called **market risk,** risk that is attributable to marketwide risk sources. Such risk is also called **systematic risk,** or **non-diversifiable risk.** In contrast, the risk that *can* be eliminated by diversification is called **unique risk, firm-specific risk, non-systematic risk,** or **diversifiable risk.**

This analysis is borne out by empirical studies. Figure 7.2 shows the effect of portfolio diversification, using data on NYSE stocks.[3] The figure shows the

---

[2] The interested reader can find a more rigorous demonstration of these points in Appendix A. That discussion, however, relies on tools developed later in this chapter.

[3] L. Fisher and J. H. Lorie, ''Some Studies of the Variability of Returns on Investments in Common Stocks,'' *Journal of Business,* 43 (April 1970).

average standard deviation of equally weighted portfolios constructed by selecting stocks at random as a function of the number of stocks in the portfolio. On average, portfolio risk does fall with diversification, but the power of diversification to reduce risk is limited by systematic or common sources of risk.

7.2   *Portfolios of Two Risky Assets*

In the last section we analyzed naive diversification, examining the risk of equally weighted portfolios of several securities. It is time now to study efficient diversification, whereby we construct risky portfolios to provide the lowest possible risk for any given level of expected return.

Constructing the optimal risky portfolio is a complicated statistical task. The *principles* we follow, however, are the same as those used to construct a portfolio from two risky assets only. We will analyze this easier process first and then backtrack a bit to see how we can generalize the technique to apply to more realistic cases.

Assume for this purpose that an investor is limited to two assets. To benefit from diversification, our investor chooses for the first asset shares in a mutual fund that maintains a broad portfolio of long-term debt securities (D), and for the second asset shares in a mutual fund that specializes in equities (E). The parameters of the joint probability distribution of returns is shown in Table 7.1.

A proportion denoted by w_D is invested in the bond fund, and the remainder, $1 - w_D$, denoted w_E, is invested in the stock fund. The rate of return on this portfolio will be

$$r_p = w_D r_D + w_E r_E$$

where r_p stands for the rate of return on the portfolio, r_D the return on investment in the debt fund, and r_E the return on investment in the equity fund.

As we noted in Chapter 5, the expected rate of return on the portfolio is a weighted average of expected returns on the component securities with portfolio proportions as weights:

$$E(r_p) = w_D E(r_D) + w_E E(r_E) \qquad (7.1)$$

TABLE 7.1   Descriptive Statistics for Two Assets

	Bonds (%)		Stocks (%)
Expected return, $E(r)$	8		13
Standard deviation, σ	12		20
Covariance, $Cov(r_D, r_E)$		72	
Correlation coefficient, ρ_{DE}		.30	

The variance of the two-asset portfolio (Rule 5 of Chapter 5) is

$$\sigma_p^2 = w_D^2 \sigma_D^2 + w_E^2 \sigma_E^2 + 2w_D w_E \text{Cov}(r_D, r_E) \tag{7.2}$$

The first observation is that the variance of the portfolio, unlike the expected return, is *not* a weighted average of the individual asset variances. To understand the formula for the portfolio variance more clearly, recall that the covariance of a variable with itself (in this case the variable is the uncertain rate of return) is the variance of that variable; that is

$$\text{Cov}(r_D, r_D) = \sum_{\text{scenarios}} \text{Pr(scenario)}[r_D - E(r_D)][r_D - E(r_D)]$$

$$= \sum_{\text{scenarios}} \text{Pr(scenario)}[r_D - E(r_D)]^2$$

$$= \sigma_D^2$$

Therefore another way to write the variance of the portfolio is as follows:

$$\sigma_p^2 = w_D w_D \text{Cov}(r_D, r_D) + w_E w_E \text{Cov}(r_E, r_E) + 2w_D w_E \text{Cov}(r_D, r_E)$$

In words, the variance of the portfolio is a weighted sum of covariances, where each weight is the product of the portfolio proportions of the pair of assets in the covariance term.

Why do we double the covariance between the two *different* assets in the last term of equation 7.2? This should become clear in the covariance matrix, Table 7.2, which is bordered by the portfolio weights.

The diagonal (from top left to bottom right) of the covariance matrix is made up of the asset variances. The off-diagonal elements are the covariances. Note that

$$\text{Cov}(r_D, r_E) = \text{Cov}(r_E, r_D)$$

so that the matrix is symmetric. To compute the portfolio variance, we sum over each term in the matrix, first multiplying it by the product of the portfolio proportions from the corresponding row and column. Thus we have *one* term for each asset variance, but twice the term for each covariance pair because each covariance appears twice.

TABLE 7.2 Bordered Covariance Matrix

		Covariances	
	Portfolio Weights	w_D	w_E
	w_D	σ_D^2	$\text{Cov}(r_D, r_E)$
	w_E	$\text{Cov}(r_E, r_D)$	σ_E^2

Concept Check

Question 1.

a. Confirm that this simple rule for computing portfolio variance from the covariance matrix is consistent with equation 7.2.

b. Consider a portfolio of three funds, X, Y, and Z, with weights w_X, w_Y, and w_Z. Show that the portfolio variance is

$$w_X^2 \sigma_X^2 + w_Y^2 \sigma_Y^2 + w_Z^2 \sigma_Z^2 + 2w_X w_Y \mathrm{Cov}(r_X, r_Y)$$
$$+ 2w_X w_Z \mathrm{Cov}(r_X, r_Z) + 2w_Y w_Z \mathrm{Cov}(r_Y, r_Z)$$

As we discussed in Chapter 5, the portfolio variance is reduced if the covariance term is negative. This is the case in the use of hedge assets. It is important to recognize that even if the covariance term is positive, thereby increasing portfolio volatility, the *portfolio* standard deviation still is less than the weighted average of the individual security standard deviations, unless the two securities are perfectly positively correlated.

To see this, recall from Chapter 5, equation 5.5, that the covariance can be written as

$$\mathrm{Cov}(r_D, r_E) = \rho_{DE} \sigma_D \sigma_E$$

Substituting into equation 7.2, we can rewrite the variance and standard deviation of the portfolio as

$$\sigma_p^2 = w_D^2 \sigma_D^2 + w_E^2 \sigma_E^2 + 2w_D w_E \sigma_D \sigma_E \rho_{DE} \tag{7.3}$$

$$\sigma_p = \sqrt{\sigma_p^2} \tag{7.4}$$

You can see from this information that the covariance term adds the most to the portfolio variance when the correlation coefficient, ρ_{DE}, is highest, that is, when it equals 1—as it would in the case of perfect positive correlation. In this case the right-hand side of equation 7.3 is a perfect square, so it may be rewritten as follows:

$$\sigma_p^2 = (w_D \sigma_D + w_E \sigma_E)^2$$

or

$$\sigma_p = w_D \sigma_D + w_E \sigma_E$$

In other words, the standard deviation of the portfolio in the case of perfect positive correlation is just the weighted average of the component standard deviations. In all other cases the correlation coefficient is less than 1, making the portfolio standard deviation *less* than the weighted average of the component standard deviations.

We know already from Chapter 5 that a hedge asset reduces the portfolio variance. This algebraic exercise adds the additional insight that the standard deviation of a portfolio of assets is less than the weighted average of the component security standard deviations, even when the assets are positively correlated. Because the portfolio expected return is always the weighted average of its component expected returns, while its standard deviation is less than the weighted average of the component standard deviations, *portfolios of less than perfectly correlated assets always offer better risk-return opportunities than the individual component securities on their own.* The less correlation between assets, the greater the gain in efficiency.

How low can portfolio standard deviation be? The lowest possible value of the correlation coefficient is −1, representing perfect negative correlation, in which case the portfolio variance is as follows:[4]

$$\sigma_p^2 = (w_D \sigma_D - w_E \sigma_E)^2$$

and the portfolio standard deviation is

$$\sigma_p = \text{Absolute value } (w_D \sigma_D - w_E \sigma_E)$$

Where $\rho = -1$, the investor has the opportunity of creating a perfectly hedged position. If the portfolio proportions are chosen as

$$w_D = \frac{\sigma_E}{\sigma_D + \sigma_E}$$

$$w_E = \frac{\sigma_D}{\sigma_D + \sigma_E} = 1 - w_D$$

the standard deviation of the portfolio will equal zero.[5]

Let us apply this analysis to the data of the bond and stock funds as presented in Table 7.1. Using these data, the formulas for the expected return, variance, and standard deviation of the portfolio are

$$E(r_p) = 8w_D + 13w_E \tag{7.5}$$

$$\sigma_p^2 = 12^2 w_D^2 + 20^2 w_E^2 + 2 \times 72 \ w_D w_E \tag{7.6}$$

$$\sigma_p = \sqrt{\sigma_p^2}$$

Now we are ready to experiment with different portfolio proportions to observe the effect on portfolio expected return and variance. Suppose we change the proportion invested in bonds. The effect on the portfolio's expected return is plotted in Figure 7.3. When the proportion invested in bonds varies from zero to one (so that the proportion in stock varies from one to zero), the portfolio expected return goes from 13 percent (the stock fund's expected return) to 8 percent (the expected return on bonds).

What happens to the right of this region, when $w_D > 1$ and $w_E < 0$? In this case portfolio strategy would be to sell the stock fund short and invest the proceeds of the short sale in bonds. This will decrease the expected return of the portfolio. For example, when $w_D = 2$ and $w_E = -1$, expected portfolio

---

[4] This expression also can be derived from equation 7.3. When $\rho_{DE} = -1$, equation 7.3 is a perfect square that can be factored as shown.

[5] It is possible to drive portfolio variance to zero with perfectly positively correlated assets as well, but this would require short sales.

FIGURE 7.3

Portfolio expected return as a function of investment proportions.

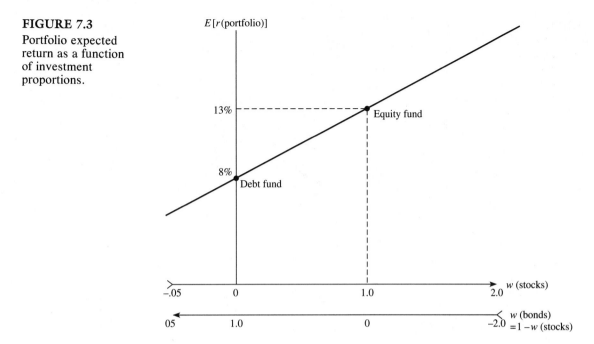

return falls to 3 percent [2 × 8 + (−1) × 13]. At this point the value of the bond fund in the portfolio is twice the net worth of the account. This extreme position is financed in part by short selling stocks equal in value to the portfolio's net worth.

The reverse happens when $w_D < 0$ and $w_E > 1$. This strategy calls for selling the bond fund short and using the proceeds to finance additional purchases of the equity fund.

Of course, varying investment proportions also has an effect on portfolio standard deviation. Table 7.3 presents portfolio standard deviations for differ-

TABLE 7.3   Portfolio Standard Deviation as a Function of Investment Proportions

		Standard Deviation (%)			
w_D	w_E	$\rho = -1$	$\rho = 0$	$\rho = 0.3$	$\rho = 1$
0	1.00	20.00	20.00	20.00	20.00
0.25	0.75	12.00	15.30	16.16	18.00
0.50	0.50	4.00	11.66	13.11	16.00
0.75	0.25	4.00	10.30	11.53	14.00
1.00	0	12.00	12.00	12.00	12.00
	minimum σ_p	0.00	10.29	11.45	—
	w_D at min σ_p	0.63	0.74	0.82	—

FIGURE 7.4
Portfolio standard
deviation as a
function of
investment
proportions.

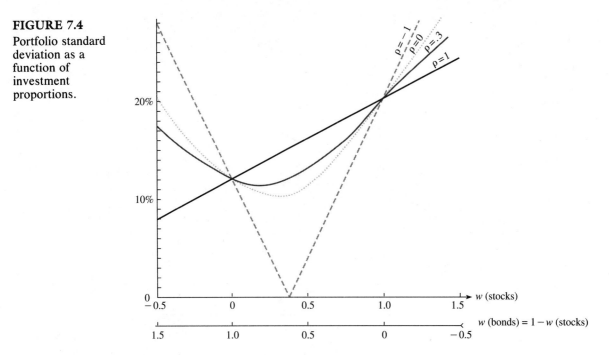

ent portfolio weights calculated from equations 7.3 and 7.4 for the assumed value of the correlation coefficient, .30, as well as for other values of ρ. Figure 7.4 shows the relationship between standard deviation and portfolio weights. Look first at the curve for $\rho = .30$. The graph shows that as the portfolio weight in the equity fund increases from zero to one, portfolio standard deviation first falls with the initial diversification from bonds into stocks, but then rises again as the portfolio becomes heavily concentrated in stocks and again is undiversified.

This pattern will generally hold as long as the correlation coefficient between the funds is not too high. For a pair of assets with a large positive correlation of returns, the portfolio standard deviation will increase monotonically from the low risk asset to the high risk asset. Even in this case, however, there is a positive (if small) value of diversification.

What is the minimum level to which portfolio standard deviation can be held? For the parameter values stipulated in Table 7.1, the portfolio weights that solve this minimization problem turn out to be:[6]

---

[6] This solution uses the minimization techniques of elementary calculus. Write out the expression for portfolio variance from equation 7.2, substitute $1 - w_D$ for w_E, differentiate the result with respect to w_D, set the derivative equal to zero, and solve for w_D. With a computer spreadsheet, however, you can obtain an accurate solution by generating a fine grid for Table 7.3 and observing the minimum.

$$w_{Min}(D) = \frac{\sigma_E^2 - \text{Cov}(r_D, r_E)}{\sigma_D^2 + \sigma_E^2 - 2\text{Cov}(r_D, r_E)} \qquad (7.7)$$

$$= \frac{20^2 - 72}{12^2 + 20^2 - 2 \times 72}$$

$$= .82$$

$$w_{Min}(E) = 1 - .82$$

$$= .18$$

This minimum variance portfolio has a standard deviation of

$$\sigma_{Min}(P) = [.82^2 \times 12^2 + .18^2 \times 20^2 + 2 \times .82 \times .18 \times 72]^{1/2}$$

$$= 11.45\%$$

as indicated in the next-to-last line of Table 7.3 for the column $\rho = .30$.

The dark line in Figure 7.4 represents the portfolio standard deviation when $\rho = .30$ as a function of the investment proportions. It passes through the two undiversified portfolios of $w_D = 1$ and $w_E = 1$. Note that the **minimum-variance portfolio** has a standard deviation smaller than that of either of the individual component assets. This highlights the effect of diversification.

The other three lines in Figure 7.4 show how portfolio risk varies for other values of the correlation coefficient, holding the variances of each asset constant. These lines plot the values in the other three columns of Table 7.3.

The straight line connecting the undiversified portfolios of all-bonds or all-stocks, $w_D = 1$ or $w_E = 1$, demonstrates portfolio standard deviation with perfect positive correlation, $\rho = 1$. In this case there is no advantage from diversification, and the portfolio standard deviation is the simple weighted average of the component asset standard deviations.

The dotted curve below the $\rho = .30$ curve depicts portfolio risk for the case of uncorrelated assets, $\rho = 0$. With lower correlation between the two assets, diversification is more effective and portfolio risk is lower (at least when both assets are held in positive amounts). The minimum portfolio standard deviation when $\rho = 0$ is 10.29 percent (see Table 7.3), again lower than the standard deviation of either asset.

Finally, the upside-down triangular broken line illustrates the perfect hedge potential when the two assets are perfectly negatively correlated ($\rho = -1$). In this case the solution for the minimum-variance portfolio is

$$w_{Min}(D; \rho = -1) = \frac{\sigma_E}{\sigma_D + \sigma_E}$$

$$= \frac{20}{12 + 20}$$

$$= .625$$

$$w_{Min}(E; \rho = -1) = 1 - .625$$

$$= .375$$

and the portfolio variance (and standard deviation) is zero.

We can combine Figures 7.3 and 7.4 to demonstrate the relationship between the portfolio's level of risk (standard deviation) and the expected rate of return on that portfolio—given the parameters of the available assets. This is done in Figure 7.5. For any pair of investment proportions, w_D, w_E, we read the expected return from Figure 7.3 and the standard deviation from Figure 7.4. The resulting pairs of portfolio expected return and standard deviation are tabulated in Table 7.4 and plotted in Figure 7.5.

The dark curve in Figure 7.5 shows the **portfolio opportunity set** for ρ = .30. We call it the *portfolio opportunity set* because it shows the combination of expected return and standard deviation of all the portfolios that can be constructed from the two available assets. The broken and dotted lines show the portfolio opportunity set for other values of the correlation coefficient. The line farthest to the right, which is the straight line connecting the undiversified portfolios, shows that there is no benefit from diversification when the correlation between the two assets is perfectly positive (ρ = 1). The opportunity set is not "pushed" to the northwest. The dotted line to the left of the dark curve shows that there is greater benefit from diversification when the correlation coefficient is zero than when it is positive.

Finally, the broken ρ = −1 lines show the effect of perfect negative correction. The portfolio opportunity set is linear, but now it offers a perfect hedging opportunity and the maximum advantage from diversification.

To summarize, although the expected rate of return of any portfolio is simply the weighted average of the asset expected returns, this is not true of the

FIGURE 7.5

Portfolio expected return as a function of standard deviation.

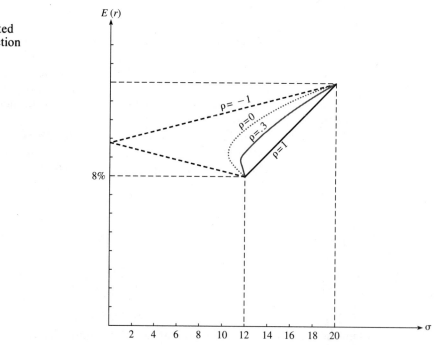

TABLE 7.4 Portfolio Expected Returns and Standard Deviations with Various Correlation Coefficients

			Portfolio Standard Deviation for Given Correlation			
w_D	w_E	$E(r_P)$	$\rho = 1$	$\rho = 0$	$\rho = 0.3$	$\rho = 1$
0	1.0	13.00	20.00	20.00	20.00	20.00
0.25	0.75	11.75	12.00	15.30	16.16	18.00
0.50	0.50	10.50	4.00	11.66	13.11	16.00
0.75	0.25	9.25	4.00	10.30	11.53	14.00
1.0	0	8.00	12.00	12.00	12.00	12.00
			Minimum Variance Portfolio			
$w_D(min)$			0.63	0.74	0.82	—
$E(r_p)$			9.875	9.32	8.90	—
σ_p			0.00	10.29	11.45	—

portfolio standard deviation. Potential benefits from diversification arise when correlation is less than perfectly positive. The lower the correlation coefficient, the greater the potential benefit of diversification. In the extreme case of perfect negative correlation, we have a perfect hedging opportunity and can construct a zero-variance portfolio.

Suppose now that an investor wishes to select the optimal portfolio from the opportunity set. The best portfolio will depend on risk aversion. Portfolios to the northeast in Figure 7.5 provide higher rates of return, but impose greater risk. The best trade-off among these choices is a matter of personal preference. Investors with greater risk aversion will prefer portfolios to the southwest, with lower expected return, but lower risk.[7]

Concept Check

Question 2. Compute and draw the portfolio opportunity set for the debt and equity funds when the correlation coefficient between them is $\rho = .25$.

---

[7] Given a level of risk aversion, one can determine the portfolio that provides the highest level of utility. Recall from Chapter 6 that we were able to describe the utility provided by a portfolio as a function of its expected return, $E(r_p)$, and its variance, σ_p^2, according to the relationship $U = E(r_p) - .005A\sigma_p^2$. The portfolio mean and variance are determined by the portfolio weights in the two funds, w_E and w_D, according to Equations 7.1 and 7.2. Using those equations, one can show using elementary calculus that the optimal investment proportions in the two funds are:

$$w_D = \frac{E(r_D) - E(r_E) + .01A(\sigma_D^2 - \sigma_E\sigma_D\rho_{DE})}{.01A(\sigma_D^2 + \sigma_E^2 - 2\sigma_D\sigma_E\rho_{DE})}$$

7.3 *Asset Allocation with Stocks, Bonds, and Bills*

The Optimal Risky Portfolio with Two Risky Assets and a Risk-Free Asset

What if we were still confined to the bond and stock funds, but now could also invest in risk-free T-bills yielding 5 percent? We start with a graphical solution. Figure 7.6 shows the opportunity set generated from the joint probability distribution of the bond and stock funds, using the data from Table 7.1.

Two possible capital allocation lines (CALs) are drawn from the risk-free rate (r_f = 5 percent) to two feasible portfolios. The first possible CAL is drawn through the minimum-variance portfolio A, which is invested 82 percent in bonds and 18 percent in stocks (equation 7.7). Portfolio A's expected return is $E(r_A)$ = 8.90 percent, and its standard deviation is σ_A = 11.45 percent. With a T-bill rate of r_f = 5 percent, the **reward-to-variability ratio,** which is the slope of the CAL combining T-bills and the minimum-variance portfolio, is

$$S_A = \frac{E(r_A) - r_f}{\sigma_A}$$

$$= \frac{8.9 - 5}{11.45}$$

$$= .34$$

Now consider the CAL that uses portfolio B instead of A. Portfolio B invests 70 percent in bonds and 30 percent in stocks. Its expected return is 9.5 percent (giving it a risk premium of 4.5 percent), and its standard deviation is 11.70 percent. Thus the reward-to-variability ratio on the CAL that is generated using portfolio B is

$$S_B = \frac{9.5 - 5}{11.7}$$

$$= .38$$

higher than the reward-to-variability ratio of the CAL that we obtained using the minimum-variance portfolio and T-bills.

If the CAL that uses portfolio B has a better reward-to-variability ratio than the CAL that uses portfolio A, then for any level of risk (standard deviation) that an investor is willing to bear, the expected return is higher with portfolio B. Figure 7.6 reflects this in showing that the CAL for portfolio B is above the CAL for portfolio A. In this sense portfolio B dominates portfolio A.

In fact, the difference between the reward-to-variability ratios is

$$S_B - S_A = .04$$

This means we get four extra basis points expected return with CAL_B for each percentage point increase in standard deviation.

FIGURE 7.6

The opportunity set of the debt and equity funds, and two feasible CALs.

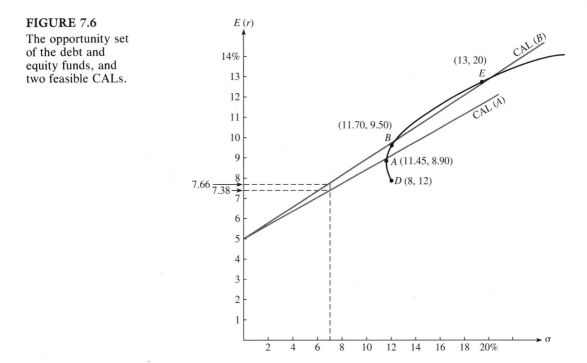

Look at Figure 7.6 again. If we are willing to bear a standard deviation of $\sigma_p = 7$ percent, we can achieve a 7.38 percent expected return with the CAL of portfolio A:

$$E(r_p)(\text{CAL}_A; \sigma_p = 7\%) = r_f + 7S_A$$

$$= 5 + 7 \times .34$$

$$= 7.38\%$$

With the CAL of portfolio B, we get expected return of 7.66 percent:

$$E(r_p)(\text{CAL}_B; \sigma_p = 7\%) = r_f + 7S_B$$

$$= 5 + 7 \times .38$$

$$= 7.66\%$$

This is a difference of $.04 \times 7 = .28$ percent or 28 basis points.

But why stop at portfolio B? We can continue to ratchet the CAL upward until it ultimately reaches the point of tangency with the investment opportunity set. This must yield the CAL with the highest feasible reward-to-variability ratio. Therefore the tangency portfolio, P, drawn in Figure 7.7, is the optimal risky portfolio to mix with T-bills. We can read the expected return and standard deviation of portfolio P from the graph in Figure 7.7.

$$E(r_P) = 11\%$$
$$\sigma_P = 14.2\%$$

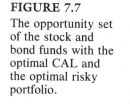

FIGURE 7.7

The opportunity set of the stock and bond funds with the optimal CAL and the optimal risky portfolio.

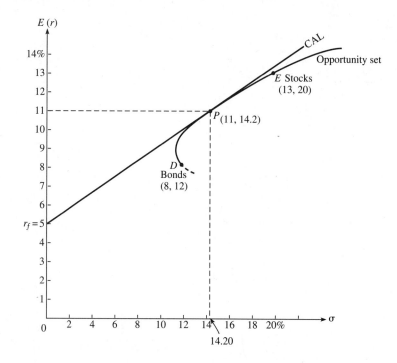

In practice, we obtain an algebraic solution to this problem with a computer program. We can describe the process briefly, however.

The objective is to find the weights w_D, w_E that result in the highest slope of the CAL (that is, the yield of the risky portfolio with the highest reward-to-variability ratio). Therefore, the objective is to maximize the slope of the CAL for any possible portfolio, p. Thus our *objective function* is the slope that we have called S_p:

$$S_p = \frac{E(r_p) - r_f}{\sigma_p}$$

For the portfolio with two risky assets, the expected return and standard deviation of portfolio p are

$$E(r_p) = w_D E(r_D) + w_E E(r_E)$$

$$= 8w_D + 13w_E$$

$$\sigma_p = [w_D^2 \sigma_D^2 + w_E^2 \sigma_E^2 + 2w_D w_E \text{Cov}(r_D, r_E)]^{1/2}$$

$$= [144w_D^2 + 400w_E^2 + 2 \times 72w_D w_E]^{1/2}$$

When we maximize the objective function, S_p, we have to satisfy the constraint that the portfolio weights sum to one (100 percent), that is $w_D + w_E = 1$. Therefore we solve a mathematical problem formally written as

$$\underset{w_i}{\text{Max }} S_p = \frac{E(r_p) - r_f}{\sigma_p}$$

subject to $\Sigma w_i = 1$. This is a standard problem in calculus.

In the case of two risky assets, the solution for the weights of the **optimal risky portfolio,** P, can be shown to be as follows:[8]

$$w_D = \frac{[E(r_D) - r_f]\sigma_E^2 - [E(r_E) - r_f]\text{Cov}(r_D, r_E)}{[E(r_D) - r_f]\sigma_E^2 + [E(r_E) - r_f]\sigma_D^2 - [E(r_D) - r_f + E(r_E) - r_f]\text{Cov}(r_D, r_E)}$$
(7.8)

$$w_E = 1 - w_D$$

Substituting our data, the solution is

$$w_D = \frac{(8 - 5)400 - (13 - 5)72}{(8 - 5)400 + (13 - 5)144 - (8 - 5 + 13 - 5)72}$$

$$= .40$$

$$w_E = 1 - .4$$

$$= .6$$

The expected return of this optimal risky portfolio is 11 percent [$E(r_p) = .4 \times 8 + .6 \times 13$]. The standard deviation is 14.2 percent:

$$\sigma_p = (.4^2 \times 144 + .6^2 \times 400 + 2 \times .4 \times .6 \times 72)^{1/2}$$

$$= 14.2\%$$

The CAL using this optimal portfolio has a slope of

$$S_P = \frac{11 - 8}{14.2} = .42$$

which is the reward-to-variability ratio of portfolio P. Notice that this slope exceeds the slope of any of the other feasible portfolios that we have considered, as it must if it is to be the slope of the best feasible CAL.

In Chapter 6 we found the optimal *complete* portfolio given an optimal risky portfolio and the CAL generated by a combination of this portfolio and T-bills. Now that we have constructed the optimal risky portfolio, P, we can use the individual investor's degree of risk aversion, A, to calculate the optimal proportion of the complete portfolio to invest in the risky component.

An investor with a coefficient of risk aversion, $A = 4$, would take a position in portfolio P of

$$y = \frac{E(r_P) - r_f}{.01 \, A\sigma_P^2}$$
(7.9)

$$= \frac{11 - 5}{.01 \times 4 \times 14.2^2}$$

$$= .7439$$

---

[8] The solution procedure is as follows. Substitute for $E(r_p)$ from equation 7.1 and for σ_p from equation 7.2. Substitute $1 - w_D$ for w_E. Differentiate the resulting expression for S_p with respect to w_D, set the derivative equal to zero, and solve for w_D.

Thus the investor will invest 74.39 percent of his or her wealth in portfolio P and 25.61 percent in T-bills. Portfolio P consists of 40% in bonds, so the percentage of wealth in bonds will be $yw_D = .4 \times .7439 = .2976$, or 29.76 percent. Similarly, the investment in stocks will be $yw_E = .6 \times .7439 = .4463$ or 44.63 percent. The graphical solution of this problem is presented in Figures 7.8 and 7.9.

Once we have reached this point, generalizing to the case of many risky assets is straightforward. Before we move on, let us briefly summarize the steps we followed to arrive at the complete portfolio.

1. Specify the return characteristics of all securities (expected returns, variances, covariances).
2. Establish the risky portfolio:
   a. Calculate the optimal risky portfolio, P (equation 7.8).
   b. Calculate the properties of portfolio P using the weights determined in step (a) and equations 7.1 and 7.2.
3. Allocate funds between the risky portfolio and the risk-free asset:
   a. Calculate the fraction of the complete portfolio allocated to portfolio P (the risky portfolio) and to T-bills (the risk-free asset) (equation 7.9).
   b. Calculate the share of the complete portfolio invested in each asset and in T-bills.

FIGURE 7.8

Determination of the optimal overall portfolio.

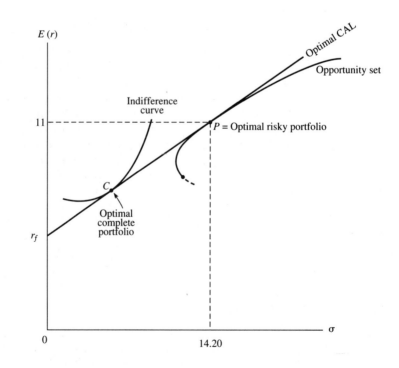

Before moving on, recall that the two assets in the asset allocation problem are already diversified portfolios. The diversification *within* each of these portfolios must be credited for most of the risk reduction, compared to undiversified single securities. For example, the standard deviation of the rate of return on an average stock is about 50 percent. In contrast, the standard deviation of our hypothetical stock index fund is only 20 percent, about equal to the historical standard deviation of the S&P 500 portfolio. This is evidence of the importance of diversification within the asset class. Asset allocation between bonds and stocks contributed incrementally to the improvement in the reward-to-volatility ratio of the complete portfolio. The CAL with stocks, bonds, and bills (Figure 7.7) shows that the standard deviation of the complete portfolio can be further reduced to 18 percent, while maintaining the same expected return of 13 percent as the stock portfolio.

FIGURE 7.9

The proportions of the optimal overall portfolio.

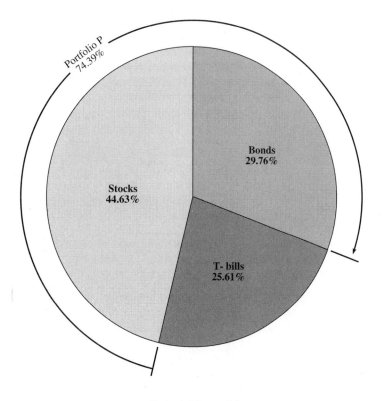

Optimal risky portfolios

Concept Check

Question 3. The universe of available securities includes two risky stock funds, *A* and *B*, and T-bills. The data for the universe are as follows:

	Expected Return	Standard Deviation
A	.10	.20
B	.30	.60
T-bills	.05	0

The correlation coefficient between funds *A* and *B* is $-.2$.

a. Draw the opportunity set of funds *A* and *B*.

b. Find the optimal risky portfolio *P* and its expected return and standard deviation.

c. Find the slope of the CAL supported by T-bills and portfolio *P*.

d. How much will an investor with $A = 5$ invest in funds *A* and *B* and in T-bills?

7.4 *The Markowitz Portfolio Selection Model*

Security Selection

Now we can generalize the portfolio construction problem to the case of many risky securities and a risk-free asset. As in the two risky assets example, the problem has three parts. First, we identify the risk-return combinations available from the set of risky assets. Next, we identify the optimal portfolio of risky assets by finding the portfolio that results in the steepest CAL. Finally, we choose an appropriate complete portfolio by mixing the risk-free asset, T-bills, with the optimal risky portfolio. Before describing the process in detail, let us first present an overview.

The first step is to determine the risk-return opportunities available to the investor. These are summarized by the **minimum-variance frontier** of risky assets. This frontier is a graph of the lowest possible portfolio variance that can be attained for a given portfolio expected return. Given the set of data for expected returns, variances, and covariances, we can calculate the minimum-variance portfolio (or equivalently, minimum standard deviation portfolio) for any targeted expected return. Performing such a calculation for many such expected return targets results in a pairing between expected returns and minimum-risk portfolios that offer those expected returns. The plot of these expected return–standard deviation pairs is presented in Figure 7.10.

Notice that all the individual assets lie to the right inside the frontier, at least

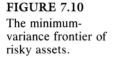

FIGURE 7.10

The minimum-variance frontier of risky assets.

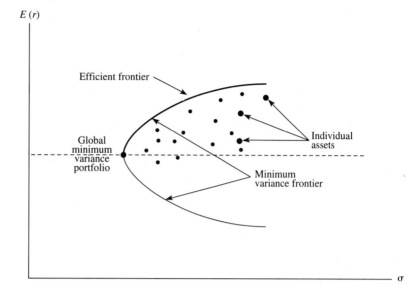

when we allow short sales in the construction of risky portfolios.[9] This tells us that risky portfolios constituted of only a single asset are inefficient. Diversifying investments leads to portfolios with higher expected returns and lower standard deviations.

All the portfolios that lie on the minimum-variance frontier, from the global minimum-variance portfolio and upward, provide the best risk-return combinations and thus are candidates for the optimal portfolio. The part of the frontier that lies above the global minimum-variance portfolio, therefore, is called the **efficient frontier.** For any portfolio on the lower portion of the minimum-variance frontier, there is a portfolio with the same standard deviation and a greater expected return positioned directly above it. Hence, the bottom part of the minimum-variance frontier is inefficient.

The second part of the optimization plan involves the risk-free asset. As before, we search for the capital allocation line with the highest reward-to-variability ratio (that is, the steepest slope) as shown in Figure 7.11.

The CAL that is supported by the optimal portfolio, *P*, is, as before, the one that is tangent to the efficient frontier. This CAL dominates all alternative feasible lines (the broken lines that are drawn through the frontier). Portfolio *P*, therefore, is the optimal risky portfolio.

Finally, in the last part of the problem the individual investor chooses the appropriate mix between the optimal risky portfolio *P* and T-bills, exactly as in Figure 7.8.

---

[9] When short sales are prohibited, single securities may lie on the frontier. For example, the security with the highest expected return must lie on the frontier, as that security represents the *only* way that one can obtain a return that high, and so it must also be the minimum-variance way to obtain that return. When short sales are feasible, however, portfolios can be constructed that offer the same expected return and lower variance. These portfolios typically will have short positions in low expected-return securities.

FIGURE 7.11
The efficient frontier
of risky assets with
the optimal CAL.

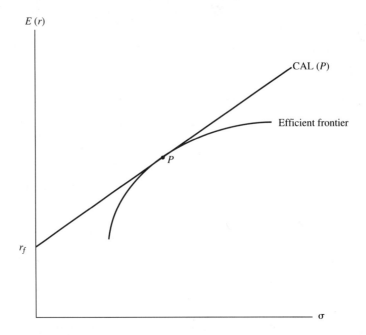

FIGURE 7.11
The efficient frontier
of risky assets with
the optimal CAL.

Now let us consider each part of the portfolio construction problem in more detail. In the first part of the problem, risk-return analysis, the portfolio manager needs, as inputs, a set of estimates for the expected returns of each security and a set of estimates for the covariance matrix. (In Part VI, Equities, we will examine the security valuation techniques and methods of financial analysis that analysts use. For now, we will assume that analysts already have spent the time and resources to prepare the inputs.)

Suppose that the horizon of the portfolio plan is one year. Therefore all estimates pertain to a one-year holding period return. Our security analysts cover n securities. As of now, time zero, we observed these security prices: $P_1^0, \ldots, P_n^0$. The analysts derive estimates for each security's expected rate of return by forecasting end-of-year (time 1) prices: $E(P_1^1), \ldots, E(P_n^1)$, and the expected dividends for the period: $E(D_1), \ldots, E(D_n)$. The set of expected rates of return is then computed from

$$E(r_i) = \frac{E(P_i^1) + E(D_i) - P_i^0}{P_i^0}$$

The covariances among the rates of return on the analyzed securities (the covariance matrix) usually are estimated from historical data. Another method is to use a scenario analysis of possible returns from all securities instead of, or as a supplement to, historical analysis.

The portfolio manager is now armed with the n estimates of $E(r_i)$ and the $n \times n$ estimates in the covariance matrix in which the n diagonal elements are estimates of the variances, σ_i^2, and the $n^2 - n = n(n - 1)$ off-diagonal elements are the estimates of the covariances between each pair of asset returns. (You can verify this from Table 7.2 for the case $n = 2$.) We know that each covariance appears twice in this table, so actually we have $n(n - 1)/2$ different covariance estimates. If our portfolio management unit covers 50 securities, our security analysts need to deliver 50 estimates of expected returns, 50 estimates of variances, and $50 \times 49/2 = 1,225$ different estimates of covariances. This is a daunting task! (We show later how the number of required estimates can be reduced substantially.)

Once these estimates are compiled, the expected return and variance of any risky portfolio with weights in each security, w_i, can be calculated from the following formulas:[10]

$$E(r_p) = \sum_{i=1}^{n} w_i E(r_i) \tag{7.10}$$

$$\sigma_p^2 = \sum_{i=1}^{n} w_i^2 \sigma_i^2 + \sum_{\substack{i=1 \\ i \neq j}}^{n} \sum_{j=1}^{n} w_i w_j \mathrm{Cov}(r_i, r_j) \tag{7.11}$$

We mentioned earlier that the idea of diversification is age-old. The phrase "don't put all your eggs in one basket" existed long before modern finance theory. It was not until 1952, however, that Harry Markowitz published a formal model of portfolio selection embodying diversification principles, ultimately earning himself the 1991 Nobel prize for economics. His model is precisely step one of portfolio management: the identification of the efficient set of portfolios, or, as it is often called, the efficient frontier of risky assets.

The principal idea behind the frontier set of risky portfolios is that, for any risk level, we are interested only in that portfolio with the highest expected return. Alternatively, the frontier is the set of portfolios that minimize the variance for any target expected return.

Indeed, the two methods of computing the efficient set of risky portfolios are equivalent. To see this, consider the graphical representation of these procedures. Figure 7.12 shows the minimum-variance frontier.

The points marked by rectangles are the result of a variance-minimization program. We first draw the constraint, that is, a horizontal line at the level of required expected return. We then look for the portfolio with the lowest standard deviation that plots on this horizontal line—we look for the portfolio that will plot farthest to the left (smallest standard deviation) on that line. When we repeat this for various levels of required expected returns, the shape of the minimum-variance frontier emerges. We then discard the bottom (dotted) half of the frontier, because it is inefficient.

In the alternative approach, we draw a vertical line that represents the standard deviation constraint. We then consider all portfolios that plot on this line (have the same standard deviation) and choose the one with the highest expected return, that is, that portfolio falling highest on this vertical line. Repeating this procedure for various vertical lines (levels of standard deviation)

---

[10] Equation 7.11 follows from our discussion in Section 7.2 on using the bordered covariance matrix to obtain each term in the formula for the variance of a portfolio.

FIGURE 7.12
The efficient
portfolio set.

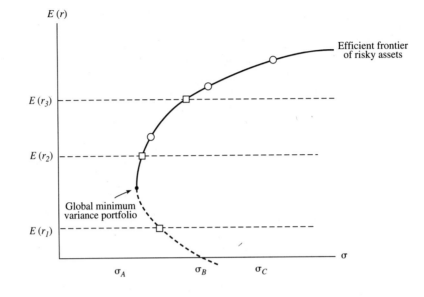

gives us the points marked by circles that trace the upper portion of the mini-mum-variance frontier, the efficient frontier.

When this step is completed, we have a list of efficient portfolios, because the solution to the optimization program includes the portfolio proportions, w_i, and the expected return, $E(r_p)$, and standard deviation, σ_p.

Let us restate what our portfolio manager has done so far. The estimates generated by the analysts were transformed into a set of expected rates of return and a covariance matrix. This group of estimates we shall call the **input list.** This input list is then fed into the optimization program.

Before we proceed to the second step of choosing the optimal risky portfolio from the frontier set, let us consider a practical point. Some clients may be subject to additional constraints. For example, many institutions are prohibited from taking short positions in any asset. For these clients the portfolio manager will add to the program constraints that rule out negative (short) positions in the search for efficient portfolios. In this special case it is possible that single assets may be, in and of themselves, efficient risky portfolios. For example, the asset with the highest expected return will be a frontier portfolio because, without the opportunity of short sales, the only way to obtain that rate of return is to hold the asset as one's entire risky portfolio.

Short-sale restrictions are by no means the only such constraints. For exam-ple, some clients may want to assure a minimal level of expected dividend yield, on the optimal portfolio. In this case the input list will be expanded to include a set of expected dividend yields $d_1, \ldots, d_n$ and the optimization program will include an additional constraint that ensures that the expected dividend yield of the portfolio will equal or exceed the desired level, d.

Portfolio managers can tailor the efficient set to conform to any desire of the client. Of course, any constraint carries a price tag in the sense that an efficient frontier constructed subject to extra constraints will offer a reward-to-variabil-

FIGURE 7.13

Capital allocation lines with various portfolios from the efficient set.

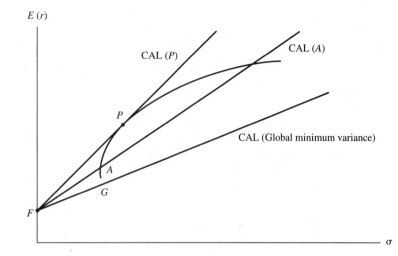

ity ratio inferior to that of a less constrained one. The client should be made aware of this cost and should reconsider constraints that are not mandated by law.

Another type of constraint that has become increasingly popular is aimed at ruling out investments in industries or countries considered ethically or politically undesirable. This is referred to as *socially responsible investing*. The nearby box contains an article from *The Globe and Mail* concerning socially responsible funds that constrain portfolio choice along several criteria. The article points out that one cost of such a policy is a potential reduction in return.

Capital Allocation and Separation Property

We are now ready to proceed to step two. This step introduces the risk-free rate. Figure 7.13 shows the efficient frontier plus three CALs representing various portfolios from the efficient set. As before, we ratchet up the CAL by selecting different portfolios until we reach portfolio *P*, which is the tangency point of a line from *F* to the efficient frontier. Portfolio *P* maximizes the reward-to-variability ratio, the slope of the line from *F* to portfolios on the efficient frontier. At this point our portfolio manager is done. Portfolio *P* is the optimal risky portfolio for the manager's clients. This is a good time to ponder our results and their implementation.

The most striking conclusion is that a portfolio manager will offer the same risky portfolio, *P*, to all clients regardless of their degree of risk aversion.[11] The degree of risk aversion of the client comes into play only in the selection of the desired point on the CAL. Thus the only difference between clients' choices is that the more risk-averse client will invest more in the risk-free asset and less in

---

[11] Clients who impose special restrictions (constraints) on the manager, such as dividend yield, will obtain another optimal portfolio. Any constraint that is added to an optimization problem leads, in general, to a different and less desirable optimum compared to an unconstrained program.

Ethical Investing Often Its Own Reward: Mixed Record Achieved by Funds That Shun Unsavoury Companies

By Eric Kirzner

"Can Canadian investors reap financial rewards while remaining true to their moral beliefs?"

This question is posed in the annual report of Investors Group Inc.'s *Summa Fund*. With assets of more than $60 million, this is the biggest of the so-called ethical funds in Canada.

The Summa Fund has a screening process that excludes certain companies as eligible investments. Excluded are companies primarily engaged in manufacturing or distributing alcohol and tobacco products; gambling; manufacturing weapons systems; and producing, importing, or distributing pornography. Also excluded are companies not practicing effective pollution control and companies supporting repressive regimes.

Other ethical funds have different exclusions. And, of course, there are problems of defining what is ethical. For example, what are repressive regimes and what constitutes supporting a repressive regime?

Common sense indicates that firms that limit their investment opportunities will earn lower returns in the long run. Defenders of ethical investment argue to the contrary—that environmentally and socially responsible companies have lower operating costs, since they have loyal clientele and don't face fines and lawsuits.

Further, defenders of ethical companies say that management may have implemented state-of-the-art operating techniques that are not only environmentally friendly but also cost-effective.

But a non-restricted fund can replicate the portfolio of an ethical fund if appropriate, while still investing in profitable and promising other companies. Thus, its performance should surpass that of the ethical fund.

The recent performance of ethical funds has been a mixed bag. Most of the smaller funds have substantially underperformed market indexes over the past few years on both a nominal and risk-adjusted return basis.

However, *Ethical Growth Fund* and Investors' Summa Fund, the two largest ethical funds in Canada, have outperformed the average for Canadian equity funds for five and three years respectively—the periods spanning the inception of each fund.

So there are at least two ethical fund managers that have overcome the barriers and done remarkably well over the past few years. Possibly these managers are particularly adroit at being first in finding and selecting innovative firms—at least for now.

The results suggest that this "first in" approach may reflect the ethical fund managers' superior effort or ability to pick stocks. It's almost as if increased skill is needed to combat the obvious operating constraints.

The bottom line: If you want to put your ethics in practice, you may pay a bit by earning a smaller return. At least that's what I expect to happen over the long term.

In practice, however, the opposite has occurred. The large ethical funds have performed well above average, which may well be a short-term fluke. But then again, maybe there is an interesting selection process taking place here. Do ethical funds attract the best managers?

In either case, the return cannot be measured strictly in dollars. Ethical investors argue that the implied social benefits are part of the return process.

From *The Globe and Mail*, November 21, 1991. Reprinted by permission of *The Globe and Mail* and the author.

the optimal risky portfolio, *P*, than will a less risk-averse client. However, both will use portfolio *P* as their optimal risky investment vehicle.

This result is called a **separation property**; it tells us that the portfolio choice problem may be separated into two independent tasks. The first task, determination of the optimal risky portfolio, *P*, is purely technical. Given the manager's input list, the best risky portfolio is the same for all clients, regardless of risk aversion. The second task, however, allocation of the complete portfolio to T-bills versus the risky portfolio, depends on personal preference. Here the client is the decision maker.

The crucial point is that the optimal portfolio *P* that the manager offers is the same for all clients. This result makes professional management more efficient and hence less costly. One management firm can serve any number of clients with relatively small incremental administrative costs.

In practice, however, different managers will estimate different input lists, thus deriving different efficient frontiers, and offer different "optimal" portfolios to their clients. The source of the disparity lies in the security analysis. It is worth mentioning here that the rule of GIGO (garbage in-garbage out) applies to security analysis too. If the quality of the security analysis is poor, a passive portfolio such as a market index fund will result in a better CAL than an active portfolio that uses low-quality security analysis to tilt the portfolio weights toward seemingly favourable (seemingly mispriced) securities.

As we have seen, the optimal risky portfolios for different clients also may vary because of portfolio constraints such as dividend-yield requirements, tax considerations, or other client preferences. Nevertheless, this analysis suggests that only a very limited number of portfolios may be sufficient to serve the demands of a wide range of investors. This is the theoretical basis of the mutual fund industry.

The (computerized) optimization technique is the easiest part of the portfolio construction problem. The real arena of competition among portfolio managers is in sophisticated security analysis.

| Concept Check | Question 4. Suppose that two portfolio managers who work for competing investment management houses each employs a group of security analysts to prepare the input list for the Markowitz algorithm. When all is completed, it turns out that the efficient frontier obtained by portfolio manager *A* dominates that of manager *B*. By domination we mean that *A*'s optimal risky portfolio lies northwest of *B*'s. Hence, given a choice, investors will always prefer the risky portfolio that lies on the CAL of *A*.
a. What should be made of this outcome?
b. Should it be attributed to better security analysis by *A*'s analysts?
c. Could it be that *A*'s computer program is superior?
d. If you were advising clients (and had an advance glimpse at the efficient frontiers of various managers), would you tell them to periodically switch their money around to the manager with the most northwesterly portfolio? |

Asset Allocation and Security Selection

As we have seen, the theories of security selection and asset allocation are identical. Both activities call for the construction of an efficient frontier, and the choice of a particular portfolio from along that frontier. The determination of the optimal combination of securities proceeds in the same manner as the analysis of the optimal combination of asset classes. Why, then, do we (and the investment community) distinguish between asset allocation and security selection?

Three factors are at work. First, as a result of greater need and ability to save (for college education, recreation, longer life in retirement and health care needs, etc.) the demand for sophisticated investment management has increased enormously. Second, the growing spectrum of financial markets and financial instruments have put sophisticated investment beyond the capacity of most amateur investors. Finally, there are strong economic returns to scale in investment management. The end result is that the size of a competitive investment company has grown with the industry, and efficiency in organization has become an important issue.

A large investment company is likely to invest both in domestic and international markets and in a broad set of asset classes, each of which requires specialized expertise. Hence, the management of each asset-class portfolio needs to be decentralized, and it becomes impossible to simultaneously optimize the entire organization's risky portfolio in one stage (although this would be prescribed as optimal on *theoretical* grounds).

The practice is therefore to optimize the security selection of each asset-class portfolio independently. At the same time, top management continually updates the asset allocation of the organization, adjusting the investment budget of each asset-class portfolio. When changed frequently in response to intensive forecasting activity, the reallocations are called *market timing*. The shortcoming of this two-step approach to portfolio construction versus the theory-based one-step optimization is the failure to exploit the covariance of the individual securities in one asset-class portfolio with the individual securities in the other asset classes. Only the covariance matrix of the securities within each asset-class portfolio can be used. However this loss might be small, due to the depth of diversification of each portfolio and the extra layer of diversification at the asset allocation level.

7.5 *Optimal Portfolios with Restrictions on the Risk-Free Investment*

The availability of a risk-free asset greatly simplifies the portfolio decision. When all investors can borrow and lend at that risk-free rate, we are led to a *unique* optimal risky portfolio that is appropriate for all investors, given a common input list. This portfolio maximizes the reward-to-variability ratio. All investors use the same risky portfolio and differ only in the proportion they invest in it and in the risk-free asset.

What if a risk-free asset is not available? Although T-bills are risk-free assets in nominal terms, their real returns are uncertain. Without a risk-free asset, there is no tangency portfolio that is best for all investors. In this case investors have to choose a portfolio from the efficient frontier of risky assets redrawn in Figure 7.14.

Each investor will now choose the optimal risky portfolio by superimposing a particular set of indifference curves on the efficient frontier, as Figure 7.14 shows. The optimal portfolio, *P*, for the investor whose risk aversion is represented by the set of indifference curves in Figure 7.14 is tangent to the highest attainable indifference curve.

Investors who are more risk averse than the one represented in Figure 7.14 would have steeper indifference curves, meaning that the tangency portfolio will be of smaller standard deviation and expected return than portfolio *P*, such as portfolio *Q*. Conversely, investors who are more risk tolerant than the one represented in Figure 7.14 would be characterized by flatter indifference curves, resulting in a tangency portfolio of higher expected return and standard deviation than portfolio *P*, such as portfolio *S*. The common feature of all these rational investors is that they choose portfolios on the efficient frontier; that is, they choose mean-variance efficient portfolios.

Even if virtually risk-free lending opportunities are available, many investors do face borrowing restrictions. They may be unable to borrow altogether, or, more realistically, they may face a borrowing rate that is significantly greater than the lending rate. Let us first consider investors who can lend without risk, but are prohibited from borrowing.

FIGURE 7.14

Individual portfolio selection without a risk-free asset.

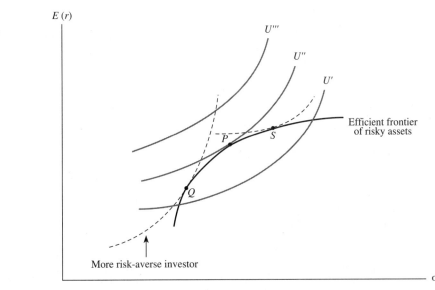

When a risk-free investment is available but an investor can take only positive positions in it (he or she can lend at r_f, but cannot borrow), a CAL exists but is limited to the line *FP*, as in Figure 7.15.

Any investors whose preferences are represented by indifference curves with tangency portfolios on the portion *FP* of the CAL, such as portfolio *A*, are unaffected by the borrowing restriction. For such investors the borrowing restriction is a nonbinding constraint, because they are net *lenders*, lending some of their money at rate r_f.

Aggressive or more risk-tolerant investors, who *would* choose portfolio *B* in the absence of the borrowing restriction, are affected, however. For them, the borrowing restriction is a binding constraint. Such investors will be driven to portfolios on the efficient frontier, such as portfolio *Q*, which have higher expected return and standard deviation than does portfolio *P* (but less than the unavailable portfolio *B*). Portfolios such as *Q*, which are on the efficient frontier of risky assets, represent a zero investment in the risk-free asset.

Finally, we consider a more realistic case, that of feasible borrowing, but at a higher rate than r_f. An individual who borrows to invest in a risky portfolio will have to pay an interest rate higher than the T-bill rate. The lender will require a premium commensurate with the probability of default. For example, the call money rate charged by brokers on margin accounts is higher than the T-bill rate.

Investors who face a borrowing rate greater than the lending rate confront a three-part CAL such as in Figure 7.16. CAL_1, which is relevant in the range

FIGURE 7.15

Individual portfolio selection with risk-free lending only.

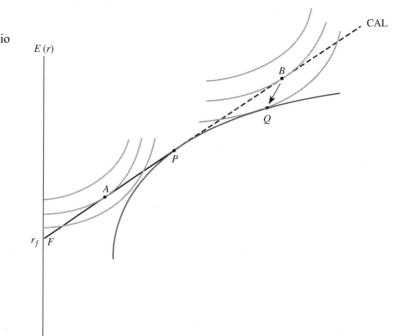

FIGURE 7.16

The investment opportunity set with differential rates for borrowing and lending.

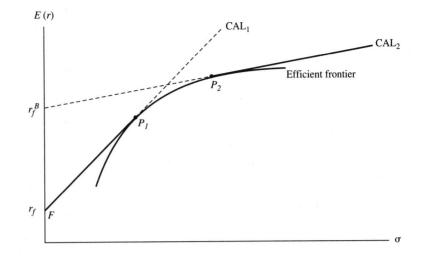

FP$_1$, represents the efficient portfolio set for defensive (risk-averse) investors. These investors invest part of their funds in T-bills at rate r_f. They find that the tangency portfolio is P_1, and they choose a complete portfolio such as portfolio *A* in Figure 7.17.

CAL$_2$, which is relevant in a range to the right of portfolio P_2, represents the efficient portfolio set for more aggressive, or risk-tolerant, investors. This line starts at the borrowing rate, r_f^B, but it is unavailable in the range $r_f^B P_2$, because *lending* (investing in T-bills) is available only at the risk-free rate r_f, less than r_f^B.

Investors who are willing to *borrow* at the higher rate, r_f^B, to invest in an optimal risky portfolio will choose portfolio P_2 as their risky investment vehicle. Such a case is described in Figure 7.18, which superimposes a relatively risk tolerant investor's indifference curve on CAL$_2$ of Figure 7.16. The investor

FIGURE 7.17

The optimal portfolio of defensive investors with differential borrowing and lending rates.

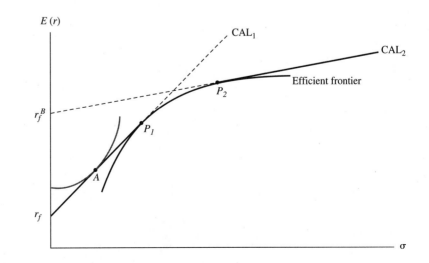

FIGURE 7.18

The optimal portfolio of aggressive investors with differential borrowing and lending rates.

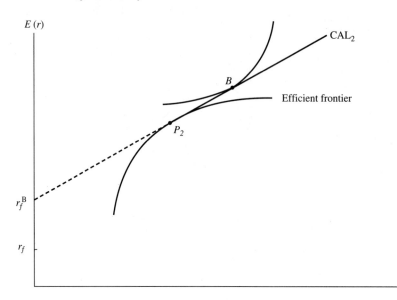

with the indifference curve in Figure 7.18 chooses portfolio P_2 as the optimal risky portfolio and borrows to invest in it, arriving at overall portfolio B.

Investors in the middle range, neither defensive enough to invest in T-bills nor aggressive enough to borrow, choose a risky portfolio from the efficient frontier in the range P_1P_2. This case is described in Figure 7.19. The indifference curve representing the investor in Figure 7.19 leads to a tangency portfolio on the efficient frontier, portfolio C.

FIGURE 7.19

The optimal portfolio of moderately risk-tolerant investors with differential borrowing and lending rates.

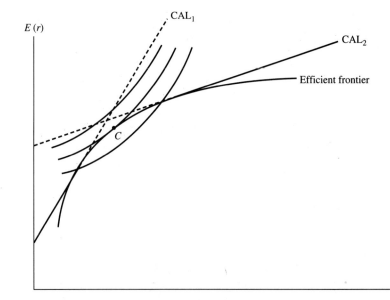

Concept Check

> Question 5. With differential lending and borrowing rates, only investors with about average degrees of risk aversion will choose a portfolio in the range P_1P_2 in Figure 7.17. Other investors will choose a portfolio on CAL_1 if they are more risk averse, or on CAL_2 if they are more risk tolerant.
> *a.* Does this mean that investors with average risk aversion are more dependent on the quality of the forecasts that generate the efficient frontier?
> *b.* Describe the trade-off between expected return and standard deviation for portfolios between P_1 and P_2 in Figure 7.17 compared with portfolios on CAL_2 beyond P_2.

Summary

1. The expected return of a portfolio is the weighted average of the component asset expected returns with the investment proportions as weights.

2. The variance of a portfolio is the weighted sum of the elements of the covariance matrix with the product of the investment proportions as weights. Thus the variance of each asset is weighted by the square of its investment proportion. Each covariance of any pair of assets appears twice in the covariance matrix, and thus the portfolio variance includes twice each covariance weighted by the product of the investment proportions in each of the two assets.

3. Even if the covariances are positive, the portfolio standard deviation is less than the weighted average of the component standard deviations, as long as the assets are not perfectly positively correlated. Thus portfolio diversification is of value as long as assets are less than perfectly correlated.

4. The greater an asset's *covariance* with the other assets in the portfolio, the more it contributes to portfolio variance. An asset that is perfectly negatively correlated with a portfolio can serve as a perfect hedge. The perfect hedge asset can reduce the portfolio variance to zero.

5. The efficient frontier is the graphical representation of a set of portfolios that maximize expected return for each level of portfolio risk. Rational investors will choose a portfolio on the efficient frontier.

6. A portfolio manager identifies the efficient frontier by first establishing estimates for the asset expected returns and the covariance matrix. This input list is then fed into an optimization program that reports as outputs the investment proportions, expected returns, and standard deviations of the portfolios on the efficient frontier.

7. In general, portfolio managers will arrive at different efficient portfolios because of difference in methods and quality of security analysis. Managers compete on the quality of their security analysis relative to their management fees.

8. If a risk-free asset is available and input lists are identical, all investors will choose the same portfolio on the efficient frontier of risky assets: the portfolio tangent to the CAL. All investors with identical input lists will hold an identical risky portfolio, differing only in how much each allocates to this optimal portfolio and to the risk-free asset. This result is characterized as the separation principle of portfolio construction.

9. When a risk-free asset is not available, each investor chooses a risky portfolio on the efficient frontier. If a risk-free asset is available but borrowing is restricted, only aggressive investors will be affected. They will choose portfolios on the efficient frontier according to their degree of risk tolerance.

Key terms

Diversification	Minimum-variance portfolio
Insurance principle	Portfolio opportunity set
Market risk	Reward-to-variability ratio
Systematic risk	Optimal risky portfolio
Non-diversifiable risk	Minimum-variance frontier
Unique risk	Efficient frontier
Firm-specific risk	Input list
Non-systematic risk	Separation property
Diversifiable risk	

Selected readings

Two frequently cited papers on the impact of diversification on portfolio risk are:
   Evans, John L.; and Archer, Stephen H. "Diversification and the Reduction of Dispersion: An Empirical Analysis." *Journal of Finance*, December 1968.
   Wagner, W. H.; and Lau, S. C. "The Effect of Diversification on Risk." *Financial Analysts Journal*, November–December 1971.
The seminal works on portfolio selection are:
   Markowitz, Harry M. "Portfolio Selection." *Journal of Finance*, March 1952.
   Markowitz, Harry M. *Portfolio Selection: Efficient Diversification of Investments.* New York: John Wiley & Sons, Inc., 1959.
Also see:
   Samuelson, Paul A. "Risk & Uncertainty: A Fallacy of Large Numbers." *Scientia* 98, 1963.

Problems

The following data apply to questions 1–8:

A pension fund manager is considering three mutual funds. The first is a stock fund, the second is a long-term government and corporate bond fund, and the third is a T-bill money market fund that yields a rate of 9 percent. The probability distribution of the risky funds is as follows:

	Expected Return	Standard Deviation
Stock fund (S)	.22	.32
Bond fund (B)	.13	.23

The correlation between the fund returns is .15.

1. What are the investment proportions of the minimum-variance portfolio of the two risky funds, and what is the expected value and standard deviation of its rate of return?
2. Tabulate and draw the investment opportunity set of the two risky funds. Use investment proportions for the stock fund of zero to 100 percent in increments of 20 percent.
3. Draw a tangent from the risk-free rate to the opportunity set. What does your graph show for the expected return and standard deviation of the optimal portfolio?
4. Solve numerically for the proportions of each asset, and for the expected return and standard deviation of the optimal risky portfolio.
5. What is the reward-to-variability ratio of the best feasible CAL?
6. You require that your portfolio yield an expected return of 15 percent, and that it be efficient on the best feasible CAL.
   a. What is the standard deviation of your portfolio?
   b. What is the proportion invested in the T-bill fund and each of the two risky funds?
7. If you were to use only the two risky funds, and still require an expected return of 15 percent, what must be the investment proportions of your portfolio? Compare its standard deviation to that of the optimized portfolio in question 6. What do you conclude?
8. Suppose that you face the same opportunity set, but you cannot borrow. You wish to construct a portfolio with an expected return of 29 percent. What are the appropriate portfolio proportions and the resulting standard deviation? What reduction in standard deviation could you attain if you were allowed to borrow at the risk-free rate?
9. Stocks offer an expected rate of return of 18 percent, with a standard deviation of 22 percent. Gold offers an expected return of 10 percent with a standard deviation of 30 percent.
   a. In light of the apparent inferiority of gold with respect to both mean return and volatility, would anyone hold gold? If so, demonstrate graphically why one would do so.
   b. Given the data above, reanswer question (a) with the additional assumption that the correlation coefficient between gold and stocks equals 1. Draw a graph illustrating why one would or would not hold gold in one's portfolio. Could this set of assumptions for expected returns, standard deviations, and correlation represent an equilibrium for the security market?
10. Suppose that there are many stocks in the market and that the characteristics of stocks A and B are given as follows:

Stock	Expected Return	Standard Deviation
A	.10	.05
B	.15	.10
	Correlation = −1	

Suppose that it is possible to borrow at the risk-free rate, r_f. True or false: in equilibrium r_f is greater than .10.

11. Assume that expected returns and standard deviations for all securities (including the risk-free rate for borrowing and lending) are known. True or false: In this case all investors will have the same optimal risky portfolio.

12. True or false: The standard deviation of the portfolio is always equal to the weighted average of the standard deviations of the assets in the portfolio.

13. Suppose that you have a project that has a .7 chance of doubling your investment in a year and a .3 chance of halving your investment in a year. What is the standard deviation of the rate of return on this investment?

14. Suppose that you have $1 million and the following two opportunities from which to construct a portfolio:

a. Risk-free asset earning .12 per year.

b. Risky asset earning .30 per year with a standard deviation of .40.

If you construct a portfolio with a standard deviation of .30, what will be the rate of return?

The following data apply to questions 15–17 (CFA Examination, Level III, 1982):

Hennessy & Associates manages a $30 million equity portfolio for the multi-manager Wilstead Pension Fund. Jason Jones, financial vice president of Wilstead, noted that Hennessy had rather consistently achieved the best record among Wilstead's six equity managers. Performance of the Hennessy portfolio had been clearly superior to that of the S&P 500 in four of the past five years. In the one less favourable year, the shortfall was trivial.

Hennessy is a "bottom-up" manager. The firm largely avoids any attempt to "time the market." It also focuses on selection of individual stocks, rather than the weighting of favoured industries.

There is no apparent conformity of style among the six equity managers. The five managers, other than Hennessy, manage portfolios aggregating $250 million made up of more than 150 individual issues.

Jones is convinced that Hennessy is able to apply superior skill to stock selection, but the favourable results are limited by the high degree of diversification in the portfolio. Over the years, the portfolio generally held 40–50 stocks, with about 2 percent to 3 percent of total funds committed to each issue. The reason Hennessy seemed to do well most years was because the firm was able to identify each year 10 or 12 issues that registered particularly large gains.

Based on this overview, Jones outlined the following plan to the Wilstead pension committee:

"Let's tell Hennessy to limit the portfolio to no more than 20 stocks. Hennessy will double the commitments to the stocks that it really favours, and eliminate the remainder. Except for this one new restriction, Hennessy should be free to manage the portfolio exactly as before."

All the members of the pension committee generally supported Jones' proposal, because all agreed that Hennessy had seemed to demonstrate superior skill in selecting stocks. Yet, the proposal was a considerable departure from previous practice, and several committee members raised questions. Respond to each of these questions:

15. Answer the following:
    a. Will the limitation of 20 stocks likely increase or decrease the risk of the portfolio? Explain.
    b. Is there any way Hennessy could reduce the number of issues from 40 to 20 without significantly affecting risk? Explain.
16. One committee member was particularly enthusiastic concerning Jones' proposal. He suggested that Hennessy's performance might benefit further from reduction in the number of issues to 10. If the reduction to 20 could be expected to be advantageous, explain why reduction to 10 might be less likely to be advantageous. (Assume that Wilstead will evaluate the Hennessy portfolio independently of the other portfolios in the fund.)
17. Another committee member suggested that, rather than evaluate each managed portfolio independently of other portfolios, it might be better to consider the effects of a change in the Hennessy portfolio on the total fund. Explain how this broader point of view could affect the committee decision to limit the holdings in the Hennessy portfolio to either 10 or 20 issues.

The following data apply to questions 18–20:
The correlation coefficients between pairs of stocks is as follows:

$$\text{Corr}(A, B) = .85; \ \text{Corr}(A, C) = .60; \ \text{Corr}(A, D) = .45$$

Each stock has an expected return of 8 percent.
18. If your entire portfolio is now comprised of stock *A* and you can add only one more, which of the following would you choose, and why?
    a. *B.*
    b. *C.*
    c. *D.*
    d. Need more data.
19. Would your answer to question 18 change for more risk-averse or risk-tolerant investors? Explain.
20. Suppose that in addition to investing in one more stock you can invest in T-bills as well. How would you change your answers to questions 18 and 19?

Appendix A: *The Power of Diversification*

Section 7.1 introduced the concept of diversification and the limits to the benefits of diversification caused by systematic risk. Given the tools we have developed, we can reconsider this intuition more rigorously and at the same time sharpen our insight regarding the power of diversification.

Recall from equation 7.11 that the general formula for the variance of a portfolio is

$$\sigma_p^2 = \sum_{i=1}^{n} w_i^2 \sigma_i^2 + \sum_{\substack{j=1 \\ j \neq i}}^{n} \sum_{i=1}^{n} w_i w_j \text{Cov}(r_i, r_j) \qquad \textbf{(7A.1)}$$

Consider now the naive diversification strategy in which an equally weighted portfolio is constructed, meaning that $w_i = 1/n$ for each security. In this case equation 7A.1 may be rewritten as follows:

$$\sigma_p^2 = \frac{1}{n} \sum_{i=1}^{n} \frac{1}{n} \sigma_i^2 + \sum_{\substack{j=1 \\ j \neq i}}^{n} \sum_{i=1}^{n} \frac{1}{n^2} \text{Cov}(r_i, r_j) \qquad \textbf{(7A.2)}$$

Note that there are n variance terms and $n(n-1)$ covariance terms in equation 7A.2.

If we define the average variance and average covariance of the securities as

$$\bar{\sigma}^2 = \frac{1}{n} \sum_{i=1}^{n} \sigma_i^2$$

$$\overline{\text{Cov}} = \frac{1}{n(n-1)} \sum_{\substack{i=1 \\ j \neq i}}^{n} \sum_{j=1}^{n} \text{Cov}(r_i, r_j)$$

we can express portfolio variance as

$$\sigma_p^2 = \frac{1}{n} \bar{\sigma}^2 + \frac{n-1}{n} \overline{\text{Cov}} \qquad \textbf{(7A.3)}$$

Now examine the effect of diversification. When the average covariance among security returns is zero, as it is when all risk is firm-specific, portfolio variance can be driven to zero. We see this from equation 7A.3: the second term on the right-hand side will be zero in this scenario while the first term approaches zero as n becomes larger. Hence, when security returns are uncorrelated, the power of diversification to limit portfolio risk is unlimited.

However, the more important case is the one in which economywide risk factors impart positive correlation among stock returns. In this case, as the portfolio becomes more highly diversified (n increases) portfolio variance remains positive. While firm-specific risk, represented by the first term in equation 7A.3, is still diversified away, the second term simply approaches $\overline{\text{Cov}}$ as n becomes greater. [Note that $(n - 1)/n = 1 - 1/n$, which approaches 1 for large n.] Thus the irreducible risk of a diversified portfolio depends on the covariance of the returns of the component securities, which in turn is a function of the importance of systematic factors in the economy.

To see further the fundamental relationship between systematic risk and security correlations, suppose for simplicity that all securities have a common standard deviation, σ, and all security pairs have a common correlation coefficient ρ. Then the covariance between all pairs of securities is $\rho\sigma^2$, and equation 7A.3 becomes

$$\sigma_p^2 = \frac{1}{n}\sigma^2 + \frac{n-1}{n}\rho\sigma^2 \qquad \text{(7A.4)}$$

The effect of correlation is now explicit. When $\rho = 0$, we again obtain the insurance principle, where portfolio variance approaches zero as n becomes greater. For $\rho > 0$, however, portfolio variance remains positive. In fact, for $\rho = 1$, portfolio variance equals σ^2 regardless of n, demonstrating that diversification is of no benefit: in the case of perfect correlation, all risk is systematic. More generally, as n becomes greater, equation 7A.4 shows that systematic risk becomes $\rho\sigma^2$.

Table 7A.1 presents portfolio standard deviation as we include ever greater numbers of securities in the portfolio for two cases: $\rho = 0$ and $\rho = .40$. The table takes σ to be 50 percent. As one would expect, portfolio risk is greater when $\rho = .40$. More surprising, perhaps, is that portfolio risk diminishes far less rapidly as n increases in the positive correlation case. The correlation among security returns limits the power of diversification.

TABLE 7A.1 Risk Reduction of Equally Weighted Portfolios in Correlated and Uncorrelated Universes

Universe Size n	Optimal Portfolio Proportion $1/n$(%)	$\rho = 0$ Standard Deviation (%)	$\rho = 0$ Reduction in σ	$\rho = .4$ Standard Deviation (%)	$\rho = .4$ Reduction in σ
1	100	50.00		50.00	
2	50	35.36	14.64	41.83	8.17
5	20	22.36		36.06	
6	16.67	20.41	1.95	35.36	.70
10	10	15.81		33.91	
11	9.09	15.08	.73	33.71	.20
20	5	11.18		32.79	
21	4.76	10.91	.27	32.73	.06
100	1	5.00		31.86	
101	.99	4.98	.02	31.86	.00

Note that, for a 100-security portfolio, the standard deviation is 5 percent in the uncorrelated case—still significant when we consider the potential of zero standard deviation. For $\rho = .40$, the standard deviation is high, 31.86%, yet it is very close to undiversifiable systematic risk in the infinite-sized universe, $\sqrt{\rho\sigma^2} = \sqrt{.4 \times .50^2} = .3162$, or 31.62 percent. At this point, further diversification is of little value.

We also gain an important insight from this exercise. When we hold diversified portfolios, the contribution to portfolio risk of a particular security will depend on the *covariance* of that security's return with those of other securities, and *not* on the security's variance. As we shall see in Chapter 8, this implies that fair risk premiums also should depend on covariances rather than total variability of returns.

Concept Check

Question 7A.1. Suppose that the universe of available risky securities consists of a large number of stocks, identically distributed with $E(r) = 15$ percent, $\sigma = 60$ percent, and a common correlation coefficient of $\rho = .5$.
a. What is the expected return and standard deviation of an equally weighted risky portfolio of 25 stocks?
b. What is the smallest number of stocks necessary to generate an efficient portfolio with a standard deviation equal to or smaller than 43 percent?
c. What is the systematic risk in this universe?
d. If T-bills are available and yield 10 percent, what is the slope of the CAL?

Appendix B: The Insurance Principle: Risk-Sharing vs. Risk-Pooling

Mean-variance analysis has taken a strong hold among investment professionals, and insight into the mechanics of efficient diversification has become quite widespread. Common misconceptions or fallacies about diversification still persist, however, and we will try to put some to rest.

It is commonly believed that a large portfolio of independent insurance policies is a necessary and sufficient condition for an insurance company to shed its risk. The fact is that a multitude of independent insurance policies is neither necessary nor sufficient for a sound insurance portfolio. Actually, an individual insurer who would not insure a single policy also would be unwilling to insure a large portfolio of independent policies.

Consider Paul Samuelson's (1963) story. He once offered a colleague 2-to-1 odds on a $1,000 bet on the toss of a coin. His colleague refused, saying, "I won't bet because I would feel the $1,000 loss more than the $2,000 gain. But I'll take you on if you promise to let me make a hundred such bets."

Samuelson's colleague, as many others, might have explained his position, not quite correctly, that "One toss is not enough to make it reasonably sure that the law of averages will turn out in my favour. But with a hundred tosses of a coin, the law of averages will make it a darn good bet."

Another way to rationalize this argument is to think in terms of rates of return. In each bet you put up $1,000 and then get back $3,000 with a probability of one half, or zero with a probability of one half. The probability distribution of the rate of return is 200 percent with $p = \frac{1}{2}$ and -100 percent with $p = \frac{1}{2}$.

The bets are all independent and identical and therefore the expected return is $E(r) = \frac{1}{2}(200) + \frac{1}{2}(-100) = 50$ percent, regardless of the number of bets. The standard deviation of the rate of return on the portfolio of independent bets is[a]

$$\sigma(n) = \frac{\sigma}{\sqrt{n}}$$

where σ is the standard deviation of a single bet:

$$\sigma = [\frac{1}{2}(200 - 50)^2 + \frac{1}{2}(-100 - 50)^2]^{1/2}$$
$$= 150\%$$

The rate of return on a sequence of bets, in other words, has a smaller standard deviation than that of a single bet. By increasing the number of bets we can reduce the standard deviation of the rate of return to any desired level. It seems at first glance that Samuelson's colleague was correct. But he was not.

The fallacy of the argument lies in the use of a rate of return criterion to choose from portfolios *that are not equal in size*. Although the portfolio is equally weighted across bets, each extra bet increases the scale of the investment by $1,000. Recall from traditional corporate finance that when choosing among mutually exclusive projects you cannot use the internal rate of return (IRR) as your decision criterion when the projects are of different sizes. You have to use the net present value (NPV) rule.

Consider the dollar profit (as opposed to rate of return) distribution of a single bet:

$$E(R) = \frac{1}{2} \times 2,000 + \frac{1}{2} \times (-1,000)$$
$$= \$500$$
$$\sigma_R = [\frac{1}{2}(2,000 - 500)^2 + \frac{1}{2}(-1,000 - 500)^2]^{1/2}$$
$$= \$1,500$$

---

[a] This follows from equation 7.11, setting $w_i = 1/n$ and all covariances equal to zero because of the independence of the bets.

These are independent bets where the total profit from n bets is the sum of the profits from the single bets. Therefore, with n bets

$$E[R(n)] = \$500n$$

$$\text{Variance} \left(\sum_{i=1}^{n} R_i \right) = n\sigma_R^2$$

$$\sigma_R(n) = \sqrt{n\sigma_R^2}$$

$$= \sigma_R \sqrt{n}$$

so that the standard deviation of the dollar return *increases* by a factor equal to the square root of the number of bets, n, in contrast to the standard deviation of the rate of return, which *decreases* by a factor of the square root of n.

As further evidence, consider the standard coin-tossing game. Whether one flips a fair coin 10 times or 1,000 times, the expected percentage of heads flipped is 50 percent. One expects the actual proportion of heads in a typical running of the 1,000-toss experiment to be closer to 50 percent than in the 10-toss experiment. This is the law of averages.

But the actual number of heads will typically depart from its expected value by a greater amount in the 1,000-toss experiment. For example, 504 heads is close to 50 percent and is 4 more than the expected number. To exceed the expected number of heads by 4 in the 10-toss game would require 9 out of 10 heads, which is a much more extreme departure from the mean. In the many-toss case, there is more volatility of the number of heads and less volatility of the percentage of heads. This is the same when an insurance company takes on more policies: the dollar variance of its portfolio increases while the rate of return variance falls.

The lesson is this: rate-of-return analysis is appropriate when considering mutually exclusive portfolios of equal size, which is what we did in all the examples so far. We applied a fixed investment budget, and we investigated only the consequences of varying investment proportions in various assets. But if an insurance company takes on more and more insurance policies, it is increasing portfolio dollar investments. The analysis that is called for in that case must be cast in terms of dollar profits, in much the same way that NPV is called for instead of IRR when we compare different-sized projects. This is why risk-pooling (that is, accumulating independent risky prospects) does not act to eliminate risk.

Samuelson's colleague should have counteroffered: "Let's make 1,000 bets, each with your $2 against my $1." Then he would be holding a portfolio of fixed size, equal to $1,000, which is diversified into 1,000 identical independent prospects. This would make the insurance principle work.

Another way for Samuelson's colleague to get around the riskiness of this tempting bet is to share the large bets with friends. Consider a firm engaging in 1,000 of Paul Samuelson's bets. In each bet the firm puts up $1,000 and receives $3,000 or nothing as before. Each bet is too large for you. Yet if you hold a 1/1,000 share of the firm, your position is exactly the same as if you were to make 1,000 small bets of $2 against $1. A 1/1,000 share of a $1,000 bet is equivalent to a $1 bet. Holding a small share of many large bets essentially allows you to replace a stake in one large bet with a diversified portfolio of manageable bets.

How does this apply to insurance companies? Investors can purchase insurance company shares in the stock market, so they can choose to hold as small a position in the overall risk as they please. No matter how great the risk of the policies, a large group of individual small investors will agree to bear the risk if the expected rate of return exceeds the risk-free rate. Thus it is the sharing of risk among many shareholders that makes the insurance industry tick.

Appendix C: The Fallacy of Time Diversification

The insurance story just discussed illustrates a misuse of rate of return analysis, specifically the mistake of comparing portfolios of different sizes. A more insidious version of this error often appears under the guise of "time diversification."

Consider the case of Mr. Frier, who has $100,000. He is trying to figure out the appropriate allocation of this fund between risk-free T-bills that yield 10 percent and a risky portfolio that yields an anual rate of return with $E(r_p) = 15$ percent and $\sigma_p = 30$ percent.

Mr. Frier took a course in finance in his youth. He likes quantitative models, and after careful introspection determines that his degree of risk aversion, A, is 4. Consequently, he calculates that his optimal allocation to the risky portfolio is

$$y = \frac{E(r_p) - r_f}{A\sigma_p^2} = \frac{.15 - .10}{4 \times .3^2}$$
$$= .14$$

That is, a 14 percent investment ($14,000) in the risky portfolio.

With this strategy, Mr. Frier calculates his complete portfolio expected return and standard deviation by

$$E(r_C) = r_f + y[E(r_p) - r_f]$$
$$= 10.70\%$$
$$\sigma_C = y\sigma_p$$
$$= 4.20\%$$

At this point, Mr. Frier gets cold feet because this fund is intended to provide the mainstay of his retirement wealth. He plans to retire in five years, and any mistake will be burdensome.

Mr. Frier calls Ms. Mavin, a highly recommended financial advisor. Ms. Mavin explains that indeed the time factor is all important. She cites academic research showing that asset rates of return over successive holding periods are independent. Therefore, she argues, returns in good years and bad years will tend to cancel out over the five-year period. Consequently, the average portfolio rate of return over the investment period will be less risky than would appear from the standard deviation of a single-year portfolio return. Because returns in each year are independent, Ms. Mavin tells Mr. Frier that a five-year investment is equivalent to a portfolio of five equally weighted independent assets. With such a portfolio, the (five-year) holding period return has a mean of

$$E[r_p(5)] = 15\% \text{ per year}$$

and standard deviation of[b]

$$\sigma_p(5) = \frac{30}{\sqrt{5}}$$
$$= 13.42\% \text{ per year}$$

Mr. Frier is relieved. He believes that the effective standard deviation has fallen from 30 percent to 13.42 percent, and that the reward-to-variability ratio is much better than his first assessment.

Is Mr. Frier's newfound sense of security warranted? Specifically, is Ms. Mavin's time diversification really a risk-reducer? Is it true that the standard deviation of the annualized *rate* of return over five years really is only 13.42 percent as Mavin claims, compared with the 30 percent one-year standard deviation?

The answer to all these questions is an emphatic no! The error in Ms. Mavin's reasoning occurs when she claims that a series of five independent annual returns is equivalent to a portfolio of five equally weighted independent assets. The weights of the five annual returns are not equal; instead they are random amounts, since each year's investment (the weight) is the result of the previous years' cumulative return. Far from reducing the variance of the final wealth, these successive annual returns on the initial investment actually increase it, both in absolute terms and compared to the mean return of total wealth.

Suppose that after one year, the realized rate of return on the risky portfolio is one standard deviation below the mean, or 15 percent − 30 percent = −15 percent. Let us compare this with the equivalent result after five years. It can be shown[c] that the standard deviation of final wealth is approximately equal to 125.6 percent with a mean rate of return of 101.14 percent ($1.15^5 - 1$); one standard deviation below the mean gives a realized five-year rate of return of 101.14 percent − 125.6 percent = −24.5 percent. There is the same chance of losing 24.5 percent of initial wealth after five years as of losing 15 percent in one year. This clearly does not suggest that "time diversification" is a benefit.

---

[b] The calculation for standard deviation is only approximate, because it assumes that the five-year return is the sum of each of the five one-year returns, and this formulation ignores compounding. The error is small, however, and does not affect the point we want to make.

[c] Let R_t denote the holding-period return during year $t = 1, \ldots, 5$. The final wealth per dollar invested is the product $R_1 \ldots R_5$, and its variance is equal to $E[R_1^2 \ldots R_5^2] - (1.15)$.[10] Since the R_t's are independent, this variance is equal to $(1.15^2 + .3^2)^5 - 4.046 = 1.577$, implying that the standard deviation is $\sqrt{1.577} = 1.256$, or 125.6 percent.

FIGURE 7C.1
Average rates of
return on common
stocks. Simulated
total return
distributions for the
period 1977–2000.
Geometric average
annual rates.

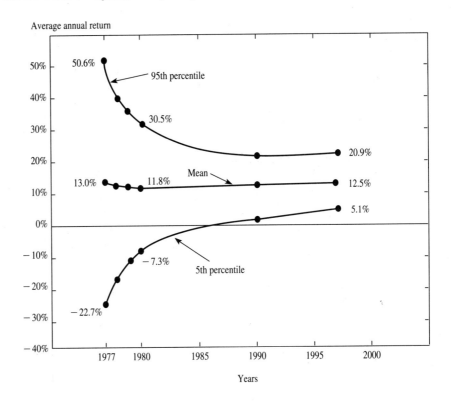

Since each successive year's investment capital depends on the previous years' results, the effect of a poor (or superior) return is compounded by time rather than averaged out. In order for time diversification to be effective, an investor must start each year with an equal amount of investment capital. In Mr. Frier's case, as for any single contribution pension fund, a low-risk strategy is indicated to reduce the possibility, that increases with time, of a single bad return. The case of additional annual contributions to previous capital requires a different analysis, and the notion of time diversification is more applicable then.

Figures 7C.1 and 7C.2 from a study by Ibbotson and Sinquefield[d] show the fallacy of time diversification. They represent simulated returns to a stock investment and show the range of possible outcomes. While the confidence band around the expected rate of return on the investment narrows with investment life, the dollar confidence band widens.

Again, the coin-toss analogy is helpful. Think of each year's investment return as one flip of the coin. After many years, the average number of heads approaches 50 percent, but the possible deviation of total heads from one half the number of flips still will be growing.

---

[d] Roger G. Ibbotson and Rex A. Sinquefield, *Stocks, Bonds, Bills, and Inflation: The Past (1926–76) and the Future (1977–2000)*, Chicago: Financial Analysts Research Foundation, 1977.

FIGURE 7C.2

Dollar returns on common stocks. Simulated distributions of nominal wealth index for the period 1977–2000 (year-end 1976 equals 1.00).

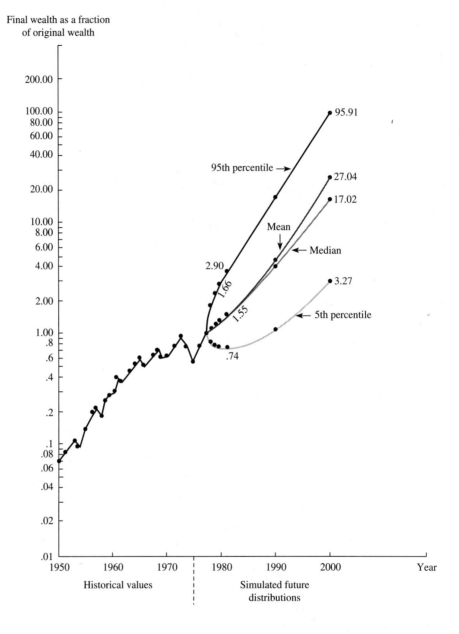

The lesson is, once again, that one should not use rate of return analysis to compare portfolios of different size. Investing for more than one holding period means that the amount at risk is growing. This is analogous to an insurer taking on more insurance policies. The fact that these policies are independent does not offset the effect of placing more funds at risk. Focus on the standard deviation of the rate of return should never obscure the more proper emphasis on the possible dollar values of a portfolio strategy.

PART III

EQUILIBRIUM IN CAPITAL MARKETS

The Capital Asset Pricing Model

The capital asset pricing model, almost always referred to as the CAPM, is a centerpiece of modern financial economics. The model gives us a precise prediction of the relationship that we should observe between the risk of an asset and its expected return. This relationship serves two vital functions. First, it provides a benchmark rate of return for evaluating possible investments. For example, if we are analyzing securities, we might be interested in whether the expected return we forecast for a stock is more or less than its "fair" return, given risk. Second, the model helps us to make an educated guess as to the expected return on assets that have not yet been traded in the marketplace. For example, how do we price an initial public offering of stock? How will a major new investment project affect the return investors require on a company's stock? Although the CAPM does not fully withstand empirical tests, it is widely used both because of the insight it offers and because its accuracy suffices for many important applications.

In this chapter we start with the basic version of the CAPM. We also show how the simple version may be extended without losing the insight and applicability of the model.

8.1   The Capital Asset Pricing Model

The capital asset pricing model is a set of predictions concerning equilibrium expected returns on risky assets. We intend to explain it in one short chapter, but do not expect this to be easy going. Harry Markowitz laid down the foundation of modern portfolio management in 1952. The CAPM was developed 12 years later in articles by William Sharpe,[1] John Lintner,[2] and Jan Mossin.[3] The time for this gestation indicates that the leap from Markowitz's portfolio selection model to the CAPM is not trivial.

We will approach the CAPM by posing the question "what if," in which the "if" part refers to a simplified world. Positing an admittedly unrealistic world allows a relatively easy leap to the "then" part. Once we accomplish this, we can add complexity to the hypothesized environment one step at a time and see how the conclusions must be amended. This process allows us to derive a reasonably realistic and comprehensible model.

We can summarize the simplifying assumptions that lead to the basic version of the CAPM in the following list. The thrust of these assumptions is that we try to ensure that individuals are as alike as possible, with the notable exceptions of initial wealth and risk tolerance. We will see that conformity of investor behaviour vastly simplifies our analysis.

1. *There are many investors, each with an endowment (wealth) that is small compared to the total endowment of all investors.* Investors are price takers, in that they act as though security prices are unaffected by their own trades. This is the usual perfect competition assumption of microeconomics.

2. *All investors plan for one identical holding period.* This behaviour sometimes is said to be myopic (short-sighted) in that it ignores everything that might happen after the end of the single-period horizon. Myopic behaviour is, in general, suboptimal.

3. *Investments are limited to a universe of publicly traded financial assets, such as stocks and bonds, and to risk-free borrowing or lending arrangements.* This assumption rules out investment in non-traded assets such as in education (human capital), private enterprises, and governmentally funded assets such as town halls and nuclear submarines. It is assumed also that investors may borrow or lend any amount at a fixed, risk-free rate.

4. *Investors pay no taxes on returns and no transaction costs (commissions and service charges) on trades in securities.* In reality, of course, we know that investors are in different tax brackets and that this may govern the type of assets in which they invest. For example, tax implications may differ depending on whether the income is from interest, dividends, or capital gains. Furthermore, trading is costly, and commissions and fees depend on the size of the trade and the good standing of the individual investor.

5. *All investors are rational mean-variance optimizers, meaning that they all use the Markowitz portfolio selection model.*

6. *All investors analyze securities in the same way and share the same economic view of the world.* The result is identical estimates of the probability

[1] Sharpe, William, "Capital Asset Prices: A Theory of Market Equilibrium," *Journal of Finance,* September 1964.

[2] Lintner, John, "The Valuation of Risk Assets and the Selection of Risky Investments in Stock Portfolios and Capital Budgets," *Review of Economics and Statistics,* February 1965.

[3] Mossin, Jan, "Equilibrium in a Capital Asset Market," *Econometrica,* October 1966.

distribution of future cash flows from investing in the available securities; that is, for any set of security prices, they all derive the same input list to feed into the Markowitz model. Given a set of security prices and the risk-free interest rate, all investors use the same expected returns and covariance matrix of security returns to generate the efficient frontier and the unique optimal risky portfolio. This assumption is often referred to as **homogeneous expectations** or beliefs.

These assumptions represent the "if" of our "what if" analysis. Obviously, they ignore many real-world complexities. With these assumptions, however, we can gain some powerful insights into the nature of equilibrium in security markets.

We can summarize the equilibrium that will prevail in this hypothetical world of securities and investors briefly. The rest of the chapter explains and elaborates on these implications.

1. All investors will choose to hold a portfolio of risky assets in proportions that duplicate representation of the assets in the **market portfolio** (*M*), which includes all traded assets. For simplicity, we shall often refer to all risky assets as stocks. The proportion of each stock in the market portfolio equals the market value of the stock (price per share multiplied by the number of shares outstanding) divided by the total market value of all stocks.

2. Not only will the market portfolio be on the efficient frontier, but it also will be the tangency portfolio to the optimal capital allocation line (CAL) derived by each and every investor. As a result, the capital market line (CML), the line from the risk-free rate through the market portfolio, *M*, is also the best attainable capital allocation line. All investors hold *M* as their optimal risky portfolio, differing only in the amount invested in it versus in the risk-free asset.

3. The risk premium on the market portfolio will be proportional to the risk of the market portfolio and the market degree of risk aversion. Mathematically,

$$E(r_M) - r_f = \overline{A} \, \sigma_M^2$$

where σ_M^2 is the variance of the market portfolio and $\overline{A}$ is the average degree of risk aversion across investors. Note that because *M* is the optimal portfolio, which is efficiently diversified across all stocks, σ_M^2 is the systematic risk of this universe.

4. The risk premium on individual assets will be proportional to the risk premium on the market portfolio, *M*, and the *beta coefficient* of the security, relative to the market portfolio. We will see that beta measures the extent to which returns on the stock and the market move together. Formally, beta is defined as

$$\beta_i = \frac{\text{Cov}(r_i, r_M)}{\sigma_M^2}$$

and we can write

$$E(r_i) - r_f = \frac{\text{Cov}(r_i, r_M)}{\sigma_M^2} [E(r_M) - r_f]$$

$$= \beta_i [E(r_M) - r_f]$$

We will elaborate on these results and their implications shortly.

Why Do All Investors Hold the Market Portfolio?

Given the assumptions of the previous section, it is easy to see that all investors will desire to hold identical risky portfolios. If all investors use identical Markowitz analysis (assumption 5) applied to the same universe of securities (assumption 3) for the same time horizon (assumption 2) and use the same input list (assumption 6), they all must arrive at the same determination of the optimal risky portfolio, the portfolio on the efficient frontier identified by the tangency line from T-bills to that frontier, as in Figure 8.1. This implies that if the weight of Seagram's (VO) stock, for example, in each common risky portfolio is 1 percent, then when we sum over all investors' portfolios to obtain the aggregate market portfolio, VO also will comprise 1 percent of the market portfolio. The same principle applies to the proportion of any stock in each investor's risky portfolio. As a result, the optimal risky portfolio of all investors is simply a share of the market portfolio, which we label *M* in Figure 8.1.

Now suppose that the optimal portfolio of our investors does not include the stock of some company such as Canadian Tire (CT). When all investors avoid CT stock, the demand is zero, and CT's price takes a free fall. As CT stock gets progressively cheaper, it becomes ever more attractive as an investment and all

FIGURE 8.1
The efficient frontier and the capital market line.

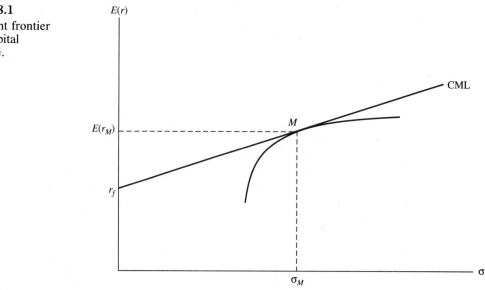

other stocks look (relatively) less attractive. Ultimately, CT reaches a price where it is profitable enough to include in the optimal stock portfolio.

Such a price adjustment process guarantees that all stocks will be included in the optimal portfolio. It shows that *all* assets have to be included in the market portfolio. The only issue is the price at which investors will be willing to include a stock in their optimal risky portfolio.

This may seem a roundabout way to derive a simple result: if all investors hold an identical risky portfolio, this portfolio has to be *M*, the market portfolio. Our intention, however, is to demonstrate a connection between this result and its underpinnings, the equilibrating process that is fundamental to security market operation.

The Passive Strategy Is Efficient

In Chapter 6 we defined the CML (capital market line) as the CAL (capital allocation line) that is constructed from either a money market account or T-bills and the market portfolio. Perhaps now you can fully appreciate why the CML is an interesting CAL. In the simple world of the CAPM, *M* is the optimal tangency portfolio on the efficient frontier. This is shown in Figure 8.1.

In this scenario the market portfolio, *M*, that all investors hold is based on the common input list, thereby incorporating all relevant information about the universe of securities. This means an investor can skip the trouble of doing specific analysis and obtain an efficient portfolio simply by holding the market portfolio. (Of course, if everyone were to follow this strategy, no one would perform security analysis, and this result would no longer hold. We discuss this issue in depth in Chapter 12 on market efficiency.)

Thus the passive strategy of investing in a market index portfolio is efficient. For this reason, we sometimes call this result a **mutual fund theorem.** The mutual fund theorem is another incarnation of the separation property discussed in Chapter 7. Assuming that all investors choose to hold a market index mutual fund, we can separate portfolio selection into two components—a technological problem, creation of mutual funds by professional managers—and a personal problem that depends on an investor's risk aversion, allocation of the complete portfolio between the mutual fund and risk-free assets.

Concept Check

Question 1. If there are only a few investors who perform security analysis, and all others hold the market portfolio *M*, would the CML still be the efficient CAL for investors who do not engage in security analysis? Why or why not?

Of course, in reality different investment managers do create risky portfolios that differ from the market index. We attribute this in part to the use of different input lists in the formation of the optimal risky portfolio. Nevertheless, the

Index Mutual Funds Thrive without Managers' Wiles

By Jade Hemeon

It doesn't always take a good portfolio manager to produce good mutual fund returns. Some funds have performed impressively without being actively managed at all.

These are index funds, and their portfolios duplicate the make-up of a particular stock or bond index, such as the Toronto Stock Exchange 300 composite or the Standard & Poor's 500.

Naturally, a fund's ability to outperform the index depends on the stock-picking acumen of its manager, and many funds do better than the index. However, many investors like the index funds because of the availability of historical statistics going back many years, which helps predict future long-term performance. Few of the hot-shot mutual funds have a track record going back 20 years.

Index mutual funds proliferate in the United States, and are widely used by pension funds. But there are only a few in Canada.

Toronto Dominion Bank sponsors two of them— the Green Line Canadian Index Fund, based on the TSE 300 composite index, and the Green Line U.S. Index Fund, based on the S & P 500. Another, the First Canadian Equity Index Fund, also based on the TSE 300, was recently introduced by Bank of Montreal.

The Royal Trust Government Bond Index Fund holds a portfolio based on McLeod Young Weir Ltd.'s long-term government bond index.

Just last week [1988], Trafalgar Capital Management, a Toronto-based pension fund manager, introduced a pooled fund for pension managers based on the Europe, Australia and Far East Index (EAFE) published by Morgan Stanley Capital International for investors seeking global exposure. The index covers about 855 companies throughout 17 countries.

Called the EAFE Index Fund, it "provides a simple and inexpensive way to access superior performance without having to go through a very complicated search for an international manager," says Tristram Lett, Trafalgar's president.

In the six months since October's market crash, the return to investors in the EAFE Index would have been 16.2 percent.

The stock index funds invest in the companies that make up the index they imitate, in the same proportion that these companies are weighted in the index. Consequently, their performance mirrors the market averages.

While this approach takes the decision making out of the hands of a fund manager, stock-pickers at the more actively managed mutual funds do not always beat the indexes.

For example, the average Canadian equity fund showed an annual 13.7 percent return over the 10 years ended April 30, while the average U.S. equity fund sold in Canada had a 14.5 percent return. Meanwhile, the TSE total return index showed a 16.6 percent return over the same period. The S & P 500 did slightly less well than the average U.S. fund, showing an 11.4 percent return.

Peter Campbell, product manager of RRSPs at the TD, speculates that index funds are hard to beat because their portfolios are composed of the larger, more established companies. Because they hold all of the companies in the index, the funds are diversified among these select companies.

Predictably, the TD's Green Line Canadian fund fell 8.8 percent for the year ended April 30, 1988—a period that included the October 19 crash. But this dismal performance was an improvement over the showing of the average Canadian equity fund, which declined 9.8 percent. The fund has assets of $37.8 million.

TD's U.S. index fund, with assets of $12.9 million, declined by 7.0 percent over the year, a vast improvement over the 14.8 percent average decline for U.S. equity funds sold in Canada.

Performances for both funds have been strong since the crash. For the six months ended April 30, the Canadian index fund rose by 11.1 percent, compared with 9.2 percent for the average equity fund. The U.S. fund rose by 5.0 percent, compared with

(Continued)

a 2.1 percent increase for the average U.S. investment fund sold in Canada.

The TD charges a lower commission on its funds, sold through TD branches, than that charged on funds sold through brokers and mutual fund dealers. Brokers may charge a commission as high as 9 percent; the TD charges 2 percent. Bank of Montreal doesn't charge any commission at all.

Unlike its equity fund counterparts, Canada's only bond index fund, the Royal Trust Bond Index Fund, has not beaten the mutual fund averages in its category. It declined by 0.79 percent in the year ended March 31, 1988, while the fixed-income group rose an average of 5 percent.

The fund invests in government bonds in the same proportion that bonds issued by federal, provincial and municipal governments are represented in the market. The fund, which has assets of $8.5 million, is sold through brokers and charges the normal commissions. However, sales have been cut off while the fund's administrators review its future direction.

"The idea of an indexed bond fund looked good, but it didn't bring in as much money as we expected," says Michael Belfie, an associate at Corporate Investment Associates (RT) Inc., a subsidiary of Royal Trust Co. "We decided to cut off further sales while we're reviewing alternatives."

Belfie says one of the alternatives may be the use of a different bond index. The long-term bond index has an average term of 15 years and "long-term bonds are not as attractive in an environment of rising interest rates."

Royal Trust also offers a savings account with a return tied to the movement of stock indexes. Unlike mutual funds, where you could lose some of your money if the stock market crashed, the savings account guarantees the principal amount invested. The principal is insured by Canada Deposit Insurance Corp.

Called the Royal Trust Guaranteed Market Index Investment (GMII), the account comes with a bull and bear market option. The return is equivalent to 40 percent of the percentage change in the TSE 35 index (composed of 35 blue-chip stocks) or the New York Stock Exchange Index over a six-month period.

You must call the market right to make any money, however. If you pick the bull market version and the market falls, there'll be no return.

From *The Financial Post*, June 6, 1988. Reprinted by permission of the author and *The Financial Post*.

significance of the mutual fund theorem is that a passive investor may view the market index as a reasonable first approximation of an efficient risky portfolio. Indeed, the accompanying box shows that index mutual funds are increasingly popular investment strategies among individual investors.

The Risk Premium of the Market Portfolio

In Chapter 6 we discussed how individual investors go about deciding how much to invest in the risky portfolio. Returning now to the decision of how much to invest in portfolio M versus in the risk-free asset, what can we deduce about the equilibrium risk premium of portfolio M?

We asserted earlier that the equilibrium risk premium on the market portfolio, $E(r_M) - r_f$, will be proportional to the average degree of risk aversion of the investor population and the risk of the market portfolio, σ_M^2. Now we can explain this result.

Recall that each individual investor chooses a proportion, y, allocated to the optimal portfolio M, such that

$$y = \frac{E(r_M) - r_f}{A\sigma_M^2} \tag{8.1}$$

In the simplified CAPM economy, risk-free investments involve borrowing and lending among investors. Any borrowing position must be offset by the lending position of the creditor. This means that net borrowing and lending across all investors must be zero, and in consequence the average position in the risky portfolio is 100 percent or $\bar{y} = 1$. Setting $y = 1$ in equation 8.1 and rearranging, we find that the risk premium on the market portfolio is related to its variance by the average degree of risk aversion:

$$E(r_M) - r_f = \bar{A}\sigma_M^2 \tag{8.2}$$

Concept Check

Question 2. Data from the period 1956–1990 for the TSE 300 index yield the following statistics: Average excess return, 2.94 percent; standard deviation, 17.5 percent.
a. To the extent that these averages approximated investor expectations for the period, what must have been the average coefficient of risk aversion?
b. If the coefficient of risk aversion were actually 1.5, what risk premium would have been consistent with the market's historical standard deviation?

Expected Returns on Individual Securities

The CAPM is built on the insight that the appropriate risk premium on an asset will be determined by its contribution to the risk of investors' overall portfolios. Portfolio risk is what matters to investors and is what governs the risk premiums they demand.

Suppose, for example, that we want to gauge the portfolio risk of Inco stock. We measure the contribution to the risk of the overall portfolio from holding Inco stock by its covariance with the market portfolio. To see why this is so, let us look again at the way the variance of the market portfolio is calculated. To calculate the variance of the market portfolio, we use the covariance matrix bordered by market portfolio weights, as discussed in Chapter 7. We highlight Inco in this depiction of the n stocks in the market portfolio.

Portfolio Weights:	w_1	w_2	$\cdots$	w_I	$\cdots$	w_n
w_1	$\text{Cov}(r_1,r_1)$	$\text{Cov}(r_1,r_2)$	$\ldots$	$\text{Cov}(r_1,r_I)$	$\ldots$	$\text{Cov}(r_1,r_n)$
w_2	$\text{Cov}(r_2,r_1)$	$\text{Cov}(r_2,r_2)$	$\ldots$	$\text{Cov}(r_2,r_I)$	$\ldots$	$\text{Cov}(r_2,r_n)$
.	.	.		.		.
.	.	.	. .	.		.
.	.	. .	.	.		.
w_I	$\text{Cov}(r_I,r_1)$		$\ldots$	$\text{Cov}(r_I,r_I)$	$\ldots$	$\text{Cov}(r_I,r_n)$
.	.	.		.		.
.	.	.		.		.
.	.	.		.		.
w_n	$\text{Cov}(r_n,r_1)$	$\text{Cov}(r_n,r_2)$	$\ldots$	$\text{Cov}(r_n,r_I)$	$\ldots$	$\text{Cov}(r_n,r_n)$

Recall that we calculate the variance of the portfolio by summing over all the elements of the covariance matrix and multiplying each element by the portfolio weights from the row and the column. The contribution of one stock to portfolio variance therefore can be expressed as the sum of all the covariance terms in the row corresponding to the stock where each covariance is multiplied by both the portfolio weight from its row and the weight from its column.[4]

For example, the contribution of Inco's stock to the variance of the market portfolio is

$$w_I[w_1\text{Cov}(r_1,r_I) + w_2\text{Cov}(r_2,r_I) + \cdots + w_I\text{Cov}(r_I,r_I) + \cdots + w_n\text{Cov}(r_n,r_I)] \tag{8.3}$$

Equation 8.3 provides a clue about the respective roles of variance and covariance in determining asset risk. It shows us that, when there are many stocks in the economy, there will be many more covariance terms than variance terms. Consequently, the covariance of a particular stock with all other stocks might be expected to have more to do with that stock's contribution to total portfolio risk than does its variance. In fact, since each stock in equation 8.3 is weighted by its share in the market portfolio, we may summarize the term in brackets in the equation simply as the covariance of Inco with the market portfolio. In other words, we can best measure the stock's contribution to the risk of the market portfolio by its covariance with that portfolio.

This should not surprise us. For example, if the covariance between Inco and the rest of the market is negative, then Inco makes a "negative contribution" to portfolio risk: by providing returns that move inversely with the rest of the market, Inco stabilizes the return on the overall portfolio. If the covariance

---

[4] An alternative and equally valid approach would be to measure Inco's contribution to market variance as the sum of the elements in the row *and* the column corresponding to Inco. In this case, Inco's contribution would be twice the sum in equation 8.3. The approach that we take in the text allocates contributions to portfolio risk among securities in a convenient manner in that the sum of the contributions of each stock equals the total portfolio variance, whereas the alternative measure of contribution would sum to twice the portfolio variance. This results from a type of double-counting, because adding both the rows and the columns for each stock would result in each entry in the matrix being added twice.

is positive, Inco makes a positive contribution to overall portfolio risk because its returns amplify swings in the rest of the portfolio.

To prove this more rigorously, note that the rate of return on the market portfolio may be written as

$$r_M = \sum_{k=1}^{n} w_k r_k$$

Therefore the covariance of the return on Inco with the market portfolio is

$$\text{Cov}(r_I, r_M) = \text{Cov}(r_I, \sum_{k=1}^{n} w_k r_k) = \sum_{k=1}^{n} w_k \text{Cov}(r_I, r_k) \qquad \textbf{(8.4)}$$

Comparing the last term of equation 8.4 to the term in brackets in equation 8.3, we can see that the covariance of Inco with the market portfolio is indeed proportional to the contribution of Inco to the variance of the market portfolio.

Having measured the contribution of Inco stock to market variance, we may determine the appropriate risk premium for Inco. We note first that the market portfolio has a risk premium of $E(r_M) - r_f$ and a variance of σ_M^2, for a reward-to-risk ratio of

$$\frac{E(r_M) - r_f}{\sigma_M^2} \qquad \textbf{(8.5)}$$

This ratio often is called the **market price of risk**[5] because it quantifies the extra return that investors demand to bear portfolio risk. The ratio of risk premium to variance tells us how much extra return must be earned per unit of portfolio risk.

Suppose that investors wish to increase their position in the market portfolio by a tiny fraction, δ, financed by borrowing at the risk-free rate. The increment to the portfolio expected excess return will be

$$\Delta E(r) = \delta[E(r_M) - r_f]$$

The portfolio variance will increase by the variance of the incremental position in the market *plus* twice its covariance with the original position (100% in the market):

$$\Delta \sigma^2 = \delta^2 \sigma_M^2 + 2\delta \text{Cov}(r_M, r_M)$$

---

[5] We open ourselves to ambiguity in using this term, because the market portfolio's reward-to-variability ratio

$$\frac{E(r_M) - r_f}{\sigma_M}$$

sometimes is referred to as the market price of risk. Note that since the appropriate risk measure of Inco is its covariance with the market portfolio (its contribution to the variance of the market portfolio), this risk is measured in percent squared. Accordingly, the price of this risk, $[E(r_M) - r_f]/\sigma^2$, is defined as the percentage of expected return per percent square of variance.

If δ is infinitesimal, then its square will be negligible,[6] leaving the incremental variance as

$$\Delta\sigma^2 = 2\delta\text{Cov}(r_M, r_M) = 2\delta\sigma_M^2$$

The trade-off between the *incremental risk premium* and *incremental risk,* referred to as the *marginal price of risk,* is given by the ratio

$$\frac{\Delta E(r)}{\Delta\sigma^2} = \frac{E(r_{\overline{M}} - r_f)}{2\sigma_M^2}$$

and equals one half the market price of risk in equation 8.5.

Now suppose that, instead, investors were to invest the increment δ in Inco stock, financed by borrowing at the risk-free rate. The increase in mean excess return is

$$\Delta E(r) = \delta[E(r_I) - r_f]$$

The increase in variance, here too, includes the variance of the incremental position in GM *plus* twice its covariance with the market:

$$\Delta\sigma^2 = \delta^2\sigma_I^2 + 2\delta\text{Cov}(r_I, r_M)$$

Dropping the negligible term, the *marginal price of risk* of Inco is

$$\frac{\Delta E(r)}{\Delta\sigma^2} = \frac{E(r_I) - r_f}{2\text{Cov}(r_I, r_M)}$$

In equilibrium, the marginal price of risk of Inco stock has to equal that of the market portfolio. Because, when the marginal price of risk of Inco is greater than the market's, investors can increase their portfolio *average* price of risk by increasing the weight of Inco in their portfolio. Moreover, as long as the price of Inco stock does not rise relative to the market, investors will keep buying Inco stock. The process will continue until stock prices adjust so that marginal price of risk of Inco equals that of the market. (The same process, in reverse, will equalize marginal prices of risk when Inco's initial marginal price of risk is less than that of the market portfolio.) Equating the marginal price of risk of Inco's stock to that of the market gets us the relationship between the risk premium of Inco and that of the market.

$$\frac{E(r_I) - r_f}{2\text{Cov}(r_I, r_M)} = \frac{E(r_M) - r_f}{2\sigma_M^2}$$

To determine the fair risk premium for Inco stock, we need only multiply the risk that Inco stock contributes to the variance of the market portfolio, which is

---

[6] For example, if δ is 1% (.01 of wealth), then its square is .0001 of wealth, one hundredth of the original value. The term $\delta\sigma_M^2$ will be smaller than $2\delta\text{Cov}(r_M, r_M)$ by an order of magnitude.

Cov(r_I,r_M), by the market price of risk. We thus find that $E(r_I) - r_f$, which is Inco's risk premium, should be

$$E(r_I) - r_f = \text{Cov}(r_I,r_M) \times \frac{E(r_M) - r_f}{\sigma_M^2}$$

Rearranging slightly, we obtain

$$E(r_I) - r_f = \frac{\text{Cov}(r_I,r_M)}{\sigma_M^2} [E(r_M) - r_f] \qquad \textbf{(8.6)}$$

The term $\text{Cov}(r_I,r_M)/\sigma_M^2$ measures the contribution of Inco stock to the variance of the market portfolio as a fraction of the total variance of the market portfolio and is referred to by the Greek letter **beta,** β. Using this measure, we can restate equation 8.6 as

$$E(r_I) = r_f + \beta_I[E(r_M) - r_f] \qquad \textbf{(8.7)}$$

This **expected return-beta relationship** is the most familiar expression of the CAPM to practitioners. We will have a lot more to say about the expected return-beta relationship shortly.

We see now why the assumptions that made individuals act similarly are so useful. If everyone holds an identical risky portfolio, then everyone will find that the beta of each asset with the market portfolio equals the asset's beta with his or her own risky portfolio. Hence everyone will agree on the appropriate risk premium for each asset.

Does this mean that the fact that few real-life investors actually hold the market portfolio implies that the CAPM is of no practical importance? Not necessarily. Recall from Chapter 7 that reasonably well-diversified portfolios shed firm-specific risk and are left with only systematic or market risk. Even if one does not hold the precise market portfolio, a well-diversified portfolio will be so very highly correlated with the market that a stock's beta relative to the market still will be a useful risk measure.

In fact, several authors have shown that modified versions of the CAPM will hold true even if we consider differences among individuals leading them to hold different portfolios. For example, Brennan[7] examines the impact of differences in investors' personal tax rates on market equilibrium, and Mayers[8] looks at the impact of nontraded assets such as human capital (earning power). Both find that, although the market is no longer each investor's optimal risky portfolio, the expected return-beta relationship still should hold in a somewhat modified form.

If the expected return-beta relationship holds for any individual asset, it must hold for any combination of assets. Suppose that some portfolio P has

[7] Michael J. Brennan, "Taxes, Market Valuation, and Corporate Finance Policy," *National Tax Journal,* December 1973.

[8] David Mayers, "Nonmarketable Assets and Capital Market Equilibrium under Uncertainty," in M. C. Jensen (editor), *Studies in the Theory of Capital Markets* (New York: Praeger, 1972).

weight w_k for stock k, where k takes on values $1, \ldots, n$. Writing out the CAPM equation 8.7 for each stock, and multiplying each equation by the weight of the stock in the portfolio, we obtain these equations, one for each stock:

$$w_1E(r_1) = w_1r_f + w_1\beta_1[E(r_M) - r_f]$$
$$+ \quad w_2E(r_2) = w_2r_f + w_2\beta_2[E(r_M) - r_f]$$
$$+ \quad \ldots = \ldots$$
$$+ \quad w_nE(r_n) = w_nr_f + w_n\beta_n[E(r_M) - r_f]$$
$$E(r_P) = r_f + \beta_P[E(r_M) - r_f]$$

Summing each column shows that the CAPM holds for the overall portfolio because $E(r_P) = \sum_k w_kE(r_k)$ is the expected return on the portfolio, and $\beta_P = \sum_k w_k\beta_k$ is the portfolio beta. Incidentally, this result has to be true for the market portfolio itself,

$$E(r_M) = r_f + \beta_M[E(r_M) - r_f]$$

Indeed, this is a tautology because $\beta_M = 1$, as we can verify by demonstrating that

$$\beta_M = \frac{\text{Cov}(r_M, r_M)}{\sigma_M^2} = \frac{\sigma_M^2}{\sigma_M^2}$$

This also establishes 1 as the weighted average value of beta across all assets. If the market beta is 1, and the market is a portfolio of all assets in the economy, the weighted average beta of all assets must be 1. Hence betas greater than 1 are considered aggressive in that investment in high-beta stocks entails above-average sensitivity to market swings. Betas below 1 can be described as defensive.

Concept Check

Question 3. Suppose that the risk premium on the market portfolio is estimated at 8 percent with a standard deviation of 22 percent. What is the risk premium on a portfolio invested 25 percent in Inco and 75 percent in Noranda, if both have a beta of 1.15?

A word of caution: we are all accustomed to hearing that well-managed firms will provide high rates of return. We agree this is true if one measures the *firm's* return on investments in plant and equipment. The CAPM, however, predicts returns on investments in the *securities* of the firm.

Let us say that everyone knows a firm is well run. Its stock price will therefore be bid up, and consequently returns to stockholders who buy at those high prices will not be excessive. Security prices, in other words, reflect public information about a firm's prospects, but only the risk of the company (as measured by beta in the context of the CAPM) should affect expected returns. In a rational market investors receive high expected returns only if they are willing to bear risk.

The Security Market Line

We can view the expected return-beta relationship as a reward-risk equation. The beta of a security is the appropriate measure of its risk because beta is proportional to the risk that the security contributes to the optimal risky portfolio.

Risk-averse investors measure the risk of the optimal risky portfolio by its variance. In this world we would expect the reward, or the risk premium on individual assets, to depend on the risk that an individual asset contributes to the portfolio. The beta of a stock measures the stock's contribution to the variance of the market portfolio as a fraction of the total portfolio variance. Hence we expect, for any asset or portfolio, the required risk premium to be a function of beta. The CAPM confirms this intuition, stating further that the security's risk premium is directly proportional to both the beta and the risk premium of the market portfolio; that is, the risk premium equals

$$\beta[E(r_M) - r_f]$$

The expected return-beta relationship can be portrayed graphically as the **security market line** (SML) in Figure 8.2. Its slope is the risk premium of the market portfolio. At the point where $\beta = 1$ on the horizontal axis (which is the market portfolio's beta), we can read off the vertical axis the expected return on the market portfolio.

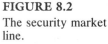
FIGURE 8.2
The security market line.

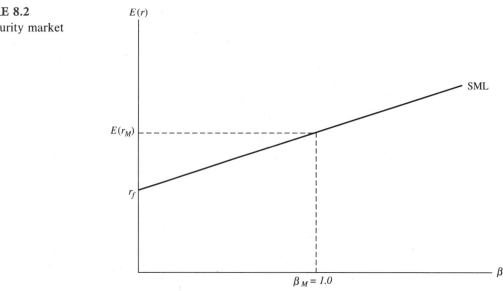

It is useful to compare the security market line to the capital market line. The CML graphs the risk premiums of efficient portfolios (that is, portfolios composed of the market and the risk-free asset) as a function of portfolio standard deviation. This is appropriate because standard deviation is a valid measure of risk for efficiently diversified portfolios that are candidates for an investor's overall portfolio. The SML, in contrast, graphs *individual asset* risk premiums as a function of asset risk. The relevant measure of risk for individual assets held as parts of well-diversified portfolios is not the asset's standard deviation or variance; it is, instead, the contribution of the asset to the portfolio variance, which we measure by the asset's beta. The SML is valid for both efficient portfolios and individual assets.

The security market line provides a benchmark for the evaluation of investment performance. Given the risk of an investment, as measured by its beta, the SML provides the required rate of return from that investment to compensate investors for risk, as well as the time value of money.

Because the security market line is the graphic representation of the expected return-beta relationship, "fairly priced" assets plot exactly on the SML; that is, their expected returns are commensurate with their risk. Given the assumptions we made in the beginning of this section, all securities must lie on the SML in market equilibrium. Nevertheless, we see here how the CAPM may be of use in the money-management industry. Suppose that the SML relation is used as a benchmark to assess the fair expected return on a risky asset. Then security analysis is performed to calculate the return actually expected. (Notice that we depart here from the simple CAPM world in that some investors now apply their own unique analysis to derive an "input list" that may differ from their competitors'.) If a stock is perceived to be a good buy, or underpriced, it will provide an expected return in excess of the fair return stipulated by the SML. Underpriced stocks, therefore, plot above the SML: given their betas, their expected returns are greater than dictated by the CAPM. Overpriced stocks plot below the SML.

The difference between the fair and actually expected rates of return on a stock is called the stock's **alpha,** denoted α. For example, if the market is expected to be 14 percent, a stock has a beta of 1.2, and the T-bill rate is 10 percent, the SML would predict an expected return on the stock of $10 + 1.2 (14 - 10) = 14.8$ percent. If one believed the stock would provide a return of 17 percent, the implied alpha would be 2.2 percent (see Figure 8.3).

Concept Check

Question 4. Stock XYZ has an expected return of 12 percent and risk of $\beta = 1$. Stock ABC has expected return of 13 percent and $\beta = 1.5$. The market's expected return is 11 percent, and $r_f = 5$ percent.
a. According to the CAPM, which stock is a better buy?
b. What is the alpha of each stock? Plot the SML and each stock's risk-return point on one graph. Show the alphas graphically.

FIGURE 8.3
The SML and a
positive-alpha stock.

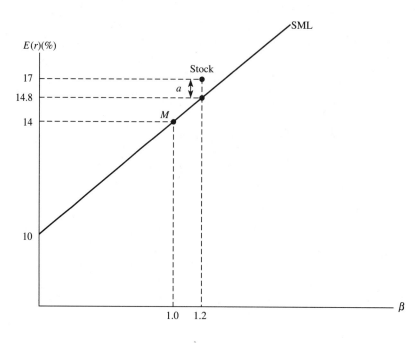

The CAPM also is useful in capital budgeting decisions. For a firm considering a new project, the CAPM can provide the return that the project needs to
yield, based on its beta, to be acceptable to investors. Managers can use the
CAPM to obtain this cutoff internal rate of return (IRR) or "hurdle rate" for the
project.

Concept Check

Question 5. The risk-free rate is 8 percent and the expected return on the
market portfolio is 12 percent. A firm considers a project that is expected
to have a beta of 1.3.
a. What is the required rate of return on the project?
b. If the expected IRR of the project is 15 percent, should it be accepted?

Yet another use of the CAPM is in utility rate-making cases. In this case, the
issue is the rate of return that a regulated utility should be allowed to earn on its
investment in plant and equipment. Suppose that the equityholders have invested $100 million in the firm and that the beta of the equity is .6. If the T-bill
rate is 6 percent and the market risk premium is 4 percent, then the fair profits
to the firm would be assessed as $6 + .6(4) = 8.4$ percent of the $100 million
investment, or $8.4 million. The firm would be allowed to set prices at a level
expected to generate these profits.

8.2 *Extensions of the CAPM*

The assumptions that allowed Sharpe to derive the simple version of the CAPM are admittedly unrealistic. Financial economists have been at work ever since the CAPM was devised to extend the model to more realistic scenarios.

There are two classes of extensions to the simple version of the CAPM. The first attempts to relax the assumptions that we outlined at the outset of the chapter. The second acknowledges the fact that investors worry about sources of risk other than the uncertain value of their securities, such as unexpected changes in relative prices of consumer goods. This idea involves the introduction of additional risk factors besides security returns, and we will discuss it further in the appendix.

The CAPM with Restricted Borrowing: The Zero-Beta Model

The CAPM is predicted on the assumption that all investors share an identical input list that they feed into the Markowitz algorithm. Thus all investors agree on the location of the efficient (minimum-variance) frontier, where each portfolio has the lowest variance among all feasible portfolios at a target expected rate of return. When all investors can borrow and lend at the safe rate, r_f, all agree on the optimal tangency portfolio and choose to hold a share of the market portfolio.

When there are constraints on risk-free lending and/or borrowing, we will see that the market portfolio is no longer the common optimal portfolio for all investors. One "restriction" on risk-free borrowing and lending is that, in a strict sense, once we account for inflation uncertainty there is no truly risk-free asset in the Canadian economy. Only Treasury securities are entirely free of default risk, but these are nominal obligations, meaning that their real values are exposed to price level risk. In this sense there is no risk-free asset in the economy. Other restrictions have to do with differences in the rates at which investors can borrow and lend.

When investors no longer can borrow or lend at a common risk-free rate, they may choose risky portfolios from the entire set of efficient frontier portfolios according to how much risk they choose to bear. The market is no longer the common optimal portfolio. In fact, with investors choosing different portfolios, it is no longer obvious whether the market portfolio, which is the aggregate of all investors' portfolios, will even be on the efficient frontier. If the market portfolio is no longer mean-variance efficient, then the expected return-beta relationship of the CAPM will no longer characterize market equilibrium.

An equilibrium expected return-beta relationship in the case of restricted risk-free investments has been developed by Fischer Black.[9] Black's model is

---

[9] Black, Fischer, "Capital Market Equilibrium with Restricted Borrowing," *Journal of Business*, July 1972.

fairly difficult and requires a good deal of facility with mathematics. Therefore, we will satisfy ourselves with a sketch of Black's argument and spend more time with its implications.

Black's model of the CAPM in the absence of a risk-free asset rests on the three following properties of mean-variance efficient portfolios:

1. Any portfolio constructed by combining efficient portfolios is itself on the efficient frontier.
2. Every portfolio on the efficient frontier has a companion portfolio on the bottom half (the inefficient part) of the minimum-variance frontier with which it is uncorrelated. Because the portfolios are uncorrelated, the companion portfolio is referred to as the **zero-beta portfolio** of the efficient portfolio.

   The expected return of an efficient portfolio's zero-beta companion portfolio can be derived by the following graphical procedure. From any efficient portfolio such as *P* in Figure 8.4 draw a tangency line to the vertical axis. The intercept will be the expected return on portfolio *P*'s zero-beta companion portfolio, denoted *Z(P)*. The horizontal line from the intercept to the minimum-variance frontier identifies the standard deviation of the zero-beta portfolio. Notice in Figure 8.4 that different efficient portfolios such as *P* and *Q* have different zero-beta companions.

   These tangency lines are only helpful constructs—they do *not* signify that one can invest in portfolios with expected return-standard deviation pairs along the line. That would be possible only by mixing a risk-free asset with the tangency portfolio. In this case, however, we assume that risk-free assets are not available to investors.

FIGURE 8.4
Efficient portfolios and their zero-beta companions.

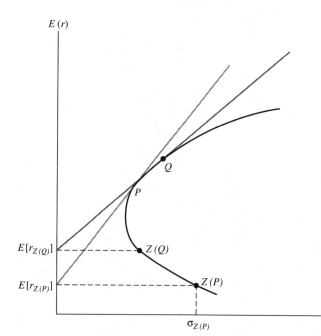

3. The expected return of any asset can be expressed as an exact, linear function of the expected return on any two frontier portfolios. Consider, for example, the minimum-variance frontier portfolios P and Q. Black shows that the expected return on any asset i can be expressed as

$$E(r_i) = E(r_Q) + [E(r_P) - E(r_Q)] \frac{\text{Cov}(r_i, r_P) - \text{Cov}(r_P, r_Q)}{\sigma_P^2 - \text{Cov}(r_P, r_Q)} \qquad (8.8)$$

Note that this last property has nothing to do with market equilibrium. It is a purely mathematical property relating frontier portfolios and individual securities.

Given these three properties, it is easy to derive Black's model. The assumption of homogeneous expectations assures us that all investors use the same input list and compute the same minimum-variance frontier. Each investor will invest in an efficient portfolio according to his or her degree of risk aversion, as in Figure 8.5. The market portfolio, which is just the aggregate of all investors' portfolios, therefore is a combination of efficient portfolios, and by property 1, must itself be an efficient portfolio.

Next, recall equation 8.8 from property 3. Instead of using the arbitrarily chosen frontier portfolios P and Q in the equation, let us instead use as our two frontier portfolios the market portfolio, M, and its zero-beta companion, $Z(M)$. This is a convenient pairing of portfolios because their mutual covariance is zero, causing equation 8.8 to simplify. Specifically, because $\text{Cov}[r_M, r_{Z(M)}] = 0$, the expected return of any asset i, using M and $Z(M)$ as the benchmark frontier portfolios, can be expressed as

$$E(r_i) = E[r_{Z(M)}] + E[r_M - r_{Z(M)}] \frac{\text{Cov}(r_i, r_M)}{\sigma_M^2} \qquad (8.9)$$

FIGURE 8.5
Portfolio selection with no risk-free assets.

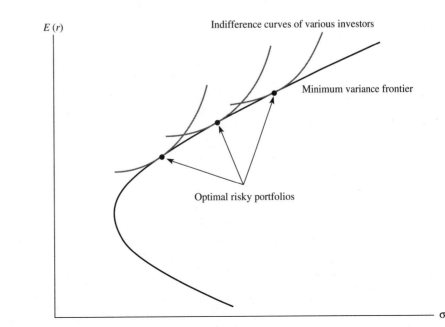

where P from equation 8.8 has been replaced by M and Q has been replaced by $Z(M)$. Note that this is a variant of the simple CAPM, in which r_f simply has been replaced with $E[r_{Z(M)}]$.

Although Black derived this variant of the CAPM for the case in which no risk-free asset exists, the approach we have taken can be applied to many related scenarios. For example, consider an economy in which investors can lend at the risk-free rate (can buy T-bills, for example) but cannot borrow funds to invest. We first explored portfolio selection for this situation in Section 7.5. Now we can explore market equilibrium.

Figure 8.6 shows that relatively conservative (risk-averse) investors will select the tangency portfolio, T, as their optimal risky portfolio, and mix T with the safe asset. Relatively aggressive investors will choose efficient portfolios like P_1 or P_2. The market portfolio, M, will be a combination of these portfolios, all of which are efficient, meaning that the market also will be an efficient portfolio. Therefore the zero-beta version of the CAPM will apply in this situation also.

A more realistic scenario is one in which the investor can lend at the risk-free rate, r_f, and can borrow at a higher rate, r_f^B. This case also was considered in Chapter 7. The same arguments that we have just employed also can be used to establish the zero-beta CAPM in this situation. Problem 18 at the end of this chapter asks you to fill in the details of the argument for this situation.

Concept Check
====

Question 6. Suppose that the zero-beta portfolio exhibits returns that are, on average, greater than the rate on T-bills. Is this fact relevant to the question of the validity of the CAPM?

Lifetime Consumption: The CAPM with Dynamic Programming

One of the restrictive assumptions of the simple version of the CAPM is that investors are myopic—they plan for one common holding period. Investors actually may be concerned with a lifetime consumption plan and a possible desire to leave a bequest to children. Consumption plans that are feasible for them depend on current wealth and future rates of return on the investment portfolio. These investors will want to rebalance their portfolios as often as required by changes in wealth.

However, Eugene Fama[10] shows that, even if we extend our analysis to a multiperiod setting, the single CAPM may still be appropriate. The key assumptions that Fama uses to replace myopic planning horizons are that investor preferences are unchanging over time and that the risk-free interest rate and probability distribution of security returns do not change unpredictably over

---

[10] Fama, Eugene F., ''Multiperiod Consumption-Investment Decisions,'' *American Economic Review, 60,* 1970.

FIGURE 8.6

Capital market
equilibrium with
risk-free lending but
no risk-free
borrowing.

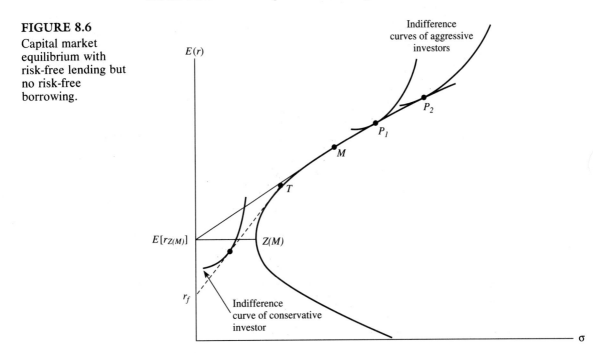

time. Of course, this latter assumption is itself somewhat unrealistic. Extensions to the CAPM engendered by considering random changes to the so-called ''investment opportunity set'' are examined in the appendix.

Summary

1. The CAPM assumes that investors are single-period planners who agree on a common input list from security analysis and seek mean-variance optimal portfolios.

    2. The CAPM assumes that security markets are ideal in the sense that:

        a. They are large, and investors are price takers.

        b. There are no taxes or transaction costs.

        c. All risky assets are publicly traded

        d. Investors can borrow and lend any amount at a fixed risk-free rate.

    3. With these assumptions, all investors hold identical risky portfolios. The CAPM holds that in equilibrium the market portfolio is the unique mean-variance efficient tangency portfolio. Thus a passive strategy is efficient.

    4. The CAPM market portfolio is a value-weighted portfolio. Each security is held in a proportion equal to its market value divided by the total market value of all securities.

5. If the market portfolio is efficient and the average investor neither borrows nor lends, then the risk premium on the market portfolio is proportional to its variance, σ_M^2, and to the average coefficient of risk aversion across investors $\overline{A}$:

$$E(r_M) - r_f = \overline{A}\sigma_M^2$$

6. The CAPM implies that the risk premium on any individual asset or portfolio is the product of the risk premium on the market portfolio and the beta coefficient:

$$E(r) - r_f = \beta[E(r_M) - r_f]$$

where the beta coefficient is the covariance of the asset with the market portfolio as a fraction of the variance of the market portfolio

$$\beta = \frac{\text{Cov}(r, r_M)}{\sigma_M^2}$$

7. When risk-free investments are restricted but all other CAPM assumptions hold, then the simple version of the CAPM is replaced by its zero-beta version. Accordingly, the risk-free rate in the expected return-beta relationship is replaced by the zero-beta portfolio's expected rate of return:

$$E(r_i) = E[r_{Z(M)}] + \beta_i E[r_M - r_{Z(M)}]$$

8. The simple version of the CAPM assumes that investors are myopic. When investors are assumed to be concerned with lifetime consumption and bequest plans, but investors' tastes and security return distributions are stable over time, the market portfolio remains efficient and the simple version of the expected return-beta relationship holds.

Key terms

Homogeneous expectations
Market portfolio
Mutual fund theorem
Market price of risk
Beta

Expected return-beta relationship
Security market line
Alpha
Zero-beta portfolio

Selected readings

A good introduction to the intuition of the CAPM is:
   Malkiel, Burton G. *A Random Walk Down Wall Street.* New York: W.W. Norton & Company, Inc., 1985.
The four articles that established the CAPM are:
   Sharpe, William. "Capital Asset Prices: A Theory of Market Equilibrium." *Journal of Finance,* September 1964.
   Lintner, John. "The Valuation of Risk Assets and the Selection of Risky Investments in Stock Portfolios and Capital Budgets." *Review of Economics and Statistics,* February 1965.
   Mossin, Jan. "Equilibrium in a Capital Asset Market." *Econometrica,* October 1966.

Treynor, Jack. "Towards a Theory of Market Value of Risky Assets." Unpublished manuscript, 1961.

A review of the simple CAPM and its variants is contained in:

Jensen, Michael C. "The Foundation and Current State of Capital Market Theory." In Michael C. Jensen (editor), *Studies in the Theory of Capital Markets.* New York: Praeger Publishers, 1972.

The zero-beta version of the CAPM appeared in:

Black, Fischer. "Capital Market Equilibrium with Restricted Borrowing." *Journal of Business,* July 1972.

Excellent practitioner-oriented discussions of the CAPM are:

Mullins, David. "Does the Capital Asset Pricing Model Work." *Harvard Business Review,* January/February 1982.

Rosenberg, Barr; and Rudd, Andrew. "The Corporate Uses of Beta." In J. M. Stern and D. H. Chew, Jr. (editors), *The Revolution in Corporate Finance.* New York: Basil Blackwell, 1986.

Problems

1. What is the beta of a portfolio with $E(r_p) = 20$ percent, if $r_f = 5$ percent and $E(r_M) = 15$ percent?

2. The market price of a security is $40. Its expected rate of return is 13 percent. The risk-free rate is 7 percent and the market risk premium is 8 percent. What will be the market price of the security if its covariance with the market portfolio doubles (and all other variables remain unchanged)? Assume that the stock is expected to pay a constant dividend in perpetuity.

3. You are a consultant to a large manufacturing corporation that is considering a project with the following net after-tax cash flows (in millions of dollars):

Years from Now	After-Tax Cash Flow
0	−20
1–9	10
10	20

   The project's beta is 1.7. Assuming that $r_f = 9$ percent and $E(r_M) = 19$ percent, what is the net present value of the project? What is the highest possible beta estimate for the project before its NPV becomes negative?

4. Are the following true or false?
   a. Stocks with a beta of zero offer an expected rate of return of zero.
   b. The CAPM implies that investors require a higher return to hold highly volatile securities.
   c. You can construct a portfolio with beta of .75 by investing .75 of the budget in bills and the remainder in the market portfolio.

5. Consider the following table, which gives a security analyst's expected return on two stocks for two particular market returns:

Market Return	Aggressive Stock	Defensive Stock
.05	.02	.035
.20	.32	.14

a. What are the betas of the two stocks?

b. What is the expected rate of return on each stock if the market return is equally likely to be 5 percent or 20 percent?

c. If the T-bill rate is 8 percent and the market return is equally likely to be 5 percent or 20 percent, draw the SML for this economy.

d. Plot the two securities on the SML graph. What are the alphas of each?

e. What hurdle rate should be used by the management of the aggressive firm for a project with the risk characteristics of the defensive firm's stock?

If the simple CAPM is valid, which of the following situations in problems 6–12 are possible? Explain. Consider each situation independently.

6.	Portfolio	Expected Return	Beta
	A	.20	1.4
	B	.25	1.2

7.	Portfolio	Expected Return	Standard Deviation
	A	.30	.35
	B	.40	.25

8.	Portfolio	Expected Return	Standard Deviation
	Risk-free	.10	0
	Market	.18	.24
	A	.16	.12

9.	Portfolio	Expected Return	Standard Deviation
	Risk-free	.10	0
	Market	.18	.24
	A	.20	.22

10.	Portfolio	Expected Return	Beta
	Risk-free	.10	0
	Market	.18	1.0
	A	.16	1.5

11.	Portfolio	Expected Return	Beta
	Risk-free	.10	0
	Market	.18	1.0
	A	.16	.9

12.	Portfolio	Expected Return	Standard Deviation
	Risk-free	.10	0
	Market	.18	.24
	A	.16	.22

In problems 13–15, assume that the risk-free rate of interest is 8 percent and the expected rate of return on the market is 18 percent.

13. A share of stock sells for $100 today. It will pay a dividend of $9 per share at the end of the year. Its beta is 1. What do investors expect the stock to sell for at the end of the year?

14. I am buying a firm with an expected cash flow of $1,000 but am unsure of its risk. If I think the beta of the firm is zero, when in fact the beta is really 1, how much *more* will I offer for the firm than it is truly worth?

15. A stock has an expected rate of return of 6 percent. What is its beta?

16. Two investment advisors are comparing performance. One averaged a 19 percent rate of return and the other a 16 percent rate of return. However, the beta of the first investor was 1.5, whereas that of the second was 1.

    a. Can you tell which investor was a better predictor of individual stocks (aside from the issue of general movements in the market)?

    b. If the T-bill rate were 6 percent and the market return during the period were 14 percent, which investor would be the superior stock selector?

    c. What if the T-bill rate were 3 percent and the market return were 15 percent?

17. In 1991, the rate of return on short-term government securities (perceived to be risk free) was about 6 percent. Suppose the expected rate of return required by the market for a portfolio with a beta measure of 1 is 11 percent. According to the capital asset pricing model (security market line):

    a. What is the expected rate of return on the market portfolio?

    b. What would be the expected rate of return on a stock with $\beta = 0$?

    c. Suppose you consider buying a share of stock at $40. The stock is expected to pay $3 dividends next year and to sell then for $41. The stock risk has been evaluated by $\beta = -.5$. Is the stock overpriced or underpriced?

18. Suppose that you can invest risk free at rate r_f but can borrow only at a higher rate, r_f^B. This case was considered in Section 7.5.

    a. Draw a minimum-variance frontier. Show on the graph the risky portfolio that will be selected by defensive investors. Show the portfolio that will be selected by aggressive investors.

    b. What portfolios will be selected by investors who neither borrow nor lend?

    c. Where will the market portfolio lie on the efficient frontier?

    d. Will the zero-beta CAPM be valid in this scenario? Explain. Show graphically the expected return on the zero-beta portfolio.

19. Consider an economy with two classes of investors. Tax-exempt investors can borrow or lend at the safe rate, r_f. Taxed investors pay tax rate t on all interest income, so their net-of-tax safe interest rate is $r_f(1 - t)$. Show that the zero-beta CAPM will apply to this economy and that $(1 - t)r_f < E[r_{Z(M)}] < r_f$.

20. Suppose that borrowing is restricted so that the zero-beta version of the CAPM holds. The expected return on the market portfolio is 17 percent, and on the zero-beta portfolio it is 8 percent. What is the expected return on a portfolio with a beta of .6?

Appendix: The Multifactor CAPM

The CAPM describes a fundamental expected return-beta relationship. Such a simple relationship implies that investors are concerned with, and hedge, only one source of risk: uncertainty about future security prices. In the real world, investors may be concerned with a number of uncertainties that affect their future consumption plans, such as the relative prices of goods and services or future investment opportunities. If it is true that investors are concerned about additional uncertainties, and if security returns are correlated with other sources of uncertainties, we would expect that investors will want to hold hedge portfolios that will reduce these uncertainties in addition to the market portfolio.

The multifactor CAPM, which is concerned with these hedging demands, describes the resulting equilibrium security returns that are consistent with such demands. The model demonstrates that individuals should be concerned with more than just the expected value and uncertainty of their wealth; they also should hedge factors that determine the future purchasing power of their wealth (relative price levels) and factors that determine the future earning power of their portfolios (such as the future level of the interest rate). Each of these additional factors requires a hedging response beyond that predicted by traditional mean-variance analysis. The result is a multifactor expected return-beta relationship that constitutes a generalized version of the CAPM.

The basic form of the CAPM uses a set of simplifying assumptions to establish that the market portfolio is efficient and that the expected excess return on any security is proportional to its covariance with the market portfolio. This is the expected return-beta relationship:

$$E(r_i) - r_f = \beta_i[E(r_M) - r_f]$$

In the main body of this chapter we discussed how relaxing some assumptions (particularly that risk-free lending and borrowing are feasible, all assets are publicly traded, and investors have a one-period investment horizon) may affect the slope of the security market line, but preserve the simple form of the expected return-beta relationship that the expected excess return on a security is proportional to its beta. Such a simple single-variable relationship, however, assumes that investors face only *one* source of risk—namely, uncertainty about future values of securities—and that the dollar value of wealth is the only determinant of economic welfare.

Obviously, there are other sources of uncertainty that real-world investors face. Some important ones are as follows:

1. Uncertainty about future tastes
2. Uncertainty about the variety of consumer goods that will be available in the future
3. Uncertainty about future investment opportunities expressed by the means, variances, and covariances of the rates of return that can be earned on investments
4. Uncertainty about labor income
5. Uncertainty about relative prices of consumption goods
6. Uncertainty about life expectancy

We have noted that the simple version of the CAPM and its various extensions treat only uncertainty about the future value of securities. The extent to which any additional uncertainty will differentially affect security prices or returns depends on whether securities can be used to hedge these uncertainties. Although these risks may be very real to investors, as long as those risks are independent of security returns they will have no bearing on portfolio choice and, therefore, should leave security prices unaffected.

For example, surely there is no financial security that could reduce the uncertainties associated with future tastes or the future variety of consumer goods. In addition, although uncertain life expectancy is a factor for all investors—life insurance was created in response to it—the event of death is reasonably statistically independent across individuals. It is unlikely that returns on securities (other than life insurance policies) would be statistically dependent on the event of an individual's death. Therefore, we would not expect life expectancy concerns to have differential effects on security prices.

The following sources of uncertainty, however, might be expected to affect security prices:

1. Uncertainty about the future values of securities
2. Uncertainty about future investment opportunities
3. Uncertainty about future labor income
4. Uncertainty about prices of consumption goods

Robert C. Merton[a] is responsible for the development of an expanded CAPM that accounts for the potential effect of these extra-market sources of uncertainty on security prices. The focal point of the model is not dollar returns per se but the consumption and investment made possible by the individual's wealth. Investors facing a broad list of risk factors must do more than hedge just the dollar value of their portfolios. Once we accept the existence of extra hedge demands, we must generalize the simple expected return-beta relationship.

---

[a] Merton, Robert C., "An Intertemporal Capital Asset Pricing Model," *Econometrica, 41,* 1973, and "A Reexamination of the CAPM," in Friend, I., and Bicksler, J. (editors), *Risk and Return in Finance,* New York: Ballinger Publishing, 1976.

Example: Hedging Oil-Price Risk

We can use an extremely simple example to illustrate the logic of the multifactor CAPM. Imagine a consumer-investor, George Green, who has reached a stage in his life where each year he consumes his labour income of $40,000 plus the return on his investment portfolio of $100,000. George subscribes to the simple version of the CAPM, and therefore uses as his risky investment vehicle a mutual fund that mimics the TSE 300. The rate of return on this fund, r_p, has an expected value of 15 percent and a standard deviation of 25 percent. The risk-free rate is 8 percent.

George's degree of risk aversion is such that he invests 50 percent of his wealth in the risky market-index mutual fund. His annual expenditure budget, B, has a mean and standard deviation of

$$E(B) = 40,000 + 100,000[r_f + y[E(r_P) - r_f]]$$
$$= 40,000 + 100,000(.08 + .5 \times .07) = \$51,500$$
$$\sigma_B = 100,000 \, y\sigma_P = 100,000 \times .5 \times .25 = \$12,500$$

Sarah Kalm points out that at current prices George spends $15,000 annually on energy-related items. Sarah figures that George's use of energy is inflexible; that is, he will consume the same amount of energy regardless of prices. Thus, if we denote the energy expenditure by F (for fuel), the consumption level, C, on "satisfying" goods is actually $C = B - F$.

Suppose that George is using 15,000 energy "units" annually at a current cost of $1 per unit. The percentage increase in the energy price has a zero expected value, but it is uncertain. Sarah estimates that the standard deviation of the rate of increase is 20 percent. Therefore, the standard deviation of the dollar expenditure on energy is $15,000 \times .20 = \$3,000$. She also believes that the correlation between the rate of oil-price increase and the portfolio return is zero. (That is a somewhat unrealistic assumption, but it simplifies calculations and does not alter the principles involved.)

Using these data, George calculates that the expected value of his consumption budget (as opposed to total expenditures including energy) is

$$E(C) = E(B) - E(F) = 51,500 - 15,000$$
$$= \$36,500$$

and that the standard deviation is

$$\sigma_C = (\sigma_B^2 + \sigma_F^2)^{1/2} = (12,500^2 + 15,000^2 \times .20^2)^{1/2}$$
$$= \$12,855$$

because the covariance between B and F is zero.

Since the standard deviation of the portfolio proceeds is $12,500, the marginal risk to George's consumption attributable to energy price uncertainty is measured by the increment of $355 over the standard deviation that he would bear if energy prices were certain.

Notice that George's problem is now more complex than the traditional mean-variance framework recognizes. Even if George were to select a risk-free portfolio, he would continue to face uncertainty in his consumption because of energy-price risk. George's risk-management techniques must account for energy-price uncertainty, as well as the usual risk of portfolio returns.

Sarah observes that George could lessen consumption risk to the pre-energy price uncertainty level in two ways. First, he could reduce his exposure to portfolio risk. Instead of investing 50 percent of his wealth in the risky mutual fund, George could decrease his position to 48.54 percent. At this position the standard deviation of the overall expenditure budget is $.4854 \times 100,000 \times .25 = \$12,135$, and the standard deviation of satisfying consumption is once again

$$\sigma_C = (12,135^2 + 3,000^2)^{1/2}$$
$$= \$12,500$$

This reduction in consumption risk to its original level comes at the expense of the risk premium on the 1.46 percent of the portfolio that is shifted from the risky portfolio to the risk-free asset. With a risk premium of 7 percent on the risky portfolio, this amounts to a loss in expected dollar consumption of $\$100,000 \times .0146 \times .07 = \$102.20$. The expected dollar expenditure on consumption items (excluding energy) becomes

$$\$40,000 + \$100,000(.08 + .4854 \times .07) - \$15,000 = \$36,397.80$$

rather than \$36,500.

Another way to eliminate the oil-price risk is by hedging. Sarah calls this a better method, maintaining that energy stocks are a natural hedge in this case. (Remember the Humanex Hospital example of Chapter 5.) Let us consider her argument.

Suppose that a mutual fund, Oilex, specializes in maintaining a portfolio of energy stocks that is perfectly positively correlated with oil prices. To simplify calculations, assume also that the Oilex fund has a zero beta so that oil prices are uncorrelated with security prices. Now, *under the simple CAPM hypothesis,* the zero-beta Oilex fund should have a zero risk premium; that is, we expect it to earn the risk-free rate of 8 percent that we have posited. Therefore, if the simple CAPM is correct and Oilex has the same expected rate of return as the risk-free asset, then investing in Oilex rather than in the risk-free asset will not affect the expected value of the consumption budget. This means that if George maintains his investment in the TSE 300 mutual fund at 50 percent of his wealth, his expected satisfying consumption level will remain at the original \$36,500, regardless of how much he invests in Oilex.

A natural choice for the proportion invested in Oilex would be the amount that minimizes risk. Since Oilex is uncorrelated with the TSE 300 fund and perfectly correlated with oil-price increases, George can use Oilex to hedge the oil-price risk completely while maintaining the (original level of) standard deviation (\$12,500) attributable to his speculative portfolio.

The hedge works as follows. On the one hand, an oil-price increase results in a loss in the consumption budget because more dollars must be spent on energy. Balancing this, however, is the fact that the rate of return on the Oilex fund increases with oil prices, thereby increasing the budget available for consumption. The net effects are offsetting, which makes the Oilex fund a perfect hedge for energy risk.

Suppose that the Oilex fund standard deviation is 22 percent. Recall that energy price uncertainty is only 20 percent, and that George will purchase 15,000 energy units at an expected price of $1 each. Because Oilex and energy prices are perfectly correlated, George fully eliminates his energy exposure by diverting $15,000 × (.20/.22) = $13,636 from T-bills to the Oilex fund. Since Oilex, by virtue of its zero beta, has the same expected rate of return as T-bills (if the CAPM is correct), George can eliminate energy risk without giving up any expected consumption. With the oil-price risk eliminated, the standard deviation of the satisfying consumption budget reverts to $12,500, as it stood before we introduced this extra source of risk.

The key point is that George has deviated from strict adherence to the tenets of traditional mean-variance analysis. His portfolio is not mean-variance efficient in terms of dollar returns—it is heavily skewed toward Oilex. But in terms of *consumption risk* (as opposed to dollar risk), George is following precisely the correct strategy. Traditional mean-variance analysis ignores this extra source of consumption risk, namely, the risk of relative prices.

The hedging strategy we show in the Oilex example is more sophisticated than the one called for in the Humanex example in Chapter 5. Humanex chose assets to hedge only the dollar rate of return on its portfolio. In this case George looks beyond dollar values to hedge extra sources of risk to his consumption. Thus he must hedge not only the dollar risk on his investment portfolio, but also the price risk of consumer goods.

Concept Check

> Question 1. Show that George's portfolio with the hedge position in Oilex is *not* mean-variance efficient in terms of portfolio rate of return. Do so by comparing the expected return and standard deviation of the portfolio rate of return of the hedging strategy with that of George's original unhedged position.
> Question 2. What does our analysis so far suggest about the appropriateness of beta as the measure of security risk? Why is beta incomplete in this scenario?

Hedging Demands and the CAPM

One way to summarize the essentials of George's problem and Sarah's solution is to say that George's optimal risky portfolio is not the market portfolio, contrary to the implications of the CAPM. Rather, it is a combination of two portfolios: the market portfolio and a hedge portfolio, in this case the energy hedge (Oilex) fund.

Note that we did not fully optimize George's portfolio because we held the proportion invested in the market index fund arbitrarily constant. Complete optimization would have included a revision of his consumption-investment plan to obtain the best investment position. We also simplified the example by assuming either zero or perfect correlations between various rates. Our point, however, is that no matter how complex the patterns of possible scenarios and how sophisticated the optimization technique, it is clear that the energy hedge portfolio will enter at least some investor portfolios.

Now consider the fact that if a significant number of investors shift their portfolios away from the market portfolio toward a specific direction such as energy stocks, the CAPM expected return-beta relationship will no longer obtain. Relative prices of securities will change to reflect this extra hedging demand for energy stocks.

Suppose, as is in fact the case, that energy is a significant component in many expenditure budgets, and that future energy prices are uncertain. Further, suppose that some combination of securities can be selected for a portfolio so as to maximize the portfolio's correlation with energy-price changes. This is the portfolio that will be the hedge portfolio in which many investors, to varying degrees, will take long positions to hedge energy-price risk. This extra demand (in excess of that predicted by the simple, single source of risk CAPM) will drive up the prices of the securities in the hedge portfolio, thereby driving down their expected rates of return. In the case of Oilex, such extra hedging demand would force its rate of return below the risk-free rate despite its (assumed) zero beta. The simple CAPM expected return-beta relationship would have to be generalized to account for the effects of this extra source of hedging demand.

We have said that the chosen hedge portfolio will be the portfolio having the maximum correlation with the source of risk it is designed to hedge. The demand for this hedge portfolio will exceed the demand predicted by the CAPM, which ignores risk sources other than the variance of the portfolio itself. The excess demand for a portfolio that hedges an extra source of uncertainty will depend on the aggregate desire of consumer-investors to hedge this source of uncertainty, and the effectiveness of the (most effective) hedge portfolio in hedging this source of uncertainty.

The equilibrium risk premium on this portfolio will be denoted $E(r_H) - r_f$, where $E(r_H)$ is the expected return on the hedge portfolio. Practically speaking, there is no way to predict the magnitude of this risk premium without information regarding the exact preferences of all investors for all consumer goods in all future periods. The most we can say is that the risk premium is smaller than the simple CAPM would predict for this portfolio when it implies that all investors ignore the extra source of risk. We are left with the result that hedge portfolios carry risk premiums that we have to assess empirically.

Concept Check

Question 3. Consider a security whose rate of return is negatively correlated with energy prices. How will the demand for this security compare with the single source of risk model? How will its expected rate of return compare to that predicted by the simple CAPM?

Extra hedging demands require generalizing the CAPM into a multifactor model. With K extra sources of risk, let $E(r_{Hk}) - r_f$ denote the risk premium on the kth hedge portfolio, and call β_{ik} the sensitivity of stock i to the kth source of extra risk. Then the risk premium on individual assets and portfolios is determined by a multifactor expected return-beta relationship:

$$E(r_i) - r_f = \beta_{iM}[E(r_M) - r_f] + \beta_{i1}[E(r_{H1}) - r_f] + \ldots + \beta_{ik}[E(r_{Hk}) - r_f] \quad \textbf{(8A.1)}$$

$$= \beta_{iM}[E(r_M) - r_f] + \sum_{k=1}^{K} \beta_{ik}[E(r_{Hk}) - r_f]$$

Note that equation 8A.1 is no more than a multifactor generalization of the one-factor security market line, which we explore further later in this appendix. Just as we can estimate beta in the traditional index model using a simple regression (the security characteristic line), we can measure the multiple "betas" in this extended model in a multiple regression that allows for several explanatory or systematic factors. Instead of regressing security returns on just market index returns, we also include, as explanatory variables, returns on those portfolios most highly correlated with each extra source of risk. These portfolios serve as indices for the extra-market risk factors.

Suppose that there exists a security, j, that has no hedge value at all, in that it is uncorrelated with all extra-market sources of risk. In that case all the β_{jk} coefficients will be zero, and this security (and only such securities) will have a risk premium that conforms to the simple version of the CAPM.

For any other security, the beta coefficient from a simple regression on the market portfolio will differ from the correct beta coefficient in the appropriate multifactor regression equation that properly identifies all hedge portfolios. Therefore, whenever extra-market risk is empirically significant, most securities will not conform to the simple CAPM expected return-beta relationship.

Note also that the magnitude of the beta coefficient of a specific security on one of the hedge portfolios represents the "importance" of this security in the hedge portfolio. A higher beta of a security means that this security return is more sensitive to the extra source of risk that this portfolio serves to hedge.

Extra Sources of Risk

Now we can again focus our attention on the extra sources of risk and ask how we might expect them to affect security prices. Our list includes (1) uncertainty about the future investment opportunity set, (2) uncertainty about labour income, and (3) uncertainty about relative prices of consumption goods.

One example of uncertainty about the future opportunity set is the future risk-free rate of interest. Although we use the T-bill rate as the risk-free rate, in reality T-bills offer risk-free returns only for short maturities. The relevant maturity depends on personal circumstances.

For example, suppose that an investor, Kay, revises her portfolio once a month. In that case the yield-to-maturity on a one-month bill (observed at the beginning of the one-month holding period) is the operational risk-free rate. Because the level of this one-month rate will change through time, Kay knows that the investment opportunities available next month are uncertain. How does this uncertainty affect the current composition of her portfolio?

Looking ahead to the next period, Kay may believe that, compared to today, the next period is riskier. As of now, the level of the next month's risk-free rate is unknown, which compounds next-period uncertainty.

If uncertainty about the future risk-free rate increases future-period uncertainty, Kay should be looking for a hedge to offset this risk. Suppose that there exists a security whose rate of return is perfectly correlated with changes in the future T-bill rate. This correlation means that if the T-bill rate next month increases from its current level, the hedge security will end the month with a higher than currently expected rate of return. If investors increase the proportion they invest in this hedge security, they will enter next month with more wealth than they would otherwise if T-bill rates go up, and less if rates go down.

Should investors take positive or negative positions in the hedge security? We cannot answer this question without knowing the exact nature of their preferences. The correct position in the interest rate hedge security (short or long) depends on whether an unexpected increase in the T-bill rate would be a pleasant or unpleasant surprise. For a net lender of funds, increases in interest rates are beneficial, whereas borrowers presumably do not welcome an increase. Those for whom an increase in interest rates is undesirable will take a long position in the hedge security so that any unpleasant increase in the T-bill rate will be offset by a pleasant increase in the return realized on the hedge asset. If the majority of investors turn out to be long hedgers, the resulting extra demand for the hedge asset will drive up its price, driving its expected return below that predicted by the one-factor CAPM.

The lesson to be learned? In some cases we cannot predict whether a hedge security will have more or less of a risk premium than will a security with no hedge value. This example of uncertainty differs from the energy price case. In that case the oil-price increase was unambiguously unpleasant to energy consumers, resulting in increased demand for hedge assets. In this case an increase in the T-bill rate is not necessarily good news or bad news, so we cannot know how most investors will try to offset this risk.

Another source of risk beyond portfolio return is uncertainty in labour income. The present value of future labour income is sometimes called "human capital." To compute the value of the human capital of a specific investor we would discount his or her expected labour income in all future periods by an appropriate discount rate. The riskier the labour income, the higher the discount rate and the less the value of this investor's human capital.

The uncertainty surrounding labour income differs across investors. Consequently, the make-up of hedge portfolios for labour income uncertainty also will differ across investors. For example, automakers are subject to different kinds of uncertainties than are physicians. Can we establish a common denominator for these hedge portfolios and thus better predict expected excess returns for securities that hedge labour income uncertainty?

To start with, we can differentiate between corporations (and their outstanding securities) on the basis of the labour intensity versus capital intensity of their production technology. For many investors, therefore, investing in firms that are relatively labour-intensive will provide a hedge for labour income uncertainty: when wages are low, the profits of these firms will be high. Thus the expected rate of return on the stocks of these firms may be pushed downward (relative to securities of capital-intensive firms) if the majority of investors desire to hedge labour income.

Finally, let us consider price risk. General price-level uncertainty (measured by price indices such as the CPI) may cause differential demand for different-maturity fixed income securities such as bonds and mortgages. Consumers reasonably differentiate among the amount they allot to broad classes of consumption (for example, housing, food, energy, transportation, clothing, and recreation). Differential demands for shares in different industries may be the result.

Concept Check	Question 4. Consider the following regression results for stock X.

$$r_x = .01 + .7 \text{ (\% change in oil prices)}$$

a. If I live in Alberta, where the local economy is heavily dependent on oil industry profits, does stock X represent a useful asset to hedge my overall economic well-being? Why or why not?

b. What if I live in Toronto, where most individuals and firms are energy *consumers*?

c. If energy consumers are far more numerous than energy producers, will high oil-beta stocks have higher or lower expected rates of return in market equilibrium than low oil-beta stocks?

What Is Gained by the Multifactor CAPM?

Merton's multifactor CAPM is a formidable theoretical construct. Consumer-investors are modelled as though they derive optimal lifetime consumption and portfolio rules when they face any number of sources of uncertainty, in addition to the uncertainty surrounding the future value of securities. The portfolio demands of these investors are in the form of desired investment proportions in "mutual funds." One of these funds is the market portfolio that hedges security price risk by diversification. The other "mutual funds" are designed to hedge each extra specific source of risk. Each "mutual fund" is a hedge portfolio designed to maximize correlation with the particular source of risk to be hedged.

We have shown that extra sources of risk do not affect all investors in the same way (and to the same degree). Therefore the positions taken in the hedge portfolios generally will not be the same for all investors. Sources of risk that are common to many investors, however, will be hedged by similar portfolios across investors. This demand will give rise to the emergence of hedge portfolios for sectors such as transportation, energy, and bond funds.

Imposing equilibrium conditions on these demands for the various portfolios gives us equation 8A.1, the generalized expected return-beta relationship of the multifactor CAPM. In equation 8A.1, β_{iM} and β_{ik} represent the sensitivity of security i to the portfolio best correlated with risk factor k. The "betas" are the measures of systematic risks.

Concept Check	Question 5. Suppose that everyone agrees that uncertainty in the relative price of coal energy versus oil energy is an important factor to hedge, but that because energy-supply companies are diversified, no securities have returns correlated with this price ratio. Would the multifactor CAPM in this case predict any departures from the simple CAPM?

FIGURE 8A.1
The multifactor
SML.

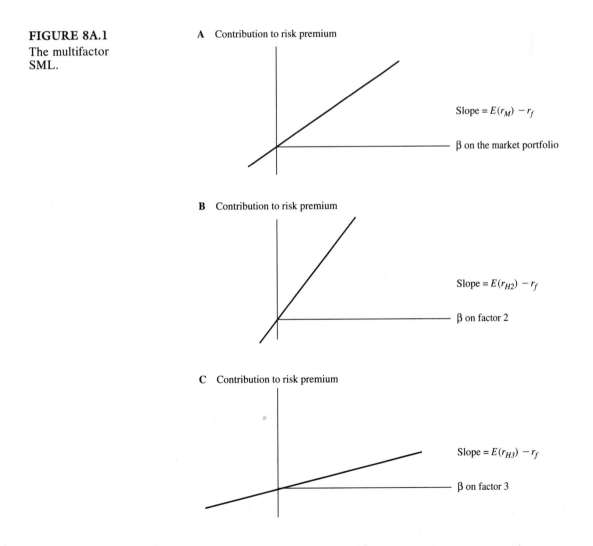

A Contribution to risk premium

Slope = $E(r_M) - r_f$

β on the market portfolio

B Contribution to risk premium

Slope = $E(r_{H2}) - r_f$

β on factor 2

C Contribution to risk premium

Slope = $E(r_{H3}) - r_f$

β on factor 3

We have noted already that the generalized expected return-beta relationship of the multifactor CAPM is really a multidimensional security market line (SML), as Figure 8A.1 shows. The horizontal axis of the market-risk SML is the market beta of the securities, β_{iM}. The vertical axis of the market-risk SML in Part **A** of Figure 8A.1 gives the part of the expected return of a security attributable to the market-risk exposure of the security as measured by the market beta. The slope of this dimension of the SML is $E(r_M) - r_f$.

The horizontal axes of the other SMLs in Figure 8A.1, **B** and **C**, are the hedge betas of the securities, β_{ik}. The vertical axes of these SMLs are the increments of the security excess returns attributable to the hedge value of the securities as given by their β_{ik} coefficients. The slopes of these SMLs are $E(r_{Hk}) - r_f$.

By suggesting what types of extra hedge factors are likely to be important to investors, the multifactor CAPM provides us with a guide as to what kind of deviations from the single source of risk CAPM we can expect for various securities. The model does not resolve all issues, however. We must determine which sources of risk are indeed priced in capital markets (that is, which ones command risk premiums), and what portfolios most efficiently hedge those risks. This adds further complexity on top of the CAPM's "old" drawback that we cannot observe the market portfolio.

With the simple version of the CAPM, we were able to finesse the difficulty posed by the unobservable market portfolio by assuming a single-factor security market, where some broad market index was assumed to be perfectly correlated with the factor. The expanded CAPM, however, directs us to a *multifactor* risk-reward trade-off.

Summary: Appendix

1. Investors are concerned with a host of extra-market sources of uncertainty pertaining to future consumption. These concerns give rise to demands for securities that hedge these extra uncertainties.

2. In order to hedge an extra-market source of uncertainty, a portfolio of securities must be correlated with this uncertainty.

3. Extra hedging demand will be reflected in security prices if many investors use similar hedge portfolios. Reasonable sources of hedging demands might revolve around the following extra-market sources of uncertainty:

    a. Uncertainty about future investment opportunities
    b. Uncertainty about future labour income
    c. Uncertainty about future relative prices of consumption goods

4. Investors will hold a number of additional portfolios to hedge extra sources of relevant uncertainty in addition to their position in the market portfolio (to hedge security price uncertainty by diversification). Each hedge portfolio is designed to maximize its correlation with one of the relevant sources of uncertainty.

5. With the extra hedging demands, equilibrium security returns will satisfy the multifactor expected return-beta relationship,

$$E(r_i) - r_f = \beta_{iM}[E(r_M) - r_f] + \sum_{k=1}^{K} \beta_{ik}[E(r_{Hk}) - r_f]$$

where the last term is the sum of the incremental risk premiums resulting from the hedge value of the security.

6. The multifactor CAPM does not explicitly predict which hedge portfolios are relevant. Any portfolio that can hedge a source of consumption uncertainty is a candidate. But a non-zero incremental risk premium will arise only if there is an aggregate desire to hedge this uncertainty *and* an effective hedge portfolio can be constructed.

Selected readings: Appendix

This material is intrinsically difficult, and most readings are correspondingly complex. A good introduction is:

Merton, Robert C. "A Reexamination of the CAPM." In I. Friend and J. Bicksler (editors), *Risk and Return in Finance*. New York: Ballinger Publishing, 1976.

A related model based explicitly on consumption uncertainty that is a useful counterpoint to Merton's treatment of the subject is:

Breeden, Douglas. "An Intertemporal Asset Pricing Model with Stochastic Consumption and Investment Opportunities." *Journal of Financial Economics* 7 (1979).

More advanced treatments of multifactor equilibrium models are:

Merton, Robert C. "An Intertemporal Capital Asset Pricing Model." *Econometrica* 41 (1973).

Cox, John C.; Ingersoll, Jonathan E.; and Ross, Stephen A. "An Intertemporal Asset Pricing Model with Rational Expectations." *Econometrica* 53 (1985).

Problems: Appendix

1. The total annual income of Don and Linda Miller is expected to be $180,000. The market value of their portfolio is $600,000, of which 40 percent is invested in a money market fund yielding a virtually risk-free rate of 7 percent. The balance is invested in a market index fund. The market index risk premium is 9 percent and has a standard deviation of 25 percent.

It occurs to Don and Linda (D&L) that their labour income has become significantly risky. They estimate its standard deviation to be 10 percent.

Assume that D&L's labour income is uncorrelated with the market portfolio, and that there exists a hedge portfolio with a standard deviation of 20 percent. The hedge portfolio is perfectly *negatively* correlated with D&L's labour income and is uncorrelated with the market portfolio.

  a. What is D&L's expected labour income (in dollars)? What is the standard deviation of this income?

b. What would be the standard deviation of total income if their labour income were risk-free?

c. How much money should be shifted from the market index fund into the money market fund to lower total risk to the level in question b? What would be D&L's expected annual income in this case?

d. If instead the funds were shifted from the money market fund to the hedge portfolio, how much should be shifted to completely eliminate labour income risk? If the (zero-beta) hedge portfolio were expected to earn the risk-free rate of 7 percent, what would be expected annual income?

e. What risk premium on the hedge portfolio would make D&L indifferent between reducing risk using the hedge portfolio compared with shifting from the market index into the money market fund? (Hint: the risk premium that results in indifference will be negative. Why?)

f. What types of securities might make up the labour income hedge portfolio? What is the likely correlation between such a portfolio and the market index?

g. How might D&L's ages affect their investment strategy?

2. Consider the following regression results for stock *X*.

$$r_X = .01 + 1.7(\text{inflation})$$

a. If I am retired and live on my pension, which provides a fixed number of dollars each month, does stock *X* represent a useful asset to hedge my overall economic well-being? Why, or why not?

b. What if I am a gold producer, and I am aware that gold prices increase when inflation accelerates?

c. If retirees are far more numerous than gold producers in this economy, will high inflation–beta stocks have higher or lower expected rates of return in market equilibrium than low inflation–beta stocks?

CHAPTER 9

Index Models and the Arbitrage Pricing Theory

The exploitation of security mispricing in such a way that risk-free economic profits may be earned is called **arbitrage.** It typically involves the simultaneous purchase and sale of equivalent securities (usually in different markets) in order to profit from discrepancies in their price relationship. The concept of arbitrage is central to the theory of capital markets. This chapter discusses the nature, and illustrates the use, of arbitrage. We show how to identify arbitrage opportunities and why investors will take as large a position as they can in arbitrage portfolios.

Perhaps the most basic principle of capital market theory is that equilibrium market prices are rational in that they rule out risk-free arbitrage opportunities. Pricing relationships that guarantee the absence of risk-free arbitrage possibilities are extremely powerful. If actual security prices allow for risk-free arbitrage, the result will be strong pressure on security prices to restore equilibrium. Only a few investors need be aware of arbitrage opportunities to bring about a large volume of trades, and these trades will bring prices back into balance.

The CAPM of the previous chapter gave us the security market line, a relationship between expected return and risk as measured by beta. The model discussed in this chapter, called the arbitrage pricing theory, or APT, also stipulates a relationship between expected return and risk, but it uses different assumptions and techniques. We explore this relationship using well-diversified portfolios, showing that these portfolios are priced to satisfy the CAPM expected return-beta relationship. Because all well-diversified portfolios have to satisfy that relationship, we show that all individual securities almost certainly satisfy this same relationship. This reasoning allows the derivation of an SML relationship that avoids reliance on the unobservable, theoretical market portfolio that is central to the CAPM. We also show how the simple single-factor APT easily can be generalized to a richer multifactor version.

The single-factor APT is based on the assumption that only one systematic common factor affects the returns of all securities. This assumption, however, was also at the origin of another class of models, known as *index* or *market models,* that predate the APT by several years. These models were initially introduced in order to simplify the computations of the Markowitz portfolio selection model. Since they also offer significant new insights into the nature of systematic risk versus firm-specific risk and constitute a good introduction to the concept of factor models of security returns, they will be examined in the first sections of this chapter.

9.1   *A Single-Index Security Market*

Systematic Risk vs. Firm-Specific Risk

The success of a portfolio selection rule depends on the quality of the input list, that is, the estimates of expected security returns and the covariance matrix. In the long run, efficient portfolios will beat portfolios with less reliable input lists and consequently inferior reward-to-risk trade-offs.

Suppose your security analysts can thoroughly analyze 50 stocks. This means that your input list will include the following:

$$n = \quad 50 \text{ estimates of expected returns}$$

$$n = \quad 50 \text{ estimates of variances}$$

$$(n^2 - n)/2 = \underline{1225} \text{ estimates of covariances}$$

$$1325 \text{ estimates}$$

This is a formidable task, particularly in light of the fact that a 50-security portfolio is relatively small. Doubling n to 100 will nearly quadruple the number of estimates to 5,150. If $n = 1,600$, roughly the number of TSE-listed stocks in 1990, we need nearly 1.3 *million* estimates.

Covariances between security returns occur because the same economic forces affect the fortunes of many firms. Some examples of common economic factors are business cycles, inflation, money-supply changes, technological changes, and prices of raw materials. All these (interrelated) factors affect almost all firms. Thus unexpected changes in these variables cause, simultaneously, unexpected changes in the rates of return on the entire stock market.

Suppose that we group all these economic factors and any other relevant common factors into one macroeconomic indicator and assume that it moves the security market as a whole. We further assume that, beyond this common effect, all remaining uncertainty in stock returns is firm-specific; that is, there is no other source of correlation between securities. Firm-specific events would include new inventions, deaths of key employees, and other factors that affect the fortune of the individual firm without affecting the broad economy in a measurable way.

We can summarize the distinction between macroeconomic and firm-specific factors by writing the return, r_i, realized on any security during some holding period as

$$r_i = E(r_i) + m_i + e_i \qquad (9.1)$$

where $E(R_i)$ is the expected return on the security as of the beginning of the holding period, m_i is the impact of unanticipated macro events on the security's return during the period, and e_i is the impact of unanticipated firm-specific events. Both m_i and e_i have zero expected values because each represents the impact of unanticipated events, which by definition must average out to zero.

We can gain further insight by recognizing that different firms have different sensitivities to macroeconomic events. Thus, if we denote the unanticipated component of the macro factor by F, and denote the responsiveness of security i to macroevents by the Greek letter beta, β_i, then equation 9.1 becomes[1]

$$r_i = E(r_i) + \beta_i F + e_i \qquad (9.2)$$

Equation 9.2 is known as a **factor model** for stock returns. It is easy to imagine that a more realistic decomposition of security returns would require more than one factor in equation 9.2. We treat this issue in subsequent sections. For now, let us examine the easy case with only one macro factor.

Of course, a factor model is of little use without specifying a way to measure the factor that is posited to affect security returns. One reasonable approach is to assert that the rate of return on a broad index of securities such as the TSE 300 is a valid proxy for the common macro factor. This approach leads to an equation similar to the factor model, which is called a **single-index model** because it uses the market index to proxy for the common or systematic factor.

According to the index model, we can separate the actual or realized rate of return on a security into macro (systematic) and micro (firm-specific) components in a manner similar to that in equation 9.2. We write the rate of return on each security as a sum of three components:

	Symbol
1. The stock's expected return if the market is neutral, that is, if the market's excess return, $r_M - r_f$, is zero	α_i
2. The component of return due to movements in the overall market; β_i is the security's responsiveness to market movements	$\beta_i(r_M - r_f)$
3. The unexpected component due to unexpected events that are relevant only to this security (firm-specific)	e_i

The holding period excess rate of return on the stock, which measures the stock's relative performance, then can be stated as

$$r_i - r_f = \alpha_i + \beta_i(r_M - r_f) + e_i$$

---

[1] You may wonder why we choose the notation β for the responsiveness coefficient, since β already has been defined in Chapter 8 in the context of the CAPM. The choice is deliberate, however. Our reason will be obvious shortly.

Let us denote security excess returns over the risk-free rate using capital R, and so rewrite this equation as

$$R_i = \alpha_i + \beta_i R_M + e_i \qquad (9.3)$$

We write the index model in terms of excess returns over r_f rather than in terms of total returns, because the level of the stock market return represents the state of the macro economy only to the extent that it exceeds or falls short of the rate of return on risk-free T-bills. For example, in the 1950s, when T-bills were yielding only a 3 percent or 4 percent rate of return, a return of 8 percent or 9 percent on the stock market would be considered good news. In contrast, in the early 1980s, when bills were yielding over 10 percent, that same 8 percent or 9 percent stock market return would signal disappointing macroeconomic news.[2]

Equation 9.3 says that each security therefore has two sources of risk: *market or "systematic" risk,* attributable to its sensitivity to macroeconomic factors as reflected in R_M, and *firm-specific risk* as reflected in e. If we denote the variance of the excess return on the market, R_M, as σ_M^2, then we can break the variance of the rate of return on each stock into two components:

	Symbol
1. The variance attributable to the uncertainty of the common macroeconomic factors	$\beta_i^2 \sigma_M^2$
2. The variance attributable to firm-specific uncertainty	$\sigma^2(e_i)$

The covariance between R_M and e_i is zero because e_i is defined as firm-specific, that is, independent of movements in the market. Hence, calling σ_i^2 the variance of the rate of return on security i, we find that

$$\sigma_i^2 = \beta_i^2 \sigma_M^2 + \sigma^2(e_i)$$

The covariance between the excess rates of return on two stocks, for example, R_i and R_j, derives only from the common factor, R_M, because e_i and e_j are each firm-specific and therefore presumed to be uncorrelated. Hence the covariance between two stocks is

$$\mathrm{Cov}(R_i, R_j) = \mathrm{Cov}(\beta_i R_M, \beta_j R_M) = \beta_i \beta_j \sigma_M^2 \qquad (9.4)$$

These calculations show that if we have

> n estimates of the expected returns, $E(R_i)$
> n estimates of the sensitivity coefficients, β_i
> n estimates of the firm-specific variances, $\sigma^2(e_i)$
> 1 estimate for the variance of the (common) macroeconomic factor, σ_M^2

---

[2] In practice, however, a "modified" index model is often used that is similar to equation 9.3 except that it uses total rather than excess returns. This practice is most common when daily data are used. In this case, the rate of return on bills is on the order of only about .02 percent per day, so total and excess returns are almost indistinguishable.

then these $(3n + 1)$ estimates will enable us to prepare the input list for this single-index security universe. Thus for a 50-security portfolio we will need 151 estimates rather than 1,325, and for a 100-security portfolio we will need only 301 estimates rather than 5,150.

It is easy to see why the index model is such a useful abstraction. For large universes of securities the data estimates required for this are only a small fraction of what otherwise would be needed. (See the accompanying box for a discussion of international indexes.)

Securities Firms Are Cooking Up Potpourri of World Stock Indexes

As investors grow hungrier for worldwide investments, demand for an accurate financial calorie counter increases as well.

As a result, some of the biggest securities firms are introducing world stock market indexes, each firm boasting it provides a comprehensive measure of world investing patterns.

Last week [1987], Salomon Brothers Inc. launched its Salomon-Russell Global Equity Index, tracing $3.565 trillion of equities worldwide. Three similar measures are already available. Laszlo Birinyi Jr., vice president for Salomon's equity market analysis group, says, "We're trying to provide reliable, consistent information on global securities."

The Salomon index has formidable competition. For most of the past 20 years, investors who wanted to compare their success, or that of their investment advisers, to markets around the world turned to the Capital International Indices, a pioneering measure computed by Capital International S.A., starting in 1968. Morgan Stanley Group Inc. acquired the index, the related data base and other publications in early 1986. The indexes, currently known as the Morgan Stanley Capital International Indices, cover equities in 2,000 companies in 21 countries.

First Boston Corp. teamed with London-based Euromoney last year to launch its Global Index. In February, Goldman, Sachs & Co. and Wood MacKenzie & Co. joined the London-based Financial Times to follow suit with the FT-Actuaries World Indices. Shearson Lehman Brothers Inc. has one in the works, too.

Designing a global index is far from easy, starting with the question of which stocks to track. Some analysts fault the Morgan Stanley index for being too inclusive, because many countries have restrictions on foreign ownership. The Morgan Stanley index, for example, counts securities in Swedish banks that can't be purchased outside Sweden. But Morgan Stanley says foreign investors can purchase these stocks by seeking permission from the company.

Some new rival indexes adjust for "cross-holdings" of one company in another, such as Seagram Co.'s 22.5 percent stake in Du Pont Co. Morgan Stanley's index, however, generally doesn't do so.

Once the universe of securities has been selected, the figures require constant recalculation and adjustment. Expensive computer resources and highly trained analysts track exchange rates, mergers, stock splits, dividend payments and changes in capitalization. New companies must be added constantly.

All this concern is the result of growing internationalization of financial markets. U.S. institutions are investing heavily abroad, and stock markets outside the United States have surged. First Boston estimates that U.S. institutions will have $45 billion to $50 billion in foreign equities by year's end, up from about $4 billion in 1980.

(Continued)

VARIATIONS ON A THEME: HOW FOUR GLOBAL STOCK INDEXES TRACK

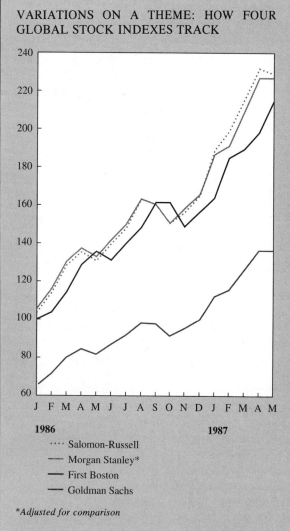

1986   1987

···· Salomon-Russell
— Morgan Stanley*
— First Boston
— Goldman Sachs

Adjusted for comparison

While the U.S. stock market, as measured by the Dow Jones Industrial Average, rose almost 23 percent in 1986, Morgan Stanley's European-Australia-Far Eastern Index, which includes the world other than the U.S., rose almost 70 percent. Salomon's International Equity Index rose 67.5 percent.

As interest in global investing rises, there is a lot of ego in getting a firm's name on a popular measuring stick. "Competitors of Morgan Stanley find it impalatable to put Morgan Stanley's name on their research," says Mark Sladkus, a vice president at Morgan Stanley.

Still, Mr. Sladkus concedes there aren't great differences in the competing measures. "They all track one another extremely closely. That would discount all claims that one is the best." He adds he is "quite certain that five years from now, there will only be two or three indexes in the market."

In addition, Mr. Sladkus says that because the Morgan Stanley index has been around much longer than competing indexes, it provides a useful historical benchmark for investors.

Tony Regan, head of international investments at Putnam Cos. in Boston, says, "Unless (competitors) can prove superiority, they've all got a problem in dislodging Morgan Stanley. It will be interesting to see if any differences in performance do emerge. Then we owe it to ourselves to see why."

However, Greg Smith, chief investment strategist for Prudential-Bache Securities Inc., says, "There'll never be a time when we have an industry standard. We're probably just splitting hairs to some people, but they're important hairs in this international market."

Another advantage is less obvious but equally important. The index model abstraction is crucial for specialization of effort in security analysis. If a covariance term had to be calculated directly for each security pair, then security analysts could not specialize by industry. For example, if one group were to specialize in the retail industry and another in the banking industry, who would have the common background to estimate the covariance *between* Canadian Tire and CIBC? Neither group would have the deep understanding of other industries necessary to make an informed judgment of co-movements among industries. In contrast, the index model suggests a simple way to compute covariances. Covariances among securities are due to the influence of the single common factor, represented by the market index return, and can be easily estimated using equation 9.4.

The simplification derived from the index model assumption is, however, not without cost. The "cost" of the model lies in the restrictions it places on the structure of asset return uncertainty. The classification of uncertainty into a simple dichotomy—macro versus micro risk—oversimplifies sources of real-world uncertainty and misses some important sources of dependence in stock returns. For example, this dichotomy rules out industry events, events that may affect many firms within an industry without substantially affecting the broad macro economy.

Statistical analysis shows that the firm-specific components of some firms are correlated. Examples are the nonmarket components of stocks in a single industry, such as retail stocks or bank stocks. At the same time, statistical significance does not always correspond to economic significance. Economically speaking, the question that is more relevant to the assumption of a single-index model is whether portfolios constructed using covariances that are estimated on the basis of the single-factor or single-index assumption are significantly different from, and less efficient than, portfolios constructed using covariances that are estimated directly for each pair of stocks. In Part IV on active portfolio management, we explore this issue further.

Concept Check

Question 1. Suppose that the index model for stocks A and B is estimated with the following results:

$$R_A = .01 + .9R_M + e_A$$

$$R_B = -.02 + 1.1R_M + e_B$$

$$\sigma_M = .20$$

$$\sigma(e_A) = .3$$

$$\sigma(e_B) = .1$$

Find the standard deviation of each stock and the covariance between them.

Estimating the Index Model

Equation 9.3 also suggests how we might go about actually measuring market and firm-specific risk. Suppose that we observe the excess return on the market index and a specific asset over a number of holding periods. We use as an example hypothetical monthly excess returns on the TSE 300 index and XYZ stock. We can summarize the results for a sample period in a **scatter diagram,** as illustrated in Figure 9.1.

FIGURE 9.1

Characteristic line for XYZ.

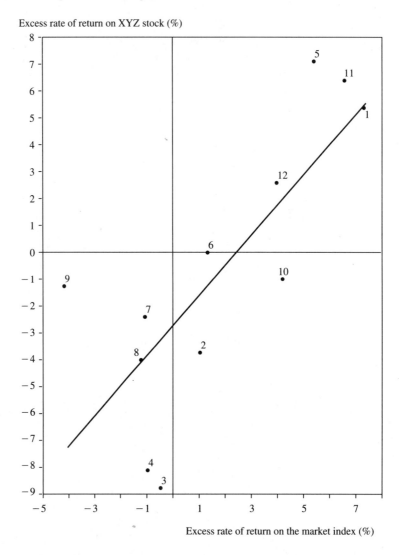

The horizontal axis in Figure 9.1 measures the excess return (over the risk-free rate) on the market index, whereas the vertical axis measures the excess return on the asset in question (XYZ stock in our example). A pair of excess returns (one for the market index, one for XYZ stock) over a holding period constitutes one point on this scatter diagram. The points are numbered 1–12, representing excess returns for the TSE 300 and XYZ for each month from January–December. The single-index model states that the relationship between the excess returns on XYZ and the TSE 300 is given by

$$R_{\text{XYZ}t} = \alpha_{\text{XYZ}} + \beta_{\text{XYZ}}R_{Mt} + e_{\text{XYZ}t}$$

Note the resemblance of this relationship to a **regression equation.**

In a single-variable linear regression equation the dependent variable plots around a straight line with an intercept α and a slope β. The deviations from the line, e_t, are assumed to be mutually independent and independent of the right-hand variable. Because these assumptions are identical to those of the index model we can look at the index model as a regression model. The sensitivity of XYZ to the market, measured by β_{XYZ}, is the slope of the regression line. The intercept of the regression line is α, and deviations of particular observations from the regression line are denoted e. These **residuals** are the parts of stock returns not explained by the independent variable (the market-index return); therefore they measure the impact of firm-specific events during the particular month. The parameters of interest, α, β, and Var(e), can be estimated using standard regression techniques.

Estimating the regression equation of the single-index model gives us the **security characteristic line** (SCL), which is plotted in Figure 9.1. (The regression results and raw data appear in Table 9.1.) The SCL is a plot of the typical excess return on a security over the risk-free rate as a function of the excess return on the market.

This sample of holding period returns is, of course, too small to yield reliable statistics. We use it only for demonstration. For this sample period we find that the beta coefficient of XYZ stock, as estimated by the slope of the regression line, is 1.1357, and that the intercept for this SCL is -2.59 percent per month.

TABLE 9.1   Characteristic Line for XYZ Stock

Month	XYZ Return	Market Return	Monthly T-Bill Rate	Excess XYZ Return	Excess Market Return
January	6.06	7.89	0.65	5.41	7.24
February	-2.86	1.51	0.58	-3.44	0.93
March	-8.18	0.23	0.62	-8.79	-0.38
April	-7.36	-0.29	0.72	-8.08	-1.01
May	7.76	5.58	0.66	7.10	4.92
June	0.52	1.73	0.55	-0.03	1.18
July	-1.74	-0.21	0.62	-2.36	-0.83
August	-3.00	-0.36	0.55	-3.55	-0.91
September	-0.56	-3.58	0.60	-1.16	-4.18
October	-0.37	4.62	0.65	-1.02	3.97
November	6.93	6.85	0.61	6.32	6.25
December	3.08	4.55	0.65	2.43	3.90
Mean	0.02	2.38	0.62	-0.60	1.75
Standard deviation	4.97	3.33	0.05	4.97	3.32
Regression results	$r_{XYZ} - r_f = \alpha + \beta (r_M - r_f)$				

	α	β
Estimated coefficient	-2.590	1.1357
Standard error of estimate	(1.547)	(0.309)
Variance of residuals = 12.601		
Standard deviation of residuals = 3.550		
R-SQR = 0.575		

For each month, our estimate of the residual, e, which is the deviation of XYZ's excess return from the prediction of the SCL, equals

$$\text{deviation} = \text{actual} - \text{predicted return}$$

$$e_{XYZt} = R_{XYZt} - (\beta_{XYZ}R_{Mt} + \alpha_{XYZ})$$

These residuals are estimates of the monthly unexpected *firm-specific* component of the rate of return on XYZ stock. Hence we can estimate the firm-specific variance by[3]

$$\sigma^2(e_{XYZt}) = \frac{1}{10}\sum_{t=1}^{12} e_t^2 = 12.60$$

Therefore, the standard deviation of the firm-specific component of XYZ's return, $\sigma(e_{XYZt})$, equals 3.55 percent per month.

The Index Model and Diversification

The index model, which was first suggested by Sharpe,[4] also offers insight into portfolio diversification. Suppose that we choose an equally weighted portfolio of n securities. The excess rate of return on each security is given by

$$R_i = \alpha_i + \beta_i R_M + e_i$$

Similarly, we can write the excess return on the portfolio of stocks as

$$R_P = \alpha_P + \beta_P R_M + e_P \tag{9.5}$$

We now show that, as the number of stocks included in this portfolio increases, the part of the portfolio risk attributable to non-market factors becomes ever smaller. This part of the risk is diversified away. In contrast, the market risk remains, regardless of the number of firms combined into the portfolio.

To understand these results, note that the excess rate of return on this equally weighted portfolio, for which $w_i = 1/n$, is

$$R_P = \sum_{i=1}^{n} w_i R_i = \frac{1}{n}\sum_{i=1}^{n} R_i = \frac{1}{n}\sum_{i=1}^{n} (\alpha_i + \beta_i R_M + e_i)$$

$$= \frac{1}{n}\sum_{i=1}^{n}\alpha_i + \left(\frac{1}{n}\sum_{i=1}^{n}\beta_i\right) R_M + \frac{1}{n}\sum_{i=1}^{n}e_i \tag{9.6}$$

Comparing equations 9.5 and 9.6, we see that the portfolio has a sensitivity to the market given by

$$\beta_P = \frac{1}{n}\sum_{i=1}^{n}\beta_i$$

---

[3] Because the mean of e_t is zero, e_t^2 is the squared deviation from its mean. The average value of e_t^2 is therefore the estimate of the variance of the firm-specific component. We divide the sum of squared residuals by the degrees of freedom of the regression, $n - 2 = 12 - 2 = 10$ to obtain an unbiased estimate of $\sigma^2(e)$.

[4] William F. Sharpe, "A Simplified Model of Portfolio Analysis," *Management Science*, January 1963.

(which is the average of the individual β_is), and has a non-market return component of a constant (intercept)

$$\frac{1}{n}\sum_{i=1}^{n}\alpha_i$$

(which is the average of the individual alphas), plus the zero mean variable

$$e_P = \frac{1}{n}\sum_{i=1}^{n}e_i$$

which is the average of the firm-specific components. Hence the portfolio's variance is

$$\sigma_P^2 = \beta_P^2\sigma_M^2 + \sigma^2(e_P) \tag{9.7}$$

The systematic risk component of the portfolio variance, which we defined as the part that depends on marketwide movements, is $\beta_P^2\sigma_M^2$ and depends on the average of the sensitivity coefficients of the individual securities. This part of the risk depends on portfolio beta and σ_M^2 and will persist regardless of the extent of portfolio diversification. No matter how many stocks are held, their common exposure to the market will be reflected in portfolio systematic risk.[5]

In contrast, the non-systematic component of the portfolio variance is $\sigma^2(e_P)$ and is attributable to firm-specific components, e_i. Because these e_is are independent, and all have zero expected value, the law of averages can be applied to conclude that as more and more stocks are added to the portfolio, the firm-specific components tend to cancel out, resulting in ever-smaller non-market risk. Such risk is thus termed *diversifiable*. To see this more rigorously, examine the formula for the variance of the equally weighted "portfolio" of firm-specific components. Because the e_is are all uncorrelated,

$$\sigma^2(e_P) = \sum_{i=1}^{n}\left(\frac{1}{n}\right)^2\sigma^2(e_i) = \frac{1}{n}\,\overline{\sigma}^2(e)$$

where $\overline{\sigma}^2(e)$ is the average of the firm-specific variances. Since this average is independent of n, when n gets large, $\overline{\sigma}^2(e_P)$ becomes negligible.

Concept Check	Question 2. Reconsider the two stocks in Concept Check 1. Suppose we form an equally weighted portfolio of A and B. What will be the non-systematic standard deviation of that portfolio?

To summarize, as diversification increases, the total variance of a portfolio approaches the systematic variance, defined as the variance of the market

---

[5] Of course, one can always construct a portfolio with zero systematic risk by mixing negative β and positive β assets. The point of our discussion is that the vast majority of securities have a positive β, implying that well-diversified portfolios with small holdings in large numbers of assets will indeed have positive systematic risk.

FIGURE 9.2

The variance of a portfolio with β in the single-factor economy.

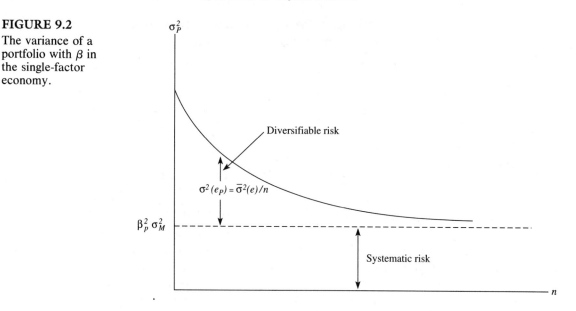

factor multiplied by the square of the portfolio sensitivity coefficient, β_P. This is shown in Figure 9.2.

Figure 9.2 shows that, as more and more securities are combined into a portfolio, the portfolio variance decreases because of the diversification of firm-specific risk. However, the power of diversification is limited. Even for very large n, risk remains because of the exposure of virtually all assets to the common, or market, factor. Therefore this systematic risk is said to be non-diversifiable.

This analysis is borne out by empirical analysis. We saw the effect of portfolio diversification on portfolio standard deviations in Figure 7.2. These empirical results are similar to the theoretical graph presented here in Figure 9.2.

The assumption that all security returns can be represented by equation 9.1 is the main assumption of the index model. It can be combined with other assumptions in order to lead to the CAPM. Alternatively, it can be used as the basis of the single-factor APT, examined in later sections.

9.2   *The Industry Version of the Index Model*

Not surprisingly, the index model has attracted the attention of practitioners. To the extent that it is approximately valid, it provides a convenient benchmark for security analysis.

A modern practitioner using the CAPM who has no special information about a security, or insight that is unavailable to the general public, will conclude that the security is "properly" priced. By "properly" priced, the analyst means that the expected return on the security is fair, given its risk, and therefore plots on the security market line. For instance, if one has no private information about Alcan's (AL) stock, then one should expect

$$E(r_{AL}) = r_f + \beta_{AL}[E(r_M) - r_f]$$

A portfolio manager who has a forecast for the market index, $E(r_M)$, and observes the risk-free T-bill rate, r_f, can use the model to determine the benchmark expected return for any stock. The beta coefficient, the market risk, σ_M^2, and the firm-specific risk, $\sigma^2(e)$, can be estimated from historical SCLs— from regressions of security excess returns on market index excess returns.

There are many sources for such regression results. For instance, the Quantitative Analysis division of Burns Fry Ltd. publishes periodic estimates of stock betas. It uses the TSE 300 index as the proxy for the market portfolio. It relies on the 54 most recent monthly observations to calculate the regression parameters. Burns Fry and most services[6] use total returns, rather than excess returns (deviations from T-bill rates), in their regressions. In this way they estimate a variant of our index model, which is

$$r = a + br_M + e^* \tag{9.8}$$

instead of

$$r - r_f = \alpha + \beta(r_M - r_f) + e \tag{9.9}$$

(Please note that "*a*" and "*b*" are regression coefficients different from "alpha" and "beta"; e^* is not a footnote, but a distinguishing symbol from the *e*.)

To see the effect of this departure, we can rewrite equation 9.9 as

$$r = r_f + \alpha + \beta r_M - \beta r_f + e = \alpha + r_f(1 - \beta) + \beta r_M + e \tag{9.10}$$

Comparing equations 9.8 and 9.10, you can see that if r_f is constant over the sample period both equations have the same independent variable, r_M, and residual, *e*. The slope coefficient will be the same in the two regressions.[7]

However, the intercept that Burns Fry calls alpha is really, using the parameters of the CAPM, an estimate of $\alpha + r_f(1 - \beta)$. The apparent justification for this procedure is that, on a monthly basis, $r_f(1 - \beta)$ is small and is apt to be swamped by the volatility of actual stock returns. However, it is worth noting that for $\beta \neq 1$, the regression intercept in equation 9.8 will not equal the CAPM alpha as it does when excess returns are used as in equation 9.9.

Company Beta Estimates

Table 9.2 illustrates some Burns Fry estimates of equation 9.8 for a number of important Canadian firms, for two different periods of 54 months. For each

---

[6] Merrill Lynch and Value Line are two well-known sources of U.S. betas; Merrill Lynch uses monthly returns and the S&P 500 for the market proxy, while Value Line uses weekly returns and the NYSE index.

[7] Actually, r_f does vary over time and so should not be grouped casually with the constant term in the regression. However, variations in r_f are tiny compared with swings in the market return. The actual volatility in the T-bill rate has only a small impact on the estimated value of beta.

TABLE 9.2   Estimates of Stock Total Return Betas

| Company | October 1984–March 1989 | | | | October 1987–March 1992 | | | |
	Beta	Alpha	% Expl. by Market	Number of Months	Beta	Alpha	% Expl. by Market	Number of Months
Alcan Aluminium	1.20	0.18	44.8	54	1.29	−0.18	67.2	54
Noranda Inc.	1.76	−1.02	62.0	54	1.67	−0.81	79.4	54
LAC Minerals	1.07	0.17	14.7	54	1.20	−1.21	26.9	54
Imperial Oil A	0.92	−0.15	35.2	54	0.56	−0.88	18.9	54
Abitibi Price	1.04	0.83	18.2	54	0.87	−0.91	32.9	54
Macmillan Bloedel	1.49	0.64	47.0	54	1.43	−0.18	62.6	54
BC Sugar Refinery	0.78	1.08	28.3	54	0.56	0.21	15.1	54
Imasco Ltd.	0.97	0.17	41.0	54	1.07	0.52	49.5	54
Seagram's	0.85	0.36	37.0	54	1.08	0.82	56.4	54
John Labatt	0.66	1.22	21.4	54	0.63	0.22	25.4	54
Magna A	1.80	−1.47	45.5	54	2.13	2.26	23.6	54
Dofasco Inc.	1.16	−0.44	55.1	54	1.08	−0.56	53.3	54
Northern Telecom	1.07	−1.38	36.8	54	0.91	1.35	33.6	54
NOVA Corp.	1.40	0.17	38.6	54	1.32	0.09	40.3	54
Laidlaw Transportation B	1.32	1.93	39.4	54	1.26	−0.51	28.4	54
BCE Inc.	0.36	0.43	24.0	54	0.40	0.78	34.6	54
Rogers Communications B	1.64	3.93	33.8	54	1.84	2.89	40.6	54
George Weston	0.89	0.64	47.9	54	0.85	−0.03	49.3	54
Royal Bank of Canada	0.72	0.46	38.0	54	0.84	1.20	48.7	54
Canadian Pacific	1.20	−0.06	51.7	54	1.05	−0.58	49.9	54

Data from the Quantitative Analysis division of Burns Fry Ltd. Reprinted by permission.

period, after the company name, the next two columns show the beta and alpha coefficients. Remember that Burns Fry's alpha is actually $\alpha + r_f(1 - \beta)$.

The next column, % Explained by Market, shows the square of the correlation coefficient, also known as *R*-square, between r_i and r_M. The *R*-square statistic, which is sometimes called the *coefficient of determination,* gives the fraction of the variance of the dependent variable (the return on the stock) that is explained by movements in the independent variable (the return on the TSE 300 index). Recall from Section 9.1 that the part of the total variance of the rate of return on an asset, σ^2, that is explained by market returns is the systematic variance $\beta^2 \sigma_M^2$. Hence the *R*-square is systematic variance over total variance, which tells us what fraction of a firm's volatility is attributable to market movements:

$$R\text{-square} = \frac{\beta^2 \sigma_M^2}{\sigma^2}$$

The firm-specific variance, $\sigma^2(e)$, is the part of the asset variance that is unexplained by the market index. Therefore, because

$$\sigma^2 = \beta^2 \sigma_M^2 + \sigma^2(e)$$

the coefficient of determination also may be expressed as

$$R^2 = 1 - \frac{\sigma^2(e)}{\sigma^2} \qquad (9.11)$$

Finally, the last column shows the number of observations, which is 54 months, unless the stock is newly listed and fewer observations are available.

The American brokerage firm Merrill Lynch provides another estimate of beta, called *adjusted beta*. The motivation for adjusting beta estimates is the observation that, on average, the beta coefficients of stocks seem to move toward 1 over time. One explanation for this phenomenon is intuitive. A business enterprise usually is established to produce a specific product or service, and a new firm may be more unconventional than an older one in many ways, from technology to management style. As it grows, however, a firm diversifies, first expanding to similar products and later to more diverse operations. As the firm becomes more conventional, it starts to resemble the rest of the economy even more. Thus, its beta coefficient will tend to change in the direction of 1.

Another explanation for this phenomenon is statistical. We know that the average beta over all securities is 1. Thus, before estimating the beta of a security our guess would be that it is 1. When we estimate this beta coefficient over a particular sample period, we sustain some unknown sampling error of the estimated beta. The greater the difference between our beta estimate and 1, the greater is the chance that we incurred a large estimation error and that, when we estimate this same beta in a subsequent sample period, the new estimate will be closer to 1.

The sample estimate of the beta coefficient is the best guess for the sample period. Given that beta has a tendency to evolve toward 1, however, a forecast of the future beta coefficient should adjust the sample estimate in that direction.

Merrill Lynch adjusts beta estimates in a simple way. They take the sample estimate of beta and average it with 1, using the weights of two thirds and one third:

Adjusted beta = ⅔ sample beta + ⅓(1)

For instance, since Seagram's (VO) is actively traded on the NYSE, Merrill Lynch will be interested in providing an adjusted beta for it. Assuming they had the same estimate for beta of .85 for the 54 months ending in March 1989, the adjusted beta for Seagram's would be .90, taking it one third of the way toward 1.

A comparison of the beta estimates between the two different periods shows that several of them were remarkably stable, even though they were estimated three years apart. For instance, Alcan's beta went from 1.20 to 1.29; Macmillan Bloedel from 1.49 to 1.43; Labatt from 0.66 to 0.63; etc. Others showed more variability: Seagram's went from 0.85 to 1.08, and Imperial Oil A from 0.92 to 0.56.

The sample period regression alpha for Seagram's for 1989 is .36. Since Seagram's beta is less than 1, we know that this means that the index model alpha estimate is somewhat smaller. As we did in equation 9.9, we have to subtract $(1 - \beta)r_f$ from the regression alpha to obtain the index model alpha.

Concept Check

Question 3. What was Seagram's CAPM alpha per month during the period covered by the Burns Fry 1989 regression if during this period the average monthly rate of return of T-bills was 0.8 percent?

More importantly, these alpha estimates are ex post (after the fact) measures. They do not mean that anyone could have forecast these alpha values ex ante (before the fact). In fact, the name of the game in security analysis is to forecast alpha values ahead of time. A well-constructed portfolio that includes long positions in future positive alpha stocks and short positions in future negative alpha stocks will outperform the market index. The key term here is *well constructed,* meaning that the portfolio has to balance concentration on high alpha stocks with the need for risk-reducing diversification. The beta and residual variance estimates from the index model regression make it possible to achieve this goal. (We examine this technique in more detail in part IV on active portfolio management.)

In the absence of special information concerning Seagram's, if our forecast for the market index is 14 percent and T-bills pay 6 percent, we learn from the Burns Fry estimates that the CAPM forecast for the rate of return on Seagram's stock is

$$E(r_{VO}) = r_f + \beta \times [E(r_M) - r_f]$$
$$= .06 + .85(.14 - .06)$$
$$= .128 = 12.8\%$$

TABLE 9.3   Estimates of Sector Total Return Betas

Sector	October 1984–March 1989				October 1987–March 1992			
	Beta	Alpha	% Expl. by Market	Number of Months	Beta	Alpha	% Expl. by Market	Number of Months
Metals and minerals	1.40	−0.04	63.6	54	1.41	0.12	76.6	54
Gold and silver	1.22	0.07	31.8	54	1.06	−1.16	31.8	54
Oil and gas	1.03	−0.51	49.3	54	0.75	−0.50	47.5	54
Paper/wood products	1.38	0.41	70.9	54	1.30	−0.53	74.6	54
Consumer products	0.91	0.12	72.8	54	1.01	0.57	78.8	54
Industrial products	1.07	−0.54	77.2	54	1.07	0.04	78.8	54
Real estate	0.94	0.80	52.9	54	1.23	−1.14	57.8	54
Transportation	1.22	0.69	48.6	54	1.29	−0.83	44.5	54
Pipelines	0.96	0.24	56.8	54	0.80	0.85	53.8	54
Utilities	0.37	0.48	32.0	54	0.40	0.76	44.1	54
Communications	0.97	0.80	62.8	54	1.09	0.28	68.8	54
Merchandising	0.81	0.58	58.9	54	0.87	0.29	73.7	54
Financial services	0.84	0.41	69.2	54	0.96	0.60	75.4	54
Management companies	1.19	0.25	74.7	54	1.14	−0.54	72.6	54

Data from the Quantitative Analysis division of Burns Fry Ltd. Reprinted by permission.

Industrial Sector Beta Estimates

In analyzing securities, it is often interesting to obtain statistical aggregates by industrial sector. Table 9.2 presented an extract from Burns Fry's calculations for the TSE 300; in compiling that they also estimate the sectoral statistics. The results for the two time periods are shown in Table 9.3; the 14 sectors are also broken down into sub-sectors in their complete analysis. Note that even by aggregation, while some betas are extremely stable, other sectors show large variations for the two periods.

9.3 *Arbitrage: Profits and Opportunities*

A risk-free arbitrage opportunity arises when an investor can construct a **zero investment portfolio** that will yield a sure profit. A zero investment portfolio means that the investor need not use any of his or her own money. Obviously, to be able to construct a zero investment portfolio one has to be able to sell short at least one asset and use the proceeds to purchase (go long on) one or more assets. Even a small investor using short positions in this fashion can take a large position in such a portfolio.

An obvious case of an arbitrage opportunity arises when the law of one price is violated, as discussed in Chapter 4. When an asset is trading at different prices in two markets (and the price differential exceeds transaction costs), a simultaneous trade in the two markets can produce a sure profit (the net price differential) without any investment. One simply sells short the asset in the high-priced market and buys it in the low-priced market. The net proceeds are positive, and there is no risk because the long and short positions offset each other.

In modern markets with electronic communications and instantaneous execution, arbitrage opportunities have become rare, but not extinct. The same technology that enables the market to absorb new information quickly also enables fast operators to make large profits by trading huge volumes at the instant that an arbitrage opportunity appears. This is the essence of program trading, to be discussed in Chapter 23.

From the simple case of a violation of the law of one price, let us proceed to a less obvious (yet just as profitable) arbitrage opportunity. Imagine that four stocks are traded in an economy with only four distinct, possible scenarios. The rates of return on the four stocks for each inflation-interest rate scenario appear in Table 9.4. The current prices of the stocks and rate of return statistics are shown in Table 9.5.

Eyeballing the rate of return data, there seems no clue to any arbitrage opportunity lurking in this set of investments. The expected returns, standard deviations, and correlations do not reveal any particular abnormality.

TABLE 9.4   Rate of Return Projections

	High Real Interest Rates		Low Real Interest Rates	
	High Inflation	Low Inflation	High Inflation	Low Inflation
Probability	.25	.25	.25	.25
Stock				
Apex (*A*)	−20	20	40	60
Bull (*B*)	0	70	30	−20
Crush (*C*)	90	−20	−10	70
Dreck (*D*)	15	23	15	36

Consider, however, an equally weighted portfolio of the first three stocks (Apex, Bull, and Crush), and contrast its possible future rates of return with those of the fourth stock, Dreck, as derived from Table 9.4.

	High Real Interest Rates		Low Real Interest Rates	
	High Inflation Rate	Low Inflation Rate	High Inflation Rate	Low Inflation Rate
Equally weighted portfolio (*A, B,* and *C*)	23.33	23.33	20.00	36.67
Dreck	15.00	23.00	15.00	36.00

This analysis reveals that in all scenarios the equally weighted portfolio will outperform Dreck. The rate of return statistics of the two alternatives are

	Mean	Standard Deviation	Correlation
Three-stock portfolio	25.83	6.40	.94
Dreck	22.25	8.58	

The two investments are not perfectly correlated; that is, they are not perfect substitutes, meaning there is no violation of the law of one price here. Nevertheless, the equally weighted portfolio will fare better under *any* circum-

TABLE 9.5   Rate of Return Statistics

Stock	Current Price	Expected Return	Standard Deviation (%)	Correlation Matrix			
				A	*B*	*C*	*D*
A	$10	25	29.58	1.00	−.15	−.29	.68
B	$10	20	33.91	−.15	1.00	−.87	−.38
C	$10	32.5	48.15	−.29	−.87	1.00	.22
D	$10	22.25	8.58	.68	−.38	.22	1.00

stances; thus any investor, no matter how risk averse, can take advantage of this dominance. All that is required is for the investor to take a short position in Dreck and use the proceeds to purchase the equally weighted portfolio.[8] Let us see how it would work.

Suppose that we sell short 300,000 shares of Dreck and use the $3 million proceeds to buy 100,000 shares each of Apex, Bull, and Crush. The dollar profits in each of the four scenarios will be as follows:

| Stock | Dollar Investment | High Real Interest Rates | | Low Real Interest Rates | |
		High Inflation Rate	Low Inflation Rate	High Inflation Rate	Low Inflation Rate
Apex	$1,000,000	$-200,000	$200,000	$400,000	$600,000
Bull	1,000,000	0	700,000	300,000	-200,000
Crush	1,000,000	900,000	-200,000	-100,000	700,000
Dreck	-3,000,000	-450,000	-690,000	-450,000	-1,080,000
Portfolio	0	$250,000	$10,000	$150,000	$20,000

The first column verifies that the net investment in our portfolio is zero. Yet this portfolio yields a positive profit according to any scenario. This is a money machine. Investors will want to take an infinite position in such a portfolio because larger positions entail no risk of losses, yet yield ever-growing profits. Theoretically, even a single investor would take such large positions that the market would react to the buying and selling pressure: the price of Dreck has to come down and/or the prices of Apex, Bull, and Crush have to go up. The arbitrage opportunity will be eliminated.

Concept Check	Question 4. Suppose that Dreck's price starts falling without any change in its per-share dollar payoffs. How far must the price fall before arbitrage between Dreck and the equally weighted portfolio is no longer possible? (Hint: what happens to the amount of the equally weighted portfolio that can be purchased with the proceeds of the short sale as Dreck's price falls?)

The idea that equilibrium market prices ought to be rational in the sense that prices will move to rule out arbitrage opportunities is perhaps the most fundamental concept in capital market theory. Violation of this restriction would indicate the grossest form of market irrationality.

---

[8] Short selling is discussed in Chapter 3.

The critical property of a risk-free arbitrage portfolio is that any investor, regardless of risk aversion or wealth, will want to take an infinite position in it so that profits will be driven to an infinite level. Because those large positions will force prices up or down until the opportunity vanishes, we can derive restrictions on security prices that satisfy the condition that no arbitrage opportunities are left in the marketplace.

There is an important difference between (risk-free) arbitrage and risk versus return dominance arguments in support of equilibrium price relationships. A dominance argument holds that when an equilibrium price relationship is violated, many investors will make portfolio changes. Each individual investor will make a limited change, though, depending on his or her degree of risk aversion. Aggregation of these limited portfolio changes over many investors is required to create a large volume of buying and selling, which in turn restores equilibrium prices. When arbitrage opportunities exist, by contrast, each investor wants to take as large a position as possible; hence it will not take many investors to bring about the price pressures necessary to restore equilibrium. For this reason, implications for prices derived from no-arbitrage arguments are stronger than implications derived from a risk versus return dominance argument.

The CAPM is an example of a dominance argument. The CAPM argues that all investors hold mean-variance efficient portfolios. If a security (or a bundle of securities) is mispriced, then investors will tilt their portfolios toward the underpriced and away from the overpriced securities. The resulting pressure on equilibrium prices results from many investors shifting their portfolios, each by a relatively small dollar amount. The assumption that a sufficiently large number of investors are mean-variance sensitive is critical, whereas the essence of the no-arbitrage condition is that even relatively few investors are enough to identify an arbitrage opportunity and then mobilize large dollar amounts to take advantage of it. Pressure on prices can result from only a few arbitrageurs.

Practitioners often use the terms *arbitrage* and *arbitrageurs* in ways other than our strict definition. *Arbitrageur* often is used to refer to a professional searching for mispriced securities in specific areas such as merger-target stocks, rather than to one who seeks strict (risk-free) arbitrage opportunities in the sense that no loss is possible. The search for mispriced securities rather than the more restrictive search for sure bets sometimes is called **risk arbitrage** to distinguish it from pure arbitrage.

To leap ahead, in Part VII we discuss "derivative" securities such as futures and options, where market values are completely determined by the prices of other securities or portfolios. For example, a call option on a stock has a value at maturity that is fully determined by the price of the stock. For such securities, strict arbitrage is a practical possibility, and the condition of no-arbitrage leads to exact pricing. In the case of stocks and other "primitive" securities (whose values are not determined strictly by a single asset or bundle of assets), no-arbitrage conditions must be obtained by appealing to diversification arguments.

9.4 *Well-Diversified Portfolios and the APT*

Stephen Ross developed the **Arbitrage Pricing Theory** (APT) in 1976.[9] As with our analysis of the CAPM, we begin with the simple version of his model, which assumes that only one systematic factor affects security returns. However, the usual discussion of the APT is concerned with the multifactor case, and we treat this richer model in Section 9.7.

Ross starts by examining a single-factor model similar in spirit to the index model introduced in Section 9.1. As in that model, uncertainty in asset returns has two sources: a common or macroeconomic factor, and a firm-specific or microeconomic cause. In the factor model the common factor is assumed to have zero expected value, and it is meant to measure new information concerning the macroeconomy. New information has, by definition, zero expected value. There is no need, however, to assume that the factor can be proxied by the return on a market index portfolio.

If we call F the deviation of the common factor from its expected value, β_i the sensitivity of firm i to that factor, and e_i, the firm-specific disturbance, the factor model states that the actual return on firm i will equal its expected return plus a (zero expected value) random amount attributable to unanticipated economywide events, plus another (zero expected value) random amount attributable to firm-specific events.

Formally,

$$r_i = E(r_i) + \beta_i F + e_i$$

where $E(r_i)$ is the expected return on stock i. All the non-systematic returns, the e_is, are uncorrelated among themselves and uncorrelated with the factor, F.

To make the factor model more concrete, consider an example. Suppose that the macro factor, F, is taken to be the unexpected percentage change in GNP, and that the consensus is that GNP will increase by 4 percent this year. Suppose also that a stock's β value is 1.2. If GNP increases by only 3 percent, then the value of F would be -1 percent, representing a 1 percent disappointment in actual growth versus expected growth. Given the stock's beta value, this disappointment would translate into a return on the stock that is 1.2 percent lower than previously expected. This macro surprise together with the firm-specific disturbance, e_i, determine the total departure of the stock's return from its originally expected value.

---

[9] Stephen A. Ross, "Return, Risk and Arbitrage," in I. Friend and J. Bicksler (editors), *Risk and Return in Finance* (Cambridge, Mass.: Ballinger, 1976).

Well-Diversified Portfolios

Now we look at the risk of a portfolio of stocks. We first show that if a portfolio is well diversified, its firm-specific or non-factor risk can be diversified away. Only factor (or systematic) risk remains. If we construct an n-stock portfolio with weights, w_i, $\Sigma w_i = 1$, then the rate of return on this portfolio is as follows:

$$r_P = E(r_P) + \beta_P F + e_P \tag{9.12}$$

where

$$\beta_P = \Sigma w_i \beta_i$$

is the weighted average of the β_i of the n securities. The portfolio non-systematic component (which is uncorrelated with F) is

$$e_P = \Sigma w_i e_i$$

which also is a weighted average, in this case of the e_i of each of the n securities.

We can divide the variance of this portfolio into systematic and non-systematic sources, as we saw in Section 9.1 (equation 9.7). The portfolio variance is

$$\sigma_P^2 = \beta_P^2 \sigma_F^2 + \sigma^2(e_P)$$

where σ_F^2 is the variance of the factor F, and $\sigma^2(e_P)$ is the non-systematic risk of the portfolio, which is given by

$$\sigma^2(e_P) = \text{Variance}(\Sigma w_i e_i) = \Sigma w_i^2 \sigma^2(e_i)$$

Note that, in deriving the non-systematic variance of the portfolio, we depend on the fact that the firm-specific e_is are uncorrelated and hence that the variance of the "portfolio" of non-systematic e_is is the weighted sum of the individual non-systematic variances (with the square of the investment proportions as weights).

If the portfolio were equally weighted, $w_i = 1/n$, then the non-systematic variance would be

$$\sigma^2\left(e_P; w_i = \frac{1}{n}\right) = \Sigma \left(\frac{1}{n}\right)^2 \sigma^2(e_i) = \frac{1}{n} \Sigma \frac{\sigma^2(e_i)}{n} = \frac{1}{n} \bar{\sigma}^2(e_i)$$

In this case, we divide the average non-systematic variance, $\bar{\sigma}^2(e_i)$, by n, so that when the portfolio gets large (in the sense that n is large and the portfolio remains equally weighted across all n stocks), the non-systematic variance approaches zero.

Concept Check

Question 5. What will be the non-systematic standard deviation of the equally weighted portfolio if the average value of $\sigma^2(e_i)$ equals .30, and (a) $n = 10$, (b) $n = 100$, (c) $n = 1,000$, and (d) $n = 10,000$? What do you conclude about the non-systematic risk of large, diversified portfolios?

The set of portfolios for which the non-systematic variance approaches zero as n gets large consists of more portfolios than just the equally weighted portfolio. Any portfolio for which each w_i becomes consistently smaller as n gets large (specifically where each w_i^2 approaches zero as n gets large) will satisfy the condition that the portfolio non-systematic risk will approach zero as n gets large.

In fact, this property motivates us to define a **well-diversified portfolio** as one that is diversified over a large enough number of securities with proportions, w_i, each small enough that for practical purposes the non-systematic variance, $\sigma^2(e_P)$, is negligible. Because the expected return of e_P is zero, if its variance also is zero, we can conclude that any realized value of e_P will be virtually zero. Rewriting equation 9.12, we conclude that for a well-diversified portfolio for all practical purposes

$$r_P = E(r_P) + \beta_P F$$

and

$$\sigma_P^2 = \beta_P^2 \sigma_F^2; \; \sigma_P = \beta_P \sigma_F$$

Large (mostly institutional) investors hold portfolios of hundreds and even thousands of securities; thus the concept of well-diversified portfolios clearly is operational in contemporary financial markets. Well-diversified portfolios, however, are not necessarily equally weighted.

As an illustration, consider a portfolio of 1,000 stocks. Let our position in the first stock be w percent. Let the position in the second stock be $2w$ percent, the position in the third $3w$ percent, and so on. In this way our largest position (in the thousandth stock) is $1,000w$ percent. Can this portfolio possibly be well diversified, considering the fact that the largest position is 1,000 times the smallest position? Surprisingly, the answer is yes.

To see this, let us determine the largest weight in any one stock, in this case, the thousandth stock. The sum of the positions in all stocks must be 100 percent; therefore

$$w + 2w + \ldots + 1,000w = 100$$

Solving for w, we find that

$$w = .0002\%$$

$$1000w = .2\%$$

Our *largest* position amounts to only .2 of 1 percent. And this is very far from an equally weighted portfolio. Yet, for practical purposes this still is a well-diversified portfolio.

Betas and Expected Returns

Because non-factor risk can be diversified away, only factor risk commands a risk premium in market equilibrium. Non-systematic risk across firms cancels out in well-diversified portfolios, so that only the systematic risk of a security can be related to its expected returns.

FIGURE 9.3

Returns as a function of the systematic factor. **A** = well-diversified portfolio (*A*); **B** = single stock (*S*).

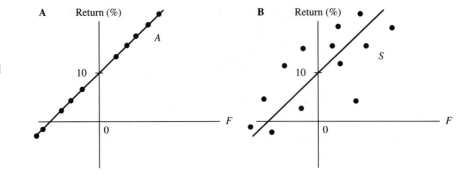

The solid line in Figure 9.3**A** plots the return of a well-diversified portfolio (*A*) with $\beta_A = 1$ for various realizations of the systematic factor. The expected return of portfolio *A* is 10 percent: this is where the solid line crosses the vertical axis. At this point the systematic factor is zero, implying no macro surprises. If the macro factor is positive, the portfolio's return exceeds its expected value; if it is negative, the portfolio's return falls short of its mean. The return on the portfolio is therefore

$$E(r_A) + \beta_A F = .10 + 1.0 \times F$$

Compare Figure 9.3**A** with Figure 9.3**B**, which is a similar graph for a single stock (*S*) with $\beta_S = 1$. The undiversified stock is subject to non-systematic risk, which is seen in a scatter of points around the line. The well-diversified portfolio's return, in contrast, is determined completely by the systematic factor.

Now consider Figure 9.4, where the dashed line plots the return on another well-diversified portfolio, portfolio *B*, with an expected return of 8 percent and β_B also equal to 1.0. Could portfolios *A* and *B* coexist with the return pattern

FIGURE 9.4

Returns as a function of the systematic factor: an arbitrage opportunity.

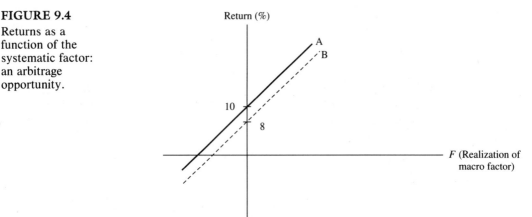

depicted? Clearly not: no matter what the systematic factor turns out to be, portfolio *A* outperforms portfolio *B*, leading to an arbitrage opportunity.

If you sell short $1 million of *B* and buy $1 million of *A*, a zero net investment strategy, your return would be $20,000, as follows:

$(.10 + 1.0 \times F) \times \$1$ million	(from long position in *A*)
$-(.08 + 1.0 \times F) \times \$1$ million	(from short position in *B*)
$.02 \times \$1$ million = \$20,000	(net proceeds)

You make a risk-free profit because the factor risk cancels out across the long and short positions. Moreover, the strategy requires zero net investment. You should pursue it on an infinitely large scale until the return discrepancy between the two portfolios disappears. Portfolios with equal betas must have equal expected returns in market equilibrium, or arbitrage opportunities exist.

What about portfolios with different betas? We show now that their risk premiums must be proportional to beta. To see why, consider Figure 9.5. Suppose that the risk-free rate is 4 percent and that well-diversified portfolio *C*, with a beta of .5, has an expected return of 6 percent. Portfolio *C* plots below the line from the risk-free asset to portfolio *A*. Consider therefore a new portfolio, *D*, composed of half of portfolio *A* and half of the risk-free asset. Portfolio *D*'s beta will be $(\frac{1}{2} \times 0 + \frac{1}{2} \times 1.0) = .5$, and its expected return will be $(\frac{1}{2} \times 4 + \frac{1}{2} \times 10) = 7$ percent. Now portfolio *D* has an equal beta but a greater expected return than does portfolio *C*. From our analysis in the previous paragraph we know that this constitutes an arbitrage opportunity.

We conclude that, to preclude arbitrage opportunities, the expected return on all well-diversified portfolios must lie on the straight line from the risk-free asset in Figure 9.5. The equation of this line will dictate the expected return on all well-diversified portfolios.

FIGURE 9.5
An arbitrage
opportunity.

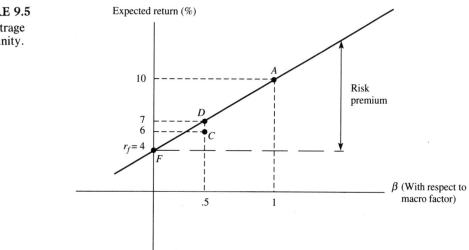

Concept Check

> Question 6. Suppose that portfolio E is well diversified with a beta of $\frac{2}{3}$ and expected return of 9 percent. Would an arbitrage opportunity exist? If so, what would be the arbitrage opportunity?

Notice in Figure 9.5 that risk premiums are indeed proportional to portfolio betas. The risk premium is depicted by the vertical arrow, which measures the distance between the risk-free rate and the expected return on the portfolio. The risk premium is zero for $\beta = 0$, and rises in direct proportion to β.

The Security Market Line

Now consider the market portfolio as a well-diversified portfolio, and let us measure the systematic factor as the unexpected return on the market portfolio. The beta of the market portfolio is 1, since that is the beta of the market portfolio with itself. Because the market portfolio is on the line in Figure 9.5, we can use it to determine the equation describing the line. As Figure 9.6 shows, the intercept is r_f, and the slope is $E(r_M) - r_f$ [rise $= E(r_M) - r_f$; run $= 1$], implying that the equation of the line is

$$E(r_P) = r_f + [E(r_M) - r_f]\beta_P \qquad \textbf{(9.13)}$$

Hence, Figures 9.5 and 9.6 are identical to the SML relation of the CAPM.

FIGURE 9.6
The security market line.

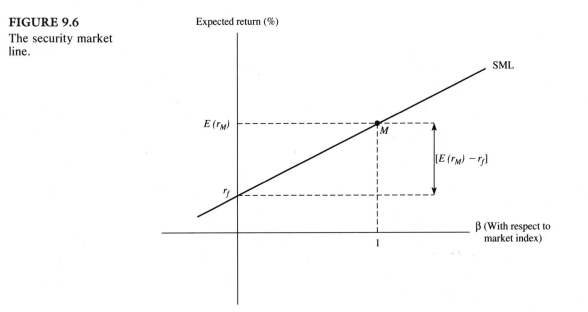

We have used the no-arbitrage condition to obtain an expected return-beta relationship identical to that of the CAPM, without the restrictive assumptions of the CAPM. This suggests that despite its restrictive assumptions the main conclusion of the CAPM, namely, the SML expected return-beta relationship, is likely to be at least approximately valid.

It is worth noting that in contrast to the CAPM the APT does not require that the benchmark portfolio in the SML relationship be the true market portfolio. Any well-diversified portfolio lying on the SML of Figure 9.5 may serve as the benchmark portfolio. For example, one might define the benchmark portfolio as the well-diversified portfolio most highly correlated with whatever systematic factor is thought to affect stock returns. Accordingly, the APT has more flexibility than does the CAPM because problems associated with an unobservable market portfolio are not a concern.

In addition, the APT provides further justification for use of the index model in the practical implementation of the SML relationship. Even if the index portfolio is not a precise proxy for the true market portfolio, which is a cause of considerable concern in the context of the CAPM, we now know that if the index portfolio is sufficiently well diversified, the SML relationship should still hold true according to the APT.

So far we have demonstrated the APT relationship for well-diversified portfolios only. The CAPM expected return-beta relationship applies to single assets, as well as to portfolios. In the next section we generalize the APT result one step further.

9.5 *Individual Assets and the APT*

We have demonstrated that, if arbitrage opportunities using well-diversified portfolios are to be ruled out, each portfolio's expected excess return must be proportional to its beta. For any two well-diversified portfolios P and Q, this can be written as

$$\frac{E(r_P) - r_f}{\beta_P} = \frac{E(r_Q) - r_f}{\beta_Q} \qquad (9.14)$$

The question is whether this relationship tells us anything about the expected rates of return on the component stocks. The answer is that if this relationship is to be satisfied by all well-diversified portfolios, it almost surely must be satisfied by all individual securities, although the proof of this proposition is somewhat difficult. We note at the outset that, intuitively, we must prove simply that non-systematic risk does not matter for security returns. The expected return-beta relationship that holds for well-diversified portfolios also must hold for individual securities.

First, we show that if individual securities satisfy equation 9.14, so will all portfolios. If for any two stocks, i and j, the same relationship holds exactly, that is,

$$\frac{E(r_i) - r_f}{\beta_i} = \frac{E(r_j) - r_f}{\beta_j} = K$$

where K is a constant for all securities, then by cross-multiplying, we can write, for any security, i,

$$E(r_i) = r_f + \beta_i K$$

Therefore for any portfolio P with security weights w_i we have

$$E(r_P) = \sum w_i E(r_i) = r_f \sum w_i + K \sum w_i \beta_i$$

Because $\sum w_i = 1$ and $\beta_P = \sum w_i \beta_i$, we have

$$E(r_P) = r_f + \beta_P K$$

Thus for all portfolios,

$$\frac{E(r_P) - r_f}{\beta_P} = K$$

and since all portfolios have the same K,

$$\frac{E(r_P) - r_f}{\beta_P} = \frac{E(r_Q) - r_f}{\beta_Q}$$

In other words, if the expected return-beta relationship holds for all single assets, then it will hold for all portfolios.

Concept Check
════════
════════

Question 7. Confirm the property expressed in equation 9.14 with a simple numerical example. Suppose that portfolio P has an expected return of 10 percent, and β of .5, whereas portfolio Q has an expected return of 15 percent and β of 1. The risk-free rate, r_f, is 5 percent.
a. Find K for these portfolios, and confirm that they are equal.
b. Find K for an equally weighted portfolio of P and Q, and show that it equals K for each individual security.

Now we show that it also is necessary that all securities satisfy the condition. To avoid extensive mathematics, we will satisfy ourselves with a less rigorous argument. Suppose that this relationship is violated for all single assets. Now create a pair of well-diversified portfolios from these assets. What are the chances that, in spite of the fact that for any two single assets this relationship

$$\frac{E(r_i) - r_f}{\beta_i} = \frac{E(r_j) - r_f}{\beta_j}$$

does not hold, the relationship *will* hold for the well-diversified portfolios as follows:

$$\frac{E(r_P) - r_f}{\beta_P} = \frac{E(r_Q) - r_f}{\beta_Q}$$

The chances are small, but it is possible that the relationships among the single securities are violated in offsetting ways so that somehow it holds for the pair of well-diversified portfolios.

Now construct yet another well-diversified portfolio. What are the chances that the violation of the relationships for single securities are such that the third portfolio also will fulfill the no-arbitrage expected return-beta relationship? Obviously, the chances are smaller still. But the relationship is possible. Continue with a fourth well-diversified portfolio, and so on. If the no-arbitrage expected return-beta relationship has to hold for infinitely many different, well-diversified portfolios, it must be virtually certain that the relationship holds for all individual securities.

We use the term *virtually certain* advisedly because we must distinguish this conclusion from the statement that all securities surely fulfill this relationship. The reason we cannot make the latter statement has to do with a property of well-diversified portfolios.

Recall that for a portfolio to qualify as well diversified it has to have very small positions in all securities. If, for example, only one security violates the expected return-beta relationship, then the effect of this violation for a well-diversified portfolio will be too small to be of importance for any practical purpose, and meaningful arbitrage opportunities will not arise. But if many securities violate the expected return-beta relationship, the relationship will no longer hold for well-diversified portfolios, and arbitrage opportunities will be available.

Consequently, we conclude that imposing the no-arbitrage condition on a single-factor security market implies maintenance of the expected return-beta relationship for all well-diversified portfolios and for all but, possibly, a *small* number of individual securities.

9.6 *The CAPM, the Index Model, and the APT*

The CAPM, the index model, and the APT all serve many of the same functions. They give us a benchmark for fair rates of return that can be used for capital budgeting, security evaluation, or investment performance evaluation. Moreover, they highlight the crucial distinction between non-diversifiable risk (factor risk), which requires a reward in the form of a risk premium, and diversifiable risk, which does not. The existence of all three models raises the question of what distinctions can be made between the assumptions and conclusions associated with each of them. In other words, what advantage is there in using any one of the models in preference to the others?

Actual Returns vs. Expected Returns

The CAPM is an elegant model. The question is whether it has real-world value—whether its implications are borne out by experience. Chapter 11 provides a range of empirical evidence on this point, but for now we will focus briefly on a more basic issue: is the CAPM testable even in principle?

For starters, one central prediction of the CAPM is that the market portfolio is a mean-variance efficient portfolio. Consider that the CAPM treats all traded risky assets. To test the efficiency of the CAPM market portfolio, we would need to construct a value-weighted portfolio of a huge size and test its efficiency. So far, this task has not been feasible. An even more difficult problem, however, is that the CAPM implies relationships among *expected* returns, whereas all we can observe are actual or realized holding period returns, and these need not equal prior expectations. Even supposing we could construct a portfolio to represent the CAPM market portfolio satisfactorily, how would we test its mean-variance efficiency? We would have to show that the reward-to-variability ratio of the market portfolio is higher than that of any other portfolio. However, this reward-to-variability ratio is set in terms of expectations, and we have no way to observe these expectations directly.

The problem of measuring expectations haunts us as well when we try to establish the validity of the second central set of CAPM predictions, the expected return-beta relationship. This relationship is also defined in terms of expected returns $E(r_i)$ and $E(r_M)$:

$$E(r_i) = r_f + \beta_i[E(r_M) - r_f] \tag{9.15}$$

The upshot is that, as elegant and insightful as the CAPM is, we must make additional assumptions to make it implementable and testable.

The Index Model and Realized Returns

We have said that the CAPM is a statement about ex ante or expected returns, whereas in practice all anyone can observe directly are ex post or realized returns. To make the leap from expected to realized returns, we can employ the index model, which we will use in excess return form as

$$R_i = \alpha_i + \beta_i R_M + e_i \tag{9.16}$$

We saw in Section 9.1 how to apply standard regression analysis to estimate equation 9.16 using observable realized returns over some sample period. Let us now see how this framework for statistically decomposing actual stock returns meshes with the CAPM.

We start by deriving the covariance between the returns on stock i and the market index. By definition, the firm-specific or non-systematic component is independent of the marketwide or systematic component, that is, $Cov(R_M,e_i) = 0$. From this relationship, it follows that the covariance of the excess rate of return on security i with that of the market index is

$$Cov(R_i,R_M) = Cov(\beta_i R_M + e_i, R_M)$$
$$= \beta_i Cov(R_M,R_M) + Cov(e_i,R_M)$$
$$= \beta_i \sigma_M^2$$

Note that we can drop α_i from the covariance terms because α_i is a constant and thus has zero covariance with all variables.

Because $Cov(R_i,R_M) = \beta_i \sigma_M^2$, the sensitivity coefficient, β_i, in equation 9.16, which is the slope of the regression line representing the index model, equals

$$\beta_i = \frac{Cov(R_i,R_M)}{\sigma_M^2}$$

The index model beta coefficient turns out to be the same beta as that of the CAPM expected return-beta relationship, except that we replace the (theoretical) market portfolio of the CAPM with the well-specified and observable market index.

Concept Check

Question 8. The data below is drawn from a three-stock financial market that satisfies the single index model.

Stock	Capitalization ($)	Beta	Mean Excess Return	Standard Deviation
A	3,000	1.0	.10	.40
B	1,940	.2	.02	.30
C	1,360	1.7	.17	.50

The single factor in this economy is perfectly correlated with the value-weighted index of the stock market. The standard deviation of the market index portfolio is 25 percent.

a. What is the mean excess return of the index portfolio?
b. What is the covariance between stock A and the index?
c. Break down the variance of stock B into its systematic and firm-specific components.

The Index Model and the Expected Return-Beta Relationship

Recall that the CAPM expected return-beta relationship is, for any asset i and the (theoretical) market portfolio,

$$E(r_i) - r_f = \beta_i[E(r_M) - r_f]$$

where $\beta_i = \text{Cov}(r_i, r_M)/\sigma_M^2$. This is a statement about the mean or expected excess return of assets relative to the mean excess return of the (theoretical) market portfolio.

Assuming that the index M in equation 9.16 represents the true market portfolio, and taking the expectation of each side of equation 9.16 shows that the index model specification is

$$E(r_i) - r_f = \alpha_i + \beta_i[E(r_M) - r_f]$$

A comparison of the index model relationship to the CAPM expected return-beta relationship shows that the CAPM predicts that α_i must be zero for all assets. The alpha of a stock is its expected return in excess of (or below) the fair expected return as predicted by the CAPM. If the stock is fairly priced, its alpha must be zero.

We emphasize again that this is a statement about expected returns on a security. After the fact, of course, some securities will do better or worse than expected and will have returns higher or lower than predicted by the CAPM relationship; that is, they will exhibit positive or negative alphas over a sample period. But this superior or inferior performance could not have been forecast in advance.

Therefore, if we estimate the index model for several firms, using equation 9.16 as a regression equation, we should find that the ex post or realized alphas (the regression intercepts) for the firms in our sample center around zero. If the initial expectation for alpha were zero, as many firms would be expected to have a positive as a negative alpha for some sample period. The CAPM states that the *expected* value of alpha is zero for all securities, whereas the index model representation of the CAPM holds that the *realized* value of alpha should average out to zero for a sample of historical observed returns.

Some interesting evidence on this property was compiled by Michael Jensen,[10] who examined the alphas realized by mutual funds over the 10-year period 1955–1964. Figure 9.7 shows the frequency distribution of these alphas, which do indeed seem to be distributed around zero.

There is yet another applicable variation on the intuition of the index model, the **market model.** Formally, the market model states that the return "surprise" of any security is proportional to the return surprise of the market, plus a firm-specific surprise:

$$r_i - E(r_i) = \beta_i[r_M - E(r_M)] + e_i$$

This equation divides returns into firm-specific and systematic components somewhat differently from the index model. If the CAPM is valid, however,

---

[10] Michael C. Jensen, "The Performance of Mutual Funds in the Period 1945–1964," *Journal of Finance* 23 (May 1968).

FIGURE 9.7

Frequency distribution of alphas.

From Michael C. Jensen, "The Performance of Mutual Funds in the Period 1945–1964," *Journal of Finance* 23 (May 1968).

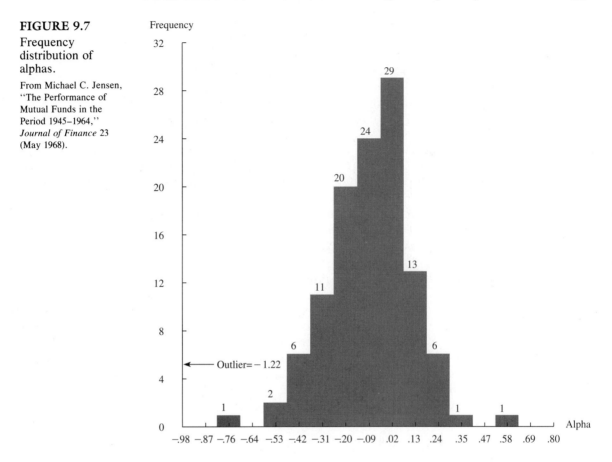

you can see that, substituting for $E(r_i)$ from equation 9.15, the market model equation becomes identical to the index model we have just presented. For this reason the terms *index model* and *market model* are sometimes used interchangeably.

Comparison with the APT

The APT is an extremely appealing model. It depends on the assumption that a rational equilibrium in capital markets precludes arbitrage opportunities. A violation of the APT's pricing relationships will cause extremely strong pressure to restore them, even if only a limited number of investors become aware of the disequilibrium.

Furthermore, the APT yields an expected return-beta relationship using a well-diversified portfolio that practically can be constructed from a large number of securities. In contrast, the CAPM is derived assuming an inherently unobservable "market" portfolio.

In spite of these appealing differences, the APT does not fully dominate the CAPM. The CAPM provides an unequivocal statement on the expected return-beta relationship for all assets, whereas the APT implies that this relationship holds for all but perhaps a small number of securities. This is an important difference, yet it is fruitless to pursue because the CAPM is not a readily testable model in the first place. A more productive comparison is between the APT and the index model.

As noted in the beginning of this chapter, the index model and the single-factor APT use virtually identical assumptions about the structure of security returns. Further, the index model relies on the assumptions of the CAPM with additional assumptions that: (1) a specified market index is virtually perfectly correlated with the (unobservable) theoretical market portfolio, and (2) the probability distribution of stock returns is stationary so that sample period returns can provide valid estimates of expected returns and variances.

The implication of the index model is that the market index portfolio is efficient and that the expected return-beta relationship holds for all assets. The assumption that the probability distribution of the security returns is stationary and the observability of the index make it possible to test the efficiency of the index and the expected return-beta relationship. The arguments leading from the assumptions to these implications rely on mean-variance efficiency; that is, if any security violates the expected return-beta relationship, then all investors (each relatively small) will tilt their portfolios so that their combined overall pressure on prices will restore an equilibrium that satisfies the relationship.

In contrast, the APT uses arbitrage arguments to obtain the expected return-beta relationship for well-diversified portfolios. Because it focuses on the no-arbitrage condition, without the further assumptions of the market or index model, the APT cannot rule out a violation of the expected return-beta relationship for any particular asset. For this, we need the CAPM assumptions and its dominance arguments.

Concept Check

Question 9. Can you sort out the nuances of the following maze of models?
a. CAPM
b. single-factor APT model
c. single index model
d. market model

9.7 *A Multifactor APT*

We have assumed all along that there is only one systematic factor affecting stock returns. This simplifying assumption is in fact too simplistic. It is easy to think of several factors that might affect stock returns: business cycles, interest rate fluctuations, inflation rates, oil prices, and so on. Presumably, exposure to any of these factors will affect a stock's perceived riskiness and appropriate expected rate of return. We can use a multifactor version of the APT to accommodate these multiple sources of risk.

Suppose that we generalize the factor model expressed in equation 9.12 to a two-factor model:

$$r_i = E(r_i) + \beta_{i1} F_1 + \beta_{i2} F_2 + e_i \tag{9.17}$$

Factor 1 might be, for example, departures of GNP growth from expectations, and factor 2 might be unanticipated inflation. Each factor has a zero expected value because each measures the surprise in the systematic variable rather than the level of the variable. Similarly, the firm-specific component of unexpected return, e_i, also has zero expected value. Extending such a two-factor model to any number of factors is straightforward.

Establishing a multifactor APT proceeds along lines very similar to those we followed in the simple one-factor case. First, we introduce the concept of a **factor portfolio,** which is a well-diversified portfolio constructed to have a beta of 1 on one of the factors and a beta of 0 on any other factor. This is an easy restriction to satisfy because we have a large number of securities to choose from, and a relatively small number of factors. Factor portfolios will serve as the benchmark portfolios for a multifactor generalization of the security market line relationship.

Suppose that the two factor portfolios, called portfolios 1 and 2, have expected returns $E(r_1) = 10$ percent and $E(r_2) = 12$ percent. Suppose further that the risk-free rate is 4 percent. The risk premium on the first factor portfolio becomes 10 percent − 4 percent = 6 percent, whereas that on the second factor portfolio is 12 percent − 4 percent = 8 percent.

Now consider an arbitrary well-diversified portfolio, portfolio A, where beta on the first factor, $\beta_{A1} = .5$, and beta on the second factor, $\beta_{A2} = .75$. The multifactor APT states that the overall risk premium on this portfolio must equal the sum of the risk premiums required as compensation to investors for each source of systematic risk. The risk premium attributable to risk factor 1 should be the portfolio's exposure to factor 1, β_{A1}, multiplied by the risk premium earned on the first factor portfolio, $E(r_1) - r_f$. Therefore the portion of portfolio A's risk premium that is compensation for its exposure to the first risk factor is $\beta_{A1}[E(r_1) - r_f] = .5 (.10 - .04) = .03$, whereas the risk premium attributable to risk factor 2 is $\beta_{A2}[E(r_2) - r_f] = .75 (.12 - .04) = .06$. The total risk premium on the portfolio should be .03 + .06 = .09. Therefore the total return on the portfolio should be .13, or 13 percent:

.04	Risk-free rate
+.03	Risk premium for exposure to factor 1
+.06	Risk premium for exposure to factor 2
.13	Total expected return

To see why the expected return on the portfolio must be 13 percent, consider the following argument. Suppose that the expected return on portfolio A were

12 percent rather than 13 percent. This return would give rise to an arbitrage opportunity. Form a portfolio from the factor portfolios with the same betas as portfolio A. This requires weights of .5 on the first factor portfolio, .75 on the second factor portfolio, and $-.25$ on the risk-free asset. This portfolio has exactly the same factor betas as portfolio A: it has a beta of .5 on the first factor because of its .5 weight on the first factor portfolio, and a beta of .75 on the second factor.

However, in contrast to portfolio A, which has a 12 percent expected return, this portfolio's expected return is $(.5 \times 10) + (.75 \times 12) - (.25 \times 4) = 13$ percent. A long position in this portfolio and a short position in portfolio A would yield an arbitrage profit. The total return per dollar long or short in each position would be

$$\begin{array}{ll} .13 + .5\,F_1 + .75\,F_2 & \text{(long position in factor portfolios)} \\ \underline{-(.12 + .5\,F_1 + .75\,F_2)} & \text{(short position in portfolio A)} \\ .01 & \end{array}$$

for a positive and risk-free return on a zero net investment position.

To generalize this argument, note that the factor exposure of any portfolio, P, is given by its betas, β_{P1} and β_{P2}. A competing portfolio formed from factor portfolios with weights β_{P1} in the first factor portfolio, β_{P2} in the second factor portfolio, and $1 - \beta_{P1} - \beta_{P2}$ in T-bills will have betas equal to those of portfolio P, and expected return of

$$\begin{aligned} E(r_P) &= \beta_{P1}\,E(r_1) + \beta_{P2}\,E(r_2) + (1 - \beta_{P1} - \beta_{P2})\,r_f \\ &= r_f + \beta_{P1}\,[E(r_1) - r_f] + \beta_{P2}\,[E(r_2) - r_f] \end{aligned} \qquad \textbf{(9.18)}$$

Hence any well-diversified portfolio with betas β_{P1} and β_{P2} must have the return given in equation 9.18 if arbitrage opportunities are to be precluded. If you compare equations 9.13 and 9.18, you will see that equation 9.18 is simply a generalization of the one-factor SML.

Finally, the extension of the multifactor SML of equation 9.18 to individual assets is precisely the same as for the one-factor APT. Equation 9.18 cannot be satisfied by every well-diversified portfolio unless it is satisfied by virtually every security taken individually. This establishes a multifactor version of the APT. Hence the fair rate of return on any stock with $\beta_1 = .5$ and $\beta_2 = .75$ is 13 percent. Equation 9.18 thus represents the multifactor SML for an economy with multiple sources of risk.

Concept Check

Question 10. Find the fair rate of return on a security with $\beta_1 = .2$ and $\beta_2 = 1.4$.

One shortcoming of the multifactor APT is that it gives no guidance concerning the determination of the risk premiums on the factor portfolios. In contrast, the single-factor CAPM implies that the risk premium on the market is determined by the market's variance and the average degree of risk aversion across investors. On the other hand, the multifactor CAPM that we saw in the appendix to the previous chapter is very similar to the multifactor APT. There are, however, some differences. We can summarize the issue of the mutual validity of the APT and the multifactor CAPM as follows:

1. As was already seen in the single-factor versions of both CAPM and APT, the expected return-beta relationship is exact for all assets in the multifactor CAPM, but only approximate for less than well-diversified portfolios in the multifactor APT. The CAPM and the multifactor CAPM require more restrictive assumptions and therefore make stronger statements; that is, the expected return-beta relationship is exact for all assets.

2. The multifactor APT predicts that all common factors affecting security returns will be priced. The multifactor CAPM, in contrast, predicts that factors that are irrelevant to consumption uncertainty *will not* be priced. Thus, an expected return-beta relationship can satisfy the APT and still be at odds with the multifactor CAPM if irrelevant factors can be shown to command risk premiums.

Can the APT and the multifactor CAPM be distinguished empirically? The answer is "Yes, in theory," but it is very doubtful whether we can prove this in the field. To reject the multifactor CAPM one must make a judgment that a priced factor is irrelevant to future consumption uncertainty. Consider, for instance, a factor such as industrial production. On the surface it would appear that uncertainty about future industrial production in and of itself is not an item affecting future consumption risk. It is conceivable, however, that industrial production, by being a proxy for the business cycle, may be related to future labour income uncertainty. More generally, seemingly irrelevant factors may appear to command risk premiums if they indirectly proxy for relevant sources of risk.

The chance that we will get an empirical verdict that the APT is valid at the same time that the multifactor CAPM is not is quite remote.

Summary

1. A single-factor model of the economy classifies sources of uncertainty as systematic (macroeconomic) factors or firm-specific (microeconomic) factors. The index model assumes that the macro factor can be represented by a broad index of stock returns.

2. The single-index model drastically reduces the necessary inputs into the Markowitz portfolio selection procedure. It also aids in specialization of labour in security analysis.

3. If the index model specification is valid, then the systematic risk of a portfolio or asset equals $\beta^2\sigma_M^2$, and the covariance between two assets equals $\beta_i\beta_j\sigma_M^2$.

4. The index model is estimated by applying regression analysis to excess rates of return. The slope of the regression curve is the beta of an asset, whereas the intercept is the asset's alpha during the sample period. The regression line is also called the security characteristic line. The regression beta is equivalent to the CAPM beta, except that the regression uses actual returns and the CAPM is specified in terms of expected returns. The CAPM predicts that the average value of alphas measured by the index model regression will be zero.

5. A risk-free arbitrage opportunity arises when two or more security prices enable investors to construct a zero net investment portfolio that will yield a sure profit.

6. Rational investors will want to take infinitely large positions in arbitrage portfolios regardless of their degree of risk aversion.

7. The presence of arbitrage opportunities and the resulting large volume of trades will create pressure on security prices. This pressure will continue until prices reach levels that preclude arbitrage. Only a few investors need to become aware of arbitrage opportunities to trigger this process because of the large volume of trades in which they will engage.

8. When securities are priced so that there are no risk-free arbitrage opportunities, we say that they satisfy the no-arbitrage condition. Price relationships that satisfy the no-arbitrage condition are important because we expect them to hold in real-world markets.

9. Portfolios are called *well diversified* if they include a large number of securities and the investment proportion in each is sufficiently small. The proportion of a security in a well-diversified portfolio is small enough so that, for all practical purposes, a reasonable change in that security's rate of return will have a negligible effect on the portfolio rate of return.

10. In a single-factor security market, all well-diversified portfolios have to satisfy the expected return-beta relationship of the security market line in order to satisfy the no-arbitrage condition.

11. If all well-diversified portfolios satisfy the expected return-beta relationship, then all but a small number of securities also must satisfy this relationship.

12. The assumption of a single-factor security market made possible by the simple version of the APT, together with the no-arbitrage condition, implies the same expected return-beta relationship as does the CAPM, yet it does not require the restrictive assumptions of the CAPM and its (unobservable) market portfolio. The price of this generality is that the APT does not guarantee this relationship for all securities at all times.

13. A multifactor APT generalizes the single-factor model to accommodate several sources of systematic risk.

14. A multifactor CAPM's predictions differ from those of the multifactor APT insofar as the former predicts that common factors affecting security returns that are unrelated to future consumption uncertainty will not be priced. The multifactor APT, on the other hand, predicts that all such common factors will be priced. This distinction, however, is not likely to be meaningful empirically.

Key terms

Arbitrage

Factor model

Single-index model

Scatter diagram

Regression equation

Residuals

Security characteristic line

Zero investment portfolio

Risk arbitrage

Arbitrage pricing theory

Well-diversified portfolio

Market model

Factor portfolio

Selected readings

The seminal paper relating the index model to the portfolio selection problem is:

Sharpe, William F. "A Simplified Model of Portfolio Analysis." *Management Science*, January 1963.

Stephen Ross developed the arbitrage pricing theory in two articles:

Ross, S. A. "Return, Risk and Arbitrage." In I. Friend and J. Bicksler (editors), *Risk and Return in Finance*. Cambridge, Mass.: Ballinger, 1976.

Ross, S. A. "Arbitrage Theory of Capital Asset Pricing." *Journal of Economic Theory*, December 1976.

Articles exploring the factors that influence common stock returns are:

Bower, D. A.; Bower, R. S.; and Logue, D. E. "Arbitrage Pricing and Utility Stock Returns." *Journal of Finance*, September 1984.

Chen, N. F.; Roll, R.; and Ross, S. "Economic Forces and the Stock Market: Testing the APT and Alternative Asset Pricing Theories." *Journal of Business*, July 1986.

Sharpe, W. "Factors in New York Stock Exchange Security Returns, 1931–1979." *Journal of Portfolio Management*, Summer 1982.

Problems

1. A portfolio management organization analyzes 75 stocks and constructs a mean-variance efficient portfolio that is constrained to these 75.
   a. How many estimates of expected returns, variances, and covariances are needed to optimize this portfolio?
   b. If one could safely assume that stock market returns closely resemble a single-index structure, how many estimates would be needed?
2. The following are estimates for two of the stocks in Question 1.

Stock	Expected Return	Beta	Firm-Specific Standard Deviation
A	.14	.6	.32
B	.25	1.3	.37

The market index has a standard deviation of .26.

a. What is the standard deviation of stocks A and B?

b. Suppose that we were to construct a portfolio with proportions:

Stock A	.33
Stock B	.38
T-bills	.29 ($r_f = 9\%$)

Compute the expected return, standard deviation, beta, and non-systematic standard deviation of the portfolio.

3. Consider the following two regression curves for stocks A and B.

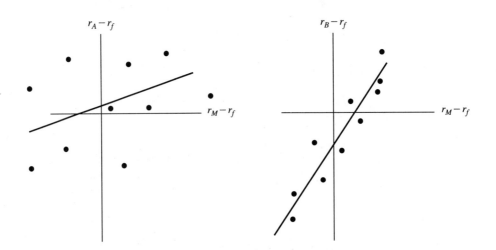

a. Which stock has higher firm specific risk?
b. Which stock has greater systematic (market) risk?
c. Which stock has higher R-square?
d. Which stock has higher alpha?
e. Which stock has higher correlation with the market?

4. Consider the two (excess return) index model regression results for stocks A and B:

$R_A = .01 + 1.2R_M$
$R^2 = .576$
$\sigma(e) = 10.3\%$

$R_B = -.02 + .8R_M$
$R^2 = .436$
$\sigma(e) = 9.1\%$

a. Which stock has more firm-specific risk?
b. Which has greater market risk?
c. For which stock does market movement explain a greater fraction of return variability?
d. Which stock had an average return in excess of that predicted by the CAPM?

e. If r_f were constant at 6 percent and the regression had been run using total rather than excess returns, what would have been the regression intercept for stock A?

Use the following data for problems 5–11. Suppose that the index model for stocks A and B is estimated with the following results:

$$R_A = .02 + .65R_M + e_A$$
$$R_B = .04 + 1.10R_M + e_B$$
$$\sigma_M = .25; \ R^2{}_A = .15; \ R^2{}_B = .30$$

5. What is the standard deviation of each stock?
6. Break down the variance of each stock to the systematic and firm-specific components.
7. What is the covariance and correlation coefficient between the two stocks?
8. What is the covariance between each stock and the market index?
9. Are the intercepts of the two regressions consistent with the CAPM? Interpret their values.
10. For portfolio P with investment proportions of .60 in A and .40 in B, rework problems 5, 6, and 8.
11. Rework problem 10 for portfolio Q with investment proportions of .50 in P, .30 in the market index, and .20 in T-bills.
12. Suppose that two factors have been identified for the Canadian economy: the growth rate of industrial production, IP, and the inflation rate, IR. IP is expected to be 4 percent, and IR 6 percent. A stock with a beta of 1 on IP and .4 on IR currently is expected to provide a rate of return of 14 percent. If industrial production actually grows by 5 percent while the inflation rate turns out to be 7 percent, what is your revised estimate of the expected rate of return on the stock?
13. Suppose that there are two independent economic factors, F_1 and F_2. The risk-free rate is 7 percent, and all stocks have independent firm-specific components with a standard deviation of 50 percent. The following are well-diversified portfolios:

Portfolio	Beta on F_1	Beta on F_2	Expected Return
A	1.8	2.1	40
B	2.0	−0.5	10

What is the expected return-beta relationship in this economy?
14. Consider the following data for a one-factor economy. All portfolios are well diversified.

Portfolio	E(r)	Beta
A	10%	1
F	4%	0

Suppose that portfolio B is well diversified with a beta of $\frac{2}{3}$ and expected return of 9 percent. Would an arbitrage opportunity exist? If so, what would be the arbitrage strategy?

15. The following is a scenario for three stocks constructed by the security analysts of Pf Inc.

Stock	Price ($)	Scenario Rate of Return (%)		
		Recession	Average	Boom
A	10	−15	20	30
B	15	25	10	−10
C	50	12	15	12

   a. Construct an arbitrage portfolio using these stocks.
   b. How might these prices change when equilibrium is restored? Give an example where a change in stock C's price is sufficient to restore equilibrium, assuming that the dollar payoffs to stock C remain the same.

16. Assume that both portfolios A and B are well diversified, that $E(r_A) = .14$, and $E(r_B) = .148$. If the economy has only one factor, and $\beta_A = 1$ whereas $\beta_B = 1.1$, what must be the risk-free rate?

17. Assume that stock market returns have the market index as a common factor, and that all stocks in the economy have a beta of 1 on the market index. Firm-specific returns all have a standard deviation of .30.

   Suppose that an analyst studies 20 stocks, and finds that one half have an alpha of 3 percent, and the other half an alpha of −3 percent. Suppose the analyst buys $1 million of an equally weighted portfolio of the positive alpha stocks, and shorts $1 million of an equally weighted portfolio of the negative alpha stocks.

   a. What is the expected profit (in dollars) and standard deviation of the analyst's profit?
   b. How does your answer change if the analyst examines 50 stocks instead of 20 stocks? 100 stocks?

18. Assume that security returns are generated by the single index model

$$R_i = \alpha_i + \beta_i R_M + e_i$$

where R_i is the excess return for security i, and R_M is the market's excess return. Suppose also that there are three securities, A, B, and C, characterized by the following data:

Security	β_i	$E(R_i)$	$\sigma^2(e_i)$
A	.8	.10	.05
B	1.0	.12	.01
C	1.2	.14	.10

   a. If $\sigma_M^2 = .04$, calculate the variance of returns of securities A, B, and C.
   b. Now assume that there are an infinite number of assets with return characteristics identical to those of A, B, and C, respectively. If one forms a well-diversified portfolio of type A securities, what will be the mean and variance of the portfolio's excess returns? What about portfolios composed only of type B or C stocks?

    c. Is there an arbitrage opportunity in this market? What is it? Analyze the opportunity graphically.

19. The SML relationship states that the expected risk premium on a security in a one-factor model must be directly proportional to the security's beta. Suppose that this were not the case. For example, suppose that expected return rises more than proportionately with beta as in the figure below.

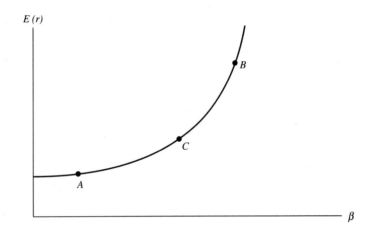

    a. How could you construct an arbitrage portfolio? (Hint: Consider combinations of portfolios A and B, and compare the resultant portfolio to C.)

    b. We will see in Chapter 11 that some researchers have examined the relationship between average return on diversified portfolios and the β and β^2 of those portfolios. What should they have discovered about the effect of β^2 on portfolio return?

20. If the APT is to be a useful theory, the number of systematic factors in the economy must be small. Why?

21. The APT itself does not provide guidance concerning the factors that one might expect to determine risk premiums. How should researchers decide which factors to investigate? Why, for example, is industrial production a reasonable factor to test for a risk premium?

22. Consider the following multifactor (APT) model of security returns for a particular stock:

Factor	Factor Beta	Factor Risk-Premium (%)
Inflation	1.2	6
Industrial production	0.5	8
Oil prices	0.3	3

    a. If T-bills currently offer a 6 percent yield, find the expected rate of return on this stock if the market views the stock as fairly priced.

    b. Suppose that the market expected the values for the three macro factors given in the middle column below, but that the actual values turn out as given in the last column. Calculate the revised expectations for the rate of return on the stock once the "surprises" become known.

Factor	Expected Rate of Change (%)	Actual Rate of Change (%)
Inflation	5	4
Industrial production	3	6
Oil prices	2	0

23. Suppose that the market can be described by the following three sources of systematic risk with associated risk premiums:

Factor	Risk Premium (%)
Industrial production (I)	6
Interest rates (R)	2
Consumer confidence (C)	4

The return on a particular stock is generated according to the following equation:

$$r = 15\% + 1.0I + .5R + .75C + e$$

Find the equilibrium rate of return on this stock using the APT. The T-bill rate is 6 percent. Is the stock over- or underpriced? Explain.

CHAPTER 10

International Diversification

Although it is common in Canada to use the TSE 300 as the market index portfolio, such practice is in some ways inappropriate. Equities actually comprise barely 10 percent of total Canadian wealth and a far smaller percentage of world wealth. In this chapter we survey the issues of extending diversification beyond the national borders. We show how international diversification can improve portfolio performance, examine exchange rate risk, and take a look at investment strategies in an international context.

10.1 *International Investments*

The World Market Portfolio

Canadian investors have shown themselves to be far less prone than their American neighbors to limit their investment horizons to the national boundaries. The presence and influence of foreign investors and markets serve to focus Canadian attention on alternatives to domestic investment; while the proximity of the United States makes it the dominant figure in our international perspective, European and Far Eastern nations already and increasingly are receiving substantial attention from investors. The internationalization of trade, beyond the traditional markets for major corporations such as Alcan, Inco, and the banks, implies that Canadians can and must diversify their portfolio holdings into foreign assets in order to hedge foreign currency and economic fluctuations.

The portfolio holdings of an investor in any country should serve to protect his or her future consumption opportunities, given the prices faced domestically; but these prices are affected by foreign economic conditions and pricing relative to the proportion that foreign trade represents in the domestic economy. Thus in the United States, where domestic production and consumption represent the vast majority of economic activity, foreign economic events have had less and later effect on domestic conditions; in contrast, Canadian conditions react swiftly and directly to external events, particularly in the United States. Canadians, therefore, have far more need to link themselves to foreign financial markets in order to hedge their portfolios and their consumption opportunties from adverse international events.

While Canadians, by nature, may be more inclined to underestimate the size of their securities markets rather than the opposite, these markets in fact represent only a small fraction of the world markets. Tables 10.1 and 10.2 present, respectively, the comparative sizes of world equity and bond markets. The Canadian market values in 1988 represented about 2.5 percent in both cases; that left about $18 trillion (U.S.) of foreign securities for investment opportunities. As we noted in Chapter 1, Canadians can easily invest in U.S. securities; but these represented only 29 percent of the equity markets and 46 percent of the bond markets. (Note that Table 10.2 refers to bonds denominated in U.S. dollars rather than issued by U.S. debtors.) Furthermore, we shall see that for Canadian portfolios, U.S. securities offer little in the way of diversification, which is the key opportunity to be exploited in considering foreign securities.

TABLE 10.1   Comparative Sizes of World Equity Markets, 1988*

Area or Country	$ Billion	% of Total
Europe	1,860	21.4
United Kingdom	718	8.3
West Germany	241	2.8
Switzerland	148	1.7
France	224	2.6
Netherlands	86	1.0
Sweden	89	1.0
Italy	135	1.6
Spain	87	1.0
Belgium	58	0.7
Other countries	74	0.9
Pacific Area	4,104	47.3
Japan	3,840	44.2
Australia	134	1.5
Singapore	43	0.5
Hong Kong	74	0.9
North America	2,702	31.1
United States	2,481	28.6
Canada	221	2.5
World	**8,680**	**100.0**

* Because of rounding error, column sums may not equal totals.
From Bruno Solnik, *International Investments* (Reading, Mass.: Addison-Wesley Publishing Co., Inc., 1990). Exhibit 4.1. Reprinted with permission.

TABLE 10.2 Size of Major Bond Markets at Year End, 1988*

Bond Market	Total Publicly Issued	Public Issues in All Markets (%)
U.S. dollar	4,517.0	46.3
Japanese yen	2,161.0	22.1
Deutsche mark	753.5	7.7
Italian lira	534.3	5.5
U.K. pound sterling	344.4	3.5
French franc	332.4	3.4
Canadian dollar	245.3	2.5
Belgian franc	187.8	1.9
Danish krone	159.7	1.6
Swedish krona	157.0	1.6
Swiss franc	156.3	1.6
Dutch guilder	133.5	1.4
Australian dollar	81.6	0.8
TOTAL	**9,763.8**	**100.0**

* Nominal value outstanding, billions of U.S. dollars equivalent.
Modified from Bruno Solnik, *International Investments* (Reading, Mass.: Addison-Wesley Publishing Co., Inc., 1990). Exhibit 6.1. Reprinted with permission.

FIGURE 10.1
International
diversification.

(Modified from B. Solnik, "Why Not Diversify Internationally Rather Than Domestically," *Financial Analysts Journal*, July/August 1974.)

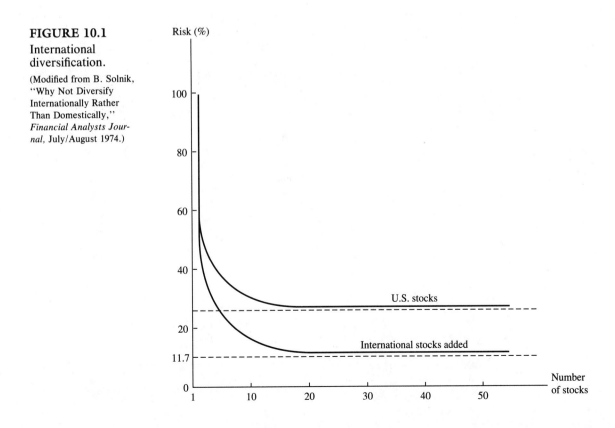

International Diversification

From our discussion of the power of diversification in Chapter 7, we know that adding to a portfolio assets that are not perfectly correlated will improve the best attainable reward-to-volatility ratio. Given increasing globalization, might not foreign securities provide a feasible way to extend diversification?

Figure 7.2 revealed the results of a classic study on U.S. equities that showed the benefits of diversification. The results of a subsequent study are summarized in Figure 10.1, which demonstrates the marked reduction in risk that can be achieved by including foreign, as well as U.S., stocks in a portfolio. The graph presents the standard deviation of equally-weighted portfolios of various sizes as a percentage of the average standard deviation of a one-stock portfolio. For example, a value of 20 means that the diversified portfolio has only 20 percent of the standard deviation of a typical stock. The graphs in Figure 10.1 are presented in terms of the standard deviation of the dollar-denominated returns to make them relevant to U.S. investors. Clearly, given the high correlation between U.S. and Canadian stocks, similar improvement can be achieved by adding foreign stocks to a Canadian portfolio.

TABLE 10.3 Correlation Coefficients of Monthly Percentage Changes in Major Stock Market Indices (Local Currencies, June 1981–September 1987)

	Australia	Austria	Belgium	Canada	Denmark	France	Germany	Hong Kong	Ireland	Italy
Austria	.219									
Belgium	.190	.222								
Canada	.568	.250	.215							
Denmark	.217	−.062	.219	.301						
France	.180	.263	.355	.351	.241					
Germany	.145	.406	.315	.194	.215	.327				
Hong Kong	.321	.174	.129	.236	.120	.201	.304			
Ireland	.349	.202	.361	.490	.387	.374	.067	.320		
Italy	.209	.224	.307	.321	.150	.459	.257	.216	.275	
Japan	.182	−.025	.223	.294	.186	.361	.147	.137	.183	.241
Malaysia	.329	−.013	.096	.274	.151	−.134	−.020	.159	.082	−.119
Mexico	.220	.018	.104	.114	−.174	−.009	.002	.149	.113	.114
Netherlands	.294	.232	.344	.545	.341	.344	.511	.395	.373	.344
New Zealand	.389	.290	.275	.230	.148	.247	.318	.352	.314	.142
Norway	.355	.009	.233	.381	.324	.231	.173	.356	.306	.042
Singapore	.374	.030	.133	.320	.133	−.085	.037	.219	.102	−.038
South Africa	.279	.159	.143	.385	−.113	.267	.007	−.095	.024	.093
Spain	.147	.018	.050	.190	.019	.255	.147	.193	.175	.290
Sweden	.327	.161	.158	.376	.131	.159	.227	.196	.122	.330
Switzerland	.334	.401	.276	.551	.283	.307	.675	.379	.290	.287
U.K.	.377	.073	.381	.590	.218	.332	.263	.431	.467	.328
United States	.328	.138	.250	.720	.351	.390	.209	.114	.380	.224

Modified from Richard Roll, "The International Crash of October 1987," *Financial Analysts Journal*, September–October 1988.

Figure 10.1 demonstrates that rational investors should invest across borders. Adding international investments to national investments enhances the power of portfolio diversification. Table 10.3 presents results from a study of equity returns showing that, although the correlation coefficients between the Canadian stock index and stock index portfolios of other large industrialized economies are positive, they are much smaller than 1. With the exception of the U.S. index, correlated at .72, most correlations are below .4. In contrast, correlation coefficients between diversified U.S. portfolios—with 40 to 50 securities, for example—typically exceed .9. The imperfect correlation across national boundaries allows for the improvement in diversification potential that shows up in Figure 10.1.

Concept Check	Question 1. What would Figure 10.1 look like if we next introduced the possibility of diversifying into bond investments in addition to foreign equity?

Japan	Malaysia	Mexico	Netherlands	New Zealand	Norway	Singapore	South Africa	Spain	Sweden	Switzerland	U.K.
.109											
−.021	.231										
.333	.151	.038									
−.111	.136	.231	.239								
.156	.262	.050	.405	.201							
.066	.891	.202	.196	.212	.280						
.225	−.013	.260	.058	.038	.156	−.056					
.248	−.071	.059	.170	.095	.075	.056	−.088				
.115	.103	.000	.324	.136	.237	.180	.070	.181			
.130	.099	.026	.570	.397	.331	.157	.112	.192	.334		
.354	.193	.068	.534	.014	.313	.250	.168	.209	.339	.435	
.326	.347	.063	.473	.083	.356	.377	.218	.214	.279	.500	.513

A different perspective on opportunities for international diversification appears in Figure 10.2. Here we examine risk-return opportunities offered by several asset classes, alone and combined into portfolios. For example, we see that world stocks plotted to the northwest of U.S. stocks for this 10-year period, offering higher average return and lower risk than U.S. stocks alone. World stocks and bonds together offered an even better risk-return combination. (All returns are calculated in terms of U.S. dollars.) Although the original study did not isolate Canadian securities, we have added the Canadian risk-return combinations. Of course, the efficient frontiers generated from these assets offer the best possible risk-return pairs; these are vastly superior to the risk-return profile of U.S. or Canadian stocks alone. A more recent study (1979–1989) by Marmer is summarized in Figure 10.3, which shows the improvement in the efficient frontier for portfolios of bills, bonds, and stocks when international assets are added to Canadian assets.

Investing in foreign markets is difficult for individual investors, due to institutional restrictions, inhibited access to the markets, and lack of information. Consequently, there has been a recent increase in the creation of both regional and single-country mutual funds; these include the Far East, Germany, Spain, Mexico, and Thailand as examples of markets in different stages of development. While these funds tend to be listed on the TSE or NYSE as closed-end funds, ordinary open-ended funds are another possibility. A study by Chua and

FIGURE 10.2

Efficient frontiers, December 1970–December 1980.

(From B. Solnik, and B. Noetzlin, "Optimal International Asset Allocation," *Journal of Portfolio Management*, Fall 1982.)

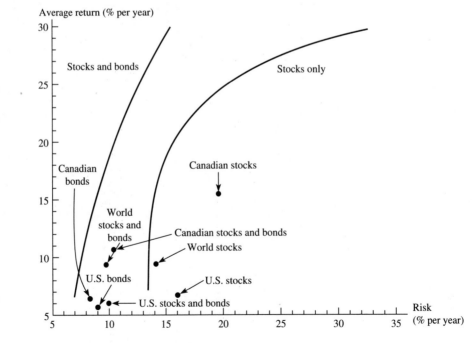

FIGURE 10.3

Canada-only efficient frontier vs. Canada and international efficient frontier, 1979–1989.

From H. S. Marmer, "International Investing: A New Canadian Perspective," *Canadian Investment Review* Vol. 4, no. 1 (Spring 1991).

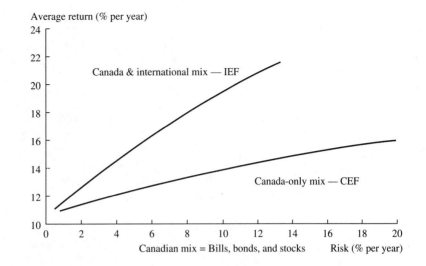

Woodward[1] has examined the opportunities for diversification by Canadian investors through investment in foreign-domiciled mutual funds, readily available from Canadian brokers. The authors examined the risk-return characteristics of portfolios of funds from Canada, the United States, and the United Kingdom, individually and in combination, and compared the results with the market indexes and efficient frontiers for those separate markets, and again in combination. They found that significant diversification benefits existed for Canadian investors who augmented their portfolios with foreign mutual funds, especially for more risk-averse investors. For the time period under consideration, 1973–1983, mutual fund performance exceeded that of the market indexes; this finding runs counter to the usual results for mutual fund performance (examined in the next chapter). Hence, the study illustrates both the advantages of international diversification and the question of active versus passive portfolio management.

Canadian interest in the international sector is evidenced by the increase in the allowable foreign assets in pension and retirement fund portfolios from 10 percent to a proposed 20 percent by 1994. Pension funds have for many years invested up to the limit; increasingly, the allowable foreign component is being filled with overseas stocks, rather than the original U.S. companies. (See the accompanying box.)

---

[1] J. H. Chua and R. S. Woodward, "International Diversification for Small Canadian Investors through Mutual Funds," *Canadian Journal of Administrative Sciences,* September 1987.

Eluding Foreign Limits on RRSPs: Some Mutual Funds Have Found Loopholes to Gain the Higher Returns of International Exposure

By Rudy Luukko

Restrictions on foreign content have long been a source of frustration for RRSP investors. If you want your savings sheltered, you've got to buy almost exclusively Canadian, though other investment pastures may seem greener. Even in this era of global investing, the federal government has made few concessions on RRSPs. The tax rules governing foreign property holdings are being eased, but only gradually. Under provisions in last year's federal budget that have yet to be enacted, the 10 percent foreign limit was to rise to 12 percent in 1990 and 14 percent in 1991, eventually reaching 20 percent by 1994. Consequently, most international mutual funds can form only part of an RRSP investor's portfolio up to the prescribed foreign property limit.

For every rule, though, there's a loophole. At least two mutual fund companies, Global Strategy Financial Inc. and the Guardian Group of Funds Ltd., offer funds that have high levels of foreign exposure but are fully RRSP-eligible. They're able to do so thanks largely to Canadian bonds denominated in foreign currencies, and foreign interest-bearing notes of Canadian issuers. And in the Global Strategy Canadian Fund, which despite its name invests mostly overseas, index options serve as a proxy for foreign equity markets.

"Investors ought to have the opportunity in the context of their RRSPs to get more diversification," says Richard Wernham, Global's president. He argues that for the same reason you shouldn't load your portfolio with a single stock, you

THE VALUE OF GLOBAL DIVERSIFICATION—OVER THE PAST DECADE, EQUITY PORTFOLIOS WITH A FOREIGN FLAVOUR EARNED HIGHER RETURNS AND WERE LESS RISKY.

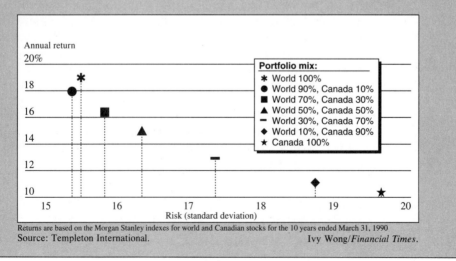

Returns are based on the Morgan Stanley indexes for world and Canadian stocks for the 10 years ended March 31, 1990
Source: Templeton International.   Ivy Wong/*Financial Times.*

(Continued)

shouldn't invest solely in a single national market. The RRSP rules force investors to give up potentially higher returns as well. To illustrate that point, Global Strategy uses the example of $3,500 invested in equities each year for 10 years during the 1980s. A representative portfolio of global stocks would have been worth $112,800 at the end of the period, compared with $71,000 for a portfolio based on the Toronto Stock Exchange 300 total-return index.

Global uses hedging strategies—combining stock index options and cash instruments—to mimic the performance of foreign equity markets. Specifically, it invests 8 percent of its Canadian Fund in options and 64 percent in cash, for a total of 72 percent in foreign equity exposure. If the equity markets stumble, the options expire worthless, but the cash component continues to generate interest and remains a currency play in relation to the Canadian dollar. Hence, the potential loss is limited.

"This is actually a less risky strategy than buying equities," says Wernham. He acknowledges that the gains are limited too; index options can only match the performance of the underlying market.

Launched in December 1987 as the Global Strategy RRSP Fund, the renamed Canadian Fund adopted its current investment mandate last January. Over the year ended November 30, it was the second-best performer among Canadian equity funds, with a return of minus 0.1 percent; its two-year compound return is still well above average at 5 percent. Global retains a London adviser to the fund, N. M. Rothschild Asset Management Ltd. An arm of the venerable British merchant bank, Rothschild is in charge of day-to-day management of the Global Strategy Income Fund and World Money Fund.

The Guardian Group, too, has a London money-management firm, Kleinwort Benson Investment Management Ltd., to run its International Income Fund. The three-year-old fund had an above-average 8.9 percent return for the 12 months ended in November, though its three-year compound return is a lacklustre 1.9 percent. "You do lose some flexibility," says adviser Richard Conyers of Kleinwort Benson. The RRSP rules restrict the choice of issuers and maturities, and also the opportunity to trade bonds of similar quality for those at more attractive prices.

But these constraints have only a slight impact on fund returns. Conyers estimates the tax rules reduce the rate of return he's able to earn by only 0.1 percent. That reflects the growing efficiency of world financial markets. With the world bond market having become so integrated, he says, there are fewer opportunities to take advantage of price anomalies.

Ultimately, the performance of an internationally oriented bond fund depends on skills other than being able to get around Canadian-content rules. A new fund launched last year by the Templeton group, the fully RRSP-eligible Templeton Heritage Bond Fund, is capable of having a high degree of foreign exposure. But so far the managers have chosen to use up only half of the current limit. "We've used only 5 percent of our foreign content right now and that's a reflection of our investment views," says Don Reed, president and CEO of Templeton Management Ltd. He says that the current high levels and firmness of the Canadian dollar make it less attractive to have foreign exposure in the fund.

For some investors, buying Canadian may well be a smart RRSP strategy. To reduce currency risk, it makes sense for Canadians to have domestic assets well represented in their RRSPs. But it's a sounder strategy if executed on its own merits, rather than because it is imposed by restrictive tax laws.

From *The Financial Times of Canada*, January 14, 1991. Reprinted by permission of the author and *The Financial Times of Canada*.

Exchange Rate Risk

International investing poses unique challenges for Canadian investors. Information in foreign markets may be less timely and more difficult to come by. In smaller economies with correspondingly smaller securities markets, one can encounter higher transaction costs and liquidity problems. There also is a need for special expertise concerning political risk. **Political risk** arises from the possibility of the expropriation of assets, changes in tax policy, the possibility of restrictions on the exchange of foreign currency for domestic currency, or other changes in the business climate of a country.

In addition to these risks, international investing entails exchange rate risk. The dollar return from a foreign investment depends not only on the returns in the foreign currency, but also on the dollar–foreign currency exchange rate.

For example, consider an investment in England in risk-free British government bills paying 10 percent annual interest in British pounds. These U.K. bills would be the risk-free asset to a British investor—but not for a Canadian investor. Suppose, for example, that the initial **exchange rate** is $2 per pound, and that the Canadian investor starts with $20,000. Those funds can be exchanged for £10,000 and invested at a risk-free 10 percent rate providing £11,000 in one year. However, what if the dollar–pound exchange rate varies over the course of the year? Suppose that the pound depreciates during the year, so that by year end only $1.80 is required to purchase £1. Despite the positive 10 percent pound-denominated return, the dollar-denominated return will be negative. The £11,000 can be exchanged at the year-end exchange rate for only $19,800 (11,000 × 1.80), resulting in a loss of $200 relative to the initial $20,000 investment, for a dollar-denominated return of −1 percent.

Let us generalize. The $20,000 is exchanged for $20,000/$E_0$ pounds, where E_0 denotes the original exchange rate ($2/£). The U.K. investment grows to $(20,000/E_0)[1 + r_f(\text{UK})]$ British pounds, where $r_f(\text{UK})$ is the risk-free rate in the United Kingdom. The pound proceeds ultimately are converted back to dollars at the subsequent exchange rate E_1, for total dollar proceeds of $20,000(E_1/E_0)[1 + r_f(\text{UK})]$. Therefore the dollar-denominated return on the investment in British bills is

$$1 + r(C) = [1 + r_f(\text{UK})]E_1/E_0 \qquad (10.1)$$

We see in equation 10.1 that the dollar-denominated return for a Canadian investor equals the pound-denominated return multiplied by the exchange rate "return." For a Canadian investor, the investment in the British bill in fact is a combination of a safe investment in the United Kingdom and a risky investment in the performance of the pound relative to the dollar. In this case the pound fared poorly, falling from a value of $2 to only $1.80. The loss on the pound more than offset the earnings on the British bill.

Concept Check

Question 2. Calculate the rate of return in dollars to a Canadian investor holding the British bill if the year-end exchange rate is:
a. $E_1 = \$2.00/£$
b. $E_1 = \$2.20/£$

In this example, the exchange rate risk could have been hedged using a forward contract in foreign exchange. Foreign currency forward contracts (to be examined in Chapter 22) establish future rates of exchange at specified dates which can be guaranteed in the present. If the forward exchange rate had been $F = \$1.93/£$ when the investment was made, the Canadian investor could have locked in a risk-free dollar-denominated return by locking in the year-end exchange rate at $\$1.93/£$. In this case, the risk-free Canadian return would have been 6.15 percent:

$$[1 + r_f(\text{UK})](F/E_0) = (1.10)(1.93/2.00)$$
$$= 1.0615$$

Let us investigate the steps that would be taken to lock in the dollar-denominated returns.

Initial Transaction	End-of-Year Proceeds in Dollars
1. Exchange $20,000 for £10,000 and invest at 10% in U.K.	£11,000 × E_1
2. Enter a contract to deliver £11,000 for dollars at the (forward) exchange rate, $1.93/£.	£11,000(1.93 − E_1)
Total	£11,000 × $1.93/£ = $21,230

The forward contract entered in step 2 exactly offsets the exchange rate risk incurred in step 1.

The Canadian investor can lock in a risk-free dollar-denominated return either by investing in the United Kingdom and hedging exchange rate risk, or by investing in risk-free Canadian assets. Because the returns on two risk-free strategies must be equal, we conclude that

$$[1 + r_f(\text{UK})]\frac{F}{E_0} = 1 + r_f(\text{C})$$
$$\frac{F}{E_0} = \frac{1 + r_f(\text{C})}{1 + r_f(\text{UK})}$$

which is the interest rate parity relationship for a single period. (This interest rate parity relationship will be explored at length in Chapter 22.)

Unfortunately, such perfect exchange rate hedging is usually not so easy. In our example, we knew exactly how many pounds to sell in the forward market because the pound-denominated proceeds in the United Kingdom were risk-free. If the U.K. investment had not been in bills but instead were in risky U.K. equity, we would not know the ultimate value in pounds of our U.K. investment or therefore how many pounds to sell forward. Thus, the hedging opportunity offered by foreign exchange forward contracts would be imperfect. To summarize, the generalization of equation 10.1 is that

$$1 + r(\text{C}) = [1 + r(\text{foreign})](E_1/E_0) \qquad \textbf{(10.2)}$$

TABLE 10.4   Domestic and Foreign Investments: Annualized Average Returns and Return Standard Deviations for 1973–1987

Period	TSE 300	Unhedged EAFE	Local EAFE	Hedged EAFE	Unhedged S&P 500	Local S&P 500	Hedged S&P 500	Canadian Paper	Canadian Bonds
1973–1987									
Return	11.0	17.7	12.0	16.0	11.8	9.8	10.7	10.8	9.7
Standard deviation	22.2	27.2	17.3	19.3	17.8	18.0	18.5	1.2	14.5
1973–1977									
Return	1.6	4.6	−0.2	0.2	1.7	−0.2	0.8	8.6	7.2
Standard deviation	12.4	21.6	18.0	19.5	18.8	18.2	19.2	1.7	8.5
1978–1982									
Return	18.3	14.5	13.8	20.8	16.8	14.0	14.5	14.0	8.1
Standard deviation	26.1	18.6	7.9	7.6	12.4	12.8	12.3	4.1	13.9
1983–1987									
Return	13.8	36.2	23.7	29.0	17.5	16.4	17.7	9.9	13.9
Standard deviation	20.4	27.1	11.6	12.4	14.4	15.5	16.0	1.5	14.9

From Robert Auger and Denis Parisien, "The Risks and Rewards of Global Investing," *Canadian Investment Review* vol. 2, no. 1 (Spring 1989).

where r(foreign) is the possibly risky return earned in the currency of the foreign investment. The only opportunity for perfect hedging is in the special case that r(foreign) is itself a known number.

Concept Check	Question 3. How many pounds would need to be sold forward to hedge exchange rate risk in the above example if *a.* r(UK) = 20% *b.* r(UK) = 30%

A study by Auger and Parisien[2] for 1973–1987 data including Canadian assets, U.S. equities (S&P 500), and international equities (Morgan Stanley's EAFE index, described in the following section) analyzes the effect of foreign currency hedging on internationally diversified portfolios for Canadian investors. While the unhedged EAFE portfolio had a slightly higher rate of return of 17.7 percent for volatility of 27.2 percent, the hedged equivalent return of 16.0 percent was obtained for a volatility of only 19.3 percent. Table 10.4, reproduced from their study, shows the returns and volatilities for various portfolios

---

[2] Robert Auger and Denis Parisien, "The Risks and Rewards of Global Investing," *Canadian Investment Review* vol. 2, no. 1 (Spring 1989).

and periods; the results show the local currency returns and the Canadian dollar equivalents, with and without hedging. Note that the TSE 300 is clearly dominated by the hedged EAFE portfolio.

Passive and Active International Investing

When we discuss investment strategies in the purely domestic context, we use a market index portfolio such as the TSE 300 as a benchmark passive equity investment. This suggests that a world market index might be a useful starting point for a passive international strategy.

Several major U.S. investment houses have composed indices of non-U.S. (actually non-North American) stocks. The most widely used index of these is the Europe, Australia, Far East, or **EAFE index** computed by Morgan Stanley. Morgan Stanley also has an alternative EAFE index using GDP rather than market value for country weighting. However, there are now several additional indices of world equity performance. Capital International Indices has published several indicators of international equity performance since 1968. Now Salomon Brothers, First Boston, and Goldman Sachs also publish world equity indices. Portfolios designed to mirror or even replicate the country, currency, and company representation of these indices would be the obvious generalization of the purely domestic passive equity strategy.

Active portfolio management in an international context also may be viewed as an extension of active domestic management. In principle, one would form an efficient frontier from the full menu of world securities, and determine the optimal risk portfolio. However, to focus on the special aspects of international investing, we more often view active management from a broader asset-allocation framework. In this case, we focus on various potential sources of abnormal returns—currency selection, country selection, stock selection within countries, and cash/bond selection within countries—and measure the contribution of each of these factors.

1. **Currency selection** measures the contribution to total portfolio performance attributable to exchange rate fluctuations relative to the investor's benchmark currency, the Canadian dollar. We can measure currency selection as the weighted average of the appreciation, E_1/E_0, of each currency represented in the portfolio, using as weights the fraction of the portfolio invested in each currency. We might use a benchmark such as the EAFE index to compare a portfolio's currency selection for a particular period to a passive benchmark. EAFE currency selection would thus be computed as the weighted average of E_1/E_0 of the currencies represented in the EAFE portfolio, using as weights the fraction of the EAFE portfolio invested in each currency.

2. **Country selection** measures the contribution to performance attributable to investing in the better-performing stock markets of the world. It can be measured as the weighted average of the *equity-index* returns of each country, using as weights the share of the manager's portfolio in each country. To measure a manager's contribution relative to a passive strategy, we

might compare country selection to the weighted average across countries of equity index returns, using as weights the share of the EAFE portfolio in each country.

3. **Stock selection** ability may be measured as the weighted average of equity returns *in excess of the equity index* in each country. In this instance, we would use local currency returns and use as weights the investments in each country.

4. **Cash/bond selection** may be measured as the excess return derived from weighting bonds and bills differently from some benchmark weights.

An example of international performance attribution is presented in Table 10.5.

Concept Check	Question 4. What would the manager's country and currency selection have been if her portfolio weights were 40 percent in Europe, 20 percent in Australia, and 40 percent in the Far East?

Under active portfolio management the problem of stock analysis and selection is much more complicated than for the domestic case. Many of the standard ratios (such as price-earnings) in foreign countries will be significantly different from the accepted norms in Canada or the United States, which are comparable. This difference may often be due to different accounting practices or institutional requirements in the foreign country, but also different levels for

TABLE 10.5   Example of Performance Attribution: International

	EAFE* Weight	Return on Equity Index	E_1/E_0	Manager's Weight	Manager's Return
Europe	.30	.10	1.10	.35	.08
Australia	.10	.05	.90	.10	.07
Far East	.60	.15	1.30	.55	.18

With the above data we can make the following calculations:

Currency selection: EAFE: .30 × 1.10 + .10 × .90 + .60 × 1.30 = 1.20 (20% appreciation)
Manager: .35 × 1.10 + .10 × .90 + .55 × 1.30 = 1.19
Loss of 1% relative to EAFE.

Country selection: EAFE: .30 × .10 + .10 × .05 + .60 × .15 = .125
Manager: .35 × .10 + .10 × .05 + .55 × .15 = .1225
Loss of .25% relative to EAFE.

Stock selection: (.08 − .10).35 + (.07 − .05).10 + (.18 − .15).55 = .0115
Contribution of 1.15% relative to EAFE.

* E, Europe; A, Australia; FE, Far East.

TABLE 10.6 Stock Market Valuation at 2/26/93*

Index	P/BV	P/CE	P/E	Yield
International Indexes (in $ U.S.)				
World index	1.94	8.9	24.2	2.7
Europe, Australia, Far East (EAFE) index	1.73	7.6	24.10	2.5
Europe index	1.72	7.1	18.5	3.7
National Indexes (in $ U.S.)				
Hong Kong	2.22	12.6	16.0	3.6
Norway	1.84	7.1	93.2	2.0
United Kingdom	2.14	10.8	20.5	4.4
Singapore/Malaysia	1.70	12.0	19.2	1.7
Australia	1.49	9.9	22.5	3.6
Canada	1.38	9.1	43.5	3.1
United States of America	2.38	10.4	23.8	2.8
New Zealand	1.22	7.2	14.3	5.1
Sweden	1.76	10.5	25.2	2.1
Netherlands	1.49	5.9	13.7	4.2
France	1.61	6.6	17.4	3.3
Japan	1.73	8.0	69.4	1.0
Belgium	1.41	5.7	15.3	4.6
Spain	1.11	4.4	10.0	5.1
Finland	0.65	22.1	−4.5	1.5
Denmark	1.51	7.8	82.7	1.8
Austria	1.62	4.1	24.9	1.9
Italy	1.15	3.0	23.0	2.7
Switzerland	1.72	9.0	16.6	2.0
Germany	1.81	4.3	16.0	3.6

* P/BV = price to book-value ratio; P/CE = price to cash-earnings (earnings + depreciation) ratio; P/E = price-earnings ratio; Yield = gross dividend yield.
From Bruno Solnik, *International Investments* (Reading, Mass.: Addison-Wesley Publishing Co., Inc., 1990). Exhibit 5.4. Reprinted with permission. This information may not be reproduced or redisseminated without prior written permission from Morgan Stanley Capital International.

ratios may reflect alternative attitudes to risk as seen in leverage and reserves for losses. Table 10.6 shows a wide range for four ratios in the more developed markets (without considering the situation for developing nations); the most widely recognized of these is the Norwegian P/E, here seen as more than 20 times the P/E of Finland.

Among the stocks available for investment there are both domestic and foreign companies, which are commonly known as *multinational firms*. Almost all large banks would qualify for this label, but there are also numerous non-financial enterprises such as Alcan, Nestlé, IBM, and Unilever. Such firms can be characterized as conducting many, if not all, of their primary activities, including obtaining raw materials, production, sales, and financing, in a large number of countries. Typically, these firms derive a majority of their profits from foreign sales. Hence, we can conclude that their financial results will depend on the economic conditions all around the world, and thus are themselves internationally diversified. Analysis of multinationals requires a more widely based approach than does analysis of purely domestic firms.[3]

Factor Models and International Investing

Analysis of stocks from an international perspective, especially of multinationals, presents a good opportunity for an application of multifactor models of security returns. Natural factors might include the following:

1. A world stock index
2. A national (domestic) stock index
3. Industrial sector indices
4. Currency movements

Solnik and de Freitas[4] use such a framework. Table 10.7 presents some of their results for several countries. The first four columns of numbers present the R^2 of various one-factor regressions. Recall that the R^2 measures the percentage of return volatility of a company's stock that can be explained by the factor treated as the independent or explanatory variable. Solnik and de Freitas estimate the factor regressions for many firms in a given country and report the average R^2 across the firms in that country. The table reveals that the domestic factor seems to be the dominant influence on stock returns. Whereas the domestic index alone generates an average R^2 of .42 across all countries, adding the three additional factors (in the last column of the table) increases average R^2 to only .46.

On the other hand, evidence of a world market factor clearly emerges from the market crash of October 1987. Despite the fact that equity returns across borders show only moderate correlation (Table 10.3), equity index returns in October in all 23 countries considered in a study by Richard Roll[5] were negative. Figure 10.4, reproduced from Roll's study, shows the value of regional equity indices (starting from a value of 1.0) during October. The correlation among returns is obvious and suggests some underlying world factor common to all economies. Roll also found that the beta of a country's equity index on a world index (estimated through September 1987) was the best predictor of that index's response to the crash, lending further support to the importance of a world factor.

---

[3] A study on the effectiveness of diversification through multinationals reveals, however, that the price of this diversification may be lower risk-adjusted performance; see S. Foerster, R. Reinders, and M. Thorfinnson, "Are Investors Rewarded for the Foreign Exposure of Canadian Corporations?" *Canadian Investment Review* vol. 5, no. 1 (Spring 1992).

[4] Bruno Solnik and A. de Freitas, "International Factors of Stock Price Behavior," CESA working paper, February 1986, cited in Bruno Solnik, *International Investments* (Reading, Mass.: Addison-Wesley Publishing Co., 1988).

[5] Richard Roll, "The International Crash of October 1987," *Financial Analyst's Journal*, September–October 1988.

TABLE 10.7 Relative Importance of World, Industrial, Currency, and Domestic Factors in Explaining Return of a Stock

	Average R^2 of Regression on Factors				
	Single-Factor Tests				Joint Test
Locality	World	Industrial	Currency	Domestic	All Four Factors
Switzerland	0.18	0.17	0.00	0.38	0.39
West Germany	0.08	0.10	0.00	0.41	0.42
Australia	0.24	0.26	0.01	0.72	0.72
Belgium	0.07	0.08	0.00	0.42	0.43
Canada	0.27	0.24	0.07	0.45	0.48
Spain	0.22	0.03	0.00	0.45	0.45
United States	0.26	0.47	0.01	0.35	0.55
France	0.13	0.08	0.01	0.45	0.60
United Kingdom	0.20	0.17	0.01	0.53	0.55
Hong Kong	0.06	0.25	0.17	0.79	0.81
Italy	0.05	0.03	0.00	0.35	0.35
Japan	0.09	0.16	0.01	0.26	0.33
Norway	0.17	0.28	0.00	0.84	0.85
Netherlands	0.12	0.07	0.01	0.34	0.31
Singapore	0.16	0.15	0.02	0.32	0.33
Sweden	0.19	0.06	0.01	0.42	0.43
ALL COUNTRIES	0.18	0.23	0.01	0.42	0.46

Modified from Bruno Solnik, *International Investments,* © 1988, Addison-Wesley Publishing Co., Inc., Reading, Massachusetts, Tables 2 and 7. Reprinted with permission.

FIGURE 10.4

Regional indices around the crash, October 14–October 26, 1987.

From Richard Roll, ''The International Crash of October 1987,'' *Financial Analysts Journal*, September–October 1988.

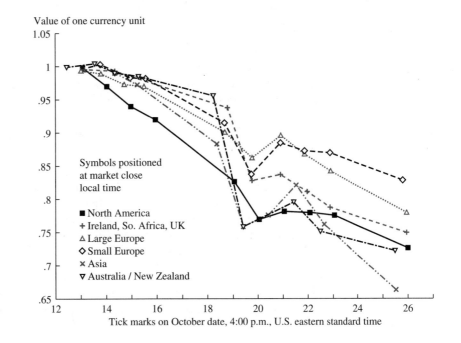

Value of one currency unit

Symbols positioned at market close local time

■ North America
+ Ireland, So. Africa, UK
△ Large Europe
◇ Small Europe
✕ Asia
▽ Australia / New Zealand

Tick marks on October date, 4:00 p.m., U.S. eastern standard time

TABLE 10.8   Equity Returns, 1960–1980

	Average Return	Standard Deviation of Return	Beta	Alpha
Australia	12.20	22.80	1.02	1.52
Austria	10.30	16.90	.01	4.86
Belgium	10.10	13.80	.45	2.44
Canada	12.10	17.50	.77	2.75
Denmark	11.40	24.20	.60	2.91
France	8.10	21.40	.50	.17
Germany	10.10	19.90	.45	2.41
Italy	5.60	27.20	.41	−1.92
Japan	19.00	31.40	.81	9.49
Netherlands	10.70	17.80	.90	.65
Norway	17.40	49.00	−.27	13.39
Spain	10.40	19.80	.04	4.73
Sweden	9.70	16.70	.51	1.69
Switzerland	12.50	22.90	.87	2.66
United Kingdom	14.70	33.60	1.47	1.76
United States	10.20	17.70	1.08	−.69

From Roger G. Ibbotson, Richard C. Carr, and Anthony W. Robinson, "International Equity and Bond Returns," *Financial Analysts Journal,* July/August 1982.

Equilibrium in International Capital Markets

As for domestic assets, we can look to the CAPM or APT to predict expected rates of return in an international capital market equilibrium. However, these models must be adapted somewhat for the international context.

For example, one might expect that a world CAPM would result simply by replacing a narrow domestic market portfolio with a broad world market portfolio, and measuring betas relative to the world portfolio. Indeed, this approach was pursued in part of a paper by Ibbotson, Carr, and Robinson,[6] who calculated betas of equity indices of several countries against a world equity index, with all returns denominated in U.S. dollars. Their results appear in Table 10.8. The betas for different countries show surprising variability.

Whereas such a straightforward generalization of the simple CAPM is a reasonable first step, it is subject to some problems:

1. Taxes, transaction costs, and capital barriers across countries make it difficult and less attractive for investors to hold a world index portfolio. Some assets are simply unavailable to foreign investors.
2. Investors in different countries view exchange rate risk from the perspective of different domestic currencies. Thus, they will not agree on the risk characteristics of various securities and, therefore, will not derive identical efficient frontiers.

---

[6] Roger G. Ibbotson, Richard C. Carr, and Anthony W. Robinson, "International Equity and Bond Returns," *Financial Analysts Journal,* July/August 1982.

3. Investors in different countries tend to consume different baskets of goods, either because of differing tastes, or because of tariffs, transportation costs, or taxes. Therefore, if relative prices of goods vary over time, the inflation risk perceived by investors in different countries also will differ.

These problems suggest that the simple CAPM will not work as well in an international context as it would if all markets were fully integrated. Indeed, some evidence suggests that assets that are less accessible to foreign investors carry higher risk premiums.[7]

The APT seems better designed for the international context, since the special risk factors that arise in this setting can be treated like any other risk factor. For example, similar to the four-factor model of Chen, Roll, and Ross for U.S. equities, returns could be described by a like number of factors, including world economic activity and currency movements for international effects, an industry-specific measure, and some measure of domestic market performance relative to world performance.

10.2   *Integration of Canadian and International Markets*

Integration vs. Segmentation in Markets

Investigation of the benefits of international investment leads immediately to the question of whether assets listed in different capital markets offer the same risk-return characteristics. Interlisting of stocks on various world exchanges makes them accessible to investors in those markets and places them in direct competition as financial assets with the domestic securities of those markets. One might suspect that the inevitable result of this would be that all assets in all markets would display the same risk-return characteristics, at least relative to some world index or common factors. Were this the case, we would describe the markets as being fully **integrated**. In contrast to this, if assets in different markets retained different risk-return characteristics or were priced according to different and country-specific factors, we would describe these markets as **segmented**.

The existence of market segmentation is ascribed to both indirect and legal barriers to investment by all potential investors in all potential assets. Indirect barriers are defined as those previously mentioned problems besetting the foreign investor, such as lack of access to financial information or ability to trade efficiently in the securities. Legal barriers include restrictions on foreign own-

[7] Vihang Errunza, and Etienne Losq, "International Asset Pricing under Mild Segmentation: Theory and Test," *Journal of Finance* 40 (March 1985).

ership or of foreign investment by individuals or institutions, such as the limitation placed on Canadian pension funds. Interlisting of securities tends to alleviate the indirect barriers, but usually cannot solve legal barriers.

We have seen in Table 10.6 that various important financial ratios have been found to vary widely across the different markets shown. This might be taken as evidence of clear segmentation of the many markets, possibly excepting the Canadian and U.S. markets with their similar ratios, given the relevance of these ratios to market valuation. Yet these statistics must be recognized as dependent upon the market conditions under which they were compiled; prices are high relative to earnings during recessions. Furthermore, the different markets are not homogeneous in terms of the firms that comprise the indexes; the Canadian market is disproportionately high in natural resource companies. Financial ratios vary appropriately across different industries, and the different comparison of specific national markets leads to a variety of aggregates of ratios.

Consideration of financial ratios is a dated approach to valuation, however, and cannot provide reliable evidence as to market segmentation. Modern financial theory prescribes the comparison of *ex post* risk-return measures and the sensitivity to market factors as evidence. Recent interest in the subject of market integration and segmentation has led to a number of theoretical and empirical studies to test which of the two descriptions is accurate. Generally, these tests involve attempts to price international assets by appeal to multifactor models, as described in the previous section; both multifactor CAPM and APT models have been used. Modelling the effects of barriers causing segmentation is difficult, however, given the problem of defining and quantifying imperfections in the markets. Hence the risk premiums for the various factors cannot be reliably established. Alternatively, theory suggests that the integration of a smaller market with larger markets will result in a lowering of expected returns in the smaller market, due to increased liquidity and demand, but more importantly, due to a lowering of the risk premium. Interlisting of securities should produce a lowering of risk premiums for these securities at least; thus the event of interlisting can be studied to test for an observed reduction as of the change.[8]

Integration of Canadian and U.S. Markets

Canadian markets offer a unique opportunity to researchers to study the question of segmentation versus integration since they are close to U.S. markets both institutionally and geographically; the economies are closely linked, corporations are governed by essentially similar rules and practices, and both debt and equity instruments of both countries are sold to and traded by investors of both countries, with interlisting of many stocks. Yet the different tax treatment of dividends in the two countries implies that ex dividend day returns should

---

[8] Gordon J. Alexander, Cheol S. Eun, and S. Janakiramanan, "Asset Pricing and Dual Listing on Foreign Capital Markets: A Note," *Journal of Finance* 42 (March 1987).

differ for stocks in the two markets; interlisted stocks were shown by Booth and Johnston[9] to behave differently from domestically traded stocks. Comparison of interlisted and domestic stocks can provide statistically significant results to demonstrate segmentation. Furthermore, a case for integration between the two markets can be made more strongly than for integration of a third market with either of the two. Statistical methods can be used to test for the different characteristics of integration as would be expected under the closely linked versus distant markets.

Empirical studies of Canadian and U.S. returns are varied and inconclusive as to whether the markets are truly integrated. Hatch and White[10] examined the comparative returns of U.S. and Canadian stock markets, and noted that U.S. stocks had a higher return than did Canadian but had a slightly lower risk; they rationalized this as resulting from a lower beta for Canadian stocks, relative to a world index. Brennan and Schwartz[11] rejected integration of the two markets over the period 1968–1980 based on a combined index, but their analysis does not correct for the substantial double counting of interlisted stocks. Extending the period to 1982, Jorion and Schwartz[12] found the same result by using a two-factor CAPM approach; the model was designed to eliminate the commonality between the domestic and international components. They found that the international index did not account for all the returns in Canadian stocks, leaving a priceable national component; hence, they concluded there was evidence of segmentation. Alexander, Eun, and Janakiramanan[13] tested the reduction in expected required returns following interlisting for the period 1969–1982. They investigated both Canadian and non-North American stocks that were listed on the NYSE, AMEX, or NASDAQ, and found a significant distinction between the Canadian and non-Canadian groups; as hypothesized, the Canadian stocks experienced a much smaller return reduction than did the others. In fact, the Canadian results were found to be insignificant, leading them to the conclusion that the foreign markets are definitely segmented from the U.S., but that the Canadian market may not have been.

In conclusion, we can say that there are institutional and sectoral explanations for an apparent segmentation of Canadian and U.S markets; at the same time, similarities and accessibility of the two markets suggest that little if any differential pricing is likely and that virtual integration is possible. Statistically, we cannot determine which of the two descriptions applies.

---

[9] L. D. Booth and D. J. Johnston, "The Ex-Dividend Day Behavior of Canadian Stock Prices: Tax Changes and Clientele Effects," *Journal of Finance* 39 (June 1984).

[10] J. E. Hatch and R. W. White, "A Canadian Perspective on Canadian and United States Capital Market Returns: 1950–1983," *Financial Analysts Journal* 42 (May–June 1986).

[11] M. J. Brennan and E. Schwartz, "Asset Pricing in a Small Economy: A Test of the Omitted Assets Model," in Spremann (ed.), *Survey of Developments in Modern Finance* (New York: Springer-Verlag, 1986).

[12] P. Jorion and E. Schwartz, "Integration vs. Segmentation in the Canadian Stock Market," *Journal of Finance* 41 (July 1986).

[13] Gordon J. Alexander, Cheol S. Eun, and S. Janakiramanan, "International Listings and Stock Returns: Some Empirical Evidence," *Journal of Financial and Quantitative Analysis* 23 (1988). This is a typical example of the event study methodology, described in Chapter 12.

Summary

1. Canadian assets comprise only a small fraction of the world wealth portfolio. International capital markets offer important opportunities for portfolio diversification with enhanced risk-return characteristics.

2. Exchange rate risk imparts an extra source of uncertainty to investments denominated in foreign currencies. Much of that risk can be hedged in foreign exchange futures or forward markets, but unless the foreign currency rate of return is known, a perfect hedge is not feasible.

3. Several world market indices can form a basis for passive international investing. Active international management can be partitioned into currency selection, country selection, stock selection, and cash/bond selection.

4. A factor model applied to international investing would include a world factor, as well as the usual domestic factors. Although some evidence suggests that domestic factors dominate stock returns, the October 1987 crash provides evidence of an important international factor.

5. Financial markets in different countries may be integrated or segmented, depending or whether the factors that influence security prices are universal or specific to the countries.

6. The benefits of international diversification are increased if market segmentation exists. Studies indicate that Canadian markets are at most mildly segmented from U.S. markets. For Canadian investors, overseas investment offers the greatest diversification opportunities.

Key terms

Political risk	Stock selection
Exchange rate	Cash/bond selection
EAFE index	Integration
Currency selection	Segmentation
Country selection	

Selected readings

Comprehensive textbooks on international facets of investing are:
Solnik, Bruno. *International Investing* (2d ed.). Reading, Mass.: Addison-Wesley Publishing, Co., Inc., 1991.
Grabbe, J. Orlin. *International Financial Markets*. New York: Elsevier Science Publishers, 1986.
A text with a greater emphasis on corporate applications and foreign exchange risk management is:
Shapiro, Alan C. *Multinational Financial Management*. Boston: Allyn & Bacon, Inc., 1986.
A good book of reading is:
Lessard, Donald R. (editor). *International Financial Management: Theory and Application*. New York: John Wiley & Sons, 1985.

Some recent Canadian empirical studies on international diversification include the works mentioned in the footnotes and:

Marmer, Harry S. "International Investing: A New Canadian Perspective." *Canadian Investment Review* vol. 4, no. 1 (Spring 1991).

Problems

1. Suppose that a Canadian investor wishes to invest in a British firm currently selling for £40 per share. The investor has $10,000 to invest, and the current exchange rate is $2/£.
   a. How many shares can the investor purchase?
   b. Fill in the table below for rates of return after one year in each of the nine scenarios.

Price per Share (£)	Pound-Denominated Return (%)	Dollar-Dominated Return for Year-End Exchange Rate		
		$1.80/£	$2/£	$2.20/£
£35				
£40				
£45				

   c. When is the dollar-denominated return equal to the pound-denominated return?
2. If each of the nine outcomes in question 1 is equally likely, find the standard deviation of both the pound- and dollar-denominated rates of return.
3. Now suppose that the investor in question 1 also sells forward £5,000 at a forward exchange rate of $2.10/£.
   a. Recalculate the dollar-denominated returns for each scenario.
   b. What happens to the standard deviation of the dollar-denominated return?
4. Calculate the contribution of total performance from currency, country, and stock selection for the following manager:

	EAFE Weight	Return on Equity Index	E_1/E_0	Manager's Weight	Manager's Return
Europe	.30	.20	.9	.35	.18
Australia	.10	.15	1.0	.15	.20
Far East	.60	.25	1.1	.50	.20

5. If the current exchange rate is $1.75/£, the one-year forward exchange rate is $1.85/£, and the interest rate on British government bills is 8 percent per year, what risk-free dollar-denominated return can be locked in by investing in the British bills?
6. If you were to invest $10,000 in the British bills of question 5, how would you lock in the dollar-denominated return?
7. (CFA Examination, Level III, 1985) A U.S. pension plan hired two offshore firms to manage the non-U.S. equity portion of its total portfolio. Each firm was free to own stocks in any country market included in Capital Interna-

tional's Europe, Australia, and Far East index (EAFE) and free to use any form of dollar and/or non-dollar cash or bonds as an equity substitute or reserve. After three years had elapsed, the records of the managers and the EAFE index were as shown below:

Summary: Contributions to Return

	Currency Selection (%)	Country Selection (%)	Stock Selection (%)	Cash/Bond Allocation (%)	Total Return Recorded (%)
Manager *A*	9.0	19.7	3.1	0.6	14.4
Manager *B*	7.4	14.2	6.0	2.8	15.6
Composite of *A & B*	8.2	16.9	4.5	1.7	15.0
EAFE index	12.9	19.9	—	—	7.0

You are a member of the plan sponsor's Pension Committee, which will soon meet with the plan's consultant to review manager performance. In preparation for this meeting, you go through the following analysis:

   a. Briefly describe the strengths and weaknesses of each manager, relative to the EAFE index data.

   b. Briefly explain the meaning of the data in the "Currency" column.

8. (Based on CFA Examination, Level III, 1986) John Irish, CFA, is an independent investment advisor who is assisting Alfred Darwin, the head of the Investment Committee of General Technology Corporation, to establish a new pension fund. Darwin asks Irish about international equities and whether the Investment Committee should consider them as an additional asset for the pension fund.

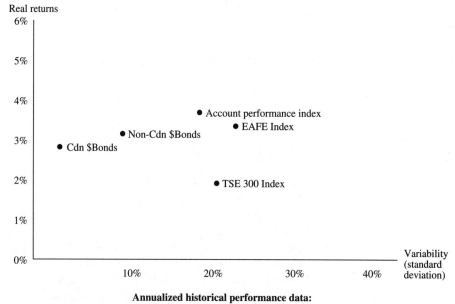

Annualized historical performance data:
14 years ended Dec. 31, 1983

a. Explain the rationale for including international equities in General's equity portfolio. Identify and describe *three* relevant considerations in formulating your answer.

b. List *three* possible arguments against international equity investment and briefly discuss the significance of each.

c. To illustrate several aspects of the performance of international securities over time, Irish shows Darwin the graph on page 348 of investment results experienced by a Canadian pension fund in the period 1970–1983. Compare the performance of the Canadian dollar and non-Canadian dollar equity and fixed-income asset categories, and explain the significance of the result of the account performance index relative to the results of the four individual asset class indices.

CHAPTER 11

Empirical Evidence on Security Returns

Before we discuss what sort of evidence supports the implications of the CAPM and APT, we must note that these implications already have been accepted in widely varying applications. Consider the following:

1. Many professional portfolio managers use the expected return-beta relationship of security returns. Furthermore, many firms rate the performance of portfolio managers according to the reward-to-variability ratios they maintain and the average of return they realize relative to the SML.
2. Regulatory commissions use the expected return-beta relationship along with forecasts of the market index return as one factor in determining the cost of capital for regulated firms.
3. Court rulings on torts cases sometimes use the expected return-beta relationship to determine discount rates to evaluate claims of lost future income.
4. Many firms use the SML to obtain a benchmark hurdle rate for capital budgeting decisions.

These practices show that the financial community has passed a favourable judgment on the CAPM and the APT, if only implicitly.

In this chapter, we consider the evidence along more explicit and rigorous lines. The first part of the chapter presents the methodology that has been deployed in testing the single-factor CAPM and APT, and assesses the results. The second part of the chapter provides an overview of current efforts to establish the validity of the multifactor versions of the CAPM and APT. Finally, we briefly report on current efforts to model the volatility of stock returns, and their contributions to tests of the validity of the CAPM/APT.

Why lump together empirical works on the CAPM and APT? The CAPM is a theoretical construct that predicts *expected* rates of return on assets, relative to a market portfolio of all risky assets. It is difficult to test these predictions empirically because both expected returns and the exact market portfolio are unobservable (see Chapter 9). To overcome this difficulty, a single- or multifactor capital market usually is postulated, where a broad-based market index portfolio (such as the TSE 300) is assumed to represent the factor, or one of the factors. Furthermore, to obtain more reliable statistics, most tests have been conducted with the rates of return on well-diversified portfolios rather than on individual securities. For both of those reasons tests that have been directed at the CAPM actually have been more suitable to establish the validity of the APT. We will see that it is more important to distinguish the empirical work on the basis of the factor structure that is assumed or estimated than to distinguish between tests of the CAPM and the APT.

11.1   *The Index Model and the Single-Factor APT*

The Expected Return-Beta Relationship

Recall that if the expected return-beta relationship holds with respect to an observable ex ante efficient index, M, the expected rate of return on any security i is

$$E(r_i) = r_f + \beta_i[E(r_M) - r_f] \tag{11.1}$$

where β_i is defined as $\text{Cov}(r_i, r_M)/\sigma_M^2$.

This is the most commonly tested implication of the CAPM. Early simple tests followed three basic steps: establishing sample data, estimating the SCL (security characteristic line), and estimating the SML (security market line).

Setting up the sample data

Determine a sample period of, for example, 60 monthly holding periods (five years). For each of the 60 holding periods collect the rates of return on 100 stocks, a market portfolio proxy (the TSE 300 or the S&P 500 for U.S. studies) and one-month (risk-free) T-bills. Your data thus consist of

r_{it} $i = 1, \ldots, 100$, and $t = 1, \ldots, 60$:
Returns on the 100 stocks over the 60-month sample
period

r_{Mt} Returns on the TSE 300 index over the sample period; and

r_{ft} Risk-free rate each month

This constitutes a table of $102 \times 60 = 6{,}120$ rates of return.

Estimating the SCL

View equation 11.1 as a security characteristic line (SCL) as in Chapter 9. For each stock, i, you estimate the beta coefficient as the slope of a **first-pass**

regression equation. (The terminology *first-pass* regression is due to the fact that the estimated coefficients will be used as input into a **second-pass regression.**)

$$r_{it} - r_{ft} = a_i + b_i(r_{Mt} - r_{ft}) + e_{it}$$

You will use the following statistics in later analysis:

$\overline{r_i - r_f}$ = Sample averages (over the 60 observations) of the excess return on each of the 100 stocks

b_i = Sample estimates of the beta coefficients of each of the 100 stocks

$\overline{r_M - r_f}$ = Sample average of the excess return of the market index

$\sigma^2(e_i)$ = Estimates of the variance of the residuals for each of the 100 stocks

The sample average excess returns on each stock and the market portfolio are taken as estimates of expected excess returns, and the values of b_i are estimates of the true beta coefficients for the 100 stocks during the sample period. The $\sigma^2(e_i)$ estimates the non-systematic risk of each of the 100 stocks.

Concept Check

Question 1.
a. How many regression estimates of the SCL do we have from the sample?
b. How many observations are there in each of the regressions?
c. To satisfy the CAPM, what should be the intercept in each of these regressions?

Estimating the SML

Now view equation 11.1 as a security market line (SML) with 100 observations for the stocks in your sample. You can estimate γ_0 and γ_1 in the following second-pass regression equation with b_i from the first pass as the independent variable:

$$\overline{r_i - r_f} = \gamma_0 + \gamma_1 b_i \quad i = 1, \ldots, 100 \tag{11.2}$$

Compare equations 11.1 and 11.2; you should conclude that if the CAPM is valid, then γ_0 and γ_1 must satisfy

$$\gamma_0 = 0 \qquad \gamma_1 = \overline{r_M - r_f}$$

In fact, however, you can go a step further and argue that the key property of the expected return-beta relationship described by the SML is that the expected excess return on securities is determined *only* by the systematic risk (as measured by beta) and should be independent of the non-systematic risk, as measured by the variance of the residuals, $\sigma^2(e_i)$, which also were estimated from the first-pass regression. These estimates can be added as a variable in equation 11.2 of an expanded SML that now looks like this:

$$\overline{r_i - r_f} = \gamma_0 + \gamma_1 b_i + \gamma_2 \sigma^2(e_i) \tag{11.3}$$

This *second-pass* regression is estimated with the hypotheses:

$$\gamma_0 = 0 \qquad \gamma_1 = \overline{r_M - r_f} \qquad \gamma_2 = 0$$

To the disappointment of early researchers, tests following this pattern consistently failed to support the index model and the results from such a test (first conducted by John Lintner[1] and later replicated by Merton Miller and Myron Scholes[2]) using annual data on 631 NYSE stocks for 10 years, 1954 to 1963, are

Coefficient:	$\gamma_0 = .127$	$\gamma_1 = .042$	$\gamma_2 = .310$
Standard error:	.006	.006	.026
Sample average:		$\overline{r_M - r_f} = .165$	

Such results are totally inconsistent with the CAPM. First, the estimated SML is "too flat"; that is, the γ_1 coefficient is too small. The slope should be $\overline{r_M - r_f} = .165$ (16.5 percent per year), but it is estimated at only .042. The difference, .122, is about 20 times the standard error of the estimate, .006, which means that the measured slope of the SML is lower than it should be by a statistically significant margin. At the same time, the intercept of the estimated SML, γ_0, which is hypothesized to be zero, in fact equals .127, which is more than 20 times it standard error of .006.

Concept Check	Question 2.
	a. What is the implication of the empirical SML being "too flat"?
	b. Do high- or low-beta stocks tend to outperform the predictions of the CAPM?

Second, and more damaging to the CAPM, is that non-systematic risk seems to predict expected excess returns. The coefficient of the variable that measures non-systematic risk, $\sigma^2(e_i)$, is .310, more than 10 times its standard error of .026.

There are, however, two principal flaws in these tests. The first is that statistical variation in stock returns introduces **measurement error** into the beta estimates, the *b* coefficients from the first-pass regressions. Using these estimates in place of the true beta coefficients in the estimation of the second-pass

---

[1] John Lintner, "Security Prices, Risk and Maximal Gains from Diversification," *Journal of Finance* 20, December 1965.

[2] Merton H. Miller and Myron Scholes, "Rate of Return in Relation to Risk: A Reexamination of Some Recent Findings," in Michael C. Jensen (editor), *Studies in the Theory of Capital Markets* (New York: Praeger Publishers, 1972).

regression for the SML biases the estimates in the direction that we have observed: the measurement errors in the beta coefficients will lead to an estimate of the SML that is too flat and that has a positive (rather than zero) intercept.

The second problem results from the fact that the variance of the residuals is correlated with the beta coefficients of stocks. Stocks that have high beta tend also to have high non-systematic risk. Add this effect to the measurement problem, and the coefficient of non-systematic risk, γ_2, in the second-pass regression will be upward biased.

Indeed, a well-controlled simulation test by Miller and Scholes (see footnote 2) confirms these arguments. In this test a random number generator simulated rates of return with covariances similar to observed ones. The average returns were made to agree exactly with the CAPM expected return-beta relationship. Miller and Scholes then used these randomly generated rates of return in the tests we have described as if they were observed from a sample of stock returns. The results of this "simulated" test were virtually identical to those reached using real data, despite the fact that the simulated returns were *constructed* to obey the SML, that is, the true γ coefficients were $\gamma_0 = 0$, $\gamma_1 = .165 = \overline{r_M} - r_f$, and $\gamma_2 = 0$.

This postmortem of the early test gets us back to square one. We can explain away the disappointing test results, but we have no positive results to support the CAPM/APT implications.

The next wave of tests was designed to overcome the measurement error problems that led to biased estimates of the SML. The innovation in these tests was to investigate the rate of return on portfolios rather than individual securities. Combining securities into portfolios diversifies away most of the firm-specific part of returns, thereby enhancing the precision of the estimates of beta and the expected rate of return on the portfolio of securities. This mitigates the statistical problems that arise from measurement error in the beta estimates.

Obviously, however, combining stocks into portfolios reduces the number of observations left for the second-pass regression. For example, suppose that we wish to group 100 stocks into portfolios of 20 stocks each. If the assumption of a single-factor market is reasonably accurate, then the residuals of the 20 stocks in each portfolio will be practically uncorrelated and hence the variance of the portfolio residual will be about one twentieth the residual variance of the average stock. Thus the portfolio beta in the first-pass regression will be estimated with far better accuracy. However, now consider the second-pass regression. With individual securities we had 100 observations to estimate the second-pass coefficients. With portfolios of 20 stocks each we are left with only five observations for the second-pass coefficients.

To get the best of this trade-off, we need to construct portfolios with the largest possible dispersion of beta coefficients. Other things being equal, a sample yields more accurate regression estimates the more widely spaced are the observations of the independent variables. Consider the first-pass regressions in the test of the CAPM where we estimate the relationship between the market's excess return and each stock's. If we have a sample with a great dispersion of market returns, we have a better shot at accurately estimating the effect of a change in the market return on the return of the stock. In our case, however, we have no control over the range of the market returns. But we can control the range of the independent variable of the second-pass regression, the portfolio betas. Rather than allocate 20 stocks to each portfolio randomly, we can rank portfolios by betas. Portfolio 1 will include the 20 highest-beta stocks and Portfolio 5 the 20 lowest-beta stocks. In that case a set of portfolios with small non-systematic components, e_P, and widely spaced betas will yield reasonably powerful tests of the SML.

A study by Black, Jensen, and Scholes[3] (BJS) pioneered this method. The researchers used an elaborate method to design the sample portfolios and estimate their betas. To illustrate, let us assume that the data set consists of 500 stocks over a long sample period. We would split the sample period into three subperiods:

Overall Sample Period of 500 Stock Returns

Subperiod I	Subperiod II	Subperiod III
Estimate *individual* stock betas and order them from highest to lowest beta. Form equally weighted portfolios of 50 stocks each, resulting in 10 portfolios from highest to lowest beta. This is a preparatory step for the first-pass regression.	Reestimate the betas of the 10 portfolios. These estimates will be used as the true betas for the SML estimates. The errors in measuring these betas are independent of the errors in the betas used to form the portfolios. This is the first-pass regression.	Use the average excess returns on the 10 portfolios from this period as estimates of the expected excess returns to regress on the betas from the previous subperiod. This is the second-pass regression.

The BJS study uses all available NYSE stock returns over the period 1931–1965. The number of available stocks increased from 582 in 1931 to 1,094 in 1965. The available stocks are allocated to 10 portfolios; thus portfolio size varies over the period from 58 to 110 stocks. The size and diversification of these portfolios reduces measurement error considerably.

Summary statistics for the 10 portfolios appear in Table 11.1. The betas of the 10 portfolios for the entire period (420 months) are shown in the first line of the table. They range from .4992 to 1.5614 and are fairly evenly spaced. The next two lines show the intercepts (denoted by α) of the SCL for each portfolio. These values are small, and the ratios of these values to their standard errors [the *t*-statistics, $t(\alpha)$] are less than 2.0 for 9 out of the 10 portfolios. The pattern of these alpha values, however, begins to tell the story of the test results. The alphas are negative for high-beta portfolios ($\beta > 1$) and positive for low-beta portfolios ($\beta < 1$). This is a clue that, contrary to what the SML would imply, lower beta portfolios earned consistently better risk-adjusted returns than higher beta portfolios.

---

[3] Fischer Black, Michael C. Jensen, and Myron Scholes, "The Capital Asset Pricing Model: Some Empirical Tests," in Michael C. Jensen (editor), *Studies in the Theory of Capital Markets* (New York: Praeger Publishers, 1972).

TABLE 11.1   Summary of Statistics for Time Series Tests (January 1931–December 1965)

Item*	Portfolio Number										$\bar{R}_M$
	1	2	3	4	5	6	7	8	9	10	
β	1.5614	1.3838	1.2483	1.1625	1.0572	0.9229	0.8531	0.7534	0.6291	0.4992	1.000
$\hat{\alpha} \cdot 10^2$	−0.0829	−0.1938	−0.0649	−0.0167	−0.0543	0.0593	0.0462	0.0812	0.1968	0.2012	
$t(\alpha)$	−0.4274	−1.9935	−0.7597	−0.2468	−0.8869	0.7878	0.7050	1.1837	2.3126	1.8684	
$\rho(\bar{R}, \bar{R}_M)$	0.9625	0.9875	0.9882	0.9914	0.9915	0.9833	0.9851	0.9793	0.9560	0.8981	
$\rho(\bar{e}_t, \bar{e}_{t-1})$	0.0549	−0.0638	0.0366	0.0073	−0.0708	−0.1248	0.1294	0.1041	0.0444	0.0992	
$\sigma(\bar{e})$	0.0393	0.0197	0.0173	0.0137	0.0124	0.0152	0.0133	0.0139	0.0172	0.0218	
$\bar{R}$	0.0213	0.0177	0.0171	0.0163	0.0145	0.0137	0.0126	0.0115	0.0109	0.0091	0.0142
σ	0.1445	0.1248	0.1126	0.1045	0.0950	0.0836	0.0772	0.0685	0.0586	0.0495	0.0891

* $\bar{R}$ = Average monthly excess returns, σ = standard deviation of the monthly excess returns. ρ = correlation coefficient. Sample size for each regression, 420.
Modified from Fischer Black, Michael C. Jensen, and Myron Scholes, "The Capital Asset Pricing Model: Some Empirical Tests," in *Studies in the Theory of Capital Markets*, Michael C. Jensen, Ed. (Praeger Publishers, New York, 1972). Copyright © 1972 by Praeger Publishers, Inc. Reprinted with permission.

The next two lines in Table 11.1 show the correlation coefficients of the portfolio returns with the market index, $\rho(R_P, R_M)$, and the serial correlation of the non-systematic component, e, of the portfolios between successive periods, $\rho(e_t, e_{t-1})$. The large size and corresponding diversification of the portfolios is such that we expect returns to be highly correlated with the market index. Indeed, the correlation coefficients range from .8981 to .9915. The non-systematic components are virtually independent from period to period: $\rho(e_t, e_{t-1})$ ranges from −.1248 to .1294, as we would expect from random noise.

From the last three lines of the table we note first that most of the risk of the 10 portfolios is systematic. The first of these lines shows the standard deviation of the residuals, our estimate of non-systematic risk, $\sigma(e)$. The bottom line shows the standard deviation of the excess rate of return, σ. For the highest-beta portfolio the monthly standard deviation was 14.45 percent per month, of which 3.93 percent is non-systematic. For the lowest-beta portfolio the standard deviation of the excess return was 4.95 percent per month, of which 2.18 percent is non-systematic.

The next-to-last line in the table shows the average monthly excess returns for the 10 portfolios and the market (NYSE) index. The market index excess return averages 1.42 percent per month, and the average excess returns for the 10 portfolios range from .91 percent to 2.13 percent per month. As we should expect from the CAPM, the portfolios with betas lower than 1 earned less than the market index, and the portfolios with betas higher than 1 earned more.

Figure 11.1 shows the second-pass regression estimate of the SML for the entire period. The upper left-hand corner of Figure 11.1 reveals the disappointing result for the CAPM hypothesis. The intercept of the estimated SML, the γ_0 coefficient, is .359 percent per month with a standard error of only .055 percent (its t-statistic is 6.53), so that the intercept, which is hypothesized by the CAPM to be zero, is positive and statistically significant.

FIGURE 11.1

The second-pass regression estimate of the security market line.

[From Fischer Black, Michael C. Jensen, and Myron Scholes, "The Capital Asset Pricing Model: Some Empirical Tests," in *Studies in the Theory of Capital Markets*, Michael C. Jensen, Ed. (Praeger Publishers, New York, 1972). Copyright © 1972 by Praeger Publishers, Inc. Reprinted with permission.]

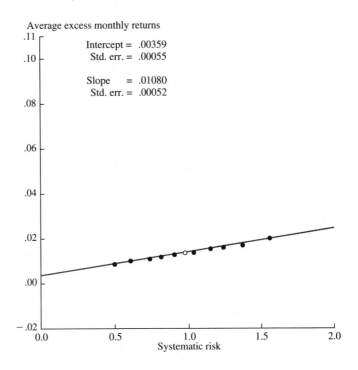

The slope of the SML is 1.08. The CAPM hypothesis is that this slope, γ_1, should equal the expected excess return on the market index. For the sample period the market index averaged 1.42 percent per month. The difference, $\gamma_1 - \overline{(r_M - r_f)}$, for this sample is thus $-.34$ percent per month. The estimated SML is too flat again. The standard error of the estimate of γ_1 is .052 percent, so the difference (.34 percent) is 6.54 times the standard error. Thus the results are inconsistent with the CAPM hypothesis for γ_1.

Breaking the analysis into subperiods, BJS found no better results. Figure 11.2 shows the estimated SMLs for four subperiods. The intercepts are positive and statistically significant in three out of the four subperiods. Worse even, in the 1957–1965 subperiod, the slope of the SML has the wrong sign.

At this point, BJS bring up the possibility that perhaps the sample results may verify the zero-beta version of the CAPM. Recall from Chapter 8 that when borrowing is restricted, the CAPM expected return-beta relationship must be amended. As it turns out, all that is called for in moving to the zero-beta version of the CAPM is replacing the risk-free rate with the expected excess return on the zero-beta portfolio (i.e., the efficient portfolio uncorrelated with the market portfolio).

The two representations of the CAPM expected return-beta relationships are as follows:

1. No restriction on risk-free investment:

$$E(r_i) - r_f = \beta_i[E(r_M) - r_f]$$

FIGURE 11.2

The estimated
security market
lines for four
subperiods.

[From Fischer Black,
Michael C. Jensen, and
Myron Scholes, "The
Capital Asset Pricing
Model: Some Empirical
Tests," in *Studies in the
Theory of Capital Mar-
kets,* Michael C. Jensen,
Ed. (Praeger Publishers,
New York, 1972). Copy-
right © 1972 by Praeger
Publishers, Inc. Reprinted
with permission.]

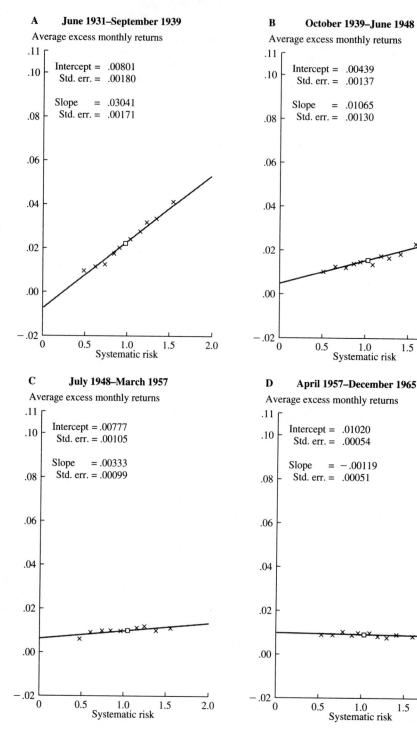

2. Restriction on risk-free investment (the zero-beta CAPM):

$$E(r_i) - E(r_{Z(M)}) = \beta_i[E(r_M) - E(r_{Z(M)})] \tag{11.4}$$

where $r_{Z(M)}$ is the rate of return on the zero-beta portfolio.

If we shift $E(r_{Z(M)})$ to the right-hand side and subtract the risk-free rate from both sides, equation 11.4 takes this form:

$$E(r_i) - r_f = E(r_{Z(M)}) - r_f + \beta_i[E(r_M) - E(r_{Z(M)})] \tag{11.5}$$

If we were to test this version of the CAPM, we would hypothesize that

$$\gamma_0 = E(r_{Z(M)}) - r_f$$
$$\gamma_1 = E(r_M) - E(r_{Z(M)})$$

To conduct their test, BJS needed to estimate returns on the zero-beta portfolio from the available data. To obtain these rates, they rearranged equation 11.5 and concluded that the actual rate of return on any stock in period t (as opposed to the expected return) would be described by

$$r_{it} = r_{Zt}(1 - \beta_i) + r_{Mt}\beta_i + e_{it} \tag{11.6}$$

Using the previously estimated beta coefficient, the zero-beta rate is *estimated* from the return of each stock by

$$r_Z = (r_{it} - \beta_i r_{Mt})/(1 - \beta_i) \tag{11.7}$$

Note that the rate of return on each stock provides one estimate of the zero-beta rate. BJS use a statistically efficient technique to average these estimates across stocks and thus obtain, for each period, an efficient estimate of the zero-beta rate.

Using the time series of the estimated zero-beta rates for each subperiod, in conjunction with the market and individual stock returns, BJS examined the validity of the zero-beta version of the CAPM. Their major conclusions follow:

1. The average return of the zero-beta portfolio is significantly greater than the risk-free rate.
2. The excess rate of return on the zero-beta portfolio explains some of the deviation of the results from the simple version of the CAPM, yet the regression estimates are not fully consistent with the zero-beta version of the CAPM either.

The fact that the average return on the zero-beta portfolio exceeds the risk-free rate is consistent with the restricted borrowing models of the CAPM presented in Chapter 8. It also is consistent with BJS's finding that the empirical SML is flatter than predicted by the simple CAPM.

Concept Check

Question 3. What should be the average return on the zero-beta portfolio in the BJS test according to the zero-beta version of the CAPM?

BJS tested the SML equation directly with negative results, with and without restrictions on risk-free lending and borrowing. They did not concern themselves with other specific implications of the CAPM, such as that expected returns are independent of non-systematic risk or that the relationship between expected returns and beta is linear.

Fama and MacBeth[4] use the BJS methodology to verify that the observed relationship between average excess returns and beta is indeed linear and that non-systematic risk does not explain average excess returns. Using 20 portfolios constructed according to the BJS methodology, Fama and MacBeth expand the estimation of the SML equation to include the square of the beta coefficient (to test for linearity of the relationship between returns and betas) and the estimated standard deviation of the residual (to test for the explanatory power of non-systematic risk). For a sequence of many subperiods they estimate, for each subperiod, the equation

$$r_i = \gamma_0 + \gamma_1\beta_i + \gamma_2\beta_i^2 + \gamma_3\sigma(e_i)$$

The term γ_2 measures potential nonlinearity of return, and γ_3 measures the explanatory power of nonsystematic risk, $\sigma(e_i)$. The Fama–MacBeth results show that the beta relationship is in fact linear (γ_2 is not significantly different from zero) and that non-systematic risk does not explain average returns (γ_3 also is insignificant). At the same time, however, the authors report that the SMLs, in general, remain too flat and have a positive significant intercept.

We can summarize these conclusions:

1. The insights that are supported by the single-factor CAPM and APT are as follows:
   a. Expected rates of return are linear and increase with beta, the measure of systematic risk.
   b. Expected rates of return are not affected by non-systematic risk.
2. The single-variable expected return-beta relationship predicted by either the risk-free rate or the zero-beta version of the CAPM is not fully consistent with empirical observation.

Thus, although the CAPM seems *qualitatively* correct, in that β matters and $\sigma(e_i)$ does not, empirical tests do not validate its *quantitative* predictions.

Concept Check

> Question 4. What would you conclude if you performed the Fama and MacBeth tests and found that the coefficients on β^2 and $\sigma(e)$ were positive?

---

[4] Eugene Fama and James MacBeth, "Test of the Multiperiod Two Parameter Model," *Journal of Financial Economics,* March 1977.

Estimating Index Models for Canadian Stocks

Relatively few studies on the SML along the lines of the previous section were done using Canadian data. The availability of data in computerized form was scarce until recent years. Furthermore, the Canadian financial markets present certain problems, not encountered in the United States.

One of the earlier estimations of the SML in Canada was by Morin,[5] who used monthly return data on 620 securities trading continuously for at least five years on the TSE during the period 1957–1971. The basic methodology was the one developed by BJS, with its extensions by Fama and MacBeth. The market index was an equally weighted average of the returns of all securities in the databank.

The general flavour of the results can be obtained by quoting from the study's conclusions: "Overall, the empirical results of this study indicate that the capital asset pricing theory, in all its forms, fares poorly in attempting to explain differential returns on Canadian equities." The return-beta relationship turned out to be weak, erratic, and non-linear, and implied unreasonably high estimates of the returns on low-risk assets.

Several other SML studies using Canadian data[6] reached conclusions that seem to confirm the basic outcome observed in the United States, namely that the single-variable expected return-beta relationship is, at best, only weakly supported by empirical work. For instance, Calvet and Lefoll[7] use monthly TSE security return data, and a value-weighted index of all stocks in their databank as a market index. Although a significant linear relationship between systematic risk and portfolio returns was found almost always, the introduction of unsystematic risk and of the squared beta coefficient in the regression, as in the Fama–MacBeth study, showed both to be significant and more important than the beta.

Empirical research in Canadian financial markets is hindered by two effects that are not present to the same extent in the United States. The first is the existence of seasonal abnormal returns that are at variance with market efficiency; these will be examined in detail in the next chapter. The second is the persistent problem of **thin trading** in a majority of Canadian securities.

Thin Trading

If transactions for many securities listed on the TSE are irregular and infrequent, then the prices quoted as closing by the exchange are unreliable and may also reflect situations that are no longer current. For instance, if a stock did not

[5] Roger A. Morin, "Market Line Theory and the Canadian Equity Market," *Journal of Business Administration* 12, no. 1 (Fall 1980).

[6] For instance, J. D. Jobson and R. M. Korkie, "Some Tests of Linear Asset Pricing with Multivariate Normality," *Canadian Journal of Administrative Sciences* 2, no. 1 (June 1985).

[7] A. L. Calvet and J. Lefoll, "Risk and Return on Canadian Capital Markets," *Canadian Journal of Administrative Sciences* 5, no. 1 (March 1988).

TABLE 11.2   Thin Trading Breakdown on TSE Listings between January 1970–December 1979

	All Securities		Securities Listed at Least 12 Months*		Securities Listed for Whole 10-Year Period		Broader "Fat" Category for 10-Year Group†	
	Number	%	Number	%	Number	%	Number	%
Fat	112	5.3	78	4.3	38	6.0	156	24.6
Moderate	744	35.3	679	37.7	328	51.7	210	33.1
Infrequent	1251	59.4	1043	58.0	268	42.3	268	42.3
TOTAL	2107	100.0	1800	100.0	634	100.0	634	100.0

* The prime difference between the all securities and the 12-month groups is that warrants and rights are largely eliminated from the latter.
† This category includes any security for which a trade could always be found in the last five days of the month.
From D. J. Fowler, C. H. Rorke, and V. M. Jog, "Thin Trading and Beta Estimation Problems on the Toronto Stock Exchange," *Journal of Business Administration* 12, no. 1 (Fall 1980). Reprinted by permission.

trade at all during a given month, then its recorded rate of return is zero during that month (in the absence of dividends). If many such securities and months occur in our database, then the statistical estimations of the SML will yield biased results.

Table 11.2 reproduces data from a study by Fowler, Rorke, and Jog[8] on the frequency of trading on the TSE during the period 1970–1979. The data base contained 120 monthly returns for each security listed on the TSE during that period. The three categories of trading frequency distinguished by the authors were defined as follows: a "fat" security showed a trade during the closing day of each month; a "moderate" security was one that traded each month, but not necessarily on the last day; an "infrequent" security was one that showed entire months without any trade. As the data show, this last category was by far the largest, accounting for 42–59 percent of the total, depending on the type of securities considered.

In addition to biases in the estimated coefficients, thinness of trading also causes heteroscedasticity,[9] that is, different variances of the residuals in the regressions. There are a number of procedures for correcting the biases arising out of thinness of trading, of which the one developed by Dimson[10] is perhaps the most popular. The Dimson method augments the single simultaneous market index term in the regression by two other terms, one with a lagged and one with a leading value of the index, each one with its own beta; an unbiased estimate of the "true" beta is equal to the sum of the three estimated betas.

[8] David J. Fowler, C. Harvey Rorke, and V. M. Jog, "Thin Trading and Beta Estimation Problems on the Toronto Stock Exchange," *Journal of Business Administration* 12, no. 1 (Fall 1980).
[9] David J. Fowler, C. Harvey Rorke, and V. M. Jog, "Heteroscedasticity, R^2 and Thin Trading on the Toronto Stock Exchange," *Journal of Finance* 34, no. 5 (December 1979).
[10] E. Dimson, "Risk Measurement When Shares Are Subject to Infrequent Trading," *Journal of Financial Economics* 7 (1979).

Another bias-correcting method was also developed by Scholes and Williams,[11] but the small-sample properties of both methods are somewhat questionable.[12]

The Efficiency of the Market Index—Roll's Critique

In 1977, while researchers were improving test methodology in an effort to conclusively endorse or reject the validity of the CAPM, Richard Roll[13] threw a monkey wrench into their machinery. In the now classic "Roll's Critique," he argues not only that the tests of the expected return-beta relationship are invalid, but also that it is doubtful that CAPM can ever be tested. Roll's critique includes the following observations:

1. There is a single testable hypothesis associated with the CAPM: that the market portfolio is mean-variance efficient.
2. All the other implications of the model, the best-known being the linear relation between expected return and beta, follow from the market portfolio's efficiency and therefore are not independently testable. There is an "if and only if" relation between the expected return-beta relationship and the efficiency of the market portfolio.
3. In any sample of observations of individual returns there will be an infinite number of ex post mean-variance efficient portfolios using the sample period returns and covariances (as opposed to the ex ante expected returns and covariances). Sample betas calculated between each such portfolio and individual assets will be exactly linearly related to sample mean returns. In other words, if betas are calculated against such portfolios, they will satisfy the SML relation exactly whether or not the true market portfolio is mean-variance efficient in an ex ante sense.
4. The CAPM is not testable unless we know the exact composition of the true market portfolio and use it in the tests. This implies that the theory is not testable unless *all* individual assets are included in the sample.
5. Using a proxy such as the TSE 300 (or the S&P 500 for U.S. studies) for the market portfolio is subject to two difficulties. First, the proxy itself might be mean-variance efficient even when the true market portfolio is not. Conversely, the proxy may turn out to be inefficient, but obviously this alone implies nothing about the true market portfolio's efficiency. Furthermore, most reasonable market proxies will be very highly correlated with each other and with the true market whether or not they are mean-variance efficient. Such a high degree of correlation will make it seem that the exact composition of the market portfolio is unimportant, whereas the use of different proxies can lead to quite different conclusions. This problem is often referred to as **benchmark error,** since it refers to the use of an incorrect benchmark (market proxy) portfolio in the tests of the theory.

[11] M. Scholes and J. Williams, "Estimating Betas from Nonsynchronous Data," *Journal of Financial Economics* 5 (1977).

[12] See Fowler, Rorke, and Jog, 1980.

[13] Richard Roll, "A Critique of the Asset Pricing Theory's Tests: Part I: On Past and Potential Testability of the Theory," *Journal of Financial Economics* 4 (1977).

Roll's criticism requires us to think in terms of two contexts and three portfolios. The contexts are as follows:

1. Ex ante expectations of rates of return and covariances.
2. Ex post (sample) averages of rates of return and estimates of covariances.

Clearly, the ex post (realized) rates of returns are random, and their measured averages and covariances are not necessarily equal to those that were expected ex ante.

Now Roll argues that we have to worry about three types of portfolios:

1. The true (unobservable) market portfolio.
2. The portfolio that happens to be ex post efficient for a given sample of realized returns.
3. The portfolio that is chosen as the proxy for the market portfolio and is used to conduct the test.

Roll argues that the third portfolio, the market proxy, will be highly correlated with the first two portfolios. Since we do not know the exact composition of the true market portfolio, even if the data seem to support the expected return-beta relationship, we cannot tell whether this is (a) because we have tested the tautology that ex post efficient portfolio (2) is indeed efficient, and therefore the expected return-beta relationship appears valid, or (b) that our index portfolio is in fact close enough to the unobservable market portfolio (1), and that *this* is the reason for the empirical finding of an expected return-beta relationship. Conversely, if we find that the results indicate that the expected return-beta relationship does not hold, we cannot tell whether the tests do not confirm the theory, or, instead, that the choice of the proxy for the market portfolio is inadequate.

Roll's critique is a serious blow to the CAPM. Indeed, it led to a now-famous article in *Institutional Investor* called "Is Beta Dead?" However, the problems in testing the CAPM should not obscure the value of the model. The accompanying box presents what we believe is a reasonably balanced view of the controversy.

With Roll's critique of the BJS and Fama–MacBeth methodology in mind, let us reassess the test results so far and consider what alternative tests might make sense. BJS used an equally weighted portfolio of all NYSE stocks as their proxy for the market portfolio. Since this portfolio included between 582 and 1,094 stocks throughout the sample period, there is no question that their market proxy was a well-diversified portfolio. The 10 test portfolios were equally weighted portfolios of between 58 and 110 stocks, also fairly well diversified. Perhaps we can view the BJS test really as a test of the APT, which applies only to well-diversified portfolios. As tests of the CAPM, however, Roll shows that the procedures are objectionable. Roll's critique tells us that all we can say about the BJS and Fama–MacBeth tests is that they, at best, constitute an attempt to verify a zero-beta version of the APT but provide no evidence about the CAPM.

Beta Is Dead! Long Live Beta!

By Jason MacQueen

Introduction

The philosophy of natural science as expounded by Karl Popper prescribes a logicoempiricist methodology for invalidating new theoretical models of the observed world, such as those hypothesized in the applied investment field by Harry Markowitz and Bill Sharpe. Their particular paradigm shift has resulted in a plethora of theoretical investment models, including the capital asset pricing model (CAPM). Recent papers by Richard Roll, however, have suggested that the CAPM may not be susceptible to invalidation by such methodological tests.

The above paragraph shows quite clearly that it is, in fact, possible to do several things at once. Several imposing names are dropped, lots of long words are used, and a relatively simple statement is made utterly confusing—all in the same paragraph. The next Guiness Book of Records will surely have a new entry in this category, awarded to the author of the 1980 *Institutional Investor (I.I.)* article entitled "Is Beta Dead?" who managed to keep up this kind of thing for seven pages, thereby utterly confusing hundreds of investment managers.

About Theories

Modern portfolio theory (MPT) developed from the work done by Harry Markowitz in 1952 on portfolio selection. In essence, it is based on the single observation that the proper task of the investment manager is not simply to maximize expected return, but to do so at an acceptable level of risk. If this were not so, portfolios would consist solely of managers' favorite stocks, instead of combining different stocks which, although all not equally attractive when considered individually, together offer the maximum expected return for a given level of risk.

This observation itself was not new. The originality of Markowitz's contribution lay in showing how investment risk could be measured and, hence, how mathematics could be used to select the best possible portfolio from all the different combinations of a chosen list of stocks.

There have been many refinements of the theory since. What is now commonly referred to as MPT is no longer a single theory, but several different theories or models, together with their applications. These models may be grouped into three main categories: versions of the market model, versions of the capital asset pricing model (CAPM), and versions of the efficient market hypothesis (EMH).

The most common misconception about MPT is that these three theoretical constructs are all part of the same one and that, therefore, they stand or fall together. While some of the applications depend on two or more of the models, the individual models themselves do not depend heavily on each other. It is thus quite possible that one could be "wrong" while the others were "right."

It is, in any case, a mistake to think in terms of theories being "right" or "wrong" absolutely. All theories are "wrong" in that sense, including, for example, Einstein's theory of relativity.

Karl Popper (see first sentence) is a philosopher of science who has pointed out that, even if a particular theory were "right," you could never actually prove it. All you can ever hope to do is prove that it is wrong. If you have a new theory, you keep testing it in as many different ways as possible to see if it doesn't work. As long as it works fairly well, you can assume that it might be right, but you will never know for sure. A good theory is generally reckoned to be one that works quite well most of the time.

Newton's theory about the way planets and stars move was considered to be a good theory for several hundred years. Then some smart engineer invented an extra-powerful telescope with a very accurate scale, and a bored astronomer who had nothing else to do one evening noticed that the orbit of Mercury, the smallest planet around these parts, wasn't quite where it should be. Suddenly, New-

(Continued)

ton's theory wasn't so hot any more, and we all had to wait a few more years for Einstein to come along and say, "Well it's nearly right, but if you put in this extra wrinkle here . . .," and so invent relativity.

Unfortunately for Einstein, smart engineers and bored astronomers are two a penny these days, even allowing for inflation, and they've already noticed one or two places where his theory is a tiny bit out.

Newton's theory is still taught in schools, and is widely used in many different applications. To give a somewhat gruesome example, it is used for ranging artillery fire. The theory may not be exactly right, but it is certainly right enough to kill people. On the other hand, Einstein's theory was used to plot the flight of the Apollo spacecraft because Newton's theory wasn't good enough to provide the rigorous degree of accuracy required.

This point about a theory being useful without needing to be right was also made about the CAPM in the *I.I.* article mentioned earlier. In that article, Barr Rosenberg was quoted as saying, "While the model is false, it's not very false." All models are false in this sense; what matters is how false they are, and to what extent this affects their application.

Much Ado About Nothing Very Much

Presumably, you may say, the *Institutional Investor* article on the demise of beta was supposed to be about something—but what exactly? The story the article was based on is actually more than five years old, and is quite simple.

In 1977 Richard Roll, the noted professor at U.C.L.A., published the first of a series of academic papers showing that there is a bit of a problem with the CAPM. The problem has to do with something else Karl Popper said about theories: namely, that any new theory that someone thinks up should not be given the time of day unless it can be tested.

In the Middle Ages any young priest who wanted to get ahead would think up a new theory about how many angels could balance on the head of a pin. Karl Popper would have said that they were all wasting their time, since there was no way of testing their theories.

What Richard Roll did was to point out that the CAPM can't be tested either. His reason was that to test it you first need to get hold of "the market," and that can't be done. A lot of so-called testing had already been done using "market proxies" such as the S&P 500. Roll pointed out, quite correctly, that using different proxies gave you different answers; and that, in any case, a proxy was merely a proxy and not what we were supposed to be testing.

The problem with using a proxy is that it is not the efficient market portfolio one would like it to be, but is an inefficient portfolio (i.e., one containing diversifiable risk), representing a subset of the market. Roll showed that one of the mathematical consequences of this was likely to be consistent errors in the betas.

It is worth pointing out that nearly everyone now agrees with this just as everyone agrees that the CAPM is clearly not true. These errors are fundamentally different from the random errors that arise from the fact that betas are estimated statistically, rather than measured directly. We might also note, en passant, that the gentlemen with calculators continue to work out discounted present values, and that stocks still tend to go up and down together. The validity of EMH and the market model, meanwhile, remains unaffected by this controversy over CAPM.

The crucial point is this: beta is supposed to measure the market-related risk of a stock or portfolio. By using the S&P 500 index as a market proxy, we are going to get betas that actually measure S&P 500-related risk. What we were hoping to do is to separate the total risk of a stock into its diversifiable and non-diversifiable components. By using a proxy that is itself an inefficient portfolio, we run the risk of not separating the total risk into the correct proportions. The S&P 500-related beta could be bigger or smaller than the "real" beta.

The "furious controversy" that the *I.I.* article described is about how important these consistent errors in the betas are. If they are small (and there are good, though complex, reasons why this is likely to be the case), then we do not have much of a problem. If they are large, then we will have to be rather careful in those applications in which it is likely to matter.

(Continued)

No doubt the "furious controversy" will continue to rage in academic circles for some time yet, and when the dust settles it may well turn out that the current version of the CAPM belongs in the same basket as theories about angels and pins. More than likely, though, academics will have thought up a different version of the CAPM that can be tested. And when some subtle variant of the present CAPM is finally vindicated, it is a fairly safe bet that beta will remain (though possibly in a different manifestation) the reigning measure of investment risk.

Is beta dead? One way to answer the question is to calculate (or buy) a few, and then watch what happens as the market goes up and down. The question then becomes fairly simply: do portfolios of high (or medium, or low) beta stocks exaggerate (or match, or dampen) market swings? Answer: yes.

The fact of the matter is that betas do work, more or less well depending mostly on how sensible we've been in calculating them. All betas are relative to one or another market proxy. According to Einstein, everything else is relative too, so this should not be too much of a problem. Naturally something's beta will change if it is measured against different market indices. It will also change if it [is] measured against hemlines, which many experienced market men believe to be a very reliable market proxy. The point is that it has to be measured against something, and it is therefore up to the user to decide which market proxy is most appropriate.

We know that these theories are not perfectly "right," but we also know that they are not too "wrong." Using MPT can provide valuable information on the risks incurred in different investment strategies. In short, while the model is false, it's not very false, and even a model that is a bit false is a great deal better than no model at all.

From Jason MacQueen, in Joel M. Stern and Donald H. Chew (editors), *The Revolution in Corporate Finance* (Oxford, England: Basil Blackwell, 1986). Originally published in *Chase Financial Quarterly,* Chase Manhattan Bank, New York. Reprinted with permission.

Another inference we can draw from Roll's critique is that one way to test the CAPM is to test the efficiency of a market proxy. If we were to verify empirically that a legitimate market proxy is the efficient portfolio, we could endorse the CAPM's validity.

This is an important, albeit confusing, point. To relate it to first principles, we need first to distinguish portfolio mean-variance efficiency from informational efficiency. The concept of informational efficiency relates to the question of whether an asset or portfolio is "fairly" priced—whether the price reflects all available information. For example, does the price of Canadian Pacific stock reflect all available information about the earning potential of the corporation that arises from its current and expected future business plans? Chapter 12 is devoted to this concept and to the empirical issue of whether capital markets are informationally efficient.

The question of the informational efficiency of capital markets cannot be divorced from the question of mean-variance efficiency of asset portfolios, however. A central assumption of the simple CAPM is that all investors deduce the same input list from security analysis and hence construct identical efficient frontiers. Under these circumstances trade leads to the mean-variance efficiency of the market portfolio. However, this means that all investors use the same information when analyzing each asset. Therefore, according to CAPM hypothesis, all assets are informationally efficiently priced.

It is possible that capital markets are *informationally* efficient, but at the same time the CAPM is not valid and the market is not a *mean-variance* efficient portfolio. Roll, in addition to providing us with his now-classic critique, realized this point and came up with a positive conclusion: studies of the performance of professionally managed portfolios that were intended to test informational efficiency also may serve as indirect tests of the CAPM. If these tests lead to the conclusion that a market proxy portfolio consistently beats all professionally managed portfolios (on a risk-adjusted basis), then we may conclude that the market proxy is mean-variance efficient and the CAPM is valid. Conversely, if a professionally managed portfolio consistently outperforms the market proxy, then either the proxy is inadequate or the CAPM is invalid.

The motivation for comparing the performance of professional portfolio managers against the market proxy portfolio is simple. Professional managers are the best qualified to choose efficient portfolios, since they spend considerable resources on selecting and revising portfolios. Yet the CAPM predicts that all their efforts will fail, that one portfolio (the market portfolio) will outperform them all. If we find that, indeed, professional managers fail to beat the market proxy, the CAPM prediction is upheld. On the other hand, if professional managers can beat the proxy, we would have to conclude that the market proxy is inadequate and/or that the CAPM must be rejected.

The evidence on the performance of professional managers relative to a market proxy is strong. Sharpe[14] pioneered this line of investigation by studying the reward-to-variability ratio of 34 U.S. mutual funds. He concludes:

We have shown that performance can be evaluated with a simple yet theoretically meaningful measure that considers both average return and risk. This measure precludes the "discovery" of differences in performance due solely to differences in objectives (e.g., the high average returns typically obtained by funds that consciously hold risky portfolios). However, even when performance is measured in this manner there are differences among funds; and such differences do not appear to be entirely transitory. To a major extent they can be explained by differences in expense ratios, lending support to the view that the capital market is highly efficient and that good managers concentrate on evaluating risk and providing diversification, spending little effort (and money) on the search for incorrectly priced securities. However, past performance per se also explains some of the differences. Further work is required before the significance of this result can be properly evaluated. But the burden of the proof may reasonably be placed on those who argue the traditional view—that the search for securities whose prices diverge from their intrinsic value is worth the expense required.

Sharpe records the annual rate of return that investors realized from 34 mutual funds over the 10-year period 1954–1963. He then measures the reward-to-variability ratio for each fund, dividing the average rate of return by the standard deviation of returns, and compares these reward-to-variability ratios to that of the Dow Jones Industrials portfolio. The results are graphed in Figure 11.3. The figure shows that only 11 out of the 34 funds outperformed the Dow

---

[14] William Sharpe, "Mutual Fund Performance," *Journal of Business, Supplement on Security Prices* 39 (January 1966).

FIGURE 11.3

Mutual fund performance compared with the Dow Jones Industrials, 1954–1963.

[From William Sharpe, "Mutual Fund Performance," *Journal of Business, Supplement on Security Prices* 39 (January 1966); published by the University of Chicago]

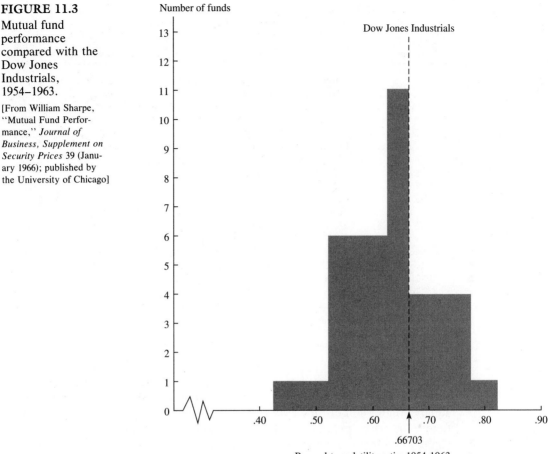

Reward-to-volatility ratio, 1954-1963

Jones Industrial portfolio, which is itself a far-from-satisfactory proxy for the theoretically efficient market portfolio.

Today, the picture is similar. Following Sharpe, several U.S. studies investigated more funds, used shorter intervals (months instead of years) to estimate variables, and, most important, included a more reasonable proxy for the market portfolio, such as the S&P 500 or the NYSE index. Their results were, overall, supportive of Sharpe's conclusions.

A similar pattern emerges from Canadian studies. One example is a study by Calvet and Lefoll[15] that uses 17 mutual fund quarterly returns over the period 1966–1975. The funds included in the study were selected because they had less than 10 percent of their capital invested in foreign securities. The market portfolio was proxied by the TSE 300 index. The study also developed its own methodology in order to evaluate performance under inflationary conditions.

---

[15] A. L. Calvet and J. Lefoll, "The CAPM under Inflation and the Performance of Canadian Mutual Funds," *Journal of Business Administration* 12, no. 1 (Fall 1980).

TABLE 11.3   Real Performances and Systematic Risks

Fund Number	α	t Value	β	t Value	R^2
1	0.0086	1.1985	0.7406	8.182	0.6379
2	−0.0049	−0.5702	0.6852	6.330	0.5133
3	−0.0030	−0.6439	0.7785	13.202	0.8210
4	−0.0051	−1.2271	0.9084	17.250	0.8867
5	−0.0048	−1.2894	0.8189	17.477	0.8893
6	−0.0055	−1.2109	0.8681	14.992	0.8553
7	−0.0084	−1.1641	0.8773	9.664	0.7107
8	−0.0016	−0.1800	1.2356	10.680	0.7500
9	0.0069	0.9520	0.9916	10.795	0.7541
10	0.0015	0.4479	0.2973	6.995	0.5628
11	0.0150	2.0603	0.5849	6.365	0.5160
12	−0.0102	−1.6300	0.9232	11.690	0.7825
13	−0.0012	−0.2904	0.9190	17.657	0.8913
14	0.0053	0.8500	0.8398	10.720	0.7515
15	−0.0015	−0.1502	1.0495	7.976	0.6260
16	−0.0016	−0.1339	1.0809	6.953	0.5598
17	0.0061	0.8401	0.9468	10.276	0.7353

$t > 2.0245$ is the value of a 5 percent two-tail test with 38 degrees of freedom.
From A.L. Calvet and J. Lefoll, "The CAPM under Inflation and the Performance of Canadian Mutual Funds," *Journal of Business Administration,* 12, no. 1 (Fall 1980). Reprinted with permission.

Results of the Calvet–Lefoll study appear in Table 11.3, which shows the Jensen alpha performance measure, the estimated constant term from the least-squares regression of fund excess returns on market excess returns, for all 17 funds. Only one fund (number 11) had a significantly positive alpha, indicating a slightly better performance than the market index if management fees are ignored. All other funds' performance measures were not significantly different from zero. These results remained virtually unchanged when performance was estimated with the "traditional" method that ignores inflation.

These results are typical of all Canadian studies.[16] The conclusion from a recent one,[17] which examined 40 Canadian mutual funds over the period 1967–1984, can be applied to all of them: ". . . Canadian mutual funds as a group were unable to perform significantly different from the market portfolio."

In the end, however, the question "How many managers beat the market portfolio over a given period" is not very informative. First, we must be convinced that each of these managers shows a *statistically significant* superior performance (after adjusting for risk). Second, we must recognize that if a large number of managers are sampled, some are expected to succeed simply by the law of large numbers.

---

[16] Dwight Grant, "Investment Performance of Canadian Mutual Funds, 1960–1974," *Journal of Business Administration* 8 (1976); and H. L. Dhingra, "Portfolio Volatility Adjustment by Canadian Mutual Funds," *Journal of Business Finance and Accounting* 5 (1978).

[17] H. Bishara, "Evaluation of the Performance of Canadian Mutual Funds (1967–1984)," *Proceedings of the Administrative Sciences Association of Canada* vol. 1, part 1 (1987), p. 18.

One way to account for the sampling problem is to subject managers' records to a test of persistence. Suppose you observe a sample of 100 managers over a period of time, splitting them in two groups of superior and inferior performers. Then you observe the same managers over the next time period, and split them again. The hypothesis is that, on average, success or failure of managers does not persist across time periods. Usually, however, a researcher obtains data on managers for a certain period. These data are first divided into two subperiods, and then managers are ranked in each period. For example, one study[18] reports the following results:

	1979–1981 Winners	1979–1981 Losers	Total
1976–1978 Winners	44	19	63
1976–1978 Losers	19	44	63
Total	63	63	126

These results (which are repeated for more subperiods with similar statistics) indicate statistically significant persistence, suggesting that some managers may be consistently outperforming the market portfolio. As it turns out, however, this method also contains severe pitfalls.

Brown, Goetzmann, Ibbotson, and Ross[19] report that the problem with studies of this type is twofold. First, they include only managers whose records are available for both subperiods and exclude managers who dropped out after the first subperiod. Some of these managers have been replaced because their performance was poor. Using simulation, the study shows that if only 5 percent of the lowest-rank managers get cut off after the first subperiod, the results of the remaining sample may show strong persistence even if managers' success is uncorrelated from one period to the next.

A further complication arises from the possibility that managers may be using similar styles, and hence their portfolios' rates of return are correlated, period by period, although each of the returns may be uncorrelated from one period to the next. Such correlation may induce seeming persistence even when no manager is cut off after the first subperiod. When the lowest-rank managers are cut off, such correlation exacerbates the survivorship bias.

11.2 *Multiple Factors in Security Returns*

Research into the multifactor nature of security returns is still in its infancy. Identifying the factors and investigating the risk premiums of securities as a function of their factor loadings (betas) present greater statistical difficulties.

[18] D. Hendricks, J. Patel, and R. Zeckhouser, "Hot Hands in Mutual Fund: The Persistence of Performance, 1974–1988," working paper, John F. Kennedy School of Government, Harvard University, 1991.

[19] Stephen J. Brown, William Goetzmann, Roger B. Ibbotson, and Stephen A. Ross, "Survivorship Bias in Performance Studies," working paper, Yale University, April 2, 1992.

Two lines of inquiry are being pursued. In the first, researchers analyze security returns statistically to discern the significant factors and construct portfolios that are highly correlated with those factors. They then estimate the average returns on these portfolios to determine whether these factors command risk premiums. The second approach is to prespecify likely economic factors and identify portfolios that are highly correlated with these factors. The risk premiums on these portfolios are then estimated from sample average returns.

Identifying Factors from Security Returns

In exploratory factor analysis the exact number of factors is not known. Typically, a model with no factors is first fit to the data. This model assumes that asset returns are mutually uncorrelated. The goodness-of-fit measure from the model serves as a base value to express the total variability in returns. The researcher then fits a succession of factor models with increasing numbers of factors, comparing the goodness-of-fit measures of the various models. As each additional factor is added, a large improvement in the goodness-of-fit measures suggests the existence of an important underlying factor that should be included. A small improvement in the fit suggests that the additional factor may have no real significance.

Factor analysis involving a large number of securities is a difficult task. In one of the most comprehensive studies to date, Lehman and Modest[20] used 750 NYSE and Amex stocks to identify the factors. They concluded that, although the test results "may be interpreted as very weak evidence in favor of a 10-factor model," the tests actually "provide very little information regarding the number of factors which underlie the APT. As the analysis suggests, the tests have little power to discriminate among models with different numbers of factors."

Studies using Canadian data yield similar and even less satisfactory results. For instance, Kryzanowski and To,[21] who analyzed both U.S. and Canadian data, found that there were a much larger number of relevant factors (18 to 20) for the Canadian data, rather than the 10 or so found for the U.S. stocks. Further, the first factor was less important and associated with fewer securities for the Canadian than for the U.S. data. Hughes[22] found that only three or four factors were priced in the market in both samples that she used in her tests, but only the first factor turned out to be the same in both samples.

Parallelling the difficulty in identifying the factor structure from security returns, it has been difficult to demonstrate significant risk premiums on the **factor portfolios** that are constructed from this analysis. Although results may

---

[20] Bruce Lehman and David Modest, "The Empirical Foundation of the Arbitrage Pricing Theory I: The Empirical Tests," *Journal of Financial Economics* 21 (1988).

[21] Lawrence Kryzanowski and Minh Chau To, "General Factor Models and the Structure of Security Returns," *Journal of Financial and Quantitative Analysis* 18, no. 1 (1983).

[22] Patricia J. Hughes, "A Test of the Arbitrage Pricing Theory Using Canadian Security Returns," *Canadian Journal of Administrative Sciences* 1, no. 2 (1984).

not be strong enough to disprove the hypothesis that the factor portfolios have insignificant risk premiums, the tests have little power to reject the hypothesis even when it is false. Reinganum and Conway[23] have developed evidence that the large number of factors identified by factor analysis techniques may be a statistical fluke. Their work uses a cross-validation technique to confirm the explanatory power of factor portfolios that are generated by factor analysis.

The cross-validation method splits the sample period rates of return into two subsamples of odd- and even-date rates of return. Factor analysis is used to identify factor portfolios from the odd-date subsample security returns. The rates of return from the even-date subsample are then used to test the explanatory power of these factor portfolios.

Suppose that the odd-date subsample produces 10 factor portfolios. We now compute the rates of return on the 10 portfolios for all the even dates. Let us assume that the first of the portfolios is the market index portfolio, r_M. Denote the other nine factor portfolio returns by $r_{P2}, \ldots, r_{P10}$. Next, we estimate 10 regression equations for all the stocks ($i = 1, \ldots, n$) using all the even-date returns ($t = 2, 4, 6, \ldots$) in the sample.

$$
\begin{aligned}
&(1) \quad r_{it} = r_{ft} + \beta_{iM}(r_{Mt} - r_{ft}) + e_{i1t} \\
&(2) \quad r_{it} = r_{ft} + \beta_{iM}(r_{Mt} - r_{ft}) + \beta_{iP2}(r_{P2} - r_{ft}) + e_{i2t} \\
&\qquad \vdots \\
&\qquad \cdots \\
&(10) \quad r_{it} = r_{ft} + \beta_{iM}(r_{Mt} - r_{ft}) + \beta_{iP2}(r_{P2} - r_{ft}) + \beta_{iP3}(r_{P3} - r_{ft}) + \cdots \\
&\qquad\qquad + \beta_{iP10}(r_{P10} - r_{ft}) + e_{i10t}
\end{aligned}
$$

For each of the 10 regressions we estimate the variance of the residual $\sigma^2(e_{ikt})$, $k = 1, \ldots, 10$. The cross-validation test requires each additional factor portfolio to reduce the residual variance significantly.

The 10 first-pass factor portfolios appear in an order determined by their significance in the factor analysis of the odd-date subsample. In the second-pass (even-date) cross-validation test, Reinganum and Conway found in their U.S. data that, of the 10, only one factor portfolio (the market index) remained significant, whereas just one other was borderline significant in explaining the variability of the residuals. In a similar spirit, a Canadian study by Abeysekera and Mahajan[24] found that the return premiums of the three to eight factors identified from their first-pass tests were not significantly different from zero. The results demonstrate the statistical difficulties in identifying the factors that drive stock returns.

By design, these factor analysis tests are in the spirit of the APT rather than the multifactor CAPM. The portfolios that researchers identify statistically as factor portfolios are not constructed with regard to any economic meaning, and the chance that any of them can be identified as an obvious hedge for some prespecified risk to future consumption is small.

---

[23] Marc Reinganum and Dolores Conway, "Cross Validation Tests of the APT," working paper, 1987.

[24] Sarath Abeysekera and Arvind Mahajan, "A Test of the APT in Pricing Canadian Stocks," *Canadian Journal of Administrative Sciences* 4, no. 2 (1987).

Tests of Multifactor Equilibrium Models with Prespecified Hedge Portfolios

The other avenue to test the multifactor equilibrium CAPM or APT is to choose portfolios that are predesigned to hedge specific risks and then test the multifactor model with these portfolios.

A full-blown test of the multifactor equilibrium model, with prespecified factors and hedge portfolios, is as yet unavailable. A test of this hypothesis requires three stages:

1. Specification of risk factors.
2. Identification of hedge portfolios.
3. Test of the explanatory power and risk premiums of the hedge portfolios.

A major step in this direction was made by Chen, Roll, and Ross,[25] who hypothesized several possible variables that might proxy for systematic factors:

1. MP = Monthly growth rate in industrial production.
2. DEI = Changes in expected inflation measured by changes in short-term (T-bill) interest rates.
3. UI = Unexpected inflation defined as the difference between actual and expected inflation.
4. UPR = Unexpected changes in borne risk premiums measured by the difference between the returns on corporate Baa bonds and long-term government bonds.
5. UTS = Unexpected changes in the term premium measured by the difference between the returns on long- and short-term government bonds.

With the identification of these potential economic factors, Chen, Roll, and Ross skip the procedure of identifying factor portfolios (the portfolios that have the highest correlation with the factors). Instead, by using the factors themselves, they implicitly assume that factor portfolios exist that are perfectly correlated with the factors. The factors are now used in a test similar to that of Fama–MacBeth.

A critical part of the methodology is the grouping of stocks into portfolios. Recall that in the single-factor tests, portfolios were constructed to span a wide range of betas to enhance the power of the tests. In a multifactor framework, the efficient criterion for grouping is less obvious. Chen, Roll, and Ross chose to group the sample stocks into 20 portfolios by market value of outstanding equity, a variable that is known to be associated with stock returns.

They first use five years of monthly data to estimate the factor betas of the 20 portfolios in a first-pass regression. This is accomplished by estimating the following regressions for each portfolio:

$$r = a + \beta_M r_M + \beta_{MP} MP + \beta_{DEI} DEI + B_{UI} UI + \beta_{URS} URS + \beta_{UTS} UTS + e$$

[25] Nai-Fu Chen, Richard Roll, and Stephen Ross, "Economic Forces and the Stock Market," *Journal of Business* 59 (1986).

where *M* stands for the stock market index. Chen, Roll, and Ross use as the market index both the value-weighted NYSE index (*VWNY*) and the equally weighted NYSE index (*EWNY*).

Using the 20 sets of first-pass estimates of factor betas as the independent variables, they now estimate the second-pass regression (with 20 observations, one for each portfolio):

$$r = \gamma_0 + \gamma_M \beta_M + \gamma_{MP} \beta_{MP} + \gamma_{DEI} \beta_{DEI} + \gamma_{UI} \beta_{UI} + \gamma_{URS} \beta_{URS} + \gamma_{UTS} \beta_{UTS} + e$$

where the gammas become estimates of the risk premiums on the factors.

Chen, Roll, and Ross ran this second-pass regression for every month of their sample period, reestimating the first-pass factor betas once every 12 months. They ran the second-pass tests in four variations. First (Table 11.4, parts **A** and **B**), they excluded the market index altogether and used two alternative measures of industrial production (*YP* based on annual growth of industrial production and *MP* based on monthly growth). Finding that *MP* is a more effective measure, they next included the two versions of the market index, *EWNY* and *VWNY*, one at a time (Table 11.4, parts **C** and **D**). The estimated risk premiums (the values for the parameters, γ) were averaged over all the second-pass regressions corresponding to each subperiod listed in Table 11.4.

Note in Table 11.4, parts **C** and **D**, that the two market indices *EWNY* (equally weighted index of NYSE) and *VWNY* (the value-weighted NYSE index) are not significant (their *t*-statistics of 1.218 and −.633 are less than 2 for the overall sample period and for each subperiod). Note also that the *VWNY* factor has the wrong sign in that it seems to imply a negative market-risk premium. Industrial production (*MP*), the risk premium on bonds (*UPR*), and unanticipated inflation (*UI*) are the factors that appear to have significant explanatory power.

A variant of the Chen, Roll, and Ross study was replicated with Canadian data by Otuteye,[26] but the results were not as satisfactory. While the exogenous variables were more or less similar to the ones used by Chen, Roll, and Ross, the market index (the return on a value-weighted portfolio of Canadian stocks) turned out to be highly significant, in contrast to the U.S. results.

The Chen, Roll, and Ross results must be treated as only preliminary in this line of enquiry, but they indicate that it may be possible to hedge some economic factors that affect future consumption risk with appropriate portfolios. A CAPM or APT multifactor equilibrium expected return-beta relationship may one day supersede the now widely used single-factor model.

It is very difficult to identify the portfolios that serve to hedge common sources of risk to future consumption opportunities. The two lines of research explore the data in search of such portfolios. Factor analysis techniques indicate the portfolios that may be providing hedge services. Researchers can then try to figure out what the source of risk is and its importance. The second line of

---

[26] E. Otuteye, "On the Specification of the Arbitrage Pricing Theory," *Proceedings of the Administrative Sciences Association of Canada* vol. 12, part 1 (1991).

TABLE 11.4   Economic Variables and Pricing (Percent per Month × 10), Multivariate Approach

A	Years	YP	MP	DEI	UI	UPR	UTS	Constant
	1958–1984	4.341	13.984	−.111	−.672	7.941	−5.87	4.112
		(.538)	(3.727)	(−1.499)	(−2.052)	(2.807)	(−1.844)	(1.334)
	1958–1967	.417	15.760	.014	−.133	5.584	.535	4.868
		(.032)	(2.270)	(.191)	(−.259)	(1.923)	(.240)	(1.156)
	1968–1977	1.819	15.645	−.264	−1.420	14.352	−14.329	−2.544
		(.145)	(2.504)	(−3.397)	(−3.470)	(3.161)	(−2.672)	(−.464)
	1978–1984	13.549	8.937	−.070	−.373	2.150	−2.941	12.541
		(.774)	(1.602)	(−.289)	(−.442)	(.279)	(−.327)	(1.911)

B	Years	MP	DEI	UI	UPR	UTS	Constant
	1958–1984	13.589	−.125	−6.29	7.205	−5.211	4.124
		(3.561)	(−1.640)	(−1.979)	(2.590)	(−1.690)	(1.361)
	1958–1967	13.155	.006	−.191	5.560	−.008	4.989
		(1.897)	(.092)	(−.382)	(1.935)	(−.004)	(1.271)
	1968–1977	16.966	−.245	−1.353	12.717	−13.142	−1.889
		(2.638)	(−3.215)	(−3.320)	(2.852)	(−2.554)	(−.334)
	1978–1984	9.383	−.140	−.221	1.679	−1.312	11.477
		(1.588)	(−.552)	(−.274)	(.221)	(−.149)	(1.747)

C	Years	EWNY	MP	DEI	UI	UPR	UTS	Constant
	1958–1984	5.021	14.009	−.128	.848	.130	−5.017	6.409
		(1.218)	(3.774)	(−1.666)	(−2.541)	(2.855)	(−1.576)	(1.848)
	1958–1967	6.575	14.936	−.005	−.279	5.747	−.146	7.349
		(1.199)	(2.336)	(−.060)	(−.558)	(2.070)	(−.067)	(1.591)
	1968–1977	2.334	17.593	−.248	−1.501	12.512	−9.904	3.542
		(.283)	(2.715)	(−3.039)	(−3.366)	(2.758)	(−2.015)	(.558)
	1978–1984	6.638	7.563	−.132	−.729	5.273	−4.993	9.164
		(.906)	(1.253)	(−.529)	(−.847)	(.663)	(−.520)	(1.245)

D	Years	VWNY	MP	DEI	UI	UPR	UTS	Constant
	1958–1984	−2.403	11.756	−.123	−.795	8.274	−5.905	10.713
		(−.633)	(3.054)	(−1.600)	(−2.376)	(2.972)	(−1.879)	(2.755)
	1958–1967	1.359	12.394	.005	−.209	5.204	−.086	9.527
		(.277)	(1.789)	(.064)	(−.415)	(1.815)	(−.040)	(1.984)
	1968–1977	−5.269	13.466	−.255	−1.421	12.897	−11.708	8.582
		(−.717)	(2.038)	(−3.237)	(−3.106)	(2.955)	(−2.299)	(1.167)
	1978–1984	−3.683	8.402	−.116	.739	6.056	−5.928	15.452
		(−.491)	(1.432)	(−.458)	(−.869)	(.782)	(−.644)	(1.867)

$VWNY$ = Return on the value-weighted NYSE index; $EWNY$ = Return on the equally weighted NYSE index; MP = Monthly growth rate in industrial production; DEI = Change in expected inflation; UI = Unanticipated inflation; UPR = Unanticipated change in the risk premium (Baa and under return—long-term government bond return); UTS = Unanticipated change in the term structure (long-term government bond return—Treasury-bill rate); and YP = Yearly growth rate in industrial production. *t*-statistics are in parentheses.
Modified from Nai-Fu Chen, Richard Roll, and Stephen Ross, "Economic Forces and the Stock Market," *Journal of Business* 59 (1986); published by the University of Chicago.

research attempts to guess the identity of economic variables that are correlated with consumption risk and determine whether they indeed explain rates of return.

Concept Check

> Question 5. Compare the strategy of prespecifying the risk factor (as in Chen, Roll, and Ross's work) with that of exploratory factor analysis.

11.3 *Time-Varying Volatility and the State of Tests of Capital Asset Prices*

In 1976, Fischer Black proposed to model the time-varying nature of asset-return volatility.[27] He suggested that such a model should include three effects. One is that the volatility depends on the stock price. (Generally, an increase in the stock price means a decrease in volatility.) A second is that the volatility tends to return to a long-term average. Finally, there are random changes in volatility. Although the idea was well received and widely cited, little was accomplished for quite a while.

In 1982, Robert F. Engle published a study[28] of U.K. inflation rates that measured their time-varying volatility. His model, named ARCH (autoregressive conditional heteroskedasticity), is based on the idea that a natural way to update a variance forecast is to average it with the most recent squared "surprise" (i.e., the deviation of the rate of return from its mean). ARCH introduced a statistically efficient algorithm to do just that.

This methodology caught fire in empirical research. A survey conducted[29] in May 1990 lists over 100 papers that employ ARCH in financial models. Moreover, an algorithm has been developed[30] to perform a joint estimation of the time-series variances and the relationship between the mean and variance of returns (ARCH-M). By applying this technique to an array of assets, tests that relate mean-asset returns to covariances can be devised.

Examination of the state of the empirical evidence on security returns reveals four facts. First, direct tests of either a single- or multifactor CAPM have

---

[27] Fischer Black, "Studies in Stock Price Volatility Changes," *Proceedings of the 1976 Business Meeting of the Business and Economic Statistics Sections, American Statistical Association,* (1976), pp. 177–181.

[28] Robert F. Engle, "Autoregressive Conditional Heteroskedasticity with Estimates of the Variance of U.K. Inflation," *Econometrica* 50 (1982), pp. 987–1008.

[29] Tim Bollerslev, Ray Y. Chou, Narayanan Jayaraman, and Kenneth F. Kroner, "ARCH Modeling in Finance: A Selective Review of the Theory and Empirical Evidence, with Suggestions for Future Research," *Journal of Econometrics* 48 (July/August, 1992).

[30] Tim Bollerslev, Robert F. Engle, and Jeffrey M. Woolridge, "A Capital Asset Pricing Model with Time Varying Covariances," *Journal of Political Economy* 96 (1989), p. 131.

rejected the mean-beta relationship. At the same time, there is no solid evidence that professional managers can persistently outperform well-diversified portfolios by exploiting the failure of security returns to price some factors or, conversely, by exploiting diversifiable risk factors.

Second, there is ample evidence that past security returns exhibit statistical "anomalies" or apparent profitable trading rules that could have been exploited by portfolio managers to produce abnormal rates of return. (More on this in Chapter 12.) Such evidence is a reflection of the noted failure of the CAPM, which predicts that security alphas must average zero. Those who take this view must expect a more general theory to better explain asset returns.

Third, tests of extensions of the CAPM (that relax one of the simplifying assumptions) usually show that asset returns do indeed conform to the prediction of the modified model. One such example is the case of dividends and taxes.[31] A careful study of the joint effect of dividend yield and taxes shows that there is a positive but non-linear association between common stock returns and dividend yields. Taxes drive investors in high tax brackets to tilt their portfolios towards lower dividend-yield stocks, creating a dividend–clientele effect. The resultant relationship between dividend yield and expected returns violates the simple CAPM.

A more interesting example is the issue of liquidity. A study of the effect of liquidity on asset returns[32] shows that once liquidity is accounted for, much of the puzzling effect of firm size on asset returns (see Chapter 12) is rendered insignificant, disposing of one anomaly. Thus, one view of the state of empirical research is that the anomalies we now observe are associated with some extensions of the CAPM. Observers of this school pin their hopes on improved specifications of tests of the CAPM.

Fourth and final, there is still a long way to go in accurate estimation of time-varying volatility (and the covariance structure) of asset returns, and in the incorporation of these estimates in the prediction of security returns.

Summary

1. Although the single-factor expected return-beta relationship has not yet been confirmed by scientific standards, its use is already commonplace in economic life.

2. Early tests of the single-factor CAPM rejected the SML, finding that non-systematic risk did explain average security returns.

---

[31] Robert H. Litzenberger and Krishna Ramaswamy, "The Effects of Dividends on Common Stock Prices, Tax Effects or Information Effects?" *Journal of Finance* vol. 37, no. 2 (1982).

[32] Y. Amihud and H. Mendelson, "Asset Pricing and the Bid-Ask Spread," *Journal of Financial Economics* 17 (1986), pp. 223–249.

3. Later tests controlling for the measurement error in beta found not only that non-systematic risk does not explain portfolio returns, but also that the estimated SML is too flat compared with what the CAPM would predict.

4. Tests using Canadian data found generally erratic results, with significant non-systematic risk and non-linear systematic risk as determinants of portfolio returns. Thin trading in the Canadian stock market can bias the tests.

5. Roll's critique implies that the usual CAPM test is a test only of the mean-variance efficiency of a prespecified market proxy and, therefore, that tests of the linearity of the expected return-beta relationship do not bear on the validity of the model.

6. Tests of the mean-variance efficiency of professionally managed portfolios against the benchmark of a prespecified market index conform with Roll's critique in that they provide evidence of the efficiency of the prespecific market index.

7. Empirical evidence suggests that most professionally managed portfolios in both Canada and the United States are outperformed by market indices, which lends weight to acceptance of the efficiency of those indices and, hence, the CAPM.

8. Factor analysis of security returns suggests that more than one factor may be necessary for a valid expected return-beta relationship. This technique, however, does not identify the economic factors behind the factor portfolios.

9. Work on prespecified economic factors is ongoing. Preliminary results suggest that factors such as unanticipated inflation do play a role in the expected return-beta relationship of security returns.

10. Volatility of stock returns is constantly changing. Empirical evidence on stock returns must account for this phenomenon. Contemporary researchers use the variations of the ARCH-M algorithm to estimate the level of volatility and its effect on mean returns.

Key terms

First-pass regression	Thin trading
Second-pass regression	Benchmark error
Measurement error	Factor portfolios

Selected readings

The key readings concerning tests of the CAPM are still:

Black, Fischer; Jensen, Michael C.; and Scholes, Myron. "The Capital Asset Pricing Model: Some Empirical Tests." In Michael C. Jensen (editor), *Studies in the Theory of Capital Markets*. New York: Praeger Publishers, 1972.

Fama, Eugene; and MacBeth, James. "Test of the Multiperiod Two Parameter Model." *Journal of Financial Economics,* March 1977.

Roll, Richard. "A Critique of the Asset Pricing Theory's Tests." *Journal of Financial Economics* 4 (1977).

Tests of the model using more recent econometric tools are:

Gibbons, Michael. "Multivariate Tests of Financial Models." *Journal of Financial Economics* 10 (1982).

Jobson, J. D.; and Korkie, R. M. "Potential Performance and Tests of Portfolio Efficiency." *Journal of Financial Economics* 10 (1982).

The factor analysis approach to testing multivariate models is treated in:

Roll, Richard; and Ross, Stephen. "An Empirical Investigation of the Arbitrage Pricing Theory." *Journal of Finance* 20 (1980).

Kryzanowski, L.; and To, M. C. "General Factor Models and the Structure of Security Returns." *Journal of Financial and Quantitative Analysis* 18, no. 1 (March 1982).

Lehman, Bruce; and Modest, David. "The Empirical Foundation of the Arbitrage Pricing Theory." *Journal of Financial Economics* 21 (1988).

A good paper that tests the APT with prespecified factors is:

Chen, Nai-Fu; Roll, Richard; and Ross, Stephen A. "Economic Forces and the Stock Market." *Journal of Business* 59 (1986).

Problems

The following annual excess rates of return were obtained for six portfolios and a market index portfolio:

		Portfolios					
Year	Market Index	A	B	C	D	E	F
1	26.4	38.1	32.6	23.6	15.2	11.9	38.0
2	17.9	21.9	20.2	17.6	14.6	11.8	19.8
3	13.4	13.4	15.1	13.0	13.2	9.0	14.4
4	10.6	9.8	10.4	11.4	12.1	11.0	9.7

1. Perform the first-pass regressions as did Black, Jensen, and Scholes, and tabulate the summary statistics as in Table 11.1.
2. Specify the hypotheses for a test of a second-pass regression for the SML.
3. Perform the second-pass SML regression by regressing the average excess return on each portfolio on its beta.
4. Summarize your test results and compare them to the reported results in the text.
5. Group the six portfolios into three, maximizing the dispersion of the betas of the three resultant portfolios. Repeat the test and explain any changes in the results.
6. Explain Roll's critique as it applies to the tests performed in problems 1–5.
7. Compare the mean variance efficiency of the six portfolios and the market index. Does the comparison support the CAPM?

Suppose that, in addition to the market factor that has been considered in problems 1–7, a second factor is considered. The values of this factor for years 1–4 were as follows:

Year	Factor Value (%)
1	13
2	17
3	−21
4	27

8. Perform the first-pass regressions as did Chen, Roll, and Ross and tabulate the relevant summary statistics. (Hint: use a multivariable regression as in the Lotus spreadsheet package. Estimate the betas of the six portfolios on the two factors.)

9. Specify the hypothesis for a test of a second-pass regression for the multi-dimensional SML.

10. Do the data suggest a two-factor economy?

11. Can you identify a factor portfolio for the second factor?

12. (CFA Examination, Level III, 1981) Richard Roll, in an article on using the capital asset pricing model (CAPM) to evaluate portfolio performance, indicated that it may not be possible to evaluate portfolio management ability if there is an error in the benchmark used.

   a. In evaluating portfolio performance, describe the general procedure, with emphasis on the benchmark employed.

   b. Explain what Roll meant by the benchmark error and identify the specific problem with this benchmark.

   c. Draw a graph showing how a portfolio that has been judged as superior relative to a ''measured'' security market line (SML) can be inferior relative to the ''true'' SML.

   d. You have been informed that a given portfolio manager has been evaluated as superior when compared to the Dow Jones Industrial Average, the S&P 500, and the NYSE Composite Index. Explain whether this consensus would make you feel more comfortable regarding the portfolio manager's true ability.

   e. While conceding the possible problem with benchmark errors as set forth by Roll, some people contend that this does not mean the CAPM is incorrect, but only that there is a measurement problem when implementing the theory. Others contend that because of benchmark errors the whole technique should be scrapped. Take and defend one of these positions.

PART IV

ACTIVE PORTFOLIO MANAGEMENT

C H A P T E R 1 2

Market Efficiency

In the 1950s, an early application of computers in economics was for analysis of economic time series. Business cycle theorists felt that tracing the evolution of several economic variables over time would clarify and predict the progress of the economy through boom and bust periods. A natural candidate for analysis was the behaviour of stock market prices over time. Assuming that stock prices reflect the prospects of the firm, recurrent patterns of peaks and troughs in economic performance ought to show up in those prices.

Maurice Kendall examined this proposition in 1953.[1] He found to his great surprise that he could identify *no* predictable patterns in stock prices. Prices seemed to evolve randomly. They were as likely to go up as they were to go down on any particular day, regardless of past performance. The data provided no way to predict price movements.

At first blush, Kendall's results were disturbing to some financial economists. They seemed to imply that the stock market is dominated by erratic market psychology, or "animal spirits"—that it follows no logical rules. In short, the results appeared to confirm the irrationality of the market. On further reflection, however, economists came to reverse their interpretation of Kendall's study.

It soon became apparent that random price movements indicated a well-functioning or efficient market, not an irrational one. In this chapter we will explore the reasoning behind what may seem a surprising conclusion. We show how competition among analysts leads naturally to market efficiency, and we examine the implications of the efficient market hypothesis for investment policy. We also consider empirical evidence that supports and contradicts the notion of market efficiency.

[1] Maurice Kendall, "The Analysis of Economic Time Series, Part I: Prices," *Journal of the Royal Statistical Society* 96 (1953).

12.1   *Random Walks and the Efficient Market Hypothesis*

Suppose Kendall had discovered that stock prices are predictable. What a gold mine this would have been for investors! If they could use Kendall's equations to predict stock prices, investors would reap unending profits simply by purchasing stocks that the computer model implied were about to increase in price and by selling those stocks about to fall in price.

A moment's reflection should be enough to convince yourself that this situation could not persist for long. For example, suppose that the model predicts with great confidence that XYZ stock price, currently at $100 per share, will rise dramatically in three days to $110. What would all investors with access to the model's prediction do today? Obviously, they would place a great wave of immediate buy orders to cash in on the prospective increase in stock price. No one holding XYZ, however, would be willing to sell. The net effect would be an *immediate* jump in the stock price to $110. The forecast of a future price increase will lead instead to an immediate price increase. In other words, the stock price will immediately reflect the "good news" implicit in the model's forecast.

This simple example illustrates why Kendall's attempt to find recurrent patterns in stock price movements was doomed to failure. A forecast about favourable *future* performance leads instead to favourable *current* performance, as market participants all try to get in on the action before the price jump.

More generally, one might say that any information that could be used to predict stock performance must already be reflected in stock prices. As soon as there is any information indicating that a stock is underpriced and therefore offers a profit opportunity, investors flock to buy the stock and immediately bid up its price to a fair level, where only ordinary rates of return can be expected. These "ordinary rates" are simply rates of return commensurate with the risk of the stock.

However, if prices are bid immediately to fair levels, given all available information, it must be that they increase or decrease only in response to new information. New information, by definition, must be unpredictable; if it could be predicted, then the prediction would be part of today's information. Thus stock prices that change in response to new (unpredictable) information also must move unpredictably.

This is the essence of the argument that stock prices should follow a **random walk,** that is, that price changes should be random and unpredictable.[2] Far from

---

[2] Actually, we are being a little loose with terminology here. Strictly speaking, we should characterize stock prices as following a submartingale, meaning that the expected change in the price can be positive, presumably as compensation for the time value of money and systematic risk. Moreover, the expected return may change over time as risk factors change. A random walk is more restrictive in that it constrains successive stock returns

a proof of market irrationality, randomly evolving stock prices are the necessary consequence of intelligent investors competing to discover relevant information on which to buy or sell stocks before the rest of the market becomes aware of that information. Indeed, if stock price movements were predictable, that would be damning evidence of stock market inefficiency, because the ability to predict prices would indicate that all available information was not already reflected in stock prices. Therefore, the notion that stocks already reflect all available information is referred to as the **efficient market hypothesis (EMH).**[3]

Competition as the Source of Efficiency

Why should we expect stock prices to reflect "all available information"? After all, if you are willing to spend time and money on gathering information, it might seem reasonable that you could turn up something that has been overlooked by the rest of the investment community. When information is costly to uncover and analyze, one would expect investment analysis calling for such expenditures to result in an increased expected return. This point has been stressed by Grossman and Stiglitz.[4] They argue that investors will have an incentive to spend time and resources to analyze and uncover new information only if such activity is likely to generate higher investment returns. Therefore, in market equilibrium it makes sense that efficient information gathering activity should be fruitful. Although we would not, therefore, go so far as to say that you absolutely cannot come up with new information, it still makes sense to consider the competition.

Consider an investment management fund currently managing a $5 billion portfolio. Suppose that the fund manager can devise a research program that could increase the portfolio rate of return by one tenth of one percent per year, a seemingly modest amount. This program would increase the dollar return to the portfolio by $5 billion $\times$ .001, or $5 million. Therefore, the fund would be willing to spend up to $5 million per year on research to increase stock returns by a mere one tenth of one percent per year. With such large rewards for such small increases in investment performance, it should not be surprising that professional portfolio managers are willing to spend large sums on industry analysts, computer support, and research effort, and therefore that price changes are, generally speaking, difficult to predict.

With so many well-backed analysts willing to spend considerable resources on research, there will not be many easy pickings in the market. Moreover, the

---

to be independent *and* identically distributed. Nevertheless, the term *random walk* is commonly used in the looser sense that price changes are essentially unpredictable. We will follow this convention.

[3] Market efficiency should not be confused with the idea of efficient portfolios introduced in Chapter 7. An informationally efficient *market* is one in which information is rapidly disseminated and reflected in prices. An efficient *portfolio* is one with the highest expected return for a given level of risk.

[4] Sanford J. Grossman and Joseph E. Stiglitz, "On the Impossibility of Informationally Efficient Markets," *American Economic Review* 70 (June 1980).

incremental rates of return on research activity are likely to be so small that only managers of the largest portfolios will find them worth pursuing.

Although it may not literally be true that "all" relevant information will be uncovered, it is virtually certain that there are many investigators hot on the trail of any leads that may improve investment performance. Competition among these many well-backed, highly paid, aggressive analysts ensures that, as a general rule, stock prices ought to reflect available information regarding their proper levels.

Versions of the Efficient Market Hypothesis

It is common to distinguish among three versions of the EMH: the weak, semistrong, and strong forms of the hypothesis. These versions differ by their notions of what is meant by the term "all available information."

The **weak-form** hypothesis asserts that stock prices already reflect all information that can be derived by examining market trading data such as the history of past prices, trading volume, or short interest. This version of the hypothesis implies that trend analysis is fruitless. Past stock price data are publicly available and virtually costless to obtain. The weak-form hypothesis holds that if such data ever conveyed reliable signals about future performance, all investors would have learned already to exploit the signals. Ultimately, the signals lose their value as they become widely known because a buy signal, for instance, would result in an immediate price increase.

The **semistrong-form** hypothesis states that all publicly available information regarding the prospects of a firm must be reflected already in the stock price. Such information includes, in addition to past prices, fundamental data on the firm's product line, quality of management, balance sheet composition, patents held, earning forecasts, and accounting practices. Again, if any investor has access to such information from publicly available sources, one would expect it to be reflected in stock prices.

Finally, the **strong-form** version of the efficient market hypothesis states that stock prices reflect all information relevant to the firm, even including information available only to company insiders. This version of the hypothesis is quite extreme. Few would argue with the notion that corporate officers have access to pertinent information long enough before public release to enable them to profit from trading on that information. Indeed, much of the activities of the provincial securities commissions is directed toward preventing insiders from profiting by exploiting their privileged situation. In Ontario, corporate officers, directors, and substantial owners are required to report trades in their firms' shares within 10 days of the end of the month in which the trade took place. These insiders, their relatives, and any associates who trade on information supplied by insiders are considered in violation of the law.

Defining insider trading is not always easy, however. After all, stock analysts are in the business of uncovering information not already widely known to market participants. As we saw in Chapter 3, the distinction between private and inside information is sometimes murky.

Concept Check	Question 1. If the weak form of the efficient market hypothesis is valid, must the strong form also hold? Conversely, does strong-form efficiency imply weak-form efficiency?

12.2 *Implications of the EMH for Investment Policy*

Technical Analysis

Technical analysis is essentially the search for recurring and predictable patterns in stock prices. Although technicians recognize the value of information that has to do with future economic prospects of the firm, they believe such information is not necessary for a successful trading strategy. Whatever the fundamental reason for a change in stock price, if the stock price responds slowly enough, the analyst will be able to identify a trend that can be exploited during the adjustment period. Technical analysis assumes a sluggish response of stock prices to fundamental supply and demand factors. This assumption is diametrically opposed to the notion of an efficient market.

Technical analysts are sometimes called *chartists* because they study records or charts of past stock prices, hoping to find patterns they can exploit to make a profit. As an example of technical analysis, consider the *relative strength* approach. The chartist compares stock performance over a recent period to performance of the market or other stocks in the same industry. A simple version of relative strength takes the ratio of the stock price to a market indicator such as the TSE 300 index. If the ratio increases over time, the stock is said to exhibit relative strength, because its price performance is better than that of the broad market. Such strength presumably may continue for a long enough period to offer profit opportunities. We will explore this technique as well as several other tools of technical analysis further in Chapter 20.

The efficient market hypothesis predicts that technical analysis is without merit. The past history of prices and trading volume is publicly available at minimal cost. Therefore, any information that was ever available from analyzing past prices has already been reflected in stock prices. As investors compete to exploit their common knowledge of a stock's price history, they necessarily drive stock prices to levels where expected rates of return are commensurate with risk. At those levels, stocks are neither bad nor good buys. They are just fairly priced, meaning one should not expect abnormal returns.

Despite these theoretical considerations, some technically oriented trading strategies would have generated abnormal profits in the past. We will consider these strategies, and technical analysis more generally, in Chapter 20.

Fundamental Analysis

Fundamental analysis uses earnings and dividend prospects of the firm, expectations of future interest rates, and risk evaluation of the firm to determine proper stock prices. Ultimately, it represents an attempt to determine the present discounted value of all the payments a stockholder will receive from each share of stock. If that value exceeds the stock price, the fundamental analyst would recommend purchasing the stock.

Fundamental analysts usually start with a study of past earnings and an examination of company balance sheets. They supplement this analysis with further detailed economic analysis, ordinarily including an evaluation of the quality of the firm's management, the firm's standing within its industry, and the prospects for the industry as a whole. The hope is to attain some insight into the future performance of the firm that is not yet recognized by the rest of the market. Chapters 18 and 19 provide a detailed discussion of the types of analyses that underlie fundamental analysis.

Once again, the efficient market hypothesis predicts that *most* fundamental analysis adds little value. If analysts rely on publicly available earnings and industry information, one analyst's evaluation of the firm's prospects is not likely to be significantly more accurate than another's. There are many well-informed, well-financed firms conducting such market research, and in the face of such competition, it will be difficult to uncover data not also available to other analysts. Only analysts with a unique insight will be rewarded.

Fundamental analysis is much more difficult than merely identifying well-run firms with good prospects. Discovery of good firms does an investor no good in and of itself if the rest of the market also knows those firms are good. If the knowledge is already public, the investor will be forced to pay a high price for those firms and will not realize a superior rate of return. The trick is not to identify firms that are good, but to find firms that are *better* than everyone else's estimate. Similarly, poorly run firms can be great bargains if they are not quite as bad as their stock prices suggest. This is why fundamental analysis is difficult. It is not enough to do a good analysis of a firm; you can make money only if your analysis is better than that of your competitors, because the market price is expected already to reflect all commonly available information.

Active vs. Passive Portfolio Management

By now it is apparent that casual efforts to pick stocks are not likely to pay off. Competition among investors ensures that any easily implemented stock evaluation technique will be used widely enough so that any insights derived will be reflected in stock prices. Only serious, time-consuming, and expensive techniques are likely to generate the *differential* insight necessary to generate trading profits.

Moreover, these techniques are economically feasible only for managers of large portfolios. If you have only $100,000 to invest, even a 1 percent per year improvement in performance generates only $1,000 per year, hardly enough to justify herculean efforts. The billion-dollar manager, however, reaps extra income of $10 million annually from the same 1 percent increment.

If small investors are not in a favoured position to conduct active portfolio management, what are their choices? The small investor probably is better off placing funds in a mutual fund. By pooling resources in this way, small investors can gain from economies of size.

More difficult decisions remain, though. Can investors be sure that even large mutual funds have the ability or resources to uncover mispriced stocks? Further, will any mispricing be sufficiently large to repay the costs entailed in active portfolio management?

Proponents of the efficient market hypothesis believe that active management is largely wasted effort and unlikely to justify the expenses incurred. Therefore, they advocate a **passive investment strategy** that makes no attempt to outsmart the market. A passive strategy aims only at establishing a well-diversified portfolio of securities without attempting to find under- or overvalued stocks. Passive management is usually characterized by a buy-and-hold strategy. Because the efficient market theory indicates that stock prices are at fair levels, given all available information, it makes no sense to buy and sell securities frequently, which generates large brokerage fees without increasing expected performance.

One common strategy for passive management is to create an **index fund.** Such a fund aims to mirror the performance of a broad-based index of stocks. For example, the Toronto Dominion Bank sponsors a mutual fund called the Green Line Canadian Index Fund, which holds stocks in direct proportion to their weight in the TSE 300 stock price index. The performance of the Green Line Canadian Index Fund therefore replicates the performance of the TSE 300. Investors in this fund obtain broad diversification with relatively low management fees. The fees can be kept to a minimum because there is no need to pay analysts for assessing stock prospects or to incur transaction costs from high portfolio turnover.

Indexing has grown in appeal considerably since 1970. Many institutional investors now hold indexed bond portfolios in addition to indexed stock portfolios. Such bond portfolios aim to replicate the features of well-known bond indices. Managers of large portfolios, such as those of pension funds, often create their own indexed funds rather than paying a mutual fund manager to do so for them. A hybrid strategy also is fairly common, where the fund maintains a *passive core,* which is an indexed position, and augments that position with one or more actively managed portfolios.

| Concept Check | Question 2. What would happen to market efficiency if *all* investors attempted to follow a passive strategy? |

The Role of Portfolio Management in an Efficient Market

If the market is efficient, why not throw darts at *The Globe and Mail*'s stock quotations page instead of trying rationally to choose a stock portfolio? This is a tempting conclusion to draw from the notion that security prices are fairly set, but it is far too facile. There is a role for rational portfolio management, even in perfectly efficient markets.

You have learned that a basic principle in portfolio selection is diversification. Even if all stocks are priced fairly, each still poses firm-specific risk that can be eliminated through diversification. Therefore, rational security selection, even in an efficient market, calls for the selection of a well-diversified portfolio providing the systematic risk level that the investor wants.

Rational investment policy also requires that tax considerations be reflected in security choice. High tax-bracket investors generally will not want the same securities that low-bracket investors find favourable. For instance, high-bracket investors might want to tilt their portfolios in the direction of capital gains as opposed to dividend or interest income, because the option to defer the realization of capital gain income is more valuable the higher the current tax bracket. Hence these investors may prefer stocks that yield lower dividends yet offer greater expected capital gain income. They also will be more attracted to investment opportunities for which returns are sensitive to tax benefits, such as real estate ventures.

A third argument for rational portfolio management relates to the particular risk profile of the investor. For example, an executive for an auto parts firm whose annual bonus depends on his firm's profits generally should not invest additional amounts in auto stocks. To the extent that his or her compensation already depends on the auto industry's well being, the executive is already overinvested in that industry and should not exacerbate the lack of diversification.

Investors of varying ages also might warrant different portfolio policies with regard to risk bearing. For example, older investors who are essentially living off savings might choose to avoid long-term bonds whose market values fluctuate dramatically with changes in interest rates (discussed in Part V). Because these investors are living off accumulated savings, they require conservation of principal. In contrast, younger investors might be more inclined toward long-term bonds. The steady flow of income over long periods of time that is locked in with long-term bonds can be more important than preservation of principal to those with long life expectancies.

In conclusion, there is a role for portfolio management even in an efficient market. Investors' optimal positions will vary according to factors such as age, tax bracket, risk aversion, and employment. The role of the portfolio manager in an efficient market is to tailor the portfolio to these needs, rather than to beat the market.

Book Values vs. Market Values

A somewhat common belief is the notion that book values are intrinsically more trustworthy than market values. Many firms, for example, are reluctant to issue additional stock when the market price of outstanding equity is lower than the book value of those shares. Issue under these circumstances is said to cause dilution of the original stockholder's ownership claim.

Perhaps this faith in book values derives from their stability. Although market values fluctuate daily, book values remain the same day in and day out. The stability of book values actually is a misleading virtue. Market prices fluctuate for a good reason: they move in response to new information about the economic prospects of the firm. The stability of book values in the face of new information is testament to their essential unreliability.

As an example of how book values can go wrong, imagine what would happen to the price of Imperial Oil stock if the price of oil were to double overnight. The stock price would increase for the very good reason that Imperial Oil's assets are now far more valuable. Yet the book value of Imperial Oil's assets would remain unchanged. Its stability in the face of changing conditions clearly shows it is not a guide to true value.

12.3 *Event Studies*

The notion of informationally efficient markets leads to a powerful research methodology. If security prices reflect all currently available information, then price changes must reflect new information. Therefore it seems that one should be able to measure the importance of an event of interest by examining price changes during the period in which the event occurs.

An **event study** describes a technique of empirical financial research that enables an observer to assess the impact of a particular event on a firm's stock price. A stock market analyst might want to study the impact of dividend changes on stock prices, for example. An event study would quantify the relationship between dividend changes and stock returns. Using the results of such a study together with a superior means of predicting dividend changes, the analyst could, in principle, earn superior trading profits.

Analyzing the impact of an announced change in dividends is more difficult than it might at first appear. On any particular day stock prices respond to a wide range of economic news such as updated forecasts for GNP, inflation rates, interest rates, or corporate profitability. Isolating the part of a stock price movement that is attributable to a dividend announcement is not a trivial exercise.

The statistical approach that researchers commonly use to measure the impact of a particular information release, such as the announcement of a dividend change, is a marriage of efficient market theory with the index model discussed in Chapter 9. We want to measure the unexpected return that results from an event. This is the difference between the actual stock return and the return that might have been expected given the performance of the market. This expected return can be calculated using the index model.

Recall that the index model holds that stock returns are determined by a market factor and a firm-specific factor. The stock return (in excess of the risk-free rate), R_t, during a given period, t, would be expressed mathematically as

$$R_t = a + bR_{Mt} + e_t \qquad (12.1)$$

where R_{Mt} is the market's excess rate of return during the period and e_t is the part of a security's return resulting from firm-specific events. The parameter b measures sensitivity to the market return, and a is the average excess rate of return the stock would realize in a period with a zero market excess return. Equation 12.1 therefore provides a decomposition of R_t into market and firm-specific factors. The firm-specific return may be interpreted as the unexpected return that results from the event.

Determination of the firm-specific return in a given period requires that we obtain an estimate of the term e_t. Therefore we rewrite equation 12.1:

$$e_t = R_t - (a + bR_{Mt}) \qquad (12.2)$$

Equation 12.2 has a simple interpretation: to determine the firm-specific component of a stock's return, subtract the return that the stock ordinarily would earn for a given level of market performance from the actual rate of return on the stock. The residual, e_t, is the stock's return over and above what one would predict based on broad market movements in that period, given the stock's sensitivity to the market.

For example, suppose that the analyst has estimated that $a = .5$ percent and $b = .8$. On a day that the market goes up by 1 percent, you would predict from equation 12.1 that the stock should rise by an expected value of .5 percent + .8 × 1 percent = 1.3 percent.[5] If the stock actually rises by 2 percent, the analyst would infer that firm-specific news that day caused an additional stock return of 2 percent − 1.3 percent = .7 percent. We sometimes refer to the term e_t in equation 12.2 as the **abnormal return**—the return beyond what would be predicted from market movements alone.

The general strategy in event studies is to estimate the abnormal return around the date that new information about a stock is released to the market and attribute the abnormal stock performance to the new information. The first step in the study is to estimate parameters a and b for each security in the study. These typically are calculated using index model regressions, as described in Chapter 9, in a period before that in which the event occurs. The prior period is used for estimation so that the impact of the event will not affect the estimates of the parameters. Next, the information release dates for each firm are recorded. For example, in a study of the impact of merger attempts on the stock prices of target firms, the **announcement date** is the date on which the public is informed that a merger is to be attempted. Finally, the abnormal returns of each firm surrounding the announcement date are computed, and the

---

[5] Actually, we should subtract the risk-free rate here to obtain excess returns, but the risk-free rate of return over one day is negligible.

statistical significance and magnitude of the typical abnormal return is assessed to determine the impact of the newly released information.

One concern that complicates event studies arises from *leakage* of information. Leakage occurs when information regarding a relevant event is released to a small group of investors before official public release. In this case, the stock price might start to increase (in the case of a "good news" announcement) days or weeks before the official announcement date. Any abnormal return on the announcement date is then a poor indicator of the total impact of the information release. A better indicator would be the **cumulative abnormal return,** which is simply the sum of all abnormal returns over the time period of interest. The cumulative abnormal return thus captures the total firm-specific stock movement for an entire period when the market might be responding to new information.

Figure 12.1 presents the results from a fairly typical event study. The authors of this study were interested in leakage of information before merger announcements and constructed a sample of 194 firms that were targets of a takeover attempt. In most takeovers, stockholders of the acquired firms sell their shares to the acquirer at substantial premiums over market value. Announcement of a takeover attempt is good news for shareholders of the target firm and therefore should cause stock prices to jump.

Figure 12.1 confirms the good-news nature of the announcements. On the announcement day, called day 0, the average cumulative abnormal return (CAR) for the sample of takeover candidates increases substantially, indicating a large and positive abnormal return on the announcement date. Notice that immediately after the announcement date the CAR no longer increases or decreases significantly. This is in accord with the efficient market hypothesis. Once the new information became public, the stock prices jumped almost immediately in response to the good news. With prices once again fairly set, reflecting the effect of the new information, further abnormal returns on any particular day are equally likely to be positive or negative. In fact, for a sample of many firms, the average abnormal return will be extremely close to zero, and thus the CAR will show neither upward nor downward drift. This is precisely the pattern shown in Figure 12.1.

The pattern of returns for the days preceding the public announcement date yields some interesting evidence about efficient markets and information leakage. If insider trading rules were perfectly obeyed and perfectly enforced, stock prices should show no abnormal returns on days before the public release of relevant news, because no special firm-specific information would be available to the market before public announcement. Instead, we should observe a clean jump in the stock price only on the announcement day. In fact, the prices of these takeover targets clearly start an upward drift 30 days before the public announcement. There are two possible interpretations of this pattern. One is that information is leaking to some market participants who then purchase the stocks before the public announcement. At least some abuse of insider trading rules is occurring.

Another interpretation is that in the days before a takeover attempt the public becomes suspicious of the attempt as it observes someone buying large

FIGURE 12.1

Cumulative abnormal returns before takeover attempts: target companies.

[From Arthur Keown and John Pinkerton, "Merger Announcements and Insider Trading Activity," *Journal of Finance* 36 (September 1981).]

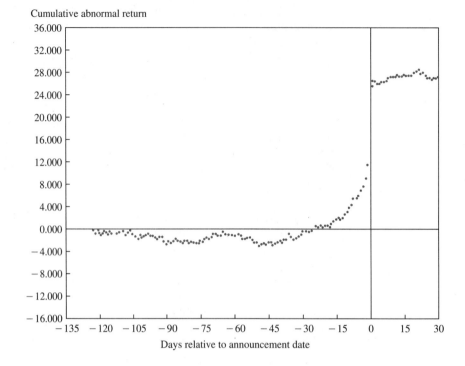

Cumulative abnormal return

blocks of stock. As acquisition intentions become more evident, the probability of an attempted merger is gradually revised upward so that we see a gradual increase in CARs. Although this interpretation is certainly a valid possibility, evidence of leakage appears almost universally in event studies, even in cases where the public's access to information is not gradual. It appears as if insider trading violations do occur.

Actually, securities commissions can take some comfort from patterns such as that in Figure 12.1. If insider trading rules were widely and flagrantly violated, we would expect to see abnormal returns earlier than they appear in these results. The CAR would turn positive as soon as acquiring firms decided on their takeover targets, because insiders would start trading immediately. By the time of the public announcement, the insiders would have bid up the stock prices of target firms to levels reflecting the merger attempt, and the abnormal returns on the actual public announcement date would be close to zero. The dramatic increase in the CAR that we see on the announcement date indicated that a good deal of these announcements are indeed news to the market and that stock prices did not already reflect complete knowledge about the takeovers. It would appear, therefore, that securities commission enforcement does have a substantial effect on restricting insider trading, even if some amount of it still persists.

Other studies, though, paint a less optimistic picture of securities trading regulation. For instance, the event studies methodology was applied by Kryzanowski[6] to investigate the effectiveness of trading suspensions in the three major Canadian stock exchanges (TSE, ME, and VSE) in arresting manipulative activities (mostly through dissemination of misleading information) on stock returns. The study identified stocks suspended from floor trading in these three exchanges over the period 1967–1973 because of alleged manipulation. It then examined the CARs in the weeks before and after the suspension event. These were significantly positive before, and significantly negative after, for up to 10 weeks around the suspension date. Hence, it appears that disseminating and exploiting misleading information about stocks is profitable. It also seems that investors were slow to react to the unfavourable information conveyed by the trading suspension.

Concept Check	Question 3. Suppose that we see negative abnormal returns (declining CARs) after an announcement date. Is this a violation of efficient markets?

12.4   *Are Markets Efficient?*

The Issues

Not surprisingly, the efficient market hypothesis does not exactly arouse enthusiasm in the community of professional portfolio managers. It implies that a great deal of the activity of portfolio managers—the search for undervalued securities—is at best wasted effort, and quite probably harmful to clients because it costs money and leads to imperfectly diversified portfolios. Consequently, the EMH has never been widely accepted among professionals, and debate continues today on the degree to which security analysis can improve investment performance. Before discussing empirical tests of the hypothesis, we want to note three factors that together imply that the debate probably never will be settled: the *magnitude issue,* the *selection bias issue,* and the *lucky event issue.*

[6] Lawrence Kryzanowski, ''Misinformation and Regulatory Actions in the Canadian Capital Markets: Some Empirical Evidence,'' *The Bell Journal of Economics* 9, no. 2 (Fall 1978), and ''The Efficacy of Trading Suspensions: A Regulatory Action Designed to Prevent the Exploitation of Monopoly Information,'' *Journal of Finance* 34 (December 1979).

The magnitude issue

Consider an investment manager overseeing a $2 billion portfolio. If she can improve performance by only one tenth of one percent per year, that effort will be worth .001 × $2 billion = $2 million annually. This manager clearly would be worth her salary! Yet can we, as observers, statistically measure her contribution? Probably not: a one tenth of one percent contribution would be swamped by the yearly volatility of the market. Remember, the annual standard deviation of the well-diversified TSE 300 index has been more than 16 percent per year. Against these fluctuations a small increase in performance would be hard to detect. Nevertheless, $2 million remains an extremely valuable improvement in performance.

All might agree that stock prices are very close to fair values, and that only managers of large portfolios can earn enough trading profits to make the exploitation of minor mispricing worth the effort. According to this view, the actions of intelligent investment managers are the driving force behind the constant evolution of market prices to fair levels. Rather than ask the qualitative question, "Are markets efficient?" we ought instead to ask a more quantitative question: "How efficient are markets?"

The selection bias issue

Suppose that you discover an investment scheme that could really make money. You have two choices: either publish your technique in *The Wall Street Journal* or *The Globe and Mail* to win fleeting fame, or keep your technique secret and use it to earn millions of dollars. Most investors would choose the latter option, which presents us with a conundrum. Only investors who find that an investment scheme cannot generate abnormal returns will be willing to report their findings to the whole world. Hence opponents of the efficient markets view of the world always can use evidence that various techniques do not provide investment rewards as proof that the techniques that do work simply are not being reported to the public. This is a problem in *selection bias:* the outcomes we are able to observe have been preselected in favour of failed attempts. Therefore we cannot fairly evaluate the true ability of portfolio managers to generate winning stock market strategies.

The lucky event issue

In virtually any month it seems we read an article about some investor or investment company with a fantastic investment performance over the recent past. Surely the superior records of such investors disprove the efficient market hypothesis.

Yet this conclusion is far from obvious. As an analogy to the investment game, consider a contest to flip the most number of heads out of 50 trials using a fair coin. The expected outcome for any person is, of course, 50 percent heads and 50 percent tails. If 10,000 people, however, compete in this contest, it would not be surprising if at least one or two contestants flipped more than 75 percent heads. In fact, elementary statistics tells us that the expected number

How to Guarantee a Successful Market Newsletter

Suppose you want to make your fortune publishing a market newsletter. You need first to convince potential subscribers that you have talent worth paying for. Ah, but what if you have no talent? The solution is simple: start eight newsletters.

In year one, let four of your newsletters predict an up-market and four a down-market. In year two, let half of the originally optimistic group of newsletters continue to predict an up-market and the other half a down-market. Do the same for the originally pessimistic group. Continue in this manner to obtain the above pattern of predictions (U = prediction of an up-market, D = prediction of a down-market).

After three years, no matter what has happened to the market, one of the newsletters would have had a perfect prediction record. This is because after three years there are $2^3 = 8$ outcomes for the market, and we have covered all eight possibilities with the eight newsletters. Now, we simply slough off the seven unsuccessful newsletters, and market the eighth newsletter based on its perfect track record. If we want to establish a newsletter with a perfect track record over a four-year period, we need $2^4 = 16$ newsletters. A five-year period requires 32 newsletters, and so on.

After the fact, the one newsletter that was always right will attract attention for your uncanny foresight and investors will rush to pay large fees for its advice. Your fortune is made, and you never even researched the market!

WARNING: This scheme is illegal! The point, however, is that with hundreds of market newsletters, you can find one that has stumbled onto an apparently remarkable string of successful predictions without any real degree of skill. After the fact, *someone's* prediction history can seem to imply great forecasting skill. This person is the one we will read about in *The Wall Street Journal* and *The Globe and Mail*; the others will be forgotten.

Newsletter Predictions

Year	1	2	3	4	5	6	7	8
1	U	U	U	U	D	D	D	D
2	U	U	D	D	U	U	D	D
3	U	D	U	D	U	D	U	D

of contestants flipping 75 percent or more heads would be two. It would be silly, though, to crown these people the "head-flipping champions of the world." Obviously, they are simply the contestants who happened to get lucky on the day of the event. (See the accompanying box.)

The analogy to efficient markets is clear. Under the hypothesis that any stock is fairly priced given all available information, any bet on a stock is simply a coin toss. There is equal likelihood of winning or losing the bet. However, if many investors using a variety of schemes make fair bets, statistically speaking, *some* of those investors will be lucky and win a great majority of the bets. For every big winner, there may be many big losers, but we never hear of these managers. The winners, though, turn up in the financial press as the latest stock market gurus; then they can make a fortune publishing market newsletters.

Our point is that after the fact there will have been at least one successful investment scheme. A doubter will call the results luck; the successful investor will call it skill. The proper test would be to see whether the successful investors can repeat their performance in another period, yet this approach is rarely taken.

With these caveats in mind, we turn now to some of the empirical tests of the efficient markets hypothesis.

Concept Check

> **Question 4.** The Fidelity Magellan Fund managed by Peter Lynch outperformed the S&P 500 in 11 of the 13 years 1976–1989. Is this performance sufficient to dissuade you from a belief in efficient markets? If not, would *any* performance record be sufficient to dissuade you?

12.5   *Tests of Predictability in Stock Market Returns*

Returns over Short Horizons

Early tests of efficient markets were tests of the weak form. Could speculators find trends in past prices that would enable them to earn abnormal profits? This is essentially a test of the efficacy of technical analysis.

The already-cited work of Kendall and of Roberts,[7] both of whom analyzed the possible existence of patterns in stock prices, suggest that such patterns are not to be found. Fama[8] later analyzed "runs" of stock prices to see whether the stock market exhibits "momentum" that can be exploited. (A run is a sequence of consecutive price increases or decreases.) For example, if the last three changes in daily stock prices were positive, could we be more confident that the next move also would be up?

Fama classified daily stock price movements of each of the 30 Dow Jones industrial stocks as positive, zero, or negative in order to test persistence of runs. He found that neither positive nor negative returns persisted to an extent that could contradict the efficient market hypothesis. Although there was some evidence of runs over very short time intervals (less than one day), the tendency for runs to persist was so slight that any attempt to exploit them would generate trading costs in excess of the expected abnormal returns.

Fama's results indicate weak serial correlation in stock market returns. *Serial correlation* refers to the tendency for stock returns to be related to past returns. Positive serial correlation means that positive returns tend to follow

---

[7] Harry Roberts, "Stock Market 'Patterns' and Financial Analysis: Methodological Suggestions," *Journal of Finance* 14 (March 1959).

[8] Eugene Fama, "The Behavior of Stock Market Prices," *Journal of Business* 38 (January 1965).

positive returns (a momentum type of property). Negative serial correlation means that positive returns tend to be followed by negative returns (a reversal or ''correction'' property).

Using more powerful statistical tools, recent tests have confirmed Fama's results. Both Conrad and Kaul[9] and Lo and MacKinlay[10] have examined weekly returns of NYSE stocks and found positive serial correlation over short horizons. However, as in Fama's study, the correlation coefficients of weekly returns tend to be fairly small, at least for large stocks for which price data are the most reliably up to date. Thus, while these studies demonstrate price trends over short periods, the evidence does not clearly suggest the existence of trading opportunities.

A more sophisticated version of trend analysis is a **filter rule.** A filter technique gives a rule for buying or selling a stock depending on past price movements. One rule, for example, might be: ''buy if the last two trades each resulted in a stock price increase.'' A more conventional one might be: ''buy a security if its price increased by 1 percent, and hold it until its price falls by more than 1 percent from the subsequent high.'' Alexander[11] and Fama and Blume[12] found that such filter rules generally could not generate trading profits.

The conclusion of the majority of weak-form tests using short-horizon returns is that the efficient market hypothesis is validated by stock market data. To be fair, however, one should note the criticism of efficient market sceptics, who argue that any filter rule or trend analysis that can be tested statistically is overly mechanical and cannot capture the finesse with which human investors can detect subtle but exploitable patterns in past prices.

Returns over Long Horizons

While studies of short-horizon returns have detected minor positive serial correlation in stock market prices, more recent tests[13,14] of long-horizon returns (i.e., returns over multiyear periods) have found suggestions of pronounced negative long-term serial correlation. The latter result has given rise to a ''fads hypothesis,'' which asserts that stock prices might overreact to relevant news. Such overreaction leads to positive serial correlation (momentum) over short time horizons. Subsequent correction of the overreaction leads to poor performance following good performance and vice versa. The corrections mean that a run of positive returns eventually will tend to be followed by negative returns,

---

[9] Jennifer Conrad and Gautam Kaul, ''Time-Variation in Expected Returns,'' *Journal of Business* 61 (October 1988), pp. 409–425.

[10] Andrew W. Lo and A. Craig MacKinlay, ''Stock Market Prices Do Not Follow Random Walks: Evidence from a Simple Specification Test,'' *Review of Financial Studies* 1 (1988), pp. 41–66.

[11] Sidney Alexander, ''Price Movements in Speculative Markets: Trends or Random Walks, No. 2,'' in Paul Cootner (editor), *The Random Character of Stock Market Prices* (Cambridge, Mass.: MIT Press, 1964).

[12] Eugene Fama and Marshall Blume, ''Filter Rules and Stock Market Trading Profits,'' *Journal of Business* 39 (Supplement) (January 1966).

[13] Eugene F. Fama and Kenneth R. French, ''Permanent and Temporary Components of Stock Prices,'' *Journal of Political Economy* 96 (April 1988), pp. 246–273.

[14] James Poterba and Lawrence Summers, ''**Mean Reversion in Stock Prices: Evidence and Implications,**'' *Journal of Financial Economics* 22 (October 1988), pp. 27–59.

leading to negative serial correlation over longer horizons. These episodes of apparent overshooting followed by correction give stock prices the appearance of fluctuating around their fair values, and suggest that market prices exhibit excessive volatility compared to intrinsic value.[15]

These long-horizon results are dramatic, but the studies offer far from conclusive evidence regarding efficient markets. First, the study results need not be interpreted as evidence for stock market fads. An alternative interpretation of these results holds that they indicate only that market risk premiums vary over time. The response of market prices to variation in the risk premium can lead one to incorrectly infer the presence of mean reversion and excess volatility in prices. For example, when the risk premium and the required return on the market rise, stock prices will fall. When the market then rises (on average) at this higher rate of return, the data convey the impression of a stock price recovery. The impression of overshooting and correction is in fact no more than a rational response of market prices to changes in discount rates.

Second, these studies suffer from statistical problems. Because they rely on returns measured over long time periods, these tests of necessity are based on few observations of long-horizon returns. Moreover, it appears that much of the statistical support for mean reversion in stock market prices derives from returns during the Great Depression. Other periods do not provide strong support for the fads hypothesis.[16]

Predictors of Broad Market Returns

Several studies have documented the ability of easily observed variables to predict market returns. For example, Fama and French[17] show that the return on the aggregate stock market tends to be higher when the dividend/price ratio, the dividend yield, is high. Campbell and Shiller[18] find that the earnings yield can predict market returns. Keim and Stambaugh[19] show that bond market data such as the spread between yields on high- and low-grade corporate bonds also help predict broad market returns.

Again, the interpretation of these results is difficult. On the one hand, they may imply that stock returns can be predicted, in violation of the efficient market hypothesis. More probably, however, these variables are proxying for

---

[15] The fads debate started as a controversy over excess volatility. See Robert J. Shiller, "Do Stock Prices Move too Much to Be Justified by Subsequent Changes in Dividends?" *American Economic Review* 71 (June 1981), pp. 421–436. However, it is now apparent that excess volatility and fads are essentially different ways of describing the same phenomenon. For a discussion of this issue, see John H. Cochrane, "Volatility Tests and Efficient Markets: A Review Essay," National Bureau of Economic Research Working Paper No. 3591, January 1991.

[16] Myung J. Kim, Charles R. Nelson, and Richard Startz, "Mean Reversion in Stock Prices? A Reappraisal of the Empirical Evidence," National Bureau of Economic Research Working Paper No. 2795, December 1988.

[17] Eugene F. Fama and Kenneth R. French, "Dividend Yields and Expected Stock Returns," *Journal of Financial Economics* 22 (October 1988), pp. 3–25.

[18] John Y. Campbell and Robert Shiller, "Stock Prices, Earnings and Expected Dividends," *Journal of Finance* 43 (July 1988), pp. 661–676.

[19] Donald B. Keim and Robert F. Stambaugh, "Predicting Returns in the Stock and Bond Markets," *Journal of Financial Economics* 17 (1986), pp. 357–390.

variation in the market risk premium. For example, given a level of dividends or earnings, stock prices will be lower and dividend and earnings yields will be higher when the risk premium (and therefore the expected market return) is larger. Thus, a high dividend or earnings yield will be associated with higher market returns. This does not indicate a violation of market efficiency—the predictability of market returns is due to predictability in the risk premium, not in risk-adjusted abnormal returns.

Fama and French[20] show that the yield spread between high- and low-grade bonds has greater predictive power for returns on low-grade bonds than for returns on high-grade bonds, and greater predictive power for stock returns than for bond returns, suggesting that the predictability in returns is in fact a risk premium rather than evidence of market inefficiency. Similarly, the fact that the dividend yield on stocks helps to predict bond market returns suggests that the yield captures a risk premium common to both markets rather than mispricing in the equity market.

12.6 *Portfolio Strategies and Market Anomalies*

Fundamental analysis calls on a much wider range of information to create portfolios than does technical analysis, and tests of the value of fundamental analysis are thus correspondingly more difficult to evaluate. They have, however, revealed a number of so-called anomalies, that is, evidence that seems inconsistent with the efficient market hypothesis. We will review several such anomalies in the following pages.

We must note before starting that one major problem with these tests is that most require risk adjustments to portfolio performance and most tests use the CAPM to make the risk adjustments. We know that, although beta seems to be a relevant descriptor of stock risk, the empirically measured quantitative trade-off between risk as measured by beta and expected return differs from the predictions of the CAPM. If we use the CAPM to adjust portfolio returns for risk, we run the risk that inappropriate adjustments will lead to the conclusion that various portfolio strategies can generate superior returns, when in fact it simply is the risk-adjustment procedure that has failed.

Another way to put this is to note that tests of risk-adjusted returns are *joint tests* of the efficient market hypothesis *and* the risk-adjustment procedure. If it appears that a portfolio strategy can generate superior returns, we must then choose between rejecting the EMH or rejecting the risk-adjustment technique. Usually, the risk-adjustment technique is based on more questionable assump-

[20] Eugene F. Fama and Kenneth R. French, ''Business Conditions and Expected Returns on Stocks and Bonds,'' *Journal of Financial Economics* 25 (November 1989), pp. 3–22.

tions than is the EMH; by opting to reject the procedure, we are left with no conclusion about market efficiency.

An example of this issue is the discovery by Basu[21] that portfolios of low price-earnings ratio stocks have higher average returns than do high P/E portfolios. The **P/E effect** holds up even if returns are adjusted for portfolio beta. Is this a confirmation that the market systematically misprices stocks according to P/E ratio? This would be an extremely surprising and, to us, disturbing conclusion, because analysis of P/E ratios is such a simple procedure. Although it may be possible to earn superior returns using hard work and much insight, it hardly seems possible that such a basic technique is enough to generate abnormal returns. One possible interpretation of these results is that the model of capital market equilibrium is at fault in that the returns are not properly adjusted for risk.

This makes sense, because if two firms have the same expected earnings, then the riskier stock will sell at a lower price and lower P/E ratio. Because of its higher risk, the low P/E stock also will have higher expected returns. Therefore, unless the CAPM beta fully adjusts for risk, P/E will act as a useful additional descriptor of risk, and will be associated with abnormal returns if the CAPM is used to establish benchmark performance.

The Small-Firm Effect

One of the most important anomalies with respect to the efficient market hypothesis is the so-called size, or **small-firm effect,** originally documented by Banz.[22] Banz found that both total and risk-adjusted rates of return tend to fall with increases in the relative size of the firm, as measured by the market value of the firm's outstanding equity. Dividing all NYSE stocks into five quintiles according to firm size, Banz found that the average annual return of firms in the smallest-size quintile was 19.8 percent greater than the average return of firms in the largest-size quintile.

This is a huge premium; imagine earning a premium of this size on a billion-dollar portfolio. Yet it is remarkable that following a simple (even simplistic) rule such as "invest in low capitalization stocks" should enable an investor to earn excess returns. After all, any investor can measure firm size at little cost. One would not expect such minimal effort to yield such large rewards.

Later studies (Keim,[23] Reinganum,[24] and Blume and Stambaugh[25]) showed that the small-firm effect occurs virtually entirely in January, in fact, in the first

---

[21] Sanjoy Basu, "The Investment Performance of Common Stocks in Relation to their Price-Earnings Ratios: A Test of the Efficient Market Hypothesis," *Journal of Finance* 32 (June 1977), pp. 663–682; and "The Relationship between Earnings Yield, Market Value, and Return for NYSE Common Stocks: Further Evidence," *Journal of Financial Economics* 12 (June 1983).

[22] Rolf Banz, "The Relationship between Return and Market Value of Common Stocks," *Journal of Financial Economics* 9 (March 1981).

[23] Donald B. Keim, "Size Related Anomalies and Stock Return Seasonality: Further Empirical Evidence," *Journal of Financial Economics* 12 (June 1983).

[24] Marc R. Reinganum, "The Anomalous Stock Market Behavior of Small Firms in January: Empirical Tests for Tax-Loss Effects," *Journal of Financial Economics* 12 (June 1983).

[25] Marshall E. Blume and Robert F. Stambaugh, "Biases in Computed Returns: An Application to the Size Effect," *Journal of Financial Economics*, 1983.

FIGURE 12.2

Average difference between daily excess returns (in percentages) of lowest-firm-size and highest-firm size deciles for each month, 1963–1979.

[Data from Donald B. Keim, "Size Related Anomalies and Stock Return Seasonality: Further Empirical Evidence," *Journal of Financial Economics* 12 (June 1983).]

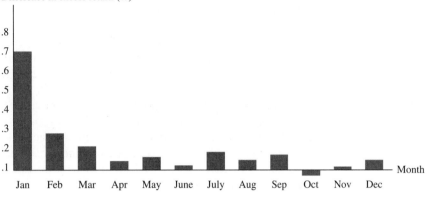

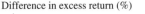

two weeks of January. The size effect is in fact a "small-firm-in-January" effect.

Figure 12.2 illustrates the January effect. Keim ranked firms in order of increasing size as measured by market value of equity and then divided them into 10 portfolios grouped by the size of each firm. In each month of the year, he calculated the difference in the average excess return of firms in the smallest-firm portfolio and largest-firm portfolio. The average monthly differences over the years 1963–1979 appear in Figure 12.2. January clearly stands out as an exceptional month for small firms, with an average small-firm premium of .714 percent per day.

The results for the first five trading days in January are even more compelling. The difference in excess returns between the smallest-firm and largest-firm portfolios for the first five trading days of the year are as follows:

Trading Day	Differential Excess Return (Average for 1963–1979)
1	3.20
2	1.68
3	1.25
4	1.14
5	0.89
TOTAL	**8.16**

The total differential return is an amazing 8.16 percent over only five trading days.

Some researchers believe that the January effect is tied to tax-loss selling at the end of the year. The hypothesis is that many people sell stocks that have declined in price during the previous months to realize their capital losses before the end of the tax year. Such investors do not put the proceeds from these sales back into the stock market until after the turn of the year. At that point the rush of demand for stock places an upward pressure on prices that results in the January effect. Indeed, Ritter[26] shows that the ratio of stock purchases to sales of individual investors reaches an annual low at the end of December and an annual high at the beginning of January. The January effect is said to show up most dramatically for the smallest firms because the small-firm group includes, as an empirical matter, stocks with the greatest variability of prices during the year. The group therefore includes a relatively large number of firms that have declined sufficiently to induce tax-loss selling.

From a theoretical standpoint, this theory has substantial flaws. First, if the positive January effect is a manifestation of buying pressure, it should be matched by a symmetric negative December effect when the tax-loss incentives induce selling pressure. Second, the predictable January effect flies in the face of efficient market theory. If investors who do not already hold these firms know that January will bring abnormal returns to the small-firm group, they should rush to purchase stock in December to capture those returns. This would push buying pressure from January to December. Rational investors should not "allow" such predictable abnormal January returns to persist. However, small firms outperform large ones in January in every year of Keim's study, 1963–1979.

Despite these theoretical objections, much empirical evidence supports the belief that the January effect is connected to tax-loss selling. For example, Reinganum found that, within size class, firms that had declined more severely in price had larger January returns. This pattern is illustrated in Figure 12.3. Reinganum divided firms into quartiles based on the extent to which stock prices had declined during the year. Big price declines would be expected to generate big January returns if these firms tend to be unloaded in December and enjoy demand pressure in January. The figure shows that the lowest quartile (biggest tax loss) portfolios within each size group show the greatest January effect.

A size effect continues to persist, however, even after adjusting for taxes. Small firms that rose in price continue to show abnormal January returns (Figure 12.3**B**), while large firms that declined in price show no special January effect. Hence, although taxes appear to be associated with the abnormal January returns (Figure 12.3**A** compared with **B, C** compared with **D**), size per se remains a factor in January (Figure 12.3**A** compared with **C, B** compared with **D**).

Several Canadian studies confirm the ambiguous nature of the conclusions drawn from the U.S. results. Berges, McConnell, and Schlarbaum[27] found a significant January effect in Canadian stock returns, and this effect was more pronounced for firms with smaller values. The abnormally high January returns, however, were present during the entire period covered by the study (1951–1980), even though Canada did not introduce a capital gains tax until

---

[26] Jay R. Ritter, "The Buying and Selling Behavior of Individual Investors at the Turn of the Year," *Journal of Finance* 43 (July 1988), pp. 701–717.

[27] Angel Berges, John J. McConnell, and Gary G. Schlarbaum, "The Turn-of-the-Year in Canada," *Journal of Finance* 39, no. 1 (March 1984)

FIGURE 12.3

Average daily returns in January for securities in the upper quartile and bottom quartile of the tax-loss selling distribution by market-value portfolio.

[From Marc R. Reinganum, "The Anomalous Stock Market Behavior of Small Firms in January: Empirical Tests for Tax-Loss Effects," *Journal of Financial Economics* 12 (June 1983).]

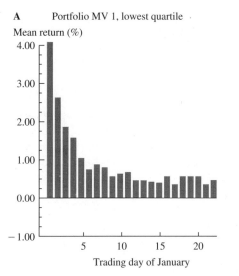

A   Portfolio MV 1, lowest quartile

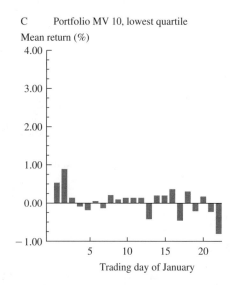

C   Portfolio MV 10, lowest quartile

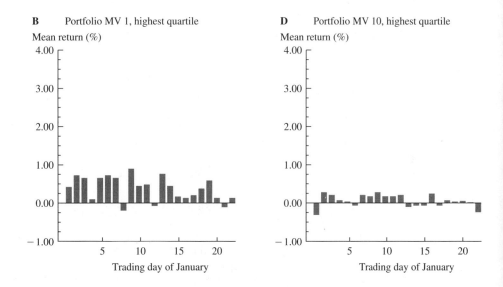

B   Portfolio MV 1, highest quartile

D   Portfolio MV 10, highest quartile

1973. Thus, there is little evidence that tax-loss selling caused the January effect. A subsequent study by Tinic, Barone-Adesi, and West[28] confirmed the fact that tax-loss selling could not be the sole cause for the high January returns. This last study, however, did find some influence of the tax laws on the seasonality of returns, since the introduction of capital gains taxation in 1972 was shown to have some influence for stocks listed solely in Canada.

---

[28] Seha M. Tinic, Giovanni Barone-Adesi, and Richard R. West, "Seasonality in Canadian Stock Prices: A Test of the 'Tax-Loss-Selling' Hypothesis," *Journal of Fininancial and Quantitative Analysis*, 21 no. 1 (March 1986).

The fundamental question is why market participants do not exploit the January effect and thereby ultimately eliminate it by bidding stock prices to appropriate levels. One possible explanation lies in segmentation of the market into two groups: institutional investors who invest primarily in large firms, and individual investors who invest disproportionately in smaller-sized firms. According to this view, managers of large institutional portfolios are the moving force behind efficient markets. It is professionals who seek out profit opportunities and bid prices to their appropriate levels. Institutional investors do not seem to buy at the small-size end of the market, perhaps because of limits on allowed portfolio positions, so the small-firm anomaly persists without the force of their participation.

Concept Check	Question 5. Does this market segmentation theory get the efficient market hypothesis off the hook, or are there still market mechanisms that, in theory, ought to act to eliminate the small firm anomaly?

The Neglected-Firm Effect

Arbel and Strebel[29] give another interpretation of the small-firm-in-January effect. Because small firms tend to be neglected by large institutional traders, information about such firms is less available. This information deficiency makes smaller firms riskier investments that command higher returns. "Brand-name" firms, after all, are subject to considerable monitoring from institutional investors that assures high-quality information, and presumably investors do not purchase "generic" stocks without the prospect of greater returns.

As evidence for the **neglected-firm effect,** Arbel[30] measures the information deficiency of firms using the coefficient of variation of analysts' forecasts of earnings. (The coefficient of variation is the ratio of standard deviation to mean and measures the dispersion of forecasts. It is a "noise-to-signal" ratio.) The correlation coefficient between the coefficient of variation and total return was .676, quite high, and statistically significant. In a related test Arbel divided firms into highly researched, moderately researched, and neglected groups based on the number of institutions holding the stock. Table 12.1 shows that the January effect was largest for the neglected firms.

Recent work by Amihud and Mendelson[31] on the effect of liquidity on stock returns might be related to both the small-firm and neglected-firm effects. They

---

[29] Avner Arbel and Paul J. Strebel, "Pay Attention to Neglected Firms," *Journal of Portfolio Management,* Winter 1983.

[30] Avner Arbel, "Generic Stocks: An Old Product in a New Package," *Journal of Portfolio Management,* Summer 1985.

[31] Yakov Amihud and Haim Mendelson, "Asset Pricing and the Bid-Ask Spread," *Journal of Financial Economics* 17 (December 1987), pp. 223–250; and "Liquidity, Asset Prices, and Financial Policy," *Financial Analysts Journal* 47 (November/December 1991), pp 56–66.

TABLE 12.1 January Effect by Degree of Neglect (1971–1980)

	Average January Return (%)	Average January Return Minus Average Return During Rest of Year (%)	Average January Return after Adjusting for Systematic Risk (%)
S&P 500 Companies			
Highly researched	2.48	1.63	−1.44
Moderately researched	4.95	4.19	1.69
Neglected	7.62	6.87	5.03
Non-S&P 500 Companies			
Neglected	11.32	10.72	7.71

From Avner Arbel, "Generic Stocks: An Old Product in a New Package," *Journal of Portfolio Management,* Summer 1985.

argue that investors will demand a rate of return premium to invest in less liquid stocks, which entail higher trading costs. Indeed, spreads for the least liquid stocks easily can be more than 5 percent of stock value. In accord with their hypothesis, Amihud and Mendelson show that these stocks show a strong tendency to exhibit abnormally high risk-adjusted rates of return. Because small and less-analyzed stocks as a rule are less liquid, the liquidity effect might be a partial explanation of their abnormal returns. However, this theory does not explain why the abnormal returns of small firms should be concentrated in January. In any case, exploiting these effects can be more difficult than it would appear.

Market-to-Book Ratios

Fama and French[32] show that a very powerful predictor of returns across securities is the ratio of the market value of the firm's equity to the book value of equity. They stratify firms into 10 groups according to market-to-book ratios and examine the average monthly rate of return of each of the 10 groups during the period July 1963–December 1990. The decile with the lowest market-to-book ratio had an average monthly return of 1.65 percent, while the highest-ratio decile averaged only 0.72 percent per month. Figure 12.4 shows the pattern of returns across deciles. The dramatic dependence of returns on market-to-book ratio is independent of beta, suggesting either that low market-to-book ratio firms are relatively underpriced, or that the market-to-book ratio is serving as a proxy for a risk factor that affects equilibrium-expected returns.

Reversals

We considered above the possibility that the aggregate stock market overreacts to economic news. Other studies have examined the overreaction hypothesis

---

[32] Eugene F. Fama and Kenneth R. French, "The Cross Section of Expected Stock Returns," manuscript, University of Chicago, 1991.

FIGURE 12.4

Average rate of return as a function of the ratio of market value to book value.

[From Eugene F. Fama and Kenneth R. French, "The Cross Section of Expected Stock Returns," manuscript, University of Chicago, 1991; Marc R. Reinganum, "The Anatomy of a Stock Market Winner," *Financial Analysts Journal*, March–April 1988, pp. 272–284.]

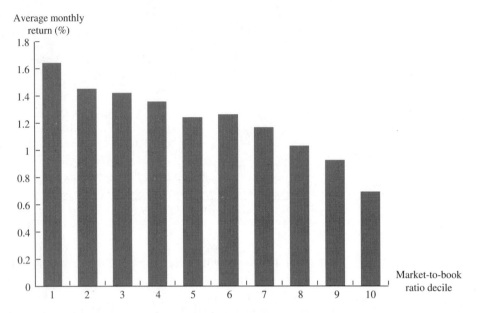

using returns on individual stocks. De Bondt and Thaler,[33] Jegadeesh,[34] and Lehman[35] all find strong tendencies for poorly performing stocks in one time period to experience sizable reversals over the subsequent period, while the best-performing stocks in a given period tend to follow with poor performance in the following period. This phenomenon, dubbed the **reversal effect,** is suggestive of overreaction of stock prices to relevant news.

It is hard to explain apparent overreaction in the cross-section of stocks by appealing to time-varying risk premiums. Moreover, these tendencies seem pronounced enough to be exploited profitably, and so present a strong challenge to market efficiency.

If the reversal effect really does offer abnormal profit opportunities, we would expect market participants to aggressively exploit it. Indeed, some funds are already attempting to exploit the reversal effect. After a short time, competition among traders should move prices to levels that reflect any information inherent in the reversal effect. At this point the profit opportunity will disappear.

In this view, market efficiency is a dynamic process. Profit opportunities occasionally arise as market participants devise as-yet unexploited trading strategies. However, as those opportunities are exploited, prices begin to reflect the trading activity and the trading rule becomes progressively less valu-

---

[33] Werner F. M. DeBondt and Richard Thaler, "Does the Stock Market Overreact?" *Journal of Finance* 40 (1985), pp. 793–805.

[34] Narasimhan Jegadeesh, "Evidence of Predictable Behavior of Security Returns," *Journal of Finance* 45 (September 1990), pp. 881–898.

[35] Bruce Lehman, "Fads, Martingales and Market Efficiency," *Quarterly Journal of Economics* 105 (February 1990), pp. 1–28.

able. Therefore, the true test of market efficiency will be to see whether the reversal effect persists now that market participants are aware of it.

The Day-of-the-Week Effect

The small-firm-in-January effect is one example of seasonality in stock market returns, a recurrent pattern of turn-of-the-year abnormal returns. Another recurrent pattern, and in several ways an even odder one, is the **weekend effect,** documented in the United States by French[36] and Gibbons and Hess,[37] and in Canada by Hindmarch et al.,[38] Jaffe and Westerfield,[39] Condoyanni et al.,[40] and Chamberlain et al.[41] These researchers studied the pattern of stock returns from close of trading on Friday afternoon to close on Monday, to determine whether the three-day return spanning the weekend would be three times the typical return on a weekday. This was to be a test of whether the market operates on calendar time or trading time.

Much to their surprise, the typical Friday-to-Monday return was not larger than that of other weekdays—in fact, it was negative! Following is the mean return of the TSE 300 portfolio for each day of the week over the period March 1978–December 1985. The Monday return is based on closing price Friday to closing price Monday, the Tuesday return is based on Monday closing to Tuesday closing, and so on:

	Monday	Tuesday	Wednesday	Thursday	Friday
Mean return	−.1512%	.0745%	.1251%	.1121%	.1378%

The negative Monday effect is extremely large. On an annualized basis, assuming 250 trading days a year, the return is −37.8 percent (−.1512 percent × 250). Chamberlain, Cheung, and Kwan report that this effect was not confined to Monday's opening trading period, but tended to persist throughout the entire day. It also tended to spill over onto Tuesday, especially whenever Monday was a stock market holiday, suggesting that the Monday effect was really a "first trading day" effect, at least in Canada. By contrast, the U.S. weekend effect does not extend beyond Monday's opening trading period.

The weekend effect poses a problem for efficient market theorists. In frictionless markets, one would expect this recurrent pattern to be "arbitraged away." Specifically, investors would sell stocks short late Friday afternoon, and repurchase them on Monday afternoon at an expected lower price, thereby

---

[36] Kenneth French, "Stock Returns and the Weekend Effect," *Journal of Financial Economics* 8 (March 1980).

[37] Michael Gibbons and Patrick Hess, "Day-of-the-Week Effects and Asset Returns," *Journal of Business* 54 (October 1981).

[38] S. Hindmarch, D. Jentsch, and D. Drew, "A Note on Canadian Stock Returns and the Weekend Effect," *Journal of Business Administration* 14 (1984).

[39] J. Jaffe and R. Westerfield, "The Weekend Effect in Common Stock Returns: The International Evidence," *Journal of Finance* 40 (June 1985).

[40] L. Condoyanni, J. O'Hanlon, and C. W. R. Ward, "Day-of-the-Week Effects on Stock Returns: International Evidence," *Journal of Business Finance and Accounting,* Summer 1987.

[41] T. W. Chamberlain, C. S. Cheung, and C. C. Y. Kwan, "Day-of-the-Week Patterns in Stock Returns: The Canadian Evidence," *Canadian Journal of Administrative Sciences* 5, no. 4 (December 1988).

capturing an abnormal return. The selling on Friday would drive prices down on Friday to a fair level in the sense that the Friday–Monday return would be expected to be positive and commensurate with the risk of the stock market.

In practice of course, such arbitrage activity would not pay. The magnitude of the weekend effect is not nearly large enough to offset the transaction costs involved in short selling and repurchasing the stocks. Hence, market frictions prevent the direct elimination of the weekend effect. Nevertheless, the effect should not be observed in efficient markets, even in the absence of direct arbitrage. If there is a predictable weekend effect, one would expect investors to shy away from purchases on Fridays, delaying them until Monday instead. Conversely, sales of stock originally scheduled for Monday optimally would be pushed up to the preceding Friday. This reshuffling of buying and selling would be enough to increase buy pressure relative to sell pressure on Mondays to the point where the weekend effect would be dissipated. The persistence of the effect seems to indicate that investors have not paid attention to the predictable price pattern.

One explanation of this anomaly is that firms may tend to release bad news to the public over the weekend, while the financial markets are closed. This is an appealing but problematic interpretation. If investors come to expect weekends to bring bad news, they will treat any weekend that passes without such news as a relief, and prices will, in response, increase on Monday morning. Averaging over the "bad-news" and "relief" weekends, one should expect mean Friday–Monday returns to be fair, and certainly not negative.

Inside Information

It would not be surprising if insiders were able to make superior profits trading in their firm's stock. The ability of insiders to trade profitably in their own stock has been documented in U.S. studies by Jaffee,[42] Seyhun,[43] Givoly and Palmon,[44] and others. Jaffee's was one of the earlier studies that documented the tendency for stock prices to rise after insiders intensively bought shares and to fall after intensive insider sales.

Similar results were also found in Canadian studies by Masse, Hanrahan, and Kushner[45] and Eckbo,[46] who examined the daily returns to companies targeted for mergers or acquisitions prior to the date of public announcement. They found evidence of significant abnormally high returns, which is consistent with the use of inside information to trade profitably in the market.

To enhance fairness, securities commissions require all insiders to register the changes in their holdings of company stock within 10 days of the end of the

---

[42] Jeffrey F. Jaffee, "Special Information and Insider Trading," *Journal of Business* 47 (July 1974).

[43] H. Nejat Seyhun, "Insiders' Profits, Costs of Trading and Market Efficiency," *Journal of Financial Economics* 16 (1986).

[44] Dan Givoly and Dan Palmon, "Insider Trading and Exploitation of Inside Information: Some Empirical Evidence," *Journal of Business* 58 (1985).

[45] Isidore Masse, Robert Hanrahan, and Joseph Kushner, "Returns to Insider Trading: The Canadian Evidence," *Canadian Journal of Administrative Sciences* 5, no. 3 (September 1988).

[46] B. Espen Eckbo, "Mergers and the Market for Corporate Control: The Canadian Evidence," *Canadian Journal of Economics* 19, no. 2 (May 1986).

month in which the changes took place. Once the insiders file the required statements, the knowledge of their trades becomes public information. At that point, if markets are efficient, fully and immediately processing the released information, an investor should no longer be able to profit from following the pattern of those trades.

Surprisingly, early studies like Jaffee's seemed to indicate that following **insider transactions**—buying after insider purchases were reported and selling after insider sales—could offer substantial abnormal returns to an outside investor. This would be a clear violation of market efficiency, as the insider trading data are publicly available. However, a more recent and extensive U.S. study by Seyhun, which carefully tracked the public release dates of the insider trading information, found that following insider transactions would be to no avail. Although there is some tendency for stock prices to increase even after public reports of insider buying, the abnormal returns are not of sufficient magnitude to overcome transaction costs.

The Canadian evidence yields similarly mixed conclusions. Baesel and Stein[47] investigated the performance of two insider groups on the TSE, ordinary insiders and insiders who were bank directors. Although both groups earned significant positive abnormal returns, the second group's such returns were higher. Fowler and Rorke[48] used monthly returns of firms listed on the TSE during the period 1967–1977 to investigate whether an outsider could realize abnormal returns by following insider transactions after they were publicly reported. They found that abnormal returns following "intense" buying or selling activity by insiders persisted for at least 12 months after the official release of the insider trading information. Moreover, the size of the returns indicated that trading profits could have been realized even after paying reasonable transactions costs. This seems to indicate a clear violation of market efficiency for the TSE, at least for the period covered by the study.

On the other hand, a study by Heinkel and Kraus[49] on the Vancouver Stock Exchange (VSE) found rather weak evidence of the ability of insider trading to generate abnormal returns for insiders. The sample of firms that Heinkel and Kraus examined over the period June 1979–June 1, 1981, was rather atypical. It consisted of small resource companies listed on the VSE, for which insiders are by far the largest shareholders. Thus, although the results could be interpreted as evidence of market efficiency of the strong form, they cannot be extrapolated to other situations.

The Value Line Enigma

The Value Line Investor Survey is an investment advisory service that ranks securities on a timeliness scale of one (best buy) to five (sell). Ranks are based

---

[47] Jerome Baesel and Garry Stein, "The Value of Information Inferences from the Profitability of Insider Trading," *Journal of Financial and Quantitative Analysis* 14 (September 1979).

[48] David J Fowler and C. Harvey Rorke, "Insider Trading Profits on the Toronto Stock Exchange, 1967–1977," *Canadian Journal of Administrative Sciences* 5, no. 1 (March 1988).

[49] Robert Heinkel and Alan Kraus, "The Effect of Insider Trading on Average Rates of Return," *Canadian Journal of Economics* 20, no. 3 (August 1987).

on relative earnings and price performance across securities, price momentum, quarterly earnings momentum, and a measure of unexpected earnings in the most recent quarter.

Several studies have examined the predictive value of the Value Line recommendations. Black[50] found that portfolio 1 (the "buy" portfolio) had a risk-adjusted excess rate of return of 10 percent, while portfolio 5 (the "sell" portfolio) had an abnormal return of −10 percent. These results imply a fantastic potential value to the Value Line forecasts. Copeland and Mayers[51] performed a similar study using a more sophisticated risk-adjustment technique, and found that the difference in the risk-adjusted performance of portfolios 1 and 5 was much smaller; portfolio 1 earned an abnormal six-month rate of return of 1.52 percent, while portfolio 5 earned an abnormal return of −2.97 percent. Even this smaller difference, however, seems to be a substantial deviation from the prediction of the efficient market hypothesis.

Given Value Line's apparent success in predicting stock performance, we would expect that changes in Value Line's timeliness rankings would result in abnormal returns for affected stocks. This seems to be the case. Stickel[52] shows that Value Line rerankings generally are followed by abnormal stock returns in the expected direction. Interestingly enough, smaller firms tend to respond with greater sensitivity to rerankings. This pattern is consistent with the neglected-firm effect in that the information contained in a reranking carries greater weight for firms that are less intensively monitored.

The Market Crash of October 1987

The market crash of October 1987 seems to be a glaring counterexample to the efficient market hypothesis. If prices reflect market fundamentals, then defenders of the EMH must look for news on the nineteenth of October consistent with the 23 percent one-day decline in stock prices. Yet no events of such importance seem to have transpired on that date. The fantastic price swing is hard to reconcile with market fundamentals. The accompanying box presents a discussion of the crash in the context of efficient market theory.

Concept Check

> Question 6. Some say that continued worry concerning the U.S. trade deficit brought down the market on October 19. Is this explanation consistent with the EMH?

---

[50] Fischer Black, "Yes, Virginia, There is Hope: Tests of the Value Line Ranking System," Graduate School of Business, University of Chicago, 1971.

[51] Thomas E. Copeland and David Mayers, "The Value Line Enigma (1965–1978): A Case Study of Performance Evaluation Issues," *Journal of Financial Economics* 11 (November 1982).

[52] Scott E. Stickel, "The Effect of Value Line Investment Survey Rank Changes on Common Stock Prices," *Journal of Financial Economics* 14 (1985).

The "Efficient Market" Was a Good Idea—and Then Came the Crash

It Launched a Revolution, but the Theory Can't Explain Why Investors Panicked on October 19

The October 19 stock market collapse crushed more than $500 billion in investor wealth. It also struck a blow against one of the most powerful ideas in finance—the efficient market theory (EMT). "It was the nail in the coffin of the theory," says economist Bruce Greenwald, a staff member on the Brady commission, which studied the crash.

That theory bucked the popular view that stocks move on the latest fad or the speculative fever of the crowd. Well-informed investors could make a bundle, went the conventional wisdom. Not so, says the EMT. The stock market is an efficient information processing machine. Investors act rationally, and stock prices reflect whatever information people have about the fundamentals, such as present and future earnings. Stock prices change only on fresh news—and that doesn't include crowd psychology.

Herd Instinct

The theory had few believers back in the early 1960s. But the EMT ended up launching a market revolution. Finance professors and math whizzes built careers on Wall Street exploiting its insights. For instance, the theory says that you can't consistently outperform the market averages, since only unexpected news moves prices. Did the EMT catch on with big money? You bet. Many pension-fund sponsors turned their backs on money managers who claimed that they could beat the market and bought some $175 billion in index funds that track the market.

Then came Bloody Monday. Efficient market theory is useless in explaining the biggest stock market calamity in 58 years. What new information jarred investors into slashing their estimate of the value of Corporate America's assets by some 23 percent in the 6½ hours the New York Stock Exchange was open? Hardly enough news came out that day, or over the weekend, to account for the plunge.

Indeed, a survey by Yale University's Robert Shiller of nearly 1,000 big and small investors showed that the reason for selling was not a change in the fundamentals. Rather, it was the declines that took place in the market itself the Thursday and Friday before, as well as the sharp sell-off on the morning of October 19. "Lots of nervous people came to believe the price drops themselves signaled a crash, and everyone tried to be the first out the door," says Shiller. Investors panicked because the market was falling like a stone. There was no rationality, only herd instinct.

The rout of the efficient markets theory holds important implications not only for investors but also for the idea that the market is the best possible way to channel capital to its most productive uses. According to this belief, investors allowed to choose in a competitive market will funnel money to those companies with the best prospects. It's no coincidence that the EMT was mainly developed at the University of Chicago, a laissez-faire bastion. Moreover, the so-called derivative securities—stock index futures and options—were conceived in the Windy City and traded on the Chicago exchanges largely because of the impetus from the university's free market theorists, who argued that the new instruments would make the stock market even more efficient.

Reason to Believe

But if crowd psychology, not rationality, rules stock prices, investors and policymakers might be getting the wrong signals from the market. Money might flow to unproductive businesses, such as junk-bond-financed leveraged buyouts. Meanwhile, companies spending a lot on future products and cultivating markets could starve for cheap capital.

(Continued)

Even Chicago's pioneering efficient-market theorist Eugene Fama admits the EMT is "a matter of belief" to him. If prices are not being set the way the theory assumes, then the free market system is not allocating resources efficiently, says Fema.

Signs that the EMT doesn't work began to show up on the stock market well before Bloody Monday. The crash is only the latest, most-dramatic, instance of the theory's failure. A cottage industry has sprung up in academe documenting market "anomalies" inconsistent with the EMT. Take the "January effect." Small-capitalization stocks repeatedly show large returns during the first five trading days of the year. According to the EMT, the January effect shouldn't persist. Sophisticated investors, anticipating the easy gains, should have bid up prices well before the beginning of the year.

Other economists believe they have found further instances of investor irrationality. A study by economists Richard Thaler and Werner De Bondt shows that a stock portfolio made up of the 35 worst-performing NYSE issues consistently outperformed the market by an average of 19.6 percent over a period of three years. The reason, explains Thaler, is that investors overreacted to the bad news and drove the dogs way down—far below what they were truly worth. Stocks again and again overshoot the fundamentals, a finding that doesn't square with the EMT.

Never Say Die

The EMT is far from dead, however. Yale University's Stephen Ross challenges the view that there was little news to account for the crash. He says volatility rose as investors became nervous about the market weeks before October 19. Under the circumstances, "only a small change in news can start an avalanche," says Ross.

The market should have been able to hold back the avalanche, says the EMT theorist, but the exchanges simply broke down. The Brady report pointed out that many NYSE specialists buckled under pressure on October 19 and 20 and were selling, not buying. At the same time, the Big Board computers could not handle the volume. The institutions that make up the market failed, not the EMT.

Still, there is evidence that the stock market is not as competitive as the efficient market theorists believe. The Brady report said that a handful of mutual and pension funds unleashed enormous selling pressure at the opening of the market on Bloody Monday, swamping the system. For the EMT to work, no one seller should be able to influence the market very much. More telling, four months after the crash, the Dow Jones industrial average is still some 800 points below its peak in August. What changes in U.S. business prospects can account for such a downgrading?

The arguments over the EMT are likely to continue. But the theory's apparent failure to explain the greatest stock market crash in history may suggest to policymakers and to the exchanges that the "market" is not all that it was cracked up to be.

Mutual Fund Performance

We have documented some of the apparent chinks in the armour of efficient market proponents. Ultimately, however, the issue of market efficiency boils down to whether skilled investors can make consistent abnormal trading profits. The best test is simply to look at the performance of market professionals to see if that performance is superior to that of a passive index fund that buys and holds the market.

Such a test was carried out in Canada by Lawson,[53] who examined filter rules for buying or selling a stock depending on the trading activity of stock market professionals. He constructed a data base of all transactions on the TSE over a 30-month period, which identified trades carried out by professional traders. The filter rules prescribed buying or selling a stock when professionals showed a corresponding "unusually high" buying or selling activity. Lawson found that his filters could not generate any trading profits, and were in fact inferior to a strategy of buying and holding the stock.

Casual evidence also does not support claims that professionally managed portfolios can beat the market. In most of the past 15 years, the S&P 500 has outperformed the median professionally managed U.S. fund. In the decade ended in 1979, about 47 percent of equity fund managers outperformed the S&P 500. In the 1980s, only 37 percent beat the market.[54] Similar results were reported in the survey of the Canadian mutual funds studies in the previous chapter.

Of course, one might argue that there are good managers and bad managers, and that the good managers can, in fact, consistently outperform the index. The real test of this notion is to see whether managers with good performance in a given year can repeat that performance in a following year. In other words, is the abnormal performance due to luck or skill? Jensen[55] performed such a test using 10 years of data on 115 mutual funds, a total of 1,150 annual observations.

Jensen first risk-adjusted all returns using the CAPM to obtain portfolio alphas, or returns in excess of required return given risk. Then he tested to see whether managers with positive alphas tended to repeat their performance in later years. If markets are efficient, and abnormal performance is due solely to the luck of the draw, the probability of following superior performance in a given year with superior performance the next year should be 50 percent: each year's abnormal return is essentially like the toss of a fair coin. This is precisely the pattern that Jensen found. Table 12.2 is reproduced from Jensen's study.

In row 1, we see that 574 positive alphas were observed out of the 1,150 observations, virtually 50 percent on the nose. Of these 574 positive alphas, 50.4 percent were followed by positive alphas. So far, it appears that obtaining a positive alpha is pure luck, like a coin toss. Row 2 shows that 312 cases of two consecutive positive alphas were observed. Of these observations, 52 percent were followed by yet another positive alpha. Continuing, we see that 53.4 percent of three-in-a-row were followed by a fourth, and 55.8 percent of four-in-a-row were followed by a fifth.

[53] William M. Lawson, "Market Efficiency: The Trading of Professionals on the Toronto Stock Exchange," *Journal of Business Administration* 12, no. 1 (Fall 1980).

[54] John C. Bogle, "Investing in the 1990s: Remembrance of Things Past, and Things Yet to Come," *Journal of Portfolio Management*, Spring 1991.

[55] Michael C. Jensen, "Risk, the Pricing of Capital Assets, and the Evaluation of Investment Portfolios," *Journal of Business* 42 (April 1969).

TABLE 12.2 Mutual Fund Performance

Number of Consecutive Positive Alphas So Far	Number of Observations	Cases in Which the Next Alpha Is Positive (%)
1	574	50.4
2	312	52.0
3	161	53.4
4	79	55.8
5	41	46.4
6	17	35.3

From Michael C. Jensen, ''Risk, the Pricing of Capital Assets, and the Evaluation of Investment Portfolios,'' *Journal of Business 42* (April 1969), published by The University of Chicago.

The results so far are intriguing. They seem to suggest that most positive alphas are indeed obtained through luck. However, as more and more stringent filters are applied, the remaining managers show greater tendency to follow good performance with more good performance. This might suggest that there are a few, rare, superior managers who can consistently beat the market. However, at this point, the pattern collapses. Only 46.4 percent of the five-in-a-row group repeats the superior performance. Yet the sample size is too small to make statistically precise inferences about the population of managers.

The ultimate interpretation of these results is thus to some extent a matter of faith. However, it seems clear that it is not wise to invest with an actively managed fund chosen at random. The average alpha of all funds was slightly negative even *before* subtracting all the costs of management.

In a more recent study, Dunn and Theisen[56] examined the performance of several institutional portfolios over the period 1973–1982. Dividing the funds into four quarters, based on total investment return for different subperiods, they posed the following question: ''Do funds that performed well in one period tend to perform well in subsequent periods?''

The answer seems to be no, suggesting that superior performance in any period is more a matter of luck than underlying consistent ability. For example, Table 12.3 shows investment results for a base period 1973–1977 and subsequent period 1978–1982. The first row shows the relative performance of the first-quartile managers from the 1973–1977 base period in the subsequent 1978–1982 period. Only 26 percent of those managers repeated their first-quartile performance; another 26 percent dropped to the *bottom* quartile in the latter period. Second quartile performers in the base period also fared poorly in the subsequent period; only 10 percent ended up in the top quartile, and 25 percent continued in the second quartile. Thus we cannot reject the hypothesis that relative rank is independent from one period to the next.

---

[56] Patricia Dunn and Rolf D. Theisen, ''How Consistently Do Active Managers Win?'' *Journal of Portfolio Management* 9 (Summer 1983).

TABLE 12.3 Quartile Comparison of Investment Results

Base Quartile Period	Subsequent Period Quartile			
	Q1	Q2	Q3	Q4
Q1	26%	37%	11%	26%
Q2	10	25	25	40
Q3	25	30	40	10
Q4	30	15	35	20

From Patricia Dunn and Rolf D. Theisen, ''How Consistently Do Active Managers Win?'' *Journal of Portfolio Management* 9 (Summer 1983).

More recent studies of the performance of mutual funds have reached mixed conclusions. Ippolito[57] examines returns of 143 mutual funds over the 1965–1984 period, and finds that returns net of expenses and fees (but not net of loads) provided an average alpha across funds of 0.83 percent. On the other hand, the performance of most funds was not statistically significantly different from that of a purely passive strategy. The alphas of 127 funds were statistically indistinguishable from zero. Four funds had significantly negative alphas and 12 had significantly positive alphas.

In contrast, Brinson, Hood, and Beebower[58] found that portfolio returns of 91 pension plans were harmed by attempts at active management. They compared actual returns to a benchmark computed by assuming plan managers had held indexed portfolios for the bond and stock sectors of their portfolios and had maintained constant weights across market sectors. They concluded that deviations from indexed positions within each market reduced average returns by .36 percent, and that attempts to time the relative performance of fixed income versus equity markets reduced average returns by .66 percent.

A recent Canadian study by Jog[59] confirms these findings for a sample of Canadian pension fund managers. The study used several different performance measures that included the alphas, and four different benchmark portfolios, one of which was the TSE 300 index. The results, however, were virtually identical for all measures and benchmark portfolios: managers of pension funds included in the sample failed to exhibit any significant or consistent ability to achieve superior risk-adjusted performance of the portfolios that they managed. Pension funds would have achieved a better risk-return combination by using combinations of suitable index funds.

---

[57] Richard A. Ippolito, ''Efficiency with Costly Information: A Study of Mutual Fund Performance, 1965–1984,'' *Quarterly Journal of Economics* 104 (February 1989), pp. 1–24.

[58] Gary P. Brinson, L. Randolph Hood, and Gilbert L. Beebower, ''Determinants of Portfolio Performance,'' *Financial Analysts Journal* 42 (July/August 1986), pp. 39–44.

[59] Vijay M. Jog, ''Investment Performance of Pension Funds—A Canadian Study,'' *Canadian Journal of Administrative Sciences* 3, no. 1 (June 1986).

Thus, the evidence on the risk-adjusted performance of professional managers is mixed at best. We conclude that the performance of professional managers is broadly consistent with market efficiency. The amounts by which professional managers as a group beat or are beaten by the market fall within the margin of statistical uncertainty. In any event, it is quite clear that performance superior to passive strategies is far from routine. Studies show either that most managers cannot outperform passive strategies, or that if there is a margin of superiority, it is small.

On the other hand, a small number of investment superstars—Peter Lynch (formerly of Fidelity's Magellan Fund), Warren Buffet (of Berkshire Hathaway), John Templeton (of Templeton Funds), and John Neff (of Vanguard's Windsor Fund) among them—have compiled career records that show a consistency of superior performance hard to reconcile with absolutely efficient markets. Nobel prize winner Paul Samuelson[60] reviews this investment hall of fame, but points out that the records of the vast majority of professional money managers offer convincing evidence that there are no easy strategies to guarantee success in the securities markets.

So, Are Markets Efficient?

There is a telling joke about two economists walking down the street. They spot a $20 bill on the sidewalk. One starts to pick it up, but the other one says, "Don't bother; if the bill were real someone would have picked it up already."

The lesson is clear. An overly doctrinaire belief in efficient markets can paralyze the investor and make it appear that no research effort can be justified. This extreme view is probably unwarranted. There are enough anomalies in the empirical evidence to justify the search for underpriced securities that clearly goes on.

The bulk of the evidence, however, suggests that any supposedly superior investment strategy should be taken with many grains of salt. The market is competitive *enough* that only differentially superior information or insight will earn money; the easy pickings have been picked. In the end it is likely that the margin of superiority that any professional manager can add is so slight that the statistician will not be able to detect it.

For the United States we can safely conclude that markets are very efficient, but that rewards to the especially diligent, intelligent, or creative may in fact be waiting. In Canada the anomalies are stronger and last longer, and the puzzle of the persistence of abnormal returns for several months following the reporting of unusual insider trading activity has not been satisfactorily explained. However, Canadian professional investment managers as a whole have shown no evidence of having exploited such inefficiencies.

---

[60] Paul Samuelson, "The Judgment of Economic Science on Rational Portfolio Management," *Journal of Portfolio Management* 16 (Fall 1989), pp. 4–12.

Summary

1. Statistical research has shown that stock prices seem to follow a random walk with no discernible predictable patterns that investors can exploit. Such findings are now taken to be evidence of market efficiency, that is, of evidence that market prices reflect all currently available information. Only new information will move stock prices, and this information is equally likely to be good news or bad news.

2. Market participants distinguish among three forms of the efficient market hypothesis. The weak form asserts that all information to be derived from past stock prices already is reflected in stock prices. The semistrong form claims that all publicly available information is already reflected. The strong form, usually taken only as a straw man, asserts that all information, including insider information, is reflected in prices.

3. Technical analysis focuses on stock price patterns and on proxies for buy or sell pressure in the market. Fundamental analysis focuses on the determinants of the underlying value of the firm, such as current profitability and growth prospects. Since both types of analysis are based on public information, neither should generate excess profits if markets are operating efficiently.

4. Proponents of the efficient market hypothesis often advocate passive as opposed to active investment strategies. The policy of passive investors is to buy and hold a broad-based market index. They expend resources neither on market research nor on frequent purchase and sale of stocks. Passive strategies may be tailored to meet individual investor requirements.

5. Event studies are used to evaluate the economic impact of events of interest, using abnormal stock returns. Such studies usually show that there is some leakage of inside information to some market participants before the public announcement date. Therefore insiders do seem to be able to exploit their access to information to at least a limited extent.

6. Empirical studies of technical analysis do not support the hypothesis that such analysis can generate superior trading profits. Only very short-term filters seem to offer any hope for profits, yet these are extremely expensive in terms of trading costs.

7. Several anomalies regarding fundamental analysis have been uncovered. These include the P/E effect, the small-firm effect, the neglected-firm effect, the weekend effect, the reversal effect, the market-to-book effect, the insider trading effect in Canada, and the Value Line Ranking System.

8. By and large, the performance record of professionally managed funds lends little credence to claims that professionals can consistently beat the market.

Key terms

Random walk	Abnormal return
Efficient market hypothesis	Announcement date
Weak-form EMH	Cumulative abnormal return
Semistrong-form EMH	Filter rule
Strong-form EMH	P/E effect
Technical analysis	Small-firm effect
Fundamental analysis	Neglected-firm effect
Passive investment strategy	Reversal effect
Index fund	Weekend effect
Event study	Insider transactions

Selected readings

One of the best treatments of the efficient market hypothesis is:

Malkiel, Burton G. *A Random Walk Down Wall Street*. New York: W.W. Norton & Co., Inc., 1990. This paperback book provides an entertaining and insightful treatment of the ideas presented in this chapter as well as fascinating historical examples of securities markets in action.

A more rigorous introduction to the theoretical underpinnings of the EMH, as well as a review of early empirical work, may be found in:

Fama, Eugene F. "Efficient Capital Markets: A Review of Theory and Empirical Work." *Journal of Finance* 25 (May 1970).

A more recent survey is:

Fama, Eugene F. "Efficient Capital Markets: II." *Journal of Finance* 46 (December 1991).

Problems

1. If markets are efficient, what should be the correlation coefficient between stock returns for two non-overlapping time periods?
2. Which of the following most appears to contradict the proposition that the stock market is *weakly* efficient? Explain.
   a. Over 25 percent of mutual funds outperform the market on average.
   b. Insiders earn abnormal trading profits.
   c. Every January, the stock market earns above-normal returns.
3. Suppose that, after conducting an analysis of past stock prices, you come up with the following observations. Which would appear to *contradict* the *weak* form of the efficient market hypothesis? Explain.
   a. The average rate of return is significantly greater than zero.
   b. The correlation between the return during a given week and the return during the following week is zero.
   c. One could have made superior returns by buying stock after a 10 percent rise in price and selling after a 10 percent fall.
   d. One could have made higher than average capital gains by holding stock with low dividend yields.

4. Which of the following statements are true if the efficient market hypothesis holds?
  a. It implies that future events can be forecast with perfect accuracy.
  b. It implies that prices reflect all available information.
  c. It implies that security prices change for no discernible reason.
  d. It implies that prices do not fluctuate.
5. Which of the following observations would provide evidence *against* the *semistrong-form* of the efficient market theory? Explain.
  a. Mutual fund managers do not on average make superior returns.
  b. You cannot make superior profits by buying (or selling) stocks after the announcement of an abnormal rise in dividends.
  c. Low P/E stocks tend to have positive abnormal returns.
  d. In any year, approximately 50 percent of pension funds outperform the market.
6. A successful firm like Seagram's has consistently generated large profits for years. Is this a violation of the EMH?
7. Suppose you find that prices of stocks before large dividend increases show on average consistently positive abnormal returns. Is this a violation of the EMH?
8. "If the business cycle is predictable, and a stock has a positive beta, the stock's returns also must be predictable." Respond.
9. Which of the following phenomena would be either consistent with or a violation of the efficient market hypothesis? Explain briefly.
  a. Nearly half of all professionally managed mutual funds are able to outperform the TSE 300 in a typical year.
  b. Money managers that outperform the market (on a risk-adjusted basis) in one year are likely to outperform in the following year.
  c. Stock prices tend to be predictably more volatile in January than in other months.
  d. Stock prices of companies that announce increased earnings in January tend to outperform the market in February.
  e. Stocks that perform well in one week perform poorly in the following week.
10. "If all securities are fairly priced, all must offer equal market rates of return." Comment.
11. An index model regression applied to past monthly excess returns in ABC Corporation's stock price produces the following estimates, which are believed to be stable over time:

$$R_{ABC} = .10\% + 1.1\ R_M$$

If the market index subsequently rises by 8 percent and ABC's stock price rises by 7 percent, what is the abnormal change in ABC's stock price? The T-bill return during the month is 1 percent.
12. The monthly rate of return on T-bills is 1 percent. The market went up this month by 1.5 percent. In addition, AmbChaser, Inc., which has an equity

beta of 2, surprisingly just won a lawsuit that awards them $1 million immediately.

   a. If the original value of AmbChaser equity were $100 million, what would you guess was the rate of return of its stock this month?

   b. What is your answer to (a) if the market had expected AmbChaser to win $2 million?

13. In a recent, closely contested lawsuit, Apex sued Bpex for patent infringement. The jury came back today with its decision. The rate of return on Apex was $r_A = 3.1$ percent. The rate of return on Bpex was only $r_B = 2.5$ percent. The market today responded to very encouraging news about the unemployment rate, and $r_M = 3$ percent. The historical relationship between returns on these stocks and the market portfolio has been estimated from index model regressions as:

$$\text{Apex: } r_A = .2\% + 1.4 \, r_M$$

$$\text{Bpex: } r_B = -.1\% + .6 \, r_M$$

   Based on these data, which company do you think won the lawsuit? (Note: On a daily basis, the rate of return on risk-free Treasury bills is close to zero.)

14. Dollar cost averaging means that you buy equal dollar amounts of a stock every period, for example, $500 per month. The strategy is based on the idea that when the stock price is low, your fixed monthly purchase will buy more shares, and when the price is high, it will buy fewer shares. Averaging over time, you will end up buying more shares when the stock is cheaper and fewer when it is relatively expensive. Therefore, by design, you will exhibit good market timing. Evaluate this strategy.

15. Steady Growth Industries has never missed a dividend payment in its 94-year history. Does this make it more attractive to you as a possible purchase for your stock portfolio?

16. We know that the market should respond positively to good news, and that good-news events such as a coming end of a recession can be predicted with at least some accuracy. Why, then, can we not predict that the market will go up as the economy recovers?

17. If prices are as likely to increase as decrease, why do investors earn positive returns from the market on average?

18. You know that firm XYZ is very poorly run. On a scale of 1 (worst) to 10 (best), you would give it a score of 3. The market consensus evaluation is that the management score is only 2. Should you buy or sell the stock?

19. Examine the figure[61] on p. 425, which presents cumulative abnormal returns both before and after dates on which insiders buy or sell shares in their firm. How do you interpret this figure? What are we to make of the pattern of CARs before and after the event date?

---

[61] From Nejat H. Seyhun, "Insiders, Profits, Costs of Trading and Market Efficiency," *Journal of Financial Economics* 16 (1986).

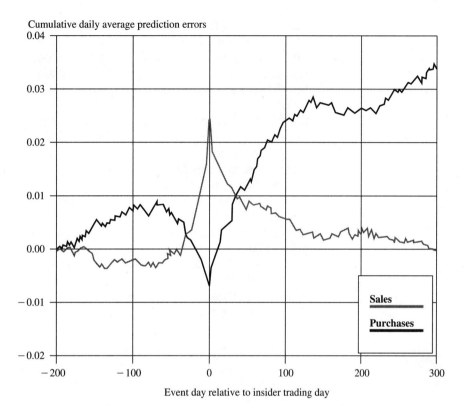

Cumulative daily average prediction errors

Event day relative to insider trading day

20. Good News Inc. just announced an increase in its annual earnings, yet its stock price fell. Is there a rational explanation for this phenomenon?

21. (Adapted from CFA Examination, Level I, 1981) Some authors contend that professional managers are incapable of outperforming the market. Others come to an opposite conclusion. Compare and contrast the assumptions about the stock market that support (a) passive portfolio management, and (b) active portfolio management.

(CFA Examination, Level III, 1985) The following information should be used in solving problems 22 and 23:

As director of research for a medium-sized investment firm, Jeff Cheney was concerned about the mediocre investment results experienced by the firm in recent years. He met with his two senior equity analysts to consider alternatives to the stock selection techniques employed in the past.

One of the analysts suggested that the current literature has examined the relationship between price earnings ratios (P/E) and securities returns. A number of studies had concluded that high P/E stocks tended to have higher betas and lower risk-adjusted returns than stocks with low P/E ratios.

The analyst also referred to recent studies analyzing the relationship between security returns and company size as measured by equity capitalization. The studies concluded that when compared to the TSE 300 index, small capitalization stocks tended to provide above-average risk-adjusted returns while large capitalization stocks tended to provide below-average risk-adjusted returns. It was further noted that little correlation was found to exist between a company's P/E ratio and the size of its equity capitalization.

Jeff's firm has employed a strategy of complete diversification and the use of beta as a measure of portfolio risk. He and his analysts were intrigued as to how these recent studies might be applied to their stock selection techniques and thereby improve their performance. Given the results of the studies indicated above:

22. Explain how the results of these studies might be used in the stock selection and portfolio management process. Briefly discuss the effects on the objectives of diversification and on the measurement of portfolio risk.

23. List the reasons and briefly discuss why this firm might *not* want to adopt a new strategy based on these studies in place of their current strategy of complete diversification and the use of beta as a measure of portfolio risk.

24. You are a portfolio manager meeting a client. During the conversation that followed your formal review of her account, your client asked the following question:

> "My grandson, who is studying investments, tells me that one of the best ways to make money in the stock market is to buy the stocks of small-capitalization firms on a Monday morning late in December and to sell the stocks one month later. What is he talking about?"

a. Identify the apparent market anomalies that would justify the proposed strategy.

b. Explain why you believe such a strategy might or might not work in the future.

CHAPTER 13

Portfolio Performance Evaluation

$\mathbf{D}$espite the theoretical predictions of market efficiency, it comes as no surprise that portfolio managers create portfolios that are not replicas of the market portfolio. In Chapter 14, we shall survey active investment strategies that managers might pursue. In this chapter, we ask how one can evaluate the performance of a portfolio manager. It turns out that even measuring average portfolio returns is not as straightforward as it might seem. In addition, difficulties lie in adjusting average returns for risk, which presents a host of other problems.

We begin with issues on measurement of portfolio returns. From there, we move on to conventional approaches to risk adjustment. We show the problems with these approaches when they are applied in a real and complex world; in this context, we examine the subject of market timing versus stock selection. We then discuss some promising developments in the theory of performance evaluation and examine evaluation procedures used in the field. We conclude with some results and discussion on the evaluation of actual performance.

13.1   *Measuring Investment Returns*

The rate of return on an investment is a simple concept in the case of a one-period investment. It is simply the total proceeds derived from the investment per dollar initially invested. Proceeds must be defined broadly to include both cash distributions and capital gains. For stocks, total returns are dividends plus capital gains. For bonds, total returns are coupon or interest paid plus capital gains.

To set the stage for discussing the more subtle issues that follow, let us start with a trivial example. Consider a stock paying a dividend of $2 annually that currently sells for $50. You purchase the stock today and collect the $2 dividend, and then you sell the stock for $53 at year-end. Your rate of return is

$$\frac{\text{Total proceeds}}{\text{Initial investment}} = \frac{\text{Income} + \text{capital gain}}{50}$$

$$= \frac{2 + 3}{50}$$

$$= .10$$

$$= 10\%$$

Another way to derive the rate of return that is useful in the more difficult multiperiod case is to set up the investment as a discounted cash flow problem. Call r the rate of return that equates the present value of all cash flows from the investment with the initial outlay. In our example, the stock is purchased for $50 and generates cash flows at year-end of $2 (dividend) plus $53 (sale of stock). Therefore we solve $50 = (2 + 53)/(1 + r)$ to find again that $r = .10$, or 10 percent.

Time-Weighted Returns vs. Dollar-Weighted Returns

When we consider investments over a period during which cash was added to or withdrawn from the portfolio, measuring the rate of return becomes more difficult. To continue our example, suppose that you were to purchase a second share of the same stock at the end of the first year, and hold both shares until the end of year 2, at which point you sell each share for $54.

Total cash outlays are

Time	Outlay
0	$50 to purchase first share
1	$53 to purchase second share a year later

Proceeds are

Time	Proceeds
1	$2 dividend from initially purchased share
2	$4 dividend from the 2 shares held in the second year, plus $108 received from selling both shares at $54 each

Using the discounted cash flow (DCF) approach, we can solve for the average return over the two years by equating the present values of the cash inflows and outflows:

$$50 + \frac{53}{1 + r} = \frac{2}{1 + r} + \frac{112}{(1 + r)^2}$$

resulting in $r = 7.117$ percent.

This value is called the internal rate of return or the **dollar-weighted rate of return** on the investment. It is "dollar weighted" because the stock's performance in the second year, when two shares of stock are held, has a greater influence on the average overall return than the first-year return, when only one share is held.

An alternative to the internal or dollar-weighted return is the **time-weighted return.** This method ignores the number of shares of stock held in each period. The stock return in the first year was 10 percent. (A $50 purchase provided $2 in dividends and $3 in capital gains.) In the second year the stock had a starting value of $53 and sold at year-end for $54, for a total one-period rate of return of $3 ($2 dividend plus $1 capital gain) divided by $53 (the stock price at the start of the second year), or 5.66 percent. The time-weighted return is the average of 10 percent and 5.66 percent, which is 7.83 percent. This average return considers only the period-by-period returns without regard to the amounts invested in the stock in each period.

Note that the dollar-weighted return is less than the time-weighted return in this example. The reason is that the stock fared relatively poorly in the second year, when the investor was holding more shares. The greater weight that the dollar-weighted average places on the second-year return results in a lower measure of investment performance. In general, dollar- and time-weighted returns will differ, and the difference can be positive or negative depending on the configuration of period returns and portfolio composition.

Which measure of performance is superior? At first, it appears that the dollar-weighted return must be more relevant. After all, the more money you invest in a stock when its performance is superior, the more money you end up with. Certainly your performance measure should reflect this fact.

Time-weighted returns have their own use, however, especially in the money management industry. This is so because in some important applications a portfolio manager may not directly control the timing or the amount of money invested in securities. Pension fund management is a good example. A pension fund manager faces cash inflows into the fund when pension contributions are made, and cash outflows when pension benefits are paid. Obviously, the amount of money invested at any time can vary for reasons beyond the manager's control. Because dollars invested do not depend on the manager's choice, it is inappropriate to weight returns by dollars invested when measuring the investment ability of the manager. Consequently, the money management industry normally uses time-weighted returns for performance evaluation.

Concept Check
─────────
─────────

> Question 1. Shares of XYZ Corp. pay a $2 dividend at the end of every year on December 31. An investor buys two shares of the stock on January 1 at a price of $20 each, sells one of those shares for $22 a year later on the next January 1, and sells the second share an additional year later for $19. Find the time- and dollar-weighted rates of return on the two-year investment.

Arithmetic Averages vs. Geometric Averages

Our example takes the arithmetic average of the two annual returns, 10 percent and 5.66 percent, as the time-weighted average, 7.83 percent. Another approach is to take a geometric average, denoted r_G. This approach would entail computing

$$1 + r_G = [(1.10)(1.0566)]^{1/2} = 1.0781$$

or

$$r_G = 7.81\%$$

The motivation for this calculation comes from the principle of compounding. If dividend proceeds are reinvested, the accumulated value of an investment in the stock will grow by a factor of 1.10 in the first year and by an additional factor of 1.0566 in the second year. The compound average growth rate is then calculated:

$$(1 + r_G)^2 = (1.10)(1.0566)$$

Taking the square root of each side gives the result. In general terms, for an n-period investment, the geometric average rate of return is given by

$$1 + r_G = [(1 + r_1)(1 + r_2) \ldots (1 + r_n)]^{1/n} \tag{13.1}$$

where r_t is the return in each time period. By contrast, the arithmetic average rate of return is given by

$$r_G = (r_1 + r_2 + \ldots + r_n) \times 1/n \tag{13.2}$$

Note that the geometric average return in this example, 7.81 percent, is slightly less than the arithmetic average return, 7.83 percent. This is a general property: geometric averages never exceed arithmetic averages, and the difference between the two becomes greater as the variability of period-by-period returns becomes greater.

For example, consider Table 13.1, which presents arithmetic and geometric returns over the period 1949–1987 for a variety of investments. The arithmetic averages all exceed the geometric averages, and the difference is greatest for stocks of small firms, where annual returns exhibit the greatest standard deviation. Indeed, the difference between the two averages falls to zero only when there is no variation in yearly returns, although the table indicates that, by the time the standard deviation falls to a level characteristic of T-bills, the difference is quite small.

Here is another return question. Which is the superior measure of investment performance, the arithmetic average or the geometric average? The geometric average has considerable appeal because it represents exactly the constant rate of return we would have needed to earn in each year to match actual performance over some past investment period. It is an excellent measure of *past* performance. However, if our focus is on future performance, then the arithmetic average is the statistic of interest because it is an unbiased estimate of the portfolio's expected future return (assuming, of course, that the expected

TABLE 13.1 Selected Canadian Annual Returns by Investment Class, 1949–1987

	Geometric Average	Arithmetic Average	Arithmetic Returns Maximum	Minimum	Standard Deviation
Equities (Value Weighted)					
Small firms	15.08	13.93	46.41	−27.85	19.61
Large firms	11.07	12.45	51.40	−26.78	17.59
All firms	11.15	12.50	51.30	−28.29	17.82
Equities (Equal Weighted)					
Small firms	20.23	23.83	80.72	−32.72	29.70
Large firms	12.22	13.93	46.41	−27.85	19.60
All firms	15.51	18.62	59.30	−27.35	23.83
Long-term industrial bonds	6.22	6.62	43.36	−7.60	9.69
Long-term Canada bonds	5.22	5.64	45.81	−5.82	10.17
Treasury bills	5.90	5.98	19.09	0.51	4.16
Inflation	4.69	4.76	12.32	−1.73	3.76

Adapted from James E. Hatch and Robert W. White, *Canadian Stocks, Bonds, Bills, and Inflation: 1950–1987*. Copyright 1988, and reprinted, with permission, The Research Foundation of the Institute of Chartered Financial Analysts, Charlottesville, Va.

return does not change over time). In contrast, because the geometric return over a sample period is always less than the arithmetic mean, it constitutes a downward-biased estimator of the stock's expected return in any future year.

To illustrate this concept, suppose that in any period a stock will either double in value ($r = 100$ percent) with probability of .5, or halve in value ($r = -50$ percent) with probability .5. The table following illustrates these outcomes:

Investment Outcome	Final Value of Each Dollar Invested	One-Year Rate of Return
Double	$2	100%
Halve	$0.50	−50%

Suppose that the stock's performance over a two-year period is characteristic of the probability distribution, doubling in one year, and halving in the other. The stock's price ends up exactly where it started, and the geometric average annual return is zero:

$$1 + r_G = [(1 + r_1)(1 + r_2)]^{1/2}$$
$$= [(1 + 1)(1 - .50)]^{1/2}$$
$$= 1$$

so that

$$r_G = 0$$

which confirms that a zero year-by-year return would have replicated the total return earned on the stock.

The expected annual future rate of return on the stock, however, is *not* zero: it is the arithmetic average of 100 percent and -50 percent: $(100 - 50)/2 = 25$ percent. To confirm this, note that there are two equally likely outcomes for each dollar invested: either a gain of \$1 (when $r = 100$ percent) or a loss of \$.50 (when $r = -50$ percent). The expected profit is $(\$1 - \$.50)/2 = \$.25$, for a 25 percent expected rate of return. The profit in the good year more than offsets the loss in the bad year, despite the fact that the geometric return is zero. The arithmetic average return thus provides the best guide to expected future returns from an investment.

This argument carries forward into multiperiod investments. Consider, for example, all the possible outcomes over a two-year period:

Investment Outcome	Final Value of Each Dollar Invested	Total Return over Two Years
Double, double	\$4	300%
Double, halve	\$1	0
Halve, double	\$1	0
Halve, halve	\$.25	−75%

The expected final value of each dollar invested is $(4 + 1 + 1 + .25)/4 = \$1.5625$ for two years, again indicating an average rate of return of 25 percent per year, equal to the arithmetic average. Note that an investment yielding 25 percent per year with certainty will yield the same final compounded value as the expected final value of this investment, as $1.25^2 = 1.5625$. The arithmetic average return on the stock is $[300 + 0 + 0 + (-75)]/4 = 56.25$ percent per two years, for an effective annual return of 25 percent, that is, $1.5625^{1/2} - 1$. In contrast, the geometric mean return is zero:

$$[(1 + 3)(1 + 0)(1 + 0)(1 - .75)]^{1/4} = 1.0$$

Again, the arithmetic average is the better guide to *future* performance.

Concept Check

Question 2. Suppose that a stock now selling for \$100 will either increase in value by 15 percent by year-end with probability .5, or fall in value by 5 percent with probability .5. The stock pays no dividends.
a. What are the geometric and arithmetic mean returns on the stock?
b. What is the expected end-of-year value of the share?
c. Which measure of expected return is superior?

13.2 *The Conventional Theory of Performance Evaluation*

Calculating average portfolio returns does not mean the task is done—returns must be adjusted for risk before they can be compared meaningfully. The simplest and most popular way to adjust returns for portfolio risk is to compare rates of return with those of other investment funds with similar risk characteristics. For example, high-yield bond portfolios are grouped into one "universe," growth stock equity funds are grouped into another universe, and so on. Then the (usually time-weighted) average returns of each fund within the universe are ordered, and each portfolio manager receives a percentile ranking depending on relative performance within the **comparison universe**. For example, the manager with the ninth-best performance in a universe of 100 funds would be the 90th percentile manager: his performance was better than 90 percent of all competing funds over the evaluation period.

These relative rankings are usually displayed in a chart such as that in Figure 13.1. The chart summarizes performance rankings over four periods: one quarter, one year, three years, and five years. The top and bottom lines of each box are drawn at the rate of return of the 95th and 5th percentile managers. The three dotted lines correspond to the rates of return of the 75th, 50th (median), and 25th percentile managers. The diamond is drawn at the average return of a particular fund and the rectangle is drawn at the return of a benchmark index such as the TSE 300. The placement of the diamond within the box is an easy-to-read representation of the performance of the fund relative to the comparison universe.

This comparison of performance with other managers of similar investment style is a useful first step in evaluating performance. However, such rankings can be misleading. For example, within a particular universe, some managers may concentrate on particular subgroups, so that portfolio characteristics are not truly comparable. For example, within the equity universe, one manager may concentrate on high-beta stocks. Similarly, within fixed-income universes, durations can vary across managers. These considerations suggest that a more precise means for risk adjustment is desirable.

Methods of risk-adjusted performance evaluation using mean-variance criteria came on stage simultaneously with the capital asset pricing model. Jack Treynor,[1] William Sharpe,[2] and Michael Jensen[3] recognized immediately the

---

[1] Jack L. Treynor, "How to Rate Management Investment Funds," *Harvard Business Review* 43 (January–February 1966).

[2] William F. Sharpe, "Mutual Fund Performance," *Journal of Business* 39 (January 1966).

[3] Michael C. Jensen, "The Performance of Mutual Funds in the Period 1945–1964," *Journal of Finance*, May 1968; and "Risk, the Pricing of Capital Assets, and the Evaluation of Investment Portfolios," *Journal of Business*, April 1969.

FIGURE 13.1
Universe
comparison (periods
ending December
31, 1991).

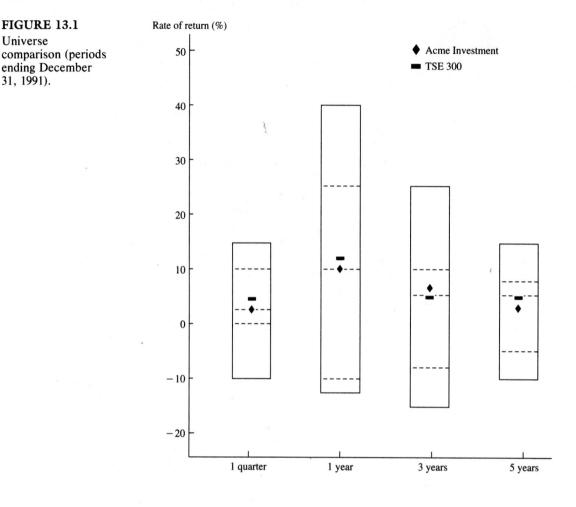

implications of the CAPM for rating the performance of managers. Within a short time, academicians were in command of a battery of performance measures, and a bounty of scholarly investigation of mutual fund performance was pouring from ivory towers. Shortly thereafter, agents emerged (A. G. Becker is one example) who were willing to supply rating services to portfolio managers eager for regular feedback. This trend has since lost some of its steam.

One explanation for the lagging popularity of risk-adjusted performance measures is the generally negative cast to the performance statistics. In nearly efficient markers it is extremely difficult for analysts to perform well enough to overcome costs of research and transaction costs. Indeed, we have seen that the most professionally managed equity funds generally underperform the TSE 300 index on both risk-adjusted and raw return measures.

Another reason mean-variance criteria may have suffered relates to intrinsic problems in these measures. We will explore these problems, as well as some innovations suggested to overcome them.[4]

For now, however, we can catalogue some possible risk-adjusted performance measures and examine the circumstances in which each measure might be most relevant.

1. *Sharpe's measure:* $(\bar{r}_P - \bar{r}_f)/\sigma_P$
   Sharpe's measure divides average portfolio excess return over the sample period by the standard deviation of returns over that period. It measures the reward to (total) volatility trade-off.[5]

2. *Treynor's measure:* $(\bar{r}_P - \bar{r}_f)/\beta_P$
   Like Sharpe's, **Treynor's measure** gives excess return per unit of risk, but uses systematic risk instead of total risk.

3. *Jensen's measure:* $\alpha_P = \bar{r}_P - [\bar{r}_f + \beta_P(\bar{r}_M - \bar{r}_f)]$
   Jensen's measure is the average return on the portfolio over and above that predicted by the CAPM, given the portfolio's beta and the average market return. Jensen's measure is the portfolio's alpha value.

4. *Appraisal ratio:* $\alpha_P/\sigma(e_P)$
   The **appraisal ratio** divides the alpha of the portfolio by the non-systematic risk of the portfolio. It measures abnormal return per unit of risk that in principle could be diversified away by holding a market index portfolio.

Each measure has some appeal. But each does not necessarily provide consistent assessments of performance, since the risk measures used to adjust returns differ substantially.

Concept Check

Question 3. Consider the following data for a particular sample period:

	Portfolio *P*	Market *M*
Average return	.35	.28
Beta	1.2	1.0
Standard deviation	.42	.30
Non-systematic risk, $\sigma(e)$	.18	0

Calculate the following performance measures for portfolio *P* and the market: Sharpe, Jensen (alpha), Treynor, appraisal ratio. The T-bill rate during the period was .06. By which measures did portfolio *P* outperform the market?

---

[4] A statistical analysis of the subject is presented in J. D. Jobson and R. M. Korkie, "Performance Hypothesis Testing with the Sharpe and Treynor Measures," *Journal of Finance* 36, no. 4 (September 1981).

[5] We place bars over r_f as well as r_P to denote the fact that since the risk-free rate may not be constant over the measurement period, we are taking a sample average, just as we do for r_P.

Sharpe's Measure as the Criterion for Overall Portfolios

Suppose that Jane d'Arque constructs a portfolio and holds it for a considerable period of time. She makes no changes in portfolio composition during the period. In addition, suppose that the daily rates of return on all securities have constant means, variances, and covariances. This assures that the portfolio rate of return also has a constant mean and variance. These assumptions are unrealistic, but they make the problem easy to analyze. They are also crucial to understanding the shortcoming of conventional applications of performance measurement.

Now we want to evaluate the performance of Jane's portfolio. Has she made a good choice of securities? This is really a three-pronged question. First, good choice compared with what alternatives? Second, in choosing between two distinct alternatives, what are the appropriate criteria to use to evaluate performance? Finally, having identified the alternatives and the performance criteria, is there a rule that will separate basic ability from the random luck of the draw?

Fortunately, our earlier chapters of this text help to determine portfolio choice criteria. If investor preferences can be summarized by a mean-variance utility function such as that introduced in Chapter 5, we can arrive at a relatively simple criterion. The particular utility function that we have used in this text is

$$U = E(r_P) - \frac{1}{2}A\sigma_P^2$$

where A is the coefficient of risk aversion. With mean-variance preferences, we have seen that Jane will want to maximize her Sharpe measure (that is, the ratio $[E(r_P) - r_f]/\sigma_P$) of her *complete* portfolio of assets. Recall that this is the criterion that led to the selection of the tangency portfolio in Chapter 7. Jane's problem reduces to that of whether her overall portfolio is the one with the highest possible Sharpe ratio.

Appropriate Performance Measures in Three Scenarios

To evaluate Jane's portfolio choice, we first ask whether she intends this portfolio to be her exclusive investment vehicle. If the answer is no, we need to know what her "complementary" portfolio is—the portfolio to which she is adding the one in question. The appropriate measure of portfolio performance depends critically on whether the portfolio is the entire investment fund or only a portion of the investor's overall wealth.

Jane's choice portfolio represents her entire risky investment fund

In this simplest case we need to ascertain only whether Jane's portfolio has the highest possible (ex ante) Sharpe measure. But how can this be done? In principle we can follow these four steps:

1. Assume that her past security performance is representative of expected future performance, meaning that security returns over Jane's holding period exhibit averages and sample covariances that Jane might have anticipated.

2. Estimate the entire efficient frontier of risk assets from return data over Jane's holding period.
3. Using the risk-free rate at the time of decision, find the portfolio with the highest Sharpe measure.
4. Compare Jane's Sharpe measure to that of the best alternative.

This comprehensive approach, however, is problematic. It requires not only an extensive data base and optimization techniques, but also exacerbates the problem of inference from sample data. We have to rely on a limited sample to estimate the means and covariances of a very large set of securities. The verdict on Jane's choice will be subject to estimation errors. The very complexity of the procedure makes it hard to assess the reliability and significance of the verdict. Is there a second-best alternative?

In fact, it makes sense to compare Jane's choice to a restricted set of alternative portfolios that were easy for her to assess and invest in at the time of her decision. An obvious first candidate for this restricted set is the passive strategy, the market index portfolio. Other candidates are professionally managed active funds. The method to use to compare Jane's portfolio to any specific alternative is the same: compare their Sharpe measures.

In essence, when Jane's portfolio represents her entire investment fund for the holding period in question, the benchmark alternative is the market index or another specific portfolio. The performance criterion is the Sharpe measure of the actual portfolio versus the benchmark portfolios.

Jane's portfolio is an active portfolio and is mixed with the passive market index portfolio

How do we evaluate the optimal mix in this case? Call Jane's portfolio P, and denote the market portfolio by M. When the two portfolios are mixed optimally, it turns out (as we shall examine more closely in Chapter 14) that the square of the Sharpe measure of the composite portfolio, C, is given by

$$S_C^2 = S_M^2 + \left[\frac{\alpha_P}{\sigma(e_P)}\right]^2$$

where α_P is the abnormal return of the active portfolio, relative to the passive market portfolio, and $\sigma(e_P)$ is the diversifiable risk. The ratio $\alpha_P/\sigma(e_P)$ is thus the correct performance measure for P for this case, since it gives the improvement in the Sharpe measure of the overall portfolio attributable to the inclusion of P.

To see the intuition of this result, recall the single-index model:

$$r_P - r_f = \alpha_P + \beta_P(r_M - r_f) + e_P$$

If P is fairly priced, the $\alpha_P = 0$, and e_P is just diversifiable risk that can be avoided. If P is mispriced, however, α_P no longer equals zero. Instead, it represents the expected abnormal return. Holding P in addition to the market portfolio thus brings a reward of α_P against the non-systematic risk voluntarily incurred, $\sigma(e_P)$. Therefore, the ratio of $\alpha_P/\sigma(e_P)$ is the natural benefit-to-cost ratio for portfolio P. This performance measurement is sometimes called the appraisal ratio:

$$AR_P = \frac{\alpha_P}{\sigma(e_P)}$$

Jane's choice portfolio is one of many portfolios combined into a large investment fund

This third case might describe the situation where Jane, as a corporate financial officer, manages the corporate pension fund. She parcels out the entire fund to a number of portfolio managers. Then she evaluates the performance of individual managers to reallocate parts of the fund to improve future performance. What is the correct performance measure?

We could continue to use the appraisal ratio if it were reasonable to assume that the complementary portfolio to P is approximately equal to the market index portfolio by virtue of its being spread among many managers and thus well diversified. The appraisal ratio is adequate in these circumstances. But you can imagine that the portfolio managers would take offense at this assumption. Jane, too, is likely to respond, "Do you think I am exerting all this effort just to end up with a passive portfolio?"

If we cannot treat this form of management as the same as investing in the index portfolio, we could make the following approximation. The benefit of portfolio P to the entire diversified fund is measured by P's alpha value. Although α_P is not a full measure of portfolio P's performance value, it will give Jane some indication of P's potential contribution to the overall portfolio. An even better solution, however, is to use Treynor's measure.

Suppose you determine that portfolio P exhibits an alpha value of 2 percent. "Not bad," you tell Jane. But she pulls out of her desk a report and informs you that another portfolio, Q, has an alpha of 3 percent. "One hundred basis points is significant," says Jane. "Should I transfer some of my funds from P's manager to Q's?"

You tabulate the relevant data, as in Table 13.2, and graph the results as in Figure 13.2. Note that we plot P and Q in the mean return-beta (rather than the mean-standard deviation) plane, because we assume that P and Q are two of many subportfolios in the fund, and thus that non-systematic risk will be largely

TABLE 13.2   Portfolio Performance

	Portfolio P	Portfolio Q	Market
Beta	.90	1.60	1.0
Excess return $(\bar{r} - \bar{r}_f)$	.11	.19	.10
Alpha*	.02	.03	0

* Alpha = Excess return − (Beta × Market excess return)
$$= (\bar{r} - \bar{r}_f) - \beta(\bar{r}_M - \bar{r}_f)$$
$$= \bar{r} - [\bar{r}_f + \beta(\bar{r}_M - \bar{r}_f)]$$

FIGURE 13.2
Treynor measure.

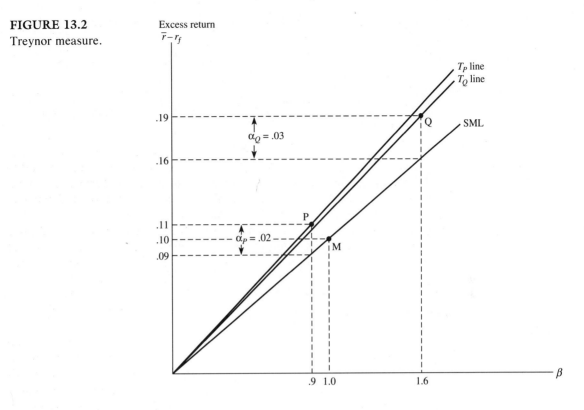

diversified away, leaving beta as the appropriate risk measure. The security market line (SML) shows the value of α_P and α_Q as the distance of P and Q above this line.

Suppose that portfolio Q can be mixed with T-bills. Specifically, if we invest w_Q in Q and $w_F = 1 - w_Q$ in T-bills, the resulting portfolio, Q^*, will have alpha and beta values proportional to Q's alpha and beta and to w_Q:

$$\alpha_{Q^*} = w_Q\alpha_Q$$
$$\beta_{Q^*} = w_Q\beta_Q$$

Thus, all portfolios Q^* generated from mixes of Q and T-bills plot on a straight line from the origin through Q. We call it the T-line for the Treynor measure, which is the slope of this line.

Figure 13.2 shows the T-line for portfolio P as well. You can see immediately that P has a steeper T-line; despite its lower alpha, P is a better portfolio in this case after all. For any *given* beta, a mixture of P with T-bills will give a better alpha than a mixture of Q with T-bills.

To see this, suppose that we choose to mix Q with T-bills to create a portfolio Q^* with a beta equal to that of P. We find the necessary proportion by solving for w_Q:

$$w_Q\beta_Q = 1.6w_Q = \beta_P = .9$$
$$w_Q = \frac{9}{16}$$

Portfolio Q^* therefore has an alpha of

$$\alpha_{Q^*} = \tfrac{9}{16} \times 3$$
$$= 1.69\%$$

which, in fact, is less than that of P.

In other words, the slope of the T-line is the appropriate performance criterion for the third case. The slope of the T-line for P, denoted by T_P, is given by

$$T_P = \frac{\bar{r}_P - \bar{r}_f}{\beta_P}$$

Treynor's performance measure is appealing in the sense that it shows that when an asset is part of a large investment portfolio, you should weight its mean excess return, $\bar{r}_P - \bar{r}_f$ against its *systematic* risk (as measured by beta) rather than against total or diversifiable risk (as measured by its standard deviation) to evaluate its contribution to performance.

Relationships among the Various Performance Measures

We have shown that under various scenarios one of four different performance measures is appropriate:

$$\text{Sharpe:} \quad \frac{E(r_P) - r_f}{\sigma_P}$$

$$\text{Treynor:} \quad \frac{E(r_P) - r_f}{\beta_P}$$

$$\text{Jensen, or Alpha:} \ \alpha_P$$

$$\text{Appraisal ratio:} \quad \frac{\alpha_P}{\sigma(e_P)}$$

It is interesting to see how these measures are related to one another. Beginning with Treynor's measure, note that as the market index beta is 1.0, Treynor's measure for the market index is

$$T_M = \bar{r}_M - \bar{r}_f$$

The mean excess return of portfolio P is

$$\bar{r}_P - \bar{r}_f = \alpha_P + \beta_P(\bar{r}_M - \bar{r}_f)$$

and thus its Treynor measure is

$$T_P = \frac{\alpha_P + \beta_P(\bar{r}_M - \bar{r}_f)}{\beta_P}$$

$$= \frac{\alpha_P}{\beta_P} + \bar{r}_M - \bar{r}_f$$

$$= \frac{\alpha_P}{\beta_P} + T_M \tag{13.3}$$

Treynor's measure compares portfolios on the basis of the alpha-to-beta ratio.[6] Note that this is very different in numerical value *and spirit* from the appraisal ratio, which is the ratio of alpha to residual risk.

The Sharpe measure for the market index portfolio is

$$S_M = \frac{\bar{r}_M - \bar{r}_f}{\sigma_M}$$

For portfolio P we have

$$S_P = \frac{\bar{r}_P - \bar{r}_f}{\sigma_P} = \frac{\alpha_P + \beta_P(\bar{r}_M - \bar{r}_f)}{\sigma_P}$$

With some algebra that relies on the fact that ρ^2 between P and M is

$$\rho^2 = \frac{\beta^2\sigma_M^2}{\beta^2\sigma_M^2 + \sigma^2(e)} = \frac{\beta^2\sigma_M^2}{\sigma_P^2}$$

we find that

$$S_P = \frac{\alpha_P}{\sigma_P} + \frac{\beta_P(\bar{r}_M - \bar{r}_f)}{\sigma_P}$$

$$= \frac{\alpha_P}{\sigma_P} + \rho S_M$$

This expression yields some insight into the process of generating valuable performance with active management. It is obvious that one needs to find significant-alpha stocks to establish potential value. A higher portfolio alpha, however, has to be tempered by the increase in standard deviation that arises when one departs from full diversification. The more we tilt toward high alpha stocks, the lower the correlation with the market index, ρ, and the greater the potential loss of performance value.

We conclude that it is important to use the performance measure that fits the relevant scenario. Evaluating portfolios by different performance measures may yield quite different results.

Actual Performance Measurement: An Example

Now that we have examined possible criteria for performance evaluation, we need to deal with a statistical issue: how can we derive an appropriate performance measure for ex ante decisions using ex post data? Before we plunge into a discussion of this problem, let us look at the rate of return on Jane's portfolio over the last 12 months. Table 13.3 shows the excess return recorded each month for Jane's portfolio P, one of her alternative portfolios Q, and the

---

[6] Interestingly, although our definition of the Treynor measure is conventional, Treynor himself initially worked with the alpha-to-beta ratio. In this form, the measure is independent of the market. Either measure will rank-order portfolio performance identically, because they differ by a constant (the market's Treynor value). Some call the ratio of alpha to beta "modified alpha" or "modified Jensen's measure," not realizing that this is really Treynor's measure.

TABLE 13.3   Excess Returns for Portfolios *P* and *Q* and the Benchmark *M* over 12 Months

Month	Jane's Portfolio P	Alternative Q	Benchmark M
1	3.58	2.81	2.20
2	−4.91	−1.15	−8.41
3	6.51	2.53	3.27
4	11.13	37.09	14.41
5	8.78	12.88	7.71
6	9.38	39.08	14.36
7	−3.66	−8.84	−6.15
8	5.56	.83	2.74
9	−7.72	.85	−15.27
10	7.76	12.09	6.49
11	−4.01	−5.68	−3.13
12	.78	−1.77	1.41
Year's average	2.76	7.56	1.63
Standard deviation	6.17	14.89	8.48

benchmark market index portfolio *M*. The last rows in Table 13.3 give sample averages and standard deviations. From these, and regressions of *P* and *Q* on *M*, we obtain the necessary performance statistics.

The performance statistics in Table 13.4 show that portfolio *Q* is more aggressive than *P*, in the sense that its beta is significantly higher (1.40 versus .69). On the other hand, *P* appears better diversified from its residual standard deviation (1.95 percent versus 8.98 percent). Both portfolios have outperformed the benchmark market index portfolio, as is evident from their larger Sharpe measures and positive alphas.

Which portfolio is more attractive, based on reported performance? If *P* or *Q* represents the entire investment fund, *Q* would be preferable on the basis of its

TABLE 13.4   Performance Statistics

	Portfolio P	Portfolio Q	Portfolio M
Sharpe's measure	.45	.51	.19
SCL regression statistics			
Alpha	1.63	5.28	.00
Beta	.69	1.40	1.00
Treynor	4.00	3.77	1.63
$\sigma(e)$	1.95	8.98	.00
Appraisal ratio	.84	.59	.00
R^2	.91	.64	1.00

higher Sharpe measure (.51 versus .45). On the other hand, as an active portfolio to be mixed with the market index, *P* is preferable to *Q*, as is evident from its appraisal ratio (.84 versus .59). For the third scenario, where *P* and *Q* are competing for a role as one of a number of subportfolios, the inadequacy of alpha as a performance measure is evident. Whereas *Q*'s alpha is larger (5.28 percent versus 1.63 percent), *P*'s beta is low enough to give it a better Treynor measure (4.00 versus 3.77), suggesting that it is superior to *Q* as one portfolio to be mixed with many others.

This analysis is based on 12 months of data only, a period too short to lend statistical significance to the conclusions. Even longer observation intervals may not be enough to make the decision clear-cut, which represents a further problem.

Realized Returns vs. Expected Returns

When evaluating a portfolio, the evaluator knows neither the portfolio manager's original expectations nor whether those expectations made sense. One can only observe performance after the fact and hope that random results are not taken for, or do not hide, true underlying ability. But risky asset returns are "noisy," which complicates the inference problem. To avoid making mistakes, we have to determine the "significance level" of a statistic to know whether a portfolio performance measure reliably indicates ability. Quite frequently, however, we can make no significant distinction about performance.

Consider Joe Dart, a portfolio manager. Suppose that his ability is such that his portfolio has an alpha value of 20 basis points per month. (This makes for a hefty 2.4 percent per year before compounding.) Let us assume that the return distribution of Joe's portfolio has a constant mean, beta, and alpha, a heroic assumption, but one that is in line with the usual treatment of performance measurement. Suppose that for the measurement period Joe's portfolio beta is 1.2 and the monthly standard deviation of the residual (non-systematic risk) is .02 (2 percent). With the market portfolio standard deviation of 6.5 percent per month (22.5 percent per year), Joe's portfolio systematic variance is

$$\beta^2 \sigma_M^2 = 1.2^2 \times .065^2 = .006084$$

and hence the correlation coefficient between his portfolio and the market index is

$$\rho = \left[\frac{\beta^2 \sigma_M^2}{\beta^2 \sigma_M^2 + \sigma^2(e)} \right]^{1/2}$$
$$= \left[\frac{.006084}{.006084 + .0004} \right]^{1/2}$$
$$= .97$$

which shows that his portfolio appears to be quite well diversified. We calculate these statistics only to show that there is nothing unusual about Joe's portfolio.

To estimate Joe's portfolio alpha, we would estimate the portfolio security characteristic line (SCL), regressing the portfolio excess returns against those of the market index. Suppose that we are in luck in the sense that over the measurement period, the regression estimates yield the true parameters. That means that our SCL estimates for the N months are:

$$\alpha = .2\%, \beta = 1.2, \sigma(e) = 2\%$$

The evaluators who run such a regression, however, do not know the true values; hence they must compute the t-statistic of the estimated alpha value to determine whether they can reject the hypothesis that Joe's alpha is zero, that is, that he has no ability.

The standard error of the alpha estimate in the SCL regression is approximately

$$\sigma(\alpha) = \frac{\sigma(e)}{\sqrt{N}}$$

where N is the number of observations and $\sigma(e)$ is the sample estimate of non-systematic risk. The t-statistic for the alpha estimate is then

$$t(\alpha) = \frac{\alpha}{\sigma(\alpha)}$$
$$= \frac{\alpha\sqrt{N}}{\sigma(e)} \tag{13.4}$$

Suppose that we require a significance level of 5 percent. This requires a $t(\alpha)$ value of 1.96 if N is large. With $\alpha = .2$ and $\sigma(e) = 2$ we solve equation 13.4 for N and find that

$$1.96 = \frac{.2\sqrt{N}}{2}$$
$$N = 384 \text{ months}$$

or 32 years!

What have we shown? Here is an analyst who has very substantial ability. The example is biased in his favour in the sense that we have assumed away statistical problems. Nothing changes in the parameters over a long period of time. Furthermore, the sample period "behaves" perfectly. Regression estimates are all perfect. Still, it will take Joe's entire working career to get to the point where statistics will confirm his true ability. We have to conclude that the problem of statistical inference makes performance evaluation extremely difficult in practice.

Concept Check

Question 4. Suppose an analyst has a measured alpha of .2 percent with a standard error of 2 percent, as in our example. What is the probability that the positive alpha is due to luck of the draw and that true ability is zero?

13.3 *Performance Measurement with Changing Portfolio Composition*

We have seen already that the high variance of stock returns requires a very long observation period to determine performance levels with any statistical significance, even if portfolio returns are distributed with constant mean and variance. Imagine how this problem is compounded when portfolio return distributions are constantly changing.

It is acceptable to assume that the return distributions of passive strategies have constant mean and variance when the measurement interval is not too long. However, under an active strategy, return distributions change by design, as the portfolio manager updates the portfolio in accordance with the dictates of financial analysis. In such a case, estimating various statistics from a sample period assuming a constant mean and variance may lead to substantial errors. Let us look at an example.

Suppose that the Sharpe measure of the passive strategy is .4. A portfolio manager is in search of a better, active strategy. Over an initial period of 52 weeks she executes a low-risk strategy with an annualized mean excess return of 1 percent and standard deviation of 2 percent. This makes for a Sharpe measure of .5, which beats the passive strategy. Over the next period of another 52 weeks this manager finds that a *high*-risk strategy is optimal, with an annual mean excess return of 9 percent standard deviation of 18 percent. Here, again, the Sharpe measure is .5. Over the two-year period our manager maintains a better-than-passive Sharpe measure.

Figure 13.3 shows a pattern of (annualized) quarterly returns that are consistent with our description of the manager's strategy over two years. In the first four quarters the excess returns are −1 percent, 3 percent, −1 percent, and 3 percent, making for an average of 1 percent and standard deviation of 2 percent. In the next four quarters the returns are: −9 percent, 27 percent, −9 percent, 27 percent, making for an average of 9 percent and a standard deviation of 18 percent. Thus *both* years exhibit a Sharpe measure of .5. However, if we take the eight-quarter sequence as a single measurement period, and measure the portfolio's mean and standard deviation over that full period, we will obtain an average excess return of 5 percent and standard deviation of 13.42 percent, making for a Sharpe measure of only .37, apparently inferior to the passive strategy!

What happened? The shift in the mean from the first four quarters to the next was not recognized as a shift in strategy. Instead, the difference in mean returns in the two years added to the *appearance* of volatility in portfolio returns. The active strategy with shifting means appears riskier than it really is and biases the estimate of the Sharpe measure downward. We conclude that for actively managed portfolios it is crucial to keep track of portfolio composition

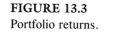

FIGURE 13.3
Portfolio returns.

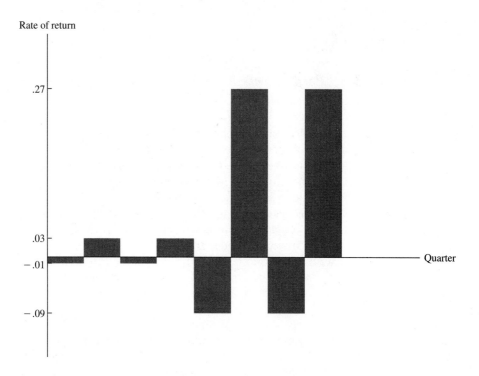

and changes in portfolio mean and risk. We will see another example of this problem in the next section, on timing.

13.4 *Timing and Selectivity*

Traditionally, portfolio managers have distinguished themselves as either market-timers or stock-pickers. In this way, some have claimed an aptitude for **timing** the broad market swings by macroeconomic analysis; others, doubting the feasibility of this, have relied on **selectivity**—identifying equities that would perform well in particular economic climates. More recently, we have seen the emergence of managers who despair of either ability and operate index funds. Researchers have attempted to answer the important question of whether these abilities, particularly timing, can be demonstrated.

In its pure form, market timing involves shifting funds between a market index portfolio and a safe asset, such as T-bills or a money market fund, depending on whether the market as a whole is expected to outperform the safe asset. In practice, of course, most managers do not shift fully between T-bills

FIGURE 13.4
Characteristic lines.
A, No market
timing, beta is
constant, **B,** Market
timing, beta
increases with
expected market
excess return. **C,**
Market timing with
only two values of
beta.

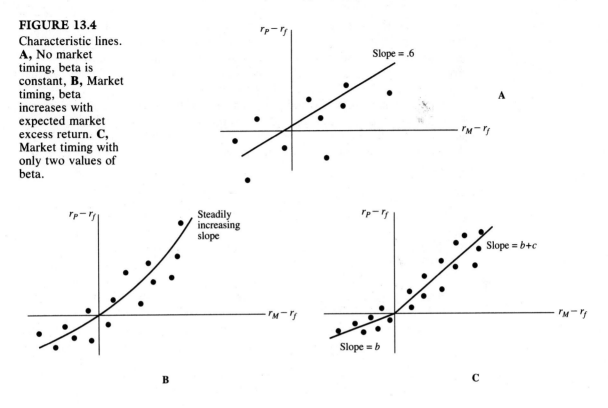

and the market. How might we measure partial shifts into the market when it is
expected to perform well?

To simplify, suppose that the investor holds only the market index portfolio
and T-bills. If the weight on the market were constant, for example, .6, then the
portfolio beta also would be constant, and the portfolio characteristic line
would plot as a straight line with slope .6, as in Figure 13.4**A**. If, however, the
investor could correctly time the market, and shift funds into it in periods when
the market does well, the characteristic line would plot as in Figure 13.4**B**. The
idea is that if the timer can predict bull and bear markets, the investor will shift
more into the market when the market is about to go up. The portfolio beta and
the slope of the characteristic line will be higher when r_M is higher, resulting in
the curved line that appears in Figure 13.4**B**.

Treynor and Mazuy[7] propose that such a line can be estimated by adding a
squared term to the usual linear index model:

$$r_P - r_f = a + b(r_M - r_f) + c(r_M - r_f)^2 + e_P$$

---

[7] Jack L. Treynor and Kay Mazuy, "Can Mutual Funds Outguess the Market," *Harvard Business Review* 43 (July–August 1966).

where r_P is the portfolio return, and *a, b,* and *c* are estimated by regression analysis. If *c* turns out to be positive, we have evidence of timing ability, because this last term will make the characteristic line steeper as $r_M - r_f$ is larger. Treynor and Mazuy estimated this equation for a number of mutual funds, but found little evidence of timing ability.

A similar and simpler methodology is proposed by Henriksson and Merton.[8] These authors suggest that the beta of the portfolio take only two values: a large value if the market is expected to do well and a small value otherwise. Under this scheme, the portfolio characteristic line appears as Figure 13.4C. Such a line appears in regression form as

$$r_P - r_f = a + b(r_M - r_f) + c(r_M - r_f)D + e_P$$

where *D* is a dummy variable that equals 1 for $r_M > r_f$ and zero otherwise. Hence the beta of the portfolio is *b* in bear markets and *b + c* in bull markets. Again, a positive value of *c* implies market timing ability.

Henriksson[9] estimates this equation for 116 mutual funds over the period 1968–1980. He finds that the average value of *c* for the funds was *negative,* and equal to −.07, although the value was not statistically significant at the conventional 5 percent level. Eleven funds had significantly positive values of *c,* while eight had significantly negative values. Overall, 62 percent of the funds had negative point estimates of timing ability. In sum, the results showed little evidence of market timing ability. Perhaps this should be expected; given the tremendous values to be reaped by a successful market timer, it would be surprising in nearly efficient markets to uncover clear-cut evidence of such skills.

The problem of identifying timing and selectivity ability has been hindered by some difficulty in defining the two skills where these tend to be related to the regression characteristics rather than to their intuitive, economic characteristics. Admati et al.[10] have presented two alternative structures for testing these abilities, based on the alternative definitions. The normal regression-based approach is identified as a portfolio approach; this stresses the use of obvious portfolios to be used for timing decisions, such as the T-bill and index fund portfolios, and examines the regression residuals for different managers. A newer approach is to use a factor model that will relate to the economic factors giving rise to timing and selection decisions. In both cases, the issue is the quality of information possessed by the manager; the information will affect the performance of individual assets and the portfolios either directly, by analysis of the assets, or through the factors that generate returns on the assets and portfolios.

[8] Roy D. Henriksson and R. C. Merton, ''On Market Timing and Investment Performance. II. Statistical Procedures for Evaluating Forecast Skills,'' *Journal of Business* 54 (October 1981).

[9] Roy D. Henriksson, ''Market Timing and Mutual Fund Performance: An Empirical Investigation,'' *Journal of Business* 57 (January 1984).

[10] A. R. Admati, S. Bhattacharya, P. Pfleiderer, and S. A. Ross, ''On Timing and Selectivity,'' *Journal of Finance* 41, no. 3 (July 1986).

Canadian studies have not focused on the timing issue, although Dhingra did find that the volatilities of fund portfolios were not stationary.[11] A recent study, however, by Weigel and Ilkiw[12] investigated market timing effected by two methods: **tactical asset allocation** (TAA) models and **swing fund management**. The latter describes the more traditional practice of switching weights in response to intuitive appraisal of the economy and asset class response. TAA is the result of computerized decision rules and relies on the use of options and other derivative instruments to effect rapid and cost-effective adjustments to the portfolio mix. The study found TAA to be a superior approach, but the authors qualified the reliability of their results due to data limitations.

To illustrate a test for market timing, return to Table 13.3. Regressing the excess returns of portfolios P and Q on the excess returns on M and the square of these returns,

$$r_P - r_f = a_P + b_P(r_M - r_f) + c_P(r_M - r_f)^2 + e_P$$
$$r_Q - r_f = a_Q + b_Q(r_M - r_f) + c_Q(r_M - r_f)^2 + e_Q$$

we derive the following statistics:

	Portfolio	
Estimate	P	Q
Alpha (a)	1.77 (1.77)	−2.29 (5.28)
Beta (b)	.70 (.70)	1.10 (1.40)
Timing (c)	.00	.10
R^2	.91 (.91)	.98 (.64)

The numbers in parentheses are the regression estimates from the single variable regression reported in Table 13.4. The results reveal that portfolio P shows no timing. It is not clear whether this is a result of Jane's making no attempt at timing or that the effort to time was in vain and served only to increase portfolio variance unnecessarily.

The results for portfolio Q, however, reveal that timing has, in all likelihood, successfully been attempted. The timing coefficient, c, is estimated at .10. This describes a successful timing effort that was offset by unsuccessful stock selection. Note that the alpha estimate, a, is now −2.29 percent, as opposed to the 5.28 percent estimate derived from the regression equation that did not allow for the possibility of timing activity.

Indeed, this is an example of the inadequacy of conventional performance evaluation techniques that assume constant mean returns and constant risk. The market timer constantly shifts beta and mean return, moving into and out of the market. Whereas the expanded regression captures this phenomenon, the simple SCL does not. The relative desirability of portfolios P and Q remains

---

[11] H. L. Dhingra, "Portfolio Volatility Adjustment by Canadian Mutual Funds," *Journal of Business Finance and Accounting* 5, no. 4 (1978).

[12] Eric J. Weigel and John H. Ilkiw, "Market Timing Skill in Canada: An Assessment," *Canadian Investment Review* vol. 4, no. 1 (Spring 1991).

unclear in the sense that the value of the timing success and selectivity failure of Q compared with P has yet to be evaluated. The important point for performance evaluation, however, is that expanded regressions can capture many of the effects of portfolio composition change that would confound the more conventional mean-variance measures.

13.5 *Performance Attribution Procedures*

Rather than focus on risk-adjusted returns, practitioners often want simply to ascertain which decisions resulted in superior or inferior performance. Superior investment performance depends on an ability to be in the "right" securities at the right time. Such timing and selection ability may be considered broadly, for instance being in equities as opposed to fixed-income securities when the stock market is performing well. Or it may be defined at a more detailed level, such as choosing the relatively better-performing stocks within a particular industry. Portfolio managers constantly make both broad-brush asset-market allocation decisions, as well as more detailed sector and security allocation decisions within markets. Performance attribution studies attempt to break down overall performance into discrete components that may be identified with a particular level of the portfolio selection process.

Recent characterizations of performance ability have extended the simpler timing–selectivity dichotomy by adding a policy variable representing asset allocation. As we have noted, market-timers do not actually switch from T-bills to index funds; rather, they have a standard or base allocation of portfolio weights to T-bills, government bonds, corporate bonds, domestic equities, foreign equities, and perhaps other assets. From this base allocation they shift weights as they see the various assets responding more favourably to changing market conditions. Assessment of managerial ability should then include their choice of base portfolio; Carlton and Osborn refute the importance of this factor.[13]

Attribution studies start from the broadest asset allocation choices and progressively focus on ever-finer details of portfolio choice. The difference between a managed portfolio's performance and that of a benchmark, or "bogey," portfolio then may be expressed as the sum of the contributions to performance of a series of decisions made at the various levels of the portfolio construction process. For example, one common attribution system breaks performance down into three components (1) broad-asset market allocation choices across equity, fixed-income, and money markets, (2) industry (sector) choice within each market, and (3) security choice within each sector.

---

[13] Colin G. Carlton and John C. Osborn, "The Determinants of Balanced Fund Performance," *Canadian Investment Review* vol. 4, no. 1 (Spring 1991).

TABLE 13.5 Performance of the Managed Portfolio

Component	Benchmark Weight	Return of Index during Month (%)
Bogey Performance and Excess Return		
Equity (TSE 300)	.60	5.81
Bonds (Scotia-McLeod)	.30	1.45
Cash (money market)	.10	0.48
Bogey = (.60 × 5.81) + (.30 × 1.45) + (.10 × 0.48) = 3.97%		
Return of managed portfolio		5.34%
Return of bogey portfolio		3.97
Excess return of managed portfolio		1.37%

To illustrate the allocation of investment results to various decisions at different levels of portfolio construction, consider the attribution results for a hypothetical portfolio. The portfolio invests in stocks, bonds, and money market securities. The attribution analysis is presented in Tables 13.5–13.8. The portfolio return over the month was 5.34 percent. A **bogey**, or benchmark performance level, is calculated based on the performances of an equity index (the TSE 300), a fixed-income index (Scotia-McLeod), and a money market index, each weighted using a notion of "usual" or neutral allocation across sectors, or alternatively, using client-specified weights. Here, the standard weights are 60 percent equity, 30 percent fixed-income, and 10 percent cash (money market securities). The bogey portfolio, composed of "investments" in each index with the 60/30/10 weights, returned 3.97 percent.

The managed portfolio's measure of extra-market performance is positive, and equal to its actual return less the return of the bogey: 5.34 − 3.97 = 1.37 percent. The next step is to allocate the 1.37 percent excess return to the separate decisions that contributed to it.

Asset Allocation Decisions

Our hypothetical managed portfolio was invested in the equity, fixed-income, and money markets with weights 70 percent, 7 percent, and 23 percent, respectively. The portfolio's performance can derive from the departure of this weighting scheme from the benchmark 60/30/10 weights, as well as from superior or inferior results *within* each of the three broad markets. To measure only the effect of the manager's asset allocation choice, we measure the performance of a hypothetical portfolio that would have invested in the *indices* for each market with weights 70/7/23. This return measures the individual effect of the shift away from the benchmark 60/30/10 weights, without allowing for any effects attributable to active management of the securities selected within each market. Superior performance relative to the bogey is achieved by overweighting investments in markets that turn out to perform relatively well, and by

TABLE 13.6   Performance Attribution

Market	(1) Actual Weight in Market	(2) Benchmark Weight in Market	(3) Excess Weight	(4) Market Return (%)	(5) = (3) × (4) Contribution to Performance (%)
A. Contribution of Asset Allocation to Performance					
Equity	.70	.60	.10	5.81	.5810
Fixed income	.07	.30	−.23	1.45	−.3335
Cash	.23	.10	.13	0.48	.0624
Contribution of asset allocation					.3099

Market	(1) Portfolio Performance (%)	(2) Index Performance (%)	(3) Excess Performance (%)	(4) Portfolio Weight	(5) = (3) × (4) Contribution (%)
B. Contribution of Selection to Total Performance					
Equity	7.28	5.81	1.47	.70	1.03
Fixed income	1.89	1.45	0.44	.07	.03
Contribution of selection within markets					1.06

underweighting poorly performing markets. The contribution of asset allocation to superior performance equals the sum over all markets of the excess weight in each market multiplied by the return of the market index.

Part **A** of Table 13.6 demonstrates that asset allocation contributed 31 basis points to the portfolio's overall excess return of 137 basis points. The major factor contributing to superior performance in this month was the heavy weighting of the equity market in a month when the equity market had an excellent return of 5.81 percent.

Sector and Security Allocation Decisions

If .31 percent of the excess performance can be attributed to advantageous asset allocation across markets, the remaining 1.06 percent must be attributable to sector and security selection within each market. Part **B** of Table 13.6 details the contribution of the managed portfolio's sector and security selection to total performance.

Part **B** shows that the equity component of the managed portfolio had a return of 7.28 percent versus a return of 5.81 percent for the TSE 300. The fixed-income return was 1.89 percent versus 1.45 percent for the Scotia-McLeod index. The superior performance in equity and fixed-income markets weighted by the portfolio proportions invested in each market sums to the 1.06 percent contribution to performance attributable to sector and security selection.

Table 13.7 documents the sources of the equity component performance by each sector within the market. The first three columns detail the allocation of funds to the sectors in the equity market compared with their (hypothetical) representation in the TSE 300. Column 4 shows the rate of return of each sector, and column 5 documents the performance of each sector relative to the return of the TSE 300. The contribution of each sector's allocation presented in column 6 equals the product of the difference in the sector weight and the sector's relative performance.

Note that good performance (a positive contribution) derives from over-weighting well-performing sectors such as energy or underweighting poorly performing sectors such as transportation. The excess return of the equity component of the portfolio attributable to sector allocation alone is 1.01 percent. Since the equity component of the portfolio outperformed the TSE 300 by 1.47 percent, we conclude that the effect of security selection within sectors must have contributed an additional $1.47 - 1.01 = .46$ percent to the performance of the equity component of the portfolio.

A similar sector analysis can be applied to the fixed-income portion of the portfolio, but we do not show those results here.

Summing Up Component Contributions

In this particular month, all facets of the portfolio selection process were successful. Table 13.8 details the contribution of each aspect of performance. Asset allocation across the major security markets contributes 31 basis points. Sector and security allocation within those markets contributes 106 basis points, for total excess portfolio performance of 137 basis points. The sector and security allocation of 106 basis points can be partitioned further. Sector allocation within the equity market results in excess performance of 100.76 basis points, and security selection within sectors contributes 46 basis points. (The total equity excess performance of 147 basis points is multiplied by the 70 percent weight in equity to obtain contribution to portfolio performance.) Similar partitioning could be done for the fixed-income sector.

TABLE 13.7 Sector Selection within the Equity Market

Sector	(1)(2) Beginning of Month Weights (%) Portfolio	TSE 300	(3) Difference in Weights	(4) Sector Return	(5) Sector Over/Under Performance*	(6) = (3) × (5) Sector Allocation Contribution
Interest-sensitive	29.72	31.99	−2.27	6.4	0.9	−2.04
Consumer	9.54	17.46	−7.92	5.4	−0.1	0.79
Resource	10.31	21.52	−11.21	3.7	−1.8	20.18
Energy	24.29	9.31	14.98	8.4	2.9	43.44
Industrial products	19.03	9.83	9.2	8.3	2.8	25.76
Transportation	2.32	3.70	−1.38	−0.2	−5.7	7.87
Management companies	4.79	6.19	−1.4	2.1	−3.4	4.76
TOTAL						**100.76 basis points**

* TSE 300 performance, excluding dividends, was 5.5 percent. Returns compared net of dividends.

TABLE 13.8   Portfolio Attribution: Summary

		Contribution (Basis Points)
1. Asset allocation		31.0
2. Selection		
a. Equity excess return		
i. Sector allocation	101	
ii. Security allocation	46	
	147 × .70 (portfolio weight) =	102.9
b. Fixed-income excess return	44 × .07 (portfolio weight) =	3.1
Total excess return of portfolio		**137.0 basis points**

13.6   *Canadian Performance Evaluation*

Evaluation of Canadian mutual funds has been carried out at two levels: professional reporting of current results for the universe of Canadian-managed funds, and academic examination of risk-adjusted performance of the funds.

Professional Performance Reporting

The most available report on mutual funds is published regularly by the major financial newspapers in Canada. For example, *The Globe and Mail*'s Report on Business survey of mutual funds appears monthly, and provides a summary of the realized performance of Canadian funds. In an attempt to provide meaningful comparisons, the funds are grouped by type, including: balanced, dividend (income), Canadian equity, U.S. equity, international equity, as well as money market, bond, mortgage, and real estate funds; the Canadian, U.S., and international equity funds ought to be growth-oriented by contrast with the balanced and dividend funds. The report also provides a measure of volatility on a one-to-five scale. The tables within the report list returns for periods ranging from three months to ten years, where these are net of management fees and include reinvestment of dividends. An average for the group is given in addition to other individual information of interest to investors, including details of sales commissions or "loads."

A far more informative appraisal is provided by firms whose primary purpose is to track performance of managers for pension funds who are their clients. Individual components of performance are measured to examine the success or failure of the manager in beating the index or the average of similar-objective funds. There are two major services that specialize in providing these analyses in Canada: SEI Financial Services and Hitchens Capital Management.

SEI has the larger client base and also has made its data available for academic study.

Software providing similar information is also available to individuals to aid in the assessment of funds. For instance, Portfolio Analytics Limited provides statistical information about mutual funds on disc through a service called "FundTrak."

Empirical Studies

A number of studies of Canadian mutual fund performance have been conducted, using a variety of techniques and investigating different phenomena. Researchers have investigated the stability of the funds' betas, the effects of inflation and fund size, performance in good and bad markets, and the general question of the value of managerial expertise.

An early study by Grant[14] used Jensen's measure to compare performance over the period 1960–1974. By examining the stability of the risk measure beta and performance, Grant found that funds were unable to satisfy the objectives that they set for themselves; that is, the revealed instability meant that an investor could not guarantee either high or low growth and risk by investing in funds with defined objectives. Similarly, Dhingra found that both average returns and volatility were unstable over time, as we previously noted.

Calvet and Lefoll[15] investigated the inflationary effect on returns and concluded that the real returns of funds were not superior to those of the TSE 300; real and nominal returns revealed that inflation did not explain the return-generating mechanism of the market or fund returns. Martel, Khoury, and M'zali[16] used a multicriterion evaluation and the Sharpe and Treynor indices in a study to determine the effect of fund size. The data were drawn from a sample of 34 funds from 1981–1986, and they identified a combined index incorporating the TSE 300, S&P 500, and the EAFE (for international effects). Their conclusion was that fund size was associated with superior performance for this sample.

Fund performance for the period 1967–1984 was analyzed by Bishara,[17] who concluded that Canadian funds could not outperform the market. He subdivided his fund universe into balanced, income, and growth funds and considered their returns over boom and recession periods. His findings concluded that while growth funds managed to match the index return, the balanced and

---

[14] D. Grant, "Investment Performance of Canadian Mutual Funds: 1960–1974," *Journal of Business Administration* 8 (Fall 1976).

[15] A. L. Calvet and J. Lefoll, "The CAPM under Inflation and the Performance of Canadian Mutual Funds," *Journal of Business Administration* 12, no. 1 (Fall 1980).

[16] Jean-Marc Martel, Nabil Khoury, and Bouchra M'zali, "Relationship between Mutual Funds' Size and Their 'Performance,'" *Finance Proceedings,* Administrative Sciences Association of Canada, vol. 8 (1987). See also J.-M. Martel, N. T. Khoury, and M. Bergeron, "An Application of a Multicriteria Approach to Portfolio Comparisons," *Journal of the Operations Research Society* 39, no. 7 (1988); and N. T. Khoury and J.-M. Martel, "The Relationship between Risk-Return Characteristics of Mutual Funds and Their Size," *Finance* 11, no. 2 (1990).

[17] Halim Bishara, "Evaluation of the Performance of Canadian Mutual Funds (1967–1984)," *Finance Proceedings,* Administrative Sciences Association of Canada, vol. 9 (1988).

income funds were inferior to the index over the whole period and during one boom.[18]

13.7   *Evaluating Performance Evaluation*

Performance evaluation has two very basic problems:

1. Many observations are needed for significant results even when portfolio mean and variance are constant.
2. Shifting parameters when portfolios are actively managed make accurate performance evaluation all the more elusive.

Although these objective difficulties cannot be overcome completely, it is clear that to obtain reasonably reliable performance measures we need to do the following:

1. Maximize the number of observations by taking more frequent return readings.
2. Specify the exact make-up of the portfolio to obtain better estimates of the risk parameters at each observation period.

Suppose an evaluator knows the exact portfolio composition at the opening of each day. Because the daily return on each security is available, the total daily return on the portfolio can be calculated. Furthermore, the exact portfolio composition allows the evaluator to estimate the risk characteristics (variance, beta, residual variance) for each day. Thus, daily risk-adjusted rates of return can be obtained. Although a performance measure for one day is statistically unreliable, the number of days with such rich data accumulates quickly. Performance evaluation that accounts for frequent revision in portfolio composition is superior by far to evaluation that assumes constant risk characteristics over the entire measurement period.

What sort of evaluation takes place in practice? Performance reports for portfolio managers traditionally have been based on quarterly data over 5–10 years. Currently, managers of mutual funds are required to disclose the exact composition of their portfolios only semiannually. Trading activity that immediately precedes the reporting date is known as "window dressing." Rumour has it that window dressing involves changes in portfolio composition to make it look as if the manager chose successful stocks. If Seagram's performed well over the quarter, for example, a portfolio manager will make sure that his or her portfolio includes a lot of Seagram's on the reporting date, whether or not it did

---

[18] These statements must be appreciated in the light of the diminishing statistical significance that accompanies sample size reduction; each of the stated results is significant.

during the quarter and whether or not Seagram's is expected to perform as well over the next quarter. Of course, portfolio managers deny such activity, and we know of no published evidence to substantiate the allegation. However, if window dressing is quantitatively significant, even the reported quarterly composition data can be misleading. Mutual funds publish portfolio values on a daily basis, which means the rate of return for each day is publicly available, but portfolio composition is not.

Moreover, mutual fund managers have had considerable leeway in the presentation of both past investment performance and fees charged for management services. The resultant non-comparability of net-of-expense performance numbers has made it difficult to meaningfully compare funds. This may be changing, however. The OSC has moved toward greater disclosure in the reporting of fees. Awareness of the fees may help to evaluate performance based on the actual invested capital.

Traditional academic research uses monthly, weekly, and, more recently, even daily data. But such research makes no use of changes in portfolio composition because the data usually are unavailable. Therefore, performance evaluation is unsatisfactory in both the academic and practitioner communities.

Portfolio managers reveal their portfolio composition only when they have to, which so far is quarterly. This is not nearly sufficient for adequate evaluation. However, current computer and communication technology makes it easy to use daily composition data for evaluation purposes. If the technology required for meaningful evaluation is in place, implementation of more accurate performance measurement techniques could improve welfare by enabling the public to identify the truly talented investment managers.

Summary

1. The appropriate performance measure depends on the role of the portfolio to be evaluated. Appropriate performance measures are as follows:
   a. *Sharpe:* when the portfolio represents the entire investment fund.
   b. *Appraisal ratio:* when the portfolio represents the active portfolio to be optimally mixed with the passive portfolio.
   c. *Treynor:* when the portfolio represents one subportfolio of many.
2. Many observations are required to eliminate the effect of the "luck of the draw" from the evaluation process, because portfolio returns commonly are very "noisy."
3. The shifting mean and variance of actively managed portfolios make it even harder to assess performance. A typical example is the attempt of portfolio managers to time the market, resulting in ever-changing portfolio betas.
4. A simple way to measure timing and selection success simultaneously is

to estimate an expanded SCL, with a quadratic term added to the usual index model.

5. Common attribution procedures partition performance improvements to asset allocation, sector selection, and security selection. Performance is assessed by calculating departures of portfolio composition from a benchmark or neutral portfolio.

6. Empirical studies of mutual fund performance have not revealed any ability to outperform the market index, nor to time market swings.

Key terms

Dollar-weighted rate of return	Appraisal ratio
Time-weighted return	Timing
Comparison universe	Selectivity
Sharpe's measure	Tactical asset allocation
Treynor's measure	Swing fund management
Jensen's measure	Bogey

Selected readings

The mean-variance based performance evaluation literature is based on early papers by:

Sharpe, William F. "Mutual Fund Performance." *Journal of Business* 39 (January 1966).

Treynor, Jack L. "How to Rate Management Investment Funds." *Harvard Business Review* 43 (January–February 1966).

Jensen, Michael C. "The Performance of Mutual Funds in the Period 1945–1964." *Journal of Finance*, May 1968.

Jensen, Michael C. "Risk, the Pricing of Capital Assets, and the Evaluation of Investment Portfolios." *Journal of Business*, April 1969.

The problems that arise when conventional mean-variance measures are calculated in the presence of a shifting-return distribution are treated in:

Dybvig, Philip H.; and Ross, Stephen A. "Differential Information and Performance Measurement Using a Security Market Line." *Journal of Finance* 40 (June 1985).

The separation of investment ability into timing versus selection activity derives from:

Fama, Eugene F. "Components of Investment Performance." *Journal of Finance* 25 (June 1970).

Key empirical papers on timing versus selection are:

Admati, A. R.; Bhattacharya, S.; Pfleiderer, P.; and Ross, S. A. "On Timing and Selectivity." *Journal of Finance* 41, no. 3 (July 1986).

Henriksson, Roy D. "Market Timing and Mutual Fund Performance: An Empirical Investigation." *Journal of Business* 57 (January 1984).

Henriksson, Roy D.; and Merton, R. C. "On Market Timing and Investment Performance. II. Statistical Procedures for Evaluating Forecast Skills." *Journal of Business* 54 (October 1981).

Kon, S. J.; and Jen, F. D. "The Investment Performance of Mutual Funds: An Empirical Investigation of Timing, Selectivity, and Market Efficiency." *Journal of Business* 52 (April 1979).

Lee, Cheng-Few; and Rahman, Shafiqur. "Market Timing, Selectivity, and Mutual Fund Performance: An Empirical Investigation." *Journal of Business* 63, no. 2 (April 1990).

Treynor, Jack, L.; and Mazuy Kay. "Can Mutual Funds Outguess the Market." *Harvard Business Review* 43 (July–August 1966).

Problems

1. Consider the rate of return of stocks ABC and XYZ.

Year	r_{ABC}	r_{XYZ}
1	.20	.30
2	.10	.10
3	.14	.18
4	.05	.00
5	.01	−.08

   a. Calculate the arithmetic average return on these stocks over the sample period.
   b. Which stock has greater dispersion around the mean?
   c. Calculate the geometric average returns of each stock. What do you conclude?
   d. If you were equally likely to earn a return of 20 percent, 10 percent, 14 percent, 5 percent, or 1 percent in each of the five annual returns for stock ABC, what would be your expected rate of return? What if the five outcomes were those of stock XYZ?

2. XYZ stock price and dividend history are as follows:

Year	Beginning of Year Price	Dividend Paid at Year-End
1991	$100	$4
1992	$110	$4
1993	$ 90	$4
1994	$ 95	$4

   An investor buys three shares of XYZ at the beginning of 1991, buys another two shares at the beginning of 1992, sells one share at the beginning of 1993, and sells all four remaining shares at the beginning of 1994.
   a. What are the arithmetic and geometric average time-weighted rates of return for the investor?
   b. What is the dollar-weighted rate of return? Hint: carefully prepare a chart of cash flows for the *four* dates corresponding to the turns of the year for January 1, 1991, to December 31, 1994. If your calculator cannot calculate internal rate of return you will have to use trial and error.

3. Based on current dividend yields and expected capital gains, the expected rates of return on portfolios *A* and *B* are .11 percent and .14 percent, respectively. The beta of A is 0.8, while that of B is 1.5. The T-bill rate is currently .06, while the expected rate of return of the TSE 300 index is .12. The standard deviation of portfolio A is .10 annually, that of B is .31, and that of the TSE 300 index is .20.

a. If you currently hold a market-index portfolio, would you choose to add either of these portfolios to your holdings? Explain.

b. If instead you could invest *only* in T-bills and *one* of these portfolios, which would you choose?

4. Consider the two (excess return) index-model regression results for stocks A and B. The risk-free rate over the period was .06, and the market's average return was .14.

(i) $r_A - r_f = .01 + 1.2(r_M - r_f)$
$R^2 = .576$
Residual standard deviation, $\sigma(e_A) = 10.3\%$
Standard deviation of $r_A - r_f = .261$

(ii) $r_B - r_f = .02 + .8(r_M - r_f)$
$R^2 = .436$
Residual standard deviation, $\sigma(e_B) = 19.1\%$
Standard deviation of $r_B - r_f = .249$

a. Calculate the following statistics for each stock:
  i. Alpha
  ii. Appraisal ratio
  iii. Sharpe measure
  iv. Treynor measure

b. Which stock is the best choice under the following circumstances?
  i. This is the only risky asset to be held by the investor.
  ii. This stock will be mixed with the rest of the investor's portfolio, currently composed solely of holdings in the market index fund.
  iii. This is one of many stocks that the investor is analyzing to form an actively managed stock portfolio.

5. Evaluate the timing and selection abilities of four managers whose performances are plotted in the following four scatter diagrams.

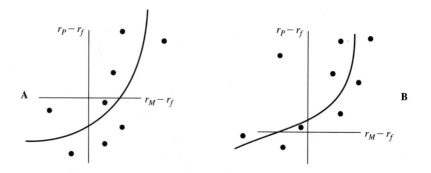

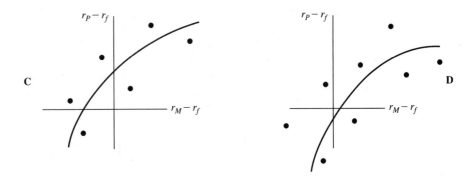

6. Consider the following information regarding the performance of a money manager in a recent month. The table presents the actual return of each sector of the manager's portfolio in column 1, the fraction of the portfolio allocated to each sector in column 2, the benchmark or neutral sector allocations in column 3, and the returns of sector indices in column 4.

	Actual Return	Actual Weight	Benchmark Weight	Index Return
Equity	.02	.70	.60	.025 (TSE 300)
Bonds	.01	.20	.30	.012 (Scotia-McLeod)
Cash	.005	.10	.10	.005

a. What was the manager's return in the month? What was her overperformance or underperformance?

b. What was the contribution of security selection to relative performance?

c. What was the contribution of asset allocation to relative performance? Confirm that the sum of selection and allocation contributions equals her total "excess" return relative to the bogey.

7. Conventional wisdom says that one should measure a manager's investment performance over an entire market cycle. What arguments support this contention? What arguments contradict it?

8. Does the use of universes of managers with similar investment styles to evaluate relative investment performance overcome the statistical problems associated with instability of beta or total variability?

9. During a particular year, the T-bill rate was 6 percent, the market return was 14 percent, and a portfolio manager with beta of .5 realized a return of 10 percent.

a. Evaluate the manager based on the porfolio alpha.

b. Reconsider your answer to part (a) in view of the Black–Jensen–Scholes finding that the security market line is too flat. Now how do you assess the manager's performance?

10. (Based on CFA Examination, Level III, 1983) The chairman provides you with the following data, covering one year, concerning the portfolios of two of the fund's equity managers (Firm *A* and Firm *B*). Although the portfolios consist primarily of common stocks, cash reserves are included in the calculation of both portfolio betas and performance. By way of perspective, selected data for the financial markets are included in the following table:

	Total Return (%)	Beta
Firm *A*	24.0	1.0
Firm *B*	30.0	1.5
TSE 300	21.0	
Scotia-McLeod Total Bond Index	31.0	
91-day Treasury bills	12.0	

   a. Calculate and compare the risk adjusted performance of the two firms relative to each other and to the TSE 300.
   b. Explain *two* reasons the conclusions drawn from this calculation may be misleading.

11. (CFA Examination, Level I, 1981) Carl Karl, a portfolio manager for the Alpine Trust Company, has been responsible since 1975 for the City of Alpine's Employee Retirement Plan, a municipal pension fund. Alpine is a growing community, and city services and employee payrolls have expanded in each of the past 10 years. Contributions to the Plan in fiscal 1980 exceeded benefit payments by a three-to-one ratio.

   The Plan's Board of Trustees directed Karl five years ago to invest for total return over the long term. However, as trustees of this highly visible public fund, they cautioned him that volatile or erratic results could cause them embarrassment. They also noted a state statute that mandated that not more than 25 percent of the plan's assets (at cost) be invested in common stocks.

   At the annual meeting of the trustees in November 1980, Karl presented the following portfolio and performance report to the board:

ALPINE EMPLOYEE RETIREMENT PLAN

Asset Mix as of 9/30/80	At Cost (Millions)		At Market (Millions)	
Fixed income assets:				
Short-term securities	$ 4.5	11.0%	$ 4.5	11.4%
Long-term bonds and mortgages	26.5	64.7	23.5	59.5
Common stocks	10.0	24.3	11.5	29.1
	$41.0	100.0%	$39.5	100.0%

INVESTMENT PERFORMANCE

	Annual Rates of Return For Periods Ending 9/30/80	
	5 Years	1 Year
Total Alpine Fund:		
Time-weighted	8.2%	5.2%
Dollar-weighted (Internal)	7.7%	4.8%
Assumed actuarial return	6.0%	6.0%
U.S. Treasury bills	7.5%	11.3%
Large sample of pension funds (average 60% equities, 40% fixed income)	10.1%	14.3%
Common stocks—Alpine Fund	13.3%	14.3%
Average portfolio beta coefficient	0.90	0.89
Standard & Poor's 500 Stock Index	13.8%	21.1%
Fixed income securities—Alpine Fund	6.7%	1.0%
Salomon Brothers' Bond Index	4.0%	−11.4%

Karl was proud of his performance, and thus was chagrined when a trustee made the following critical observations:

a. "Our one-year results were terrible, and it's what you've done for us lately that counts most."

b. "Our total fund performance was clearly inferior compared to the large sample of other pension funds for the last five years. What else could this reflect except poor management judgment?"

c. "Our common stock performance was especially poor for the five-year period."

d. "Why bother to compare your returns to the return from Treasury bills and the actuarial assumption rate? What your competition could have earned for us or how we would have fared if invested in a passive index (which doesn't charge a fee) are the only relevant measures of performance."

e. "Who cares about time-weighted return? If it can't pay pensions, what good is it!"

Appraise the merits of each of these statements, and give counterarguments that Mr. Karl can use.

CHAPTER 14

The Theory of Active
Portfolio Management

So far we have alluded to active portfolio management as an alternative to passive management by investment in the market portfolio and as an input to the Markowitz methodology of generating the optimal risky portfolio (Chapter 7). We have emphasized the theoretical result that efficient markets indicate a passive strategy. In Parts V and VI, we shall examine the approaches used professionally to obtain superior information about the bond and stock markets. You may well have wondered about the seeming contradiction between our equilibrium analysis in Part III—tempered by some of the evidence about efficient markets in Chapter 12—and the real-world environment, where profit-seeking investment managers use active management to exploit perceived market inefficiencies.

Despite the efficient market hypothesis, there are reasons to believe that active management can have effective results, and we discuss these at the outset. Next we consider the objectives of active portfolio management. We analyze two forms of active management: market timing, which is based solely on macroeconomic factors, and security selection, which includes microeconomic forecasting. At the end of the chapter we show the use of multifactor models in active portfolio management.

14.1 *The Lure of Active Management*

How can a theory of active portfolio management be reconciled with the notion that markets are in equilibrium? Market efficiency prevails when many investors are willing to depart from maximum diversification, or a passive strategy, by adding mispriced securities to their portfolios in the hope of realizing abnormal returns. The competition for such returns ensures that prices will be near their "fair" values. Most managers will not beat the passive strategy on a risk-adjusted basis. However, in the competition for rewards to investing, exceptional managers might beat the average forecasts built into market prices.

There is both economic logic and some empirical evidence to indicate that exceptional portfolio managers can beat the average forecast. Let us discuss economic logic first. We must assume that, if no analyst can beat the passive strategy, investors will be smart enough to divert their funds from strategies entailing expensive analysis to less expensive passive strategies. In that case, funds under active management will dry up, and prices will no longer reflect sophisticated forecasts. The consequent profit opportunities will lure back active managers, who once again will become successful.[1] Of course, the critical assumption is that investors allocate management funds wisely. Direct evidence on that has yet to be produced.

As for empirical evidence, consider the following: (1) some portfolio managers have produced streaks of abnormal returns that are hard to label as lucky outcomes, (2) the "noise" in realized rates is enough to prevent us from rejecting outright the hypothesis that some money managers have beaten the passive strategy by a statistically small, yet economically significant, margin, and (3) some anomalies in realized returns have been sufficiently persistent to suggest that portfolio managers who identified them in a timely fashion could have beaten the passive strategy over prolonged periods.

These conclusions persuade us that there is a role for a theory of active portfolio management. Active management has an inevitable lure even if investors agree that security markets are nearly efficient.

Suppose that capital markets are perfectly efficient, an easily accessible market index portfolio is available, and this portfolio is, for all practical purposes, the efficient risky portfolio. Clearly, in this case security selection would be a futile endeavour. You would be better off with a passive strategy of allocating funds to a money market fund (the safe asset) and the market index portfolio. Under these simplifying assumptions the optimal investment strategy seems to require no effort or know-how.

Such a conclusion, however, is too hasty. Recall that the proper allocation of investment funds to the risk-free and risky portfolios requires some analysis because the fraction, y, to be invested in the risky market portfolio, M, is given by

$$y = \frac{E(r_M) - r_f}{A\sigma_M^2} \tag{14.1}$$

where $E(r_M) - r_f$ is the risk premium on M, σ_M^2 its variance, and A is the investor's coefficient of risk aversion. Any rational allocation therefore requires an estimate of σ_M and $E(r_M)$. Even a passive investor needs to do some forecasting, in other words.

---

[1] This point is worked out fully in Sanford J. Grossman and Joseph E. Stiglitz, "On the Impossibility of Informationally Efficient Markets," *American Economic Review* 70 (June 1980).

Forecasting $E(r_M)$ and σ_M is further complicated by the existence of security classes that are affected by different environmental factors. Long-term bond returns, for example, are driven largely by changes in the term structure of interest rates, whereas equity returns depend on changes in the broader economic environment, including macroeconomic factors beyond interest rates. Once our investor determines relevant forecasts for separate sorts of investments, she might as well use an optimization program to determine the proper mix for the portfolio. It is easy to see how the investor may be lured away from a purely passive strategy, and we have not even considered temptations such as international stock and bond portfolios or sector portfolios.

In fact, even the definition of a "purely passive strategy" is problematic, since simple strategies involving only the market index portfolio and risk-free assets now seem to call for market analysis. For our purposes, we define purely passive strategies as those that use only index funds *and* weight those funds by fixed proportions that do not vary in response to perceived market conditions. For example, a portfolio strategy that always places 60 percent in a stock market index fund, 30 percent in a bond index fund, and 10 percent in a money market fund is a purely passive strategy.

More important, the lure into active management may be extremely strong because the potential profit from active strategies is enormous. At the same time, competition among the multitude of active managers creates the force driving market prices to near efficiency levels. Although enormous profits may be increasingly difficult to earn, decent profits to diligent analysts must always be the rule rather than the exception. For prices to remain efficient to some degree, some analysts must be able to eke out a reasonable profit. Absence of profits would decimate the active investment management industry, eventually allowing prices to stray from informationally efficient levels. The theory of managing active portfolios is the concern of this chapter.

14.2   *Objectives of Active Portfolios*

What does an investor expect from a professional portfolio manager, and how does this expectation affect the operation of the manager? If the client were risk neutral, that is, indifferent to risk, the answer would be straightforward. The investor would expect the portfolio manager to construct a portfolio with the highest possible expected rate of return. The portfolio manager follows this dictum and is judged by the realized average rate of return.

When the client is risk averse, the answer is more difficult. Without a normative theory of portfolio management, the manager would have to consult each client before making any portfolio decision in order to ascertain that reward (average return) is commensurate with risk. Massive and constant input would be needed from the client-investors, and the economic value of professional management would be questionable.

Fortunately, the theory of mean-variance efficient portfolio management allows us to separate the "product decision," which is how to construct a mean-variance efficient risky portfolio, and the "consumption decision," or the investor's allocation of funds between the efficient risky portfolio and the safe asset. We have seen that construction of the optimal risky portfolio is purely a technical problem, resulting in a single optimal risky portfolio appropriate for all investors. Investors will differ only in how they apportion investment to that risky portfolio and the safe asset.

Another feature of the mean-variance theory that affects portfolio management decisions is the criterion for choosing the optimal risky portfolio. In Chapter 7, we established that the optimal risky portfolio for any investor is the one that maximizes the reward-to-variability ratio, or the expected excess rate of return (over the risk-free rate) divided by the standard deviation. A manager who uses this Markowitz methodology to construct the optimal risky portfolio will satisfy all clients, regardless of risk aversion. Clients, for their part, can evaluate managers using statistical methods to draw inferences from realized rates of return to prospective, or ex ante, reward-to-variability ratios.

William Sharpe's assessment of mutual fund performance[2] is the seminal work in the area of portfolio performance evaluation. Sharpe's measure, the reward-to-variability ratio introduced in Chapter 13, is now a common criterion for tracking performance of professionally managed portfolios.

Briefly, mean-variance portfolio theory implies that the objective of professional portfolio managers is to maximize the (ex ante) Sharpe measure, which entails maximizing the slope of the CAL (capital allocation line). A "good" manager is one whose CAL is steeper than the CAL representing the passive strategy of holding a market index portfolio. Clients can observe rates of return and compute the realized Sharpe measure (the ex post CAL) to evaluate the relative performance of their manager.

Ideally, clients would like to invest their funds with the most able manager, one who consistently obtains the highest Sharpe measure and presumably has real forecasting ability. This is true for all clients, regardless of their degree of risk aversion. At the same time, each client must decide what fraction of investment funds to allocate to this manager, placing the remainder in a safe fund. If the manager's Sharpe measure is constant over time (and can be estimated by clients), the investor can compute the optimal fraction to be invested with the manager from equation 14.1, based on the portfolio long-term average return and variance. The remainder will be invested in a money market fund.

The manager's ex ante Sharpe measure from updated forecasts will be constantly varying. Clients may wish to increase their allocation to the risky port-

---

[2] William F. Sharpe, "Mutual Fund Performance," *Journal of Business, Supplement on Security Prices* 39 (January 1966).

Market Timing Is Key to Asset Allocation

By Ellen Roseman

If your stock market experience consists of buying high and selling low, you were probably intrigued by recent ads for a service that promises to get you in and out of stocks at exactly the right time.

Two companies, AGF Management Ltd. and Royal Trust Investment Services Inc., are offering an asset allocation service for RRSP investors. Using a computer model, they decide how much stocks, bonds, and cash you should hold, then move you in and out of mutual funds composed of these assets.

An asset allocation service can take extreme measures, swinging 100 per cent into each asset if market conditions warrant. This is unlike a balanced fund, which usually holds some portion of stocks, bonds, and cash at all times.

Is asset allocation for you? Here are some things to consider.

Both companies employ a U.S. computer model, which is not modified for use in Canada. They could not find a Canadian model and it doesn't matter anyway, because there is a high correlation between U.S. and Canadian markets.

But are the two markets that alike? Stock prices in the United States are setting new records, while Canadian stocks are far from their peak of August, 1987. The TSE 300 total return index went up 12 per cent last year, while the Dow Jones average went up 20 per cent and the S&P 500 index 26 per cent.

The Canadian stock market is also smaller and more illiquid. This makes it difficult for a multimillion-dollar portfolio to make quick switches from stocks to cash, or cash to stocks.

And real interest rates are several percentage points higher in Canada, which affects both bonds and cash returns.

Given these differences, do you feel comfortable about having your asset allocation decisions dictated by a signal from the United States?

Do you like investing in new products or do you prefer something with a track record? The experience in Canada is only 18 months for AGF's service, two months for Royal Trust's. Is that enough for you?

In 1991, AGF's asset allocation service had a 14-per-cent return. This compares favourably to the TSE's 12 per cent.

But bonds performed much better than Canadian stocks last year. With complete freedom to swing into bonds, shouldn't the asset allocation service have come closer to the ScotiaMcLeod bond index return of 22 per cent?

In practice, asset allocation is just market timing under a different name. We all know how hard it is to predict where the markets will go.

Professional money managers have not shown much skill in timing the markets over long periods. That's why an index fund, which buys the stocks that make up the index, usually does better than an actively managed fund. The TD Green Line Canadian Index Fund had a 10.5-per-cent return last year, while the average Canadian equity fund had a 10.1-per-cent return.

I asked the two companies if they were offering a market timing service.

"I don't like the word *timing*," said William Cameron, vice-president of AGF. "I prefer to say more active asset management. A fixed asset mix can't be the most appropriate strategy over long periods of time when conditions change."

Simon Lewis, managing partner of Royal Trust's mutual funds, says market timers use a few yardsticks, but the computer model has 125 variables. "This is market timing made scientific."

Nevertheless, there is another way to allocate your assets—without a fancy computer model or the extra costs involved.

Say you have $1,000 to invest. You decide how much in stocks, bonds and cash you want to hold, based on your age, objectives and comfort level. If you're 45, you may want $600 in stocks, $300 in bonds and $100 in cash.

Then you adjust the weightings each year. Sup-

(Continued)

pose stocks have had a big runup and your $600 investment has grown to $800. Now you have to dump $200's worth to get back down to the 60-percent level.

"If stocks have gone up dramatically, this forces you to sell high," says David Chilton, author of *The Wealthy Barber* and an advocate of old-fashioned but dependable buy and hold techniques.

Active switching or a fixed asset mix? It's your decision. But don't be fooled by advertising that promises maximum gain and minimum risk.

All the computers in the world can't tell you how to be in the right place at the right time. If so, there wouldn't be a market, since there would be no divergence of opinion on which a market depends.

From *The Globe and Mail*, January 25, 1992, by Ellen Roseman. Reprinted by permission.

folio when the forecasts are optimistic, and vice versa. However, it would be impractical to constantly communicate updated forecasts to clients and for them to constantly revise their allocation between the risky portfolios and risk-free asset.

Allowing managers to shift funds between their optimal risky portfolio and a safe asset according to their forecasts alleviates the problem. Indeed, many stock funds allow the managers reasonable flexibility to do just that (see the nearby box). Managers can be assessed on their decisions of timing, when to invest in risky or safe portfolios, and selectivity, which risky assets to choose. We examine these decisions in the following two sections.

14.3 *Market Timing*

Professor Robert Merton began a seminar with finance professors several years ago by asking them to consider the following two different investment opportunities for available U.S. securities:

1. An investor who put $1,000 in 30-day commercial paper on January 1, 1927, and rolled over all proceeds into 30-day paper (or into 30-day T-bills after they were introduced) would have ended on December 31, 1978, 52 years later, with $3,600.

2. An investor who put $1,000 in the NYSE index on January 1, 1927, and reinvested all dividends in that portfolio would have ended on December 31, 1978, with $67,500.

Suppose we define **market timing** as the ability to tell (with certainty) at the beginning of each month whether the NYSE portfolio will outperform the 30-day paper portfolio. Accordingly, at the beginning of each month, the market timer shifts all funds into either cash equivalents (30-day paper) or equities (the NYSE portfolio), whichever is predicted to do better.

Merton asked the seminar participants to estimate what, beginning with $1,000 on the same date, the perfect timer would have amassed 52 years later? Out of the collected responses, the boldest guess was a few million dollars. The correct answer: $5.36 *billion*.

Concept Check

> Question 1. What was the monthly and annual compounded rate of return for the three strategies over the period 1926–1978?

These numbers have some lessons for us. The first has to do with the power of compounding. Its effect is particularly important because more and more of the funds under management represent pension savings. The horizons of such investments may not be as long as 52 years, but by and large they are measured in decades, making compounding a significant factor.

Another result that may seem surprising at first is the huge difference between the end-of-period value of the all-safe asset strategy ($3,600) and that of the all-equity strategy ($67,500). Why would anyone invest in safe assets given this historical record? If you have internalized the lessons of previous chapters, you know the reason: risk. The average rates of return and the standard deviations on the all-bills and all-equity strategies presented by Merton are:

	Arithmetic Mean	Standard Deviation
Bills	2.55	2.10
Equities	10.70	22.14

The significantly higher standard deviation of the rate of return on the equity portfolio is commensurate with its significantly higher average return.

Can we also view the rate of return premium on the perfect-timing fund as a risk premium? The answer must be no, because the perfect timer never does worse than either bills or the market. The extra return is not compensation for the possibility of poor returns but is attributable to superior analysis. It is the value of superior information that is reflected in the tremendous end-of-period value of the portfolio.

Merton[3] pursued the issue of value of information by simulating the returns, using the actual monthly return data, given perfect timing and also incorporat-

---

[3] Robert C. Merton, "On Market Timing and Investment Performance: An Equilibrium Theory of Value for Market Forecasts," *Journal of Business*, July 1981.

ing a charge for this timing ability. The monthly rate-of-return statistics for the all-equity portfolio and the timing portfolio are

Per Month	All Equities (%)	Perfect Timer No Charge (%)	Perfect Timer Fair Charge (%)
Average rate of return	.85	2.58	.55
Average excess return over return on safe asset	.64	2.37	.34
Standard deviation	5.89	3.82	3.55
Highest return	38.55	38.55	30.14
Lowest return	−29.12	.06	−7.06
Coefficient of skewness	.42	4.28	2.84

Ignore for the moment the last column (Perfect Timer—Fair Charge). The first two rows of results are self-explanatory. The third item, standard deviation, requires some discussion. The standard deviation of the rate of return earned by the perfect market timer was 3.82 percent, far greater than the volatility of T-bill returns over the same period. Does this imply that (perfect) timing is a riskier strategy than investing in bills? No. For this analysis, standard deviation is a misleading measure of risk.

To see why, consider how you might choose between two hypothetical strategies: the first offers a sure rate of return of 5 percent; the second strategy offers an uncertain return that is given by 5 percent *plus* a random number that is zero with probability .5 and 5 percent with probability .5. The characteristics of each strategy are

	Strategy 1 (%)	Strategy 2 (%)
Expected return	5	7.5
Standard deviation	0	2.5
Highest return	5	10.0
Lowest return	5	5.0

Clearly, strategy 2 dominates strategy 1 since its rate of return is *at least* equal to that of strategy 1 and sometimes greater. No matter how risk averse you are, you will always prefer strategy 2 to strategy 1, despite the significant standard deviation of strategy 2. Compared to strategy 1, strategy 2 provides only "good surprises," so the standard deviation in this case cannot be a measure of risk.

These results are analogous to the case of the perfect timer compared with an all-equity or all-bills strategy. In every period the perfect timer obtains at least as good a return, in some cases a better one. Therefore, the timer's standard deviation is a misleading measure of risk compared to an all-equity or all-bills strategy.

Returning to the empirical results, you can see that the highest rate of return is identical for the all-equity and the timing strategies, whereas the lowest rate of return is positive for the perfect timer and disastrous for the all-equity portfolio. Another reflection of this is seen in the coefficient of skewness, which measures the asymmetry of the distribution of returns. Because the equity portfolio is almost (but not exactly) normally distributed, its coefficient of skewness is very low at .42. In contrast, the perfect timing strategy effectively eliminates the negative tail of the distribution of portfolio returns (the part below the risk-free rate). Its returns are "skewed to the right," and its coefficient of skewness is therefore quite large, 4.28.

Now for the last column, Perfect Timer—Fair Charge, which is perhaps the most interesting. Most assuredly, the perfect timer will charge clients for such a valuable service. (The perfect timer may have other-worldly predictive powers, but saintly benevolence is unlikely.)

Subtracting a fair fee from the monthly rate of return of the timer's portfolio gives us an average rate of return lower than that of the passive, all-equity strategy. However, because the fee is *assumed* to be fair, the two portfolios (the all-equity strategy and the market timing with fee strategy) must be equally attractive after risk adjustment. In this case, again, the standard deviation of the market timing strategy (with fee) is of no help in adjusting for risk, because the coefficient of skewness remains high, 2.84. In other words, standard mean-variance analysis is quite complicated for valuing market timing. We need an alternative approach.

Merton's approach to analyzing the pattern of returns to the perfect market timer was to recognize that perfect foresight is equivalent to holding a call option on the equity portfolio. We shall explore options in depth in Part VII, but for now we can identify a call option as a right, but not an obligation, to acquire an asset at a predetermined "exercise" price. The perfect timer has the option here to invest 100 percent in either the safe asset or the equity portfolio, whichever will yield the higher return. This is shown in Figure 14.1. The rate of return is bounded from below by r_f.

To see the value of information as an option, suppose that the market index currently is at S_0, and that a call option on the index has an exercise price of $X = S_0(1 + r_f)$. If the market outperforms bills over the coming period, S_T will exceed X, whereas it will be less than X otherwise. Now look at the payoff to a portfolio consisting of this option and S_0 dollars invested in bills.

	Payoff to Portfolio	
	$S_T < X$	$S_T \geq X$
Bills:	$S_0(1 + r_f)$	$S_0(1 + r_f)$
Option:	0	$S_T - X$
TOTAL	$S_0(1 + r_f)$	S_T

The portfolio pays the risk-free return when the market is bearish (that is, the market return is less than the risk-free rate), and pays the market return when the market is bullish and beats bills. Such a portfolio is a perfect market timer. Consequently, we can measure the value of perfect ability as the value of the call option, because a call enables the investor to earn the market return only when it exceeds r_f.

FIGURE 14.1

Rate of return of a perfect market timer.

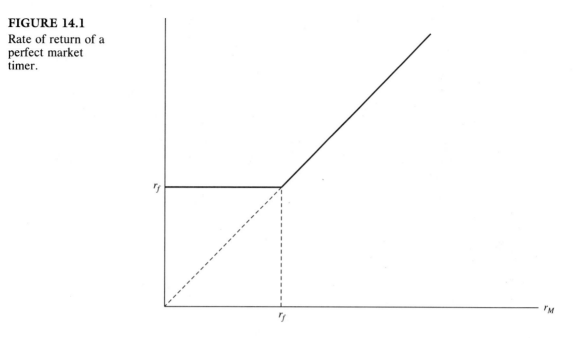

This insight lets Merton value timing ability using the theory of option valuation, and from this we calculate our fair charge for timing. Each month, we calculate the option value based on the current S_0 and r_f; this value is then subtracted from the portfolio payoff, which is converted to a rate of return to determine the monthly statistics.

The Value of Imperfect Forecasting

Unfortunately, managers are not perfect forecasters, as you and Merton know. It seems pretty obvious that if managers are right most of the time they are doing very well. However, when we say right "most of the time," we cannot refer merely to the percentage of time a manager is right. The weather forecaster in Tucson, Arizona, who *always* predicts no rain, may be right 90 percent of the time, but a high success rate for a "stopped-clock" strategy clearly is not evidence of forecasting ability.

Similarly, the appropriate measure of market forecasting ability is not the overall proportion of correct forecasts. If the market is up two days out of three and a forecaster always predicts a market advance, the two-thirds success rate is not a measure of forecasting ability. We need to examine both the proportion of bull markets ($r_M > r_f$) correctly forecast *and* the proportion of bear markets ($r_M < r_f$) correctly forecast.

If we call P_1 the proportion of the correct forecasts of bull markets and P_2 the proportion for bear markets, then $P_1 + P_2 - 1$ is the correct measure of timing ability. For example, a forecaster who always guesses correctly will have $P_1 = P_2 = 1$, and will show ability of 1 (100 percent). An analyst who always bets on a bear market will mispredict all bull markets ($P_1 = 0$), will correctly "predict" all bear markets ($P_2 = 1$), and will end up with timing ability of $P_1 + P_2 - 1 = 0$. If C denotes the (call option) value of a perfect market timer, then ($P_1 + P_2 - 1$)C measures the value of imperfect forecasting ability.

Concept Check	Question 2. What is the market timing score of someone who flips a fair coin to predict the market?

14.4   *Security Selection: The Treynor-Black Model*

Overview of the Treynor-Black Model

Security analysis is the other form of active portfolio management besides timing the overall market. Suppose that you are an analyst studying individual securities. It is quite likely that you will turn up several securities that appear to be mispriced. They offer positive anticipated alphas to the investor. But how do you exploit your analysis? Concentrating a portfolio on these securities entails a cost, namely, the firm-specific risk that you could shed by more fully diversifying. As an active manager you must strike a balance between aggressive exploitation of perceived security mispricing and diversification motives that dictate that a few stocks should not dominate the portfolio.

Treynor and Black[4] developed an optimizing model for portfolio managers who use security analysis. It represents a portfolio management theory that assumes security markets are *nearly* efficient. The essence of the model is this:

1. Security analysts in an active investment management organization can analyze in depth only a relatively small number of stocks out of the entire universe of securities. The securities not analyzed are assumed to be fairly priced.
2. For the purpose of efficient diversification, the market index portfolio is the baseline portfolio, which the model treats as the passive portfolio.
3. The macro forecasting unit of the investment management firm provides forecasts of the expected rate of return and variance of the passive (market index) portfolio.

[4] Jack Treynor and Fischer Black, "How to Use Security Analysis to Improve Portfolio Selection," *Journal of Business,* January 1973.

4. The objective of security analysis is to form an active portfolio of a necessarily limited number of securities. Perceived mispricing of the analyzed securities is what guides the composition of this active portfolio.

5. Analysts follow several steps to make up the active portfolio and evaluate its expected performance:

   a. Estimate the beta of each analyzed security and its residual risk. From the beta and the macro forecast, $E(r_M) - r_f$, determine the *required* rate of return of the security.

   b. Given the degree of mispricing of each security, determine its expected return and expected *abnormal* return (alpha).

   c. Calculate the cost of less than full diversification. The non-systematic risk of the mispriced stock, the variance of the stock's residual, offsets the benefit (alpha) of specializing in an underpriced security.

   d. Use the estimates for the values of alpha, beta, and residual risk to determine the optimal weight of each security in the active portfolio.

   e. Estimate the alpha, beta, and residual risk for the active portfolio according to the weights of the securities in the portfolio.

6. The macroeconomic forecasts for the passive index portfolio and the composite forecasts for the active portfolio are used to determine the optimal risky portfolio, which will be a combination of the passive and active portfolios.

Treynor and Black's model did not take the industry by storm. This is unfortunate for several reasons:

1. Just as even imperfect market timing ability has enormous value, security analysis of the sort Treynor and Black propose has similar potential value. Even with far from perfect security analysis, proper active management can add value.

2. The Treynor-Black model is conceptually easy to implement. Moreover, it is useful even when some of its simplifying assumptions are relaxed.

3. The model lends itself to use in decentralized organizations. This property is essential to efficiency in complex organizations.

Portfolio Construction

Assuming that all securities are fairly priced, and using the index model as a guideline for the rate of return on fairly priced securities, the rate of return on the *i*th security is given by

$$r_i = r_f + \beta_i(r_M - r_f) + e_i \tag{14.2}$$

where e_i is the zero mean, firm-specific disturbance.

Absent security analysis, Treynor and Black (TB) take equation 14.2 to represent the rate of return on all securities and assume that the market portfolio, M, is the efficient portfolio. For simplicity, they also assume that the non-systematic components of returns, e_i, are independent across securities. As for market timing, TB assume that the forecast for the **passive portfolio** already has been made, so that the expected return on the market index, r_M, as well as its variance, σ_M^2, has been assessed.

Now a portfolio manager unleashes a team of security analysts to investigate a subset of the universe of available securities. The objective is to form an active portfolio of positions in the analyzed securities to be mixed with the index portfolio. For each security, k, that is researched, we write the rate of return as

$$r_k = r_f + \beta_k(r_M - r_f) + e_k + \alpha_k \tag{14.3}$$

where α_k represents the extra expected return (called the *abnormal return*) attributable to any perceived mispricing of the security. Thus for each security analyzed the research team estimates the parameters

$$\alpha_k,\ \beta_k,\ \sigma^2(e_k)$$

If all the α_k turn out to be zero, there would be no reason to depart from the passive strategy and the index portfolio M would remain the manager's choice. However, this is a remote possibility. In general, there will be a significant number of non-zero alpha values, some positive and some negative.

One way to get an overview of the TB methodology is to examine what we should do with the active portfolio once we get it. Suppose that the **active portfolio** (**A**) has been constructed somehow and has the parameters

$$\alpha_A,\ \beta_A,\ \sigma^2(e_A)$$

Its total variance is the sum of its systematic variance, $\beta_A^2\sigma_M^2$, plus the non-systematic variance $\sigma^2(e_A)$. Its covariance with the market index portfolio, M, is

$$\text{Cov}(r_A,r_M) = \beta_A\sigma_M^2$$

Figure 14.2 shows the optimization process with the active and passive portfolios. The dashed efficient frontier represents the universe of all securities assuming that they are all fairly priced, that is, that all alphas are zero. By definition, the market index, M, is on this efficient frontier and is tangent to the (broken) capital market line (CML). In practice the analysts do not need to know this frontier. They need only to observe the market index portfolio and construct a portfolio resulting in a capital allocation line that lies above CML. Given their perceived superior analysis, they will view the market index portfolio as inefficient: the active portfolio, A, constructed from mispriced securities must lie, by design, above the CML.

To locate the active portfolio A in Figure 14.2, we need its expected return and standard deviation. The standard deviation is

$$\sigma_A = [\beta_A^2\sigma_M^2 + \sigma^2(e_A)]^{1/2}$$

Because of the positive alpha value that is forecast for A, it plots above the (broken) CML with expected return

$$E(r_A) = \alpha_A + r_f + \beta_A[E(r_M) - r_f]$$

FIGURE 14.2

The optimization
process with active
and passive
portfolios.

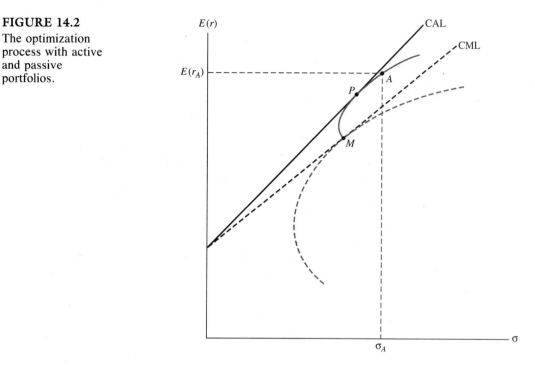

The optimal combination of the active portfolio, *A*, with the passive portfolio, *M*, is a simple application of the construction of optimal risky portfolios
from two component assets that we first encountered in Chapter 7. Because the
active portfolio is not perfectly correlated with the market index portfolio, we
need to account for their mutual correlation in the determination of the optimal
allocation between the two portfolios. This is evident from the solid efficient
frontier that passes through *M* and *A*. It supports the optimal capital allocation
line (CAL) and identifies the optimal risky portfolio, *P*, which combines portfolios *A* and *M*, and is the tangency point of the CAL to the efficient frontier. The
active portfolio *A* in this example is not the ultimately efficient portfolio, because we need to mix *A* with the passive market portfolio to achieve greater
diversification.

Let us now outline the algebraic approach to this optimization problem. If
we invest a proportion, *w*, in the active portfolio and $1 - w$ in the market index,
the portfolio return will be

$$r_p(w) = wr_A + (1 - w)r_M$$

We can use this equation to calculate Sharpe's measure (dividing the mean
excess return by the standard deviation of the return) as a function of the
weight, *w*, then find the optimal weight, w^*, that maximizes the measure. This
is the value of *w* that makes *P* the optimal tangency portfolio in Figure 14.2.

This maximization ultimately leads to the solution

$$w^* = \frac{w_0}{1 + (1 - \beta_A)w_0} \qquad (14.4)$$

where

$$w_0 = \frac{\alpha_A/\sigma^2(e_A)}{[E(r_M) - r_f]/\sigma_M^2}$$

Equation 14.4 actually is a restatement of the formula for determining the optimal weights to invest in two risky assets that you first encountered in Chapter 7. Here we state the equation in terms of portfolio alphas relative to the CAPM, but the approach is identical.

First look at w_0. This would be the optimal weight in the active portfolio *if* its beta (β_A) were 1.0. This weight is a ratio of two measures. In the numerator is the reward from the active portfolio, α_A, reflecting its mispricing, against the non-systematic risk, $\sigma^2(e_A)$, incurred in holding it. This ratio is divided by an analogous measure for the index portfolio

$$\frac{E(r_M) - r_f}{\sigma_M^2}$$

which is the ratio of the reward from holding the index $E(r_M) - r_f$ to its risk, σ_M^2.

The intuition here is straightforward. We mix the active portfolio with the index for the benefit of diversification. The position to take in the active portfolio relative to the market portfolio depends on the ratio of the active portfolio's abnormal return, α_A, to its potentially diversifiable risk, $\sigma^2(e_A)$. The optimal weights also will depend on the opportunities for diversification, which in turn depend on the correlation between the two portfolios and can be measured by β_A. To adjust the optimal weight for the fact that the beta of the active portfolio may not be 1.0, we compute w^* in equation 14.4.

What is the reward-to-variability ratio of the optimal risky portfolio once we find the best mix, w^*, of the active and passive index portfolio? It turns out that if we compute the square of Sharpe's measure of the risky portfolio, we can separate the contributions of the index and active portfolios as follows:

$$S_P^2 = S_M^2 + \frac{\alpha_A^2}{\sigma^2(e_A)}$$

$$= \left[\frac{E(r_M) - r_f}{\sigma_M}\right]^2 + \left[\frac{\alpha_A}{\sigma(e_A)}\right]^2 \qquad (14.5)$$

This decomposition of the Sharpe measure of the optimal risky portfolio, which by the way is valid *only* for the optimal portfolio, tells us how to construct the active portfolio. Look at the last equality in equation 14.5. It shows that the highest Sharpe measure for the risky portfolio will be attained when we construct an active portfolio that maximizes the value of $\alpha_A/\sigma(e_A)$. The ratio of alpha to residual standard deviation of the active portfolio will be maximized when we choose a weight for the *k*th analyzed security as follows:

$$w_k = \frac{\alpha_k/\sigma^2(e_k)}{\sum\limits_{i=1}^{n} \alpha_i/\sigma^2(e_i)} \qquad (14.6)$$

This makes sense: the weight of a security in the active portfolio depends on the ratio of the degree of mispricing, α_k, to the non-systematic risk, $\sigma^2(e_k)$, of the security. The denominator, the sum of the ratio across securities, is a scale factor to guarantee that the weights sum to one.

Note from equation 14.5 that the square of Sharpe's measure of the optimal risky portfolio is increased over the square of the Sharpe measure of the passive (market-index) portfolio by the amount

$$\left[\frac{\alpha_A}{\sigma(e_A)}\right]^2$$

The ratio of the degree of mispricing, α_A, to the non-systematic standard deviation, $\sigma(e_A)$, becomes a natural performance measure of the active component of the risky portfolio. Sometimes this is called the appraisal ratio.

We can also calculate the contribution of a single security in the active portfolio to the portfolio's overall performance. When the active portfolio contains n analyzed securities, the total improvement in the squared Sharpe measure equals the sum of the squared appraisal ratios of the analyzed securities,

$$\left[\frac{\alpha_A}{\sigma(e_A)}\right]^2 = \sum_{i=1}^{n}\left[\frac{\alpha_i}{\sigma(e_i)}\right]^2$$

The appraisal ratio for each security, $\alpha_i/\sigma(e_i)$, is a measure of the contribution of that security to the performance of the active portfolio.

The best way to illustrate the Treynor-Black process is through an example. Suppose that the macroforecasting unit of Drex Portfolio Inc. (DPF) issues a forecast for a 15 percent market return. The forecast's standard error is 20 percent. The risk-free rate is 7 percent. The macro data can be summarized as follows:

$$E(r_M) - r_f = .08 \; ; \; \sigma_M = .20$$

At the same time, the security analysis division submits to the portfolio manager the following forecast of annual returns for the three securities that it covers:

Stock	α	β	$\sigma(e)$
1	.07	1.6	.45
2	−.05	1.0	.32
3	.03	.5	.26

Note that the alpha estimates appear reasonably moderate. The estimates of the residual standard deviations are correlated with the betas, just as they are in reality. The magnitudes also reflect typical values for TSE stocks.

First, let us construct the optimal active portfolio implied by the security analyst input list. To do so we compute the appraisal ratios as follows:

Stock	$\alpha/\sigma^2(e)$	$\dfrac{\alpha_i}{\sigma^2(e_i)} \Big/ \displaystyle\sum_{i=1}^{3} \dfrac{\alpha_i}{\sigma^2(e_i)}$
1	$.07/.45^2 = \ \ .3457$	$.3457/.3012 = \ \ 1.1477$
2	$-.05/.32^2 = -.4883$	$-.4883/.3012 = -1.6212$
3	$.03/.26^2 = \ \ .4438$	$.4438/.3012 = \ \ 1.4735$
TOTAL	$.3012$	1.0000

The last column presents the optimal positions of each of the three securities in the active portfolio. Obviously, stock 2 has a negative weight. The magnitudes of the individual positions in the active portfolio (114.77 percent in stock 1, for example) seem quite extreme. However, this should not concern us because the active portfolio will later be mixed with the well-diversified market index portfolio, resulting in much more moderate positions, as we shall see shortly.

The forecasts for the stocks, together with the proposed composition of the active portfolio, lead to the following parameter estimates for the active portfolio:

$$\alpha_A = 1.1477 \times .07 + (-1.6212) \times (-.05) + 1.4735 \times .03 = .2056$$
$$\beta_A = 1.1477 \times 1.6 + (-1.6212) \times 1.0 + 1.4735 \times .5 = .9519$$
$$\sigma(e_A) = [1.477^2 \times .45^2 + (-1.6212)^2 \times .32^2 + 1.4735^2 \times .26^2]^{1/2} = .8262$$

Note that the negative weight (short position) on the negative alpha stock results in a positive contribution to the alpha of the active portfolio. Note also that because of the assumption that the stock residuals are uncorrelated, the active portfolio's residual variance is simply the weighted sum of the individual stock residual variances, with the squared portfolio proportions as weights.

The parameters of the active portfolio are now used to determine its proportion in the overall risky portfolio.

$$
\begin{aligned}
w_0 &= \frac{\alpha_A/\sigma^2(e_A)}{[E(r_M) - r_f]/\sigma_M^2} \\
&= \frac{.2056/.6826}{.08/.04} \\
&= .1506 \\
w^* &= \frac{w_0}{1 + (1 - \beta_A)w_0} \\
&= \frac{.1506}{1 + (1 - .9519) \times .1506} \\
&= .1495
\end{aligned}
$$

Although the active portfolio's alpha is impressive (20.56 percent), its proportion in the overall risky portfolio, before adjustment for beta, is only 15.06

percent, because of its large non-systematic risk (82.62 percent). Such is the importance of diversification. As it happens, the beta of the active portfolio is almost 1.0, and hence the correction for beta (from w_0 to w^*) is small, from 15.06 percent to 14.95 percent. The direction of the change makes sense. If the beta of the active portfolio is low (less than 1.0), there are more potential gains from diversification. Hence a smaller position in the active portfolio is called for. If the beta of the active portfolio were significantly greater than 1.0, a larger correction in the opposite direction would be called for.

The proportions of the individual stocks in the active portfolio, together with the proportion of the active portfolio in the overall risky portfolio, determine the proportions of each individual stock in the overall risky portfolio.

Stock	Final Position	
1	.1495 × 1.1477	= .1716
2	.1495 × (−1.6212)	= −.2424
3	.1495 × 1.4735	= .2202
Active portfolio		.1495
Market portfolio		.8505
		1.0000

The parameters of the active portfolio and market-index portfolio are now used to forecast the performance of the optimal, overall risky portfolio. When optimized, a property of the risky portfolio is that its squared Sharpe measure increases by the square of the active portfolio's appraisal ratio:

$$S_P^2 = \left[\frac{E(r_M) - r_f}{\sigma_M}\right]^2 + \left[\frac{\alpha_A}{\sigma(e_A)}\right]^2$$
$$= .16 + .0619 = .2219$$

and hence the Sharpe measure of the active portfolio is $\sqrt{.2219} = .47$, compared with .40 for the passive portfolio.

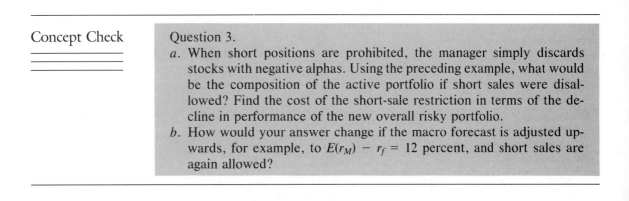

Concept Check

Question 3.
a. When short positions are prohibited, the manager simply discards stocks with negative alphas. Using the preceding example, what would be the composition of the active portfolio if short sales were disallowed? Find the cost of the short-sale restriction in terms of the decline in performance of the new overall risky portfolio.
b. How would your answer change if the macro forecast is adjusted upwards, for example, to $E(r_M) - r_f = 12$ percent, and short sales are again allowed?

14.5 *Multifactor Models and Active Portfolio Management*

Perhaps in the foreseeable future a multifactor structure of security returns will be developed and accepted as conventional wisdom. So far our analytical framework for active portfolio management seems to rest on the validity of the index model, that is, on a single-factor security model. Despite this appearance, a multifactor structure will not affect the construction of the active portfolio because the entire TB analysis focuses on the residuals of the index model. If we were to replace the one-factor model with a multifactor model, we would continue to form the active portfolio by calculating each security's alpha relative to its fair return (give its betas on *all* factors), and again would combine the active portfolio with the portfolio that would be formed in the absence of security analysis. The multifactor framework, however, does raise several new issues in portfolio management.

You saw in Chapter 9 how the index model simplifies the construction of the input list necessary for portfolio optimization programs. If

$$r_i - r_f = \alpha_i + \beta_i(r_M - r_f) + e_i$$

adequately describes the security market, then the variance of any asset is the sum of systematic and non-systematic risk: $\sigma^2(r_i) = \beta_i^2\sigma_M^2 + \sigma^2(e_i)$, and the covariance between any two assets is $\beta_i\beta_j\sigma_M^2$.

How do we generalize this rule to use in a multifactor model? To simplify, let us consider a two-factor world, and let us call the two-factor portfolios M and H. Then we generalize the index model to

$$\begin{aligned} r_i - r_f &= \beta_{iM}(r_M - r_f) + \beta_{iH}(r_H - r_f) + \alpha_i + e_i \\ &= r_\beta + e_i \end{aligned} \qquad \textbf{(14.7)}$$

β_M and β_H are the betas of the security relative to portfolios M and H. Given the rates of return on the factor portfolios, r_M and r_H, the fair excess rate of return over r_f on a security is denoted r_β and its expected abnormal return is α_i.

How can we use equation 14.7 to form optimal portfolios? Suppose that investors simply wish to maximize the Sharpe measures of their portfolios. The factor structure of equation 14.7 can be used to generate the inputs for the Markowitz portfolio selection algorithm. The variance and covariance estimates are now more complex, however:

$$\sigma^2(r_i) = \beta_{iM}^2\sigma_M^2 + \beta_{iH}^2\sigma_H^2 + 2\beta_{iM}\beta_{iH}\mathrm{Cov}(r_M, r_H) + \sigma^2(e_i)$$
$$\mathrm{Cov}(r_i, r_j) = \beta_{iM}\beta_{jM}\sigma_M^2 + \beta_{iH}\beta_{jH}\sigma_H^2 + (\beta_{iM}\beta_{jH} + \beta_{jM}\beta_{iH})\mathrm{Cov}(r_M, r_H)$$

Nevertheless, the informational economy of the factor model still is valuable, because we can estimate a covariance matrix for an *n*-security portfolio from:

n estimates of β_{iM}
n estimates of β_{iH}

$$n \text{ estimates of } \sigma^2(e_i)$$
$$1 \text{ estimate of } \sigma^2_M$$
$$1 \text{ estimate of } \sigma^2_H$$

rather than $n(n + 1)/2$ separate variance and covariance estimates. Thus the factor structure continues to simplify portfolio construction issues.

The factor structure also suggests an efficient method to allocate research effort. Analysts can specialize in forecasting means and variances of different factor portfolios. Having established factor betas, they can form a covariance matrix to be used together with expected security returns generated by the CAPM or APT to construct an optimal passive risky portfolio. If active analysis of individual stocks also is attempted, the procedure of constructing the optimal active portfolio and its optimal combination with the passive portfolio is identical to that followed in the single-factor case.

It is likely, however, that the factor structure of the market has hedging implications. This means that clients will be willing to accept an inferior Sharpe measure (in terms of dollar returns) to maintain a risky portfolio that has the desired hedge qualities. Portfolio optimization for these investors obviously is more complicated, requiring specific information on client preferences. The portfolio manager will not be able to satisfy diverse clients with one portfolio.

In the case of the multifactor market, even passive investors (meaning those who accept market prices as ''fair'') need to do a considerable amount of work. They need forecasts of the expected return and volatility of each factor return, *and* need to determine the appropriate weights on each factor portfolio to maximize their expected utility. Such a process is straightforward in principle, but quickly becomes analytically demanding.

Summary

1. A truly passive portfolio strategy entails holding the market index portfolio and a money market fund. Determining the optimal allocation to the market portfolio requires an estimate of its expected return and variance, which in turn suggests delegating some analysis to professionals.

2. Active portfolio managers attempt to construct a risky portfolio that maximizes the reward-to-variability (Sharpe) ratio.

3. The value of perfect market timing ability is considerable. The rate of return to a perfect market timer will be uncertain. However, its risk characteristics are not measurable by standard measures of portfolio risk, because perfect timing dominates a passive strategy, providing ''good surprises'' only.

4. Perfect timing ability is equivalent to the possession of a call option on the market portfolio, whose value can be determined using option valuation techniques such as the Black-Scholes formula.

5. With imperfect timing, the value of a timer who attempts to forecast whether stocks will outperform bills is given by the conditional probabilities of the true outcome given the forecasts: $P_1 + P_2 - 1$. Thus, if the value of perfect timing is given by the option value, C, then imperfect timing has the value $(P_1 + P_2 - 1)C$.

6. The Treynor-Black security selection model envisions that a macroeconomic forecast for market performance is available and that security analysts estimate abnormal expected rates of return, α, for various securities. Alpha is the expected rate of return on a security beyond that explained by its beta and the security market line.

7. In the Treynor-Black model, the weight of each analyzed security is proportional to the ratio of its alpha to its non-systematic risk, $\sigma^2(e)$.

8. Once the active portfolio is constructed, its alpha value, non-systematic risk, and beta can be determined from the properties of the component securities. The optimal risky portfolio, P, is then constructed by holding a position in the active portfolio according to the ratio of α_P to $\sigma^2(e_P)$, divided by the analogous ratio for the market index portfolio. Finally, this position is adjusted by the beta of the active portfolio.

9. When the overall risky portfolio is constructed using the optimal proportions of the active portfolio and passive portfolio, its performance, as measured by the square of Sharpe's measure, is improved (over that of the passive, market index portfolio) by the amount $[\alpha_A/\sigma(e_A)]^2$.

10. The contribution of each security to the overall improvement in the performance of the active portfolio is determined by its degree of mispricing and non-systematic risk. The contribution of each security to portfolio performance equals $[\alpha_i/\sigma(e_i)]^2$, so that for the optimal risky portfolio,

$$S_P^2 = \left[\frac{E(r_M) - r_f}{\sigma_M^2}\right]^2 + \sum_{i=1}^{n} \left[\frac{\alpha_i}{\sigma(e_i)}\right]^2$$

Key terms

Market timing   Active portfolio
Passive portfolio

Selected readings

The valuation of market timing ability using the option pricing framework was developed in:
   Robert C. Merton, "On Market Timing and Investment Performance: An Equilibrium Theory of Value for Market Forecasts." *Journal of Business,* July 1981.
The Treynor-Black model was laid out in:
   Jack Treynor and Fischer Black, "How to Use Security Analysis to Improve Portfolio Selection," *Journal of Business,* January 1973.

Problems

1. The five-year history of annual rates of return in excess of the T-bill rate for two competing stock funds is

The Bull Fund	The Unicorn Fund
−21.7	−1.3
28.7	15.5
17.0	14.4
2.9	−11.9
28.9	25.4

   a. How would these funds compare in the eye of the risk-neutral potential client?

   b. How would these funds compare by Sharpe's measure?

   c. If a risk-averse investor (with a coefficient of risk aversion $A = 3$) had to choose one of these funds to mix with T-bills, which fund would be better to choose, and how much should be invested in that fund on the basis of the available data?

2. In scrutinizing the record of two market timers, a fund manager comes up with the following table:

Number of months that $r_M > r_f$	135
Correctly predicted by timer A	78
Correctly predicted by timer B	86
Number of months that $r_M < r_f$	92
Correctly predicted by timer A	57
Correctly predicted by timer B	50

   What are the conditional probabilities, P_1 and P_2, and the total ability parameters for timers A and B?

3. A portfolio manager summarizes the input from the macro and micro forecasters in the following table:

Micro Forecasts

Asset	Expected Return (%)	Beta	Residual Standard Deviation
Stock A	20	1.3	58
Stock B	18	1.8	71
Stock C	17	.7	60
Stock D	12	1.0	55

Macro Forecasts

Asset	Expected Return (%)	Standard Deviation
T-bills	8	0
Passive equity portfolio	16	23

   a. Calculate expected excess returns, alpha values, and residual variances for these stocks.

b. Construct the optimal risky portfolio.

c. What is Sharpe's measure for the optimal portfolio, and how much of it is contributed by the active portfolio?

d. What should be the exact makeup of the complete portfolio for an investor with a coefficient of risk aversion of 2.8?

4. Recalculate problem 3 for a portfolio manager who is not allowed to short-sell securities.

   a. What is the cost in terms of Sharpe's measure of the restriction?

   b. What is the utility loss to the investor ($A = 2.8$) given his new complete portfolio?

5. A portfolio management house approximates the return-generating process by a two-factor model and uses two-factor portfolios to construct its passive portfolio. The input table that is constructed by the house analysts looks as follows:

Micro Forecasts

Asset	Expected Return (%)	Beta on M	Beta on H	Residual Standard Deviation (%)
Stock A	20	1.2	1.8	58
Stock B	18	1.4	1.1	71
Stock C	17	.5	1.5	60
Stock D	12	1.0	.2	55

Macro Forecasts

Asset	Expected Return (%)	Standard Deviation (%)
T-bills	8	0
Factor M portfolio	16	23
Factor H portfolio	10	18

The correlation coefficient between the two-factor portfolios is .6.

   a. What is the optimal passive portfolio?

   b. By how much is the optimal passive portfolio superior to the single-factor passive portfolio, M, in terms of Sharpe's measure?

   c. Analyze the utility improvement to the $A = 2.8$ investor relative to holding portfolio M as the sole risky asset that arises from the expanded macro model of the portfolio manager.

6. Construct the optimal active and overall risky portfolio with the data from problem 5 with no restrictions on short sales.

   a. What is the Sharpe measure of the optimal risky portfolio and what is the contribution of the active portfolio to that measure?

   b. Compare the risky portfolio to that from problem 3.

   c. Analyze the utility value of the optimal risky portfolio for the $A = 2.8$ investor. Compare to that of problem 3.

7. Recalculate problem 6 with a short-sale restriction. Compare the results to those from problems 4 and 6.

PART V

FIXED-INCOME SECURITIES

CHAPTER 15

Bond Prices and Yields

In the previous chapters on risk-and-return relationships, we have treated securities at a high level of abstraction. We have assumed implicitly that a prior, detailed analysis of each security already has been performed, and that its risk-and-return features have been assessed.

We turn now to specific analyses of particular security markets. We examine valuation principles, determinants of risk and return, and portfolio strategies commonly used within and across the various markets.

We begin by analyzing **fixed-income securities**. A fixed-income security is a claim on a specified periodic stream of income. Fixed-income securities have the advantage of being relatively easy to understand because much of the element of risk is absent. Because the level of payments is fixed in advance, risk considerations are minimal as long as the issuer of the security is sufficiently creditworthy. Hence these securities are a convenient starting point for our analysis of the universe of potential investment vehicles.

This chapter reviews the principles of bond pricing. It shows how bond prices are set in accordance with market interest rates, and why bond prices change with those rates. After examining the Treasury bond market, where default risk may be ignored, we move to the corporate bond sector, where we look at the determinants of credit risk and the default premium built into bond yields. Finally, we examine the impact of call and convertibility provisions on prices and yields.

15.1 Bond Prices and Yields

The basic fixed-income security is the bond. A **bond** is a simple borrowing arrangement in which the borrower issues (sells) an IOU to the investor. The arrangement obligates the issuer to make specified payments to the bondholder on specified dates. A typical *coupon bond* obligates the issuer to make semiannual payments of interest, called *coupon payments*, to the bondholder for the life of the bond, and then to repay the original **principal**, or borrowed money, at the maturity of the bond. The **coupon rate** of the bond is the coupon payment divided by the bond's **par value**. To illustrate, a bond with par value of $1,000 and coupon rate of 8 percent is sold to a buyer for a $1,000 payment. The bondholder is then entitled to payments of 8 percent of $1,000, or $80 per year, for the stated life of the bond (e.g., 30 years). That $80 payment typically comes in two semiannual installments of $40 each. After the 30-year life of the bond, the borrower (issuer) repays the original $1,000 principal to the lender (the bondholder).

Review of the Present Value Relationship

Because a bond's coupon payments and principal repayment all occur months or years into the future, the price that an investor would be willing to pay for the claim to those payments depends on the value of dollars to be received in the future compared with the dollars in hand today. The *present value* of a claim to a dollar to be paid in the future is the market price at which that claim would sell if it were traded in the securities market.

We know that the present value of a dollar to be received in the future is less than $1. This is because the time spent waiting to receive the dollar imposes an opportunity cost on the investor—if the money is not in hand today, it cannot be invested to start generating income immediately. Denoting the current market interest rate by r, the present value of a dollar to be received n years from now is $1/(1 + r)^n$.

To see why this must be, consider an example in which the interest rate is 5 percent, and $r = .05$. According to the present value rule, the value of $1 to be received in 10 years would be $1/(1.05)^{10} = \$.614$. This is precisely the amount that would be paid in the marketplace for a claim to a payment of $1 in 10 years, because an investor currently investing at the going 5 percent rate of interest realizes that only $.614 needs to be set aside now in order to provide a final value of $1 in 10 years, since $\$.614 \times 1.05^{10} = \$1$. The present value formula tells us exactly how much an investor should be willing to pay for a claim to a future cash flow. This value will be the current price of the claim.

We simplify for now by assuming that there is one interest rate that is appropriate for discounting cash flows of any maturity, but we can relax this assumption easily. In practice, there may be different discount rates for cash flows accruing in different periods. For the time being, however, we ignore this refinement until the next chapter.

Bond Pricing

In the previous example, we asserted that the 8 percent coupon bond could be sold to the public at an issue price of $1,000; that is, we assumed that the bond could be sold at its par value. This is a bit of a leap, because we do not yet know whether investors would be willing to pay $1,000 for the 60 semiannual payments of $40 and the ultimate repayment of the $1,000 in year 30. To arrive at the price they would be willing to pay for the bond, investors need to compute the present value of the cash flows they stand to receive from purchasing the bond.

In our case, the bond would indeed sell at $1,000 if the market interest rate were exactly equal to the 8 percent coupon rate, or more precisely, if the market interest rate were 4 percent per six-month period. In this event, it is easy to confirm that the present value of the bond's 60 semiannual coupon payments of $40 each would equal $904.94, while the $1,000 principal repayment would have a present value of $1,000/(1.04)^{60} = $95.06, for a total bond value of $1,000. You can perform these calculations easily on any financial calculator or use a set of present value tables.

Symbolically, we write

$$\$1,000 = \sum_{t=1}^{60} \frac{\$40}{(1.04)^t} + \frac{\$1,000}{(1.04)^{60}} \qquad (15.1)$$

The summation sign in equation 15.1 directs us to add 60 terms, each of which is $40 divided by 1.04 to a power that ranges from 1 to 60. This first expression thus gives us the present value of a $40 annuity. For expositional simplicity we can write equation 15.1 as

$$1,000 = 40 \times PA(4\%, 60) + 1,000 \times PF(4\%, 60)$$

where PA(4%, 60) represents the present value of an annuity of $1 when the interest rate is 4 percent and the annuity is to last for 60 periods, and PF (4%, 60) similarly represents the present value of a single payment of $1 to be received in 60 periods. In our example each period is six months.

Of course, if the interest rate were not equal to the bond's coupon rate, the bond would not sell at par value. For example, if the interest rate were to rise to 10 percent (5 percent per six months), the bond's price would fall by $189.29 to $810.71, as follows:

$$\$40 \times PA(5\%, 60) + \$1,000 \times PF(5\%, 60)$$
$$= \$757.17 \qquad\qquad + \$53.54$$
$$= \$810.71$$

At the higher current interest rate, the present value of the payments to be received by the bondholder is lower. This illustrates the general property that bond prices and market interest rates are inversely related.

Figure 15.1 shows the price of the 30-year, 8 percent coupon bond for a range of interest rates. The negative slope illustrates the inverse relationship between prices and yields. Note also from the figure (and from Table 15.1) that the shape of the curve implies that an increase in the interest rate results in a price decline that is smaller than the price gain resulting from a decrease of equal magnitude in the interest rate. This property of bond prices is called *convexity,* because of the convex shape of the bond price curve. This curvature reflects the fact that progressive increases in the interest rate result in progressively smaller reductions in the bond price. Therefore, the price curve becomes flatter at higher interest rates.

FIGURE 15.1
The inverse relationship between bond prices and yields.

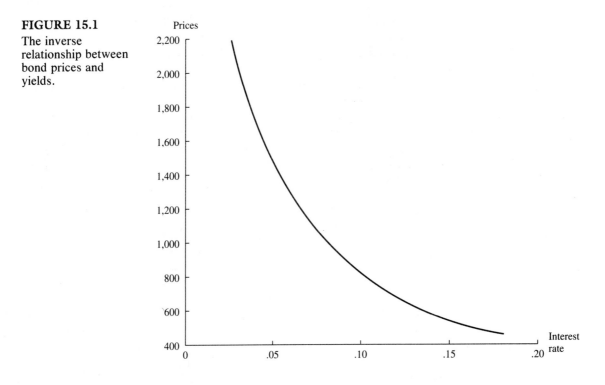

Prices

Question 1. Calculate the price of the bond for a market interest rate of 3 percent per half-year. Compare the capital gains for the interest rate decline to the losses incurred when the rate increases to 5 percent.

Corporate bonds at issue typically sell at par value. Thus, the underwriters of the bond issue (the firms that market the bonds to the public for the issuing corporation) must choose a coupon rate that very closely approximates market

TABLE 15.1 Bond Prices at Different Interest Rates (8% Coupon Bond)

Time to Maturity	Bond Price at Given Market Interest Rate				
	4%	6%	8%	10%	12%
1 year	1,038.83	1,019.13	1,000.00	981.41	963.33
10 years	1,327.03	1,148.77	1,000.00	875.38	770.60
20 years	1,547.11	1,231.15	1,000.00	828.41	699.07
30 years	1,695.22	1,276.76	1,000.00	810.71	676.77

yields. In such a primary issue the underwriters attempt to sell the newly issued bonds directly to their customers. If the coupon rate is inadequate, the bonds will not be saleable at par value.

After the bonds are issued, bondholders may buy or sell bonds in secondary markets such as the New York Bond Exchange in the United States, or the over-the-counter market, where most U.S. and all Canadian bonds trade. In these secondary markets bond prices move in accordance with market forces. The bond prices fluctuate inversely with the market interest rate.

The inverse relationship between prices and yields is a central feature of fixed-income securities. Interest rate fluctuations represent the main source of risk for this market, and we devote considerable attention in Chapter 17 to assessing the sensitivity of bond prices to market yields. For now, however, it is sufficient to highlight one key factor that determines that sensitivity, namely, the maturity of the bond.

A general rule in evaluating bond price risk is that the greater the maturity of the bond, the greater the sensitivity of price to fluctuations in the interest rate. For example, consider Table 15.1 which presents the price of an 8 percent coupon bond at different market yields and times to maturity. For any departure of the interest rate from 8 percent (the rate at which the bond sells at par value), the change in the bond price is smaller for shorter times to maturity.

This makes sense. If you buy the bond at par with an 8 percent coupon rate, and market rates subsequently rise, then you suffer a loss: you have tied up your money earning 8 percent when alternative investments offer higher returns. This is reflected in the capital loss on the bond. The longer the period for which your money is tied up, the greater the loss, and correspondingly the greater the drop in the bond price. In Table 15.1 the row for one-year maturity bonds shows little price sensitivity—with only one year's earning at stake, changes in interest rates are not too threatening. However, interest rate swings have a large impact on bond prices for 30-year maturity bonds.

This is why short-term Treasury securities such as T-bills are considered to be the safest. They are free not only of default risk, but also largely of price risk attributable to interest-rate volatility.

Yield to Maturity

In practice, an investor considering the purchase of a bond is not quoted a promised rate of return. Instead, the investor must use the bond price, maturity date, and coupon payments to infer the return offered by the bond over its life. The **yield to maturity** is a measure of the average rate of return that will be earned on a bond if it is bought now and held until maturity. To calculate the yield to maturity, we solve the bond price equation for the interest rate, given the bond's price.

For example, suppose that the 8 percent 30-year coupon bond was selling at $1,276.76. What rate of return would be earned by an investor purchasing the bond at market price? To answer this question, we solve for r in the equation following:

$$1,276.76 = \sum_{t=1}^{60} \frac{40}{(1 + r)^t} + \frac{1,000}{(1 + r)^{60}}$$

or equivalently,

$$1,276.76 = 40 \times PA(r, 60) + 1,000 \times PF(r, 60)$$

These equations have only one unknown variable, the interest rate, r. You can use a financial calculator to confirm that the solution to the equation is $r = .03$, or 3 percent per half-year.[1] This is considered the bond's yield to maturity, since the bond would be fairly priced at $1,276.76 if the fair market rate of return on the bond over its entire life were 3 percent per half-year. The bond's yield to maturity would be quoted in the financial press at an annual percentage rate (APR) of 6 percent, despite the fact that its effective annual yield is 6.09 percent ($1.03^2 - 1 = .0609$).

Notice that the bond's yield to maturity is the internal rate of return on an investment in the bond. The yield to maturity can be interpreted as the compound rate of return over the life of the bond under the assumption that all bond coupons can be reinvested at an interest rate equal to the bond's yield to maturity. If this is not the case, the yield to maturity will not be the same as the return over the bond's life. Yield to maturity is widely accepted as a proxy for average return, however, because alternative measures require forecasts of future reinvestment rates. We discuss some of the alternative measures in Chapter 16.

You should be aware that yield to maturity differs from the *current yield* of a bond. The current yield is the bond's annual coupon payment divided by the bond price. For example, for the 8 percent 30-year bond currently selling at $1,276.76, the current yield would be $80/$1,276.76 = .0627, or 6.27 percent per year. In contrast, recall that the effective annual yield to maturity is 6.09 percent. For this bond, which is selling at a premium over par value ($1,276 rather than $1,000), the coupon rate exceeds the current yield, which exceeds the yield to maturity. The coupon rate exceeds current yield because it divides the coupon payments by par value ($1,000) rather than by the bond price ($1,276). Similarly, the current yield exceeds yield to maturity because the yield to maturity accounts for the built-in capital loss on the bond: the bond bought today for $1,276 will eventually fall in value to $1,000 at maturity.

Concept Check	Question 2. What will be the relationship between coupon rate, current yield, and yield to maturity for bonds selling at discounts from par?

---

[1] Without a financial calculator we still could solve the equation, but we would need to use a trial-and-error approach.

15.2 *Bond Prices over Time*

Although bonds generally promise a fixed flow of income to their owners, that income stream is not in fact risk-free unless the investor can be sure that the issuer will not default on the obligation. All corporate bonds, for example, entail some risk of default. Even though the promised cash flows are specified when the bond is purchased, the actual bond payments are uncertain, because they depend to some extent on the ultimate financial status of the firm. In contrast, Canadian government fixed-income securities may be treated as virtually free of default risk. Because of this, these securities present fewer complicating issues for analysis. Hence, we will illustrate the properties of bond prices using Treasury securities as our example, deferring until later in the chapter the discussion of riskier non-government securities.

Zero-Coupon Bonds

Borrowers also, but less commonly, issue *original issue discount bonds* in addition to coupon bonds issued at par. These are bonds that are issued intentionally with low coupon rates, which cause the bond to sell at a discount from par value. An extreme example of this type of bond is the **zero-coupon bond**, which carries no coupons and must provide all its return in the form of price appreciation. ''Zeros'' provide only one cash flow to their owners, and that is on the maturity date of the bond.

Government of Canada Treasury bills are examples of short-term zero-coupon instruments. The Bank of Canada issues, or sells, a bill for some amount ranging from $1,000 to $1,000,000, agreeing to repay that amount at the bill's maturity. All of the investor's return comes in the form of price appreciation over time.

In addition, longer-term zero-coupon bonds can be created synthetically. Several investment banking firms buy coupon-paying Government of Canada or provincial bonds and sell rights to single payments backed by the bonds. These bonds are said to be *stripped* of coupons. The single payments are, in essence, zero-coupon bonds collateralized by the original government securities and, thus, are virtually free of default risk. They often have colorful names, like Tigrs, Cougars, or sentinels. (See the accompanying box.)

Treasury bills are issued with initial maturities of up to one year. Thus, if a bill with a six-month maturity is issued at a price of $9,600, we would determine the half-year yield to maturity over the bill's life by solving

$$\$9,600 = \$10,000/(1 + r)$$

to find that $r = .0417$, or 4.17 percent per half-year. The effective annual rate would be 8.51 percent ($1.0417^2 = 1.0851$).

A 'Tigr' That's Worth Putting in Your Investment Tank

With Interest Rates Peaking, Experts Say the Time Is Ripe to Buy Strip Bonds to Lock in High Yields. Just Hope That Rates Don't Keep Climbing

Paul Gammal

It is difficult to imagine that the old adage "every cloud has a silver lining" could apply to the Bank of Canada's unrelenting anti-inflationary stance. Yet bond strategists claim that investors can stand to capitalize on the hard-line policy. The high interest rates it has engendered, they say, provide an ideal opportunity to buy strip bonds. Known familiarly as strips or zero-coupon bonds, they traditionally come into favor during periods of high interest rates. The assumption investors make when purchasing strips is that rates are close to or at a peak. Not only do strip bonds lock in relatively high yields for investors, they also offer potential for capital appreciation should interest rates decline and bond prices rise.

Barnaby Ross, a broker with RBC Dominion Securities Inc., explains that the nomenclature for the bonds can be confusing and varied. "They can be called coupons, residuals, strips, Cougars, Tigrs, sentinels, and zeros," he explains. "But all of these are basically the same." The mechanics of the investment, however, are more straightforward. Brokerages convert government bonds into strips by detaching—or stripping—the semiannual interest coupons from the bond, and leaving the original bond, which is known as the residual. Both the strip coupons and the residual are sold separately at a discount from face value. The bonds can be purchased from brokerage firms, which generally charge up to 1.5 percent commission.

John Grant, chief economist with Wood Gundy Inc., agrees that the time is ripe to purchase strip bonds. He expects the Bank of Canada rate to soon decline from its current [1990] 13.41 percent level. Even so, Grant says, the fact that short-term interest rates are higher than long-term ones (known as an inverted yield curve) has prompted many individuals to reinvest in short-term treasury bills rather than long-term bonds. "But as interest rates gradually drop," Grant cautions, "you miss out on

an opportunity to lock in good interest rates for 20 years." His expectation is that by this June, 20-year Government of Canada bonds will decline to 9 percent, and drop drastically to the 6 percent level by 1994; last week they were 10.4 percent.

Under such a scenario, the advantages of locking in the higher yields on strips is self-evident. The risk in buying the bonds, of course, is that rates will continue to rise. Should that happen, strip-bond investors would incur bigger losses than those incurred had they invested in more conventional long-term bonds. "With strip bonds, there's more exposure to market volatility," concedes Russell Morgan, senior vice-president and director with ScotiaMcLeod Inc. The safest route, says Morgan, is to use strips as a long-term nest egg, ideally in tax-sheltered plans.

The difference between the face value and the purchase price of a strip bond is the total interest payments that will arise over the term of the bond. Unlike other bonds, strips do not make periodic interest payments and therefore provide no cash flow. With strips you make the purchase, and then wait until the time of maturity to collect. Terms on strips can vary from 6 months to 20 years. For example, the purchase price of a $10,000 Ontario Hydro strip bond maturing on February 6, 1995, with a yield of 11.15 percent is $5,960. If interest rates dropped by 2 percentage points to 9.15 percent after the first year, the market value for the bond would be $7,045.39. The total return (purchase price minus the sale price) would be $1,085.39. Of this amount, $420.85 is unrealized capital gain; the remainder is accrued compound interest.

Strips have drawn widespread attention from investors since they were first introduced in Canada in 1982. Both federal and provincial strip bonds offer a high level of security; although not protected by the Canada Deposit Insurance Corp., they are guaranteed by the issuing government. Provincial

(Continued)

THE ONTARIO HYDRO STRIP SHOW

Investors get a charge when interest rates fall—and a shock when they rise.

	5 Year	10 Year
Maturity date	Feb. 6, 1989	Feb. 6, 2000
Yield	11.15%	10.80%
Purchase price	$5,960.00	$3,624.00
Bond value	$6,793.01	$4,313.01
Interest	664.54	391.39
Capital gain	168.47	295.62
After-tax return	8.40%	13.60%
Bond value	$7,045.39	$4,661.01
Interest	664.54	391.39
Capital gain	420.85	665.62
After-tax return	12.60%	23.70%
Bond value	$6,321.25	$3,176.93
Capital loss	324.15	838.46
After-tax return	0%	−18%
Bond value	$6,100.67	$2,907.06
Capital loss	544.67	1,108.30
Interest	664.54	391.00
After-tax return	−3%	−25.18%

* Assuming a 50% marginal tax rate.
Source: Midland Capital Corp.

utility companies also offer strips. Analysts advise investors to buy only high-quality bonds—those with either an AAA or an AA bond rating. "Ontario Hydro and Quebec Hydro are safe bets," says Russell. "Don't buy something that might not be around in 20 years." There are a few corporate strips on the market, but most long-term company-issued bonds have a call feature that permits them to be redeemed by the issuer before maturity.

In an environment of rising interest rates, individuals should be prepared to hold on to a strip bond to offset risks. Indeed, strips are ideal long-term investments, says Ross. "It allows you to plan ahead," he says, "because you know the exact yield you're getting later on." Indeed, some investors prefer strips exactly because they don't require day-to-day monitoring. Says Ross: "They're basi-cally worry-free because you don't have to reinvest." The interest paid by strips is automatically reinvested annually at the prevailing rate when the coupon was purchased. With a conventional bond, the investor must reinvest every year, and may have to reinvest at a lower rate. Increased demand for strip bonds has also improved their liquidity. In fact, with sales of more than $12.2 billion, strips have more liquidity than guaranteed investment certificates.

Of course, the tax implications of purchasing strips must also be assessed. In the example cited earlier, an investor who bought a $10,000 bond for $5,960 would have to pay tax on the interest that accrues over the term of the bond—$4,040. Assuming a tax rate of 50 percent, the individual would have to prepay $2,020 in tax before seeing a penny of income.

For this reason, investors have long been advised to hold strips in self-directed RRSPs. The advice is even more valid with the introduction of a tax ruling this year that requires investors who purchased bonds after 1989 to report interest annually. Previously, individuals had the option of a three-year accrual period; under the new rule, interest can be deferred for three years only on bonds purchased before 1990.

Mark Woodruff, a tax partner with Ernst Young, says most investors will now choose to hold strips in their RRSPs, where the interest will compound tax-free. However, you might choose to keep strips outside the RRSP if you expect to be in a lower tax bracket soon, because the first $28,275 of taxable income is taxed at only 17 percent versus 26 percent for a higher income level. Says Woodruff: "To save on the 9 percent difference makes sense."

According to investment dealers, strips were particularly popular during this year's RRSP season—the period that accounts for 70 percent of annual retail strip sales. Besides retirement plans, strip bonds can also be used in registered education savings plans. Here, the long-term appeal of strips is most apparent. For instance, for a newborn child, if you pay $3,450 today for a strip bond yielding 10.5 percent, it would provide a fund of approximately $20,000 when the child is 20 years old.

From *The Financial Times of Canada*, March 12, 1990, by Paul Gammal. Reprinted by permission. Paul Gammal is a former staff writer at *The Financial Times of Canada*.

Recall from Chapter 2, however, that bill yields are quoted using the bond equivalent yield method, which is not easily comparable to the effective yield. Thus, to keep our eyes on principles rather than institutional details, we will confine our discussion to effective interest rates.

What should happen to T-bill prices as time passes? On their maturity dates, bills must sell for $10,000 because the payment of par value is imminent. Before maturity, however, bills should sell at discounts from par, as the present value of the future $10,000 payment is less than $10,000. As time passes, then, the bill's price will increase at exactly the rate of interest.

To see this, consider a Treasury bill with eight months until maturity, and suppose that the market interest rate is 1 percent per month. The price of the bill today will be $10,000/1.01^8$, or $9,234.83. Next month, with only seven months until maturity, the bill price will be $10,000/1.01^7$, or $9,327.18, a 1 percent increase over its value the previous month. Because the present value of the bill is now discounted for one less month, its price has increased by the one-month discount factor.

Figure 15.2 presents the price path of a 10-year zero-coupon bond until its maturity date for an annual market interest rate of 10 percent. Notice that the bond price rises exponentially, not linearly, until its maturity.

Revenue Canada recognizes that the "built-in" price appreciation on original issue discount (OID) bonds such as T-bills or other zero-coupon bonds in fact represents an implicit interest payment to the holder of the security. Investors are supposed to calculate a price appreciation schedule to impute interest income for any portion of the built-in appreciation that accrues to them during the tax year, even if the asset is not sold or does not mature until future years. Any additional gains or losses that arise from changes in market interest rates are treated as capital gains or losses if the OID bond is sold during the tax year. We work through an example of this procedure later in this section.

Coupon Bonds

We will use Government of Canada bonds as our prototype default-free coupon bond. Like T-bills, these bonds pose no default risk. Canada bond maturities range up to 40 years, and are issued in denominations of $1,000 or more. They make semiannual coupon payments, which are set at an initial level that enables the government to sell the securities at or near par value. Canada bonds may be *callable* for a given period; the call provision gives the issuer the right to repurchase the bond at par value.

Figure 15.3 is an excerpt from the listing of Canadian bond issues in *The Globe and Mail* of March 4, 1992. Note the bond (see the arrow) that matures in December 2001. Its coupon rate is 9.75 percent. Recall from the discussion in Chapter 2 that the quoted prices are the average of the bid and asked prices, and that although bonds are sold in denominations of $1,000 par value, the prices are quoted as a percentage of par value. Therefore, the average of the bid and asked price of the bond is 106.650 percent of par value, or $1,066.50.

As we have noted, the reported yield to maturity, 8.718 percent, is calculated by determining the six-month yield and then doubling it, rather than

FIGURE 15.2

The price of a 10-year zero-coupon bond over time. Price equals $1,000/(1.10)^t$, where t is time until maturity.

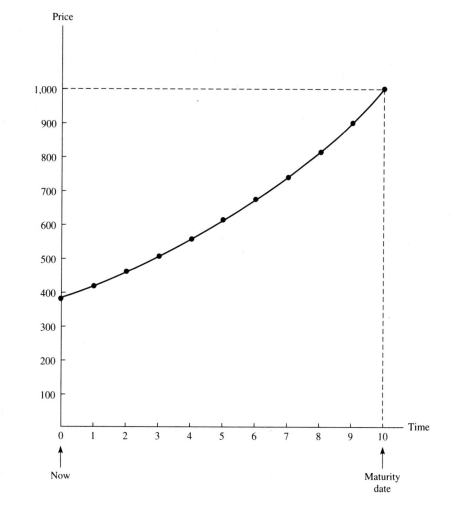

compounding it for two half-year periods. Using a simple-interest technique to annualize means that the yield is quoted on an APR basis rather than as an effective annual yield. The APR method in this context is also called the **bond equivalent yield**. As you look at Figure 15.3, you will see that the yields on most bonds are fairly similar.

The callable bonds are easily identified in Figure 15.3 because a range of the years in which the bond is callable appears in the maturity date column, and the indicator C appears in the yield column. Recall from Chapter 2 that yields on premium bonds (bonds selling above par value) are calculated as the yield to the first call date, whereas yields on discount bonds are calculated as the yield to maturity date.

In practice, a bond buyer must pay the asked price for the bond plus any accrued interest. Recall that interest payments are made every six months. If a bond is purchased between coupon payments, the buyer must pay the seller for

FIGURE 15.3

Listing of Canadian bonds.

(From *The Globe and Mail*, March 4, 1992. Reprinted by permission.)

CANADIAN BONDS

Selected quotations, with changes since the previous day, on actively traded bond issues, provided by RBC Dominion Securities. Yields are calculated to full maturity, unless marked C to indicate callable date. Price is the midpoint between final bid and ask quotations Mar. 3, 1992.

Issuer	Coupon	Maturity	Price	Yield	$ Chg	Issuer	Coupon	Maturity	Price	Yield	$ Chg
GOVERNMENT OF CANADA						NOVA SCOTIA	9.60	30 JAN 22	95.550	10.071	-0.250
CANADA	8.75	6 SEP 93	101.200	7.887	-0.100	ONTARIO HYD	10.00	8 DEC 94	103.875	8.380	-0.200
CANADA	7.00	6 DEC 93	98.700	7.797	-0.100	ONTARIO HYD	10.88	8 JAN 96	106.100	8.950	-0.250
CANADA	7.50	6 MAR 94	99.650	7.692	-0.150	ONTARIO HYD	9.63	3 AUG 99	102.075	9.229	-0.200
CANADA	9.25	1 OCT 94	102.700	8.062	-0.150	ONTARIO HYD	10.00	19 MAR 01	104.100	9.317	-0.200
CANADA	10.00	1 MAR 95	104.725	8.185	-0.150	ONTARIO HYD	8.63	6 FEB 02	95.925	9.260	-0.250
CANADA	9.25	1 OCT 96	103.300	8.362	-0.250	ONTARIO HYD	10.75	6 AUG 21	107.825	9.924	-0.300
CANADA	8.25	1 MAR 97	99.950	8.261	-0.300	ONTARIO HYD	10.13	15 OCT 21	102.025	9.910	-0.300
CANADA	7.50	1 JUL 97	97.300	8.132	-0.300	ONTARIO	8.75	16 APR 97	99.625	8.839	-0.250
CANADA	9.50	1 OCT 98	104.800	8.527	-0.200	ONTARIO	10.20	27 AUG 98	105.000	9.157	-0.200
CANADA	9.25	1 DEC 99	103.600	8.598	-0.200	ONTARIO	10.50	12 DEC 01	106.950	9.392	-0.250
CANADA	9.50	1 OCT 01	104.675	8.766	-0.200	P E I	11.00	19 SEP 11	107.150	10.151	-0.250
► CANADA	9.75	1 DEC 01	106.650	8.718	-0.250	QUEBEC	8.50	10 FEB 97	98.125	8.977	-0.250
CANADA	8.50	1 APR 02	99.850	8.521	-0.250	QUEBEC	10.25	7 APR 98	104.225	9.320	-0.400
CANADA	10.00	1 MAY 02	107.825	8.814	-0.250	QUEBEC	10.25	15 OCT 01	103.650	9.655	-0.300
CANADA	11.75	1 FEB 03	118.425	9.052	-0.250	SASKATCHEWAN	8.13	4 FEB 97	96.400	9.047	-0.250
CANADA	10.25	1 FEB 04	109.300	8.960	-0.250	SASKATCHEWAN	9.60	4 FEB 22	94.825	10.152	-0.250
CANADA	10.00	1 JUN 08	107.350	9.120	-0.300	TORONTO -MET	10.38	4 SEP 01	105.500	9.482	-0.250
CANADA	9.50	1 JUN 10	103.800	9.067	-0.300	**CORPORATE**					
CANADA	9.00	1 MAR 11	100.000	8.999	-0.300	BELL CANADA	10.35	15 DEC 09	104.750	9.778	-0.250
CANADA	10.25	15 MAR 14	109.450	9.238	-0.300	BELL CANADA	9.70	15 DEC 32	99.125	9.785	-0.250
CANADA	10.50	15 MAR 21	112.100	9.289	-0.300	BELL CDA ENT	8.50	31 JAN 97	99.375	8.656	-0.250
CANADA	9.75	1 JUN 21	105.850	9.169	-0.300	BC GAS	10.30	30 SEP 16	102.625	10.010	-0.125
CANADA	9.25	1 JUN 22	101.850	9.067	-0.250	BC TELEPHONE	10.50	12 JUN 00	106.125	9.411	-0.125
PROVINCIAL						BC TELEPHONE	10.65	19 JUN 21	107.750	9.836	-0.250
ALBERTA	9.75	8 MAY 98	103.825	8.925	-0.200	BENEFICIAL	9.63	18 MAR 97	100.125	9.592	-0.250
ALBERTA	10.25	22 AUG 01	107.000	9.127	-0.200	CONSUMER GAS	10.80	15 APR 11	106.625	10.013	-0.250
B C	9.00	9 JAN 02	99.475	9.078	-0.200	CDN IMP BANK	9.40	3 DEC 01/96	101.375	9.030C	-0.250
B C	9.50	9 JAN 12	98.475	9.671	-0.200	CDN PACIFIC	10.50	30 APR 01	103.625	9.884	-0.250
HYDRO QUEBEC	9.25	2 DEC 96	100.975	8.986	-0.250	CP SECURITIE	10.50	2 AUG 96	103.875	9.399	-0.250
HYDRO QUEBEC	10.88	25 JUL 01	107.325	9.666	-0.300	CDN UTIL	9.92	1 APR 22	100.875	9.828	-0.250
HYDRO QUEBEC	11.00	15 AUG 20	107.825	10.153	-0.400	CDN OCC PET	8.40	30 JAN 97	96.375	9.336	-0.250
HYDRO QUEBEC	10.50	15 OCT 21	103.225	10.152	-0.400	GAZ METRO	10.45	31 OCT 16	103.125	10.101	-0.250
MANITOBA	11.25	17 OCT 00	110.400	9.453	-0.250	IMPERIAL OIL	9.88	15 DEC 99	103.000	9.318	-0.250
MANITOBA	10.50	5 MAR 31	105.775	9.914	-0.300	JOHN LABATT	9.25	6 MAR 02	99.375	9.347	-0.250
NEW BRUNSWIC	9.13	1 APR 02	99.050	9.271	-0.250	MAR TEL+TEL	9.25	15 JAN 96	101.250	8.853	-0.125
NEW BRUNSWIC	10.13	31 OCT 11	102.025	9.887	-0.200	ROYAL BANK	10.50	1 MAR 02	105.875	9.572	-0.500
NEWFOUNDLAND	10.13	22 NOV 14	99.125	10.221	-0.300	THOMSON CORP	9.15	2 DEC 98	99.625	9.221	-0.125
NFLD&LAB HYD	10.75	17 SEP 01	106.125	9.747	-0.250	THOMSON CORP	10.55	10 MAY 01	105.875	9.569	-0.250
N S POWER	11.85	24 OCT 95	108.475	9.046	-0.250	SEAGRAM CO	9.00	15 DEC 98	99.625	9.070	-0.250

the prorated share of the upcoming coupon. For example, if 40 days have passed since the last coupon payment and there are 182 days in the semiannual coupon period, the seller is entitled to a payment of accrued interest of 40/182 of the semiannual coupon. The sale, or invoice price, of the bond would equal the stated price plus the accrued interest.

Figure 15.4 illustrates the pattern of bond prices over time. Assume that a bond paying annual coupons is issued at par at a coupon rate of 10 percent, and that market rates remain at 10 percent. The quoted price of the bond remains at $1,000, whereas the invoice price follows a ratchet pattern, gradually reaching $1,100 just before a coupon payment and falling back to $1,000 just after the coupon is paid.

This explains why the price of a maturing bond is listed at $1,000, rather than $1,000 plus one coupon payment. A purchaser of an 8 percent coupon bond one day before the bond's maturity would in fact receive $1,040 on the following day and therefore should be willing to pay a total price of $1,040 for the bond.

FIGURE 15.4

Invoice price of a
coupon bond over
time.

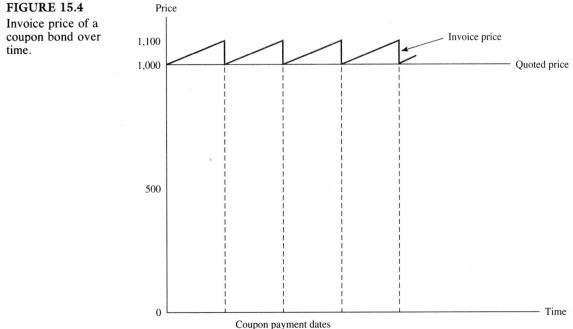

However, $40 of that total payment would constitute the accrued interest for
the preceding half-year period that is owed to the bond seller. The bond price is
quoted net of accrued interest in the financial pages and thus appears as $1,000.

As we noted earlier, a Canada bond will sell at par value when its coupon
rate equals the market interest rate. In these circumstances, the investor receives fair compensation for the time value of money in the form of the recurrent interest payments. No further capital gain is necessary to provide fair
compensation. If the coupon rate were lower than the market interest rate, the
coupon payments alone would not provide investors as high a return as they
could earn elsewhere in the market. To receive a fair return on such an investment, investors also would need to earn capital gains on their bonds to augment
the insufficient interest income. The bonds therefore would have to sell below
par value to provide a "built-in" capital gain on the investment.

To illustrate this point, suppose a bond was issued several years ago, when
the interest rate was 7 percent. The bond's annual coupon rate was thus set at 7
percent. Now, with three years left in the bond's life, the interest rate is 4
percent per half-year, slightly more than 8 percent per year compounded. The
bond's fair market price is therefore the present value of the remaining semiannual coupons plus principal repayment. If the next coupon is to be paid in six
months, that present value is

$$\$35 \times PA(4\%, 6) + \$1,000 \times PF(4\%, 6) = \$973.79$$

which is less than par value.

In six months, after the next coupon is paid, the bond would sell at

$$\$35 \times PA(4\%, 5) + \$1,000 \times PF(4\%, 5) = \$977.74$$

thereby yielding a capital gain over the six-month period of $3.95. If an investor had purchased the bond at $973.79, the total return over the six-month period would equal the coupon payment plus capital gain, or $35 + $3.95 = $38.95. This represents a six-month rate of return of 38.95/973.79, or 4 percent, exactly the current six-month rate of return available elsewhere in the market.

Concept Check	Question 3. What will the bond price be in another six months, when four half-year periods remain until maturity? What is the rate of return to an investor who purchases the bond at $977.74 and sells it in six months?

When bond prices are set according to the present value formula, any discount from par value provides an anticipated capital gain that will augment a below-market coupon rate just sufficiently to provide a fair total rate of return. Conversely, if the coupon rate exceeds the market interest rate, then the interest income by itself is greater than that available elsewhere in the market. Investors will bid up the price of these bonds above their par values. As the bonds approach maturity, they will fall in value because fewer of these above-market coupon payments remain. The resulting capital losses offset the large coupon payments so that the bondholder again receives only a fair rate of return.

Problem 5 at the end of this chapter asks you to work through the case of the high-coupon bond. Figure 15.5 traces the price paths of high- and low-coupon bonds (net of accrued interest) as time to maturity approaches. The low-coupon bond enjoys capital gains, whereas the high-coupon bond suffers capital losses.

We use these examples to make the important point that each bond offers investors the same total rate of return. Although the capital gain and income components differ, the price of each bond is set to provide competitive rates, as we should expect in well-functioning capital markets. Security returns all should be comparable on an after-tax risk-adjusted basis. If not, investors will try to sell low-return securities, thereby driving down their prices until their total return at the now-lower price is competitive with other securities. Price should continue to adjust until all securities are fairly priced in that expected returns are appropriate (given necessary risk and tax adjustments).

After-Tax Returns

We have noted that coupon payments are taxable as interest income, and that discounts from par value on original issue discount bonds are amortized and also treated as interest income. Capital gains or losses also result in tax obligations or benefits in the year they are realized. Because investors should focus

FIGURE 15.5
Price paths of
coupon bonds.

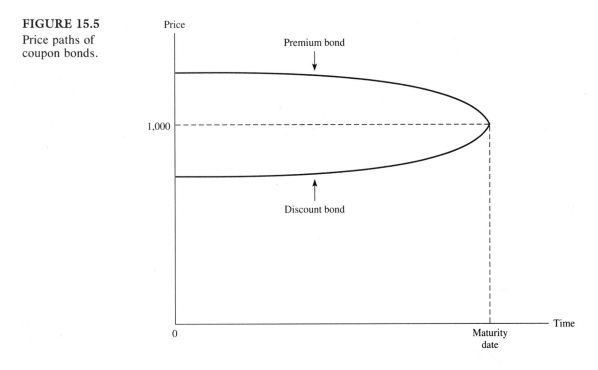

on after-tax income, we will examine the after-tax rate of return on two types of bonds: a zero-coupon bond and a par bond.

Suppose that you have a one-year investment horizon and are trying to decide between these two bonds. Both mature in 20 years. The zero-coupon bond pays $1,000 at maturity. For simplicity, assume the par bond, which has a 10 percent coupon rate, pays the $100 coupon once each year. Both bonds now offer yields to maturity of 10 percent. The 10 percent coupon bond sells at par, whereas the zero sells at $1,000/(1.10)^{20} = 148.64.

First, let us calculate after-tax returns over the coming year, assuming yields to maturity remain at 10 percent and a personal tax bracket of 40 percent. At the end of the year, the time to maturity of each bond will be 19 years. The coupon bond still will sell at par value (why?), and will have provided a $100 coupon payment. Total income is $100, and the before-tax yield is therefore 10 percent. However, the $100 coupon payment generates $40 in tax obligations and thus results in only $60 net income, providing an after-tax rate of return of 6 percent.

The zero-coupon bond will have increased in price to $1,000/(1.10)^{19} = 163.51, a pretax gain of 10 percent. However, that gain of $14.87 ($163.51 − $148.64) is treated by Revenue Canada as imputed interest, with 40 percent of it taxed away. Therefore, the net-of-tax increase in value for the zero is $10.41, for an after-tax rate of return of $8.92/148.64 = .06$, or 6 percent. Thus, for both bonds the after-tax yield equals 10 percent $\times$ (1 − .40), or 6 percent.

Now let us see what happens if the interest rate changes. Suppose the yields on each bond fall to 9 percent by next year. The price of the coupon bond will rise to $1,089.50, at which point it is sold. The pretax return on the bond will be the $100 coupon plus the capital gain of $89.50, a total return of 18.95 percent. The tax due on the bond is 40 percent of the $100 coupon plus 30 percent of $89.50, because under Canadian tax law realized capital gains are taxed at three quarters of the rate of ordinary income. Thus, taxes will be $40 + $26.85, leaving net-of-tax income of $122.65, which figures as an after-tax rate of return of 12.265 percent. Note that it is important to distinguish between capital gains and other income, not only because capital gains are taxed at a lower rate, but also because they are taxed only when realized.

The zero-coupon bond will sell at $1,000/(1.09)^{19} = $194.49 by year-end, for a pretax gain of $45.85 and a pretax rate of return of 30.85 percent. Of this total return, $14.87 will be taxed as ordinary income as the imputed or "built-in" interest at the original 10 percent yield. The remaining $30.98 income is treated as a capital gain that will be taxed if the bond is sold. Therefore, total taxes owed if the bond is sold are (.40 × $14.87) + (.30 × $30.98) = $15.24, leaving net-of-tax income of $30.61, and an after-tax rate of return of $30.61/$148.64 = 20.59 percent.

15.3   *Corporate Bonds*

Like the government, corporations borrow money by issuing bonds. Figure 15.3 also shows corporate bond listings from *The Globe and Mail*. The data presented follow the same format as Government of Canada and provincial bond listings. For example, the BC Telephone 10.50 bond pays a coupon rate of 10.50 percent and matures in 2000. Like government bonds, corporate bond listings quote the average of the bid and asked prices, as well as the APR or bond equivalent yield. By contrast, U.S. corporate bond listings quote the *current yield*, which is simply the annual coupon payment divided by the bond price. Unlike yield to maturity, the current yield ignores any prospective capital gains or losses based on the bond's price relative to par value. The last column shows the change in closing price from the previous day. Like government bonds, corporate bonds sell in units of $1,000 par value but are quoted as a percentage of par value.

Bonds are generally traded over the counter, meaning that the market for the bonds is a loosely organized network of bond dealers linked together by a computer quotation system. (See Chapter 3 for a comparison of exchange and OTC trading.) In practice, the bond market can be quite "thin," in that there are few investors interested in trading a particular bond at any particular time. On any day it might be difficult to find a buyer or seller for a particular issue, which introduces some "liquidity risk" into the bond market. It may be difficult to sell one's holdings quickly if the need arises.

Bonds issued in Canada today can be either *registered bonds* or *bearer bonds*. For registered bonds, the issuing firm keeps records of the owner of the bond and can mail interest checks to him or her. Registration of bonds is clearly helpful to tax authorities in the enforcement of tax collection. In contrast, bearer bonds are traded without any record of ownership. The investor's physical possession of the bond certificate is the only evidence of ownership.

Promised Yields vs. Expected Yields

Corporate bonds always are subject to potential default of the bond issuer. If the issuer declares bankruptcy, the bondholders will not receive all the payments that were promised to them when the bonds were issued. Because of this, we must distinguish between the bond's promised yield to maturity and its expected yield. The promised or stated yield will be realized only if the firm ultimately meets the obligations of the bond issue. Therefore, the stated yield is the maximum possible yield to maturity of the bond.[2] In contrast, the expected yield to maturity must take into account the possibility of a default.

To compensate investors for the possibility of bankruptcy, a corporate bond must offer a **default premium**. The premium is a differential in promised yield between the corporate bond and an otherwise identical government bond that is risk-free in terms of default. If the corporation remains solvent and the investor actually receives the promised yield, he or she will realize a higher total yield to maturity than can be realized from the government bond. If, however, the firm goes bankrupt, the corporate bond is likely to provide a return lower than that of the government bond. The corporate bond thus holds the possibility of both better and worse performance than the default-free Canada bond. It is important to keep in mind, therefore, that the stated yield to maturity on risky bonds is not the expected yield—it is the yield to maturity that will be realized if the corporation survives over the life of the bond.

The pattern of default premiums offered on risky bonds is sometimes called the *risk structure of interest rates*. The greater the default risk, the higher the default premium. Such default risk is measured by both Moody's and Standard & Poor's in the United States and by Canadian Bond Rating Service (CBRS) and Dominion Bond Rating Service (DBRS) in Canada; the two U.S. rating services also rate several Canadian issues. All rating agencies assign letter grades to the bonds of corporations and municipalities to reflect their assessment of the safety of the bond issue. The top rating is AAA (Standard & Poor's and DBRS), Aaa (Moody's), and A++ (CBRS). Moody's modifies each rating class with a 1, 2, or 3 suffix (e.g., Aaa1, Aaa2, Aaa3) to provide a finer gradation of ratings. S&P uses a + or − modification, and the two Canadian services use the terms (*high*) and (*low*) as modifiers.

Bonds rated BBB or above (S&P and DBRS), Baa or above (Moody's), and B++ or above (CBRS) are considered **investment grade bonds**, whereas

---

[2] The realized compound yield to maturity (see Chapter 16) can exceed the promised yield of maturity if the reinvestment rate turns out to be high. The conventional yield to maturity, however, is independent of reinvestment rates and cannot exceed the promised yield upon purchase of the bond.

lower-rated bonds are classified as **speculative grade or junk bonds**. Certain regulated institutional investors, such as insurance companies, have not always been allowed to invest in speculative grade bonds. (Some observers have expressed doubt over the value of the bond rating system; see the discussion in the accompanying box.)

Rating Services Often Overrated

John Grundy

Since their establishment in the 1970s, Canada's two credit rating agencies, Canadian Bond Rating Service Ltd. of Montreal and Dominion Bond Rating Service of Toronto, have had a growing influence on the Canadian bond scene.

Bond ratings for the relatively small Canadian market are to an extent overrated, for, if they didn't exist, the bond business would survive and in much the same way as it does now. Most experienced investors in the Canadian market can glance over a list of issues and correctly guess most of the credit ratings the agencies have assigned. The introduction of an "official" ratings system has merely served to confirm what was already evident in a marketplace that is made up of only about 150 public and private enterprises that borrow from investors.

Nonetheless, the consensus of the marketplace is obviously that the ratings established by the services are one of the key ingredients to the process of bond portfolio management. The rating and the size of a proposed new issue are the most important factors that will determine how well and how widespread the acceptance of the issue will be by the investing community.

The existence of the rating services means that even the smallest investor has access to highly competent credit analysis and has been able to introduce the essential elements of quality consideration to his investment portfolio, without making purely subjective assessments.

Prior to the creation of the Canadian raters, the bond market was alive and well and operating smoothly. Without an "official" rating system, bonds traded at yield levels that reflected the view of individual market players and it was often possi-

ble to acquire or dispose of bond holdings at prices that to the investor involved seemed inappropriate for the particular credit in question.

Such an environment also served to give a higher level of liquidity to the market, because it was relatively easy to find another market player who disagreed with your opinion. This is still the case today, with the major exception that all market players follow the "official" credit rating, thus narrowing the range of credit-worthiness opinion.

Investors should recognize that the process of managing their portfolio is a forward-looking exercise, whereas an assigned credit rating is an historical review of the enterprise being rated and a judgment as to its credit quality based on the average experience for a business cycle.

Because of this, a change in a rating is rarely "news" that affects the relative yield level of the credit in question. This is because the marketplace does not judge an enterprise based on average experience, but rather reacts immediately to the fu-

GOVERNMENT OF CANADA AVERAGE
BOND YIELDS

	Recent	Year Ago	52-Week Range High	Low
1–3 years	8.71	10.08	10.22	8.71
3–5 years	8.89	10.43	10.50	8.81
5–10 years	9.17	10.85	10.92	9.06
Over 10 years	9.24	11.03	11.13	9.17

Source: Bank of Canada.

(Continued)

ture implications of any fundamental change that takes place in a company's operations. Consequently, the relative yield level of the company's bonds usually adjusts well before the rating agencies publish their analytical conclusions.

Rather than reacting to a rating change that has usually been well discounted, investors should pay attention to continuing developments that often precede even the market's perception of the relative credit standing of a particular bond. By doing so they are in a position to trade their portfolio to advantage.

Events such as changes in corporate common stock dividends, a sudden deviation from the norm for reported profit, a perceived change in the overall status of the industry that the bond issuer operates in, management changes, particularly in the financial area, and any unusual change in the level of bank loans carried, often precede credit quality revisions.

The complexities of issuers' operating economic environments and modern accounting methods have diluted the value of traditional financial statement analysis. The creative actions of today's accounting profession have in effect reintroduced a high degree of subjectivity to the credit rating process. Much more of it will rapidly reduce the usefulness of the rating agencies and will further undermine confidence in current accounting practices.

From *The Globe and Mail*, July 26, 1986, by John Grundy. Reprinted by permission.

Figure 15.6 contains the definitions of bond rating classifications for the four bond rating agencies. Figure 15.7 shows yields to maturity of Canadian bonds of three different risk classes (federal, provincial, and corporate) since 1948. Figure 15.8 shows similar yield data for three risk classes of Canadian corporate bonds in recent years. Both Figures 15.7 and 15.8 show clear evidence of the presence of default-risk premiums on promised yields. Although yield spreads vary over time, higher promised yields clearly are associated with lower ratings.

One particular manner in which yield spreads seem to vary over time is related to the business cycle. Yield spreads tend to be wider when the economy is in a recession. Apparently, investors perceive a higher probability of bankruptcy when the economy is faltering, even holding bond ratings constant. They require a commensurately higher default premium. This is sometimes termed a *flight to quality*, meaning that investors move their funds into safer bonds unless they can obtain larger premiums on lower-rated securities.

Junk Bonds

Junk bonds are nothing more than speculative-grade (low-rated or unrated) bonds. Before 1977 almost all junk bonds were "fallen angels," that is, bonds originally issued by firms with investment-grade ratings but since downgraded. In 1977, however, firms began to issue "original-issue junk." Much of the credit for this innovation is given to Drexel Burnham Lambert, and especially its trader, Michael Milken. Drexel had long enjoyed a niche as a junk bond trader and had thereby established a network of potential investors in junk bonds. They began to market original-issue junk, so-called emerging credits, in

FIGURE 15.6
Definitions of each bond rating class.

Bond Ratings

	Very high quality	High quality	Speculative	Very poor
CBRS	A++ A+	A B++	B+ B	C D
DBRS	AAA AA	A BBB	BB B	C D
Standard & Poor's	AAA AA	A BBB	BB B	CCC D
Moody's	Aaa Aa	A Baa	Ba B	Caa C

At times all services have used adjustments to these ratings. S&P uses plus and minus signs: A+ is the strongest A rating and A− the weakest. Moody's uses a 1, 2, or 3 designation—with 1 indicating the strongest. CBRS and DBRS use a (high) for the strongest and a (low) for the weakest designations.

CBRS	DBRS	Moody's	S&P	
A++	AAA	Aaa	AAA	Debt rated Aaa and AAA has the highest rating. Capacity to pay interest and principal is extremely strong.
A+	AA	Aa	AA	Debt rated Aa and AA has a very strong capacity to pay interest and repay principal. Together with the highest rating, this group comprises the high-grade bond class.
A	A	A	A	Debt rated A has a strong capacity to pay interest and repay principal, although it is somewhat more susceptible to the adverse effects of changes in circumstances and economic conditions than debt in higher-rated categories.
B++	BBB	Baa	BBB	Debt rated Baa and BBB is regarded as having an adequate capacity to pay interest and repay principal. Whereas it normally exhibits adequate protection parameters, adverse economic conditions or changing circumstances are more likely to lead to a weakened capacity to pay interest and repay principal for debt in this category than in higher-rated categories. These bonds are medium-grade obligations.
B+	BB	Ba	BB	Debt rated in these categories is regarded, on balance, as predominantly speculative with respect to capacity to pay interest and repay principal in accordance with the terms of the obligation. BB and Ba indicate the lowest degree of speculation, and CC and Ca the highest degree of speculation. Although such debt will likely have some quality and protective characteristics, these are outweighed by large uncertainties or major risk exposures to adverse conditions. Some issues may be in default.
B	B	B	B	
C	CCC	Caa	CCC	
C	CC	Ca	CC	
C	C	C	C	This rating is reserved for income bonds on which no interest is being paid.
D	D	D	D	Debt rated D is in default, and payment of interest and/or repayment of principal is in arrears.

Data from various editions of *Standard & Poor's Bond Guide*, *Moody's Bond Guide*, *CBRS Canadian Credit Review*, and *DBRS Bond Rating*.

Modified from Stephen A. Ross and Randolph W. Westerfield, *Corporate Finance* (St. Louis: Times Mirror/Mosby College Publishing, 1988.

the belief that default rates on these bonds did not justify the large yield spreads commonly exhibited in the marketplace. Firms not able to muster an investment-grade rating were happy to have Drexel (and other investment bankers) market their bonds directly to the public, because this opened up a new source of financing. Previously, these firms had been forced to borrow from banks, and junk issues were a lower-cost financing alternative.

FIGURE 15.7
Long-term bond
yields for Canada,
provincial, and
corporate bonds,
1948–1990.

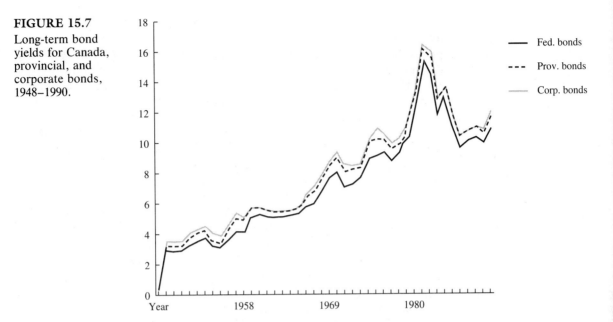

FIGURE 15.8
Canadian corporate
bond yields,
1984–1991.

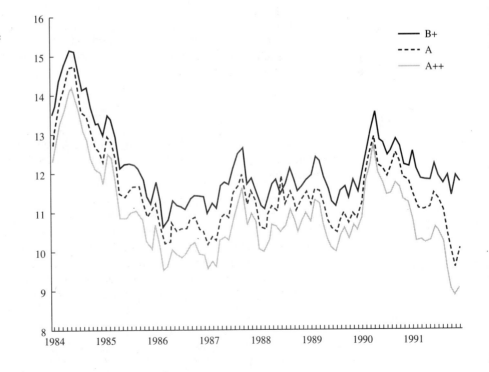

Junk bonds gained some notoriety in the 1980s, when they were used commonly as financing vehicles in leveraged buyouts and hostile takeover attempts. Although junk bonds constituted only 3.7 percent of the U.S. corporate bond market in 1977, they accounted for 23 percent of the market by 1987.[3]

Since then, however, the junk bond market has fallen on hard times. Mergers, acquisitions, and leveraged buyouts financed with junk bonds commonly involved extremely high debt ratios with consequently severe interest payment burdens. The slowdown in the U.S. economy in 1989 raised fears that these interest levels could not be supported once profit levels fell. By 1990, the default rate on junk bonds approached 10 percent.

Finally, the legal difficulties of Drexel and Michael Milken in connection with Wall Street's insider trading scandals of the late 1980s tainted the junk bond market. Milken was indicted on racketeering and security fraud charges, and eventually was sentenced to 10 years in prison. As the junk bond market tumbled in 1989, Drexel suffered large losses in its own billion-dollar portfolio of junk bonds, and filed for bankruptcy in February 1990. The speed of its demise is astounding when you consider its 1986 profits, only three years earlier, of about $500 million.

Junk bond investment performance in this period was extremely poor. While long-term U.S. Treasury bonds provided a total return of about 4 percent in the six-month period ending in mid-February 1990 (when Drexel declared bankruptcy), junk bond returns averaged about −9 percent. Prices on junk issues had fallen so severely by this time that junk bonds exceed U.S. Treasury yields by about 7.5 percentage points, the largest margin in history.

In retrospect, the early popularity of junk bonds was reinforced by the apparent low default rates on outstanding issues. This, however, was not the appropriate comparison, since the junk bond market was rapidly expanding at the time. When current defaults were compared to originally outstanding issues, the default rate was much higher.

Determinants of Bond Safety

Bond rating agencies base their quality ratings largely on an analysis of the level and trend of some of the issuer's financial ratios. The key ratios used to evaluate safety include:

1. *Coverage ratios* (ratios of company earnings to fixed costs). For example, the *times-interest-earned ratio* is the ratio of earnings before interest payments and taxes to interest obligations. The *fixed-charge coverage ratio* adds lease payments and sinking fund payments to interest obligations to arrive at the ratio of earnings to all fixed cash obligations. Low or falling coverage ratios signal possible cash flow difficulties.
2. *Leverage ratios* (debt-to-equity ratios). A too-high leverage ratio indi-

---

[3] Kevin Perry and Robert A. Taggart, "The Growing Role of Junk Bonds in Corporate Finance," *Continental Bank Journal of Applied Corporate Finance* 1 (Spring 1988).

TABLE 15.2 Rating Classes and Median Financial Ratios, 1983–1985

Rating Category	Fixed-Charge Coverage Ratio	Cash Flow to Long-Term Debt	Return on Capital (%)	Long-Term Debt to Capital (%)
AAA	7.48	3.09	25.60	8.85
AA	4.43	1.18	22.05	18.88
A	2.93	.75	18.03	24.46
BBB	2.30	.46	12.10	31.54
BB	2.04	.27	13.80	42.52
B	1.51	.19	12.01	52.04
CCC	0.75	.15	2.70	69.28

Data from Standard & Poor's *Debt Rating Criteria*, 1986.

cates excessive indebtedness, signalling the possibility that the firm will be unable to earn enough to satisfy the obligations on its bonds.

3. *Liquidity ratios.* The two common liquidity ratios are the *current ratio* (current assets/current liabilities) and the *quick ratio* (current assets excluding inventories/current liabilities). These ratios measure the firm's ability to pay bills coming due with cash currently being collected.

4. *Profitability ratios* (measures of rates of return on assets or equity). Profitability ratios are indicators of a firm's overall financial health. The *return on assets* (earnings before interest and taxes divided by total assets) is the most popular of these measures. Firms with higher return on assets should be better able to raise money in security markets because they offer prospects for better returns on the firm's investments.

5. *Cash flow to debt ratios.* These are the ratios of total cash flow to outstanding debt.

Standard & Poor's has computed three-year median values of selected ratios for firms in each of their rating classes, which we present in Table 15.2. Of course, ratios must be evaluated in the context of industry standards, and analysts differ in the weights they place on particular ratios. Nevertheless, Table 15.2 demonstrates the tendency of ratios to improve along with the firm's rating class. Direct statistical tests of the ability of financial ratios to predict bond ratings in the five top rating classes of the Canadian Bond Rating Service (CBRS) were conducted in a study by Barnes and Byng.[4] The study examined 27 financial variables that included ratios similar to those in Table 15.2, as well as variables representing the size and earnings stability of the firm. The results showed that the observed ratings assigned by CBRS in the years 1972, 1978, and 1983 could be predicted fairly accurately by an appropriate set of weights applied to the 27 variables for each year. These weights, though, tended to change from year to year, and the accuracy of one year's predictors tended to deteriorate with time.

---

[4] Tom Barnes and Tom Byng, "The Prediction of Corporate Bond Ratings: The Canadian Case," *Canadian Journal of Administrative Sciences* 5, no. 3 (September 1988).

In fact, the heavy dependence of bond ratings on publicly available financial data is evidence of an interesting phenomenon. You might think that an increase or decrease in bond rating would cause substantial bond price gains or losses, but this is not the case. Weinstein[5] finds that bond prices move in *anticipation* of rating changes, which is evidence that investors themselves track the financial status of bond issuers. This is consistent with an efficient market. Rating changes actually largely confirm a change in status that has been reflected in security prices already. Holthausen and Leftwich,[6] however, find that bond rating downgrades (but not upgrades) are associated with abnormal returns in the stock of the affected company.

Many studies have tested whether financial ratios can in fact be used to predict default risk. One of the best-known series of tests has been conducted by Edward Altman, who has used discriminant analysis to predict bankruptcy. With this technique, a firm is assigned a score based on its financial characteristics. If its score exceeds a cutoff value, the firm is deemed creditworthy. A score below the cutoff value indicates significant bankruptcy risk in the near future.

To illustrate the technique, suppose that we were to collect data on the return on equity (ROE) and coverage ratios of a sample of firms, and then keep records of any corporate bankruptcies. In Figure 15.9 we plot the ROE and coverage ratios for each firm using X for firms that eventually went bankrupt and O for those that remained solvent. Clearly, the X and O firms show different patterns of data, with the solvent firms typically showing higher values for the two ratios.

The discriminant analysis determines the equation of the line that best separates the X and O observations. Suppose that the equation of the line is $.75 = .9$ ROE $+ .4$ coverage. Each firm is assigned a ''Z-score'' equal to $.9$ ROE $+ .4$ coverage using the firm's ROE and coverage ratios. If the Z-score exceeds $.75$, the firm plots above the line and is considered a safe bet; Z-scores below $.75$ foretell financial difficulty.

The discriminant analysis method was applied to a sample of Canadian firms in a study by Altman and Lavallee,[7] who found the following equation to best separate failing and nonfailing firms:

$$Z = 0.234 \frac{\text{Sales}}{\text{Total assets}} + 0.972 \frac{\text{Net after-tax profits}}{\text{Total debt}}$$

$$+ 1.002 \frac{\text{Current assets}}{\text{Current liabilities}} - 0.531 \frac{\text{Total debt}}{\text{Total assets}}$$

$$+ 0.612 \,(\text{Rate of equity growth} - \text{Rate of asset growth})$$

---

[5] Mark I. Weinstein, ''The Effect of a Rating Change Announcement on Bond Price,'' *Journal of Financial Economics*, December 1977.

[6] Robert W. Holthausen and Richard W. Leftwich, ''The Effect of Bond Rating Changes on Common Stock Prices,'' *Journal of Financial Economics* 17 (September 1986).

[7] Edward I. Altman and Mario Y Lavalee, ''Business Failure Classification in Canada,'' *Journal of Business Administration* 12, no. 1 (Fall 1980).

FIGURE 15.9
Discriminant
analysis.

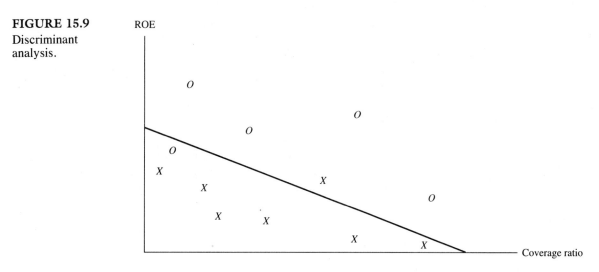

Firms with Z-scores above 1.626 were deemed safe: 81.5 percent of these were still in business in the next year. In contrast, 85.2 percent of bankrupt firms had Z-scores below 1.626 the year before they failed.

A rather more sceptical view of the ability of financial ratios to predict default risk emerges from a Canadian study of *small-business* debt (mainly bank loans) by Kryzanowski and To.[8] They found that default risk depended on variables such as the firm's size and age, the type of loan, and the project performance assessment made by the lending institution. Several important financial ratios were examined, and none of them was found to be a significant determinant of default risk. It seems, therefore, that financial ratios are not good indicators of such risk for small businesses.

Concept Check

> **Question 4.** Suppose we add to Altman's equation a new variable equal to market value of equity/book value of debt. Would you expect this variable to receive a positive or negative coefficient?

Bond Indentures

A bond is issued with an **indenture**, which is the contract between the issuer and the bondholder. Part of the indenture is a set of restrictions on the firm

---

[8] Lawrence Kryzanowski and Minh Chau To, "Small-Business Debt Financing: An Empirical Investigation of Default Risk," *Canadian Journal of Administrative Sciences* 2, no. 1 (June 1985).

issuing the bond to protect the rights of the bondholders. Such restrictions include provisions relating to sinking funds, allowed further borrowing, dividend policy, and collateral. The issuing firm agrees to these so-called *protective covenants* in order to market their bonds to investors concerned about the safety of the bond issue.

Sinking funds

Bonds call for repayment of principal at the end of the bond's life. This repayment constitutes a large cash commitment. To help ensure that the commitment does not create a cash flow crisis, the firm agrees to establish a **sinking fund** to spread the principal repayment burden over several years. The fund may operate in one of two ways:

1. The firm may repurchase a fraction of the outstanding bonds in the open market each year.
2. The firm can purchase a fraction of outstanding bonds at a special call price associated with the sinking fund provision. The firm has an option to purchase the bonds at either the market price or the sinking fund call price, whichever is lower. To fairly allocate the burden of the sinking fund call among bondholders, the bonds chosen for the call are selected at random based on serial number.[9]

The sinking fund call differs from a conventional bond call in two important ways. First, the firm can repurchase only a limited fraction of the bond issue at the sinking fund call price. At best, some indentures allow firms to use a *doubling option*, which allows repurchase of double the required number of bonds at the sinking fund call price. Second, the sinking fund call price generally is lower than the call price established by other call provisions in the indenture. The sinking fund call price often is set at the bond's par value.

Although sinking funds ostensibly protect bondholders by making principal repayment more likely, they can in fact act to hurt the investor. If interest rates fall and bond prices rise, firms will benefit from the sinking fund provision that enables them to repurchase their bonds at below-market prices. In these circumstances, the firm's gain is the bondholder's loss.

One bond issue that does not require a sinking fund is a *serial bond* issue. In a serial bond issue, the firm sells bonds with staggered maturity dates. As bonds mature sequentially, the principal repayment burden for the firm is spread out over time, just as it is with a sinking fund. Serial bonds do not include call provisions.

Subordination of further debt

One of the factors determining bond safety is total outstanding debt of the issuer. An investor purchasing a bond would be understandably distressed to

---

[9] Although it is uncommon, the sinking fund provision also may call for periodic payments to a trustee with the payments invested so that the accumulated sum can be used for retirement of the entire issue at maturity.

see the firm soon tripling its outstanding debt. The bondholder would have a bond of lower quality than it appeared when issued. To prevent firms from harming bondholders in this manner, **subordination clauses** restrict the amount of additional borrowing. Additional debt might be required to be subordinated in priority to existing debt; that is, in the event of bankruptcy, *subordinated* or *junior* debtholders will not be paid unless and until the prior senior debt is fully paid. For this reason, subordination is sometimes called a "me-first rule," meaning that the senior bondholders are to be paid first in the event of bankruptcy.

Dividend restrictions

Firms are limited in the amount of dividends that they are allowed to pay. The limitation on dividend payouts protects the bondholders, because it forces the firm to retain assets rather than paying them to stockholders. A typical restriction disallows payment of dividends if cumulative dividends paid since the firm's inception exceed cumulative net income plus proceeds from sales of stock.

Collateral

Some bonds are issued with specific collateral behind them. **Collateral** can take several forms, but it is a particular asset of the firm that the bondholders receive if the firm defaults on the bond. If the collateral is property, the bond is called a *mortgage bond*. If the collateral takes the form of other securities held by the firm, the bond is a *collateral trust bond*. If equipment is used, the bond is known as an *equipment trust certificate*. This last form of collateral is most commonly used by firms like railroads, where the equipment is fairly standard and can be easily sold to another firm should the firm default and the bondholders acquire the collateral.

Because of the specific collateral that backs them, collateralized bonds generally are considered the safest variety of corporate bonds. In contrast, general **debenture bonds** do not provide for specific collateral; they are *unsecured* bonds. They rely solely on the general earning power of the firm for their safety. If the firm defaults, debenture owners become general creditors of the firm. Because of their greater safety, collateralized bonds generally offer lower yields than do general debentures.

Callable Bonds and Convertible Bonds

Callable bonds allow the issuer to repurchase the bond at a specified price. For example, if a bond is issued with a high coupon rate when market interest rates are high, and interest rates subsequently fall, the firm might like to retire the high-priced debt and issue new bonds at a lower coupon rate, thereby reducing its interest payments. This is called *refunding*. In the absence of a call provision, the firm would have to pay fair market prices to buy back the original issue. But to the investor, those market prices reflect the increased present value of the bond's scheduled payments. The call provision, which allows the firm to repurchase the bond at the call price, lets the issuer avoid paying the full present value to the bondholders. The firm, rather than the bondholder, benefits from falls in interest rates.

Of course, the firm's benefit is the bondholder's burden. Holders of callable bonds will not reap capital gains from falls in the interest rate if the bonds are called away from them. The firm's option to call the bond at a specified price takes away from the bondholder any upside capital gains potential beyond the call price. To compensate investors, callable bonds are issued with higher coupons and promised yields to maturity than are noncallable bonds.

Figure 15.10 illustrates the risk of call to the bondholder. The straight bond line is the value at various market interest rates of a "straight" (noncallable) bond with par value $1,000, 8 percent coupon, and 30-year time to maturity. The callable bond line is the value of the same bond if it is callable at $1,100. At high interest rates the risk of call is negligible, and the values of the bonds coincide. At lower rates, however, the values of the bonds begin to diverge, the difference reflecting the value of the firm's option to reclaim the callable bond at $1,100. Finally, at very low interest rates, the bond is called, and its value simply equals $1,100.

The call price of a bond is commonly set at an initial level about par value plus one annual coupon payment. As time passes, the call price falls, gradually approaching par value.

FIGURE 15.10

Bond prices—
callable and straight
debt.

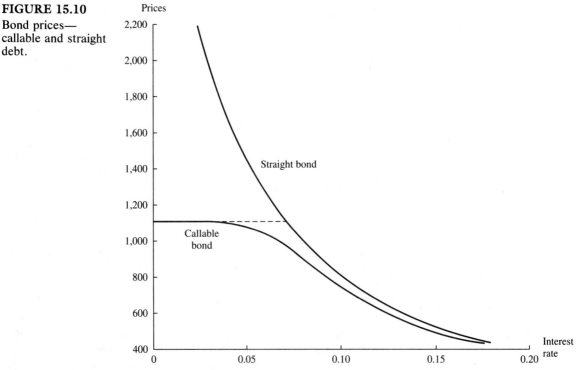

Callable bonds typically come with a period of *call protection*, an initial period during which the bonds are not callable. Such bonds are referred to as *deferred* callable bonds. An implicit form of call protection operates for bonds selling at deep discounts from their call prices. Even if interest rates fall a bit, deep-discount bonds still will sell below the call price and thus will not be subject to a call. Premium bonds that might be selling near their call prices, however, are especially apt to be called if rates fall further. If interest rates fall, a callable premium bond is likely to provide a lower return than could be earned on a discount bond whose potential price appreciation is not limited by the likelihood of a call. As a consequence, investors in premium bonds often are more interested in the bond's yield to call rather than yield to maturity, because it may appear to them that the bond will be retired at the call date.

Concept Check	Question 5. The yield to maturity on two 10-year maturity bonds currently is 7 percent. Each bond has a call price of $1,100. One bond has a coupon rate of 6 percent, the other 8 percent. Assume, for simplicity, that bonds are called as soon as the present value of their remaining payments exceeds their call price. What will be the capital gain on each bond if the market interest rate suddenly falls to 6 percent?
	Question 6. Would you expect a premium bond with the same call price as a discount bond to offer a lower, equal, or higher promised yield to maturity compared with the discount bond?

Figure 15.11 shows the terms of a callable bond issued by The Bank of Nova Scotia as described in *Moody's Bank and Finance Manual*. The bond was issued in 1977 but was not callable until 1993. After 1993, the call price falls until it eventually reaches par value after September 14, 1995. Therefore, bondholders have complete call protection until 1993. However, *limited* amounts of the bonds may be called at par value starting in 1983 as part of the provisions of the sinking fund.

A relatively new development is the **retractable bond**. Whereas the callable bond gives the issuer the option to retire the bond at the call date or to continue to the maturity date, the retractable gives the option to the bondholder. Thus, if the bond's coupon rate is below current market yields, the bondholder will choose to redeem the bond early, through retraction. If the bond's coupon rate is higher, it will be optimal not to retract. An **extendible bond**, on the other hand, allows the bondholder to retain the bond for an additional period beyond maturity, which he or she will do if the coupon exceeds current rates; such a bond is known as a *put bond* in the United States. These additional privileges granted to the bondholders are paid for by a slightly lower coupon.

Convertible bonds convey an option to bondholders to exchange each bond for a specified number of shares of common stock of the firm. The *conversion ratio* gives the number of shares for which each bond may be exchanged.

FIGURE 15.11

Callable bond issued by The Bank of Nova Scotia.

From *Moody's Bank and Finance Manual*, 1991.

17.   The Bank of Nova Scotia sinking fund debenture 9 1/2s, due 1997:

OUTSTG.—Oct. 31, 1990, C$36,375,000.

DATED—Sept. 15, 1977. DUE—Sept. 15, 1997.

INTEREST—M&S 15. Principal and interest will be payable at any branch of the Bank in Canada.

TRUSTEE—Montreal Trust Company Canada.

DENOMINATION—Coupon, $1,000, $5,000 and $25,000 registrable as to principal only and fully registered, $1,000 and full multiples thereof.

CALLABLE—As a whole or in part at any time on at least 30 days' notice to each Sept. 14 as follows:

1993. . . . . 101.50 1994. . . . . 101.00 1995. . . . .100.50

And thereafter at 100. Also callable for mandatory and optional sinking fund purposes at 100 plus accrued interest.

SINKING FUND—Annually, on Sept. 15, 1983–96, cash (or debs.), to retire $1,500,000 principal amount of debs.; plus similar optional payments.

SECURITY—Subordinate to all senior debt.

INDENTURE MODIFICATION—Indenture may be modified, except as provided, with consent of 66 2/3% of debs. outstg.

PURPOSE—Proceeds will be used to augment the Bank's general fund.

OFFERED—($50,000,000) at $100 plus accrued interest on Aug. 16, 1977 thru Wood Gundy Ltd., Burns Fry Ltd., Dominion Securities Ltd. and associates.

Suppose that a convertible bond that is issued at a par value of $1,000 is convertible into 40 shares of a firm's stock. The current stock price is $20 per share, so the option to convert is not currently profitable. However, should the stock price later rise to $30, each bond may be profitably converted into $1,200 worth of stock. The *market conversion value* is the current value of the shares for which the bonds may be exchanged. At the $20 stock price, the bond's conversion value is $800. The *conversion premium* is the excess of the bond value over the conversion value of the bond. If the bond currently were selling for $950, its premium would be $150.

Thus, convertible bonds give their holders the ability to share in price appreciation of the company's stock. Of course, this benefit comes at a price; convertible bonds offer lower coupon rates and promised yields to maturity than do non-convertible bonds. At the same time, the actual return on the convertible bond may exceed the stated yield to maturity if the option to convert becomes profitable. We discuss convertible and callable bonds further in Chapter 22.

Floating-Rate Bonds

Floating-rate bonds mimic short-term bonds in the sense that they are designed to minimize the holder's interest rate risk. As with variable-rate mortgages, the interest rate that the borrower pays is reset periodically depending on market conditions. For example, the rate paid might be adjusted annually to the current T-bill rate plus 2 percent. At each reset, the bond price should revert to par value, since the bond is now offering the current market yield. Because the bond always pays close to current market rates, its price risk is minimized. The interest rate risk of floaters is more a function of the length of the reset period than of the bond's maturity. Typically, these bonds would have a maximum and a minimum rate, known as a *cap* and a *floor*.

The yield spread on floaters is fixed over the life of the security, which may be many years, in contrast to short-term bonds or money-market instruments. Therefore, if the appropriate yield premium changes, the bond price will not revert to par value. The major risk involved in floaters has to do with changing credit conditions. The financial health of the firm may deteriorate, for example, meaning a greater yield premium is required than is offered by the security. In addition, the risk premium that the market demands for a particular risk category also may change, as in the flight-to-quality phenomenon.

Summary

1. Fixed-income securities are distinguished by their promise to pay a fixed or specified stream of income to their holders. The coupon bond is a typical fixed-income security.

2. The yield to maturity is the single interest rate that equates the present value of a security's cash flows to its price. Bond prices and yields are inversely related.

3. For premium bonds, the coupon rate is greater than the current yield, which is greater than the yield to maturity. The order of these inequalities is reversed for discount bonds.

4. Treasury bills are Canadian or U.S. government-issued zero-coupon bonds with original maturities of up to one year. Prices of zero-coupon bonds rise exponentially over time, providing a rate of appreciation equal to the interest rate. Revenue Canada treats price appreciation as an imputed interest payment to the investor.

5. Canada bonds have original maturities greater than one year. They are issued at or near par value, with their prices quoted net of accrued interest.

6. When bonds are subject to potential default, the stated yield to maturity is the maximum possible yield to maturity that can be realized by the bondholder. In the event of default, however, that promised yield will not be realized. To compensate bond investors for default risk, bonds must offer default premiums, that is, promised yields in excess of those offered by default-free government securities. If the firm remains healthy, its bonds will provide higher returns than will government bonds. Otherwise, the returns may be lower.

7. Bond safety is often measured with financial ratio analysis. Bond indentures are another safeguard to protect the claims of bondholders. Common indentures specify sinking fund requirements, collateralization of the loan, dividend restrictions, and subordination of future bond issues.

8. Callable bonds should offer higher promised yields to maturity to compensate investors for the fact that they will not realize full capital gains if the interest falls and the bonds are called away from them at the stipulated call price. Bonds often are issued with a period of call protection. In addition, discount bonds selling significantly below their call price offer implicit call protection.

9. Retractable and extendible bonds give the option to terminate early or extend the life of the bond to the bondholder rather than to the issuer.

10. Convertible bonds may be exchanged at the bondholder's discretion for a specified number of shares of stock. Convertible bondholders "pay" for this option by accepting a lower coupon rate on the security.

11. Floating-rate bonds pay a fixed premium over a reference short-term interest rate. They limit risk because the rate paid is tied to current market conditions.

Key terms

Fixed-income securities	Indenture
Bond	Sinking fund
Principal	Subordination clauses
Coupon rate	Collateral
Par value	Debenture bonds
Yield to maturity	Callable bond
Zero-coupon bond	Retractable bond
Bond equivalent yield	Extendible bond
Default premium	Convertible bonds
Investment grade bond	Floating-rate bonds
Speculative grade or junk bond	

Selected readings

A comprehensive treatment of pricing issues related to fixed-income securities is given in:
  Van Horne, James C. *Financial Market Rates and Flows*. Englewood Cliffs, N.J.: Prentice Hall, 1984.
Surveys of fixed-income instruments and investment characteristics are included in:
  Stigum, Marcia; and Fabozzi, Frank J. *Bond and Money Market Instruments*. Homewood, Ill.: Dow Jones-Irwin, 1987.
  Fabozzi, Frank J.; Fabozzi, T. Dessa; and Pollack, Irving M. *The Handbook of Fixed Income Securities*, 3rd edition. Homewood, Ill.: Business One Irwin, 1991.
Surveys of Canadian fixed-income instruments can be found in:
  Hunter, W. T. *Canadian Financial Markets*. Peterborough, Ont.: Broadview, 1988.
  Canadian Securities Institute. *The Canadian Securities Course* (annual).
Canadian references on retractable and extendible bonds include:
  Ananthanarayanan, A. L.; and Schwartz, Eduardo. "Retractable and Extendible Bonds: The Canadian Experience." *Journal of Finance* 35, no. 1 (March 1980).

Dipchand, Cecil R.; and Hanrahan, Robert J. "Exit and Exchange Option Values on Government of Canada Retractable Bonds." *Financial Management* 8, no. 3 (Autumn 1979).

Problems

1. Provincial bonds paying an 8 percent coupon rate with *semiannual* payments currently sell at par value. What coupon rate would they have to pay to sell at par if they paid their coupons *annually?*

2. A newly issued 10-year maturity, 7 percent coupon bond making *annual* coupon payments is sold to the public at a price of $850. What will be an investor's taxable income from the bond over the coming year? The bond will *not* be sold at the end of the year.

3. What is the price of a $1,000 face value bond with a coupon rate of 14 percent if the bond has an *effective* annual yield to maturity of 21 percent and 15 years until maturity? Assume that the bond pays semiannual coupons and that the next coupon payment arrives six months from now.

4. Which security has a higher *effective* annual interest rate?
   a. A three-month T-bill selling at $97,645 and par value $100,000.
   b. A coupon bond selling at par and paying a 10 percent coupon semiannually.

5. Consider a bond paying a coupon rate of 10 percent per year semiannually when the market interest rate is only 4 percent per half-year. The bond matures in three years.
   a. Find the bond's price today and six months from now, after the next coupon is paid.
   b. What is the total rate of return on the bond?

6. Assume you have a one-year investment horizon and are trying to choose among three bonds. All have the same degree of default risk and mature in 10 years. The first is a zero-coupon bond that pays $1,000 at maturity. The second has an 8 percent coupon rate and pays the $80 coupon once per year. The third has a 10 percent coupon rate and pays the $100 coupon once per year.
   a. If all three bonds are now priced to yield 8 percent to maturity, what are their prices?
   b. If you expect their yields to maturity to be 8 percent at the beginning of next year, what will their prices be then? What is your before-tax holding period return on each bond? If you are in the 30 percent marginal tax bracket, what will your after-tax rate of return be on each?
   c. Recalculate your answer to (b) under the assumption that you expect the yields to maturity on each bond to be 7 percent at the beginning of next year.

7. (Adapted from CFA Examination, Level I, 1983) Assume that two firms, PG and CLX, were concurrently to undertake private debt placements in 1987 with the following contractual details:

	PG	CLX
Issue size	$1 billion	$100 million
Issue price	100	100
Maturity	1988*	1998
Coupon	11%	12%
Collateral	First mortgage	Unsecured
First call date	1993	1990
Call price	111	106
Sinking fund, beginning	nil	1988
Sinking fund, amount	nil	$5 million/year

* Extendible at the option of the holder for an additional 10 years (to 1998) with no change in coupon rate.

Ignoring credit quality, identify four features of these issues that might account for the lower coupon on the PG debt. Explain your answers.

8. (CFA Examination, Level I, 1982) Georgia-Pacific Corporation, a large forest products manufacturer, has outstanding two Aa-rated, $150 million par amount, intermediate-term debt issues:

	10.10% Notes	Floating-Rate Notes
Maturity	1990	1987
Issued	6-12-80	9-27-79
At par to yield	10.10%	12.00%
Callable (beginning on)	6-15-86	10-01-84
Callable at	100	100
Sinking fund	None	None
Current coupon	10.10%	16.90%
Changes	Fixed	Every 6 months
Rate adjusts to	—	0.75% above 6 months Treasury bill rate
Range since issued	—	16.90%–12.00%
Current price	73⅜	97
Current yield	13.77%	17.42%
Yield to maturity	15.87%	—
Price range since issue	100–72	102–93

Based on these data:
   a. State the minimum coupon rate of interest at which Georgia-Pacific could sell a fixed rate issue at par due in 1990. Assume that the same indenture provisions as the 10.10 percent notes and disregard any tax considerations.
   b. Give two reasons why the floating-rate notes are not selling at par (offering price).
   c. State and justify whether the risk of call is high, moderate, or low for the fixed-rate issue.
   d. Assuming a decline in interest rates is anticipated, identify and justify which issue would be most appropriate for an actively managed bond portfolio where total return is the primary objective.
   e. Explain why yield to maturity is not valid for the floating-rate note.

9. (CFA Examination, Level I, 1986) You are given the following information about a convertible bond issue:

Burroughs Corp.
7¼% Due 8/1/2010

Agency rating (Moody's/S&P)	A3/A—
Conversion ratio	12.882
Market price of convertible	$102.00
Market price of common stock	$ 66.00
Dividend per share—common	$ 2.60
Call price (first call—8/1/1990)	$106.00
Estimated floor price	$ 66.50

Using this information, calculate the following data and show calculations:
  a. Market conversion value
  b. Conversion premium per common share
  c. Current yield—convertible
  d. Dividend yield—common
10. (Adapted from CFA Examination, Level III, 1982) As the portfolio manager for a large pension fund, you are offered the following bonds:

	Coupon	Maturity	Price	Call Price	Yield to Maturity
Edgar Corp. (new issue)	14.00%	2002	$101¾	$114	13.75%
Edgar Corp. (new issue)	6.00%	2002	$ 48⅛	$103	13.60%

Assuming that you expect a decline in interest rates over the next three years, identify and justify which of the bonds you would select.

The following multiple-choice problems (11–15) are based on questions that appeared in the 1986 CFA examination.

11. The spread between Treasury and BAA corporate bond yields widens when:
  a. Interest rates are low
  b. There is economic uncertainty
  c. There is a "flight from quality"
  d. All of the above
12. The market risk of an AAA-rated preferred stock relative to an AAA-rated bond is:
  a. Lower
  b. Higher
  c. Equal
  d. Unknown
13. A bond with a call feature:
  a. Is attractive because the immediate receipt of principal plus premium produces a high return
  b. Is more apt to be called when interest rates are high, because the interest savings will be greater
  c. Will usually have a higher yield than a similar non-callable bond
  d. None of the above

14. The yield to maturity on a bond is:

    a. Below the coupon rate when the bond sells at a discount, and above the coupon rate when the bond sells at a premium

    b. The discount rate that will set the present value of the payments equal to the bond price

    c. The current yield plus the average annual capital gain rate

    d. Based on the assumption that any payments received are reinvested at the coupon rate

15. A particular bond has a yield to maturity on an APR basis of 12 percent but makes equal quarterly payments. What is the effective annual yield to maturity?

    a. 11.45 percent

    b. 12.00 percent

    c. 12.55 percent

    d. 37.35 percent

CHAPTER 16

The Term Structure of Interest Rates

In Chapter 15, we assumed for the sake of simplicity that the same constant interest rate is used to discount cash flows of any maturity. In the real world, this is rarely the case. For example, in 1989 short-term bonds carried yields to maturity only slightly higher than 10.3 percent, while the longest-term bonds had yields above 15 percent. At the time when these bond prices were quoted, the longer-term securities had higher yields. This, in fact, is a common empirical pattern.

In this chapter, we explore the pattern of interest rates for different-term assets. We attempt to identify the factors that account for that pattern and determine what information may be derived from an analysis of the so-called **term structure of interest rates**, the structure of interest rates appropriate for discounting cash flows of different maturities.

16.1 *The Term Structure under Certainty*

What do you conclude from the observation that longer-term bonds offer higher yields to maturity? One possibility is that longer-term bonds are riskier and that the higher yields are evidence of a risk premium that compensates for interest rate risk. Another possibility is that investors expect interest rates to rise and that the higher average yields on long-term bonds reflect the anticipation of high interest rates in the latter years of the bond's life. We will start our analysis of these possibilities with the easiest case: a world with no uncertainty where investors already know the path of future interest rates.

Bond Pricing

The interest rate for a given year is called the **short interest rate** for that period. Suppose that all participants in the bond market are convinced that the short rates for the next four years will follow the pattern in Table 16.1. Of course, market participants cannot look up such a sequence of short rates in the daily financial press—all they observe there are prices and yields of bonds of various maturities. Nevertheless, we can think of the short-rate sequence of Table 16.1 as the series of interest rates that investors keep in the back of their minds when they evaluate the prices of different bonds. Given this pattern of rates, what prices might we observe on various maturity bonds? To keep the algebra simple, for now we will treat only a zero-coupon bond.

A bond paying $1,000 in one year would sell today for $1,000/1.08 = $925.93. Similarly, a two-year maturity bond would sell today at price

$$P = \frac{\$1,000}{(1.08)(1.10)}$$
$$= \$841.75 \qquad \text{(16.1)}$$

This is the present value of the future $1,000 cash flow, because $841.75 would need to be set aside now to provide a $1,000 payment in two years. After one year, the $841.75 set aside would grow to $841.75(1.08) = $909.09, and after the second year to $909.09(1.10) = $1,000.

In general, we may write the present value of $1 to be received after n periods as

$$\text{PV of \$1 in } n \text{ periods} = \frac{1}{(1 + r_1)(1 + r_2) \ldots (1 + r_n)}$$

where r_i is the interest rate that will prevail in year i. Continuing in this manner, we find the values of the three- and four-year bonds as shown in the first column of Table 16.2.

From the bond prices we can calculate the yield to maturity on each bond. Recall that the yield is the *single* interest rate that equates the present value of the bond's payments to the bond's price. Although interest rates may vary over time, the yield to maturity is calculated as one "average" rate that is applied to discount all of the bond's payments. For example, the yield on the two-year zero-coupon bond, which we will call y_2, is the interest rate that satisfies

$$841.75 = 1,000/(1 + y_2)^2 \qquad \text{(16.2)}$$

TABLE 16.1   Interest Rates on One-Year Bonds in Coming Years

Year	Interest Rate (%)
0 (Today)	8
1	10
2	11
3	11

TABLE 16.2 Prices and Yields of Zero-Coupon Bonds

Time to Maturity	Price ($)	Yield to Maturity (%)
1	925.93	8.000
2	841.75	8.995
3	758.33	9.660
4	683.18	9.993

which we solve for $y_2 = .08995$. We repeat the process for the two other bonds, with results as reported in the table. For example, we find y_3 by solving

$$758.33 = 1,000/(1 + y_3)^3$$

Now we can make a graph of the yield to maturity on the four bonds as a function of time to maturity. This graph, which is called the **yield curve**, appears in Figure 16.1.

The yield to maturity on zero-coupon bonds is sometimes called the **spot rate** that prevails today for a period corresponding to the maturity of the zero. The yield curve, or equivalently, the last column of Table 16.2, thus presents the spot rates for four maturities. Note that the spot rates or yields do *not* equal the one-year interest rates for each year. Instead, the yield on the two-year bond is close to the average of the short rates for years 1 and 2. This makes sense because, if the yield is a measure of the average return over the life of the bond, it should be determined by the market interest rates available in both years 1 and 2.

FIGURE 16.1
Yield curve.

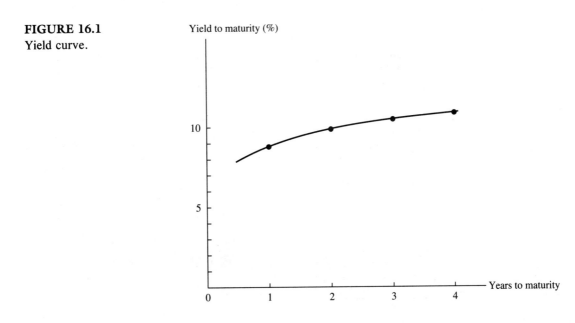

In fact, we can say more than this. Notice that equations 16.1 and 16.2 each relate the two-year bond's price to appropriate interest rates. Combining equations 16.1 and 16.2, we find

$$841.75 = \frac{1,000}{(1.08)(1.10)} = \frac{1,000}{(1 + y_2)^2}$$

so that

$$(1 + y_2)^2 = (1.08)(1.10)$$

and

$$1 + y_2 = [(1.08)(1.10)]^{1/2} = 1.08995$$

Similarly,

$$1 + y_3 = [(1 + r_1)(1 + r_2)(1 + r_3)]^{1/3}$$

and

$$1 + y_4 = [(1 + r_1)(1 + r_2)(1 + r_3)(1 + r_4)]^{1/4} \qquad \textbf{(16.3)}$$

and so on. Thus the yields are in fact related to the interest rate in each period. However, the relationship is not an arithmetic average but a geometric one.

Holding Period Returns

What is the rate of return on each of the four bonds in Table 16.2 over a one-year holding period? You might think at first that higher-yielding bonds would provide higher one-year rates of return, but this is not the case. In our simple world with no uncertainty, all bonds must offer identical rates of return over any holding period. Otherwise, at least one bond would be dominated by the others in the sense that it would offer a lower rate of return than would combinations of other bonds; consequently, the price of that bond would fall. This is no more than an application of the law of one price introduced in Chapter 4. In fact, despite their different yields to maturity, each bond will provide a rate of return over the coming year equal to this year's short interest rate.

To confirm this point, we can compute the rates of return on each bond. The one-year bond is bought today for $925.93 and matures in one year for a return of $1 + r = \$1,000/\$925.93 = 1.08$, or $r = 8$ percent. The two-year bond is bought today for $841.75. Next year the interest rate will be 10 percent, and the bond will have one year left until maturity. It will sell for $1,000/1.10 = \$909.09$. Thus the *holding period return* is defined by $1 + r = \$909.09/\$841.75 = 1.08$ for an 8 percent rate of return. Similarly, the three-year bond will be purchased for $758.33 and will be sold at year-end for $1,000/(1.10)(1.11) = \$819.00$, for a rate of return satisfying $1 + r = \$819.00/\$758.33 = 1.08$, again, an 8 percent return.

| Concept Check | Question 1. Confirm that the return on the four-year bond also will be 8 percent. |

Therefore we conclude that, when interest rate movements are known with certainty, if all bonds are fairly priced, all will provide equal one-year rates of return. The higher yields on the longer-term bonds are no more than a reflection of the fact that future interest rates are higher than are current rates, and that the longer bonds are still alive during the higher-rate period. Owners of the short-term bonds receive lower yields to maturity, but they can reinvest or "roll over" their proceeds for higher yields in later years when rates are higher. In the end, both long-term bonds and short-term rollover strategies provide equal returns over the holding period, at least in a world of interest rate certainty.

Forward Rates

Unfortunately, investors do not have access to short-term interest rate quotations for coming years. What they do have are newspaper quotations of bond prices and yields to maturity. Can they infer future short rates from the available data?

Suppose we are interested in the interest rate that will prevail during year 3, and we have access only to the data reported in Table 16.2. We start by comparing two alternatives:

1. Invest in a three-year zero-coupon bond.
2. Invest in a two-year zero-coupon bond. After two years, reinvest the proceeds in a one-year bond.

Assuming an investment of $100, under strategy 1, with a yield to maturity of 9.660 percent on three-year zero-coupon bonds, our investment would grow to $100(1.0966)^3 = 131.87. Under strategy 2, the $100 investment in the two-year bond would grow after two years to $100(1.08995)^2 = 118.80. Then in the third year it would grow by an additional factor of $1 + r_3$.

In a world of certainty, both of these strategies must yield exactly the same final payoff. If strategy 1 were to dominate strategy 2, no one would hold two-year bonds; their prices would fall and their yields rise. Likewise if strategy 2 dominated strategy 1, no one would hold three-year bonds. Therefore we can conclude that $131.87 = $118.80 (1 + r_3)$, which implies that $(1 + r_3) = 1.11$, or $r_3 = 11$ percent. This is in fact the rate that will prevail in year 3, as Table 16.1 indicates. Thus our method of obtaining the third-period interest rate does provide the correct solution in the certainty case.

More generally, the comparison of the two strategies establishes that the return on a three-year bond equals that on a two-year bond and rollover strategy:

$$100(1 + y_3)^3 = 100(1 + y_2)^2(1 + r_3)$$

so that $1 + r_3 = (1 + y_3)^3/(1 + y_2)^2$. Generalizing, for the certainty case, a simple rule for inferring a future short interest rate from the yield curve of zero-coupon bonds is to use the following formula:

$$(1 + r_n) = (1 + y_n)^n/(1 + y_{n-1})^{n-1} \tag{16.4}$$

where n denotes the period in question and y_n is the yield to maturity of a zero-coupon bond with an n-period maturity.

Of course, when future interest rates are uncertain, as they are in reality, there is no meaning to inferring "the" future short rate. No one knows today what the future interest rate will be. At best, we can speculate as to its expected value and associated uncertainty. Nevertheless, it still is common to use equation 16.4 to investigate the implications of the yield curve for future interest rates. In recognition of the fact that future interest rates are uncertain, we call the interest rate that we infer in this manner the **forward interest rate** rather than the future short rate, because it need not be the interest rate that actually will prevail at the future date.

If the forward rate for period n is f_n, we then define f_n by the equation

$$1 + f_n = (1 + y_n)^n/(1 + y_{n-1})^{n-1}$$

Equivalently, we may rewrite the equation as

$$(1 + y_n)^n = (1 + y_{n-1})^{n-1}(1 + f_n) \qquad \textbf{(16.5)}$$

In this formulation, the forward rate is *defined* as a "break-even" interest rate that equates the return on an n-period zero-coupon bond to that of an $(n - 1)$-period zero-coupon bond rolled over into a one-year bond in year n. The total returns on the two n-year strategies will be equal if the spot interest rate in year n turns out to equal f_n.

We emphasize that the interest rate that actually will prevail in the future need not equal the forward rate, which is calculated from today's data. Indeed, it is not even necessarily the case that the forward rate equals the expected value of the future short interest rate. This is an issue that we address in much detail shortly. For now, note that forward rates equal future short rates in the special case of interest rate certainty.

16.2   *Measuring the Term Structure*

Thus far we have focused on default-free zero-coupon bonds. These bonds are easiest to analyze because their maturity is given by their single payment. In practice, however, the great majority of bonds pay coupons, and most available data pertain to coupon bonds, so we must develop a general approach to calculate spot and forward rates from prices of coupon bonds. Equations 16.4 and 16.5 for the determination of the forward rate from available yields apply only to zero-coupon bonds. They were derived by equating the returns to competing investment strategies that both used zeros. If coupon bonds had been used in those strategies, we would have had to deal with the issue of coupons paid during the investment period, which complicates the analysis.

A further complication arises from the fact that bonds with different coupon rates can have different yields even if their maturities are equal. For example, consider two bonds, each with a two-year time to maturity and annual coupon payments. Bond *A* has a 3 percent coupon; bond *B* a 12 percent coupon. Using the interest rates of Table 16.1, we see that bond *A* will sell for

$$\frac{\$30}{1.08} + \frac{\$1,030}{(1.08)(1.10)} = \$894.78$$

At this price its yield to maturity is 8.98 percent. Bond *B* will sell for

$$\frac{\$120}{1.08} + \frac{\$1,120}{(1.08)(1.10)} = \$1,053.87$$

at which price its yield to maturity is 8.94 percent. Because bond *B* makes a greater share of its payments in the first year when the interest rate is lower, its yield to maturity is slightly lower. Because bonds with the same maturity can have different yields, we conclude that a single yield curve relating yields and times to maturity cannot be appropriate for all bonds.

The solution to this ambiguity is to perform all of our analysis using the yield curve for zero-coupon bonds, sometimes called the *pure yield curve*. Our goal, therefore, is to calculate the pure yield curve even if we have to use data on more common coupon-paying bonds.

The trick we use to infer the yield curve from data on coupon bonds is to treat each coupon payment as a separate "mini" zero-coupon bond. A coupon bond becomes then just a "portfolio" of many zeros. By determining the price of each of these "zeros" we can calculate the yield to that maturity date for a single-payment security and thereby construct the pure yield curve.

As a simple example of this technique, suppose that we observe an 8 percent coupon bond with one year until maturity selling at $986.10, and a 10 percent coupon bond, also with a year until maturity, selling at $1004.78. To infer the short rates for the next two six-month periods, we first attempt to find the present value of each coupon payment taken individually, that is, treated as a mini zero-coupon bond. Call d_1 the present value of $1 to be received in half a year, and d_2 the present value of a dollar to be received in one year. (The *d* stands for discounted values.) Then our two bonds must satisfy the simultaneous equations

$$986.10 = d_1 \times 40 + d_2 \times 1,040$$
$$1004.78 = d_1 \times 50 + d_2 \times 1,050$$

In each equation, the bond's price is set equal to the discounted value of all of its remaining cash flows. Solving these equations we find that $d_1 = .95694$ and $d_2 = .91137$. Thus, if r_1 is the short rate for the first six-month period, then $d_1 = 1/(1 + r_1) = .95694$, so that $r_1 = .045$, and $d_2 = 1/[(1 + r_1)(1 + f_2)] = 1/[(1.045)(1 + f_2)] = .91137$, so that $f_2 = .05$. Thus the two short rates are shown to be 4.5 percent for the first half-year period and 5 percent for the second.

Concept Check	**Question 2.** A T-bill with six-month maturity and $10,000 face value sells for $9,700. A one-year maturity Canada bond paying semiannual coupons of $40 sells for $1,000. Find the current six-month short rate, and the forward rate for the following six-month period.

When we analyze many bonds, such an inference procedure is more difficult, in part because of the greater number of bonds and time periods, but also because not all bonds give rise to identical estimates for the discounted value of a future $1 payment. In other words, there seem to be apparent error terms in the pricing relationship.[1] Nevertheless, treating these errors as random aberrations, we can use a statistical approach to infer the pattern of forward rates embedded in the yield curve.

To see how the statistical procedure would operate, suppose that we observe many coupon bonds, indexed by i, selling at prices P_i. The coupon and/or principal payment (the cash flow) of bond i at time t is denoted CF_{it}, and the present value of a $1 payment at time t, which is the implied price of a zero-coupon bond that we are trying to determine, is denoted d_t. Then for each bond we may write the following:

$$P_1 = d_1CF_{11} + d_2CF_{12} + d_3CF_{13} + \ldots + e_1$$
$$P_2 = d_1CF_{21} + d_2CF_{22} + d_3CF_{23} + \ldots + e_2$$
$$P_3 = d_1CF_{31} + d_2CF_{32} + d_3CF_{33} + \ldots + e_3$$
$$\vdots \qquad \qquad \qquad \qquad \vdots$$
$$P_n = d_1CF_{n1} + d_2CF_{n2} + d_3CF_{n3} + \ldots + e_n \qquad \textbf{(16.6)}$$

Each line of equation system 16.6 equates the price of the bond to the sum of its cash flows, discounted according to time until payment. The last term in each equation, e_i, represents the error term that accounts for the deviations of a bond's price from the prediction of the equation.

Students of statistics will recognize that equation 16.6 is a simple system of equations that can be estimated by regression analysis. The dependent variables are the bond prices, the independent variables are the cash flows, and the coefficients d_t are to be estimated from the observed data.[2] The estimates of d_t are our inferences of the present value of $1 to be paid at time t. The pattern of d_t for various times to payment is called the *discount function*, since it gives the discounted value of $1 as a function of time until payment. From the discount

---

[1] We will consider later some of the reasons for the appearance of these error terms.

[2] In practice, variations of regression analysis called "splining techniques" are usually used to estimate the coefficients. This method was first suggested by McCulloch in the following two articles: J. Huston McCulloch, "Measuring the Term Structure of Interest Rates," *Journal of Business* 44 (January 1971); and "The Tax Adjusted Yield Curve," *Journal of Finance* 30 (June 1975).

FIGURE 16.2

Yield curves for
Canada bonds: **A**
September 14, 1987;
B August 28, 1989;
C March 9, 1992.

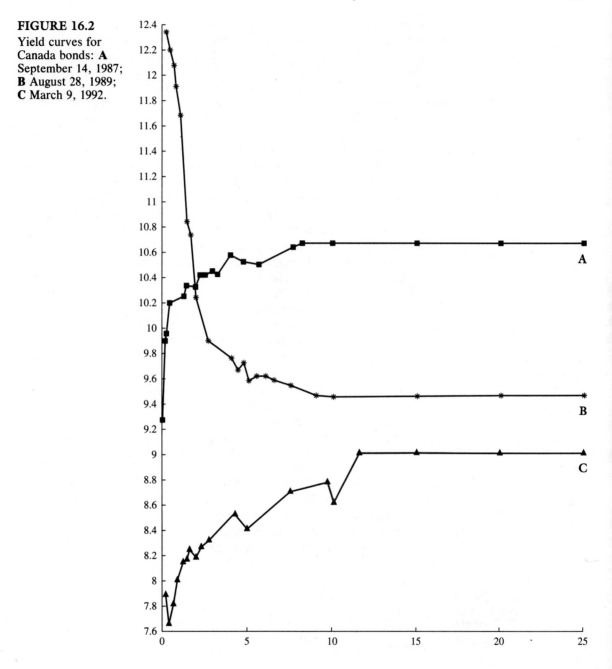

function, which is equivalent to a list of zero-coupon bond prices for various maturity dates, we can calculate the yields on pure zero-coupon bonds. We would use Treasury securities in this procedure to avoid complications arising from default risk. Figure 16.2 is a plot of the yield curve for Canada bonds as it appeared on three different dates in 1987, 1989, and 1992.[3]

Before leaving the issue of the measurement of the yield curve, it is worth pausing briefly to discuss the error terms. Why is it that all bond prices do not conform exactly to a common discount function that sets price equal to present value? The reason is that two major factors are not accounted for in the regression analysis of equation 16.6: taxes and options associated with the bond.

Taxes affect bond prices because investors care about their after-tax return on investment. Therefore, the coupon payments should be treated as net of taxes. Similarly, if a bond is not selling at par value, Revenue Canada requires that a "built-in" interest payment be imputed by amortizing the difference between the price and the par value of the bond. These considerations are difficult to capture in a mathematical formulation because different individuals are in different tax brackets, meaning that the net-of-tax cash flows from a given bond depend on the identity of the owner. Moreover, the specification of equation 16.6 implicitly assumes that the bond is held until maturity: it discounts *all* the bond's coupon and principal payments. This, of course, ignores the investor's option to sell the bond before maturity and so to realize a different stream of income from that described by equation 16.6. Moreover, it ignores the investor's ability to engage in *tax-timing options*. For example, an investor whose tax bracket is expected to change over time may benefit by realizing capital gains during the period when the tax rate is the lowest.

Another feature affecting bond pricing is the call provision. First, if the bond is callable, how do we know whether to include in equation 16.6 coupon payments in years following the first call date? Similarly, the date of the principal repayment becomes uncertain. More important, one must realize that the issuer of the callable bond will exercise the option to call only when it is profitable to do so. Conversely, the call provision is a transfer of value away from the bondholder who has "sold" the option to call to the bond issuer. The call feature, therefore, will affect the bond's price, and introduce further error terms in the simple specification of equation 16.6.

16.3 *Interest Rate Uncertainty and Forward Rates*

Let us turn now to the more difficult analysis of the term structure when future interest rates are uncertain. We have argued so far that, in a certain world,

---

[3] Note, however, that this figure is not a graph of the true term structure on zero-coupon bonds. It is simply a curve fit to yields on coupon-paying Treasury bonds of various maturities.

different investment strategies with common terminal dates must provide equal rates of return. For example, two consecutive one-year investments in zeros would need to offer the same total return as an equal-sized investment in a two-year zero. Therefore, under certainty,

$$(1 + r_1)(1 + r_2) = (1 + y_2)^2$$

What can we say when r_2 is not known today?

To be concrete, we will use an example in which the yield on one-year zero-coupon bonds is 8 percent, while that on two-year zeros is 9 percent. The implied forward rate for year 2 is given by $1 + f_2 = (1.09)^2/(1.08)$, so that $1 + f_2 = 1.10$, or $f_2 = 10$ percent.

Consider first a "short-term" investor who wishes to invest only for one year. The investor can purchase one-year maturity zero-coupon bonds with face value $100 for $100/1.08 = $92.59. The rate of return on these bonds over the year will be precisely 8 percent. Alternatively, the investor may purchase longer-term two-year zero-coupon bonds and resell them at the end of the one-year holding period.

The two-year bonds originally will cost $100/(1 + y_2)^2 = $100/(1.09)^2 = $84.17. What will they sell for next year? At that time, the year 2 interest rate will be known, and the bond will have one year until maturity. Therefore it will sell for $100/(1 + r_2)$. If the year 2 interest rate *turns out* to equal 10 percent (which is the forward rate, f_2) then the bond will sell at $100/1.10 = $90.91 and provide a one-year rate of return of 8 percent ($90.91/$84.17 = 1.08). This makes sense, since the forward rate was defined as the break-even future short rate that would equate the rates of return on different maturity bonds.

It is reasonable to assume that the expected value of r_2, which we will denote $E(r_2)$, should be equal to f_2? It is a reasonable presumption if investors do not care about the uncertainty surrounding the resale value of their two-year bonds. If $E(r_2) = f_2$, then the long-term and short-term bond strategies provide equal expected rates of return,[4] and risk-indifferent investors will be equally happy with either bond.

However, if short-term investors wish to avoid unnecessary risk, they will shy away from the long-term bond. They would not be willing to hold it unless they could anticipate an expected return greater than that offered by the one-year bond. Another way of putting this is to say that investors will require a risk premium to hold the longer-term bond. The more risk-averse investor would be willing to hold the long-term bond only if $E(r_2)$ is less than the break-even value, f_2, because the lower the expectation of r_2, the greater the anticipated return on the long-term bond.

Therefore, if most individuals are short-term investors, bonds must have prices that make f_2 greater than $E(r_2)$. The forward rate will embody a premium compared with the expected future short interest rate. This **liquidity premium**

---

[4] This condition is only approximate. The strategies would provide equal expected payoffs if $1/(1 + f_2)$ equals $E[1/(1 + r_2)]$. When interest rates are uncertain, this condition is not equivalent to $f_2 = E(r_2)$. However, for small variance of r_2 the two conditions are approximately equivalent.

compensates short-term investors for the uncertainty about the price at which they will be able to sell their long-term bonds at the end of the year.[5]

Concept Check

Question 3. Suppose that the required liquidity premium for the short-term investor is 1 percent. What must $E(r_2)$ be if f_2 is 10 percent?

Perhaps surprisingly, we also can imagine scenarios in which long-term bonds can be perceived by investors to be *safer* than short-term bonds. To see how, we now consider a "long-term" investor, who wishes to invest for a full two-year period. The investor can purchase the two-year $100 par value zero-coupon bond for $84.17 and lock in a guaranteed yield to maturity of $y_2 = 9$ percent. Alternatively, the investor can roll over two one-year investments. In this case an investment of $84.17 would grow in two years to $84.17 multiplied by $(1.08)(1 + r_2)$, which is an uncertain amount today because r_2 is not yet known. The break-even year 2 interest rate is, once again, the forward rate, 10 percent, because the forward rate is defined as the rate that equates the terminal value of the two investment strategies.

The expected value of the payoff of the rollover strategy is $84.17(1.08)[1 + E(r_2)]$. If $E(r_2)$ equals the forward rate, f_2, then the expected value of the payoff from the rollover strategy will equal the known payoff from the two-year maturity bond strategy.

Is this a reasonable presumption? Once again, it is only if the investor does not care about the uncertainty surrounding the final value of the rollover strategy. Whenever that risk is important, the long-term investor will not be willing to engage in the rollover strategy unless its expected return exceeds that of the two-year bond. In this case, the investor would require that

$$(1.08)[1 + E(r_2)] > (1.09)^2 = (1.08)(1 + f_2)$$

which implies that $E(r_2)$ exceeds f_2. The investor would require that the expected period 2 interest rate exceed the break-even value of 10 percent, which is the forward rate.

Therefore, if all investors were long-term investors, no one would be willing to hold short-term bonds unless those bonds offered a reward for bearing interest rate risk. In this situation, bond prices would be set at levels such that rolling over short bonds resulted in greater expected return than holding long bonds. This would cause the forward rate to be less than the expected future spot rate.

For example, suppose that in fact $E(r_2) = 11$ percent. The liquidity premium therefore is negative: $f_2 - E(r_2) = 10$ percent $- 11$ percent $= -1$ percent. This

---

[5] Liquidity refers to the ability to sell an asset easily at a predictable price. Because long-term bonds have greater price risk, they are considered less liquid in this context and thus must offer a premium.

is exactly opposite from the conclusion that we drew in the first case of the short-term investor. Clearly, whether forward rates will equal expected future short rates depends on investors' readiness to bear interest rate risk, as well as on their willingness to hold bonds that do not correspond to their investment horizons.

16.4   *Theories of the Term Structure*

The Expectations Hypothesis

The simplest theory of the term structure is the **expectations hypothesis**. A common version of this hypothesis states that the forward rate equals the market consensus expectation of the future short interest rate; in other words, that $f_2 = E(r_2)$, and that liquidity premiums are zero. Because $f_2 = E(r_2)$, we may relate yields on long-term bonds to expectations of future interest rates. For example, with $(1 + y_2)^2 = (1 + r_1)(1 + f_2)$ from equation 16.5, we may also write that $(1 + y_2)^2 = (1 + r_1)[1 + E(r_2)]$ if the expectations hypothesis is correct. The yield to maturity would thus be determined solely by current and expected future one-period interest rates. An upward-sloping yield curve would be clear evidence that investors anticipate increases in interest rates.

Concept Check	Question 4. If the expectations hypothesis is valid, what can we conclude about the premiums necessary to induce investors to hold bonds of different maturities from their investment horizons?

Liquidity Preference

We noted in our discussion of the long- and short-term investors that short-term investors will be unwilling to hold long-term bonds unless the forward rate exceeds the expected short interest rate, $f_2 > E(r_2)$, whereas long-term investors will be unwilling to hold short bonds unless $E(r_2)$ exceeds f_2. In other words, both groups of investors require a premium to induce them to hold bonds with maturities different from their investment horizons. Advocates of the **liquidity preference theory** of the term structure believe that short-term investors dominate the market so that, generally speaking, the forward rate exceeds the expected short rate. The excess of f_2 over $E(r_2)$, the liquidity premium, is predicted to be positive.

Concept Check

> Question 5. The liquidity premium hypothesis also holds that *issuers* of bonds prefer to issue long-term bonds. How would this preference contribute to a positive liquidity premium?

To illustrate the differing implications of these theories for the term structure of interest rates, consider a situation in which the short interest rate is expected to be constant indefinitely. Suppose that $r_1 = 10$ percent and that $E(r_2) = 10$ percent, $E(r_3) = 10$ percent, and so on. Under the expectations hypothesis, the two-year yield to maturity could be derived from the following:

$$(1 + y_2)^2 = (1 + r_1)[1 + E(r_2)]$$
$$= (1.10)(1.10)$$

so that y_2 equals 10 percent. Similarly, yields on all-maturity bonds would equal 10 percent.

In contrast, under the liquidity preference theory f_2 would exceed $E(r_2)$. For the sake of illustration, suppose that f_2 is 11 percent, implying a 1 percent liquidity premium. Then, for two-year bonds:

$$(1 + y_2)^2 = (1 + r_1)(1 + f_2)$$
$$= (1.10)(1.11)$$
$$= 1.221$$

implying that $1 + y_2 = 1.105$. Similarly, if f_3 also equals 11 percent, then the yield on three-year bonds would be determined by

$$(1 + y_3)^3 = (1 + r_1)(1 + f_2)(1 + f_3)$$
$$= (1.10)(1.11)(1.11)$$
$$= 1.35531$$

implying that $1 + y_3 = 1.1067$. The plot of the yield curve in this situation would be given as in Figure 16.3A. Such an upward-sloping yield curve is commonly observed in practice.

If interest rates are expected to change over time, then the liquidity premium may be overlaid on the path of expected spot rates to determine the forward interest rate. Then the yield to maturity for each date will be an average of the single-period forward rates. Several such possibilities for increasing and declining interest rates appear in Figure 16.3B to D.

Market Segmentation and Preferred Habitat Theories

Both the liquidity premium and expectations hypothesis theories of the term structure implicitly view bonds of different maturities as some sort of substitutes for each other. An investor considering holding bonds of one maturity possibly can be lured instead into holding bonds of another maturity by the prospect of earning a risk premium. In this sense, markets for bonds of all maturities are inextricably linked, and yields on short and long bonds are determined jointly in market equilibrium. Forward rates cannot differ from expected short rates by more than a fair liquidity premium, or else investors will reallocate their fixed-income portfolios to exploit what they perceive as abnormal profit opportunities elsewhere.

In contrast, the **market segmentation theory** holds that long- and short-maturity bonds are traded in essentially distinct or segmented markets, each of which finds its own equilibrium independently. The activities of long-term borrowers and lenders determine rates on long-term bonds. Similarly, short-term traders set short rates independently of long-term expectations. The term structure of interest rates, in this view, is determined by the equilibrium rates set in the various maturity markets.

This view of the market is not common today. Both borrowers and lenders seem to compare long and short rates, as well as expectations of future rates,

FIGURE 16.3

Yield curves. **A** Constant expected short rate. Liquidity premium of 1 percent. Result is a rising yield curve. **B** Declining expected short rates. Increasing liquidity premiums. Result is a rising yield curve despite falling expected interest rates.

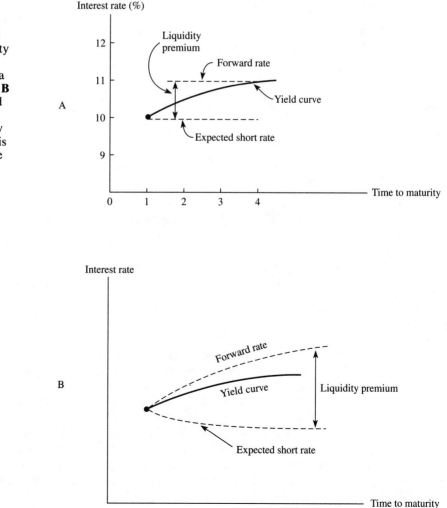

FIGURE 16.3
Continued. C
Declining expected
short rates.
Constant liquidity
premiums. Result is
a hump-shaped yield
curve. **D** Increasing
expected short
rates. Increasing
liquidity premiums.
Result is a sharply
increasing yield
curve.

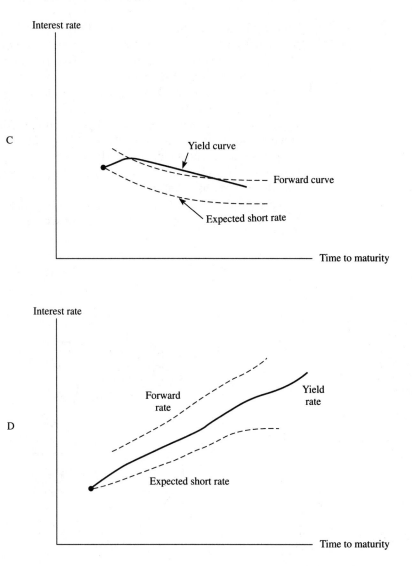

before deciding whether to borrow or lend long or short term. That they make these comparisons, and are willing to move into a particular maturity if it seems sufficiently profitable to do so, means that all-maturity bonds compete with each other for investors' attention, which implies that the rate on a bond of any given maturity is determined with an eye toward rates on competing bonds. This view of the market is called the **preferred habitat theory**: investors prefer specific maturity ranges but can be induced to switch if premiums are sufficient. Markets are not so segmented that an appropriate premium cannot attract an investor who prefers one investment horizon to consider a different one.

16.5   *Interpreting the Term Structure*

We have seen that under certainty, 1 plus the yield to maturity on a zero-coupon bond is simply the geometric average of 1 plus the future short rates that will prevail over the life of the bond. This is the meaning of equation 16.3, which we repeat here:

$$1 + y_n = [(1 + r_1)(1 + r_2) \ldots (1 + r_n)]^{1/n}$$

When future rates are uncertain, we modify equation 16.3 by replacing future short rates with forward rates:

$$1 + y_n = [(1 + r_1)(1 + f_2)(1 + f_3) \ldots (1 + f_n)]^{1/n} \qquad \textbf{(16.7)}$$

Thus, there is a direct relationship between yields on various maturity bonds and forward interest rates. This relationship is the source of the information that can be gleaned from an analysis of the yield curve.

First, we ask what factors can account for a rising yield curve. Mathematically, if the yield curve is rising, f_n must exceed y_{n-1}. In words, the yield curve is upward sloping at any point where the forward rate for the period is greater than the yield to maturity on bonds of a one-period-shorter maturity. This rule follows from the notion of the yield to maturity as an average (albeit a geometric average) of forward rates.

If the yield curve is to rise as one moves to longer maturities, it must be the case that extension to a longer maturity results in the inclusion of a "new" forward rate that is higher than the average of the previously observed rates. This is analogous to the observation that if a new student's test score is to increase the class average, that student's score must exceed the class's average without his or her score. To raise the yield to maturity, an above-average forward rate must be added to the other rates in the averaging computation.

For example, if the yield to maturity on three-year bonds is 9 percent, then the yield on four-year bonds will satisfy the following equations:

$$(1 + y_4)^4 = (1.09)^3(1 + f_4)$$

If $f_4 = .09$, then y_4 also will equal .09. (Confirm this!) If f_4 is greater than 9 percent, y_4 will exceed 9 percent, and the yield curve will slope upward.

Concept Check	Question 6. Look back at Tables 16.1 and 16.2. Show that y_4 would exceed y_3 if and only if the interest rate for period 4 had been greater than 9.66 percent, which was the yield to maturity on the three-year bond, y_3.

Given that an upward-sloping yield curve is always associated with a forward rate higher than the spot, or current, yield, we need to ask next what can account for that higher forward rate. Unfortunately, there always are two possible answers to this question. Recall that the forward rate can be related to the expected future short rate according to this equation:

$$f_n = E(r_n) + \text{Liquidity premium}$$

where the liquidity premium might be necessary to induce investors to hold bonds of maturities that do not correspond to their preferred investment horizons.

By the way, the liquidity premium need not be positive, although that is the position generally taken by advocates of the liquidity premium hypothesis. We showed previously that if most investors have long-term horizons, the liquidity premium could be negative.

In any case, the equation shows that there are two reasons that the forward rate could be high. Either investors expect rising interest rates, meaning that $E(r_n)$ is high, or they require a large premium for holding longer-term bonds. Although often it is tempting to infer from a rising yield curve that investors believe that interest rates will eventually increase, this is not a valid inference. Indeed, Figure 16.3A provides a simple counterexample to this line of reasoning. There, the spot rate is expected to stay at 10 percent forever. Yet there is a constant 1 percent liquidity premium so that all forward rates are 11 percent. The result is that the yield curve continually rises, starting at a level of 10 percent for one-year bonds, but eventually approaching 11 percent for long-term bonds as more and more forward rates at 11 percent are averaged into the yields to maturity.

Therefore, although it is true that expectations of increase in future interest rates can result in a rising yield curve, the converse is not true: a rising yield curve does not in and of itself imply expectations of higher future interest rates. This is the heart of the difficulty in drawing conclusions from the yield curve. The effects of possible liquidity premiums confound any simple attempt to extract expectations from the term structure. But estimating the market's expectations is a crucial task, because only by comparing your own expectations to those reflected in market prices can you determine whether you are relatively bullish or bearish on interest rates.

One very rough approach to deriving expected future spot rates is to assume that liquidity premiums are constant. An estimate of that premium can be subtracted from the forward rate to obtain the market's expected interest rate. For example, again making use of the example plotted in Figure 16.3A the researcher would estimate from historical data that a typical liquidity premium in this economy is 1 percent. After calculating the forward rate from the yield curve to be 11 percent, the expectation of the future spot rate would be determined to be 10 percent.

This approach has little to recommend it for two reasons. First, it is next to impossible to obtain precise estimates of a liquidity premium. The general approach to doing so would be to compare forward rates and eventually realized future short rates, and to calculate the average difference between the two.

FIGURE 16.4

Canada bond yields—five-year averages and standard deviations.

(Drawn from data in Canadian Institute of Actuaries, *Report on Canadian Economic Statistics, 1924–1991.* Reprinted by permission.)

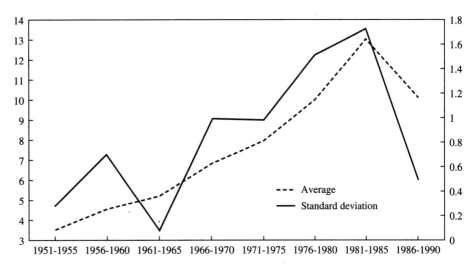

However, the deviations between the two values can be quite large and unpredictable because of unanticipated economic events that affect the realized short rate. The data do not contain enough information to calculate a reliable estimate of the expected premium. Second, there is no reason to believe that the liquidity premium should be constant. Figure 16.4 shows the averages and standard deviations of yields of long-term Canada bonds in all non-overlapping five-year intervals over the period 1951–1990. Interest rate risk fluctuated dramatically during the period, so we might expect risk premiums on various duration bonds to fluctuate. Empirical evidence from the United States suggests that term premiums do in fact fluctuate over time.[6]

Figure 16.5 presents interest rate spreads between bonds of various maturities for the 20-year period 1971–1990. The figure shows that the yield curve is usually upward sloping at all maturities: three-to-five-year Canada bonds have usually higher yields than do one-to-three-year bonds; Canada bonds of over 10-year maturities have consistently higher yields than 5-to-10-year bonds. At even longer maturities the yield curve flattens, and yield spreads between 10- and 20-year bonds fluctuate around zero and are generally quite small.

The usually observed initial upward slope for the yield curve is the empirical basis for the liquidity premium doctrine that long-term bonds offer a positive liquidity premium. In the face of this empirical regularity, perhaps it is valid to interpret a downward-sloping yield curve as evidence that interest rates are expected to decline. If **term premiums**, the spread between yields on long- and short-term bonds, are generally positive, then anticipated declines in rates could account for a downward-sloping curve.

Why might interest rates fall? There are two factors to consider: the real rate and the inflation premium. Recall that the nominal interest rate is composed of

---

[6] See, for example, Richard Startz, "Do Forecast Errors or Term Premia Really Make the Difference between Long and Short Rates?" *Journal of Financial Economics* 10 (1982).

FIGURE 16.5

Selected rate spreads.

(Drawn from data in Canadian Institute of Actuaries, *Report on Economic Statistics, 1924–1991*. Reprinted by permission.)

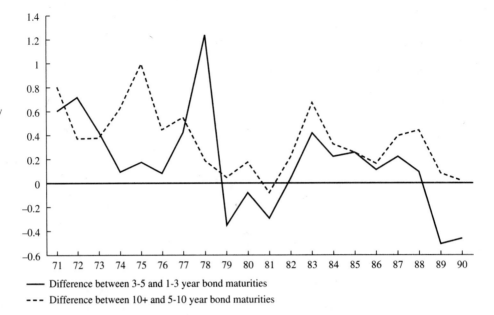

—— Difference between 3-5 and 1-3 year bond maturities

- - - Difference between 10+ and 5-10 year bond maturities

the real rate plus a factor to compensate for the effect of inflation:

$$1 + \text{Nominal rate} = (1 + \text{Real rate})(1 + \text{Inflation rate})$$

or, approximately,

$$\text{Nominal rate} \approx \text{Real rate} + \text{Inflation rate}$$

Therefore, an expected change in interest rates can be due to changes in either expected real rates or expected inflation rates. Usually, it is important to distinguish between these two possibilities because the economic environments associated with them may vary substantially. High real rates may indicate a rapidly expanding economy, high budget deficits, and tight monetary policy. Although high inflation rates also can arise out of a rapidly expanding economy, inflation also may be caused by rapid expansion of the money supply or supply-side shocks to the economy, such as interruptions in oil supplies. These factors have very different implications for investments. Even if we conclude from an analysis of the yield curve that rates will fall, we need to analyze the macroeconomic factors that might cause such a decline.

16.6   *Realized Compound Yield to Maturity*

We have noted that the yield to maturity is calculated by finding the single interest rate that makes the present value of the payments provided by a security equal to its price. This procedure is correct only if interest rates are unchanging over time, so that any intermediate cash flows from the bond can be reinvested at the bond's yield to maturity. The yield then would be the appropriate measure of the time value of money for all cash flows from the bond. When rates are not constant, however, the yield to maturity is not the appropriate discount rate for all cash flows.

Let us first examine this problem under certainty using the data shown in Table 16.1. For illustration, consider a four-year 10 percent coupon bond making annual coupon payments.

First, we compute the conventionally measured yield to maturity on the bond. The bond will sell at a price equal to the present value of all cash flows; using discount factors derived from Table 16.1 we find:

Time	Cash Flow	Discount Factor	Present Value
1	100	1.08	92.59
2	100	(1.08)(1.10)	84.18
3	100	(1.08)(1.10)(1.11)	75.83
4	1,100	(1.08)(1.10)(1.11)(1.11)	751.50
			1,004.10

The bond will sell at $1,004.10. At this price, its yield to maturity works out to 9.871 percent. This interest rate solves the following equation for y:

$$1,004.10 = 100 \times PA(y,4) + 1,000 \times PF(y,4)$$

The equation applies a single yield, y, to all cash flows.[7]

Instead of calculating yield in this manner, however, we could ask the following question: What would be the realized yield if all coupon payments from the bond are reinvested at the going market interest rate at the time of payment? Suppose that all coupons are invested short term and rolled over until the bond matures. Then the first coupon payment would grow by a factor of 1.10 in year 2, 1.11 in year 3, and 1.11 in year 4. Figure 16.6 demonstrates the total growth in invested funds over the life of the bond. By the end of year 4, the investor would have accumulated a total of $1,469.74 from the initial investment of $1,004.10. The **realized compound yield** would be computed as $1,004.10(1 + y)^4 = 1,469.74$, which implies that $y = 9.993$ percent. Thus, the realized yield differs from the conventional yield to maturity, except for zero-coupon bonds, for which there is no issue of reinvesting coupons.

---

[7] Recall from Chapter 15 that PA is the present value factor for annuities and PF is the present value factor for a one-time payment.

FIGURE 16.6
Growth of invested
funds.

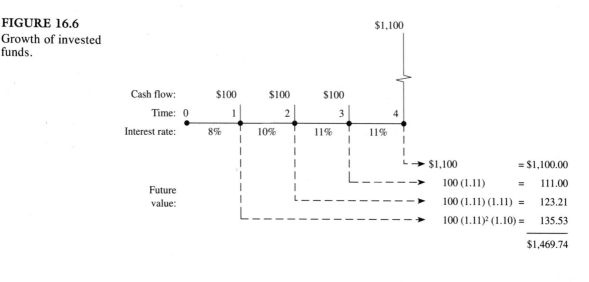

Concept Check

Question 7. Compute the conventional and realized compound yield to
maturity for a three-year 12 percent annual coupon bond using the data
from Table 16.1.

This example highlights the problem associated with using conventional yields
to maturity when the term structure is not flat. The yield to maturity is computed by mistakenly applying an "average" rate over the bond's life to all of its
payments, regardless of their timing. However, the realized yield to maturity
method—as an alternative to the conventional yield—is not a cure-all.

In an economy with future interest rate uncertainty, the rates at which
interim coupons can be reinvested are not yet known. This fact reduces much
of the attraction of the realized yield measure. In practice, we would need
either to assume a set of future interest rates at which coupons could be invested, or to use the set of forward rates implied by the yield curve as the
assumed path of rates. The appeal of either procedure is dubious, however,
because neither the assumed nor the forward rate can confidently be assumed
an accurate estimate of future short rates.

Unfortunately, although conventional yields to maturity on coupon bonds
pose problems of interpretation, realized yields to maturity raise equally difficult problems of implementation. Probably the best approach to the yield curve
is to estimate as well as possible the series of forward rates implied by the pure
yield curve, that is, the yield curve that we can plot from a series of zero-
coupon bonds. If a series of zeros is not observable, the pure yield curve may
be estimated along the lines suggested in Section 16.2. Given the series of
forward rates, the analyst must make an educated guess about their implications for future short rates and the resulting implications for portfolio composition. This is part of the art, as opposed to the science, of portfolio management.

Summary

1. The term structure of interest rates refers to the interest rates for various terms to maturity embodied in the prices of default-free zero-coupon bonds.

2. In a world of certainty all investments must provide equal total returns for any investment period. Short-term holding period returns on all bonds would be equal in a risk-free economy, and all equal to the rate available on short-term bonds. Similarly, total returns from rolling over short-term bonds over longer periods would equal the total return available from long-maturity bonds.

3. A pure yield curve could be plotted easily from a complete set of zero-coupon bonds. In practice, however, most bonds carry coupons, payable at different future times, so that yield curve estimates usually must be inferred from prices of coupon bonds. Measurement of the term structure is complicated by tax issues such as tax timing options and the different tax brackets of different investors.

4. The forward rate of interest is the break-even future interest rate that would equate the total return from a rollover strategy to that of a longer-term zero-coupon bond. It is defined by the equation

$$(1 + y_n)^n(1 + f_{n+1}) = (1 + y_{n+1})^{n+1}$$

where n is a given number of periods from today. This equation can be used to show that yields to maturity and forward rates are related by the equation

$$(1 + y_n)^n = (1 + r_1)(1 + f_2)(1 + f_3) \ . \ . \ . \ (1 + f_n)$$

5. A common version of the expectations hypothesis holds that forward interest rates are unbiased estimates of expected future interest rates. However, there are good reasons to believe that forward rates differ from expected short rates by a risk premium, also known as a liquidity premium. A liquidity premium can cause the yield curve to slope upward even if no increase in short rates is anticipated.

6. The existence of liquidity premiums makes it extremely difficult to infer expected future interest rates from the yield curve. Such an inference would be made easier if we could assume the liquidity premium remained reasonably stable over time. However, both empirical and theoretical insights cast doubt on the constancy of that premium.

7. An alternative measure to the conventional yield to maturity is the realized compound yield to maturity, computed from the total funds that would accrue if all cash flows from a fixed-income security were reinvested at going market rates. Although such a measure can be superior to conventional yield to maturity when the future path of spot rates is known, realized compound yield has no clear advantage over yield to maturity in the real world of interest rate uncertainty.

Key terms

Term structure of interest rates   Expectations hypothesis
Short interest rate   Liquidity preference theory
Yield curve   Market segmentation theory
Spot rate   Preferred habitat theory
Forward interest rate   Term premiums
Liquidity premium   Realized compound yield

Selected readings

Detailed presentations of yield curve analytics and relationships among spot rates, yields to maturity, and realized compound yields are contained in:

Homer, Sidney; and Liebowitz, Martin. *Inside the Yield Book: New Tools for Bond Market Strategy.* Englewood Cliffs, N.J.: Prentice Hall, 1972.

Abken, P. A. "Innovations in Modeling the Term Structure of Interest Rates." *Economic Review*, Federal Reserve Bank of Atlanta (July/August 1990).

A discussion of the various versions of the expectations hypothesis is:

Cox, John; Ingersoll, Jonathan; and Ross, Stephen. "A Reexamination of Traditional Hypotheses about the Term Structure of Interest Rates." *Journal of Finance* 36 (September 1981).

A test of the expectations hypothesis using survey data is:

Friedman, Benjamin. "Interest Rate Expectations versus Forward Rates: Evidence from an Expectations Survey." *Journal of Finance* 34 (September 1979).

Evidence on liquidity premiums may be found in:

Fama, Eugene. "The Information in the Term Structure." *Journal of Financial Economics* 13 (1984).

Fama, Eugene. "Forward Rates as Predictors of Future Spot Rates." *Journal of Financial Economics* 3 (1976).

Nelson, Charles. "Estimation of Term Premiums from Average Yield Differentials in the Term Structure of Interest Rates." *Econometrica*, March 1972.

Startz, Richard. "Do Forecast Errors or Term Premia Really Make the Difference between Long and Short Rates?" *Journal of Financial Economics* 10 (1982).

Problems in the measurement of the yield curve are treated in:

McCulloch, J. Houston. "Measuring the Term Structure of Interest Rates." *Journal of Business* 44 (January 1971).

McCulloch, J. Houston. "The Tax Adjusted Yield Curve." *Journal of Finance* 30 (June 1975).

Some important Canadian studies on the term structure of interest rates are:

Barber, Clarence L.; and McCallum, John S. "The Term Structure of Interest Rates and the Maturity Composition of the Government Debt." *Canadian Journal of Economics*, November 1975.

Dobson, Steven. "The Term Structure of Interest Rates and the Maturity Composition of the Government Debt: The Canadian Case." *Canadian Journal of Economics*, August 1973.

Park, Soo-Bin. "Spot and Forward Rates in the Canadian Treasury Bill Market." *Journal of Financial Economics* 10 (1982).

Pesando, James E. "The Impact of the Conversion Loan on the Term Structure of Interest Rates in Canada: Some Additional Evidence." *Canadian Journal of Economics*, May 1975.

Problems

1. (CFA Examination, Level I, 1986). Answer the following:
   a. Briefly explain why bonds of different maturities have different yields in terms of the (1) expectations, (2) liquidity, and (3) segmentation hypotheses.
   b. Briefly describe the implications of each of the three hypotheses when the yield curve is (1) upward sloping, and (2) downward sloping.
2. (CFA Examination, Level I, 1986). Which one of the following is false?
   a. The liquidity hypothesis indicates that, all other things being equal, longer maturities will have a higher yield.
   b. The basic conclusion of the expectations hypothesis is that the long-term rate is equal to the anticipated short-term rate.
   c. The expectations hypothesis indicates a flat yield curve if anticipated future short-term rates are equal to current short-term rates.
   d. The segmentation hypothesis contends that borrowers and lenders are constrained to particular segments of the yield curve.
3. The following is a list of prices for zero-coupon bonds of various maturities. Calculate the yields to maturity of each bond and the implied sequence of forward rates.

Maturity (Years)	Price of Bond ($)
1	943.40
2	898.47
3	847.62
4	792.16

4. Assuming that the expectations hypothesis is valid, compute the expected price path of the four-year bond in problem 3 as time passes. What is the rate of return of the bond in each year? Show that the expected return equals the forward rate for each year.
5. Consider an 8 percent coupon bond with three years until maturity making *annual* coupon payments. The interest rates in the next three years will be, with certainty, $r_1 = 8$ percent, $r_2 = 10$ percent, $r_3 = 12$ percent. Calculate the price, yield to maturity, and realized compound yield of the bond.
6. Would you expect the yield on a callable bond to lie above or below a yield curve fitted from non-callable bonds?
7. The current yield curve for default-free pure discount (zero-coupon) bonds is as follows:

Maturity (Years)	YTM (%)
1	10
2	11
3	12

   a. What are the implied one-year forward rates?
   b. Assume that the pure expectations hypothesis of the term structure is

correct. If market expectations are accurate, what will the pure yield curve, that is, the yields to maturity on one- and two-year pure discount bonds, be next year?

c. If you purchased a two-year pure discount bond now, what is the expected total rate of return over the next year? If it were a three-year pure discount bond? (Hint: compute the current and expected future prices.) Ignore taxes.

d. What should be the current price of the three-year maturity bond with a 12 percent coupon rate paid annually? If you purchased it at that price, what would your total expected rate of return be over the next year (coupon plus price change)? Ignore taxes.

8. Below is a list of prices for zero-coupon bonds of various maturities.

Maturity (Years)	Price of $1,000 Par Bond (Zero-Coupon)
1	943.40
2	873.52
3	816.37

a. An 8.5 percent $1,000 par bond pays an annual coupon and will mature in three years. What should the yield to maturity on the bond be?

b. If, at the end of the first year, the yield curve flattens out at 8 percent, what will be the one-year holding period return on the coupon bond?

9. Prices of zero-coupon bonds reveal the following pattern of forward rates:

Year	Forward Rate (%)
1	5
2	7
3	8

In addition to the zero-coupon bond, investors also may purchase a three-year bond making annual payments of $60 with par value $1,000.

a. What is the price of the coupon bond?

b. What is the yield to maturity of the coupon bond?

c. Under the expectations hypothesis, what is the expected realized compound yield of the coupon bond?

d. If you forecast that the yield curve in one year will be flat at 7 percent, what is your forecast for the expected rate of return on the coupon bond for the one-year holding period?

10. You observe the following term structure:

	Effective Annual YTM (%)
6-month bill	6.1
1-year zero-coupon bond	6.2
1.5-year zero-coupon bond	6.3
2-year zero-coupon bond	6.4

   a. If you believe that the term structure in six months will be the same as today's, will bills or the 2-year zeros provide a greater expected 6-month return?

   b. What if you believe in the expectations hypothesis?

11. (CFA Examination, Level II, 1983) In June 1982, when the yield to maturity (YTM) on long-term bonds was about 14 percent, many observers were projecting an eventual decline in these rates. It was not unusual to hear of customers urging portfolio managers to "lock in" these high rates by buying some new issues with these high coupons. You recognize that it is not possible to really lock in such returns for coupon bonds because of the potential reinvestment rate problem if rates decline. Assuming the following expectations for a five-year bond bought at par, compute the total realized compound yield (without taxes) for the bond below.

Coupon: 14 percent (assume annual interest payments at end of each year)
Maturity: five years
One-year reinvestment rates during:
   Year 2, 3: 10 percent
   Year 4, 5: 8 percent

C H A P T E R   1 7

Fixed-Income Portfolio Management

In this chapter, we turn to various strategies that fixed-income portfolio managers can pursue, making a distinction between passive and active strategies. A *passive investment strategy* takes market prices of securities as fairly set. Rather than attempting to beat the market by exploiting superior information or insight, passive managers act to maintain an appropriate risk/return balance given market opportunities. One special case of passive management is an immunization strategy that attempts to insulate or immunize the portfolio from interest rate risk.

An *active investment strategy* attempts to achieve returns more than commensurate with the risk borne. In the context of fixed-income management, this style of management can take two forms: active managers either use interest rate forecasts to predict movements in the entire fixed-income market, or they employ some form of intramarket analysis to identify particular sectors of the fixed-income market or particular bonds that are relatively mispriced.

We start our discussion with an analysis of the sensitivity of bond prices to interest rate fluctuations. The concept of duration, which measures interest rate sensitivity, is basic to formulating both active and passive fixed-income strategies. We turn next to passive strategies and show how duration-matching strategies can be used to immunize the holding period return of a fixed-income portfolio from interest rate risk. Finally, we explore a variety of active strategies, including intramarket analysis, interest rate forecasting, and interest rate swaps.

17.1   *Interest Rate Risk*

We have seen already that an inverse relationship exists between bond prices and yields, and we know that interest rates can fluctuate substantially. Indeed, as the accompanying box based on U.S. data (from a 1987 article in *The Wall Street Journal*) illustrates, bond volatility exceeded stock volatility for most of the 1980s. As interest rates rise and fall, bondholders experience capital losses and gains. These gains or losses make fixed-income investments risky, even if the coupon and principal payments are guaranteed, as in the case of Government of Canada obligations.

Why do bond prices respond to interest rate fluctuations? Remember that in a competitive market all securities must offer investors fair expected rates of return. If a bond is issued with an 8 percent coupon when competitive yields are 8 percent, then it will sell at par value. If the market rate rises to 9 percent, however, who would purchase an 8 percent coupon bond at par value? The bond price must fall until its expected return increases to the competitive level of 9 percent. Conversely, if the market rate falls to 7 percent, the 8 percent coupon on the bond is attractive compared to yields on alternative investments. In response, investors eager for that return would bid the bond price above its par value until the total rate of return falls to the market rate.

Interest Rate Sensitivity

It is easy to confirm with numerical examples that prices of long-term bonds generally are more sensitive to interest rate movements than are those of short-term bonds. Consider Table 17.1, which gives bond prices for 8 percent semiannual coupon bonds at different yields to maturity and times to maturity (T). The interest rates are expressed as annual percentage rates (APRs), meaning that the true six-month yield is doubled to obtain the stated annual yield.

The shortest-term bond falls in value by less than 1 percent when the interest rate increases from 8 percent to 9 percent. The 10-year bond falls by 6.5 percent, and the 20-year bond by over 9 percent. Longer-term bonds are more sensitive to interest rate increases because higher interest rates have a greater

TABLE 17.1   Prices of 8 Percent Coupon Bond

Yield to Maturity (APR)	T = 1 Year	T = 10 Years	T = 20 Years
8%	1,000	1,000	1,000
9%	990.64	934.96	907.99
Change in price (%)*	0.94%	6.50%	9.20%

* Equals value of bond at a 9% yield to maturity divided by value of bond at (the original) 8% yield, minus 1.

'Boring' Bonds?
They've Been More Volatile than Stocks

During the 1980s, the corporate bond market has been more volatile than the stock market. The fluctuation in bonds increased sharply after October 1979, when the Federal Reserve adopted a policy allowing wider moves in short-term interest rates. Since then, returns in the bond market generally have varied more than in the stock market, according to the volatility indexes compiled by Shearson Lehman Economics. The highest peak shows a period when bonds were seven times as volatile as stocks. Bonds settled down considerably in late 1986, and stocks have fluctuated more since last October [1986]. But, as fears about the dollar's decline and accelerating inflation permeate the fixed-income markets, the volatility of bonds is picking up again.

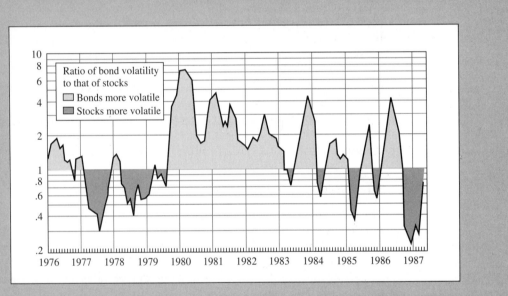

Note: Bond volatility index based on daily yields of triple-A, 20-year corporate bonds and stock volatility index based on daily changes in total return (the change in price and reinvestment of dividends) of the S&P 500 stock index; both are averaged monthly.
Source: Shearson Lehman Brothers Inc.
From *The Wall Street Journal*, May 15, 1987. Reprinted by permission of *THE WALL STREET JOURNAL*, © 1987 by Dow Jones & Company, Inc. All Rights Reserved Worldwide.

impact on more distant future payments. The one-year bond, for example, is so close to maturity that the present value of the remaining payments is hardly affected at all by the increase in the interest rate. As payments become progressively more distant, however, the effect of discounting at a higher rate becomes progressively more telling, and prices are affected much more by the increase in the interest rate.

Let us now recompute Table 17.1 using a zero-coupon bond rather than the 8 percent coupon bond. The results are shown in Table 17.2. Notice that for each

TABLE 17.2 Prices of Zero-Coupon Bond

Yield to Maturity (APR)	T = 1 Year	T = 10 Years	T = 20 Years
8%	924.56	456.39	208.29
9%	915.73	414.64	171.93
Change in price (%)*	0.96%	9.15%	17.46%

* Equals value of bond at a 9% yield to maturity divided by value of bond at (the original) 8% yield, minus 1.

maturity, there is a higher percentage decrease in the price of the zero-coupon bond, attributable to the increase in the interest rate, than for the 8 percent coupon bond. Since we know that long-term bonds are more sensitive to interest rate movements than are short-term bonds, this observation suggests that in some sense a zero-coupon bond more closely represents a longer-term bond than an equal-time-to-maturity coupon bond. In fact, this insight about effective maturity is a useful one that we can make mathematically precise.

First note that the times to maturity of the two bonds in this example are not perfect measures of the long- or short-term nature of the bonds. The 20-year bond makes many coupon payments, most of which come years before the bond's maturity date. Each of these payments may be considered to have its own "maturity date," and the effective maturity of the bond is therefore some sort of average of the maturities of *all* the cash flows paid out by the bond. The zero-coupon bond, by contrast, makes only one payment at maturity. Its time to maturity is therefore a well-defined concept.

Duration

To deal with the ambiguity of the "maturity" of a bond making many payments, we need a measure of the average maturity of the bond's promised cash flows to serve as a useful summary statistic of the effective maturity of the bond. We would like also to use the measure as a guide to the sensitivity of a bond to interest rate changes, because we have noted that price sensitivity tends to increase with time to maturity.

Frederick Macaulay[1] termed the effective maturity concept the **duration** of the bond, and suggested that duration be computed as the weighted average of the times to each coupon or principal payment made by the bond. He recommended that the weight of each payment be measured by the "importance" of that payment to the value of the bond—specifically, that the weight for each payment be the proportion of the total value of the bond accounted for by that payment. This proportion is just the present value of the payment divided by the bond price.

---

[1] Frederick Macaulay, *Some Theoretical Problems Suggested by the Movements of Interest Rates, Bond Yields, and Stock Prices in the United States since 1856* (New York: National Bureau of Economic Research, 1938).

Therefore the weight, denoted w_t, associated with the cash flow at time t (CF$_t$) would be

$$w_t = \frac{CF_t/(1 + y)^t}{\text{Bond price}}$$

where y is the bond's yield to maturity. The numerator on the right hand side of this equation is the present value of all payments forthcoming from the bond. These weights sum to 1, because the sum of the cash flows discounted at the yield to maturity equals the bond price.

Using these values to calculate the weighted average of the times until the receipt of each of the bond's payments, we obtain Macauley's duration formula:

$$D = \sum_{t=1}^{T} tw_t \qquad \qquad \text{(17.1)}$$

As an example of the application of equation 17.1, we derive in Table 17.3 the durations of 8 percent coupon and zero-coupon bonds, each with two years to maturity. We assume that the yield to maturity on each bond is 10 percent, or 5 percent per half-year.

The numbers in column 5 are the products of time to payment and payment weight. Each of these products corresponds to one of the terms in equation 17.1, which indicates that we calculate the duration of the bonds by adding the numbers in column 5. The duration of the zero-coupon bond is exactly equal to its time to maturity, two years. This makes sense, because with only one payment, the average time until payment must be the bond's maturity. In contrast, the two-year coupon bond has a shorter duration of 1.8853 years.

Duration is a key concept in fixed-income portfolio management for at least three reasons. First, it is a simple summary statistic of the effective average

TABLE 17.3 Calculating the Duration of Two Bonds

	(1) Time until Payment (in Years)	(2) Payment	(3) Payment Discounted at 5% Semiannually	(4) Weight*	(5) Column 1 Multiplied by Column 4
Bond A					
8% bond	.5	$ 40	$ 38.095	.0395	.0198
	1.0	40	36.281	.0376	.0376
	1.5	40	34.553	.0358	.0537
	2.0	1,040	855.611	.8871	1.7742
Sum:			$964.540	1.0000	1.8853
Bond B					
Zero-coupon	.5–1.5	$ 0	$ 0	0	0
bond	2.0	1,000	822.70	1.0	2
Sum:			$822.70	1.0	2

* Weight = Present value of each payment (column 3) divided by the bond price, $964.54 for bond A and $822.70 for bond B.

maturity of the portfolio. Second, it turns out to be an essential tool in immunizing portfolios from interest rate risk. (We will explore this application in Section 17.2.) Third, duration is a measure of the interest rate sensitivity of a portfolio, which we will explore here.

We have already noted that long-term bonds are more sensitive to interest rate movements than are short-term bonds. The duration measure enables us to quantify this relationship. Specifically, it can be shown that when interest rates change, the proportional change in a bond's price can be related to the change in its yield to maturity, y, according to the rule:

$$\frac{\Delta P}{P} = -D \times \left[\frac{\Delta(1 + y)}{1 + y}\right] \tag{17.2}$$

The proportional price change equals the proportional change in 1 plus the bond's yield times the bond's duration. Therefore, bond price volatility is proportional to the bond's duration, and duration becomes a natural measure of interest rate exposure.[2]

Practitioners commonly use equation 17.2 in a slightly different form. They define "modified duration" as $D^* = D/(1 + y)$, note that $\Delta(1 + y) = \Delta y$, and rewrite 17.2 as

$$\Delta P/P = -D^* \Delta y \tag{17.2A}$$

The percentage change in bond price is just the product of modified duration and the change in the bond's yield to maturity.

To confirm the relationship between duration and the sensitivity of bond price to interest rate changes, let's compare the interest rate sensitivity of the price of the two-year coupon bond in Table 17.3, which has a duration of 1.8853 years, to the sensitivity of a zero-coupon bond with maturity and duration of 1.8853 years. Both should have equal interest rate exposure if duration is a useful measure of price sensitivity.

The coupon bond sells for $964.5404 at the initial semiannual interest rate of 5 percent. If the bond's semiannual yield increases by one basis point (1/100 of a percent) to 5.01 percent, its price will fall to $964.1942, a percentage decline of .0359 percent. The zero-coupon bond has a maturity of $1.8853 \times 2 = 3.7706$ half-year periods. (Because we use a half-year interest rate of 5 percent, we also need to define duration in terms of a number of half-year periods to maintain consistency of units.) At the initial half-year interest rate of 5 percent, it sells at a price of $831.9623 ($1,000/1.05^{3.7706}$). Its price falls to $831.6636 ($1,000/1.0501^{3.7706}$) when the interest rate increases, for an identical .0359 percent capital loss. We conclude therefore that equal-duration assets are in fact equally sensitive to interest rate movements.

---

[2] Actually, equation 17.2 is only approximately valid for large changes in the bond's yield. The approximation becomes exact as one considers smaller, or localized, changes in yields. Students of calculus will recognize that duration is proportional to the derivative of the bond's price with respect to changes in the bond's yield:

$$D^* = -(1/P)(dP/dy)$$

As such, it gives a measure of the slope of the bond price curve only in the neighborhood of the current price.

Incidentally, this example confirms the validity of equation 17.2. Note that the equation predicts that the proportional price change of the two bonds should have been 3.7706 × .0001/1.05 = .000359, or .0359 percent, exactly as we found from direct computation.

Because duration is so important to fixed-income portfolio management, it is worth exploring some of its properties.[3] We have already established the following:

Rule 1 for duration

The duration of a zero-coupon bond equals its time to maturity.

We have also seen that the two-year coupon bond has a lower duration than the two-year zero, because coupons early in the bond's life lower the bond's weighted average time until payments. This illustrates another general property:

Rule 2 for duration

Holding maturity constant, a bond's duration is higher when the coupon rate is lower.

This rule is attributable to the impact of early coupon payments on the average maturity of a bond's payments. The lower these coupons, the less they reduce the weighted average maturity of the payments.

Rule 3 for duration

Holding the coupon rate constant, a bond's duration generally increases with its time to maturity. Duration always increases with maturity for bonds selling at par or at a premium to par.

This property of duration is fairly intuitive. What is surprising is that duration need not always increase with time to maturity. It turns out that for some deep-discount bonds, duration may fall with increases in maturity. However, for virtually all traded bonds it is safe to assume that duration increases with maturity.

Figure 17.1 is a graph of duration as a function of time to maturity for bonds of various coupon rates. Notice that for the zero-coupon bond, maturity and duration are equal. However, for coupon bonds, duration increases by less than a year with a year's increase in maturity. The slope of the duration graph is less than one.

Although long-maturity bonds generally will be high-duration bonds, duration is a better measure of the long-term nature of the bond because it also accounts for coupon payments. Only when the bond pays no coupons is time to maturity an adequate statistic; then maturity and duration are equal.

Compare the relative positions of the plots of the durations for the 3 percent and 15 percent coupon bonds, each yielding 15 percent. Notice also in Figure

---

[3] For more explanation of these, see G. O. Bierwag, *Duration Analysis* (Cambridge, Mass.: Ballinger Publishing Company, 1987).

FIGURE 17.1
Bond duration vs. bond maturity.

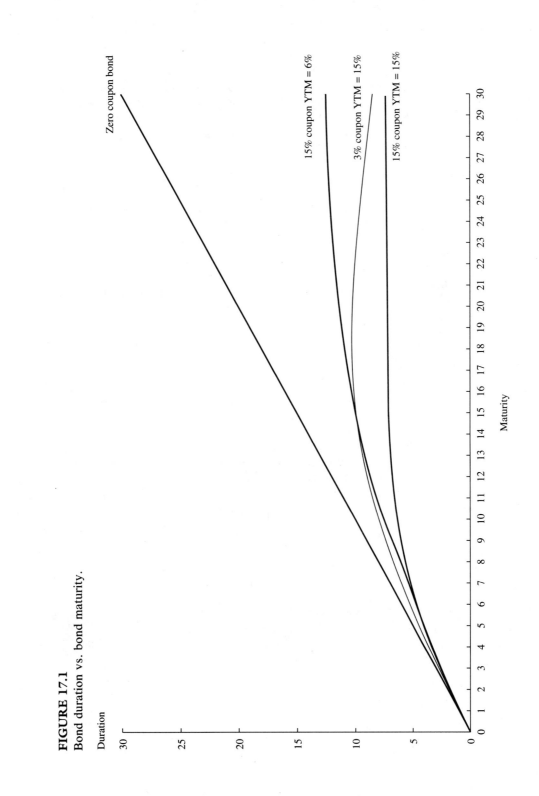

17.1 that the two 15 percent coupon bonds have different durations when they sell at different yields to maturity. The lower-yield bond has greater duration. This makes sense, because at lower yields the more distant payments made by the bond have relatively greater present values and account for a greater share of the bond's total value. Thus, in the weighted-average calculation of duration, the distant payments receive greater weights, which results in a higher duration measure. This establishes rule 4:

Rule 4 for duration

Holding other factors constant, the duration of a coupon bond is higher when the bond's yield to maturity is lower.

Rule 4 applies to coupon bonds. For zeros, of course, duration equals time to maturity, regardless of the yield to maturity.

Finally, we develop some algebraic rules for the duration of securities of special interest. These rules are derived from and consistent with the formula for duration given in equation 17.1, but may be easier to use for long-term bonds.

Rule 5 for duration

The duration of a level perpetuity is $(1 + y)/y$.

For example, at a 10 percent yield, the duration of a perpetuity that pays $100 once a year forever will equal $1.10/.10 = 11$ years, but at an 8 percent yield it will equal $1.08/.08 = 13.5$ years.

Rule 5 makes it obvious that maturity and duration can differ substantially. The maturity of the perpetuity is infinite, whereas the duration of the instrument at a 10 percent yield is only 11 years. The present-value-weighted cash flows early on in the life of the perpetuity dominate the computation of duration. Figure 17.1 also demonstrates that as their maturities become longer, the durations of the two 15 percent-yielding coupon bonds both converge to the duration of the perpetuity with the same yield, 7.67 years.

Concept Check

Question 1. Show that the duration of the perpetuity increases as the interest rate decreases in accordance with Rule 4.

Rule 6 for duration

The duration of a level annuity is equal to the following:

$$\frac{1 + y}{y} - \frac{T}{(1 + y)^T - 1}$$

where T is the number of payments and y is the annuity's yield per payment period. For example, a 10-year annual annuity with a yield of 8 percent will have duration

$$\frac{1.08}{.08} - \frac{10}{1.08^{10} - 1} = 4.87 \text{ years}$$

Rule 7 for duration

The duration of a coupon bond equals the following:

$$\frac{1 + y}{y} - \frac{(1 + y) + T(c - y)}{c[(1 + y)^T - 1] + y}$$

where c is the coupon rate per payment period, T is the number of payment periods, and y is the bond's yield per payment period. For example, a 10 percent coupon bond with 20 years until maturity, paying coupons semiannually, would have a 5 percent semiannual coupon and 40 payment periods. If the yield to maturity were 4 percent per half-year period, the bond's duration would be

$$\frac{1.04}{.04} - \frac{1.04 + 40(.05 - .04)}{.05[1.04^{40} - 1] + .04} = 19.74 \text{ half-years}$$

$$= 9.87 \text{ years}$$

This calculation reminds us again of the importance of maintaining consistency between the time units of the payment period and interest rate. When the bond pays a coupon semiannually, we must use the effective semiannual interest rate and semiannual coupon rate in all calculations. This unit of time (one half-year) is then carried into the duration measure, when we calculate duration to be 19.74 half-year periods.

Rule 8 for duration

For coupon bonds selling at par value, rule 7 simplifies to the following formula for duration:

$$\frac{1 + y}{y}\left[1 - \frac{1}{(1 + y)^T}\right]$$

Durations can vary widely among traded bonds. Table 17.4 presents durations computed from rule 7 for several bonds all assumed to pay semiannual coupons and to yield 4 percent per half-year. Notice that duration decreases as coupon rates increase, and generally increases with time to maturity. According to Table 17.4 and equation 17.2, if the interest rate were to increase from 8 percent to 8.1 percent, the **6 percent coupon 20-year bond would fall in value by about 1.01 percent (10.922 × .1 percent/1.08), while the 10 percent coupon one-year bond would fall by only 0.090 percent**. Notice also from Table 17.4 that duration is **independent of coupon rate only for the perpetual bond.**

TABLE 17.4 Bond Durations (in Years) (Initial Bond Yield = 8 percent APR)

Years to Maturity	Coupon Rates (per Year)			
	6%	8%	10%	12%
1	.985	.980	.976	.972
5	4.361	4.218	4.095	3.990
10	7.454	7.067	6.772	6.541
20	10.922	10.292	9.870	9.568
Infinite (perpetuity)	13.000	13.000	13.000	13.000

17.2 *Passive Bond Management*

Passive managers take bond prices as fairly set and seek to control only the risk of their fixed-income portfolio. Two broad classes of passive management are pursued in the fixed-income market. The first is an indexing strategy that attempts to replicate the performance of a given bond index. The second broad class of passive strategies is known as **immunization** techniques and is used widely by financial institutions such as insurance companies and pension funds. These are designed to shield the overall financial status of the institution from exposure to interest rate fluctuations. While both indexing and immunization strategies are alike in that they accept market prices as correctly set, they are very different in terms of risk exposure. A **bond index portfolio** will have the same risk-reward profile as the bond market index to which it is tied. In contrast, immunization strategies seek to establish a virtually zero-risk profile, in which interest rate movements have no impact on the value of the firm.

Bond Index Funds

In principle, bond market indexing is similar to stock market indexing. The idea is to create a portfolio that mirrors the composition of an index that measures the broad market. Thus, stock index funds will purchase shares of each firm in the TSE 300 or S&P 500 in proportion to the market value of outstanding equity, to create index portfolios. A similar strategy is used for bond index funds, but as we shall see shortly, several modifications are required because of difficulties unique to the bond market and its indices.

The major indices of the Canadian bond market are compiled by ScotiaMcLeod, their Universe Index being the relevant one. In the United States, there are three: the Salomon Brothers Broad Investment Grade (BIG) Index, the Lehman Brothers Aggregate Index, and the Merrill Lynch Domestic Master Index. These bond indices are market-value-weighted indices of total returns on both corporate and government bonds with maturities greater than one year; as time passes and the maturity of a bond falls below one year, the bond is dropped from the indices.

The first problem that arises in the formation of a bond index portfolio is that the index includes a vast number of securities (the U.S. indices include more than 4,000); hence, it is quite difficult to purchase each security in the index in proportion to its market value. Moreover, many bonds are very thinly traded, especially in Canada.

Bond index funds also present more difficult rebalancing problems than do stock index funds. Bonds are continually dropped from the index as their maturities fall below one year. Moreover, as new bonds are issued, they are added to the index. Therefore, in contrast to equity indices, the securities used to compute bond indices constantly change. As they do, the manager must update or rebalance the portfolio to ensure a close match between the composition of the portfolio and the bonds included in the index. The fact that bonds generate considerable interest income that must be reinvested further complicates the job of the index fund manager.

In practice, it is deemed infeasible to replicate precisely the broad bond indices. Instead, a stratified sampling or *cellular* approach is often pursued. The market is stratified by various characteristics such as maturity, credit risk of issuer, and coupon. Then, based on the percentage representation of the bond universe in the cells thus created, a portfolio is formed with representative bonds from each cell; the performance of the portfolio is supposed to match that of the index. Evidence from measurement of the *tracking error* between the performance of the portfolio and the index is supportive of the validity of this practice[4].

The ScotiaMcLeod bond indices are actually based only on those bonds that are considered to be available for public investment. Those bonds that are held by the Bank of Canada in particular and other institutions that buy on issue to hold to maturity are not included in calculating the value weighting. This realization points to the well-known illiquidity of the Canadian bond market, which has a bearing on the subject of index funds. In the late 1980s, ScotiaMcLeod created a Canadian bond index fund but was disappointed with the results. The same problems that make an index portfolio difficult to maintain in the U.S. market were exaggerated in Canada, such that the fund became infeasible. There also proved to be very little interest for the fund from Canadian institutional and professional investors.

As we noted, the purpose of a bond index portfolio is to limit the interest rate exposure to that of the whole market, as captured by the index. This end may be insufficient for many financial institutions, which wish to protect either the current or future values of their portfolios. For instance, banks need to maintain current net worth for regulatory reasons; pension funds need to guarantee

---

[4] Salomon Brothers found that a $100 million index fund could track the BIG index with an average absolute tracking error of only 4 basis points per month, as reported in Sharmin Mossavar-Rahmani, *Bond Index Funds* (Chicago: Probus Publishing Co., 1991).

a certain future value when liabilities will mature. Let us therefore turn to a discussion of how interest rate risk can be controlled using immunization strategies.

Net Worth Immunization

Many banks have a natural mismatch between asset and liability maturity structures. Bank liabilities are primarily the deposits owed to customers, most of which are very short term in nature and consequently of low duration. Bank assets, by contrast, are composed largely of outstanding commercial and consumer loans or mortgages. These assets are of longer duration than are deposits, and their values are correspondingly more sensitive to interest rate fluctuations. In periods when interest rates increase unexpectedly, banks can suffer serious decreases in net worth—their assets fall in value by more than their liabilities.

Flannery and James[5] have shown that prices of bank stock do in fact tend to fall when interest rates rise. In another study, Kopcke and Woglom[6] found that, when measured by market values, total liabilities exceeded total assets for some savings banks in Connecticut in several years during the 1970s, a period following significant increases in interest rates. Had these banks been required to carry their assets at market value on their balance sheets, they would have been declared insolvent. Clearly, banks are subject to interest rate risk.

The watchword in bank portfolio strategy in the 1970s and early 1980s was asset and liability management. Techniques called *gap management* were developed to limit the "gap" between asset and liability durations. Adjustable rate mortgages were one way to reduce the duration of bank asset portfolios. Unlike conventional mortgages, adjustable rate mortgages do not fall in value when market interest rates rise, because the rates they pay are tied to an index of the current market rate. Even if it is imperfect or entails lags, indexing greatly diminishes sensitivity to interest rate fluctuations. On the other side of the balance sheet, the introduction of bank certificates of deposit with fixed terms to maturity served to lengthen the duration of bank liabilities, also reducing the duration gap.

One way to view gap management is to consider that the bank is attempting to equate the durations of assets and liabilities to effectively immunize its overall position from interest rate movements. Because bank assets and liabilities are roughly equal in size, if their durations also are equal, any change in interest rates will affect the values of assets and liabilities equally. Interest rates would have no effect on net worth, in other words. Therefore, net worth immunization requires a portfolio duration of zero. This will result if assets and liabilities are equal in both magnitude and duration.

---

[5] Mark J. Flannery and Christopher M. James, "The Effect of Interest Rate Changes on the Common Stock Returns of Financial Institutions," *Journal of Finance* 39 (September 1984)

[6] Richard W. Kopcke and Geoffrey R. H. Woglom, "Regulation Q and Savings Bank Solvency—The Connecticut Experience," *The Regulation of Financial Institutions*, Federal Reserve Bank of Boston Conference Series, No. 21, 1979.

Concept Check	Question 2. If assets and liabilities are not equal, then immunization requires that $D_A A = D_L L$, where D denotes duration and A and L denote assets and liabilities, respectively. Explain why the simpler condition $D_A = D_L$ is no longer valid in this case.

Target Date Immunization

Pension funds are different from banks. They think more in terms of future commitments than current net worth. Pension funds have an obligation to provide workers with a flow of income upon their retirement, and they must have sufficient funds available to meet these commitments. As interest rates fluctuate, both the value of the assets held by the fund and the rate at which those assets generate income fluctuate. The pension fund manager therefore may want to protect or "immunize" the future accumulated value of the fund at some target date against interest rate movements.

Pension funds are not alone in this concern. Any institution with a future fixed obligation might consider immunization a reasonable risk management policy. Insurance companies, for example, also pursue immunization strategies. Indeed, the notion of immunization was introduced by F. M. Redington,[7] an actuary for a life insurance company.

The idea behind immunization is that with duration-matched assets and liabilities, the ability of the asset portfolio to meet the firm's obligations should be unaffected by interest rate movements. As an example of immunization, suppose that a pension fund is obligated to pay out $14,693.28 in five years. If the current market interest rate is 8 percent, the present value of that obligation is $10,000. The plan chooses to fund the obligation with $10,000 of 8 percent *annual* coupon bonds, selling at par value, with six years to maturity. As the duration of the bond is (from rule 8) five years, the single-payment obligation should be immunized by the bond.

Let us now investigate whether the bond can generate enough income to pay off the obligation five years from now, regardless of interest rate movements. Table 17.5 shows that if interest rates remain at 8 percent, then the accumulated funds from the bond will grow to exactly the $14,693.28 obligation. Over the five-year period, the year-end coupon income of $800 is reinvested at the prevailing 8 percent market interest rate. At the end of the period, the bonds can be sold for $10,000; they still will sell at par value because the coupon rate still equals the market interest rate. Total income after five years from reinvested coupons and the sale of the bond is precisely $14,693.28.

However, Table 17.5 shows that if interest rates fall to 7 percent, the total funds will accumulate to $14,694.05, providing a small surplus of 77 cents. If

---

[7] F. M. Redington, "Review of the Principle of Life-Office Valuations," *Journal of the Institute of Actuaries* 78 (1952).

TABLE 17.5   Terminal Value of a Bond Portfolio after Five Years (All Proceeds Reinvested)

Payment Number	Time Remaining until Obligation	Accumulated Value of Invested Payment		
Rates Remain at 8%				
1	4	$800 \times (1.08)^4$	=	$ 1,088.39
2	3	$800 \times (1.08)^3$	=	1,007.77
3	2	$800 \times (1.08)^2$	=	933.12
4	1	$800 \times (1.08)^1$	=	864.00
5	0	$800 \times (1.08)^0$	=	800.00
Sale of bond	0	10,800/1.08	=	10,000.00
				$14,693.28
Rates Fall to 7%				
1	4	$800 \times (1.07)^4$	=	$ 1,048.64
2	3	$800 \times (1.07)^3$	=	980.03
3	2	$800 \times (1.07)^2$	=	915.92
4	1	$800 \times (1.07)^1$	=	856.00
5	0	$800 \times (1.07)^0$	=	800.00
Sale of bond	0	10,800/1.07	=	10,093.46
				$14,694.05
Rates Increase to 9%				
1	4	$800 \times (1.09)^4$	=	$ 1,129.27
2	3	$800 \times (1.09)^3$	=	1,036.02
3	2	$800 \times (1.09)^2$	=	950.48
4	1	$800 \times (1.09)^1$	=	872.00
5	0	$800 \times (1.09)^0$	=	800.00
Sale of bond	0	10,800/1.09	=	9,908.26
				$14,696.02

Note: The sale price of the bond portfolio equals the portfolio's final payment ($10,800) divided by $1 + r$, because the time to maturity of the bonds will be one year at the time of sale.

rates increase to 9 percent as at the bottom of Table 17.5, the fund accumulates to $14,696.02, providing a small surplus of $2.74.

Several points are worth highlighting. First, notice that duration matching balances the trade-off between the accumulated value of the coupon payments (reinvestment rate risk) and the sale value of the bond (price risk). For example, when interest rates fall, the coupons grow less than in the base case, but the gain on the sale of the bond slightly more than offsets the coupon shortfall. When interest rates rise, the resale value of the bond falls, but the coupons more than make up for this loss with their higher accumulated interest. The net surplus in the fund is trivial, especially compared to the change in the value of the accumulated coupons or resale value taken alone. The results of duration matching are illustrated in Figure 17.2.

As we noted, immunization also can be analyzed in terms of present values as opposed to future values. Figure 17.3 presents a graph of the present values

FIGURE 17.2
Growth of invested funds. The solid curve represents the growth of portfolio value at the original interest rate. If interest rates increase at time t^*, the portfolio value falls but increases thereafter at the faster rate represented by the broken curve. At time D (duration), the curves cross.

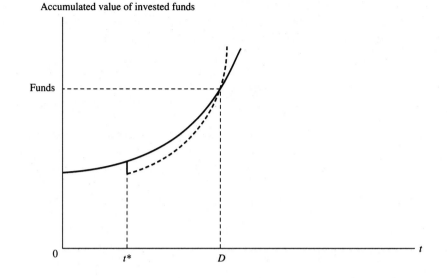

Accumulated value of invested funds

Funds

0

t^*

D

t

FIGURE 17.3
Immunization.

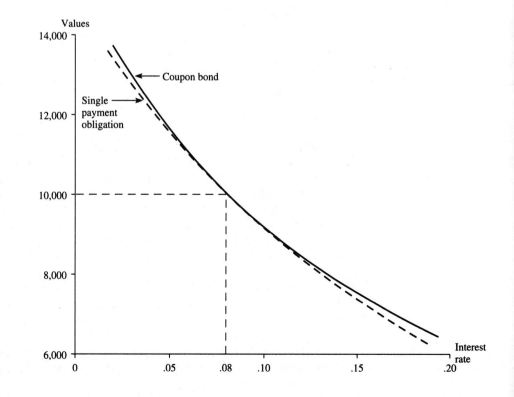

Values

14,000

Coupon bond

Single payment obligation

12,000

10,000

8,000

6,000

0 .05 .08 .10 .15 .20

Interest rate

of the bond and the single-payment obligation as a function of the interest rate. Notice that at the current rate of 8 percent the values are equal and the obligation is fully funded by the bond. Moreover, the two present value curves are tangent at $y = 8$ percent. As market yields change, the change in value of both the asset and the obligation is equal, so the obligation remains fully funded. For greater changes in the interest rate, however, the present value curves diverge. This is related to the fact that the fund actually shows some surplus in year 5 at market interest rates other than 8 percent.

Why is there any surplus in the fund? After all, we claimed that a duration-matched asset and liability mix would result in indifference to interest rate shifts. Actually, such a claim is valid only for *small* changes in the interest rate, because as bond yields change, so too does duration. (Recall rule 4 for duration and footnote 2.) In our example, although the duration of the bond is indeed equal to 5.0 years at a yield to maturity of 8 percent, it rises to 5.02 years when its yield falls to 7 percent and drops to 4.97 years at $y = 9$ percent; that is, the bond and the obligation were not duration matched *across* the interest rate shift, so that the position was not fully immunized.

This example highlights the importance of **rebalancing** immunized portfolios. As interest rates and asset durations change, a manager must rebalance the portfolio of fixed-income assets continually to realign its duration with the duration of the obligation. Moreover, even if interest rates do not change, asset durations *will* change solely because of the passage of time. Recall from Figure 17.2 that duration generally decreases less rapidly than does maturity. Thus, even if an obligation is immunized at the outset, as time passes the durations of the asset and liability will fall at different rates. Without portfolio rebalancing, durations will become unmatched and the goals of immunization will not be realized. Obviously, immunization is a passive strategy only in the sense that it does not involve attempts to identify undervalued securities. Immunization managers still actively update and monitor their positions.

As an example of the need for rebalancing, consider a portfolio manager facing an obligation of $19,487 in seven years, which, at a current market interest rate of 10 percent, has a present value of $10,000. Right now, suppose that the manager wishes to immunize the obligation by holding only three-year zero-coupon bonds and perpetuities paying annual coupons. (Our focus on zeros and perpetuities will serve to keep the algebra simple.) At current interest rates, the perpetuities have a duration of $1.10/.10 = 11$ years; the duration of the zero is simply three years.

For assets with equal yields, the duration of a portfolio is the weighted average of the durations of the assets comprising the portfolio. To achieve the desired portfolio duration of seven years, the manager would have to choose appropriate values for the weights of the zero and the perpetuity in the overall portfolio. Call w the zero's weight and $(1 - w)$ the perpetuity's weight. Then w must be chosen to satisfy the equation

$$w \times 3 \text{ years} + (1 - w) \times 11 \text{ years} = 7 \text{ years}$$

which implies that $w = 1/2$. The manager invests $5,000 in the zero-coupon bond and $5,000 in the perpetuity, providing annual coupon payments of $500 per year indefinitely. The portfolio duration is then seven years, and the position is immunized.

Next year, even if interest rates do not change, rebalancing will be necessary. The present value of the obligation has grown to $11,000, because it is one year closer to maturity. The manager's funds also have grown to $11,000: the zero-coupon bonds have increased in value from $5,000 to $5,500 with the passage of time, while the perpetuity has paid its annual $500 coupon and is still worth $5,000. However, the portfolio weights must be changed. The zero-coupon bond now will have a duration of two years, while the perpetuity remains at 11 years. The obligation is now due in six years. The weights must now satisfy the equation

$$w \times 2 + (1 - w) \times 11 = 6$$

which implies that $w = 5/9$. Now, the manager must invest a total of $11,000 \times 5/9 = $6,111.11 in the zero. This requires that the entire $500 coupon payment be invested in the zero and that an additional $111.11 of the perpetuity be sold and invested in the zero in order to maintain an immunized position.

Concept Check

> **Question 3.** What would be the immunizing weights in the second year if the interest rate had fallen to 8 percent?

Of course, rebalancing of the portfolio entails transaction costs as assets are bought or sold, so one cannot rebalance continuously. In practice, an appropriate compromise must be established between the desire for perfect immunization, which requires continual rebalancing, and the need to control trading costs, which dictates less-frequent rebalancing.

Cash Flow Matching and Dedication

The problems associated with immunization seem to have an easy solution. Why not simply buy a zero-coupon bond that provides a payment in an amount exactly sufficient to cover the projected cash outlay? If we follow the principle of **cash flow matching**, we automatically immunize the portfolio from interest rate movements because the cash flow from the bond and the obligation exactly offset each other.

Cash flow matching can be accomplished on a multiperiod basis. In this case, the manager selects either zero-coupon or coupon bonds that provide total cash flows in each period that match a series of obligations. Such a matching principle is referred to as a **dedication strategy**.

Cash flow matching is not more widely pursued probably because of the constraints that it imposes on bond selection. Immunization-dedication strategies are appealing to firms that do not wish to bet on general movements in interest rates, but these firms may want to immunize using bonds that they perceive are undervalued. Cash flow matching, however, places so many more constraints on the bond selection process that it can be impossible to pursue a dedication strategy using only "underpriced" bonds. Firms looking for under-priced bonds give up exact and easy dedication for the possibility of achieving superior returns from the bond portfolio.

Sometimes, cash flow matching is not possible. To match cash flow for a pension fund that is obligated to pay out a perpetual flow of income to current and future retirees, the pension fund would need to purchase fixed-income securities with maturities ranging up to hundreds of years. Such securities do not exist, making exact dedication infeasible. Immunization is easy, however. If the interest rate is 8 percent, for example, the duration for the pension fund obligation is $1.08/.08 = 13.5$ years (see rule 5 above). Therefore, the fund can immunize its obligation by purchasing zero-coupon bonds with maturity of 13.5 years and a market value equal to that of the pension liabilities.

Concept Check	Question 4. How would an increase in trading costs affect the attractive-ness of dedication immunization?

Other Problems with Conventional Immunization

If you look back at the definition of duration in equation 17.1, you note that it uses the bond's yield to maturity to calculate the weight applied to each coupon payment. Given this definition and limitations on the proper use of yield to maturity, it is perhaps not surprising that this notion of duration is strictly valid only for a flat yield curve for which all payments are discounted at a common interest rate.

If the yield curve is not flat, then the definition of duration must be modified and $CF_t/(1 + y)^t$ replaced with the present value of CF_t, where the present value of each cash flow is calculated by discounting with the appropriate inter-est rate from the yield curve corresponding to the date of the *particular* cash flow, instead of by discounting with the *bond's* yield to maturity. Moreover, even with this modification, duration matching will immunize portfolios only for parallel shifts in the yield curve. Clearly, this sort of restriction is unrealis-tic. As a result, much work has been devoted to generalizing the notion of duration. Multifactor duration models have been developed to allow for tilts and other distortions in the shape of the yield curve, in addition to shifts in its level. (We refer to some of this work in the suggested readings at the end of this chapter.) However, it does not appear that the added complexity of such models pays off in terms of substantially greater effectiveness.[8]

---

[8] G. O. Bierwag, G. C. Kaufman, and A. Toevs (editors), *Innovations in Bond Portfolio Management: Duration Analysis and Immunization* (Greenwich, Conn.: JAI Press, 1983).

Finally, immunization can be an inappropriate goal in an inflationary environment. Immunization is essentially a nominal notion and makes sense only for nominal liabilities. It makes no sense to immunize a projected obligation that will grow with the price level using nominal assets, such as bonds. For example, if your child will attend college in 15 years and if the annual cost of tuition is expected to be $15,000 at that time, immunizing your portfolio at a locked-in terminal value of $15,000 is not necessarily a risk-reducing strategy. The tuition obligation will vary with the realized inflation rate, whereas the asset portfolio's final value will not. In the end, the tuition obligation will not necessarily be matched by the value of the portfolio.

On this note, it is worth pointing out that immunization is a goal that may well be inappropriate for many investors who would find a zero-risk portfolio strategy unduly conservative. Full immunization is a fairly extreme position for a portfolio manager to pursue.

17.3 *Active Bond Management*

Sources of Potential Profit

Broadly speaking, there are two sources of potential value in active bond management. The first is interest rate forecasting, which tries to anticipate movements across the entire spectrum of the fixed-income market. If interest rate declines are anticipated, managers will increase portfolio duration (and vice versa). The second source of potential profit is identification of relative mispricing within the fixed-income market. An analyst, for example, might believe that the default premium on one particular bond is unnecessarily large and, therefore, that the bond is underpriced.

These techniques will generate abnormal returns only if the analyst's information or insight is superior to that of the market. One cannot profit from knowledge that rates are about to fall if everyone else in the market is aware of this. In that case, the anticipated rates are already built into bond prices in the sense that long-duration bonds are already selling at higher prices that reflect the anticipated fall in future short rates. If the analyst does not have information before the market does, it will be too late to act on that information—prices will have responded already to the news. This follows from the discussion of market efficiency.

For now, we simply repeat that valuable information is differential information. In this context it is worth noting that interest rate forecasters have a notoriously poor track record. If you consider this record, you will approach attempts to time the bond market with caution.

Homer and Liebowitz[9] have coined a popular taxonomy of active bond portfolio strategies. They characterize portfolio rebalancing activities as one of four types of *bond swaps,* as follows:

1. The **substitution swap** is an exchange of one bond for a nearly identical substitute. The substituted bonds should be of essentially equal coupon, maturity, quality, call features, sinking fund provisions, and so on. This swap would be motivated by a belief that the market has temporarily mispriced the two bonds, and that the discrepancy between the prices of the bonds represents a profit opportunity.

2. The **intermarket spread swap** is pursued when an investor believes that the yield spread between two sectors of the bond market is temporarily out of line. For example, if the current spread between corporate and government bonds is considered too wide and is expected to narrow, the investor will shift from government bonds to corporate bonds. If the yield spread does in fact narrow, corporates will outperform governments.

In these two swaps, the investor typically believes that the yield relationship between bonds or sectors is only temporarily out of alignment. When the aberration is eliminated, gains can be realized on the underpriced bond. The period of realignment is called the *workout period.*

3. The **rate anticipation swap** is pegged to interest rate forecasting. In this case, if investors believe that rates will fall, they will swap to bonds of greater duration. Conversely, when rates are expected to rise, they will swap to low-duration bonds.

4. The **pure yield pickup swap** is pursued not in response to perceived mispricing, but as a means of increasing return by holding higher-yield bonds. This must be viewed as an attempt to earn an expected term premium in higher-yield bonds. The investor is willing to bear the interest rate risk that this strategy entails.

We can add a fifth swap, called a **tax swap**, to this list. This simply refers to a swap to exploit some tax advantage. For example, an investor may swap from one bond that has decreased in price to another if realization of capital losses is advantageous for tax purposes.

Investors and analysts commonly use this classification of strategies, at least implicitly. Twenty years after Homer and Liebowitz characterized these swaps, however, the financial world's perspective requires broadening the opportunities to include derivative and foreign fixed-income assets as a sector of the bond market, and consideration of foreign interest rates in determining a bond strategy. Where Canadian analysts might earlier have examined only the U.S. prognosis, they now also compare overseas opportunities.

---

[9] Sidney Homer and Martin L. Liebowitz, *Inside the Yield Book: New Tools for Bond Market Strategy* (Englewood Cliffs, N.J.: Prentice Hall, 1972).

We can see some of these strategies reflected in the March 1992 analysis by Burns Fry, for example, revealed by the following quotations from the fixed-income sections of their recommendations:

Over the next 12 months, however, long Canada yields are expected to fall roughly 50 bps [basis points] to 8.70 percent. A drop of 40 basis points in long Treasury yields will narrow long spreads to 110 basis points. C$ weakness and political uncertainty pose risks to the near term outlook, but longer-term fundamentals continue to look constructive. A fixed-income portfolio overweighted in long Canadas and higher-quality provincials is recommended. The BFGFA [Burns Fry Gifford Fong Associates] Canada Long Bond Index has a total return potential of 12 percent compared to the BFGFA Bond Universe return of 10 percent.[10]

This analysis accompanies a recommendation that due to higher expected returns in the equity market, a slight overweighting of equities relative to bonds and a major emphasis on both relative to cash are indicated. We recognize the advice as rate anticipation, which follows from Burns Fry's overall macroeconomic analysis. Given their belief in falling rates, it recommends long asset durations.

At the end of the general analysis comes the specific intermarket spread analysis that expresses Burns Fry's view that yield relationships across the government and corporate (as included in the Bond Universe) offer better potential returns in the Canada and general government sector.

In their *Advantage* recommendation, Burns Fry reveals other examples of intermarket spread awareness and of pure yield pickup as they discuss foreign and domestic instruments and their portfolio adjustments. The accompanying box reproduces their fixed-income report. We note their preoccupation with the upward pressure on Canadian rates and downward pressure on the exchange rate value of the dollar brought on by fiscal and political problems. Domestically, they take advantage of the superior yield offered by MBSs, while other alternatives to government bonds are becoming relatively overpriced. On the other hand, in *Fixed Instrument Facts,*[11] they express some optimism by noting that the same domestic problems have pushed the risk premium on Canadas, which they refer to as an "incentive rate," to a level that will reward longer-horizon investors and recommend purchase on the basis of picking up a bonus in the yield.

Horizon Analysis

One form of interest rate forecasting is called **horizon analysis**. The analyst using this approach selects a particular holding period and predicts the yield curve at the end of that period. Given a bond's time to maturity at the end of the holding period, its yield can be read from the predicted yield curve and its end-

---

[10] Reprinted from *Asset Selection* by permission of Burns Fry Limited. Copyright 1992.

[11] *Fixed Instrument Facts,* Burns Fry Limited. Copyright 1992.

Burns Fry Fixed-Income Report

From "Canadas" to "Bunds"

We sold nearly half our Government of Canada 9.25 percent bonds of 01 Oct. 96 at $104.25.

We bought $50,000 face value of a German Bund, the Deutsche Republic 6⅜ percent of 20 Oct. 97 at 93.20 DM with an annual yield of 7.77 percent.

This is the first time we have bought a German Bund and we are proceeding cautiously.

The Deutsche Republic bonds are German government bonds rated triple A.

We chose a German government bond over a DM-pay Canadian or an ECU-denominated bond because we wanted maximum liquidity. The Deutsche Republic bonds trade like our Canadas.

Foreigns

- Faced with increased need by both federal and provincial governments to fund increasing deficits, there will be a good deal of supply in our domestic bond market putting downward pressure on bond prices.
- We may see a lower Canadian dollar as international investors become increasingly concerned with our domestic financing problems and constitutional debates.
- We may see more foreign selling of our bonds for the same reasons.
- Investors have realized strong profits in our bonds. The last year has been stellar for investors holding Canadian bonds.
- We could see Ontario bond ratings decline and many international investors, particularly Eu-

ropean, see Ontario as representative of our entire domestic market.

In summary, we have taken profits in the Canadian market and positioned ourselves to benefit from:

1. A pending bull market in Germany; rates are expected to decline through 1992, and
2. An appreciating German mark versus the Canadian dollar, with our dollar being expected to weaken somewhat through 1992 in response to economic and political woes.

Domestics

We sold our Ontario Hydro 9.75 percent of 15 Jan. 93 at $101¾ and the remaining Government of Canada 9.25 percent of 01 Oct. 96 at $104.15, a 10 basis point difference from the first sale.

It is expected that the yield curve will flatten, that short rates are at or near their lows, that inflation is under control for the time being and that long rates will drift downward but continue to be volatile.

We bought $50,000 face value of First Line Trust 8½ percent 01 Oct. 94 at $100.90 with a semi-annual yield of 7.96 percent and an annual yield of 8.12 percent. This is a three-year prepayable Mortgage Backed Security.

The MBS market for short-term maturities is trading at a substantial discount relative to other fixed income investments. Yield is currently about 1 percent over Canadas while in other fixed income areas, Corporates, Euros, and Coupons, we're seeing spreads narrowing.

of-period price calculated. Then the analyst adds the coupon income and prospective capital gain of the bond to obtain the total return on the bond over the holding period.

For example, suppose that a 20-year maturity 10 percent coupon bond currently yields 9 percent and sells at $1,092.01. An analyst with a five-year time horizon would be concerned about the bond's price and the value of reinvested coupons five years hence. At that time, the bond will have a 15-year maturity, so the analyst will predict the yield on 15-year maturity bonds at the end of the five-year period to determine the bond's expected price. Suppose that the yield is expected to be 8 percent. Then the bond's end-of-period price will be (assuming 30 semiannual coupon payments):

$$50 \times PA(4\%,30) + 1,000 \times PF(4\%,30) = \$1,172.92$$

The capital gain on the bond therefore will be $80.91.

Meanwhile, the coupons paid by the bond will be reinvested over the five-year period. The analyst must predict a reinvestment rate at which the invested coupons can earn interest. Suppose that the assumed rate is 4 percent per six-month period. If all coupon payments are reinvested at this rate, the value of the 10 semiannual coupon payments with accumulated interest at the end of the five years will be $600.31. (This amount can be solved for as the future value of a $50 annuity after 10 periods with per period interest of 4 percent.) The total return provided by the bond over the five-year period will be $80.91 + $600.31 = $681.22 for a total five-year holding period return of $681.22/ $1,092.01 = .624, or 62.4 percent.

The analyst repeats this procedure for many bonds and selects the ones promising superior holding period returns for the portfolio.

Concept Check

> **Question 5.** Consider a 30-year 8 percent coupon bond currently selling at $896.81. The analyst believes that in five years the yield on 25-year bonds will be 8.5 percent. Should she purchase the 20-year bond just discussed or the 30-year bond today?

A particular version of horizon analysis, popular among money managers, is called **riding the yield curve.** If the yield curve is upward sloping *and* if it is projected that the curve will not shift during the investment horizon, then as bond maturities fall with the passage of time, their yields also will fall as they "ride" the yield curve toward the lower yields of shorter-term bonds. The decrease in yields will contribute to capital gains on the bonds.

To illustrate, suppose that the yield to maturity on 10-year bonds currently is 9 percent, while that on nine-year bonds is 8.8 percent. A $1,000 par value 10-year zero-coupon bond can be bought today for $1,000/1.09^{10} = \$422.41$. In one year, if yields on nine-year bonds are still 8.8 percent, the bond will sell for $1,000/1.088^9 = \$468.10$, for a one-year return of 10.82 percent. In contrast, if the bond's yield remained at 9 percent, it would sell after one year for $1,000/1.09^9 = \$460.43$, offering a 9 percent rate of return.

The danger of riding the yield curve is that the yield curve will, in fact, rise over time. Indeed, according to the expectations hypothesis, an upward-sloping curve is evidence that market participants expect interest rates to be rising over time.

Contingent Immunization

Contingent immunization is a mixed passive-active strategy suggested by Liebowitz and Weinberger.[12] To illustrate, suppose that interest rates currently are 10 percent and that a manager's portfolio is worth $10 million right now. At current rates the manager could lock in, via conventional immunization techniques, a future portfolio value of $12.1 million after two years. Now suppose that the manager wishes to pursue active management but is willing to risk losses only to the extent that the terminal value of the portfolio would not drop lower than $11 million. Since only $9.09 million ($11 million/1.1^2) is required to achieve this minimum acceptable terminal value, and the portfolio currently is worth $10 million, the manager can afford to risk some losses at the outset and might start off with an active strategy rather than immediately immunizing.

The key is to calculate the funds required to lock in via immunization a future value of $11 million at current rates. If T denotes the time left until the horizon date, and r is the market interest rate at any particular time, then the value of the fund necessary to guarantee an ability to reach the minimum acceptable terminal value is $11 million/$(1 + r)^T$, because this size of portfolio, if immunized, will grow risk-free to $11 million by the horizon date. This value becomes the trigger point: if and when actual portfolio value dips to the trigger point, active management will cease. *Contingent* upon reaching the trigger, an immunization strategy is initiated instead, guaranteeing that the minimal acceptable performance can be realized.

Figure 17.4 illustrates two possible outcomes in a contingent immunization strategy. In Figure 17.4**A**, the portfolio falls in value and hits the trigger at time t^*. At that point, immunization is pursued and the portfolio rises smoothly to the $11 million terminal value. In Figure 17.4**B**, the portfolio does well, never reaches the trigger point, and is worth more than $11 million at the horizon date.

Concept Check

> Question 6. What would be the trigger point with a three-year horizon, an interest rate of 12 percent, and a minimum acceptable terminal value of $10 million?

An Example of a Fixed-Income Investment Strategy

As an example of an analytical fixed-income portfolio strategy, we might consider the approach of RBC Dominion Securities presented in its New Year 1990 *Strategy* book. The initial discussion concerned the macroeconomic analysis for Canada, as influenced by the U.S. economy. On this basis, it predicted

---

[12] Martin L. Liebowitz and Alfred Weinberger, "Contingent Immunization—Part I: Risk Control Procedures," *Financial Analysts Journal* 38 (November–December 1982).

FIGURE 17.4
Contingent
immunization.

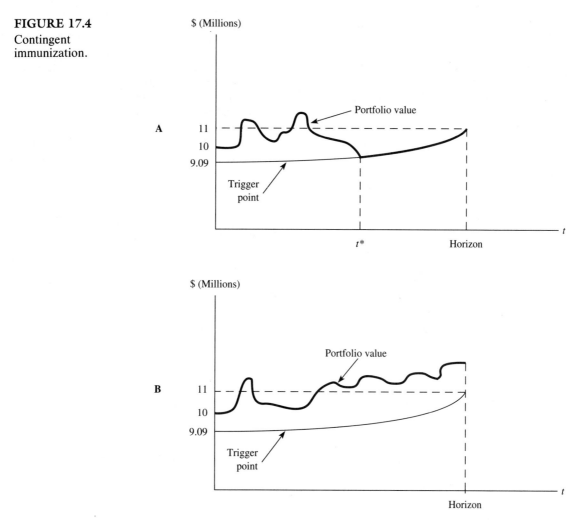

easier Bank of Canada monetary policy due to slow economic growth, but only after evidence of reduced inflationary pressure. An inverted yield curve was expected to return to normal. Risks to this prediction were then advanced, including the escape of the U.S. economy from recession (which of course did not materialize), the danger of reduced rate spreads with respect to the United States and of dollar devaluation, and the resultant threat of foreign partial withdrawal from the Canadian bond market.

Given the uncertainties, RBC outlined three scenarios (optimistic, pessimistic, and most likely) for interest rates at the end of the year and assigned them probabilities. This projection then allowed them to calculate the expected one-year HPR from following alternative portfolio strategies. From this analysis, they concluded:

Under these sets of conditions, Canada 9.50 percent September 1, 1993 offers the best potential for maximizing year-over-year rate of return with an indicated holding period yield of 12.59 percent, marginally ahead of the 12.52 percent weighted return projected for Canada 9.75 percent October 1, 1997 and well ahead of the weighted 11.03 percent return forecast for Canada 9.50 percent June 1, 2010. Given our outlook for 1990, it is difficult to justify term commitments beyond the three- to four-year period unless current yields move back up to higher levels. [They mean *before* investing.] At this juncture we would advocate commitments be limited to the 1993 area and, consequently, recommend new investments be focused on Canada 9.50 percent September 1, 1993. Containment of weighted duration to 2.92 years is consistent with this approach, as additional return, only attainable under the "optimistic" scenario, would require a doubling or more in term and duration.[13]

To summarize the key features of RBC's strategy, we can make the following observations:

1. The firm recognizes the difficulty in attempting to forecast interest rate moves given the uncertain conditions, and also appreciates the dependence on U.S. factors. It expressly observes the need for the Canadian yield premium necessary to attract foreign capital.
2. The firm believes in the use of expected value analysis and simulation of portfolio payoffs to determine the effects of choosing a strategy.
3. Consistent with this unpredictable future and cautious approach, it recommends a portfolio that minimizes potential loss and gain associated with a longer duration.

17.4   *Interest Rate Swaps*

Interest rate swaps recently have emerged as a major fixed-income tool. They arose originally as a means of managing interest rate risk. Since 1980, the volume of swaps has increased from virtually zero to about $2.3 trillion in 1991. (Interest rate swaps do not have anything to do with the Homer/Liebowitz bond swap taxonomy set out earlier; other similar-type swaps are explained in detail in Chapter 23.)

A typical risk management swap is between two parties exposed to opposite types of interest rate risk. For example, on one side may be a trust company (Trustco) with short-term variable-rate liabilities (deposits) and long-term fixed-rate assets, such as conventional mortgages. Trustco will suffer losses if interest rates rise. On the other side of the swap might be a corporation (Adcorp) that has issued long-term non-callable fixed rate bonds and has invested in short-term or variable-rate assets. Adcorp will lose if interest rates fall.

A swap would work as follows. Trustco would agree to make fixed-rate payments to Adcorp based on some *notional* principal amount and fixed inter-

---

[13] Reprinted from *Strategy*, vol. 10, no. 1, by permission of RBC Dominion Securities. Copyright 1990.

est rate. For example, with a fixed rate of 10 percent, and notional principal of $10 million, Trustco would pay $1 million per year for the period of the swap. On the other side, Adcorp pays an agreed-upon short-term interest rate multiplied by the notional principal to Trustco. Typically, that short rate is tied to the London Interbank Offered Rate (LIBOR), which is an interest rate at which banks borrow from each other in the Eurodollar market. For example, Adcorp may pay LIBOR plus 50 basis points. (A basis point is 1/100 of 1 percent, so that 50 points is a half-percentage point premium.) If LIBOR currently is 8 percent, Adcorp initially will pay 8.5 percent of the notional principal, or $850,000 per year to Trustco. As LIBOR changes, so too will Adcorp's payments.

How does a swap affect the net interest rate exposure of each party? Trustco started with long-term fixed-rate assets and variable-rate liabilities. The swap imposes a long-term fixed-rate liability on Trustco, but brings variable-rate inflows from Adcorp. Trustco's net interest rate exposure has thus been reduced or eliminated. Adcorp has done the reverse. It can fund its variable-rate obligation under the swap arrangement with its short-term assets, and can use the fixed-rate payments received from the swap to make the coupon payments on its long-term debt.

Table 17.6 depicts the balance sheets of the two parties before and after the swap. Note that although each party is maturity-mismatched before the swap, each has both short- and long-term assets and liabilities after the swap, which eliminates the original mismatch.

Note also that the swap arrangement does not mean that a new loan has been made. The participants have agreed only to exchange a fixed cash flow for variable cash flow stream. In practice, participants to a swap do not deal with each other directly. Instead, each usually trades with a dealer who acts as an intermediary. The dealer makes a market in swaps, entering one side of a swap with one party and the other side with another party. In some cases swaps are brokered, meaning that the two parties are matched up directly instead of each trading with a dealer.

TABLE 17.6 Interest Rate Swap

Bank		Corporation	
Assets	**Liabilities**	**Assets**	**Liabilities**
Before the Swap			
Long-term loans	Short-term deposits	Variable-rate or short-term assets	Long-term bonds
	Net worth		Net worth
After the Swap			
Long-term loans	Short-term deposits	Short-term assets	Long-term bonds
Claim to variable-rate cash flows	Obligation to make fixed cash payments	Claim to fixed cash flows	Obligation to make variable-rate payments
	Net worth		Net worth

Concept Check

Question 7. A pension fund holds a portfolio of money market securities that the analyst believes are providing excellent interest rates. What type of swap will mitigate the fund's interest rate risk?

One might ask why firms go to the trouble of arranging these swaps. Why didn't the corporation originally borrow short term instead of borrowing long and entering a swap? When the U.S. swap market first developed, the answer seemed to lie in systematic differences in the perceived credit ratings in different markets. Participants in these markets claimed that European banks placed more weight than U.S. banks on a firm's size, name recognition, and product line compared with its credit rating. Thus, it could have paid for a firm that wanted to borrow long term to instead borrow short term in the United States and swap into long-term obligations with a European trading partner. The practice exploited a type of market inefficiency—specifically, differences in credit assessments across national markets. Now, however, these inefficiencies seem to have been arbitraged away. Swaps simply provide a means to restructure balance sheets and manage risk very quickly with small transaction costs.

Swaps create an interesting problem for financial statement analysis. Firms are not required to disclose interest rate swaps in corporate financial statements unless they have a "material impact" on the firm, and even then they appear only in the footnotes. Therefore, the firm's true net obligations may be quite different from its apparent or presented debt structure.

Summary

1. Even default-free bonds such as Canada issues are subject to interest rate risk. Longer-term bonds generally are more sensitive to interest rate shifts than are short-term bonds. A measure of the average life of a bond is Macaulay's duration, defined as the weighted average of the times until each payment made by the security, with weights proportional to the present value of the payment.

2. Duration is a direct measure of the sensitivity of a bond's price to a change in its yield. The proportional change in a bond's price equals the negative of duration multiplied by the proportional change in $1 + y$.

3. Immunization strategies are characteristic of passive fixed-income portfolio management. Such strategies attempt to render the individual or firm immune from movements in interest rates. This may take the form of immunizing net worth or, instead, immunizing the future accumulated value of a fixed-income portfolio.

4. Immunization of a fully funded plan is accomplished by matching the durations of assets and liabilities. To maintain an immunized position as time passes and interest rates change, the portfolio must be periodically rebalanced. Classic immunization also depends on parallel shifts in a flat yield curve. Given that this assumption is unrealistic, immunization generally will be less than complete. To mitigate this problem, multifactor duration models can be used to allow for variation in the shape of the yield curve.

5. A more direct form of immunization is dedication, or cash flow matching. If a portfolio is perfectly matched in cash flow with projected liabilities, rebalancing will be unnecessary.

6. Active bond management consists of interest rate forecasting techniques and intermarket spread analysis. One popular taxonomy classifies active strategies as substitution swaps, intermarket spread swaps, rate anticipation swaps, or pure yield pickup swaps.

7. Horizon analysis is a type of interest rate forecasting. In this procedure, the analyst forecasts the position of the yield curve at the end of some holding period, and from that yield curve predicts corresponding bond prices. Bonds then can be ranked according to expected total returns (coupon plus capital gain) over the holding period.

8. Interest rate swaps are major recent developments in the fixed-income market. In these arrangements, parties trade the cash flows of different securities without actually exchanging any securities directly. This is a useful tool to manage the duration of a portfolio. It also has been used by corporations to borrow at advantageous interest rates in foreign credit markets that are viewed as more hospitable than domestic credit markets.

Key Terms

Duration	Rate anticipation swap
Immunization	Pure yield pickup swap
Bond index portfolio	Tax swap
Rebalancing	Horizon analysis
Cash flow matching	Riding the yield curve
Dedication strategy	Contingent immunization
Substitution swap	Interest rate swaps
Intermarket spread swap	

Selected Readings

Duration and immunization are analyzed extensively in the literature. Good treatments are:

Bierwag, G. O. *Duration Analysis*. Cambridge, Mass.: Ballinger Publishing Company, 1987.

Weil, Roman. "Macaulay's Duration: An Appreciation." *Journal of Business* 46 (October 1973).

Useful general references to techniques of fixed-income portfolio management may be found in a book of readings used by the Institute of Chartered Financial Analysts:

Fong, H. Gifford. "Portfolio Construction—Fixed Income." In John L. Maginn and

Donald L. Tuttle, (editors), *Managing Investment Portfolios: A Dynamic Process,* 2d edition. Boston: Warren, Gorham & Lamont, 1990.

Active bond management strategies are discussed in:

Homer, Sidney; and Liebowitz, Martin L. *Inside the Yield Book: New Tools for Bond Market Strategy.* Englewood Cliffs, N.J.: Prentice Hall, 1972.

Liebowitz, Martin L. "Horizon Analysis: A New Analytic Framework for Managed Bond Portfolios." *Journal of Portfolio Management,* Spring 1975.

Bond indexing is treated in:

Mossavar-Rahmani, Sharmin. *Bond Index Funds.* Chicago: Probus Publishing Co., 1991.

For a detailed analysis of swaps, see:

Beidleman, Carl R. *Interest Rate Swaps.* Homewood, Ill.: Business One Irwin, 1991.

Problems

1. A nine-year bond has a yield of 10 percent and a duration of 7.194 years. If the market yield changes by 50 basis points, what is the percentage change in the bond's price?

2. Find the duration of a 6 percent coupon bond making *annual* coupon payments if it has three years until maturity and has a yield to maturity of 6 percent. What is the duration if the yield to maturity is 10 percent?

3. Find the duration of the bond in problem 2 if the coupons are paid semiannually.

4. Rank the durations of the following pairs of bonds:

    a. Bond *A* is an 8 percent coupon bond, with a 20-year time to maturity selling at par value. Bond *B* is an 8 percent coupon bond, with a 20-year maturity time selling below par value.

    b. Bond *A* is a 20-year non-callable coupon bond with a coupon rate of 8 percent, selling at par. Bond *B* is a 20-year callable bond with a coupon rate of 9 percent, also selling at par.

5. (1985 CFA Examination, Level I) Rank the following bonds in order of descending duration:

Bond	Coupon (%)	Time to Maturity (Years)	Yield to Maturity (%)
A	15	20	10
B	15	15	10
C	0	20	10
D	8	20	10
E	15	15	15

6. Currently, the term structure is as follows: one-year bonds yield 7 percent, two-year bonds yield 8 percent, three-year bonds and greater maturity bonds all yield 9 percent. An investor is choosing between one-, two-, and three-year maturity bonds all paying *annual* coupons of 8 percent, once a year. Which bond should she buy if she strongly believes that at year-end the yield curve would be flat at 9 percent?

7. You will be paying $10,000 a year in tuition expenses at the end of the next two years. Bonds currently yield 8 percent.

   a. What is the present value and duration of your obligation?

   b. What maturity zero-coupon bond would immunize your obligation?

   c. Suppose you buy a zero-coupon bond with value and duration equal to your obligation. Now suppose that rates immediately increase to 9 percent. What happens to your net position, that is, to the difference between the value of the bond and that of your tuition obligation? What if rates fall to 7 percent?

8. What types of interest rate swaps would be appropriate for a corporation holding long-term assets that it funded with floating-rate bonds?

9. You are managing a portfolio of $1 million. Your target duration is 10 years, and you can choose from two bonds: a zero-coupon bond with maturity of five years and a perpetuity, each currently yielding 5 percent.

   a. How much of each bond will you hold in your portfolio?

   b. How will these fractions change *next year* if target duration is now nine years?

10. My pension plan will pay me $10,000 once a year for a 10-year period. The first payment will come in exactly five years. The pension fund wants to immunize its position.

   a. What is the duration of its obligation to me? The current interest rate is 10 percent per year.

   b. If the plan uses five-year and 20-year zero-coupon bonds to construct the immunized position, how much money ought to be placed in each bond? What will be the *face value* of the holdings in each zero?

11. (1983 CFA Examination, Level III) The ability to *immunize* a bond portfolio is very desirable for bond portfolio managers in some instances.

   a. Discuss the components of interest rate risk—that is, assuming a change in interest rates over time, explain the two risks faced by the holder of a bond.

   b. Define immunization and discuss why a bond manager would immunize his portfolio.

   c. Explain why a duration-matching strategy is a superior technique to a maturity-matching strategy for the minimization of interest rate risk.

   d. Explain in specific terms how you would use a zero-coupon bond to immunize a bond portfolio. Discuss why a zero-coupon bond is an ideal instrument in this regard.

   e. Explain how contingent immunization, another bond portfolio management technique, differs from *classical immunization*. Discuss why a bond portfolio manager would engage in *contingent immunization*.

12. (1981 CFA Examination, Level I) You are the manager for the bond portfolio of a pension fund. The policies of the fund allow for the use of active strategies in managing the bond portfolio. It appears that the economic cycle is beginning to mature, inflation is expected to accelerate, and in an effort to contain the economic expansion central bank policy is moving toward constraint. For each of the situations below, *state* which one of the two bonds you would prefer. *Briefly justify* your answer in each case.

   a. Government of Canada (Canadian pay), 10 percent due in 1984 and priced at 98.75 to yield 10.50 percent to maturity; or Government of Canada

(Canadian pay), 10 percent due in 1995 and priced at 91.75 to yield 11.19 percent to maturity.

b. Texas Power and Light Co., 7½ due in 2002, rated AAA, and priced at 62 to yield 12.78 percent to maturity; or Arizona Public Service Co., 7.45 due in 2002, rated A−, and priced at 56 to yield 14.05 percent to maturity.

c. Commonwealth Edison, 2¾ due in 1999, rated Baa, and priced at 25 to yield 14.9 percent to maturity; or Commonwealth Edison, 15⅜ due in 2000, rated Baa, and priced at 102.75 to yield 14.9 percent to maturity.

d. Shell Oil Co., 8½ sinking fund debentures due in 2000, rated AAA (sinking fund begins 9/80 at par), and priced at 69 to yield 12.91 percent to maturity; or Warner-Lambert, 8⅞ sinking fund debentures due in 2000, rated AAA (sinking fund begins 4/86 at par), and priced at 75 to yield 12.31 percent to maturity.

e. Bank of Montreal (Canadian pay), 12 percent certificates of deposit due in 1985, rated AAA, and priced at 100 to yield 12 percent to maturity; or Bank of Montreal (Canadian pay), floating rate notes due in 1991, rated AAA. Coupon currently set at 10.65 percent and priced at 100 (coupon adjusted semiannually to .5 percent above the three-month Government of Canada Treasury bill rate).

13. (1983 CFA Examination, Level I) Active bond management, as contrasted with a passive buy and hold strategy, has gained increased acceptance as investors have attempted to maximize the total return on bond portfolios under their management. The following bond swaps could have been made in recent years as investors attempted to increase the total return on their portfolio. From the information presented below, identify the reason(s) investors may have made each swap.

	Action		Call	Price	YTM (%)
a.	Sell	Baa1 Georgia Pwr. 1st mtg. 11⅝% due 2000	108.24	75⅝	15.71
	Buy	Baa1 Georgia Pwr. 1st mtg. 7⅜% due 2001	105.20	51⅛	15.39
b.	Sell	Aaa Amer. Tel & Tel notes 13¼% due 1991	101.50	96⅛	14.02
	Buy	U.S. Treasury notes 14¼% due 1991	NC	102.15	13.83
c.	Sell	Aa1 Chase Manhattan zero-coupon due 1992	NC	25¼	14.37
	Buy	Aa1 Chase Manhattan float rate notes due 2009	103.90	90¼	—
d.	Sell	A1 Texas Oil & Gas 1st mtg. 8¼% due 1997	105.75	60	15.09
	Buy	U.S. Treasury bond 8¼% due 2005	NC	65.60	12.98
e.	Sell	A1 K mart convertible deb. 6% due 1999	103.90	62¾	10.83
	Buy	A2 Lucky Stores S.F. deb. 11¾% due 2005	109.86	73	16.26

PART VI

EQUITIES

Security Analysis

The dilemma for the portfolio manager and the investor is whether to follow the implication of the empirical evidence and the theory of market efficiency or to ignore it; should one accept a passive investment strategy of an index fund or will the effort and expense of active management provide a superior portfolio? You saw in our discussion of market efficiency that finding undervalued securities is hardly easy. At the same time, there are enough doubts about the accuracy of the efficient market hypothesis that the search for such securities should not be dismissed out of hand. Moreover, it is the continuing search for mispriced securities that maintains a nearly efficient market. Even infrequent discoveries of minor mispricing justify the salary of a stock market analyst.

The area of security analysis can be divided into fundamental analysis and technical analysis. **Fundamental analysis** refers to the search for information concerning the current and prospective profitability of a company in order to discover its fair market value. **Technical analysis** embraces the use of information contained in stock market data to identify trends that will uncover trading opportunities. Empirical evidence suggests that neither of these approaches, especially the latter, is fruitful on the whole, but both are widely practiced and must be understood.

Fundamental analysis has various aspects to it, including an economic analysis of how the firm will react to potential future conditions that will affect earnings; alternatively, the analyst can examine the recent financial results of the firm in the hope of finding unrecognized value. In this chapter, we see how to predict earnings and cash flows and use these figures in models to determine the corresponding firm value. In the following two chapters, we examine financial statement analysis and technical analysis.

We start with a discussion of alternative measures of the value of a company. From there, we progress to quantitative tools called *dividend discount models* that security analysts commonly use to measure the value of a firm as a lasting entity. Next, we turn to price/earnings (or P/E) ratios, both explaining why they are of such interest to analysts and at the same time highlighting some of their shortcomings. We explain how P/E ratios are tied to dividend growth models and, more generally, to the growth prospects of the firm. Finally, we examine the broader issue of how economic conditions affect the prospects of the firm—first, we analyze the effect of inflation, and then we identify key macroeconomic variables and discuss business cycles; from there we consider industry analysis and the sensitivity of the firm to the general environment.

18.1 *Balance Sheet Valuation Methods*

A common valuation measure is **book value**, which is the net worth of a company as shown on the balance sheet. Table 18.1 gives the balance sheet totals for Northern Telecom, to illustrate how to calculate book value per share. Book value of Northern Telecom stock on December 31, 1990, was $13.36 per share ($3,253 million divided by 243,516,231 shares). On that same date, Northern Telecom stock had a market price of $32.50. Would it be fair then to say that Northern Telecom stock was overpriced?

If you think further, you will recognize that the book value is the result of applying a set of arbitrary accounting rules to spread the acquisition cost of assets over a specified number of years, whereas the market price of a stock takes account of the firm's value as a going concern. In other words, the market price reflects the present value of its expected future cash flows. It would, therefore, be unusual if the market price of Northern Telecom stock were exactly equal to its book value.

Can book value represent a "floor" for the stock's price, below which level the market price can never fall? Although Northern Telecom's book value per share on December 31, 1990, was less than its market price, other evidence disproves this notion. At the end of 1990, Canadian Pacific stock had a book value of $24.55 per share and a market price of $19.75. Clearly, book value cannot always be a floor for the stock's price.

A better measure of a floor for the stock price is the **liquidation value** per share of the firm. This represents the amount of money that could be realized by breaking up the firm, selling its assets, repaying its debt, and distributing the remainder to the shareholders. The reasoning behind this concept is that if the market price of equity drops below the liquidation value of the firm, the firm becomes attractive as a takeover target. A corporate raider such as Carl Icahn or T. Boone Pickens would find it profitable to buy enough shares to gain

TABLE 18.1 Northern Telecom Balance Sheet, December 31, 1990 ($ million)

Assets	Liabilities and Owners' Equity	
4,435	Liabilities	1,236
	Common Equity	3,253
	(243,516,231 shares outstanding)	

control and then actually liquidate, because the liquidation value exceeds the value of the business as a going concern.

Another balance sheet concept that is of interest in valuing a firm is the **replacement cost** of its assets less its liabilities. Some analysts believe that the market value of the firm cannot get too far above its replacement cost because, if it did, competitors would try to replicate the firm. The competitive pressure of other similar firms entering the same industry would drive down the market value of all firms until they came into equality with replacement cost.

This idea is popular among economists, and the ratio of market price to replacement cost of a firm's common stock is known as **Tobin's q**.[1] In the long run, according to this view, the ratio of market price to replacement cost will tend toward 1, but the evidence is that this ratio can differ significantly from 1 for very long periods of time.[2]

Although focusing on the balance sheet can give some useful information about a firm's liquidation value or its replacement cost, the analyst must usually turn to the expected future cash flows for a better estimate of the firm's value as a going concern. We now examine the quantitative models that analysts use to value common stock in terms of the future earnings and dividends the firm will yield.

18.2 *Intrinsic Value vs. Market Price*

The most popular model for assessing the value of a firm as a going concern takes off from the observation that an investor in stock expects a return consisting of cash dividends and capital gains or losses. We begin by assuming a one-year holding period and supposing that ABC stock has an expected dividend per share, $E(D_1)$, of $4; the current price of a share, P_0, is $48; and the expected price at the end of a year, $E(P_1)$, is $52.

The holding period return the investor expects is $E(D_1)$ plus the expected price appreciation, $E(P_1) - P_0$, all divided by the current price P_0:

$$
\begin{aligned}
\text{Expected HPR} &= E(r) \\
&= \frac{E(D_1) + [E(P_1) - P_0]}{P_0} \\
&= \frac{4 + (52 - 48)}{48} \\
&= 0.167 \\
&= 16.7\%
\end{aligned}
$$

[1] The ratio is named after the Nobel prize-winning economist James Tobin. For a discussion of Tobin's q and its role in monetary theory, see James Tobin, "A General Equilibrium Approach to Monetary Theory," *Journal of Money, Credit, and Banking*, February 1969.

[2] See, for example, Lawrence H. Summers, "Taxation and Corporate Investment: A q-Theory Approach," *Brookings Papers on Economic Activity*, 1981.

Note that $E(\ )$ denotes an expected future value. Thus, $E(P_1)$ represents the expectation today of the stock price one year from now. $E(r)$ is referred to as the stock's expected holding period return. It is the sum of the expected dividend yield, $E(D_1)/P_0$, and the expected rate of price appreciation, the capital gains yield, $[E(P_1) - P_0]/P_0$.

But what is the investor's *required* rate of return on the stock? From the CAPM we know that the required rate, k, is equal to $r_f + \beta[E(r_M) - r_f]$. Suppose $r_f = 6$ percent, $\beta = 1.2$, and $E(r_M) - r_f = 5$ percent. Then the value of k is

$$k = 6\% + 1.2 \times 5\%$$
$$= 12\%$$

For ABC, the rate of return the investor expects exceeds the required rate based on ABC's risk by a margin of 4.7 percent. Naturally, the investor will want to include more of ABC stock in the portfolio than a passive strategy would dictate.

Another way to see this is to compare the intrinsic value of a share of stock to its market price. The **intrinsic value**, denoted V_0, of a share of stock is defined as the present value of all cash payments to the investor in the stock, including dividends as well as the proceeds from the ultimate sale of the stock, discounted at the appropriate risk-adjusted rate, k. Whenever the intrinsic value, or the investor's own estimate of what the stock is really worth, exceeds the market price, the stock is considered undervalued and a good investment. In the case of ABC, using a one-year investment horizon and a forecast that the stock can be sold at the end of the year at price $P_1 = \$52$, the intrinsic value is

$$V_0 = \frac{E(D_1) + E(P_1)}{1 + k}$$
$$= \frac{\$4 + \$52}{1.12}$$
$$= \$50$$

Because intrinsic value, \$50, exceeds current price, \$48, we conclude the stock is undervalued in the market. We again conclude investors will want to buy more ABC than they would following a passive strategy.

If the intrinsic value turns out to be lower than the current market price, investors should buy less of it than under the passive strategy. It might even pay to go short on ABC stock, as we discussed in Chapter 7.

In market equilibrium, the current market price will reflect the intrinsic value estimates of all market participants. This means the individual investor whose V_0 estimate differs from the market price, P_0, in effect must disagree with some or all of the market consensus estimates of $E(D_1)$, $E(P_1)$, or k. A common term for the market consensus value of the required rate of return, k, is the **market capitalization rate**, which we use often throughout this chapter.

Concept Check
=====
=====

> Question 1. You expect the price of IBX stock to be $59.77 per share a
> year from now. Its current market price is $50, and you expect it to pay a
> dividend one year from now of $2.15 a share.
>   *a.* What is the stock's expected dividend yield, rate of price appreciation,
>   and holding period return?
>   *b.* If the stock has a beta of 1.15, the risk-free rate is 6 percent per year,
>   and the expected rate of return on the market portfolio is 14 percent
>   per year, what is the required rate of return on IBX stock?
>   *c.* What is the intrinsic value of IBX stock, and how does it compare to
>   the current market price.

18.3 *Dividend Discount Models*

Consider an investor who buys a share of Steady State Electronics stock,
planning to hold it for one year. The intrinsic value of the share is the present
value of the dividend to be received at the end of the first year, D_1, and the
expected sales price, P_1. We will henceforth use the simpler notation P_1 instead of $E(P_1)$ to avoid clutter. Keep in mind, though, future prices and dividends are unknown, and we are dealing with expected values, not certain
values. We've already established

$$V_0 = \frac{D_1 + P_1}{1 + k} \qquad (18.1)$$

While dividends are fairly predictable given a company's history, you might
ask how we can estimate P_1, the year-end price. According to Equation 18.1,
V_1 (the year-end value) will be

$$V_1 = \frac{D_2 + P_2}{1 + k}$$

If we assume the stock will be selling for its intrinsic value next year, then $V_1 =
P_1$, and we can substitute this value for P_1 into Equation 18.1 to find

$$V_0 = \frac{D_1}{1 + k} + \frac{D_2 + P_2}{(1 + k)^2}$$

This equation may be interpreted as the present value of dividends plus sales
price for a two-year holding period. Of course, now we need to come up with a
forecast of P_2. Continuing in the same way, we can replace P_2 by $(D_3 + P_3)/
(1 + k)$, which relates P_0 to the value of dividends plus the expected sales price
for a three-year holding period.

More generally, for a holding period of H years, we can write the stock value as the present value of dividends over the H years, plus the ultimate sale price, P_H.

$$V_0 = \frac{D_1}{1 + k} + \frac{D_2}{(1 + k)^2} + \cdots + \frac{D_H + P_H}{(1 + k)^H} \qquad \textbf{(18.2)}$$

Note the similarity between this formula and the bond valuation formula developed in Chapter 15. Each relates price to the present value of a stream of payments (coupons in the case of bonds, dividends in the case of stocks) and a final payment (the face value of the bond, or the sales price of the stock). The key differences in the case of stocks are the uncertainty of dividends, the lack of a fixed maturity date, and the unknown sales price at the horizon date. Indeed, one can continue to substitute for price indefinitely to conclude

$$V_0 = \frac{D_1}{1 + k} + \frac{D_2}{(1 + k)^2} + \frac{D_3}{(1 + k)^3} + \cdots \qquad \textbf{(18.3)}$$

Equation 18.2 states the stock price should equal the present value of all expected future dividends into perpetuity. This formula is called the **dividend discount model (DDM)** of stock prices.

It is tempting, but incorrect, to conclude from Equation 18.3 that the DDM focuses exclusively on dividends and ignores capital gains as a motive for investing in stock. Indeed, we assume explicitly in Equation 18.1 that capital gains (as reflected in the expected sales price, P_1) are part of the stock's value. At the same time, the price at which you can sell a stock in the future depends on dividend forecasts at that time.

The reason only dividends appear in Equation 18.3 is not that investors ignore capital gains. It is instead that those capital gains will be determined by dividend forecasts at the time the stock is sold. That is why in Equation 18.2 we can write the stock price as the present value of dividends plus sales price for *any* horizon date. P_H is the present value at time H of all dividends expected to be paid after the horizon date. That value is then discounted back to today, time 0. The DDM asserts that stock prices are determined ultimately by the cash flows accruing to stockholders, and those are dividends.[3]

The Constant Growth DDM

Equation 18.3 as it stands is still not very useful in valuing a stock, because it requires dividend forecasts for every year into the indefinite future. For a more structured valuation approach, we need to introduce some simplifying assumptions. A useful first pass at the problem is to assume that Steady State Electronics dividends are trending upward at a stable growth rate, which we will call g.

---

[3] If investors never expected a dividend to be paid, then this model implies that the stock would have no value. To reconcile the fact that non-dividend-paying stocks do have a market value with this model, one must assume that investors expect that some day it may pay out some cash, even if only a liquidating dividend.

Then if $g = .05$, and the most recently paid dividend was $D_0 = 3.81$, expected future dividends are

$$D_1 = D_0(1 + g) = 3.81 \times 1.05 = 4.00$$
$$D_2 = D_0(1 + g)^2 = 3.81 \times (1.05)^2 = 4.20$$
$$D_3 = D_0(1 + g)^3 = 3.81 \times (1.05)^3 = 4.41 \text{ etc.}$$

Using these dividend forecasts in Equation 18.3, we solve for intrinsic value as

$$V_0 = \frac{D_0(1 + g)}{1 + k} + \frac{D_0(1 + g)^2}{(1 + k)^2} + \frac{D_0(1 + g)^3}{(1 + k)^3} + \cdots$$

This equation can be simplified to

$$V_0 = \frac{D_0(1 + g)}{k - g} = \frac{D_1}{k - g} \tag{18.4}$$

Note in Equation 18.4 that we divide D_1 (not D_0) by $k - g$ to calculate intrinsic value. If the market capitalization rate for Steady State is 12 percent, now we can use Equation 18.4 to show that the intrinsic value of a share of Steady State stock is

$$\frac{\$400}{.12 - .05} = \$57.14$$

Equation 18.4 is called the **constant growth DDM** or the *Gordon model*, after Myron J. Gordon, who popularized the model. It should remind you of the formula for the present value of a perpetuity. If dividends were expected not to grow, then the dividend stream would be a simple perpetuity, and the valuation formula would be $P_0 = D_1/k$. Equation 18.4 is a generalization of the perpetuity formula to cover the case of a *growing* perpetuity. As g increases, the stock price also rises.[4]

---

[4] Proof that the intrinsic value, V_0, of a stream of cash dividends growing at a constant rate, g, is equal to $\frac{D_1}{k - g}$:

By definition,

$$V_0 = \frac{D_1}{1 + k} + \frac{D_1(1 + g)}{(1 + k)^2} + \frac{D_1(1 + g)^2}{(1 + k)^3} + \cdots \tag{a}$$

Multiplying through by $(1 + k)/(1 + g)$, we obtain

$$\frac{(1 + k)}{(1 + g)} V_0 = \frac{D_1}{(1 + g)} + \frac{D_1}{(1 + k)} + \frac{D_1(1 + g)}{(1 + k)^2} + \cdots \tag{b}$$

Subtracting equation a from equation b, we find that

$$\frac{(1 + k)}{(1 + g)} V_0 - V_0 = \frac{D_1}{(1 + g)}$$

which implies

$$\frac{(k - g)V_0}{(1 + g)} = \frac{D_1}{(1 + g)}$$

$$V_0 = \frac{D_1}{k - g}$$

The constant growth DDM is valid only when g is less than k. If dividends were expected to grow forever at a rate faster than k, the value of the stock would be infinite. If an analyst derives an estimate of g that is greater than k, that growth rate must be unsustainable in the long run. The appropriate valuation model to use in this case is a multistage DDM such as that discussed below.

The constant growth DDM is so widely used by stock market analysts that it is worth exploring some of its implications and limitations. The constant growth rate DDM implies that a stock's value will be greater:

1. The larger its expected dividend per share.
2. The lower the market capitalization rate, k.
3. The higher the expected growth rate of dividends.

Another implication of the constant growth model is that the stock price is expected to grow at the same rate as dividends. To see this, suppose Steady State stock is selling at its intrinsic value of $57.14, so that $V_0 = P_0$. Then,

$$P_0 = \frac{D_1}{k - g}$$

Note that price is proportional to dividends. Therefore, next year, when the dividends paid to Steady State stockholders are expected to be higher by $g = 5$ percent, price also should increase by 5 percent. To confirm this, note

$$D_2 = \$4(1.05) = \$4.20$$
$$P_1 = D_2/(k - g) = \$4.20/(.12 - .05) = \$60.00$$

which is 5 percent higher than the current price of $57.14. To generalize,

$$P_1 = \frac{D_2}{k - g} = \frac{D_1(1 + g)}{k - g} = \frac{D_1}{k - g}(1 + g)$$
$$= P_0(1 + g)$$

Therefore, the DDM implies that in the case of constant growth of dividends, the rate of price appreciation in any year will equal that constant growth rate, g. Note that for a stock whose market price equals its intrinsic value ($V_0 = P_0$) the expected holding period return will be

$$E(r) = \text{Dividend yield} + \text{Capital gains yield}$$
$$= \frac{D_1}{P_0} + \frac{P_1 - P_0}{P_0} \qquad\qquad (18.5)$$
$$= \frac{D_1}{P_0} + g$$

This formula offers a means to infer the market capitalization rate of a stock, for if the stock is selling at its intrinsic value, then $E(r) = k$, implying that $k = D_1/P_0 + g$. By observing the dividend yield, D_1/P_0, and estimating the growth rate of dividends, we can compute k. This equation is also known as the *discounted cash flow (DCF) formula*.

This is an approach often used in rate hearings for regulated public utilities. The regulatory agency responsible for approving utility pricing decisions is mandated to allow the firms to charge just enough to cover costs plus a "fair" profit, that is, one that allows a competitive return on the investment the firm has made in its productive capacity. In turn, that return is taken to be the expected return investors require on the stock of the firm. The $D_1/P_0 + g$ formula provides a means to infer that required return.

Concept Check

Question 2.
a. IBX's stock dividend at the end of this year is expected to be $2.15, and it is expected to grow at 11.2 percent per year forever. If the required rate of return on IBX stock is 15.2 percent per year, what is its intrinsic value?
b. If IBX's current market price is equal to this intrinsic value, what is next year's expected price?
c. If an investor were to buy IBX stock now and sell it after receiving the $2.15 dividend a year from now, what is the expected capital gain (i.e., price appreciation) in percentage terms? What is the dividend yield, and what would be the holding period return?

Convergence of Price to Intrinsic Value

Now suppose that the current market price of ABC stock is only $48 per share and, therefore, that the stock now is undervalued at $2 per share. In this case, the expected rate of price appreciation depends on an additional assumption about whether the discrepancy between the intrinsic value and the market price will disappear, and if so, when.

One fairly common assumption is that the discrepancy will never disappear and that the market price will continue to grow at rate g forever. This implies that the discrepancy between intrinsic value and market price also will grow at that same rate. In our example:

Now	Next Year
$V_0 = \$50$	$V_1 = \$50 \times 1.04 = \$52$
$P_0 = \$48$	$P_1 = \$48 \times 1.04 = \$49.92$
$V_0 - P_0 = \$2$	$V_1 - P_1 = \$2 \times 1.04 = \$2.08$

Under this assumption, the expected HPR will exceed the required rate, because the dividend yield is higher than it would be if P_0 were equal to V_0. In our example, the dividend yield would be 8.33 percent instead of 8 percent, so that the expected HPR would be 12⅓ percent rather than 12 percent.

$$E(r) = \frac{D_1}{P_0} + g$$
$$= \frac{\$4}{\$48} + .04$$
$$= .0833 + .04$$
$$= 12\frac{1}{3}\% \text{ per year}$$

An investor who identifies this undervalued stock can get an expected dividend yield that exceeds the required yield by 33 basis points. This excess return is earned each year, and the market price never catches up to intrinsic value.[5]

A second possible assumption is that the gap between market price and intrinsic value will disappear by the end of the year. In that case we would have $P_1 = V_1 = \$52$, and

$$r = \frac{D_1}{P_0} + \frac{P_1 - P_0}{P_0}$$
$$= \frac{4}{48} + \frac{52 - 48}{48}$$
$$= .0833 + .0833$$
$$= .1667 = 16\frac{2}{3}\% \text{ per year}$$

The assumption of complete catchup to intrinsic value produces a much larger one-year HPR. In future years, the stock is expected to generate only fair rates of return.

Many stock analysts assume that a stock's price will approach its intrinsic value gradually over time—for example, over a five-year period. This puts their expected one-year HPR somewhere between the bounds of 12⅓ percent and 16⅔ percent.

Stock Prices and Investment Opportunities

Consider two companies, No-Opps and Good-Opps, each with expected earnings in the coming year of $5 per share. Both companies could in principle pay out all of these earnings as dividends, maintaining a perpetual dividend flow of $5 per share. If the market capitalization rate were $k = 12.5$ percent, both companies would then be valued at $D_1/k = \$5/.125 = \$40$ per share. Neither firm would grow in value, because with all earnings paid out as dividends, and no earnings reinvested in the firm, both companies' capital stock and earnings capacity would remain unchanged over time; earnings and dividends would not grow.

Actually, we are referring here to earnings net of the funds necessary to maintain the productivity of the firm's capital, that is, earnings net of "eco-

---

[5] Closed-end investment companies selling at a discount to their net asset value (discussed in Chapter 3) are an example.

nomic depreciation.'' In other words, the earnings figure should be interpreted as the maximum amount of money the firm could pay out each year in perpetuity without depleting its productive capacity. For this reason, the net earnings number may be quite different from the accounting earnings figure that the firm reports in its financial statements. (We explore this further in the next chapter.)

Now suppose one of the firms, Good-Opps, engages in projects that generate a return on investment of 15 percent, which is greater than the required rate of return, $k = 12.5$ percent. It would be foolish for such a company to pay out all of its earnings as dividends. If Good-Opps retains or plows back some of its earnings into its highly profitable projects, it can earn a 15 percent rate of return for its shareholders, while if it pays out all earnings as dividends, it forgoes the projects, leaving shareholders to invest the dividends in other opportunities at a fair market rate of only 12.5 percent. Suppose, therefore, Good-Opps lowers its **dividend payout ratio** (the fraction of earnings paid out as dividends) from 100 percent to 40 percent, maintaining a **plowback ratio** (the fraction of earnings reinvested in the firm) at 60 percent. The plowback ratio is also referred to as the **earnings retention ratio.**

Concept Check

> Question 3. What must be the sum of the payout and plowback ratios?

The dividend of the company, therefore, will be $2 (40 percent of $5 earnings) instead of $5. Will share price fall? No—it will rise! Although dividends initially fall under the earnings reinvestment policy, subsequent growth in the assets of the firm because of reinvested profits will generate growth in future dividends, which will be reflected in today's share price.

How much growth will be generated? Suppose Good-Opps starts with plant and equipment of $100 million and is all equity financed. With a return on investment or equity (ROE) of 15 percent, total earnings are ROE $\times$ $100 million $= .15 \times$ $100 million $=$ $15 million. There are 3 million shares of stock outstanding, so earnings per share are $5, as posited above. If 60 percent of the $15 million in this year's earnings is reinvested, then the value of the firm's capital stock will increase by $0.60 \times$ $15 million $=$ $9 million, or by 9 percent. The percentage increase in the capital stock is the rate at which income was generated (ROE) times the plowback ratio (the fraction of earnings reinvested in more capital), which we will denote as b.

Now endowed with 9 percent more capital, the company earns 9 percent more income, and pays out 9 percent higher dividends. The growth rate of the dividends, therefore, is

$$g = \text{ROE} \times b$$
$$= .15 \times .60$$
$$= .09.$$

If the stock price equals its intrinsic value, it should sell at

$$P_0 = \frac{D_1}{k - g} = \frac{\$2}{.125 - .09} = \$57.14$$

When Good-Opps pursued a no-growth policy and paid out all earnings as dividends, the stock price was only \$40. When it reduced current dividends and plowed funds back into the company, the growth rate increased enough to cause the stock price to increase.

The difference between the no-growth price of \$40 and the actual price of \$57.14 can be ascribed to the present value of the company's excellent investment opportunities. One way to think of the company's value is to describe its stock price as the sum of the no-growth value (the value of current earnings per share, E_1, in perpetuity) plus the present value of these growth opportunities, which we will denote as PVGO. In terms of the example we have been following, PVGO = 17.14:

$$P_0 = \frac{E_1}{k} + \text{PVGO}$$
$$57.14 = 40 + 17.14. \tag{18.6}$$

It is important to recognize that growth per se is not what investors desire. Growth enhances company value only if it is achieved by investments in projects with attractive profit opportunities (i.e., with ROE > k). To see why, let's now consider Good-Opps' unfortunate sister company, No-Opps. No-Opps' ROE is only 12.5 percent, just equal to the required rate of return, k. The NPV of its investment opportunities is zero. We've seen that following a zero-growth strategy with $b = 0$ and $g = 0$, the value of No-Opps will be $E_1/k = \$5/.125 = \$40$ per share. Now suppose that No-Opps chooses a plowback ratio of $b = .60$, the same as Good-Opps' plowback. Then g would be

$$\begin{aligned} g &= \text{ROE} \times b \\ &= 0.125 \times 0.60 \\ &= 0.075, \end{aligned}$$

and the stock price becomes

$$P_0 = \frac{D_1}{k - g} = \frac{\$2}{.125 - .075} = \$40$$

no different from the no-growth strategy.

In the case of No-Opps, the dividend reduction used to free funds for reinvestment in the firm generates only enough growth to maintain the stock price at the current level. This is as it should be: If the firm's projects yield only what investors can earn on their own, shareholders cannot be made better off by a high reinvestment rate policy. This demonstrates that "growth" is not the same as growth opportunities. To justify reinvestment, the firm must engage in projects with better prospective returns than those shareholders can find elsewhere. Notice also that the PVGO of No-Opps is zero: PVGO = $P_0 - E_1/k = 40 - 40 = 0$. With ROE = k, there is no advantage to plowing funds back into the firm; this shows up as PVGO of zero.

Concept Check

> **Question 4.**
> *a.* Calculate the price of a firm with a plowback ratio of 0.60 if its ROE is 20 percent. Current earnings, E_1, will be $5 per share, and $k = 12.5$ percent.
> *b.* What if ROE is 10 percent, less than the market capitalization rate? Compare price in this instance to that of a firm with the same ROE and E_1, but a plowback ratio $b = 0$.

Multistage Dividend Discount Models

A major limitation of the constant growth model is that it fails to capture the real-world pattern of dividends of many firms. Some firms go through periods in which they pay no dividends at all, while others see periods of very rapid growth in dividends, which cannot be sustained forever. To allow for this variation, stock analysts use multistage dividend discount models.

The simplest of the multistage DDMs is the two-stage model, where an initial stage of dividend growth at rate g_1 lasts for a limited number of years and is followed thereafter by constant growth at a lower rate, g_2. We can illustrate the two-stage model with an example for which there are no dividends at all in the first stage.

Consider what we will call Growth Dynamics (GD), a young firm experiencing rapid growth, reinvesting all its earnings, and paying no dividends. Its most recent earnings per share were $1, and its ROE is 25 percent per year.

Analysts assume that GD's high ROE will fall to 15 percent per year three years from now, and that at that point GD's management will start paying out all earnings as dividends. If the required rate of return, k, on GD stock is 12 percent per year, what can we say about GD's current and future intrinsic values?

Since its ROE in the first three years is expected to be 25 percent per year and the plowback ratio is 1.0, the growth rate of earnings, g, is 25 percent per year. Earnings per share will grow from the current value of $1 to $1.953125 in year 3. Starting in year 3, GD will pay annual dividends of $1.953125 per share forever, at which point further growth is zero, since plowback into the firm is zero.

The pattern of expected future earnings and dividends is as follows:

t:	0	1	2	3	4	5
E_t	$1	$1.25	$1.5625	$1.953125	$1.953125	→
D_t	0	0	0	$1.953125	$1.953125	→

The firm is expected to reach a constant growth phase 2 years from now (with $g = 0$). At this point, we can obtain its price from the discounted dividend model. The expected price of a share two years from now, P_2, is therefore simply D_3/k, or $1.953125/.12 = $16.2760. Therefore, its value today is the present value of that expected future price, discounted at 12 percent per year, which is $16.2760/(1.12)^2 = $12.9752.

Between now and three years from now, the investor's return will be entirely in the form of price appreciation at a rate of 12 percent per year. Starting in year three the return will come entirely in the form of a 12 percent per year dividend yield.

The $12.9752 present value of expected future dividends represents our DDM intrinsic value estimate for GD stock, assuming a 12 percent per year market capitalization rate. But how do we estimate the *expected* rate of return on the stock, given its current market price?

Suppose the current market price is $10 per share. According to the DDM, the stock is worth $12.9752, or $2.9752 more than this. As in the earlier constant growth rate DDM, the expected rate of return to stockholders depends on how rapidly the market price will converge to its intrinsic value.

One measure of expected return we can derive from analogy with bond returns is a yield to maturity measure, which is the discount rate that would make the present value of all expected future dividends equal to the current market price.

In the case of GD, the expected future flow of dividends is $1.953125 per year starting three years from now and lasting forever. The yield to maturity analogue y can be found by solving for y:

$$P_0 = \$10 = \frac{1}{(1 + y)^2}\frac{D_3}{y}$$
$$= \frac{1.953125}{(1 + y)^2 y} \tag{18.7}$$

This equation sets the current price equal to the present value of the expected perpetual stream of dividends. The present value of the perpetuity equals D_3/y discounted for an extra two years, because the dividend stream starts in three years rather than in one year, as is usually the case. Solving this equation by a trial-and-error procedure, we find that $y = 14.81$ percent per year.[6]

Note that y is the expected rate of return for someone who will hold the stock in perpetuity. It is not, in general, the same as the expected HPR for shorter time horizons, because y is analogous to the yield to maturity on a bond.

Alternatively, we can assume, as we did in the case of the constant growth rate DDM, that the market price will converge to its intrinsic value by the end of the first year.

The intrinsic value one year from now is

$$\frac{P_2}{1 + k} = \frac{16.2760}{1.12}$$
$$= \$14.5321$$

as the expected price at time 2 is now one year closer.

---

[6] The value of *y* that satisfies this equation is found by an iterative search procedure. The general procedure is to start with an initial guess, and then through a systematic trial-and-error process make progressively better approximations.

The expected HPR is thus

$$E(r) = \frac{P_1 - P_0}{P_0}$$
$$= \frac{\$14.5321 - \$10}{\$10}$$
$$= .45321 = 45.32\% \text{ per year}$$

This high one-year HPR is generated by the immediate "catchup" of market price to intrinsic value.

Two points are worth noting about this example of a multistage DDM. The first is that, even when the market price equals the intrinsic value, the expected rate of price appreciation is not equal to the growth rate of earnings until the final stage, where g once again is constant. This feature differentiates the multistage from the constant growth DDM. The second point, which is true of any DDM, is that when market price equals intrinsic value the expected HPR, the sum of the expected dividend yield plus the expected rate of price appreciation equals the market capitalization rate.

If the GD stock is priced at its intrinsic value, we have $P_0 = \$12.9752$, and the expected rate of capital appreciation in the first stage is 12 percent [($14.53 − $12.98)/$12.98], which is the market capitalization rate. In the second stage the growth rate is expected to fall to zero, and all earnings are paid out as dividends. Price is expected to remain constant at $16.276 per year.

Note that in both stages of GD's growth the sum of expected dividend yield and price appreciation is 12 percent per year. In stage one it is all price appreciation; in stage two it is all dividend yield.

You might well ask how realistic this example is. Market history shows many cases of firms that proceeded through an early growth stage when they paid no dividends and then subsequently started to pay cash dividends that have grown at a roughly constant rate. Perhaps the best-known case is IBM. Still other companies are in the first stage, yet to pay a cash dividend. Digital Equipment Corporation is one example.

More generally, however, we can allow for dividends to be paid in both stages of growth. To see how an analyst would actually apply the two-stage DDM to a stock that is currently paying a cash dividend, let us now use it to value the stock of Northern Telecom Corporation.

Our assumptions are:

1. Next year's earnings per share: $2.40
2. Earnings per share three years from now: $3.195
3. The dividend payout ratio: .16
4. Return on equity three years from now: 14 percent
5. β: 1.20

Let us assume that the risk-free rate is 6 percent per year and the risk premium on the market portfolio 6 percent per year. We will assume that earnings and dividends grow smoothly at a rate of 10 percent per year between now and three years from now, since that is the growth rate implied by assumptions 1 and 2.

Under these assumptions, the ultimate growth rate beyond year 4 is 11.76 percent per year ($b \times ROE = .84 \times 14$ percent), and the market capitalization rate 13.2 percent ($r_f + \beta[E(r_M) - r_f] = 6$ percent $+ 1.20 \times 6$ percent). The cash flow diagram is therefore

t:	0	1	2	3	4 ...
E_t	—	$2.40	$2.64	$2.90	$3.19 ...
D_t	—	$0.384	$0.422	$0.465	$0.511 ...

The estimated price at $t = 3$ is:

$$P_3 = D_4/(k - g)$$
$$= \$0.511/(.132 - .1176) = \$35.49$$

The intrinsic value is the present value (PV) of dividends in years 1 through 3 plus the PV of P_3.

$$V_0 = (\$0.384/1.132) + (\$0.422/1.132^2) + (\$0.465 + 35.49)/1.132^3 = \$25.46$$

Concept Check

Question 5. The Two-Stage Corporation just paid a dividend of $2 per share, and it is expected to grow by 10 percent per year for the next three years. Starting at the end of year 3, the dividend growth rate is expected to fall to 4 percent per year and to stay there forever. The appropriate market capitalization rate for Two-Stage stock is 12 percent per year.
a. What should be the price of the stock?
b. What is its expected price one year from now?
c. What is the expected dividend yield and rate of capital appreciation?

In practice, the multistage DDMs that security analysts use often are more complex than our two-stage model. Usually, they allow for a more gradual transition from the initial high-growth stage to the ultimate steady state. In addition, computers make it relatively easy to generate patterns of expected future dividends that conform to any plausible scenario, and to estimate the corresponding intrinsic value and expected rate of return.

There is, however, one multistage DDM that does not require computer aid and still allows the assumed growth rate of dividends to start high and to fall gradually over time to a long-run steady state level. The so-called *H*-model is gaining in popularity because of its relative simplicity.[7]

---

[7] For a detailed exposition of this model, see R. J. Fuller and C. C. Hsia, "A Simplified Model for Estimating Stock Prices for Growth Firms," *Financial Analysts Journal*, September–October 1984.

The H model assumes that the dividend growth rate starts at a level g_a and declines linearly over $2H$ years to a long-run constant growth rate of g_n. Therefore, at H years the growth rate is halfway between g_a and g_n.

Under these assumptions, the equation for the stock's price is:

$$P_0 = \frac{D_0(1 + g_n)}{k - g_n} + \frac{D_0 H(g_a - g_n)}{k - g_n}$$

The first term on the right-hand side of equation 18.8 represents the value of a share if dividends were expected to grow at the long-run growth rate, g_n, starting with the very first period. The second term is the premium because of higher than g_n growth rates expected during the first $2H$ years. The longer the half-life of the period of higher growth (H) and the higher the initial growth rate (g_a), the more the premium is.

To demonstrate how the H-model works, suppose the stream of future dividends per share of the HIJ Corporation is expected to start at $1 per share, with an initial growth rate of 25 percent per year that falls to a long-run rate of 5 percent per year after 10 years. In this case

$$D_0 = \$1$$
$$g_a = .25$$
$$g_n = .05$$
$$H = 5 \text{ years}$$

Assume further that its market capitalization rate is 10 percent per year.

$$P_0 = \frac{1.05}{.1 - .05} + \frac{1.0 \times 5(.25 - .05)}{.1 - .05}$$
$$= 21 + 20$$
$$= \$41.00 \text{ per share}$$

The H model also has a simple expression for the expected yield to maturity (y) on the expected dividend stream, given its market price. Recall that y is the discount rate that makes the present value of all expected future dividends equal to the current market price. For the H model it is given by

$$y = \frac{D_0}{P_0} [1 + g_n + H(g_a - g_n)] + g_n$$

If the market price of a share of HIJ is $20, the expected yield to maturity is

$$y = \frac{1}{20} [(1.05) + 5(.25 - .05)] + .05$$
$$= \frac{2.05}{20} + .05$$
$$= .1525$$
$$= 15.25\% \text{ per year}$$

If the market price were $41 rather than $20 per share, y would be 10 percent per year, which is the market capitalization rate.

Concept Check

Question 6. The Unlimited Corporation is a rapidly growing retailer of women's clothing. Its most recent dividend per share was $2, and its market capitalization rate is 12 percent per year. You are an analyst who believes that Unlimited's dividend growth rate will be 35 percent this year and will decline gradually to 6 percent per year 20 years from now. Thereafter, growth will level off at 6 percent per year forever.

a. What is your estimate of the intrinsic value of a share of Unlimited's stock?

b. If the market price of a share is currently $100, what is the expected yield to maturity on an investment in the stock?

18.4 *Price/Earnings Ratios*

The Price/Earnings Ratio and Growth Opportunities

Much of the real-world discussion of stock market valuation concentrates on the firm's **price/earnings multiple**, the ratio of price per share to earnings per share. Our discussion of growth opportunities shows why stock market analysts focus on this multiple, commonly called the *P/E ratio*. Both companies considered, No-Opps and Good-Opps, had earnings per share, EPS, of $5, but Good-Opps reinvested 60 percent of earnings in prospects with an ROE of 15 percent, while No-Opps paid out all earnings as dividends. No-Opps had a price of $40, giving it a P/E multiple of 40/5 = 8.0, while Good-Opps sold for $57.14, giving it a multiple of 57.14/5 = 11.4. This observation suggests the P/E ratio might serve as a useful indicator of expectations of growth opportunities. We can see this explicitly by rearranging Equation 18.6 to

$$\frac{P_0}{E_1} = \frac{1}{k}\left[1 + \frac{\text{PVGO}}{E_1/k}\right] \tag{18.9}$$

When PVGO = 0, Equation 18.9 shows that $P_0 = E_1/k$. The stock is valued like a non-growing perpetuity of EPS_1. The P/E ratio is just $1/k$. However, as PVGO becomes an increasingly dominant contributor to price, the P/E ratio can rise dramatically. The ratio of PVGO to E/k has a simple interpretation. It is the ratio of the component of firm value due to growth opportunities to the component of value due to assets already in place (i.e., the no-growth value of the firm, E/k). When future growth opportunities dominate the estimate of total value, the firm will command a high price relative to current earnings. Thus, a high P/E multiple appears to indicate a firm is endowed with ample growth opportunities.

TABLE 18.2   Effect of ROE and Plowback on Growth and the P/E Ratio

ROE (%)	Plowback Rate(b)			
	0	.25	.50	.75
A Growth rate, g(%)				
10	0	2.5	5.0	7.5
12	0	3.0	6.0	9.0
14	0	3.5	7.0	10.5
B P/E Ratio				
10	8.33	7.89	7.14	5.56
12	8.33	8.33	8.33	8.33
14	8.33	8.82	10.00	16.67

Assumption: $k = 12$ percent per year.

Clearly, it is differences in expected growth opportunities that justify particular differentials in P/E ratios across firms. The P/E ratio actually is a reflection of the market's optimism concerning a firm's growth prospects. In their use of a P/E ratio, analysts must decide whether they are more or less optimistic than the market. If they are more optimistic, they will recommend buying the stock.

There is a way to make these insights more precise. Look again at the constant growth DDM formula, $P_0 = D_1/(k - g)$. Now recall that dividends equal the earnings that are *not* reinvested in the firm: $D_1 = E_1(1 - b)$. Recall also that $g = \text{ROE} \times b$. Hence, substituting for D_1 and g, we find that

$$P_0 = \frac{E_1(1 - b)}{k - \text{ROE} \times b}$$

implying the P/E ratio is

$$\frac{P_0}{E_1} = \frac{1 - b}{k - \text{ROE} \times b} \qquad \qquad \textbf{(18.10)}$$

It is easy to verify that the P/E ratio increases with ROE. This makes sense, because high ROE projects give the firm good opportunities for growth.[8] We also can verify that the P/E ratio increases for higher b as long as ROE exceeds k. This too makes sense. When a firm has good investment opportunities, the market will reward it with a higher P/E multiple if it exploits those opportunities more aggressively by plowing back more earnings into those opportunities.

Remember we noted, however, that growth is not desirable for its own sake. Examine Table 18.2 where we use Equation 18.10 to compute both growth rates and P/E ratios for different combinations of ROE and b. While growth always increases with the plowback rate (move across the rows in Table 18.2**A**), the

---

[8] Note that Equation 18.10 is a simple rearrangement of the DDM formula, with $\text{ROE} \times b = g$. Because that formula requires that $g < k$, Equation 18.10 is valid only when $\text{ROE} \times b < k$.

P/E ratio does not (move across the rows in panel **B**). In the top row of Table 18.2**B**, the P/E falls as the plowback rate increases. In the middle row, it is unaffected by plowback. In the third row, it increases.

This pattern has a simple interpretation. When the expected ROE is less than the required return, k, investors prefer that the firm pay out earnings as dividends rather than reinvest earnings in the firm at an inadequate rate of return. That is, for ROE lower than k, the value of the firm falls as plowback increases. Conversely, when ROE exceeds k, the firm offers superior investment opportunities, so the value of the firm is enhanced as those opportunities are more fully exploited by increasing the plowback rate.

Finally, where ROE just equals k, the firm offers "break-even" investment opportunities with a fair rate of return. In this case, investors are indifferent between reinvestment of earnings in the firm or elsewhere at the market capitalization rate, because the rate of return in either case is 12 percent. Therefore, the stock price is unaffected by the plowback rate.

One way to summarize these relationships is to say the higher the plowback rate, the higher the growth rate, but a higher plowback rate does not necessarily mean a higher P/E ratio. A higher plowback rate increases P/E only if investments undertaken by the firm offer an expected rate of return higher than the market capitalization rate. Otherwise, higher plowback hurts investors because it means more money is sunk into prospects with inadequate rates of return.

Concept Check

> Question 7. ABC stock has an expected ROE of 12 percent per year, expected earnings per share of $2, and expected dividends of $1.50 per share. Its market capitalization rate is 10 percent per year.
> *a.* What are its expected growth rate, its price, and its P/E ratio?
> *b.* If the plowback rate were 0.4, what would be the expected dividend per share, the growth rate, price, and the P/E ratio?

Pitfalls in P/E Analysis

No description of P/E analysis is complete without mentioning some of its pitfalls. First, consider that the denominator in the P/E ratio is accounting earnings, which are influenced by somewhat arbitrary accounting rules such as the use of historical cost in depreciation and inventory valuation. In times of high inflation, historic cost depreciation and inventory costs will tend to underrepresent true economic values because the replacement cost of both goods and capital equipment will rise with the general level of prices. Historically, P/E ratios have tended to be lower when inflation has been higher. This reflects the market's assessment that earnings in these periods are of "lower quality," artificially distorted by inflation, and warranting lower P/E ratios.

Another confounding factor in the use of P/E ratios is related to the business cycle. We were careful in deriving the DDM to define earnings as being net of *economic* depreciation, that is, the maximum flow of income that the firm could pay out without depleting its productive capacity. And reported earnings, as we note above, are computed in accordance with generally accepted accounting principles and need not correspond to economic earnings. Beyond this, however, notions of a normal or justified P/E ratio, as in Equations 18.9 or 18.10, assume implicitly that earnings rise at a constant rate, or, put another way, on a smooth trend line. In contrast, reported earnings can fluctuate dramatically around a trend line over the course of the business cycle.

Another way to make this point is to note that the "normal" P/E ratio predicted by Equation 18.10 is the ratio of today's price to the trend value of future earnings, E_1. The P/E ratio reported in the financial pages of the newspaper, by contrast, is the ratio of price to the most recent *past* accounting earnings. Current accounting earnings can differ considerably from future economic earnings. Because ownership of stock conveys the right to future as well as current earnings, the ratio of price to most recent earnings can vary substantially over the business cycle, as accounting earnings and the trend value of economic earnings diverge by greater and lesser amounts.

Because the market values the entire stream of future dividends generated by the company, when earnings are temporarily depressed, the P/E ratio should tend to be high—that is, the denominator of the ratio responds more sensitively to the business cycle than the numerator. This is why analysts must be careful in using P/E ratios. There is no way to say a P/E ratio is overly high or low without referring to the company's long-run growth prospects, as well as to current earnings per share relative to the long-run trend line.

18.5 *Capitalized Earnings Models*

Equity valuation often focuses on earnings rather than dividends. As you know from earlier discussion, the relationship between earnings and dividends in any period t, assuming no external equity financing, is

$$\text{Dividends}_t = \text{Earnings}_t - \text{Reinvested earnings}_t$$

It follows that the present value of all expected dividends must equal the present value of expected earnings minus the present value of expected reinvested earnings. Therefore

$$V_0 = \sum_{t=1}^{\infty} \frac{D_t}{(1 + k)^t} = \sum_{t=1}^{\infty} \frac{E_t}{(1 + k)^t} - \sum_{t=1}^{\infty} \frac{I_t}{(1 + k)^t} \qquad \textbf{(18.11)}$$

Recognize that equation 18.11 does *not* imply that the value of a firm is equal to the PV of expected future earnings. It says that the firm's value equals the PV of expected future earnings *less* the PV of the earnings reinvested in the firm.

If the expected ROE on reinvested earnings is equal to k, then even the most complicated multistage DDM reduces to the simplest capitalized earnings model:

$$V_0 = E(E_1)/k$$

The reason is that in this special case the net present value of all new investment is zero, so the firm is worth the same as if it paid all earnings out as dividends and was not expected to grow at all.

For example, let us return to our two-stage growth model of Northern Telecom stock. We assumed that the ROE in years 4 and beyond was going to be 14 percent per year, while the market capitalization rate was 13.2%. Had we assumed that the ROE in years 4 and beyond was going to be 13.2 percent rather than 14 percent per year, then our estimate of P_3 would be $E(E_4)/k = \$3.19/.132 = \$24.17$, rather than \$35.49. The resulting intrinsic value would therefore be \$17.65, rather than \$25.46.

Note that if Northern Telecom continues to plow back 84 percent of its earnings in years 4 and beyond, the growth rate of earnings and dividends will be 11.09 percent per year ($.84 \times 13.2$ percent). The expected price of a share at $T = 3$, however, will be the same as if it paid out all earnings as dividends.

$$P_3 = E(D_4)/(k - g) = \$0.511/(.132 - .1109) = \$24.22$$

Many analysts employ a simple two-step earnings-based approach to equity valuation. First, they forecast earnings per share, and then they multiply this forecast by an "appropriate" earnings multiplier. Usually, this multiplier is chosen according to some ad hoc empirical rule. The simplest such rule would be to apply the P/E multiple for the TSE 300.

For example, if our estimate of Northern Telecom's next earnings per share is \$2.40, and the P/E multiple for the TSE 300 is 12, then our estimate of the intrinsic value of a share of Northern Telecom stock would be \$28.80. A more sophisticated version of this approach is to compute P/E multiples by industry group. Thus, we might find that for companies in the electrical equipment industry the average P/E multiple is 14. When we apply this multiplier to Northern Telecom's estimated EPS of \$2.40, we get an intrinsic value of \$33.60 per share.

An even more sophisticated approach would be to base the multiplier on factors such as the firm's beta, its expected growth rate of earnings, and its dividend payout ratio. If done in the way described in earlier sections of this chapter, the resultant estimate of intrinsic value will be the same as that produced by the DDM. Usually, however, analysts who employ the earnings multiplier approach do not worry about whether their results are consistent with the DDM.

18.6 *Corporate Finance and the Free Cash Flow Approach*

In both the discounted dividend and capitalized earnings approaches to equity valuation we made the assumption that the only source of financing of new equity investment in the firm was retained earnings. How would our results be affected if we allowed external equity financing of new investments? How would they be affected if we assumed debt financing of new investments? In other words, how do dividend policy and capital structure affect the value of a firm's shares?

The classic answer to these questions was provided by Modigliani and Miller (MM) in a series of articles that have become the foundation for the modern theory of corporate finance,[9] and we will briefly explain the main points of their theory.[10]

MM claim that if we take as given a firm's future investments, then the value of its existing common stock is not affected by how those investments are financed. Therefore, neither the firm's dividend policy nor its capital structure should affect the value of a share of its equity.

The basic reasoning underlying the MM theory is that the intrinsic value of the equity in a firm is the present value of the net cash flows to shareholders that can be produced by the firm's existing assets plus the net present value of any investments to be made in the future. Given those existing and expected future investments, the firm's dividend and financing decisions will affect only the form in which existing shareholders will receive their future returns, that is, as dividends or capital gains, but not their present value.

As a by-product of their proof of these propositions, MM show the equivalence of three seemingly different approaches to valuing the equity in a firm. The first two are the discounted dividend and capitalized earnings approaches presented in the earlier parts of this chapter. The third is the free cash flow approach.

This third approach starts with an estimate of the value of the firm as a whole and derives the value of the equity by subtracting the market value of all non-equity claims. The estimate of the value of the firm is found as the present value of cash flows, assuming all-equity financing plus the net present value of tax shields created by using debt. This approach is similar to that used by the firm's

---

[9] The original two papers are M. Miller and F. Modigliani, "Dividend Policy, Growth and the Valuation of Shares," *Journal of Business,* October 1961; and F. Modigliani and M. Miller, "The Cost of Capital, Corporation Finance, and the Theory of Investment," *American Economic Review,* June 1958. Miller has revised his views in "Debt and Taxes," *Journal of Finance,* May 1976, and Modigliani his in "Debt, Dividend Policy, Taxes, Inflation and Market Valuation," *Journal of Finance,* May 1982.

[10] For a more complete treatment see Stephen A. Ross and Randolph W. Westerfield, *Corporate Finance* (St. Louis: Times Mirror/Mosby, 1988), Chapters 14 and 15.

own management in capital budgeting, or the valuation approach that another firm would use in assessing the firm as a possible acquisition target.

For example, consider the MiMo Corporation. Its cash flow from operations before interest and taxes was $1 million in the year just ended, and it expects that this will grow by 6 percent per year forever. To make this happen, the firm will have to invest an amount equal to 15 percent of pretax cash flow each year. The tax rate is 30 percent. Depreciation was $100,000 in the year just ended and is expected to grow at the same rate as the operating cash flow. The appropriate market capitalization rate for the unleveraged cash flow is 10 percent per year, and the firm currently has debt of $2 million outstanding.

MiMo's projected free cash flow for the coming year is

Before-tax cash flow from operations	$1,060,000
Depreciation	106,000
Taxable income	954,000
Taxes (at 30%)	286,200
After-tax unleveraged income	667,800
After-tax cash flow from operations (after-tax unlevered income plus depreciation)	773,800
New investment (15% of cash flow from operations)	159,000
Free cash flow (after-tax cash flow from operations minus new investment)	614,800

It is important to realize that this projected free cash flow is what the firm's cash flow would be under all-equity financing. It ignores the interest expense on the debt, as well as any tax savings resulting from the deductibility of the interest expense.

The present value of all future free cash flows is

$$V_0 = \frac{C_1}{k - g}$$
$$= \frac{\$614,800}{.1 - .06} = \$15,370,000$$

Thus the value of the whole firm, debt plus equity, is $15,370,000. Since the value of the debt is $2 million, the value of the equity is $13,370,000.

If we believe that the use of financial leverage enhances the total value of the firm, then we should add to the $15,370,000 estimate of the firm's unleveraged value the gain from leverage. Thus, if in our example we believe that the tax shield provided by the deductibility of interest payments on the debt increases the firm's total value by $.5 million, the value of the firm would be $15,870,000 and the value of the equity $13,870,000.

In reconciling this free cash flow approach with either the discounted dividend or the capitalized earnings approaches, it is important to realize that the capitalization rate to be used in the present value calculation is different. In the free cash flow approach it is the rate appropriate for unleveraged equity, whereas in the other two approaches it is the rate appropriate for leveraged equity. Since leverage affects the stock's beta, these two capitalization rates will be different.

18.7   *Inflation and Equity Valuation*

What about the effects of inflation on stock prices? We can study that by starting with the sample case where the current price is unaffected by inflation, then explore the ways in which reality might differ.

Consider the case of Inflatotrend, a firm that in the absence of inflation pays out all earnings as dividends. Earnings and dividends per share are $1, and there is no growth. We will use asterisked (*) letters to denote variables in the no-inflation case, or what represents the real value of variables. We again consider an equilibrium capitalization rate, k^*, of 10 percent per year. The price per share of this stock should be $10:

$$P_0 = \frac{\$1}{.1} = \$10$$

Now imagine that inflation (i) is 6 percent per year, but that the values of the other economic variables adjust so as to leave their real values unchanged. Specifically, the *nominal* interest or capitalization rate, k, becomes $(1 + k^*)$ $(1 + i) - 1 = 1.10 \times 1.06 - 1 = .166$ or 16.6 percent, and the expected nominal growth rate of dividends, g, is now 6 percent, which is necessary to maintain a constant level of real dividends. The *nominal* dividend expected at the end of this year is therefore $1.06 per share.

If we apply the constant growth DDM to these nominal variables we get the same price as in the no-inflation case:

$$P_0 = \frac{E(D_1)}{k - g}$$
$$= \frac{\$1.06}{.166 - .060}$$
$$= \frac{\$1.06}{.106}$$
$$= \$10$$

Thus, as long as real values are unaffected, the stock's current price is unaffected by inflation.

Note that the expected nominal dividend yield, $E(D_1)/P_0$, is 10.6 percent and the expected nominal capital gains rate, $[E(P_1) - P_0]/P_0$ is 6 percent. Almost the entire 6.6 percent increase in nominal HPR comes in the form of expected capital gains. A capital gain is necessary if the real value of the stock is to remain unaffected by inflation.

Let us see how these assumptions affect the other variables: earnings and the plowback ratio. To illuminate what otherwise may be confusing implications, we can explore a simplified story behind the examples above.

Inflatotrend produces a product that requires purchase of inventory at the beginning of each year, processing, and sale of the finished product at the end of the year. Last year there was no inflation. The inventory cost $10 million. Labour, rent, and other processing costs (paid at year-end) were $1 million, and revenue was $12 million. Assuming no taxes, earnings were $1 million.

Revenue	$12 million
−Labour and rent	1 million
−Cost of goods sold	10 million
Earnings	$1 million

All earnings are distributed as dividends to the 1 million shareholders. Because the only invested capital is the $10 million in inventory, the ROE is 10 percent.

This year inflation of 6 percent is expected, and all prices are expected to rise at that rate. As inventory is paid for at the beginning of the year it will still cost $10 million. However, revenue will be $12.72 million instead of $12 million, and other costs will be $1.06 million.

Nominal Earnings	
Revenue	$12.72 million
−Labour and rent	1.06 million
−Cost of goods sold	10.00 million
Earnings	$1.66 million
ROE	16.6%

Note that the amount required to replace inventory at year's end is $10.6 million, rather than the beginning cost of $10 million, so the amount of cash available to distribute as dividends is $1.06 million, not the reported earnings of $1.66 million.

A dividend of $1.06 million would be just enough to keep the real value of dividends unchanged and at the same time allow for maintenance of the same real value of inventory. The reported earnings of $1.66 million overstate true economic earnings, in other words.

We thus have the following set of relationships:

	No Inflation	6% Inflation
Dividends	$1 million	$1.06 million
Reported earnings	$1 million	$1.06 million
ROE	10%	16.6%
Plowback ratio	0	.36145
Price of a share	$10	$10
P/E ratio	10	6.0241

There are some surprising findings in this case of "neutral" inflation, that is, inflation that leaves the real interest rate and real earnings unaffected. While nominal dividends rise at the rate of inflation, 6 percent, reported earnings increase initially by 66 percent. In subsequent years, as long as inflation remains at a constant rate of 6 percent, earnings will grow at 6 percent.

Note also that the plowback ratio rises from 0 to .36145. Although plowback in the no-inflation case was zero, positive plowback of reported earnings now becomes necessary to maintain a constant value real inventory level. Inventory must rise from a nominal level of $10 million to a level of $10.6 million to maintain its real value. This inventory investment requires reinvested earnings of $.6 million.

Thus, the proportion of reported income that must be retained and reinvested to keep the real growth rate of earnings at zero is .36145 if inflation is 6 percent per year. Multiplying this plowback ratio by the nominal ROE of 16.6 percent produces a nominal growth rate of dividends of 6 percent, which is equal to the inflation rate:

$$g = b \times \text{ROE}$$
$$= .36145 \times 16.6\%$$
$$= 6\% \text{ per year}$$

More generally, the relationship between nominal and real variables is:

Variable	Real	Nominal
Growth rate	g^*	$g = (1 + g^*)(1 + i) - 1$
Capitalization rate	k^*	$k = (1 + k^*)(1 + i) - 1$
Return on equity	ROE^*	$\text{ROE} = (1 + \text{ROE}^*)(1 + i) - 1$
Expected dividend	$E(D_1^*)$	$E(D_1) = (1 + i)E(D_1^*)$
Plowback ratio	b^*	$b = \dfrac{(1 + b^* \times \text{ROE}^*)(1 + i) - 1}{(1 + \text{ROE}^*)(1 + i) - 1}$

Note that it is not true that $E(E_1) = (1 + i)E(E_1^*)$. That is, expected reported earnings do not, in general, equal expected real earnings times one plus the inflation rate. The reason, as you have seen, is that stated earnings do not accurately measure the cost of replenishing assets.

For example, cost of goods sold is treated as if it were $10 million, even though it now costs $10.6 million to replace the inventory. Original cost accounting in this case distorts the measured cost of goods sold, which in turn distorts the reported earnings figures. We will return to this point in Chapter 19.

Note also the effect of inflation on the P/E ratio. In our example, the P/E ratio drops from 10 in the no-inflation scenario to 6.0241 in the 6 percent inflation scenario. This is entirely a result of the fact that the reported earnings figure gets distorted by inflation and overstates true economic earnings.

This is true in the real world too, not just in our simplified example. Many companies show gains in reported earnings during inflationary periods, even though real earnings may be unaffected. This is one reason analysts must interpret data on the past behaviour of P/E ratios over time with greater care.

For many years, financial economists considered stocks to be an inflation-neutral investment in the sense that we have described. They believed, and many of them still believe, that changes in the rate of inflation, whether expected or unexpected, have no effect on the expected real rate of return on common stocks.

Recent empirical research, however, seems to indicate that real rates of return are negatively correlated with inflation. In terms of the simple constant growth rate DDM, this would mean that an increase in inflation is associated

Concept Check

> Question 8. Assume that Inflatotrend has a 4 percent annual expected constant growth rate of earnings if there is no inflation. $E(E_1^*) = \$1$ per share; ROE* = 10 percent per year; $b^* = .4$; and $k^* = 10$ percent per year.
>
> *a.* What is the current price of a share ex-dividend?
> *b.* What are the expected real dividend yield and rate of capital appreciation?
> *c.* If the firm's real revenues and dividends are unaffected by inflation, and expected inflation is 6 percent per year, what should be the nominal growth rate of dividends, the expected nominal divided yield, the expected ROE, and the nominal plowback ratio?

with (but is not necessarily caused by) either a decrease in $E(D_1)$, an increase in k, a decrease in g, or some combination of all three.

One school of thought[11] believes that economic "shocks" such as the OPEC oil price hikes have caused a simultaneous increase in the inflation rate and decline of expected real earnings (and dividends). This would demonstrate a negative correlation between inflation and real stock returns.

A second view[12] is that the higher the rate of inflation, the riskier real stock returns are perceived to be. The reasoning here is that higher inflation is associated with greater uncertainty about the economy, which tends to induce a higher required rate of return on equity. In addition, a higher k implies a lower level of stock prices.

A third perspective[13] is that higher inflation results in lower real dividends because our tax system causes lower after-tax real earnings as the inflation rate rises.

Finally, there is the view[14] that most investors in the stock market suffer from a form of "money illusion." Investors mistake the rise in the nominal rate of interest for a rise in the real rate. As a result, they undervalue stocks in a period of higher inflation.

We will have more to say about the behaviour of the aggregate stock market in the face of inflation and the hypotheses advanced to account for it in Section 18.9.

---

[11] See Eugene F. Fama, "Stock Returns, Real Activity, Inflation, and Money," *American Economic Review,* September 1981.

[12] See Burton Malkiel, *A Random Walk Down Wall Street,* 4th edition. (New York: W.W. Norton & Co., Inc., 1985).

[13] See Martin Feldstein, "Inflation and the Stock Market," *American Economic Review,* December 1980.

[14] See Franco Modigliani and Richard Cohn, "Inflation, Rational Valuation, and the Market," *Financial Analysts Journal,* March–April 1979.

18.8 *Macroeconomic Analysis*

The Macro Economy

An investment analysts must understand the macro economy because it determines the environment in which all firms operate. The ability to forecast the macro economy can translate into spectacular investment performance, but it is not sufficient to forecast the macro economy well—to earn abnormal profits, one must forecast it better than one's competitors.

Some of the key variables that analysts use to assess the state of the macro economy include the *gross domestic product* (GDP), the *unemployment rate, inflation, interest rates,* and the *budget deficit.* The GDP measures the total production of goods and services and allows the tracking of the rate of growth in the economy; this can be more narrowly focused on industrial production. Employment statistics and capacity utilization rates help analysts determine whether the economy may be overheating. This is closely related to the inflation rate, where various precise measures are used to identify the cause and probable course of inflationary pressures. The perceived trade-off between inflation and unemployment is at the heart of many macroeconomic policy disputes. Interest rates generally respond to inflation, but they are managed by the central bank policy as well. They also follow from the budget deficit, which is the difference between government spending and revenues. Government borrowing as a result of deficits puts upward pressure on interest rates; excessive borrowing will "crowd out" private borrowing by forcing up interest rates.

In an export-dependent economy, such as Canada's, the international variables of the *exchange rate* and the *current account* are crucial. Exchange rates, primarily against the U.S. dollar, determine the balance between exports and imports; they also affect inflation through the domestic cost of imported goods. The current account is determined by the difference between the value of imports and exports and by international transfers of investment funds; these transfers depend greatly on the investment decisions of foreigners holding Canadian assets and Canadians holding foreign assets. Persistent trade deficits (the major component of the current account) will cause the dollar to depreciate. Thus, we have a complex interplay of forces affecting interest rates, inflation, and exchange rates resulting from government policies and private investment and production decisions.

Demand and Supply Shocks and Government Policy

A useful way to organize the analysis of the factors that might influence the macro economy is to classify any impact as a demand or supply shock. A

demand shock is an event that affects the demand for goods and services. Examples of positive demand shocks are reductions in tax rates, increases in the money supply, increases in government spending, or increases in foreign export demand. A **supply shock** is an event that influences production capacity and costs. Examples of supply shocks are droughts that might reduce quantities of crops, changes in the immigration policies that increase the number of skilled labourers, or changes in the labour code governing wage rates or union activity.

Demand shocks are usually characterized by aggregate output moving in the same direction as interest rates and inflation. Thus, an increase in government spending will stimulate the economy and increase GDP, with a likely increase in borrowing, interest rates, and even inflation. A supply shock has the opposite effect—aggregate output usually moves counter to interest rates and inflation. Increases in world prices of oil increase production costs and prices of finished goods; the inflationary pressure results in higher interest rates and lower production as individuals are less able to purchase more expensive goods.

The federal government has two broad classes of macroeconomic tools with which to attempt to regulate the economy—those that affect demand and those affecting supply. **Fiscal policy** includes taxation and government spending, and has a pronounced effect on demand. Increases in taxes directly restrict consumption and rapidly rein in the economy. An increase in government spending, on the other hand, fuels demand and can cause a prompt increase in production. An increase in one without a corresponding increase in the other changes the deficit; thus a stimulative or restrictive shock can be given to the economy.

The other tool of demand-side policy is **monetary policy**, which refers to the manipulation of the money supply and works mainly through its impact on interest rates. The money supply is increased or decreased by the purchase or sale of securities by the Bank of Canada; the money paid for a security by the bank is a direct increase to the money supply. The bank can also raise or lower the bank rate to make borrowing more or less costly, thereby affecting investment. These tools are easier to implement but less effective than fiscal policy. Many economists believe that an increased money supply leads only to inflation in the long run.

The failure of economic policy to manage the economy of most western nations in past decades, as evidenced by high inflation, high deficits, and high unemployment, as well as severe recessions induced by restrictive monetary policies, has been blamed on the inadequacies of demand-side policies. Consequently, the 1980s saw the emergence of supply-side economics. This approach focuses on the productive capacity of the economy. Its goal is to create an environment in which workers and owners of capital have the maximum incentive and ability to produce and develop goods. Hence, the emphasis is on tax policy and the incentives that it defines; lower tax rates lead to more incentives to provide capital and labour, thereby enhancing economic growth.

TABLE 18.3   Components of Leading Economic Indicators' Composite Index

Retail Sales	**Manufacturing**
Furniture and appliances	New orders—durables
Other durable sales	Ratio of shipments to stocks
	Average work week
Financial	Business and personnel services employment
Real money supply	
Toronto stock market (TSE 300)	**House Spending**
	U.S. Index

Business Cycles

The economy recurrently experiences periods of expansion and contraction, although the length and depth of those cycles can be irregular. This pattern of recession and recovery is called the **business cycle**. Given this cyclical nature, it is not surprising that the cycle can be predicted. Statistics Canada has developed a set of cyclical indicators to help forecast and measure short-term fluctuations in economic activity. **Leading economic indicators** are those economic series that tend to rise or fall in advance of the rest of the economy.

Ten series are grouped into a widely followed composite index of leading economic indicators, as specified in Table 18.3. Figure 18.1 on page 622 graphs percent changes in the composite leading indicator series against changes in the GDP and the coincident series of industrial production for the years 1986–1992. It is not at all apparent that the leading indicator series is earning its title over this period!

The stock market price index is a leading indicator.[15] As the accompanying box shows, the relationship is far from reliable, but stock prices should lead because they are forward-looking estimates of future profitability. Unfortunately, this makes the series of leading indicators much less useful for investment policy—by the time the series predicts an upturn, the market has already made its move. While the business cycle may be somewhat predictable, the stock market may not be. This is one more manifestation of the efficient market hypothesis.

---

[15] See, for example, Stanley Fischer and Robert C. Merton, "Macroeconomics and Finance: The Role of the Stock Market," *Carnegie-Rochester Conference Series on Public Policy* 21 (1984).

The Stock Market Is a Lousy Economic Forecaster

People wait anxiously for the other shoe to drop: The stock market has crashed [1987]—508 points in one day, 983 points over two months. Now, what happens to the economy? Will it, too, crash or at least take a nasty spill?

If the history of the past six decades is a guide, the answer is probably not. Barrie A. Wigmore of Goldman, Sachs & Co. is author of *The Crash and Its Aftermath*, a definitive economic history of the early 1930s. Here's what he says: "This year's boom has had little to do with the underlying strength of the U.S. economy. So why should the recent crash?" *Forbes* has dusted off the history books and picked the nine great market breaks be-ginning with 1929. What we found confirms Wigmore's view of this tenuous relationship. Our conclusion: no depression, probably no recession. At least not now.

Forbes researchers identified the nine occasions when the stock market crashed by 25 percent or more as measured by the Dow Jones industrials. Four of these "crashes" were followed by strong economic advances. Three were followed by short economic downturns. One was followed by a big, fat depression—1929.

That's not much of a forecasting record.

September 3, 1929 to July 8, 1932. A market collapse that altogether wiped out 89 percent of the

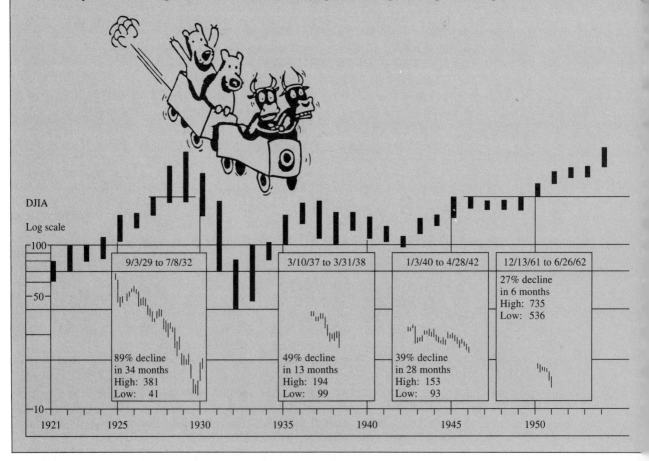

Dow industrials' value, the greatest peacetime economic loss in modern history. As we know now, that crash ushered in the Great Depression. But people didn't know that then. In two months the Dow industrials lost 48 percent of their value, but the economy kept on growing and ended the year with GNP substantially above year-earlier levels. Even business writer Alexander Dana Noyes, who had been predicting the bust for months, believed the selling was overdone.

Unfortunately, the first wave of selling was followed by another collapse in 1930 (April to December), when the stock market lost 47 percent of its value. In the third sell-off (February 1931 to December 1931) the Dow lost 62 percent in value. By now the economy, too, was on the ropes. By year's end, the GNP had dropped 7.7 percent below 1930 levels in constant dollars, and unemployment stood at 25 percent of the labour force.

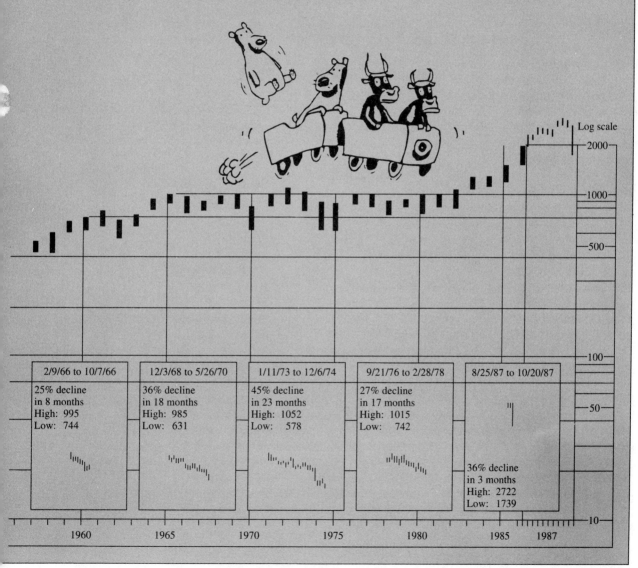

Log scale

2/9/66 to 10/7/66	12/3/68 to 5/26/70	1/11/73 to 12/6/74	9/21/76 to 2/28/78	8/25/87 to 10/20/87
25% decline in 8 months High: 995 Low: 744	36% decline in 18 months High: 985 Low: 631	45% decline in 23 months High: 1052 Low: 578	27% decline in 17 months High: 1015 Low: 742	36% decline in 3 months High: 2722 Low: 1739

1960   1965   1970   1975   1980   1985 1987

(Continued)

The fourth slide (March to July 1932) wiped out 54 percent of what little value the Dow averages still retained. But any brave soul who bought stocks at this point would have come out a rich man. This fourth collapse was followed by a sustained five-year bull market, in which the Dow averages rose 372 percent.

March 10, 1937 to March 31, 1938, the so-called Roosevelt recession. Here the stock market did accurately predict a slowdown. Ironically, that slowdown came when Roosevelt yielded to pressures similar to those now weighing on Washington and cut spending to balance the budget. Waves of strikes ensued as the economy began slowly to reverse course and slide back into recession. The downturn lasted for about a year, ending when the administration began some Keynesian pump-priming.

January 3, 1940 to April 28, 1942. During this 28-month period, Dow stocks lost an average of 39 percent in value, as investors blamed everything from Roosevelt's health to the danger that Germany and Japan might win the war. Through it all, the economy kept on growing, with the GNP nearly doubling from 1940 to 1943, while war mobilization cut unemployment from 8.1 percent to 1.1 percent over the same period.

December 13, 1961 to June 26, 1962. The so-called Kennedy correction. During the six-month period, Dow stocks lost 27 percent in value. Many investors at the time blamed the administration's confrontation with the steel industry, leaving fears of an antibusiness era. There was growing international tension with the Bay of Pigs and the Berlin Wall. But whatever the cause, the economy remained strong. Already in the second year of an advance, it continued right on growing, racking up gains of 4 percent or more in GNP annually through the rest of the decade. This was the longest period of sustained economic growth since the end of World War II.

February 9, 1966 to October 7, 1966. During this eight-month period, Dow stocks dropped 25 percent in value as investors grew wary of Lyndon Johnson's guns-and-butter economic strategy. But even rising interest rates and tight money from William McChesney Martin Jr. at the Federal Reserve failed to halt growth, and by early 1967, stocks were once again rising smartly.

December 3, 1968 to May 26, 1970. The Nixon slide, 36 percent. During this 18-month period, Wall Street's speculative excesses of the Johnson era were wiped out, creating a long list of famous casualties, from James Ling of LTV to Bernie Cornfeld of IOS. Corporate casualties included Penn Central Corp., F.I. du Pont & Co. and a host of lesser names on Wall Street.

Then, as now, prophets of doom were not lacking. In May of 1970, at the very trough of the decline, liberal economist John Kenneth Galbraith reportedly likened the year to 1929, suggesting that even more wrenching declines lay ahead. Anyone who listened to Harvard's sage soon regretted doing so. Though the economy declined throughout the remainder of 1970, the stock market took off on a two-year advance.

January 11, 1973 to December 6, 1974. This 23-month bear market, which knocked 45 percent off the Dow industrials, did precede a recession. But the steepest drop (March to December 1974) came as a consequence of a recession. The economy was already reeling from rising petroleum prices when investors began pulling their money out of Wall Street. Hardest hit: the so-called Nifty Fifty blue-chip stocks like Polaroid and Avon, which had gotten wildly overpriced in the previous bull market and now lost, in some cases, 90 percent of their value.

The recession—which started before the steepest market collapse—lasted 16 months, until spring 1975. But anyone watching economic indicators for when to return to the market would have missed out. The Dow industrials had begun to improve three months earlier, indicating what wise investors have known all along: The market is a much better predictor of recoveries than of recessions.

September 21, 1976 to February 28, 1978. The economy had been relentlessly advancing since the spring of 1975 when Wall Street grew wary that Jimmy Carter might defeat Gerald Ford and unleash a round of Democratically inspired runaway spending in Washington. Carter did defeat Ford, spending did balloon, inflation did explode, and the stock market did plunge 27 percent in the following 17 months. Yet through it all, the economy continued to advance for another five years.

The fact is that the stock market often responds to its own internal momentum and, at other times, to a misapprehension of what lies ahead. Take the "Dow theory collapse" that lasted from May to October of 1946. This was not quite rough enough to make our list of crashes, but it was a nasty one all the same. During this five-month period, the Dow industrials dropped 23 percent, and jittery investors fretted that a new depression was just over the horizon. In fact, as a subsequent study by the Securities & Exchange Commission showed, much of the selling was caused by large numbers of investors reacting to the Dow theory "sell signal" and dumping stocks when the Dow industrial average dropped down through 186.02, a presumed support level.

Does the October crash foreshadow an economic collapse? Only one in nine major crashes has done so in 60 years. The odds are slightly better that it may foreshadow a recession of some kind. But the odds are highest that it presages nothing more severe than correction of the market's own previous excesses on the upside.

18.9   *The Aggregate Stock Market and Industry Analysis*

Explaining Past Behaviour

Most scholars and serious analysts would agree that, although the stock market appears to have a substantial life of its own, responding perhaps to bouts of mass euphoria and then panic, economic events and the anticipation of such events do have a substantial effect on stock prices.[16] Perhaps the two factors with the greatest impact are interest rates and corporate profits.

Figure 18.2 shows the behaviour of the difference between the yield to maturity on long-term Canada bonds and earnings-to-price ratio (i.e., the earnings yield) of the TSE 300 stock index over the 35-year period 1955–1990. Our discussion of valuation models earlier in this chapter gives us some insights into the relationship between these two yields.

In the absence of inflation and assuming that the expected ROE on future real investments in the corporate sector is equal to the equity capitalization rate and that current earnings per share equal expected future earnings per share, the earnings yield on the TSE 300 represents the expected real rate of return on the stock market. This should be equal to the yield to maturity on Canada bonds plus a risk premium, which may change slowly over time.

Inflation will alter this relationship for several reasons. First, as shown earlier in this chapter, even in the case of neutral inflation reported earnings tend to rise in a period of high inflation. Thus, at least part of the sharp drop in

---

[16] For a discussion of the current debate on the rationality of the stock market, see the suggested readings at the end of this chapter.

Annual percent change

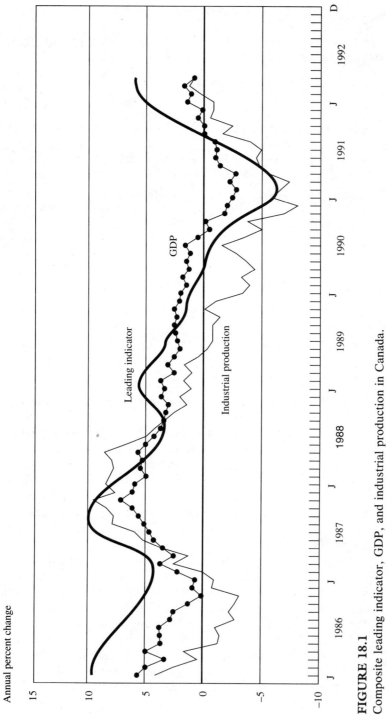

FIGURE 18.1

Composite leading indicator, GDP, and industrial production in Canada.

[Source: *Canadian Economic Observer*, Statistics Canada, Cat. No. 11-010 (July 1992). Reproduced with the permission of the Minister of Industry, Science, and Technology, 1992.]

the 1970s from the graph in Figure 18.2 can be attributed to the sharp rise in the rate of inflation during that period.

However, a more important fact is that the yield to maturity on long-term bonds is a nominal rate that embodies the inflation expectations of market participants. The earnings yield on common stocks, on the other hand, is a real yield. Thus, if stocks are inflation neutral, the difference between the earnings yield on stocks and the yield to maturity on Canada bonds will reflect both the risk premium on stocks and the expected long-run inflation rate. This implies that when the expected rate of inflation is low, the earnings yield on stocks should exceed the yield to maturity on bonds, and when the expected rate of inflation is high, the reverse should be true.

For example, suppose that in the absence of inflation the earnings yield on stocks is 9 percent per year and the yield to maturity on bonds 3 percent per year, implying an equity risk premium of 6 percent per year. As you can see in Figure 18.2, this appeared to be the case in the late 1960s and early 1970s, until (approximately) the first oil shock of 1973. Now suppose the expected rate of inflation is 8 percent per year. If stocks are inflation neutral, the earnings yield will still be 9 percent. (If, as some have suggested, stocks are perceived to be riskier when the inflation rate rises, then the earnings yield will be higher.) But the yield to maturity on bonds, since it is a nominal rate, will jump to 11 percent per year. Thus, the yield to maturity on bonds will exceed the earnings yield on stocks by 2 percent per year, the difference between the expected rate of inflation (8 percent per year) and the equity risk premium (6 percent per year). These hypothetical relationships are summarized in Table 18.4.

Something like this appears to be what actually happened in the 1980s. Of course, other things that might have affected stock and bond yields were happening during this period as well. Perhaps the most important were changes in the relative risk of stocks and bonds. Long-term bonds, in particular, became much riskier during this period as a result of changes in Bank of Canada monetary policy and the variability in the inflation rate.

FIGURE 18.2

Long-term bond yield minus earnings yield of TSE 300. (From Burns Fry Limited Equity Investment Strategy Group, September, 1990. By permission of Burns Fry Ltd.)

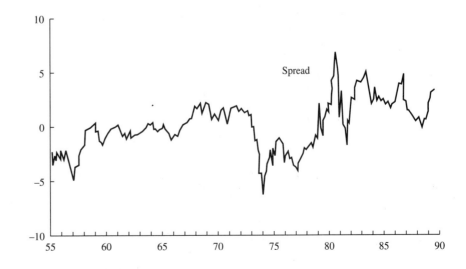

TABLE 18.4   Effect of Inflation on Stock and Bond Yields

Rate of Inflation	Earnings Yield on Stocks (% per Year)	Yield to Maturity on Bonds (% per Year)
0	9	3
8%	9	11

Forecasting the Stock Market

What can we learn from all of this about the future rate of return on stocks? First, a note of optimism. Although timing the stock market is a very difficult and risky game, it is not impossible.

In the early 1980s, several serious scholars of the stock market were predicting that as the rate of inflation came down the stock market would do extraordinarily well. For example, in the fourth edition of his classic book, *A Random Walk Down Wall Street*, Malkiel[17] predicted a compound rate of return of 17 percent per year during the decade of the 1980s. In fact, the average compound rate of return on the S&P 500 during the five-year period 1982–1987 was 17 percent per year. (The equivalent rate on the TSE 300 during the same period was 13.8 percent per year.)

In addition, by the summer of 1987 (on the eve of the October 1987 stock market crash), many market analysts were warning that the market was seriously overvalued. The ensuing debacle is now history.

However, if market history teaches us anything at all, it is that the market has great variability. In the language of statistics, the standard deviation is quite large. Thus, although we can use a variety of methods to derive a best-point forecast of the expected holding period return on the market, the standard error of that forecast will always be high.

The most popular approach to forecasting the stock market is the earnings multiplier approach applied at the aggregate level. The first step is to forecast corporate profits for the coming period (either a quarter or a full year). Then an estimate of the earnings multiplier is derived, based on a forecast of long-term interest rates. The product of the two forecasts is the point forecast of the end-of-period level of the market. Table 18.5 illustrates an application of this method.

Other analysts use an aggregate version of the discounted dividend model. All of these models rely heavily on forecasts of such macroeconomic variables as GNP, interest rates, and the rate of inflation, which are themselves very difficult to predict accurately.

An alternative approach is to extrapolate past rates of return on the stock market. The simplest version of this approach is to take the current Treasury

---

[17] Burton Malkiel, *A Random Walk Down Wall Street*, 4th edition (New York: W. W. Norton Co., 1985.)

TABLE 18.5   TSE 300 Price Targets under Various Scenarios

	9–12 Month Target	Other Interest Rate Possibilities		The Bull Scenario
Canada bond interest rate*	10.75%	10.25%	10.00%	9.50%
P/E ratio	11.4x†	12.1x	12.5x	13.3x
EPS (midpoint of 1988 and 1989 estimates)	$275	$275	$275	$310
TSE price target one year out	3143	3328	3438	4123

* Forecast year-end Canada bond.
† Assumes a TSE 300 earnings yield 100 basis points below the bond yield. Our reasoning is that, even though the earnings yield exceeded the bond yield for most of the post-World War II era, the earnings yield has been below the bond yield for most of the recent period, beginning with the high-inflation era and extending into the current time. We believe one of the explanations for this current relationship is the abundant liquidity that is buoying the market. In recognition of the market's willingness to accept a lower earnings yield, we assume an 8.7 percent earnings yield, which implies a P/E of 11.5x. Other tests validate this type of number.

bill rate plus the historical average risk premium on equity as the forecast value of the expected HPR on the stock market. This is the approach adopted by Ibbotson and Sinquefield.[18]

There are many variants of this approach. Perhaps the most innovative is a Bayesian approach proposed by Merton. Merton uses past data to estimate the expected HPR return on the stock market, but imposes the reasonable Bayesian "prior" that the risk premium can never be negative.[19]

Industry Analysis

Whatever the means an analyst uses to forecast the macro economy, it is necessary to determine the implication of that forecast for specific industries. Not all industries are equally sensitive to the business cycle. For example, consider Figure 18.3, which shows how various sectors of the economy responded to the recession in 1990 and 1991. While the traditional industries of transportation, construction, and manufacturing contracted, the emerging industry of communications and the evolving financial sector kept expanding through the recession.

Three factors will determine the sensitivity of a firm's earnings to the business cycle. First is the sensitivity of sales. Necessities such as food, drugs, and medical services will show little sensitivity to business conditions. Other industries with low sensitivity will be those for which income is not a crucial determinant of demand, such as tobacco products. In contrast, firms in industries such as machine tools, steel, autos, and transportation are highly sensitive to the state of the economy.

---

[18] See R. G. Ibbotson and R. A. Sinquefield, *Stocks, Bonds, Bills and Inflation: The Past and the Future*, Financial Analysts Research Foundation, 1977.
[19] See Robert C. Merton, "On Estimating the Expected Return on the Market," *Journal of Financial Economics* 8 (1980).

FIGURE 18.3

Sectoral response to
the recession.

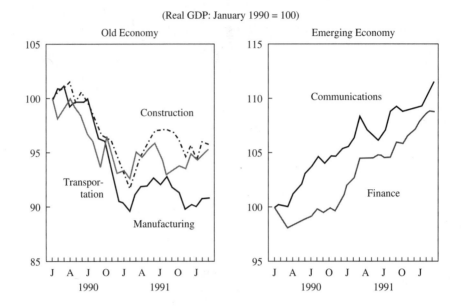

(Real GDP: January 1990 = 100)

The second factor determining business cycle sensitivity is operating lever-age, which refers to the division between fixed and variable costs. (Fixed costs are those the firm incurs regardless of its production levels. Variable costs are those that rise or fall as the firm produces more or less product.) Firms with variable as opposed to fixed costs will be less sensitive to business conditions, because in economic downturns these firms can reduce costs as output falls in response to falling sales. Profits for firms with high fixed costs will swing more widely with sales because costs do not move to offset revenue variability. Firms with high fixed costs are said to have high operating leverage, as small swings in business conditions can have large impacts on profitability.

An example might help illustrate this concept. Consider two firms operating in the same industry with identical revenues in all phases of the business cycle: recession, normal, and expansion. Firm A has short-term leases on most of its equipment and can reduce its lease expenditures when production slackens. It has fixed costs of $5 million and variable costs of $1 per unit of output. Firm B has long-term leases on most of its equipment and must make lease payments regardless of economic conditions. Its fixed costs are higher, $8 million, but its variable costs are only $.50 per unit. Table 18.6 shows that firm A will do better in recessions than firm B, but not as well in expansions. A's costs move in conjunction with its revenues to help performance in downturns and impede performance in upturns.

The third factor influencing business cycle sensitivity is financial leverage, which is the use of borrowing. Interest payments on debt must be paid regard-less of sales. They are fixed costs that also increase the sensitivity of profits to business conditions. We will have more to say about financial leverage in Chapter 19.

TABLE 18.6   Operating Leverage

	Recession Scenario		Normal Scenario		Expansion Scenario	
	Firm A	Firm B	Firm A	Firm B	Firm A	Firm B
Sales (million units)	5	5	6	6	7	7
Price per unit	$ 2	$ 2	$ 2	$ 2	$ 2	$ 2
Revenue ($ million)	10	10	12	12	14	14
Fixed costs ($ million)	5	8	5	8	5	8
Variable costs ($ million)	5	2.5	6	3	7	3.5
Total costs ($ million)	$10	$10.5	$11	$11	$12	$11.5
Profits	$ 0	$(0.5)	$ 1	$ 1	$ 2	$ 2.5

Investors should not always prefer industries with lower sensitivity to the business cycle. Firms in sensitive industries will have high-beta stocks and are riskier. But while they swing lower in downturns, they also swing higher in upturns. As always, the issue you need to address is whether the expected return on the investment is fair compensation for the risks borne.

Concept Check	Question 9. What will be profits in the three scenarios for firm C with fixed costs of $2 million and variable costs of $1.50 per unit? What are your conclusions regarding operating leverage and business risk?

18.1   *Contingent Claims Approach to Equity Valuation*

In recent years, the theory of contingent claims pricing has been applied to common stocks.[20] This approach can be a useful adjunct to the valuation models presented earlier—especially the free cash flow model—if a firm has substantial debt in its capital structure. In this approach, common stock is viewed as a call option on the assets of the firm, with an exercise price equal to the face value of the debt.

For example, suppose the Hidett Corporation has assets worth $100 million and debt with a face value of $100 million. Although the book value of the

---

[20] See Scott Mason and Robert C. Merton, "The Role of Contingent Claims Analysis in Corporate Finance," in Altman and Subramanyam (editors), *Recent Advances in Corporate Finance* (Homewood, Ill.: Richard D. Irwin, Inc., 1985).

equity may be zero, the common stock may still have a substantial market value. The equity is a call option in the sense that if the shareholders pay off the debt at its face value at maturity, then they can keep the firm's assets; otherwise assets will belong to the creditors.

Viewing the equity of Hidett Corporation as a call option on the assets of the firm gives considerable insight into the determinants of its value, as well as a well-known methodology for estimating it. A detailed exposition of the techniques used is contained in Part VII, but one insight is worth mentioning now.

How will the value of Hidett's common stock be affected if the riskiness of the firm's assets (as measured by the standard deviation of their market value) increases? The answer is that the value of the common stock will increase, just as the price of an option increases when the standard deviation of the underlying security increases.

Summary

1. One approach to estimating intrinsic value is to focus on the firm's book value, either as it appears on the balance sheet or as adjusted to reflect current replacement cost of assets or liquidation value. Another approach is to focus on the present value of expected future dividends, earnings, or free cash flow.

2. The dividend discount model (DDM) holds that the price of a share of stock should equal the present value of all future dividends per share, discounted at an interest rate commensurate with the risk of the stock.

3. The constant growth version of the DDM asserts that if dividends are expected to grow at a constant rate forever, then the intrinsic value of a share is determined by the formula:

$$V_0 = D_1/(k - g)$$

The more realistic DDMs allow for several stages of earnings growth. Usually there is an initial stage of rapid growth, followed by a final stage of constant growth at a lower sustainable rate.

4. Stock market analysts devote considerable attention to a company's price to earnings ratio. The P/E ratio is a useful measure of the market's assessment of the firm's growth opportunities. Firms with no growth opportunities should have a P/E ratio that is just the reciprocal of the capitalization rate, k. As growth opportunities become a progressively more important component of the value of the firm, the P/E ratio will increase.

5. You can relate any DDM to a simple capitalized earnings model by comparing the expected ROE on future investments to the market capitalization rate, k. If the two rates are equal, then the stock's intrinsic value reduces to expected earnings per share (EPS) divided by k.

6. Many analysts form their estimate of a stock's value by multiplying their forecast of next year's EPS by a P/E multiple derived from some empirical rule. This rule can be consistent with some version of the DDM, although often it is not.

7. The free cash flow approach is the one used most often in corporate finance. The analyst first estimates the value of the entire firm as the present value of expected future free cash flows, assuming all-equity financing, then adds the value of tax shields arising from debt financing, and finally subtracts the value of all claims other than equity. This approach will be consistent with the DDM and capitalized earnings approaches as long as the capitalization rate is adjusted to reflect financial leverage.

8. We explored the effects of inflation on stock prices in the context of the constant growth DDM. Although traditional theory has been that inflation has a neutral effect on real stock returns, recent historical evidence shows a striking negative correlation between inflation and real stock market returns. There are four different explanations that may account for this negative correlation:

   a. Economic ''shocks'' that simultaneously produce higher inflation and lower real earnings.
   b. Increased riskiness of stocks in a more inflationary environment.
   c. Lower real after-tax earnings and dividends attributable to inflation-induced distortions in the tax system.
   d. Money ''illusion.''

9. Macroeconomic analysis plays a major role in fundamental analysis; economists identify supply and demand shocks to the macro economy and the business cycle and use these in predicting future returns in the markets.

10. The models presented in this chapter can be used to explain and to forecast the behaviour of the aggregate stock market. The key macroeconomic variables that determine the level of stock prices in the aggregate are interest rates and corporate profits. The response of different sectors of the market to macroeconomic changes is called industry analysis.

11. The modern theory of contingent claims pricing has been used to value common stocks by viewing them as a call option on the assets of the firm. This approach is especially useful for valuing the equity of highly leveraged firms, where the probability of default is significant.

Key terms

Fundamental analysis	Dividend payout ratio
Technical analysis	Plowback ratio
Book value	Earnings retention ratio
Liquidation value	Price/earnings multiple
Replacement cost	Demand shock
Tobin's q	Supply shock
Intrinsic value	Fiscal policy
Market capitalization rate	Monetary policy
Dividend discount model (DDM)	Business cycle
Constant growth DDM	Leading economic indicators

Selected readings

For the key issues in the recent debate about the rationality of the stock market, see:
Cutler, David M.; Poterba, James M.; and Summers, Lawrence H., "What Moves Stock Prices?" *Journal of Portfolio Management* 15, no. 3 (1989).
Merton, Robert C. "On the Current State of the Stock Market Rationality Hypothesis." In Dornbusch, Rudiger; Fischer, Stanley; and Bossons, John (editors), *Macroeconomics and Finance, Essays in Honor of Franco Modigliani.* Cambridge, Mass.: MIT Press, 1986.
West, Kenneth D. "Bubbles, Fads, and Stock Price Volatility Tests: A Partial Evaluation." Cambridge, Mass.: National Bureau of Economic Research Working Paper No. 2574, May 1988.

Problems

1. The P/E ratio of the Bank of Nova Scotia is currently 7, while the P/E ratio of the TSE 300 is 12. How might you account for the difference?
2. According to the discounted dividend approach, the value of a firm's equity is the present value of expected future dividends. But according to many analysts, a firm's dividend policy does not affect the value of its equity. How can you reconcile these seemingly contradictory points of view?
3. "Since the value of the firm increases with the growth rate of dividends, firms should increase the plowback ratio to a value of 1.0 in order to maximize g." Under what circumstances, if any, is this statement true?
4. The FI Corporation's dividends per share are expected to grow indefinitely by 5 percent per year.
   a. If this year's year-end dividend is $8 and the market capitalization rate is 10 percent per year, what must the current stock price be according to the DDM?
   b. If the expected earnings per share are $12, what is the implied value of the ROE on future investment opportunities?
   c. How much is the market paying per share for growth opportunities (i.e., for an ROE on future investments that exceeds the market capitalization rate)?
5. (Based on the 1987 CFA Examination, Level I) Using the data provided, discuss whether the common stock of Dominion Tobacco Company is attractively priced based on at least three different valuation approaches. (Hint: use the asset value, DDM, and earnings multiplier approaches.)

	Dominion Tobacco	TSE 300
Recent price	$27.00	2900
Book value per share	$ 6.42	
Liquidation value per share	$ 4.90	
Replacement costs of assets per share	$ 9.15	
Anticipated next year's dividend	$ 1.20	$87.50
Estimated annual growth in dividends and earnings	10.0%	7.0%
Required return	13.0%	
Estimated next year's EPS	$ 2.40	$16.50
P/E ratio based on next year's earnings	11.3	17.6
Dividend yield	4.4%	3.0%

6. The risk-free rate of return is 10 percent, the required rate of return on the market is 15 percent, and High-Flyer stock has a beta coefficient of 1.5.
   a. If the dividend per share expected during the coming year, D_1, is $2.50 and $g = 5$ percent, at what price should a share sell?
   b. If it is selling at $18 per share, what is the expected HPR to a potential investor? (Assume first that the price converges to intrinsic value by the end of the holding period, and then assume that price never converges to intrinsic value.)
7. Your preliminary analysis of two stocks has yielded the information set forth below. The market capitalization rate for both stock A and stock B is 10 percent per year.

	Stock A	Stock B
Expected return on equity	14%	12%
Estimated earnings per share	$ 2.00	$ 1.65
Estimated dividends per share	$ 1.00	$ 1.00
Current market price per share	$27.00	$25.00

   a. What are the expected dividend payout ratios for the two stocks?
   b. What are the expected dividend growth rates for each?
   c. What is the intrinsic value of each stock?
   d. In which, if either, of the two stocks would you choose to invest?
   e. What is the expected one-year HPR on each of the stocks if:
      i. The market prices grow at the same rate as dividends?
      ii. The market prices converge to their intrinsic values by the end of the year?
8. (Based on the 1988 CFA Examination, Level I) The Tennant Company, founded in 1870, has evolved into the leading producer of large-sized floor sweepers and scrubbers, which are ridden by their operators. Its latest dividend per share was $.96, its earnings per share were $1.85, and its ROE was 16.9 percent.
   a. Based on these data, calculate a value for Tennant common stock by applying the constant growth dividend discount model. Assume that an investor's required rate of return is a five percentage point premium over the current risk-free rate of return of 7 percent.
   b. To your disappointment, the calculation that you completed in part *a* results in a value below the stock's current market price. Consequently, you apply the constant growth DDM with the same required rate of return as in your calculation for part *a*, but using the company's stated goal of earning 20 percent per year on stockholders' equity and maintaining a 35 percent dividend payout ratio. However, you find that you are unable to calculate a meaningful answer. Explain why this is so, and identify an alternative DDM that may provide a meaningful answer.
9. (Based on the 1986 CFA Examination, Level I) You are a portfolio manager considering the purchase of XYZ common stock. XYZ is an important Canadian steel company, which produces a limited number of products,

primarily for the construction market. You are provided the following information:

XYZ Corporation	
Stock price (Dec. 30, 1985)	$53.00
1985 estimated earnings	$ 4.25
1985 estimated book value	$25.00
Indicated dividend	$ 0.40
Beta	1.10
Risk-free return	7.0%
High-grade corporate bond yield	9.0%
Risk premium—stocks over bonds	5.0%

  a. Calculate the expected stock market return. Show your calculations.
  b. Calculate the implied total return of XYZ stock.
  c. Calculate the required return of XYZ stock using the security market line model.
  d. Briefly discuss the attractiveness of XYZ based on these data.
 10. The stock of Nogro Corporation is currently selling for $10 per share. Earnings per share in the coming year are expected to be $2. The company has a policy of paying out 50 percent of its earnings each year in dividends. The rest is retained and invested in projects that earn a 20 percent rate of return per year. This situation is expected to continue indefinitely.
  a. Assuming the current market price of the stock reflects its intrinsic value as computed using the constant growth rate DDM, what rate of return do Nogro's investors require?
  b. By how much does its value exceed what it would be if all earnings were paid as dividends and nothing were reinvested?
  c. If Nogro were to cut its dividend payout ratio to 25 percent, what would happen to its stock price? What if Nogro eliminated the dividend altogether?
  d. Suppose that Nogro wishes to maintain its current 50 percent dividend payout policy but that it also wishes to invest an amount each year equal to that year's total earnings. All the money would be invested in projects earning 20 percent per year. One way that Nogro could do so would be to issue an amount of new stock each year equal to one-half that year's earnings. What do you think would be the effect of this policy on the current stock price?
 11. The Digital Electronic Quotation System (DEQS) Corporation pays no cash dividends currently and is not expected to for the next five years. Its latest EPS was $10, all of which was reinvested in the company. The firm's expected ROE for the next five years is 20 percent per year, and during this time it is expected to continue to reinvest all of its earnings. Starting six years from now the firm's ROE on new investments is expected to fall to 15 percent, and the company is expected to start paying out 40 percent of its earnings in cash dividends, which it will continue to do forever after. DEQS' market capitalization rate is 15 percent per year.

    a. What is your estimate of DEQS' intrinsic value per share?

    b. Assuming its current market price is equal to its intrinsic value, what do you expect to happen to its price over the next year? The year after?

    c. What effect would it have on your estimate of DEQS' intrinsic value if you expected DEQS to pay out only 20 percent of earnings starting in year 6?

12. Microhard, Inc., is a computer hardware company that has been growing rapidly in recent years. You are an analyst who thinks that over the next 10 years its dividend growth rate will go from 20 percent per year to a long-run constant rate of 4 percent per year. The latest dividend per share was $3, and you think the appropriate capitalization rate is 15 percent per year.

    a. What is your estimate of Microhard's intrinsic value per share?

    b. If its current market price is $40 per share, what is the expected yield to maturity?

    c. If all expectations are realized, and Microhard's stock price moves to its new intrinsic value, what should its price be one year from now?

13. The Duo Growth Company just paid a dividend of $1 per share. The dividend is expected to grow at a rate of 25 percent per year for the next three years and then level off to 5 percent per year forever after. You think the appropriate market capitalization rate is 20 percent per year.

    a. What is your estimate of the intrinsic value of a share of the stock?

    b. If the market price of a share is equal to this intrinsic value, what is the expected dividend yield?

    c. What do you expect its price to be one year from now? Is the implied capital gain consistent with your estimate of the dividend yield and the market capitalization rate?

14. The risk-free rate of return is 8 percent, the expected rate of return on the market portfolio is 15 percent, and the stock of Xyrong Corporation has a beta coefficient of 1.2. Xyrong pays out 40 percent of its earnings in dividends, and the latest earnings announced were $10 per share. Dividends were just paid and are expected to be paid annually. You expect that Xyrong will earn an ROE of 20 percent per year on all reinvested earnings forever.

    a. What is the intrinsic value of a share of Xyrong stock?

    b. If the market price of a share is currently $100, and you expect the market price to be equal to the intrinsic value one year from now, what is your expected one-year holding period return on Xyrong stock?

15. You are a different analyst trying to evaluate Xyrong stock. You agree with the previous analyst's assessments of everything except Xyrong's future earnings and dividends. You decide to apply the *H* model, and you assume that the growth rate of dividends will start at 12 percent per year and decline linearly to a long-run rate of 4 percent per year over the next 20 years.

    a. What is your assessment of the intrinsic value of a share of Xyrong stock?

    b. If the current market price of Xyrong stock is $100 per share, what is your estimate of the yield to maturity?

c. If you expect the market price to be equal to the intrinsic value one year from now, what is your expected one-year holding period return on Xyrong stock?

16. The Generic Genetic (GG) Corporation pays no cash dividends currently and is not expected to for the next four years. Its latest EPS was $5, all of which was reinvested in the company. The firm's expected ROE for the next four years is 20 percent per year, during which time it is expected to continue to reinvest all of its earnings. Starting five years from now, the firm's ROE on new investments is expected to fall to 15 percent per year. GG's market capitalization rate is 15 percent per year.

a. What is your estimate of GG's intrinsic value per share?

b. Assuming its current market price is equal to its intrinsic value, what do you expect to happen to its price over the next year?

17. The MoMi Corporation's cash flow from operations before interest and taxes was $2 million in the year just ended, and it expects that this will grow by 5 percent per year forever. To make this happen, the firm will have to invest an amount equal to 20 percent of pretax cash flow each year. The tax rate is 34 percent. Depreciation was $200,000 in the year just ended and is expected to grow at the same rate as the operating cash flow. The appropriate market capitalization rate for the unleveraged cash flow is 12 percent per year, and the firm currently has debt of $4 million outstanding. Use the free cash flow approach to value the firm's equity.

18. The CPI Corporation is expected to pay a real dividend of $1 per share this year. Its expected growth rate of real dividends is 4 percent per year, and its current market price per share is $20.

a. Assuming the constant growth DDM is applicable, what must be the real market capitalization rate for CPI?

b. If the expected rate of inflation is 6 percent per year, what must be the nominal capitalization rate, the nominal dividend yield, and the growth rate of nominal dividends?

c. If the expected real earnings per share are $1.80, what would be your estimate of intrinsic value if you used a simple capitalized earnings model?

d. If you inflated the above estimate of EPS using the 6 percent per year inflation rate and discounted it using the nominal capitalization rate, what estimate of intrinsic value would you get? What conclusion can you draw about adjusting the simple capitalized earnings model for inflation?

19. (Based on the 1986 CFA examination, Level II) You are Paul R. Overlook, CFA, and investment advisor for a large endowment fund. You have recently read about a basic valuation model that values an asset according to the present value of the asset's expected cash flows. You now are using this valuation framework to explain to the fund's trustees how inflation affects the rates of return on stocks. After your presentation, the trustees ask the following:

a. "If common stocks are attractive for hedging inflation, why did stocks perform so poorly in the 1970s when the inflation rate was increasing?"

b. "If stocks are attractive inflation hedges, it seems that stock prices should rise the most when inflation increases. Why then did stock prices appreciate so much from 1982 to 1986 when the inflation rate was declining?"

Explain your response to each of these questions in the context of the valuation model you have just read about.

20. You are trying to forecast the expected level of the aggregate Toronto stock market for the next year. Suppose the current three-month Treasury bill rate is 8 percent, the yield to maturity on 10+-year Canada bonds is 10 percent per year, the expected rate of inflation is 5 percent per year, and the expected EPS for the TSE 300 is $300. What is your forecast, and why?

CHAPTER 19

Financial Statement Analysis

In the previous chapter, we explored equity valuation techniques. These techniques take as inputs the firm's dividends and earnings prospects. While the valuation analyst is interested in economic earnings streams, only financial accounting data are readily available. What can we learn from a company's accounting data that can help us estimate the intrinsic value of its common stock?

In this chapter, we show how investors can use financial data as inputs into stock valuation analysis. We start by reviewing the basic sources of such data—the income statement, the balance sheet, and the statement of cash flows. We next discuss the difference between economic and accounting earnings. While economic earnings are more important for issues of valuation, we examine evidence suggesting that, whatever their shortcomings, accounting data still are useful in assessing the economic prospects of the firm. We show how analysts use financial ratios to explore the sources of a firm's profitability and evaluate the "quality" of its earnings in a systematic fashion. We also examine the impact of debt policy on various financial ratios. Finally, we conclude with a discussion of the limitations of financial statement analysis as a tool in uncovering mispriced securities. Some of these limitations are due to differences in firms' accounting procedures, while others arise from inflation-induced distortions in accounting numbers.

19.1 *The Major Financial Statements*

The Income Statement

The **income statement** is a summary of the profitability of the firm over a period of time, such as a year. It presents revenues generated during the operating period, the expenses incurred during that same period, and the company's net income, which is simply the difference between revenues and expenses.

It is useful to distinguish four broad classes of expense: cost of goods sold (COGS), which is the direct cost attributable to producing the product sold by the firm; salaries, advertising, and other costs of operating the firm that are not directly attributable to production; interest expense on the firm's debt; and taxes on earnings owed to federal and local governments.

Typically, this simple breakdown is not immediately recognizable in the income statement of larger firms. Table 19.1 presents a 1991 consolidated income statement for BCE Inc., the parent company of Bell Canada and of other subsidiaries; as a holding company, BCE has consolidated the financial results from various subsidiaries. The first three major kinds of operations list alternative means of presentation. Telecommunications services includes overhead in operating expenses to arrive directly at net revenues. Equipment manufacturing lists cost of goods sold separately from general and administrative ex-

TABLE 19.1 Consolidated Income Statement (For the Years Ended December 31)

		$ Millions		
		1991	1990	1989
Total revenues		19,884	18,373	16,681
Telecommunications services	Operating revenues	8,597	8,468	8,011
	Operating expenses	6,332	6,284	5,976
	Net revenues—telecommunications services	2,265	2,184	2,035
Telecommunications equipment manufacturing	Revenues	9,343	7,851	7,161
	Cost of revenues	5,420	4,707	4,340
	Selling, general, administrative, and other expenses	2,962	2,357	2,198
	Net revenues—	8,382	7,064	6,538
	telecommunications equipment manufacturing	961	787	623
Financial services	Revenues—investment and loan income	1,325	1,387	851
	—fees and commissions	162	188	134
		1,487	1,575	985
	Less: interest expenses	1,141	1,208	730
	operating expenses	311	306	197
		1,452	1,514	927
	Net revenues—financial services	35	61	58
Other operations	Operating revenues	457	479	524
	Operating expenses	436	452	506
	Net revenues—other operations	21	27	18
	Total net revenues	3,282	3,059	2,734

TABLE 19.1   Continued

		$ Millions		
		1991	1990	1989
Other income	Equity in net income of associated companies	103	155	173
(expense)	Allowance for funds used during construction	33	41	39
	Interest—long-term debt	(860)	(730)	(661)
	—other debt	(206)	(222)	(208)
	Unrealized foreign currency gains (losses)	2	(3)	2
	Miscellaneous—net	151	(176)	156
		(777)	(935)	(499)
	Income before income taxes and minority interest	2,505	2,124	2,235
	Income taxes	803	628	733
	Income before minority interest	1,702	1,496	1,502
	Minority interest	373	349	301
	Income from continuing operations	1,329	1,147	1,201
	Loss from discontinued real estate operations	—	—	(440)
	Net income	1,329	1,147	761
	Dividends on preferred shares	94	85	37
	Net income applicable to common shares	1,235	1,062	724
Earnings per share	Continuing operations	4.01	3.50	3.91
	Discontinued real estate operations (loss)	—	—	(1.48)
	Earnings per common share	4.01	3.50	2.43
	Dividends declared per common share	2.57	2.53	2.49
	Average number of common shares outstanding (thousands)	307,649	303,813	297,508

penses. Financial services identifies interest expenses separately from operating expenses; these are direct interest payments made on funds used in loans, rather than interest on BCE debt.

Aggregating net revenues from the major divisions and other sources gives total net revenues, often called *operating income*. At this point, peripheral sources of income or expense are included with other adjustments to obtain earnings before interest and taxes (EBIT); BCE has not calculated this item separately, but has proceeded to income before income taxes and minority interest. We can reconstruct EBIT, as an item of interest, from this last figure as $2,505 million *plus* interest expense of $1,066 million; thus, EBIT was $3,571 million. This is what the firm would have earned if not for obligations to its creditors and the tax authorities, and is a measure of the profitability of the firm's operations ignoring the cost of debt financing. Finally, the effect of income tax and income from a minority interest, which is accounted for as a net adjustment after taxes, leads to net income, the "bottom line" of the income statement; for purposes of comparison, profit and loss from discontinued operations are recorded separately, as in 1989.

The Balance Sheet

While the income statement provides a measure of the profitability over a period of time, the **balance sheet** provides a "snapshot" of the financial condition of the firm at a particular point in time. The balance sheet is a list of the firm's assets and liabilities at that moment. The difference in assets and liabilities is the net worth of the firm, also called *shareholders' equity*. Like income statements, balance sheets are reasonably standardized in presentation. Table 19.2 is the balance sheet of BCE for year-end 1991.

TABLE 19.2 Consolidated Balance Sheet (at December 31)

		\$ Millions	
ASSETS		1991	1990
Current assets	Cash and temporary cash investments	323	308
	Accounts receivable	3,932	3,930
	Inventories	1,066	1,043
	Other (principally prepaid expenses)	545	480
		5,866	5,761
Financial services	Short-term securities	820	1,028
	Loans receivable	9,648	9,442
	Bonds, stocks, and other investments	1,738	1,493
		12,206	11,963
Investments	Associated companies (at equity)	1,255	2,338
	Other investments	991	948
		2,246	3,286
Property, plant, and equipment	At cost	31,520	29,087
	Less: accumulated depreciation	11,469	10,513
		20,051	18,574
Other assets	Long-term notes and receivables	1,269	1,333
	Deferred charges		
	—unrealized foreign currency losses, less amortization	6	15
	—other	814	373
	Cost of shares in subsidiaries in excess of underlying net assets, less amortization	3,246	682
		5,335	2,403
TOTAL ASSETS		45,704	41,987

TABLE 19.2 Continued

LIABILITIES AND SHAREHOLDERS' EQUITY		$ Millions	
		1991	1990
Current liabilities	Accounts payable	4,180	2,659
	Advance billing and payments	175	183
	Dividends payable	239	217
	Taxes accrued	196	180
	Interest accrued	244	297
	Debt due within one year	2,247	1,878
		7,281	5,414
Financial services	Demand deposits	1,189	1,071
	Investment certificates and borrowings	10,711	10,655
		11,900	11,726
Long-term debt	Long-term debt	7,971	7,431
Deferred credits	Income taxes	2,297	2,425
	Other	547	389
		2,844	2,814
Minority interest in subsidiary companies	Preferred shares	1,446	1,309
	Common shares	2,303	1,968
		3,749	3,277
Preferred shares	Preferred shares	1,232	1,235
Common shareholders' equity	Common shares	5,614	5,407
	Common share purchase warrants	39	39
	Contributed surplus	1,034	1,034
	Retained earnings	4,165	3,727
	Foreign exchange adjustment	(125)	(117)
		10,727	10,090
TOTAL LIABILITIES AND SHAREHOLDERS' EQUITY		45,704	41,987

The first section of the balance sheet gives a listing of the assets of the firm. Current assets are presented first. These are cash and other items such as accounts receivable or inventories that will be converted into cash within one year. Because of its financial and other subsidiaries, BCE next lists related liquid assets before the typical listing of long-term assets, which generally corresponds to the company's property, plant, and equipment. The sum of current and long-term assets, plus other adjustments, gives total assets, the last line of the assets side of the balance sheet.

The liability and shareholders' equity side is similarly arranged. First come short-term or current liabilities such as accounts payable, accrued taxes, and debts due within one year, plus (in this case) financial services liabilities. Following this is long-term debt and other liabilities due in more than a year, as well as other adjustments. The difference between total assets and total liabilities is shareholders' equity. This is the net worth or book value of the firm. Shareholders' equity is divided between preferred and common shareholders. The latter section is usually divided into value of common shares, contributed surplus (additional paid-in capital), and retained earnings; the first two of these represent the proceeds realized from the sale of shares to the public, while retained earnings derive from the buildup of equity from profits plowed back into the firm.

The Statement of Changes in Financial Position

The **statement of changes in financial position** is also referred to as a *statement of cash flows* or *flow of funds statement*. It is a report of the cash flow generated by the firm's operations, investments, and financial activities. The income statement and balance sheet are based on accrual methods of accounting, which means revenues and expenses are recognized when incurred, even if no cash has yet been exchanged; this third statement, however, recognizes only the results of transactions in which cash changes hands. For example, if goods are sold now, with payment due in 60 days, the income statement will treat the revenue as generated when the sale occurs, and the balance sheet will be immediately augmented by accounts receivable less inventory; but the statement of changes in financial position will not recognize the transaction until the bill is paid and the cash is in hand.

Table 19.3 is the 1991 consolidated statement of changes in financial position for BCE. The first entry listed under cash provided from operations is income from continuing operations. The next entries modify that figure by components of income that have been recognized, but for which cash has not yet been exchanged. Increase in accounts receivable, for example, means income has been claimed on the income statement, but cash has not yet been collected. Hence, increases in accounts receivable reduce the cash flows realized from operations in this period. Similarly, increases in accounts payable mean expenses have been incurred, but cash has not yet left the firm. Any payment delay increases the company's net cash flows in this period.

Another major difference between the income statement and the statement of changes in financial position involves depreciation, which is a major addition to income in the adjustment section of cash provided in Table 19.3. The income statement attempts to "smooth" large capital expenditures over time to reflect a measure of profitability not distorted by large infrequent expenditures. The depreciation expense on the income statement is a way of doing this by recognizing capital expenditures over a period of many years rather than at the specific time of those expenditures.

The statement of cash flows, however, recognizes the cash implication of a capital expenditure when it occurs. It will ignore the depreciation "expense" over time, but will account for the full capital expenditure when it is paid in the second section, entitled cash flows from investing activities.

Rather than smooth or allocate expenses over time, as in the income statement, the statement of cash flows reports cash flows separately for operations, investing, and financing activities. This way, any large cash flows (such as those for big investments) can be recognized explicitly as non-recurring, without affecting the measure of cash flow generated by operating activities.

The second section of the statement of cash flows is the accounting of cash flows from investing activities. These entries are investments in the capital stock necessary for the firm to maintain or enhance its productive capacity.

Finally, the last section of the statement lists the cash flows realized from financing activities. Issuance of securities will contribute positive cash flows. For example, BCE issued $1,139 million more in long-term debt than it retired in 1991, which was a major source of cash flow. In contrast, payments of dividends and redemption of preferred shares reduced net cash flow. Notice

TABLE 19.3 Consolidated Statement of Changes in Financial Position (For the years ended December 31)

	$ Millions		
	1991	1990	1989
Cash Provided from (Used for) Operations			
Income from continuing operations	1,329	1,147	1,201
Items not affecting cash			
Depreciation	2,219	2,018	1,813
Minority interest	373	349	301
Deferred income taxes	26	70	88
Equity in net income of associated companies			
in excess of dividends received	(5)	(49)	(69)
Allowance for funds used during construction	(33)	(41)	(39)
Other items	(46)	68	(74)
Changes in working capital other than cash and debt			
(Increase) decrease in current assets:			
Accounts receivable	(2)	(319)	(463)
Inventories	(23)	57	(29)
Other current assets	(65)	(17)	(123)
Income and other taxes receivable	—	—	103
Increase (decrease) in current liabilities:			
Accounts payable	1,183	158	83
Advance billing and payments	(8)	21	(269)
Dividends payable	22	2	6
Taxes accrued	16	11	166
Interest accrued	(53)	6	79
Net cash provided from operations	**4,933**	**3,481**	**2,774**

TABLE 19.3 Continued

	$ Millions		
	1991	**1990**	**1989**
Cash Provided from (Used for) Investments			
Capital expenditures (net)	**(3,270)**	(3,312)	(3,191)
Investments—acquisition of STC Limited (net of cash			
acquired of $1,284)	**(1,717)**	—	—
—proceeds on disposal of			
businesses of STC Limited	**407**	—	—
—acquisition of Montreal Trustco Inc.	**—**	—	(874)
—other	**(162)**	(372)	(526)
Sales of investments in TCPL and Encor	**—**	710	—
Long-term notes and receivables	**58**	(29)	6
Net securities and loans—financial services			
Short-term securities	**208**	(92)	313
Loans receivable	**(206)**	(1,093)	(661)
Bonds, stocks, and other investments	**(245)**	(36)	(275)
Other items	**(331)**	51	149
Net cash used for investments	**(5,258)**	(4,173)	(5,059)
Cash Provided from (Used for) Financing			
Addition to long-term debt	**3,105**	656	1,233
Reduction of long-term debt	**(1,966)**	(372)	(239)
Issues of preferred shares	**—**	371	847
Issues of common shares			
Acquisition of Montreal Trustco Inc.	**—**	—	336
Other issues	**202**	126	132
Issues of preferred and common shares by subsidiaries			
to minority shareholders	**310**	236	463
Redemption of preferred shares by subsidiaries	**(10)**	(79)	(51)
Notes payable and bank advances	**(285)**	(358)	61
Net deposits and borrowings—financial services			
Demand deposits	**118**	30	80
Investment certificates and borrowings	**56**	1,296	560
Other items	**(147)**	(36)	(90)
Net cash provided from financing	**1,383**	1,870	3,332
Dividends Declared			
By BCE Inc.			
Preferred shares	**(94)**	(85)	(37)
Common shares	**(791)**	(769)	(743)
By subsidiaries to minority shareholders	**(158)**	(157)	(139)
Total dividends declared	**(1,043)**	(1,011)	(919)

that while dividends paid are included in the cash flows from financing, interest payments on debt are included with operating activities, presumably because unlike dividends, interest payments are not discretionary.

The statement of cash flows provides evidence on the well-being of a firm. If a company cannot pay its dividends and maintain the productivity of its capital stock out of cash flow from operations, for example, and it must resort to borrowing to meet these demands, this is a serious warning that the firm cannot maintain dividend payout at its current level in the long run. The statement of cash flows will reveal this developing problem, when it shows that cash flow from operations is inadequate and that borrowing is being used to maintain dividend payments at unsustainable levels.

19.2 *Accounting vs. Economic Earnings*

We've seen that stock valuation models require a measure of economic earnings or sustainable cash flow that can be paid out to stockholders without impairing the productive capacity of the firm. In contrast, **accounting earnings** are affected by several conventions regarding the valuation of assets, such as inventories (e.g., LIFO versus FIFO treatment), and by the way some expenditures, such as capital investments, are recognized over time (as depreciation expenses). We will discuss problems with some of these accounting conventions in greater detail later in the chapter. In addition to these accounting issues, as the firm makes its way through the business cycle, its earnings will rise above or fall below the trend line that might more accurately reflect sustainable **economic earnings.** This introduces an added complication in interpreting net income figures. One might wonder how closely accounting earnings approximate economic earnings and, correspondingly, how useful accounting data might be to investors attempting to value the firm.[1]

In fact, the net income figure on the firm's income statement does convey considerable information concerning a firm's prospects. We see this in the fact that stock prices tend to increase when firms announce earnings greater than market analysts or investors had anticipated. There are several studies to this effect.

In one study, Niederhoffer and Regan[2] formed three groups of stock: the 50 stocks with the greatest price increases in 1970, the 50 with the greatest price decreases, and 50 randomly selected stocks. In the worst-performing group,

[1] In "The Trouble with Earnings," *Financial Analysts Journal,* September–October 1972, Jack Treynor points out some important difficulties with the accounting concept of earnings. In particular, he argues that the trouble stems from accountants' attempts to measure the value of assets.

[2] Victor Niederhoffer and Patrick Regan, "Earnings Changes, Analysts Forecasts, and Stock Prices," *Financial Analysts Journal,* May/June 1972.

earnings declined by 83 percent (compared with analysts' forecasts of a 15.3 percent *increase*), while in the best-performing group, earnings increased 21.4 percent (the analysts had forecast a 7.7 percent increase). The implication is that deviation of actual earnings from projected earnings is the driving force behind abnormal stock returns.

In a more recent study, Foster, Olsen, and Shevlin[3] used time series of earnings for many firms to forecast the coming quarter's earnings announcement. They estimated an equation for more than 2,000 firms between 1974 and 1981:

$$E_{i,t} = E_{i,t-4} + a_i(E_{i,t-1} - E_{i,t-5}) + g_i$$

where

$$E_{i,t} = \text{Earnings of firm } i \text{ in quarter } t$$
$$a_i = \text{Adjustment factor for firm } i$$
$$g_i = \text{Growth factor for firm } i$$

The rationale is that this quarter's earnings, $E_{i,t}$, will equal last year's earnings for the same quarter, $E_{i,t-4}$, plus a factor representing recent above-trend earnings performance as measured by the difference between last quarter's earnings and the corresponding quarter's earnings a year earlier, plus another factor that represents steady earnings growth over time. Regression techniques are used to estimate a_i and g_i. Given these estimates, the equation is used together with past earnings to forecast future earnings.

Now it is easy to determine earnings surprises. Simply take the difference between actual earnings and forecasted or expected earnings, and see whether earnings surprises correlate with subsequent stock price movements.

Before doing so, however, these researchers introduced an extra refinement (first suggested by Latane and Jones[4]). Instead of using the earnings forecast error itself as the variable of interest, they first divided the forecast errors for each period by the standard deviation of forecast errors calculated from earlier periods; they effectively deflated the earnings surprise in a particular quarter by a measure of the typical surprise in an average quarter. This discounts forecast errors for firms with historically very unpredictable earnings. A large error for such firms might not be as significant as for a firm with typically very predictable earnings. The resulting "normalized" forecast error commonly is called the "standardized unexpected earnings" (SUE) measure. SUE is the variable that was correlated with stock price movements.

Each earnings announcement was placed in one of 10 deciles ranked by the magnitude of SUE, and the abnormal returns of the stock in each decile were calculated. The abnormal return in a period is the portfolio return after adjusting for both the market return in that period and the portfolio beta. It measures

[3] George Foster, Chris Olsen, and Terry Shevlin, "Earnings Releases, Anomalies, and the Behavior of Security Returns," *The Accounting Review* 59, no. 4 (October 1984).

[4] H. A. Latane and C. P. Jones, "Standardized Unexpected Earnings—1971–1977," *Journal of Finance*, June 1979.

FIGURE 19.1

Cumulative abnormal returns in response to earnings announcements.

(From H. A. Latane and C. P. Jones, "Standardized Unexpected Earnings—1971–1977, *Journal of Finance* June 1979.)

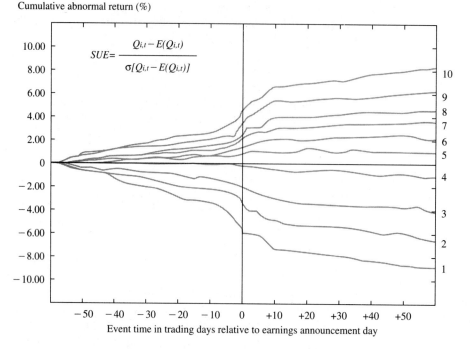

Cumulative abnormal return (%)

$$SUE = \frac{Q_{i,t} - E(Q_{i,t})}{\sigma[Q_{i,t} - E(Q_{i,t})]}$$

Event time in trading days relative to earnings announcement day

return over and above what would be expected given market conditions in that period. Figure 19.1 is a graph of the cumulative abnormal returns.

The results of this study are dramatic. The correlation between SUE ranking and abnormal returns across deciles is as predicted. There is a large abnormal return (a large increase in cumulative abnormal return) on the earnings announcement day (time 0). The abnormal return is positive for high-SUE and negative for low-SUE (actually negative-SUE) firms.

The more remarkable, and disturbing, result of the study concerns stock price movements *after* the announcement date. The cumulative abnormal returns of high-SUE stocks continue to grow even after the earnings information becomes public, while the low-SUE firms continue to suffer negative abnormal returns. The market appears to adjust to the earnings information only gradually, resulting in a sustained period of abnormal returns.

Evidently, one can earn abnormal profits simply by waiting for earnings announcements and purchasing a stock portfolio of high-SUE companies. These are precisely the types of predictable continuing trends that ought to be impossible in an efficient market. This finding is not unique. Many earnings announcement studies have found similar results.

Analysts' Forecasts and Stock Returns

You might wonder whether security analysts can predict earnings more accurately than can mechanical time series equations. After all, analysts have access to these statistical equations and to other qualitative and quantitative data.

The evidence seems to be that analysts in fact do outperform such mechanical forecasts. Two recent Canadian studies analyzed the effect on stock prices of the release of estimated earnings by analysts and of revisions to forecasts announced by analysts. Their findings were consistent with earlier U.S. studies.[5] Both studies used the data contained in publicly available summary reports of analysts' forecasts.

In a test of market efficiency, Brown, Richardson, and Trzcinka[6] determined that there is positive correlation between analysts' forecasts and abnormal returns in individual stocks. The forecasts of stock prices, presumably based on earnings estimates, are reported in the Research Evaluation Service of the *Financial Post Information Service*. The authors found that use of the service in a trading strategy led to significant excess returns, net of transactions costs. They also tested the significance of the benchmark for risk adjustment and concluded that the result was independent of the choice of a CAPM or APT approach; hence, they demonstrated that use of the simpler CAPM methodology was justified in this context.

L'Her and Suret[7] examined the reaction to earnings revisions by measuring abnormal returns. Using the information in the *Institutional Brokers Estimate System* (IBES), they divided earnings revisions into quintiles by magnitude of the percentage change from greatest downward revision (quintile 1) to greatest upward revision (quintile 5). The findings were remarkably similar to those in the Latane and Jones study. Cumulative average residuals were recorded for the nine-month periods preceding and following the release by IBES of the revisions, as shown in Figure 19.2. Although most of the price reaction occurred in anticipation of the announcement, the extreme cases (quintiles 5 and 1) showed that abnormal returns persisted for nine months following release for upward revisions, but only three months for downward revisions. (On the other hand, the reaction to unfavourable revisions was much more pronounced over the 18-month period.) Findings such as these may lead one to suspect the causality; it is possible that analysts revise their forecasts in response to price changes, which they interpret as inside information.

In an interesting observation, L'Her and Suret note that segregating the data by industrial sector gave varied results. Using a three-sector classification, they found that the primary sector, with unpredictable commodity prices determining earnings, did not react to earnings revisions, while the other two sectors did; the secondary sector had a major reaction, such that purchase or sale of stock, including commissions, after an announced revision yielded significant gains. They also noted that if the revision occurs close to the end of the fiscal year, the signal is more reliable.

[5] A good survey of American studies is given in D. Givoly and J. Lakonishok, "Properties of Analysts' Forecasts of Earnings: A Review and Analysis of the Research," *Journal of Accounting Literature,* 1984.

[6] Lawrence Brown, Gordon Richardson, and Charles Trzcinka, "Strong-Form Efficiency on the Toronto Stock Exchange: An Analysis of Analyst Price Forecasts," *Contemporary Accounting Research,* Spring 1991.

[7] Jean-Francois L'Her and Jean-Marc Suret, "The Reaction of Canadian Securities to Revisions of Earnings," *Contemporary Accounting Research,* Spring 1991.

FIGURE 19.2

Cumulative average residuals in response to forecast revisions.

(From Jean-Francois L'Her and Jean-Marc Suret, "The Reaction of Canadian Securities to Revisions of Earnings," *Contemporary Accounting Research,* Spring 1991.)

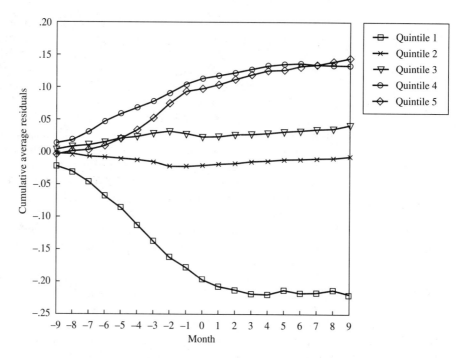

The *Value Line Investment Survey* is an influential service that provides reports of most of the recognized publicly traded stocks in the United States, including many large Canadian firms. Brown and Rozeff[8] compared earnings forecasts from Value Line with those made using a sophisticated statistical technique called a Box-Jenkins model. The Value Line forecasts generally were more accurate. Whereas 54 percent of the Box-Jenkins forecasts were within 25 percent of the realized values, and 26.5 percent were within 10 percent, 63.5 percent of the Value Line forecasts were within 25 percent and 23 percent were within 10 percent. Apparently, the qualitative data and firm-specific fundamental analysis that analysts bring to bear are of value.[9]

19.3   *Return on Equity*

Past vs. Future ROE

We noted in Chapter 18 that **return on equity** (ROE) is one of the two basic factors in determining a firm's growth rate of earnings. There are two sides to

---

[8] Lawrence D. Brown and Michael Rozeff, "The Superiority of Analysts' Forecasts as Measures of Expectations: Evidence from Earnings," *Journal of Finance,* March 1978.
[9] See Section 20.5 for more on Value Line.

using ROE. Sometimes it is reasonable to assume that future ROE will approximate its past value, but a high ROE in the past does not necessarily imply a firm's future ROE will be high.

A declining ROE, on the other hand, is evidence that the firm's new investments have offered a lower ROE than its past investments. The best forecast of future ROE in this case may be lower than the most recent ROE. The vital point for an analyst is not to accept historical values as indicators of future values. Data from the recent past may provide information regarding future performance, but the analyst should always keep an eye on the future. It is expectations of future dividends and earnings that determine the intrinsic value of the company's stock.

Financial Leverage and ROE

An analyst interpreting the past behaviour of a firm's ROE or forecasting its future value must pay careful attention to the firm's debt-equity mix and to the interest rate on its debt. An example will show why. Suppose Nodett is a firm that is all equity financed and has total assets of $100 million. Assume it pays corporate taxes at the rate of 40 percent of taxable earnings.

Table 19.4 shows the behaviour of sales, earnings before interest and taxes, and net profits under three scenarios representing phases of the business cycle. It also shows the behaviour of two of the most commonly used profitability measures: operating **return on assets** (ROA), which equals EBIT/assets, and ROE, which equals net profits/equity.

Somdett is an otherwise identical firm to Nodett, but $40 million of its $100 million of assets are financed with debt bearing an interest rate of 8 percent. It pays annual interest expense of $3.2 million. Table 19.5 shows how Somdett's ROE differs from Nodett's.

Note that annual sales, EBIT, and therefore ROA for both firms are the same in each of the three scenarios, that is, business risk for the two companies is identical. It is their financial risk that differs. Although Nodett and Somdett have the same ROA in each scenario, Somdett's ROE exceeds that of Nodett in normal and good years and is lower in bad years.

TABLE 19.4   Nodett's Profitability over the Business Cycle

Scenario	Sales ($ millions)	EBIT ($ millions)	ROA (% per year)	Net Profit ($ millions)	ROE (% per year)
Bad year	80	5	5	3	3
Normal year	100	10	10	6	6
Good year	120	15	15	9	9

TABLE 19.5 Impact of Financial Leverage on ROE

Scenario	EBIT ($ millions)	Nodett		Somdett	
		Net Profits ($ millions)	ROE (%)	Net Profits* ($ millions)	ROE† (%)
Bad year	5	3	3	1.08	1.8
Normal year	10	6	6	4.08	6.8
Good year	15	9	9	7.08	11.8

* Somdett's after-tax profits are given by .6(EBIT − $3.2 million).
† Somdett's equity is only $60 million.

We can summarize the exact relationship among ROE, ROA, and leverage in the following equation:[10]

$$\text{ROE} = (1 - \text{Tax rate}) \left[\text{ROA} + (\text{ROA} - \text{Interest rate}) \frac{\text{Debt}}{\text{Equity}} \right] \qquad \textbf{(19.1)}$$

The relationship has the following implications. If there is no debt or if the firm's ROA equals the interest rate on its debt, its ROE will simply equal (1 − the tax rate) × ROA. If its ROA exceeds the interest rate, then its ROE will exceed (1 − the tax rate) × ROA by an amount that will be greater the higher the debt-to-equity ratio.

This result makes intuitive sense: if ROA exceeds the borrowing rate, the firm earns more on its money than it pays out to creditors. The surplus earnings are available to the firm's owners, the equity holders, which raises ROE. If, on the other hand, ROA is less than the interest rate, then ROE will decline by an amount that depends on the debt-to-equity ratio.

To illustrate the application of equation 19.1, we can use the numerical example in Table 19.5. In a normal year, Nodett has an ROE of 6 percent, which is .6 (1 − the tax rate) × its ROA of 10 percent. However, Somdett,

---

[10] The derivation of equation 19.1 is as follows:

$$\text{ROE} = \frac{\text{Net profit}}{\text{Equity}}$$

$$= \frac{\text{EBIT} - \text{Interest} - \text{Taxes}}{\text{Equity}}$$

$$= \frac{(1 - \text{Tax rate})(\text{EBIT} - \text{Interest})}{\text{Equity}}$$

$$= (1 - \text{Tax rate}) \frac{(\text{ROA} \times \text{Assets} - \text{Interest rate} \times \text{Debt})}{\text{Equity}}$$

$$= (1 - \text{Tax rate}) \left[\text{ROA} \times \frac{(\text{Equity} + \text{Debt})}{\text{Equity}} - \text{Interest Rate} \times \frac{\text{Debt}}{\text{Equity}} \right]$$

$$= (1 - \text{Tax rate}) \left[\text{ROA} + (\text{ROA} - \text{Interest rate}) \frac{\text{Debt}}{\text{Equity}} \right]$$

which borrows at an interest rate of 8 percent and maintains a debt/equity ratio of ⅔, has an ROE of 6.8 percent. The calculation using equation 19.1 is

$$ROE = .6[10\% + (10\% - 8\%)⅔]$$
$$= .6[10\% + ⁴⁄₃\%]$$
$$= 6.8\%$$

The important point to remember is that increased debt will make a positive contribution to a firm's ROE only if the firm's ROA exceeds the interest rate on the debt.

Note also that financial leverage increases the risk of the equityholder returns. Table 19.5 shows that ROE on Somdett is worse than that of Nodett in bad years. Conversely, in good years, Somdett outperforms Nodett because the excess of ROA over ROE provides additional funds for equity holders. The presence of debt makes Somdett more sensitive to the business cycle than Nodett. Even though the two companies have equal business risk (reflected in their identical EBITs in all three scenarios), Somdett carries greater financial risk than Nodett.

Even if financial leverage increases the expected ROE of Somdett relative to Nodett (as it seems to in Table 19.5), this does not imply the market value of Somdett's equity will be higher.[11] Financial leverage increases the risk of the firm's equity as surely as it raises the expected ROE.

Concept Check

> Question 1. Mordett is a company with the same assets as Nodett and Somdett but a debt-to-equity ratio of 1.0 and an interest rate of 9 percent. What would its net profit and ROE be in a bad year, a normal year, and a good year?

19.4 *Ratio Analysis*

Decomposition of ROE

To understand the factors affecting a firm's ROE, including its trend over time and its performance relative to competitors, analysts often "decompose" ROE into the product of a series of ratios. Each component ratio is in itself meaningful, and the process serves to focus the analyst's attention on the separate factors influencing performance.[12]

---

[11] This is the essence of the debate on the Modigliani–Miller theorems regarding the effect of financial leverage on the value of the firm. For a discussion of the issues and evidence, see footnotes 9 and 10 in Chapter 18.

[12] This kind of decomposition of ROE is often called the *Dupont system.*

One useful decomposition of ROE is

$$\text{ROE} = \frac{\text{Net profit}}{\text{Pretax profit}} \times \frac{\text{Pretax profit}}{\text{EBIT}} \times \frac{\text{EBIT}}{\text{Sales}} \times \frac{\text{Sales}}{\text{Assets}} \times \frac{\text{Assets}}{\text{Equity}}$$

$$(1) \quad \times \quad (2) \quad \times \quad (3) \quad \times \quad (4) \quad \times \quad (5)$$

Table 19.6 shows all these ratios for Nodett and Somdett Corporations under the three different economic scenarios.

Let us first focus on factors 3 and 4. Notice that their product, EBIT/Assets, gives us the firm's ROA.

Factor 3 is known as the firm's operating **profit margin** or **return on sales** (ROS). ROS shows operating profit per dollar of sales. In an average year, Nodett's ROS is 0.10, or 10 percent; in a bad year, it is 0.0625, or 6.25 percent, and in a good year, .125, or 12.5 percent.

Factor 4, the ratio of sales to assets, is known as **asset turnover** (ATO). It indicates the efficiency of the firm's use of assets in the sense that it measures the annual sales generated by each dollar of assets. In a normal year, Nodett's ATO is 1.0 per year, meaning that sales of $1 per year were generated per dollar of assets. In a bad year, this ratio declines to 0.8 per year, and in a good year, it rises to 1.2 per year.

Comparing Nodett and Somdett, we see that factors 3 and 4 do not depend on a firm's financial leverage. The firms' ratios are equal to each other in all three scenarios.

Similarly, factor 1, the ratio of net income after taxes to pretax profit, is the same for both firms. We call this the *tax-burden ratio*. Its value reflects both the government's tax code and the policies pursued by the firm in trying to mini-

TABLE 19.6   Ratio Decomposition Analysis for Nodett and Somdett

	ROE	(1) Net Profit / Pretax Profit	(2) Pretax Profit / EBIT	(3) EBIT / Sales (ROS)	(4) Sales / Assets (ATO)	(5) Assets / Equity	(6) Compound Leverage Factor (2) × (5)
Bad Year							
Nodett	.030	.6	1.000	.0625	.800	1.000	1.000
Somdett	.018	.6	.360	.0625	.800	1.667	.600
Normal Year							
Nodett	.060	.6	1.000	.100	1.000	1.000	1.000
Somdett	.068	.6	.680	.100	1.000	1.667	1.134
Good Year							
Nodett	.090	.6	1.000	.125	1.200	1.000	1.000
Somdett	.118	.6	.787	.125	1.200	1.667	1.311

mize its tax burden. In our example, it does not change over the business cycle, remaining a constant .6.

While factors 1, 3, and 4 are not affected by a firm's capital structure, factors 2 and 5 are. Factor 2 is the ratio of pretax profits to EBIT. The firm's pretax profits will be greatest when there are no interest payments to be made to debt holders. In fact, another way to express this ratio is

$$\frac{\text{Pretax profits}}{\text{EBIT}} = \frac{\text{EBIT} - \text{Interest expense}}{\text{EBIT}}$$

We will call this factor the *interest-burden* (IB) *ratio*. It takes on its highest possible value, 1, for Nodett, which has no financial leverage. The higher the degree of financial leverage, the lower the IB ratio. Nodett's IB ratio does not vary over the business cycle. It is fixed at 1.0, reflecting the total absence of interest payments. For Somdett, however, because interest expense is fixed in dollar amount while EBIT varies, the IB ratio varies from a low of 0.36 in a bad year to a high of 0.787 in a good year.

Factor 5, the ratio of assets to equity, is a measure of the firm's degree of financial leverage. It is called the **leverage ratio** and is equal to 1 + the debt-to-equity ratio.[13] In our numerical example in Table 19.6, Nodett has a leverage ratio of 1 while Somdett's is 1.667.

From our discussion in Section 19.2, we know that financial leverage helps boost ROE only if ROA is greater than the interest rate on the firm's debt. How is this fact reflected in the ratios of Table 19.6?

The answer is that to measure the full impact of leverage in this framework, the analyst must take the product of the IB and leverage ratios (that is, factors 2 and 5, shown in Table 19.6 as column 6). For Nodett, factor 6, which we call the *compound leverage factor,* remains a constant 1.0 under all three scenarios. But for Somdett, we see that the compound leverage factor is greater than 1 in normal years (1.134) and in good years (1.311), indicating the positive contribution of financial leverage to ROE. It is less than 1 in bad years, reflecting the fact that when ROA falls below the interest rate, ROE falls with increased use of debt.

We can summarize all of these relationships as follows: ROE = tax burden × interest burden × margin × turnover × leverage. Because

$$\text{ROA} = \text{Margin} \times \text{Turnover}$$

and

$$\text{Compound leverage factor} = \text{Interest burden} \times \text{Leverage}$$

we can decompose ROE equivalently as follows:

$$\text{ROE} = \text{Tax burden} \times \text{ROA} \times \text{Compound leverage factor}$$

---

[13] $\dfrac{\text{Assets}}{\text{Equity}} = \dfrac{\text{Equity} + \text{Debt}}{\text{Equity}} = 1 + \dfrac{\text{Debt}}{\text{Equity}}$

TABLE 19.7   Differences between ROS and ATO across Industries

	ROS	x	ATO	=	ROA
Supermarket chain	.02		5.0		.10
Utility	.20		0.5		.10

Table 19.6 compares firms with the same ROS and ATO but different degrees of financial leverage. Comparison of ROS and ATO usually is meaningful only in evaluating firms in the same industry. Cross-industry comparisons of these two ratios are often meaningless and can even be misleading.

For example, let us take two firms with the same ROA of 10 percent per year. The first is a supermarket chain; the second is a gas utility.

As Table 19.7 shows, the supermarket chain has a "low" ROS of 2 percent and achieves a 10 percent ROA by "turning over" its assets five times per year. The capital-intensive utility, on the other hand, has a "low" ATO of only 0.5 times per year and achieves its 10 percent ROA by having an ROS of 20 percent. The point here is that a "low" ROS or ATO ratio need not indicate a troubled firm. Each ratio must be interpreted in light of industry norms.

Even within an industry, ROS and ATO sometimes can differ markedly among firms pursuing different marketing strategies. In the retailing industry, for example, Holt-Renfrew pursues a high-margin, low-ATO policy compared to Zellers, which pursues a low-margin, high-ATO policy.

Concept Check	Question 2. Do a ratio decomposition analysis for the Mordett corporation of question 1, preparing a table similar to Table 19.6.

Turnover and Other Asset Utilization Ratios

It is often helpful in understanding a firm's ratio of sales to assets to compute comparable efficiency-of-utilization, or turnover, ratios for subcategories of assets. For example, fixed-asset turnover would be

$$\frac{\text{Sales}}{\text{Fixed assets}}$$

This ratio measures sales per dollar of the firm's money tied up in fixed assets.

To illustrate how you can compute this and other ratios from a firm's financial statements, consider Growth Industries, Inc. (GI). GI's income statement and opening and closing balance sheets for the years 19X1, 19X2, and 19X3 appear in Table 19.8.

GI's total asset turnover in 19X3 was 0.303, which was below the industry average of 0.4. To understand better why GI underperformed, we decide to

TABLE 19.8 Growth Industries Financial Statements, 19X1–19X3 ($ thousands)

	19X0	19X1	19X2	19X3
Income Statements				
Sales revenue		$100,000	$120,000	$144,000
Cost of goods sold (including depreciation)		55,000	66,000	79,200
Depreciation		15,000	18,000	21,600
Selling and administrative expenses		15,000	18,000	21,600
Operating income		30,000	36,000	43,200
Interest expense		10,500	19,095	34,391
Taxable income		19,500	16,905	8,809
Income tax (40% rate)		7,800	6,762	3,524
Net income		11,700	10,143	5,285
Balance sheets (End of Year)				
Cash and marketable securities	$ 50,000	$ 60,000	$ 72,000	$ 86,400
Accounts receivable	25,000	30,000	36,000	43,200
Inventories	75,000	90,000	108,000	129,600
Net plant and equipment	150,000	180,000	216,000	259,200
Total assets	$300,000	$360,000	$432,000	$518,400
Accounts payable	$ 30,000	$ 36,000	$ 43,200	$ 51,840
Short-term debt	45,000	87,300	141,957	214,432
Long-term debt (8% bonds maturing in 19X7)	75,000	75,000	75,000	75,000
Total liabilities	$150,000	$198,300	$260,157	$341,272
Shareholders' equity (1 million shares outstanding)	$150,000	$161,700	$171,843	$177,128
Other Data				
Market price per common share at year-end		$93.60	$61.00	$21.00

compute asset utilization ratios separately for fixed assets, inventories, and accounts receivable.

GI's sales in 19X3 were $144 million. Its only fixed assets were plant and equipment, which were $216 million at the beginning of the year and $259.2 million at year's end. Average fixed assets for the year were, therefore, $237.6 million [($216 million + $259.2 million)/2]. GI's fixed asset turnover for 19X3 was $144 million per year/$237.6 million = .606 per year. In other words, for every dollar of fixed assets, there were $.606 in sales during the year 19X3.

Comparable figures for the fixed-asset turnover ratio for 19X1 and 19X2 and the 19X3 industry average are

19X1	19X2	19X3	19X3 Industry Average
.606	.606	.606	.700

GI's fixed asset turnover has been stable over time and below the industry average.

Whenever a financial ratio includes one item from the income statement, which covers a period of time, and another from the balance sheet, which is a "snapshot" at a particular time, the practice is to take the average of the beginning and end-of-year balance sheet figures. Thus, in computing the fixed-asset turnover ratio you divide sales (from the income statement) by average fixed assets (from the balance sheet).

Another widely followed turnover ratio is the inventory turnover ratio, which is the ratio of cost of goods sold per dollar of inventory. It is usually expressed as cost of goods sold (instead of sales revenue) divided by average inventory. It measures the speed with which inventory is turned over.

In 19X1, GI's cost of goods sold (less depreciation) was $40 million, and its average inventory was $82.5 million [($75 million + $90 million)/2]. Its inventory turnover was 0.485 per year ($40 million/$82.5 million). In 19X2 and 19X3, inventory turnover remained the same and continued below the industry average of 0.5 per year.

Another measure of efficiency is the ratio of accounts receivable to sales. The accounts receivable ratio usually is computed as average accounts receivable/sales × 365. The result is a number called the **average collection period,** or **days receivables,** which equals the total credit extended to customers per dollar of daily sales. It is the number of days' worth of sales tied up in accounts receivable. You can also think of it as the average lag between the date of sale and the date payment is received.

For GI in 19X3, this number was 100.4 days:

$$\frac{(\$36 \text{ million} + \$43.2 \text{ million})/2}{\$144 \text{ million}} \times 365 = 100.4 \text{ days}$$

The industry average was 60 days.

In summary, use of these ratios lets us see that GI's poor total asset turnover relative to the industry is in part caused by lower-than-average fixed-asset turnover and inventory turnover and higher than average days receivables. This suggests GI may be having problems with excess plant capacity along with poor inventory and receivables management procedures.

Liquidity and Coverage Ratios

Liquidity and interest coverage ratios are of great importance in evaluating the riskiness of a firm's securities. They aid in assessing the financial strength of the firm.

Liquidity ratios include the current ratio, quick ratio, and interest coverage ratio.

1. **Current ratio:** current assets/current liabilities. This ratio measures the ability of the firm to pay off its current liabilities by liquidating its current assets (i.e., turning them into cash). It indicates the firm's ability to avoid insolvency in the short run. GI's current ratio in 19X1, for example, was (60 + 30 + 90)/(36 + 87.3) = 1.46. In other years, it was

19X1	19X2	19X3	19X3 Industry Average
1.46	1.17	.97	2.0

This represents an unfavourable time trend and poor standing relative to the industry.

2. **Quick ratio:** (cash + receivables)/current liabilities. This ratio is also called the **acid test ratio.** It has the same denominator as the current ratio, but its numerator includes only cash, cash equivalents, and receivables. The quick ratio is a better measure of liquidity than the current ratio for firms whose inventory is not readily convertible into cash. GI's quick ratio shows the same disturbing trends as its current ratio:

19X1	19X2	19X3	19X3 Industry Average
.73	.58	.49	1.0

3. **Interest coverage ratio:** EBIT/interest expense. This ratio is often called **times interest earned.** It is closely related to the interest-burden ratio discussed in the previous section. A high coverage ratio tells the firm's shareholders and lenders that the likelihood of bankruptcy is low because annual earnings are significantly greater than annual interest obligations. It is widely used by both lenders and borrowers in determining the firm's debt capacity and is a major determinant of the firm's bond rating. GI's interest coverage ratios are

19X1	19X2	19X3	19X3 Industry Average
2.86	1.89	1.26	5

GI's interest coverage ratio has fallen dramatically over this three-year period, and by 19X3 it is far below the industry average. Probably its credit rating has been declining as well, and no doubt GI is considered a relatively poor credit risk in 19X3.

Market Price Ratios

There are two market price ratios: the market-to-book-value ratio and the price/earnings ratio.

The **market-to-book-value ratio** (P/B) equals the market price of a share of the firm's common stock divided by its *book value,* that is, shareholders' equity per share. Analysts sometimes consider the stock of a firm with a low market-to-book value to be a "safer" investment, seeing the book value as a "floor" supporting the market price.

Analysts presumably view book value as the level below which market price will not fall because the firm always has the option to liquidate, or sell, its assets for their book values. However, this view is questionable. In fact, some firms, such as Digital, do sometimes sell for less than book value. Nevertheless, low market-to-book-value ratio is seen by some as providing a "margin of safety," and some analysts will screen out or reject high P/B firms in their stock selection process.

Proponents of the P/B screen would argue that, if all other relevant attributes are the same for two stocks, the one with the lower P/B ratio is safer.

Although there may be firms for which this approach has some validity, book value does not necessarily represent liquidation value, which renders the margin of safety notion unreliable.

The theory of equity valuation offers some insight into the significance of the P/B ratio. A high P/B ratio is an indication that investors think a firm has opportunities of earning a rate of return on their investment in excess of the market capitalization rate, k.

To illustrate this point, we can return to the numerical example in Chapter 18, Section 18.4 and its accompanying table. That example assumes the market capitalization rate is 12 percent per year. Now add the assumptions that the book value per share is $8.33, and that the coming year's expected EPS is $1, so that in the case for which the expected ROE on future investments also is 12 percent, the stock will sell at $1/.12 = $8.33, and the P/B ratio will be 1.

Table 19.9 shows the P/B ratio for alternative assumptions about future ROE and plowback ratio.

Reading down any column, you can see how the P/B ratio changes with ROE. The numbers reveal that, for a given plowback ratio, the higher the expected ROE, the higher is the P/B ratio. This makes sense, because the greater the expected profitability of the firm's future investment opportunities, the greater its market value as an ongoing enterprise compared with the cost of acquiring its assets.

We've noted that the **price/earnings ratio** that is based on the firm's financial statements and reported in newspaper stock listings is not the same as the price/earnings multiple that emerges from a discounted dividend model. The numerator is the same (the market price of the stock), but the denominator is different. The P/E ratio uses the most recent past accounting earnings, while the P/E multiple predicted by valuation models uses expected future economic earnings.

Many security analysts pay careful attention to the accounting P/E ratio in the belief that among low P/E stocks they are somehow more likely to find bargains than with high P/E stocks. The idea is that you can acquire a claim on

TABLE 19.9   Effect of ROE and Plowback Ratio on P/B

| | Plowback Ratio (b) | | | |
ROE	0	25%	50%	75%
10%	1.00	.95	.86	.67
12%	1.00	1.00	1.00	1.00
14%	1.00	1.06	1.20	2.00

The assumptions and formulas underlying this table are: E_1 = $1; book value per share = $8.33; k = 12% per year.

$$g = b \times \text{ROE}$$
$$P_0 = \frac{(1 - b)E}{k - g}$$
$$\text{P/B} = P_0/\$8.33$$

a dollar of earnings more cheaply if the P/E ratio is low. For example, if the P/E ratio is 8, you pay $8 per share per $1 of *current* earnings, while if P/E is 12, you must pay $12 for a claim on $1 of current earnings.

Note, however, that current earnings may differ substantially from future earnings. The higher P/E stock still may be a bargain relative to the low P/E stock if its earnings and dividends are expected to grow at a faster rate. Our point is that ownership of the stock conveys the right to future earnings, as well as to current earnings. An exclusive focus on the commonly reported accounting P/E ratio can be shortsighted, because by its nature it ignores future growth in earnings.

An efficient markets adherent will be skeptical of the notion that a strategy of investing in low P/E stocks would result in an expected rate of return greater than that of investing in high or medium P/E stocks having the same risk. The empirical evidence on this question is mixed, but if the strategy had worked in the past, it almost surely would not work in the future because too many investors would be following it.[14]

Before leaving the P/B and P/E ratios, it is worth pointing out the relationship among these ratios and ROE:

$$\text{ROE} = \frac{\text{Earnings}}{\text{Book value}}$$
$$= \frac{\text{Market price}}{\text{Book value}} \div \frac{\text{Market price}}{\text{Earnings}}$$
$$= \text{P/B ratio} \div \text{P/E ratio}$$

By rearranging the terms, we find that a firm's **earnings yield**, the ratio of earnings to price, is equal to its ROE divided by the market-book value ratio:

$$\frac{E}{P} = \frac{\text{ROE}}{\text{P/B}}$$

Thus, a company with a high ROE can have a relatively low earnings yield because its P/B ratio is high. This indicates a high ROE does not in and of itself imply the stock is a good buy: the price of the stock already may be bid up to reflect an attractive ROE. If so, the P/B ratio will be above 1.0, and the earnings yield to stockholders will be below the ROE, as the equation demonstrates. The relationship shows that a strategy of investing in the stock of high ROE firms may produce a lower holding period return than investing in those with a low ROE.

Clayman[15] has found that investing in the stocks of 29 "excellent" companies, with mean reported ROE of 19.05 percent during the period 1976 to 1980, produced results much inferior to investing in 39 "unexcellent" companies, those with a mean ROE of 7.09 percent during the period. An investor putting equal dollar amounts in the stocks of the unexcellent companies would have earned a portfolio rate of return over the 1981–1985 period that was 11.3 per-

---

[14] See the discussion of this point in Chapter 12, on market efficiency.

[15] Michelle Clayman, "In Search of Excellence: The Investor's Viewpoint," *Financial Analysts Journal*, May/June 1987.

cent higher per year than the rate of return on a comparable portfolio of excellent company stocks.

Concept Check	Question 3. What were GI's ROE, P/E, and P/B ratios in the year 19X3? How do they compare to the industry average ratios, which were: ROE = 8.64% P/E = 8 P/B = .69 How does GI's earnings yield in 19X3 compare to the industry's average?

19.5   *An Illustration of Financial Statement Analysis*

In her 19X3 annual report to the shareholders of Growth Industries, Inc., the president wrote: "19X3 was another successful year for Growth Industries. As in 19X2, sales, assets, and operating income all continued to grow at a rate of 20%."

Is she right?

We can evaluate her statement by conducting a full-scale ratio analysis of Growth Industries. Our purpose is to assess GI's performance in the recent past, to evaluate its future prospects, and to determine whether its market price reflects its intrinsic value.

Table 19.10 shows the key financial ratios we can compute from GI's financial statements. The president is certainly right about the growth in sales, assets, and operating income. Inspection of GI's key financial ratios, however, contradicts her first sentence: 19X3 was not another successful year for GI—it appears to have been another miserable one.

TABLE 19.10   Key Financial Ratios of Growth Industries, Inc.

Year	ROE	(1) $\dfrac{\text{Net Profit}}{\text{Pretax Profit}}$	(2) $\dfrac{\text{Pretax Profit}}{\text{EBIT}}$	(3) $\dfrac{\text{EBIT}}{\text{Sales}}$ (ROS)	(4) $\dfrac{\text{Sales}}{\text{Assets}}$ (ATO)	(5) $\dfrac{\text{Assets}}{\text{Equity}}$	(6) Compound Leverage Factor (2) × (5)	(7) ROA (3) × (4)	P/E	P/B
19X1	7.51%	.6	.650	30%	.303	2.117	1.376	9.09%	8	.58
19X2	6.08	.6	.470	30	.303	2.375	1.116	9.09	6	.35
19X3	3.03	.6	.204	30	.303	2.723	.556	9.09	4	.12
Industry average	8.64%	.6	.800	30%	.400	1.500	1.200	12.00%	8	.69

ROE has been declining steadily from 7.51 percent in 19X1 to 3.03 percent in 19X3. A comparison of GI's 19X3 ROE to the 19X3 industry average of 8.64 percent makes the deteriorating time trend appear especially alarming. The low and falling market-to-book-value ratio and the falling price/earnings ratio indicate investors are less and less optimistic about the firm's future profitability.

The fact that ROA has not been declining, however, tells us that the source of the declining time trend in GI's ROE must be inappropriate use of financial leverage. And we see that, while GI's leverage ratio climbed from 2.117 in 19X1 to 2.723 in 19X3, its interest-burden ratio fell from 0.650 to 0.204—with the net result that the compound leverage factor fell from 1.376 to 0.556.

The rapid increase in short-term debt from year to year and the concurrent increase in interest expense make it clear that, to finance its 20 percent growth rate in sales, GI has incurred sizable amounts of short-term debt at high interest rates. The firm is paying rates of interest greater than the ROA it is earning on the investment financed with the new borrowing. As the firm has expanded, its situation has become ever more precarious.

In 19X3, for example, the average interest rate on short-term debt was 20 percent versus an ROA of 9.09 percent. (We compute the average interest rate on short-term debt by taking the total interest expense of $34,391,000, subtracting the $6 million in interest on the long-term bonds, and dividing by the beginning-of-year short-term debt of $141,957,000.)

GI's problems become clear when we examine its statement of cash flows in Table 19.11. The statement is derived from the income statement and balance

TABLE 19.11   Growth Industries Statement of Cash Flows ($ Thousands)

	19X1	19X2	19X3
Cash Flow from Operating Activities			
Net income	$ 11,700	$ 10,143	$ 5,285
+ Depreciation	15,000	18,000	21,600
+ Decrease (increase) in accounts receivable	(5,000)	(6,000)	(7,200)
+ Decrease (increase) in inventories	(15,000)	(18,000)	(21,600)
+ Increase in accounts payable	6,000	7,200	8,640
	$ 12,700	$ 11,343	$ 6,725
Cash Flow from Investing Activities			
Investment in plant and equipment*	$(45,000)	$(54,000)	$(64,800)
Cash Flow from Financing Activities			
Dividends paid†	$ 0	$ 0	$ 0
Short-term debt issued	$ 42,300	$ 54,657	$ 72,475
Change in cash and marketable securities‡	$ 10,000	$ 12,000	$ 14,400

* Gross investment equals increase in net plant and equipment plus depreciation.
† We can conclude that no dividends are paid because stockholders' equity increases each year by the full amount of net income, implying a plowback ratio of 1.0.
‡ Equals cash flow from operations plus cash flow from investment activities plus cash flow from financing activities. Note that this equals the yearly change in cash and marketable securities on the balance sheet.

sheet in Table 19.8. GI's cash flow from operations is falling steadily, from $12,700,000 in 19X1 to $6,725,000 in 19X3. The firm's investment in plant and equipment, by contrast, has increased greatly. Net plant and equipment (i.e., net of depreciation) rose from $150,000,000 in 19X0 to $259,200,000 in 19X3. This near doubling of the capital assets makes the decrease in cash flow from operations all the more troubling.

The source of the difficulty is GI's enormous amount of short-term borrowing. In a sense, the company is being run as a pyramid scheme. It borrows more and more each year to maintain its 20 percent growth rate in assets and income. However, the new assets are not generating enough cash flow to support the extra interest burden of the debt, as the falling cash flow from operations indicates. Eventually, when the firm loses its ability to borrow further, its growth will be at an end.

At this point, GI stock might be an attractive investment. Its market price is only 12 percent of its book value, and with a P/E ratio of 4 its earnings yield is 25 percent per year. GI is a likely candidate for a takeover by another firm that might replace GI's management and build shareholder value through a radical change in policy.

Concept Check

Question 4. You have the following information for IBX Corporation for the years 1991 and 1988 (all figures are in $ millions):

	1991	1988
Net income	$ 253.7	$ 239.0
Pretax income	411.9	375.6
EBIT	517.6	403.1
Average assets	4,857.9	3,459.7
Sales	6,679.3	4,537.0
Shareholders' equity	2,233.3	2,347.3

What is the trend in IBX's ROE, and how can you account for it in terms of tax burden, margin, turnover, and financial leverage?

19.6   *Comparability*

The Problem

Financial statement analysis gives us a good amount of ammunition for evaluating a company's performance and future prospects, but comparing financial results of different companies is not so simple. There is more than one acceptable way to represent various items of revenue and expense according to generally accepted accounting principles (GAAP). This means that two firms may have exactly the same economic income yet very different accounting incomes.

Furthermore, interpreting a single firm's performance over time is complicated when inflation distorts the dollar measuring rod. Comparability problems are especially acute in this case, because the impact of inflation on reported results often depends on the particular method the firm adopts to account for inventories and depreciation. The security analyst must adjust the earnings and the financial ratio figures to a uniform standard before attempting to compare financial results across firms and over time.

Comparability problems can arise out of the flexibility of GAAP guidelines in accounting for inventories and depreciation and in adjusting for the effects of inflation. Other important potential sources of noncomparability include the capitalization of leases and other expenses and the treatment of pension costs, but they are beyond the scope of this book. Analysts may also choose to include or exclude non-recurring items such as write-offs, reserves, and gains or losses from discontinued operations in reporting earnings. Similarly, analysts may treat intangibles differently when estimating book value.

Inventory Valuation

There are two commonly used ways to value inventories: **LIFO** (last-in, first-out) and **FIFO** (first-in, first-out). The difference is best explained using a numerical example. Suppose Generic Products, Inc. (GPI), has a constant inventory of 1 million units of generic goods. The inventory turns over once per year, meaning that the ratio of cost of goods sold to inventory is 1.

The LIFO system calls for valuing the million units used up during the year at the current cost of production, so that the last goods produced are considered the first ones to be sold. The FIFO system assumes that the units used up or sold are the ones that were added to inventory first, and therefore that goods sold should be valued at original cost. If the price of generic goods were constant, for example, at the level of $1, the book value of inventory and the cost of goods sold would be the same $1 million under both systems. But suppose the price of generic goods rises by 10 cents during the year as a result of general inflation. LIFO accounting would result in a cost of goods sold of $1.1 million, while the end-of-year balance sheet value of the 1 million units in inventory remains $1 million. The balance sheet value of inventories is measured as the cost of the goods still in inventory. Under LIFO, the last goods produced are assumed to be sold at the current cost of $1.10; the goods remaining are thus the previously produced goods, at a cost of only $1. You can see that although LIFO accounting accurately measures the cost of goods sold, it understates the current value of the remaining inventory in an inflationary environment.

In contrast, under FIFO accounting the cost of goods sold would be $1 million, and the end-of-year balance sheet value of the inventory would be $1.1 million. The result is that the LIFO firm has both a lower profit and a lower balance sheet of inventories than the FIFO firm.

LIFO is to be preferred to FIFO in computing economic earnings (i.e., real sustainable cash flow), because it uses up-to-date prices to evaluate the cost of goods sold. However, LIFO accounting induces balance sheet distortions when it values investment in inventories at original cost. This practice results in an upward bias in ROE, since the investment base on which return is earned is undervalued.

Canadian tax law requires that firms use FIFO accounting in determining their taxable income, but they are free to use LIFO in their internal or annual reporting. In the case of a discrepancy between accounting methods used, an adjustment must be made for the deferred tax credit or liability that is created with respect to the reported financial statements.

Depreciation

Depreciation comparability problems include one more wrinkle. A firm can use different depreciation methods for tax purposes than for other reporting purposes. Canadian firms must use an accelerated depreciation method (declining balance for most depreciable assets) to calculate the capital cost allowance (CCA) for tax purposes; they are free, however, to use straight-line CCA in published financial statements. There are also differences across firms in their estimates of the depreciable life of plant, equipment, and other depreciable assets.

The major problem related to depreciation, however, is caused by inflation. Because conventional depreciation is based on historical costs rather than on the current replacement cost of assets, measured depreciation in periods of inflation is understated relative to replacement cost, and *real* economic income (sustainable cash flow) is correspondingly overstated.

The situation is similar to what happens in FIFO inventory accounting. Conventional depreciation and FIFO both result in an inflation-induced overstatement of real income, because both use original cost instead of current cost to calculate income. For example, suppose Generic Products, Inc., has a machine with a three-year useful life that originally cost $3 million. Annual straight-line depreciation is $1 million, regardless of what happens to the replacement cost of the machine. Suppose inflation in the first year turns out to be 10 percent. Then the true annual depreciation expense is $1.1 million in current terms, while conventionally measured depreciation remains fixed at $1 million per year. Accounting income therefore overstates *real* economic income by the inflation factor, $100,000. Again, if firms use straight-line depreciation for reported statements while using declining balance for tax purposes, a discrepancy with respect to tax liability is created; consequently, the appropriate adjustment must be noted in the statements.

Inflation and Interest Expense

If inflation can cause distortions in the measurement of a firm's inventory and depreciation costs, it has perhaps an even greater effect on calculation of *real* interest expense. Nominal interest rates include an inflation premium that compensates the lender for inflation-induced erosion in the *real* value of principal. From the perspective of both lender and borrower, part of what is conventionally measured as interest expense should be treated more properly as repayment of principal.

For example, suppose Generic Products has debt outstanding with a face value of $10 million, paying 10 percent per year. Interest expense, as conventionally measured, is therefore $1 million per year. However, suppose inflation during the year is 6 percent, so that the real interest rate is 4 percent. Then $600,000 of what appears as interest expense on the income statement is really an inflation premium, or compensation for the anticipated reduction in the real value of the $10 million principal; only $400,000 is *real* interest expense. The $600,000 reduction in the purchasing power of the outstanding principal may be thought of as repayment of principal, rather than as an interest expense. Real income of the firm is therefore understated by $600,000. Mismeasurement of real interest means that inflation deflates the statement of real income. The effects of inflation on the reported values of inventories and depreciation that we have discussed work in the opposite direction.

These distortions might by chance cancel each other out, so that the reported income figure is an unbiased estimate of real economic income. Although this seems extremely improbable for any individual firm, there is some evidence that these distortions have approximately offset one another for the aggregate corporate sector of the U.S. economy during the past 20 years.[16] Both in Canada and the United States, the responsible accounting bodies (in Canada, the Canadian Institute of Chartered Accountants, or CICA) have tried to impose a requirement for inflation-adjusted accounting reports as supplements to regular statements. Reportedly, however, security analysts by and large ignore the inflation-adjusted data, particularly since this adds another element of non-comparability. Consequently, the requirement has been dropped in both jurisdictions.

Concept Check

> Question 5. In a period of rapid inflation, companies ABC and XYZ have the same *reported* earnings. ABC uses LIFO inventory accounting, has relatively fewer depreciable assets, and has more debt than XYZ. XYZ uses FIFO inventory accounting. Which company has the higher *real* income, and why?

---

[16] See F. Modigliani and R. Cohn, "Inflation, Rational Valuation and the Market," *Financial Analysts Journal*, March/April 1979.

19.7   *Value Investing: The Graham Technique*

No presentation of fundamental security analysis would be complete without a discussion of the ideas of Benjamin Graham, the greatest of the investment "gurus." Until the evolution of modern portfolio theory in the latter half of this century, Graham was the single most important thinker, writer, and teacher in the field of investment analysis. His influence on investment professionals remains very strong.

Graham's magnum opus is *Security Analysis*, written with Columbia Professor David Dodd in 1934. Its message is similar to the ideas presented in this chapter. By analyzing a firm's financial statements carefully, Graham felt one could identify bargain stocks. Over the years, he developed many different rules for determining the most important financial ratios and the critical values for judging a stock to be undervalued. Through its many editions, his book has had a profound influence on investment professionals. It has been so influential and successful, in fact, that widespread adoption of Graham's techniques has led to the elimination of the very bargains they are designed to identify.

In a 1976 seminar, Graham said:

I am no longer an advocate of elaborate techniques of security analysis in order to find superior value opportunities. This was a rewarding activity, say, 40 years ago, when our textbook "Graham and Dodd" was first published; but the situation has changed a good deal since then. In the old days any well-trained security analyst could do a good professional job of selecting undervalued issues through detailed studies; but in the light of the enormous amount of research now being carried on, I doubt whether in most cases such extensive efforts will generate sufficiently superior selections to justify their cost. To that very limited extent I'm on the side of the "efficient market" school of thought now generally accepted by the professors.[17]

Nonetheless, in that same seminar Graham suggested a simplified approach to identify bargain stocks:

My first, more limited, technique confines itself to the purchase of common stocks at less than their working-capital value, or net current-asset value, giving no weight to the plant and other fixed assets, and deducting all liabilities in full from the current assets. We used this approach extensively in managing investment funds, and over a 30-odd-year period we must have earned an average of some 20 percent per year from this source. For a while, however, after the mid-1950s, this brand of buying opportunity became very scarce because of the pervasive bull market. But it has returned in quantity since the 1973–1974 decline. In January 1976 we counted over 100 such issues in the Standard & Poor's *Stock Guide*—about 10 percent of the total. I consider it a foolproof method of systematic investment—once again, not on the basis of individual results but in terms of the expectable group outcome.

---

[17] As cited by John Train in *Money Masters* (New York: Harper & Row, Publishers, Inc., 1987). Graham is reported to have attributed his success in investing to the purchase of growth stocks rather than to reliance on fundamental analysis.

There are two convenient sources of information for those interested in trying out the Graham technique. Both Standard & Poor's *Outlook* and *The Value Line Investment Survey* carry lists of stocks selling below net working capital value.

Summary

1. The primary focus of the security analyst should be the firm's real economic earnings rather than its reported earnings. Accounting earnings as reported in financial statements can be a biased estimate of real economic earnings, although empirical studies reveal that reported earnings convey considerable information concerning a firm's prospects.

2. A firm's ROE is a key determinant of the growth rate of its earnings. ROE is affected profoundly by the firm's degree of financial leverage. An increase in a firm's debt-to-equity ratio will raise its ROE and hence its growth rate only if the interest rate on the debt is less than the firm's return on assets.

3. It is often helpful to the analyst to decompose a firm's ROE ratio into the product of several accounting ratios and to analyze their separate behaviour over time and across companies within an industry. A useful breakdown is

$$\text{ROE} = \frac{\text{Net profits}}{\text{Pretax profits}} \times \frac{\text{Pretax profits}}{\text{EBIT}} \times \frac{\text{EBIT}}{\text{Sales}} \times \frac{\text{Sales}}{\text{Assets}} \times \frac{\text{Assets}}{\text{Equity}}$$

4. Other accounting ratios that have a bearing on a firm's profitability and/or risk are fixed asset turnover, inventory turnover, days receivables, and current, quick, and interest coverage ratios.

5. Two ratios that make use of the market price of the firm's common stock in addition to its financial statements are the ratio of market-to-book value and the price-earnings ratio. Analysts sometimes take low values for these ratios as a margin of safety or a sign that the stock is a bargain.

6. A strategy of investing in stocks with high reported ROE seems to produce a lower rate of return to the investor than investing in low ROE stocks. This implies that high reported ROE stocks are overpriced compared with low ROE stocks.

7. A major problem in the use of data obtained from a firm's financial statements is comparability. Firms have a great deal of latitude in how they choose to compute various items of revenue and expense. It is therefore necessary for the security analyst to adjust accounting earnings and financial ratios to a uniform standard before attempting to compare financial results across firms.

8. Comparability problems can be acute in a period of inflation. Inflation can create distortions in accounting for inventories, depreciation, and interest expense.

Key terms

Income statement
Balance sheet
Statement of changes in financial
  position
Accounting earnings
Economic earnings
Return on equity
Return on assets
Profit margin
Return on sales
Asset turnover
Leverage ratio

Average collection period (Days
  receivables)
Current ratio
Quick ratio (Acid test ratio)
Interest coverage ratio (Times
  interest earned)
Market-to-book-value ratio
Price-earnings ratio
Earnings yield
LIFO
FIFO

Selected readings

The classic book on the use of financial statements in equity valuation, now in its fifth edition, is:

   Cottle, S.; Murray, R.; and Block, F. *Graham and Dodd's Security Analysis.* New York: McGraw-Hill, Inc., 1988.

Problems

1. The Crusty Pie Co., which specializes in the production of apple turnovers, has a return on sales higher than the industry average, yet its ROA is the same as the industry average. How can you explain this?
2. The ABC Corporation has a profit margin on sales below the industry average, yet its ROA is above the industry average. What does this imply about its asset turnover?
3. Firm A and firm B have the same ROA, yet firm A's ROE is higher. How can you explain this?
4. (1988 CFA Examination, Level I) Which of the following *best* explains a ratio of "net sales to average net fixed assets" that *exceeds* the industry average?
    a. The firm expanded its plant and equipment in the past few years.
    b. The firm makes less efficient use of its assets than other firms.
    c. The firm has a lot of old plant and equipment.
    d. The firm uses straight line depreciation.
5. (1988 CFA Examination, Level I) The rate of return on assets is equivalent to:
    a. Profit margin × Total asset turnover
    b. Profit margin × Total asset turnover × Leverage ratio/Interest expense

    c. Net income + Interest expense net of income tax +

$$\frac{\text{Minority interest in earnings}}{\text{Average total assets}}$$

    d. $\dfrac{\text{Net income + Minority interest in earnings}}{\text{Average total assets}}$

       i. a only
      ii. a and c
      iii. b only
      iv. b and d

6. (1988 CFA Examination, Level I) Which one of the following is *true*?

    a. During inflation, LIFO makes the income statement less representative than if FIFO were used.

    b. During inflation, FIFO makes the balance sheet less representative than if LIFO were used.

    c. After inflation ends, distortion due to LIFO will disappear as inventory is sold.

    d. None of the above.

7. (1987 CFA Examination, Level I) The financial statements for Seattle Manufacturing Corporation are to be used to compute the following ratios for 1986 (Tables 19A and 19B)

    a. Return on total assets

    b. Earnings per share of common stock

    c. Acid test ratio

    d. Interest coverage ratio

    e. Receivables collection period

    f. Leverage ratio

TABLE 19A Seattle Manufacturing Corp. Consolidated Balance Sheet, as of December 31 ($ Millions)

	1985	1986
Assets		
Current assets		
Cash	$ 6.2	$ 6.6
Short-term investment in commercial paper	20.8	15.0
Accounts receivable	77.0	93.2
Inventory	251.2	286.0
Prepaid manufacturing expense	1.4	1.8
Total current assets	**$356.6**	**$402.6**
Leased property under capital leases net of accumulated amortization	181.4	215.6
Other	6.2	9.8
Total assets	**$544.2**	**$628.0**

TABLE 19A   Continued

	1985	1986
Liabilities		
Current liabilities		
Accounts payable	$143.2	$161.0
Dividends payable	13.0	14.4
Current portion of long-term debt	12.0	16.6
Current portion of obligations under capital leases	18.8	22.6
Estimated taxes on income	10.8	9.8
Total current liabilities	**$197.8**	**$224.4**
Long-term debt	86.4	107.0
Obligations under capital leases	140.8	165.8
Total liabilities	**$425.0**	**$497.2**
Shareholder's Equity		
Common stock, $10 par value: 4,000,000 shares authorized, 3,000,000 and 2,680,000 outstanding, respectively	$ 26.8	$ 30.0
Cumulative preferred stock, Series A 8%; $25 par value; 1,000,000 authorized; 600,000 outstanding	15.0	15.0
Additional paid-in capital	26.4	27.0
Retained earnings	51.0	58.8
Total shareholders' equity	**$119.2**	**$130.8**
Total liabilities and shareholders' equity	**$544.2**	**$628.0**

TABLE 19B   Seattle Manufacturing Corp. Income Statement, Years Ending December 31 ($ Millions)

	1985	1986
Sales	$1,166.6	$1,207.6
Other income, net	12.8	15.6
Total revenues	**$1,179.4**	**$1,223.2**
Cost of sales	$ 912.0	$ 961.2
Amortization of leased property	43.6	48.6
Selling and administrative expense	118.4	128.8
Interest expense	16.2	19.8
Total costs and expenses	**$1,090.2**	**$1,158.4**
Income before income tax	$ 89.2	$ 64.8
Income tax	19.2	10.4
Net income	**$ 70.0**	**$ 54.4**

8. (1986 CFA Examination, Level I) The financial statements for Chicago Refrigerator Inc. are to be used to compute the following ratios for 1985 (Tables 19C and 19D).
   a. Quick ratio
   b. Return on assets
   c. Return on common shareholders' equity
   d. Earnings per share of common stock
   e. Profit margin
   f. Times interest earned
   g. Inventory turnover
   h. Leverage ratio

TABLE 19C   Chicago Refrigerator Inc. Balance Sheet, as of December 31 ($ Thousands)

	1984	1985
Assets		
Current assets		
Cash	$ 683	$ 325
Accounts receivable	1,490	3,599
Inventories	1,415	2,423
Prepaid expenses	15	13
Total current assets	$3,603	$6,360
Property, plant, equipment, net	1,066	1,541
Other	123	157
Total assets	$4,792	$8,058
Liabilities		
Current liabilities		
Notes payable to bank	$ —	$ 875
Current portion of long-term debt	38	116
Accounts payable	485	933
Estimated income tax	588	472
Accrued expenses	576	586
Customer advance payment	34	963
Total current liabilities	$1,721	$3,945
Long-term debt	122	179
Other liabilities	81	131
Total liabilities	$1,924	$4,255
Shareholder's Equity		
Common stock, $1 par value: 1,000,000 shares authorized; 550,000 and 829,000 outstanding, respectively	$ 550	$ 829
Preferred stock, Series A 10%; $25.00 par value; 25,000 authorized; 20,000 and 18,000 outstanding, respectively	500	450
Additional paid-in capital	450	575
Retained earnings	1,368	1,949
Total shareholders' equity	$2,868	$3,803
Total liabilities and shareholders' equity	$4,792	$8,058

TABLE 19D   Chicago Refrigerator Inc. Income Statement, Years Ending December 31 ($ Thousands)

	1984	1985
Net sales	$7,570	$12,065
Other income, net	261	345
Total revenues	**$7,831**	**$12,410**
Cost of goods sold	$4,850	$ 8,048
General administrative and market-		
ing expense	1,531	2,025
Interest expense	22	78
Total costs and expenses	**$6,403**	**$10,151**
Net income before tax	$1,428	$ 2,259
Income tax	628	994
Net income	**$ 800**	**$ 1,265**

9. (1985 CFA Examination, Level I) The financial statements for Atlas Corporation are to be used to compute the following ratios for 1984 (Tables 19E and 19F).
   a. Acid-test ratio
   b. Inventory turnover
   c. Earnings per share
   d. Interest coverage
   e. Leverage
10. (Based on the 1987 CFA Examination, Level I) The profit growth of United States Tobacco Company has been excellent over the past 10 years. Identify the five sources of corporate internal earnings growth, and from the data appearing in Tables 19G, 19H, and 19I state whether each has or has not contributed to the profit progress of United States Tobacco Co. over the past 10 years.
11. (Based on the 1984 CFA Examination, Level I) The Coca-Cola Company (KO) and PepsiCo, Inc. (PEP), are the leading companies in the worldwide market for soft drinks and snack foods. Return on shareholders' equity is a prime measure of management's performance and can be analyzed using turnover, leverage, profit margin, and income tax rate. Use the ratios and company data provided in Tables 19J–19M below to:
    a. Calculate the return on average common equity for KO and PEP for the two years 1977 and 1983.
    b. Identify the ratios that account for the level and trend of ROE for each company in these two years.

TABLE 19E   Atlas Corporation Consolidated Balance Sheet, as of December 31 ($ Millions)

	1983	1984
Assets		
Current assets		
Cash	$ 3.1	$ 3.3
Short-term investment in commercial paper	2.9	—
Accounts receivable	38.5	46.6
Inventory	125.6	143.0
Prepaid manufacturing expense	.7	.9
Total current assets	**$170.8**	**$193.8**
Leased property under capital leases net of accumulated amortization	$ 90.7	$107.8
Other	3.1	4.9
Total assets	**$264.6**	**$306.5**
Liabilities		
Current liabilities		
Accounts payable	$ 71.6	$ 81.7
Dividends payable	6.5	6.0
Current portion of long-term debt	6.0	8.3
Current portion of obligation under capital leases	9.4	11.3
Estimated taxes on income	5.4	4.9
Total current liabilities	**$ 98.9**	**$112.2**
Long-term debt	$ 43.2	$ 53.5
Obligations under capital leases	70.4	82.9
Total liabilities	**$212.5**	**$248.6**
Shareholders' Equity		
Common stock, $10 par value: 2,000,000 shares authorized; 1,340,000 and 1,500,000 outstanding, respectively	$ 13.4	$ 15.0
Additional paid-in capital	13.2	13.5
Retained earnings	25.5	29.4
Total shareholders' equity	**$ 52.1**	**$ 57.9**
Total liabilities and shareholders' equity	**$264.6**	**$306.5**

TABLE 19F   Atlas Corporation Income Statement, Years Ending December 31 ($ Millions)

	1983	1984
Sales	$583.3	$603.8
Other income, net	6.4	2.8
Main revenues	**$589.7**	**$606.6**
Cost of sales	$456.0	$475.6
Amortization of leased property	21.8	24.3
Selling and administrative expense	59.2	64.4
Interest expense	8.1	9.9
Total costs and expenses	**$545.1**	**$574.2**
Income before income tax	$ 44.6	$ 32.4
Income tax	9.6	5.2
Net income	**$ 35.0**	**$ 27.2**

TABLE 19G　The United States Tobacco Company, Historic Income Statement Data ($ Thousands)

	Revenues	Income before Interest and Taxes		Interest Expense	Income before Taxes		Taxes		Net Income		Earnings per Share	
		Amount	% of Revs.		Amount	% of Revs.	Amount	Tax Rate	Amount	% Increase	Amount	% Increase
1986	$517,996	$200,274	38.7%	$5,534	$194,740	37.6%	$90,802	46.6%	$103,938	11.1%	$1.79	9.1%
1985	480,021	177,122	36.9	5,898	171,224	35.7	77,695	45.4	93,529	11.7	1.64	14.7
1984	443,792	165,053	37.2	5,147	159,906	36.0	76,179	47.6	83,727	18.5	1.43	19.2
1983	382,783	141,228	36.9	4,688	136,540	35.7	65,892	48.3	70,648	27.7	1.21	19.8
1982	320,448	110,266	34.4	6,575	103,691	32.4	48,356	46.6	55,335	21.2	1.01	20.2
1981	280,229	92,277	32.9	3,622	88,655	31.6	42,993	48.5	45,662	21.2	0.84	20.0
1980	265,762	80,677	30.4	5,149	75,528	28.4	37,842	50.1	37,686	17.6	0.70	16.7
1979	233,262	67,662	29.0	6,943	60,719	26.0	28,685	47.2	32,034	15.1	0.60	3.2
1978	205,861	59,006	28.7	4,766	54,240	26.4	26,412	48.7	27,828	14.3	0.53	12.8
1977	181,033	49,508	27.4	3,807	45,701	25.2	21,354	46.7	24,347	25.6	0.47	23.7
1976	166,405	42,159	25.3	3,403	38,726	23.3	19,342	50.0	19,384	21.0	0.38	11.1
Compound Annual Growth Rates												
1976–86	12%	17%		5%	18%		17%		18%		17%	

TABLE 19H　The United States Tobacco Company, Historic Asset and Equity Analysis
　　　　　　　　($ Thousands)

	Average Total Assets	Revenues/ Average Total Assets	Average Total Equity	Net Income as % of Average Total Equity	Average Total Equity as % of Total Average Capitalization
1986	$496,026	1.04	$347,468	30%	75%
1985	438,295	1.10	302,233	31	73
1984	390,654	1.14	270,563	31	79
1983	352,800	1.08	239,405	30	75
1982	306,810	1.04	202,154	27	74
1981	271,959	1.03	173,821	26	75
1980	252,491	1.05	151,871	25	73
1979	230,072	1.01	133,274	24	71
1978	197,658	1.04	117,316	24	69
1977	166,729	1.09	102,788	24	69
1976	145,820	1.14	89,643	22	66

TABLE 19I The United States Tobacco Company, Historic Dividend and Retained Earnings Analysis ($ Thousands)

	Dividends		Retained Earnings	
	Amount	% of Net Income	Amount	% of Net Income
1986	$54,744	53%	$49,194	47%
1985	47,835	51	45,694	49
1984	40,494	48	43,233	52
1983	32,493	46	38,155	54
1982	25,722	46	29,613	54
1981	21,892	48	23,770	52
1980	18,863	50	18,823	50
1979	16,395	51	15,639	49
1978	14,144	51	13,684	49
1977	12,257	50	12,090	50
1976	9,492	49	9,892	51

TABLE 19J Selected Financial Ratios

Fiscal Year	EBIT ÷ Assets		Total Assets ÷ Common Equity		Net Earnings ÷ Pretax Earnings		Net Sales ÷ Total Assets	
	KO	PEP	KO	PEP	KO	PEP	KO	PEP
1983 (est.)	21.1%	14.7%	1.78x	2.56x	56.0%	58.0%	1.33x	1.82
1982	23.7	16.9	1.68	2.57	55.0	57.2	1.47	1.82
1981	24.3	17.7	1.60	2.53	55.4	58.5	1.69	1.89
1980	24.3	18.3	1.59	2.39	55.1	56.5	1.77	1.90
1979	26.2	18.5	1.51	2.20	55.4	59.8	1.70	1.92
1978	27.8	19.8	1.46	2.13	54.4	56.1	1.69	1.89
1977	27.9	20.1	1.41	2.31	54.0	55.4	1.59	1.83
1976	28.3	16.9	1.39	2.55	53.4	54.4	1.57	1.77
Averages								
1980–1983	23.3%	16.9%	1.66x	2.51x	55.4%	57.5%	1.57x	1.84x
1976–1979	27.6	18.8	1.44	2.30	54.3	56.4	1.64	1.85
1976–1983	25.4	17.9	1.55	2.41	54.8	57.0	1.60	1.86

Average of beginning- and end-of-year assets and equity used where applicable in computing ratios.

TABLE 19K   Selected Financial Ratios

Fiscal Year	Pretax Earnings ÷ Net Sales		Net Earnings ÷ Total Assets		Net Earnings ÷ Common Equity		Dividends ÷ Net Earnings	
	KO	PEP	KO	PEP	KO	PEP	KO	PEP
1983 (est.)	14.8%	6.4%	11.0%	6.5%	19.6%	16.6%	64.6%	53.1%
1982	14.9	7.1	12.1	7.4	20.3	18.9	62.8	48.9
1981	13.7	7.2	12.8	8.0	20.6	20.3	59.5	44.1
1980	13.1	7.7	12.8	8.3	20.3	19.8	63.2	44.1
1979	15.2	8.2	14.3	9.4	21.6	20.8	57.6	40.9
1978	16.2	9.2	14.9	9.8	21.8	20.9	57.4	40.6
1977	17.5	9.7	15.1	9.9	21.3	22.8	57.5	38.6
1976	18.0	9.6	15.1	9.2	21.1	23.4	55.7	35.4
Averages								
1980–1983	14.1%	7.1%	12.2%	7.6%	20.2%	18.9%	62.5%	47.6%
1976–1979	16.7	9.2	14.9	9.6	21.4	22.0	57.1	38.9
1976–1983	15.4	8.1	13.5	8.6	20.8	20.4	59.8	43.2

Average of beginning- and end-of-year assets and equity used where applicable in computing ratios.

TABLE 19L   Selected Financial Statistics, The Coca-Cola Company ($ Millions)

	Fiscal Year							
	1983 (Est.)	1982	1981	1980	1979	1978	1977	1976
Operations								
Sales	6,820.0	6,249.0	5,889.0	5,621.0	4,689.0	4,095.0	3,394.0	2,989.0
Depreciation	180.0	148.9	136.9	131.0	110.0	91.0	80.0	70.0
Interest	73.0	74.6	38.3	35.1	10.7	7.8	NA	NA
Income taxes	444.0	419.8	360.2	330.4	318.0	303.0	273.0	251.0
Net earnings	565.0	512.2	447.0	406.0	395.0	361.0	321.0	288.0
Financial Position								
Cash	616.4	311.0	393.0	289.0	209.0	369.0	418.0	403.0
Receivables	831.3	751.8	483.5	523.1	435.1	338.3	279.9	237.3
Current assets	2,444.2	2,076.6	1,636.2	1,622.3	1,305.6	1,236.6	1,103.5	1,027.3
Total assets	5,331.0	4,923.3	3,564.8	3,406.0	2,938.0	2,582.8	2,254.5	2,007.0
Current liabilities	1,702.7	1,326.8	1,006.3	1,061.6	884.2	744.0	596.3	506.4
Long-term debt	475.0	462.3	137.3	133.2	31.0	15.2	15.3	11.0
Common equity	2,990.0	2,778.7	2,270.8	2,074.7	1,918.7	1,739.6	1,578.0	1,434.0

TABLE 19M   Selected Financial Statistics, PepsiCo, Inc.* ($ Millions)

	Fiscal Year							
	1983 (Est.)	1982	1981	1980	1979	1978	1977	1976
Operations								
Sales	7,700.0	7,499.0	7,027.0	5,975.0	5,089.0	4,300.0	3,649.0	3,109.0
Depreciation	260.0	230.4	205.5	172.9	142.1	117.0	93.7	79.1
Interest	156.0	166.2	149.7	114.7	73.1	52.0	46.0	45.0
Income taxes	206.0	226.8	210.8	200.8	168.2	174.3	158.3	135.3
Net earnings	285.0	303.7†	297.5	260.7	250.4	223.0	196.7	161.7
Financial Position								
Cash and equivalents	397.3	280.3	239.0	232.0	205.0	167.0	256.0	231.0
Receivables	785.7	746.1	741.4	596.7	557.2	433.6	374.4	324.5
Current assets	1,739.4	1,590.6	1,762.5	1,326.5	1,201.4	1,010.5	997.0	903.7
Total assets	4,588.9	4,197.5	4,040.0	3,399.9	2,888.9	2,416.8	2,130.3	1,853.6
Current liabilities	1,440.0	1,345.6	1,430.7	1,005.3	843.6	650.7	574.5	478.9
Long-term debt	786.7	864.2	816.1	781.7	619.0	479.1	427.9	278.6
Common equity	1,786.3	1,650.5	1,556.3	1,381.0	1,247.0	1,165.0	971.9	753.0

* Amounts for 1978–1981 restated to reflect overstatement of net income aggregating $92.1 million.
† Before unusual charge of $79.4 million.

CHAPTER 20

Technical Analysis

In the two previous chapters, we examined fundamental analysis of equity, considering how the general macroeconomic environment and the specific prospects of the firm or industry might affect the present value of the dividend stream the firm can be expected to generate. In this chapter, we examine technical analysis. Technical analysis focuses more on past price movements of a company than on the underlying fundamental determinants of future profitability. Technicians believe that past price and volume data signal future price movements.

Such a view is diametrically opposed to that of the efficient market hypothesis, which holds that all historical data must be reflected in stock prices already. As we lay out the basics of technical analysis in this chapter, we will point out the contradiction between the assumptions on which these strategies are based and the notion of well-functioning capital markets with rational and informed traders.

20.1 *Technical Analysis*

Technical analysis is, in most instances, an attempt to exploit recurring and predictable patterns in stock prices to generate abnormal trading profits. Technicians do not necessarily deny the value of fundamental information such as we have discussed in the past two chapters. Many technical analysts believe stock prices eventually "close in" on their fundamental values. Technicians believe, nevertheless, that shifts in market fundamentals can be discerned before the impact of those shifts is fully reflected in prices. As the market adjusts to a new equilibrium, astute traders can exploit these price trends.

Technicians also believe that market fundamentals can be perturbed by irrational factors. More or less random fluctuations in price will accompany any underlying trend. If these fluctuations dissipate slowly, they can be taken advantage of for abnormal profits.

These presumptions, of course, clash head-on with those of the efficient market hypothesis (EMH) and with the logic of well-functioning capital markets. According to the EMH, a shift in market fundamentals should be reflected in prices immediately. According to technicians, though, that shift will lead to a gradual price change that can be recognized as a trend. Such easily exploited trends in stock market prices would be damning evidence against the EMH, as they would indicate profit opportunities that market participants had left unexploited.

A more subtle version of technical analysis holds that there are patterns in stock prices that can be exploited, but that once investors identify and attempt to profit from these patterns their trading activity affects prices, thereby altering price patterns. This means the patterns that characterize market prices will be constantly evolving, and only the best analysts who can identify new patterns earliest will be rewarded. We call this phenomenon *self-destructing* patterns and explore it further later in the chapter.

The notion of evolving patterns is consistent with almost but not quite efficient markets. It allows for the possibility of temporarily unexploited profit opportunities, but it also views market participants as aggressively exploiting those opportunities once they are uncovered. The market is continually groping toward full efficiency, but it is never quite there.

This is in some ways an appealing middle position in the ongoing debate between technicians and proponents of the EMH. Ultimately, however, it is an untestable hypothesis. Technicians will always be able to identify trading rules that would have worked in the past but need not work any longer. Is this evidence of a once viable trading rule that has now been eliminated by competition? Perhaps. But it is far more likely that the trading rule could have been identified only after the fact.

Until technicians can prove rigorous evidence that their trading rules provide *consistent* trading profits, we must doubt the viability of those rules. As you saw in the chapter on the efficient market hypothesis, the evidence on the performance of professionally managed funds does not support the efficacy of technical analysis.

20.2 *Charting*

Technical analysts are sometimes called *chartists* because they study records or charts of past stock prices and trading volume, hoping to find patterns they can exploit to make a profit. In this section, we examine several specific charting strategies.

The Dow Theory

The **Dow theory**, named after its creator Charles Dow (who established *The Wall Street Journal*), is the most famous of technical analyses. The aim of the Dow theory is to identify long-term trends in stock market prices. The two indicators used are the Dow Jones Industrial Average (DJIA) and the Dow Jones Transportation Average (DJTA). The DJIA is the key indicator of underlying trends, while the DJTA usually serves as a check to confirm or reject that signal.

The Dow theory posits three forces simultaneously affecting stock prices:

1. The *primary trend* is the long-term movement of prices, lasting from several months to several years.
2. *Secondary* or *intermediate trends* are caused by short-term deviations of prices from the underlying trend line. These deviations are eliminated via *corrections* when prices revert back to trend values.
3. *Tertiary* or *minor trends* are daily fluctuations of little importance.

Figure 20.1 represents these three components of stock price movements. In this figure, the primary trend is upward, but intermediate trends result in short-lived market declines lasting a few weeks. The intraday minor trends have no long-run impact on price.

Figure 20.2 depicts the course of the DJIA during 1988. The primary trend is upward, as evidenced by the fact that each market peak is higher than the previous peak (point F versus D versus B). Similarly, each low is higher than the previous low (E versus C versus A). This pattern of upward-moving "tops" and "bottoms" is one of the key ways to identify the underlying primary trend. Notice in Figure 20.2 that, despite the upward primary trend, intermediate trends still can lead to short periods of declining prices (points B through C, or D through E).

The Dow theory incorporates notions of support and resistance levels in stock prices. A **support level** is a value below which the market is relatively unlikely to fall. A **resistance level** is a value above which it is difficult to rise.

FIGURE 20.1

Dow theory trends.

(From Melanie F. Bowman and Thom Hartle, "Dow Theory," *Technical Analysis of Stocks and Commodities,* September 1990, p. 690.)

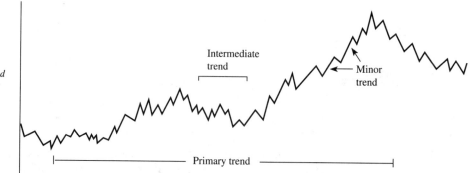

The primary trend is typically measured in years and the intermediate trend is measured in weeks to months, while the minor trend will last from days to weeks.

FIGURE 20.2

Dow Jones
Industrial Average,
January–November
1988.

(From Melanie F. Bowman and Thom Hartle, "Dow Theory," *Technical Analysis of Stocks an Commodities,* September 1990, p. 690.)

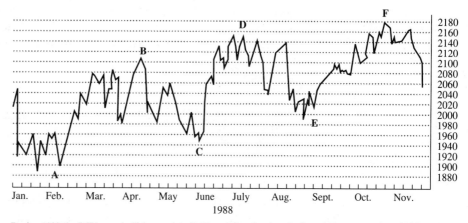

During 1988 the DJIA was bullish as points B, D, and F and points A, C, and E were a series of higher highs and higher lows, respectively.

Support and resistance levels are determined by the recent history of prices. In Figure 20.3, the price at point C would be viewed as a resistance level because the recent intermediate-trend high price was unable to rise above C. Hence, piercing the resistance point is a bullish signal. The fact that the transportation index also pierces its resistance level at point D confirms the bull market signal.

Technicians see resistance and support levels as resulting from common psychological investor traits. Consider, for example, stock XYZ, which traded for several months at a price of $72 and then declined to $65. If the stock eventually begins to increase in price, $72 is a natural resistance level because the many investors who bought originally at $72 will be eager to sell their shares

FIGURE 20.3

Dow theory
signals—confirmation
simulation.

(From Melanie F. Bowman and Thom Hartle, "Dow Theory," *Technical Analysis of Stocks and Commodities,* September 1990, p. 690.)

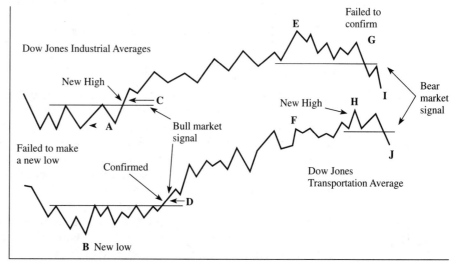

A simulated example of confirmation and non-confirmation by the DJIA and the DJTA.

as soon as they can break even on their investment. Whenever prices near $72, a wave of selling pressure would develop. Such activity imparts to the market a type of ''memory'' that allows past price history to influence current stock prospects.

Concept Check	Question 1. Describe how technicians might explain support levels.

At point G, the DJIA fails to move to a higher high when the DJTA reaches a higher high at point H. This contradictory signal, called a *non-confirmation,* is a warning sign. At points I and J, both indexes fall below the low points of the previous trading range, which is taken as a signal of the end of the primary bull market.

In evaluating the Dow theory, don't forget the lessons of the efficient market hypothesis. The Dow theory is based on a notion of predictably recurring price patterns. Yet the EMH holds that if any pattern is exploitable, many investors would attempt to profit from such predictability, which would ultimately move stock prices and cause the trading strategy to self-destruct. While Figure 20.2 certainly appears to describe a classic upward primary trend, one always must wonder whether we can see that trend only *after* the fact. Recognizing patterns as they emerge is far more difficult.

A recent variation on the Dow theory is the Elliott wave theory. Like the Dow theory, the idea behind Elliott waves is that stock prices can be described by a set of wave patterns. Long-term and short-term wave cycles are superimposed and result in a complicated pattern of price movements, but by interpreting the cycles, one can, according to the theory, predict broad movements. Robert Prechter is a famous advocate of this technique. The accompanying box reproduces a profile of Prechter from *The Wall Street Journal.*

Other Charting Techniques

The Dow theory posits a particular, and fairly simple, type of pattern in stock market prices: long-lasting trends with short-run deviations around those trends. Not surprisingly, several more involved patterns have been identified in stock market prices. Figure 20.4 illustrates several of these patterns. If stock prices actually follow any of these patterns, profit opportunities would result. The patterns are reasonably straightforward to discern, meaning future prices could be extrapolated from current prices.

A variant on pure trend analysis is the *point and figure chart* depicted in Figure 20.5. This figure has no time dimension. It simply traces significant upward or downward moves in stock prices without regard to their timing. The data for Figure 20.5 come from Table 20.1.

FIGURE 20.4

Chart representation of market bottoms and tops.

[From Irwin Shishko, "Techniques of Forecasting Commodity Prices," *Commodity Yearbook* (New York: Commodity Research Bureau, 1965), p. 4.]

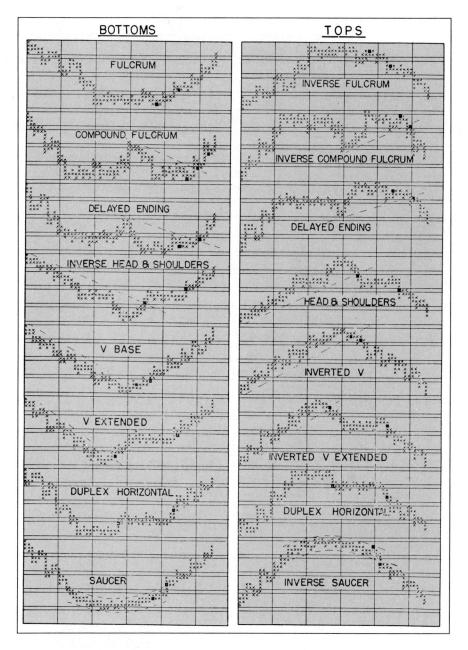

Suppose, as in Table 20.1, that a stock's price is currently $40. If the price rises by at least $2, you put an X in the first column at $42 in Figure 20.5. Another increase of at least $2 calls for placement of another X in the first column, this time at the $44 level. If the stock then falls by at least $2, you start a new column and put an O next to $42. Each subsequent $2 price fall results in another O in the second column. When prices reverse yet again and head

TABLE 20.1   Stock Price History

Date	Price	Date	Price
January 2	40	February 1	40*
January 3	40½	February 2	41
January 4	41	February 5	40½
January 5	42*	February 6	42*
January 8	41½	February 7	45*
January 9	42½	February 8	44½
January 10	43	February 9	46*
January 11	43¾	February 12	47
January 12	44*	February 13	48*
January 15	45	February 14	47½
January 16	44	February 15	46†
January 17	41½†	February 16	45
January 18	41	February 19	44*
January 19	40*	February 20	42*
January 22	39	February 21	41
January 23	39½	February 22	40*
January 24	39¾	February 23	41
January 25	38*	February 26	40½
January 26	35*	February 27	38*
January 29	36†	February 28	39
January 30	37	March 1	36*
January 31	39*	March 2	34*

upward, you begin the third column with an X denoting each consecutive $2 price increase.

The asterisks in Table 20.1 mark an event resulting in the placement of a new X or O in the chart. The daggers denote price movements that result in the start of a new column of Xs or Os.

FIGURE 20.5

Point and figure chart for Table 20.1.

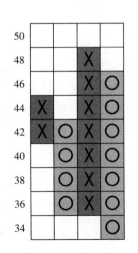

FIGURE 20.6

Point and figure chart with sell signal, buy signal, and congestion areas.

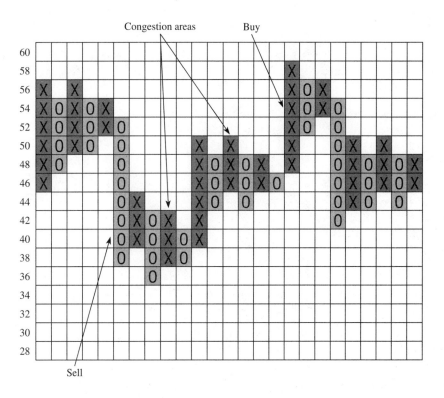

Sell signals are generated when the stock price *penetrates* previous lows, and buy signals occur when previous high prices are penetrated. A *congestion area* is a horizontal band of Xs and Os created by several price reversals. These three regions are indicated in Figure 20.6.

One can devise point and figure charts using price increments other than $2, but it is customary in setting up a chart to require reasonably substantial price changes before marking pluses or minuses.

Concept Check

Question 2. Draw a point and figure chart using the history in Table 20.1 with price increments of $3.

A Warning

The search for patterns in stock market prices is nearly irresistible, and the ability of the human eye to discern apparent patterns is remarkable. Unfortunately, it is possible to perceive patterns that really don't exist. Consider Fig-

Wave Theory Wins Robert Prechter
Title of Wall Street Guru

Cynthia Crossen

Technical Analyst Is Successor to Granville, Mendelson; Preparing for a Cataclysm
GAINESVILLE, Ga.—Outside the window is rural Georgia, a vista of leggy pines surrounding a sprawling lake.

Inside is bedlam.

A brisk round of buying has just sent the Dow Jones Industrial Average up sharply [1987], and Robert R. Prechter and some of his staff are trying to figure out what's going on. A half-dozen phone lines blink impatiently as subscribers to Mr. Prechter's consulting service wait for marching orders. Other employees process newsletter subscriptions and bills on computer terminals. As the day wears on, the noise level in the room rises to a dull roar, not unlike the din heard on Wall Street trading desks more than 800 miles away.

A Market Rosetta Stone

This is the home of the Elliott wave principle, an arcane system of technical analysis that thousands of investors have come to believe is the Rosetta stone of the stock market. Mr. Prechter, 37 years old, is the theory's champion and oracle, and his influence on the market extends far beyond the subscribers to his newsletter, the *Elliott Wave Theorist*.

Rumors about Mr. Prechter's latest calls galvanize traders across the country. As a result, he is often credited, or blamed, for sudden shifts in the stock market and praised for his prescience. Early last July, Mr. Prechter advised his subscribers to take profits on short-term positions. When the Dow Jones Industrial Average lost more than 79 points the following week, many people held Mr. Prechter responsible. In early September, he issued another warning, and the average dropped more than 120 points a short time later. Monday before last, when the market fell more than 28 points in the first 15

minutes of trading, market watchers noted that Mr. Prechter had told hot-line subscribers the previous Friday night that the market was vulnerable to a correction.

Of course, Mr. Prechter has also made many wrong calls, most notably in the short-term stock market and in bonds. So far, his Wall Street followers have dismissed them as minor flaws in an exceptional record, but the role of market guru is difficult to sustain for long. Wall Street is fickle, and some of Mr. Prechter's predecessors, like Joseph Granville, Henry Kaufman, and John A. Mendelson, know that a few bad calls can turn the public's adulation to derision. "No one can be right 100 percent of the time," says Mr. Granville.

Mr. Prechter's popularity comes at a time when technical analysis, the system of predicting stock prices using past price and volume statistics, has been making a comeback on Wall Street. The technicians' rivals, the fundamentalists, have been unable to explain how the current economic situation justifies a 20 percent gain in the stock market since the beginning of the year. The startling volatility of the market has also undermined the fundamentalists' view that investors behave rationally.

But technical analysis continues to be regarded skeptically by many academicians and money managers. Hundreds of studies of market patterns have failed to find one that can make consistently accurate predictions. Furthermore, critics say, if such a system could be found, it would be neutralized very quickly by the rush of investors using it.

"I tend to classify technical analysis like Tarot," says Stephen Figlewski, a professor of finance at New York University. "The people who use it successfully—if there are such people—bring a lot more to it than just charts."

Some also argue that a record as good as Mr. Prechter's may well be pure chance. "Most people

(Continued)

don't understand that with stochastic [random] systems, you can get lucky and have a long string of good calls," says James B. Ramsey, a professor of economics at New York University. "It's a low-probability event, but it's not a zero-probability event."

Like other technicians, Mr. Prechter favors one kind of chart but uses others to support or challenge his initial conclusions. His primary system is based on patterns first discerned—or, some would say, fabricated—in the late 1930s by Ralph N. Elliott, an accountant who had lost some of his savings in the 1929 stock-market crash.

The idea behind the Elliott principle is that stock prices are a barometer of the national mood and that the mood moves in predictable waves between optimism and pessimism. The waves, which are based on stock market data, unfold in specific sequences. For example, the waves in a bull market rally will go up, down, up, down, and up, followed by a correction in which waves will go down, up, down. Each wave contains smaller series of waves so that, for example, between January and July of 1984, the market was in a second wave on one scale and a fifth wave on another. A single large wave can last as long as several centuries; one that occurs within other waves can last as short a time as an hour.

In what Elliott and Mr. Prechter call the Grand Supercycle, or the largest scale identified so far, the market is now in a fifth wave, and it won't end until the Dow Jones Industrial Average hits 3686 sometime in 1988. After that, Mr. Prechter says, expect a cataclysm worse than the 1929 crash. Then, if history repeats itself, and Mr. Prechter firmly believes it does, a depression and major war will follow.

Although most people remember only his accurate calls, Mr. Prechter has also had his share of blunders. He himself concedes that beginning in 1985, he consistently called the bond market wrong for more than a year. "I shorted bonds three times on the way up," he says. Other investors contend that his gold forecasts have cost them money.

Mr. Prechter says that his interpretations, not the charts he uses, should be blamed for the bad calls. Furthermore, he says, anyone could take the same charts and, with a certain amount of discipline, do what he does. "Nobody needs me," he says. "All I do is take Elliott's observations and using those patterns and guidelines, I rank the probabilities of the likely paths of the market. It's just a matter of memorizing the patterns and their implications."

Nobody may need him, but Mr. Prechter makes his living from those who think they do. His monthly newsletter, with occasional interim reports, costs $233 a year, and a third or more of his roughly 15,000 subscribers pay an additional $377 a year for his thrice-weekly hot-line. Subscribers may also call one of his three assistants for instant advice at the rate of $30 a minute.

To the critics who wonder why a person who is so smart about the market makes his living—albeit a good one—writing a newsletter, Mr. Prechter quotes a friend who also writes a newsletter. "I want other people to know how smart I am," he says.

As certain as Mr. Prechter is of the Elliott wave principle, he also knows that "hot hands" in the market often have short lives. "I'm probably going to be wrong about something in some big way around the top," he says. "Undoubtedly the top will take too long and probably I'll put out caution too early, in which case people will say baloney on this crash stuff."

In the meantime, Mr. Prechter feels that he is a target for all those who dislike technical analysis in general and hot technicians specifically. "There are people who hate the idea that anyone can be successful at predicting the market," he says. "I just try to avoid them. But sometimes you walk out on the dusty street at noon, and there's some guy standing there with his guns."

ure 20.7, which presents simulated and actual values of the Dow Jones Industrial Average during 1956 taken from a famous study by Harry Roberts.[1] In Figure 20.7**B**, it appears as though the market presents a classic head-and-shoulders pattern where the middle hump (the head) is flanked by two shoulders. When the price index "pierces the right shoulder"—a technical trigger point—it is believed to be heading lower, and it is time to sell your stocks. Figure 20.7**A** also looks like a "typical" stock market pattern.

Can you tell which of the two graphs is constructed from the real value of the Dow and which from the simulated data? Figure 20.7**A** is based on the real data. The graph in **B** was generated using "returns" created by a random number generator. These returns *by construction* were patternless, but the simulated price path that is plotted appears to follow a pattern much like that of **A**.

Figure 20.8 shows the weekly price changes behind the two panels in Figure 20.7. Here the randomness in both series—the stock price as well as the simulated sequence—is obvious.

A problem related to the tendency to perceive patterns where they don't exist is data mining. After the fact, you can always find patterns and trading rules that would have generated enormous profits. If you test enough rules, some will have worked in the past. Unfortunately, picking a theory that would have worked after the fact carries no guarantee of future success.

In this regard, consider a curous investment rule that has worked with uncanny precision since 1967. In years that an original National Football League team wins the Superbowl (played in January), bet on the stock market rising for the rest of the year. In years that a team from the American Football Conference that was not originally an NFL team wins, bet on a market decline.

Between 1967 and 1990, the NYSE index rose in the year following the Superbowl 15 of the 17 times that an NFC or original NFL team won. The market fell in six out of seven years that an AFC team won. Despite the overwhelming past success of this rule, would you use it to invest your money? We suspect not.

In evaluating trading rules, you should always ask whether the rule would have seemed reasonable *before* you looked at the data. If not, you might be buying into the one arbitrary rule among many that happened to have worked in the recent past. The hard but crucial question is whether there is reason to believe that what worked in the past should continue to work in the future.

---

[1] Harry Roberts, "Stock Market 'Patterns' and Financial Analysis: Methodological Suggestions," *Journal of Finance* 14 (March 1959), pp. 701–717.

FIGURE 20.7

Actual and simulated levels for stock market prices of 52 weeks.

(From Harry Roberts, "Stock Market 'Patterns' and Financial Analysis: Methodological Suggestions," *Journal of Finance,* March 1959, pp. 5–6.)

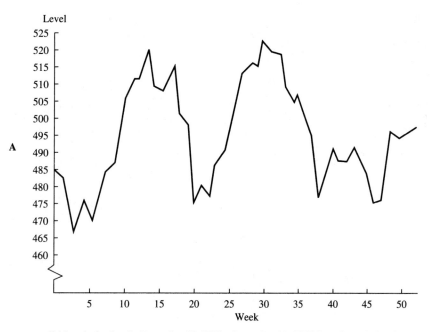

Friday closing levels, December 30, 1955—December 28, 1956, Dow Jones Industrial Average

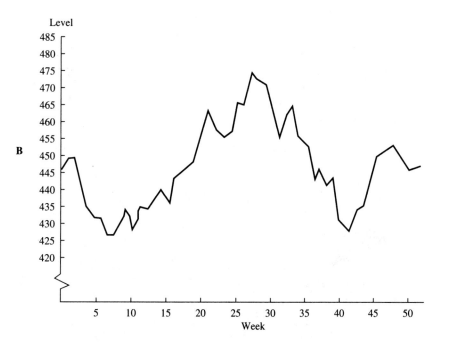

FIGURE 20.8

Actual and simulated changes in weekly stock prices for 52 weeks.

(From Harry Roberts, "Stock Market 'Patterns' and Financial Analysis: Methodological Suggestions," *Journal of Finance,* March 1959, pp. 5–6.)

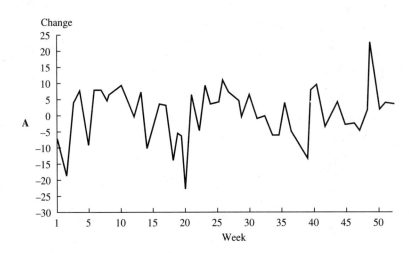

Changes from Friday to Friday (closing) January 6, 1956—December 28, 1956. Dow Jones Industrial Average

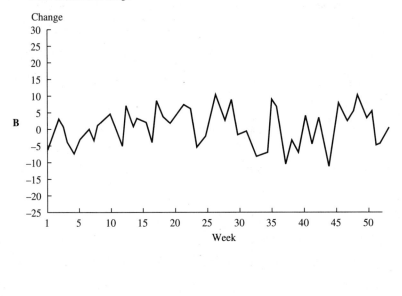

20.3   *Technical Indicators*

Technical analysts use technical indicators besides charts to assess prospects for market declines or advances. We will examine some popular indicators in this section.

Market volume is sometimes used to measure the strength of a market rise or fall. Increased investor participation in a market advance or retreat is viewed as a measure of the significance of the movement. Technicians consider market advances to be a more favourable omen of continued price increases when they are associated with increased trading volume. Similarly, market reversals are considered more bearish when associated with higher volume. The **trin** statistic is the ratio of the number of advancing to declining issues divided by the ratio of volume in advancing versus declining issues:

$$\text{Trin} = \frac{\text{Number advancing/Number declining}}{\text{Volume advancing/Volume declining}}$$

This expression can be rearranged as:

$$\text{Trin} = \frac{\text{Volume declining/Number declining}}{\text{Volume advancing/Number advancing}}$$

Therefore, trin is the ratio of average volume in declining issues to average volume in advancing issues. Ratios above 1.0 are considered bearish because the falling stocks would then have higher average volume than the advancing stocks, indicating net selling pressure. *The Wall Street Journal* reports trin every day in the market diary section, as in Figure 20.9.

Note, however, for every buyer, there must be a seller of stock. Rising volume in a rising market should not necessarily indicate a larger imbalance of buyers versus sellers. For example, a trin statistic above 1.0, which is considered bearish, could equally well be interpreted as indicating that there is more *buying* activity in declining issues.

The **breadth** of the market is a measure of the extent to which movement in a market index are reflected widely in the price movements of all the stocks in the market. The most common measure of breadth is the spread between the num-

FIGURE 20.9
Market diary.

(From *The Wall Street Journal,* October 18, 1990. Reprinted by permission of *The Wall Street Journal,* © 1990 Dow Jones & Company, Inc. All Rights Reserved Worldwide.)

DIARIES

NYSE	WED	TUES	WK AGO
Issues traded	1,981	1,988	1,990
Advances	659	487	356
Declines	833	1,077	1,200
Unchanged	489	424	434
New highs	6	5	1
New lows	248	276	278
zAdv vol (000)	68,047	29,694	25,874
zDecl vol (000)	74,617	105,139	129,075
zTotal vol (000)	161,260	149,570	167,890
Closing tick[1]	−418	−111	−378
Closing trin[2]	.87	1.60	1.48
zBlock trades	3,503	3,077	3,558

[1]The net difference of the number of stocks closing higher than their previous trade from those closing lower; NYSE trading only.
[2]A comparison of the number of advancing and declining issues with the volume of shares rising and falling. Generally, a trin of less than 1.00 indicates buying demand; above 1.00 indicates selling pressure.
z-NYSE or Amex only.

ber of stocks that advance and decline in price. If advances outnumber declines by a wide margin, then the market is viewed as being stronger because the rally is widespread. A standard indicator of the current breadth is the **tick**, computed as the net difference between the number of stocks trading higher than their previous trade price and the number trading lower. These breadth numbers also are reported daily in *The Wall Street Journal* (see Figure 20.9).

Some analysts cumulate breadth data each day, as in Table 20.2. The cumulative breadth for each day is obtained by adding that day's net advances (or declines) to the previous day's total. The direction of the cumulated series is then used to discern broad market trends.

Short interest is the total number of shares of stock currently sold short in the market. Some technicians interpret short interest as bullish, some as bearish. The bullish perspective is that because all short sales must be covered (i.e., short-sellers eventually must purchase shares to return the ones they have borrowed), short interest represents latent future demand for the stocks. As short sales are covered, the demand created by the share purchase will force prices up.

The bearish interpretation of short interest is based on the fact that short-sellers tend to be larger, more sophisticated investors. Accordingly, increased short interest reflects bearish sentiment by those investors "in the know," which would be a negative signal of the market's prospects.

Just as short-sellers tend to be larger institutional traders, odd-lot traders are almost always small individual traders. (An odd lot is a transaction of fewer than 100 shares; 100 shares is one round lot.) The **odd-lot theory** holds that these small investors tend to miss key market turning points, typically buying stocks after a bull market has already run its course and selling too late into a bear market. Therefore, the theory suggests that when odd-lot traders are widely buying, you should sell, and vice versa.

The Wall Street Journal publishes odd-lot trading data every day. You can construct an index of odd-lot trading by computing the ratio of odd-lot purchases to sales. A ratio substantially above 1.0 is bearish because it implies small traders are net buyers.

Barron's computes a confidence index using data from the bond market. The presumption is that actions of bond traders reveal trends that will emerge soon in the stock market.

TABLE 20.2   Breadth

Day	Advances	Declines	Net Advances	Cumulative Breadth
1	802	748	54	54
2	917	640	277	331
3	703	772	−69	262
4	512	1122	−610	−348
5	633	1004	−371	−719

Note: The sum of advances and declines varies across days because some stock prices are unchanged.

The **confidence index** is the ratio of the average yield on 10 top-rated corporate bonds divided by the average yield on 10 intermediate-grade corporate bonds. The ratio will always be below 100 percent because higher-rated bonds will offer lower promised yields to maturity. When bond traders are optimistic about the economy, however, they might require smaller default premiums on lower-rated debt. Hence, the yield spread will narrow, and the confidence index will approach 100 percent. Therefore, higher values of the confidence index are bullish signals.

Concept Check	**Question 3. Yields on lower-rated debt will rise after fears of recession have spread through the economy. This will reduce the confidence index. Should the stock market now be expected to fall or will it already have fallen?**

Relative strength measures the extent to which a security has outperformed or underperformed either the market as a whole or its particular industry. Relative strength is computed by calculating the ratio of the price of the security to a price index for the industry. For example, the relative strength of IBM versus the computer industry would be measured by movements in the ratio of Price (IBM)/Price (computer industry index). A rising ratio implies IBM has been outperforming the rest of the industry. If relative strength can be assumed to persist over time, then this would be a signal to buy IBM.

Similarly, the relative strength of an industry relative to the whole market can be computed by tracking the ratio of the industry price index to the market price index.

Some technical indicators are depicted in charts of individual stocks, industry groups, or the entire market. Thus charting services may include graphs of the relative strength and of the **advance-decline line**, which is the common indicator of market breadth. In addition to these, **moving averages** computed on 13-week, 26-week, or 200-day periods are watched closely by many technicians; failure of the current price to break through a moving average line is interpreted to indicate that the existing trend in the price graph will prevail, while a convincing breakthrough implies that a reversal and thus a new trend are being established.

20.4 *Technical Analysis for Canadian Investors*

The subject of technical analysis followed in Canada can be divided along macro and micro lines. Broadly, the market in Canada can be viewed as following that in the United States, as evidenced by the high degree of correlation between them. In response to this, a brokerage house can predict the direction of the market by performing technical analysis on the S&P 500 or by following the Dow theory. If market timing is the objective, then either an in-house analysis can be pursued or predictions can be obtained from U.S. affiliates or other sources.

At the level of the individual company, there is an important dichotomy. For those companies that are actively traded on the NYSE, such as Northern Telecom or Alcan, information is likely to be available from U.S. sources; the relevant price behaviour to follow is that on the NYSE, at least as much as that on the TSE. For smaller companies, however, Canadian investment advisors must perform their own technical analysis. This will be done using the same measures as are used in the United States, such as relative strength and charts displaying patterns and trends.

The information on Canadian stocks available to investors is somewhat more limited. Brokers may have displayed on their screens the technical indicators such as the trin and tick for the NYSE; more recently, trin and tick have also been available for TSE stocks. This will enable traders (if they so believe) to speculate on short-run movements in the market, for either Canadian or U.S. securities. Other U.S. indicators like odd-lot trading and the confidence index are not computed, although short interest figures are available.

The *Globe and Mail* gives a daily report of market breadth for Canadian markets as well as the three major U.S. markets, as illustrated in Figure 20.10; in addition, there are daily price and volume charts for the TSE 300, as illustrated in Figure 20.11, and the block trade report (shown in Chapter 2). Investors can also consult the *Graphoscope,* available by subscription or at libraries. This document presents charts on Canadian stocks, commodities, indices, and foreign markets and currencies, giving the advance-decline line and the moving average. The *Independent Survey Co.* gives similar information, including relative strength.

One area where academics are less inclined to reject technical analysis is in commodity trading. For whatever reasons, chart patterns seem to offer infor-

FIGURE 20.10
Market breadth.

(From *The Globe and Mail,* August 27, 1992. Reprinted by permission.)

MARKET BREADTH

	Volume in 1,000s									
	Trading	Adv.	Decl.	Transactions	Issues	Adv.	Decl.	Unch.	New high	New low
Toronto	20864	9537	6239	10972	804	274	234	296	19	18
Industrials	14041	7067	3545	8730	551	195	156	200	12	16
Mines	4206	1296	1664	1255	153	35	52	66	0	0
Oils	2617	1175	1030	987	100	44	26	30	7	2
Montreal	4976	2327	1306	3255	360	135	101	124	10	9
Vancouver	12956	7194	3828	3241	608	200	231	177	14	30
Alberta	3420	1759	620	777	137	52	36	49	10	6
New York	172562	96547	51508	106052	2294	978	723	593	26	33
American	9857	4520	3572	7511	703	228	254	221	7	22
NASDAQ NMS	154618	80647	48612	69463	3478	1300	1133	1045	170	349

FIGURE 20.11
TSE 300 Index and
market volume.

(From *The Globe and
Mail*, August 27, 1992.
Reprinted by permission.)

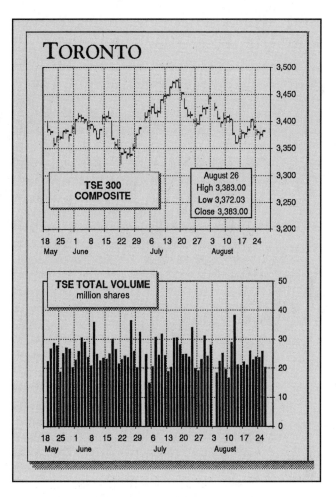

mation about future prices. In Figure 20.12, the chart pattern for the relative
performance of the TSE gold index versus gold illustrates how the analysis may
be applied.

20.5 *The Value Line System*

The Value Line ranking system may be the most celebrated and well-documented example of successful stock analysis. Value Line is the largest investment advisory service in the world. Besides publishing the *Value Line Investment Survey,* which provides information on investment fundamentals for

FIGURE 20.12

TSE Gold Index vs. gold (daily relative performance).

(From Burns Fry Investment Research, *Gold Chart Book,* December 1991. Reprinted by permission of Burns Fry Ltd.)

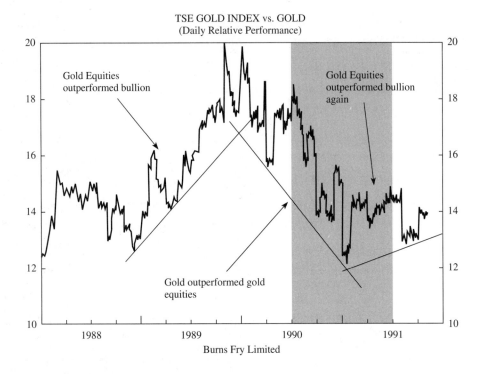

TSE GOLD INDEX vs. GOLD
(Daily Relative Performance)

Gold Equities outperformed bullion

Gold Equities outperformed bullion again

Gold outperformed gold equities

Burns Fry Limited

approximately 1,700 publicly traded companies, Value Line also ranks each of these stocks according to their anticipated price appreciation over the next 12 months. Stocks ranked in group 1 are expected to perform the best, while those in group 5 are expected to perform the worst. Value Line calls this "ranking for timeliness."

Figure 20.13 shows the performance of the Value Line ranking system over the 25 years from 1965 to March 1990. Over the total period, the different groups performed just as the rankings would predict, and the differences were quite large. The total 25-year price appreciation for the group 1 stocks was 3,083 percent (or 14.8 percent per year) compared to 15 percent (or 0.5 percent per year) for group 5.

How does the Value Line ranking system work? As Bernhard[2] explains it, the ranking procedure has three components: (1) relative earnings momentum, (2) earnings surprise, and (3) a value index. Most (though not all) of the Value Line criteria are technically oriented, relying on either price momentum or relative strength. Points assigned for each factor determine the stock's overall ranking.

The relative earnings momentum factor is calculated as each company's year-to-year change in quarterly earnings divided by the average change for all stocks.

---

[2] See the suggested readings.

FIGURE 20.13

Record of Value Line ranking for timeliness (without allowing for changes in rank, 1965–1990).

(From *Value Line Selection & Opinion,* April 20, 1990.)

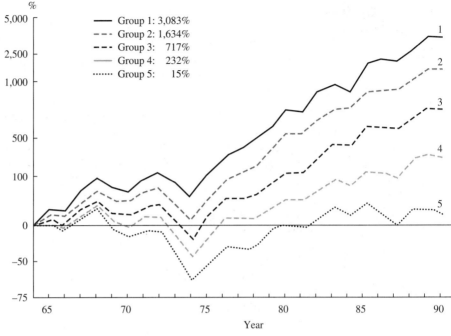

The earnings surprise factor has to do with the difference between actual reported quarterly earnings and Value Line's estimate. The points assigned to each stock increase with the percentage difference between reported and estimated earnings.

The value index is calculated from the following regression equation:

$$V = a + b_1 x_1 + b_2 x_2 + b_3 x_3$$

where

x_1 = A score from 1 to 10 depending on the relative earnings momentum ranking, compared with the company's rank for the last 10 years;

x_2 = A score from 1 to 10 based on the stock's relative price, with ratios calculated in a similar way to the earnings ratio;

x_3 = The ratio of the stock's latest 10-week average relative price (stock price divided by the average price for all stocks) to its 52-week average relative price;

and a, b_1, b_2, and b_3 are the coefficients from the regression estimated on 12 years of data.

Finally, the points for each of the three factors are added, and the stocks are classified into five groups according to the total score.

Investing according to this system does seem to produce superior results on paper, as Figure 20.13 shows. Yet as the box on pages 699–700 points out, in practice, things are not so simple—Value Line's own mutual funds have not kept up even with the broad market averages. The box illustrates that even apparently successful trading rules can be difficult to implement in the market.

20.6   *Can Technical Analysis Work in Efficient Markets?*

Self-Destructing Patterns

It should be abundantly clear from our presentation that most of technical analysis is based on ideas totally at odds with the foundations of the efficient market hypothesis. The EMH follows from the idea that rational profit-seeking investors will act on new information so quickly that prices will nearly always reflect all publicly available information. Technical analysis, on the other hand, posits the existence of long-lived trends that play out slowly and predictably. Such patterns, if they exist, would violate the EMH notion of essentially unpredictable stock price changes.

An interesting question is whether a technical rule that seems to work will continue to work in the future once it becomes widely recognized. A clever analyst may occasionally uncover a profitable trading rule, but the real test of efficient markets is whether the rule itself becomes reflected in stock prices once its value is discovered.

Suppose, for example, the Dow theory predicts an upward primary trend. If the theory is widely accepted, it follows that many investors will attempt to buy stocks immediately in anticipation of the price increase; the effect would be to bid up prices sharply and immediately rather than at the gradual, long-lived pace initially expected. The Dow theory's predicted trend would be replaced by a sharp jump in prices. It is in this sense that price patterns ought to be *self-destructing*. Once a useful technical rule (or price pattern) is discovered, it ought to be invalidated once the mass of traders attempt to exploit it.

For the prediction of a technical indicator to work, enough believers must trade correspondingly to bring about the anticipated price behaviour. In this sense, the trading rule may become self-fulfilling. If everyone were to believe, however, the necessary anticipation of the price movement would eliminate any potential gain. Technicians are happy to admit that they rely on enough believers to produce the effect, but enough skeptics to allow it to continue; alternatively, smaller investors can follow the rules, but institutional investors moving large blocks of stock are unable to profit from technical strategies.

An instructive example of this phenomenon is the evidence by Jegadeesh[3] and Lehmann[4] that stock prices seem to obey a reversal effect; specifically, the best-performing stocks in one week or month tend to fare poorly in the following period, while the worst performers follow up with good performance. Such a phenomenon can be used to form a straightforward technically based trading strategy: buy shares that recently have done poorly and sell shares that re-

---

[3] Narasimhan Jegadeesh, "Evidence of Predictable Behavior of Security Prices," *Journal of Finance* 45 (September 1990), pp. 881–898.

[4] Bruce Lehmann, "Fads, Martingales and Market Efficiency," *Quarterly Journal of Economics* 105 (February 1990), pp. 1–28.

Paying the Piper

On Paper, Value Line's Performance in Picking Stocks Is Nothing Short of Dazzling . . . for an Investor to Capitalize on That Performance Is a Different Matter

Value Line, Inc., publishes the *Value Line Investment Survey,* that handy review of 1,652 companies. Each week the survey rates stocks from I (best buys) to V (worst). Can you beat the market following these rankings? Value Line tracks the performance of group I from April 1965, when a new ranking formula went into effect. If you bought group I then and updated your list every week, you would have a gain of 15,391 percent by June 30. That means $10,000 would have grown to about $1.5 million, dividends excluded. The market is up only 245 percent since 1965, dividends excluded.

Quite an impressive record. There is only one flaw: It ignores transaction costs. Do transaction costs much matter against a performance like that? What does the investor lose in transaction costs? A percentage point a year? Two percent?

None other than Value Line provides an answer to this question, and the answer is almost as startling as the paper performance. Since late 1983, Value Line has run a mutual fund that attempts to track group I precisely. Its return has averaged a dismal 11 percentage points a year worse than the hypothetical results in group I. The fund hasn't even kept up with the market (see chart).

What went wrong? "Inefficiencies and costs of implementation," says Mark Tavel, manager of the fund, Value Line Centurion.

This is not to denigrate Value Line's undeniably impressive stock-picking record. Far from it: one of the funds run for Value Line by Tavel, Leveraged Growth Investors, shines on Forbes' mutual fund honor roll. (Leveraged Growth and the flagship Value Line Fund use the ranking system, but not as closely as Centurion.)

The point here is to illustrate the folly of constant trading. It's a familiar story, but one that investors are prone to forget in the middle of a bull market. It costs money to run the racetrack, and the fellow who steps up to the betting window pays. Wall Street's revenues top $50 billion a year. People who trade pay the bill, and people who try to beat the market with a lot of trading pay dearly.

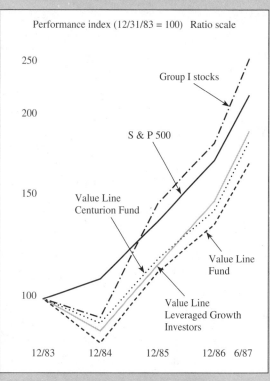

Performance index (12/31/83 = 100) Ratio scale

The Value Line Centurion Fund's turnover is 200 percent a year. That's quite a bit of turnover—although by no means the highest in the business. The turnover is high because in a typical week, 4 of the 100 group I stocks drop down in rank and have to be replaced with new group I stocks. It's not impossible for traders like Centurion to beat the market, but they start out with a handicap.

All of which means that paper performance can be pretty fanciful. "Anytime hypothetical returns are offered as proof of a particular investing style, one should also swallow a large grain of salt," says Cam Schmidt of Potomac Investment Management, a money manager in Bethesda, Maryland, that brought the Value Line discrepancy to *Forbes'* attention.

(Continued)

What are these inefficiencies and costs? And what do they tell investors about the perils of in-and-out trading?

Fund overhead is not a big item. At the $244 million Centurion, which is available only through variable life and annuity policies sold by Guardian Life, the annual expense ratio averages 0.6 percent. Nor are brokerage commissions large. Funneled at about 5 cents a share mostly to a captive Value Line broker, commissions eat up to 0.4 percent of Centurion's assets per year.

So far we have 1 percent. Where's the other 10 percent of the shortfall? Bid-ask spreads, for one. A stock quoted at 39 to sellers might cost a buyer 39½—or even 41 or 42 if the buyer wants a lot of it. With about 95 of the 100 group I stocks at any given time in the Centurion portfolio, Tavel needs to amass an average $2.5 million position in each. Some of these companies have $150 million or less in outstanding shares. The very smallest Tavel doesn't even try to buy.

Timing explains some of the gulf between hypothetical and actual results. The hypothetical performance assumes a purchase at the Wednesday close before publication of the new rankings. Most subscribers get their surveys on Friday morning, however, and buy at the Friday opening—if they are lucky. An internal Value Line rule forbids the funds to act on rank changes before Friday morning.

Why, then, are Wednesday prices used in the performance claims? Because, says Samuel Eisenstadt, Value Line's chief of statistics, until recently that was all Value Line had in its data base. Wednesday prices were gathered because it takes nine days to compute, print, and mail the results. The hypothetical buy, then, would come a week after the closing prices used to calculate the rankings, and a day and a half before a real buyer could act on the advice. Eisenstadt says a conversion to Friday night scoring is under way and will no doubt depress reported performance.

A day makes all the difference. A 1985 study by Scott Stickel, now an assistant professor at Wharton, showed that almost all of the excess return on a group I stock is concentrated on three days, almost evenly divided: the Friday when subscribers read about the stock's being promoted into group I,

the Thursday before and the Monday following. Wait until Tuesday to buy and you might as well not subscribe.

Why are prices moving up on Thursday, the day before publication? Eisenstadt suspects the Postal Service of acting with uncharacteristic efficiency in some parts of the country, giving a few subscribers an early start. Another reason for an uptick: Enough is known about the Value Line formula for smart investors to anticipate a rank change by a few days. The trick is to watch group II (near-top) stocks closely. If a quarterly earnings report comes in far better than the forecast published in *Value Line*, grab the stock. "What happens if you're wrong? You're stuck with a group II stock with terrific earnings," says Eisenstadt.

Come Friday at 9:30 A.M., the throng is at the starting gate. Tavel says he often gets only a small portion of his position established before the price starts to run away from him. How are the individual investors faring? Probably no better. True, a 200-share order is not by itself going to move the market the way Tavel's 20,000-share order will. But if both orders arrive at the opening bell, the small investor is in no position to get a good price. Individuals aren't paying the fund overhead, but then they pay higher commissions than Tavel.

What of the future? Value Line's magic was built on its computer-quick response to favourable earnings reports. Now computers are nothing special. Significantly, they're becoming a lot more common among individual investors, the people who buy the small-cap stocks where the ranking system has shown its strength. Eisenstadt concedes: "Everyone's playing this earnings surprise game now." But he insists that there's no firm evidence yet that the ranking system is falling apart.

Even if the ranking system loses some of its effectiveness, however, it would be premature to write off Value Line, which trades over the counter near 27. Many of the survey's 120,000 subscribers pay $495 a year just to get the detailed financial histories of the companies in it. Indeed, considering that subscriptions are on the upswing and that it costs maybe $50 to print and mail one, favourable earnings surprises may be in store. If you don't like the horses, buy stock in the track.

cently have done well. Lehmann shows such a strategy would have been extremely profitable in the past.

The reversal effect is at odds with market efficiency and at the same time consistent with the viability of technical analysis. The real test of the trading rule will come now that the potential of the strategy has been uncovered. Lehmann notes that Rosenberg Institutional Equity Management and the College Retirement Equity Fund now use return reversal strategies in their actively managed portfolios. These activities presumably should eliminate existing profit opportunities by forcing prices to their "correct" levels.

Thus, the market dynamic is one of a continual search for profitable trading rules, followed by destruction by overuse of those rules found to be successful, followed by more search for yet-undiscovered rules.

A New View of Technical Analysis

Brown and Jennings[5] offer a rigorous foundation for the potential efficacy of technical analysis. They envision an economy where many investors have private information regarding the ultimate value of a stock. Moreover, as time passes, each investor acquires additional information. Each investor can infer something of the information possessed by other traders by observing the price at which securities trade. The entire sequence of past prices can turn out to be useful in the inference of the information held by other traders. In this sense, technical analysis can be useful to traders even if all traders rationally use all information available to them.

Most discussions of the EMH envision public information commonly available to all traders and ask only if prices reflect that information. In this sense, the Brown and Jennings framework is more complex. Here, different individuals receive different private signals regarding the value of a firm. As prices unfold, each trader infers the good-news or bad-news nature of the signals received by other traders and updates assessments of the firm accordingly. Prices *reveal* as well as *reflect* information and become useful data to traders. Without addressing specific technical trading rules, the Brown and Jennings model is an interesting and innovative attempt to reconcile technical analysis with the usual assumption of rational traders participating in efficient markets.

Summary

1. Technical analysis is the search for recurring patterns in stock market prices. It is based essentially on the notion that market prices adjust slowly to new information and, thus, is at odds with the efficient market hypothesis.

[5] David Brown and Robert H. Jennings, "On Technical Analysis," *Review of Financial Studies* 2 (1989), pp. 527–552.

2. The Dow theory is the earliest chart-based version of technical analysis. The theory posits the existence of primary, intermediate, and minor trends that can be identified on a chart and acted on by an analyst before the trends fully dissipate. Other trend-based theories are based on relative strength and the point and figures chart.

3. Technicians believe high volume and market breadth accompanying market trends add weight to the significance of a trend.

4. Odd-lot traders are viewed as uninformed, which suggests informed traders should pursue trading strategies in opposition to their activity. In contrast, short-sellers are viewed as informed traders, lending credence to their activity.

5. Value Line's ranking system uses technically based data and has shown great ability to discriminate between stocks with good and poor prospects, but the Value Line mutual fund that uses this system most closely has been only a mediocre performer, suggesting that implementation of the Value Line timing system is difficult.

6. New theories of information dissemination in the market suggests there may be a role for the examination of past prices in formulating investment strategies. They do not, however, support the specific charting patterns currently relied on by technical analysts.

Key terms

Dow theory	Short interest
Support level	Odd-lot theory
Resistance level	Confidence index
Trin	Relative strength
Breadth	Advance-decline line
Tick	Moving average

Selected readings

A magazine devoted to technical analysis is Technical Analysis of Stocks and Commodities.

The Value Line method is described in:

Bernhard, Arnold. *Value Line Methods of Evaluating Common Stocks.* New York: Arnold Bernhard and Co., 1979.

Problems

1. Consider the graph of stock prices over a two-year period in Figure 20.14. Identify likely support and resistance levels.

2. Use the data from *The Globe and Mail* in Figure 20.10 to construct the trin ratio for the market. Is the trin ratio bullish or bearish?

3. Calculate market breadth using the same data as in Problem 2. Is the signal bullish or bearish?

4. Collect data on the TSE 300 for a period covering a few months. Try to identify primary trends. Can you tell whether the market currently is in an upward or downward trend?

FIGURE 20.14
Simulated stock
prices over time.

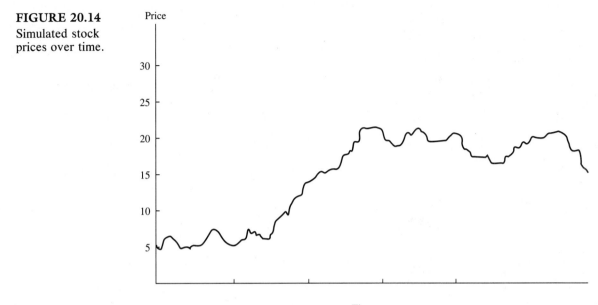

5. The ratio of put to call options outstanding is viewed by some as a technical indicator. Do you think a high ratio is viewed as bullish or bearish? Should it be?

6. Using Figure 20.11 from *The Globe and Mail*, determine whether market price movements and volume patterns were bullish or bearish around the following dates: June 17; June 29; July 20; July 27. In each instance, compare your prediction to the subsequent behaviour of the DJIA in the following few weeks.

PART VII

DERIVATIVE ASSETS: OPTIONS AND FUTURES

CHAPTER 21

An Introduction to Options Markets

Trading of standardized options contracts on a national exchange started in the United States in 1973, when the Chicago Board Options Exchange (CBOE) began listing call options. These contracts were almost immediately a great success, crowding out the over-the-counter trading in stock options that had preceded the inception of the formal exchange. Today, options contracts are traded on several exchanges in the United States, and the CBOE is the second-largest securities market in the United States in terms of the value of traded securities (only the New York Stock Exchange is larger).

In Canada, organized exchange trading of standardized option contracts began in 1975–1976 in Montreal and Toronto. The following year the two exchanges merged their options-clearing corporations, forming TransCanada Options Inc. (TCO). The Vancouver Stock Exchange joined TCO in 1984.

Traded option contracts are written on common stock, stock indices, foreign exchanges, agricultural commodities, precious metals, and interest rate futures. Popular and potent tools in modifying portfolio characteristics, options have become essential elements that a portfolio manager must understand.

This chapter is an introduction to options markets. It explains how puts and calls work and examines their investment characteristics. Popular option strategies are considered next. Finally, the chapter provides a brief overview of option valuation issues.

21.1 The Option Contract

A **call option** gives its holder the right to purchase an asset for a specified price, called the **exercise price** or **strike price,** on or before a specified expiration date.

For example, a July call option on Seagram's stock with an exercise price of $130 entitles its owner to purchase Seagram's stock for a price of $130 at any time up to and including the expiration date in July. The holder of the call is not required to exercise the option. Only if the market value of the asset to be purchased exceeds the exercise price will it be profitable for the holder to exercise it. When the market price does exceed the exercise price, the option holder may either sell the option, or "call away" the asset for the exercise price and reap a profit. Otherwise, the option may be left unexercised. If it is not exercised before the expiration date of the contract, a call option simply expires and no longer has value.

The purchase price of the option is called the *premium*. It represents the compensation the purchaser of the call must pay for the ability to exercise the option if it becomes profitable. Sellers of call options, who are said to *write* calls, receive premium income now as payment against the possibility that they will be forced at some later date to deliver the asset in return for an exercise price lower than the market value of the asset. If the option is left to expire because the exercise price remains above the market price of the asset, then— aside from transaction costs—the writer of the call clears a profit equal to the premium income derived from the initial sale of the option.

A **put option** gives its holder the right to *sell* an asset for a specified exercise or strike price on or before a given expiration date. A July put on Seagram's with exercise price $130 thus entitles its owner to sell Seagram's stock to the put writer at a price of $130 at any time before expiration in July, even if the market price of Seagram's is less than $130. Whereas profits on call options increase when the asset increases in value, profits on put options increase when the asset value falls. The put is exercised only if its holder can deliver an asset with market value less than the exercise price in return for the exercise price.

Options and futures contracts are sometimes called *derivative securities*. Their values derive from the values of the underlying primary security. For example, the value of a Seagram's option depends on the price of Seagram's stock. For this reason, options and futures contracts also are called *contingent claims:* payoff is contingent on prices of other securities.

An option is said to be **in the money** when its exercise would produce profits for its holder; an option is **out of the money** when exercise would be unprofitable. A call option is in the money when the exercise price is below the asset's value, because purchase at the exercise price would be profitable. It is out of the money when the exercise price exceeds the asset value; no one would exercise the right to purchase for the exercise price an asset worth less than that price. Conversely, put options are in the money when the exercise price exceeds the asset's value because delivery of the lower-valued asset in exchange for the exercise price would be profitable.

Some options trade on over-the-counter (OTC) markets. An OTC market offers the advantage that the terms of the option contract—the exercise price, maturity date, and number of shares committed—can be tailored to the needs of the traders. The costs of establishing an OTC option contract, however, are quite high. Today, virtually all option trading takes place on organized exchanges.

Options contracts traded on exchanges are standardized by allowable maturity dates and exercise prices for each listed option. Each stock option contract provides for the right to buy or sell 100 shares of stock. (If stock splits occur after the contract is listed, adjustments are required. We discuss adjustments in option contract terms later in this section.)

Standardization of the terms of listed option contracts means that all market participants trade in a limited and uniform set of securities. This increases the depth of trading in any particular option, which lowers trading costs and results in a more competitive market. Therefore, exchanges offer two important benefits: ease of trading, which flows from a central marketplace where buyers and sellers or their representatives congregate; and a liquid secondary market, where buyers and sellers of options can establish and trade their positions quickly and cheaply.

Figure 21.1 is a reproduction of listed stock option quotations from *The Globe and Mail;* only the options that traded that day are quoted. Note the option listed (arrow) for shares of Inco Ltd. In the first line, following the company name and the letter C, it is indicated that the last recorded price on the Toronto Stock Exchange for Inco stock was \$33½ per share. Options are traded on Inco at exercise prices varying in \$2.5 increments. These values are also called *strike prices* and are given in the first column of numbers, next to the expiration month.

The exchanges offer options on stocks with exercise prices that bracket the stock price. Exercise prices generally are set at intervals of either \$2.5 or \$5, depending on whether the price of the stock is below or above \$35; however, tighter intervals can also be set for low stock prices. If the stock price moves outside the range of exercise prices of the existing set of options, new options with appropriate exercise prices may be offered. Therefore, at any time both in-the-money and out-of-the-money options will be listed, as in the Inco example.

The next four groups of rows of numbers provide the bid, asked, and closing prices of call and put options on Inco shares that traded that day, with expiration dates of April, May, August, and November. The contracts expire on the Saturday following the third Friday of the month. Notice that the prices of Inco call options decrease as one moves down each column, toward progressively higher exercise prices. This makes sense, because the right to purchase a share at a given exercise price is worth less as that exercise price increases. At an exercise price of \$35, the May Inco call had a closing price of \$.90, whereas the option to purchase for an exercise price of \$40 sold for only \$.05.

Many options may go an entire day without trading. Because trading is infrequent (especially in Canada), it is not unusual to find option prices that appear out of line with other prices. You might find, for example, two calls with different exercise prices that seem to sell for equal prices. This discrepancy arises because the last trades for these options may have occurred at different times during the day. At any moment the call with the lower exercise price must be worth more than an otherwise-identical call with a higher exercise price.

Several rows, distinguished by a P, report prices of put options with various strike prices and times to maturity. Notice that, in contrast to call options, put

FIGURE 21.1

Listed Trans Canada Options quotations.

(From *The Globe and Mail,* April 1, 1992. Reprinted by permission.)

TRANS CANADA OPTIONS

Trans Canada Options combine Montreal, Toronto and Vancouver option trading. P is a put.

[Figure 21.1 reproduces a full page of Trans Canada Options quotations from The Globe and Mail*, April 1, 1992, listing Series, Bid, Ask, Last, Vol, and Op Int columns for numerous option classes. Inco Ltd is marked with an arrow. Total contract volume 8,236; Total open interest 271,442.]*

prices increase with the exercise price. The right to sell a share of Inco at a price of $35 obviously is less valuable than the right to sell it at $37.5.

American and European Options

An **American option** allows its holder to exercise the right to purchase (call) or sell (put) the underlying asset on *or before* the expiration date. A **European option** allows for exercise of the option only on the expiration date. American options, because they allow more leeway than do their European counterparts, generally will be more valuable. Virtually all traded options in Canada and the United States are American. Foreign currency options and stock index options traded on the Chicago Board Options Exchange in the United States, and stock index options traded on the Toronto Stock Exchange in Canada, are notable exceptions to this rule, however.

Adjustments in Option Contract Terms

Because options convey the right to buy or sell shares at a stated price, stock splits would radically alter their value if the terms of the option contract were not adjusted to account for the stock split. For example, reconsider the Inco call options in Figure 21.1. If Inco were to announce a ten-for-one split, its share price would fall from $33½ to about $3.30. A call option with exercise price $35 would be just about worthless, with virtually no possibility that the stock would sell at more than $35 before the option expired.

To account for a stock split, the exercise price is reduced by the factor of the split, and the number of options held is increased by that factor. For example, the original Inco call option with exercise price of $35 would be altered after a ten-for-one split to ten new options, with each option carrying an exercise price of $3.5. A similar adjustment is made for stock dividends of more than 10 percent; the number of shares covered by each option is increased in proportion to the stock dividend, and the exercise price is reduced by that proportion.

Concept Check	Question 1. Suppose that Inco's stock price at the exercise date is $40, and the exercise price of the call $35. What is the profit on one option contract? After a ten-for-one split, the stock price is $4, the exercise price is $3.5, and the option holder now can purchase 1,000 shares. Show that the split leaves option profits unaffected.

In contrast to stock dividends, cash dividends do not affect the terms of an option contract. Because payment of a cash dividend reduces the selling price of the stock without inducing offsetting adjustments in the option contract, the value of the option is affected by dividend policy. Other things being equal, call option values are lower for high dividend-payout policies, because such policies slow the rate of increase of stock prices; conversely, put values are higher for high dividend payouts. (Of course, the option values do not rise or fall on the dividend payment or ex-dividend dates. Dividend payments are anticipated, so the effect of the payment already is built into the original option price.)

The Option Clearing Corporation

The Option Clearing Corporation (OCC) is jointly owned by the exchanges on which stock options are traded. It is the clearinghouse for options trading. In Canada, it is called TransCanada Options Inc. (TCO) and is owned by the Montreal, Toronto, and Vancouver Stock Exchanges.

Buyers and sellers of options who agree on a price will consummate the sale of the option. At this point the OCC steps in, by placing itself between the two traders and becoming the effective buyer of the option from the writer and the effective writer of the option to the buyer. All individuals, therefore, deal only with the OCC, which effectively guarantees contract performance.

When an option holder exercises an option, the OCC arranges for a member firm with clients who have written that option to make good on the option obligation. The member firm, in turn, selects from its clients who have written that option to fulfill the contract. The selected client must either deliver 100 shares of stock at a price equal to the exercise price for each call option contract written, or purchase 100 shares at the exercise price for each put option contract written.

Because the OCC guarantees contract performances, option writers are required to post margin amounts to guarantee that they can fulfill their obligations under the option contract. The margin required is determined, in part, by the amount by which the option is in the money, because that value is an indicator of the potential obligation of the option writer upon exercise of the option. When the required margin exceeds the posted margin, the writer will receive a margin call. The holder of the option need not post margin, because the holder will exercise the option only if it is profitable to do so. After purchasing the option, no further money is at risk.

Margin requirements are determined, in part, by the other securities held in the investor's portfolio. For example, a call option writer owning the stock against which the option is written can satisfy the margin requirement simply by allowing a broker to hold that stock in the brokerage account. The stock is then guaranteed to be available for delivery should the call option be exercised. If the underlying security is not owned, however, the margin requirement is determined by both the value of the underlying security and the amount by which the option is in or out of the money. Out-of-the-money options require less margin from the writer, because expected payouts are lower.

Other Listed Options

Options on assets other than stocks are also widely traded, especially in the United Sates. These include options on market and industry indices; foreign currency; and even the future prices of agricultural products, gold, silver, fixed-income securities, and stock indices. We will discuss these in turn.

Index options

An index option is a call or put based on a stock market index such as the TSE 35 or the New York Stock Exchange Index. Index options are traded on several broad-based indices, as well as on a few industry-specific indices. We discussed many of these indices in Chapter 2.

The construction of the indices can vary across contracts or exchanges. For example, the TSE 35 index is a value-weighted average of 35 major Canadian stocks in the TSE 300 stock group. The weights are proportional to the market value of outstanding equity for each stock. The Major Market Index, by contrast, is a price-weighted average of 20 U.S. stocks, most of which are in the Dow Jones Industrial Average group, whereas the Value Line Index is an equally weighted arithmetic average of roughly 1,700 U.S. stocks.

In contrast to stock options, index options do not require that the call writer actually "deliver the index" upon exercise, or that the put writer "purchase the index." Instead, a cash settlement procedure is used. The profits that would accrue upon exercise of the option are calculated, and the option writer simply pays that amount to the option holder. The profits are equal to the difference between the exercise price of the option and the value of the index. For example, if the TSE 35 index is at $190 when a call option on the index with exercise price $180 is exercised, the holder of the call receives a cash payment of $10 multiplied by the contract multiplier of 100, or $1,000 per contract. The TSE 35 traded options are listed at the end of Figure 21.1. Figure 21.2 is a sample listing of various index options from *The Wall Street Journal*.

Foreign currency options

A currency option offers the right to buy or sell a quantity of foreign currency for a specified amount of domestic currency. Several foreign currency options were introduced by the Montreal Exchange in the 1980s, but met with little success and were subsequently withdrawn. In the United States, foreign currency options have traded on the Philadelphia Stock Exchange since December 1982. Since then, the Chicago Board Options Exchange and Chicago Mercantile Exchange have also listed foreign currency options.

Currency option contracts on U.S. exchanges call for purchase or sale of the currency in exchange for a specified number of U.S. dollars. Contracts are quoted in cents or fractions of a cent per unit of foreign currency. Figure 21.3 shows a listing from *The Wall Street Journal* of the contracts traded on the Philadelphia Exchange. The size of each option contract is specified for each listing. The call option on the British pound, for example, entitles its holder to purchase 12,500 pounds for a specified number of cents per pound on or before the expiration date. The June call option with strike price of 185 cents sells for 2.15 cents, which means that each contract costs $.0215 × 12,500 = $268.75. In the figure, the current exchange rate is 186.02 cents per pound. Therefore, the option is in the money by 1.02 cents, the difference between the current exchange rate (186.02 cents) and the exercise price of 185 cents per pound.

Futures options

Futures options give their holders the right to buy or sell a specified futures contract, using as a futures price the exercise price of the option. Although the delivery process is slightly complicated, the terms of futures options contracts are designed, in effect, to allow the option to be written on the futures price itself. The option holder receives upon exercise a profit equal to the difference between the current futures price on the specified asset and the exercise price of the option. Thus, if the futures price is, for example, $37, and the call has an

FIGURE 21.2
Listing of various index options.

(From *The Wall Street Journal,* May 30, 1988. Reprinted by permission of *The Wall Street Journal.* © Dow Jones & Company Inc. 1988. All Rights Reserved Worldwide.)

INDEX OPTIONS

Friday, May 27, 1988

Chicago Board

S&P 100 INDEX

Strike	Calls–Last			Puts–Last		
Price	Jun	Jul	Aug	Jun	Jul	Aug
220	....	22	....	½	1¾	3⅛
225	....	....	....	⅞	2½	4⅜
230	12¼	15¾	....	1 9/16	3⅝	5⅝
235	8¾	12	....	2 9/16	5⅛	7¼
240	5⅜	8⅜	10½	4½	7⅛	9¼
245	2 15/16	5¾	8	7⅛	9¼	11¾
250	1 7/16	3⅝	6	11	12¼	....
255	⅝	2 1/16	3¾	15¼	16	....
260	¼	1⅛	2⅝	20¼	21½	....
265	⅛	⅝	1 7/16	....	....	....
270	1/16	5/16	⅞	....	....	....
275	....	3/16	....	....	....	....

Total call volume 39,754 Total call open int. 278,352
Total put volume 41,239 Total put open int. 227,762
The index: High 241.96; Low 240.02; Close 240.72, −1.24

S&P 500 INDEX

Strike	Calls–Last			Puts–Last		
Price	Jun	Jul	Sep	Jun	Jul	Sep
195	....	....	60	....	....	⅞
200	....	....	54½	1/16	....	1 1/16
205	....	....	49½	....	....	1 1/16
210	....	....	44¾	1/16	....	1½
215	....	....	....	1/16	....	1¾
220	33½	....	....	¼	....	....
225	....	....	....	5/16	....	....
230	....	25½	....	7/16	1¾	4¾
235	....	....	....	¾	....	....
240	14¾	....	....	1	3½	....
245	....	13	....	2⅛	4½	....
250	6⅝	9¾	....	3½	6¼	10
255	3⅝	6¾	....	5⅜	7⅞	....
260	2¼	4¾	....	9¼	....	....
265	1 1/16	3	....	12⅜	....	....
270	7/16	1 13/16	5¼	....	....	....
275	....	....	3½	....	....	....
280	1/16	....	....	....	....	....
295	....	....	....	41⅞	....	....
315	....	....	....	61½	....	....

Total call volume 29,729 Total call open int. 165,580
Total put volume 6,694 Total put open int. 217,332
The index: High 254.63; Low 252.74; Close 253.42, −1.21.

Philadelphia Exchange

GOLD/SILVER INDEX

Strike	Calls–Last			Puts–Last		
Price	Jun	Jul	Aug	Jun	Jul	Aug
95	5⅜	....	....	1⅛	2⅛	....
100	2 9/16	....	....	2⅞	....	....
110	3/16	....	....	....	....	....

Total call volume 21 Total call open int. 583
Total put volume 29 Total put open int. 493
The index: High 99.84; Low 98.88; Close 99.02, −0.78

VALUE LINE INDEX OPTIONS

Strike	Calls–Last			Puts–Last		
Price	Jun	Jul	Aug	Jun	Jul	Aug
205	....	....	....	....	....	2⅜
210	....	....	....	....	....	2⅝
215	....	....	....	....	....	3¾
220	....	....	....	....	....	5⅛
235	....	3¼	....	....	....	....

Total call volume 50 Total call open int. 667
Total put volume 40 Total put open int. 180
The index: High 227.80; Low 227.03; Close 227.36, −0.36
Based on Value Line arithmetic average.

NATIONAL O-T-C INDEX

Total call volume 0 Total call open int. 9
Total put volume 0 Total put open int. 92
The index: High 237.86; Low 236.68; Close 237.37, −0.49

UTILITIES INDEX

Strike	Calls–Last			Puts–Last		
Price	Jun	Jul	Aug	Jun	Jul	Aug
170	7	....	....	....	....	....
175	2½	....	....	....	....	....
180	....	1½	....	....	....	....

Total call volume 58 Total call open int. 2,583
Total put [illegible] Total put open int. 1,424

N.Y. Stock Exchange

NYSE INDEX OPTIONS

Strike	Calls–Last			Puts–Last		
Price	Jun	Jul	Aug	Jun	Jul	Aug
130	....	....	....	¼	⅞	....
135	....	....	....	9/16	1 9/16	....
137½	7	....	....	15/16	....	....
140	5½	7	....	1 11/16	3⅛	....
145	1 13/16	3 9/16	....	3½	....	6½
150	½	1 11/16	....	7¼	8¼	....
155	1/16	9/16	....	....	....	....

Total call volume 1,178. Total call open int. 7,910.
Total put volume 463. Total put open int. 7,491.
The index: High 144.17; Low 143.35; Close 143.66, −0.57.

Pacific Exchange

FINANCIAL NEWS COMPOSITE INDEX

Strike	Calls–Last			Puts–Last		
Price	Jun	Jul	Sep	Jun	Jul	Sep
155	17¾	....	....	....	....	....
160	13½	....	....	....	....	....
165	8⅞	....	....	....	2 7/16	....
170	5	7⅜	....	2 3/16	4	....
175	2⅜	....	....	4⅜	....	....
180	....	....	....	7¾	....	....
185	....	....	....	12⅜	....	....
190	....	....	....	17¼	....	....
205	....	....	....	32⅜	....	....

Total call volume 186 Total call open int. 3,835
Total put volume 589 Total put open int. 3,216
The index: High 173.82; Low 172.34; Close 172.89, −0.92

American Exchange

MAJOR MARKET INDEX

Strike	Calls–Last			Puts–Last		
Price	Jun	Jul	Aug	Jun	Jul	Aug
350	....	....	....	11/16	2⅞	....
355	....	....	....	1 1/16	3⅝	....
360	22	....	....	1 9/16	4¾	....
365	18	....	....	2 7/16	....	....
370	14½	....	....	3½	7¼	11½
375	10¼	....	19	5⅛	8⅞	13¾
380	7¼	12¼	....	7⅜	11⅜	....
385	5	....	13½	11⅛	....	17½
390	3¼	7⅜	....	13⅛	19⅜	....
395	2	5⅜	8¼	16½	19⅜	....
400	1⅛	4	7⅛	20½	....	....
405	9/16	2 15/16	5½	....	....	....
410	⅜	1 15/16	4	....	....	....
415	....	1⅛	....	....	....	....
420	⅛	13/16	....	....	....	....
425	1/16	½	....	....	....	....
430	....	¼	....	....	....	....

Total call volume 6,328 Total call open int. 21,125
Total put volume 3,402 Total put open int. 17,812
The index: High 382.15; Low 378.79; Close 379.92, −2.19.

COMPUTER TECHNOLOGY INDEX

Strike	Calls–Last			Puts–Last		
Price	Jun	Jul	Aug	Jun	Jul	Aug
120	....	⅜	....	....	....	....

Total call volume 30 Total call open int. 386
Total put volume 0 Total put open int. 245
The index: High 104.39; Low 103.99; Close 103.99, −0.40.

OIL INDEX

Strike	Calls–Last			Puts–Last		
Price	Jun	Jul	Aug	Jun	Jul	Aug
175	....	....	....	....	4⅝	....
180	1½	....	....	....	....	....
185	½	2¼	....	....	....	....

Total call volume 9 Total call open int. 150
Total put volume 20 Total put open int. 713
The index: High 177.69; Low 175.43; Close 175.82, −1.87.

INSTITUTIONAL INDEX

Strike	Calls–Last			Puts–Last		
Price	Jun	Jul	Aug	Jun	Jul	Aug
[illegible]	....	....		⅜		

FIGURE 21.3

Foreign currency option contracts traded on the Philadelphia exchange.

(From *The Wall Street Journal,* May 18, 1988. Reprinted by permission of *The Wall Street Journal,* © Dow Jones & Company, Inc. 1988. All Rights Reserved Worldwide.)

FOREIGN CURRENCY OPTIONS

Tuesday, May 17, 1988

Philadelphia Exchange

Option & Underlying	Strike Price	Calls—Last			Puts—Last		
		May	Jun	Sep	May	Jun	Sep
50,000 Australian Dollars-cents per unit.							
ADollr	...75	r	1.74	2.53	r	0.32	1.76
76.53	...76	r	1.03	1.62	r	0.68	r
76.53	...77	r	0.50	1.21	r	1.08	r
76.53	...78	r	0.30	0.98	r	r	r
76.53	...79	r	0.11	0.80	r	r	r
50,000 Australian Dollars-European Style.							
76.53	...79	r	0.14	r	r	r	r
12,500 British Pounds-cents per unit.							
BPound	182½	r	r	5.90	r	0.30	r
186.02	.185	r	2.15	r	r	1.05	r
186.02	187½	r	0.75	3.15	r	2.15	r
186.02	.190	r	0.20	2.35	r	4.20	r
186.02	192½	r	0.15	1.85	r	r	r
186.02	195	r	r	r	r	9.40	r
12,500 British Pounds-European Style.							
186.02	182½	r	4.20	r	r	r	r
50,000 Canadian Dollars-cents per unit.							
CDollr	...79	r	1.84	r	s	r	r
80.84	...81	r	r	r	r	0.60	r
80.84	.81½	r	0.16	r	r	r	r
62,500 West German Marks-cents per unit.							
DMark	.. 56	r	2.75	r	r	0.01	r
58.58	...57	r	r	r	r	0.05	0.40
58.58	...58	r	0.98	r	r	0.14	0.66
58.58	...59	r	0.28	1.42	r	0.56	1.03
58.58	...60	r	0.04	0.90	r	1.40	r
58.58	...61	r	0.05	0.60	r	2.40	2.40
58.58	...62	r	r	0.42	r	r	r
58.58	...63	r	0.03	0.25	r	r	r
58.58	...64	r	r	0.26	r	r	r
6,250,000 Japanese Yen-100ths of a cent per unit.							
JYen	... 73	r	r	r	r	r	0.12
79.49	...75	r	r	r	r	0.01	r
79.49	...76	r	3.50	r	r	0.02	r
79.49	...77	r	r	r	r	0.06	0.51
79.49	...78	r	2.32	r	r	0.09	r
79.49	...79	r	0.92	r	r	0.27	r
79.49	...80	r	0.36	1.80	r	0.66	r
79.49	...81	r	0.13	1.28	r	1.56	2.05
79.49	...82	r	0.05	0.94	r	r	r
79.49	...83	r	0.01	r	r	r	r
79.49	...85	r	r	0.31	r	r	r
62,500 Swiss Francs-cents per unit.							
SFranc	..69	r	r	r	r	0.09	r
70.28	...70	r	r	r	r	0.26	1.02
70.28	...71	r	0.32	r	r	0.71	r
70.28	...72	r	0.10	r	r	1.65	1.94
70.28	...73	r	0.07	r	r	2.32	s
70.28	...74	r	r	r	r	3.32	r
62,500 Swiss Francs-European Style.							
70.28	...73	r	r	r	r	2.14	r

Total call vol. 37,694 Call open int. 529,299
Total put vol. 32,914 Put open int. 506,575
r—Not traded. s—No option offered.
Last is premium (purchase price).

exercise price of $35, the holder who exercises the call option on the futures gets a payoff of $2.

Interest rate options

Options on Canada bonds are traded on the Montreal and Toronto exchanges via TCO. Figure 21.1 shows three such bonds (denoted by CDA in the listing) traded that particular day.

Options on particular U.S. Treasury notes and bonds are listed on the American Exchange and the CBOE. Options also are traded on Treasury bills, certificates of deposit, and GNMA pass-through certificates. Options on Treasury bond and Treasury note futures also trade on the Chicago Board of Trade.

21.2 *Values of Options at Expiration*

Call Options

Recall that a call option gives the right to purchase a security at the exercise price. If you hold a call option on Seagram's stock with an exercise price of $130 and Seagram's currently sells at $140, you can exercise your option to purchase the stock at $130 and simultaneously sell the shares at the market price of $140, clearing $10 per share. On the other hand, if the shares sell below $130, you can sit on the option and do nothing, realizing no further gain or loss. The value of the call option at expiration equals:

$$\text{Payoff to call holder} = \begin{array}{ll} S_T - X & \text{if } S_T > X \\ 0 & \text{if } S_T \le X \end{array}$$

where S_T is the value of the stock at expiration and X is the exercise price. This formula emphasizes the option property, because the payoff cannot be negative. That is, the option is exercised only if S_T exceeds X. If S_T is less than X, exercise does not occur and the option expires with zero value. The loss to the option holder in this case equals the price originally paid for the right to buy at the exercise price.

The value at expiration of the call on Seagram's with exercise price $130 is given by the following schedule:

Seagram's value:	$120	$130	$140	$150	$160
Option value:	0	0	$ 10	$ 20	$ 30

For Seagram's prices at or below $130, the option is worthless. Above $130, the option is worth the excess of Seagram's price over $130. The option's value increases by $1 for each dollar increase in the Seagram's stock price. This relationship can be depicted graphically, as in the solid (top) line of Figure 21.4.

The solid line of Figure 21.4 depicts the value of the call at maturity. The net *profit* to the holder of the call equals the gross payoff less the initial investment in the call. Suppose the call cost $14. Then the profit to the call holder would be as given in the broken (bottom) line of Figure 21.4. At option expiration, the investor has suffered a loss of $14 if the stock price is less than $130. Profits do not become positive unless the stock price at expiration exceeds $144. The break-even point is $144, because at that point the payoff to the call, $S_T - X =$

FIGURE 21.4

Payoff and profit to call option at expiration.

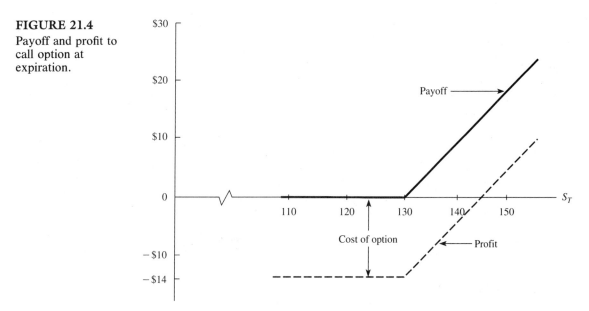

$144 - \$130 = \$14$, equals the cost paid to acquire the call. Hence, the call holder profits only if the stock price is higher.

Conversely, the writer of the call incurs losses if the stock price is high. In that scenario, the writer will receive a call and will be obligated to deliver a stock worth S_T for only X dollars:

$$\text{Payoff to call writer} = \begin{array}{ll} -(S_T - X) & \text{if } S_T \geq X \\ 0 & \text{if } S_T < X \end{array}$$

The call writer, who is exposed to losses if Seagram's stock increases in price, is willing to bear this risk in return for the option premium. Figure 21.5 depicts the payoff and profit diagrams for the call writer. Notice that these are just the mirror images of the corresponding diagrams for call holders. The break-even point for the option writer also is $144. The (negative) payoff at that point just offsets the premium originally received when the option was written.

Put Options

A put option conveys the right to sell an asset at the exercise price. In this case, the holder will not exercise the option unless the asset sells for *less* than the exercise price. For example, if Seagram's shares were to fall to $110, a put option with exercise price $120 could be exercised to give a $10 profit to its holder. The holder would purchase a share of Seagram's for $110, and simultaneously deliver it to the put option writer for the exercise price of $120.

The value of a put option at expiration is

$$\text{Payoff to call holder} = \begin{array}{ll} X - S_T & \text{if } S_T \leq X \\ 0 & \text{if } S_T > X \end{array}$$

FIGURE 21.5
Payoff and profit to
call writers at
expiration.

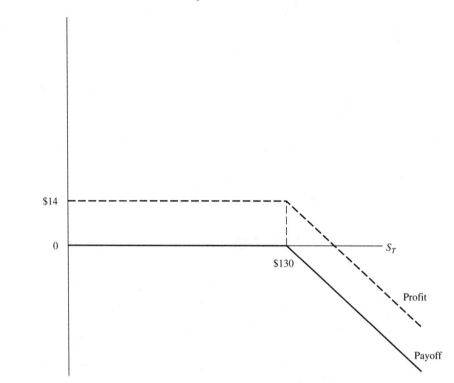

The solid (top) line in Figure 21.6 illustrates the payoff at maturity to the holder of a put option on Seagram's stock with an exercise price of $130. If the stock price at option maturity is above $130, the put has no value, because the right to sell the shares at $130 would not be exercised. Below a price of $130, the put value at expiration increases by $1 for each dollar that the stock price falls. The dashed (bottom) line in Figure 21.6 is a graph of the put option owner's profit at expiration, net of the initial cost of the put.

Concept Check	Question 2. Analyze the strategy of put writing.
	a. What is the payoff to a put writer as a function of the stock price?
	b. What is the profit?
	c. Draw the payoff and profit graphs.
	d. When do put writers do well? When do they do poorly?

Writing puts *naked* (i.e., writing a put without an offsetting position in the stock for hedging purposes) exposes the writer to losses if the market falls. Writing

FIGURE 21.6
Payoff and profit to
put option at
expiration.

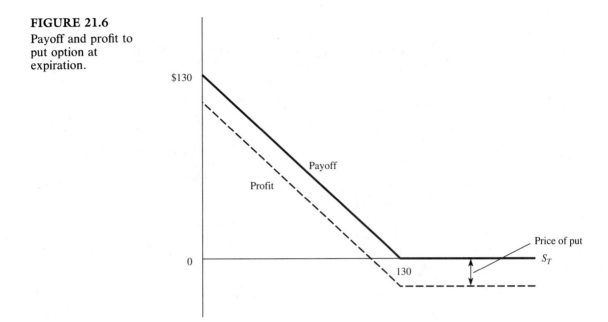

naked out-of-the-money puts was once considered an attractive way to generate income, since it was believed that as long as the market did not fall sharply
before the option expiration, the option premium could be collected without the
put holder ever exercising the option against the writer. Because only sharp
drops in the market could result in losses to the writer of the put, the strategy
was not viewed as overly risky. However, as the accompanying box makes
clear, in the wake of the market crash of October 1987 such put writers suffered
huge losses. Participants now perceive much greater risk to this strategy.

Options vs. Stock Investments

Call options are bullish investments; that is, they provide profits when stock
prices increase. Puts, in contrast, are bearish investments. Symmetrically,
writing calls is bearish and writing puts is bullish. Because option values depend on market movements, purchase of options may be viewed as a substitute
for direct purchase or sale of a stock. Why might an option strategy be preferable to direct stock transactions?

For example, why would you purchase a call option rather than buy Seagram's stock directly? Maybe you have some information that leads you to
believe that Seagram's stock will increase in value from its current level, which
in our examples we will take to be $140. You know your analysis could be
incorrect, and that Seagram's also could fall in price. Suppose that a six-month
maturity call option with exercise price $135 currently sells for $14, and that the
six-month interest rate is 5 percent. Consider these three strategies for invest-

The Black Hole: How Some Investors Lost All Their Money in the Market Crash

Their Sales of "Naked Puts" Quickly Come to Grief, Damage Suits Are Filed

When Robert O'Connor got involved in stock-index options, he hoped his trading profits would help put his children through college. His broker, Mr. O'Connor explains, "said we would make about $1,000 a month, and if our losses got to $2,000 to $3,000, he would close out the account."

Instead, Mr. O'Connor, the 46-year-old owner of a small medical X-ray printing concern in Grand Rapids, Michigan, got caught in one of the worst investor blowouts in history. In a few minutes on October 19 [1987], he lost everything in his account plus an *additional* $91,000—a total loss of 175 percent of his original investment.

"If I had been told what the real risks were, I would never have done this. We're not big rollers," Mr. O'Connor says. "That's my life savings. That's not money to play with."

Scene of Disaster

For Mr. O'Connor and hundreds of other investors, a little-known corner of the Chicago Board Options Exchange was the "black hole" of Black Monday's market crash. In a strategy marketed by brokers nationwide as a sure thing, these customers had sunk hundreds of millions of dollars into "naked puts"—unhedged, highly leveraged bets that the stock market was in no danger of plunging. Most of these naked puts seem to have been options on the Standard & Poor's 100 stock index, which are traded on the CBOE.

Lulled into complacency by the market's long surge, hundreds of brokers marketed naked puts to ill-informed investors ranging from a retired civil servant in Virginia to a quadriplegic woman in Texas. When stocks crashed, many traders with unhedged positions got margin calls for several times their original investment.

Risky options trades are emerging as the leading single source of investor complaints following the crash, regulators say. Unlike the huge stock market losses, which remain mostly on paper, individuals' losses on stock-index options were suddenly forced on them at the time of the crash and involved immediate losses of real money. The losses are estimated at several hundred million dollars, and a rash of lawsuits and countersuits between brokers and investors seem certain.

Suitability Questioned

"There are some very serious suitability questions about which investors were put into options," says Scott Staph, the communications director for the North American Securities Administrators Association in Washington. "It's much more dramatic than anything in stocks."

The carnage has sparked investigations by the Chicago Board Options Exchange and the American Stock Exchange, which also has trading in stock-index options. Also scheduled are hearings by several congressional committees. They may press for tighter regulation and stiffer margin requirements, which are regulated by the Securities and Exchange Commission, to curb speculative activity.

The blowout underscores one of the biggest regulatory breakdowns exposed by the market crash: brokers' failure to recognize the riskiness of certain options positions and to require adequate margins, or security deposits. Traders say as much as 25 percent of the CBOE's stock-index option trades were unhedged—that is, not backed by holdings of the underlying stocks or offsetting trades.

The "Put" Strategy

The losses were especially sharp in "naked, out-of-the-money puts." A seller of puts agrees to buy stock or stock-index contracts at a set price before the put expires. These contracts are usually sold "out of the money"—priced at a level below current market prices that makes it unprofitable to exercise the option so long as the market rises or stays flat. The seller pockets a small amount per contract.

But if the market plunges, as it did October 19, the option swings into the money. The seller, in effect, has to pay pre-plunge stock prices to make good on his contract—and he takes a big loss.

Moreover, many investors were required to post margin money equal to only 5 percent to 10 percent of the face value of the options contracts—a minuscule amount compared with their exposure to loss. That kind of leverage more resembles Russian roulette than the "risk-free" trading that many customers thought they were doing in naked options, says Robert Gordon, the president of Twenty-First Securities Corp., a New York investment firm.

Brokers across the nation are still smarting as well. In San Francisco, Charles Schwab Corp. said a single trader's activity in stock-index options accounted for $15 million of its $22 million in losses in October. Bear, Stearns & Co. and other big Wall Street houses took heavy hits. Options-related losses sank H.B. Shaine & Co., the Grand Rapids brokerage firm where Mr. O'Connor did business. Some $90 million of losses at First Options of Chicago Inc. may drag its parent company, Continental Illinois Corp., into the red in the fourth quarter. And in London, too, a 23-year-old trainee accountant lost nearly one million pounds (about $1.75 million) trading options, according to British press reports.

"You have to recognize that there is unlimited potential for disaster" in selling naked options, says Peter Thayer, executive vice-president of Gateway Investment Advisors Inc., a Cincinnati-based investment firm that trades options to hedge its stock portfolios. Last September, Gateway bought out-of-the-money put options on the S&P 100 stock index on the CBOE at $2 to $3 a contract as "insurance" against a plunging market. By October 20, the day after the crash, the value of those contracts had soared to $130. Although Gateway profited handsomely, the parties on the other side of the trade were clobbered.

In many cases, brokers played down the risks to attract more customers to a big-commission business. "Brokers were selling these things like annuities," says Elisabeth Richards, a broker and strategic analyst with Heritage Financial Investments Corp. of Falls Church, Virginia.

In Texas, the 56-year-old quadriplegic, who asked not to be named, says she lost her entire $35,000 nest egg trading naked stock-index options. "It was far too risky for me," she says. She adds that now she is left with only Social Security.

Flying Blind

The North American Securities Administrators Association, which has been fielding investors' post-crash complaints on a new telephone hot line, heard from a Mendocino, California, investor who lost $1.3 million in naked puts without even knowing what his position was in the market. The man told association officials that he had switched recently to an aggressive broker who assured him that he would "fill him in as they went along." In a phone call to the association, Mr. Staph says, the man "was asking me what puts and calls are." (A call is an option to buy at a specified price within a specified period.)

Neither the CBOE nor the Amex passes judgment on the riskiness of particular trading strategies. But to help traders caught in sharp moves, the CBOE recently adopted an accelerated opening procedure aimed at starting trading more quickly during heavy volume; it wants to avoid a replay of the morning of October 20, when a huge influx of orders kept some options from trading for an hour and a half.

Firm Sued

Brokers who were pushing naked options assumed that the stock market wouldn't plunge into uncharted territory. Frank VanderHoff, one of the two main brokers who put 50 to 70 H.B. Shaine clients into stock-index options, says he told clients that the strategy's risk was "moderate barring a nuclear attack or a crash like 1929. It wasn't speculative. The market could go up or down, but not *substantially* up or down. If the crash had only been as bad as '29," he adds, "we would have made it." Mr. VanderHoff says that all his customers read and signed option-trading risk-disclosure documents and that he never promised that accounts would have strictly limited losses.

Nevertheless, Mr. O'Connor and other customers are suing the firm in state court in Grand Rapids. They allege that they weren't fully in-

(Continued)

formed of the risks and that Shaine acted negligently by selling out their options accounts without authority from them. The complaint says that the defendants lost about $100,000 each and that they should be reimbursed the amount, plus $500,000 each in damages.

The public's enthusiasm for options trading seems sure to wane. Harry Fluke of Alexandria, Virginia, was trading naked puts and calls in an arcane strategy known as a "strangle" when the market wiped out the $54,000 in his account. He still owes his brokerage firm $318,500. "It just killed me," he says.

Mr. Fluke's broker, Thomson-McKinnon Securities Inc., contends in a suit filed in federal court in Alexandria to collect money from him that he was well aware of the risks. Mr. Fluke concedes that he had been trading naked puts and calls for several years, but he says nothing had prepared him for the impact of the stock market's unprecedented volatility.

Similarly, a retired engineer in Niagara Falls, New York, who asked that his name be withheld, set up a trust for his daughter and grandson 10 years ago, with himself as trustee. The 76-year-old retiree says he lost nearly $360,000 on Black Monday when he was forced to buy back the stock-index options and the trust account was left about $140,000 in debt to Bear Stearns.

His experience is typical: On October 16, he sold 40 S&P 100 stock-index put options for $1,550 each, or a total of $62,000. In essence, he was betting that after the 108.35 point drop in the Dow Jones Industrial Average that Friday, the market wasn't likely to drop much further and probably would soon rally.

But Black Monday's plunge forced him to buy back the puts to cover his margin calls. Meanwhile, the price of the options had jumped 600 percent to $10,500 a contract—costing him $420,000 for the 40 contracts that he had sold for $62,000 just three days earlier.

Professional Battered

Some professional traders didn't fare much better. On Black Monday, Hwalin Lee took his accustomed place in the CBOE's stock-index options pit,
but unbeknown to other traders, the Taiwan native was already $5 million to $7 million in debt from the Friday plunge. He was under orders from his clearing firm and lender, First Options of Chicago, to close out his big positions in naked puts—to buy back options that he had previously sold. First Options even sent an official variously described in market parlance as a "leg breaker" or "sheriff" onto the CBOE floor with him to make sure he did so. But it was too late. The trader single-handedly lost $52 million.

Mr. Lee, 55, had consistently taken huge positions and a dozen times since 1978 had been sanctioned by the CBOE for violating trading limits. First Options didn't shun risk, either. Just a month before, its computers had simulated a 450-point drop in the industrial average. But the computer model assumed that the options market would keep functioning, allowing traders to close out losing positions.

On Black Monday, it didn't. Few were willing to step in front of an oncoming train, and none took the opposite side of Mr. Lee's trades. As the market hit bottom, his losses ballooned.

Mr. Lee couldn't be reached to comment, and officials at Continental Illinois and its options-clearing unit recently declined to be interviewed. However, Jim R. Porter, First Options' chairman, does say another 500-point drop in the industrial average wouldn't cost his firm money because its traders are operating under stricter trading standards and are putting up more margin cash.

Nevertheless, First Options still lets customers, such as James F. Hart, trade in naked, out-of-the-money puts and calls. Mr. Hart says First Options hasn't sought to rein him in. Other brokerage firms, however, have curbed or halted unhedged options trading since the crash.

For small investors such as Mr. Fluke, it's too late. Though not disputing the facts laid out in his broker's suit against him, he is still reeling. He won't comment on his plans, but a lawyer familiar with his case says the former federal employee may file for personal bankruptcy. Mr. Fluke says, "I wish someone had sat down with me and said the risk is greater than you—a retired civil servant—can risk."

ing a sum of money, for example, $14,000. For simplicity, suppose that Seagram's will not pay any dividends until after the six-month period.

Strategy A: purchase 100 shares of Seagram stock.

Strategy B: purchase 1,000 call options on Seagram's with exercise price $135. (This would require 10 contracts, each for 100 shares.)

Strategy C: purchase 100 call options for $1,400. Invest the remaining $12,600 in six-month T-bills, to earn 5 percent interest.

Let us trace the possible values of these three portfolios when the options expire in six months as a function of Seagram's stock price at that time.

Seagram's Price	$120	$130	$140	$150	$160
Value of portfolio A:	$12,000	$13,000	$14,000	$15,000	$16,000
Value of portfolio B:	0	0	5,000	15,000	25,000
Value of portfolio C:	13,230	13,230	13,730	14,730	15,730

Portfolio *A* will be worth 100 times the share value of Seagram's. Portfolio *B* is worthless unless Seagram's sells for more than the exercise price of the call. Once that point is reached, the portfolio is worth 1,000 times the excess of the stock price over the exercise price. Finally, portfolio *C* is worth $13,230 from the investment in T-bills ($12,600 × 1.05 = $13,230) plus any profits from the 100 call options. Remember that each of these portfolios involves the same $14,000 initial investment. The rates of return on these three portfolios are as follows:

Seagram's Price	$120	$130	$140	$150	$160
A (all stock)	−14.3%	−7.1%	0.0%	7.1%	14.3%
B (all options)	−100.0%	−100.0%	−64.3%	7.1%	78.6%
C (options plus bills)	−5.5%	−5.5%	−1.9%	5.2%	12.4%

These rates of return are illustrated in Figure 21.7.

Comparing the returns to portfolios *B* and *C* to those of the simple investment in Seagram's stock represented by portfolio *A*, we see that options offer two interesting features. First, an option offers leverage. Compare the returns of portfolios *B* and *A*. When Seagram's stock falls in price even moderately to $130, the value of portfolio *B* falls precipitously to zero, a rate of return of −100 percent. Conversely, if the stock price increases by 14.3 percent, from $140 to $160, the all-option portfolio jumps in value by a disproportionate 78.6 percent. In this sense, calls are a leveraged investment on the stock. Their values respond more than proportionately to changes in the stock value. Figure 21.7 vividly illustrates this point. The slope of the all-option portfolio is far steeper than the all-stock portfolio, reflecting its greater proportional sensitivity to the value of the underlying security. The leverage factor is the reason that investors (illegally) exploiting inside information commonly choose options as their investment vehicle.

The potential insurance value of options is the second interesting feature, as portfolio *C* shows. The T-bill plus option portfolio cannot be worth less than

FIGURE 21.7
Rates of return to three strategies.

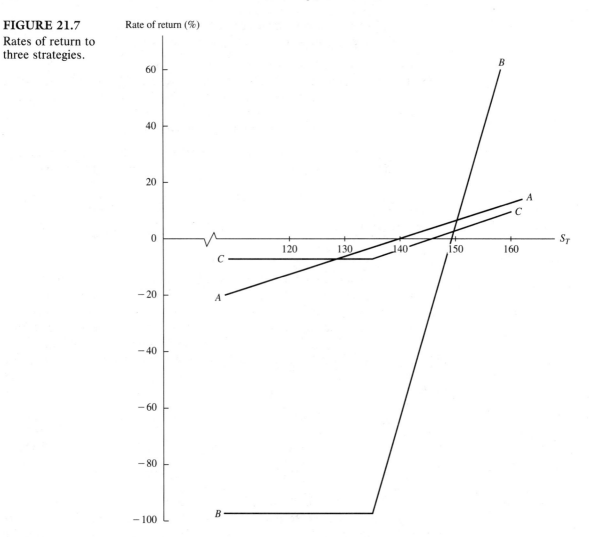

$13,230 after six months, since the option can always be left to expire worthless. The worst possible rate of return on portfolio C is -5.5 percent, compared to a (theoretically) worst possible rate of return on Seagram's stock of -100 percent if the company were to go bankrupt. Of course, this insurance comes at a price: when Seagram's does well, portfolio C does not perform quite as well as portfolio A.

The Put-Call Parity Relationship

Suppose that you buy a call option and write a put option, each with the same exercise price, X, and the same expiration date, T. At expiration, the payoff on your investment will equal the payoff to the call, minus the payoff that must be made on the put. The payoff for each option will depend on whether the ultimate stock price, S_T, exceeds the exercise price at contract expiration.

	$S_T \leq X$	$S_T > X$
Payoff of call held	0	$S_T - X$
Payoff of put written	$-(X - S_T)$	0
TOTAL	$S_T - X$	$S_T - X$

Figure 21.8 illustrates this payoff pattern. Compare the payoff to that of a portfolio made up of the stock plus a borrowing position, where the money to be paid back will grow, with interest, to X dollars at the maturity of the loan. Such a position, in fact, is a *leveraged* equity position in which $X/(1 + r_f)^T$ dollars is borrowed today (so that X will be repaid at maturity) and S_0 dollars is

FIGURE 21.8

The payoff pattern of a long call–short put position.

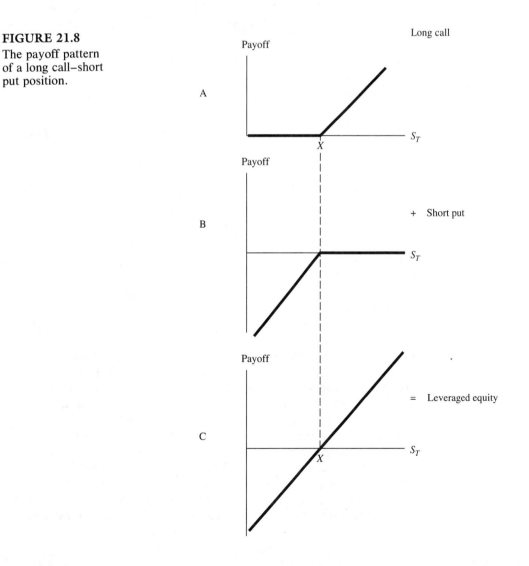

invested in the stock. The total payoff of the leveraged equity position is $S_T - X$, the same as that of the option strategy. Thus the long call–short put position replicates the leveraged equity position. Again, we see that option trading allows us to construct artificial leverage.

Because the option portfolio has a payoff identical to that of the leveraged equity position, the costs of establishing them must be equal. The net cost of establishing the option position is $C - P$; the call is purchased for C, while the written put generates premium income of P. Likewise, the leveraged equity position requires a net cash outlay of $S_0 - X/(1 + r_f)^T$, the cost of the stock less the proceeds from borrowing. Equating these costs, we conclude that

$$C - P = S_0 - X/(1 + r_f)^T \qquad \textbf{(21.1)}$$

Equation 21.1 is called the **put-call parity theorem** because it represents the proper relationship between put and call prices. If the parity relation is ever violated, an arbitrage opportunity arises. For example, suppose that you confront these data for a certain stock:

Stock price	$110
Call price (6-month maturity, X = $105)	$ 17
Put price (6-month maturity, X = $105)	$ 5
Risk-free interest rate:	10.25 percent annual yield, or 5% per 6 months

We use these data in the put-call parity theorem to see if parity is violated:

$$
\begin{aligned}
C - P &\overset{?}{=} S_0 - X/(1 + r_f)^T \\
17 - 15 &\overset{?}{=} 110 - 105/1.05 \\
12 &\overset{?}{=} 10
\end{aligned}
\qquad \textbf{(21.2)}
$$

Parity is violated. To exploit the mispricing, you can buy the relatively cheap portfolio (the stock plus borrowing position represented on the right-hand side of equation 21.2) and sell the relatively expensive portfolio (the long call–short put position corresponding to the left-hand side—i.e., write a call and buy a put).

Let us examine the payoff to this strategy. In six months, the stock will be worth S_T. The $100 borrowed will be paid back with interest, resulting in a cash outflow of $105. The written call will result in a cash outflow of $S_T - \$105$ if S_T exceeds $105.

Table 21.1 summarizes the outcome. The immediate cash inflow is $2. In six months, the various positions provide exactly offsetting cash flows: the $2 inflow is thus realized without any offsetting outflows. This is an arbitrage opportunity that will be pursued on a large scale until buying and selling pressure restores the parity condition expressed in equation 21.1.

The parity condition actually applies only to options on stocks that pay no dividends before the maturity date of the options. It also applies only to European options, because the cash flow streams from the two portfolios represented by the two sides of equation 21.1 will match only if each position is held until maturity. If a call and a put may be optimally exercised at different times before their common expiration date, then the equality of payoffs cannot be

TABLE 21.1   Arbitrage Strategy

Position	Immediate Cash Flow	Cash Flow in 6 Months	
		$S_T \leq 105$	$S_T > 105$
Buy stock	−110	S_T	S_T
Borrow $X/(1 + r_f)^T = \$100$	+100	−105	−105
Sell call	+ 17	0	$-(S_T - 105)$
Buy put	− 5	$105 - S_T$	0
TOTAL	2	0	0

ensured, or even expected, and the portfolios will have different values. We will return to these issues in Chapter 22.

For now, however, let's see how well parity works with real data from Figure 21.1, using Inco options since few Seagram's options traded that day. The May call on Inco with exercise price $35 and time to expiration of 45 days cost $0.90, while the put cost $2.05. Inco was selling for $33.50, and the annualized interest rate on this date for 39-day T-bills was 7.2 percent. According to parity, we should find that

$$\$0.90 - \$2.05 = \$33.50 - \$35/(1.072)^{45/365}$$
$$\$1.15 = \$1.20$$

In this case, parity is violated by only 5 cents per share, far too small an amount to outweigh the brokerage fees involved in attempting to exploit the minor mispricing. Moreover, given the infrequent trading of options that we have noted, this small discrepancy from parity could be due to "stale prices." Indeed, we note from Figure 21.1 that the last recorded prices for both call and put used in this example lie outside their corresponding bid and asked prices, implying that the last recorded trades in both options took place before the bid and asked prices took their closing values.

Combination of Options

An unlimited variety of payoff patterns can be achieved by combining puts and calls with various exercise prices. The following subsections explain the motivation and structure of some of the more popular methods.

Protective put

Imagine that you would like to invest in a stock, for example, Seagram's, but that you are unwilling to bear potential losses beyond some given level. Investing in the stock alone is quite risky, because in principle you could lose all the money you invest. You might consider instead investing in stock together with a put option on the stock. Table 21.2 illustrates the total value of your portfolio at option expiration.

TABLE 21.2   Payoff to Protective Put Strategy

	$S_T \leq X$	$S_T > X$
Stock	S_T	S_T
Put	$X - S_T$	0
TOTAL	X	S_T

FIGURE 21.9
Value of a
protective put
position at
expiration.

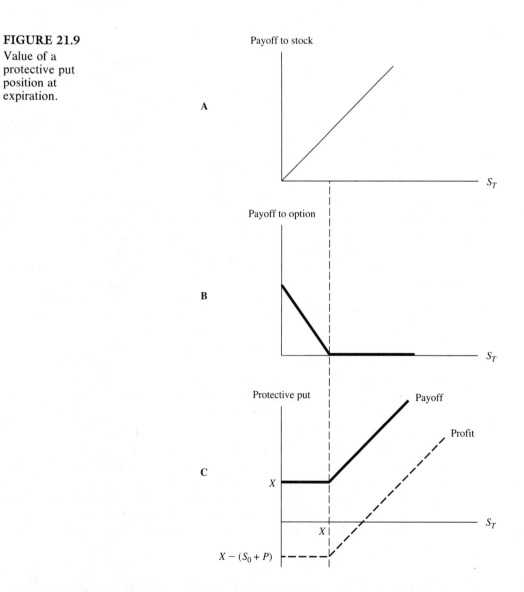

Whatever happens to the stock price, you are guaranteed a payoff equal to the put option's exercise price because the put gives you the right to sell Seagram's for the exercise price even if the stock price is below that value.

Figure 21.9 illustrates the payoff and profit to this **protective put** strategy. The solid line in Figure 21.9**C** is the total payoff; the dashed line is displaced downward by the cost of establishing the position, $S_0 + P$. Notice that potential losses are indeed limited.

It is instructive to compare the profit to the protective put strategy with that of the stock investment. For simplicity, consider an at-the-money protective put, so that $X = S_0$. Figure 21.10 compares the profits for the two strategies. The profit on the stock is zero if the stock price remains unchanged, and $S_T = S_0$. It rises or falls by \$1 for every \$1 swing in the ultimate stock price. The profit on the stock plus put portfolio is negative and equal to the cost of the put if S_T is below S_0. The profit on the overall protective put position increases one for one with increases in the stock price, once S_T exceeds S_0.

Figure 21.10 makes it clear that the protective put offers some insurance against stock price declines in that it limits losses. Indeed, as we shall see in Chapter 22, protective put strategies are the conceptual basis for the portfolio insurance industry. The cost of the protection is that, in the case of stock price

FIGURE 21.10
Protective put versus stock investment.

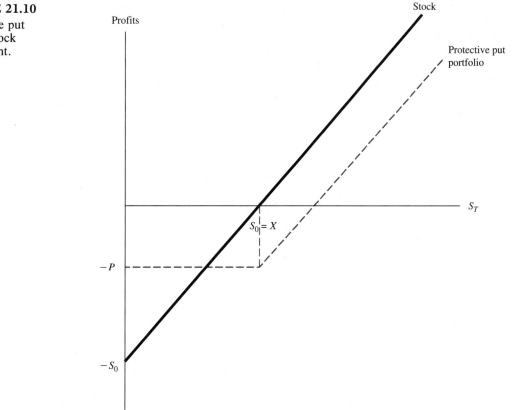

Protective Puts vs. Stop-Loss Orders

We have seen that protective puts guarantee that the end-of-period value of a portfolio will equal or exceed the put's exercise price. As a specific example, consider a share of stock protected by a European put option with one-year maturity and an exercise price of $40. Even if the stock at year-end is selling below $40, the put can be exercised and the stock can be sold for the exercise price. The stock-plus-put position will be worth $40, regardless of how far the stock price falls.

Another common tool to protect a portfolio position is the stop-loss order. This is an order to your broker to sell your stock when and if its price falls to some lower boundary, such as $40 per share. Thus, should the stock price fall substantially, your shares will be sold before losses mount, so that your proceeds will not fall below $40 per share.

It would seem from this analysis that the stop-loss order provides the same stock price insurance offered by the protective put. The protective put, however, must be obtained by paying for the option, whereas the stop-loss order can be executed by your broker for no extra cost. Does this mean that the stop-loss order is effectively a free put option? What does the put option offer that the stop-loss order does not?

To resolve this seeming paradox, look at Figure 21.11, which graphs one possible path for the stock price over the course of the year. Notice that, al-though the stock price falls below $40 at time *t*, it ultimately recovers and ends the year selling at $60. The protective put combination in this circumstance will end the year worth $60—the put will expire worthless, but the stock will be worth $60. The stop-loss order, however, has required that the stock be sold at time *t* as soon as its price falls below $40. This strategy will yield by year-end only $40 plus any interest accumulated between time *t* and the end of the year, far less than the payoff on the protective put strategy.

The protective put strategy does offer an advantage over the stop-loss strategy. With a stop-loss order in force, the investor realizes the $40 lower bound if the stock price *ever* reaches that boundary because the stock is sold as soon as the boundary is reached. Whenever the stock price rebounds from the $40 limit, the investor using the stop-loss order will not share in the gain. The holder of the put option, on the other hand, does not have to exercise when the stock hits $40. Instead, the option holder may wait until the end of the year to exercise the option, knowing that the $40 exercise price is guaranteed regardless of how far the stock falls, but that, should the stock price recover, the stock still will be held and any gain will be captured. This is the advantage that justifies the cost required to purchase the protective put option.*

* Another disadvantage of the stop-loss order, which is of a more practical nature, is that the selling price is not guaranteed. Problems in executing trades could lead to a transaction at a price lower than $40.

increases, your profit is reduced by the cost of the put, which turned out to be unneeded. The accompanying box discusses the relative merits of protective puts versus stop-loss orders.

Covered call

A **covered call** position is the purchase of a share of stock with a simultaneous sale of a call on that stock. The position is "covered" because the obligation to deliver the stock is covered by the stock held in the portfolio. Writing an option without an offsetting stock position is called, by contrast, *naked option writing*. The payoff to a covered call, presented in Table 21.3, equals the stock value

FIGURE 21.11
Stop-loss versus
protective put.

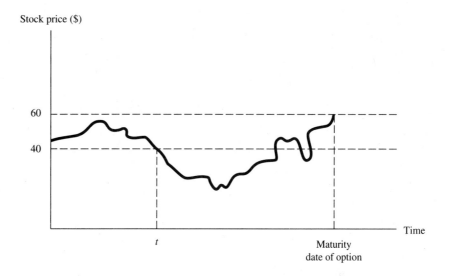

minus the payoff of the call. The call payoff is subtracted because the covered call position involves issuing a call to another investor who can choose to exercise it to profit at your expense.

The solid line in Figure 21.12C illustrates the payoff pattern. We see that the total position is worth S_T when the stock price at time T is below X, and rises to a maximum of X when S_T exceeds X. In essence, the sale of the call option means that the call writer has sold the claim to any stock value above X in return for the initial premium (the call price). Therefore, at expiration the position is worth, at most, X. The dashed line of Figure 21.12C is the net profit to the covered call.

Writing covered call options has been a popular investment strategy among institutional investors. Consider the managers of a fund invested largely in stocks. They might find it appealing to write calls on some or all of the stock in order to boost income by the premiums collected. Although they thereby forfeit potential capital gains should the stock price rise above the exercise price, if they view X as the price at which they plan to sell the stock anyway, then the call may be viewed as enforcing a kind of "sell discipline." The written call guarantees that the stock sale will take place as planned.

For example, assume a pension fund is holding 1,000 shares of Seagram's stock, with a current price of $130 per share. Suppose that management intends to sell all 1,000 shares if the share price hits $140, and that a call expiring in 90

TABLE 21.3 Payoff to a Covered Call

	$S \leq X$	$S > X$
Payoff of stock	S_T	S_T
−Payoff of call	−0	$-(S_T - X)$
TOTAL	S_T	X

FIGURE 21.12
Value of a covered
call position at
expiration.

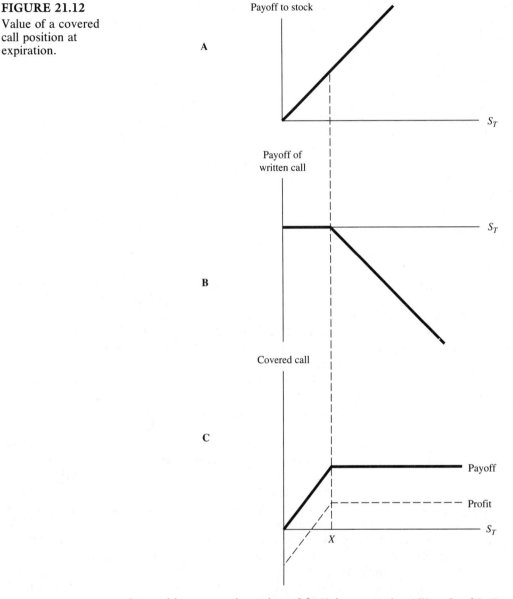

days with an exercise price of $140 is currently selling for $5. By writing 10
Seagram's call contracts (100 shares each) the fund can pick up $5,000 in extra
income. The fund would lose its share of profits from any movement of Seagram's stock above $140 per share, but given that it would have sold its shares
at $140, it would not have realized those profits anyway.

Straddle

A **straddle** is established by buying both a call and a put on a stock, each with
the same exercise price, X, and the same expiration date, T. Straddles are

TABLE 21.4 Payoff to a Straddle

	$S_T \leq X$	$S_T > X$
Payoff of call	0	$S_T - X$
+Payoff of put	$+(X - S_T)$	$+0$
TOTAL	$X - S_T$	$S_T - X$

useful strategies for investors who believe that a stock will move a lot in price, but are uncertain about the direction of the move. For example, suppose you believe that an important court case that will make or break a company is about to be settled, and the market is not yet aware of the situation. The stock will either double in value if the case is settled favourably, or will drop by half if the settlement goes against the company. The straddle position will do well regardless of the outcome, because its value is highest when the stock price makes extreme upward or downward moves from X.

The kiss of death for a straddle is no movement in the stock price. If S_T equals X, both the call and the put expire worthless, and the investor's outlay for the purchase of the two positions is lost. Straddle positions, in other words, are bets on volatility. An investor who establishes a straddle must view the stock as more volatile than the market does. The payoff to a straddle is presented in Table 21.4.

The solid line in Figure 21.13C illustrates this payoff. Notice that the portfolio payoff is always positive, except at the one point where the portfolio has zero value, $S_T = X$. You might wonder why all investors do not pursue such a no-lose strategy. Remember, however, that the straddle requires that both the put and call be purchased. The value of the portfolio at expiration, although never negative, still must exceed the initial cash outlay for the investor to clear a profit.

The broken line in Figure 21.13C is the profit to the straddle. The profit line lies below the payoff line by the cost of purchasing the straddle, $P + C$. It is clear from the diagram that the straddle position generates a loss unless the stock price deviates substantially from X. The stock price must depart from X by the total amount expended to purchase the call and the put for the purchaser of the straddle to clear a profit.

Strips and *straps* are variations of straddles. A strip is two puts and one call on a security with the same exercise price and maturity date. A strap is two calls and one put.

Concept Check	Question 3. Graph the profit and payoff diagrams for strips and straps.

FIGURE 21.13
Payoff and profit to
a straddle at
expiration.

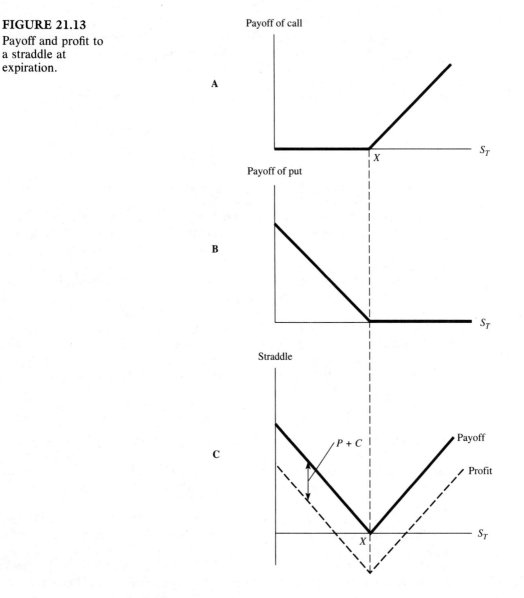

Spreads

A **spread** is a combination of two or more call options (or two or more puts) on the same stock with differing exercise prices or times to maturity. Some options will be held long, while others are written. A *vertical* or *money spread* involves the purchase of one option and the simultaneous sale of another with a different exercise price. A *horizontal* or *time* spread refers to the sale and purchase of options with differing expiration dates.

The vertical and horizontal spreads take their names from the way options are listed in the newspaper. Going vertically down a column of option listings such as in Figure 21.1, we find options with identical maturities but different

TABLE 21.5 Payoff to a Bullish Vertical Spread

	$S_T \leq X_1$	$X_1 < S_T \leq X_2$	$S_T > X_2$
Payoff of call, exercise price = X_1	0	$S_T - X_1$	$S_T - X_1$
$-$Payoff of call, exercise price = X_2	-0	-0	$-(S_T - X_2)$
TOTAL	0	$S_T - X_1$	$X_2 - X_1$

exercise prices. Moving horizontally across the row are options with identical exercise prices but different maturities.

Consider a vertical spread in which one call option is bought with an exercise price X_1, while another call with an identical expiration date but higher exercise price, X_2, is written. The payoff to this position will be the difference in the value of the call held and the value of the call written, as shown in Table 21.5.

Notice that we now have three instead of two outcomes to distinguish: the lowest-price region where S_T is below both exercise prices, a middle region where S_T is between the two exercise prices, and a high-price region where S_T exceeds both exercise prices. Figure 21.14 illustrates the payoff and profit to this strategy, which is called a *bullish spread* because the payoff either increases or is unaffected by stock price increases. Holders of bullish spreads benefit from stock price increases.

A bullish spread would be appropriate for an investor who has a target-wealth goal in mind, but is unwilling to risk losses beyond a certain level. If you are contemplating buying a house for $150,000, for example, you might set this figure as your goal. Your current wealth may be only $145,000, and you are unwilling to risk losing more than $10,000. A bullish spread on 1,000 shares (10 option contracts) with $X_1 = \$135$ and $X_2 = \$150$ would give you a good chance to realize the $5,000 capital gain without risking a loss of more than $10,000.

Another motivation for a bullish spread might be that the investor believes that one option is overpriced relative to another. For example, if the investor believes that the $X = \$135$ call is cheap compared to the $X = \$150$ call, he or she might establish the spread, even without a strong desire to take a bullish position in the stock.

21.3 *Option Valuation*

Consider a call option that is out of the money currently, with the stock price below the exercise price. Does this mean that the option is altogether value-less? Clearly not. Even though immediate exercise would be unprofitable, the call retains positive value because there is always a chance that the stock price

FIGURE 21.14
Value of a bullish
spread position at
expiration.

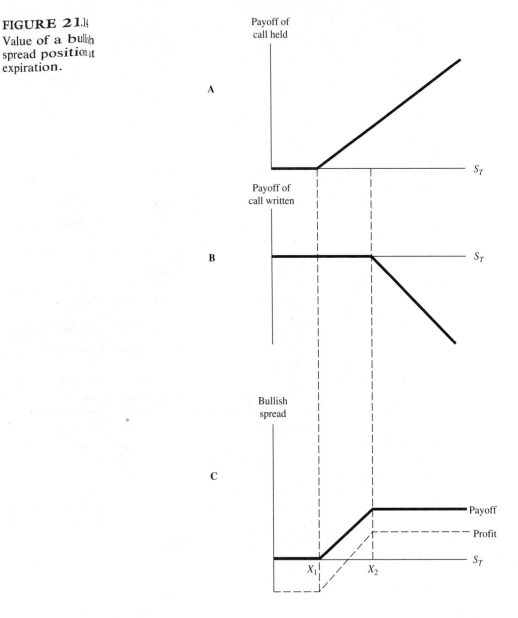

will increase sufficiently by the expiration date to allow for profitable exercise. If not, the worst that can happen is that the option will expire with zero value.

The value $S_0 - X$ is sometimes called the **intrinsic value** of in-the-money options, because it gives the profit that could be obtained by immediate exercise. Intrinsic value is set equal to zero for out-of-the-money options. The difference between the actual call price and the intrinsic value is commonly called the **time value** of the option. "Time value" is an unfortunate choice of terminology, because it may confuse the option's time value with the time value of money. Time value in the options context simply refers to the difference between the option's price and the value the option would have if it were expiring immediately. It is the part of the option's value that may be attributable to the fact that it still has positive time to expiration.

Most of an option's time value is in fact a type of "volatility value." As long as the option holder can choose not to exercise, the payoff cannot be worse than zero. Even if a call option is out of the money now, it still will sell for a positive price because it offers the potential for a profit if the stock price increases while imposing no risk of additional loss should the stock price fall. The volatility value lies in the value of the right not to exercise the option if that action would be unprofitable. The option to exercise, as opposed to the obligation to exercise, provides insurance against poor stock price performance.

As the stock price increases substantially, it becomes more likely that the option will be exercised by expiration. In this case, with exercise all but assured, the volatility value becomes minimal. As the stock price gets ever greater, the option value approaches the "adjusted" intrinsic value, the stock price minus the present value of the exercise price, $S_0 - PV(X)$.

Why should this be? If you *know* that the option will be exercised and the stock purchased for X dollars, it is as though you own the stock already. The stock certificate might as well be sitting in your safe deposit box now, because it will be there in only a few months. You just have not paid for it yet. The present value of your obligation is the present value of X, so your net position is $S_0 - PV(X)$.

Figure 21.15 illustrates the call option valuation function. Notice that the option always increases in value with the stock price. The slope is greatest, however, when the option is deep in the money. In this case exercise is all but assured, and the option increases in value one for one with the stock price.

Determinants of the Value of a Call Option

We can identify at least six factors that should affect the value of a call option: the stock price, the exercise price, the volatility of the stock price, the time to expiration, the interest rate, and the dividend rate of the stock. The call option should increase in value with the stock price and decrease in value with the exercise price because the payoff to a call, if exercised, equals $S_T - X$. The magnitude of the expected payoff from the call increases with the difference of $S_0 - X$.

Call option value also increases with the volatility of the underlying stock price. To see why, consider circumstances where possible stock prices at expiration may range from $10 to $50 compared with a situation where stock prices may range only from $20 to $40. In both cases the expected stock price will be $30. Suppose that the exercise price on a call option is also $30. What are the option payoffs?

High-Volatility Scenario				
Stock price	$10	$20	$30	$40	$50
Option payoff	0	0	0	$10	$20

FIGURE 21.15
Call option value
before expiration.

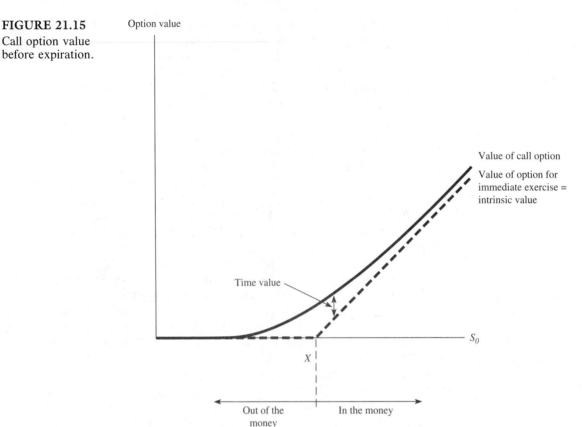

If each outcome is equally likely, with probability .2, the expected payoff to the option under high-volatility conditions will be $6.

	Low-Volatility Scenario				
Stock price	$20	$25	$30	$35	$40
Option payoff	0	0	0	$ 5	$10

Again, with equally likely outcomes, the expected payoff to the option is half as much, only $3.

Despite the fact that the average stock price in each scenario is $30, the average option payoff is greater in the high-volatility scenario. The source of this extra value is the limited loss that an option holder can suffer, or the volatility value of the call. No matter how far below $30 the stock price drops, the option holder will get zero. Obviously, extremely poor stock price performance is no worse for the call option holder than is moderately poor performance. In the case of good stock performance, however, the option will expire in the money, and it will be more profitable the higher the stock price. Thus, extremely good stock outcomes can improve the option payoff without limit, but extremely poor outcomes cannot worsen the payoff below zero. This asym-

TABLE 21.6 Determinants of Call Option Values

	Variable Increases	Value of Call Option
	Stock price, S	Increases
	Exercise price, X	Decreases
	Volatility, σ	Increases
	Time to expiration, T	Increases
	Interest rate, r_f	Increases
	Cash dividend payouts	Decreases

metry means that volatility in the underlying stock price increases the expected payoff to the option, thereby enhancing its value.[1]

Concept Check

> **Question 4. Should a put option also increase in value with the volatility of the stock?**

Similarly, longer time to expiration increases the value of a call option. For more distant expiration dates, the range of likely stock prices expands, which has an effect similar to that of increased volatility. Moreover, as time to expiration increases, the present value of the exercise price falls, thereby benefiting the call option holder and increasing the option value. As a corollary to this issue, call option values are higher when interest rates rise (holding the stock price constant), because higher interest rates also reduce the present value of the exercise price.

Finally, the dividend payout policy of the firm affects option values. A high-dividend payout policy puts a drag on the rate of growth of the stock price. For any expected total rate of return on the stock, a higher dividend yield must imply a lower expected rate of capital gain. This drag on stock price appreciation decreases the potential payoff from the call option, thereby lowering the call value. Table 21.6 summarizes these relationships.

Concept Check

> **Question 5. How should the value of a put option respond to the firm's dividend payout policy?**

---

[1] Strictly speaking, our demonstration shows only that the expected payoff from the call increases with stock volatility. It does not *necessarily* follow that the price of the call will be greater. This issue is treated in Ravi Jagannathan, "Call Options and the Risk of Underlying Securities," *Journal of Financial Economics* 13 (September 1984).

The Black-Scholes Formula

Financial economists searched for years for a workable option-pricing model before Black and Scholes[2] and Merton[3] derived a formula for the value of a call option. Now widely used by option-market participants, the **Black-Scholes formula** is

$$C_0 = S_0 N(d_1) - Xe^{-rT}N(d_2) \qquad \textbf{(21.3)}$$

where

$$d_1 = \frac{\ln(S_0/X) + (r + \sigma^2/2)T}{\sigma\sqrt{T}}$$
$$d_2 = d_1 - \sigma\sqrt{T}$$

and where

C_0 = Current option value

S_0 = Current stock price

X = Exercise price

r = Risk-free interest rate (the annualized continuously compounded rate on a safe asset with the same maturity as the expiration of the option, which is to be distinguished from r_f, the discrete period interest rate)

T = Time to maturity of options in years

σ = Standard deviation of the annualized continuously compounded rate of return of the stock

ln = Natural logarithm function

e = 2.71828, the base of the natural log function

$N(d)$ = The probability that a random draw from a standard normal distribution will be less than d. This equals the percentage of the area under the normal curve up to d, as shown in Figure 21.16.

Notice one thing that the option value does not depend on: the expected rate of return on the stock. In a sense this information is already built into the formula with inclusion of the stock price, which itself depends on the stock's risk-and-return characteristics. This version of the Black-Scholes formula is predicated on the assumption that the stock pays no dividends. (We address this issue in Chapter 22).

Although you may find the Black-Scholes formula intimidating, we can explain it first at a somewhat intuitive level. The trick is to view the $N(d)$ terms (loosely!) as risk-adjusted probabilities that the call option will expire in the money. First, look at equation 21.3 when both $N(d)$ terms are close to 1, indicating a very high probability that the option will be exercised. Then the call

---

[2] Fischer Black and Myron Scholes, "The Pricing of Options and Corporate Liabilities," *Journal of Political Economy* 81 (May/June 1973).

[3] Robert C. Merton, "Theory of Rational Option Pricing," *Bell Journal of Economics and Management Science* 4 (Spring 1973).

FIGURE 21.16
A standard normal curve.

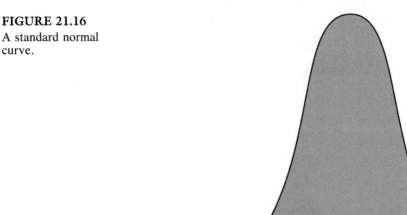

$N(d)$ = Shaded area

d

option value is equal to $S_0 - Xe^{-rT}$, which is what we called earlier the adjusted intrinsic value, $S_0 - PV(X)$. This makes sense: if exercise is certain, we have a claim on a stock with current value S_0 and an obligation with present value $PV(X)$, or, with continuous compounding, Xe^{-rT}.

Now look at equation 21.3 when the $N(d)$ terms are close to zero, meaning that the option almost certainly will not be exercised. Then the equation confirms that the call is worth nothing. For middle-range values of $N(d)$ between 0 and 1, equation 21.3 tells us that the call value can be viewed as the present value of the call's potential payoff adjusting for the probability of in-the-money expiration.

How do the $N(d)$ terms serve as risk-adjusted probabilities? This question quickly leads us into advanced statistics. Notice, however, that d_1 and d_2 both increase as the stock price increases. Therefore, $N(d_1)$ and $N(d_2)$ also increase with higher stock prices. This is the property we would desire of our "probabilities." For higher stock prices relative to exercise prices, future exercise is more likely.

In fact, you can use the Black-Scholes formula fairly easily. Suppose that you want to value a call option under the following circumstances:

Stock price	$S_0 = 100$
Exercise price	$X = 95$
Interest rate	$r = .10$
Time to expiration	$T = .25$ (one-fourth year)
Standard deviation	$\sigma = .5$

First calculate

$$d_1 = \frac{\ln(100/95) + (.10 + .5^2/2) \times .25}{.5\sqrt{.25}} = .43$$

$$d_2 = .43 - .5\sqrt{.25} = .18$$

Next find $N(d_1)$ and $N(d_2)$. The values of the normal distribution are tabulated and may be found in many statistics textbooks. A table of $N(d)$ is provided here as Table 21.7. The table reveals (using interpolation) that

$$N(.43) = .6664$$
$$N(.18) = .5714$$

Thus the value of the call option is

$$C = 100 \times .6664 - (95e^{-.10 \times .25}) \times .5714$$
$$= 66.64 - 52.94 = \$13.70$$

TABLE 21.7   Cumulative Normal Distribution

d	N(d)	d	N(d)	d	N(d)
−3.00	.0013	−1.80	.0359	−1.20	.1151
−2.95	.0016	−1.78	.0375	−1.18	.1190
−2.90	.0019	−1.76	.0392	−1.16	.1230
−2.85	.0022	−1.74	.0409	−1.14	.1271
−2.80	.0026	−1.72	.0427	−1.12	.1314
−2.75	.0030	−1.70	.0446	−1.10	.1357
−2.70	.0035	−1.68	.0465	−1.08	.1401
−2.65	.0040	−1.66	.0485	−1.06	.1446
−2.60	.0047	−1.64	.0505	−1.04	.1492
−2.55	.0054	−1.62	.0526	−1.02	.1539
−2.50	.0062	−1.60	.0548	−1.00	.1587
−2.45	.0071	−1.58	.0571	−0.98	.1635
−2.40	.0082	−1.56	.0594	−0.96	.1685
−2.35	.0094	−1.54	.0618	−0.94	.1736
−2.30	.0107	−1.52	.0643	−0.92	.1788
−2.25	.0122	−1.50	.0668	−0.90	.1841
−2.20	.0139	−1.48	.0694	−0.88	.1894
−2.15	.0158	−1.46	.0721	−0.86	.1949
−2.10	.0179	−1.44	.0749	−0.84	.2005
−2.05	.0202	−1.42	.0778	−0.82	.2061
−2.00	.0228	−1.40	.0808	−0.80	.2119
−1.98	.0239	−1.38	.0838	−0.78	.2177
−1.96	.0250	−1.36	.0869	−0.76	.2236
−1.94	.0262	−1.34	.0901	−0.74	.2297
−1.92	.0274	−1.32	.0934	−0.72	.2358
−1.90	.0287	−1.30	.0968	−0.70	.2420
−1.88	.0301	−1.28	.1003	−0.68	.2483
−1.86	.0314	−1.26	.1038	−0.66	.2546
−1.84	.0329	−1.24	.1075	−0.64	.2611
−1.82	.0344	−1.22	.1112	−0.62	.2676

TABLE 21.7   Continued

d	N(d)	d	N(d)	d	N(d)
−0.60	.2743	0.42	.6628	1.44	.9251
−0.58	.2810	0.44	.6700	1.46	.9279
−0.56	.2877	0.46	.6773	1.48	.9306
−0.54	.2946	0.48	.6844	1.50	.9332
−0.52	.3015	0.50	.6915	1.52	.9357
−0.50	.3085	0.52	.6985	1.54	.9382
−0.48	.3156	0.54	.7054	1.56	.9406
−0.46	.3228	0.56	.7123	1.58	.9429
−0.44	.3300	0.58	.7191	1.60	.9452
−0.42	.3373	0.60	.7258	1.62	.9474
−0.40	.3446	0.62	.7324	1.64	.9495
−0.38	.3520	0.64	.7389	1.66	.9515
−0.36	.3594	0.66	.7454	1.68	.9535
−0.34	.3669	0.68	.7518	1.70	.9554
−0.32	.3745	0.70	.7580	1.72	.9573
−0.30	.3821	0.72	.7642	1.74	.9591
−0.28	.3897	0.74	.7704	1.76	.9608
−0.26	.3974	0.76	.7764	1.78	.9625
−0.24	.4052	0.78	.7823	1.80	.9641
−0.22	.4129	0.80	.7882	1.82	.9656
−0.20	.4207	0.82	.7939	1.84	.9671
−0.18	.4286	0.84	.7996	1.86	.9686
−0.16	.4365	0.86	.8051	1.88	.9699
−0.14	.4443	0.88	.8106	1.90	.9713
−0.12	.4523	0.90	.8159	1.92	.9726
−0.10	.4602	0.92	.8212	1.94	.9738
−0.08	.4681	0.94	.8264	1.96	.9750
−0.06	.4761	0.96	.8315	1.98	.9761
−0.04	.4841	0.98	.8365	2.00	.9772
−0.02	.4920	1.00	.8414	2.05	.9798
0.00	.5000	1.02	.8461	2.10	.9821
0.02	.5080	1.04	.8508	2.15	.9842
0.04	.5160	1.06	.8554	2.20	.9861
0.06	.5239	1.08	.8599	2.25	.9878
0.08	.5319	1.10	.8643	2.30	.9893
0.10	.5398	1.12	.8686	2.35	.9906
0.12	.5478	1.14	.8729	2.40	.9918
0.14	.5557	1.16	.8770	2.45	.9929
0.16	.5636	1.18	.8810	2.50	.9938
0.18	.5714	1.20	.8849	2.55	.9946
0.20	.5793	1.22	.8888	2.60	.9953
0.22	.5871	1.24	.8925	2.65	.9960
0.24	.5948	1.26	.8962	2.70	.9965
0.26	.6026	1.28	.8997	2.75	.9970
0.28	.6103	1.30	.9032	2.80	.9974
0.30	.6179	1.32	.9066	2.85	.9978
0.32	.6255	1.34	.9099	2.90	.9981
0.34	.6331	1.36	.9131	2.95	.9984
0.36	.6406	1.38	.9162	3.00	.9986
0.38	.6480	1.40	.9192	3.05	.9989
0.40	.6554	1.42	.9222		

What if the option price were in fact $15? Is the option mispriced? Maybe, but before betting your fortune on that, you may want to reconsider the valuation analysis. First, like all models, the Black-Scholes formula is based on some simplifying abstractions that make the formula only approximately valid. We consider some of these shortcomings in Chapter 22.

Second, even within the context of the model, you must be sure of the accuracy of the parameters used in the formula. Four of these—S_0, X, T, and r—are straightforward. The stock price, exercise price, and time to maturity may be read directly from the option pages. The interest rate used is the money market rate for a maturity equal to that of the option. The last input, however, the standard deviation of the stock return, is not directly observable. It must be estimated from historical data, from scenario analysis, or from the prices of other options, as we will describe momentarily. Because the standard deviation must be estimated, it is always possible that discrepancies between an option price and its Black-Scholes value are simply artifacts of error in the estimation of the stock's volatility.

In fact, market participants often give the option valuation problem a different twist. Rather than calculating a Black-Scholes option value for a given stock standard deviation, they ask instead, "What standard deviation would be necessary for the option price that I can see to be consistent with the Black-Scholes formula?" This is called the **implied volatility** of the option, the volatility level for the stock that the option price implies. From the implied standard deviation investors judge whether they think the actual stock standard deviation exceeds the implied volatility. If it does, the option is considered a good buy; if actual volatility seems greater than the implied volatility, its fair price would exceed the observed price.

Concept Check

Question 6. Consider the option in the example selling for $15 with Black-Scholes value of $13.70. Is its implied volatility more or less than .5?

Another variation is to compare two options on the same stock with equal expiration dates but different exercise prices. The option with the higher implied volatility would be considered relatively expensive, because a higher standard deviation is required to justify its price. The analyst might consider buying the option with the lower implied volatility and writing the option with the higher implied volatility.

Put Option Valuation

We have concentrated so far on call option valuation. We can derive Black-Scholes European put option values from call option values using the put-call parity theorem. To value the put option, we simply calculate the value of the corresponding call option in equation 21.3 from the Black-Scholes formula, and solve for the put option value:

$$P = C + PV(X) - S_0 \qquad \textbf{(21.4)}$$

The data from our Black-Scholes call option example are $C = \$13.70$, $X = \$95$, $S = \$100$, $r = .10$, and $T = .25$. Using these data, we find a European put option on that stock with identical exercise price and time to maturity is worth[4]

$$P = \$13.70 + (\$95e^{-.10 \times .25}) - \$100 = \$6.35$$

As noted, we might then compare this formula value to the actual put price as one step in formulating a trading strategy.

Equation 21.4 is valid for European puts on non-dividend-paying stocks. Listed put options are American options that offer the opportunity of early exercise, however. Because an American option allows its owner to exercise at any time before the expiration date, it must be worth at least as much as the corresponding European option. Therefore, equation 21.4 describes only the lower bound on the true value of the American put. We will consider American options further in Chapter 22.

21.4 *Recent Innovations: Bull and Bear CDs and Protected Index Notes*

A recent innovation is the bond, note, or certificate of deposit that allows its holder to participate in an equity index growth. Such certificates of deposit are sometimes known as *bull* CDs. Unlike conventional CDs, which pay a fixed rate of interest, *bull CDs* pay depositors a specified fraction of the increase in the rate of return on a market index such as the S&P 500, while guaranteeing a minimum rate of return should the market fall.

The protected index notes (PINs) are a Canadian variant of bull CDs. They are discount notes issued by the Export Development Corporation (EDC) and denominated in U.S. dollars. Unlike conventional notes, the PINs are redeemable at any time prior to maturity at the larger of the following prices: the original par price, or the par price multiplied by the ratio of the S&P 500 index at redemption time to 1.05 times the value of the index at the time of issuance.

This arrangement is clearly a type of call option. If the market rises, the investor profits according to the relative rise in the index; if the market falls, the

---

[4] Notice that we discount the exercise price using continuous compounding rules in accord with the Black-Scholes formula. See the Appendix to Chapter 4 for a review of continuous compounding.

FIGURE 21.17
Bull CD.

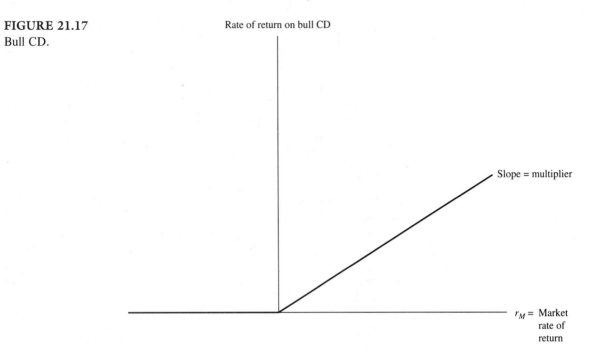

investor is guaranteed to receive at least the par value. The return to the prospective investor is at least equal to the ratio of par value to purchase value, and can increase in proportion to the rise of the S&P index. Just as clearly, the issuer offering these notes is in effect writing call options and can hedge its position by buying index calls in the U.S. options market. Figure 21.17 shows the nature of the issuer's obligation to its depositors.

Bull CDs are similar to the PINs, except that the holder may receive only a fraction (say 70 percent) of the growth in the index; this fraction is known as the *participation rate* or *multiplier*, and is set by the issuer. The PIN is essentially a bull CD with a multiplier equal to 1/1.05. In valuing PINs we are especially interested in the *inverse multiplier*, equal in this example to 1.05.

How can one value a PIN or bull CD at any time prior to expiration? To answer this, note various features of the option:

1. At exercise the PIN holder receives the par value, or (1/1.05) times (par value) times the realized return on the S&P 500 index, whichever is greater. If the PIN sells at par at issuance, then the payoff at exercise time per dollar invested is equal to the larger of 1, and (1/1.05) times (1 plus the market rate of return r_M as measured by the index).

2. Suppose that we want to replicate this pattern of payments, by using call options on the index and a riskless investment (say a T-bill or a conventional CD) with rate of return r_f. If C is the value of a call option on one unit of the index, with exercise price equal to 1.05 times the value S_0 of the index at issuance, then the ratio $C/(1.05S_0)$ is the value of a contingent claim that pays at exercise time the larger of 0, and/or (1/1.05) times $(1 + r_M)$ minus 1.

Hence, a portfolio of this contingent claim plus an amount $1/(r_f + 1)$ invested in the riskless investment pays the larger of 1, or $(1/1.05)$ times $(1 + r_M)$, same as the PIN. To avoid arbitrage, this portfolio must, therefore, have a value equal to that of the PIN at issuance, divided by the par value.

3. To determine whether the PIN should sell at par at issuance it suffices, therefore, to evaluate the quantity $C/(1.05S_0) + 1/(r_f + 1)$: if it is equal to 1, then the PIN should sell at par; it should sell above or below par if the above quantity is respectively greater or smaller than 1.

As an example, suppose that $r_f = 6$ percent per year (3 percent for six months), and that the index is currently at $240, implying that $1.05S_0 = 252$. The six-month maturity calls on the market index with an exercise price of \$252 are currently valued at \$10. Then the test quantity is equal to \$10/\$252 + $1/1.03 = 1.011$ per dollar of par value. Therefore, the PIN should sell at slightly above par.

This PIN is a bull CD with a multiplier equal to $1/1.05$. This version of the bull CD has several variants. Investors can purchase bull CDs that guarantee a positive minimum return, perhaps in combination with a smaller multiplier. In this case, the bull CD per unit par value is replicated by an index call option (with value C) plus riskless investment portfolio. The call option has exercise price equal to the inverse multiplier times $(r_{min} + 1)$ times the value of the index at issuance, where r_{min} is the guaranteed minimum return; the riskless investment is $(1 + r_{min})/(1 + r_f)$. The test quantity, the riskless investment plus C divided by the inverse multiplier times the index at issuance, is again compared to one to determine whether the instrument should be sold at par. Another variant is the *bear CD*, which pays depositors a fraction of any *fall* in the market index. For example, a bear CD might offer a rate of return of .6 times any percentage decline in the S&P 500.

Concept Check

> Question 7. Continue to assume that $r_f = 6$ percent, the appropriate calls sell for \$10, the multiplier is still $1/1.05$, and the market index is at 240. What would be the value of bull CDs per unit par value if they offer a guaranteed minimum return of 1 percent on a six-month deposit?

Summary

1. A call option is the right to buy an asset at an agreed-upon exercise price. A put option is the right to sell an asset at a given exercise price.

2. American options allow exercise on or before the expiration date. European options allow exercise only on the expiration date. Most traded options are American in nature.

3. Options are traded on stocks, stock indices, foreign currencies, fixed-income securities, and several futures contracts.

4. Options can be used either to increase an investor's exposure to an asset price, or to provide insurance against volatility of asset prices. Popular option strategies include covered calls, protective puts, straddles, and spreads.

5. The put-call parity theorem relates the prices of put and call options. If the relationship is violated, arbitrage opportunities will result. Specifically, the relationship that must be satisfied is that

$$C + PV(X) = S_0 + P$$

where X is the exercise price of both the call and the put options, and $PV(X)$ is the present value of a claim to X dollars to be paid at the expiration date of the options.

6. Option values may be viewed as the sum of intrinsic value plus time or "volatility" value. The volatility value is the right to choose not to exercise if the stock price moves against you. Thus, option holders cannot lose more than the cost of the option, regardless of stock price performance.

7. Call options are more valuable when the exercise price is lower, the stock price is higher, the interest rate is higher, the time to maturity is greater, the stock's volatility is greater, and dividends are lower.

8. Put option values can be derived using call option values and the put-call parity theorem. For American-style options, such values are only approximate.

9. Bull and bear CDs are in fact options, and may be valued by comparing them to the prices of market-traded options.

Key terms

Call option	Protective put
Exercise price (Strike price)	Covered call
Put option	Straddle
In the money	Spread
Out of the money	Intrinsic value
American option	Time value
European option	Black-Scholes formula
Put-call parity theorem	Implied volatility

Selected readings

An upper-level textbook that gives a comprehensive treatment of option markets, institutions, and valuation is:

Cox, John; and Rubinstein, Mark. *Options Markets*. Englewood Cliffs, N.J.: Prentice Hall, 1985.

A good treatment of the institutional organization of option markets in the United States and Canada is:

Chicago Board Options Exchange. *Reference Manual.* (The CBOE also publishes a *Margin Manual* that provides an overview of margin requirements on many option positions.)

TransCanada Options Inc. *Exchange Traded Put and Call Options.* Prospectus, July 11, 1980.

An excellent discussion of option trading strategies is:

Black, Fischer. "Fact and Fantasy in the Use of Options." *Financial Analysts Journal,* July/August 1975.

The results of several simulations of various trading strategies are reported in:

Merton, Robert C.; Scholes, Myron; and Gladstein, Matthew. "The Returns and Risk of Alternative Call Option Portfolio Strategies." *Journal of Business* 51 (April 1978).

Merton, Robert C., Scholes, Myron; and Gladstein, Matthew. "The Returns and Risks of Alternative Put-Option Portfolio Investment Strategies." *Journal of Business* 55 (January 1982).

A description and empirical evaluation of several characteristics of Canadian option markets is in:

Mandron, Alix. "Some Empirical Evidence about Canadian Stock Options, Part I: Valuation; Part II: Market Structure." *Canadian Journal of Administrative Sciences* 5, no. 2 (June 1988).

Problems

1. Suppose you think ABC stock is going to appreciate substantially in value in the next six months. Also suppose that the stock's current price, S_0, is $100, and the call option expiring in six months has an exercise price, X, of $100 and is selling at a price, C, of $10. With $10,000 to invest, you are considering three alternatives.

a. Invest all $10,000 in the stock, buying 100 shares

b. Invest all $10,000 in 1,000 options (10 contracts)

c. Buy 100 options (one contract) for $1,000, and invest the remaining $9,000 in a money market fund paying 4 percent in interest over six months (8 percent per year)

What is your rate of return for each alternative for four stock prices six months from now? Summarize your results in the following table and diagram.

Rate of Return on Investment

	Price of Stock 6 Months from Now			
Stock Price:	80	100	110	120
a. All stocks (100 shares)				
b. All options (1,000 shares)				
c. Bills + 100 options				

Rate of return

0 S_T

2. The common stock of the PUTT Corporation has been trading in a narrow price range for the past month, and you are convinced that it is going to break far out of that range in the next three months. You do not know whether it will go up or down, however. The current price of the stock is $100 per share, and the price of a three-month call option at an exercise price of $100 is $10.
   a. If the risk-free interest rate is 10 percent per year, what must be the price of a three-month put option on PUTT stock at an exercise price of $100?
   b. What would be a simple options strategy to exploit your conviction about the stock price's future movement? How far would it have to move in either direction for you to make a profit on your initial investment?
3. The common stock of the C.A.L.L. Corporation has been trading in a narrow range around $50 per share for months, and you are convinced that it is going to stay in that range for the next three months. The price of a three-month put option with an exercise price of $50 is $4.
   a. If the risk-free interest rate is 10 percent per year, what must be the price of a three-month call option on C.A.L.L. stock at an exercise price of $50 if it is at the money?
   b. What would be a simple options strategy using a put and a call to exploit your conviction about the stock price's future movement? What is the most money you can make on this position? How far can the stock price move in either direction before you lose money?
   c. How can you create a position involving a put, a call, and risk-free lending that would have the same payoff structure as the stock at expiration? What is the net cost of establishing that position now?
4. (Based on the 1984 CFA Examination, Level III) Upon the death of his grandmother several years ago, Bill Melody received as a bequest from her estate 2,000 shares of General Motors (GM) common stock. The price of

the stock at time of distribution from the estate was $75 a share, and this became the cost basis of Melody's holding. Late in 1983, Melody agreed to purchase a new condominium for his parents at a total cost of $160,000, payable in full upon its completion in March 1984. Melody planned to sell the General Motors stock to raise funds to purchase the condominium. At year-end 1983, GM's market price was around $75 a share, but it appeared to be weakening. This concerned Melody, because if the price of the stock were to drop by a significant amount before he sold, the proceeds would not be sufficient to cover the purchase of the condominium the following March. Melody visited with three different investment counselling firms to seek advice in developing a strategy that, at a minimum, would protect the value of his principal at or near $150,000 ($75 a share). Ideally, the strategy would enhance the value to $160,000 so Melody would have the total cost of the condominium. Four alternatives were discussed:

a. Melody's own opinion was to sell the General Motors stock at $75 a share and invest the proceeds in a 10 percent certificate of deposit maturing in three months.

b. Anderson Investment Advisors suggested that Melody write a March 1984 call option on his General Motors holding at a strike price of $80. The March 1984 calls were quoted at $2.

c. Cole Capital Management suggested that Melody purchase March 1984 at-the-money put contracts on General Motors, now quoted at $2.

d. MBA Associates suggested that Melody keep the stock, purchase March 1984 at-the-money put contracts on GM, and finance the purchase by selling March calls with a strike price of $80.

Disregarding transaction costs, divided income, and margin requirements, rank the four alternatives in terms of their likelihood of fulfilling the strategy of at least preserving the value of Melody's principal at $150,000, and preferably increasing the value to $160,000 by March 1984. Support your conclusions by showing the payoff structure of each alternative.

5. Construct graphs for the following two situations:

a. A butterfly spread is the purchase of one call at exercise price X_1, the sale of two calls at exercise price X_2, and the purchase of one call at exercise price X_3. X_1 is less than X_2, and X_2 is less than X_3 by equal amounts, and all calls have the same expiration date. Graph the payoff diagram to this strategy.

b. A vertical combination is the purchase of a call with exercise price X_2, and a put with exercise price, X_1, with X_2 greater than X_1. Graph the payoff to this strategy.

6. A bearish spread is the purchase of a call with exercise price X_2 and the sale of a call with exercise price X_1, with X_2 greater than X_1. Graph the payoff to this strategy and compare it to Figure 21.14.

7. We showed in the chapter that the value of a call option increases with the volatility of the stock. Is this also true of put option values? Use the put-call parity theorem, as well as a numerical example, to confirm your answer.

8. Use the Black-Scholes formula to find the value of a call option on the following stock:

$$\begin{array}{ll} \text{Time to maturity} & = \text{6 months} \\ \text{Standard deviation} & = \text{50\% per year} \\ \text{Exercise price} & = \$50 \\ \text{Stock price} & = \$50 \\ \text{Interest rate} & = \text{10\% per year} \end{array}$$

9. Recalculate the value of the option in problem 8, successively substituting each one of the following changes (only one at a time) while keeping the other parameters as in problem 8:

$$\begin{array}{ll} \text{Time to maturity} & = \text{3 months} \\ \text{Standard deviation} & = \text{25\% per year} \\ \text{Exercise price} & = \$55 \\ \text{Stock price} & = \$55 \\ \text{Interest rate} & = \text{15\%} \end{array}$$

Consider each scenario independently. Confirm that the option value changes in accordance with the prediction of Table 21.6.

10. If a call option on a non-dividend-paying stock selling at $25 with exercise price $25 and time to maturity of six months sells for $2.13, while the corresponding put option sells for $1.39, find the present value of $25 to be paid in six months.

11. In each of the following questions you are asked to compare two options with parameters as given. The risk-free interest rate for *all* cases should be assumed to be 6 percent. Assume that the stocks on which these options are written pay no dividends.

a.

Put	T	X	σ	Price of Option
A	.5	50	.20	$10
B	.5	50	.25	$10

Which *put* option is written on the stock with the *lower* price?
    i. A
   ii. B
  iii. Not enough information

b.

Put	T	S	σ	Price of Option
A	.5	50	.20	$10
B	.5	50	.20	$12

Which *put* option must be written on the stock with the *lower* price?
    i. A
   ii. B
  iii. Not enough information

c.

Call	S	X	σ	Price of Option
A	50	50	.20	$12
B	55	50	.20	$10

Which *call* option must have the *lower* time to maturity?
 i. A
 ii. B
 iii. Not enough information

d.

Call	T	X	S	Price of Option
A	.5	50	55	$10
B	.5	50	55	$12

Which *call* option is written on the stock with *higher* volatility?
 i. A
 ii. B
 iii. Not enough information

e.

Call	T	X	S	Price of Option
A	.5	50	55	$10
B	.5	55	55	$ 7

Which *call* option is written on the stock with *higher* volatility?
 i. A
 ii. B
 iii. Not enough information

12. I am attempting to formulate an investment strategy. On the one hand, I think that there is great upward potential in the stock market and would like to participate in the upward move if it in fact materializes. However, I am not able to afford substantial stock market losses and so cannot run the risk of a stock market collapse, which I also think is a possibility. My investment advisor suggests a protective put position: buy both shares in a market-index stock fund and put options on those shares with three-month maturity and exercise price of $260. The stock index is currently selling for $300. However, my uncle suggests that I instead buy a three-month call option on the index fund with exercise price $280, and buy three-month T-bills with face value $280.

 a. On the same graph, draw the *payoffs* to each of these strategies as a function of the stock-fund value in three months. (Hint: think of the options as being on one "share" of the stock-index fund, with the current price of each share of the index equal to $300.)

 b. Which portfolio must require a greater initial outlay to establish? (Hint: does either portfolio provide a final payoff that is always at least as great as the payoff of the other portfolio?)

 c. Suppose that the market prices of the securities are as follows:

Stock fund	$300
T-bill (face value $280)	$270
Call (exercise price $280)	$ 40
Put (exercise price $260)	$ 2

   i. Make a table of the profits realized for each portfolio for the following values of the stock price in three months: $S_T = 0$, \$260, \$280, \$300, and \$320.

   ii. Graph the profits to each portfolio as a function of S_T on a single graph.

d. Which strategy is riskier? Which should have a higher beta?

   Explain why the prices for the securities given in part c do *not* violate the put-call parity relationship.

13. Consider a bear CD with a minimum return of zero, and a promise to pay a specified fraction of any percentage fall in the S&P 500 index after a six-month period. If six-month maturity at-the-money puts on the index cost \$15, the conventional CD rate is 8 percent per year, and the index is at 250, what multiplier can the bear CD offer?

CHAPTER 22

Options Markets: A Closer Look

This chapter presents more advanced material on option strategies and valuation. We start with a closer look at option pricing. In Chapter 21 we showed some qualitative properties of option pricing and demonstrated one particular valuation formula, the famous Black-Scholes model. Arguably the most significant breakthrough in finance theory in the last three decades, the model still suffers from some unrealistic simplifying assumptions. Two in particular are that the option is exercised only at the exercise date and that the underlying stock pays no dividends. In this chapter we will examine the impact of relaxing these assumptions. Then we will look at some of the more important applications of option pricing theory. We will see how an option hedge ratio can be used in portfolio management and control. One of the most controversial applications of this analysis has been the use of the option hedge ratio in the provision of portfolio insurance.

Option pricing theory also has implications for the valuation of several option-like securities, such as callable bonds, convertible bonds, and warrants. We examine an alternative approach to exact option valuation called ''two-state'' or ''binomial'' option pricing. Finally, we explore the option pricing implications of relaxing the assumptions of this last approach.

22.1 *More on Option Valuation*

The Black-Scholes formula is extremely useful but, like many theoretical constructs, it relies on several simplifying assumptions. You might wonder which properties of option values are truly general and which depend on the particular simplifications. To start with, we will consider some of the more important general properties of option prices. Some of these properties have important implications for the effect of stock dividends on option values and the possible profitability of early exercise of an American option.

Restrictions on the Value of a Call Option

The most obvious restriction on the value of a call option is that its value must be zero or positive. Because the option need not be exercised, it cannot impose any liability on its holder; moreover, as long as there is any possibility that at some point the option can be exercised profitably, the option will command a positive price. Its payoff must be zero at worst, and possibly positive, so that investors are willing to pay a positive amount to purchase it.

We can place another lower bound on the value of a call option. Suppose that the stock will pay a dividend of D dollars just before the expiration date of the option, denoted by T (where today is time zero). Now compare two portfolios, one consisting of a call option on one share of stock and the other a leveraged equity position consisting of that share and borrowing of $(X + D)/(1 + r_f)^T$ dollars. The loan repayment is $X + D$ dollars, due on the expiration date of the option. For example, for a half-year maturity option with exercise price $70, dividends to be paid of $5, and effective annual interest of 10 percent, you would purchase one share of stock and borrow $75/(1.10)^{1/2} = \$71.51$. In six months, when the loan matures, the payment due is $75.

At that time, the payoff to the leveraged equity position would be

	In General	Our Numbers
Stock value	$S_T + D$	$S_T + 5$
−Payback of loan	$-(X + D)$	-75
TOTAL	$S_T - X$	$S_T - 70$

where S_T denotes the stock price at the option expiration date. Notice that the payoff to the stock is the ex-dividend stock value plus dividends received. Whether the total payoff to the stock-plus-borrowing position is positive or negative depends on whether S_T exceeds X. The net cash outlay required to establish this leveraged equity position is $S_0 - \$71.51$, or, more generally, $S_0 - (X + D)/(1 + r_f)^T$, that is, the current price of the purchased stock, S_0, less the initial cash inflow from the borrowing position.

The payoff to the call option will be $S_T - X$ if the option expires in the money and zero otherwise. Thus, the option payoff is equal to the leveraged equity payoff when that payoff is positive and is greater when the leveraged equity position has a negative payoff. Because the option payoff always is greater than or equal to that of the leveraged equity position, the option price must exceed the cost of establishing that position.

In our case the value of the call must be greater than $S_0 - (X + D)/(1 + r_f)^T$, or, more generally,

$$C \geq S_0 - PV(X) - PV(D)$$

where $PV(X)$ denotes the present value of the exercise price and $PV(D)$ is the present value of the dividends the stock will pay at the option's expiration. More generally, we can interpret $PV(D)$ as the present value of any and all dividends to be paid prior to the option expiration date. Because we know already that the value of a call option must be non-negative, we may conclude that C is greater than the *maximum* of either 0 or $S_0 - PV(X) - PV(D)$.

We also can place an upper bound on the possible value of the call: simply the stock price. No one would pay more than S_0 dollars for the right to purchase a stock currently worth S_0 dollars. Thus, $C \le S_0$.

Figure 22.1 demonstrates graphically the range of prices that is ruled out by these upper and lower bounds for the value of a call option. Any option value outside the shaded area is not possible according to the restrictions we have derived. Before expiration, the call option value normally will be *within* the allowable range, touching neither the upper nor lower bounds, as in Figure 22.2.

Early Exercise and Dividends

A call option holder who wants to close out that position has two choices: exercise the call or sell it. If the holder exercises at time t, the call will provide a profit of $S_t - X$, assuming, of course, that the option is in the money. We have just seen that the option can be sold for at least $S_t - PV(X) - PV(D)$. Therefore, for an option on a non-dividend-paying stock, C is greater than $S_t - PV(X)$. Because the present value of X is less than X itself, it follows that

$$C \ge S_t - PV(X) \ge S_t - X$$

The implication here is that the proceeds from a sale of the option (at price C) must exceed the proceeds from an exercise ($S_t - X$). It is economically more effective to keep the call option ''alive'' rather than ''killing'' it through

FIGURE 22.1

Range of possible call option values.

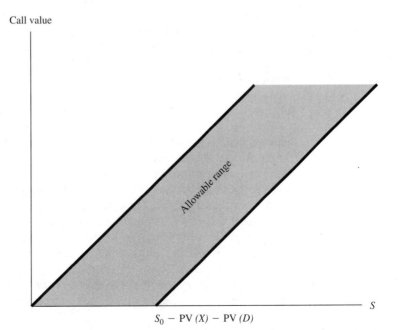

Call value

Allowable range

S

$S_0 - PV(X) - PV(D)$

FIGURE 22.2

Call option value as a function of the stock price.

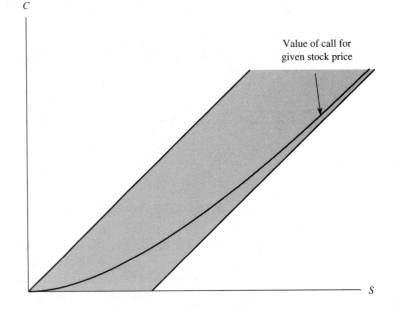

Value of call for given stock price

early exercise. In other words, calls on non-dividend-paying stocks are worth more alive than dead.

If it never pays to exercise a call option before maturity, the right to exercise early actually must be valueless. The right of the American call holder to exercise early is irrelevant because it will never pay to exercise early. We have to conclude that the values of otherwise-identical American and European call options on stocks paying no dividends are equal. If we can find the value for the European call, we also will have found the value of the American call. Therefore, the Black-Scholes formula for European call options will apply as well to American calls on non-dividend-paying stocks.

As most stocks do pay dividends, you may wonder whether this result is just a theoretical curiosity. It is not: reconsider our argument and you will see that all that we really require is that the stock pay no dividends *until the option expires*. This condition will be true for many real-world options.

For American *put options,* however, the optimality of early exercise is most definitely a possibility. To see why, consider a simple example. Suppose that you purchase a put option on a stock. Soon the firm goes bankrupt, and the stock price falls to zero. Of course you want to exercise now, because the stock price can fall no lower. Immediate exercise gives you immediate receipt of the exercise price, which can be invested to start generating income. Delay in exercise means a time-value-of-money cost. The right to early exercise of a put option must have value.

Now suppose instead that the firm is only nearly bankrupt, with the stock selling at just a few cents. Immediate exercise may still be optimal. After all, the stock price can fall by only a very small amount, meaning that the proceeds from future exercise cannot be more than a few cents greater than the proceeds from immediate exercise. Against this possibility of a tiny increase in proceeds must be weighed the time-value-of-money cost of deferring exercise. Clearly, there is some stock price below which early exercise is optimal.

Concept Check	Question 1. In light of this discussion, explain why the put-call parity relationship is valid only for European options on non-dividend-paying stocks. If the stock pays no dividends, what *inequality* for American options would correspond to the parity theorem?

Dividends and Call Option Valuation

We noted in Chapter 21 that the Black-Scholes call option formula applies to stocks that do not pay dividends. When dividends are to be paid before the option expires, we need to adjust the formula. The payment of dividends raises the possibility of early exercise, and for most realistic dividend payout schemes the valuation formula becomes significantly more complex than the already-intimidating Black-Scholes equation.

We can apply some simple rules of thumb to approximate the option value, however. One popular approach, originally suggested by Black,[1] calls for adjusting the stock price downward by the present value of any dividends that are to be paid before option expiration. Such an adjustment will take dividends into account by reflecting their eventual impact on the stock price. The option value then may be computed as before, assuming that the option will be held to expiration.

This procedure would yield a very good approximation of option value for European call options that must be held until maturity, but it does not allow for the fact that the holder of an American call option might choose to exercise the option just before a dividend. The current value of a call option, assuming that the option will be exercised just before the ex-dividend date, might be greater than the value of the option—assuming it will be held until maturity. Although holding the option until maturity allows greater effective time to expiration, which increases the option value, it also entails more dividend payments, lowering the expected stock price at maturity and thereby lowering the current option value.

---

[1] Fischer Black, "Fact and Fantasy in the Use of Options," *Financial Analysts Journal* 31 (July–August 1975).

For example, suppose that a stock selling at $20 will pay a $1 dividend in four months, whereas the call option on the stock does not expire for six months. The effective annual interest rate is 10 percent, so that the present value of the dividend is $1/(1.10)^{1/3} = $0.97. Black suggests that we can compute the option value in one of two ways:

1. Apply the Black-Scholes formula assuming early exercise, thus using the actual stock price of $20 and a time to expiration of four months (the time until the dividend payment).
2. Apply the Black-Scholes formula assuming no early exercise, using the dividend-adjusted stock price of $20 − $0.97 = $19.03 and a time to expiration of six months.

The greater of the two values is the estimate of the option value, recognizing that early exercise might be optimal. In other words, the so-called *pseudo-American* call option value is the maximum of the value derived by assuming that the option will be held until expiration and the value derived by assuming that the option will be exercised just before an ex-dividend date. Even this technique is not exact, however, for it assumes that the option holder makes an irrevocable decision now on when to exercise, when in fact the decision is not binding until exercise notice is given.[2]

American Put Option Valuation

We saw from the put-call parity theorem for European options with identical maturities and exercise prices written on non-dividend-paying stocks, that the put value can be related to the call value as follows:

$$P = C - S_0 + PV(X) \qquad (22.1)$$

We have demonstrated that if the stock pays no dividends the American call has the same value as its European counterpart, whereas the American put is worth more than its European counterpart. Therefore, American puts on non-dividend-paying stocks must be worth more than the expression on the right-hand side of equation 22.1. Exact put option valuation, however, is difficult because of the complexities associated with the possibility of early exercise. When the stock pays dividends, valuation is even more complicated. In this case, both American put options and call options are worth more than their European counterparts.

---

[2] An exact formula for American call valuation on dividend-paying stocks has been developed in Richard Roll, "An Analytic Valuation Formula for Unprotected American Call Options on Stocks with Known Dividends," *Journal of Financial Economics* 5 (November 1977). The technique has been discussed and revised in Robert Geske, "A Note on an Analytical Formula for Unprotected American Call Options on Stocks with Known Dividends," *Journal of Financial Economics* 7 (December 1979); Robert E. Whaley, "On the Valuation of American Call Options on Stocks with Known Dividends," *Journal of Financial Economics* 9 (June 1981); and Giovanni Barone-Adesi and Robert E. Whaley, "Efficient Analytic Approximations of American Option Values," *Journal of Finance* 42, no. 2 (June 1987). Note that these are difficult papers, however.

22.2 *Using the Black-Scholes Formula*

Hedge Ratios and the Black-Scholes Formula

In Chapter 21 we considered two investments in Seagram's: 1,000 shares of Seagram's stock or 10,000 call options on Seagram's. We saw that the call option position was more sensitive to swings in Seagram's stock price than the all-stock position. To analyze the overall exposure to a stock price more precisely, however, it is necessary to quantify these relative sensitivities. A tool that enables us to summarize the overall exposure of portfolios of options with various exercise prices and times to maturity is the **hedge ratio**. An option's hedge ratio is the change in the price of an option for a $1 increase in the stock price. Therefore, a call option has a positive hedge ratio and a put option has a negative hedge ratio. The hedge ratio is commonly called the option's **delta**.

If you were to graph the option value as a function of the stock value as we have done for a call option in Figure 22.3, the hedge ratio is simply the slope of the value function evaluated at the current stock price.[3] For example, suppose that the slope of the curve at $S_0 = \$120$ equals .60. As the stock increases in value by $1, the option increases by approximately $.60, as the figure shows.

For every call option written, .60 shares of stock would be needed to hedge the investor's portfolio. For example, if one writes 10 options and holds six shares of stock, according to the hedge ratio of .6, a $1 increase in stock price will result in a gain of $6 on the stock holdings, whereas the loss on the 10 options written will be $10 \times \$0.60$, an equivalent $6. The stock price movement leaves total wealth unaltered, which is what is required of a hedged position. The investor holding the stock and option in proportions dictated by their relative price movements hedges the portfolio.

Black-Scholes hedge ratios are particularly easy to compute. It turns out that the hedge ratio for a call is $N(d_1)$, and the hedge ratio for a put is $N(d_1) - 1$. We defined $N(d_1)$ as part of the Black-Scholes formula (equation 21.3). Recall that $N(d)$ stands for the area under the standard normal curve up to d. Therefore, the call option hedge ratio must be positive and less than 1, whereas the put option hedge ratio is negative and of smaller absolute value than 1.

Figure 22.3 verifies the insight that the slope of the call option valuation function is indeed less than 1, approaching 1 only as the stock price becomes extremely large. This tells us that option values change less than one-for-one with changes in stock prices. Why should this be? Suppose that an option is so far in the money that you are absolutely certain it will be exercised. In that case, every dollar increase in the stock price would indeed increase the option

---

[3] Students of calculus will recognize that the hedge ratio also may be viewed as the partial derivative of the formula for the value of the call with respect to the stock price.

FIGURE 22.3
Call option value
and hedge ratio.

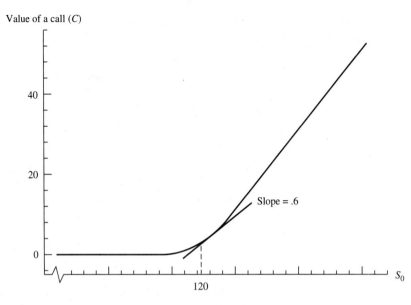

value by $1. However, if there is a reasonable chance that the call option will expire out of the money even after a moderate stock price gain, a $1 increase in the stock price will not necessarily increase the ultimate payoff to the call; therefore, the call price will not respond by a full dollar.

The fact that hedge ratios are less than 1 does not conflict with our earlier observation that options offer leverage and are quite sensitive to stock price movements. Although *dollar* movements in option prices are slighter than dollar movements in the stock price, the *rate of return* volatility of options remains greater than stock return volatility because options sell at smaller prices. In our example, with the stock selling at $120 and a hedge ratio of 0.6, an option with exercise price $120 may sell for $5. If the stock price increases to $121, the call price would be expected to increase by only $.60 to $5.60. The percentage increase in the option value is $.60/$5.00 = 12 percent, however, whereas the stock price increase is only $1/$120 = .83 percent. In this case, we would say that the **elasticity** of the option is 12 percent/.83 percent = 14.4. For every 1 percent increase in the stock price, the option price increases by 14.4 percent.

Concept Check

> Question 2. What is the elasticity of a put option currently selling for $4, with exercise price $120 and hedge ratio −.4, if the stock price is currently $122?

The hedge ratio is an essential tool in portfolio management and control. An example will illustrate.

Consider two portfolios, one holding 750 Seagram's calls and 200 shares of Seagram's, and the other holding 800 shares of Seagram's. Which portfolio has greater dollar exposure to Seagram's price movements? You can answer this question easily using the hedge ratio.

Each option changes in value by H dollars for each dollar change in stock price, where H stands for the hedge ratio. Thus, if H equals 0.6, the 750 options are equivalent to 450 ($.6 \times 750$) shares in terms of the response of their market value to Seagram's stock price movements. The first portfolio has less dollar sensitivity to Seagram's, because the 450 share-equivalents of the options plus the 200 shares actually held are less than the 800 shares held in the second portfolio.

This is not to say, however, that the first portfolio is less sensitive to Seagram's in terms of its rate of return. As we noted in discussing option elasticities, the first portfolio may be of lower total value than the second, so despite its lower sensitivity in terms of total market value, it might have greater rate of return sensitivity. Because a call option has a lower market value than the stock, its price changes more than proportionally with stock price changes, even though its hedge ratio is less than 1.

Portfolio Insurance

In Chapter 21 we showed that protective put strategies offer a sort of insurance policy on an asset. The protective put has proved to be extremely popular with investors. Even if the asset price falls, the put conveys the right to sell the asset for the exercise price, which is a way to lock in a minimum portfolio value. With an at-the-money put ($X = S_0$), the maximum loss that can be realized is the cost of the put. The asset can be sold for X, which equals its original value, so even if the asset price falls, the investor's net loss over the period is just the cost of the put. If the asset value increases, however, upside potential is unlimited. Figure 22.4 graphs the profit or loss on a protective put position as a function of the change in the value of the underlying asset.

Although the protective put is a simple and convenient way to achieve **portfolio insurance**, there are practical difficulties in trying to insure a portfolio of stocks. First, unless the investor's portfolio corresponds to a standard market index for which puts are traded, a put option on the portfolio will not be available for purchase. In addition, if index puts are used to protect a non-indexed portfolio, tracking error can result. For example, if the portfolio falls in value while the market index rises, the put will fail to provide the intended protection. Tracking error limits the investor's freedom to pursue active stock selection, because such error will be greater as the managed portfolio departs more substantially from the market index.

Moreover, the desired horizon of the insurance program must match the maturity of a traded put option in order to establish the appropriate protective put position. Whereas most insurance programs have horizons of several years, traded puts in Canada have been limited to maturities of less than one year. In the United States, however, the CBOE has recently initiated trading in European index options with longer maturities. Rolling over a sequence of short-term puts, which might be viewed as a response to this problem, introduces

FIGURE 22.4

Return characteristics for a portfolio with a protective put.

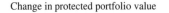
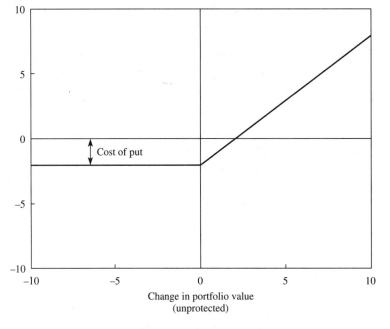

new risks because the prices at which successive puts will be available in the future are not known today.

Providers of portfolio insurance with horizons of several years, therefore, cannot rely on the simple expedient of purchasing protective puts for their clients' portfolios. Instead, they follow trading strategies that replicate the payoffs to the protective put position.

Here is the general idea: Even if a put option on the desired portfolio with the desired expiration date does not exist, a theoretical option pricing model (such as the Black-Scholes model) can be used to determine how that option's price would respond to the portfolio's value if the option did in fact trade. For example, if stock prices were to fall, the put option would increase in value. The option model could quantify this relationship. The net exposure of the (hypothetical) protective put portfolio to swings in stock prices is the sum of the exposures of the two components of the portfolio, the stock and the put. The net exposure of the portfolio equals the equity exposure less the (offsetting) put option exposure. We can create "synthetic" protective put positions by holding a quantity of stocks with the same net exposure to market swings as the hypothetical protective put position. The key to this strategy is the option's delta, or hedge ratio, that is, the change in the price of the protective put option per change in the value of the underlying stock portfolio.

An example will clarify the procedure. Suppose that a portfolio is currently valued at $100 million. An at-the-money put option on the portfolio might have a hedge ratio or delta of −.6, meaning that the option's value swings $.60 for every dollar change in portfolio value, but in an opposite direction. Suppose the stock portfolio falls in value by 2 percent. The profit on a hypothetical protective put position (if the put existed) would be as follows (in millions of dollars):

Loss on stocks: 2% of $100 = $2.00
Gain on put: .6 × $2   = $1.20
Net loss: = $ .80

We create the synthetic option position by selling a proportion of shares equal to the put option's delta (that is, selling 60 percent of the shares), and placing the proceeds in risk-free T-bills. The rationale is that the hypothetical put option would have offset 60 percent of any change in the stock portfolio's value, so one must reduce portfolio risk directly by selling off 60 percent of the equity and putting the proceeds into a risk-free asset. Total return on a synthetic protective put position with $60 million in risk-free investments, such as T-bills, and $40 million in equity is

Loss on stocks: 2% of $40 = $.80
Loss on bills: =   0
Net loss: = $ .80

The synthetic and actual protective put positions have equal returns. We conclude that if you sell a proportion of shares equal to the put option's delta and place the proceeds in cash equivalents, your exposure to the stock market will equal that of the desired protective put position.

The difficulty with this procedure is that deltas constantly change. Figure 22.5 shows that, as the stock price falls, the magnitude of the appropriate hedge ratio increases. Therefore, market declines require extra hedging, that is, addi-

FIGURE 22.5

Hedge ratios change as the stock price fluctuates.

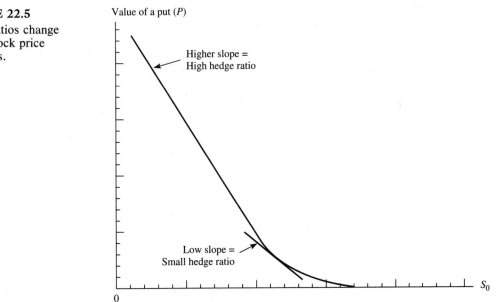

Value of a put (P)

Higher slope =
High hedge ratio

Low slope =
Small hedge ratio

S_0

0

tional conversions of equity into cash. This constant updating of the hedge ratio is called **dynamic hedging**.

Dynamic hedging is one reason portfolio insurance has been said to contribute to market volatility. Market declines trigger additional sales of stock as portfolio insurers strive to increase their hedging. These additional sales are seen as reinforcing or exaggerating market downturns.

In practice, portfolio insurers do not actually buy or sell stocks directly when they update their hedge positions. Instead, they minimize trading costs by buying or selling stock index futures as a substitute for sale of the stocks themselves. As you will see in the following chapters, stock prices and index futures prices usually are very tightly linked by cross-market arbitrageurs so that futures transactions can be used as reliable proxies for stock transactions. Instead of selling equities based on the put option's delta, insurers will sell an equivalent number of futures contracts.[4]

Several U.S. portfolio insurers suffered great setbacks on October 19, 1987, when the Dow Jones Industrial Average fell by more than 500 points. We can describe what happened then so you can appreciate the complexities of applying a seemingly straightforward hedging concept:

1. Market volatility was much greater than ever encountered before. Put option deltas based on historical experience were too low, and insurers underhedged, held too much equity, and suffered excessive losses.
2. Prices moved so fast that insurers could not keep up with the necessary rebalancing. They were chasing deltas that kept getting away from them. In addition, the futures market saw a "gap" opening, where the opening price was nearly 10 percent below the previous day's close. The price dropped before insurers could update their hedge ratios.
3. Execution problems were severe. First, current market prices were unavailable, with the trade execution and price quotation system hours behind, which made computation of correct hedge ratios impossible. Moreover, trading in stocks and stock futures ceased altogether during some periods. The continuous rebalancing capability that is essential for a viable insurance program simply vanished during the precipitous market collapse.
4. Future prices traded at steep discounts to their proper levels compared to reported stock prices, thereby making the sale of futures (as a proxy for equity sales) to increase hedging seem expensive. Although we will see in the next chapter that stock index futures prices normally exceed the value of the stock index, Figure 22.6 shows that on October 19, 1987, futures sold far below the stock index level. The so-called cash-to-futures spread was negative most of the day. When some insurers gambled that the futures price would recover to its usual premium over the stock index, and chose to defer sales, they remained underhedged. As the market fell further, their portfolios experienced substantial losses.

---

[4] Notice, however, that the use of index futures reintroduces the problem of tracking error between the portfolio and the market index.

FIGURE 22.6

S&P 500 cash-to-futures spread in points at 15-minute intervals.

(From *The Wall Street Journal*. Reprinted by permission of *The Wall Street Journal*, © Dow Jones & Company, Inc. 1987. All Rights Reserved Worldwide.)

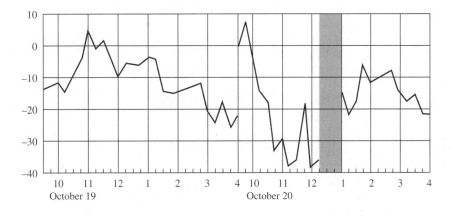

Many observers believe the portfolio insurance industry will never recover from the market crash. Participants are now far more sensitive to the practical difficulties of successfully implementing an insurance program. Direct, rather than synthetic, option strategies now appear more attractive. In this regard, it is noteworthy that the CBOE has introduced longer-term index options, called LEAPS, with maturities of a few years.

In Canada, portfolio insurance is virtually non-existent. There are too few derivative instruments and too little liquidity in the markets to allow efficient dynamic hedging of Canadian stock portfolios. The accompanying box explores some of these reasons in more depth.

22.3 *Option-Like Securities*

Even if you never trade an option directly, you still need to appreciate the properties of options in formulating any investment plan. Why? Many other financial instruments and agreements have features that convey implicit or explicit options to one or more parties. If you are to value and use these securities correctly, you must understand these option attributes.

Callable Bonds

You know from Chapter 15 that many corporate bonds are issued with call provisions entitling the issuer to buy bonds back from bondholders at some time in the future at a specified call price. This provision conveys a call option to the issuer, where the exercise price is equal to the price at which the bond can be repurchased. A callable bond arrangement is essentially a sale of a *straight bond* (a bond with no option features such as callability or convertibil-

Program Trade Problems Seen Unlikely in Canada

By Douglas Goold

Program trading and portfolio insurance received black eyes in the U.S. for contributing to the October 19 [1987] crash, but they haven't encountered the same criticism in Canada.

Program trading is a general term for using computers to execute split-second trades involving large baskets of stocks, usually offset by trades in the stock index futures market.

Portfolio insurance is a technique used by large institutions to hedge their stock holdings in a falling market. Computers are programmed to sell either stocks or futures once the market falls a certain amount, usually 3 percent. Between US $60 billion and US$90 billion worth of stock was covered by portfolio insurance prior to the crash.

Brought Collapse

Several U.S. studies have concluded that these strategies helped bring Wall Street to the brink of collapse on October 19 and 20.

The computers turned a market retreat into a rout and vastly increased volatility, the studies say. Critics claim computer programs are taking the place of human decision making and that "derivative" markets of futures and options are supplanting the underlying equity markets. It's a case of the tail wagging the dog, they say.

While U.S. authorities are wringing their hands over what to do, the New York Stock Exchange has ruled that member firms cannot use its automated order system for computer program trading when the Dow Jones industrial average is up or down more than 50 points in a day.

Canada didn't suffer problems with program trading last October and is unlikely to face them, "because the futures market here is so illiquid you couldn't get the same size transaction," says Michael Simms, vice-president of options marketing at Nesbitt Thomson Deacon Inc.

That isn't to say program trades are impossible here. A big institution could hold all 35 stocks in the TSE 35, which was introduced last May to make hedging possible.

If the Toronto Stock Exchange 300 composite index started to plummet, the institution could hedge its portfolio by selling futures contracts on the Toronto Futures Exchange, rather than by dumping all 35 stocks on the market.

By introducing the TSE 35, "the Toronto Stock Exchange bit off a hell of a lot more than they could chew" since any serious hedging can be accomplished far more easily by turning to the markets south of the border, Simms says.

Simms maintains that whatever controls the United States introduces are bound to spread to Canada. Already the TSE has followed New York's example in increasing to 10 percent from 5 percent the margin requirements on index options, with some firms upping the requirement to as much as 30 percent.

Program trading "is used very, very little in Canada," agrees Marshall Beyer, a financial futures analyst with Richardson Greenshields of Canada Ltd.

And given the bad name portfolio insurance strategies in the United States have received, "I don't think there's much chance of any increase of portfolio insurance or arbitrage strategies in Canada."

Beyer said his firm looked at and then rejected using the TSE 35 for hedging purposes. None of the controls the United States is looking at are needed in Canada, he says. If the New York exchange keeps its 50-point rule, its effects will spill over into the Canadian markets and help lessen volatility here, he says.

Canada Slow

Gurney Watson, technical analyst with Prudential-Bache Securities Canada Ltd., believes program trading, not fundamental economic problems, almost brought Wall Street to a grinding halt last October. But just as Canada was slow to introduce options, it has been slow to get involved in program trading. "There aren't very many players here," he says.

(Continued)

In any case, the TSE has long had controls on program trades. "We've done a number of things here which are way ahead of the United States," said Andrew Clademenos, director of the TSE's derivative markets.

The maximum a firm can execute for its house account is one program trade of 10 futures contracts, the equivalent of about $800,000 of stock, every five minutes. Clademenos says the TSE is now looking at whether it should implement controls similar to New York's 50-point limit.

From *The Financial Post*, March 21, 1988, by Douglas Goold. Reprinted by permission.

ity) to the investor and the concurrent sale of a call option by the investor to the bond-issuing firm.

There must be some compensation for offering this implicit call option to the firm. If the callable bond were issued with the same coupon rate as a straight bond, we would expect it to sell at a discount to the straight bond equal to the value of the call. To sell callable bonds at par, firms must issue them with coupon rates higher than the coupons on straight debt. The higher coupons are the investor's compensation for the call option retained by the issuer. Coupon rates usually are selected so that the newly issued bond will sell at par value.

Figure 22.7 illustrates the option-like property of a callable bond. The horizontal axis is the value of a straight bond with terms otherwise identical to the callable bond. The 45-degree dashed line represents the value of straight debt.

FIGURE 22.7
Values of callable bonds compared with straight bonds.

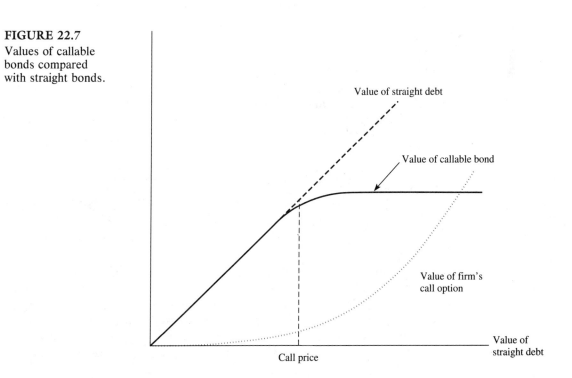

The solid line is the value of the callable bond, and the dotted line is the value of the call option retained by the firm. A callable bond's potential for capital gains is limited by the firm's option to repurchase at the call price.

| Concept Check | Question 3. How is a callable bond similar to a covered call strategy on a straight bond? |

The option inherent in callable bonds is actually more complex than an ordinary call option, because usually it may be exercised only after some initial period of call protection. Also, the price at which the bond is callable may change over time. Unlike exchange-listed options, these features are defined in the initial bond offering and will depend on the needs of the issuing firm and its perception of the market's tastes.

| Concept Check | Question 4. Suppose that the period of call protection is extended. How will the coupon rate that is required for the bond to sell at par value change? |

Convertible Securities

Convertible bonds and convertible preferred stock convey options to the holder of the security rather than to the issuing firm. The convertible security typically gives its holder the right to exchange each bond or share of preferred stock for a fixed number of shares of common stock, regardless of the market prices of the securities at the time.

| Concept Check | Question 5. Should a convertible bond issued at par value have a higher or lower coupon rate than a non-convertible bond issued at par? |

For example, a bond with a conversion ratio of 10 allows its holder to convert one bond of par value $1,000 into 10 shares of common stock. Alternatively, the conversion price in this case is $100: to receive 10 shares of stock, the investor sacrifices bonds with face value $1,000, or $100 of face value per share. If the present value of the bond's scheduled payments is less than 10 times the value of one share of stock, it may pay to convert; that is, the conversion option is in the money. A bond worth $950 with a conversion ratio of 10 could be converted profitably if the stock were selling above $95, since the value of the 10 shares received for each bond surrendered would exceed $950. Most convertible bonds are issued "deep out of the money"; that is, the issuer sets the conversion ratio so that conversion will not be profitable unless there is a substantial increase in stock prices and/or decrease in bond prices from the time of issue.

A bond's conversion value equals the value it would have if you converted it into stock immediately. Clearly, a bond must sell for at least its conversion value. If it did not, you could purchase the bond, convert it immediately, and clear a risk-free profit. This condition could never persist, because all investors would pursue such a strategy, which ultimately would bid up the price of the bond.

The straight bond value or "bond floor" is the value the bond would have if it were not convertible into stock. The bond must sell for more than its straight bond value because a convertible bond is in fact a straight bond plus a valuable call option. Therefore the convertible bond has two lower bounds on its market price: the conversion value and the straight bond value.

Figure 22.8**A** illustrates the value of the straight debt as a function of the stock price of the issuing firm. For healthy firms the straight debt value is almost independent of the value of the stock because default risk is small. However, if the firm is close to bankruptcy (stock prices are low), default risk increases, and the straight bond value falls. Figure 22.8**B** shows the conversion value of the bond, and **C** compares the value of the convertible bond to these two lower bounds.

When stock prices are low, the straight bond value is the effective lower bound, and the conversion option is nearly irrelevant. The convertible will trade like straight debt. When stock prices are high, the bond's price is determined by its conversion value. With conversion all but guaranteed, the bond is essentially equity in disguise.   .

We can illustrate with two examples:

	Bond A	Bond B
Annual coupon	$80	$80
Maturity date	10 years	10 years
Quality rating	Baa	Baa
Conversion ratio	20	25
Stock price	$30	$50
Conversion value	$600	$1,250
Market yield on 10-year Baa-rated bonds	8.5%	8.5%
Value as straight debt	$967	$967
Actual bond price	$972	$1,255
Reported yield to maturity	8.42%	4.76%

Bond A has a conversion value of only $600. Its value as straight debt, in contrast, is $967. This is the present value of the coupon and principal payments at a market rate for straight debt of 8.5 percent. The bond's price is $972, so the premium over straight bond value is only $5, reflecting the low probability of conversion. Its reported yield to maturity based on scheduled coupon

FIGURE 22.8
Value of a
convertible bond as
a function of stock
price. **A**—straight
debt value, or
bond floor. **B**—
conversion value of
the bond. **C**—total
value of convertible
bond.

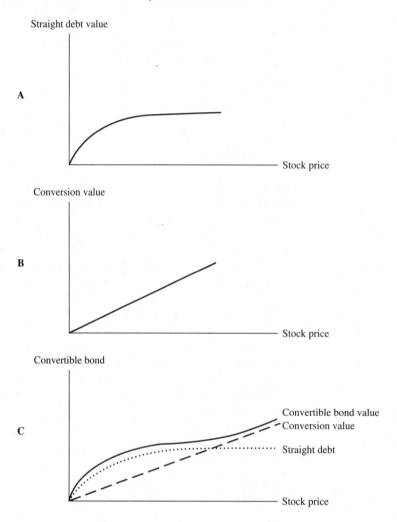

payments and the market price of $972 is 8.42 percent, close to that of straight debt.

The conversion option on Bond B is in the money. Conversion value is $1,250, and the bond's price, $1,255, reflects its value as equity (plus $5 for the protection the bond offers against stock price declines). The bond's reported yield is 4.76 percent, far below the comparable yield on straight debt. The big yield sacrifice is attributable to the far greater value of the conversion option. In theory, we could value convertible bonds by treating them as straight debt plus call options. In practice, however, this approach is often impractical for several reasons:

1. The conversion price frequently increases over time, which means the exercise price for the option changes.
2. Stocks may pay several dividends over the life of the bond, further complicating the option valuation analysis.

3. Most convertibles also are callable at the discretion of the firm. In essence, the investor and the firm hold options on each other. If the firm exercises its call option to repurchase the bond, the bondholders typically have a month during which they still can convert. When firms use a call option, while knowing that bondholders will choose to convert, the firm is said to have *forced a conversion*. These conditions together mean that the actual maturity of the bond is indeterminate.

Warrants

Warrants are essentially call options issued by the firm. One important difference between calls and warrants is that exercise of a warrant requires the firm to issue a new share of stock to satisfy its obligation—the total number of shares outstanding increases. Exercise of a call option requires only that the writer of the call deliver an already-issued share of stock to discharge the obligation. In this case, the number of shares outstanding remains fixed. Also unlike call options, warrants result in a cash flow to the firm when the exercise price is paid by the warrant holder. These differences mean that warrant values will differ somewhat from the values of call options with identical terms.

Like convertible debt, warrant terms may be tailored to meet the needs of the firm. Also like convertible debt, warrants generally are protected against stock splits and dividends in that the exercise price and the number of warrants held are adjusted to offset the effects of the split.

Warrants are often issued in conjunction with another security. Bonds, for example, may be packaged together with a warrant "sweetener," frequently a warrant that may be sold separately. This is called a *detachable warrant*.

Issue of warrants and convertible securities creates the potential for an increase in outstanding shares of stock if exercise occurs. Exercise obviously would affect financial statistics that are computed on a per-share basis, so annual reports must provide earnings-per-share (EPS) figures under the assumption that all convertible securities and warrants are exercised. These figures are called *fully diluted* earnings per share.[5]

Collateralized Loans

Most loan arrangements require that the borrower put up collateral to guarantee that the loan will be paid back. In the event of default, the lender takes possession of the collateral. A non-recourse loan gives the lender no recourse beyond the right to the collateral; that is, the lender may not sue the borrower for further payment if the collateral turns out not to be valuable enough to repay the loan.

This arrangement, it turns out, gives an implicit call option to the borrower. The borrower, for example, is obligated to pay back L dollars at the maturity of

---

[5] We should note that the exercise of a convertible bond need not reduce EPS. Diluted EPS will be less than undiluted EPS only if interest saved (per share) on the converted bonds is less than the prior EPS.

the loan. The collateral will be worth S_T dollars at maturity. (Its value today is S_0.) The borrower has the option to wait until loan maturity and repay the loan only if the collateral is worth more than the L dollars he or she borrowed. If the collateral is worth less than L, the borrower can default on the loan, discharging the obligation by forfeiting the collateral, which is worth only S_T.

Another way of describing such a loan is to view the borrower as, in effect, turning over collateral to the lender but retaining the right to reclaim it by paying off the loan. The transfer of the collateral with the right to claim it is equivalent to a payment of S_0 dollars, less a future recovery of a sum that resembles a call option with exercise price L. Basically, the borrower turns over collateral and keeps an option to "repurchase" it for L dollars at the maturity of the loan if L turns out to be less than S_T. This is, of course, a call option.

A third way to look at a collateralized loan is to assume the borrower will repay the L dollars with certainty, but also retain the option to sell the collateral to the lender for L dollars, even if S_T is less than L. In this case, the sale of the collateral would generate the cash necessary to satisfy the loan. The ability to "sell" the collateral for a price of L dollars represents a put option, which guarantees that the borrower can raise enough money to satisfy the loan by turning over the collateral.

It is strange to think that we can describe the same loan as involving either a put option or a call option, since the payoffs to calls and puts are so different. Yet the equivalence of the two approaches is nothing more than a reflection of the put-call parity relationship. In our call option description of the loan, the value of the borrower's liability is $S_0 - C$: the borrower turns over the asset, which is a transfer of S_0 dollars, but retains a call, which is worth C dollars. In the put option description the borrower is obligated to pay L dollars but retains the put, which is worth P: the present value of this net obligation is $L/(1 + r_f)^T - P$. Because these alternative descriptions are equivalent ways of viewing the same loan, the value of the obligations must be equal:

$$S_0 - C = L/(1 + r_f)^T - P \qquad (22.2)$$

Treating L as the exercise price of the option, equation 22.2 is simply the put-call parity relationship.

Figure 22.9**A** illustrates the value of the payment to be received by the lender, which equals the minimum of S_T or L. Figure 22.9**B** shows that this amount can be expressed as S_T minus the payoff of the call implicitly written by the lender and held by the borrower. Figure 22.9**C** shows that it also can be viewed as a receipt of L dollars minus the proceeds of the put option.

Leveraged Equity and Risky Debt

Investors holding stock in incorporated firms are protected by limited liability, which means that if the firm cannot pay its debts, the firm's creditors may attach only the firm's assets, not sue the corporation's equity holders for further payment. In effect, any time the corporation borrows money, the maximum possible collateral for the loan is the total of the firm's assets. If the firm

FIGURE 22.9
Collateralized loan.

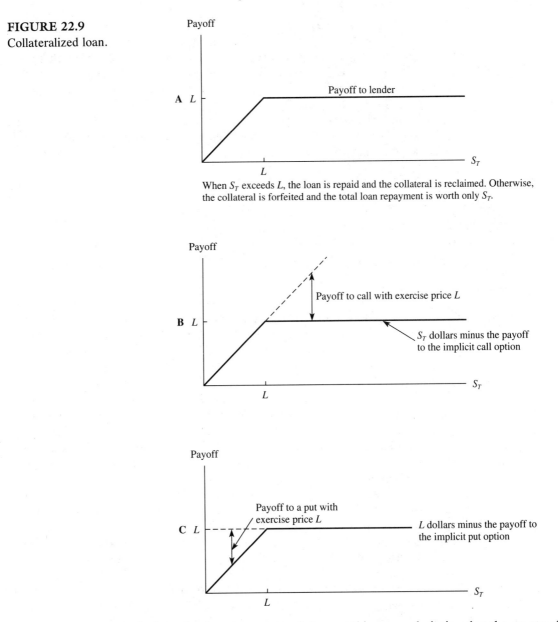

When S_T exceeds L, the loan is repaid and the collateral is reclaimed. Otherwise, the collateral is forfeited and the total loan repayment is worth only S_T.

declares bankruptcy, we can interpret this as an admission that the assets of the firm are insufficient to satisfy the claims against it. The corporation may discharge its obligations by transferring ownership of the firm's assets to the creditors.

Just as with non-recourse collateralized loans, the required payment to the creditors represents the exercise price of the implicit option, while the value of the firm is the underlying asset. The equity holders have a put option to transfer their ownership claims on the firm to the creditors in return for the face value of the firm's debt.

Alternatively, we may view the equity holders as retaining a call option. They have, in effect, already transferred their ownership claim on the firm to the creditors but have retained the right to reacquire the ownership claims on the firm by paying off the loan. Hence, the equity holders have the option to "buy back" the firm for a specified price—they have a call option.

The significance of this observation is that the values of corporate bonds can be estimated using option pricing techniques. The default premium required of risky debt, in principle, can be estimated using Black-Scholes or more sophisticated option valuation models.

22.4 *Binomial Option Pricing*

Two-State Option Pricing

A complete understanding of the Black-Scholes formula is difficult without a substantial mathematics background. Nevertheless, we can develop valuable insight into option valuation by considering a particularly simple special case. Assume that a stock price can take only two possible values at option expiration: the stock will either increase to a given higher price or decrease to a given lower price. Although this may seem an extreme simplification, it allows us to come closer to understanding more complicated and seemingly more realistic models. Moreover, we can extend this approach to accept far more reasonable specifications of stock price behaviour. In fact, several major financial firms employ variants of this simple model to value options and securities with option-like features.

Suppose that the stock currently sells at $100 and that by year-end the price will either double to $200 or be cut in half to $50. A call option on the stock might specify an exercise price of $125 and a time to expiration of one year. Suppose the interest rate is 8 percent. At year-end, the payoff to the holder of the call option will be either zero if the stock falls or $75 if the stock price goes to $200.

Compare this payoff to that of a portfolio consisting of one share of the stock and borrowing of $46.30 at the interest rate of 8 percent. The payoff to this portfolio also depends on the stock price at year-end:

	$50	$200
Value of stock	$50	$200
−Repayment of loan with interest	−$50	−$ 50
TOTAL	$ 0	$150

The payoff of this portfolio is exactly twice the option value regardless of the stock price. In other words, two call options will exactly replicate the payoff to the portfolio; two call options, therefore, should have the same price as the cost of establishing the portfolio. We know the cost of establishing the portfolio is

$100 for the stock, less the $46.30 proceeds from borrowing. Hence, the two calls should sell at

$$2C = \$100 - \$46.30$$

or each call should sell at $C = \$26.85$. Thus, given the stock price, exercise price, interest rate, and volatility of the stock price (as represented by the magnitude of the up or down movements), we can derive the fair value for the call option.

This valuation approach relies heavily on the notion of replication. With only two possible end-of-year values of the stock, the returns to the leveraged stock portfolio replicate the returns to the call option, and so need to command the same market price. This notion of replication is behind most option pricing formulas. For more complex price distributions for stocks, the replication technique is correspondingly more complex, but the principles remain the same.

One way to view the role of replication is to note that, using the numbers assumed for this example, a portfolio made up of one share of stock and two call options written is perfectly hedged. Its year-end value is independent of the ultimate stock price:

Stock value	$50	$200
−Obligations from two calls written	− 0	−$150
Net payoff	$50	$ 50

The investor has formed a risk-free portfolio, with a payout of $50. Its value must be the present value of $50, or $50/1.08 = $46.30. The value of the portfolio, which equals $100 from the stock held long, minus $2C$ from the two calls written, should equal $46.30. Hence, $100 − 2C = $46.30, or $C = $26.85.

The ability to create a perfect hedge is the key to this argument. The hedge guarantees the end-of-year payout, which can be discounted using the risk-free interest rate. To find the value of the option in terms of the value of the stock, we do not need to know the option's or the stock's beta or expected rate of return. (Recall that this also was true of Black-Scholes option valuation.) The perfect hedging, or replication, approach enables us to express the value of the option in terms of the current value of the stock without this information. With a hedged position the final stock price does not affect the investor's payoff, so the stock's risk-and-return parameters have no bearing.

The hedge ratio of this example is one share of stock to two calls, or one half. For every option written, one-half share of stock must be held in the portfolio to hedge away risk. This ratio has an easy interpretation in this context: it is the ratio of the range of the values of the option to those of the stock across the two possible outcomes. The option is worth either zero or $75, for a range of $75. The stock is worth either $50 or $200, for a range of $150. The ratio of ranges, 75/150, is one half, which is the hedge ratio we have established.

The hedge ratio equals the ratio of ranges because the option and stock are perfectly correlated in this two-state example. When the returns of the option and stock are perfectly correlated, a perfect hedge requires that option and stock be held in a fraction determined only by relative volatility.

The generalization of the hedge ratio for the other two-state option problems is

$$H = \frac{C^+ - C^-}{S^+ - S^-}$$

where C^+ and C^- refer to the call option's value when the stock goes up or down, respectively, and S^+ and S^- are the stock prices in the two states. The hedge ratio, H, is thus the ratio of the swings in the possible end-of-period values of the option and the stock. If the investor writes one option and holds H shares of stock, the value of the portfolio will be unaffected by the stock price. In this case, option pricing is easy: simply set the value of the hedged portfolio equal to the present value of the known payoff.

Concept Check	Question 6. Intuitively, would you expect the hedge ratio to be higher or lower when the call option is more in the money? (You can confirm your intuition in problem 2 at the end of the chapter.)

Using our example, the option pricing technique would proceed as follows:

1. Given the possible end-of-year stock prices, $S^+ = 200$ and $S^- = 50$, and the exercise price of 125, calculate that $C^+ = 75$ and $C^- = 0$. The stock price range is thus 150, while the option price range is 75.
2. Find that the hedge ratio is $75/150 = 5$.
3. Find that a portfolio made up of .5 shares with one written option would have an end-of-year value of $25 with certainty.
4. Show that the present value of $25 with a one-year interest rate of 8 percent is $23.15.
5. Set the value of the hedged position to the present value of the certain payoff.

$$.5S_0 - C_0 = 23.15$$
$$\$50 - C_0 = \$23.15$$

6. Solve for the call's value, $C_0 = \$26.85$.

What if the option were overpriced, perhaps selling for $30? Then you can make arbitrage profits. Here is how:

	Initial Cash Flow	CF in 1 Year for Each Possible Stock Price	
		S = 50	S = 200
1. Write two options	60	0	−150
2. Purchase one share	−100	50	200
3. Borrow $40 at 8% interest, and repay in 1 year	40	−43.20	−43.20
TOTAL	0	6.80	6.80

Although the net initial investment is zero, the payoff in one year is positive and riskless. If the option were underpriced, one would simply reverse this arbitrage strategy: buy the option, and shortsell the stock to eliminate price risk. Note, by the way, that the present value of the profit to the arbitrage strategy above exactly equals twice the amount by which the option is over-priced. The present value of the risk-free profit of $6.80 at an 8 percent interest rate is $6.30. With two options written in this strategy, this translates to a profit of $3.15 per option, exactly the amount by which the option was overpriced: $30 versus the "fair value" of $26.85.

Generalizing the Two-State Approach

Although the two-state stock price model seems simplistic, we can generalize it to incorporate more realistic assumptions. To start, suppose that we were to break up the year into two six-month segments, and then assert that over each half-year segment the stock price could take on two values. In this case we will say it can increase 10 percent or decrease 5 percent. A stock initially selling at 100 could follow these possible paths over the course of the year:

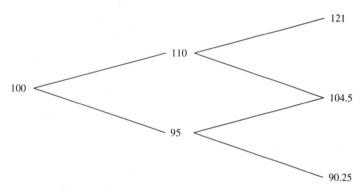

The midrange value of 104.5 can be attained by two paths: an increase of 10 percent followed by a decrease of 5 percent, or a decrease of 5 percent followed by a 10 percent increase.

There are now three possible end-of-year values for the stock and three for the option.

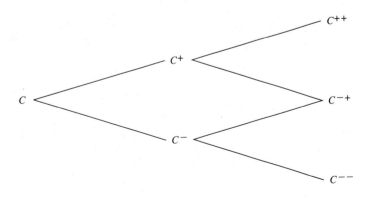

Using methods similar to those we followed above, we could value C^+ from knowledge of C^{++} and C^{+-}, then value C^- from knowledge of C^{-+} and C^{--}, and finally value C from knowledge of C^+ and C^-. There is no reason to stop at six-month intervals. We could next break up the year into 4 three-month units, or 12 one-month units, or 365 one-day units, each of which would be posited to have a two-state process. Although the calculations become quite numerous and correspondingly tedious, they are easy to program into a computer, and such computer programs are used widely by participants in the securities market.

As we break the year into progressively finer subintervals, the range of possible year-end stock prices expands and, in fact, will ultimately take on a lognormal distribution.[6] This can be seen from an analysis of the event tree for the stock for a period with three subintervals:

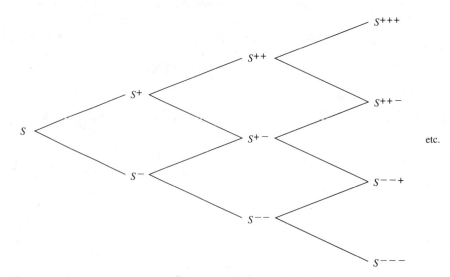

First, notice that as the number of subintervals increases the number of possible stock prices also increases. Second, notice that extreme events such as S^{+++} or S^{---} are relatively rare, since they require either three consecutive increases or decreases in the three subintervals. More moderate, or midrange, results such as S^{++-} can be arrived at by more than one path—any combination of two price increases and one decrease will result in stock price S^{++-}. Thus the midrange values will be more likely, and the stock price distribution

---

[6] Actually, more complex considerations enter here. The limit of this process is lognormal only if we assume also that stock prices move continuously, by which we mean that over small time intervals only small price movements can occur. This rules out rare events such as sudden, extreme price moves in response to dramatic information (like a takeover attempt). For a treatment of this type of "jump process," see John C. Cox and Stephen A. Ross, "The Valuation of Options for Alternative Stochastic Processes," *Journal of Financial Economics* 3 (January–March 1976), or Robert C. Merton, "Option Pricing When Underlying Stock Returns Are Discontinuous," *Journal of Financial Economics* 3 (January–March 1976).

will acquire the familiar bell-shaped pattern discussed in Chapter 5. The probability of each outcome is described by the binomial distribution, and this multiperiod approach to option pricing is therefore called the **binomial model.**

For example, using our initial stock price of $100, equal probability of stock price increases or decreases, and three intervals for which the possible price increase is 5 percent and decrease is 3 percent, we would obtain the probability distribution of stock prices from the following calculations. There are eight possible combinations for the stock price movements in the three periods: $+ + +, + + -, + - +, - + +, + - -, - + -, - - +, - - -$. Each has probability of $\frac{1}{8}$. Therefore the probability distribution of stock prices at the end of the last interval would be as follows:

Event	Probability	Stock Price	
3 up movements	$\frac{1}{8}$	100×1.05^3	$= 115.76$
2 up and 1 down	$\frac{3}{8}$	$100 \times 1.05^2 \times .97$	$= 106.94$
1 up and 2 down	$\frac{3}{8}$	$100 \times 1.05 \times .97^2$	$= 98.79$
3 down movements	$\frac{1}{8}$	$100 \times .97^3$	$= 91.27$

The midrange values are three times as likely to occur as the extreme values. Figure 22.10**A** is a graph of the frequency distribution for this example. Notice that the graph is beginning to take on the familiar appearance of the bell-shaped curve. In fact, as the number of intervals increases, as in Figure 22.10**B** the frequency distribution progressively approaches the lognormal distribution rather than the normal distribution. (Recall our discussion in the appendix to Chapter 5 on why the lognormal distribution is superior to the normal as a means of modeling stock prices.)

Suppose that we were to continue subdividing the interval in which stock prices are posited to move up or down. Eventually, each node of the event tree would correspond to an infinitesimally small time interval. The possible stock price movement within that time interval would be correspondingly small. As those many intervals passed, the end-of-period stock price would more and more closely resemble a lognormal distribution. Thus the apparent oversimplification of the two-state model can be overcome by progressively subdividing any period into many subperiods.

At any node, one still could set up a portfolio that would be perfectly hedged over the next tiny time interval. Then, at the end of that interval, upon reaching the next node, a new hedge ratio could be computed and the portfolio composition could be revised to remain hedged over the coming small interval. By continuously revising the hedge position, the portfolio would remain hedged and would earn a risk-free rate of return over each interval. This is dynamic hedging, which calls for continued updating of the hedge ratio as time passes. In fact, Black and Scholes used a dynamic hedge approach to derive their option valuation formula, and you saw in our discussion of portfolio insurance that a dynamic hedge strategy is required for the stock plus bills portfolio to replicate the payoff to a protective put.

FIGURE 22.10
Probability
distributions.
A—possible
outcomes and
associated
probabilities for
stock prices after
three periods. The
stock price starts at
$100, and in each
period it can
increase by 5% or
decrease by 3%.
B—each period is
subdivided into two
smaller subperiods.
Now there are six
periods, and in each
of these the stock
price can increase
by 2.5% or fall by
1.5%. Notice that as
the number of
periods increases
the stock price
distribution
approaches the
familiar bell-shaped
curve.

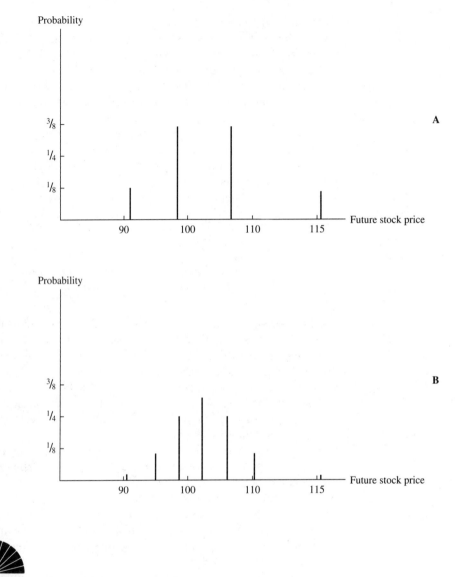

22.5 *Multinomial Option Pricing*

Complete and Incomplete Markets

The binomial model described in the previous section assumes that in every subinterval the stock price can take exactly two possible values, up or down by given amounts. We saw that in such a model it is possible to replicate the option with a portfolio containing exactly two assets, the stock and a riskless loan at the prevailing rate of interest. This correspondence of available assets and possible stock values in every subinterval is crucial to the use of the model for option pricing.

Consider again the example of the previous section, where a stock that sells at $100 can by year-end either double to $200 or be cut in half to $50. Now, however, suppose that there is also a third possibility, that the stock keeps the original price of $100. If the interest rate is 8 percent, can we still use the replication method to value the option with exercise price of $125 and one year time to expiration?

The answer to this question is no. At year-end, the option payoff is either zero if the stock falls or stays the same or $75 if it rises. The portfolio that we examined in the previous section, with one share of the stock and borrowing of $46.30 at 8 percent now yields the following contingent payoffs:

Value of stock	$50	$100	$200
Repayment of loan with interest	−50	−50	−50
TOTAL	$0	$50	$150

The holder of this portfolio would get twice the option value when the stock goes up or down, *plus* $50 whenever the stock stays the same. Hence, the value of the portfolio can no longer be equal to twice that of the option, since it is clearly greater.

In fact, it can be shown that there is no portfolio involving only the stock and borrowed funds capable of replicating this option. Suppose that a replicating portfolio contains x shares and y of borrowed funds. Its future value must be equal to that of the option for all possible values of the stock. This means that:

$$50x - 1.08y = 0, \ 100x - 1.08y = 0, \ 200x - 1.08y = 75$$

This system has no solution, since it has three equations and only two unknowns. This implies that there is no portfolio capable of replicating the option. The reason for this is that there are more possible future values of the stock than there are assets to form a replicating portfolio.

In the binomial model, there are only two future "states of the world" as far as the stock price is concerned. In our example, the stock can only go down to $50 (state 1), or up to $200 (state 2). Suppose also that we have two assets, also numbered 1 and 2, each one of them yielding a payoff equal to $1 if the corresponding state occurs, and 0 otherwise; their respective values are v_1 and v_2. These assets are known as *elementary* or *primitive* securities, and they are a very convenient analytical tool in valuing options or other derivative assets.

With these elementary assets we can now replicate every other asset in our binomial model. Thus, the stock is equivalent to a portfolio of 50 units of asset 1 and 200 units of asset 2, and any riskless investment corresponds to portfolios having equal numbers of units of assets 1 and 2. This helps us determine the two elementary assets' values, v_1 and v_2:

$$50v_1 + 200v_2 = 100$$
$$v_1 + v_2 = 1/1.08$$

Solving this system, we find $v_1 = 0.5679$, $v_2 = 0.358$. With these prices it is now very easy to price the option with exercise price $125: it is simply equal to $75v_2 = 75 \times 0.358 = 26.85$, which is the value found in the previous section.

We can now see why the notion of replication can be applied to the binomial model, but breaks down when there is a third "state of the world." In such a case we have three elementary assets, each one paying $1 when the corresponding state of the world occurs, and zero otherwise. Let us number them 1, 2, and 3, corresponding to the ascending order of future stock price, and denote their corresponding values by v_1, v_2, and v_3; then one share would be equivalent to a portfolio of 50 units of asset 1, 100 units of asset 2, and 200 units of asset 3. However, we now have only *two* equations to determine the three unknown elementary asset values v_1, v_2, v_3:

$$50v_1 + 100v_2 + 200v_3 = 100$$
$$v_1 + v_2 + v_3 = 1/1.08 \qquad \textbf{(22.3)}$$

Here, the observable stock price and rate of interest are insufficient to give us unique values of the three elementary assets. There are more states of the world (and, hence, elementary assets) than there are observable assets. This indeterminacy is the mirror image of the impossibility to find a portfolio replicating a given option.

A market that has as many independent observable assets as there are future states of the world is said to be *complete*. By contrast, **incomplete markets** are those that have fewer such assets than there are states of the world; real-world markets are generally assumed to be incomplete.[7] The binomial model is the only complete market model if our states of the world are classified by a stock's future payoffs, and if we observe only the optioned stock and the riskless rate of interest.

Generalizing the Binomial Option Pricing

A unique set of elementary asset values consistent with the observed stock price and rate of interest does not exist in incomplete markets. Consequently, a unique option price cannot be derived by the replication method. For instance, there are infinitely many values of v_3, the elementary asset that pays $1 when the stock goes up and zero otherwise, that satisfy the two equations 22.3 corresponding to the stock price and rate of interest. Each one of these v_3 values would yield a different value of the option with exercise price equal to $125, since the option's payoff is zero in all other states of the world.

This indeterminancy is rather disturbing, given that a stock price model with three (or more) states is otherwise very similar to the two-state model. In both types of models we can subdivide the year into progressively finer subintervals, approaching at the limit *the same* lognormal distribution. For such a distribution the appropriate option value is given by the Black-Scholes formula. Do all admissible option values, derived from the values of v_3 satisfying the equations 22.3, similarly approach the Black-Scholes option price at the limit?

The answer is again no. While there are infinitely many option values consistent with the observed stock price and rate of interest, only a given subset of

---

[7] See the remarks in W. Sharpe, *Investments,* 2d edition (Englewood Cliffs, N.J.: Prentice Hall, 1988), pp. 99–101.

them, contained between an upper and a lower bound, converge at the limit to the Black-Scholes option value. This set of option values constitutes, therefore, the appropriate generalization of the binomial model when the number of possible future stock prices exceeds two.

The two bounds that define the appropriate option values depend not only on the size of the future stock prices, but also on their probabilities. Suppose, for instance, that in our previous example the stock price could either double or be cut in half, each with probability equal to ¼, and could stay the same with probability equal to ½. The expected value of the stock price would be equal to

$$.25 \times 50 + .5 \times 100 + .25 \times 200 = 112.5$$

This corresponds to a return of 12.5 percent, which is higher than the rate on interest of 8 percent. For stock price distributions with expected returns higher than the rate of interest, it can be shown that upper and lower bounds on the admissible option values are equal to the expected present values of the call payoff with the expectations taken over transformed[8] stock price distributions. In this example, the transformed probabilities for the upper bound are .304, .464, and .232 for stock prices of 50, 100, and 200; they give an upper bound equal to $75 \times .232/1.08 = \$16.11$. The corresponding transformed probabilities for the lower bound are .263, .526, and .211, yielding a lower bound equal to $75 \times .211/1.08 = \$15.86$.

Thus, option prices with an exercise price of \$125 must lie between \$15.86 and \$16.11 in this three-state option pricing model. As we subdivide the time period into increasingly finer partitions, the distance between the two bounds tends to decrease. At the limit, both bounds become equal to the Black-Scholes option value.

22.6   *Empirical Evidence*

There have been an enormous number of empirical tests of the option pricing model. For the most part, the results of the studies have been positive in that the Black-Scholes model generates option values fairly close to the actual prices at which options trade. At the same time, some regular empirical failures

---

[8] Let p_1, p_2, and p_3 denote the three probabilities corresponding to the down, stay-the-same, and up states, respectively. Then for the upper bound the probabilities are transformed into $p_1 = Q + (1 - Q)p_1$, $p_2 = (1 - Q)p_2$, $p_3 = (1- Q)p_3$, where Q is equal to $(112.5 - 108)/(112.5 - 50)$ in our example, the ratio of the difference between the expected future stock price and the rate of interest, to the difference between the expected stock price and the lowest possible stock value. The transformation for the lower bound is slightly more complicated. See S. Perrakis, "Preference-Free Option Prices When the Stock Return Can Go Up, Go Down, or Stay the Same," *Advances in Futures and Options Research,* 1988

of the model have been noted. Geske and Roll[9] have argued that these empirical results can be attributed to the failure of the Black-Scholes model to account for the possible early exercise of American calls on stocks that pay dividends. Indeed, they show that the theoretical bias induced by this failure exactly corresponds to the actual "mispricing" observed empirically.

Whaley[10] examines the performance of the Black-Scholes formula relative to that of the pseudo-American and true American option formulas. His findings also indicate that formulas that allow for the possibility of early exercise do better at pricing than does the Black-Scholes formula. Whaley's results indicate that the Black-Scholes formula performs worst for options on stocks with high dividend payouts. The true American call option formula, on the other hand, seemed to fare equally well in the prediction of option prices on stocks with high or low dividend payouts.

A more sceptical view of the Black-Scholes formula or, indeed, of any other option pricing formula presented in the literature, comes out of the tests performed by Rubinstein.[11] He found that all formulas exhibited systematic biases in their predictions, in terms of both the exercise price and the time to expiration of the options. Fortunately these biases were not, in most cases, sufficiently large to have major economic consequences for option holders using the Black-Scholes formula as if it were the true option value.

A different type of empirical test on option pricing examines whether the observed call option prices satisfy the general restrictions stated in the first section of this chapter. These restrictions are independent of any particular option pricing model. The major difficulty in carrying out the tests is the simultaneous observation of corresponding stock and option prices. A Canadian study by Halpern and Turnbull[12] examined whether traded stock and call option prices on the TSE, together with the prevailing rates of interest, did satisfy the appropriate conditions in 1978–1979. They found several violations of these restrictions, which should have allowed traders to realize riskless profits. There are, however, indications that these violations were due to the comparative novelty of option trading on the TSE, and did not persist in more recent years.

---

[9] Robert Geske and Richard Roll, "On Valuing American Call Options with the Black-Scholes European Formula," *Journal of Finance* 39 (June 1984).

[10] Robert E. Whaley, "Valuation of American Call Options on Dividend-Paying Stocks: Empirical Tests," *Journal of Financial Economics* 10 (1982).

[11] M. Rubinstein, "Nonparametric Tests of Alternative Option Pricing Models Using All Reported Trades and Quotes on the 30 Most Active CBOE Option Classes from August 23, 1976 through August 31, 1978," *Journal of Finance* 40 (June 1985).

[12] Paul Halpern and Stuart Turnbull, "Empirical Tests of Boundary Conditions for Toronto Stock Exchange Options," *Journal of Finance* 40, no. 2 (June 1985).

Summary

1. Call options must sell for at least the stock price less the present value of the exercise price and dividends to be paid before maturity. This implies that a call option on a non-dividend-paying stock may be sold for more than the proceeds from immediate exercise. Thus, European calls are worth as much as American calls on stocks that pay no dividends because the right to exercise the American call early has no value.

2. The Black-Scholes formula is valid for options on stocks that pay no dividends. Dividend adjustments may be adequate to price European calls on dividend-paying stocks, but the proper treatment of American calls on dividend-paying stocks requires more complex formulas.

3. Put options may be exercised early whether the stock pays dividends or not. Therefore, American puts generally are worth more than are European puts.

4. European put values can be derived from the call value and the put-call parity relationship. This technique cannot be applied to American puts for which early exercise is a possibility.

5. The hedge ratio is the number of shares of stock required to hedge the price risk involved in writing one option. Hedge ratios are near zero for deep out-of-the-money call options, and approach 1 for deep in-the-money calls.

6. Although hedge ratios are less than 1, call options have elasticities greater than 1. The rate of return on a call (as opposed to the dollar return) responds more than one-for-one with stock price movements.

7. Portfolio insurance can be obtained by purchasing a protective put option on an equity position. When the appropriate put is not traded, portfolio insurance entails a dynamic hedge strategy in which a fraction of the equity portfolio equal to the desired put option's delta is sold and placed in risk-free securities.

8. Many commonly traded securities embody option characteristics. Examples of these securities are callable bonds, convertible bonds, and warrants. Other arrangements such as collateralized loans and limited-liability borrowing can be analyzed as conveying implicit options to one or more parties.

9. Options may be priced relative to the underlying stock price using a simple two-period, two-state pricing model. As the number of periods increases, we may approximate more realistic stock price distributions. The Black-Scholes formula may be seen as a limiting case of the binomial option model as the holding period is divided into progressively smaller subperiods.

10. The simple two-state pricing model is the only model where an exact option price can be derived from the stock and the rate of interest. If there are more than two possible stock prices, then only an upper and a lower bound on admissible option values can be defined. However, both bounds become, at the limit, equal to the Black-Scholes formula, as the holding period is subdivided into progressively finer subintervals.

Key terms

Hedge ratio	Dynamic hedging
Delta	Warrants
Elasticity	Binomial model
Portfolio insurance	Incomplete markets

Selected readings

The breakthrough articles in option pricing are:

Black, Fischer; and Scholes, Myron. "The Pricing of Options and Corporate Liabilities." *Journal of Political Economy* 81 (May–June 1973).

Merton, Robert C. "Theory of Rational Option Pricing." *Bell Journal of Economics and Management Science* 4 (Spring 1973).

A good review of these, as well as an interesting treatment of earlier attempts to value options, appears in:

Smith, Clifford W., Jr. "Option Pricing: A Review." *Journal of Financial Economics* 3 (January–March 1976).

Good articles on portfolio insurance and replication strategies are:

McCallum, John S. "On Portfolio Insurance, the Stock Market Crash, and Avoiding a Repeat." *Business Quarterly* 53, no. 2 (Fall 1989).

Perold, Andre F.; and Sharpe, William F. "Dynamic Strategies for Asset Allocation." *Financial Analysts Journal,* January–February 1988.

Rubinstein, Mark; and Leland, Hayne. "Replicating Options with Positions in Stock and Cash." *Financial Analysts Journal,* July–August 1981.

The January–February 1988 edition of *Financial Analysts Journal* is devoted to issues surrounding portfolio insurance.

Several applications of option-type analysis to various financial instruments are surveyed in:

Hull, John; and White, Alan. "An Overview of Contingent Claims Pricing." *Canadian Journal of Administrative Sciences* 5, no. 3 (September 1988).

Smith, Clifford. "Applications of Option-Pricing Analysis." In James L. Bicksler (editor), *Handbook of Financial Economics.* New York: North-Holland Publishing Co., 1979.

Other relevant references are:

Bigger, Nahum; and Hull, John. "The Valuation of Currency Options." *Financial Management* 12 (1983).

Boyle, Phelim; and Kirzner, Eric P. "Pricing Complex Options: Echo-Bay Ltd. Gold Purchase Warrants." *Canadian Journal of Administrative Sciences* 2, no. 4 (December 1985).

Hull, John; and White, Alan. "Hedging the Risks from Writing Foreign Currency Options." *Journal of International Money and Finance,* June 1987.

Reich, Allan L. "Market Efficiency of IOCC Gold Options Traded on the Montreal Exchange." *International Options Journal* 1, no. 1 (Fall 1984).

The two-state approach was first suggested in:

Sharpe, William F. *Investments.* Englewood Cliffs, N.J.: Prentice Hall, 1978.

The approach was developed more fully in:

Cox, John C.; Ross, Stephen A.; and Rubinstein, Mark. "Option Pricing: A Simplified Approach." *Journal of Financial Economics* 7 (September 1979).

Rendleman, Richard J. Jr.; and Bartter, Brit J. "Two-State Option Pricing." *Journal of Finance* 34 (December 1979).

The extension of the two-state option pricing was introduced in:

Perrakis, Stylianos; and Ryan, Peter. "Option Pricing Bounds in Discrete Time." *Journal of Finance* 39 (June 1984).

Ritchken, Peter. "On Option Pricing Bounds." *Journal of Finance* 40 (September 1985).

The approach was developed more fully in:

Perrakis, Stylianos. "Option Pricing Bounds in Discrete Time: Extensions and the Pricing of the American Put." *Journal of Business* 59 (February 1986).

Perrakis, Stylianos. "Preference-Free Option Pricing When the Stock Returns Can Go Up, Go Down, or Stay the Same." *Advances in Futures and Options Research* 3 (1988).

Ritchken, Peter; and Kuo, S. "Option Bounds with Finite Revision Opportunities." *Journal of Finance* 43 (June 1988).

A summary of the empirical evidence on the accuracy of the option pricing formula may be found in:

Galai, Dan. "A Survey of Empirical Tests of Option Pricing Models." In Menachem Brenner (editor), *Option Pricing*. Lexington, Mass.: Heath, 1983.

Interesting later work includes:

Geske, Robert; and Roll, Richard. "On Valuing American Call Options with the Black-Scholes European Formula." *Journal of Finance* 39 (June 1984).

Rubinstein, Mark. "Nonparametric Tests of Alternative Option Pricing Models Using All Reported Trades and Quotes on the 30 Most Active CBOE Option Classes from August 23, 1976 through August 31, 1978." *Journal of Finance* 40 (June 1985).

Whaley, Robert E. "Valuation of American Call Options on Dividend-Paying Stocks: Empirical Tests." *Journal of Financial Economics* 10 (1982).

Empirical work in Canadian option markets is contained in:

Halpern, Paul; and Turnbull, Stuart. "Empirical Tests on Boundary Conditions for Toronto Stock Exchange Options." *Journal of Finance* 40, no. 3 (June 1985).

Mandron, Alix. "Some Empirical Evidence about Canadian Stock Options, Part I: Valuation." *Canadian Journal of Administrative Sciences* 5, no. 2 (June 1988).

Problems

1. Let $p(S,T,X)$ denote the value of a European put on a stock selling at S dollars, with time to maturity T and exercise price X, and let $P(S,T,X)$ be the value of an American put.
   a. Evaluate $p(O,T,X)$
   b. Evaluate $P(O,T,X)$
   c. Evaluate $p(S,T,0)$
   d. Evaluate $P(S,T,0)$
   e. What does your answer to part b tell you about the possibility that American puts may be exercised early?

2. Reconsider the determination of the hedge ratio in the two-state model in Section 22.4 where we showed that one-half share of stock would hedge one option. What is the hedge ratio at the following exercise prices: 115, 100, 75, 50, 25, 10? What do you conclude about the hedge ratio as the call option becomes progressively more in the money?

3. Show that Black-Scholes call option hedge ratios also increase as the stock price increases. Consider a one-year option with exercise price $50 on a stock with annual standard deviation 20 percent. The T-bill rate is 8 percent per year. Find $N(d_1)$ for stock prices $45, $50, and $55.

4. Imagine that you are a provider of portfolio insurance. You are establishing a four-year program. The portfolio you manage is currently worth $100 million, and you hope to provide a minimum return of 0 percent. The equity portfolio has a standard deviation of 25 percent per year, and T-bills pay 5 percent per year risk-free. Assume for simplicity that the portfolio pays no dividends (or that all dividends are reinvested).

   a. What fraction of the portfolio should be placed in bills? What fraction in equity?

   b. What should the manager do if the stock portfolio falls by 3 percent on the first day of trading?

5. In-The-Money Financial Services Corporation (ITM) is a small firm whose securities are not publicly traded. You are an analyst trying to estimate the value of ITM's common stock and bonds. You have estimated the market value of the firm's assets to be $2 million. The face value of its debt, all of which is going to mature one year from now, is $2 million. You estimate the standard deviation of the proportional change in the value of the assets to be .3 per year, and the riskless rate of interest is 10 percent per year.

   a. Write out the payoff to the equity holders at the maturity of the debt. In what way is the equity value like a call option?

   b. Use the Black-Scholes option pricing methodology and formula to price ITM's debt and equity, assuming that the total market value of the firm is currently $2 million.

   c. What would the be the effect of an increase in the standard deviation of the change in asset value on the values of the debt and equity, holding constant the value of the assets and the risk-free interest rate? A numerical answer is not required; just give the direction of change and your explanation.

6. Would you expect a $1 increase in a call option's exercise price to lead to a decrease in the option's value of more or less than $1?

7. The agricultural price support system guarantees farmers a minimum price for their output. Describe the program provisions as an option. What is the asset? The exercise price?

8. In what way is owning a corporate bond similar to writing a put option? A call option?

9. An executive compensation scheme might provide a bonus to a manager of $1,000 for every dollar by which the company's stock price exceeds some cutoff level. In what way is this arrangement equivalent to issuing the manager call options on the firm's stock?

10. We will derive a two-state *put* option value in this problem. Data: $S_0 = 100$; $X = 120$; $1 + r = 1.1$. The two possibilities for S_T are 140 and 80.

    a. Show that the range of S is 60 while that of P is 40 across the two states. What is the hedge ratio of the put?

b. Form a portfolio of two shares of stock and three puts. What is the (non-random) payoff to this portfolio? What is the present value of the portfolio?

c. Given that the stock currently is selling at 100, solve for the value of the put.

d. Would you exercise this put early?

e. Given your answers to parts c and d, what is the true value of the put?

f. What do you conclude about the possibility of early exercise?

11. (1987 CFA Examination, Level III) You are considering the sale of a call option with an exercise price of $100 and one year to expiration. The underlying stock pays no dividends, its current price is $100, and you believe it has a 50 percent chance of increasing to $120 and a 50 percent chance of decreasing to $80. The risk-free rate of interest is 10 percent.

a. Describe the specific steps involved in applying the binomial option pricing model to calculate the call option's value.

b. Compare the binomial option pricing model to the Black-Scholes option pricing model.

12. XYZ Corp. will pay a $2 per share dividend in two months. Its stock price currently is $60 per share. A call option on XYZ has an exercise price of $55 and three-month time to maturity. The risk-free interest rate is .5 percent per month, and the stock's volatility (standard deviation) = 7 percent per month. Find the pseudo-American option value. (Hint: Try defining one "period" as a month, rather than as a year.)

13. Suppose that the risk-free interest rate is zero. Would an American put option ever be exercised early. Explain.

14. You would like to be holding a protective put position on the stock of XYZ Co. to lock in a guaranteed minimum value of $100 at year-end. XYZ currently sells for $100. Over the next year the stock price will increase by 10 percent or decrease by 10 percent. The T-bill rate is 5 percent. Unfortunately, no put options are traded on XYZ Co.

a. Suppose that the desired put option is traded. How much would it cost to purchase?

b. What would have been the cost of the protective put portfolio?

c. What portfolio position in stock and T-bills will ensure you a payoff equal to the payoff that would be provided by a protective put with $X = 100$? Show that the payoff to this portfolio and the cost of establishing the portfolio match those of the desired protective put portfolio.

15. These three *put* options all are written on the same stock. One has a delta of $-.9$, one a delta of $-.5$, and one a delta of $-.1$. Assign deltas to the three puts by filling in this table:

Put	X	Delta
A	10	
B	20	
C	30	

16. You are *very* bullish (optimistic) on stock EFG, much more so than the rest of the market. In each question choose the portfolio strategy that will give you the greatest dollar profit if your bullish forecast turns out to be correct. Explain your answer.

   a. Choice A: $10,000 invested in calls with $X = 50$; choice B: $10,000 invested in EFG stock

   b. Choice A: 10 call options contracts (for 100 shares each), with $X = 50$; choice B: 1,000 shares of EFG stock

Futures and Forward Markets

$\mathbf{F}$utures and forward contracts are similar to options in that they specify purchase or sale of some underlying security at some future date. The key difference is that the holder of an option to buy is not compelled to buy and will not do so if it is to his or her disadvantage. A futures or forward contract, on the other hand, carries the obligation to go through with the agreed-on transaction. To see how futures and forwards work and how they might be useful, consider the portfolio diversification problem facing a farmer of a single crop, for example, wheat. The entire planting season's revenue depends critically upon the highly volatile crop price. The farmer cannot easily diversify his or her position because virtually his or her entire wealth is tied up in the crop.

The miller who must purchase wheat for processing faces a portfolio problem that is the mirror image of the farmer's. He or she is subject to profit uncertainty because of the unpredictable future cost of the wheat.

Both parties can reduce this source of risk if they enter into a **forward contract** requiring the farmer to deliver the wheat when harvested at a price agreed on now, regardless of the market price at harvest time. No money need change hands at this time. A forward contract is simply a deferred delivery sale of some asset with the sales price agreed on now. All that is required is that each party be willing to lock in the ultimate price to be paid or received for delivery of the commodity. A forward contract protects each party from future price fluctuations.

A forward contract is not an investment in the strict sense that funds are paid for an asset—it is only a commitment today to transact in the future. Forward arrangements are part of our study of investments, however, because they offer powerful means to hedge other investments and generally modify portfolio characteristics, as this farming example illustrates.

Forward markets for future delivery of various commodities go back at least to ancient Greece. Organized *futures markets*, though, are a relatively modern development, dating only to the nineteenth century. Futures markets replace informal forward contracts with highly standardized, exchange-traded securities.

This chapter describes the workings of futures markets, and the mechanics of trading in these markets. We show how futures contracts are useful investment vehicles for both hedgers and speculators, and how the futures price relates to the spot price of an asset. This chapter deals with both principles of futures markets in general and specific futures markets in some detail.

23.1   *The Futures Contract*

Futures markets formalize and standardize forward contracting. Buyers and sellers do not have to rely on fortuitous matching of their interests; they can trade in a centralized futures market. The futures exchange standardizes the types of **futures contract** that may be traded; it establishes contract size, the acceptable grade of commodity, contract delivery dates, and so forth. Although standardization eliminates much of the flexibility available in informal forward contracting, it has the offsetting advantage of liquidity. Futures contracts also differ from forward contracts in that they call for a daily settling of any gains or losses on the contract. In contrast, in forward contracts no money is exchanged until the delivery date.

In a centralized market, buyers and sellers can trade through brokers without personally searching for trading partners. The standardization of contracts and the depth of trading in each contract allow futures positions to be easily liquidated through a broker, rather than personally renegotiated with the other party to the contract. Because the exchange guarantees the performance of each party to the contract, costly credit checks on other traders are not necessary. Instead, each trader simply posts a good faith deposit, called the *margin*, to guarantee contract performance.

The Basics of Futures Contracts

The futures contract calls for delivery of a commodity at a specified delivery or maturity date, for an agreed-on price (called the *futures price*), to be paid at contract maturity. The contract specifies precise requirements for the commodity. For agricultural commodities, allowable grades (e.g., No. 2 hard winter wheat, or No. 1 soft red wheat) are set by the exchange. The place or means of delivery of the commodity is specified as well. For agricultural commodities, delivery is made by transfer of warehouse receipts issued by approved warehouses. For financial futures, delivery may be made by wire transfer; in the case of index futures, delivery may be accomplished by a cash settlement procedure similar to those for index options. (Although the futures contract technically calls for delivery of an asset, delivery in fact rarely occurs. Instead, traders much more commonly close out their positions before contract maturity, taking gains or losses in cash. We will examine how this is done shortly.)

Because the futures exchange completely specifies the terms of the contract, the traders need bargain only over the futures price. The trader taking the **long position** commits to purchasing the commodity on the delivery date, while the trader who takes the **short position** commits to delivering the commodity at contract maturity. The trader in the long position is said to ''buy'' a contract; the short-side trader ''sells'' a contract. We are using the words *buy* and *sell* loosely, because a contract is not really bought or sold like a stock or bond, but entered into by mutual agreement. At the time the contract is entered into, no money changes hands.

Figure 23.1 shows prices for several agricultural futures contracts on the Winnipeg Commodity Exchange as they appear in *The Globe and Mail*. The boldface line lists the commodity, the contract size, and the pricing unit. The first contract listed is for wheat. Each contract calls for delivery of 20 metric tons, and prices are quoted in dollars per ton. The next several rows detail price data for contracts expiring on various dates. The July 1992 maturity wheat contract, for example, opened during the day at a futures price of $102.90 per ton. The highest futures price during the day was $103.90, the lowest was $102.90, and the settlement price (a representative trading price during the last few minutes of trading) was $103.40. The settlement price increased by 30 cents from the previous trading day. The highest futures price over the contract's life to date was $119.80, and the lowest was $96. Finally, open interest, or the number of outstanding contracts, was 4,810. Similar information is given for each maturity date for all seven commodities traded on the exchange.

The trader holding the long position, who will purchase the good, profits from price increases. Suppose that in July the price of wheat turns out to be $105 per ton. The long-position trader who entered into the contract at the futures price of $103.40 on April 30 would pay the agreed-on $103.40 per ton to

FIGURE 23.1

Prices for Canadian commodity futures.

(From *The Globe and Mail*, May 1, 1992. Reprinted by permission.)

receive wheat that, at contract maturity, is worth $105 per ton in the market. Since each contract calls for delivery of 20 tons, ignoring brokerage fees, the profit to the long position equals 20($105 − $103.40) = $32. Conversely, the short position must deliver 20 tons of wheat, each with value $105, for the previously agreed-on futures price of only $103.40. The short position's loss equals the long position's gain.

To summarize, at maturity:

Profit to long = Spot price at maturity − Original futures price
Profit to short = Original futures price − Spot price at maturity

where the spot price is the actual market price of the commodity at the time of delivery.

Concept Check

Question 1. Graph the profit realized by an investor who enters the long side of a futures contract as a function of the price of the asset on the maturity date. Compare this graph to a graph of the profits realized by the purchaser of the asset itself. Next, try the same exercise for a short futures position and a short sale of the asset.

The futures contract is therefore a zero-sum game, with losses and gains to all positions netting out to zero. Every long position is offset by a short position. The aggregate profits to futures trading, summing over all investors, also must be zero, as is the net exposure to changes in the commodity price. For this reason, the establishment of a futures market in a commodity should not have a major impact on the spot market for that commodity. That is, a futures market in Canadian Tire stock, were it to be established, should not affect Canadian Tire's ability to raise money in the equity market.

Concept Check

Question 2. What is the difference between the futures price and the value of the futures contract?
Question 3. Evaluate the criticism that futures markets siphon off capital from more productive uses.

Existing Contracts

Futures and forward contracts are traded in the United States and other financial centres on a wide variety of goods in four broad categories: agricultural commodities, metals and minerals (including energy commodities), foreign cur-

TABLE 23.1 Futures Contracts, 1992

Foreign Currencies	Agricultural	Metals and Energy	Financial Futures
British pound	Corn	Copper	Eurodollars
Canadian dollar	Oats	Aluminum	Treasury bonds
Japanese yen	Soybeans	Gold	Treasury bills
Swiss franc	Soybean meal	Platinum	Treasury notes
French franc	Soybean oil	Palladium	Municipal bond index
Deutsche mark	Wheat	Silver	LIBOR
U.S. dollar index	Barley	Crude oil	S&P 500 index
European currency unit	Flaxseed	Heating oil	S&P mid-cap index
Australian dollar	Canola	Gas oil	NYSE index
Mark/yen cross rate	Rye	Natural gas	Value Line index
	Cattle (feeder)	Gasoline	Major market index
	Cattle (live)	Propane	OTC index
	Hogs	CRB index*	Nikkei index
	Pork bellies		Short gilt†
	Cocoa		Long gilt†
	Coffee		
	Cotton		
	Orange juice		
	Sugar		
	Lumber		
	Rice		

* The Commodity Research Bureau's index of futures prices of agricultural as well as metal and energy prices.
† Gilts are British government bonds.

From *Commodity Trading Manual*, Chicago Board of Trade, 1992.

rencies, and financial futures (fixed-income securities and stock market indices). The financial futures contracts are recent innovations, for which trading was introduced in 1975. Innovation in financial futures has been quite rapid and is ongoing. Table 23.1 enumerates the various contracts trading in the United States in 1992.

In Canada, futures contracts for several major agricultural commodities have been trading for a long time at the Winnipeg Commodity Exchange (WCE). The early 1980s saw the introduction of several precious metal, stock index, and interest rate futures, together with options on stock indices, foreign currencies, and bonds. By the end of the decade, most of these instruments had failed (see the accompanying box). By 1991, apart from the WCE the only active futures trading in Canada was in TSE 35 contracts in Toronto, and bankers' acceptances, Canada bond futures, and options on Canada bond futures in Montreal. Low liquidity, thin trading, and the ready availability of comparable financial instruments in the United States are major reasons for the relative failure of financial innovations in Canadian futures markets.[1]

---

[1] A more extensive treatment of the reasons for the failure of many new Canadian futures instruments can be found in E. Kirzner, "The Unfolding Derivative Securities Story: Abroad and in Canada," *Canadian Investment Review* 1, no. 1 (Fall 1988).

Montreal Exchange to Draw on Past for Futures

By Bud Jorgensen

Those who believe this country really needs commodity markets find a paradox in an apparent lack of interest by potential customers. After all, Canadians are supposed to be averse to risk.

Ken Broaderip, vice-president and national futures manager out of Toronto for Nesbitt Thomson Deacon, summed it up this way at a conference in Montreal a while back: "What's happened in Canada is somewhat of an embarrassment to our industry."

When compared with investors and financial managers in other countries, Canadians seem to have been slow to find advantages in commodity markets. Investment dealers will quickly reach this conclusion when they observe how much markets in Chicago and Philadelphia expanded during the 1980s. Meanwhile, Canadian efforts to develop commodity markets have produced extremely limited results.

Mr. Broaderip was delivering his assessment in Montreal because the Montreal Exchange has been the most persistent in trying to establish commodity markets. It used to be called the stock exchange, but the title was shortened to reflect this broader interest. The ME sponsors an annual gathering that attracts a respectable collection of experts in commodity trading from the major centres.

By apologizing before such a group, Mr. Broaderip seemed so, well, Canadian. His point, though, is a good one. Why are Canadians so seemingly slow to adopt a type of market that grew so rapidly elsewhere during the past decade?

Part of the answer is probably in the nature of the growth in commodity markets. The hot items were financial commodities. This was a direct result of the unpegging of convertible currencies.

Interestingly, the Canadian government was a pioneer in allowing the value of its currency to float against those of its trading partners. But such a move became significant to the world economy only when major currencies were set adrift.

Abandoning the fixed-rate system introduced massive uncertainties into world trade. The inevitable result was the development of ways to hedge against currency swings.

Futures or options on currencies quickly became an integral part of most trading arrangements. Strategies to hedge against changes in currency values are commonplace. It's now possible to buy a mutual fund containing securities in one country and a built-in hedge to ease the mind of an investor in another country.

Because currency reasons were the base for the growth in commodity markets, the fast-growing markets were in the major industrial countries. The dominant commodity markets in North America are in Chicago.

The Montreal Exchange tried during the 1980s to develop a futures market in Canadian dollars. Exchanges in Chicago and Philadelphia offered competing products. The U.S. exchanges won hands down. They had a head start in picking off the market on a secondary currency because they already had traders in commodity pits handling large volumes in futures or options on the major currencies.

When trying to develop the market in Canadian dollar futures, the ME made mistakes in design and strategy. Based on that experience, the ME has been much more thorough in its current efforts to develop futures and options contracts on Canadian government bonds.

Simply put, futures and options on bonds are a way of hedging against interest rate swings. This time, the ME is out in front with a contract that is similar to those for other government bonds and the ME's odds for success are greater.

As for the currency markets, the Canadian experience involves the history of the banking system. Canadian bankers had much more experience internationally than most of their American counterparts. With their large branch networks, the Cana-

(Continued)

dian banks were able to deliver foreign exchange expertise to businesses in small towns.

Treasurers at large Canadian companies learned to deal directly with brokers in financial commodities. It used to be common for Canadian companies to report losses on currency transactions, but no more. Institutional fund managers have become equally adept at hedging currency risk.

Somehow, domestic demand was never concentrated enough to get the Canadian financial institutions into the business at home in a big way. Domestic brokers were either not active in financial commodities or became minor players in foreign commodity markets.

Financial commodity markets may have been more efficient in providing currency hedges, but for smaller businesses, the banks were already there with long-established ways of dealing in currencies.

Now that the banks have investment dealer subsidiaries—thus employing about 80 percent of the brokers—they may take a different view of commodity markets.

From *The Globe and Mail*, January 23, 1991, by Bud Jorgensen. Reprinted by permission.

Outside the futures markets, a fairly developed network of banks and brokers has established a forward market in foreign exchange. This forward market is not a formal exchange in the sense that the exchange specifies the terms of the traded contract. Instead, participants in a forward contract may negotiate for delivery of any quantity of goods, as distinguished from futures markets where contract size is set by the exchange. In forward arrangements, banks and brokers simply negotiate contracts for clients (or themselves) as needed.

23.2 *Mechanics of Trading in Futures Markets*

The Clearinghouse and Open Interest

Trading in futures contracts is more complex than making ordinary stock transactions. If you want to make a stock purchase, your broker simply acts as an intermediary to enable you to buy shares from or sell to another individual through the stock exchange. In futures trading, however, the exchange plays a more active role.

When an investor contacts a broker to establish a futures position, the brokerage firm wires the order to the firm's trader on the floor of the futures exchange. In contrast to stock trading, which involves specialists or market makers in each security, futures trades take place among floor traders in the "trading pit" for each contract. Traders use voice or hand signals to signify their desire to buy or sell. Once a trader willing to accept the opposite side of a trade is located, the trade is recorded and the customer is notified.

At this point, just as is true for options contracts, the **clearinghouse** enters the picture. Rather than having the long and short traders hold contracts with each other, the clearinghouse becomes the seller of the contract for the long position and the buyer of the contract for the short position. The clearinghouse is obligated to deliver the commodity to the long position, and to pay for delivery from the short; consequently, the clearinghouse's position nets to zero. This arrangement makes the clearinghouse the trading partner of each trader, both long and short. The clearinghouse, bound to perform on its side of each contract, is the only party that can be hurt by the failure of any trader to fulfill the obligations of the futures contract. This arrangement is necessary, because a futures contract calls for future performance, which cannot be guaranteed as easily as an immediate stock transaction.

Figure 23.2**A** illustrates what would happen in the absence of the clearinghouse. The trader in the long position would be obligated to pay the futures price to the short position trader; the trader in the short position would be obligated to deliver the commodity. Figure 23.2**B** shows how the clearinghouse becomes an intermediary, acting as the trading partner for each side of the contract. The clearinghouse's position is neutral, since it takes a long and a short position for each transaction.

The existence of the clearinghouse enables traders to liquidate positions easily. If you are currently long in a contract and want to undo your position, you simply instruct your broker to enter the short side of a contract to close out your position. This is called a **reversing trade**. The exchange nets out your long and short positions, reducing your net position to zero. Your zero net position with the clearinghouse eliminates the need to fulfill at maturity either the original long or the reversing short position.

The **open interest** on the contract is the number of contracts outstanding. (Long and short positions are not counted separately, meaning that open interest can be defined as the number of either long or short contracts outstanding.)

FIGURE 23.2

A—trading without the clearinghouse.
B—trading with a clearinghouse.

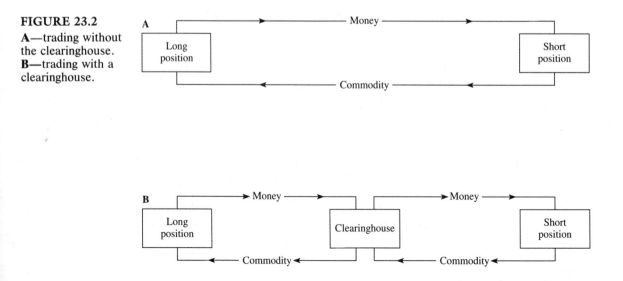

The clearinghouse's position nets out to zero, of course, and so is not counted in the computation of open interest. When contracts begin trading, open interest is zero. As time passes, open interest increases as progressively more contracts are entered. Almost all traders, however, liquidate their positions before the contract maturity date. Instead of actually taking or making delivery of the commodity, virtually all traders enter reversing trades to cancel their original positions, thereby realizing the profits or losses on the contract. Actual deliveries and purchases of commodities are then made via regular channels of supply. The percentage of contracts that result in actual delivery is estimated to range from less than 1 percent to 3 percent, depending on the commodity and the activity in the contract. The image of a trader awakening one delivery date with a hog in the front yard is amusing, but unlikely.

You can see the typical pattern of open interest in Figure 23.1. In the wheat or barley contracts, for example, the May delivery contracts are close to maturity and open interest is relatively small; most contracts have been reversed already. The next few maturities have significant open interest. Finally, the most distant maturity contract has little open interest, because the contract has only recently been available for trading.

Marking to Market and the Margin Account

Anyone who saw the film *Trading Places* knows that Eddie Murphy as a trader in orange juice futures had no intention of purchasing or delivering orange juice. Traders simply bet on the future price of juice. The total profit or loss realized by the long trader who buys a contract at time zero and closes, or reverses, it at time t is just the change in the futures price over the period $F_t - F_0$. Symmetrically, the short trader earns $F_0 - F_t$.

The process by which profits or losses accrue to traders is called **marking to market**. At initial execution of a trade, each trader establishes a margin account. The margin is a security account consisting of cash and/or near-cash securities, such as Treasury bills, which ensure that the trader is able to satisfy the obligations of the futures contract. Because both parties to a futures contract are exposed to losses, both must post margin. This is in contrast to options, where only the option writer has an obligation and thus needs to post margin. Because the margin may be satisfied with interest-earning securities, posting the margin does not impose a significant opportunity cost of funds on the trader. The initial margin is usually set between 5 percent and 10 percent of the total value of the contract. Contracts written on assets with more volatile prices require higher margins.

On any day that futures markets trade, futures prices may rise or fall. An increase in price benefits long positions that agreed to purchase the good at the lower price that was established when the contract was initiated; conversely, the price increase harms short positions that still must deliver the good at the originally agreed-on futures price. Instead of waiting until the maturity date for traders to realize all gains and losses, the clearinghouse requires all positions to recognize profits as they accrue daily. If the futures price of wheat at the WCE rises from $103 to $105 per ton, the clearinghouse credits the margin account of the long position for 20 tons (which is the standard size of the wheat-futures contract) multiplied by $2 per ton, or $40 per contract. Conversely, for the short position the clearinghouse takes this amount from the margin account for each contract held. This daily settling is marking to market.

Therefore, the maturity date of the contract does not govern realization of profit or loss. Marking to market ensures that, as futures prices change, the proceeds accrue to the trader's margin account immediately.

Concept Check	Question 4. What must be the net inflow or outlay from marking to the market for the clearinghouse? (Hint: what is the net position of the clearinghouse?)

If a trader accrues sustained losses from marking to market, the margin account may fall below a critical value called the **maintenance margin** or **variation margin**. Once the value of the account falls below this value, the trader receives a margin call. Either new funds must be transferred into the margin account, or the broker will close out enough of the trader's position to reduce the required margin for that position to a level at or below the trader's remaining margin. This procedure safeguards the position of the clearinghouse. Positions are closed out before the margin account is exhausted—any losses suffered by the trader are thereby covered.

Marking to market is the major way in which futures and forward contracts differ, besides contract standardization. Futures follow a pay- (or receive) as-you-go-method. Forward contracts are simply held until maturity, and no funds are transferred until that date, although the contracts may be traded.

It is important to note that the futures price on the delivery date will equal the spot price of the commodity on that date. Since a maturing contract calls for immediate delivery, the futures price on that day must equal the spot price— the cost of the commodity from the two competing sources is equalized in a competitive market.[2] You may obtain the delivery of the commodity either by purchasing it directly in the spot market or by entering the long side of a futures contract.

A commodity available from two sources (spot or futures market) must be priced identically, or else investors will rush to purchase it from the cheap source in order to sell it in the higher-priced market. Such arbitrage activity could not persist without prices adjusting to eliminate the arbitrage opportunity. Therefore, the futures price and spot price must converge at maturity. This is called the **convergence property**.

---

[2] Small differences between the spot and futures prices at maturity may persist because of transportation costs, but this is a minor factor.

Because of convergence, the profits realized over the life of futures and forward contracts are quite similar. Call f_0 the forward price at contract inception and P_T the spot price of the commodity on the maturity date T. The profit to the long position of the forward contract is $P_T - f_0$, that is, the difference between the value of the good received and the price that was contracted to be paid for it. The futures contract, by contrast, uses daily marking to market. The sum of all daily settlements will equal $F_T - F_0$, where F_T stands for the futures price at contract maturity. We have noted, however, that the futures price at maturity equals the spot price, so total futures profits also may be expressed as $P_T - F_0$. Summing the daily mark-to-market settlements results in a profit formula identical to that of the forward contract.

Because these payments accrue continually, we should not, strictly speaking, simply add them up to obtain total profits without first adjusting for interest on interim payments. Some empirical evidence, however, suggests that interest earnings on daily settlements have only a small effect on the determination of futures and forward prices. For this reason, we often ignore this fine point and simply take the profits or losses on a futures contract held to maturity to be $P_T - F_0$ for the long position, and $F_0 - P_T$ for the short. Section 23.4 explores this issue in greater detail.

Concept Check	Question 5. If futures prices are equally likely to go up as to go down on each trading day, what are the expected proceeds from marking to market? The expected interest earnings on those proceeds?

To illustrate the time profile of returns to a futures contract, consider an example for which the current futures price for silver for delivery five days from today is $7.60 per ounce (in U.S. dollars). Suppose that over the next five days the futures price evolves as follows:

Day	Futures Price
0 (today)	$7.60
1	$7.70
2	$7.75
3	$7.68
4	$7.68
5 (delivery)	$7.71

The spot price of silver on the delivery day is $7.71: the convergence property implies that the price of silver in the spot market must equal the futures price on delivery day.

The daily mark-to-market settlements for each contract held by the long position will be as follows:

Day	Profit (Loss) per Ounce	× 1,000 Ounces/Contract = Daily Proceeds
1	7.70 − 7.60 = .10	$100
2	7.75 − 7.70 = .05	$ 50
3	7.68 − 7.75 = −.07	−$ 70
4	7.68 − 7.68 = 0	0
5	7.71 − 7.68 = .03	$ 30
		$110

The profit on day 1 is the increase in the futures price from the previous day, or ($7.70 − $7.60) per ounce. Because each silver contract on the Chicago Board of Trade calls for purchase and delivery of 1,000 ounces, the total profit per contract is 1,000 multiplied by $.10, or $100. On day 3, when the futures price falls, the long position's margin account will be debited by $70. By day 5, the sum of all daily proceeds is $110. This is exactly equal to 1,000 times the difference between the final futures price of $7.71 and original futures price of $7.60. Thus the sum of all the daily proceeds (per ounce of silver held long) equals $P_T - F_0$.

Cash vs. Actual Delivery

Most futures markets call for delivery of an actual commodity, such as a particular grade of wheat or a specified amount of foreign currency, if the contract is not reversed before maturity. For agricultural commodities where quality of the delivered good may vary, the exchange sets quality standards as part of the futures contract. In some cases, contracts may be settled with higher- or lower-grade commodities. In these cases, a premium or discount is applied to the delivered commodity to adjust for the quality difference.

The availability of different grade commodities for delivery reduces the possibility of a *squeeze*. A squeeze occurs when enough long positions hold their contracts to maturity and demand actual delivery that supplies of the commodity are insufficient to cover all contracts. The longs in that case "corner the market." Squeezes have been quite rare in practice, and their legal implications for traders and the exchange are not yet settled. A short squeeze occurs when shorts accumulate a position and threaten to deliver some commodity that is costly to store.

Some futures contracts call for **cash delivery**. An example is a stock index futures contract where the underlying asset is an index such as the TSE 35 or the S&P 500 index. Delivery of every stock in the index clearly would be impractical. Hence the contract calls for "delivery" of a cash amount equal to the value that the index attains on the maturity date of the contract. The sum of all the daily settlements from marking to market results in the long position realizing total profits or losses of $S_T - F_0$, where S_T is the value of the stock index on the maturity date T, and F_0 is the original futures price. Cash settlement closely mimics actual delivery, the only difference being that the cash value of the asset rather than the asset itself is delivered by the short position in exchange for the futures price.

More concretely, the TSE 35 index contract calls for delivery of $500 multiplied by the value of the index. At maturity, the index might list at 200, a market value-weighted index of the prices of all 35 stocks in the index. The cash settlement contract calls for delivery of $500 × 200, or $100,000, in return for 500 times the futures price. This yields exactly the same profit as would result from directly purchasing 500 units of the index for $100,000 and then delivering it for 500 times the original futures price.

Regulations

Futures markets in Canada are under the jurisdiction of the provincial securities commissions, with the exception of grain futures traded on the WCE, which are subject to federal law. Most futures trading is self-regulated, although some provinces have passed commodity futures acts.

In the United States, futures markets are regulated by the Commodities Futures Trading Commission (CFTC), a federal agency. The CFTC sets capital requirements for member firms of the futures exchanges, authorizes trading in new contracts, and oversees maintenance of daily trading records.

The futures exchange sets limits on the amount by which futures prices may change from one day to the next. For example, the price limit on the TSE 35 futures contract is $4,500, corresponding to a change of 9 ($4500/$500) in the index. This means that if TSE 35 futures close today at 200, trades tomorrow in the TSE 35 index may vary only between 191 and 209. Likewise, the price limit on silver contracts traded on the Chicago Board of Trade is 20 cents, which means that if silver futures close today at $7.40 per ounce, trades in silver tomorrow may vary only between $7.20 and $7.60 per ounce. The exchanges may increase or reduce price limits in response to perceived increases or decreases in price volatility of the contract. Price limits are often eliminated as contracts approach maturity, usually in the last month of trading.

Price limits traditionally are viewed as a means to limit violent price fluctuations. This reasoning seems dubious. Suppose that an international monetary crisis overnight drives up the spot price of silver to $8.50. No one would sell silver futures at prices for future delivery as low as $7.40. Instead, the futures price would rise each day by the 20-cent limit, although the quoted price would represent only an unfilled bid order—no contracts would trade at the low quoted price. After several days of limit moves of 20 cents per day, the futures price would finally reach its equilibrium level, and trading would occur again. This process means no one could unload a position until the price reached its equilibrium level. This example shows that price limits offer no real protection against price fluctuation.

Taxation

Because of the mark-to-market procedure, investors do not have control over the tax year in which they realize gains or losses. Instead, price changes are realized gradually, with each daily settlement. Therefore, taxes are paid at year-end on accumulated profits or losses, regardless of whether the position has been closed out.

23.3   *Futures Markets Strategies*

Hedging and Speculating

Hedging and speculating are two polar uses of futures markets. A speculator uses a futures contract to profit from movements in futures prices; a hedger, to protect against price movement.

If speculators believe that prices will increase, they will take a long position for expected profits. Conversely, they exploit expected price declines by taking a short position. As an example of a speculative strategy, suppose someone thinks that silver futures prices, currently at $7.20 U.S. per ounce, will rise to $7.50 by month's end. Each silver contract on the Chicago Board of Trade (CBT) calls for delivery of 1,000 ounces. If the silver futures price does in fact increase to $7.50, the speculator profits by 1,000 multiplied by $.30, or $300 per contract. If the forecast is incorrect and silver prices decline, the investor loses 1,000 times the decrease in the futures price for each contract purchased. Speculators bet on the direction of futures price movements.

Why does a speculator buy a silver futures contract? Why not buy silver directly? One reason lies in transaction costs, which are far smaller in futures markets. Another reason is storage costs. Holding silver in inventory directly and insuring it is needlessly expensive when futures contracts may be used instead. A third reason is the leverage that futures trading provides. Each silver contract calls for delivery of 1,000 ounces of silver, worth about $7,200 in our example. The initial margin required for this account might be only $1,000. The $300 per contract gain on the silver translates into a 30 percent ($300/$1,000) return, despite the fact that the silver futures price increases only 4.2 percent ($.30/$7.20). Futures margins, therefore, allow speculators to achieve much greater leverage than is available from direct trading in the commodity.

Hedgers, by contrast, use futures markets to immunize themselves from price movements. Holders of silver (e.g., jewelers) might want to protect the value of their inventory against price fluctuations. In this case, they have no desire to bet on price movements in either direction. To achieve such protection, a hedger takes a short position in silver futures, which obligates the hedger to deliver silver at the contract maturity date for the current futures price. This locks in the sales price for the silver and guarantees that the total value (per ounce) of the silver-plus-futures position at the maturity date is the current futures price.

For illustration, suppose that the futures price for delivery next year is $7.80, and that the only three possible year-end prices per ounce are $7.40,

$7.80, and $8.20. If investors currently hold 10,000 ounces of silver, they would take short positions in 10 contracts, each for 1,000 ounces. Protecting the value of an asset with short futures positions is called *short hedging*. Note that the futures position requires no current investment. (We can ignore the margin requirement in the initial investment because it is small relative to the size of the contract, and because it may be posted in interest-bearing securities and so does not present a time-value or opportunity cost.)

Next year, the profits from the short futures position will be 10,000 times any decrease in the futures price, or the sum of the mark-to-market settlements. At maturity the final futures price will equal the spot price of silver because of convergence. Hence the futures profit will be 10,000 times $(F_0 - P_T)$, where P_T is the price of silver on the delivery date and F_0 is the original futures price, $7.80. For the three possible price outcomes, the total portfolio value equals:

	Silver Price at Year-End		
	$7.40	**$7.80**	**$8.20**
Silver holdings (value = 1,000 P_T)	$74,000	$78,000	$82,000
Futures profits or losses	$ 4,000	0	-$ 4,000
TOTAL	$78,000	$78,000	$78,000

Note that the total portfolio value is unaffected by the year-end silver price. The gains or losses on the silver holdings are exactly offset by those on the ten contracts held short. For example, if silver prices fall to $7.40 per ounce, the losses on the silver inventory are offset by the $4,000 gain on the futures contracts. That profit equals the difference between the futures price on the maturity date (which is the spot price of $7.40) and the originally contracted futures price of $7.80. For short contracts, a profit of $.40 per ounce is realized from the fall in the spot price. Because each contract calls for delivery of 10,000 ounces, this results in a $4,000 gain that offsets the decline in the value of silver held. A hedger, in contrast to a speculator, is indifferent to the ultimate price of the spot commodity. The short-hedger who has arranged to sell the commodity for an agreed-on price need not be concerned about further developments in the market price.

To generalize this numerical example, you can note that the silver will be worth P_T at maturity, while the profit on the futures contract is $F_0 - P_T$. The sum of the two positions is therefore F_0 dollars, which is independent of the eventual silver price.

A *long hedge* is the analogue to a short hedge for a purchaser of a commodity. A company that will purchase silver at year-end can lock in the total cost of the purchase by entering the long side of a contract, which commits it to purchasing at the currently determined futures price.

Exact futures hedging may be impossible for some goods because the necessary futures contract is not traded. For example, producers of bauxite, the ore from which aluminum is made, might like to trade in bauxite futures but cannot. Because bauxite and aluminum prices are highly correlated, however, a close hedge may be established by shorting aluminum futures. Hedging a position using futures on another commodity is called *cross hedging*.

Concept Check	Question 6. What are the sources of risk to an investor who uses aluminum futures to hedge an inventory of bauxite?

Futures contracts may be used also as general portfolio hedges. Bodie and Rosansky[3] show that commodity futures returns have had a negative correlation with the stock market. Investors may add a diversified portfolio of futures contracts to a diversified stock portfolio to lower the standard deviation of the overall rate of return. Moreover, the average rate of increase in commodity futures prices has been roughly the same as for common stocks as these figures show:

	1950–1976	
	Average Annual Return (%)	Annual Standard Deviation (%)
Portfolio of T-bills and 23 commodity futures	13.85	22.43
S&P 500 index	13.05	18.95

The correlation coefficient between the two portfolios during the estimation period was $-.24$. This implies that long positions in commodity futures would add substantial diversification benefits to a stock portfolio.

To illustrate, suppose that you invest a fraction of your total wealth in stocks and use the remainder to invest in commodity futures contracts, posting 100 percent margin with T-bills. The stock-futures-bills portfolio presents you with substantial reduction in risk and no sacrifice in expected return. Bodie and Rosansky found that a portfolio composed of 60 percent stock and 40 percent T-bills with futures would have had a return of 13.36 percent and standard deviation of only 12.68 percent: virtually an unchanged average return from either portfolio taken alone, but with roughly a one-third reduction in standard deviation.

Commodity futures are also inflation hedges. When commodity prices increase because of unanticipated inflation, returns from long futures positions will increase because the contracts call for delivery of goods for the price agreed on before the high inflation rate became a reality. A more direct means of hedging inflation is offered by a new contract on the Consumer Price Index, to be discussed later in this chapter.

---

[3] Zvi Bodie and Victor Rosansky, "Risk and Return in Commodity Futures," *Financial Analysts Journal*, May/June 1980.

Basis Risk and Hedging

The **basis** is the difference between the futures price and the spot price. As we have noted, on the maturity date of a contract the basis must be zero: the convergence property implies that $F_T - P_T = 0$. Before maturity, however, the futures price for later delivery may differ substantially from the current spot price.

We discussed the case of a short hedger who holds an asset and a short position to deliver that asset in the future. If the asset and futures contract are held until maturity, the hedger bears no risk, because the ultimate value of the portfolio on the delivery date is determined completely by the current futures price. Risk is eliminated because the futures price and spot price at contract maturity must be equal: gains and losses on the futures and the commodity position will exactly cancel. If the contract and asset are to be liquidated early, however, the hedger bears **basis risk**, because the futures price and spot price need not move in perfect lockstep at all times before the delivery date. In this case, gains and losses on the contract and the asset need not exactly offset each other.

Some speculators try to profit from movements in the basis. Rather than betting on the direction of the futures or spot prices per se, they bet on the changes in the difference between the two. A long spot–short futures position will profit when the basis narrows. For example, consider an investor holding 1,000 ounces of silver, who is short one silver futures contract. Silver might sell for $7.20 per ounce, while the futures price for next-year delivery is $7.80. The basis is therefore 60 cents. Tomorrow, the silver spot price might increase to $7.24, while the futures price might increase to $7.81. The basis has narrowed from 60 cents to 57 cents. The investor realizes a capital gain of 4 cents per ounce on her silver holdings, and a loss of 1 cent per ounce from the increase in the futures price. The net gain is the decrease in basis, or 3 cents per ounce.

A related strategy is a **spread** position where the investor takes a long position in a futures contract of one maturity and a short position in a contract on the same commodity, but with a different maturity. Profits accrue if the difference in futures prices between the two contracts changes in the hoped-for direction; that is, if the futures price on the contract held long increases by more (or decreases by less) than the futures price on the contract held short.

23.4   *The Determination of Futures Prices*

The Spot-Futures Parity Theorem

We have seen that a futures contract can be used to hedge changes in the value of the underlying asset. If the hedge is perfect, meaning that the asset-plus-futures portfolio has no risk, then the hedged position must provide a rate of return equal to the rate on other risk-free investments. Otherwise, there will be arbitrage opportunities that investors will exploit until prices are brought back into line. This insight can be used to derive the theoretical relationship between a futures price and the price of its underlying asset.

Suppose, for example, that the TSE 35 index currently is at 200 and an investor who holds $200 in a mutual fund indexed to the TSE 35 wishes to temporarily hedge her exposure to market risk. Assume that the indexed portfolio pays dividends totaling $4 over the course of the year and, for simplicity, that all dividends are paid at year end. Finally, assume that the futures price for year-end delivery on the TSE 35 contract is 208.[4] Let's examine the end-of-year proceeds for various values of the stock index if the investor hedges her portfolio by entering the short side of the futures contract.

Value of stock portfolio	$195	$200	$205	$210	$215	$220
Payoff from short futures position	13	8	3	−2	−7	−12
(equals $F_0 - F_T = \$208 - S_T$)						
Dividend income	4	4	4	4	4	4
TOTAL	$212	$212	$212	$212	$212	$212

The payoff from the short futures position equals the difference between the original futures price, $208, and the year-end stock price. This is due to convergence: the futures price at contract maturity will equal the stock price at that time.

Notice that the overall position is perfectly hedged. Any increase in the value of the indexed stock portfolio is offset by an equal decrease in the payoff of the short futures position, resulting in a final value independent of the stock price. The $212 payoff is the sum of the current futures price, $F_0 = \$208$, and the $4 dividend. It is as though the investor arranged to sell the stock at year-end for the current futures price, thereby eliminating price risk and locking in total proceeds equal to the sales price plus dividends paid before the sale.

What rate of return is earned on this riskless position? The stock investment requires an initial outlay of $200, while the futures position is established without an initial cash outflow. Therefore, the $200 portfolio grows to a year-end value of $212, providing a rate of return of 6 percent. More generally, a total investment of S_0, the current stock price, grows to a final value of $F_0 + D$, where D is the dividend payout on the portfolio. The rate of return is therefore

$$\text{Rate of return on perfectly hedged stock portfolio} = \frac{(F_0 + D) - S_0}{S_0}$$

This return is essentially riskless. We observe F_0 at the beginning of the period when we enter the futures contract. While dividend payouts are not perfectly riskless, they are highly predictable over short periods, especially for diversi-

---

[4] Actually, the futures contract calls for delivery of $500 times the value of the TSE 35 index, so that each contract would be settled for $500 times 208. We will simplify by assuming that you can buy a contract for one unit rather than 500 units of the index. In practice, one contract would hedge about $500 × 200 = $100,000 worth of stock. Of course, institutional investors would consider a stock portfolio of this size to be quite small.

fied portfolios. Any uncertainty is *extremely* small compared to the uncertainty in stock prices.

Presumably, 6 percent must be the rate of return available on other riskless investments. If not, then investors would face two competing risk-free strategies with different rates of return, a situation that could not last. Therefore, we conclude that

$$\frac{(F_0 + D) - S_0}{S_0} = r_f.$$

Rearranging, we find that the futures price must be

$$F_0 = S_0(1 + r_f) - D = S_0(1 + r_f - d) \qquad \qquad \textbf{(23.1)}$$

where d is the dividend yield on the stock portfolio, defined as D/S_0. This result is called the **spot-futures parity theorem.** It gives the normal or theoretically correct relationship between spot and futures prices.

Suppose that parity were violated. For example, suppose the risk-free interest rate in the economy were only 5 percent, so that according to parity, the futures price should be $\$200(1 + .05) - \$4 = \$206$. The actual futures price, $F_0 = \$208$, is \$2 higher than its "appropriate" value. This implies that an investor can make arbitrage profits by shorting the relatively overpriced futures contract, and buying the relatively underpriced stock portfolio using money borrowed at the 5 percent market interest rate. The proceeds from this strategy would be as follows:

Action	Initial Cash Flow	Cash Flow in One Year
Borrow $200, repay with interest in one year	+$200	$-200(1.05) = -\$210$
Buy stock for $200	−$200	$S_T + \$4$ dividend
Enter short futures position ($F_0 = \$208$)	0	$\$208 - S_T$
TOTAL	0	$2

The net initial investment of the strategy is zero. But its cash flow in one year is positive and riskless. The payoff is \$2 regardless of the stock price. This payoff is precisely equal to the mispricing of the futures contract relative to its parity value.

When parity is violated, the strategy to exploit the mispricing produces an arbitrage profit—a riskless profit requiring no initial net investment. If such an opportunity existed, all market participants would rush to take advantage of it. The results? The stock price would be bid up, and/or the futures price offered down until equation 23.1 is satisfied. A similar analysis applies to the possibility that F_0 is less than \$206. In this case, you simply reverse the strategy above to earn riskless profits. We conclude, therefore, that in a well-functioning market in which arbitrage opportunities are competed away, $F_0 = S_0(1 + r_f) - D$.

The parity relationship also is called the **cost-of-carry relationship** because it asserts that the futures price is determined by the relative costs of buying a stock with deferred delivery in the futures market versus buying it in the spot market with immediate delivery and ''carrying'' it in inventory. If you buy the stock now, you tie up your funds and incur a time-value-of-money cost of r_f per period. On the other hand, you receive dividend payments with a current yield of d. The net carrying-cost advantage of deferring delivery of the stock is therefore $r_f - d$ per period. This advantage must be offset by a differential between the futures price and the spot price. The price differential just offsets the cost-of-carry advantage when $F_0 = S_0(1 + r_f - d)$.

The parity relationship is easily generalized to multiperiod applications. We simply recognize that the difference between the futures and spot prices will be larger as the maturity of the contract is longer. This reflects the longer period to which we apply the net cost of carry. For contract maturity of T periods, the parity relationship is

$$F_0 = S_0(1 + r_f - d)^T \qquad \textbf{(23.2)}$$

While we have described parity in terms of stocks and stock index futures, it should be clear that the logic applies as well to any financial futures contract. For gold futures, for example, we would simply set the dividend yield to zero. For bond contracts, we would let the coupon income on the bond play the role of dividend payments. In both cases, the parity relationship would be essentially the same as equation 23.2.

The arbitrage strategy described above should convince you that these parity relationships are more than just theoretical results. Any violations of the parity relationship give rise to arbitrage opportunities that can provide large profits to traders. We will see shortly that index arbitrage in the stock market is a tool to exploit violations of the parity relationship for stock index futures contracts.

| Concept Check | Question 7. What are the three steps of the arbitrage strategy if F_0 is equal to \$205? Work out the cash flows of the strategy now and in one year in a table like the one on page 811. |

Spreads

Just as we can predict the relationship between spot and futures prices, there are similar methods to determine the proper relationships among futures prices for contracts of different maturity dates. These relationships are simple generalizations of the spot-futures parity relationship. We will restrict ourselves to stock futures in this discussion, and thus avoid the additional complications that arise from non-interest carrying costs.

Call $F(T_1)$ the current futures price for delivery at date T_1, and $F(T_2)$ the futures price for delivery at T_2. Let d be the dividend yield of the stock between

CHAPTER 23 Futures and Forward Markets 813

T_1 and T_2. We know from the parity equation 23.2 that

$$F(T_1) = S_0(1 + r_f - d)^{T_1}$$
$$F(T_2) = S_0(1 + r_f - d)^{T_2}$$

As a result,

$$F(T_2)/F(T_1) = (1 + r_f - d)^{(T_2 - T_1)}$$

Therefore, the basic parity relationship for spreads is

$$F(T_2) = F(T_1)(1 + r_f - d)^{(T_2 - T_1)} \tag{23.3}$$

Note that equation 23.3 is quite similar to the spot-futures parity relationship. The major difference is in the substitution of $F(T_1)$ for the current spot price. The intuition is also similar. Delaying delivery from T_1 to T_2 provides the long position with the knowledge that the stock will be purchased for $F(T_2)$ dollars at T_2 but does not require that money be tied up in the stock until T_2. The savings realized are the cost of carry between T_1 and T_2 of the money that would have been paid at T_1. Delaying delivery from T_1 until T_2 frees up $F(T_1)$ dollars, which earn risk-free interest at rate r_f. The delayed delivery of the stock also results in the lost dividend yield between T_1 and T_2. The net cost of carry saved by delaying the delivery is thus $r_f - d$. This gives the proportional increase in the futures price that is required to compensate market participants for the delayed delivery of the stock and postponement of the payment of the futures price. If the parity condition for spreads is violated, arbitrage opportunities will arise. (Problem 5 at the end of the chapter explores this phenomenon.)

To see how to use equation 23.3, consider the following data for a hypothetical contract:

Contract Maturity Date	Futures Price
January	105
March	106

Suppose that the effective annual T-bill rate is expected to persist at 10 percent and that the dividend yield is 4 percent per year. The "correct" March futures price relative to the January price is, according to equation 23.3,

$$105(1 + .1 - .04)^{1/6} = 106.025$$

The actual March futures price is 106, meaning that the March futures is slightly underpriced compared to the January futures, and that, aside from transaction costs, an arbitrage opportunity seems to be present.

Equation 23.3 shows that futures prices should all move together. Actually, it is not surprising that futures prices for different maturity dates move in unison, because all are linked to the same spot price through the parity relationship. Figure 23.3 plots futures prices on gold for three maturity dates. It is apparent that the prices move in virtual lockstep and that the more distant delivery dates require higher futures prices, as equation 23.3 predicts.

FIGURE 23.3

Futures prices in
January 1986 for
kilo gold contracts
maturing in
February, June, and
December 1986.

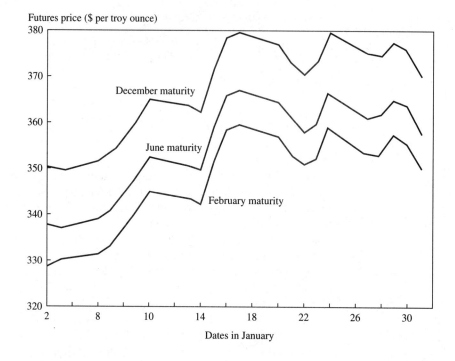

Forward vs. Futures Pricing

Until now we have paid little attention to the differing time profile of returns of
futures and forward contracts. Instead, we have taken the sum of daily mark-
to-market proceeds to the long position as $P_T - F_0$ and assumed for convenience that the entire profit to the futures contract accrues on the delivery date.
The parity theorems we have derived apply strictly to forward pricing because
they are predicated on the assumption that contract proceeds are realized only
on delivery. Although this treatment is appropriate for a forward contract, the
actual timing of cash flows influences the determination of the futures price.

Futures prices will deviate from parity values when marking to market gives
a systematic advantage to either the long or short position. If marking to market
tends to favour the long position, for example, the futures price should exceed
the forward price, since the long position will be willing to pay a premium for
the advantage of marking to market.

When will marking to market favour either the long or short trader? A trader
will benefit if daily settlements are received when the interest rate is high, and
paid when the interest rate is low. Receiving payments when the interest rate is
high allows investment of proceeds at a high rate; traders therefore prefer a
high correlation between the level of the interest rate and the payments received from marking to market. The long position will benefit if futures prices
tend to rise when interest rates are high. In such circumstances, the long trader
will be willing to accept a higher futures price. Whenever there is a positive
correlation between interest rates and changes in futures prices, the "fair"
futures price will exceed the forward price. Conversely, a negative correlation

means that marking to market favours the short position and implies that the equilibrium futures price should be below the forward price.

In practice, however, it appears that the covariance between futures prices and interest rates is low enough so that futures prices and forward prices differ by negligible amounts. In estimating the theoretically appropriate difference in futures and forward prices on foreign exchange contracts, Cornell and Reinganum[5] found that the mark-to-market premium is so small that contracts as quoted do not carry enough decimal points to reflect the predicted difference in the two prices.

23.5 *Futures Prices vs. Expected Spot Prices*

So far we have considered the relationship between futures prices and the current spot price. One of the oldest controversies in the theory of futures pricing concerns the relationship between futures price and the expected value of the spot price of the commodity at some *future* date. Three traditional theories have been put forth: the expectations hypothesis, normal backwardation, and contango. Today's consensus is that all of these traditional hypotheses are subsumed by the insights provided by modern portfolio theory. Figure 23.4 shows the expected path of futures prices under the three traditional hypotheses.

Expectations Hypothesis

The *expectations hypothesis* is the simplest theory of futures pricing. It states that the futures price equals the expected value of the future spot price of the asset: $F_0 = E(P_T)$. Under this theory, the expected profit to either position of a futures contract would equal zero: the short position's expected profit is $F_0 - E(P_T)$, while the long's is $E(P_T) - F_0$. With $F_0 = E(P_T)$, the expected profit to either side is zero. This hypothesis relies on a notion of risk neutrality. If all market participants are risk neutral, they should agree on a futures price that provides an expected profit of zero to all parties.

The expectations hypothesis bears a resemblance to market equilibrium in a world with no uncertainty; that is, if prices of goods at all future dates are currently known, then the futures price for delivery at any particular date would simply equal the currently known future spot price for that date. It is a tempting but incorrect leap to assert next that under uncertainty the futures price should equal the currently expected spot price. This view ignores the risk

[5] Bradford Cornell and Marc R. Reinganum, "Forward and Futures Prices: Evidence from the Foreign Exchange Markets," *Journal of Finance* 36 (December 1981).

FIGURE 23.4

Futures price for delivery at the end of the harvest, in the special case that the expected spot price remains unchanged.

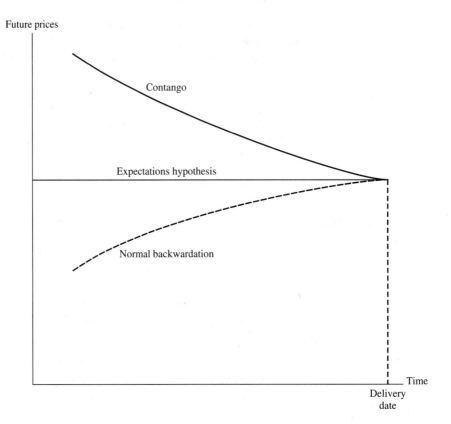

premiums that must be built into futures prices when ultimate spot prices are uncertain.

Normal Backwardation

This theory is associated with the famous British economists, John Maynard Keynes and John Hicks. They argued that for most commodities there are natural hedgers who desire to shed risk. For example, wheat farmers will desire to shed the risk of uncertain wheat prices. These farmers will take short positions to deliver wheat in the future at a guaranteed price; they will short hedge. In order to induce speculators to take the corresponding long positions, the farmers need to offer them an expectation of profit. Speculators will enter the long side of the contract only if the futures price is below the expected spot price of wheat, for an expected profit of $E(P_T) - F_0$. The speculator's expected profit is the farmer's expected loss, but farmers are willing to bear the expected loss on the contract in order to shed the risk of uncertain wheat prices. The theory of *normal backwardation* thus suggests that the futures price will be bid down to a level below the expected spot price, and will rise over the life of the contract until the maturity date, at which point $F_T = P_T$.

Although this theory recognizes the important role of risk premiums in futures markets, it is based on total variability rather than on systematic risk.

(This is not surprising, as Keynes wrote almost 40 years before the development of modern portfolio theory.) The modern view refines the measure of risk used to determine appropriate risk premiums.

Contango

The polar hypothesis to backwardation holds that the natural hedgers are the purchasers of a commodity, rather than the suppliers. In the case of wheat, for example, we would view grain processors as willing to pay a premium to lock in the price that they must pay for wheat. These processors hedge by taking a long position in the futures market; they are long hedgers, as opposed to farmers, who are short hedgers. Because long hedgers will agree to pay high futures prices to shed risk, and because speculators must be paid a premium to enter into the short position, the *contango* theory holds that F_0 must exceed $E(P_T)$.

It is clear that any commodity will have both natural long hedgers and short hedgers. The compromise traditional view, called the *net hedging hypothesis*, is that F_0 will be less than $E(P_T)$ when short hedgers outnumber long hedgers, and vice versa. The strong side of the market will be the side (short or long) that has more natural hedgers. The strong side must pay a premium to induce speculators to enter into enough contracts to balance the "natural" supply of long and short hedgers.

Modern Portfolio Theory

The three traditional hypotheses all envision a mass of speculators willing to enter either side of the futures market if they are sufficiently compensated for the risk they incur. Modern portfolio theory fine-tunes this approach by refining the notion of risk used in the determination of risk premiums. Simply put, if commodity prices pose positive systematic risk, futures prices must be lower than expected spot prices.

As an example of the use of modern portfolio theory to determine the equilibrium futures price, consider once again a stock paying no dividends. If $E(P_T)$ denotes today's expectation of the time T price of the stock, and k denotes the required rate of return on the stock, then the price of the stock today must equal the present value of its expected future payoff as follows:

$$P_0 = \frac{E(P_T)}{(1 + k)^T} \tag{23.4}$$

We also know from the spot-futures parity relationship that

$$P_0 = \frac{F_0}{(1 + r_f)^T} \tag{23.5}$$

Therefore, the right-hand sides of equation 23.4 and 23.5 must be equal. Equating these terms allows us to solve for F_0:

$$F_0 = E(P_T) \left(\frac{1 + r_f}{1 + k} \right)^T \tag{23.6}$$

You can see immediately from equation 23.6 that F_0 will be less than the expectation of P_T whenever k is greater than r_f, which will be the case for any positive-beta asset. This means that the long side of the contract will make an expected profit [F_0 will be lower than $E(P_T)$] when the commodity exhibits positive systematic risk (k is greater than r_f).

Why should this be? A long futures position will provide a profit (or loss) of $P_T - F_0$. If the ultimate realization of P_T involves positive systematic or non-diversifiable risk, the profit to the long position also involves such risk. Speculators with well-diversified portfolios will be willing to enter long futures positions only if they receive compensation for bearing that risk in the form of positive expected profits. Their expected profits will be positive only if $E(P_T)$ is greater than F_0. The converse is that the short position's profit is the negative of the long's and will have negative systematic risk. Diversified investors in the short position will be willing to suffer an expected loss in order to lower portfolio risk and will be willing to enter the contract even when F_0 is less than $E(P_T)$. Therefore, if P_T has positive beta, F_0 must be less than the expectation of P_T. The analysis is reversed for negative-beta commodities.

Concept Check

> **Question 8.** What must be true of the risk of the spot price of an asset if the futures price is an unbiased estimate of the ultimate spot price?

23.6   *Stock Index Futures*

The Contracts

In contrast to most futures contracts, which call for delivery of a specified commodity, stock index contracts are settled by a cash amount equal to the value of the stock index in question on the contract maturity date times a multiplier that scales the size of the contract. The total profit to the long position is $S_T - F_0$, where S_T is the value of the stock index on the maturity date. Cash settlement avoids the costs that would be incurred if the short trader had to purchase the stocks in the index and deliver them to the long position, and if the long position then had to sell the stock for cash. Instead, the long trader's profit is $S_T - F_0$ dollars, and the short trader's is $F_0 - S_T$ dollars. These profits duplicate those that would arise with actual delivery.

As noted earlier, the only index futures contract currently trading in Canada is the TSE 35, which trades in the Toronto Futures Exchange (TFE) with a multiplier equal to $500. Several other index futures were introduced in the past by the TFE and the Montreal Exchange (ME), but did not meet with any success. Table 23.2 shows the evolution of the trading volume of the various

TABLE 23.2 Toronto Futures Exchange Trading, 1985–1990

Volume Traded in	1990	1989	1988	1987	1986	1985
91-day T-bills	0	0	0	0	9,802	9,463
Long-term bond 18 Yr*	0	0	0	0	13	25,224
Long-term bond II 15 Yr	0	0	0	1	2,315	9,036
U.S. dollar	0	0	0	0	18	9,032
Silver options	956	5,325	7,188	35,186	21,132	75,856
11¾% bond options	0	0	0	5,663	39,389	6,309
9% bond options	0	0	0	19,532	3,833	
8¾% bond options	0	0	0	184	244	
TSE 300 composite index	0	0	0	6,373	51,491	25,050
TSE 300 spot index	22	1,191	654	25,187	75,081	23,680
Toronto 35 index†	52,687	34,814	27,284	35,524		
TSE oil & gas index	0	0	0	0	795	3,307
TSE oil and gas spot index	0	0	0	12	67	424
Continental BK mortgage WT‖	0	0	30	7	11,586	48,164
National Bank WT§	0	0	0	0	3,358	4,877
Bank of British Columbia WT‡	0	0	0	0	8,000	42,900
TOTAL	53,665	41,330	35,156	127,669	227,124	283,322
Total transactions	19,700	17,294	12,537	35,378	30,361	23,728
Average daily volume traded	213	165	140	508	901	1,124
Average volume per trade	2.7	2.4	2.8	3.6	7.5	11.9
TFE open interest at year-end	890	1,850	1,429	2,270	3,637	4,754
Number of TFE members	193	198	196	194	192	195
Number of active dealer-members	23	26	26	26	21	22

* Delisted February 1986
† Listed May 27, 1987
‡ Delisted August 29, 1988
§ Delisted February 20, 1990
‖ Delisted January 23, 1990

Source: Toronto Stock Exchange, *1990 Official Trading Statistics*.

futures and other derivatives traded on the TFE from 1985 to the end of 1990, by which time only the TSE 35 index futures contract still had any appreciable trading volume.

In the United States, however, there are several stock index futures contracts currently traded. Table 23.3 lists the major ones, showing under contract size the multiplier used to calculate contract settlements. An S&P 500 contract, for example, with a futures price of 250 and a final index value of 255 would result in a profit for the long side of $500 \times (255 - 250) = \$2,500$.

The broad-based U.S. stock market indices are all highly correlated. Table 23.4 presents a correlation matrix for four indices calculated over the 20-year period ending in 1981. The only index whose correlation with the others is below .90 is the Value Line index. This index uses an equally weighted average of 1,700 firms, as opposed to the NYSE or S&P indices, which use market value weights. This means that the Value Line contract overweights small firms compared to the other indices, which may explain the lower observed correlation.

TABLE 23.3   Stock Index Futures

Contract	Underlying Market Index	Contract Size	Exchange
S&P 500	Standard & Poor's 500 index. A value-weighted arithmetic average of 500 stocks.	$500 times the S&P 500 index	Chicago Mercantile Exchange
Value Line	Value Line Composite Average. An equally weighted average of about 1,700 firms.	$500 times the Value Line index	Kansas City Board of Trade
NYSE	NYSE Composite Index. Value-weighted arithmetic average of all stocks listed on the NYSE.	$500 times the NYSE index	New York Futures Exchange
Major Market	Price-weighted arithmetic average of 20 blue-chip stocks. Index is designed to track the Dow Jones Industrial Average.	$250 times the Major Market Index	Chicago Board of Trade
S&P Mid-Cap	Index of 400 firms of mid-range market value.	$500 times the Index	Chicago Mercantile Exchange
National Over-the-Counter	Value-weighted arithmetic average of 100 of the largest over-the-counter stocks.	$500 times the OTC index	Philadelphia Board of Trade
Nikkei	Nikkei 225 stock average.	$5 times the Nikkei Index	Chicago Mercantile Exchange
FT-SE 100	Financial Times-Share Exchange Index of 100 U.K. firms.	£25 times the FT-SE index	London International Financial Futures Exchange
FT-SE Eurotrack 100	Index of 100 non-U.K. European firms.	50 Deutschemarks times the Index	London International Financial Futures Exchange

Creating Synthetic Stock Positions

One reason why stock index futures are so popular is that they substitute for holdings in the underlying stocks themselves. Index futures let investors participate in broad market movements without actually buying or selling large numbers of stocks.

TABLE 23.4   Correlation of Stock Market Indices

	Dow Jones	Value Line	S&P 500	NYSE
Dow Jones	1.00	.86	.94	.94
Value Line	.86	1.00	.86	.90
S&P 500	.94	.86	1.00	.98
NYSE	.94	.90	.98	1.00

Modified from David Modest and Mahadevan Sundaresan, ''The Relationship between Spot and Futures Prices in Stock Index Futures Markets: Some Preliminary Evidence,'' *Journal of Futures Markets* 3 (Spring 1983). © John Wiley & Sons, Inc., 1983.

Because of this, we say futures represent "synthetic" holdings of the market portfolio. Instead of holding the market directly, the investor takes a long futures position in the index. Such a strategy is attractive because the transaction costs involved in establishing and liquidating futures positions are much lower than taking actual spot positions. Investors who wish to frequently buy and sell market positions find it much less costly and easier to play the futures market rather than the underlying spot market. "Market timers," who speculate on broad market moves rather than on individual securities, are large players in stock index futures for this reason.

One means to market time, for example, is to shift between Treasury bills and broad-based stock market holdings. Timers attempt to shift from bills into the market before market upturns, and to shift back into bills to avoid market downturns, thereby profiting from broad market movements. Market timing of this sort, however, can result in huge brokerage fees with the frequent purchase and sale of many stocks. An attractive alternative is to invest in Treasury bills and hold varying amounts of market index futures contracts.

The strategy works like this: when timers are bullish, they will establish many long futures positions that they can liquidate quickly and cheaply when expectations turn bearish. Rather than shifting back and forth between T-bills and stocks, they buy and hold T-bills, and adjust only the futures position. This minimizes transaction costs. An advantage of this technique for timing is that investors can implicitly buy or sell the market index in its entirety, whereas market timing in the spot market would require the simultaneous purchase or sale of all the stocks in the index. This is technically difficult to coordinate and can lead to slippage in execution of a timing strategy.

You can construct a T-bill plus index futures position that duplicates the payoff to holding the stock index itself. Here is how:

1. Hold as many market index futures contracts long as you need to purchase your desired stock position. A desired holding of $1,000 multiplied by the TSE 35 index, for example, would require the purchase of two contracts because each contract calls for delivery of $500 multiplied by the index.
2. Invest enough money in T-bills to cover the payment of the futures price at the contract's maturity date. The necessary investment will equal the present value of the futures price that will be paid to satisfy the contracts. The T-bill holdings will grow by the maturity date to a level equal to the futures price.

For example, suppose that an institutional investor wants to invest $20 million in the Canadian equity market for one month and, to minimize trading costs, chooses to buy the TSE 35 futures contract as a substitute for actual stock holdings. If the index is now at 200, the one-month delivery futures price is 202, and the T-bill rate is 1 percent per month, it would buy 200 contracts. (Each contract controls $500 × 200 = $100,000 worth of stock, and $20 million/ $100,000 = 200.) The institution thus has a long position of 100,000 × the TSE 35 index (200 contracts × the contract multiplier of $500). To cover payment of the futures price, it must invest 100,000 × the present value of the futures price in T-bills. This equals $100,000 \times (202/1.01) = \$20$ million market value of bills. Notice that the $20 million outlay in bills is precisely equal to the amount that would have been needed to buy the stock directly. The bills will increase in value in one month to $20.2 million.

This is an artificial, or synthetic, stock position. What is the value of this portfolio at the maturity date? Call S_T the value of the stock index on the maturity date T, and, as usual, let F_0 be the original futures price:

	In General (Per Unit of the Index)	Our Numbers
1. Profits from contract	$S_T - F_0$	$100,000(S_T - 202)$
2. Value of T-bills	F_0	$20,200,000$
TOTAL	S_T	$100,000 S_T$

The total payoff on the contract maturity date is exactly proportional to the value of the stock index. In other words, adopting this portfolio strategy is equivalent to holding the stock index itself, aside from the issue of interim dividend distributions and tax treatment.

Concept Check	Question 9. This result implies something about the relative cost of pursuing this strategy compared to that of purchasing the index directly. As the payoffs are identical, so should be the costs. What does this say about the spot-futures parity relationship?

The bills-plus-futures strategy may be viewed as a 100 percent stock strategy. At the other extreme investing in zero futures results in a 100 percent bills position. Moreover, a short futures position will result in a portfolio equivalent to that obtained by short selling the stock market index, because in both cases the investor gains from decreases in the stock price. Bills-plus-futures mixtures clearly allow for a flexible and low transaction-cost approach to market timing. The futures positions may be established or reversed quickly and cheaply. Also, since the short futures position allows the investor to earn interest on T-bills, it is superior to a conventional short sale of the stock, where the investor typically earns no interest on the proceeds of the short sale.

Empirical Evidence on Pricing of Stock Index Futures

Recall equation 23.2, the spot-futures parity relationship between the futures and spot stock price:

$$F_0 = S_0(1 + r_f - d)^T$$

Several investigators have tested this relationship empirically. The general procedure has been to calculate the theoretically appropriate futures price

FIGURE 23.5

Dividend
distribution, Dow
Jones 30 Industrials.

[From Gregory M. Kipnis
and Steve Tsang, ''Classi-
cal Theory, Dividend
Dynamics and Stock
Index Futures Pricing,'' in
Frank J. Fabozzi and
Gregory M. Kipnis,
(editors), *Stock Index
Futures* (Homewood, Ill.:
Dow Jones-Irwin, 1982).]

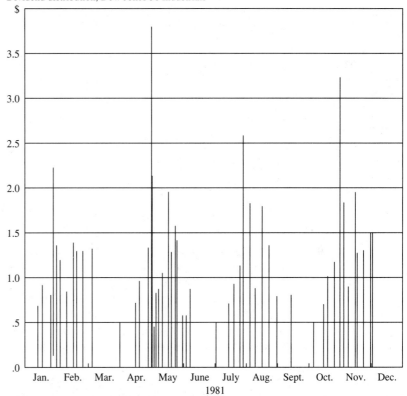

Dividend distribution, Dow Jones 30 Industrials

using the current value of the stock index and equation 23.2. The dividend yield of the index in question is approximated using historical data. Although dividends of individual securities may fluctuate unpredictably, the annualized dividend yield of a broad-based index such as the S&P 500 is fairly stable, usually in the neighbourhood of 3 percent to 4 percent per year. The yield is seasonal with regular and predictable peaks and troughs, however, so the dividend yield for the relevant months must be the one used. Figure 23.5 illustrates the dividend distributions of the Dow Jones Industrial stocks during 1981.

If the actual futures price deviates from the value dictated by the parity relationship, then (forgetting transaction costs) an arbitrage opportunity arises. Given an estimate of transaction costs, we can bracket the theoretically correct futures price within a band. If the actual futures price lies within that band, the discrepancy between the actual and the proper futures price is too small to exploit because of the transaction costs; if the actual price lies outside the no-arbitrage band, profit opportunities are worth exploiting.

Modest and Sundaresan[6] constructed such a test using the April and June 1982 S&P 500 contracts. Figure 23.6 replicates an example of their results. The

---

[6] David Modest and Mahadevan Sundaresan, ''The Relationship between Spot and Futures Prices in Stock Index Futures Markets: Some Preliminary Evidence,'' *Journal of Futures Markets* 3 (Spring 1983).

FIGURE 23.6

Prices of S&P 500 contract maturing June 1982. Data plotted for April 21–June 16, 1982.

[From David Modest and Mahadevan Sundaresan, "The Relationship between Spot and Futures Prices in Stock Index Futures Markets: Some Preliminary Evidence," *Journal of Futures Markets* 3, (Spring 1983). © John Wiley & Sons, Inc., 1983.]

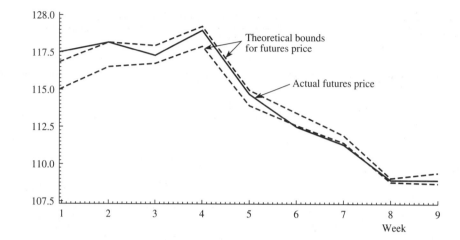

figure shows that the futures prices generally did lie in the theoretically determined no-arbitrage band, but that profit-opportunities occasionally were possible for low-cost transactors.

Such opportunities presented themselves more often in the early years of trading in the contract. Recently, sustained deviations from parity have been far less frequent. This has led some observers[7] to suggest that early deviations from parity are symptomatic of a learning process for market participants; as learning progresses, deviations become rarer. Indeed, the rapid growth of index arbitrage, which attempts to exploit temporary deviations from the parity relationship, is evidence of a dramatic increase in the sophistication of market participants.

Modest and Sundaresan point out that much of the cost of short selling shares is attributable to the investor's inability to invest the entire proceeds from the short sale. Proceeds must be left on margin account, where they do not earn interest. Arbitrage opportunities, or the width of the no-arbitrage band, therefore depend on assumptions regarding the use of short-sale proceeds. Figure 23.6 assumes that one half of the proceeds are available to the short seller.

Concept Check

> Question 10. What (if anything) would happen to the top of the no-arbitrage band if short sellers could obtain full use of the proceeds from the short sale? What would happen to the low end of the band? (Hint: when do violations of parity call for a long futures–short stock position, versus short futures–long stock?)

---

[7] Stephen Figlewski, "Explaining the Early Discounts on Stock Index Futures: The Case for Disequilibrium," *Financial Analysts Journal,* July/August 1984.

Watching the Witching

A Primer on Program Trading for Investors

By Patrick Bloomfield

Yes, Virginia, there is program trading in Canada— and a double witching hour on the third Friday of each month.

But before elaborating on those statements, it is as well as to explain what program trading is all about.

A computer trading program is not, repeat not, a complicated formula fed into a computer to enable it to flash buy and sell signals.

It is simply a simultaneous trade of a number of stocks.

The stocks traded are known as a "basket" of stocks.

A basket can be any number of stocks assembled to mimic the performance of a particular stock index.

In most instances, the computer's role is limited to adding up the price of every stock in the basket, which it can do much faster than any human being.

The investor concerned then has control of a basket of stocks that will move up and down in line with a particular stock index.

He can then trade that basket of stocks against a futures contract in that same index, profiting from differences in price between the two.

Program trading got its start as a trading mechanism in the mid-1980s when the New York Stock Exchange first allowed program traders to put through their trades at the close of the day, giving them the leeway to negotiate the prices at which they were going to do a program trade in advance.

Since those early days, program trading has broadened into a whole spectrum of trading strategies that can influence prices on the NYSE at any time of the day.

Program trading is a somewhat less visible feature of the Toronto-market, but, like Everest, it is there and can have some unpredictable effects on stock prices from one hour to another.

It is at its most noticeable on the third Friday of any month when the option (TXO) and futures (TXF) contracts on the TSE 35 index for that month expire.

The TSE 35 index is made up of 35 household-name stocks to be found in just about every major institutional portfolio.

As a result, institutional investors can use the TXO and TXF contracts to sharpen their performance.

For instance, the TXOs or TXFs can be used as an insurance policy against the TSE 35 declining. Or a private investor can buy them as a means of participating in an expected market rally.

Between these two very simple approaches lies a host of more arcane strategies that are often based as much on market mathematics as on expectations of the market moving one way or the other.

Managers of index funds (portfolios limited to all the stocks in one particular stock index) use the futures and options markets to try to beat the performance of that particular index.

Not a few institutions holding the stocks in the TSE 35 index in their basic portfolios seek to improve their return by selling TXO calls, being the right to the cash amount of any increase in the value of a particular TXO option in the period to expiry date.

The selling institution pockets the premium that the buyer pays for the call, and can cover any potential loss in a fast-rising market by taking some profits from TSE 35 stocks in its own portfolios.

Whatever the strategy, all the buyers and sellers concerned have to decide how they are going to close out their positions ahead of the expiry of each month's TXO and TXF contracts, which is based on the opening prices of all 35 stocks in the TSE 35 index on expiry Friday.

That is when the trading programs begin to roll in, generally leading to a very significant increase in volume for the first hour of trading.

Thomas Briant, the TSE officer responsible for options and futures market surveillance, tells this

(Continued)

column that trading volumes in the opening hour of an expiry Friday can amount to as much as 40 percent of the total volume of trading that day, compared with a level nearer 20 percent on other days.

There can also be significant difference between the level at which the TSE 35 closes on the Thursday night, and its level for the first five or 10 minutes of trading on expiry Friday morning.

In turn, this can also do some funny things to the value of the TXO options contract, which has become by far the largest option contract traded in Canada.

The sharpest overnight change in the TSE 35 on an expiry Friday in Briant's records is 2.42 (equivalent to 1¼ percent of the index) the Friday the March 1991 contracts closed.

The sharpest overnight change in 1990 was 2.18.

Expiry Friday can also bring significant order imbalances (say, far more orders to buy a particular stock than orders to sell it).

It is a time when an individual investor with market orders to be filled should be keeping a close watch on what is going on.

The TSE requires members firms putting through program trades to notify it in advance.

It then puts out on its tape 20 minutes before the start of trading on an expiry Friday a list of indicated order imbalances.

The basic idea is to alert institutional investors of potential trading opportunities and to encourage them [to] put in orders to lessen these imbalances.

But make sure your broker knows about them, too.

If institutions are going to be given the fortituous opportunity to get a particularly good deal on a sale of BCE Inc. stock, so should you.

At the very least, check out that your broker is watching the ticker for those imbalances and keeps you briefed.

From *The Financial Post,* April 2, 1991, by Patrick Bloomfield. Reprinted by permission.

Index Arbitrage and the Triple Witching Hour

Whenever the actual futures price falls outside the no-arbitrage band, there is an opportunity for profit. This is why the parity relationships are so important. Far from being theoretical academic constructs, they are in fact a guide to trading rules that can generate large profits. One of the most notable developments in trading activity has been the advent of **index arbitrage,** an investment strategy that exploits divergences between the actual futures price and its theoretically correct parity value (see the accompanying box).

In theory, index arbitrage is simple. If the futures price is too high, short the futures contract and buy the stocks in the index. If it is too low, go long in futures and short the stocks. You can perfectly hedge your position and should earn arbitrage profits equal to the mispricing of the contract.

In practice, however, index arbitrage can be difficult to implement. The problem lies in buying "the stocks in the index." Selling or purchasing shares in all stocks in an index is impractical for two reasons. The first is transaction costs, which may outweigh any profits to be made from the arbitrage. Second, it is extremely difficult to buy or sell stock of many different firms simultaneously, and any lags in the execution of such a strategy can destroy the effectiveness of a plan to exploit temporary price discrepancies.

In the real world, most arbitrageurs devise portfolios with a small number of stocks that closely mimic the broader market index. These subportfolios are called *baskets,* and the traders who develop them are called *basket weavers.* Their trades on the spot market are made in this proxy portfolio only, which reduces the execution problems in getting trades off quickly. The substitution, however, creates tracking or basis risk because the futures price on a broad stock index will not correlate as closely with the value of the proxy portfolio as it will with the index itself.

Arbitrageurs need to trade an entire portfolio of stocks quickly and simultaneously if they hope to exploit disparities between the futures price and its corresponding stock index. For this they need a coordinated trading program; hence the term **program trading**, which refers to coordinated purchases or sales of entire portfolios of stocks. The response has been the designated order turnaround (DOT) system, which enables traders to send coordinated buy or sell programs to the floor of the stock exchange via computer.

Index arbitrage seems to have had its own effect on market movements. Four times a year, for example, the TSE 35 futures contract expires at the same time as the TSE 35 index option contract and option contracts on individual stocks. The great volatility of the market at these periods has led people to call the simultaneous expirations the **triple witching hour**.

Expiration-day volatility can be explained by program trading to exploit arbitrage opportunities. Suppose that before a stock index future contract matures, the futures price is a little above its parity value. Arbitrageurs will attempt to lock in superior profits by buying the stocks in the index (the program trading buy order) and taking an offsetting short futures position. If and when the pricing disparity reverses, the position can be unwound at a profit. Alternatively, arbitrageurs can wait until contract maturity day and realize a profit by closing out the offsetting stock and futures positions with "market-on-close" orders, that is, closing out both positions at prices in the closing range of the day. By waiting until the close of the maturity day, arbitrageurs can be assured that the futures price and stock index price will be aligned—they rely on the convergence property.

Obviously, when many program traders follow such a strategy at market close, a wave of program selling passes over the market. The result? Prices go down. This is the expiration-day effect. If execution of the arbitrage strategy calls for a sale (or short sale) of stocks, unwinding on expiration day requires repurchase of the stocks, with the opposite effect: prices will increase.

The success of these arbitrage positions and associated program trades depends on only two things: the relative levels of spot and futures prices and synchronized trading in the two markets. Because arbitrageurs exploit disparities in futures and spot prices, absolute price levels are unimportant. This means that large buy or sell programs can hit the floor even if stock prices are at "fair" levels, that is, at levels consistent with fundamental information. The markets in individual stocks may not be sufficiently deep to absorb the arbitrage-based program trades without significant price movements, despite the fact that those trades are not informationally motivated.

In an investigation of expiration day effects, Stoll and Whaley[8] found that the market is in fact more volatile at contract expirations. For example, the standard deviation of the last-hour return on the S&P 500 index is .641 on expirations of the S&P 500 futures contract, whereas it is only .211 on non-expiration days. Interestingly, the last-hour volatility of non-S&P 500 stocks appears unaffected by expiration days, consistent with the hypothesis that the effect is related to program trading of the stocks in the index.

23.7   Foreign Exchange Futures

The Markets

Exchange rates between currencies vary continually and often quite substantially. This variability can be a source of concern for anyone involved in international business. A Canadian exporter who sells goods in England, for example, will be paid in British pounds, and the dollar value of those pounds depends on the exchange rate at the time payment is made. Until that date, the Canadian exporter is exposed to foreign exchange rate risk. This risk, however, is easily hedged through currency futures or forward markets.

The forward market in foreign exchange is fairly informal. It is simply a network of banks and brokers that allows customers to enter forward contracts to purchase or sell currency in the future at a currently agreed-on rate of exchange. Unlike those in futures markets, these contracts are not standardized in a formal market setting. Instead, each is negotiated separately. Moreover, there is no marking to market as would occur in futures markets. The contracts call only for execution at the maturity date.

For currency futures, however, there are formal markets. As already noted, trading in such futures was introduced by the Montreal Exchange, but did not meet with any success, and by 1991 had been eliminated. Elsewhere, however, currency futures markets were established by the Chicago Mercantile Exchange (International Monetary Market), the London International Financial Futures Exchange, and the MidAmerican Commodity Exchange. In these exchanges, contracts are standardized by size, and daily marking to market is observed. Moreover, there are standard clearing arrangements that allow traders to enter or reverse positions easily. The resulting liquidity of these contracts is a major advantage of trading in these markets rather than in forward markets. Of course, the standardization that allows for liquidity correspondingly does not permit the flexibility of contract design that is available in forward markets.

---

[8] Hans R. Stoll and Robert E. Whaley, "Program Trading and Expiration Day Effects," *Financial Analysts Journal*, March–April 1987.

Figure 23.7 reproduces a listing of foreign exchange spot and forward rates from *The Globe and Mail*. The listing gives the number of both Canadian and U.S. dollars required to purchase some unit of foreign currency. Figure 23.8 reproduces futures listings from *The Wall Street Journal*, which show the number of dollars needed to purchase a given unit of foreign currency. In Figure 23.7 both spot and forward exchange rates are listed for various delivery dates for several major currencies. The forward quotations always apply to delivery in 30, 90, 180, or 360 days. Thus, tomorrow's forward listings will apply to a maturity date one day later than today's listing. In contrast, the futures contracts mature in March, June, September, and December, and these four maturity days are the only dates each year when futures contracts settle.

FIGURE 23.7

Foreign exchange listing.

(From *The Globe and Mail*, May 1, 1992. Reprinted by permission.)

FOREIGN EXCHANGE

Mid-market rates in Toronto at noon, April 30, 1992. Prepared by the Bank of Montreal Treasury Group.

		$1 U.S. in Cdn.$ =	$1 Cdn. in U.S.$ =
U.S./Canada spot		1.1959	0.8362
1 month forward		1.1985	0.8344
2 months forward		1.2013	0.8324
3 months forward		1.2040	0.8306
6 months forward		1.2122	0.8249
12 months forward		1.2269	0.8151
3 years forward		1.2869	0.7771
5 years forward		1.3109	0.7628
7 years forward		1.3434	0.7444
10 years forward		1.3809	0.7242
Canadian dollar	High	1.1402	0.8770
in 1992:	Low	1.2004	0.8331
	Average	1.1797	0.8477

Country	Currency	Cdn. $ per unit	U.S. $ per unit
Britain	Pound	2.1221	1.7745
1 month forward		2.1147	1.7645
2 months forward		2.1084	1.7551
3 months forward		2.1026	1.7464
6 months forward		2.0876	1.7222
12 months forward		2.0675	1.6852
Germany	Mark	0.7235	0.6050
1 month forward		0.7214	0.6019
3 months forward		0.7178	0.5962
6 months forward		0.7131	0.5883
12 months forward		0.7075	0.5767
Japan	Yen	0.008965	0.007496
1 month forward		0.008978	0.007491
3 months forward		0.009011	0.007484
6 months forward		0.009069	0.007481
12 months forward		0.009206	0.007503
Algeria	Dinar	0.0543	0.0454
Antigua, Grenada and St. Lucia	E.C.Dollar	0.4437	0.3711
Argentina	Peso	1.23263	1.03072
Australia	Dollar	0.9088	0.7599
Austria	Schilling	0.10261	0.08580
Bahamas	Dollar	1.1959	1.0000
Barbados	Dollar	0.5953	0.4978
Belgium	Franc	0.03511	0.02936
Bermuda	Dollar	1.1959	1.0000
Brazil	Cruzeiro	0.00052	0.00044
Bulgaria	Lev	0.0660	0.0552
Chile	Peso	0.0034	0.0029
China	Renminbi	0.2170	0.1815
Cyprus	Pound	2.5718	2.1505
Czechoslovakia	Koruna	0.0411	0.0344
Denmark	Krone	0.1870	0.1564
Egypt	Pound	0.3720	0.3111

Country	Currency	Cdn. $ per unit	U.S. $ per unit
Fiji	Dollar	0.7983	0.6675
Finland	Markka	0.2655	0.2220
France	Franc	0.2144	0.1793
Greece	Drachma	0.00617	0.00516
Hong Kong	Dollar	0.1542	0.1289
Hungary	Forint	0.01494	0.01250
Iceland	Krona	0.02013	0.01684
India	Rupee	0.04237	0.03543
Indonesia	Rupiah	0.00059	0.00049
Ireland	Punt	1.9270	1.6113
Israel	N. Shekel	0.49326	0.41246
Italy	Lira	0.000962	0.000804
Jamaica	Dollar	0.05089	0.04255
Jordan	Dinar	1.7207	1.4388
Lebanon	Pound	0.00077	0.00065
Luxembourg	Franc	0.03511	0.02936
Malaysia	Ringgit	0.4739	0.3963
Mexico	Peso	0.00039	0.00032
Netherlands	Guilder	0.6433	0.5379
New Zealand	Dollar	0.6432	0.5378
Norway	Krone	0.1848	0.1545
Pakistan	Rupee	0.04791	0.04006
Philippines	Peso	0.04591	0.03839
Poland	Zloty	0.00009	0.00007
Portugal	Escudo	0.00859	0.00718
Romania	Leu	0.0061	0.0051
Russia	Ruble	0.0120	0.0100
Saudi Arabia	Riyal	0.3190	0.2667
Singapore	Dollar	0.7214	0.6032
South Africa	Rand	0.4159	0.3478
South Korea	Won	0.001536	0.001284
Spain	Peseta	0.01150	0.00962
Sudan	Pound	0.0133	0.0111
Sweden	Krona	0.2005	0.1677
Switzerland	Franc	0.7883	0.6592
Taiwan	Dollar	0.0478	0.0400
Thailand	Baht	0.0468	0.0392
Trinidad, Tobago	Dollar	0.2817	0.2356
Venezuela	Bolivar	0.01844	0.01542
Yugoslavia	Dinar	0.008729	0.007299
Zambia	Kwacha	0.0088	0.0074
European Currency Unit		1.4805	1.2380
Special Drawing Right		1.6381	1.3698

The U.S. dollar closed at $1.1912 in terms of Canadian funds, down $0.0036 from Wednesday. The pound sterling closed at $2.1174, down $0.0004.

In New York, the Canadian dollar closed up $0.0025 at $0.8395 in terms of U.S. funds. The pound sterling was up $0.0050 to $1.7775.

FIGURE 23.8
Foreign exchange
futures.

(From *The Wall Street
Journal*, June 7, 1991.
Reprinted by permission
of *The Wall Street Jour-
nal*, © 1991 Dow Jones &
Company, Inc. All Rights
Reserved Worldwide.)

CURRENCY TRADING

FUTURES

	Open	High	Low	Settle	Change	Lifetime High	Low	Open Interest
JAPAN YEN (IMM)—12.5 million yen; $ per yen (.00)								
June	.7184	.7190	.7171	.7180	+ .0006	.8010	.6645	43,213
Sept	.7160	.7163	.7146	.7155	+ .0006	.7995	.7032	9,631
Dec	.7138	.7143	.7138	.7140	+ .0006	.7770	.7038	1,712
Mr92	....	....		.7141	+ .0005	.7540	.7095	1,192
June	....	....		.7143	+ .0006	.7220	.7150	1,470
Est vol 13,545; vol Wed 25,148; open int 57,218, +1,563.								
DEUTSCHEMARK (IMM)—125,000 marks; $ per mark								
June	.5708	.5717	.5689	.5698	— .0013	.6870	.5601	72,017
Sept	.5667	.5676	.5648	.5657	— .0013	.6810	.5561	18,340
Dec	.5634	.5634	.5620	.5621	— .0013	.6670	.5538	469
Est vol 33,764; vol Wed 49,650; open int 90,834, +3,327.								
CANADIAN DOLLAR (IMM)—100,000 dlrs.; $ per Can $								
June	.8720	.8722	.8708	.8715	— .0009	.8733	.7995	27,143
Sept	.8667	.8667	.8655	.8661	— .0009	.8677	.7985	6,211
Dec	.8609	.8617	.8609	.8611	— .0009	.8625	.8175	472
Mr92	....	....		.8568	— .0009	.8578	.8253	987
June	.8530	.8530	.8530	.8527	— .0009	.8533	.8330	173
Est vol 3,766; vol Wed 5,815; open int 35,008, +397.								
BRITISH POUND (IMM)—62,500 pds.; $ per pound								
June	1.6882	1.6920	1.6792	1.6940	—.0064	1.9610	1.6550	24,409
Sept	1.6680	1.6720	1.6582	1.6634	—.0064	1.9360	1.6346	4,803
Dec	1.6460	1.6514	1.6460	1.6472	—.0064	1.7900	1.6200	713
Est vol 13,340; vol Wed 14,971; open int 29,925, +800.								
SWISS FRANC (IMM)—125,000 francs; $ per franc								
June	.6675	.6676	.6635	.6639	— .0038	.8084	.6635	35,761
Sept	.6641	.6643	.6605	.6607	— .0037	.8055	.6605	9,278
Dec	.6600	.6600	.6585	.6583	— .0037	.8090	.6585	162
Est vol 22,587; vol Wed 31,603; open int 45,266, +2,338.								
AUSTRALIAN DOLLAR (IMM)—100,000 dlrs.; $ per A.$								
June	.7510	.7522	.7493	.7494	— .0086	.7815	.7493	1,685
Sept	.7435	.7445	.7415	.7420	— .0085	.7730	.7415	1,076
Est vol 1,433; vol Wed 492; open int 2,761, —154.								
U.S. DOLLAR INDEX (FINEX)—500 times USDX								
June	93.70	94.03	93.60	93.92	+ .25	95.19	81.45	5,339
Sept	94.71	95.00	94.69	94.91	+ .26	96.02	83.17	1,885
Dec	...	....	....	95.71	+ .27	96.62	67.20	492
Est vol 3,740; vol Wed 1,787; open int 7,716, +144.								
The index: High 93.86; Low 93.52; Close 93.75 +.24								

—OTHER CURRENCY FUTURES—

Settlement prices of selected contracts. Volume and open
interest of all contract months.

British Pound (MCE) 12,500 pounds; $ per pound
   Sep 1.6634 — .0064; Est. vol. 110; Open Int. 239
Japanese Yen (MCE) 6.25 million yen; $ per yen (.00)
   Sep .7155 +.0006; Est. vol. 110; Open Int. 226
Swiss Franc (MCE) 62,500 francs; $ per franc
   Sep .6607 —.0037; Est. vol. 300; Open Int. 575
Deutschemark (MCE) 62,500 marks; $ per mark
   Sep .5657 —.0013; Est. vol. 220; Open Int. 1,140
   FINEX—Financial Instrument Exchange, a division of
the New York Cotton Exchange. IMM—International Mone-
tary Market at the Chicago Mercantile Exchange. MCE—
MidAm━━ ━━by Exchan━━

Interest Rate Parity

As is true of stocks and stock futures, there is a spot-futures exchange rate
relationship that will prevail in well-functioning markets. Should this so-called
interest rate parity relationship be violated, arbitrageurs will be able to make
risk-free profits in foreign exchange markets with zero net investment. Their
actions will force futures and spot exchange rates back into alignment.

We can illustrate the **interest rate parity theorem** by using two currencies,
the Canadian dollar and the British (U.K.) pound. Call E_0 the current exchange
rate between the two currencies, that is, E_0 dollars are required to purchase one

pound. F_0, the forward price, is the number of dollars that is agreed to today for purchase of one pound at time T in the future. Call the risk-free interest rates in Canada and the United Kingdom r_{CAN} and r_{UK}, respectively.

The interest rate parity theorem then states that the proper relationship between E_0 and F_0 is given as

$$F_0 = E_0 \left(\frac{1 + r_{CAN}}{1 + r_{UK}}\right)^T \tag{23.7}$$

For example, if $r_{CAN} = .06$ and $r_{UK} = .05$ annually, while $E_0 = \$2.10$ per pound, then the proper futures price for a one-year contract would be

$$\$2.10 \left(\frac{1.06}{1.05}\right) = \$2.12 \text{ per pound}$$

Consider the intuition behind this result. If r_{CAN} is greater than r_{UK}, money invested in Canada will grow at a faster rate than money invested in the United Kingdom. If this is so, why wouldn't all investors decide to invest their money in Canada? One important reason why not is that the dollar may be depreciating relative to the pound. Although dollar investments in Canada grow faster than pound investments in the United Kingdom, each dollar is worth progressively fewer pounds as time passes. Such an effect will exactly offset the advantage of the higher Canadian interest rate.

To complete the argument, we need only determine how a depreciating dollar will show up in equation 23.7. If the dollar is depreciating, meaning that progressively more dollars are required to purchase each pound, then the forward exchange rate F_0 (which equals the dollars required to purchase one pound for delivery in one year) must exceed E_0, the current exchange rate. This is exactly what equation 23.7 tells us: when r_{CAN} exceeds r_{UK}, F_0 must exceed E_0. The depreciation of the dollar embodied in the ratio of F_0 to E_0 exactly compensates for the difference in interest rates available in the two countries. Of course, the argument also works in reverse; if r_{CAN} is less than r_{UK}, then F_0 is less than E_0.

What if the interest rate parity relationship is violated? For example, suppose the futures price is \$2.11 instead of \$2.12. You could adopt the following strategy to reap arbitrage profits. In this example, let E_1 denote the exchange rate that will prevail in one year. E_1 is, of course, a random variable from the perspective of today's investors.

Action	Initial Cash Flow ($)	CF in One Year ($)
1. Borrow one U.K. pound in London. Convert to dollars.	2.10	$-E_1(1.05)$
2. Lend \$2.10 in Canada.	-2.10	$2.10(1.06)$
3. Enter a contract to purchase 1.05 pounds at a (futures) price of $F_0 = \$2.11$.	0	$1.05(E_1 - 2.11)$
TOTAL	0	\$.0105

In stage 1, you exchange the one pound borrowed in the United Kingdom for $2.10 at the current exchange rate. After one year you must repay the pound borrowed with interest. Since the loan is made in the United Kingdom at the U.K. interest rate, you would repay 1.05 pounds, which would be worth $E_1(1.05)$ dollars. The Canadian loan in step 2 is made at the Canadian interest rate of 6 percent. The futures position in step 3 results in receipt of 1.05 pounds, for which you would first pay F_0 dollars each, and then trade into dollars at rate E_1.

Note that the exchange rate risk here is exactly offset between the pound obligation in step 1 and the futures position in step 3. The profit from the strategy is therefore risk-free and requires no net investment.

To generalize this strategy:

Action	Initial CF ($)	CF in One Year ($)
1. Borrow one U.K. pound in London. Convert to $.	$\$E_0$	$-\$E_1(1 + r_{UK})$
2. Use proceeds of borrowing in London to lend in Canada.	$-\$E_0$	$\$E_0(1 + r_{CAN})$
3. Enter $(1 + r_{UK})$ futures positions to purchase one pound for F_0 dollars	0	$(1 + r_{UK})(E_1 - F_0)$
TOTAL	0	$E_0(1 + r_{CAN}) - F_0(1 + r_{UK})$

Let us again review the stages of the arbitrage operation. The first step requires borrowing one pound in the United Kingdom. With a current exchange rate of E_0, the one pound is converted into E_0 dollars, which is a cash inflow. In one year the British loan must be paid off with interest, requiring a payment in pounds of $(1 + r_{UK})$, or in dollars of $E_1(1 + r_{UK})$. In the second step the proceeds of the British loan are invested in Canada. This involves an initial cash outflow of $\$E_0$, and a cash inflow of $\$E_0(1 + r_{CAN})$ in one year. Finally, the exchange risk involved in the British borrowing is hedged in step 3. Here, the $(1 + r_{UK})$ pounds that will need to be delivered to satisfy the British loan are purchased ahead in the futures contract.

The net proceeds to the arbitrage portfolio are risk-free and given by $E_0(1 + r_{CAN}) - F_0(1 + r_{UK})$. If this value is positive, borrow in the United Kingdom, lend in Canada, and enter a long futures position to eliminate foreign exchange risk. If the value is negative, borrow in Canada, lend in the United Kingdom, and take a short position in pound futures. When prices are aligned properly to preclude arbitrage opportunities, the expression must equal zero. If it were positive, investors would pursue the arbitrage portfolio. If it were negative, they would pursue the reverse positions.

Rearranging this expression gives us the relationship

$$F_0 = \frac{1 + r_{CAN}}{1 + r_{UK}} E_0 \qquad \textbf{(23.8)}$$

which is the interest rate parity theorem for a one-year horizon, known also as the **covered interest arbitrage relationship**.

Concept Check

> Question 11. What are the arbitrage strategy and associated profits if the initial futures price is $F_0 = \$2.14/\text{pound}$?

Ample empirical evidence bears out this theoretical relationship. For two other currencies, for example, on May 1, 1992, *The Globe and Mail* listed the six-month U.S. interest rate at 1.925 percent and the six-month Canadian rate at 3.488 percent. The U.S. dollar was then worth 1.1959 Canadian dollars. Substituting these values into equation 23.8 gives $F_0 = 1.1959(1.03488/1.01925) = 1.2142$. The actual forward price at that time for six-month delivery was $1.2122 per U.S. dollar, so close to the parity value that transaction costs would prevent arbitrageurs from profiting from the discrepancy.

23.8 *Interest Rate Futures*

The Markets

The late 1970s and 1980s saw a dramatic increase in the volatility of interest rates, leading to investor desire to hedge returns on fixed-income securities against changes in interest rates. Similarly, thrift institutions that had loaned money on home mortgages before 1975 suffered substantial capital losses on those loans when interest rates later increased. An interest rate futures contract could have protected banks against such large swings in yields. Demonstration of these losses has spurred trading in interest rate futures.

As with other futures contracts, several Canadian interest rate futures were introduced by the TFE and Montreal Exchange. Very few of them survive today. Figure 23.9 shows the futures contracts that traded on the Montreal Exchange in May 1992. Only bankers' acceptances and Canada bond futures had survived by that date.

Interest rate futures contracts call for delivery of a bond, bill, or note. Should interest rates rise, the market value of the security at delivery will be less than the original futures price, and the deliverer will profit. Hence, the short position in the interest rate futures contract gains when interest rates rise.

In the United States, the major interest rate contracts currently traded are on Eurodollars, Treasury bills, Treasury notes, Treasury bonds, and a municipal bond index. These securities thus provide an opportunity to hedge against a wide spectrum of maturities from very short (T-bills) to long term (T-bonds). In addition, futures contracts tied to interest rates in Germany and the United Kingdom trade on the London International Financial Futures Exchange and are listed in the major U.S. financial publications.

FIGURE 23.9

Canadian interest rate futures.

(From *The Globe and Mail*, May 1, 1992. Reprinted by permission.)

MONTREAL FUTURES

Bankers' acceptances; $1-million; pts of 100%.
Change of 0.01 equals $25 a contract.

Season			Settle				Open
High	Low	Month	High	Low	Price	Change	Interest
93.44	88.20	Jun	93.13	93.06	93.12	— 0.03	6845
93.40	89.82	Sep	92.95	92.87	92.93	— 0.06	5868
93.10	89.43	Dec	92.57	92.45	92.57	+ 0.02	4839
92.86	89.25	Mar	91.97	91.95	92.03	— 0.10	2583
92.40	88.99	Jun	91.55	91.55	91.55	— 0.03	1654
92.18	89.88	Sep	0.00	0.00	91.07	— 0.03	910
91.90	89.85	Dec	90.70	90.70	90.78	— 0.17	225

Estimated volume: 1,362
Previous day's volume: 1,225
Previous day's open interest: 22,924

One-month bankers' acceptances
$3-million; pts of 100%.
Change of 0.01 equals $25 a contract.

Season			Settle				Open
High	Low	Month	High	Low	Price	Change	Interest
93.47	93.20	May	0.00	0.00	93.34		353
93.39	93.17	Jun	93.30	93.30	93.30	— 0.02	175
93.29	93.07	Jul	93.15	93.12	93.15		60
93.21	92.90	Aug	93.02	93.02	93.02	— 0.04	55

Estimated volume: 55
Previous day's volume: 70
Previous day's open interest: 643

Government of Canada bond futures
$100,000; pts of 100%.

Season			Settle				Open
High	Low	Month	High	Low	Price	Change	Interest
101.42	95.78	Jun		98.25	97.95	98.24	— 0.03	4496

Estimated volume: 2,404
Previous day's volume: 1,903
Previous day's open interest: 4,496

Canada bond futures option; $100,000; pts of 100%

Strike	Calls			Puts		
Price	Jun	Sep	Dec	Jun	Sep	Dec
94	4.22	3.92	0.00	0.05	0.28	0.00
95	3.22	3.13	0.00	0.05	0.47	0.00
96	2.24	2.42	0.00	0.07	0.74	0.00
97	1.36	1.81	0.00	0.14	1.11	0.00
98	0.67	1.31	0.00	0.45	1.58	0.00
99	0.30	0.91	0.00	1.03	2.16	0.00
100	0.09	0.60	0.00	1.84	2.83	0.00
101	0.06	0.39	0.00	2.78	3.59	0.00
102	0.05	0.24	0.00	3.78	4.42	0.00
103	0.05	0.14	0.00	4.78	5.30	0.00

Estimated volume: 75
Prev. call volume: 75   Prev. call open interest: 386
Prev. put volume: 25   Prev. put open interest: 158

Bond Futures Strategies

Bond futures can be useful hedging vehicles for bond dealers or underwriters. Suppose, for instance, that an underwriting syndicate brings out a bond issue on behalf of a corporate client. As is typical in such cases, the syndicate quotes an interest rate at which it guarantees that the bonds can be sold. In essence, the syndicate buys the company's bonds at an agreed-on price and then takes the responsibility of reselling them in the open market. If interest rates increase before the bonds can be sold to the public, the syndicate, not the issuer, bears the capital loss from the fall in the value of the bonds. This loss can be hedged through bond futures.

How can the underwriters construct the proper hedge ratio, that is, the proper number of futures contracts per bond held in its inventory? Suppose that the Canada bond futures contract nominally calls for delivery of an 8 percent coupon 20-year maturity federal government bond in return for the futures price. (In practice, other bonds may be substituted for this standard bond to settle the contract, but we will use the 8 percent bond for illustration.) Suppose that the market interest rate is 10 percent and that the syndicate is holding $100 million worth of bonds, with a coupon rate of 10 percent, and 20-year time to maturity. The bonds currently sell at par value of $1,000. If the interest rate were to jump to 11 percent, the bonds would fall to a market value of $919.77, a loss of $8.02 million. (We use semiannual compounding in this calculation.)

To hedge this risk, the underwriters would need to short enough futures so that the profits on the futures position would offset the loss on the bonds. The 8 percent 20-year bond of the futures contract would sell for $828.41 if the interest rate were 10 percent. If the interest rate were to jump to 11 percent, the bond price would fall to $759.31, and the fall in the price of the 8 percent bond, $69.10, would approximately equal the profit on the short futures position per bond to be delivered.[9] Because each contract calls for delivery of $100,000 par value of bonds (100 bonds at par value of $1,000), the gain on each short position would equal $6,910. Thus, to offset the $8.02 million loss on the value of the bonds, the syndicate would need to hold $8.02 million/$6,910 = 1,161 contracts short. The total gain on the contracts would offset the loss on the bonds and leave the underwriters unaffected by interest rate swings.

The actual hedging problem is more difficult for several reasons: (1) the syndicate probably would hold more than one issue of bonds in its inventory, and (2) interest rates on government and corporate bonds will not be equal and need not move in lockstep (and a corporate bond contract does not exist in Canada), (3) the Canada bond contract may be settled with any of several bonds instead of the 8 percent benchmark bond, and (4) taxes could complicate the picture. Nevertheless, the principles illustrated here underlie all hedging activity.

23.9 *Commodity Futures Pricing*

Commodity futures prices are governed by the same general considerations as stock futures. One difference, however, is that the cost of carrying commodities, especially those subject to spoilage, is greater than the cost of carrying financial assets. Moreover, spot prices for some commodities demonstrate marked seasonal patterns that can affect futures pricing.

Pricing with Storage Costs

The cost of carrying commodities includes (in addition to interest costs) storage costs, insurance costs, and an allowance for spoilage of goods in storage. To price commodity futures, let us reconsider the earlier arbitrage strategy that calls for holding both the asset and a short position in the futures contract on the asset. In this case, we will denote the price of the commodity at time T as P_T, and assume for simplicity that all non-interest carrying costs (C) are paid in

---

[9] We say "approximately" because the exact figure depends on the time to maturity of the contract. We assume here that the maturity date is less than a month away, so that the futures price and band price move in virtual lockstep.

one lump sum at time T, the contract maturity. Carrying costs appear in the final cash flow.

Action	Initial Cash Flow	CF at Time T
Buy asset; pay carrying costs at T	$-P_0$	$P_T - C$
Borrow P_0; repay with interest at time T	P_0	$-P_0(1 + r_f)$
Short futures position	0	$F_0 - P_T$
TOTAL	0	$F_0 - P_0(1 + r_f) - C$

Because market prices should not allow for arbitrage opportunities, the terminal cash flow of this zero net investment, risk-free strategy should be zero.

If the cash flow were positive, this strategy would yield guaranteed profits for no investment. If the cash flow were negative, the reverse of this strategy also would yield profits. In practice, the reverse strategy would involve a short sale of the commodity. This is unusual but may be done as long as the short sale contract appropriately accounts for storage costs.[10] Thus we conclude that

$$F_0 = P_0(1 + r_f) + C$$

Finally, if we call $c = C/P_0$, and interpret c as the percentage "rate" of carrying costs, we may write

$$F_0 = P_0(1 + r_f + c) \tag{23.9}$$

which is a (one-year) parity relationship for futures involving storage costs. Compare equation 23.9 to the first parity relation for stocks, equation 23.2, and you will see that they are extremely similar. In fact, if we think of carrying costs as a "negative dividend," the equations are identical. This treatment makes intuitive sense because, instead of receiving a dividend yield of d, the storer of the commodity must pay a storage cost of c. Obviously, this parity relationship is simply an extension of those we have seen already.

It is vital to note that we derive equation 23.9 assuming that the asset will be bought and stored; it therefore applies only to goods that currently *are* being stored. Two kinds of commodities cannot be expected to be stored. The first is highly perishable goods, such as strawberries, for which storage is technologically not feasible. The second includes goods that are not stored for economic reasons. For example, it would be foolish to buy wheat now, planning to store it for ultimate use in three years. Instead, it is clearly preferable to delay the purchase of the wheat until after the harvest of the third year. The wheat is then obtained without incurring the storage costs. Moreover, if the wheat harvest in the third year is comparable to this year's, you could obtain it at roughly the same price as you would pay this year. By waiting to purchase, you avoid both interest and storage costs.

In fact, it is generally not reasonable to hold large quantities of agricultural goods across a harvesting period. Why pay to store this year's wheat, when

---

[10] Robert A. Jarrow and George S. Oldfield, "Forward Contracts and Futures Contracts," *Journal of Financial Economics* 9 (1981).

you can purchase next year's wheat when it is harvested? Maintaining large wheat inventories across harvests makes sense only if such a small wheat crop is forecast that wheat prices will not fall when the new supply is harvested.

Concept Check	Question 12. People are willing to buy and "store" shares of stock despite the fact that their purchase ties up capital. Most people, however, are not willing to buy and store wheat. What is the difference in the properties of the expected evolution of stock prices versus wheat prices that accounts for this result?

Because storage across harvests is costly, equation 23.9 should not be expected to apply for holding periods that span harvest times, nor should it apply to perishable goods that are available only "in season." You can see that this is so if you look at the U.S. futures markets page of the newspaper. Figure 23.10, for example, gives futures prices for several times to maturity for soybeans and for gold. Whereas the futures price for gold, which is a stored commodity, increases steadily with the maturity of the contract, the futures price for soybeans is seasonal; it rises within a harvest period as equation 23.9 would predict, but the price then falls across harvests as new supplies become available.

Futures pricing across seasons requires a different approach that is not based on storage across harvest periods. In place of general no-arbitrage restrictions we rely instead on risk premium theory and discounted cash flow (DCF) analysis.

FIGURE 23.10

Futures prices for soybeans and gold.

(From *The Wall Street Journal,* June 8, 1988. Reprinted by permission of *The Wall Street Journal.* © Dow Jones & Company, Inc. 1988. All Rights Reserved Worldwide.)

	Open	High	Low	Settle	Change	Lifetime High	Low	Open Interest
			–GRAINS AND OILSEEDS–					
	SOYBEANS (CBT) 5,000 bu.; cents per bu.							
July	900	909	866	882	+ 3	909	488½	57,494
Aug	904½	911	874	887	+ 2½	911	512	15,568
Sept	912	913	879	886½	+ 1	913	503	7,852
Nov	910	918	875	890½	– 3½	918	499¼	75,909
Ja89	924	924	882	896½	– 4½	924	553	8,757
Mar	924	925	885	901¼	– 3¾	925	579	3,962
May	914	914	876	889½	– 9	914	647	1,574
July	900	900	874	875½	– 10½	900	684	2,044
Nov	718	730	716	716	– 18¼	734¼	677	1,360
	Est vol 80,000; vol Mon 19,774; open int 174,521, +1,934.							

Dec			....	/9.2u	– 2.6u	62.20	11.n.	.17
	Est vol 8,500; vol Mon 9,885; open int 33,133, +152.							
	GOLD (CMX)–100 troy oz.; $ per troy oz.							
June	463.10	465.50	460.00	460.00	– 2.90	523.00	399.00	2,687
July	....	....		461.60	– 3.30	467.50	458.40	305
Aug	468.50	470.00	464.60	464.80	– 3.30	527.00	425.00	62,648
Oct	473.30	475.50	469.70	470.00	– 3.40	533.50	429.00	11,366
Dec	479.50	481.20	475.00	475.40	– 3.40	546.00	430.00	24,322
Fb89	484.50	485.00	481.00	480.80	– 3.30	549.50	446.00	10,109
Apr	....	....		486.30	– 3.20	550.00	451.00	7,134
June	....	....		492.00	– 3.10	570.00	455.50	10,425
Aug	....	....		498.00	– 3.00	575.00	482.20	6,299
Oct	....	....		504.40	– 2.90	575.50	466.30	7,080
Dec	....	....		510.90	– 2.80	514.50	472.50	5,569
Fb90	....	....		517.40	– 2.70	516.00	502.00	2,323
Apr	525.80	525.80	525.80	524.00	– 2.60	525.80	525.80	346
	Est vol 55,000; vol Mon 33,720; open int 150,613, +507.							

Discounted Cash Flow Analysis for Commodity Futures

We have said that most agricultural commodities follow seasonal price patterns; prices rise before a harvest and then fall at the harvest when the new crop becomes available for consumption. Figure 23.11 graphs this pattern. The price of the commodity following the harvest must rise at the rate of the total cost of carry (interest plus non-interest carrying costs) to induce holders of the commodity to store it willingly for future sale instead of selling it immediately. Inventories will be run down to near zero just before the next harvest.

Clearly, this pattern differs sharply from financial assets such as stocks or gold, for which there is no seasonal price movement. For financial assets, the current price is set in market equilibrium at a level that promises an expected rate of capital gains plus dividends equal to the required rate of return on the asset. Financial assets are stored only if their economic rate of return compensates for the cost of carry. In other words, financial assets are priced so that storing them produces a fair return. Agricultural prices, by contrast, are subject to steep periodic drops as each crop is harvested, which makes storage across harvests consequently unprofitable.

Of course, neither the exact size of the harvest nor the demand for the good is known in advance, so the spot price of the commodity cannot be perfectly predicted. As weather forecasts change, for example, the expected size of the crop and the expected future spot price of the commodity are updated continually.

Given the current expectation of the spot price of the commodity at some future date and a measure of the risk characteristics of that price, we can measure the present value of a claim to receive the commodity at that future

FIGURE 23.11
Typical commodity price pattern over the season. Prices adjusted for inflation.

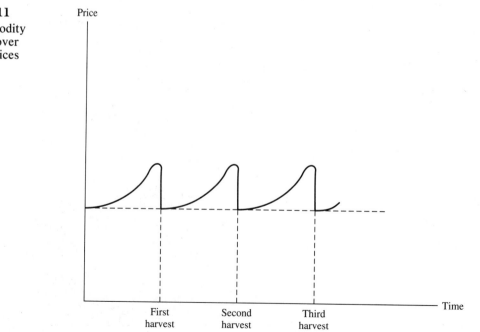

date. We simply calculate the appropriate risk premium from a model such as the CAPM or APT and discount the expected spot price at the appropriate risk-adjusted interest rate.

Table 23.5, which presents betas on a variety of commodities, shows that the beta of orange juice, for example, was estimated to be .117 over the period. If the T-bill rate is currently 7 percent, and the historical market risk premium has been about 8.5 percent, the appropriate discount rate for orange juice would be given by the CAPM as

$$7\% + .117(8.5\%) = 7.99\%$$

If the expected spot price for orange juice six months from now is $1.75 per pound, the present value of a six-month deferred claim to a pound of orange juice is simply

$$\$1.75/(1.0799)^{1/2} = \$1.68$$

What would the proper futures price for orange juice be? The contract calls for the ultimate exchange of orange juice for the futures price. We have just shown that the present value of the juice is $1.68. This should equal the present value of the futures price that will be paid for the juice. A commitment to a

TABLE 23.5 Commodity Betas

Commodity	Beta
Wheat	−0.370
Corn	−0.429
Oats	0.000
Soybeans	−0.266
Soybean oil	−0.650
Soybean meal	0.239
Broilers	−1.692
Plywood	0.660
Potatoes	−0.610
Platinum	0.221
Wool	0.307
Cotton	−0.015
Orange juice	0.117
Propane	−3.851
Cocoa	−0.291
Silver	−0.272
Copper	0.005
Cattle	0.365
Hogs	−0.148
Pork bellies	−0.062
Egg	−0.293
Lumber	−0.131
Sugar	−2.403

From Zvi Bodie and Victor Rosansky, "Risk and Return in Commodity Futures," *Financial Analysts Journal* 36 (May–June 1980).

payment of F_0 dollars in six months has a present value of $F_0/(1.07)^{1/2} = .967 \times F_0$. (Note that the discount rate is the risk-free rate of 7 percent, because the promised payment is fixed and therefore independent of market conditions.)

To equate the present values of the promised payment of F_0 and the promised receipt of orange juice, we would set

$$.967F_0 = \$1.68$$

or

$$F_0 = \$1.74.$$

The general rule, then, to determine the appropriate futures price is to equate the present value of the future payment of F_0 and the present value of the commodity to be received. This gives us

$$\frac{F_0}{(1 + r_f)^T} = \frac{E(P_T)}{(1 + k)^T}$$

or   (23.10)

$$F_0 = E(P_T) \left(\frac{1 + r_f}{1 + k}\right)^T$$

where k is the required rate of return on the commodity, which may be obtained from a model of asset market equilibrium such as the CAPM.

Note that equation 23.10 is perfectly consistent with the spot-futures parity relationship. For example, apply equation 23.10 to the futures price for a stock paying no dividends. Because the entire return on the stock is in the form of capital gains, the expected rate of capital gains must equal k, the required rate of return on the stock. Consequently, the expected price of the stock will be its current price times $(1 + k)^T$, or $E(P_T) = P_0(1 + k)^T$. Substituting this expression into equation 23.10 results in $F_0 = P_0(1 + r_f)^T$, which is exactly the parity relationship. This equilibrium derivation of the parity relationship simply reinforces the no-arbitrage restrictions we derived earlier. The spot-futures parity relationship may be obtained from the equilibrium condition that all portfolios earn fair expected rates of return.

Concept Check

> Question 13. Suppose that the systematic risk of orange juice were to increase, holding the expected time T price of juice constant. If the expected spot price is unchanged, would the futures price change? In what direction? What is the intuition behind your answer?

The advantage of the arbitrage proofs that we have explored is that they do not rely on the validity of any particular model of security market equilibrium. The absence of arbitrage opportunities is a much more robust basis for argument than the CAPM, for example. Moreover, arbitrage proofs clearly demonstrate how an investor can exploit any misalignment in the spot-futures relationship.

To their disadvantage, arbitrage restrictions may be less precise than desirable in the face of storage costs or costs of short selling.

We can summarize by saying that the actions of arbitrageurs force the futures prices of financial assets to maintain a precise relationship with the price of the underlying financial asset. This relationship is described by the spot-futures parity formula. Opportunities for arbitrage are more limited in the case of commodity futures, because such commodities often are not stored. Hence, to make a precise prediction for the correct relationship between futures and spot prices, we must rely on a model of security market equilibrium such as the CAPM or APT and estimate the unobservables, the expected spot price, and the appropriate interest rate. Such models will be perfectly consistent with the parity relationships in the benchmark case where investors willingly store the commodity.

23.10 *Swaps*

We noted in Chapter 17 that interest rate swaps have become common tools for interest rate risk management. Since their inception in 1981, swaps have grown to a North American market of well over $1 trillion in notional principal. A large and active market of several hundred billion dollars also exists for foreign exchange swaps. Recall that a swap arrangement obligates two counterparties to exchange cash flows at one or more future dates. To illustrate, a **foreign exchange swap** might call for one party to exchange $1.6 million for 1 million British pounds in each of the next five years. An **interest rate swap** with notional principal of $1 million might call for one party to exchange a variable cash flow equal to $1 million times the LIBOR rate for $1 million times a fixed rate of 8 percent. In this way, the two parties exchange the cash flows corresponding to interest payments on a fixed-rate 8 percent coupon bond for those corresponding to payments on a floating-rate bond paying LIBOR.

As we saw in Chapter 17, an interest rate swap agreement is a cheap and quick way to restructure the balance sheet. The swap does not entail trading costs to buy back outstanding bonds or underwriting fees and lengthy registration procedures to issue new debt. In addition, if the firm perceives price advantages in either the fixed or floating rate market, the swap market allows it to issue its debt in the cheaper of the two markets, and then "convert" to the financing mode it feels best suits its business needs.

Foreign exchange swaps also enable the firm to quickly and cheaply restructure its balance sheet. Suppose, for example, that the firm issues $10 million in debt at 8 percent, but it actually prefers that its interest obligations be denominated in British pounds. For example, the issuing firm might be a British corporation that perceives advantageous financing opportunities in Canada but prefers pound-denominated liabilities. Then the firm, whose debt currently obliges it to make dollar-denominated payments of $800,000, can agree to swap a given number of pounds each year for $800,000. By so doing, it effectively covers its dollar obligation and replaces it with a new pound-denominated obligation.

How can the fair swap rate be determined? For example, do we know that an exchange of LIBOR is a fair trade for a fixed rate of 8 percent? Or what is the fair swap rate between dollars and pounds for the foreign exchange swap we considered? To answer these questions we can exploit the analogy between a swap agreement and a forward or futures contract.

Consider a swap agreement to exchange dollars for pounds for one period only. Next year, for example, one might exchange $1 million for £.5 million. This is no more than a simple forward contract in foreign exchange. The dollar-paying party is contracting to buy British pounds in one year for a number of dollars agreed to today. The forward exchange rate for one year delivery is $F_1 = \$2.00/\text{pound}$. We know from the interest rate parity relationship that this forward price should be related to the spot exchange rate, E_0, by the formula $F_1 = E_0(1 + r_{CAN})/(1 + r_{UK})$. Because a one-period swap is in fact a forward contract, the fair swap rate is also given by the parity relationship.

Now consider an agreement to trade foreign exchange for two periods. This agreement could be structured as a portfolio of two separate forward contracts. If so, the forward price for the exchange of currencies in one year would be $F_1 = E_0(1 + r_{CAN})/(1 + r_{UK})$, while the forward price for the exchange in the second year would be $F_2 = E_0[(1 + r_{CAN})/(1 + r_{UK})]^2$. As an example, suppose that $E_0 = \$2.038/\text{pound}$, $r_{CAN} = 5$ percent, and $r_{UK} = 7$ percent. Then, using the parity relationship, we would have prices for forward delivery of $F_1 = \$2.038/£ \times (1.05/1.07) = \$2.00/£$ and $F_2 = \$2.038/£ \times (1.05/1.07)^2 = \$1.9625/£$. Figure 23.12**A** illustrates this sequence of cash exchanges assuming that the swap calls for delivery of one pound in each year. While the dollars to be paid in each of the two years are known today, they vary from year to year.

In contrast, a swap agreement to exchange currency for two years would call for a fixed exchange rate to be used for the duration of the swap. This means that the same number of dollars would be paid per pound in each year, as illustrated in Figure 23.12**B**. Because the forward prices for delivery in each of the next two years are $2.00/£ and $1.9625/£, the fixed exchange rate that makes the two-period swap a fair deal must be between these two values. Therefore, the dollar payer underpays for the pound in the first year (compared to the forward exchange rate) and overpays in the second year. Thus, the swap can be viewed as a portfolio of forward transactions, but instead of each transaction being priced independently, one forward price is applied to all of the transactions.

Given this insight, it is easy to determine the fair swap price. If we were to purchase one pound per year for two years using two independent forward rate agreements, we would pay F_1 dollars in one year and F_2 dollars in two years. If, instead, we enter a swap, we pay a constant rate of F^* dollars per pound. Because both strategies must be equally costly, we conclude that

$$\frac{F_1}{1 + y_1} + \frac{F_2}{(1 + y_2)^2} = \frac{F^*}{1 + y_1} + \frac{F^*}{(1 + y_2)^2}$$

FIGURE 23.12
Forward contracts versus swaps.
A—Two forward contracts, each priced independently;
B—Two-year swap agreement.

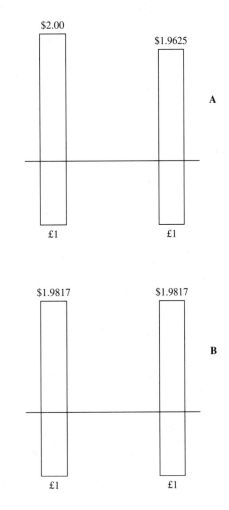

where y_1 and y_2 are the appropriate yields from the yield curve for discounting dollar cash flows of one and two years maturity, respectively. In our example, where we have assumed a flat Canadian yield curve at 5 percent, we would solve

$$\frac{2.00}{1.05} + \frac{1.9625}{1.05^2} = \frac{F^*}{1.05} + \frac{F^*}{1.05^2}$$

which implies that $F^* = 1.9817$. The same principle would apply to a foreign exchange swap of any other maturity. In essence, we need to find the level annuity, F^*, with the same present value as the sequence of annual cash flows that would be incurred in a sequence of forward rate agreements.

Interest rate swaps can be subjected to precisely the same analysis. Here, the forward contract is on an interest rate. For example, if you swap LIBOR for an 8 percent fixed rate with notional principal of $100, then you have entered a forward contract for delivery of $100 times r_{LIBOR} for a fixed "forward" price of

$8. If the swap agreement is for many periods, the fair spread will be determined by the entire sequence of interest rate forward prices over the life of the swap.

23.11   *Other Developments in Futures Markets*

As it becomes apparent that investors want to speculate on or hedge against a source of uncertainty, the futures exchanges respond by introducing new contracts to satisfy investor demands. The exchanges profit in proportion to the volume of trading on the contract, so it pays them to seek out new contracts with wide appeal to investors. We have seen that Canadian futures exchanges did not have much success with the introduction of new instruments. U.S. exchanges, on the other hand, have successfully introduced several new types of contracts in recent years. One example is the recent establishment of futures contracts on the U.S. dollar, the U.S. Dollar Index Futures traded on the New York Cotton Exchange. The dollar index contracts allow investors to bet on (or hedge against) changes in the value of the dollar relative to a bundle of foreign currencies rather than bet on the value of the dollar relative to a particular foreign currency. Various energy futures similarly arose when oil prices became volatile in the 1970s.

The CPI contract, an inflation futures contract, is an example of an unsuccessful U.S. financial innovation introduced in 1985 by the Economic Index Market of the Coffee, Sugar, and Cocoa Exchange. The inflation measure originally was based on the Consumer Price Index for Urban Wage Earners and Clerical Workers (CPI-W), which is the index used for wage, lease, and Social Security cost-of-living adjustments. (The U.S. government also publishes a CPI-U index for all urban consumers.) The CPI-W contract sets the 1967 price level equal to 100. A price level of 110 means that the average cost of goods is 10 percent higher than it was in 1967. The level of the CPI-W in September 1987 was 339, which means that goods then cost on average 3.39 times what they did in 1967.

The CPI contract called for *cash delivery* from the long to the short position of the difference between the original futures price and the value of the CPI-W index at contract maturity. A scaling index of $1,000 was used, so that a futures price of 350 and a CPI-W index of 348 at maturity would have resulted in payment of $1,000 \times (350 - 348) = $2,000 from the long to the short position. An inflation futures contract such as this has obvious appeal in a period of uncertain inflation. It can be used to lock in a real rate of return on nominal contracts. Notably, the longest contract maturity on a CPI contract was roughly three years, which is just the length of most collective bargaining wage agreements.

To show how such a contract locked in real values, consider this example. Suppose that the nominal interest rate is 9 percent, and the current level of the CPI is 380. You lend $366,972 today and will be repaid $400,000 in one year. This gives you a 9 percent nominal rate of return. The purchasing power of that payment and the real rate of return on the loan, however, are uncertain, because prices next year depend on inflation experience during the coming year.

The $366,972 that you lend today has a "real value" of $96,572 ($366,972/3.80), meaning that the purchasing power of $366,972 today, when the price level is 380, is equivalent to the purchasing power that $96,572 had in 1967. Real value may be thought of as the price-level adjusted value of your dollar investment. The real value of the $400,000 that you will be repaid will equal $400,000 adjusted for the price level in one year.

Consider now the establishment of a long position in the CPI-W contract. If the futures price is 400, the payoff to the long position will be (CPI − 400) × 1,000. Your total portfolio (loan plus futures position) will be:

Loan repayment	400,000
Futures profit	(CPI × 1,000) − 400,000
TOTAL	CPI × 1,000

Note that the portfolio's value is exactly proportional to the price level. In essence, you have sold your original claim to a $400,000 nominal payment for a claim to a payment of 1,000 times the CPI. Your final payment is exactly proportional to the general level of prices, which gives you known purchasing power.

The payment is constant in real terms. Because the CPI is set equal to 100 in 1967, a payment of 1,000 times the CPI has a purchasing power of 1,000 times the purchasing power of $100 in 1967. This is 100,000 real dollars. Thus your original loan of $96,572 in "constant dollars" of 1967 will grow with certainty to a real value of 100,000 constant dollars, thereby yielding a guaranteed real rate of return of 3.55 percent. The CPI futures contract provided the ability to eliminate completely the effect of inflation on the real rate of return. The real interest rate that could be locked in using CPI futures was essentially the nominal interest rate paid on bonds adjusted for the implicit inflation forecast built into the CPI futures price.

When it was introduced, economists such as Nobel laureate Milton Friedman hailed the inflation contract. They felt the ability to hedge price risk was of great value and would attract much trading interest. The interest, however, never materialized, and the instrument was eventually withdrawn. We speculate that some reasons for the failure of the contract are as follows:

1. Inflation has been low and fairly stable since the contract was introduced, reducing the need for hedging.
2. The contract may have been too difficult for many traders to understand.
3. The value of the "spot commodity," the CPI, is released only monthly. Because the daily value is not known and cannot be traded directly, the spot-futures trading strategies that contribute to volume in other contracts never developed.

4. Many firms already may be inflation hedged, since the prices they pay and charge for goods and services already increase with the general level of prices.

5. Demand for true inflation hedging is more likely to arise to protect long-term interests, such as nominal pension benefits. The CPI contract's three-year maximum maturity is insufficient to hedge these values.

We conclude that ingredients that contribute to successful futures contracts are the presence of natural hedging demands by investors, a closely related spot market for the commodity and the ability to engage in spot-futures arbitrage strategies, and an easily understood contract design.

Summary

1. Forward contracts are arrangements that call for future delivery of an asset at a currently agreed-on price. The long trader is obligated to purchase the good, and the short trader is obligated to deliver it. If the price of the asset at the maturity of the contract exceeds the forward price, the long side benefits by virtue of acquiring the good at the contract price.

2. A futures contract is similar to a forward contract, differing most importantly in the aspects of standardization and marking to market, which is the process by which gains and losses on futures contract positions are settled daily. In contrast, forward contracts call for no cash transfers until contract maturity.

3. Futures contracts are traded on organized exchanges that standardize the size of the contract, the grade of the deliverable asset, the delivery date, and the delivery location. Traders negotiate only over the contract price. This standardization creates increased liquidity in the marketplace and means buyers and sellers can easily find many traders for a desired purchase or sale.

4. The clearinghouse represents an intermediary between each pair of traders, acting as the short position for each long, and as the long position for each short. In this way, traders need not be concerned about the performance of the trader on the opposite side of the contract. In turn, traders post margins to guarantee their own performance on the contracts.

5. The gain or loss to the long side for a futures contract held between time 0 and t is $F_t - F_0$. Because $F_T = P_T$, the long's profit if the contract is held until maturity is $P_T - F_0$, where P_T is the spot price at time T and F_0 is the original futures price. The gain or loss to the short position is $F_0 - P_T$.

6. Futures contracts may be used for hedging or speculating. Speculators use the contracts to take a stand on the ultimate price of an asset. Short hedgers take short positions in contracts to offset any gains or losses on the value of an asset already held in inventory. Long hedgers take long positions to offset gains or losses in the purchase price of a good.

7. The spot-futures parity relationship states that the equilibrium futures price on an asset providing no services or payments (such as dividends) is $F_0 = P_0(1 + r_f)^T$. If the futures price deviates from this value, then market participants can earn arbitrage profits.

8. If the asset provides services or payments with yield d, the parity relationship becomes $F_0 = P_0(1 + r_f - d)^T$. This model is also called the cost-of-carry model, because it states that the futures price must exceed the spot price by the net cost of carrying the asset until maturity date T.

9. The equilibrium futures price will be less than the currently expected time T spot price if the spot price exhibits systematic risk. This provides an expected profit for the long position that bears the risk and imposes an expected loss on the short position that is willing to accept that expected loss as a means to shed risk.

10. Futures contracts calling for cash settlement are traded on the TSE 35 in Canada and in various U.S. stock market indices. Stock index contracts may be mixed with Treasury bills to construct artificial equity positions, which makes them potentially valuable tools for market timers. Market index contracts are used also by arbitrageurs who attempt to profit from violations of the parity relationship.

11. Foreign exchange futures trade in the U.S. on several foreign currencies, as well as on a European currency index. The interest rate parity relationship for foreign exchange futures is

$$F_0 = E_0 \left(\frac{1 + r_{\text{US}}}{1 + r_{\text{foreign}}} \right)^T$$

Deviations of the futures price from this value imply arbitrage opportunity. Empirical evidence, however, suggests that generally the parity relationship is satisfied.

12. Interest rate futures allow for hedging against interest rate fluctuations in several different markets. Few of them are currently actively traded in Canada.

13. Commodity futures pricing is complicated by costs for storage of the underlying commodity. When the asset is willingly stored by investors, then the storage costs enter the futures pricing equation as follows:

$$F_0 = P_0(1 + r_f + c)^T$$

The non-interest carrying costs, c, play the role of a "negative dividend" in this context.

14. When commodities are not stored for investment purposes, the correct futures price must be determined using general risk-return principles. In this event

$$F_0 = E(P_T) \left(\frac{1 + r_f}{1 + k} \right)^T$$

The equilibrium (risk-return) and the no-arbitrage predictions of the proper futures price are consistent with one another.

15. Swaps, which call for the exchange of a series of cash flows, may be viewed as portfolios of forward contracts. Each transaction may be viewed as a separate forward agreement. However, instead of pricing each exchange independently, the swap sets one "forward price" that applies to all of the transactions. Therefore, the swap price will be an average of the futures prices that would prevail if each exchange were priced separately.

16. As new hedging demands arise among consumers, futures exchanges respond by introducing new contracts, not always successfully. Recent examples of some unsuccessful and successful contracts are the CPI contract, dollar index contracts, and various energy futures contracts.

Key terms

Forward contract	Basis risk
Futures contract	Spread
Long position	Spot-futures parity theorem
Short position	Cost-of-carry relationship
Clearinghouse	Index arbitrage
Reversing trade	Program trading
Open interest	Triple witching hour
Marking to market	Interest rate parity theorem
Maintenance margin (Variation margin)	Covered interest arbitrage relationship
Convergence property	Foreign exchange swap
Cash delivery	Interest rate swap
Basis	

Selected readings

Extensive treatments of the institutional background of several futures markets in the United States and Canada are provided in:

Hore, John E. *Trading on Canadian Futures Markets*, 3rd edition. The Canadian Securities Institute, 1987.

Kolb, Robert W. *Understanding Futures Markets*. Glenview, Ill.: Scott, Foresman, and Co., 1985.

Excellent, although challenging, treatments of the differences between futures and forward markets and the pricing of each type of contract are in:

Black, Fischer. "The Pricing of Commodity Contracts." *Journal of Financial Economics* 3 (January–March 1976).

Cox, John; Ingersoll, Jonathan; and Ross, Stephen A. "The Relation between Forward Prices and Futures Prices." *Journal of Financial Economics* 9 (December 1981).

Jarrow, Robert; and Oldfield, George. "Forward Contracts and Futures Contracts." *Journal of Financial Economics* 9 (December 1981).

Textbooks covering both theoretical and institutional aspects of U.S. and Canadian futures markets are:

Khoury, Nabil; and Laroche, Pierre. *Options et Contrats à Terme* (in French). Québec: Les Presses de l'Université Laval, 1988.

Siegel, Daniel R.; and Siegel, Diane F. *Futures Markets*. Hinsdale, Ill.: Dryden Press, 1990.

A survey of the issues involved in the regulation of futures markets is provided in:

Edwards, Franklin. "Futures Markets in Transition: The Uneasy Balance between Government and Self-Regulation." *Journal of Futures Markets* 3 (Summer 1983).

For treatments of the backwardation/contango debate, see:

Cootner, Paul H. "Speculation and Hedging." Stanford, Calif.: Food Research Institute Studies, Supplement, 1967.

Hicks, J. R. *Value and Capital*, 2d ed. London: Oxford University Press, 1946.

Keynes, John Maynard. *Treatise on Money*, 2d ed. London: Macmillan, 1930.

Working, Holbrook. "The Theory of Price of Storage." *American Economic Review* 39 (December 1949).

The economics of hedging and spreading is discussed in:

Scholes, Myron. "The Economics of Hedging and Spreading in Futures Markets." *Journal of Futures Markets* 1 (Summer 1981).

An excellent treatment of stock index futures is:

Modest, David; and Sundaresan, Mahadevan. "The Relationship between Spot and Futures Prices in Stock Index Futures Markets: Some Preliminary Evidence." *Journal of Futures Markets* 3 (Spring 1983).

A good set of readings on index futures is:

Fabozzi, Frank J.; and Kipnis, Gregory M. (editors). *Stock Index Futures*. Homewood, Ill.: Dow Jones-Irwin, 1984.

A useful introduction to foreign exchange markets may be found in:

Chrystal, K. Alex. "A Guide to Foreign Exchange Markets." *Federal Reserve Bank of St. Louis,* March 1984.

Two analyses of the use of financial futures to hedge interest rate risk are:

Fortin, Michel, and Khoury, Nabil. "Hedging Interest Rate Risks with Financial Futures." *Canadian Journal of Administrative Sciences* 1, no. 2 (December 1984).

Kolb, Robert; and Gay, Gerald. "Immunizing Bond Portfolios with Interest Rate Futures." *Financial Management* 11 (Summer 1982).

A survey of the U.S. financial futures market with much institutional detail is:

Powers, Mark J. *Inside the Financial Futures Markets*. New York: John Wiley & Sons, 1984.

Analyses of risk and return in commodity futures are in:

Bodie, Zvi; and Rosansky, Victor. "Risk and Return in Commodity Futures." *Financial Analysts Journal* 36 (May–June 1980).

Dusak, Katherine. "Futures Trading and Investor Returns: An Investigation of Commodity Market Risk Premiums." *Journal of Political Economy* 81 (December 1973).

Khoury, Nabil T.; and Martel, Jean-Marc. "Optimal Futures Hedging in the Presence of Asymmetric Information." *Journal of Futures Markets* 5, no. 4 (1985).

The issue of the storage of commodities is treated in:

Brennan, Michael. "The Supply of Storage." *American Economic Review* 47 (March 1958).

Khoury, Nabil T.; and Martel, Jean-Marc. "A Supply of Storage Theory with Asymmetric Information." *Journal of Futures Markets* 9, no. 6 (1989).

Empirical studies on Canadian futures markets include:

Khoury, Nabil T.; and Yourougou, Pierre. "Price Discovery Performance and Maturity Effect in the Canadian Feed Wheat Market." *Review of Futures Markets* 8, no. 3 (1989).

———. "The Informational Content of the Basis: Evidence from Canadian Barley, Oats, and Canola Futures Markets." *Journal of Futures Markets* 11, no. 1 (1991).

Problems

1. Why is there no futures market in cement?

2. Why might persons purchase futures contracts rather than the underlying asset?

3. What is the difference in cash flow between short selling an asset and entering a short futures position?

4. Consider a stock that will pay a dividend of D dollars in one year, which is when a futures contract matures. Consider the following strategy: buy the stock, short a futures contract on the stock, and borrow S_0 dollars, where S_0 is the current price of the stock.
   a. What are the cash flows now and in one year?
   b. Show that the equilibrium futures price must be $F_0 = S_0(1 + r) - D$ to avoid arbitrage.
   c. Call the dividend yield $d = D/S_0$, and conclude that $F_0 = S_0(1 + r - d)$.

5. Consider this arbitrage strategy to derive the parity relationship for spreads: (1) enter a long futures position with maturity date T_1 and futures price $F(T_1)$; (2) enter a short position with maturity T_2 and futures price $F(T_2)$; and (3) at T_1, when the first contract expires, buy the asset and borrow $F(T_1)$ dollars at rate r_f; pay back the loan with interest at time T_2.
   a. What are the total cash flows to this strategy at times 0, T_1, and T_2?
   b. Why must profits at time T_2 be zero if no arbitrage opportunities are present?
   c. What must the relationship between $F(T_1)$ and $F(T_2)$ be for the profits at T_2 to be equal to zero? This relationship is the parity relationship for spreads.

6. Suppose that an investor in a 50 percent tax bracket purchases three soybean futures contracts at a price of $5.40 a bushel and closes them out at price $5.80. What are the after-tax profits to the position?

7. These questions address stock futures contracts:
   a. A hypothetical futures contract on a non-dividend-paying stock with current price $150 has a maturity of one year. If the T-bill rate is 8 percent, what is the futures price?
   b. What should the futures price be if the maturity of the contract is three years?
   c. What if the interest rate is 12 percent and the maturity of the contract is three years?

8. You suddenly receive information that indicates to you that the stock market is about to rise substantially. The market is unaware of this information. What should you do?

9. (1982 CFA Examination, Level III) In each of the following cases discuss how you, as a portfolio manager, would use financial futures to protect the portfolio.
   a. You own a large position in a relatively illiquid bond that you want to sell.

b. You have a large gain on one of your long Treasuries and want to sell it, but would like to defer the gain until the next accounting period, which begins in four weeks.

c. You will receive a large contribution next month that you hope to invest in long-term corporate bonds on a yield basis as favourable as is now available.

10. Suppose the value of the TSE 35 stock index is currently 250. If the one-year T-bill rate is 8 percent and the expected dividend yield on the TSE 35 is 5 percent, what should the one-year maturity futures price be?

11. It is now January. The interest rate is currently 8 percent annually. The June futures price for gold is $346.30, while the December futures price is $360. Is there an arbitrage opportunity here? If so, how would you exploit it?

12. The Toronto Futures Exchange has just introduced a new futures contract on Brandex stock, a company that currently pays no dividends. Each contract calls for delivery of 1,000 shares of stock in one year. The T-bill rate is 6 percent per year.

a. If Brandex stock now sells at $120 per share, what should be the futures price?

b. If Brandex stock immediately decreases by 3 percent, what will be the change in the futures price and the change in the investor's margin account?

c. If the margin on the contract is $12,000, what is the percentage return on the investor's position?

13. (Based on the 1986 CFA Examination, Level III) Your client, for whom you are underwriting a $400 million bond issue, is concerned that market conditions will change before the issue is brought to market. He has heard that it may be possible to reduce the risk exposure by hedging in the Montreal Exchange's Canada bond futures market. Specifically, he asks you to:

a. Briefly explain how the hedge works.

b. Describe *three* practical problems that would limit the effectiveness of the hedge.

14. (1986 CFA Examination, Level III) Futures contracts and options on a futures contract can be used to modify risk. Identify the fundamental distinction between a futures contract and an option on a futures contract, and briefly explain the difference in the manner that futures and options modify *portfolio* risk.

15. Consider the futures contract written on the S&P 500 index and maturing in six months. The interest rate is 5 percent per six-month period, and the future value of dividends expected to be paid over the next six months is $8. The current index level is 127.5. Assume that you can short sell the S&P 500 index.

a. Suppose the expected rate of return on the market is 10 percent per six-month period. What is the expected level of the index in six months?

b. What is the theoretical no-arbitrage price for a six-month futures contract on the S&P 500 stock index?

c. Suppose the futures price is 124. Is there an arbitrage opportunity here? If so, how would you exploit it?

16. Consider these futures market data for the June delivery S&P 500 contract, exactly six months hence. The S&P 500 index is at 249.32, and the June maturity contract is at $F_0 = 250.70$.

a. If the current interest rate is 3.25 percent semiannually, and the average dividend rate of the stocks in the index is 1.5 percent semiannually, what fraction of the proceeds of stock short sales would you need to be available to you to earn arbitrage profits?

b. Suppose that you, in fact, have access to 90 percent of the proceeds from a short sale. What is the lower bound on the futures price that rules out arbitrage opportunities? By how much does the actual futures price fall below the no-arbitrage bound? Formulate the appropriate arbitrage strategy, and calculate the profits to that strategy.

17. You manage a $3 million portfolio, currently all invested in equities, and believe that you have extraordinary market timing skills. You believe that the market is on the verge of a big but short-lived downturn; you would move your portfolio temporarily into T-bills, but you do not want to incur the transaction costs of liquidating and reestablishing your equity position. Instead, you decide to temporarily hedge your equity holdings with TSE 35 index futures contracts.

a. Should you be long or short on the contracts? Why?

b. If your equity holdings are invested in a market-index fund, into how many contracts should you enter? The TSE 35 index is now at 300 and the contract multiplier is 500.

c. How does your answer to question b change if the beta of your portfolio is .6?

18. Suppose that the spot price of the Swiss franc is currently 80 cents. The one-year futures price is 84 cents. Is the interest rate higher in Canada or Switzerland?

19. Consider the following information:

$$r_{Can} = 15\%$$
$$r_{UK} = 17\%$$
$$E_0 = 2.0 \text{ dollars per pound}$$
$$F_0 = 1.97 \text{ (one-year delivery)}$$

where the interest rates are annual yields on Canadian or U.K. bills. Given this information:

a. Where would you lend?

b. Where would you borrow?

c. How could you arbitrage?

20. (Based on the 1983 CFA Examination, Level III) The United Dominion Co. is considering the sale in February 1983 of $100 million in 10-year debentures that probably will be rated AAA, like the firm's other bond issues. The firm is eager to proceed at today's rate of 10.5 percent. As treasurer, you know that it will take about 12 weeks (until May 1983) to get the issue registered and sold. Therefore, you suggest that the firm hedge the pending bond issue using Canada bond futures contracts. (Each Canada bond contract is for $100,000.) Explain how you would go about hedging the bond issue, and describe the results, assuming that the following two sets of future conditions actually occur. (Ignore commissions and margin costs, and assume a one-to-one hedge ratio.) Show all calculations.

	Case 1	Case 2
Current Values—February 1983		
Bond rate	10.5%	10.5%
June 1983 Canada bond futures	78.875	78.875
Estimated Values—May 1983		
Bond rate	11.0%	10.0%
June 1983 Canada bond futures	75.93	81.84

21. A trust company is underwriting an issue of 30-year zero-coupon corporate bonds with a face value of $100 million and a current market value of $5.354 million (a yield of 5 percent per six-month period). The firm must hold the bonds for a few days before issuing them to the public, which exposes it to interest rate risk. The company wishes to hedge its position by using T-bond futures contracts. The current T-bond futures price is $90.80 per $100 par value, and the T-bond contract will be settled using a 20-year 8 percent coupon bond paying interest semiannually. The contract is due to expire in a few days, so the T-bond price and the T-bond futures price are virtually identical. The yield implied on the bond is therefore 4.5 percent per six-month period. (Confirm this as a first step.) Assume that the yield curve is flat and that the corporate bond will continue to yield 0.5 percent more than T-bonds per six-month period, even if the general level of interest rates should change. What hedge ratio should the underwriter use to hedge its bond holdings against possible interest rate fluctuations over the next few days?

22. If the spot price of gold is $350 per troy ounce, the risk-free interest rate is 10 percent, and storage and insurance costs are zero, what should the forward price of gold be for delivery in one year? Use an arbitrage argument to prove your answer, and include a numerical example showing how you could make risk-free arbitrage profits if the forward price exceeded its upper bound value.

23. If the wheat harvest today is poor, would you expect this fact to have any effect on today's futures prices for wheat to be delivered (post-harvest) two years from today? Under what circumstances will there be no effect?

24. Suppose that the price of corn is risky, with a beta of .5. The monthly storage cost is $.03, and the current spot price is $2.75, with an expected spot price in three months of $2.94. If the expected rate of return on the market is 1.8 percent per month, with a risk-free rate of 1 percent per month, would you store corn for three months?

PART VIII

PLAYERS AND STRATEGIES

CHAPTER 24

Portfolio Management Policy

The investment process is a chain of considerations and actions for an individual, from thinking about investing to placing buy/sell orders for investment assets such as stocks and bonds. Likewise, for institutions such as insurance companies and pension funds, the investment process starts with a mission and a budget and ends with a detailed investment portfolio.

Establishing a clear hierarchy of the investment process is useful. The first step is to determine the investor's objectives. The second step is to identify all the constraints, that is, the qualifications and requirements of the resultant portfolio. Finally, the objectives and constraints must be translated into investment policies. These steps are necessary for both individual and institutional investors.

Individuals' objectives and constraints are greatly affected by their household's stage in the life cycle. A young father's goals are very different from a retired widow's. Institutional investors do the lion's share of investing, however. Their constraints are often compounded by legal restrictions and regulations.

24.1 *Making Investment Decisions*

Translating the aspirations and circumstances of diverse households into desirable investment decisions is a daunting task. Accomplishing the same task for institutions with many stakeholders, which are regulated by various authorities, is equally perplexing. Put simply, the investment process is not easily programmable into an efficient procedure.

A natural place to look for quality investment procedures is in the offices of professional investors. Better yet, we chose to examine the approach of the

Association for Investment Management and Research (AIMR), which was established by a merger of the Financial Analysts Federation (FAF) with the Institute of Chartered Financial Analysts (ICFA).

The AIMR administers three examinations for those who wish to be certified as chartered financial analysts (CFAs). To become a CFA, a candidate must pass exams at Levels I, II, and III, and show a satisfactory record of experience. The AIMR helps CFA candidates by organizing classes and compiling reading materials. Our analysis in this chapter is compiled along the lines of the AIMR model.

The basic idea is to subdivide the major steps (objectives, constraints, and policies) into concrete considerations of the various aspects, making the task of organization more tractable. The standard format appears in Table 24.1. In the next sections, we elaborate briefly (there is a lot more to be said than this text will allow) on the construction of the three parts of the investment process, along the lines of Table 24.1.

Objectives

Portfolio objectives centre on the risk-return trade-off between the expected return the investors want (*return requirements* in the first column of Table 24.1) and how much risk they are willing to assume (*risk tolerance*). Investment managers must know the level of risk that can be tolerated in the pursuit of a better rate of return. Table 24.2 lists factors governing return requirements and risk attitudes for each of the seven major investor categories discussed.

Individual Investors

Individual investors are, simply, households. The basic factors affecting individual investors' return requirements and risk tolerance are life-cycle stage and individual preferences. We will have much more to say about individual investor objectives in Chapter 25.

Personal Trusts

Personal trusts are established when an individual confers legal title to property to another person or institution (the trustee) to manage that property for

TABLE 24.1   Determination of Portfolio Policies

Objectives	Constraints	Policies
Return requirements	Liquidity	Asset allocation
Risk tolerance	Horizon	Diversification
	Regulations	Risk positioning
	Taxes	Tax positioning
	Unique needs	Income generation

TABLE 24.2 Matrix of Objectives

Type of Investor	Return Requirement	Risk Tolerance
Individual and personal trusts	Life cycle (education, children, retirement)	Life cycle (younger are more risk tolerant)
Mutual funds	Variable	Variable
Pension funds	Assumed actuarial rate	Depends on proximity of payouts
Endowment funds	Determined by current income needs and need for asset growth to maintain real value	Generally conservative
Life insurance companies	Should exceed new money rate by sufficient margin to meet expenses and profit objectives; also actuarial rates important	Conservative
Non-life insurance companies	No minimum	Conservative
Banks	Interest spread	Variable

one or more beneficiaries. Beneficiaries customarily are divided into **income beneficiaries,** who receive the interest and dividend income from the trust during their lifetimes, and **remaindermen,** who receive the principal of the trust when the income beneficiary dies and the trust is dissolved. The trustee is usually a trust company, a lawyer, or an investment professional. Investment of a trust is subject to provincial trust laws, as well as "prudent man" rules that limit the types of allowable trust investment to those that a prudent person would select.

Objectives in the case of personal trusts normally are more limited in scope than those of the individual investor. Because of their fiduciary responsibility, personal trust managers typically are more risk-averse than are individual investors. Certain asset classes such as options and futures contracts, for example, and strategies such as short selling or buying on margin are ruled out, although the sale of calls against stocks is an acceptable, conservative strategy.

When there are both income beneficiaries and remaindermen, the trustee faces a built-in conflict between the interests of the two sets of beneficiaries, because greater current income inherently entails a sacrifice of future capital gain. For the typical case where the life beneficiary has substantial income requirements, there is pressure on the trustee to invest heavily in fixed-income securities or high dividend-yielding common stocks.

Mutual Funds

Mutual funds are firms that manage pools of investors' money. They invest it in ways specified in their prospectuses and issue shares to investors entitling them to a pro rata portion of the income generated by the funds. The objectives of a mutual fund are spelled out in its prospectus. We discussed mutual funds in detail in Chapter 3.

Pension Funds

Pension fund objectives depend on the type of pension plan. There are two basic types: **defined contribution plans** and **defined benefit plans.** Defined contribution plans are, in effect, tax-deferred retirement savings accounts established by the firm in trust for its employees, with the employee bearing all the risk and receiving all the return from the plan's assets.

The largest pension funds, however, are defined benefit plans. In these plans, the assets serve as collateral for the liabilities that the firm sponsoring the plan owes to the plan beneficiaries. The liabilities are life annuities, earned during the employee's working years, that start at the plan participant's retirement. The sponsoring firm's pension actuary makes an assumption about the rate of return that will be earned on the plan's assets and uses this assumed rate to compute the amount that the firm must contribute regularly to fund the plan's liabilities.

If the pension fund's actual rate of return exceeds the actuarial assumed rate, then the firm's shareholders experience an unanticipated gain, since the excess can be used to reduce future contributions.[1] If the plan's actual rate of return falls short of the assumed rate, the firm eventually will have to increase future contributions. Thus, it is the sponsoring firm's shareholders who bear the risk in a defined benefit pension plan, so it is natural to assume that a main objective of the plan will be to reward the shareholders for bearing this risk.

Many firms try to match the risk of the pension assets with the risk of their pension liabilities. Often a distinction is made between the firm's liability to already-retired participants, which is a known flow of money fixed in nominal amount, and its liability to active participants, which is tied to the employee's final wage or salary under most benefit formulas. The firm can hedge its known liability to retired workers by investing in fixed-income securities, but it cannot completely hedge the pension benefits it owes to active workers because this liability is effectively linked directly to future wages, which are not known in advance.[2]

Many pension plans view their assumed actuarial rate of return as their target rate of return and consider their tolerance for earning less than that rate to be quite low. We discuss pension plans more fully in Chapter 25.

Endowment Funds

Endowment funds are organizations chartered to use their money for specific non-profit purposes. They are financed by gifts from one or more sponsors and are typically managed by educational, cultural, and charitable organizations or by independent foundations established solely to carry out the fund's specific purposes. Generally, the investment objectives of an endowment fund are to

---

[1] See the box in Chapter 25 for a discussion on the ownership of pension fund surpluses.

[2] This statement is not entirely correct, because a pension fund can transfer all of its pension liabilities to a life insurance company. In such a case the plan is called an *insured pension plan.*

produce a steady flow of income subject to only a moderate degree of risk. Trustees of an endowment fund, however, can specify other objectives as dictated by the circumstances of the particular endowment fund.

Life Insurance Companies

Life insurance companies generally try to invest so as to hedge their liabilities, which are defined by the policies they write. Thus, there are as many objectives as there are distinct types of policies. Until a decade or so ago there were only two types of life insurance policies available for individuals: whole-life and term. A **whole-life insurance policy** combines a death benefit with a kind of savings plan that provides for a gradual buildup of cash value that the policyholder can withdraw at a later point in life, usually at age 65. **Term insurance,** on the other hand, provides death benefits only, with no buildup of cash value.

The interest rate that is imbedded in the schedule of cash value accumulation promised under a whole-life policy is a fixed rate, and life insurance companies try to hedge this liability by investing in long-term bonds. Often, the insured individual has the right to borrow at a prespecified fixed interest rate against the cash value of the policy.

During the inflationary years of the 1970s and early 1980s, when many older whole-life policies carried contractual borrowing rates as low as 4 percent or 5 percent per year, policyholders borrowed heavily against the cash value to invest in money market mutual funds paying double-digit yields. Other actual and potential policyholders abandoned whole-life policies and took out term insurance, investing the difference in the premiums on their own. From 1970–1980, term insurance rose from approximately 29 percent to 50 percent of individual life insurance policies purchased, before insurance companies reacted to the decrease in the more profitable form.

In response to the public's change in tastes, the insurance industry came up with some new policy types, of which two are of particular interest to investors: **variable life** and **universal life.**[3] Under a variable life policy, the insured's premium buys a fixed death benefit plus a cash value that can be invested in a variety of mutual funds from which the policyholder can choose. With a universal life policy, policyholders can increase or reduce the premium or death benefit according to their changing needs. Furthermore, the interest rate on the cash value component changes with market interest rates. These two plans effectively unbundle the charges for insurance and savings.

The great advantage of variable and universal life insurance policies is that earnings on the cash value are not taxed until the money is withdrawn, although the 1981 federal budget imposed tax liability on policies that provided too much cash value; this enabled the government to identify and tax excessive tax-sheltered savings plans.[4]

---

[3] A third type was *adjustable life,* which enabled the policyholder to vary benefits and premiums according to his or her changing needs.

[4] Investment contracts with insurance features also may be protected against seizure in bankruptcy.

The life insurance industry also provides services or products in the pension area, these being the sale of annuities and pension fund management service. Prior to the introduction of the Registered Retirement Savings Plan (RRSP) for individual retirement planning, the monopolistic sale by insurance companies of annuities was a major source of income. The insurance industry must now compete with other financial intermediaries for the sale of RRSPs. The RRSP must, however, be collapsed into an annuity or a Registered Retirement Income Fund (RRIF); since RRIFs are less popular than annuities, which may only be offered by insurance companies, the industry has benefited from the wide adoption of RRSPs.

Since the cash flow characteristics of life insurance and pensions are quite similar, insurance companies have developed expertise in fund management that is transferable to the pension industry. One example of this is the **insured defined benefit pension.** A firm sponsoring a pension plan enters into a contractual agreement by which an insurance company assumes all liability for the benefits accrued under the plan. This guarantee is given in return for an annual premium based on the benefit formula, and the number and characteristics of the employees covered by the plan.

Life insurance companies may be organized as either mutual companies or stock companies. In principle, the organizational form should affect the investment objectives of the company. Mutual companies are supposed to be run solely for the benefit of their policyholders, whereas stock companies have as their objective the maximization of shareholder value. In actuality, it is hard to discern from its investment policies which organizational form a particular insurance company has. Some examples of mutual insurance companies are Sun Life and Manufacturers; examples of stock companies include London Life and Great-West.

Non-Life Insurance Companies

Non-life insurance companies such as property and casualty insurers have investable funds primarily because they pay claims *after* they collect policy premiums. Typically, they are conservative in their attitude toward risk. As with life insurers, non-life insurance companies can be either stock companies or mutual companies.

Banks and Trust Companies

The defining characteristic of banks is that most of their investments are loans to businesses and consumers, and most of their liabilities are accounts of depositors. As investors, the objective of banks is to try to match the risk of assets to liabilities while earning a profitable spread between the lending and borrowing rates. Although trust companies have a different clientele, their objectives parallel those of banks. Other savings institutions such as credit unions and caisses populaires also have the same aims but have less of a matching problem.

24.2 *Constraints*

Both households and institutional investors restrict their choice of investment assets. These restrictions arise from their specific circumstances. Identifying these restrictions/constraints will affect the choice of investment policy. Five common types of constraints are described below.

Liquidity

Liquidity is the ease (speed) with which an asset can be sold and still fetch a fair price. It is a relationship between the time dimension (how long will it take to dispose) and the price dimension (what discount from fair market price) of an investment asset.

When an actual concrete measure of liquidity is necessary, one thinks of the discount when an immediate sale is unavoidable.[5] Cash and money market instruments such as Treasury bills and commercial paper, where the bid-ask spread is a fraction of 1 percent, are the most liquid assets, and real estate is among the least liquid. Office buildings and manufacturing structures can easily be assessed a 50 percent liquidity discount.

Both individual and institutional investors must consider how likely they are to dispose of assets at short notice. From this likelihood, they establish the minimum level of liquid assets they want in the investment portfolio.

Investment Horizon

This is the *planned* liquidation date of the investment or part of it. Examples of an individual **investment horizon** could be the time to fund college education or the retirement date for a wage earner. For a university endowment, an investment horizon could relate to the time to fund a major campus construction project. Horizon needs to be considered when investors choose between assets of various maturities, such as bonds, which pay off at specified future dates.

Regulations

Only professional and institutional investors are constrained by regulations. First and foremost is the already-mentioned **prudent man** law. That is, professional investors who manage other people's money have a fiduciary responsibility to restrict investment to assets that would have been approved by a prudent investor. The law is purposefully non-specific. Every professional in-

---

[5] In most cases, it is impossible to know the liquidity of an asset with certainty, before it is put up for sale. In dealer markets (described in Chapter 4), however, the liquidity of the traded assets can be observed from the bid-ask spread that is quoted by the dealers, that is, the difference between the "bid" quote (the lower price the dealer will pay the owner), and the "ask" quote (the higher price a buyer would have to pay the dealer).

vestor must stand ready to defend an investment policy in a court of law, and interpretation may differ according to the standards of the times.

Also, specific regulations apply to various institutional investors. For instance, Canadian pension portfolios are limited to a maximum proportion (rising to 20 percent in 1994) of foreign assets. Similarly, provincial legislation governs mutual fund holdings, imposing a maximum on the percentage of ownership in a single corporation; this regulation keeps professional investors from getting involved in the actual management of corporations.

Tax Considerations

Tax consequences are central to investment decisions. The performance of any investment strategy should be measured by how much it yields (jargon for what its rate of return is expected to be) in real (constant purchasing power) after-tax investment returns. For household and institutional investors who face significant tax rates, tax sheltering and deferral of tax obligations may be pivotal in their investment strategy.

Unique Needs

Virtually every investor faces special circumstances. Imagine husband-and-wife aeronautical engineers holding high-paying jobs in the same aerospace corporation. The entire human capital of that household is tied to a single player in a rather cyclical industry. This couple would need to hedge the risk (find investment assets that yield more when the risk materializes, thus partly insuring against the risk) of a deterioration in the economic well-being of the aerospace industry.

An example of a unique need for an institutional investor is a university whose trustees let the administration use only cash income from the endowment fund. This constraint would translate into a preference for high-dividend-paying assets.

Table 24.3 presents a summary of the importance of each of the general constraints to each of the seven types of investors.

TABLE 24.3   Matrix of Constraints

Type of Investor	Liquidity	Horizon	Regulatory	Taxes
Individuals and personal trusts	Variable	Life cycle	None	Variable
Mutual funds	Low	Short	Little	None
Pension funds	Young, low; mature, high	Long	Some (federal)	None
Endowment funds	Little	Long	Little	None
Life insurance companies	Low	Long	Complex	Yes
Non-life insurance companies	High	Short	Little	Yes
Banks	Low	Short	Changing	Yes

24.3 *Asset Allocation*

Consideration of their objectives and constraints leads investors to a set of investment policies. The policies column of Table 24.1 lists the various dimensions of portfolio management policy making—asset allocation, diversification, risk and tax positioning, and income generation. By far the most important part of policy determination is asset allocation, that is, deciding how much of the portfolio to invest in each major asset category.

We can view the process of asset allocation as consisting of the following steps:

1. *Specify asset classes to be included in the portfolio.* The major classes usually considered are the following:
   a. Money market instruments (usually called cash).
   b. Fixed-income securities (usually called bonds)
   c. Stocks.
   d. Real estate.
   e. Precious metals.
   f. Other.

Institutional investors will rarely invest in more than the first four categories, whereas individual investors frequently will include precious metals and other more exotic types of investments in their portfolios.

2. *Specify capital market expectations.* This step consists of using both historical data and economic analysis to determine your expectations of future rates of return over the relevant holding period on the assets to be considered for inclusion in the portfolio.
3. *Derive the efficient portfolio frontier.* This step consists of finding portfolios that achieve the maximum expected return for any given degree of risk.
4. *Find the optimal asset mix.* This step consists of selecting the efficient portfolio that best meets your risk and return objectives while satisfying the constraints you face.

Let us illustrate how the process works by considering a simple example. We start the process by initially restricting our portfolio to cash, bonds, and stocks. Later we will consider how much of an improvement we can achieve by adding real estate and other asset classes.

Specifying Capital Market Expectations

Having decided to restrict ourselves to cash, bonds, and stocks, we must specify our expectations of the holding period returns on these asset classes over the period until our next planned revision in the asset mix. Although

TABLE 24.4 Probability Distribution of HPR on Stocks, Bonds, and Cash

State of Economy	Probability	Holding Period Return		
		Stocks (%)	Bonds (%)	Cash (%)
Boom with low inflation	.1	74	4	6
Boom with high inflation	.2	20	−10	6
Normal growth	.4	14	9	6
Recession with low inflation	.2	0	35	6
Recession with high inflation	.1	−30	0	6
Expected return	E(r)	14.0	9.0	6
Standard deviation	σ	24.5	14.8	0

Correlation coefficient between stocks and bonds is −.2372.

professional investors revise their asset mix every three months, when they receive new information about the state of the economy, market developments may cause us to revise more frequently.[6] In our example, we will express all rates of return in annualized terms, but the holding period should be thought of as three months.

The set of capital market expectations must be in a form that allows assessment of both expected rates of return and risk. Sometimes investors will make only point forecasts of holding period returns on assets. These may serve as measures of expected rates of return, but they do not allow assessment of risks.

There are two sources of information relevant to forming capital market expectations: historical data on capital market rates and economic forecasts. The investment professional must exercise considerable judgment when deciding how much to rely on each of these two sources.

For example, suppose that, based entirely on economic forecasts derived from careful analysis of all the information we can assemble, we have determined the probability distribution of holding period returns exhibited in Table 24.4. Our assessment of the HPR on bonds comes from a consideration of a 30-year Canada bond with a 9 percent coupon. If there is normal growth, then we expect interest rates to remain at their current level and we will experience neither capital gains nor losses on the bond. Our HPR will simply equal the coupon rate of 9 percent.

If there is a boom, then we think interest rates will rise and the price of the bond will fall. The amount by which interest rates will rise depends on whether there is a low or a high rate of inflation. With low inflation interest rates will rise a little bit, causing a capital loss of only 5 percent on bonds, for a net HPR of 4 percent. However, if inflation is high, interest rates will rise a lot, causing a capital loss of 19 percent, for a net HPR of −10 percent on bonds.

If there is a recession, then we think that the direction of interest rates will depend on inflation. If there is low inflation interest rates will fall, but if there is high inflation they will rise despite the recession. In the low-inflation recession-

---

[6] Many statistics, such as the CPI for inflation, are released monthly.

ary scenario bonds will do very well, with an HPR of 35 percent. But in the high-inflation recessionary scenario, the bond price will fall by 9 percent, leaving an HPR of 0.

The assessment of the rates of return on stocks for each scenario is evident from Table 24.4. Stocks are expected to do best in a non-inflationary boom and worst in an inflationary recession.

To the extent that these parameter estimates—either the means, the standard deviations, or the correlation coefficient—differ from what they have been in the past, we may want to adjust their values so that they conform more to historical experience. In the rest of our example, however, we will use the unadjusted numbers calculated in Table 24.4.

Concept Check

Question 1. Suppose that you revised your assessment of the probabilities of each of the five economic scenarios in Table 24.4 as follows:

State of Economy	Probability	Holding Period Return Stocks (%)	Bonds (%)	Cash (%)
Boom with low inflation	.05	74	4	6
Boom with high inflation	.2	20	−10	6
Normal growth	.5	14	9	6
Recession with low inflation	.2	0	35	6
Recession with high inflation	.05	−30	0	6

What are your new estimates of expected returns, standard deviations, and correlations?

Deriving the Efficient Portfolio Frontier

Given the probability distribution of holding period returns in Table 24.4, what is the efficient portfolio frontier? Since we are considering only two risky assets for inclusion in the portfolio, we can use the formula presented in Chapter 7 to find the optimal combination of stocks and bonds to be combined with the risk-free asset.

The formula is reproduced here as equation 24.1:

$$w^* = \frac{[E(r_s) - r_f]\sigma_b^2 - [E(r_b) - r_f]\text{cov}(r_s,r_b)}{[E(r_s) - r_f]\sigma_b^2 + [E(r_b) - r_f]\sigma_s^2 - [E(r_s) - r_f + E(r_b) - r_f]\text{cov}(r_s,r_b)}$$

(24.1)

where w^* is the proportion of stocks and $1 - w^*$ is the proportion of bonds. Substituting in this equation we find that $w^* = .45$:

$$w^* = \frac{(14 - 6) \times 218 - (9 - 6) \times (-86)}{8 \times 218 + 3 \times 600 - (8 + 3)(-86)} = .45$$

Thus the optimal stock-bond portfolio to be combined with cash is 45 percent stocks and 55 percent bonds.

Its expected HPR, $E(r^*)$, and standard deviation, σ^*, are

$$
\begin{aligned}
E(r^*) &= w^*E(r_s) + (1 - w^*)E(r_b) \\
&= .45 \times 14\% + .55 \times 9\% \\
&= 11.25\% \\
\sigma^{*2} &= w^{*2}\sigma_s^2 + (1 - w^*)^2\sigma_b^2 + 2\,w^*(1 - w^*)\mathrm{cov}(r_s,r_b) \\
&= .45^2 \times 600 + .55^2 \times 218 + 2 \times .45 \times .55 \times (-86) \\
&= 144.875 \\
\sigma^* &= 12.0\%
\end{aligned}
$$

Figure 24.1 displays the efficient portfolio frontier.

Point F represents 100 percent invested in cash, point B 100 percent in bonds, and point S 100 percent in stocks. Point O^* is the optimal combination of stocks and bonds (45 percent stocks and 55 percent bonds) to be combined with cash to form the investor's final portfolio. All efficient portfolios rest along the straight line connecting points F and O^*. The slope of this efficient frontier, the reward to variability ratio, is:

$$
\begin{aligned}
S^* &= \frac{E(r^*) - r_f}{\sigma^*} \\
&= \frac{11.25\% - 6\%}{12.0\%} \\
&= .4375
\end{aligned}
$$

The fact that we have drawn the segment of the efficient frontier to the right of O^* with the same slope as to the left reflects the assumption that we can borrow at a risk-free rate of 6 percent per year to buy the O^* portfolio on

FIGURE 24.1

The risk-reward trade-off for portfolios of stocks, bonds, and cash.

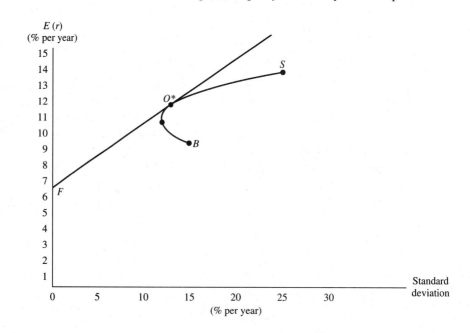

margin. If the borrowing rate is higher than 6 percent per year, then the slope to the right of point O^* will be lower than to the left.

If we rule out buying the O^* portfolio on margin altogether, then the segment of the efficient frontier to the right of O^* will be the curve linking points O^* and S. This indicates that, to achieve an expected HPR higher than $E(r^*)$ in the absence of borrowing, we would have to increase the proportion of our portfolio invested in stocks and reduce the proportion in bonds relative to their proportions in O^*. The maximum expected HPR under these circumstances would be the expected HPR on stocks, achieved by investing 100 percent in stocks.

Concept Check	Question 2. What is the O^* portfolio for the set of revised capital market parameters you derived in question 1?

The Optimal Mix

Our choice of where to be on the efficient frontier will depend on our degree of risk aversion, as shown in Chapters 5–7. We reproduce here as equation 24.2 the formula for the optimal proportion to invest in portfolio O^*:

$$y^* = \frac{E(r^*) - r_f}{A\sigma^{*2}} \qquad \textbf{(24.2)}$$

where A is our coefficient of risk aversion.

For example, we might wonder how risk-averse we need to be to want to hold the portfolio O^* itself, with nothing invested in cash. To find the answer, we set y^* equal to 1 and solve for A. The answer is $A = 3.65$.

Diversifying into Different Asset Classes

Diversification is a good thing in asset allocation. But can there be too much of a good thing? After all, there are many different asset categories. Should you have some of each in your portfolio: stocks, bonds, real estate, precious metals, art, collectibles, and so on? And if so, how much?

The basic principle of efficient diversification suggests that you can never be made worse off by broadening the set of assets included in your portfolio. However, when we quantify the improvement in portfolio efficiency resulting from including additional assets, we often find that it is not large enough to justify the additional time, trouble, and other transaction costs associated with implementing it.

For example, let us consider whether we should add real estate to our portfolio in the example above. The first thing we need is the mean, standard deviation, and the correlations of the HPR on real estate with the returns on stocks and bonds. One way to derive them is from an expansion of the scenario

TABLE 24.5   Capital Market Expectations: Stocks, Bonds, and Real Estate

	Stocks	Bonds	Real Estate	Cash
Expected HPR $E(r)$	14.0%	9.0%	10.0%	6%
Standard deviation σ	24.5%	14.8%	20.0%	0
Correlation Coefficients				
Stocks	1.0	−.24	0	
Bonds		1.0	0	
Real estate			1.0	

analysis presented earlier in this chapter. Another way is by looking at past data.

Data on real estate holding period returns is not as readily available as data on stock and bond returns. One feasible approach, however, is to gather data on a few publicly traded real estate investment companies[7] and treat them as representative of real estate as a whole. The advantage of doing so is that we can then invest in the shares of those same REITs when it comes time to implement our investment policy.

Let us assume that we have used one or more of these methods to derive the following set of capital market parameters for real estate:

$$E(r_r) = 10\% \text{ per year}$$
$$\sigma_r = 20\%$$
$$\rho_{RE,s} = 0 \text{ (correlation between real estate and stock returns)}$$
$$\rho_{RE,b} = 0 \text{ (correlation between real estate and bond returns)}$$

In addition, let us use the parameters for stocks, bonds, and cash as we did in Table 24.4:

$$r_f = 6\%$$
$$E(r_s) = 14\% \; \sigma_s = 24.5\%$$
$$E(r_b) = 9\% \; \sigma_b = 14.8\%$$
$$\rho_{sb} = -.24 \text{ (correlation between stock and bond returns)}$$

Table 24.5 presents a convenient summary of these capital market assumptions.

We use a computer-based optimization program to find the optimal combination of risky assets to combine with cash.[8] Table 24.6 shows the new O^* portfolio composition and characteristics, as well as the old.

Thus the reward-to-variability ratio that we face is .480, compared with .438 in the case without real estate. The optimal portfolio for an investor whose coefficient of risk aversion is 3.65 and who previously would have chosen to

---

[7] Opportunities for real estate investment were discussed in Chapter 3.
[8] The software diskette provided with this text contains such a program.

TABLE 24.6 The Optimal Combination of Risky Assets (O^*) with and without Real Estate

	New	Old
Portfolio Proportions		
Stocks	35%	45%
Bonds	43%	55%
Real estate	22%	
Parameters of O* Portfolio		
Expected HPR $E(r^*)$	11.0%	11.25%
Standard deviation σ^*	10.4%	12.0%
Reward-to-variability ratio S^*	.480	.438

hold the old O^* portfolio with no cash would be:

$$y^* = \frac{E(r^*) - r_f}{A\sigma^2}$$
$$= \frac{.11 - .06}{3.65 \times .0108}$$
$$= 1.27$$

Thus, if this were you and if you had $100,000 of your own money to invest, you should invest $127,000 in the O^* mutual fund, borrowing the other $27,000 at an interest rate of 6 percent per year.

The mean and standard deviation of your optimal portfolio would be

$$E(r) = r_f + 1.27[E(r^*) - r_f]$$
$$= 6\% + 1.27(11\% - 6\%)$$
$$= 12.35\%$$
$$\sigma = 1.27\sigma^*$$
$$= 1.27 \times 10.4\%$$
$$= 13.21\%$$

And your certainty-equivalent HPR would be

$$U = E(r) - \tfrac{1}{2}A\sigma^2$$
$$= .1235 - .5 \times 3.65 \times .0175$$
$$= .092$$
$$= .92\% \text{ per year}$$

This is .6 percent per year higher than the comparable certainty-equivalent HPR of 8.6 percent per year that you would have if you excluded real estate from your portfolio.

What can we conclude from all of this about the value of adding real estate to stocks, bonds, and cash in creating your investment portfolio? Is it worth the effort?

The first thing to point out is that the specific results we got are very sensitive to the specific assumptions that we made about the parameters of the probability distribution of the HPR on real estate. In our example, the reward-to-variability ratio goes up from .438 to .480, but had we assumed different numbers for the means, standard deviations, and correlation coefficients, the results could have been very different.

For example, had we assumed a higher value for the expected HPR on real estate, the optimization program would have indicated that we should invest much more heavily in it. The resultant increase in the reward-to-variability ratio would have been higher too. By experimenting with the optimization program that accompanies this text, you can gain a feel for the contribution that real estate would make to improving the efficiency of your portfolio under a variety of assumptions about the relevant parameter values.

Whenever we add an asset class, the process is identical to the one described for real estate. We first must specify the mean and standard deviation of the HPR and its correlation with the other asset classes. Our optimization program then tells us what the optimal proportions of all risky assets are in the O^* portfolio. We then can compute $E(r^*)$, σ^*, and S^*, and decide which combination of the risk-free asset and the new, expanded O^* mutual fund is optimal for us.

For example, suppose we are thinking of adding gold to our portfolio. Suppose that we think that its $E(r)$ is 7 percent, its σ is 20 percent, and its correlation with the other three risky assets is zero. Table 24.7 summarizes our capital market assumptions. What is the composition of the new O^* portfolio, and how much do we gain by diversifying into gold?

Our portfolio optimization program tells us that the new O^* has the following portfolio proportions:

Stocks	33%
Bonds	41%
Real estate	21%
Gold	5%

The expected return and risk of this new O^* portfolio are

$$E(r^*) = 10.76\%$$
$$\sigma^* = 9.87\%$$

TABLE 24.7 Capital Market Expectations: Stocks, Bonds, Real Estate, and Gold

	Stocks	Bonds	Real Estate	Gold	Cash
Expected HPR $E(r)$	14.0%	9.0%	10.0%	7.0%	6%
Standard deviation σ	24.5%	14.8%	20.0%	20.0%	0
Correlation Coefficients					
Stocks	1.0	−.24	0	0	
Bonds		1.0	0	0	
Real estate			1.0	0	
Gold				1.0	

and the new reward-to-variability ratio is

$$S^* = .482$$

This compares with a reward-to-variability ratio of .480 for the previous case without gold. It would appear that the gain from adding gold to the portfolio is slight.

In general it seems to be true that, unless you can identify an additional asset that has a high expected HPR, the gain from further diversification will be slight. You can explore the gains from additional diversification, using your own capital market assumptions, with the aid of the portfolio optimization program provided with this book.

Taxes and Asset Allocation

Until this point, we have completely ignored the issue of income taxes in discussing asset allocation. Of course, to the extent that you are a tax-exempt investor such as a pension fund, or if all of your investment portfolio is in a tax-sheltered account such as an RRSP, then taxes are irrelevant to your portfolio decisions.

But let us say that at least some of your investment income is subject to income taxes at a rate of 50 percent (the highest marginal rate). You are interested in the after-tax HPR on your portfolio. At first glance it might appear to be a simple matter to figure out what the after-tax HPRs on stocks, bonds, and cash are if you know what they are before taxes. However, there are several complicating factors.

The first is the fact that you can choose between common or preferred shares and bonds. We discussed this issue in Chapter 2 and concluded there that the dividend treatment may cause you to invest in preferred shares rather than bonds if your personal tax rate is such that the after-tax yield on dividends is more than that on interest, although a risk adjustment must be considered.

The second complication is not quite so easy to deal with. It arises from the fact that part of your HPR is in the form of a capital gain or loss. Under the current tax system, you pay income taxes on a capital gain only if you *realize* it by selling the asset during the holding period. This applies to bonds, as well as stocks, and makes the after-tax HPR a function of whether the security will actually be sold at the end of the holding period. Sophisticated investors time the realization of their sales of securities to maximize their tax advantage. This often calls for selling securities that are losing money at the end of the tax year and holding on to those that are making money.

For the time being, at least, tax rates cause dividends on stocks to be taxable at approximately the same rate as capital gains; hence, other things being equal, the after-tax HPR on stocks will not depend on the dividend payout policy of the corporations that issued the stock.

Given that the concept of an RRSP allows capital to accumulate tax-free within the account until withdrawals are made, and accepting that financial instruments are priced competitively on a risk-adjusted, after-tax basis, taxable bonds are better vehicles for RRSP investment than preferred or common shares. For an investor with a balanced portfolio of assets held both inside and outside the RRSP, it is clear that bonds should be placed within the RRSP before any equities are; thus, the portfolio could have the RRSP holding exclusively bonds, with bonds and equities outside, or have the outside portion holding exclusively equities, with bonds and equities inside the RRSP, but never both kinds of securities inside and outside the RRSP.

These tax complications make the process of portfolio selection for a taxable investor a lot harder than for the tax-exempt investor. There is a whole branch of the money management industry that deals with ways to avoid paying taxes through special investment strategies. Unfortunately, many of these strategies contradict the principles of efficient diversification. We will discuss these and related issues in greater detail in Chapter 25.

24.4 *Hedging against Inflation*

An inflation hedge is an asset that enables investors to reduce the risk of loss of purchasing power stemming from uncertainty about the prices of consumer goods. Those most vulnerable to such losses are individuals on fixed incomes, such as retirees living on pension annuities. Such individuals face inflation risk, and if they are risk-averse, they will want to hedge at least some of it. This section analyzes the effectiveness and cost of various types of inflation hedges, including index-linked bonds, floating-rate bonds, common stocks, and commodities.

Index-Linked Financial Instruments

For pensioners, the perfect inflation hedge is an annuity denominated in terms of a basket of consumption goods, but few of these are available. In 1980, the U.K. government began issuing bonds whose principal and interest are linked to that country's official retail price index (RPI) with a lag of six months. In 1991, the Canadian government offered similar bonds, called Real Return Bonds, with a maturity of 30 years; these bonds pay a real return of 4.25 percent with respect to the inflation rate defined by the consumer price index.

Index-linked bonds are not the only perfect inflation hedge. A forward or a futures contract on the consumer price index (CPI) can serve as well. Let us illustrate with a forward contract on the CPI. A buyer of a CPI forward contract receives compensation for inflation only if the CPI at the contract maturity date exceeds the forward price at the time the contract is entered into. Thus, for a one-year contract, the forward price might be 5 percent higher than the current CPI. If the CPI rises by more than 5 percent during the year, the buyer of the forward contract receives the difference from the seller. But if the CPI rises by less than 5 percent, the buyer must pay the seller the difference.

By combining such a CPI forward contract with a conventional Treasury bond, an investor can synthesize an index-linked bond. The guaranteed real rate of interest on a synthetic index-linked bond is the difference between the interest rate on the Treasury bill and the inflation rate embodied in the forward price. Thus, in our example, if the one-year Treasury bill rate is 8 percent and the inflation rate implied by the CPI forward contract is 5 percent, the real rate on the synthetic index-linked bond is 3 percent. A CPI futures contract works essentially the same way as a CPI forward contract. As we saw in the previous chapter, the Coffee, Sugar, and Cocoa Exchange in New York created a market for CPI futures contracts in 1985, but eventually abandoned the effort due to lack of trading volume.

CPI forward and futures contracts are symmetric in their treatment of inflation: the buyer receives money if the rate of inflation exceeds the forward rate or pays money if the rate of inflation is less than the forward rate. By contrast, an inflation insurance policy allows people to eliminate only downside inflation risk. The insured party receives money if the rate of inflation exceeds some specified rate but pays nothing otherwise. An inflation insurance policy is equivalent to a call option on the CPI.[9]

The rate of interest on U.K. index-linked bonds (the risk-free real rate) has averaged about 3 percent per year since they began trading in 1981. The interest rate on conventional U.K. Treasury bonds of comparable maturity (the risk-free nominal rate) has been considerably greater. While the spread between the risk-free nominal and real rates reflects a variety of tax and other features that are different for the two types of bonds, part of the spread is certainly due to inflation expectations. Finance theory suggests that for any given maturity, the spread between the nominal interest rate on a default-free nominal bond and the real rate on a default-free real bond will equal the sum of the expected rate of inflation and a risk premium. According to the CAPM, the size of this risk premium depends on the correlation between the rate of inflation and the real rate of return on the market portfolio.

Floating-Rate Bonds

Where index-linked bonds or CPI futures contracts do not exist, it is natural to consider alternatives that are imperfect inflation hedges. In contrast to CPI-linked bonds, floating-rate bonds tie interest payments to the current level of interest rates, as measured by some reference rate. The reference rate of interest might be the rate on U.S. Treasury obligations of a specified maturity, LIBOR, or some other indicator of current interest rates.

If the reference rate of interest changes only because of changes in the rate of inflation, then floating rate bonds are an effective inflation hedge. More formally, if interest rates are perfectly correlated with inflation, then floating rate bonds are a perfect inflation hedge. While economic theory offers some

---

[9] For a full development of this subject, see Zvi Bodie, "Inflation Insurance," *Journal of Risk and Insurance,* December 1990.

reason to believe that nominal interest rates adjust to reflect changes in expected inflation (the "Fisher effect"), that reasoning does not directly carry over to the connection between nominal interest rates and actual inflation. Empirical studies show that interest rates in many countries have been positively correlated with inflation in the past, but the correlation is far from perfect.

Common Stocks as an Inflation Hedge

When some people suggest that common stocks are a good inflation hedge, they have in mind a definition different from ours. Often what they mean is that the real rate of return on common stocks is unaffected by the rate of inflation. The reasoning behind this view is that stocks are an ownership claim over real physical capital. Real profits are either unaffected or enhanced when there is inflation, so owners of real capital should not be hurt by it. Thus, in a regression of nominal stock returns against the rate of inflation, the slope coefficient should be 1.

Even if this proposition is true, however, it does not imply that stocks can be used effectively to hedge inflation risk in our earlier sense. The slope coefficient merely determines the proportion of an inflation hedger's portfolio that should be devoted to the proposed hedge asset. Its effectiveness in reducing inflation risk is determined by its degree of correlation with inflation—the R^2 in the regression. Empirical studies show that stock returns in the United States have been negatively correlated with inflation in the past, but the degree of correlation is small.[10]

There is yet another sense in which common stocks have been said to be a good inflation hedge. Some investment advisers, in comparing stocks to bonds and other fixed-income securities, state that stocks are a good long-term inflation hedge. They claim that over a long holding period—say 20 years—stocks are very likely to offer a higher rate of return than fixed-income securities, and are therefore especially suitable as an investment for retirement funds. Upon analysis, this proposition turns out to mean no more than that common stocks have a significantly higher expected rate of return than fixed-income securities. In investment portfolio selection, however, risk must be considered as well as expected return. Unfortunately, some of these advisers tend to understate the long-term risk of common stocks. No matter how attractive they may be in terms of expected returns, common stocks are not a completely safe asset even in the long run.

Gold, Commodities, and Real Estate

It has sometimes been suggested that investors can use gold or commodities to hedge against inflation risk. The empirical evidence, however, indicates that while price changes of gold and commodities traded on futures markets are

---

[10] See Zvi Bodie, "Common Stocks as a Hedge against Inflation," *Journal of Finance*, May 1976.

TABLE 24.8 Probability Distribution of Inflation and the Nominal HPR on Stocks and Bonds

State of Economy	Probability	Holding Period Return		
		Stocks	Bonds	Inflation
Boom with low inflation	.1	74%	4%	1%
Boom with high inflation	.2	20%	−10%	9%
Normal growth	.4	14%	9%	5%
Recession with low inflation	.2	0	35%	1%
Recession with high inflation	.1	−30%	0	9%
Expected return	E(r)	14.0%	9.0%	5.0%
Standard deviation	σ	24.49%	14.76%	3.1%
Correlation				
Stocks			−.238	

positively correlated with consumer price changes, the degree of correlation is not very great.[11] The same is true of real estate. Thus, although they may be desirable investments because of their high expected rates of return in certain periods, they are not very effective inflation hedges in the conventional finance sense of being useful in eliminating inflation risk.

Effectiveness of Real-Return Instruments

We can analyze the benefit to investors from having this new investment alternative. We first analyze the difference between portfolio optimization using nominal rates of return and real rates of return and measure the loss in portfolio efficiency from failing to take account of inflation risk. We then show how introduction of bonds offering a real risk-free rate of interest can improve portfolio efficiency.

Let us first consider the probability distribution of inflation and the distribution of nominal HPRs presented in Table 24.8. When we do the portfolio optimization in nominal terms using a risk-free rate of 6 percent, we find that the O* portfolio consists of 45 percent stocks and 55 percent bonds.

Now let us consider the portfolio optimization in real terms. Table 24.9 shows the probability distribution of real holding period returns implied by Table 24.8. The real HPR is defined in this case as the nominal HPR minus the rate of inflation.

Table 24.10 compares the parameters of the nominally efficient portfolios with those of the real efficient portfolios derived under the assumption that short sales and buying securities on margin are not permitted. Table 24.10 shows that the asset mixes that were efficient in nominal terms are not efficient

---

[11] See Zvi Bodie, "Commodity Futures as an Inflation Hedge," *Journal of Portfolio Management*, Spring 1983.

TABLE 24.9   Probability Distribution of the Real HPR on Stocks and Bonds and Cash

		Holding Period Return		
State of Economy	Probability	Stocks	Bonds	Cash
Boom with low inflation	.1	73%	3%	5%
Boom with high inflation	.2	11%	−19%	−3%
Normal growth	.4	9%	4%	1%
Recession with low inflation	.2	−1%	34%	5%
Recession with high inflation	.1	−39%	−9%	−3%
Expected return	$E(r)$	9.0%	4.0%	1.0%
Standard deviation	σ	25.71%	17.40%	3.10%
Correlation Coefficient				
Stocks			−.0295	.442
Bonds				.875

in real terms, but the differences are not large. In fact, they are so small that optimization in nominal terms appears to be a satisfactory substitute for optimization in real terms.

For a portfolio with a mean real holding period return of 2 percent, for example, the standard deviation of the efficient portfolio (12 percent stocks, 4 percent bonds, and 84 percent cash) is 5.14 percent, whereas that of the nominally efficient portfolio is 5.34 percent, a difference of only 20 basis points. And this is the largest difference reported in the table.

The restriction on short sales means that for portfolios with a mean real HPR greater than 6.5 percent the real and nominal efficient portfolios are the same,

TABLE 24.10   Real vs. Nominal Efficient Portfolios*

	Real Efficient Portfolios				Nominal Efficient Portfolios			
		Portfolio Weights (%)				Portfolio Weights (%)		
Mean (%)	σ(%)	Stocks	Bonds	Cash	σ(%)	Stocks	Bonds	Cash
1.0	3.10	0	0	100.0	3.10	0	0	100.0
2.0	5.14	11.9	3.6	84.5	5.34	9.1	11.1	79.8
4.0	9.58	28.4	24.2	47.4	9.68	25.7	31.4	42.9
5.0	12.06	37.7	35.6	26.7	12.13	35.0	42.7	22.3
6.0	14.27	45.9	45.8	8.3	14.34	43.3	52.9	3.8
6.23	14.67	47.4	47.7	4.9	14.76	44.6	55.4	0
6.5	15.31	50.0	50.0	0	15.31	50.0	50.0	0
7.0	16.74	60.0	40.0	0	16.74	60.0	40.0	0
9.0	25.71	100.0	0	0	25.71	100.0	0	0

* No real risk-free asset and no short selling or borrowing.

FIGURE 24.2

The efficient frontier
in real terms, no
real risk-free asset,
and no short selling
or borrowing.

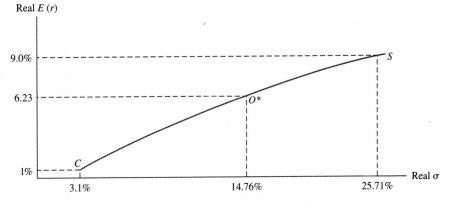

and consist only of stocks and bonds. It also means that the minimum risk portfolio is 100 percent cash. If short sales were permitted, this portfolio would be −7.1 percent stocks, −20.1 percent bonds, and 127.2 percent cash and it would have a mean of −.17 percent and a σ of .49 percent.

Figure 24.2 shows the risk-return trade-off in real terms graphically.

When we add a real risk-free asset offering a real interest rate of 3 percent to the other assets, it completely displaces cash. The optimal combination of risky assets (O^{**}) is 71.2 percent stocks and 28.8 percent bonds. The mean real HPR of this portfolio is 7.56 percent per year, and the standard deviation 18.84 percent. There is a substantial gain in portfolio efficiency for portfolios with means below that of O^{**}. The lower the mean, the greater the gain.

The situation is best described with the help of Figure 24.3 and Table 24.11, which show the efficient frontier in real terms and compare it to points corresponding to the previous efficient frontier in the absence of a real risk-free asset.

FIGURE 24.3

Real efficient
trade-off line with
real risk-free asset.

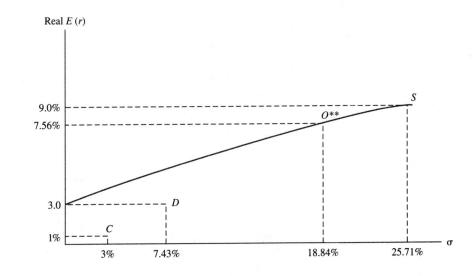

TABLE 24.11   Real Efficient Portfolios with and without a Real Risk-Free Asset*

| | | Without Risk-Free Asset | | | | With Risk-Free Asset | | |
| | | Portfolio Weights (%) | | | | Portfolio Weights (%) | | |
Mean (%)	σ(%)	Stocks	Bonds	Cash	σ(%)	Stocks	Bonds	Riskless Asset
1.0	3.10	0	0	100.0	—	—	—	—
2.0	5.14	11.9	3.6	84.5	—	—	—	—
3.0	7.43	20.4	14.2	65.4	0	0	0	100
4.0	9.58	28.4	24.2	47.4	4.13	15.6	6.3	78.1
5.0	12.06	37.7	35.6	26.7	8.26	31.2	12.6	56.1
6.0	14.27	45.9	45.8	8.3	12.40	46.8	18.9	34.2
6.5	15.31	50.0	50.0	0	14.46	54.6	22.1	23.2
7.0	16.74	60.0	40.0	0	16.53	62.5	25.3	12.3
7.56	18.84	71.2	28.8	0	18.84	71.2	28.8	0
9.0	25.71	100.0	0	0	25.71	100.0	0	0

* No short selling and no borrowing.

Note that a risk-averse investor, who would hold a portfolio with a mean real HPR of 3 percent per year, stands to gain the most from holding the real risk-free asset. Using stocks, bonds, and cash, the σ of the portfolio would be 7.43 percent per year (point *D* in Figure 24.3), as opposed to zero risk using the real risk-free asset. The less risk-averse the investor, that is, the smaller the proportion invested in cash in the absence of a real risk-free asset, the smaller the gain from adding CPI-linked bonds to the menu of assets.

Summary

1. When discussing the principles of portfolio management, it is useful to distinguish among seven classes of investors:
   a. Individual investors and personal trusts.
   b. Mutual funds.
   c. Pension funds.
   d. Endowment funds.
   e. Life insurance companies.
   f. Non-life insurance companies.
   g. Banks.
In general, these groups have somewhat different investment objectives, constraints, and portfolio policies.

2. To some extent, most institutional investors seek to match the risk and return characteristics of their investment portfolios to the characteristics of their liabilities. Thus, a pension fund of a mature company with a large number of retired employees receiving dollar-fixed annuities may seek to hold an immunized portfolio of fixed-income securities. On the other hand, the pension fund of a young company whose plan participants are far from retirement may choose to invest heavily in equities.

3. The process of asset allocation consists of the following steps:

a. Specification of the asset classes to be included.

b. Specification of capital market expectations.

c. Finding the efficient portfolio frontier.

d. Determining the optimal mix.

4. For investors who must pay taxes on their investment income, the process of asset allocation is complicated by the fact that they pay different rates of income tax on different investment income. However, the really difficult part of the tax effect to deal with is the fact that capital gains are taxable only if realized through the sale of an asset during the holding period. Investment strategies designed to avoid taxes may contradict the principles of efficient diversification.

5. For investors concerned about risk and return in real as opposed to nominal terms, there can be substantial gains from including a real risk-free asset in the portfolio mix. The gains are greatest for the most risk-averse investors.

Key terms

Personal trusts

Income beneficiaries

Remaindermen

Defined contribution plans

Defined benefit plans

Endowment funds

Whole-life insurance policy

Term insurance

Variable life

Universal life

Insured defined benefit pension

Liquidity

Investment horizon

Prudent man

Selected readings

For a collection of essays presenting the Institute of Chartered Financial Analysts approach to portfolio management, see:

Ambachtsheer, Keith P. "Strategic Approaches to Asset Allocation." *Asset Allocation for Institutional Portfolios,* The Institute of CFAs, 1988.

Maginn, John L.; and Tuttle, David L. (editors). *Managing Investment Portfolios: A Dynamic Analysis,* 2d edition. Boston: Warren, Gorham, & Lamont, 1990.

Good discussions of asset allocation in practice include:

Brinson, G. P.; Diermeier, J. J.; and Schlarbaum, G. G. "A Composite Portfolio Benchmark for Pension Plans." *Financial Analysts Journal,* March–April 1986.

Sharpe, William F. "Integrated Asset Allocation." *Financial Analysts Journal,* September–October 1987.

A number of interesting articles appear under the collective theme "Investment Management: A New Look" in the special edition of:
Canadian Investment Review 4, no. 1 (Spring 1991).

Problems

1. (1988 CFA Examination, Level I) Several discussion meetings have provided the following information about one of your firm's new advisory clients, a charitable endowment fund recently created by means of a one-time $10,000,000 gift:

   Objectives
   - *Return requirement.* Planning is based on a minimum total return of 8 percent per year, including an initial current income component of $500,000 (5 percent on beginning capital). Realizing this current income target is the endowment fund's primary return goal. (See "Unique needs," following.)

   Constraints
   - *Time horizon.* Perpetuity, except for requirement to make an $8,500,000 cash distribution on June 30, 1998. (See "Unique needs.")
   - *Liquidity needs.* None of a day-to-day nature until 1998. Income is distributed annually after year-end. (See "Unique needs," below.)
   - *Tax considerations.* None; this endowment fund is exempt from taxes.
   - *Legal and regulatory considerations.* Minimal, but the prudent man rule applies to all investment actions.
   - *Unique needs, circumstances, and preferences.* The endowment fund must pay out to another tax-exempt entity the sum of $8,500,000 in cash on June 30, 1988. The assets remaining after this distribution will be retained by the fund in perpetuity. The endowment fund has adopted a "spending rule" requiring a first-year current income payout of $500,000; thereafter, the annual payout is to rise by 3 percent in real terms. Until 1998, annual income in excess of that required by the spending rule is to be reinvested; after 1998, the spending rate will be reset at 5 percent of the then-existing capital.

   With this information and information found in this chapter, do the following:

   a. Formulate an appropriate investment policy statement for the endowment fund.
   b. Identify and briefly explain three major ways in which your firm's initial asset allocation decisions for the endowment fund will be affected by the circumstances of the account.

2. (1988 CFA Examination, Level I) Your client says, "With the unrealized gains in my portfolio, I have almost saved enough money for my daughter to go to college in eight years, but educational costs keep going up." Based on this statement alone, which one of the following appears to be least important to your client's investment policy?

   a. Time horizon.
   b. Purchasing power risk.

    c. Liquidity.

    d. Taxes.

3. (1988 CFA Examination, Level I) The aspect least likely to be included in the portfolio management process is

    a. Identifying an investor's objectives, constraints, and preferences.

    b. Organizing the management process itself.

    c. Implementing strategies regarding the choice of assets to be used.

    d. Monitoring market conditions, relative values, and investor circumstances.

4. (Adapted from the 1988 CFA Examination, Level I) Investors in high marginal tax brackets probably would be least interested in a

    a. Portfolio of diversified stocks.

    b. Tax-deferred retirement fund.

    c. Commodity pool.

    d. High-income bond fund.

5. (1988 CFA Examination, Level II) Sam Short, CFA, has recently joined the investment management firm of Green, Spence, and Smith (GSS). For several years, GSS has worked for a broad array of clients, including employee benefit plans, wealthy individuals, and charitable organizations. Also, the firm expresses expertise in managing stocks, bonds, cash reserves, real estate, venture capital, and international securities. To date, the firm has not utilized a formal asset allocation process but instead has relied on the individual wishes of clients or the particular preferences of its portfolio managers. Short recommends to GSS management that a formal asset allocation process would be beneficial, and emphasizes that a large part of a portfolio's ultimate return depends on asset allocation. He is asked to take his conviction an additional step by making a proposal to executive management.

    a. Recommend and justify an approach to asset allocation that could be used by GSS.

    b. Apply the approach to a middle-aged, wealthy individual characterized as a fairly conservative investor (sometimes referred to as a "guardian investor").

6. (1987 CFA Examination, Level II) John Oliver, formerly a senior partner of a large management consulting firm, has been elected president of Mid-South Trucking Company. He has contacted you, a portfolio manager for a large investment advisory firm, to discuss the company's defined benefit pension plan. Upon assuming his duties, Oliver learned that Mid-South's pension plan was 100 percent in bonds, with a maximum maturity of 10 years. He believes that "a pension plan should be managed so as to maximize return within well-defined risk parameters," and "anyone can buy bonds and sit on them." Mr. Oliver has suggested that he meet with you, as an objective advisor, and the plan's actuary to discuss possible changes in plan asset mix. To aid you in preparing for the meeting, Mr. Oliver has provided the current portfolio (Table 24.12). He also has provided the following information about the company and its pension plan.

TABLE 24.12   Current Portfolio

	Cost	Market Value	Current Yield	Yield to Maturity
Short-term reserves	$ 10,000,000	$ 10,000,000	5.8%	5.8%
Notes, 90 days to 1 year	25,000,000	25,500,000	6.5	6.4
Notes, 1 to 5 years	110,000,000	115,000,000	8.0	7.8
Bonds, 5 to 10 years	115,000,000	127,500,000	8.8	8.5
TOTAL	$260,000,000	$278,000,000	8.1%	7.9%

- *Company* Mid-South is the eighth-largest domestic trucking company, with annual revenues of $500 million. Revenues have grown about 8 percent per year over the past five years, with one down year. The company employs about 7,000 people, compared with 6,500 five years ago. The annual payroll is about $300 million. The average age of the workforce is 43 years. Company profits last year were $20 million, compared with $12 million five years ago.
- *Pension plan* Mid-South's pension plan is a defined benefit plan that was established in 1965. The company annually contributes 7 percent of payroll to fund the plan. During the past five years, portfolio income has been used to meet payments for retirees, while company contributions have been available for investment. Although the plan is adequately funded on a current basis, unfunded past service liabilities are equal to 40 percent of plan assets. This liability is to be funded over the next 35 years. Plan assets are valued annually on a rolling four-year average for actuarial purposes. Whereas FASB No. 87 requires an annual reassessment of the assumed rate of return, for purposes of this analysis Mid-South's management, in consultation with the actuary, has decided to use an assumed annual rate of 7 percent. This compares with actual plan results that have averaged 10 percent per year over the past 20 years. Wages and salaries are assumed to increase 5 percent per year, identical with past company experience. Before the meeting, you review your firm's investment projections, dated March 31, 1987. Your firm believes that continued prosperity is the most likely outlook for the next three to five years but has allowed for two alternatives: first, a return to high inflation; or second, a move into deflation/depression. The details of the projections are shown in Table 24.13.
- a. Based on this information, create an investment policy statement for the Mid-South Trucking Company's pension plan. Based upon your policy statement and the expectations shown, recommend an appropriate asset allocation strategy for Mid-South Trucking Company's pension plan limited to the same asset classes shown. Justify your changes, if any, from the current portfolio. Your allocation must sum to 100 percent.
- b. At the meeting, the actuary suggests that Mid-South consider terminating the defined benefit plan, purchasing annuities for retirees and vested employees with the proceeds, and establishing a defined contribution plan. The company would continue to contribute 7 percent of payroll to

TABLE 24.13 Investment Projections

Scenarios	Expected Annual Total Return (%)
Continued Prosperity (60% Probability)	
Short-term reserves (Treasury bills)	6.0
Stocks (S&P 500 index)	12.0
Bonds (S&P high-grade bond index)	8.0
High-Inflation Scenario (25% Probability)	
Short-term reserves (Treasury bills)	10.0
Stocks (S&P 500 index)	15.0
Bonds (S&P high-grade bond index)	3.0
Deflation/Depression Scenario (15% Probability)	
Short-term reserves (Treasury bills)	2.0
Stocks (S&P 500 index)	−6.0
Bonds (S&P high-grade bond index)	12.0

the defined contribution plan. Compare the key features of a defined benefit plan and a defined contribution plan. Assuming Mid-South were to adopt and retain responsibility for a defined contribution plan, briefly explain any revisions to your asset allocation strategy developed in part *a* above. Again, your allocation must sum to 100 percent and be limited to the same asset classes shown.

7. (1981 CFA Examination, Level II) You are a portfolio manager and senior executive vice-president of Advisory Securities Selection, Inc. Your firm has been invited to meet with the trustees of the Wood Museum Endowment Funds. Wood Museum is a privately endowed charitable institution that is dependent on the investment return from a $25 million endowment fund to balance the budget. The treasurer of the museum has recently completed a budget that indicates a need for cash flow of $3 million in 1982, $3.2 million in 1983, and $3.5 million in 1984 from the endowment fund to balance the budget in those years. At the present time the entire endowment portfolio is invested in Treasury bills and money market funds because the trustees fear a financial crisis. The trustees do not anticipate any further capital contributions to the fund. The trustees are all successful business people, and they have been critical of the fund's previous investment advisors because they did not follow a logical decision-making process. In fact, several previous managers were dismissed because of their inability to communicate with the trustees and their preoccupation with the fund's relative performance rather than the cash flow needs. Advisory Securities Selection, Inc., has been contacted by the trustees because of its reputation for understanding and relating to its clients' needs. The trustees have asked you, as a prospective portfolio manager for the Wood Museum Endowment Fund, to prepare a written report in response to the following questions. Your report will be circulated to the trustees before the initial interview on June 15, 1981. Explain in detail how each of the following

relates to the determination of either investor objectives or investor constraints that can be used to determine the portfolio policies for this three-year period for the Wood Museum Endowment Fund.

a. Liquidity requirements.

b. Return requirements.

c. Risk tolerance.

d. Time horizon.

e. Tax considerations.

f. Regulatory and legal considerations.

g. Unique needs and circumstances.

8. (1985 CFA Examination, Level III) Mrs. Mary Atkins, age 66, has been your firm's client for five years, since the death of her husband, Dr. Charles Atkins. Dr. Atkins had built a successful newspaper business that he sold two years before his death to Merit Enterprises, a publishing and broadcasting conglomerate, in exchange for Merit common stock. The Atkinses had no children, and their wills provide that upon their deaths the remaining assets shall be used to create a fund for the benefit of Good Samaritan Hospital, to be called the Atkins Endowment Fund. Good Samaritan is a 180-bed, not-for-profit hospital with an annual operating budget of $12.5 million. In the past, the hospital's operating revenues have often been sufficient to meet operating expenses and occasionally even generate a small surplus. In recent years, however, rising costs and declining occupancy rates have caused Good Samaritan to run a deficit. The operating deficit has averaged $300,000–$400,000 annually over the last several years. Existing endowment assets (i.e., excluding the Atkins' estate) of $7.5 million currently generate approximately $375,000 of annual income, up from less than $200,000 five years ago. This increased income has been the result of somewhat higher interest rates, as well as a shift in asset mix toward more bonds. To offset operating deficits, the Good Samaritan Board of Governors has determined that the endowment's current income should be increased to approximately 6 percent of total assets (up from 5 percent currently). The hospital has not received any significant additions to its endowment assets in the past five years. Identify and describe an appropriate set of investment objectives and constraints for the Atkins Endowment Fund to be created after Mrs. Atkins' death.

9. (1982 CFA Examination, Level III) You have been named as investment advisor to a foundation established by Dr. Walter Jones with an original contribution consisting entirely of the common stock of Jomedco, Inc. Founded by Dr. Jones, Jomedco manufactures and markets medical devices invented by the doctor and collects royalties on other patented innovations. All of the shares that made up the initial contribution to the foundation were sold at a public offering of Jomedco common stock, and the $5 million proceeds will be delivered to the foundation within the next week. At the same time, Mrs. Jones will receive $5 million in proceeds from the sale of her stock in Jomedco. Dr. Jones' purpose in establishing the Jones Foundation was to "offset the effect of inflation on medical school tuition for the maximum number of worthy students." You are preparing for a

TABLE 24.14   Capital Market Expectations: Stocks, Bonds, and Real Estate

	Stocks	Bonds	Real Estate	Cash
Expected HPR $E(r)$	14%	9%	11%	6%
Standard deviation σ	24.5%	14.8%	20.0%	0
Correlation Coefficients				
Stocks	1.0	−.24	0	
Bonds		1.0	0	
Real estate			1.0	

meeting with the foundation's trustees to discuss investment policy and asset allocation.

a. Define and give examples that show the differences between an investment objective, an investment constraint, and investment policy.

b. Identify and describe an appropriate set of investment objectives and investment constraints for the Jones Foundation.

c. Based on the investment objectives and investment constraints identified in part *b*, prepare a comprehensive investment policy statement for the Jones Foundation to be recommended for adoption by the trustees.

10. (Use the computer-based portfolio optimization program to do this problem.) Assume the set of capital market expectations regarding stocks, bonds, real estate, and cash given in the Table 24.14. What is the composition of the O^* portfolio, its mean, standard deviation, and the reward-to-variability ratio?

CHAPTER 25

Individual Investors and Retirement Savings

The overriding consideration in individual investor goal setting is one's stage in the life cycle. Most young people start their adult lives with only one asset—their earning power. In this early stage of the life cycle, an individual may not have much interest in investing in stocks and bonds. The needs for liquidity and preserving safety of principal dictate a conservative policy of putting savings in a bank or a money market fund. If and when a person gets married, the purchase of life and disability insurance will be required to protect the value of human capital.

When a married couple's labour income grows to the point at which insurance and housing needs are met, the couple may start to save for their children's college education and their own retirement, especially if the government provides tax incentives for retirement savings. Retirement savings typically constitute a family's first pool of investable funds. This is money that can be invested in stocks, bonds, and real estate (other than the primary home). It is the issue of how to allocate these investable funds that we address in this chapter.

First, we examine the particular circumstances that the individual faces and how these affect the individual investment decision. Then, we focus on the institutional forms that private retirement savings can take and how they should be invested. By far the most important institution in the retirement income system is the employer-sponsored pension plan. These plans vary in form and complexity, but there are certain universal characteristics. In general, investment strategy depends on the type of plan.

25.1 *The Life Cycle and the Risk-Return Trade-Off*

Human Capital and Insurance

The first significant investment decision for most individuals concerns education, building up their human capital. The major asset most people have during their early working years is the earning power that draws on their human capital. In these circumstances, the risk of illness or injury is far greater than the risk associated with their financial wealth.

The most direct way of hedging human capital risk is to purchase insurance. Viewing the combination of your labour income and a disability insurance policy as a portfolio, the rate of return on this portfolio is less risky than the labour income by itself. Life insurance is a hedge against the complete loss of income as a result of death of any of the family's income earners.

Investment in Residence

The first major economic asset many people acquire is their own house. Deciding to buy rather than rent a residence qualifies as an investment decision.

An important consideration in assessing the risk-and-return aspects of this investment is the value of a house as a hedge against two kinds of risk. The first kind is the risk of increases in rental rates. If you own a house, any increase in rental rates will increase the return on your investment.

The second kind of risk is that the particular house or apartment where you live may not always be available to you. By buying, you guarantee its availability.

Saving for Retirement and the Assumption of Risk

People save and invest money to provide for future consumption and leave an estate. The primary aim of lifetime savings is to allow maintenance of the customary standard of living after retirement. Life expectancy, when one makes it to retirement at age 65, approaches 85 years, so the average retiree needs to prepare a 20-year nest egg and sufficient savings to cover unexpected health-care costs. Investment income may also increase the welfare of one's heirs, favourable charity, or both.

The leisure that investment income can be expected to produce depends on the degree of risk the household is willing to take with its investment portfolio. Empirical observation summarized in Table 25.1 indicates a person's age and stage in the life cycle affect attitude toward risk.

The evidence in Table 25.1 supports the life-cycle view of investment behaviour. Questionnaires suggest that attitudes shift away from risk tolerance and toward risk aversion as investors near retirement age. With age, individuals lose the potential to recover from a disastrous investment performance. When

TABLE 25.1 Amount of Risk That Investors Said They Were Willing to Take (by Age)

	Under 35	35–54	55 and Over
No risk	54%	57%	71%
A little risk	30%	30%	21%
Some risk	14%	18%	8%
A lot of risk	2%	1%	1%

From Market Facts, Inc., Chicago, Ill.

they are young, investors can respond to a loss by working harder and saving more of their income. But as retirement approaches, investors realize there will be less time to recover. Hence, the shift to safe assets.

Concept Check	Question 1. *a.* Think about the financial circumstances of your closest relative in your parents' generation (preferably your parents' household, if you are fortunate enough to have them around). Write down the objectives and constraints for their investment decisions. *b.* Now consider the financial situation of your closest relative who is in his or her 30s. Write down the objectives and constraints that would fit his or her investment decision. *c.* How much of the difference between the two statements is due to the age of the investors?

Manage Your Own Portfolio or Rely on Others?

Lots of people have assets such as social security benefits, pension and group insurance plans, and savings components of life insurance policies. Yet they exercise limited control, if any, on the investment decisions of these plans. The funds that secure pension and life insurance plans are managed by institutional investors.

Outside of the "forced savings" plans, however, individuals can manage their own investment portfolios. As the population grows richer, more and more people face this decision.

Managing your own portfolio *appears* to be the lowest-cost solution. Conceptually, there is little difference between managing one's own investments and professional financial planning/investment management.

Against the fees and charges that financial planners and professional investment managers impose, you will want to offset the value of your time and energy expended on diligent portfolio management. People with a suitable background may even look at investment as recreation. Most of all, you must recognize the *potential* difference in investment results.

Diversity Is More Than Stocks and Bonds

By Barbara Donnelly

Every investor has heard about how crucial it is to diversify, but many people—even some with varied stock and bond holdings—probably don't realize how *un*diversified they really are.

"Individuals rarely take an overall view" when it comes to diversification, says Michael Lipper, who heads Lipper Analytical Services. "They think of it in terms of different chunks of money" they have invested in stocks, bonds, cash, and other assets. In reality, "securities are only one part of the total [diversification] picture—and not even the most important one at that."

Take the case of a young Wall Street executive with a mortgaged cooperative apartment in lower Manhattan. A diversified stock portfolio would actually compound, not lessen, such an individual's risk because all those "assets"—job, home, and savings—are heavily exposed to the vagaries of the stock market.

In a similar vein, Lawrence Manchester, head of the private-client group at Standish, Ayer & Wood, says he would advise a client who owns a car agency to avoid long-term bonds, utilities, and insurance stocks. Those investments, just like the car business, are "very interest-rate sensitive," he says. For that client diversification means "fixing it so that when his company goes in the dumper every four years, he's protected in his portfolio."

The way the professionals see it, diversification for individuals isn't driven by fancy theories about market volatility. Instead, they say, it starts with a basic grasp of personal economic risk.

"I'd always ask myself at the start of the analysis, 'What's the worst that could happen to me? And the next worst?—and build a portfolio strategy based on that," says Russell Fogler of Aronson + Fogler, a Philadelphia money management firm. "It's a sequential process."

At different points in an individual's investing lifetime, diversification has two roles to play, the pros say. Initially, its function is to protect the individual from being hit hard by losses in basic "assets," such as job, home, and purchasing power.

"Most people don't think of their job as their No. 1 investment," says Mr. Lipper. "But over their lifetime, it's salary, insurance, and pension benefits that will wind up setting their whole investment picture."

The second purpose of diversification is to protect against the long-term risk of "outliving one's capital" once the job ends, says Mr. Lipper. In this context, says Owen Quattlebaum, head of personal financial services at Brown Brothers Harriman & Co., diversification means "branching out into other, risky assets" such as stocks and bonds. In other words, it becomes "something genuinely defined as a way to make money," he says.

What strategies should the individual use to hedge these risks? The pros offer some advice:

Job Risk

At the end of a long economic expansion, especially in this age of corporate restructurings and increasing foreign competition, job risk—unemployment and other factors that threaten income and benefits—is relatively high. In such a hazardous environment, individuals should safeguard their option of seeking new opportunity elsewhere.

Depending on how marketable a person's skills are and how vulnerable his or her industry is, everyone should hold between three months' and a year's worth of after-tax salary in short-term cash investments, such as bank deposits and money market funds, the specialists say.

Additionally, says Mr. Lipper, an individual should hedge against the loss of 3 to 12 months of pension and other benefits—a sum usually equal to about a third of pre-tax salary. That money should be invested in risky assets, such as stocks and long-term bonds. "In this barbell strategy, individuals should be as aggressive as they can stomach on the far end," he says.

(Continued)

House Risk

A mortgaged home is probably the individual's major exposure to "the factors in the local area that will vibrate with the job risk and, in effect, double up the job risk," says Mr. Quattlebaum of Brown Brothers.

The risk of having to meet house payments while searching for a new job would probably be covered by the cash reserves mentioned above. However, says Mr. Lipper, people who think they might have to sell their home and move to find employment in another area should consider protecting themselves against potential losses.

Today's "short-term weakness in housing prices might entail a 10 percent to 20 percent hit to the equity in your house," compared with what it would cost to buy a comparable home in a more-vibrant area, he says. He recommends setting aside money to cover that potential shortage and buying "intermediate bonds of one to five years' maturity and roll them over—so that you get a reasonable interest rate."

In the years ahead, houses—and real-estate assets generally—present another risk: "They will not be as effective a hedge against inflation as in the 1970s because the country is so overbuilt," says Barry Berlin, vice-president at First Wachovia Capital Management. Rolled-over positions in intermediate bonds, as well as stocks and foreign securities, could help offset that risk.

Source: Barbara Donnelly, "Diversity Is More Than Stocks and Bonds," *The Wall Street Journal,* September 14, 1989. Reprinted by permission of *The Wall Street Journal,* © 1989 Dow Jones & Company, Inc. All Rights Reserved Worldwide.

Besides the need to deliver better-performing investments, professional managers face two added difficulties. First, getting clients to communicate their objectives and constraints requires considerable skill. This is not a one-time task, because objectives and constraints are forever changing. Second, the professional needs to articulate the financial plan and keep the client abreast of outcomes. Professional management of large portfolios is complicated further by the need to set up an efficient organization where decisions can be decentralized and information properly disseminated.

The task of life-cycle financial planning is a formidable one for most individuals. Therefore, it is not surprising that a whole industry has grown in recent years to provide personal financial advice.[1] The "right" portfolio for an individual also depends on unique circumstances. The accompanying box discusses some of these.

Growth vs. Income

There is a strong tendency in the popular investments literature to talk as if the investor must use only dividend and interest income for current consumption spending and reserve appreciation in security prices (i.e., growth) for future spending. The only sensible justification behind such a policy would be the existence of significant transaction costs for selling securities, because in fact expenses can be met by selling securities just as easily as by collecting and dispensing the cash from dividends or interest.

For example, suppose you have $100,000 in assets and expect to spend $8,000 this year. You are trying to decide between two mutual funds that have

---

[1] For a review of the Canadian financial planning industry, see Gisele H. Delente, "The Financial Planning Industry: Does Canada Have One?" *Canadian Investment Review* volume II, no. 2 (Fall 1989).

the same expected return and risk. Income Fund offers an expected dividend yield of 8 percent and zero expected capital gains, while Growth Fund offers a dividend yield of 5 percent and expected capital gains of 3 percent. You can meet your planned $8,000 current expenditure in two ways:

	Invest in Income Fund	Invest in Growth Fund
Expected rate of return	8%	8%
Dividends	$ 8,000	$ 5,000
Sale of shares	0	$ 3,000
TOTAL	$ 8,000	$ 8,000
Portfolio Value		
Before sale of shares	$100,000	$103,000
Sale of shares	0	–$ 3,000
End-of-year value	**$100,000**	**$100,000**

Note that in both cases the $8,000 for current spending is derived from portfolio returns and the end-of-year portfolio is worth the same $100,000. Whether the $8,000 comes from dividends or capital gains is irrelevant.

The classification of stocks into income versus growth stocks really represents an implicit assessment about risk. Mutual funds termed "income funds" tend to have lower risk and lower expected returns than so-called "growth funds." The choice between income and growth funds really should be viewed in terms of the risk-return trade-off. The purpose to which investment returns will be applied is irrelevant.

25.2 *Tax Sheltering*

In this section, we explain three important tax-sheltering options that can radically affect optimal asset allocation for individual investors. The first is the tax-deferral option, which arises from the fact that you do not have to pay tax on a capital gain until you choose to realize the gain. The second is tax-deferred retirement plans such as Registered Retirement Savings Plans, and the third is tax-deferred annuities offered by life insurance companies.

The Tax-Deferral Option

A fundamental feature of the Income Tax Act is that tax on a capital gain on an asset is payable only when the asset is sold;[2] this is its **tax-deferral option**. The

---

[2] The only exception to this rule occurs in futures investing, where National Revenue treats a gain as taxable in the year it occurs, regardless of whether the investor closes his or her position. Note also that on pure discount bonds imputed interest is taxable, even though no interest payment is received until sale or maturity. Additionally, note that both the principal residence and the first $100,000 of capital gains are exempted from taxation.

investor, therefore, can control the timing of the tax payment. From a tax perspective, this option makes stocks in general preferable to fixed-income securities.

To see this, compare Seagram's stock with a Seagram's bond. Both offer an expected total return of 15 percent this year. The stock has a dividend yield of 5 percent and an expected appreciation in price of 10 percent, whereas the bond has an interest rate of 15 percent. The bond investor must pay tax on the bond's interest in the year it is earned, whereas the Seagram's stockholder pays tax only on the dividend and defers paying tax on the capital gain until the stock is sold.

Suppose the investor is investing $2,000 for five years and is in a 51 percent tax bracket. An investment in the bond will earn an after-tax return of 7.35 percent per year (.49 × 15 percent). The yield after taxes at the end of five years is:

$$\$1,000 \times 1.0735^5 = \$1,424.64$$

For the stock, dividend yield after taxes will be 2.479 percent per year ([1 − (.51 × 1.25) + .1333] × 5 percent). Because no taxes are paid on the capital gain until year 5, the return before paying the capital gains tax is

$$\$1,000 \times (1 + .02479 + .10)^5 = 1,000(1.1245)^5 = \$1,800.35$$

In year 5, the capital gain is

$$\$1,800.35 - \$1,000(1.02479)^5 = 1,800.35 - 1,130.25 = \$670.10$$

Taxes due are $256.46, leaving $1,543.88, which is $119.24 more than the bond investment yields. Deferral of the capital gains tax allows the investment to compound at a faster rate until the tax is actually paid.

Note that the more of one's total return that is in the form of price appreciation, the greater the value of the tax-deferral option.

Tax-Deferred Retirement Plans

Recent years have seen establishment of **tax-deferred retirement plans** in which investors can choose how to allocate assets. Such plans would include self-directed RRSPs and employer-sponsored "tax-qualified" defined contribution plans. A feature they all have in common is that contributions and earnings are subject to neither federal nor provincial income tax until the individual withdraws them as benefits.

Typically, an individual may have some investment in the form of such qualified retirement accounts and some in the form of ordinary taxable accounts. The basic investment principle that applies is to keep whatever bonds you want to hold in the retirement account while placing equities in the ordinary account. You maximize the tax advantage of the retirement account by holding in it the security that is the least tax advantaged.

To see this point, consider the following example. Suppose Eloise has $200,000 of wealth, $100,000 of it in a tax-qualified retirement account. She has decided to invest half of her wealth in bonds and half in stocks, so she allocates half of her retirement account and half of her non-retirement funds to each. By doing this, Eloise is not maximizing her after-tax returns. She could reduce her tax bill with no change in before-tax returns by simply shifting her bonds into the retirement account and holding all her stocks outside the retirement account.

Concept Check	Question 2. Suppose Eloise earns a 10 percent per year rate of interest on bonds and 15 percent per year on stocks, all in the form of price appreciation. In five years she will withdraw all her funds and spend them. By how much will she increase her final accumulation if she shifts all bonds into the retirement account and holds all stocks outside the retirement account? She is in a 28 percent tax bracket.

Deferred Annuities

Deferred annuities are essentially tax-sheltered accounts offered by life insurance companies. They combine the same kind of deferral of taxes available on RRSPs with the option of withdrawing one's funds in the form of a life annuity. Variable annuity contracts offer the additional advantage of mutual fund investing. One major difference between an RRSP and a variable annuity contract is that whereas the amount one can contribute to an RRSP is tax deductible and extremely limited as to maximum amount, the amount one can contribute to a deferred annuity is unlimited, but not tax deductible.

The defining characteristic of a life annuity is that its payments continue as long as the recipient is alive, although virtually all deferred annuity contracts have several withdrawal options, including a lump sum of cash paid out at any time. You need not worry about running out of money before you die. Like Canada Pension Plan (CPP), therefore, life annuities offer longevity insurance and, therefore, would seem to be an ideal asset for someone in the retirement years. Indeed, theory suggests that where there are no bequest motives, it would be optimal for people to invest heavily in actuarially fair life annuities.[3]

There are two types of life annuities, **fixed annuities** and **variable annuities**. A fixed annuity pays a fixed nominal sum of money per period (usually each month), whereas a variable annuity pays a periodic amount linked to the investment performance of some underlying portfolio.

In pricing annuities, insurance companies use **mortality tables** that show the probabilities that individuals of various ages will die within a year. These tables enable the insurer to compute with reasonable accuracy how many of a large number of people in a given age group will die in each future year. If it sells life

---

[3] For an elaboration of this point, see Laurence J. Kotlikoff and Avia Spivak, "The Family as an Incomplete Annuities Market," *Journal of Political Economy* 89 (April 1981).

annuities to a large group, the insurance company can estimate fairly accurately the amount of money it will have to pay in each future year to meet its obligations.

Variable annuities are structured so that the investment risk of the underlying asset portfolio is passed through to the recipient, much as shareholders bear the risk of a mutual fund. There are two stages in a variable annuity contract: an accumulation phase and a payout phase. During the *accumulation* phase, the investor contributes money periodically to one or more open-end mutual funds and accumulates shares. The second, or *payout,* stage usually starts at retirement, when the investor typically has several options, including the following:

1. Taking the market value of the shares in a lump-sum payment
2. Receiving a fixed annuity until death
3. Receiving a variable amount of money each period that is computed according to a certain procedure

This procedure is best explained by the following example. Assume that, at retirement, John Shortlife has $100,000 accumulated in a variable annuity contract. The initial annuity payment is determined by setting an assumed investment return (AIR), 4 percent per year in this example, and an assumption about mortality probabilities. In Shortlife's case we assume he will live for only three years after retirement and will receive three annual payments starting one year from now.

The benefit payment in each year, B_t, is given by the recursive formula:

$$B_t = B_{t-1}[(1 + R_t)/(1 + \text{AIR})] \tag{25.1}$$

where R_t is the actual holding period return on the underlying portfolio in year t. In other words, each year the amount Shortlife receives equals the previous year's benefit multiplied by a factor that reflects the actual investment return compared with the assumed investment return. In our example, if the actual return equals 4 percent, the factor will be one, and this year's benefit will equal last year's. If R_t is greater than 4 percent, the benefit will increase, and if R_t is less than 4 percent, the benefit will decrease.

The starting benefit is found by computing a hypothetical constant payment with a present value of $100,000 using the 4 percent AIR to discount future values and multiplying it by the first year's performance factor. In our example, the hypothetical constant payment is $36,035.

The accompanying box summarizes the computation and shows what the payment will be in each of three years if R_t is 6 percent, then 2 percent, and finally 4 percent. The last column shows the balance in the fund after each payment.

This method guarantees that the initial $100,000 will be sufficient to pay all benefits due, regardless of what actual holding period returns turn out to be. In this way, the variable annuity contract passes all portfolio risk through to the annuitant.

By selecting an appropriate mix of underlying assets, such as stocks, bonds, and cash, an investor can create a stream of variable annuity payments with a

Illustration of a Variable Annuity

Starting accumulation = $100,000

R_t = Rate of return on underlying portfolio in year t

Assumes investment return (AIR) = 4 percent per year

B_t = Benefit received at end of year t

$$= B_{t-1} \frac{1 + R_t}{1 + AIR}$$

B_o = $36,035. This is the hypothetical constant payment, which has a present value of $100,000, using a discount rate of 4 percent per year.

A_t = Remaining balance after B_t is withdrawn

t	R_t	B_t	Remaining Balance = $A_t = A_{t-1} \times (1 + R_t) - B_t$
0			$100,000
1	6%	36,728	69,272
2	2%	36,022	34,635
3	4%	36,022	0

wide variety of risk-return combinations. Naturally, the investor wants to select a combination on the efficient frontier, that is, a combination that offers the highest expected level of payments for any specified level of risk.[4]

Concept Check

Question 3. Assume Victor is now 75 years old and is expected to live until age 80. He has $100,000 in a variable annuity account. If the assumed investment return is 4 percent per year, what is the initial annuity payment? Suppose the annuity's asset base is the TSE 300 equity portfolio and its holding period return for the next five years is each of the following: 4 percent, 10 percent, −8 percent, 25 percent, and 0. How much would Victor receive each year? Verify that the insurance company would wind up using exactly $100,000 to fund Victor's benefits.

Variable and Universal Life Insurance

Variable life insurance is another tax-deferred investment vehicle offered by the life insurance industry. A variable life insurance policy combines life insurance with the tax-deferred annuities described earlier.

[4] For an elaboration on possible combinations see Zvi Bodie, "An Innovation for Stable Real Retirement Income," *Journal of Portfolio Management,* Fall 1980; and Zvi Bodie and James E. Pesando, "Retirement Annuity Design in an Inflationary Climate," Chapter 11 in Zvi Bodie and J. B. Shoven (editors), *Financial Aspects of the United States Pension Systems* (Chicago: University of Chicago Press, 1983).

To invest in this product, you pay either a single premium or a series of premiums. In each case there is a stated death benefit, and the policyholder can allocate the money invested to several portfolios, which generally include a money market fund, a bond fund, and at least one common stock fund. The allocation can be changed at any time.

A variable life policy has a cash surrender value equal to the investment base minus any surrender charges. Typically, there is a surrender charge (about 5 percent of the purchase payments) if you surrender the policy during the first several years, but not thereafter. At policy surrender, income taxes become due on all investment gains.

Variable life insurance policies offer a death benefit that is the greater of the stated face value or the market value of the investment base. In other words, the death benefit may rise with favourable investment performance, but it will not go below the guaranteed face value. Furthermore, the surviving beneficiary is not subject to income tax on the death benefit.

The policyholder can choose from a number of income options to convert the policy into a stream of income, either on surrender of the contract or as a partial withdrawal. In all cases, income taxes are payable on the part of any distribution representing investment gains.

The insured can gain access to the investment without having to pay income tax by borrowing against the cash surrender value. Policy loans of up to 90 percent of the cash value are available at any time at a contractually specified interest rate.

A universal live insurance policy is similar to a variable life policy, except that instead of having a choice of portfolios to invest in, the policyholder earns a rate of interest that is set by the insurance company and changed periodically as market conditions change. The disadvantage of universal life insurance is that the company controls the rate of return to the policyholder and, although companies may change the rate in response to competitive pressures, changes are not automatic. Different companies offer different rates, so it often pays to shop around for the best.

25.3 *Pension Funds*

Defined Contribution vs. Defined Benefit Plans

Although employer pension programs vary in design, they are usually classified into two broad types: defined contribution and defined benefit. Under a defined contribution (DC) plan, each employee has an account into which the employer and the employee (in a contributory plan) make regular contributions. Benefit levels depend on the total contributions and investment earnings of the accumulation in the account. Defined contribution plans are, in effect, tax-deferred savings accounts held in trust for the employees.

In a defined benefit (DB) plan, the employee's pension benefit entitlement is determined by a formula that takes into account years of service for the employer and, in most cases, wage or salary. Many defined benefit formulas also take into account the CPP benefit to which an employee is entitled. These are called "integrated" plans.

Defined Contribution Plans

The DC arrangement is conceptually simpler. The employer, and sometimes also the employee, makes regular contributions into the employee's retirement account. The contributions usually are specified as a predetermined fraction of salary, although that fraction need not be constant over the course of a career.

Contributions from both parties are tax deductible, and investment income accrues tax-free. Often, the employee has some choice as to how the account is to be invested. In principle, contributions may be invested in any security, although in practice most plans limit investment options to various bond, stock, and money market funds. At retirement, the employee typically receives an annuity whose size depends on the accumulated value of the funds in the retirement account. The employee bears all the investment risk; the retirement account is by definition fully funded, and the firm has no obligation beyond making its periodic contribution.

Defined Benefit Plans

A typical DB plan determines the employee's benefit as a function of both years of service and wage history. As a representative plan, consider one in which the employee receives retirement income equal to 1 percent of final salary multiplied by the number of years of service. Thus, an employee retiring after 40 years of service with a final salary of $15,000 per year would receive a retirement benefit of 40 percent of $15,000, or $6,000 per year.

The annuity promised to the employee is the employer's liability. The present value of this liability represents the amount of money that the employer must set aside today to fund the deferred annuity that commences upon the employee's retirement.

Concept Check

Question 4. An employee is 40 years old and has been working for the firm for 15 years. If normal retirement age is 65, the interest rate is 8 percent, and the employee's life expectancy is 80, what is the present value of the accrued pension benefit?

Alternative perspectives on DB plans

Defined benefit pension funds are pools of assets that serve as collateral for firms' pension liabilities. Traditionally, these funds have been viewed as separate from the corporation. Funding and asset allocation decisions are supposed to be made in the beneficiaries' best interests, regardless of the financial condition of the sponsoring corporation.

Beneficiaries presumably want corporate pension plans to be as well funded as possible. Their preferences with regard to asset allocation policy, however, are less clear. If beneficiaries could not share in any windfall gains—if the defined benefit liabilities were really fixed in nominal terms—rationally, they would prefer that the funds be invested in the least risky assets. If beneficiaries had a claim on surplus assets, however, the optimal asset allocation could in principle include virtually any mix of stocks and bonds.

Another way to view the pension fund investment decision is as an integral part of overall corporate financial policy. Seen in this perspective, defined benefit liabilities are part and parcel of the firm's other fixed financial liabilities, and pension assets are part of the firm's assets. From this point of view, any plan surplus or deficit belongs to the firm's shareholders. The firm thus manages an extended balance sheet, which includes both its normal assets and liabilities and its pension assets and liabilities, in the best interests of *shareholders*.

The question of who should benefit from surpluses in pension funds, due partially to good performance in the market, became a subject of much controversy towards the end of the 1980s, as described in the accompanying box.

Asset allocation in DB pension plans

The practitioner literature seems to view a firm's pension liabilities as divided into two parts—retired and active. Benefits owed to retired participants are nominal, and benefits accruing to active participants are real. The nominal benefits can be immunized by investing in fixed-income securities with the same duration or even exactly the same pattern of cash flows as the pension annuities. Accruing benefits, on the other hand, call for a very different investment policy.

The essence of that policy can be summarized as follows. In estimating the liabilities to active participants, the firm's actuaries make an "actuarial interest rate" assumption that should become the target rate for the pension asset portfolio. The pension fund should view the possibility of receiving a rate of return below the actuarial assumption as having a greater negative weight than the positive weight associated with a return above the actuarial assumption. This factor will affect the asset allocation decision.

Portfolio insurance is a new investment strategy that has developed recently in response to this view. It calls for maintaining an asset portfolio with a truncated and positively skewed probability distribution of returns. The probability of getting returns below the actuarial rate is zero, whereas the probabilities of returns above the actuarial rate are positive.

Portfolio insurance can be provided in a number of ways. The most direct method is to invest in common stocks and buy protective puts on them, which eliminates downside risk while maintaining upside potential. Of course, the

Battle Rages over Pension Surplus Ownership

By Bruce Gates

Companies and their employees are locked in a high-stakes struggle for control over pension plan surpluses.

Legal battles have been won and lost on both sides, but there has yet to be a final resolution to the fundamental question:

Who owns the surplus?

There's no simple answer, and the uncertainty over ownership is "bad for the health of pension plans," says John Christie, chairman of the Canadian Institute of Actuaries' task force on pension surpluses.

In the absence of clear legislation outlining the rules of the game, the courts in many provinces have steered clear of making definitive rulings. Instead, they've taken each case on its own merits.

Ownership in the courts' eyes may depend to some extent on how the plan was created. An employer may have a better case for keeping the surplus if it contributed all of the money to the pension plan—less so if employees contributed a portion.

However, as with anything that involves lawyers and judges, nothing is quite that simple.

Opposing Viewpoints

A great deal has depended on the availability of documentation, and how the rules of the plan were interpreted by the judges.

However, if you listen to labour groups, such as the Canadian Labour Congress and the United Steelworkers of America, the surplus belongs to the workers. Labour groups consider surpluses to be deferred wages.

But if you listen to companies that take the trouble of setting up and administering employee pension plans, they should keep the surplus for taking the risk.

They say that because they assume the burden of setting up and administering these plans, as well as picking up any deficits, or "downside risk," that may occur, they should be entitled to any surplus.

There are two problems with that argument, says one analyst who asked not to be named.

"First, much of the downside risk taking is eliminated through the choice of actuarial assumptions when the plan is being set up.

"The second problem is that employers are able to shift some of the downside risk to employees during collective bargaining. For example, employers may take any amortization costs associated with rescuing a pension plan into account in determining employee wages during collective bargaining."

The arguments over who should get the surplus could be ended in the next few years as provinces introduce legislation to address the issue. As this is provincial legislation, each will address the issue in its own way.

In Quebec, for example, a consultation paper tabled in the national assembly last December [1990] by Manpower & Income Security Minister André Bourbeau suggested one possible solution would be some kind of sharing arrangement between employers and employees who contributed to a pension plan.

The paper was discussed at a parliamentary commission last month. However, a representative of Bourbeau says it's uncertain whether there will be any new legislation during this session of the assembly.

"It's possible, but not definite."

Manitoba's pension commission launched a discussion paper in February. It proposes allowing employers to keep any surplus if they satisfy a number of criteria. These include having a plan whose language clearly stipulates that surpluses accrue to the employer.

New Brunswick is awaiting proclamation of its first pension benefits act, which was passed in 1987. The act would allow companies to claim surpluses, if their pension plan documentation so stated. Otherwise, the money would go to the employees.

(Continued)

For its part, Ontario is also preparing to resolve the issue.

Officials at the Ministry of Financial Institutions are briefing the new minister, Brian Charlton, but it's still too early to say what will be in any discussion paper that will follow.

"We're working to decide where we go from here," says Robert Simpson, the deputy minister.

But if the new rules reflect the musings of Ontario Premier Bob Rae, it may be bad news for many companies sitting on hefty surpluses.

"Contribution Holidays"

Last November, when he promised new legislation, Rae said the surpluses belonged to the employees, and should be used to improve the benefits for plan members. He also objected to "contribution holidays," a practice whereby companies use up their surpluses by not contributing any new money to employee pension plans.

Rae's words may be cause for concern among Ontario companies, whose employees make up about 40 percent of Canada's pension members. They also fear legislation that may override their present arrangements with employees.

"If a plan is very specific one way or another, it wouldn't really be fair for legislation to retroactively override it," says Stephen Donald, a consulting actuary with A. Foster Higgins in Toronto.

Proposed government legislation in Ontario and other provinces also bothers benefits consultant William M. Mercer Ltd. and others who warn that too much tinkering by government could affect future pension plans.

David Stouffer, a principal with Toronto-based Mercer, says if legislation were to deny the recovery of employers' overcontributions to a defined benefit pension plan, they would put as little as possible into their plans. If they won't have access to the surplus, they won't let one develop.

The implication for employees is they could end up with a smaller pension plan than they would had employers been allowed to deal with the surplus as they saw fit.

In an article in Mercer's February newsletter, Stouffer adds that employers with defined benefit plans should be free to negotiate with employees the ownership of any excess assets.

"In plans where the employer has retained the right to surplus assets, he should be free to use those assets as he chooses, provided his actions don't jeopardize the security of the benefits."

As provinces move toward legislation, the Canadian Institute of Actuaries' Christie hopes they "won't take precipate action until we have had a chance to put forward our views for debate."

The actuaries' task force is in the midst of preparing a final paper on the issue. The paper is expected this year.

It's been an arduous process, Christie says, because the issue is so complicated, that even actuaries can't fully agree on the best solution.

"We're trying to put forward an unbiased professional view and contribute to the public debate that's going on."

From *The Financial Post*, April 5, 1991, by Bruce Gates. Reprinted by permission.

guaranteed minimum return on such a policy will always be lower than the risk-free rate. Another method is to invest in T-bills and buy call options. The third way of providing portfolio insurance is to pursue a dynamic hedging strategy with stocks and T-bills. The strategy involves continuous portfolio revision to replicate the payoff structure of the two previous strategies. It involves selling stocks when their price falls and buying them when their price rises.[5]

---

[5] For a more complete discussion of dynamic hedging, see Chapter 22. In addition, see Mark Rubinstein, "Alternative Paths to Portfolio Insurance," *Financial Analysts Journal,* July–August 1985.

The Black-Dewhurst Proposal

In 1981, Fischer Black and Moray Dewhurst created a stir among pension plan finance specialists by making a proposal that carried to a logical extreme the notion that a pension plan is a way to shelter investment income from corporate income taxes.[6] They claimed that, to maximize the value of a firm to its shareholders, a firm should fully fund its pension plan and invest the entire amount in bonds.

They propose the firm arbitrage taxes by substituting bonds for stocks in the pension fund. The simple form of the plan consists of four operations carried out at the same time:

1. Sell all equities, $X, in the pension fund.
2. Purchase on pension account $X of bonds of the same risk as the firm's own bonds.
3. Issue new debt in an amount equal to $X.
4. Invest $X in equities on corporate account.

The net effect of these operations will be that the firm will have more debt outstanding owed on corporate account and more bonds owned on pension account. The market value of the firm's own shares should thereby go up by as much as the corporate tax rate multiplied by the amount of new debt taken on in the manoeuvre.

The plan adds value because the firm earns close to the pretax rate of return on the bonds in the fund while paying the after-tax rate on the debt issued to support the procedure. Because the dividends from the common stock are not taxable and the tax on the capital gains can be deferred indefinitely by not selling appreciated stock, the effective tax rate on the equities held on corporate account will be very low. Thus, the after-tax return on the equities will not fall significantly if they are switched from pension account to corporate account. If all value accrues to the firm's shareholders, the effective corporate tax rate on equities is zero, and the stocks held on corporate account are equivalent to the stocks previously held by the pension fund, then the gain to shareholders has a present value of $TX, where T is the marginal corporate income tax rate faced by the firm.

To clarify this proposal, let us take a specific example. The Hi-Tek Corporation is a relatively new company, with a young workforce and a fully funded defined benefit pension plan. Hi-Tek's total corporate assets are worth $50 million, and its capital structure is 20 percent debt and 80 percent equity. Its pension assets consist entirely of a well-diversified portfolio of common stocks indexed to the TSE 300 and worth $10 million. The present value of its pension liabilities is $10 million. The corporate balance sheet is presented in Table 25.2, part **A**, and the pension fund's balance sheet in Table 25.2, part **B**.

---

[6] See Fischer Black and M. P. Dewhurst, "A New Investment Strategy for Pension Funds," *Journal of Portfolio Management,* Summer 1981.

TABLE 25.2   Hi-Tek Corp. Balance Sheets before Black-Dewhurst Manoeuvre

Assets		Liabilities and Owners' Equity	
A. Corporate Balance Sheet ($ million)			
Current assets	$ 2	Debt	$10
Property, plant, and equipment	48	Owners' equity	40
Total assets	**$50**	**Total liabilities**	**$50**
B. Pension Fund Balance Sheet ($ million)			
Stocks	$10	PV of accrued benefits	$10
		Fund balance	0

Hi-Tek's treasurer, who is in charge of the pension fund, has read the Black-Dewhurst article and decides to implement the proposal. The pension fund sells its entire $10 million stock portfolio to the corporation and invests the proceeds in corporate bonds issued by other high-technology companies. The corporation pays for the stock by issuing $10 million of new bonds. The resulting new balance sheets are presented in Table 25.3.

According to Black and Dewhurst, the result of these transactions should be an increase in the market value of owners' equity of as much as $10 million multiplied by the corporate tax rate, currently 40 percent. In other words, the market value of the outstanding shares of Hi-Tek's common stock should increase by $3.4 million.[7]

To see why, let r be the interest rate on the debt. As a result of the previous four operations, the company will now be earning $r \times \$10$ million per year in interest on the bonds it bought on pension account, and paying from its after-tax cash flow $(1 - T)r \times \$10$ million per year on the debt it issued on corporate account. The net cash flow to the firm will be $.34r \times \$10$ million per year, the tax saving on the interest. The present value of this saving in perpetuity is $3.4 million:

$$(.34r \times \$10 \text{ million})/r = \$3.4 \text{ million}$$

Note that even though Hi-Tek's debt ratio has increased from .2 to .3, the overall risk of the firm has not changed. If we accept the theory that the pension fund assets and liabilities belong to the shareholders, the risk of the assets does not change when the $10 million of stock in the pension fund is, in effect, transferred to a corporate account.

This plan implies that the company should increase its contributions to the pension fund up to the limits allowed by National Revenue. This is because for every dollar of assets added to the pension fund, invested in bonds, and supported by issuing new bonds, the tax saving increases by rT per year and the PV

---

[7] If the corporate tax rate on equities is greater than zero, the gain in shareholders' equity will be smaller than $3.4 million.

TABLE 25.3 Hi-Tek Corp. Balance Sheets after Black-Dewhurst Manoeuvre

Assets		Liabilities and Owners' Equity	
A. Corporate Balance Sheet ($ million)			
Current assets	$ 2	Debt	$20
Property, plant, and equipment	48	Owners' equity	40
Stocks	10		
Total assets	60	**Total liabilities**	60
B. Pension Fund Balance Sheet ($ million)			
Bonds	$10	PV of accrued benefits	$10
		Fund balance	0

of shareholders' equity increases by T. Thus, if T is .34, shareholders' equity rises by $.34 for every dollar added to pension assets or for every dollar switched out of stocks into bonds.

Summary

1. The life-cycle approach to the management of an individual's investment portfolio views the individual as passing through a series of stages, becoming more risk-averse in later years. The rationale underlying this approach is that as we age, we use up our human capital and have less time remaining to recoup possible portfolio losses through increased labour supply.

2. People buy life and disability insurance during their prime earning years to hedge against the risk associated with loss of their human capital, that is, their future earning power.

3. A major investment for most people is the purchase of a house. Home ownership provides a hedge against unanticipated increases in the cost of shelter, so the discount rate to use in a discounted cash flow analysis should be lower than would normally be the case.

4. There are three ways to shelter investment income from federal income taxes. The first is by investing in assets whose returns take the form of appreciation in value, such as common stocks or real estate. As long as capital gains taxes are not paid until the asset is sold, the tax can be deferred indefinitely. The second way of tax sheltering is through investing in tax-deferred retirement plans, such as RRSPs. The general investment rule is to hold the least tax-advantaged assets in the plan and the most tax-advantaged assets outside of it. The third way of sheltering is to invest in the tax-advantaged products offered by the life insurance industry—tax-deferred annuities and variable and universal life insurance. They combine the flexibility of mutual fund investing with the tax advantages of tax deferral.

5. Distinguishing between income and growth in investment returns is justified only to the extent that transaction costs of selling assets are significant.

6. Pension plans are either defined contribution plans or defined benefit plans. Defined contribution plans are, in effect, retirement funds held in trust for the employee by the employer. The employees in such plans bear all the risk of the plan's assets and often have some choice in the allocation of those assets. Defined benefit plans give the employees a claim to a money-fixed annuity at retirement. The annuity level is determined by a formula that takes into account years of service and the employee's wage or salary history.

7. A popular investment strategy employed by managers of defined benefit funds is portfolio insurance, which is designed to guarantee downside protection while maintaining upside potential.

8. Black and Dewhurst have proposed a strategy that allows a firm with a defined benefit pension plan to exploit the tax arbitrage opportunity provided by the tax-exempt status of the plan's assets. A firm should shift all the stocks in its pension fund to a corporate account, and replace them with an equal amount of bonds financed by issuing new corporate debt. By doing so, the firm can earn the before-tax interest rate on the bonds while paying the after-tax rate of interest. The market value of the firm's common stock should increase substantially as a result.

Key terms

Tax-deferral option   Variable annuities
Tax-deferred retirement plans   Mortality tables
Deferred annuities   Portfolio insurance
Fixed annuities

Selected readings

For a further discussion of the theory and evidence regarding the investment policies of corporate defined benefit pension plans, see:

Bodie, Z. "Managing Pension and Retirement Assets: An International Perspective." *Journal of Financial Services Research,* December 1990.

Bodie, Z.; Light, J.; Morck, R.; and Taggart, R. A. "Corporate Pension Policy: An Empirical Investigation." *Financial Analysts Journal* 41, no. 5 (September–October 1985).

Problems

1. Your neighbour has heard that you have just successfully completed a course in investments and has come to seek your advice. She and her husband are both 50 years old. They have just finished making their last payments for their condominium and their children's college education and are planning for retirement. Until now they have not been able to set aside any savings for retirement and so have not participated in their employers' voluntary tax-sheltered savings plan, nor have they opened RRSPs. Both of them work, and their combined after-tax income last year was $50,000. They are both in the 42 percent marginal tax bracket. They plan to retire at age 65 and would like to maintain the same standard of living in retirement as they had before.

a. Devise a simple plan for them on the assumption of a combined CPP income of $10,000 per year. How much should they start saving? (Assume they will live to age 80, can shelter as much retirement savings as they want from tax, and will earn a zero real rate of return.)

b. Redo part *a* with the following changes:
   i. The real interest rate is assumed to be 3 percent per year.
   ii. Your neighbours are 40 years old instead of 50.
   iii. The tax bracket after retirement drops to 15 percent.

c. What advice on investing their retirement savings would you give them? If they are very risk-averse, what would you advise.

2. (Based on the 1985 CFA Examination, Level II) You are Faye Trotter, assistant treasurer of Ednam Products Company, a firm that recently terminated its defined benefit (pension) retirement plan in favour of a new defined contribution (profit-sharing) retirement plan. Termination proceeds were used to purchase an annuity for each employee, with normal retirement at age 65. Before termination, Ednam has also sponsored a generous savings plan under which many employees have accumulated sizable participations. These accumulations have been incorporated into the employees' individual accounts as an integral part of the new plan, which meets all requirements for protecting employee tax benefits that are part of this arrangement.

Each employee is now responsible for investment decisions in his or her own personal plan account. This includes selection of the vehicles of implementation, current disposition of the accumulated monies now awaiting investment, and ongoing monitoring and adjustment of account exposure, as well as disposition of future company profit-sharing contributions. This decision-making requirement is a totally new experience for most employees and is one about which many concerns have been expressed to Ednam management.

Responding to these concerns, the company has made five investment alternatives available under the plan and has designated you as a resource person for interested employees.

Your role is to provide information about the plan and its investment alternatives, the no-load mutual funds selected by the company as investment vehicles, consensus capital market expectations, and the fundamentals of investing. Although Ednam management realizes that this response falls short of being a complete counselling program, they believe that the combination of a wide range of investment vehicles and continuing access to an objective and experienced person should enable employees to make intelligent investment choices. Moreover, the plan provides that allocations to any or all of the five investment vehicles may be changed at six-month intervals. Employees have been told that investing is a process that requires their continuing participation, with particular attention to adjustment of market exposures as personal and external conditions change through time.

Overall, employee reactions have been enthusiastic and three individuals already have requested appointments with you. The following background information on the three individuals has been made available to you:

- Tom Davis, sales manager, age 58; intends to retire at age 62; married; no children; wife employed. Owns $150,000 house (no mortgage) and $100,000 portfolio of growth stocks. No family health problems; no major indebtedness. Amount accumulated in plan investment account: $160,000.
- Margaret Custer, assistant director of market research, age 30; single; excellent health; buying condominium (heavily mortgaged) and car. Amount accumulated in plan investment account: $40,000.
- Glenn Abbott, plant supervisor, age 42; widower; two children, ages 14 and 10; buying $130,000 house ($80,000 mortgage). No other indebtedness except regular heavy use of credit cards. Amount accumulated in plan investment account: $110,000.

You expect that each of these individuals will want to discuss allocation of their account accumulations, as well as details of the plan and the no-load mutual fund investment vehicles described here:

- *Money market fund.* Average maturity typically is 30 days.
- *High-grade bond fund.* Average duration maintained at 15 years.
- *Index stock fund.* A TSE 300 proxy. Beta of 1.00.
- *Growth stock fund.* Portfolio beta maintained at 1.30.
- *Real estate equity fund.* Owns diversified portfolio of commercial properties. Holds no mortgages; not a tax-shelter fund.

As part of your preparation, you have determined that consensus risk and return expectations for the various asset classes over the next several years are in line with average historical experience, accompanied by modest inflation levels.

Utilizing this information and your own assessment of the risk-bearing capacities of Tom, Margaret, and Glenn, do the following:

a. Identify and discuss the differences in investor life cycle position and in investment objectives and constraints that exist among the three individuals. Frame the identification part of your answer in the matrix format shown below:

Investment Considerations	Tom	Margaret	Glenn

    b. Prepare a normal, long-term allocation of the accumulated monies in each of the three individual accounts and justify the resulting asset mix. Your allocations should sum to 100 percent in each case and be based on your conclusions to part *a*. Do not base your answer on any qualitative considerations related to current or expected market considerations as you perceive them.

3. George More is a participant in a defined contribution pension plan that offers a fixed-income fund and a common stock fund as investment choices. He is 40 years old and has an accumulation of $100,000 in each of the funds. He currently contributes $1,500 per year to each. He plans to retire at age 65, and his life expectancy is age 80.

    a. Assuming a 3 percent per year real earnings rate for the fixed-income fund and 6 percent per year for common stocks, what will be George's expected accumulation in each account at age 65?

    b. What will be the expected real retirement annuity from each account, assuming these same real earnings rates?

    c. If George wanted a retirement annuity of $30,000 per year from the fixed-income fund, by how much would he have to increase his annual contributions?

4. A firm has a defined benefit pension plan that pays an annual retirement benefit of 1.5 percent of final salary per year of service. Jane Loyal is 60 years old and has been working for the firm for the last 35 years. Her current salary is $40,000 per year.

    a. If normal retirement age is 65, the interest rate is 8 percent, and Jane's life expectancy is 80, what is the present value of her accrued pension benefit?

    b. If Jane wanted to retire now, what would be an actuarially fair annual pension benefit? (Assume the first payment would be made one year from now.)

5. Unlimited Horizons, Inc. (UH), has corporate assets of $100 million and conventional debt of $40 million. Its defined benefit pension plan has assets (50 percent stocks and 50 percent bonds) with a current market value of $10 million, and the present value of accrued benefits is $12 million. UH is in the 34 percent tax bracket.

    a. What do its corporate and pension fund balance sheets look like? What is the net worth on its corporate account, and what is its total net worth, including its pension plan?

    b. According to Black and Dewhurst, what could the firm do to increase the value of shareholders' equity?

    c. What would its corporate and pension fund balance sheets look like after implementation of the Black and Dewhurst plan?

6. (Adapted from the 1983 CFA Examination, Level III) You are R. J. Certain, a retired C.F.A., who formerly was the chief investment officer of a major investment management organization. Although you have over 30 years of experience in the investment business, you have kept up with the literature and developed a reputation for your knowledge and ability to blend modern portfolio theory and traditional portfolio methods.

The chairman of the board of Morgan Industries has asked you to serve as a consultant to him and the other members of the board of trustees of the company's pension fund. Since you are interested in developing a consulting practice and keeping actively involved in the investment management business, you welcome the opportunity to develop a portfolio management decision-making process for Morgan Industries that you could apply to all types of investment portfolios.

Morgan Industries is a company in transition. Its long-established business, dating back to the early years of the century, is the production of steel. Since the 1970s, however, Morgan has gradually built a highly profitable stake in the domestic production of oil and gas.

Most of the company's 1992 sales of $4 billion were still derived from steel operations. Because Morgan occupies a relatively stable niche in a specialized segment of the steel industry, its losses on steel during the 1992 recession were moderate compared to industry experience. At the same time, profit margins for Morgan's oil and gas business remained satisfactory despite all the problems in the world oil market. This segment of the company's operations accounted for the entire 1992 net profit of $150 million. Even when steel operations recover, oil and gas operations are expected to contribute, on average, over half of Morgan's annual profits.

Based on the combination of the two segments of the company's operations, the overall cyclicality of company earnings appears to be approximately the same as that of the TSE 300. Several well-regarded security analysts, citing the outlook for recovery in steel operations as well as further gains in the oil and gas production, project earnings progress for Morgan over the next five years at about the same rate as for the TSE 300. Debt comprises about 35 percent of the long-term capital structure, and the beta (market risk) for the company's common stock is also about the same as for the TSE 300.

Morgan's defined benefit pension plan covers 25,000 active employees, vested and unvested, and 15,000 retired employees, with the latter projected to exceed 20,000 in five years. The burden of pension liabilities is large, because the steel industry has long been labour-intensive and the company's current labour force in this area of operations is not as large as it was some years ago. The oil and gas operations, although growing at a significant rate, account for only 10 percent of the active plan participants and for even less of the retired beneficiaries.

Pension assets amounted to $1 billion of market value at the end of 1992. For the purpose of planning investment policy, the present value of the unfunded pension liability is calculated at $500 million. Although the company's outstanding debt is $600 million, it is clear that the unfunded pension liability adds significantly to the leverage in the capital structure.

Pension expenses charged to company income—and reflected in company contributions to the pension trust—were $80 million in 1992. The level of expenses, which are projected to rise with payroll, reflects current assumptions concerning inflation, the rate of return on pension assets, wage and salary increases, and benefits changes. If these assumptions were to prove completely correct, the current method of funding would amortize the unfunded pension liability over 20 years. Since assumptions are subject to change in the light of new information, they must be reviewed periodically. Revision by one percentage point in the assumed rate of investment return, for example, would require a current change in the level of pension expenses by $15 million before taxes, or about $7 million after taxes. The current actuarially assumed rate of return is 8.5 percent.

Pension investment policy, through its influence on pension expenses, unfunded pension liability, and the company's earnings progress, is a critical issue of Morgan management. The chairman is strongly committed to the corporate goal of achieving a total investment return for shareholders superior to that of other large industrial companies. He recognizes that a more aggressive pension investment policy—if successful—would facilitate attainment of the corporate goal through a significant reduction in pension expenses and unfunded pension liability. He also worries, however, that a significant drop in the market value of the company's pension fund—now $1 billion—could result in a major setback in the company's growth strategy. Current pension investment policy is based on an asset mix of approximately 50 percent common stocks and 50 percent fixed-income securities. The chairman is concerned about the overall investment management and direction of the pension fund and is very interested in your informed and objective evaluation.

What recommendations would you make to the chairman, and why?

APPENDIX

Quantitative Review

Students in management and investment courses typically come from a variety of backgrounds. Some, who have had strong quantitative training, may feel perfectly comfortable with formal mathematical presentation of material. Others, who have had less technical training, may easily be overwhelmed by mathematical formalism.

Most students, however, will benefit from some coaching to make the study of investments easier and more efficient. If you had a good introductory quantitative methods course, and liked the text that was used, you may want to refer to it whenever you feel in need of a refresher. If you feel uncomfortable with standard quantitative texts, this reference is for you. Our aim is to present the essential quantitative concepts and methods in a self-contained, non-technical, and intuitive way. Our approach is considered structured in line with requirements for the CFA program. The material included is relevant to investment management by the ICFA, the Institute of Chartered Financial Analysts. We hope you find this appendix helpful. Use it to make your venture into investments more enjoyable.

Note: If you do not already have a financial calculator, we strongly advise you get one. Most financial calculators have a statistical mode that allows you to compute expected values, standard deviations, and regressions with ease. Actually, working through the user manual is a helpful exercise by itself. If you are interested in investments, you should look at a financial calculator as a good initial investment.

A.1 *Probability Distributions*

Statisticians talk about "experiments," or "trials," and refer to possible outcomes as "events." In a roll of a die, for example, the "elementary events" are the numbers 1 through 6. Turning up one side represents the most disaggregate *mutually exclusive* outcome. Other events are *compound,* that is, they consist of more than one elementary event, such as the result "odd number" or "less than 4." In this case "odd" and "less than 4" are not mutually exclusive. Compound events can be mutually exclusive outcomes, however, such as "less than 4" and "equal to or greater than 4."

In decision making, "experiments" are circumstances in which you contemplate a decision that will affect the set of possible events (outcomes) and their likelihood (probabilities). Decision theory calls for you to identify optimal decisions under various sets of circumstances (experiments), which you may do by determining losses from departures from optimal decisions.

When the outcome of a decision (experiment) can be quantified, that is, when a numerical value can be assigned to each elementary event, the decision outcome is called a *random variable*. In the context of investment decision making, the random variable (the payoff to the investment decision) is denominated either in dollars or as a percentage rate of return.

The set or list of all possible values of a random variable, *with* their associated probabilities, is called the *probability distribution* of the random variable. Values that are impossible for the random variable to take on are sometimes listed with probabilities of zero. All possible elementary events are assigned values and probabilities, and thus the probabilities have to sum to 1.0.

Sometimes the values of a random variable are *uncountable,* meaning that you cannot make a list of all possible values. For example, suppose you roll a ball on a line and report the distance it rolls before it comes to a rest. Any distance is possible, and the precision of the report will depend on the need of the roller and/or the quality of the measuring device. Another uncountable random variable is one that describes the weight of a newborn baby. Any positive weight (with some upper bound) is possible.

We call uncountable probability distributions "continuous," for the obvious reason that, at least within a range, the possible outcomes (those with positive probabilities) lie anywhere on a continuum of values. Because there is an infinite number of possible values for the random variable in any continuous distribution, such a probability distribution has to be described by a formula that relates the values of the random variable and their associated probabilities, instead of by a simple list of outcomes and probabilities. We discuss continuous distributions later in this section.

Even countable probability distributions can be complicated. For example, on the New York Stock Exchange stock prices are quoted in eighths. This means the price of a stock at some future date is a *countable* random variable. Probability distributions of countable random variables are called *discrete distributions*. Although a stock price cannot dip below zero, it has no upper bound. Therefore a stock price is a random variable that can take on infinitely many values, even though they are countable, and its discrete probability distribution will have to be given by a formula just like a continuous distribution.

There are random variables that are both discrete and finite. When the probability distribution of the relevant random variable is countable and finite, decision making is tractable and relatively easy to analyze. One example is the decision to call a coin toss "heads" or "tails," with a payoff of zero for guessing wrong and one for guessing right. The random variable of the decision to guess "heads" has a discrete, finite probability distribution. It can be written as

Event	Value	Probability
Heads	1	.5
Tails	0	.5

This type of analysis usually is referred to as "scenario analysis." Because scenario analysis is relatively simple, it is used sometimes even when the actual random variable is infinite and uncountable. You can do this by specifying values and probabilities for a set of compound, yet exhaustive and mutually exclusive, events. Because it is simple and has important uses, we handle this case first.

Here is a problem from the 1988 CFA examination.

Mr. Arnold, an Investment Committee member, has confidence in the forecasting ability of the analysts in the firm's research department. However, he is concerned that analysts may not appreciate risk as an important investment consideration. This is especially true in an increasingly volatile investment environment. In addition, he is conservative and risk averse. He asks your risk analysis for Anheuser-Busch stock.

1. Using Table A.1, calculate the following measures of dispersion of returns for Anheuser-Busch stock under each of the three outcomes displayed. Show calculations.
   a. Range.
   b. Variance: $\Sigma \Pr(i)[r_i - E(r)]^2$
   c. Standard deviation
   d. Coefficient of variation: $CV = \dfrac{\sigma}{E(r)}$
2. Discuss the usefulness of each of the four measures listed in quantifying risk.

The examination questions require very specific answers. We use the questions as a framework for exposition of scenario analysis.

Table A.1 specifies a three-scenario decision problem. The random variable is the rate of return on investing in Anheuser-Busch stock. However, the third column that specifies the value of the random variable does not say simply "Return"—it says "Expected Return." This tells us that the scenario description is a compound event consisting of many elementary events, as is almost always the case. We streamline or simplify reality in order to gain tractability.

TABLE A.1 Anheuser-Busch Companies, Inc., Dispersion of Potential Returns

Outcome	Probability	Expected Return*
Number 1	.20	20%
Number 2	.50	30%
Number 3	.30	50%

* Assume for the moment that the expected return in each scenario will be realized with certainty. This is the way returns were expressed in the original question.

Analysts who prepare input lists must decide on the number of scenarios with which to describe the entire probability distribution, as well as the rates of return to allocate to each one. This process calls for determining the probability of occurrence of each scenario *and* the expected rate of return *within* (conditional on) each scenario, which governs the outcome of each scenario. Once you become familiar with scenario analysis, you will be able to build a simple scenario description from any probability distribution.

Expected returns

The expected value of a random variable is the answer to the question, "What would be the value of the variable if the 'experiment' (the circumstances and the decision) were repeated infinitely?" In the case of an investment decision, your answer is meant to describe the reward from making the decision.

Note that the question is hypothetical and abstract. It is hypothetical because, practically, the exact circumstances of a decision (the "experiment") often cannot be repeated even once, much less infinitely. It is abstract because, even if the experiment were to be repeated many times (short of infinitely), the *average* rate of return may not be one of the possible outcomes. To demonstrate, suppose that the probability distribution of the rate of return on a proposed investment project is +20 percent or −20 percent, with equal probabilities of .5. Intuition indicates that repeating this investment decision will get us ever closer to an average rate of return of zero. But a one-time investment cannot produce a rate of return of zero. Is the "expected" return still a useful concept when the proposed investment represents a one-time decision?

One argument for using expected return to measure the reward from making investment decisions is that, although a specific investment decision may be made only once, the decision maker will be making many (though different) investment decisions over time. Over time, then, the average rate of return will come close to the average of the expected values of all the individual decisions. Another reason for using the expected value is that admittedly we lack a better measure.[1]

The probabilities of the scenarios in Table A.1 predict the relative frequencies of the outcomes. If the current investment in Anheuser-Busch could be replicated many times, a 20 percent return would occur 20 percent of the time, a 30 percent return would occur 50 percent of the time, and a 50 percent return would occur the remaining 30 percent of the time. This notion of probabilities and the definition of the expected return tells us how to calculate the expected return:[2]

$$E(r) = .20 \times .20 + .50 \times .30 + .30 \times .50 = .34 \text{ (or 34\%)}$$

---

[1] Another case where we use a less-than-ideal measure is the case of yield to maturity on a bond. The YTM measures the rate of return from investing in a bond *if* it is held to maturity and *if* the coupons can be reinvested at the same yield to maturity over the life of the bond.

[2] We will consistently perform calculations in decimal fractions to avoid confusion.

Labeling each scenario $i = 1,2,3$, and using the summation sign, Σ, we can write the formula for the expected return:

$$E(r) = \Pr(1)r_1 + \Pr(2)r_2 + \Pr(3)r_3 \qquad \textbf{(A.1)}$$

$$= \sum_{i=1}^{3} \Pr(i)r_i.$$

The definition of the expectation in equation A.1 reveals two important properties of random variables. First, if you add a constant to a random variable, its expectation is also increased by the same constant. If, for example, the return in each scenario in Table A.1 were increased by 5 percent, the expectation would increase to 39 percent. Try this, using equation A.1. If a random variable is multiplied by a constant, its expectation will change by that same proportion. If you multiply the return in each scenario by 1.5, $E(r)$ would change to $1.5 \times .34 = .51$ (or 51 percent).

Second, the deviation of a random variable from its expected value is itself a random variable. Take any rate of return r_i in Table A.1 and define its deviation from the expected value by

$$d_i = r_i - E(r)$$

What is the expected value of d? $E(d)$ is the expected deviation from the expected value, and by equation A.1 it is necessarily zero because

$$E(d) = \Sigma \Pr(i)d_i = \Sigma \Pr(i)[r_i - E(r)]$$
$$= \Sigma \Pr(i)r_i - E(r)\Sigma \Pr(i)$$
$$= E(r) - E(r) = 0$$

Measures of dispersion: the range

Assume for a moment that the expected return for each scenario in Table A.1 will be realized with certainty in the event that scenario occurs. Then the set of possible return outcomes is unambiguously 20 percent, 30 percent, and 50 percent. The *range* is the difference between the maximum and the minimum values of the random variable, 50 percent − 20 percent = 30 percent in this case. Range is clearly a crude measure of dispersion. Here it is particularly inappropriate because the scenario returns themselves are given as expected values, and therefore the true range is unknown. There is a variant of the range, the *interquartile range,* that we explain in the discussion of descriptive statistics.

Measures of dispersion: the variance

One interpretation of variance is that it measures the "expected surprise." Although that may sound like a contradiction in terms, it really is not. First, think of a surprise as a deviation from expectation. The surprise is not in the *fact* that expectation has not been realized, but rather in the *direction* and *magnitude* of the deviation.

In our example Table A.1 leads us to *expect* a rate of return of 34 percent from investing in Anheuser-Busch stock. A second look at the scenario returns, however, tells us that we should stand ready to be surprised because the probability of earning exactly 34 percent is zero. Being sure that our expectation will not be realized does not mean that we can be sure what the realization is going to be. The element of surprise lies in the direction and magnitude of the deviation of the actual return from expectation, and that is the relevant random variable for the measurement of uncertainty. Its probability distribution adds to our understanding of the nature of the uncertainty that we are facing.

We measure the reward by the expected return. Intuition suggests that we measure uncertainty by the expected *deviation* of the rate of return from expectation. We showed in the previous section, however, that the expected deviation from expectation must be zero. Positive deviations, when weighted by probabilities, are exactly offset by negative deviations. To get around this problem, we replace the random variable "deviation from expectations" (denoted earlier by d) with its square, which must be positive even if d itself is negative.

We define the *variance,* our measure of surprise or dispersion, by the *expected squared deviation of the rate of return from its expectation*. With the Greek letter sigma square denoting variance, the formal definition is

$$\sigma^2(r) = E(d^2) = E[r_i - E(r)]^2 = \Sigma \Pr(i)[r_i - E(r)]^2 \qquad \textbf{(A.2)}$$

Squaring each deviation eliminates the sign, which eliminates the offsetting effects of positive and negative deviations.

In the case of Anheuser-Busch, the variance of the rate of return on the stock is

$$\sigma^2(r) = .2(.20 - .34)^2 + .5(.30 - .34)^2 + .3(.50 - .34)^2 = .0124$$

Remember that if you add a constant to a random variable, the variance does not change at all. This is because the expectation also changes by the same constant, and hence deviations from expectation remain unchanged. You can test this by using the data from Table A.1.

Multiplying the random variable by a constant, however, *will* change the variance. Suppose that each return is multiplied by the factor k. The new random variable, kr, has expectation of $E(kr) = kE(r)$. Therefore the deviation of kr from its expectation is

$$d(kr) = kr - E(kr) = kr - kE(r) = k[r - E(r)] = kd(r)$$

If each deviation is multiplied by k, the squared deviations are multiplied by the square of k:

$$\sigma^2(kr) = k^2\sigma^2(r)$$

To summarize, adding a constant to a random variable does not affect the variance. Multiplying a random variable by a constant, though, will cause the variance to be multiplied by the square of that constant.

Measures of dispersion: the standard deviation

A closer look at the variance will reveal that its dimension is different from that of the expected return. Recall that we squared deviations from the expected return in order to make all values positive. This alters the *dimension* (units of measure) of the variance to "square percents." To transform the variance into terms of percentage return, we simply take the square root of the variance. This measure is the *standard deviation*. In the case of Anheuser-Busch's stock return, the standard deviation is

$$\sigma = (\sigma^2)^{1/2} = \sqrt{.0124} = .1114 \text{ (or 11.14\%)} \qquad \textbf{(A.3)}$$

Note that you always need to calculate the variance first before you can get the standard deviation. The standard deviation conveys the same information as the variance but in a different form.

We know already that adding a constant to *r* will not affect its variance, and it will not affect the standard deviation either. We also know that multiplying a random variable by a constant multiplies the variance by the square of that constant. From the definition of the standard deviation in equation (A.3), it should be clear that multiplying a random variable by a constant will multiply the standard deviation by the (absolute value of this) constant. The absolute value is needed because the sign of the constant is lost through squaring the deviations in the computation of the variance. Formally,

$$\sigma(kr) = \text{Abs}(k)\,\sigma(r)$$

Try a transformation of your choice using the data in Table A.1.

Measures of dispersion: the coefficient of variation

To evaluate the magnitude of dispersion of a random variable, it is useful to compare it to the expected value. The ratio of the standard deviation to the expectation is called the *coefficient of variation*. In the case of returns on Anheuser-Busch stock, it is

$$CV = \frac{\sigma}{E(r)} = \frac{.1114}{.3400} = .3275 \qquad \textbf{(A.4)}$$

This standard deviation of the Anheuser-Busch return is about one third of the expected return (reward). Whether this value for the coefficient of variation represents a big risk depends on what can be obtained with alternative investments.

The coefficient of variation is far from an ideal measure of dispersion. Suppose that a plausible expected value for a random variable is zero. In this case, regardless of the magnitude of the standard deviation, the coefficient of variation will be infinite. Clearly, this measure is not applicable in all cases. Generally, the analyst must choose a measure of dispersion that fits the particular decision at hand. In finance, the standard deviation is the measure of choice in most cases where overall risk is concerned. (For individual assets, the measure β, explained in the text, is the measure used.)

Skewness

So far, we have described the measures of dispersion as indicating the size of the average surprise, loosely speaking. The standard deviation is not exactly equal to the average surprise though, because squaring deviations, and then taking the square root of the average square deviation, results in greater weight (emphasis) placed on larger deviations. Other than that, it is simply a measure that tells us how big a deviation from expectation can be expected.

Most decision makers agree that the expected value and standard deviation of a random variable are the most important statistics. However, once we calculate them another question about risk (the nature of the random variable describing deviations from expectations) is pertinent: are the larger deviations (surprises) more likely to be positive? Risk-averse decision makers worry about bad surprises, and the standard deviation does not distinguish good from bad ones. Most risk avoiders are believed to prefer random variables with likely *small negative surprises* and *less* likely *large positive surprises,* to the reverse, likely *small good surprises* and *less* likely *large bad surprises.* More than anything, risk is really defined by the possibility of disaster (large bad surprises).

One measure that distinguishes between the likelihood of large good-versus-bad surprises is the ''third moment.'' It builds on the behavior of deviations from the expectation, the random variable we have denoted by d. Denoting the *third moment* by M_3, we define it:

$$M_3 = E(d^3) = E[r_i - E(r)]^3 = \Sigma \ \Pr(i)[r_i - E(r)]^3 \qquad \textbf{(A.5)}$$

Cubing each value of d (taking it to the third power) magnifies larger deviations more than smaller ones. Raising values to an odd power causes them to retain their sign. Recall that the sum of all deviations multiplied by their probabilities is zero because positive deviations weighted by their probabilities exactly offset the negative. When *cubed* deviations are multiplied by their probabilities and then added up, however, large deviations will dominate. The sign will tell us in this case whether *large positive* deviations dominate (positive M_3) or whether *large negative* deviations dominate (negative M_3).

Incidentally, it is obvious why this measure of skewness is called the third moment; it refers to cubing. Similarly, the variance is often referred to as the second moment, because it requires squaring.

Returning to the investment decision described in Table A.1, with the expected value of 34 percent, the third moment is

$$M_3 = .2(.20 - .34)^3 + .5(.30 - .34)^3 + .3(.50 - .34)^3 = .000648$$

The sign of the third moment tells us that larger *positive* surprises dominate in this case. You might have guessed this by looking at the deviations from expectation and their probabilities; that is, the most likely event is a return of 30 percent, which makes for a small negative surprise. The other negative surprise (20 percent − 34 percent = −14 percent) is smaller in magnitude than the positive surprise (50 percent − 34 percent = 16 percent) *and* in also *less* likely (probability .20) relative to the positive surprise, 50 percent (probability .30). The difference appears small, however, and we do not know whether the third moment may be an important issue for the decision to invest in Anheuser-Busch.

It is difficult to judge the importance of the third moment, here .000648, without a benchmark. Following the same reasoning we applied to the standard deviation, we can take the *third root* of M_3 (which we denote m_3) and compare it to the standard deviation. This yields $m_3 = .0865 = 8.65$ percent, which is not trivial compared with the standard deviation (11.14 percent).

Another example: options on Anheuser-Busch stock

Suppose that the current price of Anheuser-Busch stock is $30. A call option on the stock is selling for 60 cents, and a put is selling for $4. Both have an exercise price of $42 and maturity date to match the scenarios in Table A.1.

The call option allows you to buy the stock at the exercise price. You will choose to do so if the call ends up "in the money," that is, the stock price is above the exercise price. The profit in this case is the difference between the stock price and the exercise price, less the cost of the call. Even if you exercise the call, your profit may still be negative if the cash flow from the exercise of the call does not cover the initial cost of the call. If the call ends up "out of the money," that is, the stock price is below the exercise price, you will let the call expire worthless and suffer a loss equal to the cost of the call.

The put option allows you to sell the stock at the exercise price. You will choose to do so if the put ends up "in the money," that is, the stock price is below the exercise price. Your profit is then the difference between the exercise price and the stock price, less the initital cost of the put. Here, again, if the cash flow is not sufficient to cover the cost of the put, the investment will show a loss. If the put ends up "out of the money," you again let it expire worthless, taking a loss equal to the initial cost of the put.

The scenario analysis of these alternative investments is described in Table A.2.

The expected rates of return on the call and put are

$$E(r_{\text{call}}) = .2(-1) + .5(-1) + .3(4) = .5 \quad (\text{or } 50\%)$$
$$E(r_{\text{put}}) = .2(.5) + .5(-.25) + .3(-1) = -.325 \quad (\text{or } -32.5\%)$$

The negative expected return on the put may be justified by the fact that it is a hedge asset, in this case an insurance policy against losses from holding Anheuser-Busch stock. The variance and standard deviation of the two investments are

$$\sigma^2_{\text{call}} = .2(-1 - .5)^2 + .5(-1 - .5)^2 + .3(4 - .5)^2 = 5.25$$
$$\sigma^2_{\text{put}} = .2[.5 - (-.325)]^2 + .5[-.25 - (-.325)]^2 + .3[-1 - (-.325)]^2 = .2756$$
$$\sigma_{\text{call}} = \sqrt{5.25} = 2.2913 \quad (\text{or } 229.13\%)$$
$$\sigma_{\text{put}} = \sqrt{.2756} = .525 \quad (\text{or } 52.5\%)$$

These are very large standard deviations. Comparing the standard deviation of the call's return to its expected value, we get the coefficient of variation:

$$\text{CV}_{\text{call}} = \frac{2.2913}{.5} = 4.5826$$

TABLE A.2   Scenario Analysis for Investment in Options
on Anheuser-Busch Stock

	Scenario 1	Scenario 2	Scenario 3
Probability	.20	.50	.30
Event			
1. Return on stock	20%	30%	50%
Stock price	$36.00	$39.00	$45.00
(initial price = $30)			
2. Cash flow from call	0	0	$3.00
(exercise price = $42)			
Call profit	−$.60	−$.60	$2.40
(initial price = $.60)			
3. Call rate of return	−100%	−100%	400%
Cash flow from put	$6.00	$3.00	0
(exercise price = $42)			
Put profit	$2.00	−$1.00	−$4.00
(initial price = $4)			
Put rate of return	50%	−25%	−100%

Refer back to the coefficient of variation for the stock itself, .3275, and it is clear that these instruments have high standard deviations. This is quite common for stock options. The negative expected return of the put illustrates again the problem in interpreting the magnitude of the "surprise" indicated by the coefficient of variation.

Moving to the third moments of the two probability distributions:

$$M_3(\text{call}) = .2(-1 - .5)^3 + .5(-1 - .5)^3 + .3(4 - .5)^3 = 10.5$$
$$M_3(\text{put}) = .2[.5 - (-.325)]^3 + .5[-.25 - (-.325)]^3 + .3[-1 - (-.325)]^3$$
$$= .02025$$

Both instruments are positively skewed, which is typical of options and one part of their attractiveness. In this particular circumstance the call is more skewed than the put. To establish this fact, note the third root of the third moment:

$$m_3(\text{call}) = M_3(\text{call})^{1/3} = 2.1898 \text{ (or 218.98\%)}$$
$$m_3(\text{put}) = .02^{1/3} = .2725 \text{ (or 27.25\%)}$$

Compare these figures to the standard deviations, 229.13 percent for the call and 52.5 percent for put, and you can see that a large part of the standard deviation of the option is driven by the possibility of large good surprises instead of by the more likely, yet smaller, bad surprises.[3]

---

[3] Note that the expected return of the put is −32.5 percent; hence the worst surprise is −67.5 percent, and the best is 82.5 percent. The middle scenario is also a positive deviation of 7.5 percent (with a high probability of .50). These two elements explain the positive skewness of the put.

So far we have described discrete probability distributions using scenario analysis. We shall come back to decision making in a scenario analysis framework in Section A.3 on multivariate statistics.

Continuous Distributions: Normal and Lognormal Distributions

When a compact scenario analysis is possible and acceptable, decisions may be quite simple. Often, however, so many relevant scenarios must be specified that scenario analysis is impossible for practical reasons. Even in the case of Anheuser-Busch, as we were careful to specify, the individual scenarios considered actually represented compound events.

When many possible values of the rate of return have to be considered, we must use a formula that describes the probability distribution (relates values to probabilities). As we noted earlier, there are two types of probability distributions: discrete and continuous. Scenario analysis involves a discrete distribution. However, the two most useful distributions in investments, the normal and lognormal, are continuous. At the same time they are often used to approximate variables with distributions that are known to be discrete, such as stock prices. The probability distribution of future prices and returns is discrete—prices are quoted in eighths. Yet the industry norm is to approximate these distributions by the normal or lognormal distribution.

Standard normal distribution

The normal distribution, also known as Gaussian (after the mathematician Gauss) or bell-shaped, describes random variables with the following properties and is shown in Figure A.1:

- The expected value is the mode (the most frequent elementary event) and also the median (the middle value in the sense that half the elementary events are greater and half smaller). Note that the expected value, unlike the median or mode, requires weighting by probabilities to produce the concept of central value.
- The normal probability distribution is symmetric around the expected value. In other words, the likelihood of equal absolute-positive and nega-

FIGURE A.1
Probabilities under
the normal density.

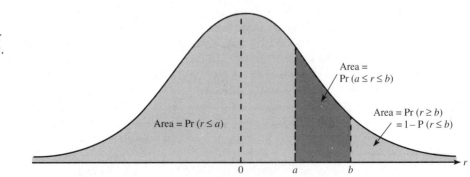

tive deviations from expectation is equal. Larger deviations from the expected value are less likely than are smaller deviations. In fact, the essence of the normal distribution is that the probability of deviations decreases exponentially with the magnitude of the deviation (positive and negative alike).

- A normal distribution is identified completely by two parameters, the expected value and the standard deviation. The property of the normal distribution that makes it most convenient for portfolio analysis is that any weighted sum of normally distributed random variables produces a random variable that also is normally distributed. This property is called stability. It is also true that if you add a constant to a "normal" random variable (meaning a random variable with a normal probability distribution) or multiply it by a constant, then the transformed random variable also will be normally distributed.

Suppose that n is any random variable (not necessarily normal), with expectation μ and standard deviation σ. As we showed earlier, if you add a constant c to n, the standard deviation is not affected at all, but the mean will change to $\mu + c$. If you multiply n by a constant b, its mean and standard deviation will change by the same proportion to $b\mu$ and $b\sigma$. If n is normal, the transformed variable also will be normal.

Stability, together with the property that a normal variable is completely characterized by its expectation and standard deviation, implies that if we know one normal probability distribution with a given expectation and standard deviation, we know them all.

Thus, the *standard normal distribution* has an expectation of zero, and both variance and standard deviation equal to 1.0. Formally, the relationship between the value of the standard normal random variable, z, and its probability, f, is given by

$$f(z) = \frac{1}{\sqrt{2\pi}} \exp\left(\frac{-z^2}{2}\right) \tag{A.6}$$

where "exp" is the quantity e to the power of the expression in the brackets. The quantity e is an important number just like the well-known π that also appears in the function. It is important enough to earn a place on the keyboard of your financial calculator, mostly because it is used also in continuous compounding.

Probability functions of continuous distributions are called *densities* and denoted by f, rather than by the "Pr" of scenario analysis. The reason is that the probability of any of the infinitely many possible values of z is infinitesimally small. Density is a function that allows us to obtain the probability of a *range of values* by integrating it over a desired range. In other words, whenever we want the probability that a standard normal variate (a random variable) will fall in the range from $z = a$ to $z = b$, we have to add up the density values, $f(z)$ for all zs from a to b. There are infinitely many zs in that range, regardless how close a is to b. *Integration* is the mathematical operation that achieves this task.

Consider first the probability that a standard normal variate will take on a value less than or equal to a, that is, z is in the range $[-\infty, a]$. We have to integrate the density from ∞ to a. The result is called the *cumulative (normal) distribution*, and denoted by $N(a)$. When a approaches infinity, any value is allowed for z; hence the probability that z will end up in that range approaches 1.0. It is a property of any density that when it is integrated over the entire range of the random variable, the cumulative distribution is 1.0.

In the same way, the probability that a standard normal variate will take on a value less than or equal to b is $N(b)$. The probability that a standard normal variate will take on a value in the range $[a,b]$ is just the difference between $N(b)$ and $N(a)$. Formally,

$$\Pr(a \leqq z \leqq b) = N(b) - N(a)$$

These concepts are illustrated in Figure A.1. The graph shows the normal density. It demonstrates the symmetry of the normal density around the expected value (zero for the standard normal variate, which is also the mode and the median), and the smaller likelihood of larger deviations from expectation. As is true for any density, the entire area under the density graph adds up to 1.0. The values a and b are chosen to be positive, so they are to the right of the expected value. The left-most shaded area is the proportion of the area under the density for which the value of z is less than or equal to a. Thus this area yields the cumulative distribution for a, the probability that z will be smaller than or equal to a. The dark shaded area is the area under the density graph between a and b. If we add that area to the cumulative distribution of a, we get the entire area up to b, that is, the probability that z will be anywhere to the left of b. Thus, the area between a and b has to be the probability that z will fall between a and b.

Applying the same logic, we find the probability that z will take on a value greater than b. We know already that the probability that z will be smaller than or equal to b is $N(b)$. The compound events "smaller than or equal to b" and "greater than b" are mutually exclusive *and* "exhaustive," meaning that they include all possible outcomes. Thus, their probabilities sum to 1.0, and the probability that z is greater than b is simply equal to one minus the probability that z is less than or equal to b. Formally, $\Pr(z > b) = 1 - N(b)$.

Look again at Figure A.1. The area under the density graph between b and infinity is just the difference between the entire area under the graph (equal to 1.0), and the area between minus infinity and b, that is, $N(b)$.

The normal density is sufficiently complex that its cumulative distribution, its integral, does not have an exact formulaic closed-form solution. It must be obtained by numerical (approximation) methods. These values are produced in tables that give the value $N(z)$ for any z, such as Table 21.7 of this text.

To illustrate, let us find the following probabilities for a standard normal variate:

$\Pr(z \leqq -.36) = N(-.36) =$ Probability that z is less than or equal to .36
$\Pr(z \leqq .94) = N(.94) =$ Probability that z is less than or equal to .94
$\Pr(-.36 \leqq z \leqq .94) = N(.94) - N(-.36) =$ Probability that z will be in the range $[-.36, .94]$
$\Pr(z > .94) = 1 - N(.94) =$ Probability that z is greater than .94

Appendix

FIGURE A.2
Probabilities and the
cumulative normal
distribution.

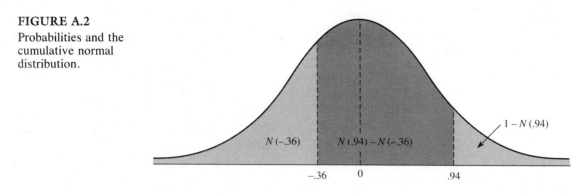

Use Table 19.7 of the cumulative standard normal (sometimes called the area under the normal density) and Figure A.2. The table shows that

$$N(-.36) = .3594$$
$$N(.94) = .8264$$

In Figure A.2 the area under the graph between $-.36$ and $.94$ is the probability that z will fall between $-.36$ and $.94$. Hence,

$$\Pr(-.36 \leq z \leq .94) = N(.94) - N(-.36) = .8264 - .3594 = .4670$$

The probability that z is greater than $.94$ is the area under the graph in Figure A.2, between $.94$ and infinity. Thus it is equal to the entire area (1.0) less the area from minus infinity to $.94$. Hence,

$$\Pr(z > .94) = 1 - N(.94) = 1 - .8264 = .1736$$

Finally, one can ask, "what is the value, a, so that z will be smaller than or equal to a with probability P?" The notion for the function that yields the desired value of a is $\Phi(P)$ so that

$$\text{If } \Phi(P) = a, \text{ then } P = N(a) \tag{A.7}$$

For instance, suppose the question is, "which value has a cumulative density of .50?" A glance at Figure A.2 reminds us that the area between minus infinity and zero (the expected value) is .5. Thus we can write

$$\Phi(.5) = 0, \text{ because } N(0) = .5$$

Similarly,

$$\Phi(.8264) = .94 \text{ because } N(.94) = .8264$$

and

$$\Phi(.3594) = -.36$$

For practice, confirm with Table 21.7 that $\Phi(.6554) = .40$, meaning that the value of z with a cumulative distribution of .6554 is $z = .40$.

Non-standard normal distributions

Suppose that the monthly rate of return on a stock is closely approximated by a normal distribution with a mean of .015 (1.5 percent per month), and standard deviation of .127 (12.7 percent per month). What is the probability that the rate of return will fall below zero in a given month? Recall that because the rate is a normal variate, its cumulative density has to be computed by numerical methods. The standard normal table can be used for any normal variate.

Any random variable, x, may be transformed into a new standardized variable, x^*, by the following rule:

$$x^* = \frac{x - E(x)}{\sigma(x)} \qquad \textbf{(A.8)}$$

Note that all that we have done to x was (1) *subtract* its expectation and (2) *multiply* by one over its standard deviation, $1/[\sigma(x)]$. According to our earlier discussion, the effect of transforming a random variable by adding and multiplying by a constant is such that the expectation and standard deviation of the transformed variable are

$$E(x^*) = \frac{E(x) - E(x)}{\sigma(x)} = 0; \; \sigma(x^*) = \frac{\sigma(x)}{\sigma(x)} = 1 \qquad \textbf{(A.9)}$$

From the stability property of the normal distribution we also know that if x is normal, so is x^*. A normal variate is characterized completely by two parameters: its expectation and standard deviation. For x^*, these are zero and 1.0, respectively. When we subtract the expectation and then divide a normal variate by its standard deviation, we standardize it; that is, we transform it to a standard normal variate. This trick is used extensively in working with normal (and approximately normal) random variables.

Returning to our stock, we have learned that if we subtract .15 and then divide the monthly returns by .127, the resultant random variable will be standard normal. We can now determine the probability that the rate of return will be zero or less in a given month. We know that

$$z = \frac{r - .015}{.127}$$

where z is standard normal and r the return on our stock. Thus, if r is zero, z has to be

$$z(r = 0) = \frac{0 - .015}{.127} = -.1181$$

For r to be zero, the corresponding standard normal has to be -11.81 percent, a negative number. The event "r will be zero or less" is identical to the event "z will be $-.1181$ or less." Calculating the probability of the latter will solve our problem. That probability is simply $N(-.1181)$. Visit the standard normal table and find that

$$N(-.1181) = \Pr(r \leq 0) = .5 - .047 = .453$$

The answer makes sense. Recall that the expectation of r is 1.5 percent. Thus, whereas the probability that r will be 1.5 percent or less is .5, the probability that it will be *zero* or less has to be close, but somewhat less.

Confidence intervals

Given the large standard deviation of our stock, it is logical to be concerned about the likelihood of extreme values for the monthly rate of return. One way to quantify this concern is to ask: "What is the interval (range) within which the stock return will fall in a given month, with a probability of .95?" Such an interval is called the *95 percent confidence interval*.

Logic dictates that this interval be centered on the expected value, .015, because r is a normal variate (has a normal distribution), which is symmetric around the expectation. Denote the desired interval by

$$[E(r) - a, E(r) + a] = [.015 - a, .015 + a]$$

which has a length of $2a$. The probability that r will fall within this interval is described by the following expression:

$$Pr(.015 - a \leq r \leq .015 + a) = .95$$

To find this probability, we start with a simpler problem, involving the standard normal variate, that is, a normal with expectation of zero and standard deviation of 1.0.

What is the 95 percent confidence interval for the standard normal variate, z? The variable will be centered on zero, so the expression is

$$Pr(-a^* \leq z \leq a^*) = N(a^*) - N(-a^*) = .95$$

You might best understand the substitution of the difference of the appropriate cumulative distributions for the probability with the aid of Figure A.3. The probability of falling outside of the interval is $1 - .95 = .05$. By the symmetry of the normal distribution, z will be equal to or less than $-a^*$ with probability of

FIGURE A.3

Confidence intervals and the standard normal density.

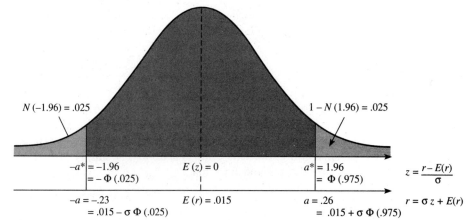

$N(-1.96) = .025$

$1 - N(1.96) = .025$

$-a^* = -1.96$ $E(z) = 0$ $a^* = 1.96$ $z = \dfrac{r - E(r)}{\sigma}$
$= -\Phi(.025)$ $= \Phi(.975)$

$-a = -.23$ $E(r) = .015$ $a = .26$ $r = \sigma z + E(r)$
$= .015 - \sigma \Phi(.025)$ $= .015 + \sigma \Phi(.975)$

.025, and with probability .025, z will be greater than a^*. Thus, we solve for a^* using

$$-a^* = \Phi(.025) \text{ which is equivalent to } N(-a^*) = .025$$

We can summarize the chain that we have pursued so far as follows. If we seek a $P = .95$ level confidence interval, we define α as the probability to fall outside the confidence interval. Because of the symmetry, α will be split so that half of it is the probability of falling to the right of the confidence interval, while the other half of α is the probability of falling to the left of the confidence interval. Therefore the relation between α and P is

$$\alpha = 1 - P = .05; \quad \frac{\alpha}{2} = \frac{1 - P}{2} = .025$$

We use $\alpha/2$ to indicate that the area that is excluded for r is equally divided between the tails of the distributions. Each tail that is excluded for r has an area of $\alpha/2$. The value, $\alpha = 1 - P$, represents the entire value that is excluded for r.

To find $z = \Phi(\alpha/2)$, which is the lower boundary of the confidence interval for the standard normal variate, we have to locate the z value for which the standard normal cumulative distribution is .025, finding $z = -1.96$. Thus, we conclude that $-a^* = -1.96$ and $a^* = 1.96$. The confidence interval for z is

$$[E(z) - \Phi(\alpha/2), E(z) + \Phi(\alpha/2) = [-\Phi(.025), \Phi(0.25)]$$
$$= [-1.96, 1.96]$$

To get the interval boundaries for the non-standard normal variate r, we transform the boundaries for z by the usual relationship, $r = z\sigma(r) + E(r) = \Phi(\alpha/2)\sigma(r) + E(r)$. Note that all we are doing is setting the expectation at the center of the confidence interval and extending it by a number of standard deviations. The number of standard deviations is determined by the probability that we allow for falling outside the confidence interval (α), or equivalently, the probability of falling in it (P). Using minus and plus 1.96 for $z = \pm\Phi(0.25)$, the distance on each side of the expectation is $\pm 1.96 \times .127 = .249$. Thus, we obtain the confidence interval

$$[E(r) - \sigma(r)\Phi(\alpha/2), E(r) + \sigma(r)\Phi(\alpha/2) = [E(r) - .249, E(r) + .249]$$
$$= [-.234, .264]$$

so that

$$P = 1 - \alpha = \Pr[E(r) - \sigma(r)\Phi(\alpha/2) \leq r \leq E(r) + \sigma(r)\Phi(\alpha/2)]$$

which, for our stock (with expectation .015 and standard deviation .127) amounts to

$$\Pr[-.234 \leq r \leq .264] = .95$$

Note that, because of the large standard deviation of the rate of return on the stock, the 95 percent confidence interval is 49 percent wide.

To reiterate with a variation on this example, suppose we seek a 90 percent confidence interval for the annual rate of return on a portfolio, r_p, with a monthly expected return of 1.2 percent and standard deviation of 5.2 percent.

The solution is simply

$$\Pr\left[E(r) - \sigma(r)\Phi\left(\frac{1-P}{2}\right) \leq r_p \leq E(r) + \sigma(r)\Phi\left(\frac{1-P}{2}\right)\right]$$
$$= \Pr[.012 - (.052 \times 1.645) \leq r_p \leq .012 + (.052 \times 1.645)]$$
$$= \Pr[-.0735 \leq r_p \leq .0975] = .90$$

Since the portfolio is of low risk this time (and we allow a 90 percent rather than a 95 percent probability of falling within the interval), the 90 percent confidence interval is only 2.4 percent wide.

The lognormal distribution

The normal distribution is not adequate to describe stock prices and returns for two reasons. First, whereas the normal distribution admits any value, including negative values, actual stock prices cannot be negative. Second, the normal distribution does not account for compounding. The lognormal distribution addresses these two problems.

The lognormal distribution describes a random variable that grows, *every instant,* by a rate that is a normal random variable. Thus the progression of a lognormal random variable reflects continuous compounding.

Suppose that the *annual continuously compounded* (ACC) rate of return on a stock is normally distributed with expectation $\mu = .12$ and standard deviation $\sigma = .42$. The stock price at the beginning of the year is $P_0 = \$10$. With continuous compounding (see appendix to Chapter 4), if the ACC rate of return, r_C, turns out to be .23, then the end-of-year price will be

$$P_1 = P_0\exp(r_C) = 10e^{.23} = \$12.586$$

representing an effective annual rate of return of

$$r = \frac{P_1 - P_0}{P_0} = e^{r_C} - 1 = .2586 \text{ (or } 25.86\%)$$

This is the practical meaning of r, the annual rate on the stock, being lognormally distributed. Note that however negative the ACC rate of return (r_C) is, the price, P_1, cannot become negative.

Two properties of lognormally distributed financial assets are important: their expected return and the allowance for changes in measurement period.

Expected return of a lognormally distributed asset

The expected annual rate of return of a lognormally distributed stock (as in our example) is

$$E(r) = \exp(\mu + \tfrac{1}{2}\sigma^2) - 1 = \exp(.12 + \tfrac{1}{2} \times .42^2) - 1 = e^{.2082} - 1$$
$$= .2315 \text{ (or } 23.15\%)$$

This is just a statistical property of the distribution. For this reason, a useful statistic is

$$\mu^* = \mu + \tfrac{1}{2}\sigma^2 = .2082$$

Often, when analysts refer to the expected ACC return on a lognormal asset, they are really referring to μ^*. Often, the asset is said to have a normal distribution of the ACC return with expectation μ^* and standard deviation σ.

Change of frequency of measured returns

The lognormal distribution allows for easy change of the holding period of returns. Suppose that we want to calculate returns monthly instead of annually. We use the parameter t to indicate the fraction of the year that is desired, in the case of monthly periods $t = 1/12$. To transform the annual distribution to a t-period (monthly) distribution, it is necessary merely to multiply the expectation and variance of the ACC return by t (in this case, 1/12).

The monthly continuously compounded return on the stock in our example has the expectation and standard deviation of

$$\mu(\text{monthly}) = .12/12 = .01 \ (1\% \text{ per month})$$
$$\sigma(\text{monthly}) = .42/\sqrt{12} = .1212 \ (\text{or } 12.12\% \text{ per month})$$
$$\mu^*(\text{monthly}) = .2082/12 = .01735 \ (\text{or } 1.735\% \text{ per month})$$

Note that we divide variance by 12 when changing from annual to monthly frequency; the standard deviation therefore is divided by the square root of 12.

Similarly, we can convert a non-annual distribution to an annual distribution by following the same routine. For example, suppose that the weekly continuously compounded rate of return on a stock is normally distributed with $\alpha = .003$ and $\sigma = .07$. Then the ACC return is distributed with

$$\mu^* = 52 \times .003 = .156 \ (\text{or } 15.6\% \text{ per year})$$
$$\sigma = \sqrt{52} \times .07 = .5048 \ (\text{or } 50.48\% \text{ per year})$$

In practice, to obtain normally distributed, continuously compounded returns, R, we take the log of 1.0 plus the raw returns:

$$r_C = \log(1 + r)$$

For short intervals, raw returns are small, and the continuously compounded returns, R, will be practically identical to the raw returns, r. The rule of thumb is that this conversion is not necessary for periods of one month or less. That is, approximating stock returns as normal will be accurate enough. For longer intervals, however, the transformation may be necessary.

A.2 *Descriptive Statistics*

Our analysis so far has been forward looking, or, as economists like to say, ex ante. We have been concerned with probabilities, expected values, and surprises. We made our analysis more tractable by assuming that decision outcomes are distributed according to relatively simple formulas, and that we know the parameters of these distributions.

Investment managers must satisfy themselves that these assumptions are reasonable, which they do by constantly analyzing observations from relevant random variables that accumulate over time. Distribution of past rates of return on a stock is one element they need to know in order to make optimal decisions. True, the distribution of the rate of return itself changes over time. However, a sample that is not too old does yield information relevant to the next period probability distribution and its parameters. In this section we explain descriptive statistics, or the organization and analysis of such historic samples.

Histograms, Boxplots, and Time Series Plots

Table A.3 shows the annual excess returns (over the T-bill rate) for two major classes of assets, the S&P 500 index and a portfolio of long-term government bonds, for the period 1926 to 1987.

One way to understand the data is to present it graphically, commonly in a *histogram* or frequency distribution. Histograms of the 62 observations in Table A.3 are shown in Figure A.4. We construct a histogram according to the following principles:

- The range (of values) of the random variable is divided into a relatively small number of equal-sized intervals. The number of intervals that makes sense depends on the number of available observations. The data in Table A.3 provide 62 observations, and thus deciles (10 intervals) seem adequate.

TABLE A.3 Excess Return (Risk Premiums) on Stocks and Long-Term Treasury Bonds (Maturity Premiums)

Date	Equity Risk Premium	Maturity Premium
1926	0.0835	0.045
1927	0.3437	0.0581
1928	0.4037	−0.0314
1929	−0.1317	−0.0133
1930	−0.2731	0.0225
1931	−0.4441	−0.0638
1932	−0.0915	0.1588
1933	0.5369	−0.0038
1934	−0.016	0.0986
1935	0.475	0.0481
1936	0.3374	0.0733
1937	−0.3534	−0.0008
1938	0.3114	0.0555
1939	−0.0043	0.0592
1940	−0.0978	0.0609
1941	−0.1165	0.0087

TABLE A.3 Continued

Date	Equity Risk Premium	Maturity Premium
1942	0.2007	0.0295
1943	0.2555	0.0173
1944	0.1942	0.0248
1945	0.3611	0.104
1946	−0.0842	−0.0045
1947	0.0521	−0.0313
1948	0.0469	0.0259
1949	0.1769	0.0535
1950	0.3051	−0.0114
1951	0.2253	−0.0543
1952	0.1671	−0.005
1953	−0.0281	0.0181
1954	0.5176	0.0633
1955	0.2999	−0.0287
1956	0.041	−0.0805
1957	−0.1392	0.0431
1958	0.4182	−0.0764
1959	0.0901	−0.0521
1960	−0.0219	0.1112
1961	0.2476	−0.0116
1962	−0.1146	0.0416
1963	0.1968	−0.0191
1964	0.1294	−0.0003
1965	0.0852	−0.0322
1966	−0.1482	−0.0111
1967	0.1977	−0.134
1968	0.0585	−0.0547
1969	−0.1508	−0.1166
1970	−0.0252	0.0557
1971	0.0992	0.0884
1972	0.1514	0.0184
1973	−0.2159	−0.0804
1974	−0.3447	−0.0365
1975	0.314	0.0339
1976	0.1876	0.1167
1977	−0.123	−0.0579
1978	−0.0062	−0.0834
1979	0.0806	−0.116
1980	0.2118	−0.1519
1981	−0.1962	−0.1286
1982	0.1087	0.2981
1983	0.1371	−0.0812
1984	−0.0358	0.0558
1985	0.2444	0.2325
1986	0.1231	0.1828
1987	−0.0024	−0.0816
Average	0.0833	0.0106
Standard deviation	0.2106	0.0798
Minimum	−0.4441	−0.1519
Maximum	0.5369	0.2981

Data from the Center for Research of Security Prices, University of Chicago, Chicago, Illinois.

FIGURE A.4
A, Histogram of the equity risk premium.
B, Histogram of the bond maturity premium.

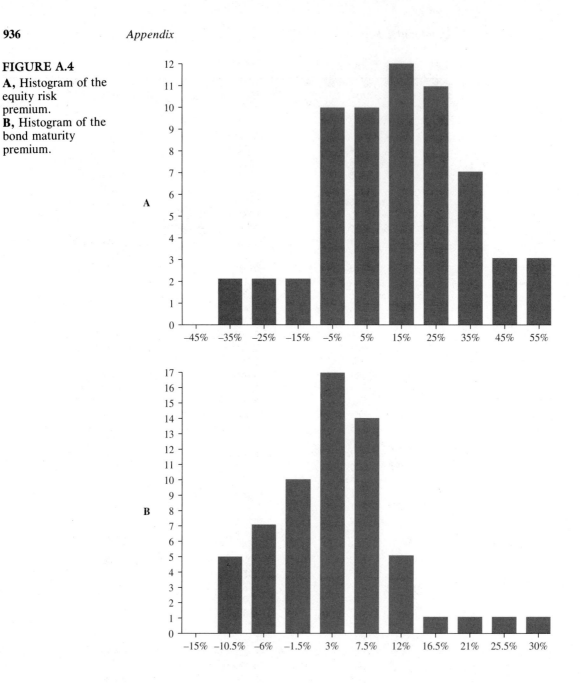

- A rectangle is drawn over each interval. The height of the rectangle represents the frequency of observations for each interval.
- If the observations are concentrated in one part of the range, the range may be divided into unequal intervals. In that case the rectangles are scaled so that their *area* represents the frequency of the observations for each interval. (This is not the case in our samples, however.)

- If the sample is representative, the shape of the histogram will reveal the probability distribution of the random variable. In our case 62 observations are not a large sample, but a look at the histogram does suggest that the returns may be reasonably approximated by a normal or lognormal distribution.

Another way to represent sample information graphically is by *boxplots*. Figure A.5 is an example that uses the same data as in Table A.3. Boxplots are most useful to show the dispersion of the sample distribution. A commonly used measure of dispersion is the *interquartile range*. Recall that the range, a crude measure of dispersion, is defined as the distance between the largest and smallest observations. By its nature, this measure is unreliable because it will be determined by the two most extreme outliers of the sample.

FIGURE A.5

Boxplots of annual equity risk premium and long-term bond (maturity) risk premium (1926–1987).

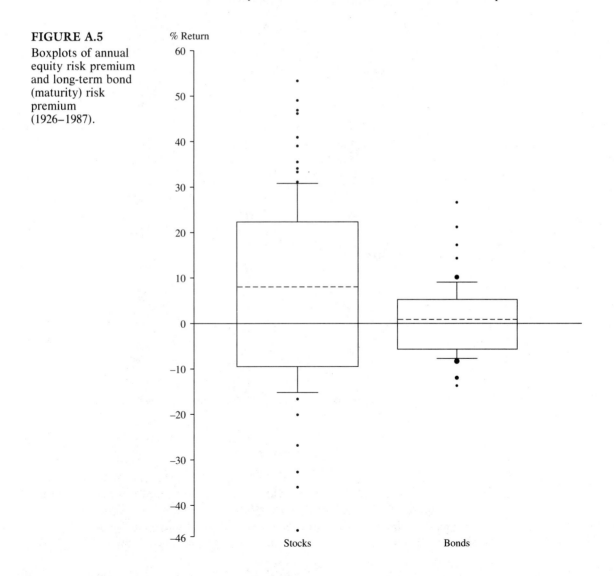

The interquartile range, a more satisfactory variant of the simple range, is defined as the difference between the lower and upper quartiles. Below the *lower* quartile lies 25 percent of the sample; similarly, above the *upper* quartile lies 25 percent of the sample. The interquartile range therefore is confined to the central 50 percent of the sample. The greater the dispersion of a sample, the greater the distance between these two values.

In the boxplot the horizontal broken line represents the median, the box the interquartile range, and the vertical lines extending from the box the range. The vertical lines representing the range often are restricted (if necessary) to extend only to 1.5 times the interquartile range, so that the more extreme observations can be shown separately (by points) as outliers.

As a concept check, verify from Table A.3 that the points on the boxplot of Figure A.5 correspond to the following list:

	Equity Risk Premium	Bond (Maturity) Risk Premium
Lowest extreme		
points	−43.94	−13.66
	−35.23	−12.85
	−31.92	−11.21
	−26.66	−10.94
	−20.19	−10.50
	−17.10	−7.85
		−7.74
		−7.52
		−7.52
		−7.46
Lowest quartile	−8.39	−5.06
Median	8.15	1.30
Highest quartile	22.19	5.29
Highest extreme		
points	31.14	9.85
	33.32	10.37
	33.68	10.82
	35.99	11.11
	39.10	15.73
	41.19	17.22
	47.19	21.58
	47.42	26.96
	51.31	
	53.53	
Interquartile range	30.58	10.35
1.5 times the		
interquartile range	45.87	15.53
From:	−14.79	−6.46
To:	31.09	9.06

Finally, a third form of graphing is time series plots, which are used to convey the behavior of economic variables over time. Figure A.6 shows a time series plot of the excess returns on stocks and bonds from Table A.3. Even though the human eye is apt to see patterns in randomly generated time series, examining time series evolution over a long period does yield some informa-

FIGURE A.6
A, Equity risk premium, 1926–1987.
B, Bond maturity premium, 1926–1987.

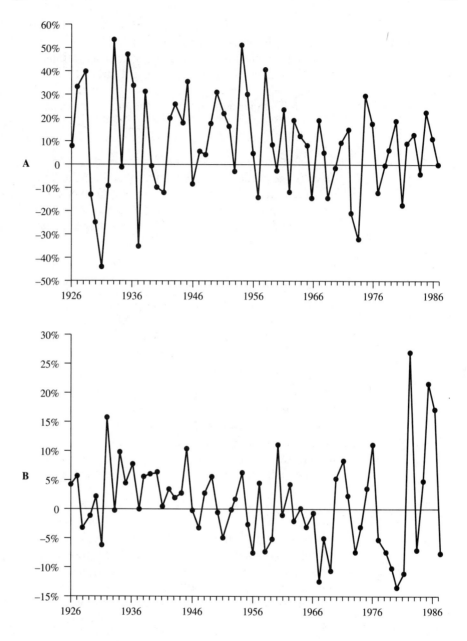

tion. Sometimes, such examination can be as revealing as that provided by formal statistical analysis.

Sample Statistics

Suppose we can assume that the probability distribution of stock returns has not changed over the past 62 years. We wish to draw inferences about the probability distribution of stock returns from the sample of 62 observations of annual stock excess returns in Table A.3.

A central question is whether given observations represent independent observations from the underlying distribution. If they are, statistical analysis is quite straightforward. Our analysis assumes that this is indeed the case. Empiricism in financial markets tends to confirm this assumption in most cases.

Estimating expected returns from the sample average

The definition of expected returns suggests that the sample average be used as an estimate of the expected value. Indeed, one definition of the expected return is the average of a sample when the number of observations tends to infinity.

Denoting the sample returns in Table A.3 by R_t, $t = 1, \ldots, T = 62$, the estimate of the annual expected excess rate of return is

$$\bar{r} = \frac{1}{T} \Sigma R_t = 8.33\%$$

The bar over the r is a common notation for an estimate of the expectation. Intuition suggests that the larger the sample the greater the reliability of the sample average, and the larger the standard deviation of the measured random variable, the less reliable the average. We discuss this property more fully later.

Estimating higher moments

The principle of estimating expected values from sample averages applies to higher moments as well. Recall that higher moments are defined as expectations of some power of the deviation from expectation. For example, the variance (second moment) is the expectation of the squared deviation from expectation. Accordingly, the sample average of the squared deviation from the average will serve as the estimate of the variance, denoted by s^2:

$$s^2 = \frac{1}{T - 1} \Sigma(R_t - \bar{R}^2) = \frac{1}{61} \Sigma(R_t - .0833)^2 = .04436 \ (s = 21.06\%)$$

where $\bar{R}$ is the estimate of the sample average. The average of the squared deviation is taken over $T - 1 = 61$ observations for a technical reason. If we were to divide by T, the estimate of the variance will be downward-biased by the factor $(T - 1)/T$. Here too, the estimate is more reliable the larger the sample and the smaller the true standard deviation.

A.3 *Multivariate Statistics*

Building portfolios requires combining random variables. The rate of return on a portfolio is the weighted average of the individual returns. Hence understanding and quantifying the interdependence of random variables is essential to portfolio analysis. In the first part of this section we return to scenario analysis. Later we return to making inferences from samples.

The Basic Measure of Association: Covariance

Table A.4 summarizes what we have developed so far for the scenario returns on Anheuser-Busch stock and options. We know already what happens when we add a constant to one of these return variables, or multiply by a constant. But what if we combine any two of them? Suppose that we add the return on the stock to the return on the call. We create a new random variable that we denote by $r(s + c) = r(s) + r(c)$, where $r(s)$ is the return on the stock and $r(c)$ is the return on the call.

From the definition, the expected value of the combination variable is

$$E[r(s + c)] = \Sigma \Pr(i) r_i(s + c) \qquad \textbf{(A.10)}$$

Substituting the definition of $r(s + c)$ into equation A.10 we have

$$E[r(s + c)] = \Sigma \Pr(i)[r_i(s) + r_i(c)] = \Sigma \Pr(i) r_i(s) + \Sigma \Pr(i) r_i(c) \qquad \textbf{(A.11)}$$
$$= E[r(s)] + E[r(c)]$$

In words, the expectation of the sum of two random variables is just the sum of the expectations of the component random variables. Can the same be true about the variance? The answer is "no," which is, perhaps, the most important fact in portfolio theory. The reason lies in the statistical association between the combined random variables.

As a first step, we introduce the *covariance,* the basic measure of association. Although the expressions that follow may look intimidating, they are merely squares of sums; that is, $(a + b)^2 = a^2 + b^2 + 2ab$, and $(a - b)^2 = a^2 +$

TABLE A.4 Probability Distribution of Anheuser-Busch Stock and Options

	Scenario 1	Scenario 2	Scenario 3
Probability	.20	.50	.30
Rates of Return (%)			
Stock	20	30	50
Call option	−100	−100	400
Put option	50	−25	−100

	E(r)	σ	σ²
Stock	.34	.1114	.0124
Call option	.50	2.2913	5.25
Put option	−.325	.5250	.2756

$b^2 - 2ab$, where the *a*s and *b*s might stand for random variables, their expectations, or their deviations from expectations. From the definition of the variance

$$\sigma_{s+c}^2 = E[r_{s+c} - E(r_{s+c})]^2 \tag{A.12}$$

To make equations A.12 through A.20 easier to read, we will identify the variables by subscripts *s* and *c* and drop the subscript *i* for scenarios. Substitute the definition of $r(s + c)$ and its expectation into equation A.12:

$$\sigma_{s+c}^2 = E[r_s + r_c - E(r_s) - E(r_c)]^2 \tag{A.13}$$

Changing the order of variables within the brackets in equation A.13.

$$\sigma_{s+c}^2 = E[r_s - E(r_s) + r_c - E(r_c)]^2$$

Within the square brackets we have the sum of the deviations from expectations of the two variables, which we denote by *d*. Writing this out,

$$\sigma_{s+c}^2 = E[(d_s + d_c)^2] \tag{A.14}$$

Equation A.14 is the expectation of a complete square. Taking the square we find

$$\sigma_{s+c}^2 = E(d_s^2 + d_c^2 + 2d_sd_c) \tag{A.15}$$

The term in the brackets in equation A.15 is the summation of three random variables. Since the expectation of a sum is the sum of the expectations, we can write equation A.15 as

$$\sigma_{s+c}^2 = E(d_s^2) + E(d_c^2) + 2E(d_sd_c) \tag{A.16}$$

In equation A.16 the first two terms are the variance of the stock (the expectation of its squared deviation from expectation) plus the variance of the call. The third term is twice the expression that is the definition of the covariance discussed in equation A.17. (Note that the expectation is multiplied by 2 because expectation of twice a variable is twice the variable's expectation.)

In other words, the variance of a sum of random variables is the sum of the variances, *plus* twice the covariance, which we denote by $Cov(r_s, r_c)$, or the covariance between the return on *s* and the return on *c*. Specifically,

$$Cov(r_s,r_c) = E(d_sd_c) = E\{[r_s - E(r_s)][r_c - E(r_c)]\} \tag{A.17}$$

The sequence of the variables in the expression for the covariance is of no consequence. Since the order of multiplication makes no difference, the definition of the covariance in equation A.17 shows that it will not affect the covariance either.

We use the data in Table A.4 to set up the input table for the calculation of the covariance, as shown in Table A.5.

First, we analyze the covariance between the stock and the call. In scenarios 1 and 2, both assets show *negative* deviations from expectation. This is an indication of *positive co-movement*. When these two negative deviations are multiplied, the product, which eventually contributes to the covariance between the returns, is positive. Multiplying deviations leads to positive covariance when the variables move in the same direction, and negative covariance

TABLE A.5 Deviations, Squared Deviations, and Weighted Products of Deviations from Expectations of Anheuser-Busch Stock and Options

	Scenario 1	Scenario 2	Scenario 3	Probability-Weighted Sum
Probability	.20	.50	.30	
Deviation of stock	−.14	−.04	.16	
Squared deviation	.0196	.0016	.0256	.0124
Deviation of call	−1.50	−1.50	3.50	
Squared deviation	2.25	2.25	12.25	5.25
Deviation of put	.825	.075	−.675	
Squared deviation	.680625	.005625	.455635	.275628
Product of deviations $(d_s d_c)$	.21	.06	.56	.24
Product of deviations $(d_s d_p)$	−.1155	−.003	−.108	−.057
Product of deviations $(d_c d_p)$	−1.2375	−.1125	−2.3625	−1.0125

when they move in the opposite direction. In scenario 3 both assets show *positive* deviations, reinforcing the inference that the co-movement is positive. The magnitude of the products of the deviations, weighted by the probability of each scenario, when added up, results in a covariance that shows not only the direction of the co-movement (by its sign) but also the degree of the co-movement.

The covariance is a variance-like statistic. Whereas the variance shows the degree of the movement of a random variable about its expectation, the covariance shows the degree of the co-movement of two variables about their expectations. It is important for portfolio analysis that the covariance of a variable with itself is equal to its variance. You can see this by substituting the appropriate deviations in equation A.17; the result is the expectation of the variable's squared deviation from expectation.

The first three values in the last column of Table A.5 are the familiar variances of the three assets, the stock, the call, and the put. The last three are the covariances; two of them are negative. Examine the covariance between the stock and the put, for example. In the first two scenarios the stock realizes negative deviations, while the put realizes positive deviations. When we multiply such deviations, the sign becomes negative. The same happens in the third scenario, except that the stock realizes a positive deviation and the put a negative one. Again, the product is negative, adding to the inference of negative co-movement.

With other assets and scenarios the product of the deviations can be negative in some scenarios, in others positive. The *magnitude* of the products, when *weighted* by the probabilities, determines which co-movements dominate. However, whenever the sign of the products varies from scenario to scenario, the results will offset one another, contributing to a small, close-to-zero covariance. In such cases we may conclude that the returns have either a small, or no, average co-movement.

Covariance between transformed variables

Since the covariance is the expectation of the product of deviations from expectation of two variables, analyzing the effect of transformations on deviations from expectation will show the effect of the transformation on the covariance.

Suppose that we add a constant to one of the variables. We know already that the expectation of the variable increases by that constant; so deviations from expectation will remain unchanged. Just as adding a constant to a random variable does not affect its variance, it also will not affect its covariance with other variables.

Multiplying a random variable by a constant also multiplies its expectation, as well as its deviation from expectation. Therefore the covariance with any other variable will also be multiplied by that constant. Using the definition of the covariance, check that this summation of the foregoing discussion is true:

$$\text{Cov}[a_1 + b_1 r_s, \, a_2 + b_2 r_c] = b_1 b_2 \text{Cov}(r_s, r_c) \qquad \textbf{(A.18)}$$

The covariance allows us to calculate the variance of sums of random variables, and eventually the variance of portfolio returns.

A Pure Measure of Association: The Correlation Coefficient

If we tell you that the covariance between the rates of return of the stock and the call is .24 (see Table A.5), what have you learned? Because the sign is positive, you known that the returns generally move in the same direction. However, the number .24 adds nothing to your knowledge of the degree of co-movement of the stock and the call.

To obtain a measure of association that conveys the degree of intensity of the co-movement, we relate the covariance to the standard deviations of the two variables. Each standard deviation is the square root of the variance. Thus, the product of the standard deviations has the dimension of the variance that is also shared by the covariance. Therefore, we can define the correlation coefficient, denoted by ρ, as

$$\rho_{sc} = \frac{\text{Cov}(r_s, r_c)}{\sigma_s \sigma_c} \qquad \textbf{(A.19)}$$

where the subscripts on ρ identify the two variables involved. Since the order of the variables in the expression of the covariance is of no consequence, equation A.19 shows that the order does not affect the correlation coefficient either.

We use the covariances from Table A.5 to show the *correlation matrix* for the three variables:

	Stock	Call	Put
Stock	1.0	.94	-.97
Call	.94	1.0	-.84
Put	-.97	-.84	1.0

The highest (in absolute value) correlation coefficient is between the stock and the put, $-.97$, although the absolute value of the covariance between them is the lowest by far. The reason is attributable to the effect of the standard deviations. The following properties of the correlation coefficient are important:

- Because the correlation coefficient, just as the covariance, measures only the degree of association, it tells us nothing about causality. The direction of causality has to come from theory and be supported by specialized tests.
- The correlation coefficient is determined completely by deviations from expectations, as are the components in equation A.19. We expect, therefore, that it is not affected by adding constants to the associated random variables. However, the correlation coefficient is invariant also to multiplying the variables by constants. You can verify this property by referring to the effect of multiplication by a constant on the covariance and standard devation.
- The correlation coefficient can vary from -1.0, perfect negative correlation, to 1.0, perfect positive correlation. This can be seen by calculating the correlation coefficient of a variable with itself. You expect it to be 1.0. Recalling that the covariance of a variable with itself is its own variance, you can verify this using equation A.19. The more ambitious can verify that the correlation between a variable and the negative of itself is equal to -1.0. First, find from equation A.17 that the covariance between a variable and its negative equals the negative of the variance. Then check equation A.19.

Since the correlation between x and y is the same as the correlation between y and x, the *correlation matrix is symmetric about the diagonal*. The diagonal consists of 1.0s because it represents the correlation of the returns with themselves. Therefore, it is customary to present only the lower triangle of the correlation matrix.

Reexamine equation A.16. You can invert it so that the covariance is presented in terms of the correlation coefficient and the standard deviations as in equation A.20:

$$\text{Cov}(r_s, r_c) = \rho_{sc}\sigma_s\sigma_c \qquad \textbf{(A.20)}$$

This formulation can be useful, because many think in terms of correlations rather than covariances.

Estimating correlation coefficients from sample returns

Assuming that a sample consists of independent observations, we assign equal weights to all observations and use simple averages to estimate expectations. When estimating variances and covariances, we get an average by dividing by the number of observations minus one.

Suppose that you are interested in estimating the correlation between stocks and long-term default-free (government) bonds. Assume that the sample of 62 annual excess returns for the period 1926 to 1987 in Table A.3 is representative.

Using the definition for the correlation coefficient in equation A.19, you estimate the following statistics (using the subscripts s for stocks, b for bonds, and t for time):

$$\bar{R}_s = \frac{1}{62} \sum_{t=1}^{62} R_{s,t} = .08334; \quad \bar{R}_b = \frac{1}{62} \sum R_{b,t} = .01058$$

$$\sigma_s = \left[\frac{1}{61} \sum (R_{s,t} - \bar{R}_s)^2 \right]^{1/2} = .21064$$

$$\sigma_b = \left[\frac{1}{61} \sum (R_{b,t} - \bar{R}_b)^2 \right]^{1/2} = .07977$$

$$\text{Cov}(R_s, R_b) = \frac{1}{61} \sum [(R_{s,t} - \bar{R}_s)(R_{b,t} - \bar{R}_b)] = .00257$$

$$\rho_{sb} = \frac{\text{Cov}(R_s, R_b)}{\sigma_s \sigma_b} = .15295$$

Here is one example of how problematic estimation can be. Recall that we predicate our use of the sample on the assumption that the probability distributions have not changed over the sample period. To see the problem with this assumption, suppose that we reestimate the correlation between stocks and bonds over a more recent period—for example, beginning in 1965, about the time of onset of government debt financing of both the war in Vietnam and the Great Society programs.

Repeating the previous calculations for the period 1965 to 1987, we find:

$$\bar{R}_s = .0312; \quad \bar{R}_b = -.00317$$
$$\sigma_s = .15565; \quad \sigma_b = .11217$$
$$\text{Cov}(R_s, R_b) = .0057; \quad \rho_{sb} = .32647$$

A comparison of the two sets of numbers suggests that it is likely, but by no means certain, that the underlying probability distributions have changed. The variance in the rates of return and the size of the samples are why we cannot be sure. We shall return to the issue of testing the sample statistics shortly.

Regression Analysis

We will use a problem from the CFA examination (Level I, 1986) to represent the degree of understanding of regression analysis that is required for the ground level. However, first let us develop some background.

In analyzing measures of association so far, we have ignored the question of causality, identifying simply *independent* and *dependent* variables. Suppose that theory (in its most basic form) tells us that all asset excess returns are driven by the same economic force, whose movements are captured by a broad-based market index, such as excess return, on the S&P 500 stock index.

Suppose further that our theory predicts a simple, linear relationship between the excess return of any asset and the market index. A linear relationship, one that can be described by a straight line, takes on this form:

$$R_{j,t} = a_j + b_j R_{M,t} + e_{j,t} \tag{A.21}$$

where the subscript j represents any asset, M represents the market index (the S&P 500), and t represents variables that change over time. (In the following discussion we omit subscripts when possible.) On the left-hand side of equation A.21 is the dependent variable, the excess return on asset j. The right-hand side has two parts, the explained and unexplained (by the relationship) components of the dependent variable.

The explained component of R_j is the $a + bR_M$ part. It is plotted in Figure A.7. The quantity a, also called the *intercept,* gives the value of R_j when the *independent* variable is zero. This relationship assumes that it is a constant. The second term in the explained part of the return represents the driving force, R_M, times the sensitivity coefficient, b, that transmits movements in R_M to movements in R_j. The term b is also assumed to be constant. Figure A.7 shows that b is the slope of the regression line.

The unexplained component of R_j is represented by the *disturbance* term, e_j. The disturbance is assumed to be uncorrelated with the explanatory variable, R_M, and of zero expectation. Such a variable is also called a noise variable, because it contributes to the variance but not to the expectation of the dependent variable, R_j.

A relationship such as that shown in equation A.21 applied to data, with coefficients estimated, is called a *regression equation*. A relationship including only one explanatory variable is called *simple regression*. The parameters a and b are called (simple) *regression coefficients*. Since every value of R_j is explained by the regression, the expectation and variance of R_j are also deter-

FIGURE A.7

Simple regression estimates and residuals. The intercept and slope are chosen so as to minimize the sum of the squared deviations from the regression line.

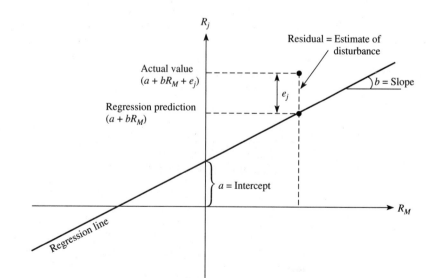

mined by it. Suppose we use the expectation of the expression in equation A.21:

$$E(R_j) = a + bE(R_M) \tag{A.22}$$

The constant a has no effect on the variance of R_j. Because the variables r_M and e_j are uncorrelated, the variance of the sum, $bR_M + e$, is the sum of the variances. Accounting for the parameter b multiplying R_M, the variance of R_j will be

$$\sigma_j^2 = b^2\sigma_M^2 + \sigma_e^2 \tag{A.23}$$

Equation A.23 tells us that the contribution of the variance of R_M to that of R_j depends on the regression (slope) coefficient b. The term $(b\sigma_M)^2$ is called the *explained variance*. The variance of the disturbance makes up the *unexplained* variance.

The covariance between R_j and R_M is also given by the regression equation. Setting up the expression, we have

$$\begin{aligned} \text{Cov}(R_j, R_M) &= \text{Cov}(a + bR_M + e, R_M) \\ &= \text{Cov}(bR_M, R_M) = b\text{Cov}(R_M, R_M) = b\sigma_M^2 \end{aligned} \tag{A.24}$$

The intercept, a, is dropped because a constant added to a random variable does not affect the covariance with any other variable. The disturbance term e is dropped because it is, by assumption, uncorrelated with the market return.

Equation A.24 shows that the slope coefficient of the regression, b, is equal to

$$b = \frac{\text{Cov}(R_j, R_M)}{\sigma_M^2}$$

The slope thereby measures the co-movement of j and M as a fraction of the movement of the driving force, the explanatory variable.

One way to measure the explanatory power of the regression is by the fraction of the variance of R_j that it explains. This fraction is called the *coefficient of determination,* and denoted by ρ^2.

$$\rho_{jM}^2 = \frac{b^2\sigma_M^2}{\sigma_j^2} = \frac{b^2\sigma_M^2}{b_M^2\sigma_M^2 + \sigma_e^2} \tag{A.25}$$

Note that the unexplained variance, σ_e^2, has to make up the difference between the coefficient of determination and 1.0. Therefore, another way to represent the coefficient of determination is by

$$\rho_{jM}^2 = 1 - \frac{\sigma_e^2}{\sigma_j^2}$$

Some algebra shows that the coefficient of determination is the square of the correlation coefficient. Finally, squaring the correlation coefficient tells us what proportion of the variance of the dependent variable is explained by the independent (the explanatory) variable.

Estimation of the regression coefficients a and b is based on minimizing the sum of the square deviation of the observations from the estimated regression line (see Figure A.7). Your calculator, as well as any spreadsheet program, can compute regression estimates.

The CFA 1986 examination for Level I included this question:

Question.

Pension plan sponsors place a great deal of emphasis on universe rankings when evaluating money managers. In fact, it appears that sponsors assume implicitly that managers who rank in the top quartile of a representative sample of peer managers are more likely to generate superior relative performance in the future than managers who rank in the bottom quartile.

The validity of this assumption can be tested by regressing percentile rankings of managers in one period on their percentile rankings from the prior period.

1. Given that the implicit assumption of plan sponsors is true to the extent that there is perfect correlation in percentile rankings from one period to the next, list the numerical values you would expect to observe for the slope of the regression, and the R-squared of the regression.
2. Given that there is no correlation in percentile rankings from period to period, list the numerical values you would expect to observe for the intercept of the regression, the slope of the regression, and the R-squared of the regression.
3. Upon reforming such a regression, you observe an intercept of .51, a slope of $-.05$, and an R-squared of .01. Based on this regression, state your best estimate of a manager's percentile ranking next period if his [or her] percentile ranking this period were .15.
4. Some pension plan sponsors have agreed that a good practice is to terminate managers who are in the top quartile and to hire those who are in the bottom quartile. State what those who advocate such a practice expect implicitly about the correlation and slope from a regression of the managers' subsequent ranking on their current ranking.

Answer.

1. Intercept $= 0$
   Slope $= 1$
   R-squared $= 1$
2. Intercept $= .50$
   Slope $= 0.0$
   R-squared $= 0.0$
3. 50th percentile, derived as follows:
   $y = a + bx$
   $ = .51 - 0.05(.15)$
   $ = .51 - .0075$
   $ = .5025$
   Given the very low R-squared, it would be difficult to estimate what the manager's rank would be.
4. Sponsors who advocate firing top-performing managers and hiring the poorest implicitly expect that both the correlation and slope would be significantly negative.

Multiple Regression Analysis

In many cases, theory suggests that a number of independent, explanatory variables drive a dependent variable. This concept becomes clear enough when demonstrated by a two-variable case. A real estate analyst offers the following regression equation to explain the return on a nationally diversified real estate portfolio:

$$RE_t = a + b_1RE_{t-1} + b_2NVR_t + e_t \qquad \textbf{(A.26)}$$

The dependent variable is the period t real estate portfolio return, RE_t. The model specifies that the explained part of that return is driven by two independent variables. The first is the previous period return, RE_{t-1} representing persistence or momentum. The second explanatory variable is the current national vacancy rate (NVR_t).

As in the simple regression, a is the intercept, representing the value that RE is expected to take when the explanatory variables are zero. The (slope) regression coefficients, b_1 and b_2, represent the *marginal* effect of the explanatory variables.

The coefficient of determination is defined exactly as before. The ratio of the variance of the disturbance, e, to the total variance of RE is 1.0 *minus* the coefficient of determination. The regression coefficients are estimated here, too, by finding coefficients that minimize the sum of squared deviations of the observations from the prediction of the regression.

A.4   *Hypothesis Testing*

The central hypothesis of investment theory is that nondiversifiable (systematic) risk is rewarded by a higher *expected* return. But do the data support the theory? Consider the data on the excess return on stocks in Table A.3. The estimate of the expected excess return (the sample average) is 8.33 percent. This appears to be a hefty risk premium, but so is the risk—the estimate of the standard deviation for the same sample is 21.06 percent. Could it be that the positive average is just the luck of the draw? Hypothesis testing supplies probabilistic answers to such concerns.

The first step in hypothesis testing is to state the claim that is to be tested. This is called the *null hypothesis* (or the null for short), denoted by H_0. Against the null, an alternative claim (hypothesis) is stated, which is denoted by H_1. The objective of hypothesis testing is to decide whether to reject the null in favor of the alternative, while identifying the probabilities of the possible errors in the determination.

A hypothesis is *specified* if it assigns a value to a variable. A claim that the risk premium on stocks is zero is one example of a specified hypothesis. Often, however, a hypothesis is general. A claim that the risk premium on stocks is not zero would be a completely general alternative against the specified hypothesis that the risk premium is zero. It amounts to "anything but the null." The alternative that the risk premium is *positive*, while not completely general, is still unspecified. Although it is sometimes desirable to test two unspecified hypotheses (for instance, the claim that the risk premium is zero or negative, against the claim that it is positive), unspecified hypotheses complicate the task of determining the probabilities of errors in judgment.

What are the possible errors? There are two, called type I and type II errors. Type I is the event that we will *reject* the null when it is *true*. The probability of type I error is called the *significance level*. Type II is the event that we will *accept* the null when it is *false*.

Suppose we set a criterion for acceptance of H_0 that is so lax that we know for certain we will accept the null. In doing so we will drive the significance level to zero (which is good). If we will never reject the null, we will also never reject it when it is true. At the same time the probability of type II error will become 1 (which is bad). If we will accept the null for certain, we must also do so when it is false.

The reverse is to set a criterion for acceptance of the null that is so stringent that we know for certain that we will reject it. This drives the probability of type II error to zero (which is good). By never accepting the null, we avoid accepting it when it is false. Now, however, the significance level will go to 1 (which is bad). If we always reject the null, we will reject it even when it is true.

To compromise between the two evils, hypothesis testing fixes the significance level; that is, it limits the probability of type I error. Then, subject to this preset constraint, the ideal test will minimize the probability of type II error. If we *avoid* type II error (accepting the null when it is false) we actually *reject* the null when it is indeed *false*. The probability of doing so is *one minus the probability of type II error,* which is called the *power of the test.* Minimizing the probability of type II error maximizes the power of the test.

Testing the claim that stocks earn a risk premium, we set the hypotheses as

$$H_0: \quad E(R) = 0 \quad \text{The expected return is zero.}$$
$$H_1: \quad E(R) > 0 \quad \text{The expected return is positive.}$$

H_1 is an *unspecified alternative*. When a null is tested against a completely general alternative, it is called a *two-tailed test* because you may reject the null in favor of both greater or smaller values.

When both hypotheses are unspecified, the test is difficult because the calculation of the probabilities of type I and II errors is complicated. Usually, at least one hypothesis is simple (specified) and set as the null. In that case it is relatively easy to calculate the significance level of the test. Calculating the power of the test that assumes the *unspecified* alternative is true remains complicated; often it is left unsolved.

As we will show, setting the hypothesis that we wish to reject, $E(R) = 0$ as the null (the ''straw man''), makes it harder to accept the alternative that we favor, our theoretical bias, which is appropriate.

In testing $E(R) = 0$, suppose we fix the significance level at 5 percent. This means that we will reject the null (and accept that there is a positive premium) *only* when the data suggest that the probability the null is true is 5 percent or less. To do so, we must find a critical value, denoted z_α (or critical values in the case of two-tailed tests) that corresponds to $\alpha = .05$, which will create two regions, an acceptance region and a rejection region. Look at Figure A.8 as an illustration.

If the sample average is to the right of the critical value (in the rejection region), the null is rejected; otherwise, it is accepted. In the latter case it is too likely (e.g., the probability is greater than 5 percent) that the sample average is positive simply because of sampling error. If the sample average is greater than the critical value, we will reject the null in favor of the alternative. The probability that the positive value of the sample average results from sampling error is 5 percent or less.

If the alternative is one-sided (one-tailed), as in our case, the acceptance region covers the entire area from minus infinity to a positive value, above which lies 5 percent of the distribution (see Figure A.8). The critical value is z_α in Figure A.8. When the alternative is two-tailed, the area of 5 percent lies at both extremes of the distribution and is equally divided between them, 25 percent on each side. A two-tailed test is more stringent (it is harder to reject the null). In a one-tailed test the fact that our theory predicts the direction in which the average will deviate from the value under the null is weighted in favor of the alternative. The upshot is that for a significance level of 5 percent, with a one-tailed test, we use a confidence interval of $\alpha = .05$, instead of $\alpha/2 = .025$ as with a two-tailed test.

Hypothesis testing requires assessment of the probabilities of the test statistics, such as the sample average and variance. Therefore, it calls for some assumption about the probability distribution of the underlying variable. Such an assumption becomes an integral part of the null hypothesis, often an implicit one.

In this case we assume that the stock portfolio excess return is normally distributed. The distribution of the test statistic is derived from its mathematical definition and the assumption of the underlying distribution for the random variable: In our case the test statistic is the sample average.

The sample average is obtained by summing all observations ($T = 62$), and then multiplying by $1/T = 1/62$. Each observation is a random variable, drawn independently from the same underlying distribution, with an unknown expectation μ and standard deviation σ. The expectation of the sum of all observa-

FIGURE A.8
Under the null hypothesis the sample average excess return should be distributed around zero. If the actual average exceeds z_α, we conclude that the null hypothesis is false.

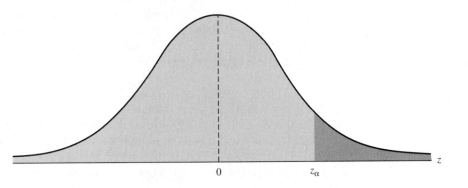

tions is the sum of the T expectations (all equal to μ) divided by T, therefore equal to the population expectation. The result is 8.33 percent, which is equal to the true expectation *plus* sampling errors. Under the null hypothesis, the expectation is zero, and the entire 8.33 percent constitutes sampling errors.

To calculate the variance of the sample average, recall that we assume d observations were independent, or uncorrelated. Hence the variance of the sum is the sum of the variances, that is, T times the population variance. However, we also transform the sum, multiplying it by $1/T$; therefore we have to divide the variance of the sum $T\sigma^2$ by T^2. We end up with the variance of the sample average as the population variance divided by T. The standard deviation of the sample average, which is called the *standard error*, is

$$\sigma(\text{average}) = \left(\frac{1}{T^2} \Sigma\sigma^2\right)^{1/2} = \left(\frac{1}{T^2} T\sigma^2\right)^{1/2} = \frac{\sigma}{\sqrt{T}} = \frac{.21064}{\sqrt{62}} = .02675 \qquad \textbf{(A.27)}$$

Our test statistic has a standard error of 2.675 percent. It makes sense that the more the number of observations, the *smaller* the *standard error* of the estimate of the expectation. However, note that it is the variance that goes down by the proportion $T = 62$. The standard error goes down by a much smaller proportion, $\sqrt{T} = 7.87$.

Now that we have the sample mean, 8.33 percent, its standard deviation, 2.675 percent, and know that the distribution under the null is normal, we are ready to perform the test. We want to determine whether 8.33 percent is significantly positive. We achieve this by standardizing our statistic, which means that we subtract from its expected value under the null hypothesis and divide by its standard deviation. This standardized statistic can now be compared to z values from the standard normal tables. We ask whether

$$\frac{\bar{R} - E(R)}{\sigma} > z_\alpha$$

We would be finished except for another caveat. The assumption of normality is all right in that the test statistic is a weighted sum of normals (according to our assumption about returns). Therefore it is also normally distributed. However, the analysis also requires that we *know* the variance. Here we are using a sample variance that is only an *estimate* of the true variance.

The solution to this problem turns out to be quite simple. The normal distribution is replaced with the *student-t* (or t, for short) *distribution*. Like the normal, the t distribution is symmetric. It depends on degrees of freedom, that is, the number of observations less one. Thus, here we replace z_α with $t_{\alpha,T-1}$.

The test is then

$$\frac{\bar{R} - E(R)}{s} > t_{\alpha,T-1}$$

When we substitute in sample results, the left-hand side is a standardized statistic and the right-hand side is a t-value derived from t tables for $\alpha = .05$ and $T - 1 = 62 - 1 = 61$. We ask whether the inequality holds. If it does, we *reject* the null hypothesis with a 5 percent significance level; if it does not we *cannot reject* the null hypothesis. Proceeding, we find that

$$\frac{.0833 - 0}{.02675} = .3114 > 1.671$$

In our sample the inequality holds, and we reject the null hypothesis in favor of the alternative that the risk premium is positive.

A repeat of the test of this hypothesis for the 1965–1987 period may make a skeptic out of you. For that period the sample average is 3.12 percent, the sample standard deviation is 15.57 percent, and there are $23 - 1 = 22$ degrees of freedom. Does that give you second thoughts?

The *t*-test of regression coefficients

Suppose that we apply the simple regression model (equation A.21), to the relationship between the long-term governmental bond portfolio and the stock market index, using the sample in Table A.3. The estimation result (percent per year) is

$$a = .5668, \, b = .0589, \, R\text{-squared} = .0242$$

We interpret these coefficients as follows. For periods when the excess return on the market index is zero, we expect the bonds to earn an excess return of 56.68 basis points. This is the role of the intercept. As for the slope, for each percentage return of the stock portfolio in any year, the bond portfolio is expected to earn, *additionally*, 5.89 basis points. With the average equity risk premium for the sample period of 8.33 percent, the sample average for bonds is $.5668 + .0589 \times 8.33 = 1.058$ percent. From the squared correlation coefficient you know that the variation in stocks explains 2.42 percent of the variation in bonds.

Can we rely on these statistics? One way to find out is to set up a hypothesis test, presented here for the regression coefficient b.

H_0: $b = 0$ The regression slope coefficient is zero, meaning that changes in the independent variable do not explain changes in the dependent variable.

H_1: $b > 0$ The dependent variable is sensitive to changes in the independent variable (with a *positive* covariance).

Any decent regression software supplies the statistics to test this hypothesis. The regression customarily assumes that the dependent variable and the disturbance are normally distributed, with an unknown variance that is estimated from the sample. Thus, the regression coefficient b is normally distributed. Because once again the null is that $b = 0$, all we need is an estimate of the standard error of this statistic.

The estimated standard error of the regression coefficient is computed from the estimated standard deviation of the disturbance and the standard deviation of the explanatory variable. For the regression at hand, that estimate is, $s(b) = .0479$. Just as in the previous exercise, the critical value of the test is

$$s(b)t_{\alpha, T-1}$$

Compare this value to the value of the estimated coefficient b. We will reject the null in favor of $b > 0$ if

$$b > s(b)t_{\alpha,T-1}$$

which, because the standard deviation $s(b)$ is positive, is equivalent to the following condition:

$$\frac{b}{s(b)} > t_{\alpha,T-1}$$

The t-test reports the ratio of the estimated coefficient to its estimated standard deviation. Armed with this t-*ratio,* the number of observations, T, and a table of the student-t distribution, you can perform the test at the desired significance level.

The t-ratio for our example is $.0589/.0479 = 1.2305$. The t-table for 61 degrees of freedom shows we cannot reject the null at a significance level of 5 percent, for which the critical value is 1.671.

A question from the CFA 1987 level exam calls for understanding of regression analysis and hypothesis testing.

Question.

An academic suggests to you that the returns on common stocks differ based on a company's market capitalization, its historical earnings growth, the stock's current yield, and whether or not the company's employees are unionized. You are skeptical that there are any attributes other than market exposure as measured by beta that explain the differences in returns across a sample of securities.

Nonetheless, you decide to test whether or not these other attributes account for the differences in returns. You select the S&P 500 stocks as your sample, and regress their returns each month for the past 5 years against the company's market capitalization at the beginning of each month, the company's growth in earnings throughout the previous 12 months, the prior year's dividend divided by the stock price at the beginning of each month, and a dummy variable that has a value of 1 if employees are unionized and 0 if not.

1. The average R-squared from the regressions is .15, and it varies very little from month-to-month. Discuss the significance of this result.
2. You note that all of the coefficients of the attributes have t-statistics greater than 2 in most of the months in which the regressions were run. Discuss the significance of these attributes in terms of explaining differences in common stock returns.
3. You observe in most of the regressions that the coefficient of the dummy variable is $-.14$, and that the t-statistic is -4.74. Discuss the implication of the coefficient regarding the relationship between unionization and the return on a company's common stock.

Answer.

1. Differences in the attributes' values together explain about 15% of the differences in return among the stocks in the S&P 500 index. The remaining unexplained differences in return may be attributable to omitted attributes, industry affiliations, or stock-specific factors. This information by itself is not sufficient to form any qualitative conclusions. The fact that the R-squared varied little from month-to-month implies that the relationship is stable and the observed results are not sample specific.

2. Given a *t*-statistic greater than 2 in most of the months, one would regard the attribute coefficients as statistically significant. If the attribute coefficients were not significantly different from zero, one would expect *t*-statistics greater than 2 in fewer than 5 percent of the regressions for each attribute coefficient. Since the *t*-statistics are greater than 2 much more frequently, one should conclude that they are definitely significant in terms of explaining differences in stock returns.

3. Since the coefficient for the dummy variable representing unionization has persistently been negative and since it persistently has been statistically significant, one would conclude that disregarding all other factors, unionization lowers a company's common stock return. That is, everything else being equal, non-unionized companies will have higher returns than companies whose employees are unionized. Of course, one would want to test the model further to see if there are omitted variables or other problems that might account for this apparent relationship.

Solutions to Concept Checks

I Introduction

Chapter 1—The Investment Environment

1. The real assets are patents, customer relations, and the college education. These assets enable individuals or firms to produce goods or services that yield profits or income. Lease obligations are simply claims to pay or receive income and do not in themselves create new wealth. Similarly, the $5 bill is only a paper claim on the government and does not produce wealth.

2. The car loan is a primitive security. Payments on the loan depend only on the solvency of the borrower.

3. The borrower has a financial liability, the loan owed to the bank. The bank treats the loan as a financial asset.

4. *a.* Used cars trade in direct search markets when individuals advertise in local newspapers, and in dealer markets at used-car lots or automobile dealers.

   b. Paintings trade in broker markets when clients commission brokers to buy or sell art for them, in dealer markets at art galleries, and in auction markets.

   c. Rare coins trade mostly in dealer markets in coin shops, but they also trade in auctions and in direct search markets when individuals advertise they want to buy or sell coins.

5. Creative unbundling can separate interest or dividend from capital gains income. Dual funds do just this. In tax regimes where capital gains are taxed at lower rates than other income, or where gains can be deferred, such unbundling may be a way to attract different tax clienteles to a security.

Chapter 2—Markets and Instruments

1. The bond equivalent yield is 8.08. Therefore

$$P = 10,000/[1 + .0808 \times (182/365)] = \$9,612.71$$

2. If the bond is selling below par, it is unlikely that the government will find it optimal to call the bond at par, when it can instead buy the bond in the secondary market for less than par. Therefore, it makes sense to assume that the bond will remain alive until its maturity date. In contrast, premium bonds are vulnerable to call because the government can acquire them by paying only par value. Hence it is likely that the bonds will repay principal at the first call date, and the yield to first call is the statistic of interest.

3. *a.* You are entitled to a prorated share of Alcan's dividend payments and to vote in any of Alcan's stockholder meetings.

   b. Your potential gain is unlimited because Alcan's stock price has no upper bound.

   c. Your outlay was $50 × 100 = $5,000. Because of limited liability, this is the most you can lose.

4. The price-weighted index increases from 62.5 [(100 + 25)/2] to 65 [(110 + 20)/2)], a gain of 4 percent. An investment of one share in each company requires an outlay of $125 that would increase in value to $130, for a return of 4 percent (5/125), which equals the return to the price-weighted index.

5. The market value–weighted index return is calculated by computing the increase in value of the stock portfolio. The portfolio of the two stocks starts with an initial value of $100 million + $500 million = $600 million and falls in value to $110 million + $400 million = $510 million, a loss of 90/600 = .15 or 15 percent. The index portfolio return is a weighted average of the returns on each stock with weights of 1/6 on XYZ and 5/6 on ABC, (weights proportional to relative investments). Because the return on XYZ is 10 percent, while that on ABC is −20 percent, the index portfolio return is 1/6 × 10% + 5/6 × (−20%) = −15%, equal to the return on the market value–weighted index.

6. The payoff to the option is $2 per share at maturity. The option cost $1.00 share. The dollar profit is therefore $1.00. The put option expires worthless. Therefore, the investor's loss is the cost of the put, or $2.10.

Chapter 3—How Securities Are Traded

1.
$$\frac{100P - \$4,000}{100P} = .4$$
$$100P - \$4,000 = 40P$$
$$60P = \$4,000$$
$$P = \$66.67 \text{ per share}$$

2. The investor will purchase 150 shares, with a rate of return as follows:

Year-End Change in Price	Year-End Value of Shares	Repayment of Principal and Interest	Investor's Rate of Return
30%	19,500	$5,450	40.5%
No change	15,000	5,450	−4.5%
−30%	10,500	5,450	−49.5%

3.

$$\frac{\$150,000 - 1,000P}{1,000P} = .4$$
$$\$150,000 - 1,000P = 400P$$
$$1,400P = \$150,000$$
$$P = \$107.14 \text{ per share}$$

Chapter 4—Concepts and Issues

1. *a.*

$$1 + r = (1 + R)(1 + i)$$
$$= (1.03)(1.08)$$
$$= 1.1124$$
$$r = 11.24\%$$

b.
$$1 + r = (1.03)(1.10)$$
$$= 1.133$$
$$r = 13.3\%$$

2.
$$R = (.12 - .13)/.13$$
$$= -.00885 \text{ or } -.885\%$$

When the inflation rate exceeds the nominal interest rate, the real rate of return is negative.

II Portfolio Theory

Chapter 5—Risk and Risk Aversion

1. The expected rate of return on the risky portfolio is $22,000/$100,000 = .22, or 22 percent. The T-bill rate is 5 percent. The risk premium therefore is 22 percent − 5 percent = 17 percent.

2. The investor is taking on exchange rate risk by investing in a pound-denominated asset. If the exchange rate moves in the investor's favor, the investor will benefit and will earn more from the U.K. bill than the Canadian bill. For example, if both the Canadian and U.K. interest rates are 5 percent, and the current exchange rate is $2.00 per pound, a $2.00

investment today can buy one pound, which can be invested in England at a certain rate of 5 percent, for a year-end value of 1.05 pounds. If the year-end exchange rate is $2.10 per pound, the 1.05 pounds can be exchanged for $1.05 \times \$2.10 = \$2.205$ for a rate of return in dollars of $1 + r = \$2.205/\$2.00 = 1.1025$ or 10.25%, more than is available from Canadian bills. Therefore, if the investor expects favorable exchange rate movements, the U.K. bill is a speculative investment. Otherwise, it is a gamble.

3. For the $A = 4$ investor the utility of the risky portfolio is

$$U = .20 - \tfrac{1}{2} \times 4 \times .2^2$$
$$= .12$$

while the utility of bills is

$$U = .07 - \tfrac{1}{2} \times 4 \times 0$$
$$= .07$$

The investor will prefer the risky portfolio to bills. (Of course, a mixture of bills and the portfolio might be even better, but that is not a choice here.)

For the $A = 8$ investor, the utility of the risky portfolio is

$$U = .20 - \tfrac{1}{2} \times 8 \times .2^2$$
$$= .04$$

while the utility of bills is again .07. The more risk-averse investor therefore prefers the risk-free alternative.

4. The less risk-averse investor has a shallower indifference curve. An increase in risk requires less increase in expected return to restore utility to the original level.

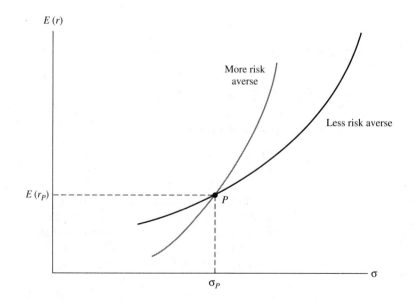

5. Despite the fact that gold investments *in isolation* seem dominated by the stock market, gold still might play a useful role in a diversified portfolio. Because gold and stock market returns have very low correlation, stock investors can reduce their portfolio risk by placing part of their portfolios in gold.

6. *a.* With the given distribution for SugarBeet, the scenario analysis looks as follows:

	Normal Year for Sugar		Abnormal Year
	Bullish Stock Market	**Bearish Stock Market**	**Sugar Crisis**
Probability	.5	.3	.2
	Rate of Return (%)		
Best Candy	.25	.10	−.25
SugarBeet	.07	−.05	.20
T-bills	.05	.05	.05

The expected return and standard deviation of SugarBeet is now

$$E(r_{SugarBeet}) = .5 \times .07 + .3(-.05) + .2 \times .20$$
$$= .06$$
$$\sigma_{SugarBeet} = [.5(.07 - .06)^2 + .3(-.05 - .06)^2 + .2(.20 - .06)^2]^{1/2}$$
$$= .0872$$

The covariance between the returns of Best and SugarBeet is

$$Cov(SugarBeet, Best) = .5(.07 - .06)(.25 - .105)$$
$$+ .3(-.05 - .06)(.10 - .105) + .2(.20 - .06)(-.25 - .105) = -.00905$$

and the correlation coefficient is

$$\rho_{(SugarBeet, Best)} = \frac{Cov(SugarBeet, Best)}{\sigma_{(SugarBeet)}\sigma_{(Best)}}$$
$$= \frac{-.00905}{.0872 \times .1890}$$
$$= -.55$$

The correlation is negative, but less than before (−.55 instead of −.86) so we expect that SugarBeet will now be a less powerful hedge than before. Investing 50% in SugarBeet and 50% in Best will result in a portfolio probability distribution of

Probability	.5	.3	.2
Portfolio return	.16	.025	−.025

resulting in a mean and standard deviation of

$$E(r_{\text{Hedged portfolio}}) = .5 \times .16 + .3 \times .025 + .2(-.025)$$
$$= .0825$$
$$\sigma_{\text{Hedged portfolio}} = [.5(.16 - .0825)^2 + .3(.025 - .0825)^2 + .2(-.025 - .0825)^2]^{1/2}$$
$$= .0794.$$

    b. It is obvious that even under these circumstances the hedging strategy dominates the risk-reducing strategy that uses T-bills (which results in $E(r) = 7.75$ percent, $\sigma = 9.45$ percent). At the same time, the standard deviation of the hedged position (7.94 percent) is not as low it was using the original data.

c, d. Using Rule 5 for portfolio variance, we would find that

$$\sigma^2 = .5^2 \times \sigma_{\text{Best}}^2 + .5^2 \times \sigma_{\text{Beet}}^2 + 2 \times .5 \times .5 \times \text{Cov(SugarBeet,Best)}$$
$$= .5^2 \times .189^2 + .5^2 \times .0872^2 + 2 \times .5 \times .5 \times (-.00905)$$
$$= .006306$$

which implies that $\sigma = .0794$, precisely the same result that we obtained by analyzing the scenarios directly.

A.1. Investors appear to be more sensitive to extreme outcomes relative to moderate outcomes than variance and higher *even* moments can explain. Casual evidence suggests that investors are eager to insure extreme losses and express great enthusiasm for highly, positively skewed lotteries. This hypothesis is, however, extremely difficult to prove with properly controlled experiments.

A.2. The better diversified the portfolio, the smaller is its standard deviation, as the sample standard deviations of Table 5A.1, p. 165, confirm. When we draw from distributions with smaller standard deviations, the probability of extreme values shrinks. Thus, the expected smallest and largest values from a sample get closer to the expected value as the standard deviation gets smaller. This expectation is confirmed by the samples of Table 1 for both the sample maximum and minimum annual rate.

B.1. *a.* $U(W) = \sqrt{W}$
$$U(50,000) = \sqrt{50,000}$$
$$= 223.61$$
$$U(150,000) = 387.30$$

    b. $E(U) = .5 \times 223.61 + .5 \times 387.30$
$$= 305.45$$

    c. We must find W_{CE} that has utility level 305.45. Therefore
$$\sqrt{W_{CE}} = 305.45$$
$$W_{CE} = 305.45^2$$
$$= \$93,301$$

    d. Yes. The certainty equivalent of the risky venture is less than the expected outcome of $100,000.

    e. The certainty equivalent of the risky venture to this investor is greater than it was for the log utility investor considered in the text. Hence this utility function displays less risk aversion.

Chapter 6—Capital Allocation Between the Risky Asset and the Risk-Free Asset

1. Holding 50 percent of your invested capital in Ready Assets means that your investment proportion in the risky portfolio is reduced from 70 percent to 50 percent.

   Your risky portfolio is constructed to invest 54 percent in VO and 46 percent in CT. Thus, the proportion of VO in your overall portfolio is .5 × .54 = 27 percent, and the dollar value of your position in VO is $300,000 × .27 = $81,000.

2. In the expected return-standard deviation plane all portfolios that are constructed from the same risky and risk-free funds (with various proportions) lie on a line from the risk-free rate through the risky fund. The slope of this CAL (capital allocation line) is the same everywhere; hence the reward-to-variability ratio is the same for all of these portfolios. Formally, if you invest in a proportion, y, in a risky fund with expected return, $E(r_P)$, and standard deviation, σ_P, and the remainder, $1 - y$, in a risk-free asset with a sure rate, r_f, then the portfolio's expected return and standard deviation are

$$E(r_C) = r_f + y[E(r_P) - r_f]$$
$$\sigma_C = y\sigma_P$$

and, therefore, the reward-to-variability ratio of this portfolio is

$$S_C = \frac{E(r_C) - r_f}{\sigma_C} = \frac{y[E(r_P) - r_f]}{y\sigma_P} = \frac{E(r_P) - r_f}{\sigma_P}$$

which is independent of the proportion, y.

3. The lending and borrowing rates are unchanged at: $r_f = 7$ percent, $r_f^B = 9$ percent. The standard deviation of the risky portfolio is still 22 percent, but its expected rate of return shifts from 15 percent to 17 percent.

   The slope of the two-part CAL is

$$\frac{E(r_P) - r_f}{\sigma_P} \quad \text{for the lending range}$$
$$\frac{E(r_P) - r_f^B}{\sigma_P} \quad \text{for the borrowing range}$$

Thus, in both cases the slope increases: from 8/22 to 10/22 for the lending range, and from 6/22 to 8/22 for the borrowing range.

4. *a.* The parameters are: $r_f = .07$, $E(r_P) = .15$, $\sigma_P = .22$. With these parameters an investor with a degree of risk aversion, A, will choose a proportion, y, in the risky portfolio of

$$y = \frac{E(r_P) - r_f}{A\sigma_P^2}$$

With $A = 3$ we find that

$$y = \frac{.15 - .07}{3 \times .0484} = .55$$

When the degree of risk aversion decreases from the original value of four to the new value of three, investment in the risky portfolio increases from 41 percent to 55 percent. Accordingly, the expected return and standard deviation of the optimal portfolio increase.

$$E(r_C) = .07 + .55 \times .08 = .114 \quad \text{(before: .1028)}$$
$$\sigma_C = .55 \times .22 = .121 \quad \text{(before: .0902)}$$

b. All investors whose degree of risk aversion is such that they would hold the risky portfolio in a proportion equal to 100 percent or less ($y < 1.00$) are lending rather than borrowing, and so are unaffected by the borrowing rate. The least risk-averse of these investors hold 100 percent in the risky portfolio ($y = 1$). We can solve for the degree of risk aversion of these "cut off" investors, from the parameters of the investment opportunities:

$$y = 1 = \frac{E(r_P) - r_f}{A\sigma_P^2} = \frac{.08}{.0484A}$$

which implies

$$A = \frac{.08}{.0484} = 1.65$$

Any investor who is more risk tolerant (that is, with A less than 1.65) would borrow if the borrowing rate were 7 percent. For borrowers,

$$y = \frac{E(r_P) - r_f^B}{A\sigma_P^2}$$

Suppose, for example, an investor has an A of 1.1. When $r_f = r_f^B = 7$ percent, this investor chooses to invest in the risky portfolio.

$$y = \frac{.08}{1.1 \times .0484} = 1.50$$

which means that the investor will borrow 50 percent of the total investment capital. Raise the borrowing rate, in this case to $r_f^B = 9$ percent, and the investor will invest less in the risky asset. In that case,

$$y = \frac{.06}{1.1 \times .0484} = 1.13$$

and "only" 13 percent of his or her investment capital will be borrowed. Graphically, the line from r_f to the risky portfolio shows the CAL for lenders. The dashed part *would* be relevant if the borrowing rate equaled the lending rate. When the borrowing rate exceeds the lending rate, the CAL is kinked at the point corresponding to the risky portfolio.

The following figure shows indifference curves of two investors. The steeper indifference curve portrays the more risk-averse investor, who chooses portfolio C_0, which involves lending. This investor's choice is unaffected by the borrowing rate.

The more risk-tolerant investor is portrayed by the shallower-sloped indifference curves. If the lending rate equaled the borrowing rate, this investor would choose portfolio C_1 on the dashed part of the CAL. When the borrowing rate goes up, this investor chooses portfolio C_2 (in the borrowing range of the kinked CAL), which involves less borrowing than before. This investor is hurt by the increase in the borrowing rate.

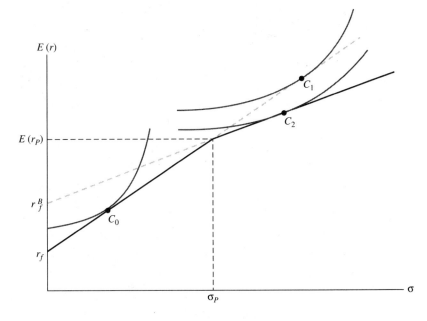

5. If all the investment parameters remain unchanged, the only reason for an investor to decrease the investment proportion in the risky asset is an increase in the degree of risk aversion. If you think that this is unlikely, then you have to reconsider your faith in your assumptions. Perhaps the TSE 300 is not a good proxy for the optimal risky portfolio. Perhaps investors expect a higher real rate on T-bills (inflation is ignored in this model).

Chapter 7—Optimal Risky Portfolios

1. *a.* The first term will be $w_D \times w_D \times \sigma_D^2$, since this is the element in the top corner of the matrix (σ_D^2) times the term on the column border (w_D) times the term on the row border (w_D). Applying this rule to each term of the covariance matrix results in the sum $w_D^2 \sigma_D^2 + w_D w_E \text{Cov}(r_E, r_D) + w_E w_D \text{Cov}(r_D, r_E) + w_E^2 \sigma_E^2$, which is the same as equation 7.2, since $\text{Cov}(r_E, r_D) = \text{Cov}(r_D, r_E)$.

b. The bordered covariance matrix is

	w_X	w_Y	w_Z
w_X	σ_X^2	$\text{Cov}(r_X,r_Y)$	$\text{Cov}(r_X,r_Z)$
w_Y	$\text{Cov}(r_Y,r_X)$	σ_Y^2	$\text{Cov}(r_Y,r_Z)$
w_Z	$\text{Cov}(r_Z,r_X)$	$\text{Cov}(r_Z,r_Y)$	σ_Z^2

There are nine terms in the covariance matrix. Portfolio variance is calculated from these nine terms:

$$\begin{aligned}
\sigma_P^2 &= w_X^2\sigma_X^2 + w_Y^2\sigma_Y^2 + w_Z^2\sigma_Z^2 \\
&+ w_X w_Y \, \text{Cov}(r_X,r_Y) + w_Y w_X \, \text{Cov}(r_Y,r_X) \\
&+ w_X w_Z \, \text{Cov}(r_X,r_Z) + w_Z w_X \, \text{Cov}(r_Z,r_X) \\
&+ w_Y w_Z \, \text{Cov}(r_Y,r_Z) + w_Z w_Y \, \text{Cov}(r_Z,r_Y) \\
&= w_X^2\sigma_X^2 + w_Y^2\sigma_Y^2 + w_Z^2\sigma_Z^2 \\
&+ 2w_X w_Y \, \text{Cov}(r_X,r_Y) + 2w_X w_Z \, \text{Cov}(r_X,r_Z) + 2w_Y w_Z \, \text{Cov}(r_Y,r_Z)
\end{aligned}$$

2. The parameters of the opportunity set are $E(r_D) = .20$, $E(r_E) = .15$, $\sigma_D = .45$, $\sigma_E = .32$, and $\rho(D,E) = .25$. From the standard deviations and the correlation coefficient we generate the covariance matrix:

Fund	D	E
D	.2025	.0360
E	.0360	.1024

The *global minimum-variance* portfolio is constructed so that

$$\begin{aligned}
w_D &= [\sigma_E^2 - \text{Cov}(r_D,r_E)] \div [\sigma_D^2 + \sigma_E^2 - 2\,\text{Cov}(r_D,r_E)] \\
&= (.1024 - .0360) \div (.2205 + .1024 - 2 \times .0360) = .2851 \\
w_E &= 1 - w_D = .7149.
\end{aligned}$$

Its expected return and standard deviation are

$$\begin{aligned}
E(r_P) &= .2851 \times .20 + .7149 \times .15 = .1643 \\
\sigma_P &= [w_D^2\sigma_D^2 + w_E^2\sigma_E^2 + 2w_D w_E \, \text{Cov}(r_D,r_E)]^{1/2} \\
&= [.2851^2 \times .2025 + .7149^2 \times .1024 + 2 \times .2851 \times .7149 \times .0360]^{1/2} \\
&= .2289
\end{aligned}$$

For the other points we simply increase w_D from .10 to .90 in increments of .10; accordingly, w_E ranges from .90 to .10 in the same increments. We substitute these portfolio proportions in the formulas for expected return and standard deviation. Note that for w_D or w_E equal to 1.0, the portfolio parameters equal those of the fund.

We then generate the following table:

w_D	w_E	$E(r)$	σ
.00	1.00	.1500	.3200
.10	.90	.1550	.3024
.20	.80	.1600	.2918
.2851	.7149	.1643	.2889(min)

W_D	W_E	$E(r)$	σ
.30	.70	.1650	.2890
.40	.60	.1700	.2942
.50	.50	.1750	.3070
.60	.40	.1800	.3264
.70	.30	.1850	.3515
.80	.20	.1900	.3811
.90	.10	.1950	.4142
1.00	.00	.2000	.4500

You can now draw your graph.

3. *a.* The computations of the opportunity set of the two stock funds are like those of Question 2 and will not be shown here. You should perform these computations, however, in order to give a graphical solution to part a. Note that the covariance between the funds is

$$Cov(r_A, r_B) = \rho(A,B) \times \sigma_A \times \sigma_B$$
$$= -.2 \times .20 \times .60 = -.0240$$

b. The proportions in the optimal risky portfolio are given by

$$w_A = \frac{(.10 - .05).60^2 - (.30 - .05)(-.0240)}{(.10 - .05).60^2 + (.30 - .05).20^2 - .30(-.0240)}$$
$$= .6818$$
$$w_B = 1 - w_A = .3182$$

The expected return and standard deviation of the optimal risky portfolio are

$$E(r_P) = .6818 \times .10 + .3182 \times .30 = .1636$$
$$\sigma_P = [.6818^2 \times .20^2 + .3182^2 \times .60^2 + 2 \times .6818 \times .3182(-.0240)]^{1/2}$$
$$= .2113$$

Note that in this case the standard deviation of the optimal risky portfolio is smaller than the standard deviation of fund *A*. Note also that portfolio *P* is not the global minimum variance portfolio. The proportions of the latter are given by

$$w_A = [.60^2 - (-.0240)] \div [.60^2 + .20^2 - 2(-.0240)] = .8571$$
$$w_B = 1 - w_A = .1429$$

With these proportions, the standard deviation of the minimum variance portfolio is

$$\sigma(\text{min}) = [.8571^2 \times .20^2 + .1429^2 \times .60^2 + 2 \times .8571 \times .1429 \times (-.0240)]^{1/2}$$
$$= .1757$$

which is smaller than that of the optimal risky portfolio.

c. The CAL is the line from the risk-free rate through the optimal risky portfolio. This line represents all efficient portfolios that combine T-bills with the optimal risky portfolio. The slope of the CAL is

$$S = [E(r_P) - r_f]/\sigma_P$$
$$= (.1636 - .05)/.2113 = .5376$$

d. Given a degree of risk aversion, A, an investor will choose a proportion, y, in the optimal risky portfolio of

$$y = [E(r_P) - r_f]/(A\sigma_P^2)$$
$$= (.1636 - .05)/(5 \times .2113^2) = .5089$$

This means that the optimal risky portfolio, with the given data, is
attractive enough for an investor with $A = 5$ to invest 50.89 percent of
his or her wealth in it. Since fund A makes up 68.18 percent of the
risky portfolio and fund B 31.82 percent, the investment proportions
for this investor are

Fund A: $.5089 \times 68.18 = 34.70\%$
Fund B: $.5089 \times 31.82 = \underline{16.19\%}$

TOTAL   50.89%

4. Efficient frontiers derived by portfolio managers depend on forecasts of
   the rates of return on various securities and estimates of risk, that is, the
   covariance matrix. The forecasts themselves do not control outcomes.
   Thus, preferring managers with rosier forecasts (northwesterly frontiers)
   is tantamount to rewarding the bearers of good news and punishing the
   bearers of bad news. What we should do is reward bearers of *accurate*
   news. Thus, if you get a glimpse of the frontiers (forecasts) of portfolio
   managers on a regular basis, what you want to do is develop the track
   record of their forecasting accuracy and steer your advisees toward the
   more accurate forecaster. Their portfolio choices will, in the long run,
   outperform the field.

5. Portfolios that lie on the CAL are combinations of the tangency (risky)
   portfolio and the risk-free asset. Hence they are just as dependent on the
   accuracy of the efficient frontier as portfolios that are on the frontier
   itself. If we judge forecasting accuracy by the accuracy of the reward-to-
   volatility ratio, then all portfolios on a CAL will be exactly as accurate as
   the tangency portfolio.

A.1 The parameters are $E(r) = .15$, $\sigma = .60$, and the correlation between
   any pair of stocks is $\rho = .5$.

a. The portfolio expected return is invariant to the size of the portfolio
   because all stocks have identical expected returns. The standard
   deviation of a portfolio with $n = 25$ stocks is

$$\sigma_P = [\sigma^2(1/n) + \rho \times \sigma^2(n - 1)/n]^{1/2}$$
$$= [.60^2/25 + .5 \times .60^2 \times 24/25]^{1/2} = .4327$$

b. Because the stocks are identical, efficient portfolios are equally
   weighted. To obtain a standard deviation of 43 percent, we need to
   solve for n:

$$.43^2 = .60^2/n + .5 \times .60^2(n - 1)/n$$
$$.1849n = .3600 + .1800n - .1800$$
$$n = \frac{.1800}{.0049} = 36.73$$

Thus, we need 37 stocks and will come in slightly under the target.

c. As n gets very large, the variance of an efficient (equally weighted) portfolio diminishes, leaving only the variance that comes from the covariances among stocks, that is

$$\sigma_P = \sqrt{\rho \times \sigma^2} = \sqrt{.5 \times .60^2} = .4243$$

Note that with 25 stocks we came within 84 basis points of the systematic risk, that is, the non-systematic risk of a portfolio of 25 stocks is 84 basis points. With 37 stocks the standard deviation is .4300, of which non-systematic risk is 57 basis points.

d. If the risk-free rate is 10 percent, then the risk premium on any size portfolio is $15 - 10 = 5$ percent. The standard deviation of a well-diversified portfolio is (practically) 42.43 percent; hence the slope of the CAL is

$$S = 5/42.43 = .1178$$

III *Equilibrium in Capital Markets*

Chapter 8—The Capital Asset Pricing Model

1. We can characterize the entire population by two representative investors. One is the "uninformed" investor, who does not engage in security analysis and holds the market portfolio, whereas the other optimizes using the Markowitz algorithm with input from security analysis. The uninformed investor does not know what input the informed investor uses to make portfolio purchases. The uninformed investor knows, however, that if the other investor is informed the market portfolio proportions will be optimal. Therefore, to depart from these proportions would constitute an uninformed bet, which will, on average, reduce the efficiency of diversification with no compensating improvement in expected returns.

2. a. Substituting the historical mean and standard deviation in equation 8.2 yields a coefficient of risk aversion of

$$\bar{A} = \frac{E(r_M) - r_f}{\sigma_M^2} = \frac{.0294}{.175^2} = .96$$

b. This relationship also tells us that for the historical standard deviation and a coefficient of risk aversion of 1.5 the risk premium would be

$$E(r_M) - r_f = \bar{A}\sigma_M^2 = 1.5 \times .175^2 = .0459 \ (4.59\%)$$

3. $\beta_I = \beta_{NOR} = 1.15$. Therefore, whatever the investment proportions, w_I, w_{NOR}, the portfolio β, which is

$$\beta_P = w_I\beta_I + w_{NOR}\beta_{NOR}$$

will equal 1.15.

As the market risk premium, $E(r_M) - r_f$, is .08, the portfolio risk premium will be

$$E(r_P) - r_f = \beta_P[E(r_M) - r_f]$$
$$= 1.15 \times .08 = .092$$

4. The alpha of a stock is its expected return in excess of that required by the CAPM.

$$\alpha = E(r) - [r_f + \beta[E(r_M) - r_f]]$$
$$\alpha_{XYZ} = .12 - [.05 + 1.0(.11 - .05)] = .01$$
$$\alpha_{ABC} = .13 - [.05 + 1.5(.11 - .05)] = -.01$$

ABC plots below the SML, while *XYZ* plots above.

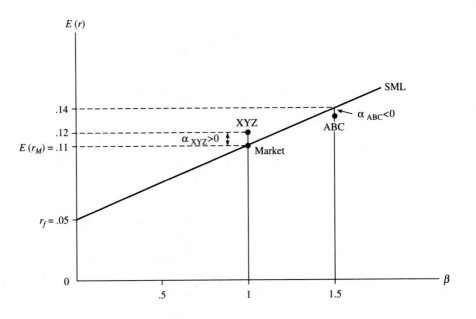

5. The project-specific required expected return is determined by the project beta coupled with the market risk premium and the risk-free rate. The CAPM tells us that an acceptable expected rate of return for the project is

$$E(r_f) + \beta[E(r_M) - r_f] = 8 + 1.3(12 - 8) = 13.2\%$$

which becomes the project's hurdle rate. If the IRR of the project is 15 percent, then it is desirable. Any project with an IRR equal to or less than 13.2 percent should be rejected.

6. If the basic CAPM holds, any zero-beta asset must be expected to earn on average the risk-free rate. Hence the posited performance of the zero-beta portfolio violates the simple CAPM. It does not, however, violate the zero-beta CAPM. Since we know that borrowing restrictions do exist, we expect the zero-beta version of the model is more likely to hold, with the zero-beta rate differing from the virtually risk-free T-bill rate.

A1. In George's original position, the portfolio is divided equally between risky portfolio P [with $E(r_P) = .15$, $\sigma = .25$] and T-bills (with $r_f = .07$). The complete portfolio has expected return and standard deviation:

$$E(r) = .50 \times .15 + .50 \times .07 = .11$$
$$\sigma = .50 \times .25 = .125$$

In the hedging strategy, energy price risk is offset by holdings of Oilex stock. Of the portfolio, 50 percent remains in the risky portfolio P, 13.64 percent is placed in Oilex (which is assumed to be uncorrelated with P and has expected return .07), and 36.36 percent is left in bills. Therefore

$$E(r) = .50 \times .15 + .1364 \times .07 + .3636 \times .07 = .11$$
$$\sigma^2 = .50^2 \times .25^2 + .1364^2 \times .22^2 = .0165$$
$$\sigma = .1286$$

George's hedge strategy portfolio has the same expected return as the original portfolio, but a higher standard deviation. Hence it cannot be mean-variance efficient with respect to portfolio rates of return. Nevertheless, the hedge strategy is an improvement over the original position because more than rate of return is important here. George cares about energy prices as well as about his portfolio value, and he must hedge both sources of risk.

A2. Since the beta of the one-factor CAPM measures the sensitivity of portfolio returns to the market return, and ignores other hedging motives, it will be inadequate as a complete description of security risk in this more general context.

A3. The security will be held *short* in the hedge portfolio. The extra hedge demand, therefore, will drive down demand for the security and will drive up its expected rate of return relative to the simple CAPM.

A4. *a.* For Alberta residents, the stock is not a hedge. When their economy does poorly (low oil prices) the stock also does poorly, thereby aggravating their problems.

b. For Toronto residents, the stock is a hedge. When energy prices increase, the stock will provide greater wealth with which to purchase energy.

c. If energy consumers (who are willing to bid up the price of the stock for its hedge value) dominate the economy, then high oil–beta stocks will have low expected rates of return.

A5. Although people will want to hedge this source of risk, the lack of correlation between security returns and the risk factor will make such hedging impossible. Because security returns are uncorrelated with the

risk factor, the securities cannot serve to offset the uncertainty surrounding that factor. Hence there is no reason for investors to tilt their
portfolios toward or away from any security for hedging in connection
with the factor.

Chapter 9—Index Models and the Arbitrage Pricing Theory

1. The variance of each stock is $\beta^2\sigma_M^2 + \sigma^2(e)$.
For stock A, we obtain

$$\sigma_A^2 = .9^2(.20)^2 + .3^2 = .1224$$
$$\sigma_A = .35$$

For stock B,

$$\sigma_B^2 = 1.1^2(.20)^2 + .1^2 = .0584$$
$$\sigma_B = .24$$

The covariance is

$$\beta_A\beta_B\sigma_M^2 = .9 \times 1.1 \times .2^2 = .0396$$

2.
$$\sigma^2(e_P) = (\tfrac{1}{2})^2[\sigma^2(e_A) + \sigma^2(e_B)]$$
$$= \tfrac{1}{4}(.3^2 + .1^2)$$
$$= \tfrac{1}{4}(.09 + .01)$$
$$= .025$$

Therefore

$$\sigma(e_P) = .158$$

3. Burns Fry's alpha is related to the CAPM alpha by

$$\alpha_{BF} = \alpha_{CAPM} + (1 - \beta)r_f$$

For Seagram's, $\alpha_{BF} = .36\%$, $\beta = .85$, and we are told that r_f was .8%.
Thus

$$\alpha_{CAPM} = .36 - (1 - .85).8$$
$$= .24\%$$

Seagram's still performed well relative to the market and the index
model. It beat its "benchmark" return by an average of .24 percent per
month.

4. The least profitable scenario currently yields a profit of $10,000 and
gross proceeds from the equally weighted portfolio of $700,000. As the
price of Dreck falls, less of the equally weighted portfolio can be purchased from the proceeds of the short sale. When Dreck's price falls by
more than a factor of 10,000/700,000, arbitrage no longer will be feasible,
because the profits in the worst state will be driven below zero.

To see this, suppose that Dreck's price falls to $10 \times (1 - \frac{1}{70})$. The
short sale of 300,000 shares now yields $2,957,142, which allows dollar
investments of only $985,714 in each of the other shares. In the high real
interest rate—low inflation scenario, profits will be driven to zero:

Stock	Dollar Investment	Rate of Return	Dollar Return
Apex	$985,714	.20	197,143
Bull	985,714	.70	690,000
Crush	985,714	−.20	−197,143
Dreck	−2,957,142	.23	−690,000
TOTAL	0		0

At any price for Dreck stock *below* $10 × (1 − 1/70) = $9.857, profits are negative, which means this arbitrage opportunity is eliminated. (*Note:* $9.857 is not the equilibrium price of Dreck. It is simply the upper bound on Dreck's price that rules out the simple arbitrage opportunity.)

5. $\sigma(e_P) = \sqrt{\sigma^2(e_i)/n}$

   a. $\sqrt{30/10} = 1.732\%$

   b. $\sqrt{30/100} = .548\%$

   c. $\sqrt{30/1,000} = .173\%$

   d. $\sqrt{30/10,000} = .055\%$

   We conclude that non-systematic volatility can be driven to arbitrarily low levels in well-diversified portfolios.

6. A portfolio consisting of two thirds of portfolio *A* and one third of the risk-free asset will have the same beta as portfolio *E*, but an expected return of (1/3 × 4 + 2/3 × 10) = 8 percent, less than that of portfolio *E*. Therefore, one can earn arbitrage profits by shorting the combination of portfolio *A* and the safe asset, and buying portfolio *E*.

7. *a.* For portfolio *P*,

$$K = \frac{E(r_P) - r_f}{\beta_P} = \frac{.10 - .05}{.5} = .10$$

For portfolio *Q*,

$$K = \frac{.15 - .05}{1} = .10$$

   b. The equally weighted portfolio has an expected return of 12.5 percent and a beta of .75. $K = (.125 − .05)/.75 = .10$.

8. *a.* Total market capitalization is 3000 + 1940 + 1360 = 6300. Therefore the mean excess return of the index portfolio is

$$\frac{3000}{6300} \times .10 + \frac{1940}{6300} \times .02 + \frac{1360}{6300} \times .17 = .10$$

   b. The covariance between stock *A* and the index portfolio equals,

$$\text{Cov}(R_A, R_M) = \beta_A \sigma_M^2 = .1 \times .25^2 = .0625$$

   c. The variance of *B* equals

$$\sigma_B^2 = \text{Var}(\beta_B R_M + e_B) = \beta_B^2 \sigma_M^2 + \sigma^2(e_B)$$

   Thus, the firm specific variance of *B* equals

$$\sigma_B^2 - \beta_B^2 \sigma_M^2 = .30^2 - .2^2 \times .25^2 = .0875$$

9. The CAPM is a model that relates expected rates of return to risk. It results in the expected return-beta relationship where the expected excess return on any asset is proportional to the expected excess return on the market portfolio with beta as the proportionality constant. As such the model is impractical for two reasons: (a) expectations are unobservable, and (b) the theoretical market portfolio includes every publicly traded risky asset and is in practice unobservable. The next three models incorporate assumptions that overcome these problems.

The single factor APT model assumes that one economic factor, denoted F, exerts the only common influence on security returns. Beyond it, security returns are driven by independent, firm-specific factors. Thus, for any security i,

$$r_i = a_i + b_iF + e_i$$

The single index model assumes that in the single factor model, the factor, F, is perfectly correlated with and therefore can be replaced by a broad-based index of securities that can proxy for the CAPM's theoretical market portfolio.

At this point is should be said that many interchange the meaning of the index and market models. The concept of the market model is that rate of return surprises on a stock are proportional to corresponding surprises on the market index portfolio, again with proportionality constant β.

10. Using equation 9.18, the expected return is $.04 + .2(.06) + 1.4(.08) = .164$.

Chapter 10—International Diversification

1. The graph would asymptote to a lower level, as shown in the following figure on page 975, reflecting the improved opportunities for diversification. However, there still would remain a positive level of non-diversifiable risk.

2. $1 + r(\text{Cdn}) = [(1 + r_f(\text{UK})] \times (E_1/E_0)$
   a. $1 + r(\text{Cdn}) = 1.1 \times 1.0 = 1.10$ $r(\text{Cdn}) = 10\%$
   b. $1 + r(\text{Cdn}) = 1.1 \times 1.1 = 1.21$ $r(\text{Cdn}) = 21\%$

3. You must sell forward the number of pounds that you will end up with at the end of the year. However, this value cannot be known with certainty unless the rate of return of the pound-denominated investment is known.
   a. $10,000 \times 1.20 = 12,000$ pounds
   b. $10,000 \times 1.30 = 13,000$ pounds

4. *Country selection:*

$$(.40 \times .10) + (.20 \times .05) + (.40 \times .15) = .11$$

This is a loss of .015 (1.5 percent) relative to the EAFE passive benchmark.

Currency selection:

$$(.40 \times 1.10) + (.20 \times .9) + (.40 \times 1.30) = 1.14$$

This is a los of 6 percent relative to the EAFE benchmark.

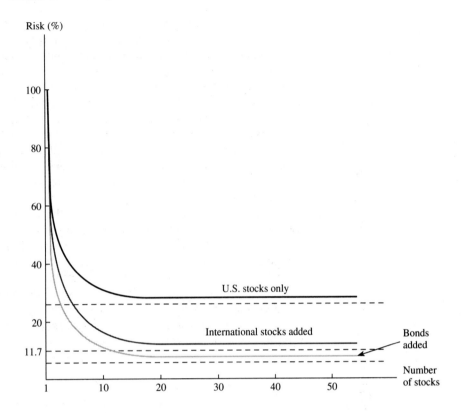

Risk (%)

100

80

60

40

20

11.7

U.S. stocks only

International stocks added

Bonds added

Number of stocks

1   10   20   30   40   50

Chapter 11—*Empirical Evidence on Security Returns*

1. The SCL is estimated for each stock; hence we need to estimate 100 equations. Our sample consists of 60 monthly rates of return for each of the 100 stocks and for the market index. Thus, each regression is estimated with 60 observations. Equation 11.1 in the text shows that when stated in excess return form, the SCL should pass through the origin, that is, have a zero intercept.

2. When the SML has a positive intercept and its slope is less than the mean excess return on the market portfolio, it is flatter than predicted by the CAPM. Low beta stocks therefore have yielded returns that, on average, were more than they should have been on the basis of their beta. Conversely, high beta stocks were found to have yielded, on average, less than they should have on the basis of their betas.

3. The intercept of the SML was .00359 (36 basis points) instead of zero as it should have been according to the simple CAPM. Equation 11.5 in the text shows that if the zero-beta version of the CAPM is valid because of restrictions on borrowing, and the SCL and SML are estimated from excess returns over the risk-free rate (rather than over the zero-beta rate), then the intercept will be the difference between the zero-beta rate and the risk-free rate. Thus, if BJS had found that the average risk premium of

the zero-beta portfolio was 36 basis points (per month), the zero-beta version of the CAPM would have been supported. Similarly, the slope of the estimated SML should equal the difference between the market mean return and that of the zero-beta portfolio. The market index risk premium averaged 1.42 percent per month, and the slope of the SML was estimated as 1.08 percent. Here, a risk premium of 34 basis points would have supported the zero-beta version of the CAPM.

4. A positive coefficient on beta-squared would indicate that the relationship between risk and return is nonlinear. High beta securities would provide expected returns more than proportional to risk. A positive coefficient on $\sigma(e)$ would indicate that firm-specific risk affects expected return, a direct contradiction of the CAPM and APT.

5. It is very difficult to identify the portfolios that serve to hedge systematic sources of risk to future consumption opportunities. Both lines of research explore the data in search of such portfolios. Factor analysis techniques indicate the portfolios that may be providing hedge services. Researchers can then try to figure out what the source of risk is and show how important it is. The second line of attack attempts to use theoretical arguments to guess at the identity of economic variables that may be correlated with consumption risk and then determines whether these variables do indeed explain rates of return.

IV *Active Portfolio Management*

Chapter 12—Market Efficiency

1. The information sets that pertain to the weak, semistrong, and strong form of the EMH can be described by the following illustration:

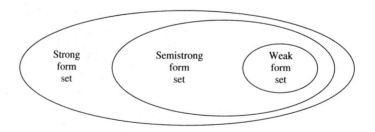

The weak-form information set includes only the history of prices and volumes. The semistrong-form set includes the weak-form set *plus* all publicly available information. In turn, the strong-form set includes the semistrong set *plus* insiders' information. It is illegal to act on the incremental information (insiders' private information). The direction of *valid* implication is

Strong-form EMH $\Rightarrow$ Semistrong-form EMH $\Rightarrow$ Weak-form EMH

The reverse direction implication is *not* valid. For example, stock prices may reflect all past price data (weak-form efficiency) but may not reflect relevant fundamental data (semistrong-form inefficiency).

2. If *everyone* follows a passive strategy, sooner or later prices will fail to reflect new information. At this point there are profit opportunities for active investors who uncover mispriced securities. As they buy and sell these assets, prices again will be driven to fair levels.

3. Predictably declining CARs do violate the EMH. If one can predict such a phenomenon, a profit opportunity emerges: sell (or short sell) the affected stocks on an event date just before their prices are predicted to fall.

4. The answer depends on your prior beliefs about market efficiency. Magellan's record has been incredibly strong. On the other hand, with so many funds in existence, it is less surprising that *some* fund would appear to be consistently superior after the fact. The answer really depends more on faith than inference.

5. If profit opportunities can be made, one would expect mutual funds specializing in small stocks to spring into existence. Moreover, one wonders why buyers of small stocks do not compete for those stocks in December and bid up their prices before the January rise.

6. Concern over the deficit was an ongoing issue in 1987. No significant *new* information concerning the deficit was released on October 19. Hence this explanation for the crash is not consistent with the EMH.

Chapter 13—*Portfolio Performance Evaluation*

1.

Time	Action	Cash Flow
0	Buy two shares	−40
1	Collect dividends; then sell one of the shares	4 + 22
2	Collect dividend on remaining share, then sell it	2 + 19

a. Dollar-weighted return:

$$-40 + \frac{26}{1 + r} + \frac{21}{(1 + r)^2} = 0$$
$$r = .1191 = 11.91\%$$

b. Time-weighted return:
  The rates of return on the stock in the two years were

$$r_1 = \frac{2 + (22 - 20)}{20} = .20$$
$$r_2 = \frac{2 + (19 - 22)}{22} = -.045$$
$$(r_1 + r_2)/2 = .077, \text{ or } 7.7\%$$

2. *a.* $E(r_A) = [.15 + (-.05)]/2 = .05$
$\qquad E(r_G) = [(1.15)(.95)]^{1/2} - 1 = .045$
$\quad$ *b.* The expected stock price is $(115 + 95)/2 = 105$
$\quad$ *c.* The expected rate of return on the stock is 5 percent, equal to r_A.

3. Sharpe: $(\bar{r} - \bar{r}_f)/\sigma$

$$S_P = (.35 - .06)/.42 = .69$$
$$S_M = (.28 - .06)/.30 = .733$$

Alpha: $\bar{r} - [r_f + \beta(\bar{r}_M - \bar{r}_f)]$

$$\alpha_P = .35 - [.06 + 1.2(.28 - .06)] = .026$$
$$\alpha_M = 0$$

Treynor: $(\bar{r} - \bar{r}_f)/\beta$

$$T_P = (.35 - .06)/1.2 = .242$$
$$T_M = (.28 - .06)/1.0 = .22$$

Appraisal ratio: $\alpha/\sigma(e)$

$$A_P = .026/.18 = .144$$
$$A_M = 0$$

4. The t-statistic on α is $.2/2 = .1$. The probability that a manager with a true alpha of zero could obtain a sample period alpha with a t-statistic of .1 or better by pure luck can be calculated approximately from a table of the normal distribution. The probability is 46 percent.

Chapter 14—The Theory of Active Portfolio Management

1. We show the answer for the annual compounded rate of return for each strategy and leave you to compute the monthly rate.

Beginning-of-period fund:

$$F_0 = \$1,000$$

End-of-period fund for each strategy:

$$F_1 = \begin{cases} 3,600 & \text{Strategy = Bills only} \\ 67,500 & \text{Strategy = Market only} \\ 5,360,000,000 & \text{Strategy = Perfect timing} \end{cases}$$

Number of periods: $N = 52$ years
Annual compounded rate:

$$[1 + r_A]^N = \frac{F_1}{F_0}$$

$$r_A = \left(\frac{F_1}{F_0}\right)^{1/N} - 1$$

$$r_A = \begin{cases} 2.49\% & \text{Strategy = Bills only} \\ 8.44\% & \text{Strategy = Market only} \\ 34.71\% & \text{Strategy = Perfect timing} \end{cases}$$

2. The timer will guess bear or bull markets completely randomly. One half of all bull markets will be preceded by a correct forecast, and similarly for bear markets. Hence, $P_1 + P_2 - 1 = \frac{1}{2} + \frac{1}{2} - 1 = 0$.

3. *a.* When short positions are prohibited, the analysis is identical except that negative alpha stocks are dropped from the list. In that case, the sum of the ratios of alpha to residual variance for the remaining two stocks is .7895. This leads to the new composition of the active portfolio:

$$x_1 = .3457/.7895 = .4379$$
$$x_2 = .4438/.7895 = .5621$$

The alpha, beta, and residual standard deviation of the active portfolio are now:

$$\alpha_A = .4379 \times .07 + .5621 \times .03 = .0475$$
$$\beta_A = .4379 \times 1.6 + .5621 \times .5 = .9817$$
$$\sigma(e_A) = [.4379^2 \times .45^2 + .5621^2 \times .26^2]^{1/2} = .2453$$

The cost of the short sale restriction is already apparent. The alpha has shrunk from 20.56 percent to 4.75 percent, while the reduction in the residual risk is more moderate, from 82.62 percent to 24.53 percent. In fact, a negative alpha stock is potentially more attractive than a positive alpha one: since most stocks are positively correlated, the negative position that is required for the negative alpha stock creates a better diversified active portfolio.

The optimal allocation of the new active portfolio is:

$$w_0 = \frac{.0475/.6019}{.08/.04} = .3946$$
$$w^* = \frac{.3946}{1 + (1 - .9817) \times .3946} = .3918$$

Here, too, the beta correction is essentially irrelevant because the portfolio beta is so close to 1.0.

Finally, the performance of the overall risky portfolio is estimated at

$$S_P^2 = .16 + \left[\frac{.0475}{.2453}\right]^2 = .1975; \; S_P = .44$$

It is clear that in this we have lost about half of the original improvement in the Sharpe measure. Note, however, that this is an artifact of the small coverage of the security analysis division. When more stocks are covered, then a good number of positive alpha stocks will keep the residual risk of the active portfolio low. This is the key to extracting large gains from the active strategy.

b. When the forecast for the market index portfolio is more optimistic, the position in the active portfolio will be smaller and the contribution of the active portfolio to the Sharpe measure of the risky portfolio will be of a smaller magnitude. In the original example the allocation to the active portfolio would be

$$w_0 = \frac{.2056/.6826}{.12/.04} = .1004$$

$$w^* = \frac{.1004}{1 + (1 - .9519) \times .1004} = .0999$$

Although the Sharpe measure of the market is now better, the improvement derived from security analysis is smaller:

$$S_P^2 = \left(\frac{.12}{.20}\right)^2 + \left(\frac{.2056}{.8262}\right)^2 = .4219$$

$$S_P = .65; \; S_M = .60$$

V *Fixed-Income Securities*

Chapter 15—Bond Prices and Yields

1. At a semiannual interest rate of 3 percent, the bond is worth $40 \times PA(3$ percent, 60$) + \$1,000 \times PF(3$ percent, 60$) = \$1,276.75$, which results in a capital gain of \$276.75. This exceeds the capital loss of \$189.29 (\$1,000 − \$810.71) when the interest rate increased to 5 percent.

2. Yield to maturity exceeds current yield, which exceeds coupon rate. An example is the 8 percent coupon bond with a yield to maturity of 10 percent per year (5 percent per half-year). Its price is \$810.71, and therefore its current yield is 80/810.77 = .0987 or 9.87 percent, which is higher than the coupon rate but lower than the yield to maturity.

3. Price $= \$35 \times PA(4$ percent, 4$) + \$1,000 \times PF(4$ percent, 4$) = \$981.85$

$$\text{Rate of return to investor} = \frac{\$35 + (\$981.85 - \$977.74)}{\$977.74} = .040 \text{ or } 4.0\%$$

4. It should receive a negative coefficient. A high ratio of liabilities to assets is a poor omen for a firm that should lower its credit rating.

5. The bond with the 6 percent coupon rate currently sells for $30 \times PA(3.5$ percent, 20$) + 1,000 \times PF(3.5$ percent, 20$) = \$928.94$. If the interest rate immediately drops to 6 percent (3 percent per half-year), the bond price will rise to \$1,000, for a capital gain of \$71.06, or 7.65 percent. The 8 percent coupon bond currently sells for \$1,071.06. If the interest rate falls to 6 percent, the present value of the *scheduled* payments increases to \$1,148.77. However, the bond will be called at \$1,100, for a capital gain of only \$28.94, or 2.70 percent.

6. The premium bond should offer a higher promised yield in compensation for its greater susceptibility to being called.

Chapter 16—The Term Structure of Interest Rates

1. The bond sells today for $683.18 (from Table 16.2). Next year, it will sell for $1,000 ÷ [(1.10)(1.11)(1.11)] = $737.84, for a return $1 + r$ = 737.84/683.18 = 1.08, or 8 percent.

2. The data pertaining to the T-bill imply that the six-month interest rate is $300/$9,700 = .03093, or 3.093 percent. To obtain the forward rate, we look at the one-year T-bond: The pricing formula

$$1,000 = \frac{40}{1.03093} + \frac{1040}{(1.03093)(1 + f)}$$

implies that f = .04952, or 4.952 percent.

3. 9 percent.

4. The risk premium will be zero.

5. If issuers wish to issue long-term bonds, they will be willing to accept higher expected interest costs on long bonds over short bonds. This willingness combines with investors' demands for higher rates on long-term bonds to reinforce the tendency toward a positive liquidity premium.

6. If r_4 equaled 9.66 percent, then the four-year bond would sell for $1,000/[(1.08)(1.10)(1.11)(1.0966)] = $691.53. The yield to maturity would satisfy the equation $691.53(1 + y_4)^4$ = 1,000, or y_4 = 9.66 percent. At a lower value of r_4, the bond would sell for a higher price and offer a lower yield. At a higher value of r_4, the yield would be greater.

7.

Time	Cash Flow	Discount Factor	Present Value
1	120	1.08	111.11
2	120	(1.08)(1.10)	101.01
3	1,120	(1.08)(1.10)(1.11)	849.33
			1,061.45

The bond will sell for $1061.45, and so offer a conventional yield to maturity satisfying:

$$\$1061.45 = \$120 \times PA(y, 3) + 1000 \times PF(y, 3)$$

or y = 9.55 percent. The realized compound yield is determined from the accumulated future value of all reinvested coupons

Time	Cash Flow	Growth Factor	Future Value
1	120	(1.10)(1.11)	146.52
2	120	(1.11)	133.20
3	1,120	1	1,120.00
			1,399.72

The realized compound yield is the solution to

$$1061.45 \times (1 + y)^3 = 1399.72$$

so that $y = 9.66$ percent.

Chapter 17—Fixed-Income Portfolio Management

1. The duration of a level perpetuity is $(1 + y)/y$ or $1 + 1/y$, which clearly falls as y increases. Tabulating duration as a function of r we get

y	D
.01	101 years
.02	51
.05	21
.10	11
.20	6
.25	5
.40	3.5

2. Potential gains and losses are proportional to both duration *and* portfolio size. The dollar loss on a fixed-income portfolio resulting from an increase in the portfolio's yield to maturity is, from equation 17.2, $D \times P \times \Delta y/(1 + y)$, where P is the initial market value of the portfolio. Hence $D \times P$ must be equated for immunization.

3. The perpetuity's duration now would be $1.08/.08 = 13.5$. We need to solve the following equation for w:

$$w \times 2 + (1 - w) \times 13.5 = 6$$

Therefore, $w = .6522$

4. Dedication would be more attractive. Cash flow matching eliminates the need for rebalancing and thus saves transaction costs.

5. The 30-year 8 percent coupon bond will provide a stream of coupons of $40 per half-year, which invested at the assumed rate of 4 percent per half-year will accumulate to $480.24. The bond will sell in five years at a price equal to $40 × PA(4.25 percent, 50) + $1,000 × PF(4.25 percent, 50), or $948.52, for a capital gain of $51.71. The total five-year income is $51.71 + $480.24 = $531.95, for a five-year return of $531.95/$896.81 = .5932, or 59.32 percent. Based on this scenario, the 20-year 10 percent coupon bond offers a higher return for a five-year horizon.

6. The trigger point is $10M/(1.12)^3 = $7.118M$.

7. The fund has long-term liabilities and short-term assets. If interest rates fall, it will suffer, as the value of the liabilities will rise by more than the value of the assets. To offset this duration mismatch, the fund should swap an obligation to make variable rate payments in return for receipt of fixed cash flows. The swap gives the fund a long-term asset and a short-term liability.

VI *Equities*

Chapter 18—Security Analysis

1. *a.* Dividend yield = $2.15/50 = 4.3 percent
Capital gains yield = (59.77 − 50)/50 = 19.54 percent
Total return = 4.3 percent + 19.54 percent = 23.84 percent
b. k = 6 percent + 1.15 (14 percent − 6 percent) = 15.2 percent
c. V_0 = ($2.15 + $59.77)/1.152 = $53.75, which exceeds the market price. This would indicate a "buy" opportunity.

2. *a.* $E(D_1)/(k − g)$ = $2.15/(.152 − .112) = $53.75
b. $E(P_1) = P_0(1 + g)$ = $53.75(1.112) = $59.77
c. The expected capital gain equals $59.77 − $53.75 = $6.02, for a percentage gain of 11.2 percent. The dividend yield is $E(D_1)/P_0$ = $2.15/53.75 = 4 percent, for an HPR of 4 percent + 11.2 percent = 15.2 percent.

3. The payout and plowback ratios are complementary fractions of earnings; their sum is unity.

4. *a.*
$$g = ROE \times b = .20 \times .60 = .12$$
$$D_1 = (1 − b)E_1 = (1 − .60) \times \$5 = \$2$$
$$P_0 = D_1/(k − g) = \$2/(.125 − .12) = \$400$$
b.
$$g = .10 \times .60 = .06$$
$$P_0 = \$2/(.125 − .06) = \$30.77$$

or, with $g = b = 0$,

$$P_0 = D_1/k = E_1/k = \$5/.125 = \$40$$

5. *a.* The cash flow diagram is:

t	0	1	2	3	4 . . .
D_t	$2.00	$2.20	$2.42	$2.662	$2.76848 . . .

The estimated price at t = 3 is

$$P_3 = \frac{D_4}{k − g} = \frac{\$2.76848}{.12 − .04} = \$34.606$$

The current price should be the PV of dividends in years 1 through 3 plus the PV of P_3.

$$P_0 = \frac{\$2.20}{1.12} + \frac{\$2.42}{1.12^2} + \frac{\$2.662 + 34.606}{1.12^3} = \$30.42$$

b. The expected price one year from now is the PV of dividends in years 2 and 3 plus the PV of P_3:

$$P_1 = \frac{\$2.42}{1.12} + \frac{\$2.662 + 34.606}{1.12^2} = \$31.87$$

c. The expected dividend yield is $\$2.20/\$30.42 = .0723$, or 7.23 percent. The expected rate of capital appreciation is $\dfrac{\$31.87 - 30.42}{\$30.42} = .0477$ or 4.77 percent. Note that they sum to k, or 12 percent.

6. *a.*
$$
\begin{aligned}
V_0 &= \frac{D_0(1 + g_n)}{k - g_n} + \frac{D_0 H(g_a - g_n)}{k - g_n} \\
&= \frac{2(1.06)}{.12 - .06} + \frac{2 \times 10(.35 - .06)}{.12 - .06} \\
&= 35.333 + 96.667 \\
&= \$132
\end{aligned}
$$

b.
$$
\begin{aligned}
y &= \frac{D_0}{P_0}[(1 + g_n) + H(g_a - g_n)] + g_n \\
&= \frac{2}{100}[(1.06) + 10(.35 - .06)] + .06 \\
&= .1392, \text{ or } 13.92\% \text{ per year}
\end{aligned}
$$

7. *a.* ROE = 12%
$b = \$.50/\$2 = .25$
$g = \text{ROE} \times b = 12\% \times .25 = 3\%$
$P_0 = D_1/(k - g) = \$1.50/(.10 - .03) = \$21.43$
$P_0/E(E_1) = \$21.43/\$2 = 10.71$

b. If $b = .4$, then $.4 \times \$2 = \$.80$ would be reinvested and the remainder of earnings, or \$1.20, paid as dividends.

$$
\begin{aligned}
g &= 12\% \times .4 = 4.8\% \\
P_0 &= E(D_1)/(k - g) = \$1.20/(.10 - .048) = \$23.08 \\
P_0/E(E_1) &= \$23.08/\$2.00 = 11.54
\end{aligned}
$$

8. *a.*
$$P_0 = \frac{(1 - b)E(E_1)}{k - g} = \frac{.6 \times \$1}{.1 - .04} = \$10$$

b.
$$\frac{E(D_1^*)}{P_0} = \frac{(1 - b)E(E_1^*)}{P_0} = \frac{(1 - .4) \times \$1}{\$10} = .06, \text{ or } 6 \text{ percent per year}$$

The rate of price appreciation $= g^* = b^* \times \text{ROE}^* = 4$ percent per year

c. i. $g = (1.04)(1.06) - 1 = 1.024$, or 10.24 percent;

ii. $\dfrac{E(D_1)}{P_0} = \dfrac{E(D_1^*)(1 + i)}{P_0} = .06 \times 1.06 = .0636$, or 6.36 percent

iii. ROE = 16.6 percent

iv. $b = \dfrac{g}{\text{ROE}} = \dfrac{.1024}{.166} = .6169$

9. With fixed costs of $2 million and variable costs of $1.5 million, firm C has variable costs of $7.5, $9, and $10.5 million in each scenario; the corresponding total costs are $9.5, $11, and $12.5 million. Thus, the profits for firm C are $.5, $1, and $1.5 million under recession, normal, and expansion scenarios. We conclude that the higher the operating leverage, the higher is the resulting business risk; operating leverage increases the sensitivity of operating income to economic conditions.

Chapter 19—Financial Statement Analysis

1. A debt/equity ratio of 1 implies that Mordett will have $50 million of debt and $50 million of equity. Interest expense will be .09 × $50 million, or $4.5 million per year. Mordett's net profits and ROE over the business cycle will, therefore, be

		Nodett		Mordett	
Scenario	EBIT	Net profits	ROE	Net profits[a]	ROE[b]
Bad year	$5M	$3 million	3%	$.3 million	.6%
Normal year	10M	6	6%	3.3	6.6%
Good year	15M	9	9%	6.3	12.6%

[a] Mordett's after-tax profits are given by: .6(EBIT − $4.5 million).
[b] Mordett's equity is only $50 million.

2.

		Ratio Decomposition Analysis for Mordett Corporation					
		(1) Net profit / Pretax profit	(2) Pretax profit / EBIT	(3) EBIT / Sales	(4) Sales / Assets	(5) Assets / Equity	(6) Combined leverage factor
	ROE			(ROS)	(ATO)		(2) × (5)
a. *Bad year*							
Nodett	.030	.6	1.000	.0625	.800	1.000	1.000
Somdett	.018	.6	.360	.0625	.800	1.667	.600
Mordett	.006	.6	.100	.0625	.800	2.000	.200
b. *Normal year*							
Nodett	.060	.6	1.000	.100	1.000	1.000	1.000
Somdett	.068	.6	.680	.100	1.000	1.667	1.134
Mordett	.066	.6	.550	.100	1.000	2.000	1.100
c. *Good year*							
Nodett	.090	.6	1.000	.125	1.200	1.000	1.000
Somdett	.118	.6	.787	.125	1.200	1.667	1.311
Mordett	.126	.6	.700	.125	1.200	2.000	1.400

3. GI's ROE in 19X3 was 3.03 percent, computed as follows:

$$\text{ROE} = \frac{\$5,285}{.5(\$171,843 + 177,128)} = .303, \text{ or } 3.03\%$$

Its P/E ratio was $4 = \dfrac{\$21}{\$5.285}$

and its P/B ratio was $.12 = \dfrac{\$21}{\$177}$

Its earnings yield was 25 percent compared with an industry average of 12.5 percent.

Note that in our calculations the earnings yield will not equal ROE/ (*P/B*) because we have computed ROE with average shareholders' equity in the denominator and *P/B* with end-of-year shareholders' equity in the denominator.

4.

Honeywell Ratio Analysis

Year	ROE	(1) Net profit / Pretax profit	(2) Pretax profit / EBIT	(3) EBIT / Sales (ROS)	(4) Sales / Assets (ATO)	(5) Assets / Equity	(6) Combined leverage factor (2) × (5)	(7) ROA (3) × (4)
1987	11.4%	.616	.796	7.75%	1.375	2.175	1.731	10.65%
1984	10.2%	.636	.932	8.88%	1.311	1.474	1.374	11.65%

ROE went up despite a decline in operating margin and a decline in the tax burden ratio because of increased leverage and turnover. Note that ROA declined from 11.65 percent in 1984 to 10.65 percent in 1987.

5. LIFO accounting results in lower reported earnings than does FIFO. Fewer assets to depreciate results in lower reported earnings because there is less bias associated with the use of historic cost. More debt results in lower reported earnings because the inflation premium in the interest rate is treated as part of interest expense and not as repayment of principal. If ABC has the same reported earnings as XYZ despite these three sources of downward bias, its real earnings must be greater.

Chapter 20—Technical Analysis

1. Suppose a stock had been selling in a narrow trading range around $50 for a substantial period and later increased in price. Now the stock falls back to a price near $50. Potential buyers might recall the price history of the stock and remember that the last time the stock fell so low, they missed an opportunity for large gains when it later advanced. They might then view $50 as a good opportunity to buy. Therefore, buying pressure will materialize as the stock price falls to $50, which will create a support level.

2.

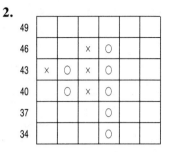

49					
46			×	○	
43	×	○	×	○	
40		○	×	○	
37				○	
34				○	

3. By the time the news of the recession affects bond yields, it also ought to affect stock prices. The market should fall *before* the confidence index signals that the time is ripe to sell.

VII *Derivative Assets: Options and Futures*

Chapter 21—*An Introduction to Options Markets*

1. Before the split, profits would have been 100 × ($40 − $35) = $500. After the split, profits are 1,000 × ($4 − $3.5) = $500. Profits are unaffected.

2. *a.* Payoff to put writer = $\begin{cases} 0 & \text{if } S_T > X \\ -(X - S_T) & \text{if } S_T \le X \end{cases}$

b. Profit = Initial premium realized + Ultimate payoff

$$= \begin{cases} P & \text{if } S_T > X \\ P - (X - S_T) & \text{if } S_T \le X \end{cases}$$

c. Put written

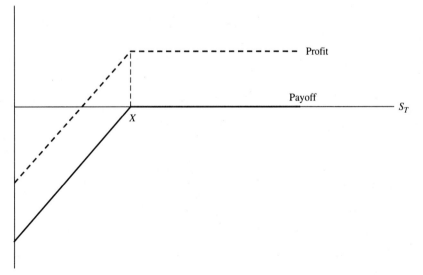

    d. Put writers do well when the stock price increases and poorly when it falls.

3.

Payoff to a Strip		
	$S_T \leq X$	$S_T > X$
2 puts	$2(X - S_T)$	0
1 call	0	$S_T - X$

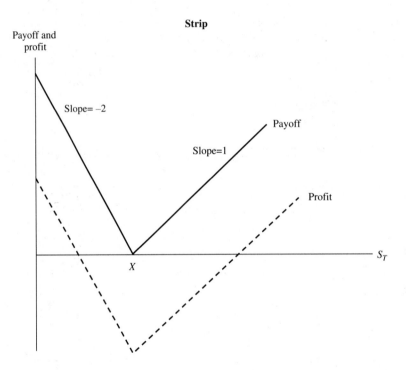

Strip

Payoff to a Strap

	$S_T < X$	$S_T > X$
1 put	$X - S_T$	0
2 calls	0	$2(S_T - X)$

Strap

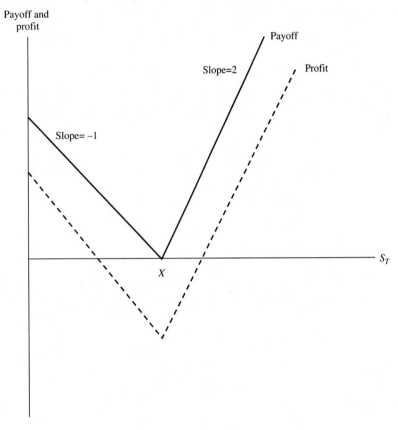

4. Yes. Consider the same scenarios as for the call:

Stock price	$10	$20	$30	$40	$50
Put payoff	$20	$10	$ 0	$ 0	$ 0

Stock price	$20	$25	$30	$35	$40
Put payoff	$10	$ 5	$ 0	$ 0	$ 0

The low volatility scenario yields a lower expected payoff.

5. Puts should be more valuable for higher dividend policies. These policies reduce future stock prices, which will increase the expected payout from the put.

6. Implied volatility exceeds .5. Given a standard deviation of .5, the option value is $13.70. A higher volatility is needed to justify the actual $15 price.

7. The appropriate calls to replicate the bull CDs have exercise price equal to $1.05 \times 240 \times 1.005$, and the riskless investment is $1.005/1.03$. Investing in a portfolio of $\$10/(240 \times 1.05)$ in calls and $1.005/1.03$ in the riskless asset yields the largest of 1.005 and $(1 + r_M)/1.05$, which corresponds to the bull CDs' return per dollar par value. The value of the portfolio is $10/252 + 1.005/1.03 = 1.0154$, which is the value of the bull CD per unit par value.

Chapter 22—Options Markets: A Closer Look

1. The parity relationship assumes that all options are held until expiration and that there are no cash flows until expiration. These assumptions are valid only in the special case of European options on non-dividend-paying stocks. If the stock pays no dividends, the American and European calls are equally valuable, whereas the American put is worth more than the European put. Therefore, although the parity theorem for European options states that

$$P = C + S_0 - PV(X)$$

in fact, P will be *greater* than this value if the put is American.

2. A $1 increase in stock price is a percentage increase of $1/122 = .82$ percent. The put option will fall by $(.4 \times \$1) = \$.40$, a percentage decrease of $\$.40/\$4 = 10$ percent. Elasticity is $-10/.82 = -12.2$.

3. The covered call strategy would consist of a straight bond with a call written on the bond. The value of the strategy at option expiration as a function of the value of the straight bond is given in the following figure, which is virtually identical to Figure 22.7.

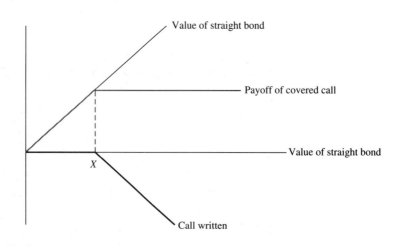

4. The call option is worth less as call protection is expanded. Therefore, the coupon rate need not be as high.

5. Lower. Investors will accept a lower coupon rate in return for the conversion option.

6. Higher. For deep out-of-the-money options, an increase in the stock price still leaves the option unlikely to be exercised. Its value increases only fractionally. For deep in-the-money options, exercise is likely, and option holders benefit by a full dollar for each dollar increase in the stock, as though they already own the stock.

Chapter 23—Futures and Forward Markets

1.

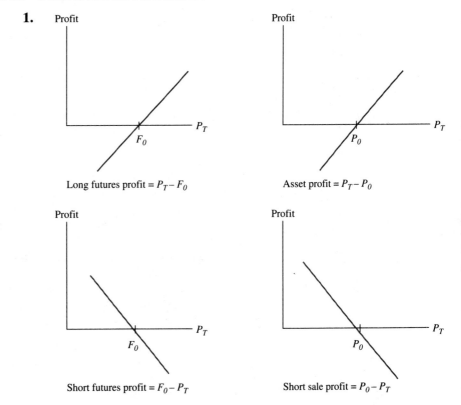

Long futures profit = $P_T - F_0$

Asset profit = $P_T - P_0$

Short futures profit = $F_0 - P_T$

Short sale profit = $P_0 - P_T$

2. The futures price is the agreed-upon price for deferred delivery of the asset. If that price is fair, then the *value* of the agreement ought to be zero; that is, the contract will be a zero-NPV agreement for each trader.

3. Because long positions equal short positions, futures trading *must* entail a "canceling out" of bets on the asset. Moreover, no cash is transacted at the inception of futures trading. Thus, there should be minimal impact on the spot market for the asset, and futures trading should not be expected to reduce capital available for other uses.

4. The clearinghouse has a zero net position in all contracts. Its long and short positions are offsetting, so that net cash flow from marking to market must be zero.

5. Zero. Zero.

6. The risk would be that aluminum and bauxite prices do not move perfectly together. Thus, basis risk involving the spread between the futures price and bauxite spot prices could persist even if the aluminum futures price were set perfectly relative to aluminum itself.

7.

Action	Initial CF	Time-T CF
Lend $200	−$200	+$200 × 1.05 = $210
Short stock	$200	−$S_T − $4
Long futures	0	$S_T − $205
	0	$1

8. It must have zero beta. If the futures price is an unbiased estimator, then we infer that it has a zero risk premium, which means that beta must be zero.

9. As the payoffs to the two strategies are identical, so should the costs of establishing them. The synthetic stock strategy costs $F_0/(1 + r_f)^T$ to establish, this being the present value of the futures price. The stock index purchased directly costs S_0. Therefore, we conclude that $S_0 = F_0/(1 + r_f)^T$, or $F_0 = S_0(1 + r_f)^T$, which is the parity relationship.

10. If the futures price is above the parity level, investors would sell futures and buy stocks. Short selling would not be necessary. Therefore, the top of the no-arbitrage band would be unaffected by the use of the proceeds. If the futures price is too low, investors would want to short sell stocks and buy futures. Now the costs of short selling are important. If proceeds from the short sale become available, short selling becomes less costly and the bottom of the band will move up.

11. According to interest rate parity, F_0 should be $2.12. Since the futures price is too high, we should reverse the arbitrage strategy just considered.

	CF Now ($)	CF in 1 Year
1. Borrow $2.10 in Canada. Convert to one pound.	+2.10	−2.10(1.06)
2. Lend the one pound in the U.K.	−2.10	1.05 E_1
3. Enter a contract to sell 1.05 pounds at a futures price of $2.14.	0	$(1.05)(2.14 − E_1)$
TOTAL	0	.021

12. Stocks offer a total return (capital gain plus dividends) large enough to compensate investors for the time value of the money tied up in the stock. Wheat prices do not necessarily increase over time. In fact, across a harvest, wheat prices will fall. The returns necessary to make storage economically attractive are lacking.

13. If systematic risk were higher, the appropriate discount rate, k, would increase. Referring to equation 23.10, we conclude that F_0 would fall. Intuitively, the claim to 1 pound of orange juice is worth less today if its expected price is unchanged, but the risk associated with the value of the claim increases. Therefore, the amount investors are willing to pay today for future delivery is lower.

VIII *Players and Strategies*

Chapter 24—Portfolio Management Policy

1. The new estimates are as follows:

| | | Holding Period Return | | |
State of Economy	Probability	Stocks	Bonds	Cash
Boom with low inflation	.05	74%	4%	6%
Boom with high inflation	.2	20%	−10%	6%
Normal growth	.5	14%	9%	6%
Recession with low inflation	.2	0	35%	6%
Recession with high inflation	.05	−30%	0	6%
Expected return	$E(r)$	13.2%	9.7%	6%
Standard deviation	σ	17.96%	14.57%	0

Correlation coefficient between stocks and bonds is $-.3449$.

2. To find the composition of the optimal combination of stocks and bonds to be combined with cash we use the following formula:

$$w^* = \frac{[E(r_s) - r_f]\sigma_b^2 - [E(r_b) - r_f]\mathrm{Cov}(r_b, r_s)}{[E(r_s) - r_f]\sigma_b^2 + [E(r_b) - r_f]\sigma_s^2 - [E(r_s) - r_f + E(r_b) - r_f]\mathrm{Cov}(r_b, r_s)}$$

where w^* is the proportion of stocks in portfolio O^* and $1 - w^*$ is the proportion of bonds. Substituting in the formula we get

$$w^* = \frac{(13.2 - 6)212.2849 - (9.7 - 6)(90.2525)}{7.2 \times 212.2849 + 3.7 \times 322.5616 + (7.2 + 3.7)90.2525}$$

$$= \frac{1194.5}{1738.2} = .687$$

So the proportion of stocks in the O^* portfolio changes from 45 percent to 69 percent.

Chapter 25—Individual Investors and Retirement Savings

1. Individual reader's response.

$$C \sum_{t=1}^{55} \frac{1}{1.03^t} = 25,000 \sum_{t=1}^{35} \frac{1}{1.03^t} + 8,000 \sum_{t=36}^{55} \frac{1}{1.03^t}$$

$$26.7744C = 25,000 \times 21.4872 + 8,000 \times 5.2873 = 537,180.50 + 42,297.66$$

$$C = \frac{577,478.16}{26.7744} = \$21,463 \text{ per year}$$

Saving is: $S = 25,000 - C = 25,000 - 21,643 = \$3,357$ per year

2. If Eloise keeps her present asset allocation, she will have the following amounts to spend after taxes five years from now:

Tax-qualified account

Bonds:	$50,000 (1.1)^5 \times .72$	= $ 57,978.36
Stocks:	$50,000 (1.15)^5 \times .72$	= $ 72,408.86
	Subtotal	**$130,387.22**

Nonretirement account

Bonds:	$50,000 (1.072)^5$	= $ 70,785.44
Stocks:	$50,000 (1.15)^5 - .28 \times [50,000(1.15)^5 - 50,000]$	= $ 86,408.86
	Subtotal	**$157,194.30**
	TOTAL	**$287,581.52**

If Eloise shifts all of the bonds into the retirement account and all of the stock into the non-retirement account she will have the following amounts to spend after taxes five years from now:

Tax-qualified account

Bonds:	$100,000 (1.1)^5 \times .72$	=	$115,957

Nonretirement account

Stocks:	$100,000 (1.15)^5 - .28[100,000(1.15)^5 - 100,000]$	=	$172,817.72
	TOTAL		**$288,774.72**

Her spending budget will increase by $1,193.20.

3. $B_0 \times$ PA(4 percent, 5 years) = 100,000 implies that $B_0 = \$22,462.71$.

t	R_t	B_t	A_t
0			$100,000.00
1	4%	$22,462.71	$ 81,537.29
2	10%	$23,758.64	$ 69,923.38
3	−8%	$21,017.26	$ 39,640.53
4	25%	$25,261.12	$ 24,289.54
5	0	$24,289.54	0

4. He has accrued an annuity of $.01 \times 15 \times 15,000 = \$2,250$ per year for 15 years, starting in 25 years. The PV of this annuity is $2,812.13. PV = 2,250 PA (8 percent, 15) × PF (8 percent, 25).

Glossary

Abnormal return. Return on a stock beyond what would be predicted by market movements alone. Cumulative abnormal return (CAR) is the total abnormal return for the period surrounding an announcement or the release of information.

Accounting earnings. Earnings of a firm as reported on its income statement.

Acid test ratio. See Quick ratio.

Active management. Attempts to achieve portfolio returns more than commensurate with risk, either by forecasting broad market trends or by identifying particular mispriced sectors of a market or securities in a market.

Active portfolio. In the context of the Treynor-Black model, the portfolio formed by mixing analyzed stocks of perceived non-zero alpha values. This portfolio is ultimately mixed with the passive market index portfolio.

Adjustable-rate mortgage. A mortgage whose interest rate varies according to some specified measure of the current market interest rate.

Advance-decline line. A graph of the net difference between the number of stock prices advancing and the number declining; a technical indicator of market breadth.

Agency problem. Conflicts of interest among stockholders, bondholders, and managers.

Alpha. The abnormal rate of return on a security in excess of what would be predicted by an equilibrium model like the CAPM or APT.

American option, European option. An American option can be exercised before and up to its expiration date. Compare with a *European option*, which can be exercised only on the expiration date.

Announcement date. Date on which particular news concerning a given company is announced to the public. Used in *event studies*, which researchers use to evaluate the economic impact of events of interest.

Appraisal ratio. The signal-to-noise ratio of an analyst's forecasts. The ratio of alpha to residual standard deviation.

Arbitrage. A zero-risk, zero-net investment strategy that still generates profits.

Arbitrage pricing theory. An asset pricing theory that is derived from a factor model, using diversification and arbitrage arguments. The theory describes the relationship between expected returns on securities, given that there are no opportunities to create wealth through risk-free arbitrage investments.

Asked price. The price at which a dealer will sell a security.

Asset allocation decision. Choosing among broad asset classes such as stocks versus bonds.

Asset turnover (ATO). The annual sales generated by each dollar of assets (sales/assets).

Auction market. A market where all traders in a good meet at one place to buy or sell an asset. The NYSE is an example.

Average collection period, or days' receivables. The ratio of accounts receivable to sales, or the total amount of credit extended per dollar of daily sales (average AR/sales × 365).

Balance sheet. A financial statement of the assets, liabilities, and net worth of the firm as of a particular date.

Bank discount yield. An annualized interest rate assuming simple interest, a 360-day year, and using the face value of the security rather than purchase price to compute return per dollar invested.

Banker's acceptance. A money market asset consisting of an order to a bank by a customer to pay a sum of money at a future date.

Basis. The difference between the futures price and the spot price.

Basis risk. Risk attributable to uncertain movements in the spread between a futures price and a spot price.

Benchmark error. Use of an inappropriate proxy for the true market portfolio.

Beta. The measure of the systematic risk of a security. The tendency of a security's returns to respond to swings in the broad market.

Bid price. The price at which a dealer is willing to purchase a security.

Bid-asked spread. The difference between a dealer's bid and asked price.

Binomial model. An option valuation model predicated on the assumption that stock prices can move to only two values over any short time period.

Black-Scholes formula. An equation to value a call option that uses the stock price, the exercise price, the risk-free interest rate, the time to maturity, and the standard deviation of the stock return.

Block house. Brokerage firms that help to find potential buyers or sellers of large block trades.

Block sale. A transaction of more than 10,000 shares of stock.

Block transactions. Large transactions in which at least 10,000 shares of stock are bought or sold. Brokers or "block houses" often search directly for other large traders rather than bringing the trade to the stock exchange.

Board lot. A standard volume of traded securities, generally equal to 100 shares. It can be larger (smaller) for low-priced (high-priced) securities.

Bogey. The return an investment manager is compared to for performance evaluation.

Bond. A security issued by a borrower that obligates the issuer to make specified payments to the holder over a specific period. A *coupon bond* obligates the issuer to make interest payments called coupon payments over the life of the bond, then to repay the *principal* at maturity.

Bond equivalent yield. Bond yield calculated on an annual percentage rate method. Differs from effective annual yield.

Bond index portfolio. A portfolio of bonds stratified to include representatives of available grades, coupons, and maturities in weights proportional to the actual bond universe.

Book value. An accounting measure describing the net worth of common equity according to a firm's balance sheet.

Breadth. A technical indicator measuring the extent to which movement in a market index is reflected in the price movements of all stocks.

Brokered market. A market where an intermediary (a broker) offers search services to buyers and sellers.

Bull CD, bear CD. A *bull CD* pays its holder a specified percentage of the increase in return on a specified market index while guaranteeing a minimum rate of return. A *bear CD* pays the holder a fraction of any fall in a given market index.

Bullish, bearish. Words used to describe investor attitudes. *Bullish* means optimistic; *bearish* means pessimistic. Also used in bull market and bear market.

Bundling, unbundling. A trend allowing creation of securities either by combining primitive and derivative securities into one composite hybrid or by separating returns on an asset into classes.

Business cycle. The sequence of expansion and contraction of activity in the economy, observable after the fact.

Call option. The right to buy an asset at a specified exercise price on or before a specified expiration date.

Call protection. An initial period during which a callable bond may not be called.

Callable bond. A bond that the issuer may repurchase at a given price in some specified period.

Capital allocation decision. The choice of the proportion of the overall portfolio to place in safe money market securities, versus risky but higher-return securities like stocks.

Capital allocation line (CAL). A graph showing all feasible risk-return combinations of a risky and risk-free asset.

Capital gains. The amount by which the sale price of a security exceeds the purchase price.

Capital market line (CML). A capital allocation line provided by the market index portfolio.

Capital markets. Includes longer-term, relatively riskier securities.

Cash delivery. The provision of some futures contracts that requires not delivery of the underlying assets (as in agricultural futures) but settlement according to the cash value of the asset.

Cash equivalents. Short-term money-market securities.

Cash flow matching. A form of immunization, matching cash flows from a bond with an obligation.

Cash/bond selection. Asset allocation in which the choice is between short-term cash equivalents and longer-term bonds.

CDN system (COATS). The automated quotation system for the Canadian OTC market, the equivalent of NASDAQ in the United States.

Certainty equivalent. The certain return providing the same utility as a risky portfolio.

Certificate of deposit. A bank time deposit.

Clearinghouse. Established by exchanges to facilitate transfer of securities resulting from trades. For options and futures contracts, the clearinghouse may interpose itself as a middleman between two traders.

Closed-end (mutual) fund. A fund whose shares are traded through brokers at market prices; the fund will not redeem shares at their net asset value. The market price of the fund can differ from the net asset value.

Collateral. A specific asset pledged against possible default on a bond. *Mortgage* bonds are backed by claims on property. *Collateral trust bonds* are backed by claims on other securities. *Equipment obligation bonds* are backed by claims on equipment.

Collateralized mortgage obligation (CMO). A mortgage pass-through security that partitions cash flows from underlying mortgages into successive maturity groups, called *tranches*, that receive principal payments according to different maturities.

Commercial paper. Short-term unsecured debt issued by large corporations.

Commission broker. A broker on the floor of the exchange who executes orders for other members.

Common stock. Equities, or equity securities, issued as ownership shares in a publicly held corporation. Shareholders have voting rights and may receive dividends based on their proportionate ownership.

Comparison universe. The collection of money managers of similar investment style used for assessing relative performance of a portfolio manager.

Complete portfolio. The entire portfolio, including risky and risk-free assets.

Concentration (of control). The holding by a few individuals of controlling blocks of shares in companies representing a large segment of the Canadian economy.

Confidence index. The ratio of the average yield on 10 top-rated corporate bonds divided by the average yield on 10 intermediate-grade corporate bonds; a technical indicator that is bullish when the index approaches 100 percent, implying low risk premiums.

Constant growth model. A form of the dividend discount model that assumes dividends will grow at a constant rate.

Contango theory. Holds that the futures price must exceed the expected future spot price.

Contingent claim. Claim whose value is directly dependent on or is contingent on the value of some underlying assets.

Contingent immunization. A mixed passive-active strategy that immunizes a portfolio if necessary to guarantee a minimum acceptable return but otherwise allows active management.

Convergence property. The convergence of futures prices and spot prices at the maturity of the futures contract.

Convertible bond. A bond with an option allowing the bondholder to exchange the bond for a specified number of shares of common stock in the firm. A *conversion ratio* specifies the number of shares. The *market conversion price* is the current value of the shares for which the bond may be exchanged. The *conversion premium* is the excess of the bond's value over the conversion price.

Corporate bonds. Long-term debt issued by private corporations typically paying semiannual coupons and returning the face value of the bond at maturity.

Correlation coefficient. A statistic that scales the covariance to a value between minus one (perfect negative correlation) and plus one (perfect positive correlation).

Cost-of-carry relationship. See Spot-futures parity theorem.

Country selection. A type of active international management that measures the contribution to performance attributable to investing in the better-performing stock markets of the world.

Coupon rate. A bond's interest payments per dollar of par value.

Covariance. A measure of the degree to which returns on two risky assets move in tandem. A positive covariance means that asset returns move together. A negative covariance means they vary inversely.

Covered call. A combination of selling a call on a stock together with buying the stock.

Covered interest arbitrage relationship. See Interest rate parity theorem.

Credit enhancement. Purchase of the financial guarantee of a large insurance company to raise funds.

Cross hedge. Hedging a position in one asset using futures on another commodity.

Cumulative abnormal return. See Abnormal return.

Currency selection. Asset allocation in which the investor chooses among investments denominated in different currencies.

Current ratio. A ratio representing the ability of the firm to pay off its current liabilities by liquidating current assets (current assets/current liabilities).

Day order. A buy order or a sell order expiring at the close of the trading day.

Day's receivables. See Average collection period.

Dealer market. A market where traders specializing in particular commodities buy and sell assets for their own accounts. The OTC market is an example.

Debenture or unsecured bond. A bond not backed by specific collateral.

Dedication strategy. Refers to multiperiod cash flow matching.

Default premium. A differential in promised yield that compensates the investor for the risk inherent in purchasing a corporate bond that entails some risk of default.

Deferred annuities. Tax-advantaged life insurance product. Deferred annuities offer deferral of taxes with the option of withdrawing one's funds in the form of a life annuity.

Defined benefit plans. Pension plans in which retirement benefits are set according to a fixed formula.

Defined contribution plans. Pension plans in which the corporation is committed to making contributions according to a fixed formula.

Delta (of option). See Hedge ratio.

Demand shock. An event affecting the aggregate demand for goods and services, thereby influencing the state of the economy.

Derivative asset/contingent claim. Securities providing payoffs that depend on or are contingent on the values of other assets such as commodity prices, bond and stock prices, or market index values. Examples are futures and options.

Derivative security. See Primitive security.

Detachable warrant. A warrant entitles the holder to buy a given number of shares of stock at a stipulated price. A detachable warrant is one that may be sold separately from the package it may have originally been issued with (usually a bond).

Direct search market. Buyers and sellers seek each other directly and transact directly.

Discount function. The discounted value of $1 as a function of time until payment.

Discounted dividend model (DDM). A formula to estimate the intrinsic value of a firm by figuring the present value of all expected future dividends.

Discretionary account. An account of a customer who gives a broker the authority to make buy and sell decisions on the customer's behalf.

Diversifiable risk. Risk attributable to firm-specific risk, or non-market risk. Non-diversifiable risk refers to systematic or market risk.

Diversification. Spreading a portfolio over many investments to avoid excessive exposure to any one source of risk.

Dividend payout ratio. Percentage of earnings paid out as dividends.

Dollar-weighted return. The internal rate of return on an investment.

Doubling option. A sinking fund provision that may allow repurchase of twice the required number of bonds at the sinking fund call price.

Dow theory. A long-standing approach to forecasting stock market direction by identification of long-term trends; the Dow Jones Industrial and Transportation Averages were used by Charles Dow to identify and confirm underlying trends.

Dual funds. Funds in which income and capital shares on a portfolio of stocks are sold separately.

Duration. A measure of the average life of a bond, defined as the weighted average of the times until each payment is made, with weights proportional to the present value of the payment.

Dynamic hedging. Constant updating of hedge positions as market conditions change.

EAFE index. The European, Australian, Far East index, computed by Morgan, Stanley, is a widely used index of non-U.S. stocks.

Earnings retention ratio. Plowback ratio.

Earnings yield. The ratio of earnings to price, E/P.

Economic earnings. The real flow of cash that a firm could pay out forever in the absence of any change in the firm's productive capacity.

Effective annual yield. Annualized interest rate on a security computed using compound interest techniques.

Efficient diversification. The organizing principle of modern portfolio theory, which maintains that any risk-averse investor will search for the highest expected return for any level of portfolio risk.

Efficient frontier. Graph representing a set of portfolios that maximize expected return at each level of portfolio risk.

Efficient market hypothesis. The prices of securities fully reflect available information. Investors buying securities in an efficient market should expect to obtain an equilibrium rate of return. Weak-form EMH asserts that stock prices already reflect all information contained in the history of past prices. The semi-strong-form hypothesis asserts that stock prices already reflect all publicly available information. The strong-form hypothesis asserts that stock prices reflect all relevant information including insider information.

Elasticity (of an option). Percentage change in the value of an option accompanying a 1 percent change in the value of a stock.

Endowment funds. Organizations chartered to invest money for specific purposes.

Eurodollars. Dollar-denominated deposits at foreign banks or foreign branches of American banks.

European option. A European option can be exercised only on the expiration date. Compare with an American option, which can be exercised before, up to, and including its expiration date.

Event study. Research methodology designed to measure the impact of an event of interest on stock returns.

Exchange rate. Price of a unit of one country's currency in terms of another country's currency.

Exchanges. National or regional auction markets providing a facility for members to trade securities. A seat is a membership on an exchange.

Exercise or strike price. Price set for calling (buying) an asset or putting (selling) an asset.

Expectations hypothesis (of interest rates). Theory that forward interest rates are unbiased estimates of expected future interest rates.

Expected return. The probability weighted average of the possible outcomes.

Expected return-beta relationship. Implication of the CAPM that security risk premiums (expected excess returns) will be proportional to beta.

Extendible bond. A bond that the holder may choose either to redeem for par value at maturity, or to extend for a given number of years; it is known as a put bond in the United States.

Factor model. A way of decomposing the factors that influence a security's rate of return into common and firm-specific influences.

Factor portfolio. A well-diversified portfolio constructed to have a beta of 1.0 on one factor and a beta of zero on any other factor.

Fair game. An investment prospect that has a zero-risk premium.

FIFO. The first-in first-out accounting method of inventory valuation.

Filter rule. A technical analysis technique stated as a rule for buying or selling stock according to past price movements.

Financial assets. Financial assets such as stocks and bonds are claims to the income generated by real assets or claims on income from the government.

Financial intermediary. An institution such as a bank, mutual fund, investment company, or insurance company that serves to connect the household and business sectors so households can invest and businesses can finance production.

Firm-specific risk. See Diversifiable risk.

First-pass regression. A time series regression to estimate the betas of securities or portfolios.

Fiscal policy. The use of taxes and government spending to affect aggregate demand as well as other objectives of macroeconomic policy.

Fixed annuities. Annuity contracts in which the insurance company pays a fixed dollar amount of money per period.

Fixed-charge coverage ratio. Ratio of earnings to all fixed cash obligations, including lease payments and sinking fund payments.

Fixed-income security. A security such as a bond that pays a specified cash flow over a specific period.

Flight to quality. Describes the tendency of investors to require larger default premiums on investments under uncertain economic conditions.

Floating-rate bond. A bond whose interest rate is reset periodically according to a specified market rate.

Floor broker. A member of the exchange who can execute orders for commission brokers.

Flower bond. Special Treasury bond (no longer issued) that may be used to settle federal estate taxes at par value under certain conditions.

Forced conversion. Use of a firm's call option on a callable convertible bond when the firm knows that bondholders will exercise their option to convert.

Foreign exchange market. An informal network of banks and brokers that allows customers to enter forward contracts to purchase or sell currencies in the future at a rate of exchange agreed upon now.

Foreign exchange swap. The exchange of cash flows denominated in one currency for cash flows denominated in another currency, in order to manage the foreign exchange risk.

Forward contract. An arrangement calling for future delivery of an asset at an agreed-upon price. Also see Futures contract.

Forward interest rate. Rate of interest for a future period that would equate the total return of a long-term bond with that of a strategy of rolling over shorter-term bonds. The forward rate is inferred from the term structure.

Fourth market. Direct trading in exchange-listed securities between one investor and another without the benefit of a broker.

Fully diluted earnings per share. Earnings per share expressed as if all outstanding convertible securities and warrants have been exercised.

Fundamental analysis. Research to predict stock value that focuses on such determinants as earnings and dividends prospects, expectations for future interest rates, and risk evaluation of the firm.

Futures contract. Obliges traders to purchase or sell an asset at an agreed-upon price on a specified future date. The long position is held by the trader who commits to purchase. The short position is held by the trader who commits to sell. Futures differ from forward contracts in their standardization, exchange trading, margin requirements, and daily settling (marking to market).

Futures option. The right to enter a specified futures contract at a futures price equal to the stipulated exercise price.

Globalization. Tendency toward a worldwide investment environment, and the integration of national capital markets.

Guaranteed insurance contract. A contract promising a stated nominal rate of interest over some specific time period, usually several years.

Hedge ratio (for an option). The number of stocks required to hedge against the price risk of holding one option. Also called the option's delta.

Hedging. Investing in an asset to reduce the overall risk of a portfolio.

Holding period return. The rate of return over a given period.

Homogenous expectations. The assumption that all investors use the same expected returns and covariance matrix of security returns as inputs in security analysis.

Horizon analysis. Interest rate forecasting that uses a forecast yield curve to predict bond prices.

Immunization. A strategy that matches durations of assets and liabilities so as to make net worth unaffected by interest rate movements.

Implied volatility. The standard deviation of stock returns that is consistent with an option's market value.

In the money. In the money describes an option whose exercise would produce profits. Out of the money describes an option where exercise would not be profitable.

Income beneficiary. One who receives income from a trust.

Income fund. A mutual fund providing for liberal current income from investments.

Income statement. A financial statement summarizing the profitability of the firm over a period of time, such as a year; revenues and expenses are listed and their difference is calculated as net income.

Incomplete markets. Financial markets in which the number of available independent securities is less than the number of distinct future states of the world.

Indenture. The document defining the contract between the bond issuer and the bondholder.

Index arbitrage. An investment strategy that exploits divergences between actual futures prices and their theoretically correct parity values to make a profit.

Index fund. A mutual fund holding shares in proportion to their representation in a market index such as the S&P 500.

Index model. A model of stock returns using a market index such as the S&P 500 to represent common or systematic risk factors.

Index option. A call or put option based on a stock market index.

Indifference curve. A curve connecting all portfolios with the same utility according to their means and standard deviations.

Initial public offering. Stock issued to the public for the first time by a formerly privately owned company.

Input list. The set of estimates of expected rates of return and covariances for the securities that will constitute portfolios forming the efficient frontier.

Inside information. Non-public knowledge about a corporation possessed by corporate officers, major owners, or other individuals with privileged access to information about a firm.

Insider trading. Trading by officers, directors, major stockholders, or others who hold private inside information allowing them to benefit from buying or selling stock.

Insider transactions. Transactions by officers, directors, and major stockholders in their firm's securities; these transactions must be reported publicly at regular intervals.

Insurance principle. The law of averages. The average outcome for many independent trials of an experiment will approach the expected value of the experiment.

Integration. The condition in which two distinct financial markets can be analysed as if they were a single market.

Interest coverage ratio, or times interest earned. A financial leverage measure (EBIT divided by interest expense).

Interest rate. The number of dollars earned per dollar invested per period.

Interest rate parity theorem. The spot-futures exchange rate relationship that prevails in well-functioning markets.

Interest rate swaps. A method to manage interest rate risk where parties trade the cash flows corresponding to different securities without actually exchanging securities directly.

Intermarket spread swap. Switching from one segment of the bond market to another (from Treasuries to corporates, for example).

Intrinsic value (of a firm). The present value of a firm's expected future net cash flows discounted by the required rate of return.

Intrinsic value of an option. Stock price minus exercise price, or the profit that could be attained by immediate exercise of an in-the-money option.

Investment company. Firm managing funds for investors. An investment company may manage several mutual funds.

Investment dealers. Firms that specialize in the sale of new securities to the public, typically by underwriting the issue; they are known as investment bankers in the United States.

Investment grade bond. Bond rated BBB and above or Baa and above. Lower-rated bonds are classified as speculative-grade or junk bonds.

Investment horizon. The planned liquidation date of an investment portfolio or part of it; it plays a role in the choice of assets.

Investment portfolio. Set of securities chosen by an investor.

Jensen's measure. The alpha of an investment.

Junk bond. See Speculative grade bond.

Law of one price. The rule stipulating that equivalent securities or bundles of securities must sell at equal prices to preclude arbitrage opportunities.

Leading economic indicators. A collection of economic series shown to precede changes in overall economic activity; these include retail sales, financial, manufacturing, house sales measures, and the U.S. index.

Leakage. Release of information to some persons before official public announcement.

Leverage ratio. Measure of debt to total capitalization of a firm.

LIFO. The last-in first-out accounting method of valuing inventories.

Limit order. An order specifying a price at which an investor is willing to buy or sell a security.

Limited liability. The fact that shareholders have no personal liability to the creditors of the corporation in the event of failure.

Liquidation value. Net amount that could be realized by selling the assets of a firm after paying the debt.

Liquidity. The ease with which an asset can be sold at a fair price, relating time and value to the asset.

Liquidity preference theory. Theory that the forward rate exceeds expected future interest rates.

Liquidity premium. Forward rate minus expected future short interest rate.

Load fund. A mutual fund with a sales commission, or load.

London Interbank Offered Rate (LIBOR). Rate that most creditworthy banks charge one another for large loans of Eurodollars in the London market.

Long position or long hedge. Protecting the future cost of a purchase by taking a long futures position to protect against changes in the price of the asset.

Maintenance, or variation, margin. An established value below which a trader's margin cannot fall. Reaching the maintenance margin triggers a margin call.

Margin. Describes securities purchased with money borrowed from a broker. Current maximum margin is 50 percent.

Market capitalization rate. The market-consensus estimate of the appropriate discount rate for a firm's cash flows.

Market model. Another version of the index model that breaks down return uncertainty into systematic and non-systematic components.

Market or systematic risk, firm-specific risk. Market risk is risk attributable to common macroeconomic factors. Firm-specific risk reflects risk peculiar to an individual firm that is independent of market risk.

Market order. A buy or sell order to be executed immediately at current market prices.

Market portfolio. The portfolio for which each security is held in proportion to its market value.

Market price of risk. A measure of the extra return, or risk premium, that investors demand to bear risk. The reward-to-risk ratio of the market portfolio.

Market segmentation or preferred habitat theory. The theory that long- and short-maturity bonds are traded in essentially distinct or segmented markets and that prices in one market do not affect those in the other.

Market timer. An investor who speculates on broad market moves rather than on specific securities.

Market timing. Asset allocation in which the investment in the market is increased if one forecasts that the market will outperform T-bills.

Market value–weighted index. An index of a group of securities computed by calculating a weighted average of the returns of each security in the index, with weights proportional to outstanding market value.

Market-book ratio. Market price of a share divided by book value per share.

Marking to market. Describes the daily settlement of obligations on futures positions.

Mean-variance analysis. Evaluation of risky prospects based on the expected value and variance of possible outcomes.

Mean-variance criterion. The selection of portfolios based on the means and variances of their returns. The choice of the higher expected return portfolio for a given level of variance or the lower variance portfolio for a given expected return.

Measurement error. Errors in measuring an explanatory variable in a regression that lead to biases in estimated parameters.

Membership or seat on an exchange. A limited number of exchange positions that enable the holder to trade for the holder's own accounts and charge clients for the execution of trades for their accounts.

Minimum variance frontier. Graph of the lowest possible portfolio variance that is attainable for a given portfolio expected return.

Minimum variance portfolio. The portfolio of risk assets with lowest variance.

Modern portfolio theory (MPT). Principles underlying analysis and evaluation of rational portfolio choices based on risk-return trade-offs and efficient diversification.

Monetary policy. The manipulation of the money supply to influence economic activity and the level of interest rates.

Money market. Includes short-term, highly liquid, and relatively low-risk debt instruments.

Mortality tables. Tables of probabilities that individuals of various ages will die within a year.

Mortgage-backed security. Ownership claim in a pool of mortgages or an obligation that is secured by such a pool. Also called a *pass-through*, because payments are passed along from the mortgage originator to the purchaser of the mortgage-backed security.

Moving average. A rolling average of stock prices, based on a short, intermediate, or long period, serving as a reference point for the current price; displayed on a chart.

Multifactor CAPM. Generalization of the basic CAPM that accounts for extra-market hedging demands.

Municipal bonds. Tax-exempt bonds issued by state and local governments in the United States, generally to finance capital improvement projects. General obligation bonds are backed by the general taxing power of the issuer. Revenue bonds are backed by the proceeds from the project or agency they are issued to finance.

Mutual fund. A firm pooling and managing funds of investors.

Mutual fund theorem. A result associated with the CAPM, asserting that investors will choose to invest their entire risky portfolio in a market-index mutual fund.

Naked option writing. Writing an option without an offsetting stock position.

NASDAQ. The automated quotation system for the OTC market, showing current bid-asked prices for thousands of stocks.

Neglected-firm effect. That investments in stock of less well-known firms have generated abnormal returns.

Non-systematic risk. Non-market or firm-specific risk factors that can be eliminated by diversification. Also called unique risk or diversifiable risk. Systematic risk refers to risk factors common to the entire economy.

Normal backwardation theory. Holds that the futures price will be bid down to a level below the expected spot price.

Odd-lot theory. Assessment of market tops and bottoms by observation of the net buying and selling of odd-lots (shares sold in less than round or board lots); used as a contrarian measure so that odd-lot buying suggests a top.

Open (good-till-canceled) order. A buy or sell order remaining in force for up to six months unless canceled.

Open interest. The number of futures contracts outstanding.

Open-end (mutual) fund. A fund that issues or redeems its own shares at their net asset value (NAV).

Optimal risky portfolio. An investor's best combination of risky assets to be mixed with safe assets to form the complete portfolio.

Option elasticity. The percentage increase in an option's value given a 1 percent change in the value of the underlying security.

Original issue discount bond. A bond issued with a low coupon rate that sells at a discount from par value.

Out of the money. Out of the money describes an option where exercise would not be profitable. In the money describes an option where exercise would produce profits.

Over-the-counter market. An informal network of brokers and dealers who negotiate sales of securities (not a formal exchange).

Par value. The face value of the bond.

Pass-through security. Pools of loans (such as home mortgage loans) sold in one package. Owners of pass-throughs receive all principal and interest payments made by the borrowers.

Passive investment strategy. See Passive management.

Passive management. Buying a well-diversified portfolio to represent a broad-based market index without attempting to search out mispriced securities.

Passive portfolio. A market index portfolio.

Passive strategy. See Passive management.

P/E effect. That portfolios of low P/E stocks have exhibited higher average risk-adjusted returns than high P/E stocks.

Personal trust. An interest in an asset held by a trustee for the benefit of another person.

Plowback ratio. The proportion of the firm's earnings that is reinvested in the business (and not paid out as dividends). The plowback ratio equals 1 minus the dividend payout ratio.

Political risk. Possibility of the expropriation of assets, changes in tax policy, restrictions on the exchange of foreign currency for domestic currency, or other changes in the business climate of a country.

Portfolio insurance. The practice of using options or dynamic hedge strategies to provide protection against investment losses while maintaining upside potential.

Portfolio management. Process of combining securities in a portfolio tailored to the investor's preferences and needs, monitoring that portfolio, and evaluating its performance.

Portfolio opportunity set. The possible expected return-standard deviation pairs of all portfolios that can be constructed from a given set of assets.

Preferred habitat theory. Holds that investors prefer specific maturity ranges but can be induced to switch if premiums are sufficient.

Preferred stock. Non-voting shares in a corporation, paying a fixed or variable stream of dividends.

Premium. The purchase price of an option.

Price-earnings multiple. See Price-earnings ratio.

Price-earnings ratio. The ratio of a stock's price to its earnings per share. Also referred to as the P/E multiple.

Primary market. New issues of securities are offered to the public here.

Primitive security, derivative security. A *primitive security* is an instrument such as a stock or bond for which payments depend only on the financial status of its issuer. A *derivative security* is created from the set of primitive securities to yield returns that depend on factors beyond the characteristics of the issuer and that may be related to prices of other assets.

Principal. The outstanding balance on a loan.

Profit margin. See Return on sales.

Program trading. Coordinated buy orders and sell orders of entire portfolios, usually with the aid of computers, often to achieve index arbitrage objectives.

Prospectus. A final and approved registration statement including the price at which the security issue is offered.

Protective convenant. A provision specifying requirements of collateral, sinking fund, dividend policy, etc., designed to protect the interests of bondholders.

Protective put. Purchase of stock combined with a put option that guarantees minimum proceeds equal to the put's exercise price.

Proxy. An instrument empowering an agent to vote in the name of the shareholder.

Prudent man. A phrase implying the conduct of conservative investment practices by professional and institutional investors when managing others' funds.

Public offering, private placement. A *public offering* consists of bonds sold in the primary market to the general public; a *private placement* is sold directly to a limited number of institutional investors.

Pure yield pickup swap. Moving to higher yield bonds.

Put option. The right to sell an asset at a specified exercise price on or before a specified expiration date.

Put-call parity theorem. An equation representing the proper relationship between put and call prices. Violation of parity allows arbitrage opportunities.

Quick ratio. A measure of liquidity similar to the current ratio except for exclusion of inventories (cash plus receivables divided by current liabilities).

Random walk. Describes the notion that stock price changes are random and unpredictable.

Rate anticipation swap. A switch made in response to forecasts of interest rates.

Real assets, financial assets. *Real assets* are land, buildings, and equipment that are used to produce goods and services. *Financial assets* are claims such as securities to the income generated by real assets.

Real interest rate. The excess of the interest rate over the inflation rate. The growth rate of purchasing power derived from an investment.

Realized compound yield. Yield assuming that coupon payments are invested at the going market interest rate at the time of their receipt and rolled over until the bond matures.

Rebalancing. Realigning the proportion of assets in a portfolio as needed.

Registered bond. A bond whose issuer records ownership and interest payments. Differs from a bearer bond, which is traded without record of ownership and whose possession is its only evidence of ownership.

Registered trader. A trader who makes a market in the shares of one or more firms and who maintains a "fair and orderly market" by dealing personally in the stock; registered traders are known as specialists in the United States.

Registration statement. Required to be filed with the SEC to describe the issue of a new security.

Regression equation. An equation that describes the average relationship between a dependent variable and a set of explanatory variables.

REIT. Real estate investment trust, which is similar to a closed-end mutual fund. REITs invest in real estate or loans secured by real estate and issue shares in such investments.

Relative strength. The ratio of an individual stock price to a price index for the relevant industry; a technical indicator of the out- or underperformance of a company relative to the industry or market.

Remainderman. One who receives the principal of a trust when it is dissolved.

Replacement cost. Cost to replace a firm's assets. "Reproduction" cost.

Repurchase agreements (repos). Short-term, often overnight, sales of government securities with an agreement to repurchase the securities at a slightly higher price. A *reverse repo* is a purchase with an agreement to resell at a specified price on a future date.

Residual claim. Refers to the fact that shareholders are at the bottom of the list of claimants to assets of a corporation in the event of failure or bankruptcy.

Residuals. Parts of stock returns not explained by the explanatory variable (the market-index return). They measure the impact of firm-specific events during a particular period.

Resistance level. A price level above which it is supposedly difficult for a stock or stock index to rise.

Restricted shares. A special type of shares that have no voting rights, or only limited voting rights, but otherwise participate fully in the financial benefits of share ownership.

Retractable bond. A bond that gives the right to the holder to redeem early at par value, instead of holding it till maturity date.

Return on assets (ROA). A profitability ratio; earnings before interest and taxes divided by total assets.

Return on equity (ROE). An accounting ratio of net profits divided by equity.

Return on sales (ROS), or profit margin. The ratio of operating profits per dollar of sales (EBIT divided by sales).

Reversal effect. A tendency of stocks that perform unusually poorly or unusually well during one period to follow with the opposite performance during the next period.

Reversing trade. Entering the opposite side of a currently held futures position to close out the position.

Reward-to-volatility ratio. Ratio of excess return to portfolio standard deviation.

Riding the yield curve. Buying long-term bonds in anticipation of capital gains as yields fall with the declining maturity of the bonds.

Risk arbitrage. Speculation on perceived mispriced securities, usually in connection with merger and acquisition targets.

Risk-averse, risk-neutral, risk-lover. A *risk-averse* investor will consider risky portfolios only if they provide compensation for risk via a risk premium. A *risk-neutral* investor finds the level of risk irrelevant and considers only the expected return of risk prospects. A *risk-lover* is willing to accept lower expected returns on prospects with higher amounts of risk.

Risk-free asset. An asset with a certain rate of return; often taken to be short-term T-bills.

Risk-free rate. The interest rate that can be earned with certainty.

Risk lover. See Risk averse.

Risk neutral. See Risk averse.

Risk premium. An expected return in excess of that on risk-free securities. The premium provides compensation for the risk of an investment.

Risk-return trade-off. If an investor is willing to take on risk, there is the reward of higher expected returns.

Risky asset. An asset with an uncertain rate of return.

Seasoned new issue. Stock issued by companies that already have stock on the market.

Second-pass regression. A cross-sectional regression of portfolio returns on betas. The estimated slope is the measurement of the reward for bearing systematic risk during the period.

Secondary market. Already existing securities are bought and sold on the exchanges or in the OTC market.

Securitization. Pooling loans for various purposes into standardized securities backed by those loans, which can then be traded like any other security.

Security analysis. Determining correct value of a security in the marketplace.

Security characteristic line. A plot of the expected excess return on a security over the risk-free rate as a function of the excess return on the market.

Security market line. Graphical representation of the expected return-beta relationship of the CAPM.

Security selection. See Security selection decision.

Security selection decision. Choosing the particular securities to include in a portfolio.

Segmentation. The state of relative independence of different financial markets, as characterized by different responses to specific factors.

Selectivity. The ability to select individual stocks that will perform well in particular economic climates.

Semistrong-form EMH. See Efficient market hypothesis.

Separation property. The property that portfolio choice can be separated into two independent tasks: (1) determination of the optimal risky portfolio, which is a purely technical problem, and (2) the personal choice of the best mix of the risky portfolio and the risk-free asset.

Serial bond issue. An issue of bonds with staggered maturity dates that spreads out the principal repayment burden over time.

Settlement date. The date at which capital gains are recognized for tax purposes; usually five business dates after the actual trade date.

Sharpe's measure. Reward-to-volatility ratio; ratio of portfolio excess return to standard deviation.

Shelf registration. Advance registration of securities with the SEC for sale up to two years following initial registration.

Short interest. The total number of shares of stock held short in the market; considered bullish in that short holdings must be covered by purchases (latent demand), but bearish in that sophisticated traders (who are more likely to short) predict better.

Short interest rate. A one-period interest rate.

Short position or hedge. Protecting the value of an asset held by taking a short position in a futures contract.

Short sale. The sale of shares not owned by the investor but borrowed through a broker and later repurchased to replace the loan. Profit comes from initial sale at a higher price than the repurchase price.

Simple prospect. An investment opportunity where a certain initial wealth is placed at risk and only two outcomes are possible.

Single index model. A model of stock returns that decomposes influences on returns into a systematic factor, as measured by the return on a broad market index, and firm-specific factors.

Sinking fund. A procedure that allows for the repayment of principal at maturity by calling for the bond issuer to repurchase some proportion of the outstanding bonds either in the open market or at a special call price associated with the sinking fund provision.

Skip-day settlement. A convention for calculating yield that assumes a T-bill sale is not settled until two days after quotation of the T-bill price.

Small-firm effect. That investments in stocks of small firms appear to have earned abnormal returns.

Speculation. Undertaking a risky investment with the objective of earning a positive profit compared with investment in a risk-free alternative (a risk premium)

Speculative grade bond. Bond rated Ba or lower by Moody's, or BB or lower by Standard & Poor's, or an unrated bond.

Spot rate. The current interest rate appropriate for discounting a cash flow of some given maturity.

Spot-futures parity theorem, or cost-of-carry relationship. Describes the theoretically correct relationship between spot and futures prices. Violation of the parity relationship gives rise to arbitrage opportunities.

Spread (futures). Taking a long position in a futures contract of one maturity and a short position in a contract of different maturity, both on the same commodity.

Spread (options). A combination of two or more call options or put options on the same stock with differing exercise prices or times to expiration. A vertical or money spread refers to a spread with different exercise price; a horizontal or time spread refers to differing expiration date.

Squeeze. The possibility that enough long positions hold their contracts to maturity that supplies of the commodity are not adequate to cover all contracts. A *short squeeze* describes the reverse: short positions threaten to deliver an expensive-to-store commodity.

Standard deviation. Square root of the variance.

Statement of changes in financial position. A listing of the sources and uses of funds through operations, financing, and investments; over the specific time period, the net addition to the cash position is determined.

Stock exchanges. Secondary markets where already issued securities are bought and sold by members.

Stock selection. An active portfolio management technique that focuses on advantageous selection of particular stocks rather than on broad asset allocation choices.

Stock split. Issue by a corporation of a given number of shares in exchange for the current number of shares held by stockholders. Splits may go in either direction, either increasing or decreasing the number of shares outstanding. A *reverse split* decreases the number outstanding.

Stop-loss order. A sell order to be executed if the price of the stock falls below a stipulated level.

Straddle. A combination of buying both a call and a put, each with the same exercise price and expiration date. The purpose is to profit from expected volatility in either direction.

Straight bond. A bond with no option features such as callability or convertibility.

Street name. Describes securities held by a broker on behalf of a client but registered in the name of the firm.

Strike price. See Exercise price.

Strip, strap. Variants of a straddle. A *strip* is two puts and one call on a stock; a *strap* is two calls and one put, both with the same exercise price and expiration date.

Stripped of coupons. Describes the practice of some investment banks that sell "synthetic" zero-coupon bonds by marketing the rights to a single payment backed by a coupon-paying Treasury bond.

Strong-form EMH. See Efficient market hypothesis.

Subordination clause. A provision in a bond indenture that restricts the issuer's future borrowing by subordinating the new lenders' claims on the firm to those of the existing bond holders. Claims of *subordinated* or *junior* debtholders are not paid until the prior debt is paid.

Substitution swap. Exchange of one bond for a bond with similar attributes but more attractively priced.

Supply shock. An event affecting the aggregate supply of goods and services, thereby influencing the state of the economy.

Support level. A price level below which it is supposedly difficult for a stock or stock index to fall.

Swing fund management. The practice of active portfolio management through the switching of weights for asset classes in response to predictions of economic changes.

Systematic risk. Risk factors common to the whole economy, for example non-diversifiable risk; see Market risk.

Tactical asset allocation. Active portfolio management achieved by the use of options and derivatives to alter the response of asset classes to economic changes; rapid and cost-effective changes to asset class sensitivity are produced by computer analysis.

Tax anticipation notes. Short-term municipal debt to raise funds to pay for expenses before actual collection of taxes.

Tax deferral option. The feature of the U.S. Internal Revenue Code that the capital gains tax on an asset is payable only when the gain is realized by selling the asset.

Tax swap. Swapping two similar bonds to receive a tax benefit.

Tax-deferred retirement plans. Employer-sponsored and other plans that allow contributions and earnings to be made and accumulate tax free until they are paid out as benefits.

Tax-timing option. Describes the investor's ability to shift the realization of investment gains or losses and their tax implications from one period to another.

Technical analysis. Research to identify mispriced securities that focuses on recurrent and predictable stock price patterns and on proxies for buy or sell pressure in the market.

Tender offer. An offer from an outside investor to shareholders of a company to purchase their shares at a stipulated price, usually substantially above the market price, so that the investor may amass enough shares to obtain control of the company.

Term insurance. Provides a death benefit only, no buildup of cash value.

Term premiums. Excess of the yields to maturity on long-term bonds over those of short-term bonds.

Term structure of interest rates. The pattern of interest rates appropriate for discounting cash flows of various maturities.

Thin trading. Persistently infrequent trading, including long intervals without any recorded transactions, for a given security.

Third market. Trading of exchange-listed securities on the OTC market.

Tick. The net difference between the number of stocks trading higher than their previous trade prices and the number trading lower; a technical indicator of market breadth.

Time value (of an option). The part of the value of an option that is due to its positive time to expiration. Not to be confused with present value or the time value of money.

Time-weighted return. An average of the period-by-period holding period returns of an investment.

Times interest earned. See Interest coverage ratio.

Timing. The ability to predict the changes in market trends; timing is used to switch funds between asset classes to increase returns.

Tobin's *q*. Ratio of market value of the firm to replacement cost.

Tranche. See Collateralized mortgage obligation.

Treasury bill. Short-term, highly liquid government securities issued at a discount from the face value and returning the face amount at maturity.

Treasury bond or note. Debt obligations of the U.S. federal government that make semiannual coupon payments and are sold at or near par value in denominations of $1,000 or more.

Treynor's measure. Ratio of excess return to beta.

Trin. The ratio of the number of advancing to declining stocks divided by the ratio of volume in advancing versus declining stocks; a technical indicator of market strength that is bullish when the value is less than one.

Triple-witching hour. The four times a year that the S&P 500 futures contract expires at the same time as the S&P 100 index option contract and option contracts on individual stocks.

Unbundling. See Bundling.

Underwriting, underwriting syndicate. Underwriters (investment bankers) purchase securities from the issuing company and resell them. Usually a syndicate of investment bankers is organized behind a lead firm.

Unique risk. See Diversifiable risk.

Unit investment trust. Money invested in a portfolio whose composition is fixed for the life of the fund. Shares in a unit trust are called redeemable trust certificates, and they are sold at a premium above NAV.

Universal life policy. An insurance policy that allows for a varying death benefit and premium level over the term of the policy, with an interest rate on the cash value that changes with market interest rates.

Uptick, or zero-plus tick. A trade resulting in a positive change in a stock price, or a trade at a constant price following a preceding price increase.

Utility. The measure of the welfare or satisfaction of an investor.

Utility value. The welfare a given investor assigns to an investment with a particular return and risk.

Variable annuities. Annuity contracts in which the insurance company pays a periodic amount linked to the investment performance of an underlying portfolio.

Variable life policy. An insurance policy that provides a fixed death benefit plus a cash value that can be invested in a variety of funds from which the policyholder can choose.

Variance. A measure of the dispersion of a random variable. Equals the expected value of the squared deviation from the mean.

Variation margin. See Maintenance margin.

Warrant. An option issued by the firm to purchase shares of the firm's stock.

Weak-form EMH. See Efficient market hypothesis.

Weekend effect. The common recurrent negative average return from Friday to Monday in the stock market.

Well-diversified portfolio. A portfolio spread out over many securities in such a way that the weight in any security is close to zero.

Whole-life insurance policy. Provides a death benefit and a kind of savings plan that builds up cash value for possible future withdrawal.

Workout period. Realignment period of a temporary misaligned yield relationship.

Writing a call. Selling a call option.

Yield curve. A graph of yield to maturity as a function of time to maturity.

Yield to maturity. A measure of the average rate of return that will be earned on a bond if held to maturity.

Zero-beta portfolio. The minimum-variance portfolio uncorrelated with a chosen efficient portfolio.

Zero-coupon bond. A bond paying no coupons that sells at a discount and provides payment of the principal only at maturity.

Zero-investment portfolio. A portfolio of zero net value, established by buying and shorting component securities, usually in the context of an arbitrage strategy.

Name Index

Subject Index